ATTENTION-DEFICIT HYPERACTIVITY DISORDER

A Handbook for Diagnosis and Treatment

Second Edition

RUSSELL A. BARKLEY

THE GUILFORD PRESS
New York London

© 1998 The Guilford Press
A Division of Guilford Publications, Inc.
72 Spring Street, New York, NY 10012
http://www.guilford.com

Printed in the United States of America

This book is printed on acid-free paper.

Last digit is print number: 9   8   7   6   5   4   3   2

Library of Congress Cataloging-in-Publication Data

Barkley, Russell A., 1949–
    Attention-deficit hyperactivity disorder : a handbook for
diagnosis and treatment / Russell A. Barkley. — 2nd ed.
      p. cm.
    Includes bibliographical references and index.
    ISBN 1-57230-275-5
    1. Attention-deficit hyperactivity disorder—Handbooks, manuals,
etc.   2. Attention-deficit hyperactivity disorder—Treatment—
Handbooks, manuals, etc.   3. Behavior therapy for children—
Handbooks, manuals, etc.   I. Title.
    [DNLM: 1. Attention Deficit Disorder with Hyperactivity—
diagnosis.   2. Attention Deficit Disorder with Hyperactivity—
therapy.   3. Attention Deficit Disorder with Hyperactivity—
etiology.   WS 350.8.A8 B256a 1998]
RJ496.A86B37   1998
616.85'89—dc21
DNLM/DLC
for Library of Congress   97-52762
                                                    CIP

Once again, with love,
to my sons, Steve and Ken, and my wife, Pat

CONTRIBUTORS

Arthur D. Anastopoulos, PhD, Associate Professor of Psychology, University of North Carolina at Greensboro, Greensboro, North Carolina

Russell A. Barkley, PhD, Director of Psychology and Professor of Psychiatry and Neurology, University of Massachusetts Medical Center, Worcester, Massachusetts

Joseph Biederman, MD, Professor of Psychiatry, Harvard Medical School, and Chief of the Pediatric Psychopharmacology Unit, Massachusetts General Hospital, Boston, Massachusetts

Daniel F. Connor, MD, Assistant Professor of Psychiatry, Chief, Pediatric Psychopharmacology Clinic, University of Massachusetts Medical Center, Worcester, Massachusetts

Charles E. Cunningham, PhD, Professor of Psychology, Department of Psychiatry, Chedoke–McMaster Hospitals, McMaster University Medical Centre, Hamilton, Ontario, Canada

Lesley J. Cunningham, MSW, Board of Education, City of Hamilton, Ontario, Canada

Jodi K. Dooling-Litfin, PhD, Children's Hospital of Alabama, Birmingham, Alabama

George J. DuPaul, PhD, Associate Professor of School Psychology, Department of Counseling Psychology, School Psychology, and Special Education, Lehigh University, Bethlehem, Pennsylvania

Gwenyth Edwards, PhD, Assistant Professor of Psychiatry and Chief of the Child ADHD Clinic, University of Massachusetts Medical Center, Worcester, Massachusetts

Michael Gordon, PhD, Professor of Psychiatry and Director of the ADHD Clinics, State University of New York Health Sciences Center at Syracuse, New York

William Hathaway, PhD, Assistant Professor of Psychology, Regents University, Norfolk, Virginia

Kevin R. Murphy, PhD, Assistant Professor of Psychiatry and Chief of the Adult ADHD Clinic, University of Massachusetts Medical Center, Worcester, Massachusetts

Linda J. Pfiffner, PhD, Assistant Professor of Psychiatry, University of Chicago, Chicago, Illinois

Arthur L. Robin, PhD, Director of Psychology, Children's Hospital of Michigan, and Professor of Psychiatry, Wayne State University Medical Center, Detroit, Michigan

Julianne M. Smith, graduate student, Department of Psychology, University of North Carolina at Greensboro, Greensboro, North Carolina

Thomas J. Spencer, MD, Assistant Professor of Psychiatry, Harvard Medical School and the Massachusetts General Hospital, Boston, Massachusetts

Emily E. Wien, graduate student, Department of Psychology, University of North Carolina at Greensboro, Greensboro, North Carolina

Timothy Wilens, MD, Assistant Professor of Psychiatry, Harvard Medical School and the Massachusetts General Hospital, Boston, Massachusetts

PREFACE

The intention of this book remains the same as that of its two predecessors (Barkley, 1981, 1990): to wring from the research literature as much clinically useful information as possible about the nature, diagnosis, assessment, and treatment of Attention-Deficit/Hyperactivity Disorder (ADHD). We have nearly a century of clinical papers and scientific research that serve to guide this endeavor, and we need to take advantage of it for every ounce of clinically useful information it may yield. But like the two earlier volumes, this volume is not intended as an exhaustive or a critical review of the research literature, its methodologies, or its findings on ADHD. Nevertheless, our contributors cite many research findings here that bear on clinically important information or on critical issues that arise in clinical practice with those who have ADHD. And even more than in the prior editions, this text takes a life span perspective on ADHD; a perspective made all the easier as a consequence of the increasing pace of research into the nature of ADHD as it occurs both in ADHD children followed to adulthood and in clinic-referred adults with ADHD.

The cornerstone of this text continues to be that ADHD must be viewed as a developmental disorder of behavioral inhibition, inattention, and self-regulation. New to this volume, however, is the belief that the developmental delay in inhibition gives rise to deficits in the executive functions that subserve self-regulation (Chapter 7). It is these secondary deficits that result in the inattentive, distractible, impersistent, and poorly regulated behavior of those with ADHD. The evidence accumulated over the past 20 years suggests that this view is a more accurate and heuristic one than that ADHD represents simply an attention deficit (Barkley, 1997a, 1997b). My own ongoing follow-up study with Mariellen Fischer, PhD, of more than 158 ADHD children, reviewed later in this text, resoundingly supports this perspective more than any other professional experience of my career. One cannot help but be affected by the plight of these children, the struggles of their families in coping with and managing the disorder, and the successes of many in overcoming their limitations when personally following them for a decade of their development. More strongly than before, I continue to appreciate the striking and reciprocal interplay between environmental demands and the handicapped capacities of these individuals, between social prejudice and family advocacy, and between the sincere desire to be good and the strong pull of disinhibition within these children in defining where, when, and for how long their condition will disable them. ADHD continues to cry out for broad societal recognition as a neuropsychological disorder of self-regulation with substantial genetic contributions that is shaped to its final form by the individual's unique environmental experiences. It is past the time that ADHD receive such recognition, yet it is repeatedly challenged by some members of society and the media who continue to struggle with and even deny the notion that individuals can have developmental disorders of self-regulation that are of biological origin rather than the result of purely personal, social, moral, or child-rearing factors. As long as this gross disparity exists between the deeply held societal beliefs about the purely personal and social origins of self-control and the scientific findings that contradict it, people with ADHD will continue to struggle to have their developmental disorder respected as such.

The voluminous research on ADHD continued to require that I take on for this volume the expert assistance of some of my friends and colleagues to accomplish the intended goal of this text. I am very grateful to those new contributors who agreed to prepare chapters within their areas of expertise: Gwenyth Edwards, PhD, Kevin Murphy, PhD, Michael Gordon, PhD, Tim Wilens, MD, Thomas Spencer, MD, Joseph Biederman, MD, Daniel F. Connor, MD, Jodi Dooling-Litfin, PhD, William Hathaway, PhD, Julianne Smith, and Emily Wien. And I extend my sincere appreciation to those opting to revise their original contributions: Charles Cunningham, PhD, Arthur Anastopoulos, PhD, Arthur Robin, PhD, Linda Pfiffner, PhD, and George DuPaul, PhD.

Behind any extensive endeavor such as this stands the support of one's family, and mine continues to be no exception. I remain deeply indebted to my wife and love of 29 years, Pat Gann, and my sons, Ken and Steve, for their patience with the demands of this project, for their encouragement to see it through this revision, and for the insights they give me on children and on family life. I also remain eternally grateful to the many families of ADHD children, now numbering in the thousands, whom I have had the honor and pleasure to serve over the past 25 years of clinical research and practice. As with the earlier volumes, their influence is an integral part of the fabric of this text.

During the preparation of this book, I was financially supported, in part, by grants from the National Institute of Mental Health (Nos. MH45714 and MH41583). I was also financially supported during this time by funds from the Department of Psychiatry, University of Massachusetts Medical Center. The contents of this book, however, are solely my responsibility and do not necessarily represent the official views of institutions. For all of this financial support, I am most grateful.

And finally, I must once again express my continual gratitude to Seymour Weingarten and Robert Matloff of Guilford Publications for their support of and patience with this revision, for their friendship and kindness over the past two decades, and for the highly competent and tireless work of their staff in bringing this text to fruition. There is no more attentive, supportive, enthusiastic, and professional a publishing house than this one.

RUSSELL A. BARKLEY
Worcester, Massachusetts

REFERENCES

Barkley, R. A. (1981). *Hyperactive children: A handbook for diagnosis and treatment*. New York: Guilford Press.

Barkley, R. A. (1990). *Attention-deficit hyperactivity disorder: A handbook for diagnosis and treatment*. New York: Guilford Press.

Barkley, R. A. (1997a). Behavioral inhibition, sustained attention, and executive functions: Constructing a unifying theory of attention-deficit hyperactivity disorder. *Psychological Bulletin, 121*, 65–94.

Barkley, R. A. (1997b). *ADHD and the nature of self-control*. New York: Guilford Press.

CONTENTS

ঽ

PART III. TREATMENT

Part I

NATURE AND DIAGNOSIS

Chapter 1

HISTORY

ε**ટ**

Attention-Deficit/Hyperactivity Disorder (ADHD) is the most recent diagnostic label for children presenting with significant problems with attention, impulsiveness, and overactivity. Children with ADHD represent a heterogeneous population who display considerable variation in the degree of their symptoms, in the situational pervasiveness of those symptoms, and in the extent to which other disorders occur in association with it. The disorder represents one of the most common reasons children are referred to mental health practitioners in the United States and is one of the most prevalent childhood psychiatric disorders. This chapter presents an overview of the history of this disorder; a history that spans nearly a century of clinical and scientific publications on the disorder. In this history resides the nascent concepts that serve as the foundation for the current conceptualizations of the disorder and its treatment. Such a history is important for any serious student of the disorder to appreciate for it shows that many themes concerning the nature of the disorder recurred throughout this century as clinical scientists strove for a clearer, more accurate understanding of the very essence of this condition. Other sources provide additional discussions of the history of this disorder also (Kessler, 1980; Ross & Ross, 1976, 1982; Schachar, 1986; Werry, 1992).

THE PERIOD 1900 TO 1950: THE AGE OF THE BRAIN-DAMAGED CHILD

Although one of the first references to a hyperactive or ADHD child (Fidgety Phil) seems to have been in the poems of the German physician Heinrich Hoffman in 1865, credit is typically awarded to George Still and Alfred Tredgold as being the first authors to focus serious scientific attention on the behavioral condition in children that most closely approximates what is today known as ADHD.

Still's Description

In his series of three published lectures to the Royal College of Physicians, Still (1902) described 43 children in his clinical practice who were often aggressive, defiant, resistant to discipline, and excessively emotional or "passionate" and who showed little "inhibitory vo-

3

lition." These children also manifested "lawlessness," spitefulness, cruelty, and dishonesty. He proposed the immediate gratification of the self as being the "keynote" quality of these and other attributes of the children. And among all of them, passion (or heightened emotionality) was the most commonly observed attribute and the most noteworthy. Still noted further that an insensitivity to punishment characterized many of these cases for they would be punished, evenly physically, yet engage in the same infraction within a matter of hours. And Still was particularly impressed by the serious problems with sustained attention that these cases often manifested, agreeing with William James (1890) that such attention may be another important element in the moral control of behavior. Most were also quite overactive.

Still believed these children displayed a major "defect in moral control" in their behavior that was relatively chronic in most cases. In some cases, these children acquired the defect secondary to an acute brain disease, and it might remit on recovery from the disease. In the chronic cases, research noted a higher risk for criminal acts in later development in some, though not all. Although this defect could be associated with intellectual retardation, as it was in 23 of the cases, it could also arise in children of near normal intelligence as it seemed to do in the remaining 20.

To Still (1902), the moral control of behavior meant "the control of action in conformity with the idea of the good of all" (p. 1008). Moral control was thought to arise out of a cognitive or conscious comparison of the individual's volitional activity with that of the good of all; a comparison he termed "moral consciousness." For purposes that shall become evident later, it is important to realize here that to make such a comparison inherently involves the capacity to hold in mind forms of information about oneself and one's actions, along with information on context. Those forms of information involve the action being proposed by the individual, the context, and the moral principle or rule against which it must be compared. This notion may link up Still's views with the contemporary concepts of self-awareness, working memory, and rule-governed behavior discussed later in this text. Still did not specifically identify these inherent aspects of the comparative process, but they are clearly implied in the manner in which he uses the term "conscious" in describing this process. He stipulated that this process of comparison of proposed action to a rule concerning the greater good involved the critical element of the conscious or cognitive relation of individuals to their environment, or self-awareness. Intellect was recognized as playing a part in moral consciousness but just as or more important was the notion of volition. The latter is where Still believed the impairment arose in many of those with defective moral control who suffered no intellectual delay. Volition was viewed as being primarily inhibitory in nature, that a stimulus to act must be overpowered by the stimulus of the idea of the greater good of all.

Both volitional inhibition and the moral regulation of behavior founded on it were believed to develop gradually in children; therefore younger children would find it more difficult to resist the stimulus to act on impulse than would older children. Thus, judging a child defective in volitional inhibition and moral control of behavior meant making a comparison to same-age normal children and taking into account the degree of appeal of the stimulus. Even at the same age, inhibition and moral control varied across children, in part owing to environmental factors, but also, Still proposed, to innate differences in these capacities. Still (1902) concluded that a defect in moral control could arise as a function of three distinct impairments: "(1) defect of cognitive relation to the environment; (2) defect of moral consciousness; and (3) defect in inhibitory volition" (p. 1011). He placed these impairments in a hierarchical relation to each other in the order shown, arguing that impairments in lower levels would affect those levels above it and ultimately the moral control of behavior.

Much as today, a greater proportion of males than females existed in Still's cases (3:1) and their disorder appeared to arise in most cases before 8 years of age and frequently in early childhood. Many of Still's cases displayed a higher incidence of minor anomalies in their physical appearance, or "stigmata of degeneration," such as abnormally large head size, malformed palate, or increased epicanthal fold. A proneness to accidental injuries was reported in these children as was an increased threat to the safety of other children because of their aggressive or violent behavior. Alcoholism, criminality, and affective disorders such as depression and suicide were noted to be more common among their biological relatives. Some of the children displayed a history of significant brain damage or convulsions, while others did not. A few had associated tic disorders, or "microkinesia," perhaps the first time tic disorders and ADHD were noted to be comorbid conditions. We now recognize that as many as 70% of children with tic disorders and Tourette syndrome have associated ADHD (Barkley, 1988).

Although many children were reported to have a chaotic family life, others came from households with seemingly adequate upbringing. In fact, Still believed that when poor child rearing was clearly involved, the children should be exempt from the category of lack of moral control—reserving it instead only for children who displayed a morbid failure of moral control despite adequate training. He proposed a biological predisposition to this behavioral condition that was probably hereditary in some children while the result of pre- or postnatal injury in others. In keeping with the theorizing of William James (1890), Still hypothesized that the deficits in inhibitory volition, moral control, and sustained attention were causally related to each other and to the same underlying neurological deficiency. He cautiously speculated on the possibility of either a decreased threshold for inhibition of responding to stimuli or a cortical disconnection syndrome where intellect was dissociated from "will" that may be due to neuronal cell modification. Any biologically compromising event that could cause significant brain damage (cell modification) and retardation could, he conjectured, in its milder forms lead only to this defective moral control.

Later Tredgold (1908), and much later Pasamanick, Rogers, and Lilienfeld (1956), would use such a theory of early, mild, and undetected damage to account for these developmentally late arising behavioral and learning deficiencies. Temporary improvements in conduct might be achieved by alterations in the environment or by medications, both Still and Tredgold found, but they stressed the relative permanence of the defect even in these cases. The need for special educational environments for these children was strongly emphasized. We see here the origins of many later and even current notions about ADHD and oppositional–defiant children, although it would take almost 70 years to return to the more heuristic among them. The children whom Still and Tredgold described would likely now be diagnosed as having not only ADHD but also Oppositional Defiant Disorder (ODD), or Conduct Disorder, and most likely a learning disability as well (see Chapter 6, this volume, for diagnostic criteria for these disorders).

North American Interest in ADHD

The history of interest in the precursors of ADHD in North America is frequently traced to the outbreak of an encephalitis epidemic in 1917–1918 when clinicians were presented with a number of children who survived this brain infection yet were left with significant behavioral and cognitive sequelae (Cantwell, 1981; Kessler, 1980; Stewart, 1970). Numerous papers reported these sequelae (Ebaugh, 1923; Strecker & Ebaugh, 1924; Stryker, 1925), and they included many of the characteristics we now incorporate into the concept of ADHD. Such children were described as being impaired in attention, regulation of activity, and impulsivity, as well as other cognitive abilities, including memory, and were often noted to be socially disruptive. Symptoms of oppositional and defiant behavior as well as delinquency and conduct disorder also arose in some cases. Postencephalitic Behavior Disorder, as it was called, was clearly the result of brain damage. The large number of children affected resulted in significant professional and educational interest. The severity of this behavioral syndrome was such that many children were recommended for care and education outside the home and normal educational facilities. Despite a rather pessimistic view of the prognosis of these children, some facilities reported significant success in their treatment using simple behavior modification programs and increased supervision (Bender, 1942; Bond & Appel, 1931).

The Origins of a Brain-Damage Syndrome

This association of a brain disease with behavioral pathology apparently led early investigators to study other potential causes of brain injury in children and their behavioral manifestations. Birth trauma (Shirley, 1939); other infections such as measles (Meyer & Byers, 1952), lead toxicity (Byers & Lord, 1943), epilepsy (Levin, 1938), and head injury (Blau, 1936; Werner & Strauss, 1941) were studied in children and were found to be associated with numerous cognitive and behavioral impairments, including the triad of ADHD symptoms noted earlier. Other terms introduced during this era for children displaying these behavioral characteristics were "organic driveness" (Kahn & Cohen, 1934) and "restlessness" syndrome (Childers, 1935; Levin, 1938). Many of the children seen in these samples were also mentally retarded or more seriously behaviorally disordered than are children who are today called ADHD. It would be some time before investigators would attempt to parse out the separate contributions of intellectual delay, learning disabilities, or other neuropsychological deficits from those of the behavioral deficits to the maladjustment of these children. Even so, scientists at this time would discover that activity level was often inversely related to intelligence in children, increasing as intelligence declined in a sample—a finding supported in many subsequent studies (Rutter, 1989). It should also be noted that a large number of children in these older studies were, in fact, brain damaged or had signs of such damage (epilepsy, hemiplegias, etc.).

Notable during this era was also the recognition of the striking similarity between hyperactive children and the behavioral sequelae of frontal lobe lesions in primates (Blau, 1936; Levin, 1938). Frontal lobe ablation studies of monkeys had been done since 1876 (Ferrier, 1876) and the lesions were known to result in excessive restlessness, poor ability to sustain interest in activities, aimless wandering, and excessive appetite, among other behavioral changes. Several investigators, such as Levin (1938), would use these similarities to postulate that severe restlessness in children was likely the result of pathological defects in the forebrain structures, although gross evidence of such was not always apparent in many of these children. Later investigators (e.g., Chelune, Ferguson, Koon, & Dickey, 1986; Lou, Henriksen, & Bruh, 1984; Lou, Henriksen, Bruhn, Borner, & Nielsen, 1989; Mattes, 1980) would return to this notion but with greater evidence to substantiate their claims. Milder forms of hyperactivity, in contrast, were attributed in this era to psychological causes, such as "spoiled" child-rearing practices or delinquent family environments. This theme would also be resurrected again in the 1970s and beyond.

Over the next decade, it became fashionable to consider most children hospitalized in psychiatric facilities with this symptom picture to have suffered from some type of brain damage, such as encephalitis or pre-/perinatal trauma, whether or not the clinical history of the case contained evidence of such. The concept of the "brain-injured child" was to be born in this era (Strauss & Lehtinen, 1947) and applied to children with these behavioral characteristics, many of whom had insufficient or no evidence of brain pathology. In fact, Strauss argued that the psychological disturbances alone were, de facto, evidence of brain injury as the etiology. This term would later evolve into the concept of minimal brain damage and, eventually minimal brain dysfunction (MBD) by the 1950s and 1960s. Even so, a few early voices, such as Childers (1935), would raise serious questions about the notion of brain damage in these children when no historical documentation of damage existed. Substantial recommendations for educating these "brain-damaged" children were made in the classic text by Strauss and Lehtinen (1947), which included placement in smaller, more regulated classrooms and reducing the amount of distracting stimulation in the environment. Strikingly austere classrooms were developed in which teachers could not wear jewelry or brightly colored clothing and few pictures could adorn the walls.

Although the population served by the Pennsylvania center in which Strauss, Werner, and Lehtinen worked principally contained mentally retarded children, their neuropsychological findings were later extended to cerebral palsied children of near-normal or normal intelligence by the work of Cruickshank and his students (Dolphin & Cruickshank, 1951a, 1951b, 1951c). This extension resulted in the extrapolation of the educational recommendations of Strauss to nonretarded children who manifested behavioral or perceptual disturbances (Cruickshank & Dolphin, 1951; Strauss & Lehtinen, 1947). Echoes of these recommendations are still commonplace today in most educational plans for ADHD or learning-disabled children, despite the utter lack of scientific support for their efficacy (Kessler, 1980; Routh, 1978; Zentall, 1985). These classrooms are historically significant as they were the predecessors as well as instigators of the types of educational resources that would be incorporated into the initial U.S. Public Law 94-142 mandating the special education of learning-disabled and behaviorally disorder children in 1977 and its later reauthorization, the Individuals with Disabilities in Education Act (IDEA; 1991).

Beginnings of Child Psychopharmacology with ADHD

Another significant series of papers on the treatment of hyperactive children appeared in 1937–1941. These papers were to mark the beginnings of medication therapy for behaviorally disordered children specifically as well as the field of child psychopharmacology in general (Bradley, 1937; Bradley & Bowen, 1940; Molitch & Eccles, 1937). They revealed the efficacy of the amphetamines in reducing the disruptive behavior and improving the academic performance of behaviorally disordered children hospitalized at the Emma Pendleton Bradley Home in Providence, Rhode Island. Later studies would also confirm such a positive drug response in half or more of hyperactive hospitalized children (Laufer, Denhoff, & Solomons, 1957). As a result, by the 1970s, stimulant medications had become the treatment of choice for the characteristics of ADHD. And so they remain today.

The Emergence of a Hyperkinetic Syndrome

In the 1950s, researchers began a number of investigations into the neurological mechanisms underlying these behavioral symptoms, the most famous of which was probably that by Laufer et al. (1957). These writers referred to ADHD children as having Hyperkinetic Impulse Disorder and reasoned that the central nervous system (CNS) deficit occurred in the thalamic area. Here, poor filtering of stimulation occurred, allowing an excess of stimulation to reach the brain. Their evidence was based on a study of the effects of the photo-Metrozol method in which the drug Metrozol is administered while flashes of light are presented to the child. The amount of drug required to induce a muscle jerk of the forearms along with a spike-wave pattern on the electroencephalogram serves as the measure of interest. Laufer et al. (1957) found that hyperactive inpatient children required less Metrozol than nonhyperactive inpatient children to induce this pattern of response. This finding suggested that hyperactive children had a lower threshold for stimulation in the thalamic area. The study would never be replicated, and it is unlikely that such research would pass today's standards of ethical conduct in research required by institutional review boards on research with human subjects. Nevertheless, it remains a milestone in the history of the disorder for its delineation of a more specific mechanism that might give rise to hyperactivity (cortical overstimulation). Others at the time also conjectured that an imbalance between cortical and subcortical areas existed such that there was diminished control of subcortical areas responsible for sensory filtering that permitted excess stimulation to reach the cortex (Knobel, Wolman, & Mason, 1959).

By the end of this era it seemed well-accepted that hyperactivity was a brain-damage syndrome, even when evidence of damage was lacking. The disorder was best treated through educational classrooms characterized by reduced stimulation or through residential centers. Its prognosis was considered fair to poor. The possibility that a relatively new class of medications, the stimulants, might hold promise for its treatment was only beginning to be appreciated.

THE PERIOD 1960 TO 1969: THE GOLDEN AGE OF HYPERACTIVITY

The Decline of MBD

In the late 1950s and early 1960s, critical reviews began appearing questioning the concept of a unitary syndrome of brain damage in children. They also pointed out the logical fallacy that if brain damage resulted in some of these behavioral symptoms, these symptoms could be pathognomonic of brain damage without any other corroborating evidence of CNS lesions. Chief among these critical reviews were those of Birch (1964), Herbert (1964), and Rapin (1964), who questioned the validity of applying the concept of brain damage to children who had only equivocal signs of neurological involvement, not necessarily damage. A plethora of research followed on MBD children (see Rie & Rie, 1980, for reviews); in addition, a task force by the National Institute of Neurological Diseases and Blindness (Clements, 1966) recognized at least 99 symptoms for this disorder. The concept of MBD would die a slow death as it eventually became recognized as vague, overinclusive, of little or no prescriptive value, and without much neurological evidence (Kirk, 1963). Its value remained in its emphasis on neurological mechanisms over the often excessive, pedantic, and convoluted environmental mechanisms proposed at that time, particularly those etiological hypotheses stemming from psychoanalytical theory, which blamed parental and family factors entirely for these problems (Hertzig, Bortner, & Birch, 1969; Kessler, 1980; Taylor, 1983). The term "MBD" would eventually be replaced by more specific labels applying to somewhat more homogeneous populations of cognitive, learning, and behavioral disorders, such as dyslexia, language disorders, learning disabilities, and hyperactivity. These new labels were based on the observable and descriptive deficits of the children rather than on some underlying unobservable etiological mechanism in the brain.

The Hyperactive Child Syndrome

As dissatisfaction with the term "MBD" was occurring, concurrently the concept of a hyperactive child syndrome arose, described in the classic papers by Laufer and Denhoff (1957) and Chess (1960) and other papers of this era (Burks, 1960; Ounsted, 1955; Prechtl & Stemmer, 1962). Chess defined hyperactivity as follows: "The hyperactive child is one who carries out activities at a higher than normal rate of speed than the average child, or who is constantly in motion, or both" (p. 239). Chess's article was historically significant for several reasons: (1) it emphasized activity as the defining feature of the disorder, as other scientists of the time would also do, (2) it stressed the need to consider objective evidence of the symptom beyond the subjective reports of parents or teachers, (3) it took the blame for the child's problems away from the parents, and (4) it separated the syndrome of hyperactivity from the concept of a brain-damaged syndrome. Other scientists of this era would emphasize similar points (Werry & Sprague, 1970). It would now be recognized that hyperactivity was a behavioral syndrome that could arise from organic pathology but could also occur in its absence. Even so, it would continue to be viewed as the result of some biological difficulty rather than due solely to environmental causes.

Chess described the characteristics of 36 children diagnosed with "physiological hyperactivity" from a total of 881 children seen in a private practice. The ratio of males to females was approximately 4:1 and many children were referred prior to 6 years of age, intimating a relatively earlier age of onset than other childhood behavioral disorders. Educational difficulties were common in this group, particularly scholastic underachievement, and many displayed oppositional–defiant behavior and poor peer relationships. Impulsive and aggressive behavior as well as poor attention span were commonly associated characteristics. Chess believed that the hyperactivity could also be associated with mental retardation, organic brain damage, or serious mental illness such as schizophrenia. Similar findings in later research would lead others to question the specificity and hence the utility of this symptom for the diagnosis of ADHD (Douglas, 1972). Echoing many of today's prescriptions, a multimodal treatment approach incorporating parent counseling, behavior modification, psychotherapy, medication, and special education was recommended. Unlike Still, Chess and others writing in this era stressed the relatively benign nature of these ADHD symptoms and claimed that in most cases it resolved by puberty (Laufer & Denhoff, 1957; Solomons, 1965).

Also noteworthy in this era was the definition of hyperactivity given in the official diagnostic nomenclature at the time, second edition of the *Diagnostic and Statistical Manual of Mental Disorders* (DSM-II; American Psychiatric Association, 1968). It employed only a single sentence describing the hyperkinetic reaction of childhood disorder and, following the lead of Chess, stressed the view that the disorder was developmentally benign: "The disorder is characterized by overactivity, restlessness, distractibility, and short attention span, especially in young children; the behavior usually diminishes by adolescence" (p. 50).

Europe and North America Part Company

It is perhaps during this period, or even earlier, that the perspective of hyperactivity in North America began to diverge from that in Europe, and particularly Great Britain. In North America, hyperactivity would become a behavioral syndrome recognized chiefly by greater-than-normal levels of activity, would be viewed as a relatively common disturbance of childhood, would not necessarily be associated with demonstrable brain pathology or mental retardation, and would be more of an extreme degree in the normal variation of temperament in children. In Great Britain, the narrower view would continue into the 1970s that hyperactivity or hyperkinesis was an extreme state of excessive activity of almost driven quality, was highly uncommon, and usually occurred in conjunction with other signs of brain damage, such as epilepsy, hemiplegias, retardation, or a clearer history of brain insult, such as trauma or infection (Taylor, 1988). The divergence in views would lead to large discrepancies between North America and Europe in their estimations of the prevalence of the disorder, their diagnostic criteria, and their preferred treatment modalities. A rapprochement between these views would not occur until well into the 1980s (Rutter, 1988, 1989; Taylor, 1986, 1988).

The Prevailing View by 1969

As Ross and Ross (1976) noted, the perspective on hyperactivity in this era was that it remained a brain-dysfunction syndrome, although of a milder magnitude than previously believed. The disorder was no longer ascribed to brain damage; instead a focus on brain mechanisms prevailed. The disorder was also viewed as having a predominant relatively homogeneous set of symptoms, chief among which was excessive activity level or hyperactivity. Its prognosis was now felt to be relatively benign as it was often outgrown by puberty. The recommended treatments now consisted of stimulant medication and psychotherapy in addition to the minimum-stimulation types of classrooms recommended in earlier years.

THE PERIOD 1970 TO 1979: THE ASCENDANCE OF ATTENTION DEFICITS

Research in this decade on the disorder took a quantum leap forward, with more than 2,000 published studies existing by the time the decade ended (G. Weiss & Hechtman, 1979). Numerous clinical and scientific textbooks (Cantwell, 1975; Safer & Allen, 1976; Trites, 1979; Wender, 1971) appeared along with a most thorough and scholarly review of the literature by Ross and Ross (1976). Special journal issues were devoted to the topic (Douglas, 1976; Barkley, 1978), along with numerous scientific gatherings (Knights & Bakker, 1976, 1980). Clearly, hyperactivity had become a subject of serious professional, scientific, and popular attention.

By the early 1970s, the defining features of the hyperactive or hyperkinetic child syndrome were broadened to include what investigators previously felt to be only associated characteristics, including impulsivity, short attention span, low frustration tolerance, distractibility, and aggressiveness (Marwitt & Stenner, 1972; Safer & Allen, 1976). Others (Wender, 1971, 1973) persisted with the excessively inclusive concept of MBD in which even more features, such as motor clumsiness, cognitive impairments, and parent–child conflict, were viewed as hallmarks of the syndrome and in which hyperactivity was unnecessary for the diagnosis. As noted earlier, the diagnostic term "MBD" would fade from clinical and scientific usage by the end of this decade, the result in no small part of the scholarly tome by Rie and Rie (1980) and critical reviews by Rutter (1977, 1982). These writings emphasized the lack of evidence for such a broad syndrome in that the symptoms were not well defined, did not correlate significantly among themselves, had no well-specified etiology, and displayed no common course and outcome. The heterogeneity of the disorder was overwhelming and more than a few took note of the apparent hypocrisy in defining an MBD syndrome with statements that there was often little or no evidence of neurological abnormality (Wender, 1971). Moreover, even in cases of well-established cerebral damage, the behavioral sequelae were not uniform across cases and hyperactivity was seen in only a minority. Hence, contrary to 25 years of theorizing to this point, hyperactivity was not a common sequelae of brain damage, truly brain-damaged children did not display a uniform pattern of behavioral deficits, and children with hyperactivity rarely had substantiated evidence of neurological damage (Rutter, 1989).

Wender's Theory of MBD

This decade was notable for the development of two different models of the nature of ADHD (see also Barkley, 1998): Wender's theory of MBD and Douglas's model of attention and impulse control in hyperactive children (next section). At the start of this decade, Wender

(1971) described the essential psychological characteristics of children with MBD as consisting of six clusters of symptoms: (1) motor behavior, (2) attentional–perceptual cognitive function, (3) learning difficulties, (4) impulse control, (5) interpersonal relations, and (6) emotion. Many of the characteristics first reported by Still were echoed by Wender within these six domains of functioning:

1. Within the realm of motor behavior, the essential features were noted to be hyperactivity and poor motor coordination. Excessive speech, colic, and sleeping difficulties were thought to be related to the hyperactivity. Foreshadowing the later official designation of a group of children with attentional problems who would not be hyperactive (ADD without Hyperactivity; American Psychiatric Association, 1980), Wender expressed the opinion that some of these children were hypoactive and listless while still demonstrating attentional disturbance. He argued that they should be included within this syndrome because of their manifestation of many of the other difficulties thought to characterize it.

2. Short attention span and poor concentration were described as the most striking deficit in the domain attentional and perceptual–cognitive functioning. Distractibility and daydreaming were also included with these attentional disturbances, as was poor organization of ideas or percepts.

3. Learning difficulties were the third domain of dysfunction, with most of these children observed to be doing poorly in their academic performance. A large percentage were described as having specific difficulties with learning to read, with handwriting, and with reading comprehension and arithmetic.

4. Impulse-control problems, or a decreased ability to inhibit behavior, were identified as a fourth characteristic of most MBD children. Within this general category, Wender included low frustration tolerance; an inability to delay gratification; antisocial behavior; lack of planning, forethought, or judgment; and poor sphincter control leading to enuresis and encopresis. Disorderliness, or lack of organization, and recklessness, particularly with regard to bodily safety, were also listed within this domain of dysfunction.

5. In the area of interpersonal relations, Wender singled out the unresponsiveness of these children to social demands as the most serious. Extroversion, excessive independence, obstinence, stubbornness, negativism, disobedience, noncompliance, sassiness, and an imperviousness were some of the characteristics that instantiated the problem with interpersonal relations.

6. Finally, within the domain of emotional difficulties, Wender included increased lability of mood, altered reactivity, increased anger, aggressiveness, and temper outbursts, as well as dysphoria. The dysphoria of these children involved the specific difficulties of anhedonia, depression, low self-esteem, and anxiety. A diminished sensitivity to both pain and punishment were also felt to typify this area of dysfunction in children with MBD. All these symptoms bear a striking resemblance to the case descriptions Still earlier had provided in his lectures to support his contention that a defect in moral control and volitional inhibition could exist in children apart from intellectual delay.

Wender theorized that these six domains of dysfunction could be best accounted for by three primary deficits: (1) a decreased experience of pleasure and pain, (2) a generally high and poorly modulated level of activation, and (3) extroversion. A consequence of item (1) is that MBD children would prove less sensitive to both rewards and punishments, making them less susceptible to social influence. The generally high and poorly modulated level of activation were thought to be aspects of poor inhibition. Hyperactivity, of course, was the consummate demonstration of this high level of activation. The problems with poor sustained attention and distractibility were conjectured to be secondary aspects of high activation.

Emotional overreactivity, low frustration tolerance, quickness to anger, and temper outbursts resulted from the poor modulation of activation. These three primary deficits, then, created a cascading of effects into the larger social ecology of the child, resulting in numerous interpersonal problems and academic performance difficulties.

Like Still (1902), Wender gives a prominent role to the construct of poor inhibition. He believes it to explain both the activation difficulties and the attentional problems that stem from them, as well as the excessive emotionality, low frustration tolerance, and hot temperedness of these children. It is therefore quite puzzling as to why deficient inhibition was not made to be a primary symptom in this theory in place of high activation and poor modulation of activation.

Unlike Still's attempt at a theory, however, Wender does not say much about normal developmental processes with respect to the three primary areas of deficit and thus does not clarify more precisely what may be going awry in them to give rise to these characteristics of MBD. The exception is his discussion of a diminished sensitivity of those with ADHD to the reasonably well-understood processes of reinforcement and punishment. A higher than normal threshold for pleasure and pain, as noted earlier, was thought to create these insensitivities to behavioral consequences.

Wender's theory is also unclear about a number of issues. For instance, how do the three primary deficits account for the difficulties with motor coordination that occurred alongside hyperactivity in his category of motor control problems? It is doubtful that a high level of activation that is said to cause the hyperactivity also causes these motor deficits. Nor is it clear just how the academic achievement deficits in reading, math, and handwriting can arise from the three primary deficits in the model. It is also unclear why the construct of extroversion needs to be proposed at all if what is meant by its use is reduced social inhibition. This model might be just as parsimoniously explained by the deficit in behavioral inhibition already posited. And the meaning of the term "activation" in the model is not very clearly specified. Does it refer to excessive behavior, in which case hyperactivity would have sufficed? Or does it refer to level of CNS arousal, in which case ample subsequent evidence has not found this to be the case (Hastings & Barkley, 1978; Rosenthal & Allen, 1978)? To his credit, Wender recognized the abstract nature of the term "activation" as he employed it in this theory but retained it as he felt it could be used to incorporate both the hyperactive and hypoactive child. It is never made clear just how this could be the case, however.

From the advantage of hindsight and subsequent research over the past 26 years since the formulation of this theory, it is also evident that Wender is combining the symptoms of ODD (and even Conduct Disorder) with those of ADHD to form a single disorder. Still (1902) did very much the same thing, which is understandable given that clinic-referred cases were the starting point for both theories, and many clinic-referred cases are comorbid for both disorders (ADHD/ODD). Sufficient evidence now exists, however, to show that these are not the same disorder (August & Stewart, 1983; Hinshaw, 1987; Stewart, deBlois, & Cummings, 1980).

The Emergence of Attention Deficits

At this time, disenchantment with the exclusive focus on hyperactivity developed as the *sine qua non* of this disorder (Werry & Sprague, 1970). Significant at this historical juncture would be the presidential address of Virginia Douglas to the Canadian Psychological Association (Douglas, 1972), in which she argued that deficits in sustained attention and impulse control were more likely to account for the difficulties seen in these children than just hyperactivity. These other symptoms were also seen as the major areas of impact of the stimulant medications used to treat the disorder. Douglas's paper is historically significant in other ways as well. Her extensive and thorough battery of objective measures of various behavioral and cognitive domains allowed her to rule in or out various characteristics felt to be typical for these children in earlier clinical and scientific lore. For instance, Douglas found that hyperactive children were not necessarily more reading or learning disabled, did not perseverate on concept learning tasks, did not manifest auditory or right–left discrimination problems, and had no difficulties with short-term memory. Most important, she and Susan Campbell demonstrated that hyperactive children were not more distractible than normal children and that the sustained attention problems could emerge in conditions in which no significant distractions existed.

The McGill research team repeatedly demonstrated that hyperactive children had some of their greatest difficulties on tasks assessing vigilance, or sustained attention, such as the continuous performance test (CPT). These findings would be repeatedly reconfirmed over the next 20 years of research using CPTs (Corkum & Siegel, 1993). This test would eventually be standardized and commercially marketed for diagnosis of the disorder (Conners, 1995; Gordon, 1983; Greenberg & Waldman, 1992). Douglas remarked on the extreme degree of variability demonstrated during task performances by these children—a characteristic that would later be advanced as one of the defining features of the disorder. The McGill team (Freibergs, 1965; Freibergs & Douglas, 1969; Parry & Douglas, 1976) also found that hyperactive children could perform at normal or near-normal levels of sustained attention under conditions of continuous and immediate reinforcement but their performance deteriorated dramatically when partial reinforcement was introduced, particularly at schedules below 50% reinforcement. Campbell (Campbell, Douglas, & Morgenstern, 1971) further demonstrated substantial problems with impulse control and field dependence in the cognitive styles of hyperactive children. Like George Still 70 years earlier, Douglas commented on the probable association between deficits in attention/impulse control and deficiencies in moral development that were plaguing her subjects, particularly in their adolescent years. The research of the McGill team showed dramatic improvements in these attention deficiencies during stimulant medication treatment, as did the research at other laboratories at the time (Conners & Rothschild, 1968; Sprague, Barnes, & Werry, 1970). Finally, of substantial significance were the observations of Douglas's colleague, Gabrielle Weiss, from her follow-up studies (see G. Weiss & Hechtman, 1986) that although the hyperactivity of these children often diminished by adolescece, their problems with poor sustained attention and impulsivity persisted. This persistence of the disabilities and the risk for greater academic and social maladjustment would be sounded by other research teams from their own follow-up investigations (Mendelson, Johnson, & Stewart, 1971) and would be better substantiated by more rigorous studies in the next decade (see Barkley, Fischer, Edelbrock, & Smallish, 1990; Brown & Borden, 1986; Gittelman, Mannuzza, Shenker, & Bonagura 1985).

Douglas's Model of Attention Deficits

Douglas (1980a, 1980b, 1983; Douglas & Peters, 1979) later elaborated, refined, and further substantiated her model of hyperactivity; thus, her model culminated in the view that four major deficits could account for symptoms of ADHD: (1) the investment, organization, and maintenance of attention and effort; (2) the inhibition of impulsive responding; (3) the modulation of arousal levels to meet situational demands; and (4) an unusually strong inclination to seek immediate reinforcement. This perspective initiated or guided a substantial amount of research over the next 15 years, including my own (Barkley, 1977, 1989; Barkley & Ullman, 1975), constituting a model as close to a scientific paradigm as the field of hyperactivity is likely to have in its history to date. Yet, over the next 10 years results emerged that were somewhat at odds with this perspective. Scientists began to seriously question the adequacy of an attentional model in accounting for the behavioral deficits seen in ADHD children as well as for the effects of stimulant medications on them (Barkley, 1981, 1984; Draeger, Prior, & Sanson, 1986; Haenlein & Caul, 1987; van der Meere & Sergeant, 1988a, 1988b).

Douglas's paper and the subsequent research published by the team of students and colleagues working with her at McGill University were so influential that they were probably the major reason the disorder was renamed Attention-Deficit Disorder (ADD) in 1980 with the publication of DSM-III (American Psychiatric Association, 1980). In this revised official taxonomy, deficits in sustained attention and impulse control were formally recognized as of greater significance in the diagnosis than hyperactivity. The shift to attention deficits rather than hyperactivity as the major difficulty of these children was useful, at least for a time, because of the growing evidence that hyperactivity was not specific to this particular condition but could be noted in other psychiatric disorders (anxiety, mania, autism, etc.), that there was no clear delineation between normal and abnormal levels of activity, that activity was in fact a multidimensional construct, and that the symptoms of hyperactivity were quite situational in nature in many children (Rutter, 1989). But this approach only corrected the problem of definition for little over a decade before these same concerns also began to be raised about the construct of attention (multidimensional, situationally variable, etc.). Yet, some research would show that at least deficits in vigilance or sustained attention could be used to discriminate this disorder from other psychiatric disorders (Werry, 1988).

Other Historical Developments

A number of other historical developments during this period deserve mention.

The Rise of Medication Therapy

One of these developments was the rapidly increasing use of stimulant medication with school-age hyperactive children. This use was no doubt spawned by the significant increase in research on the effects, often dramatic, of stimulants on hyperactive children. A second development was the use of much more rigorous scientific methodology in drug studies, due in large measure to the early studies by C. Keith Conners then working with Leon Eisenberg at Harvard, and somewhat later to the research of Robert Sprague at the University of Illinois, Virginia Douglas at McGill University, and John Werry in New Zealand. This body of literature became voluminous (Barkley, 1977; Ross & Ross, 1976), with more than 120 studies published through 1976 and more than twice this number by 1995 (Swanson, McBurnett, Christian, & Wigal, 1995), making this treatment approach the most well-studied therapy in child psychiatry. Despite the proven efficacy of this approach, public and professional misgivings about its increasingly widespread use with children emerged. In an incident in Omaha, Nebraska (Maynard, 1970), news accounts reported that as many as 5–10% of the children in grade schools were receiving behavior-modifying drugs. These estimates of drug treatment would later be shown to be grossly exaggerated by as much as tenfold. And, this is certainly not the last instance of the media's penchant for hyperbole and scandal in their accounts of stimulant medication treatments for ADHD—a penchant that seems to only have increased over the past 28 years. Yet the public interest that arose around the initial reports led to a congressional review of the use of psychotropic medications for schoolchildren. At this same time, the claim was being advanced that hyperactivity was a "myth" arising from intolerant teachers and parents and an inadequate educational system (Conrad, 1975; Schrag & Divoky, 1975).

Environment as Etiology

Almost simultaneous with this backlash against "drugging" schoolchildren for behavior problems came another significant development in this decade: a growing belief that hyperactivity was a result of environmental causes. It is not just coincidental that this development occurred at the same time the United States was experiencing a popular interest in natural foods, health consciousness, and the extension of life expectancy via environmental manipulations. An extremely popular view was that allergic or toxic reaction to food additives, such as dyes, preservatives, and salicylates (Feingold, 1975), caused hyperactive behavior. It was claimed that more than half of all hyperactive children had developed their difficulties because of their diet. Effective treatment could be had if families of these children would buy or make foods that did not contain the offending substances. This view became so widespread that organized parent groups, or Feingold associations, composed mainly of parents advocating Feingold's diet, were established in almost every state within the United States, and legislation was introduced, although not passed, in California requiring that all school cafeteria foods be prepared without these substances. A sizable number of research investigations were undertaken (see Conners, 1980, for a review), the more rigorous of which found these substances to have little if any effect on children's behavior. A National Advisory Committee on Hyperkinesis and Food Additives (1980) was convened to review this literature and concluded more strongly than Conners that the evidence available clearly refuted Feingold's claims. Nevertheless, it would be more than 10 years before this notion receded in popularity, to be replaced by the equally unsupported hypothesis that refined sugar was more to blame for hyperactivity than were food additives (see Milich, Wolraich, & Lindgren, 1986; Wolraich, Wilson, & White, 1995, for reviews).

The emphasis on environmental causes, however, spread to possible sources other than diet. Block (1977) advanced the notion that technological development and more rapid cultural change would result in an increasing societal "tempo" causing growing excitation or environmental stimulation. This excitation or stimulation would interact with a predisposition in some children toward hyperactivity, making it manifest. It was felt that this theory explained the apparently increasing incidence of hyperactivity in developed cultures. Ross and Ross (1982) provided an excellent critique of the theory and concluded that there was insufficient evidence in support of it and some that would contradict it. Little evidence suggested that hyperactivity was increasing or that its prevalence varied as a function of societal development. Instead, Ross and Ross proposed that cultural effects on hyperactivity have more to do with whether important institutions of enculturation are consistent or inconsistent in the demands made and standards set for child behavior and development. These cultural views it is said determine the threshold for deviance that will be tolerated in children as well as exaggerate a predisposition to hyperactivity in some children. Consistent cultures will have fewer children diagnosed with hyperactivity as they minimize individual differences among children and provide clear and consistent expectations and consequences for behavior that conforms to the expected norms. Inconsistent cultures by contrast will have more children diagnosed as hyperactive as they maximize or stress individual differences and provide ambiguous expectations and consequences to children regarding appropriate conduct. This intriguing hypothesis remains unstudied. However, on these grounds an equally compelling case could be made for the opposite effects of cultural influences in that in highly consistent, high conforming cultures, hyperactive behavior will be considerably more obvious in children as they are unable to conform to these societal expectations, whereas inconsistent and low-conforming cultures might tolerate deviant behavior to a greater degree.

A different environmental view was advanced by schools of psychology/psychiatry at diametrically opposite poles—that poor child rearing generally and child behavior management specifically lead to hyperactivity. Both psychoanalysts (Bettelheim, 1973; Harticollis, 1968) and behaviorists (Willis & Lovaas, 1977) promulgated this view, the former claiming that parents who are intolerant of negative or hyperactive temperament in their infants would react with excessively negative, demanding parental responses giving rise to clinical levels of hyperactivity. The latter, behavioral view stressed poor conditioning of children to stimulus control by commands and instructions that would give rise to noncompliant and hyperactive behavior. Both could derive some support from prospective studies that found negative mother–child interactions in the preschool years to be associated with the continuation of hyperactivity into the late childhood (Campbell, 1987) and adolescent (Barkley et al., 1990) years. However, such correlational data do not prove that poor child rearing or negative parent–child interactions cause hyperactivity but are only associated with its persistence. It could just as easily be that the severity of hyperactivity elicits greater maternal negative reactions, and it is this severity that is related to persistence of the disorder over time. Supporting this interpretation are the studies of stimulant drug effects on the interactions of mothers and their hyperactive children, which show that mothers' negative and directive behavior is greatly reduced when stimulant medication is used to reduce the hyperactivity in their children (Barkley, 1989b; Barkley & Cunningham, 1979; Barkley, Karlsson, Pollard, & Murphy, 1985; Danforth, Barkley, & Stokes, 1991). Moreover, follow-up studies also show that the degree of hyperactivity in childhood is predictive of its persistence into later childhood and adolescence (Barkley et al., 1990; Campbell & Ewing, 199). And given the dramatic hereditary contribution to ADHD, it is also just as likely that the more negative, impulsive, emotional, and inattentive behavior of mothers with their hyperactive children in part stems from the parents' own ADHD, a factor that has never been taken into account in the analysis of such data or in interpreting findings in this area. Nevertheless, family context would still prove to be important in predicting the outcome of hyperactive children, even though the mechanism of its action was not yet specified (G. Weiss & Hechtman, 1986). Furthermore, parent training in child behavior management would be increasingly recommended as an important therapy in its own right (Dubey & Kaufman, 1978; Pelham, 1977) despite a paucity of studies concerning its actual efficacy at the time (Barkley, 1989a).

The Passage of Public Law 94-142

Another significant development was the passage of Public Law 94-142 in 1975, mandating special educational services for handicapping and behavioral disabilities of children in addition to those already available for mental retardation (see Henker & Whalen, 1980, for a review of the legal precedents leading up to this law). Although many of its recommendations were foreshadowed by Section 504 of the Rehabilitation Act of 1973 (PL 93-112), it was the financial incentives for the state associated with the adoption of Public Law 94-142 that probably encouraged its immediate and widespread implementation by the states. Programs for learning disabilities, behavioral–emotional disturbance, language disorders, physical handicaps, and motor disabilities, among others, were now required to be provided to all eligible children in all public schools in the United States. The full impact of these widely available educational treatment programs on hyperactive children cannot yet be completely appreciated for several reasons. First, hyperactivity, by itself, was overlooked in the criteria set forth for behavioral and learning disabilities warranting eligibility for these special classes. Such children must typically also have another condition, such as a learning disability, language delay, or emotional disorder, to receive exceptional educational services. The effects of special educational resources on the outcome of hyperactivity are difficult to assess given this confounding of multiple disorders. It was only in 1991 that the Department of Education and its Office of Special Education chose to reinterpret its regulations, thereby allowing

ADHD children to receive special educational services for this disorder under the "Other Health Impaired" category of this law. And, second, the mandated services have little more than a decade of existence, thus, long-term outcome studies begun in the late 1970s are only now being reported. Those that were reported (Barkley et al., 1990) suggest that over 35% of ADHD children receive some type of special educational placement. Although the availability of these services seems to have reduced the percentage of ADHD children being retained in grade for their academic problems when compared to earlier followup studies, the rates of school suspensions and expulsions have not declined appreciably from pre-1977 rates. A more careful analysis of the effects of Public Law 94-142, and its more recent reauthorization as the IDEA, is in order before its efficacy for ADHD children can be judged.

The Rise of Behavior Modification

This growing emphasis on educational intervention for behavioral- and learning-disordered children was accompanied by a plethora of research on the use of behavior modification techniques in the management of disruptive classroom behavior, particularly as an alternative to stimulant medication (Allyon, Layman, & Kandel, 1975; O'Leary, Pelham, Rosenbaum, & Price, 1976). Although the studies demonstrated considerable efficacy of these techniques in the management of inattentive and hyperactive behavior, they were not found to achieve the same degree of behavioral improvement as the stimulants (Gittelman-Klein et al., 1976) and so did not replace them as a treatment of choice. Nevertheless, a growing opinion would be that the stimulant drugs should never be used as a sole intervention but should be combined with parent training and behavioral intervention in the classroom.

Developments in Assessment

Another hallmark of this era was the widespread adoption of the parent and teacher rating scales developed by C. Keith Conners (1969) for the assessment of symptoms of hyperactivity, particularly during trials on stimulant medication. For at least 20 years, these simply constructed ratings of behavioral items would be the "gold standard" for selecting children as hyperactive for both research purposes and treatment with medication. Large-scale normative data were collected, particularly for the teacher scale, and epidemiological studies throughout the world relied on them for assessing the prevalence of hyperactivity in their populations. Their use moved the practice of diagnosis and assessment of treatment effects from that of clinical impression alone to one in which at least some more structured and semiobjective and quantitative measure of behavioral deviance was employed. These scales would later be criticized for their confounding of hyperactivity with aggression. This confounding called into question whether the findings of research that relied on the scales were the result of oppositional–defiant–hostile (aggression) features of the population or of their hyperactivity (Ullmann, Sleator, & Sprague, 1984). Nevertheless, the widespread adoption of these rating scales in this era marks an historical turning point toward the use of structured, quantitative assessment methods that can be empirically tested and can assist in determining developmental deviance.

Also significant during this decade was the effort to study the social–ecological impact of hyperactive/inattentive behavior. This line of research set about evaluating the effects produced on family interactions by the hyperactive child. Originally initiated by Campbell (1973, 1975), this line of inquiry dominated my own research over the next decade (Barkley & Cunningham, 1979; Cunningham & Barkley, 1978, 1979; Danforth et al., 1991), particularly evaluating the effects of stimulant medication on these social exchanges. These studies showed that hyperactive children were much less compliant and more oppositional during parent–

child exchanges than normal children and that their mothers were more directive, command-ing, and negative than mothers of normal children. These difficulties would increase sub-stantially when the situation changed from free play to task-oriented demands. Studies also demonstrated that stimulant medication resulted in significant improvements in child com-pliance and decreases in maternal control and directiveness. Simultaneously, Humphries, Kinsbourne, and Swanson (1978) reported similar effects of stimulant medication, all of which suggested that much of parental controlling and negative behavior toward hyperac-tive children was the result rather than the cause of the children's poor self-control and in-attention. At the same time, Carol Whalen and Barbara Henker at the University of Califor-nia, Irvine, demonstrated similar interactional conflicts between hyperactive children and their teachers and peers as well as similar effects of stimulant medication on these social in-teractions (Whalen & Henker, 1980; Whalen, Henker, & Dotemoto, 1980). This line of re-search would increase substantially in the next decade.

A Focus on Psychophysiology

The 1970s also were noteworthy for an explosion in the number of research studies on the psychophysiology of hyperactivity in children. Numerous studies were published measur-ing galvanic skin response, heart rate acceleration and deceleration, various parameters of the electroencephalogram, electropupillography, averaged evoked responses, and other as-pects of electrophysiology in hyperactive children. Many were investigating the evidence for theories of over- or underarousal of the CNS in hyperactivity that grew out of the specula-tions in the 1950s on cortical overstimulation. Most studies were seriously methodologically flawed, difficult to interpret, and often contradictory in their findings. Two influential re-views at the time (Hastings & Barkley, 1978; Rosenthal & Allen, 1978) were highly critical of most investigations but concluded that if there was any consistency across findings, it might be that hyperactive children showed a sluggish or underreactive electrophysiologi-cal response to stimulation. This view laid to rest the belief in an overstimulated cerebral cortex as the cause of the symptoms in hyperactive children but did little to suggest a spe-cific neurophysiological mechanism for this underreactivity. Further advances in the contributions of psychophysiology to understanding hyperactivity would await further re-finements in instrumentation and in definition and diagnosis of the disorder along with advances in computer-assisted analysis of electrophysiological measures.

An Emerging Interest in Adult MBD/Hyperactivity

Finally, this decade should be credited with the emergence of clinical and research interests in the existence of MBD or hyperactivity in adult clinical patients. Initial interest in adult MBD can be traced back to the latter part of the 1960s, seemingly arising as a result of two events. The first of these was the publication of several early follow-up studies demonstrat-ing persistence of symptoms of hyperactivity/MBD into adulthood in many cases (Mendelson et al., 1971; Menkes, Rowe, & Menkes, 1967). The second was the publication by Harticollis (1968) of the results of neuropsychological and psychiatric assessments of 15 adolescent and young adult patients (ages 15–25) seen at the Menninger Clinic whose neuropsychological performance suggested evidence of moderate brain damage. Their behavioral profile sug-gested many of the symptoms that Still initially identified in ADHD children, particularly impulsiveness, overactivity, concreteness, mood lability, and proneness to aggressive behavior and depression. Some of the cases appeared to have demonstrated this behavior uniformly since childhood. Horticollis speculated that this condition arose from an early and possibly congenital defect in the ego apparatus in interaction with busy, action-oriented, successful parents.

The following year, Quitkin and Klein (1969) reported on two behavioral syndromes in adults that may be related to MBD. The authors studied 105 patients at the Hillside Hospital in Glen Oaks, New York, for behavioral signs of organicity (brain damage), behavioral syndromes that might be considered soft neurological signs of CNS impairment, as well as the results of electroencephalogram (EEG), psychological testing, and clinical presentation and history that might differentiate these patients from other types of adult psychopathology. From this group of patients, the authors selected those having a childhood history that suggested CNS damage, including early hyperactive and impulsive behavior. These subjects were further sorted into three groups based on current behavioral profiles: those having socially awkward and withdrawn behavior ($N = 12$), those having impulsive and destructive behavior ($N = 19$), and a "borderline" group that did not fit neatly into these other two groups ($N = 11$). The results indicated that nearly twice as many of these "organic" groups had EEG abnormalities and impairments on psychological testing indicating organicity as did the control group. Early history of hyperactive–impulsive–inattentive behavior was highly predictive of placement in the adult impulsive–destructive group, implying a persistent course of this behavioral pattern from childhood to adulthood. Of the 19 patients in the impulsive–destructive group, 17 had received a clinical diagnosis of Character Disorder (primarily emotionally unstable types) as compared to only 5 in the socially awkward group (which were of the schizoid and passive dependent types).

The results were interpreted as being in conflict with the widely held beliefs at the time that hyperactive–impulsive behavior tends to wane in adolescence, instead arguing that some of these children continued into young adulthood with this specific behavioral syndrome. Quitkin and Klein (1969) also took issue with Harticollis's hypothesis that demanding, perfectionistic child rearing by parents was associted with this syndrome as their impulsive–destructive patients did not uniformly experience such an upbringing. In keeping with Still's original belief that family environment could not account for this syndrome, the authors hypothesized "that such parents would intensify the difficulty, but are not necessary to the formation of the impulsive–destructive syndrome" (p. 140) and that the "illness shaping role of the psycho-social environment may have been over-emphasized by other authors" (p. 141). Treatment with a well-structured set of demands and educational procedures as well as with phenothiazine medication was thought to be indicated.

Later into this decade, Morrison and Minkoff (1975) similarly argued that adult patients with explosive personality disorder or episodic dyscontrol syndrome may well be the adult sequel to the hyperactive child syndrome. They also suggested that antidepressant medications might be useful in their management, echoing the same suggestion made earlier by Huessy (1974) in a letter to the editor of a journal that both antidepressants and stimulants may be the most useful medications for the treatment of these hyperkinetic or MBD adults. But the first truly scientific evaluation of the efficacy of stimulants with adults having MBD must be credited to Wood, Reimherr, Wender, and Johnson (1976), who used a double-blind, placebo-controlled method to assess response to methylphenidate in 11 of 15 adults with MBD followed by an open trial of pemoline, imipramine, and amitryptiline. The authors found that 8 of the 11 tested on methylphenidate had a favorable response whereas 10 of the 15 tested in the open trial showed a positive response to either the stimulants or antidepressants. Others in this decade and into the next would also make the case for the existence of an adult equivalent of childhood hyperkinesis or MBD and the efficacy of using stimulants and antidepressants for its management (Gomez, Janowsky, Zetin, Huey, & Clopton, 1981; Mann & Greenspan, 1976; Packer, 1978; Pontius, 1973; Rybak, 1977; Shelley & Reister, 1972).

Yet it would not be until the 1990s that the clinical practice of adult psychiatry would begin to recognize the adult equivalent of childhood ADHD on a more widespread basis and to recommend stimulant or antidepressant treatment in these cases (Spencer et al., 1995; Wender, 1995), but even then not without its skeptics (Shaffer, 1994).

The work of Pontius (1973) in this decade is historically notable for her proposition that many cases of adult MBD demonstrating hyperactive and impulsive behavior may arise from frontal lobe and caudate dysfunction. Such dysfunction would lead to "an inability to construct plans of action ahead of the act, to sketch out a goal of action, to keep it in mind for some time (as an overriding idea) and to follow it through in actions under the constructive guidance of such planning" (p. 286). Moreover, if adult MBD arises from dysfunction in this frontal-caudate network, it should also be associated with an inability "to re-program an ongoing activity and to shift within *principles* of action whenever necessary" (p. 286). She went on to show that indeed adults with MBD demonstrated such deficits indicative of dysfunction in this brain network. Such observations would prove quite prophetic when, 23 years later, research demonstrated reduced size in the prefrontal–caudate network in children with ADHD (Castellanos et al., 1996; Filipek et al., 1997) and theories of ADHD argued that the neuropsychological deficits associated with it involved the executive functions, such as planning, the control of behavior by mentally represented information, rule-governed behavior, and response fluency and flexibility, among others (Barkley 1997a, 1997b).

The Prevailing View by 1979

The decade closed with the prevailing view that hyperactivity was not the only or most important behavioral deficit seen in hyperactive children but poor attention span and impulse control were equally if not more important in explaining their problems. Brain damage was relegated to an extremely minor role as a cause of the disorder, at least in the realm of childhood hyperactivity/MBD, although other brain mechanisms, such as underarousal or underreactivity, brain neurotransmitter deficiencies (Wender, 1971), or neurological immaturity (Kinsbourne, 1977) were viewed as promising. A greater appreciation for potential environmental causes or irritants emerged, particularly diet and child rearing. Thus, the most recommended therapies for hyperactivity were not only stimulant medication but widely available special education programs, classroom behavior modification, dietary management, and parent training in child management skills. A greater appreciation for the effects of hyperactive children on their immediate social ecology was beginning to emerge, as was the impact of stimulant medication in altering these social conflicts. However, the sizable discrepancy in North American and European views of the disorder remained, with North American professionals continuing to recognize the disorder as more common, in need of medication, and more likely being an attentional deficit while those in Europe viewed it as uncommon, defined by severe overactivity, and associated with brain damage. Those children in North America being diagnosed as hyperactive or attention deficit would likely be diagnosed as conduct disorder in Europe where treatment would be psychotherapy, family therapy, and parent training in child management and medication would be little used. Nevertheless, the view that attentional deficits were equally as important in the disorder as hyperactivity was beginning to make its way into European taxonomies (e.g., *International Classification of Diseases*, ninth revision [ICD-9], World Health Organization, 1978). Finally, some recognition occurred in this decade that there were adult equivalents of childhood hyperactivity or MBD that they might be indicative of frontal-caudate dysfunction, and that these cases responded to the same medication treatments that had earlier been suggested for childhood ADHD—the stimulants and antidepressants.

THE PERIOD 1980 TO 1989: THE AGE
OF DIAGNOSTIC CRITERIA AND THE RISE
AND FALL OF ATTENTION DEFICITS

The exponential increase in research on hyperactivity characteristic of the 1970s continued unabated into the 1980s, making hyperactivity the most well-studied childhood psychiatric disorder in existence. More books were written, conferences convened, and scientific papers presented during this decade than in any previous historical period. This decade would become known for its emphasis on attempts to develop more specific diagnostic criteria, the differential conceptualization and diagnosis of hyperactivity from other psychiatric disorders, and, later in the decade, critical attacks on the notion that inability to sustain attention was the core behavioral deficit in ADHD.

The Creation of an ADD Syndrome

Marking the beginning of this decade was the publication of DSM-III (American Psychiatric Association, 1980) and its radical reconceptualization (from that in DSM-II) of Hyperkinetic Reaction of Childhood to Attention-Deficit Disorder (with or without Hyperactivity). These criteria are set forth in Table 1.1. The new diagnostic criteria were noteworthy not only for their greater emphasis on inattention and impulsivity as defining features of the disorder but also for their creation of much more specific symptom lists, numerical cutoff scores for symptoms, guidelines for age of onset and duration of symptoms, and the exclusion of other childhood psychiatric conditions as essential to defining the disorder. This was also a radical departure from the ICD–9 criteria set forth by the World Health Organization (1978) in its own taxonomy of child psychiatric disorders which continued to emphasize pervasive hyperactivity as a hallmark of this disorder.

Even more controversial was the creation of subtypes of ADD based on the presence or absence of hyperactivity (+H/–H) in the DSM-III criteria. Little, if any, empirical research had existed at the time these subtypes were formulated. Their creation in the official nomenclature of psychiatric disorders would, by the end of this decade, initiate numerous research studies into the validity and utility of this subtyping approach along with a search for other useful ways of subtyping ADD (situational pervasiveness, presence of aggression, stimulant drug response, etc.). Although at times conflicting, the trend in the findings of these studies was that children with ADD–H differed from those with ADD+H in important domains of current adjustment. Those with ADD–H were characterized as more daydreamy, hypoactive, lethargic, and learning disabled in academic achievement but substantially less aggressive and less rejected by their peers (Barkley, Grodzinsky, & DuPaul, 1992; Carlson, 1986; Goodyear & Hynd, 1992; Lahey & Carlson, 1992). Unfortunately, this research came too late to be considered in the subsequent revision of DSM.

In DSM-III-R (American Psychiatric Association, 1987), shown later in Table 1.2, only diagnostic criteria for ADD+H were stipulated. ADD–H would no longer be officially recognized as a subtype of ADD but would be relegated to a minimally defined category: Undifferentiated ADD. This reorganization was associated with an admonition that far more research on the utility of this subtyping approach was necessary before its place in this taxonomy could be identified. Despite the controversy that arose over the demotion of ADD–H in this fashion, it would actually be a prudent gesture on the part of the committee asked to formulate these criteria. At the time, the committee had little available research to guide its deliberations in this matter. There was simply no indication whether ADD–H had a similar or qualitatively different type of attentional deficit, which would make it a separate childhood psychiatric disorder

TABLE 1.1. DSM-III Diagnostic Criteria for Attention Deficit Disorder with and without Hyperactivity

The child displays, for his or her mental and chronological age, signs of developmentally inappropriate inattention, impulsivity, and hyperactivity. The signs must be reported by adults in the child's environment, such as parents and teachers. Because the symptoms are typically variable, they may not be observed directly by the clinician. When the reports of teachers and parents conflict, primary consideration should be given to the teacher reports because of greater familiarity with age-appropriate norms. Symptoms typically worsen in situations that require self-application, as in the classroom. Signs of the disorder may be absent when the child is in a new or a one-to-one situation.

The number of symptoms specified is for children between the ages of eight and ten, the peak age for referral. In younger children, more severe forms of the symptoms and a greater number of symptoms are usually present. The opposite is true of older children.

A. *Inattention.* At least three of the following:

    (1) often fails to finish things he or she starts
    (2) often doesn't seem to listen
    (3) easily distracted
    (4) has difficulty concentrating on schoolwork or other tasks requiring sustained attention
    (5) has difficulty sticking to a play activity

B. *Impulsivity.* At least three of the following:

    (1) often acts before thinking
    (2) shifts excessively from one activity to another
    (3) has difficulty organizing work (this not being due to cognitive impairment).
    (4) needs a lot of supervision
    (5) frequently calls out in class
    (6) has difficulty awaiting turn in games or group situations

C. *Hyperactivity.* At least two of the following:

    (1) runs about or climbs on things excessively
    (2) has difficulty sitting still or fidgets excessively
    (3) has difficulty staying seated
    (4) moves about excessively during sleep
    (5) is always "on the go" or acts as if "driven by a motor"

D. Onset before the age of seven.

E. Duration of at least six months.

F. Not due to Schizophrenia, Affective Disorder, or Severe or Profound Mental Retardation.

Note. From American Psychiatric Association (1980). Copyright 1980 by the American Psychiatric Association. Reprinted by permission.

in its own right. Rather than continue to merely conjecture about the nature of the subtype and how it should be diagnosed, the committee essentially placed the concept in abeyance until more research was available to its successor committee to guide its definition. Notable in the construction of DSM-III-R was its emphasis on the empirical validation of its diagnostic criteria through a field trial that guided the selection of items for the symptom list and the recommended cutoff score on that list (Spitzer, Davies, & Barkley, 1990).

The Development of Research Diagnostic Criteria

At the same time that the DSM-III criteria for ADD (+/–H) were gaining in recognition, others attempted to specify research diagnostic criteria (Barkley, 1982; Loney, 1983). My own efforts in this endeavor were motivated by the rather idiosyncratic and highly variable approach to diagnosis being used in clinical practice up to that time, the vague or often unspecified criteria used in published research studies, and the lack of specificity in current theoretical writings on the disorder up to 1980. There was also the more pragmatic consideration that as a young scientist attempting to select hyperactive children for research studies, I had no operational or consensus criteria available for doing so. Therefore, I set forth a more operational definition of hyperactivity, or ADD+H, which not only required the usual parent and/or teacher complaints of inattention, impulsivity, and overactivity but also stipulated that these symptoms had to (1) be deviant for the child's mental age as measured by well-standardized child behavior rating scales, (2) be relatively pervasive within the jurisdiction of the major caregivers in the child's life (parent/home and teacher/school), (3) have developed by 6 years of age, and (4) have lasted at least 12 months (Barkley, 1982).

Concurrently, Loney (1983) and her colleagues had been engaged in a series of historically important studies that would differentiate the symptoms of hyperactivity or ADD+H from those of aggression or conduct problems (Loney, Langhorne, & Peternite, 1978; Loney & Milich, 1982). Following an empirical/statistical approach to developing research diagnostic criteria, Loney demonstrated that a relatively short list of symptoms of hyperactivity could be empirically separated from a similarly short list of aggression symptoms. Empirically derived cutoff scores on these symptom ratings by teachers could create these two semi-independent constructs. These constructs would prove highly useful in accounting for much of the heterogeneity and disagreement across studies in their findings. Among other things, it would become well-established that many of the negative outcomes of hyperactivity in adolescence and young adulthood were actually due to the presence and degree of aggression that coexisted with the hyperactivity. Purely hyperactive children would be shown to display substantial cognitive problems with attention and overactivity whereas purely aggressive children did not. Previous findings of greater family psychopathology in hyperactive children would also be shown to be primarily a function of the degree of aggression or conduct disorder in the children (August & Stewart, 1983; Lahey et al., 1988). Furthermore, hyperactivity would be found to be associated with signs of developmental and neurological delay or immaturity whereas aggression was more likely to be associated with environmental disadvantage and family dysfunction (Hinshaw, 1987; Milich & Loney, 1979; Paternite & Loney, 1980; Rutter, 1989; Werry, 1988; G. Weiss & Hechtman, 1986). The need for future studies to clearly specify the makeup of their samples along these two dimensions was now obvious and the raging debate as to whether hyperactivity was separate from or merely synonymous with conduct problems would be settled by this important research discovery (Ross & Ross, 1982). These findings would also lead to the demise of the commonplace use of the Conners 10-item Hyperactivity Index to select children as hyperactive. It would now be shown that many of these items actually assessed aggression rather than hyperactivity, resulting in samples of children with mixed disorders (Ullmann et al., 1984).

The laudable drive toward greater clarity, specificity, and operationalization of diagnostic criteria would continue throughout this decade. Pressure would now be exerted from experts within the field (Quay, 1987; Rutter, 1983, 1989; Werry, 1988) to demonstrate that the symptoms of ADHD could distinguish it from other childhood psychiatric disorders—a crucial test for the validity of a diagnostic entity—rather than continuing simply to demonstrate differences from normal populations. The challenge would not be easily met. Eric Taylor (1986) and colleagues in Great Britain made notable advances in further refining the criteria and their measurement along more empirical lines. Taylor's (1989) statistical approach to studying clusters of behavioral disorders resulted in the recommendation that a syndrome of hyperactivity could be valid and distinctive from other disorders, particularly conduct problems. This distinction required that the symptoms of hyperactivity and inattention be excessive and handicapping to the children, occur in two of three broadly defined settings (e.g., home, school, and clinic), be objectively measured rather than subjectively rated by parents and teachers, develop before age 6, last at least 6 months, and exclude children with autism, psychosis, or affective disorders (depression, anxiety, mania, etc.).

Efforts to develop research diagnostic criteria for ADHD eventually led to an international symposium on the subject (Sergeant, 1988) and a general consensus that subjects selected for research on ADHD should at least meet the following criteria: (1) reports of problems with activity and attention by at least two independent sources (home, school, clinic), (2) at least three of four difficulties with activity and three of four with attention being endorsed, (3) onset before 7 years of age, (4) duration of 2 years, (5) significantly elevated scores on parent/teacher ratings of these ADHD symptoms, and (6) exclusion of autism and psychosis. The proposed criteria are quite similar to others proposed earlier in the decade (Barkley, 1982) but provide for greater specificity of symptoms of overactivity and inattention and a longer duration of symptoms.

Subtyping of ADD

Also important was the attempt to identify useful approaches to subtyping other than those just based on the degree of hyperactivity (+H/–H) or aggression associated with ADD. A significant though underappreciated line of research by Roscoe Dykman and Peggy Ackerman at the University of Arkansas distinguished between ADD children with and without learning disabilities, particularly reading impairments. Their research (Ackerman, Dykman, & Oglesby, 1983; Dykman, Ackerman, & Holcomb, 1985) and that of others (McGee, Williams, Moffit, & Anderson, 1989) showed that some of the cognitive deficits (verbal memory, intelligence, etc.) formerly attributed to ADHD were actually more a function of the presence and degree of language/reading difficulties than ADHD. And, although some studies showed that ADHD children with reading disabilities are not a distinct subtype of ADHD (Halperin, Gittelman, Klein, & Rudel, 1984), the differential contributions of reading disorders to the cognitive test performance of ADHD require that subsequent research studies either carefully select subjects with pure ADHD not associated with reading disability or at least identify the degree to which reading disorders exist in the sample and partial out its effects on the cognitive test results.

Others in this era attempted to distinguish between pervasive and situational hyperactivity where the former was determined by the presence of hyperactivity at home and school and the latter referred to hyperactivity in only one of these settings (Schachar, Rutter, & Smith, 1981). It would be shown that pervasively hyperactive children were likely to have more severe behavioral symptoms, greater aggression and peer relationship problems, and poor academic achievement. A revision of DSM-III (DSM-III-R; American Psychiatric Association, 1987) incorporated this concept into an index of severity of ADHD, and British scientists viewed pervasiveness as an essential criteria for the diagnosis of a distinct syndrome of hyperactivity (see earlier). However, research appearing at the end of the decade (Costello, Loeber, Stoutheimer-Loeber, 1991) demonstrated that such group differences were more likely the result of differences in the source of the information used to classify the children (parents versus teachers) than to actual behavioral differences between the situational and pervasive subgroups. This did not mean that symptom pervasiveness might not be a useful means of subtyping or diagnosing ADHD but that more objective means of establishing it were needed than just comparing parent and teacher ratings on a questionnaire.

A different and relatively understudied approach were the subtypes of ADHD created by the presence or absence of significant anxiety/depression or affective disturbance. Several studies demonstrated that ADHD children with significant problems with anxiety or affective disturbance were likely to show poor or adverse responses to stimulant medication (Taylor, 1983; Voelker, Lachar, & Gdowski, 1983) and would perhaps respond better to antidepressant medications (Pliszka, 1987). The utility of this latter subtyping approach would be investigated and supported further in the next decade (DuPaul, Barkley, & McMurray, 1994; Tannock, in press).

ADD Becomes ADHD

Later in the decade, in an effort to further improve the criteria for defining this disorder, DSM was revised (American Psychiatric Association, 1987), resulting in the renaming of the disorder Attention-Deficit Hyperactivity Disorder. These revised diagnostic criteria are shown in Table 1.2. The revisions were significant in several respects. First, a single item list of symptoms and a single cutoff score replaced the three separate lists (inattention, impulsivity, and hyperactivity) and cutoff score in DSM-III. Second, the item list was now based more on empirically derived dimensions of child behavior from behavior rating scales and the items and cutoff score underwent a large field trial to determine their sensitivity, specificity, and discriminating power to distinguish ADHD from other psychiatric disorders and normal children (Spitzer et al., 1990). Third, the need to establish the symptoms as developmentally inappropriate for the child's mental age were stressed more emphatically. Fourth, the coexis-

---

TABLE 1.2. DSM-III-R Diagnostic Criteria for Attention-Deficit Hyperactivity Disorder

---

A. A disturbance of at least six months during which at least eight of the following are present:
  (1) often fidgets with hands or feet or squirms in seat (in adolescents, may be limited to subjective feelings of restlessness)
  (2) has difficulty remaining seated when required to do so
  (3) is easily distracted by extraneous stimuli
  (4) has difficulty awaiting turn in games or group situations
  (5) often blurts out answers to questions before they have been completed
  (6) has difficulty following through on instructions from others (not due to oppositional behavior or failure of comprehension), e.g., fails to finish chores
  (7) has difficulty sustaining attention in tasks or play activities
  (8) often shifts from one uncompleted activity to another
  (9) has difficulty playing quietly
  (10) often talks excessively
  (11) often interrupts or intrudes on others, e.g., butts into other children's games
  (12) often does not seem to listen to what is being said to him or her
  (13) often loses things necessary for tasks or activities at school or at home (e.g., toys, pencils, books, assignments)
  (14) often engages in physically dangerous activities without considering possible consequences (not for the purpose of thrillseeking), e.g., runs into street without looking

Note: The above items are listed in descending order of discriminating power based on the data from a national field trial of the DSM-III-R criteria for Disruptive Behavior Disorders.

B. Onset before the age of seven

C. Does not meet the criteria for a Pervasive Developmental Disorder.

Criteria for severity of Attention-Deficit Hyperactivity Disorder:

Mild: Few if any, symptoms in excess of those required to make the diagnosis **and** only minimal or no impairment in school and social functioning.

Moderate: Symptoms or functional impairment intermediate between "mild" and "severe."

Severe: Many symptoms in excess of those required to make the diagnosis **and** pervasive impairment in functioning at home and school and with peers.

---

tence of affective disorders with ADHD no longer excluded the diagnosis of ADHD. And, more controversially, the subtype of ADD without Hyperactivity was removed as a subtype and relegated to a vaguely defined category, Undifferentiated ADD, which was in need of greater research on its merits. ADHD was now classified with two other behavioral disorders (Oppositional Defiant Disorder and Conduct Disorder) in a supraordinate category known as the Disruptive Behavior Disorders in view of their substantial overlap or comorbidity in clinic-referred populations of children.

ADHD as a Motivation Deficit Disorder

One of the most profound conceptual developments in this decade only began to emerge in the latter half of the period. This was the nascent and almost heretical view that ADHD was not actually a disorder of attention. Doubt as to the central importance of attention to the disorder crept in late in the 1970s as some researchers more fully plumbed the depths of the attentional construct while others took note of the striking situational variability of the symptoms (Douglas & Peters, 1979; Rosenthal & Allen, 1978; Routh, 1978; Sroufe, 1975). As more rigorous and technical studies of attention in ADHD children appeared in the 1980s, an increasing number failed to find evidence of problems with attention under some experimental conditions while observing them under others (see Douglas, 1983, 1988, for reviews; Barkley, 1984; Draeger et al., 1986; Sergeant, 1988; Sergeant & van der Meere, 1989; van der Meere & Sergeant, 1988a, 1988b). Moreover, if attention was conceptualized as involving the perception, filtering, and processing of information, no substantial evidence could be found in these studies for any such deficits. These findings, coupled with the realization that both instructional and motivational factors in an experiment played a strong role in determining the presence and degree of ADHD symptoms, led some investigators to hypothesize that deficits in motivation may be a better model for explaining the symptoms seen in ADHD children (Glow & Glow, 1979; Rosenthal & Allen, 1978; Sroufe, 1975). Following this line of reasoning, others pursued a behavioral or functional analysis of these symptoms, resulting in hypothesized deficits in the stimulus control over behavior, particularly by rules and instructions. I argued that such deficits arose from neurological factors (Barkley, 1988) whereas others argued that they arose from poor training of the child by parents (Willis & Lovaas, 1977).

I initially raised the possibility that rule-governed behavior might account for many of the deficits in ADHD but later amended this view to include the strong probability that response to behavioral consequences might also be impaired and could conceivably account for the problems with rule following (Barkley, 1981, 1984, 1990). Others independently advanced the notion that a deficit in responding to behavioral consequences, not attention, was the difficulty in ADHD (Benninger, 1989; Haenlein & Caul, 1987; Quay, 1988; Sagvolden, Wultz, Moser, Moser, & Morkrid, 1989; Sergeant, 1988; van der Meere & Sergeant, 1988b). That is, ADHD arises out of an insensitivity to consequences, reinforcement, punishment, or both. This insensitivity was viewed as neurological in origin. Yet this idea was not new, having been advanced some 10 to 20 years earlier by investigators in Australia (Glow & Glow, 1979) and those studying conduct problem children (see Patterson, 1982, for a review) and by Wender (1971) in his classic text on MBD. What was original in these more recent ideas was a greater specificity of their hypotheses and increasing evidence supporting them. Others continued to argue against the merits of a Skinnerian, or functional, analysis of the deficits in ADHD (Douglas, 1989) and for the continued explanatory value of cognitive models of attention in accounting for the deficits in ADHD children.

The appeal of the motivational model came from several different sources: (1) its greater explanatory value in accounting for the more recent research findings on situational variability in attention in ADHD, (2) its consistency with neuroanatomical studies suggesting decreased activation of brain reward centers and their cortical–limbic regulating circuits (Lou et al., 1984; Lou et al., 1989), (3) its consistency with studies of the functions of dopamine pathways in regulating locomotor behavior and incentive or operant learning (Benninger, 1989), and (4) its greater prescriptive power in suggesting potential treatments for the ADHD symptoms. Whether or not ADHD would be labeled a motivational deficit, there was little doubt that these new theories based on a the construct of motivation required altering the way in which this disorder was to be conceptualized. From here on, any attempts at theory construction would need to incorporate some components and processes that dealt with motivation or effort.

Other Historical Developments of the Era

The Increasing Importance of Social Ecology

This decade also witnessed considerably greater research into the social-ecological impact of ADHD symptoms on the children, their parents (Barkley, 1989b; Barkley, Karlsson, & Pollard, 1985; Mash & Johnston, 1982), teachers (Whalen et al., 1980, 1981), siblings (Mash & Johnston, 1983), and peers (Cunningham, Siegel, & Offord, 1985; Henker & Whalen, 1980). These investigators further explored the effects of stimulant medications on these social systems as well as buttressing the conclusion that ADHD children elicit significant negative, controlling, and hostile or rejecting interactions from others which can be greatly reduced by stimulant medication. From these studies emerged the view that handicaps associated with ADHD do not rest solely in the child but in the interface between the child's capabilities and the environmental demands made within the social-ecological context in which that child must perform (Whalen & Henker, 1980). Changing the attitudes, behaviors, and expectations of caregivers as well as the demands they make on ADHD children in their care should result in changes in the degree to which the ADHD children are disabled by their behavioral deficits.

Theoretical Advances

During this decade, Herbert Quay adopted Jeffrey Gray's neuropsychological model of anxiety (Gray, 1982, 1987, 1994) to explain the origin of the poor inhibition evident in ADHD (Quay, 1987, 1988, 1997). Gray identified both a behavioral inhibition system as well as a behavioral activation system as being critical to understanding emotion. He also stipulated mechanisms for basic nonspecific arousal and for the appraisal of incoming information that must be critical elements of any attempt to model the emotional functions of the brain. According to this theory, signals of reward serve to increase activity in the behavioral activation system (BAS), thus giving rise to approach behavior and the maintenance of such behavior. Active avoidance and escape from aversive consequences (negative reinforcement) likewise activate this system. Signals of impending punishment (particularly conditioned punishment) as well as frustrative nonreward increase activity in the behavioral inhibition system (BIS). Another system is the fight–flight system, which reacts to unconditioned punitive stimuli.

Quay's use of this model for ADHD states that the impulsiveness characterizing the disorder arises from diminished activity in the brain's BIS. This model predicts that those with ADHD should prove less sensitive to such signals, particularly in passive avoidance paradigms (Quay, 1987). The theory also specifies predictions that can be used to test and even falsify the model as it applies to ADHD. For instance, Quay (1987, 1988) predicted that there should be greater resistance to extinction following periods of continuous reinforcement in those with ADHD but less resistance when training conditions involved partial reward. They should also demonstrate a decreased ability to inhibit behavior in passive avoidance paradigms when avoidance of the punishment is achieved through the inhibition of responding. And those with ADHD should also demonstrate diminished inhibition to signals of pain and novelty as well as to conditioned signals of punishment. Finally, Quay predicted increased rates of responding by those with ADHD under fixed-interval or fixed-ratio schedules of consequences. Some of these predictions are supported by subsequent research; others either remain to be investigated more fully and rigorously or have not been completely supported by the available evidence (see Milich, Hartung, Martin, & Haigler, 1994; Quay, 1997). Nevertheless, the theory remains a viable one for explaining the origin of the inhibitory deficits in ADHD and continues to be deserving of further research.

Further Developments in Nature, Etiology, and Course

Another noteworthy development in this decade was the greater sophistication of research designs attempting to explore the unique features of ADHD relative to other psychiatric conditions rather than just in comparison to normal. As Rutter (1983, 1989) noted repeatedly, the true test of the validity of a syndrome of ADHD is the ability to differentiate its features from other psychiatric disorders of children, such as affective or anxiety disorders, learning disorders, and particularly conduct disorders. Those studies that undertook such comparisons indicated that situational hyperactivity was not consistent in discriminating among psychiatric populations but that difficulties with attention and pervasive (home and school) hyperactivity were more reliable in doing so and were often associated with patterns of neurocognitive immaturity (Firestone & Martin, 1979; Gittelman, 1988; McGee, Williams, & Silva, 1984a, 1984b; Rutter, 1989; Taylor, 1988; Werry, 1988).

The emerging interest in comparing ADD children with and without Hyperactivity (+/–H) furthered this line of inquiry by demonstrating relatively unique features of each disorder in contrast to each other (see Chapter 3) and to groups of learning-disabled and normal children (Barkley, DuPaul, & McMurray, 1990, 1991). Further strengthening the position of ADHD as a psychiatric syndrome was evidence from family aggregation studies that relatives of ADHD children had a different pattern of psychiatric disturbance from those children with Conduct Disorder or mixed ADHD and Conduct Disorder (Biederman, Munir, & Knee, 1987; Lahey et al., 1988). Purely ADHD children were more likely to have relatives with ADHD, academic achievement problems, and dysthymia, whereas those children with Conduct Disorder had a greater prevalence of Conduct Disorder, antisocial behavior, substance abuse, depression, and marital dysfunction among their relatives. This finding led to speculations that ADHD had a different etiology from conduct disorder. The former is said to arise out of a biologically based disorder of temperament or a neurocognitive delay; the latter springs from inconsistent, coercive, and dysfunctional child rearing and management frequently associated with parental psychiatric impairment (Hinshaw, 1987; Loeber, 1990; Patterson, 1982, 1986).

Equally elegant research was done on potential etiologies of ADHD. Several studies on cerebral blood flow revealed patterns of underactivity in the prefrontal areas of the CNS and their rich connections to the limbic system via the striatum (Lou et al., 1984; Lou et al., 1989). Other studies (Hunt, Cohen, Anderson, & Minderaa, 1988; Rapoport & Zametkin, 1988; Shaywitz, Shaywitz, Cohen, & Young, 1983; Shekim, Glaser, Horwitz, Javaid, & Dylund, 1987; Zametkin & Rapoport, 1986) on brain neurotransmitters provided further evidence that deficiencies in dopamine, norepinephrine, or both may be involved in explaining these patterns of brain underactivity—patterns arising in precisely those brain areas in which dopamine and norepinephrine are most involved. Drawing these lines of evidence together even further was the fact that these brain areas are critically involved in response inhibition, motivational learning, and response to reinforcement. More rigorous studies on the hereditary transmission of ADHD were published (Goodman & Stevenson, 1989), indicating a strong heritability for ADHD symptoms.

Follow-up studies appearing in this decade were also more methodologically sophisticated and hence more revealing of not only widespread maladjustment in children with ADHD as they reached adolescence and adulthood but of potential mechanisms involved in the differential courses shown within this population (Barkley, Fischer, Edelbrock, & Smallish, 1990, 1991; Fischer, Barkley, Edelbrock, & Smallish, 1990; Gittelman et al., 1985; Lambert, 1988; G. Weiss & Hechtman, 1993). These findings are discussed in Chapter 4. Again, neurocognitive delays, the presence and pervasiveness of early aggression, and mother–child conflict were associated with a different, and more negative, outcome in later childhood and adolescence than was ADHD alone (Campbell, 1987; Paternite & Loney, 1980).

There was also a movement during this decade away from the strict reliance on clinic-referred samples of ADHD children to the use of community-derived samples. This change was prompted by the widely acknowledged bias that occurs among clinic samples of ADHD children as a result of the process of referral itself. It is well-known that children who are referred are often more, though not always the most, impaired, have more numerous comorbid conditions, are likely to have associated family difficulties, and are skewed toward those socioeconomic classes that value the utilization of mental health care resources. Such biases can create findings that are not representative of the nature of the disorder in its natural state. For instance, it has been shown that the ratio of boys to girls within clinic-referred samples of ADHD children may range from 6:1 to 9:1 and that girls with ADHD within these samples are as likely to be aggressive or oppositional as boys (see Chapter 2). In contrast, in samples of ADHD children derived from community- or school-based samples, the ratio of boys to girls is only 2.5:1 and girls with ADHD are considerably less likely to be aggressive than boys. For these and other reasons, a greater emphasis on studying epidemiological samples of children and the rates and nature of ADHD within them (Offord et al., 1987) arose toward the latter half of the 1980s.

Developments in Assessment

The 1980s also witnessed some advances in the tools of assessment in addition to those for treatment. The Child Behavior Checklist (CBCL; Achenbach & Edelbrock, 1983, 1986) emerged as a more comprehensive, more rigorously developed, and better-normed alternative to the Conners Rating Scales (Barkley, 1987). It would become widely adopted in research on child psychopathology in general, not just in ADHD, by the end of this decade. Other rating scales more specific to ADHD were also developed, such as the ACTeRS (Ullmann et al., 1984), the Home and School Situations Questionnaires (Barkley & Edelbrock, 1987; DuPaul & Barkley, 1992), the Child Attention Profile (see Barkley, 1987), and the ADHD Rating Scale (DuPaul, 1991).

Gordon (1983) developed, normed, and commercially marketed a small, portable, computerized device that administered two tests believed to be sensitive to the deficits in ADHD. One was a CPT measuring vigilance and impulsivity and the other was a direct reinforcement of low rates (DRL) test assessing impulse control. This test became the first commercially available objective assessment device for evaluating ADHD children. Although the DRL test showed some promise in early research (Gordon, 1979), it was subsequently shown to be insensitive to stimulant medication effects (Barkley, Fischer, Newby, & Breen, 1988) and was eventually deemphasized as useful in the diagnosis in ADHD. The CPT task, by contrast, showed satisfactory discrimination of ADHD from normal groups and was sensitive to medication effects (Barkley et al., 1988; Gordon & Mettelman, 1988). Although cautionary statements would be made that more research evidence was needed to evaluate the utility of the instrument (Milich, Pelham, & Hinshaw, 1985) and that its false-negative rate (misses of legitimate ADHD children) might be greater than that desired in a diagnostic tool, the device and others like it (Conners, 1995; Greenberg & Waldman, 1992) found a wide clinical following by the next decade.

Greater emphasis was also given to developing direct behavioral observation measures of ADHD symptoms that could be taken in the classroom or clinic and would be more objective and useful adjuncts to the parent and teacher rating scales in the diagnostic process. Abikoff, Gittelman-Klein, and Klein (1977) and O'Leary (1981) developed classroom observation codes with some promise for discriminating ADHD from normal and non-ADHD children (Gittelman, 1988). Roberts (1979), drawing on the earlier work of Routh and Schroeder (1976) and Kalverboer (1988), refined a laboratory playroom observation procedure that would be found to discriminate ADHD not only from normal children but also from aggressive or mixed aggressive–ADHD children (see Chapter 10). This coding system had excellent 2-year stability coefficients. Somewhat later I streamlined the system (Barkley, 1988) for more convenient clinical or classroom use and found it to be sensitive to stimulant medication effects (Barkley et al., 1988), to differentiate between ADD children with and without Hyperactivity (Barkley, Dupaul, & McMurray, 1991), and to correlate well with parent and teacher ratings of ADHD symptoms (Barkley, 1991). Nevertheless, problems with developing normative data and the practical implementation of such a procedure in busy clinic practices remained hindrances to its widespread adoption.

Developments in Therapy

Developments also continued in the realm of treatments for ADHD. Comparisons of single versus combined treatments were more common during the decade (Barkley, 1989c), as was the use of more sophisticated experimental designs (Hinshaw, Henker, & Whalen, 1984; Pelham, Schnedler, Bologna, & Contreras, 1980) and mixed interventions (Satterfield, Satterfield, & Cantwell, 1981). Several of these developments in treatment require historical mention. The first was the emergence of a new approach to the treatment of ADHD: cognitive-behavioral modification (Camp, 1980; Douglas, 1980a; Kendall & Braswell, 1985; Meichenbaum, 1988). Founded on the work of Russian neuropsychologists (Vygotsky and Luria), North American developmental and cognitive psychologists (Flavell, Beach, & Chinsky, 1966), and early cognitive-behavioral theories (Meichenbaum, 1977), these approaches stressed the need to develop self-directed speech in impulsive children to guide their definition of and attention to immediate problem situations, to generate solutions to these problems, and to guide their behavior as the solutions were performed. Self-evaluation, correction, and consequation at task completion were also viewed as important (Douglas, 1980a, 1980b). Although first reports of the efficacy of this approach appeared in the late 1960s and the 1970s (Bornstein & Quevillon, 1976; Meichenbaum & Goodman, 1979), it was not until this decade that the initial claims of success with nonclinical populations of impulsive children were more fully tested in clinical populations of ADHD children. The results were disappointing (Abikoff, 1987; Gittelman & Abikoff, 1989). Generally, they indicated some degree of improvement in impulsiveness on cognitive laboratory tasks but insufficient to be detected in teacher or parent ratings of school and home ADHD behaviors and certainly not as effective as stimulant medication (Brown, Wynne, & Medenis, 1985). Many continued to see some promise in these techniques (Barkley, 1981, 1989b; Meichenbaum, 1988; Whalen, Henker, & Hinshaw, 1985), particularly when they are implemented in natural environments by important caregivers (parents and teachers); others ended the decade with a challenge to those who persisted in their support of this approach to provide further evidence for its efficacy (Gittelman & Abikoff, 1989). Later, even the conceptual basis for the treatment came under attack as being inconsistent with Vygotsky's theory of the internalization of language (Diaz & Berk, 1995).

A second development in treatment was the publication of a specific parent-training format for families with ADHD and oppositional children. A specific set of steps for training parents of ADHD children in child behavior management skills was developed (Barkley, 1981) and refined (Barkley, 1987, 1997b). The approach was founded on a substantial research literature (Barkley, 1997b; Forehand & McMahon, 1981; Patterson, 1982) demonstrating the efficacy of differential attention and time-out procedures for treating oppositional behavior in children—a behavior frequently associated with ADHD. These two procedures were coupled with additional components based on a theoretical formulation of ADHD as a developmental disorder that is typically chronic and associated with decreased rule-governed behavior and an insensitivity to certain consequences, particularly mild or social reinforcement. These components included counseling parents to conceptualize ADHD as a developmentally handicapping condition; implementing more powerful home token economies to reinforce behavior rather than relying on attention alone; using shaping techniques to develop nondisruptive, independent play; and training parents in cognitive-behavioral skills to teach their children during daily management encounters, particularly in managing disruptive behavior in public places (Anastopoulos & Barkley, 1990; see Chapter 12 for a detailed description of this program). Because of the demonstrated impact of parental and family dysfunction on the severity of children's ADHD symptoms, their greater risk for developing oppositional–defiant behavior and conduct disorders, and the responsiveness of their parents to treatments for the children, clinicians began to pay closer attention to intervening in family systems rather than just in child management skills. Noteworthy among these attempts were the modifications to the previously described parent-training program by Charles Cunningham at McMaster University Medical Center (Cunningham, 1990; see Chapter 13 for a detailed description of this approach). Arthur Robin at Wayne State University and the Children's Hospital of Michigan and Sharon Foster at West Virginia University (Robin & Foster, 1989) also emphasized the need for work on family systems as well as on problem-solving and communication skills in treating the parent–adolescent conflicts so common in families with ADHD teenagers (see Chapter 14 for a discussion of this approach).

A similar increase in more sophisticated approaches occurred in this era in relation to the classroom management of ADHD children (Barkley, Copeland, & Sivage, 1980; Pelham et al., 1980; Pfiffner & O'Leary, 1987; Whalen & Henker, 1980). These developments were based on earlier promising studies in the 1970s with contingency management methods in hyperactive children (Allyon et al., 1975; see Chapter 15 for the details of such an approach). Although these methods may not produce the degree of behavioral change seen in the stimulant medications (Gittelman et al., 1980), they provide a more socially desirable intervention that can be a useful alternative when children have mild ADHD and cannot take stimulants or their parents decline the prescription, or as an adjunct to medication therapy to further enhance academic achievement.

The fourth area of treatment development was in the area of social skills training for ADHD children. Hinshaw and his colleagues (Hinshaw, Henker, & Whalen, 1984) developed a program for training ADHD children in anger-control techniques. This program demonstrated some initial short-term effectiveness in assisting these children to deal with this common deficit in their social skills and emotional control (Barkley et al., 1997). Related approaches to social skills training with ADHD children also showed promising results (Pfiffner & McBurnett, 1997).

Finally, medication treatments for ADHD expanded to include the use of the tricyclic antidepressants, particularly for those ADHD children with characteristics that contraindicated using a stimulant medication (e.g., tic disorders or Tourette syndrome) or for ADHD children with anxiety/depression (Pliszka, 1987). The work of Joseph Biederman and his colleagues at Massachusetts General Hospital (Biederman, Gastfriend, & Jellinek, 1986; Biederman, Baldessarini, Wright, Knee, & Harmatz, 1989) on the safety and efficacy of the tricyclic medications encouraged the rapid adoption of these drugs by many practitioners (see Ryan, 1990), particularly when the stimulants, such as Ritalin (methylphenidate), were receiving such negative publicity in the popular media (see the next section). Simultaneously, initially positive research reports appeared on the use of the antihypertensive drug, clonidine, in the treatment of ADHD children, particularly those with very high levels of hyperactive–impulsive behavior and aggression (Hunt, Caper, & O'Connell, 1990; Hunt, Minderaa, & Cohen, 1985).

Developments in Public Awareness

Several noteworthy developments also occurred in the public forum during this decade. Chief and most constructive among these was the blossoming of numerous parent support associations for families with ADHD. Although less than a handful existed in the early 1980s, within 9 years there would be well over 100 such associations throughout the United States alone. These would begin to organize into a national network and political action organization by 1989 known as CHADD (Children and Adults with ADD) and the Attention Deficit Disorders Association (ADDA). With this greater public/parent activism, initiatives were taken to have state laws and federal laws reevaluated and, it was hoped, changed to include ADHD as an educational disability in need of special educational services in public schools.

When Public Law 94-142 was passed in 1975, it included the concept of minimal brain dysfunction under the category of learning disabilities that would be eligible for special educational services. But it overlooked the inclusion of ADD or ADHD in its description of learning or behavioral disorders eligible for mandated special services in public schools—an oversight that would lead many public schools to deny access for children with ADD/ADHD to such services and to much parental and teacher exasperation in trying to get educational recognition and assistance for this clearly academically handicapping disorder. Other parents would initiate lawsuits against private schools for learning-disabled students for educational malpractice in failing to provide special services for ADHD children (Skinner, 1988). By the early part of the next decade, these lobbying efforts would be partially successful in getting the Department of Education to reinterpret Public Law 94-142 as including ADHD children under the category of Other Health Impaired because of their difficulties in alertness and attention. Upon the reauthorization of this special education act as the Individuals with Disabilities in Education Act, ADHD would continue to be interpreted as eligible for special educational services provided that it resulted in a significant impairment in academic performance. As should be evident from this text, I am fully supportive of these efforts to obtain special educational resources for ADHD children and adolescents in view of their tremendous risk for academic underachievement, failure, retention, suspension, and expulsion, not to mention negative social and occupational outcomes (Barkley, Fischer, et al., 1990, 1991; Cantwell & Satterfield, 1978; G. Weiss & Hechtman, 1986).

The Church of Scientology Campaign

Yet with this increased public activism also came, in my view, a tremendously destructive trend in the United States primarily fueled by the Church of Scientology and its Citizens Commission on Human Rights (CCHR). This campaign capitalized on a general media tendency to uncritically publish alarming or scintillating anecdotes and a public gullibility for them. Drawing on evidence of an increase in stimulant medication use with school children as well as on the extant public concern over drug abuse, members of CCHR effectively linked these events together to play on the public's general concern for using behavior-modifying drugs with children. What is more, reminiscent of the gross overstatement seen in the earlier "reefer madness" campaign by the U.S. government against marijuana, members of CCHR selectively focused on the rare cases of adverse reactions to stimulants and greatly exaggerated both the number and degree of them to persuade the public that these reactions were commonplace. They also argued that massive overprescribing was posing a serious threat to our school children. By picketing scientific and public conferences on ADHD, actively distributing leaflets to parents and students in many North American cities, seeking out appearances on many national television talk shows, and placing numerous letters to newspapers decrying the evils of Ritalin and the myth of ADHD (Bass, 1988; CCHR, 1987; Cowart, 1988; Dockx, 1988), CCHR members and others took this propaganda directly to the public. Ritalin, they claimed, was a dangerous and addictive drug often used as a chemical straitjacket to subdue normally exuberant children because of intolerant educators and parents and money-hungry psychiatrists (Clark, 1988; CCHR, 1987; Dockx, 1988). Dramatic, exaggerated, or unfounded claims were made that Ritalin could frequently result in violence or murder, suicide, Tourette syndrome, permanent brain damage or emotional disturbance, sezures, high blood pressure, confusion, agitation, and depression (CCHR, 1987; Clark, 1988; Dockx, 1988; Laccetti, 1988; "Ritalin Linked," 1988; Toufexis, 1989; Williams, 1988). It was also claimed that the increasing production of Ritalin and its prescription was leading to increased abuse of these drugs (Associated Press, 1988; Cowart, 1988; "Rise in Ritalin Use," 1988). Great controversy was said to exist among the scientific and professional practice communities on this disorder and the use of medication. No evidence was presented in these articles, however, that ever demonstrated a rise in Ritalin abuse or linked it with the increased prescribing of the medication. Moreover, close inspection of professional journals and conferences revealed that no major or widespread controversy ever existed within the professional or scientific fields over the nature of the disorder or the effectiveness of stimulant medication. Yet, lawsuits were threatened, initiated, or assisted by the CCHR against practitioners for medical negligence and malpractice and against schools for complicity in "pressuring" parents to have their children placed on these medicines (Bass, 1988; Cowart, 1988; Henig, 1988; *Nightline*, 1988; Twyman, 1988). A major lawsuit ($125 million) was also filed by the CCHR against the American Psychiatric Association for fraud in developing the criteria for ADHD (Henig, 1988; "Psychiatrist Sued," 1987), though the suit would later be dismissed.

So effective was this national campaign by the CCHR, so widespread were newspaper and television stories on adverse Ritalin reactions, and so easily could public sentiment be misled about a disorder and its treatment by a fringe religious group and overzealous, scandal-mongering journalists that within 1 year the public attitude toward Ritalin was dramatically altered. Ritalin was seen as a dangerous and overprescribed drug and the public believed that there was tremendous professional controversy over its use. The minor benefits to come out of this distorted reporting were that some practitioners would become more rigorous in their assessments and more cautious in their prescribing of medication. Schools also became highly sensitized to the percentage of their enrollment receiving stimulant medication and in some cases encouraged exploration of alternative behavioral means of managing children.

Yet, even the few modestly positive effects of this campaign were greatly outweighed by the damaging effects on parents and children. Many parents were scared into unilaterally discontinuing the medication with their children without consulting their treating physicians. Others rigidly refused to consider the treatment as one part of their child's treatment plan if recommended or were harassed into doing so by well-meaning relatives misled by the distorted church propaganda and media reports. Some ADHD adolescents began refusing the treatment, even if beneficial to them, after being alarmed by these stories. Some physicians stopped prescribing the medications altogether out of concern for the threats of litigation, thereby depriving many children within their care of the clear benefits of this treatment approach. Most frustrating to watch was the unnecessary anguish created for parents whose children were already on the medication or were contemplating its use. The psychological damage done to those children whose lives could have been improved by this treatment was incalculable. The meager, poorly organized, and sporadically disseminated response of the mental health professions was primarily defensive in nature (Barkley, 1988; Weiner, 1988) and, as usual, too little, too late to change the tide of public opinion. It would take several years to reverse this regression in public opinion toward ADHD and its treatment by medication as well as the chilling effect all this had on physician prescribing of the medication.

The Prevailing View at the End of the 1980s

This decade closed with the professional view of ADHD being that it was a developmentally handicapping condition generally chronic in nature, having a strong biological or hereditary predisposition, and having a significant negative impact on academic and social outcomes for many ADHD children. However, its severity, comorbidity, and outcome were viewed as significantly affected by environmental, particularly familial, factors. Growing doubts about the central role of attention deficits in the disorder arose late in the decade while increasing interest focused on possible motivational factors or reinforcement mechanisms as the core difficulty in ADHD. Effective treatment was now viewed as requiring multiple methods and professional disciplines working in concert over longer time intervals with periodic reintervention as required to improve the long-term prognosis for ADHD. The view that environmental causes were involved in the genesis of the disorder was weakened by increasing evidence for the heritability of the condition and its neuroanatomical localization. Even so, evidence that familial/environmental factors were associated with type of outcome was further strengthened. Developments in treatment would expand the focus of interventions to parental disturbances and family dysfunction as well as to the children's anger control and social skills. A potentially effective role for the use of tricyclic antidepressants and antihypertensive medications was also demonstrated, expanding the armamentarium of symptomatic interventions for helping ADHD children.

Despite these tremendous developments in the scientific and professional fields, the general public became overly sensitized to and excessively alarmed by the increasing use of stimulant medication as a treatment for this disorder. Fortunately, the explosive growth of parent support/political action associations for ADHD arose almost simultaneously with this public controversy over Ritalin and promised to counteract its effects as well as to make the education of ADHD children a national political priority at the start of this last decade of the 20th century. These associations also offered the best hope that the general public could be provided with a more accurate depiction of ADHD and its treatment. Perhaps now the public could be made to understand that hyperactive, disruptive child behaviors could arise out of a biologically based disability that can be diminished or amplified by the social environment rather than being entirely due to the simplistic yet pervasive societal view of bad parenting and diet as its cause.

THE PERIOD 1990 TO 1998: THE DECADE OF NEUROIMAGING, GENETICS, AND ADULT ADHD

Since 1990, and the last edition of this text, a number of noteworthy developments have occurred in the history of this disorder, chief among them being the increase in research on the neurological and genetic basis of the disorder and on ADHD as it occurs in clinic-referred adults.

Neuroimaging Research

Researchers have long-suspected that ADHD was associated in some way with abnormalities or developmental delays in brain functioning. Supporting such an interpretation are numerous neuropsychological studies showing deficits in performance by ADHD children on tests that were presumed to assess frontal lobe or executive functions (Barkley, 1997b; Barkley et al., 1992; Goodyear & Hynd, 1992, for reviews). Moreover, psychophysiological research in earlier decades had suggested brain underactivity, particularly in functioning related to the frontal lobes (Hastings & Barkley, 1978; Klorman, 1992). And thus there is good reason to suspect that delayed or disturbed functioning in the brain, and particularly the frontal lobes, may be involved in this disorder.

In 1990, Alan Zametkin and his colleagues at the National Institute of Mental Health (NIMH; Zametkin et al., 1990) published a landmark study. The authors evaluated brain metabolic activity in 25 adults with ADHD who had a childhood history of the disorder and who also had children with the disorder. The authors used positron emission tomography (PET), an exceptionally sensitive technique for detecting states of brain activity and its localization within the cerebral hemispheres. The results of this study indicated significantly reduced brain metabolic activity in adults with ADHD relative to a control group, primarily in frontal and striatal regions. Such results were certainly consistent in many, though not all, respects with the earlier demonstrations of reduced cerebral blood flow in the frontal and striatal regions in children with ADHD (Lou et al., 1984, 1989). Significant in the Zametkin et al. (1990) study, however, was its use of a much better defined sample of ADHD patients and its focus on adults with ADHD. Although later attempts by this research team to replicate their original results using teenagers with ADHD were consistent with these initial results for girls with ADHD, no differences were found in boys with ADHD (see Ernst, 1996, for a review). Sample sizes in these studies were quite small, however, almost ensuring some difficulties with the reliable demonstration of the original findings. Despite these difficulties, the original report stands out as one of the clearest demonstrations to date of reduced brain activity, particularly in the frontal regions, in ADHD.

At the same time as the NIMH research using PET scans was appearing, other researchers were employing magnetic resonance imaging (MRI) to evaluate brain structures in children with ADHD. Hynd and his colleagues were the first to use this method and they focused on the total brain volume as well as specific regions in the anterior and posterior brain sections. Children with ADHD were found to have abnormally smaller anterior cortical regions, especially on the right side, and they lacked the normal right–left frontal asymmetry (Hynd, Semrud-Clikeman, Lorys, Novey, & Eliopulis, 1990). Subsequent research by this team focused on the size of the corpus callosum, finding that both the anterior and posterior portions were smaller in children with ADHD (Hynd et al., 1991); however, in a later study, only the posterior region was significantly smaller (Semrud-Clikeman et al., 1994).

Additional studies were reported by Hynd et al. (1993), who found a smaller left caudate region in children with ADHD, and Giedd et al., (1994), who found smaller anterior regions of the corpus callosum (rostrum and rostral body).

Most recently, two research teams published studies using MRI with considerably larger samples of ADHD children (Castellanos et al., 1994, 1996; Filipek et al., 1997). These studies documented significantly smaller right prefrontal lobe and striatal regions in children with ADHD. Castellanos et al. (1996) also found smaller right-sided regions of structures in the basal ganglia, such as the striatum, as well as the right cerebellum. Filipek et al. (1997) observed the left striatal region to be smaller than the right. Despite some inconsistencies across these studies, most have implicated the prefrontal-striatal network as being smaller in children with ADHD with the right prefrontal region being smaller than the left. Such studies have placed on a considerably firmer foundation the view that ADHD does, indeed, involve impairments in the development of the brain, particularly in the prefrontal-striatal regions, and that the origin of these differences from normal are likely to have occurred in embryological development (Castellanos et al., 1996). Advances in neuroimaging technology will continue to provide exciting and revealing new developments in the search for the structural differences in the brain that underlie this disorder. For instance, the advent of functional MRI with its greater sensitivity for localization of activity has already resulted in a number of newly initiated investigations into possible impairments in these brain regions in children and adults with ADHD.

Genetic Research

Since the 1970s, studies have indicated that children with hyperactivity or ADHD seem to have parents with a greater frequency of psychiatric disorders, including ADHD. Cantwell (1975) and Morrison and Stewart (1973) both reported higher rates of hyperactivity in the biological parents of hyperactive children than in adoptive parents of such children. Yet, both studies were retrospective and both failed to study the biological parents of the adopted hyperactive children as a comparison group (Pauls, 1991). In the 1990s, a number of studies, particularly those by Biederman and colleagues, clarified and strengthened this evidence of the familial nature of ADHD. Between 10% and 35% of the immediate family members of children with ADHD were found to have the disorder, with the risk to siblings of the ADHD children being approximately 32% (Biederman, Faraone, & Lapey, 1992; Biederman, Keenan, & Faraone, 1990; Pauls, 1991; Welner, Welner, Stewart, Palkes, & Wish, 1977). Even more striking, recent research shows that if a parent has ADHD, the risk to the offspring is 57% (Biederman et al., 1995). Thus, family aggregation studies find that ADHD clusters among biological relatives of children or adults with the disorder, strongly implying a hereditary basis to this condition.

At the same time that these studies were appearing, a number of studies of twins were being reported that focused on the heritability of the dimension(s) of behavior underlying ADHD, that being hyperactive–impulsive–inattentive behavior, or on the clinical diagnosis of ADHD itself. Large-scale twin studies on this issue have been quite consistent in their findings of a high heritability for this trait or for the clinical diagnosis with minimal or no contribution made by the shared environment (Edelbrock, Rende, Plomin, & Thompson, 1995; Levy & Hay, 1992). For instance, Gilger, Pennington, and DeFries (1992) found that if one twin was diagnosed as ADHD, the concordance for the disorder was 81% in monozygotic twins and 29% in dizygotic twins. Stevenson (1994) summarized the status of twin studies on symptoms of ADHD by stating that the average heritability is .80 for symptoms of this disorder (range .50–.98). More recent large-scale twin studies are remarkably consistent with this conclusion, demonstrating that the majority of variance (70–90%) in the trait of hyperactivity–impulsivity is due to genetic factors (averaging approximately 80%) and that such a genetic contribution may increase the more extreme the scores along this trait happen to be, although this latter point is debatable (Faraone, 1996; Gjone, Stevenson, & Sundet, 1996; Gjone, Stevenson, Sundet, & Eilertsen, 1996; Rhee, Waldman, Hay, & Levy, 1995; Silberg et al., 1996; Thapar, Hervas, & McGuffin, 1995; van den Oord, Verhulst, & Boomsma, 1996). Thus, twin studies add substantially more evidence to that already found in family aggregation studies supporting a strong genetic basis to ADHD and its behavioral symptoms. Equally as important is the evidence consistently appearing in such research that what environmental contributions may exist to ADHD symptoms fall more within the realm of unique (nonshared) environmental effects rather than effects of the common or shared environment.

Also in this decade, a few studies began to be published that used molecular genetic techniques to analyze DNA taken from ADHD children and their family members to identify genes that may be associated with the disorder. The focus of research initially was on the dopamine type 2 gene given findings of its increased association with alcoholism, Tourette syndrome, and ADHD (Blum, Cull, Braverman, & Comings, 1996; Comings et al., 1991), but others failed to replicate this finding (Gelernter et al., 1991; Kelsoe et al., 1989). More recently, the dopamine transporter gene was implicated in ADHD (Cook et al., 1995; Cook, Stein, & Leventhal, 1997). Another gene related to dopamine, the D4RD (repeater gene) was recently found to be overrepresented in the seven-repetition form of the gene in children with ADHD (Lahoste et al., 1996). The latter finding has been replicated in two ongoing studies by Swanson and colleagues (James Swanson, personal communication, November 1996) and Biederman and colleagues (Joseph Biederman, personal communication, November 8, 1977). Clearly research into the molecular genetics involved in the transmission of ADHD across generations promises to be an exciting and fruitful area of research endeavor over the next decade as the human genome is mapped and better understood. Such research offers not only the promise of the eventual development of genetic tests for and subtyping of ADHD into potentially more homogenous and useful genotypes but also the promise of developing more specific pharmacological agents for treating ADHD.

ADHD in Adults

Although papers dealing with the adult equivalents of childhood hyperactivity/MBD date back to the late 1960s and the 1970s, they did not seem to initiate widespread acceptance of these adult equivalents in the field of adult psychiatry and clinical psychology. It was not until the 1990s that more serious and more rigorous scientific research was conducted on adults with ADHD. Also, at this time the greater clinical professional community began to consider the disorder a legitimate clinical condition worthy of differential diagnosis and treatment (Goldstein, 1997; Nadeau, 1995; Wender, 1995). This broadening acceptance of ADHD adults continues to the present time and is only likely to further increase in the decade ahead. It seems to be due in some part to the repeated publications throughout this decade of follow-up studies that documented the persistence of the disorder into adolescence in up to 70% and into adulthood in up to as many as 66% of childhood cases (Barkley, Fischer, et al., 1990; Mannuzza, Gittelman-Klein, Bessler, Malloy, & LaPadula, 1993; Fischer, 1997; G. Weiss & Hechtman, 1993). And it can be attributed as well to published studies on clinically referred adults diagnosed with the disorder (Biederman et al., 1993; Murphy & Barkley, 1996; Shekim, Asarnow, Hess, Zaucha, & Wheeler, 1990; Spencer, Biederman, Wilens, & Faraone, 1994). But more likely it largely resulted from pressure from the general public that was made more cognizant of this disorder in adults through various media. These media included the publication of best-selling popular books on the subject (Hallowell & Ratey, 1994; Kelly & Ramundo, 1992; Murphy & LeVert, 1994; L. Weiss, 1992), numerous media accounts of the condition in adults, the efforts of large-scale parent support groups discussed earlier, such as CHADD, to promote greater public awareness of this issue, and the advent of Internet chatrooms, Web pages, and bulletin boards devoted to this topic (Gordon, 1997). Adults who obtan such information and seek out evaluation and treatment for their condition are simply not satisfied any longer with outdated opinions from adult mental health specialists that the disorder does not exist in adults and is commonly outgrown by adolescence, as was the widespread belief in the 1960s.

Also notable in this decade has been the publication of more rigorous studies that demonstrate the efficacy of the stimulants (Spencer et al., 1995) and the antidepressants (Wilens et al., 1996) in the management of adult ADHD. Such studies confirmed the initial clinical speculations in the 1970s as well as the earlier, smaller studies of Paul Wender and his colleagues in the 1970s (see earlier) and 1980s that such medications were efficacious for this disorder in adults (Wender, Reimherr, & Wood, 1981; Wender, Reimherr, Wood, & Ward, 1985). Thus, the adult form of the disorder was found not only to share many of the same patterns of symptoms and comorbid disorders as did the childhood form but also to respond just as well to the same medications that proved themselves so useful in the management of childhood ADHD.

Other Developments

The 1990s has been marked with other significant developments in the field of ADHD. In 1994, new diagnostic criteria for the disorder were set forth in DSM-IV (American Psychiatric Association, 1994). These criteria contained several improvements over those in the earlier DSM-III-R. These criteria are discussed critically in the next chapter (see Table 2.1), but suffice it to say here that they reintroduced criteria for the diagnosis of a purely inattentive form of ADHD similar to ADD without hyperactivity which first appeared in DSM-III. The diagnostic criteria also now require evidence of symptom pervasiveness across settings as well as the demonstration of impairment in a major domain of life functioning (home, school, work). Based on a much larger field trial than any of its predecessors, the DSM-IV criteria are the most empirically based in the history of this disorder.

A further development during this decade was the undertaking by the NIMH of a multisite study of ADHD that focused on various combinations of long-term treatments (Arnold et al., 1997). This study hopes to determine what combinations of treatments are most effective for what types of ADHD based on those treatment strategies that have the greatest empirical support in the prior treatment literature. The results will be very important to the field and should be available within the next few years. In the interim, other long-term treatment studies recently reported findings of great significance to the field. The Swedish government commissioned the longest treatment study of stimulant medication treatment ever undertaken, the results of which indicated that amphetamine treatment remained effective for the entire 15 months of the investigation. More sobering was the recent report that an intensive, year-long treatment program using primarily cognitive-behavioral treatment strategies produced no substantial treatment effects either at posttreatment or at follow-up (Braswell et al., 1997). Similarly, a year-long intensive early intervention program for hyperactive–aggressive children found no significant impact of parent training either at posttreatment or at 2-year follow-up (Barkley et al., 1997); the school-based portion of this multimethod program produced some immediate treatment gains, but by 2-year follow-up these had dissipated (Shelton et al., 1997). Finally, a multisite study of stimulant medication with and without intensive behavioral and psychosocial interventions was reported to have found that the psychosocial interventions added little or nothing to treatment outcome beyond that achieved by stimulant medication alone (Abikoff & Hechtman, 1995). Although these studies do not so much undermine the earlier studies on the effectiveness of behavioral interventions with ADHD children, they do sggest that some of those interventions produce minimal or no improvement when used on a large-scale basis, that the extent of improvement is difficult to detect when adjunctive stimulant medication is also used, and that treatment effects may not be able to be maintained over time following treatment termination.

This decade also witnessed the emergence of trends that are likely to further develop over the next decade. These trends include a renewed interest in theory development related to ADHD (Barkley, 1997a, 1997b; Quay, 1988, 1997; Sergeant & van der Meere, 1994; van der Meere, in press) as well as an expanding recognition and treatment of the disorder in countries outside the United States and Canada (Fonseco et al., 1995; Shalev, Hartman, Stavsky, & Sergeant, 1995; Toone & van der Linden, 1997; Vermeersch & Fombonne, 1995). A new stimulant medication, Adderall, appeared on the market in this decade that shows promise as being as effective for ADHD as the other stimulants (Swanson et al., 1997), and at least three new nonstimulant medications and an additional stimulant were in development or in Phase II clinical trials by several pharmaceutical companies as of this writing. There also appeared to be an increasing interest in the use of peers as treatment agents in several new behavioral intervention programs for academic performance and peer conflict in school settings (see Cunningham & Cunningham, Chapter 16, this volume; DuPaul & Henningson, 1993). These developments, when combined with those surely to continue in molecular genetics, neuroimaging, and adult ADHD, as well as other trends under way in the field of ADHD, are likely to make the next decade as or more exciting than the present one and will surely further our understanding of the nature, diagnosis, and management of this prevalent disorder in children and adults.

The Prevailing View at the End of the 1990s

Although this decade is not yet over as of this writing, it seems clear that a shift is under way back viewing ADHD as far more influenced by neurological and genetic factors than by social or environmental ones. Clearly, the interaction of these sources of influence are generally well accepted by professionals at this time, but greater emphasis is now being placed on the former more than the latter in understanding the potential causation of the disorder. Moreover, evidence began accruing that the influence of the environment on the symptoms of the disorder fall chiefly in the realm of unique or nonshared factors rather than among the more oft-considered but now weakly supported common or shared environment.

There was also a discernible shift over this decade in the recognition that deficits in behavioral inhibition may be the most distinguishing characteristic of this disorder from other mental and developmental disorders (Barkley, 1997b; Pennington & Ozonoff, 1996; Schachar, Tannock, & Logan, 1993), and that this deficit is associated with a significant disruption in the development of normal self-regulation. It is also noteworthy that the subtype of ADHD comprising chiefly inattention without impulsive–hyperactive behavior may possibly be a qualitatively distinct disorder entirely from those children who have hyperactive–impulsive behavior (Barkley et al., 1992; Goodyear & Hynd, 1992; Lahey & Carlson, 1992). The issue of comorbidity became an increasingly important one in subgrouping ADHD children, leading to greater understanding in the manner in which disorders coexisting with ADHD may influence family functioning, academic success, developmental course and outcome, and even treatment response. In contrast to the attitudes apparent in the middle of this century, the view of ADHD at the close of the century is a less developmentally benign one owing in large part to multiple follow-up studies that documented the pervasiveness of difficulties with adaptive functioning that occurred in the adult lives of many, though by no means all, cases clinically diagnosed in childhood.

And there is little doubt that the use of pharmacology in the management of the disorder will continue its dramatic rise in popularity, owing in no small part to the repeated demonstration of the efficacy of stimulants in the treatment of the disorder, the greater recognition of subtypes of ADHD as well as girls and adults with ADHD, and the rather discouraging results of multimethod intensive psychosocial intervention programs of late. Even so, combinations of medication with psychosocial and educational treatment programs remained the norm in recommendations for the management of the disorder across this decade, much as they were in the 1980s.

The expansion, solidification, and increased political activity and power of the patient and family support organizations, such as CHADD, across this decade were indeed a marvel to behold. They clearly led to far wider public recognition of the disorder, as well as to controversies over its existence, definition, and treatment with stimulant medications, but the general trend toward greater public acceptance of ADHD as a developmental disability remains a largely optimistic one. Moreover, such political activity resulted in increased eligibility of those with ADHD for entitlements, under the IDEA, and legal protections, under the Americans with Disabilities Act of 1990 (Public Law 101-336).

ADHD has undoubtedly become a mature disorder and field of scientific study, widely accepted throughout the mental health and pediatric profession as a legitimate developmental disability. At the close of this century it is unmistakably one of the most well-studied childhood disorders and the object of renewed research initiatives into its adult counterparts, which should eventually lead to as widespread an acceptance of adult ADHD as has occurred for the childhood version of the disorder. Further discoveries into its nature, causes, and developmental course promise tremendous advances in our insight not only into this disorder but also into the very nature and development of human self-regulation more generally and its rather substantial neurological, genetic, and unique environmental underpinnings.

REFERENCES

Abikoff, E. (1987). An evaluation of cognitive behavior therapy for hyperactive children. In B. Lahey & A. Kazdin (Eds.), *Advances in clinical child psychology* (Vol. 10, pp. 171–216). New York: Plenum.

Abikoff, H., Gittelman-Klein, R., & Klein, D. (1977). Validation of a classroom observation code for hyperactive children. *Journal of Consulting and Clinical Psychology, 45,* 772–783.

Abikoff, H., & Hechtman, L. (1995, June). *Multimodal treatment study of children with attention deficit hyperactivity disorder.* Paper presented at the International Society for Research in Child and Adolescent Psychopathology, London.

Achenbach, T. M., & Edelbrock, C. S. (1983). *Manual for the Child Behavior Profile and Child Behavior Checklist.* Burlington, VT: Author.

Achenbach, T. M., & Edelbrock, C. S. (1986). Empirically based assessment of the behavioral/emotional problems of 2- and 3-year-old children. *Journal of Abnormal Child Psychology, 15,* 629–650.

Ackerman, P. T., Dykman, R. A., & Oglesby, D. M. (1983). Sex and group differences in reading and attention disordered children with and without hyperkinesis. *Journal of Learning Disabilities, 16,* 407–415.

Allyon, T., Layman, D. & Kandel, H. (1975). A behavioral–educational alternative to drug control of hyperactive children. *Journal of Applied Behavior Analysis, 8,* 137–146.

American Psychiatric Association. (1968). *Diagnostic and statistical manual of mental disorders* (2nd ed.). Washington, DC: Author.

American Psychiatric Association. (1980). *Diagnostic and statistical manual of mental disorders* (3rd ed.). Washington, DC: Author.

American Psychiatric Association. (1987). *Diagnostic and statistical manual of mental disorders* (3rd ed., rev.). Washington, DC: Author.

American Psychiatric Association. (1994). *Diagnostic and statistical manual of mental disorders* (4th ed.). Washington, DC: Author.

Anastopoulos, A. D., & Barkley, R. A. (1990). Counseling and parent training. In R. A. Barkley, *Attention-deficit hyperactivity disorder: A handbook for diagnosis and treatment* (pp. 397–431). New York: Guilford Press.

Arnold, L. E., Abikoff, H. B., Cantwell, D. P., Connors, C. K., Elliott, G., Greenhill, L. L., Hechtman, L., Hinshaw, S. P., Hoza, B., Jensen, P. S., Kraemer, H. C., March, J. S., Newcorn, J. H., Pelham, W. E., Richters, J. E., Schiller, E., Severe, J. B., Swanson, J. M., Vereen, D., & Wells, K. C. (1997). National Institute of Mental Health collaborative multimodal treatment study of children with ADHD (the MTA). *Archives of General Psychiatry, 54*, 865–870.

Associated Press. (1988, January). To many, Ritalin is a "chemical billy club." *Worcester Telegram and Gazette.*

August, G. J., & Stewart, M. A. (1983). Family subtype of childhood hyperactivity. *Journal of Nervous and Mental Disease, 171*, 362–368.

Barkley, R. A. (1977). A review of stimulant drug research with hyperactive children. *Journal of Child Psychology and Psychiatry, 18*, 137–165.

Barkley, R. A. (Ed). (1978). Special issue on hyperactivity. *Journal of Pediatric Psychology, 3.*

Barkley, R. A. (1981). *Hyperactive children: A handbook for diagnosis and treatment.* New York: Guilford Press.

Barkley, R. A. (1982). Guidelines for defining hyperactivity in children (attention deficit disorder with hyperactivity). In B. Lahey & A. Kazdin (Eds.), *Advances in clinical child psychology* (Vol. 5, pp. 137–180). New York: Plenum.

Barkley, R. A. (1984). *Do as we say, not as we do: The problem of stimulus control and rule-governed behavior in attention deficit disorder with hyperactivity.* Paper presented at the Highpoint Hospital Conference on Attention Deficit and Conduct Disorders, Toronto, Canada.

Barkley, R. A. (1987). Child behavior rating scales and checklists. In M. Rutter, A. H. Tuma, & I. Lann (Eds.), *Assessment and diagnosis in child psychopathology* (pp. 113–155). New York: Guilford Press.

Barkley, R.A. (1988). Tic disorders and Tourette's syndrome. In E. J. Mash & L. G. Terdal (Eds.), *Behavioral assessment of childhood disorders* (2nd ed., pp. 552–585). New York: Guilford Press.

Barkley, R. A. (1989a). The problem of stimulus control and rule-governed behavior in children with attention deficit disorder with hyperactivity. In J. Swanson & L. Bloomingdale (Eds.), *Attention deficit disorders* (pp. 203–234). New York: Pergamon Press.

Barkley, R. A. (1989b). Hyperactive girls and boys: Stimulant drug effects on mother–child interactions. *Journal of Child Psychology and Psychiatry, 30*, 379–390.

Barkley, R. A. (1989c). Attention-deficit hyperactivity disorders. In E. J. Mash & R. A. Barkley (Eds.), *Treatment of childhood disorders* (pp. 39–72). New York: Guilford Press.

Barkley, R. A. (1990). *Attention-deficit hyperactivity disorder: A handbook for diagnosis and treatment.* New York: Guilford Press.

Barkley, R. A. (1991). The ecological validity of laboratory and analogue assessments of ADHD Symptoms. *Journal of Abnormal Child Psychology, 19*, 149–178.

Barkley, R. A. (1997a). Inhibition, sustained attention, and executive functions: Constructing a unifying theory of ADHD. *Psychological Bulletin, 121*, 65–94.

Barkley, R. A. (1997b). *ADHD and the nature of self-control.* New York: Guilford Press.

Barkley, R., Copeland, A., & Sivage, C. (1980). A self-control classroom for hyperactive children. *Journal of Autism and Developmental Disorders, 10*, 75–89.

Barkley, R. A., & Cunningham, C. E. (1979). The effects of methylphenidate on the mother–child interactions of hyperactive children. *Archives of General Psychiatry, 36*, 201–208.

Barkley, R. A., DuPaul, G. J., & McMurray, M.B. (1990). A comprehensive evaluation of attention deficit disorder with and without hyperactivity. *Journal of Consulting and Clinical Psychology, 58*, 775–789.

Barkley, R. A., DuPaul, G. J., & McMurray, M.B. (1991). Attention deficit disorder with and without hyperactivity: Clinical response to three doses of methylphenidate. *Pediatrics, 87*, 519–531.

Barkley, R. A., & Edelbrock, C. S. (1987). Assessing situational variation in children's behavior problems: The Home and School Situations Questionnaires. In R. Prinz (Ed.), *Advances in behavioral assessment of children and families* (Vol. 3, pp. 157–176). Greenwich, CT: JAI Press.

Barkley, R. A., Fischer, M., Edelbrock, C. S., & Smallish, L. (1990). The adolescent outcome of hyperactive children diagnosed by research criteria: I. An 8-year prospective followup study. *Journal of the American Academy of Child and Adolescent Psychiatry, 29*, 546–557.

Barkley, R. A., Fischer, M., Edelbrock, C. S., & Smallish, L. (1991). The adolescent outcome of hyperactive children diagnosed by research criteria: III. Mother–child interactions, family conflicts, and maternal psychopathology. *Journal of Child Psychology and Psychiatry, 32*, 233–256.

Barkley, R. A., Fischer, M., Newby, R., & Breen, M. (1988). Development of a multi-method clinical protocol for assessing stimulant drug responses in ADHD children. *Journal of Clinical Child Psychology, 17*, 14–24.

Barkley, R. A., Grodzinsky, G., & DuPaul, G. (1992). Frontal lobe functions in attention deficit disorder with and without hyperactivity: A review and research report. *Journal of Abnormal Child Psychology, 20*, 163–188.

Barkley, R. A., Karlsson, J., & Pollard, S. (1985). Effects of age on the mother–child interactions of hyperactive children. *Journal of Abnormal Child Psychology, 13*, 631–638.

Barkley, R. A., Karlsson, J., Pollard, S., & Murphy, J.V. (1985). Developmental changes in the mother–child interactions of hyperactive boys: Effects of two dose levels of Ritalin. *Journal of Child Psychology and Psychiatry and Allied Disciplines, 26*, 705–715.

Barkley, R. A., Shelton, T. L., Crosswait, C., Moorehouse, M., Fletcher, K., Barrett, S., Jenkins, L., & Metevia, L. (1997). *An early behavioral and educational intervention program for aggressive and hyperactive–impulsive children.* Manuscript submitted for publication.

Barkley, R. A., & Ullman, D. G. (1975). A comparison of objective measures of activity level and distractibility in hyperactive and nonhyperactive children. *Journal of Abnormal Child Psychology, 3*, 213–244.

Bass, A. (1988, March 28). Debate over Ritalin is heating up: Experts say critics are lashing out for all the wrong reasons. *Boston Globe*, pp. 36–38.

Bender, L. (1942). Postencephalitic behavior disorders in children. In J. B. Neal (Ed.), *Encephalitis: A clinical study.* New York: Grune & Stratton.

Benninger, R. J. (1989). Dopamine and learning: Implications for attention deficit disorder and hyperkinetic syndrome. In T. Sagvolden & T. Archer (Eds.), *Attention deficit disorder: Clinical and basic research* (pp. 323–338). Hillsdale, NJ: Erlbaum.

Bettelheim, B. (1973). Bringing up children. *Ladies Home Journal*, p. 23.

Biederman, J., Baldessarini, R. J., Wright, V., Knee, D., & Harmatz, J. S. (1989). A double-blind placebo controlled study of desimpramine in the treatment of ADD: I. Efficacy. *Journal of the American Academy of Child and Adolescent Psychiatry, 28*, 777–784.

Biederman, J., Faraone, S. V., & Lapey, K. (1992). Comorbidity of diagnosis in attention-deficit hyperactivity disorder. In G. Weiss (Ed.), *Child and adolescent psychiatric clinics of North America: Attention-deficit hyperactivity disorder* (pp. 335–360). Philadelphia: Saunders.

Biederman, J., Faraone, S. V., Mick, E., Spencer, T., Wilens, T., Kiely, K., Guite, J., Ablon, J. S., Reed, E., Warburton, R. (1995). High risk for attention deficit hyperactivity disorder among children of parents with childhood onset of the disorder: A pilot study. *American Journal of Psychiatry, 152*, 431–435.

Biederman, J., Faraone, S. V., Spencer, T., Wilens, T., Norman, D., Lapey, K. A., Mick, E., Lehman, B. K., & Doyle, A. (1993). Patterns of psychiatric comorbidity, cognition, and psychosocial functioning in adults with attention deficit hyperactivity disorder. *American Journal of Psychiatry, 150*, 1792–1798.

Biederman, J., Gastfriend, D. R., & Jellinek, M. S. (1986). Desipramine in the treatment of children with attention deficit disorder. *Journal of Clinical Psychopharmacology, 6*, 359–363.

Biederman, J., Keenan, K., & Faraone, S. V. (1990). Parent-based diagnosis of attention deficit disorder predicts a diagnosis based on teacher report. *American Journal of Child and Adolescent Psychiatry, 29*, 698–701.

Biederman, J., Munir, K., & Knee, D. (1987). Conduct and Oppositional Defiant Disorder in clinically referred children with Attention Deficit Disorder: A controlled family study. *Journal of the American Academy of Child and Adolescent Psychiatry, 26*, 724–727.

Birch, H. G. (1964). *Brain damage in children: The biological and social aspects.* Baltimore: Williams & Wilkins.

Blau, A. (1936). Mental changes following head trauma in children. *Archives of Neurology and Psychiatry, 35,* 722–769.

Block, G. H. (1977). Hyperactivity: a cultural perspective. *Journal of Learning Disabilities, 110,* 236–240.

Blum, K., Cull, J. G., Braverman, E. R., & Comings, D. E. (1996). Reward deficiency syndrome. *American Scientist, 84,* 132–145.

Bond, E. D., & Appel, K. E. (1931). *The treatment of behavior disorders following encephalitis.* New York: Commonwealth Fund.

Bornstein, P. H., & Quevillon, R. P. (1976). The effeects of a self-instructional package on overactive preschool boys. *Journal of Applied Behavior Analysis, 9,* 179–188.

Bradley, W. (1937). The behavior of children receiving benzedrine. *American Journal of Psychiatry, 94,* 577–585.

Bradley, W., & Bowen, C. (1940). School performance of children receiving amphetamine (benzedrine) sulfate. *American Journal of Orthopsychiatry, 10,* 782–788.

Braswell, L., August, G. J., Bloomquist, M. L., Realmuto, G. M., Skare, S. S., & Crosby, R. D. (1997). School-based secondary prevention for children with disruptive behavior: Initial outcomes. *Journal of Abnormal Child Psychology, 25,* 197–208.

Brown, R. T., & Borden, K. A. (1986). Hyperactivity in adolescence: Some misconceptions and new directions. *Journal of Clinical Child Psychology, 15,* 194–209.

Brown, R. T., Wynne, M. E., & Medinis, R. (1985). Methylphenidate and cognitive therapy: A comparison of treatment approaches with hyperactive boys. *Journal of Abnormal Child Psychology, 13,* 69–88.

Burks, H. (1960). The hyperkinetic child. *Exceptional Children, 27,* 18.

Byers, R. K., & Lord, E. E. (1943). Late effects of lead poisoning on mental development. *American Journal of Diseases of Children, 66,* 471–494.

Camp, B. W. (1980). Two psychoeducational treatment programs for young aggressive boys. In C. Whalen & B. Henker (Eds.), *Hyperactive children: The social ecology of identification and treatment* (pp. 191–220). New York: Academic Press.

Campbell, S. B. (1973). Mother–child interaction in reflective, impulsive, and hyperacative children. *Developmental Psychology, 8,* 341–349.

Campbell, S. B. (1975). Mother-child interactions: A comparison of hyperactive, learning disabled, and normal boys. *American Journal of Orthopsychiatry, 45,* 51–57.

Campbell, S. B. (1987). Parent-referred problem three-year olds: Developmental changes in symptoms. *Journal of Child Psychology and Psychiatry, 28,* 835–846.

Campbell, S. B., Douglas, V. I., & Morganstern, G. (1971). Cognitive styles in hyperactive children and the effect of methylphenidate. *Journal of Child Psychology and Psychiatry, 12,* 55–67.

Campbell, S. B., & Ewing, L. J. (1990). Follow-up of hard-to-manage preschoolers: Adjustment at age nine years and predictors of continuing symptoms. *Journal of Child Psychology and Psychiatry, 31,* 891–910.

Cantwell, D. (1975). *The hyperactive child.* New York: Spectrum.

Cantwell, D. (1981). Foreword. In R. A. Barkley, *Hyperactive children: A handbook for diagnosis and treatment.* New York: Guilford Press.

Cantwell, D. P., & Satterfield, J. H. (1978). The prevalence of acdemic underachievement in hyperactive children. *Journal of Pediatric Psychology, 3,* 168–171.

Carlson, C. (1986). Attention deficit disorder without hyperactivity: A review of preliminary experimental evidence. In B. Lahey & A. Kazdin (Eds.), *Advances in clinical child psychology* (Vol. 9, pp. 153–176). New York: Plenum.

Castellanos, F. X., Giedd, J. N., Eckburg, P., Marsh, W. L., Vaituzis, C., Kaysen, D., Hamburger, S. D., & Rapoport, J. L. (1994). Quantitative morphology of the caudate nucleus in attention deficit hyperactivity disorder. *American Journal of Psychiatry, 151,* 1791–1796.

Castellanos, F. X., Giedd, J. N., Marsh, W. L., Hamburger, S. D., Vaituzis, A. C., Dickstein, D. P., Sarfatti, S. E., Vauss, Y. C., Snell, J. W., Lange, N., Kaysen, D., Krain, A. L., Ritchhie, G. F., Rajapakse, J. C., & Rapoport, J. L. (1996). Quantitative brain magnetic resonance imaging in attention-deficit hyperactivity disorder. *Archives of General Psychiatry, 53,* 607–616.

Chelune, G. J., Ferguson, W., Koon, R., & Dickey, T. O. (1986). Frontal lobe disinhibition in attention deficit disorder. *Child Psychiatry and Human Development, 16,* 221–234.

Chess, S. (1960). Diagnosis and treatment of the hyperactive child. *New York State Journal of Medicine, 60,* 2379–2385.

Childers, A. T. (1935). Hyper-activity in children having behavior disorders. *American Journal of Orthopsychiatry, 5,* 227–243.

Citizens Commission on Human Rights. (1987). *Ritalin: A warning to parents.* Los Angeles: Church of Scientology.

Clark, D. (1988, January). [Guest on the syndicated television show *Sally Jessy Raphael*]. New York: Multimedia Entertainment.

Clements, S. D. (1966). *Task Force One: Minimal brain dysfunction in children* (National Institute of Neurological Diseases and Blindness, Monograph No. 3). Rockville, MD: U.S. Department of Health, Education, and Welfare.

Comings, D. E., Comings, B. G., Muhleman, D., Dietz, G., Shahbahrami, B., Tast, D., Knell, E., Kocsis, P., Baumgarten, R., Kovacs, B. W., Levy, D. L., Smith, M., Borison, R. L., Evans, D. D., Klein, D. N., MacMurry, J., Tosk, J. M., Sverd, J., Gysin, R., & Flanagan, S. D. (1991). The dopamine D2 receptor locus as a modifying gene in neuropsychiatric disorders. *Journal of the American Medical Association, 266,* 1793–1800.

Conners, C. K. (1969). A teacher rating scale for use in drug studies with children. *American Journal of Psychiatry, 126,* 884–888.

Conners, C. K. (1980). *Food additives and hyperactive children.* New York: Plenum.

Conners, C. K. (1995). *The Conners Continuous Performance Test.* North Tonawanda, NY: MultiHealth Systems.

Conners, C. K., & Rothschild, G. H. (1968). Drugs and learning in children. In J. Hellmuth (Ed.), *Learning disorders* (Vol. 3, pp. 191–223). Seattle, WA: Special Child.

Conrad, P. (1975). The discovery of hyperkinesis: Notes on the medicalization of deviant behavior. *Social Problems, 23,* 12–21.

Cook, E. H., Stein, M. A., Krasowski, M. D., Cox, N. J., Olkon, D. M., Kieffer, J. E., & Leventhal, B. L. (1995). Association of attention deficit disorder and the dopamine transporter gene. *American Journal of Human Genetics, 56,* 993–998.

Cook, E. H., Stein, M. A., & Leventhal, D. L. (1997). Family-based association of attention-deficit/hyperactivity disorder and the dopamine transporter. In K. Blum (Ed.), *Handbook of psychiatric genetics* (pp. 297–310). New York: CRC Press.

Corkum, P. V., & Siegel, L. S. (1993). Is the continuous performance task a valuable research tool for use with children with attention-deficit–hyperactivity disorder? *Journal of Child Psychology and Psychiatry, 34,* 1217–1239.

Costello, E. J., Loeber, R., & Stouthamer-Loeber, M. (1991). Pervasive and situational hyperactivity—Confounding effect of informant: A research note. *Journal of Child and Psychiatry, 32,* 367–376.

Cowart, V. S. (1988). The Ritalin controversy: What's made this drug's opponents hyperactive? *Journal of the American Medical Association, 259,* 2521–2523.

Cruickshank, W. M., & Dolphin, J. E. (1951). The educational implications of psychological studies of cerebral palsied children. *Exceptional Children, 18,* 3–11.

Cunningham, C. E. (1990). A family systems approach to parent training. In R. A. Barkley, *Attention-deficit hyperactivity disorder: A handbook for diagnosis and treatment* (pp. 432–461). New York: Guilford Press.

Cunningham, C. E., & Barkley, R. (1978). The effects of Ritalin on the mother–child interactions of hyperkinetic twin boys. *Developmental Medicine and Child Neurology, 20,* 634–642.

Cunningham, C. E., & Barkley, R. A. (1979). The interactions of hyperactive and normal children with their mothers during free play and structured task. *Child Development, 50,* 217–224 .

Cunningham, C. E., Siegel, L. S., & Offord, D. R. (1985). A developmental dose response analysis of the effects of methylphenirtate on the peer interactions of attention deficit disordered boys. *Journal of Child Psychology and Psychiatry, 26,* 955–971.

Danforth, J. S., Barkley, R. A., & Stokes, T. F. (1991). Observations of parent–child interactions with hyperactive children: Research and clinical implications. *Clinical Psychology Review, 11,* 703–727.

Diaz, R. M., & Berk, L. E. (1995). A Vygotskian critique of self-instructional training. *Development and Psychopathology, 7,* 369–392.

Dockx, P. (1988, January 11). Are schoolchildren getting unnecessary drugs? *Woonsocket, RI, Sun Chronicle*, p. 15.

Dolphin, J. E., & Cruickshank, W. M. (1951a). The figure background relationship in children with cerebral palsy. *Journal of Clinical Psychology, 7*, 228–231.

Dolphin, J. E., & Cruickshank, W. M. (1951b). Pathology of concept formation in children with cerebral palsy. *American Journal of Mental Deficiency, 56*, 386–392.

Dolphin, J. E., & Cruickshank, W. M. (1951c). Visuo-motor perception of children with cerebral palsy. *Quarterly Journal of Child Behavior, 3*, 189–209.

Douglas, V. I. (1972). Stop, look, and listen: The problem of sustained attention and impulse control in hyperactive and normal children. *Canadian Journal of Behavioural Science, 4*, 259–282.

Douglas, V. I. (Ed.). (1976). Special issue on hyperactivity. *Journal of Abnormal Child Psychology, 4*.

Douglas, V. I. (1980a). Higher mental processes in hyperactive children: Implications for training. In R. Knights & D. Bakker (Eds.), *Treatment of hyperactive and learning disordered children* (pp. 65–92). Baltimore: University Park Press.

Douglas, V. I. (1980b). Treatment and training approaches to hyperactivity: Establishing internal or external control. In C. Whalen & B. Henker (Eds.), *Hyperactive children: The social ecology of identification and treatment* (pp. 283–318). New York: Academic Press.

Douglas, V. I. (1983). Attention and cognitive problems. In M. Rutter (Ed.), *Developmental neuropsychiatry* (pp. 280–329). New York: Guilford Press.

Douglas, V. I. (1988). Cognitive deficits in children with attention deficit disorder with hyperactivity. In. L. M. Bloomingdale & J. A. Sergeant (Eds.), *Attention deficit disorder: Criteria, cognition, intervention* (pp. 65–82). London: Pergamon Press.

Douglas, V. I. (1989). Can Skinnerian psychology acount for the deficits in attention deficit disorder? A reply to Barkley. In L. Bloomingdale & J. Sergeant (Eds.), *Attention deficit disorder* (Vol. 6, pp. 235–253). New York: Pergamon Press.

Douglas, V. I., & Peters, K. G. (1979). Toward a clearer definition of the attentional deficit of hyperactive children. In G. A. Hale & M. Lewis (Eds.), *Attention and the developments of cognitive skills* (pp. 173–248). New York: Plenum.

Draeger, S., Prior, M., & Sanson, A. (1986). Visual and auditory attention performance in hyperactive children: Competence or compliance. *Journal of Abnormal Child Psychology, 14*, 411–424.

Dubey, D. R., & Kaufman, K. F. (1978). Home management of hyperkinetic children. *Journal of Pediatrics, 93*, 141–146.

DuPaul, G. J. (1991). Parent and teacher ratings of ADHD symptoms: Psychometric properties in a community-based sample. *Journal of Clinical Child Psychology, 20*, 242–253.

DuPaul, G. J., & Barkley, R. A. (1992). Situational variability of attention problems: Psychometric properties of the Revised Home and School Situations Questionnaires. *Journal of Clinical Child Psychology, 21*, 178–188.

DuPaul, G. J., Barkley, R. A., & McMurray, M. B. (1994). Response of children with ADHD to methylphenidate: Interaction with internalizing symptoms. *Journal of American Academy of Child and Adolescent Psychiatry, 93*, 894–903.

DuPaul, G. J., & Henningson, P. N. (1993). Peer tutoring effects on the classroom performance of children with attention-deficit hyperactivity disorder. *School Psychology Review, 22*, 134–143.

Dykman, R. A., Ackerman, P. T., & Holcomb, P. J. (1985). Reading disabled and ADD children: Similarities and differences. In D. B. Gray & J. F. Kavanaugh (Eds.), *Biobehavioral measures of dyslexia* (pp. 47–62). Parkton, MD: Your Press.

Ebaugh, F. G. (1923). Neuropsychiatric sequelae of acute epidemic encephalitis in children. *American Journal of Diseases of Children, 25*, 89–97.

Edelbrock, C. S., Rende, R., Plomin, R., & Thompson, L. (1995). A twin study of competence and problem behavior in childhood and early adolescence. *Journal of Child Psychology and Psychiatry, 36*, 775–786.

Ernst, M. (1996). Neuroimaging in attention-deficit/hyperactivity disorder. In G. R. Lyon & J. M. Rumsey (Eds.), *Neuroimaging: A window to the neurological foundations of learning and behavior in children* (pp. 95–118). Baltimore, MD: Paul H. Brookes.

Faraone, S. V. (1996). Discussion of: "Genetic influence on parent-reported attention-related problems in a Norwegian general population twin sample." *Journal of the American Academy of Child and Adolescent Psychiatry, 35,* 596–598.

Feingold, B. (1975). *Why your child is hyperactive.* New York: Random House.

Ferrier, D. (1876). *The functions of the brain.* New York: Putnam.

Filipek, P. A., Semrud-Clikeman, M., Steingard, R. J., Renshaw, P. F., Kennedy, D. N., & Biederman, J. (1997). Volumetric MRI analysis comparing subjects having attention-deficit hyperactivity disorder with normal controls. *Neurology, 48,* 589–601.

Firestone, P., & Martin, J. E. (1979). An analysis of the hyperactive syndrome: A comparison of hyperactive, behavior problem, asthmatic, and normal children, *Journal of Abnormal Child Psychology, 7,* 261–273.

Fischer, M. (1997). Persistence of ADHD in adulthood: It depends on whom you ask. *ADHD Report, 5*(4), 8–10.

Fischer, M., Barkley, R. A., Edelbrock, C.S., & Smallish, L. (1990). The adolescent outcome of hyperactive children diagnosed by research criteria: II. Academic, attentional, and neuropsychological status. *Journal of Consulting and Clinical Psychology, 58,* 580–588.

Flavell, J. H., Beach, D. R., & Chinksy, J. M. (1966). Spontaneous verbal rehearsal in a memory task as a function of age. *Child Development, 37,* 283–299.

Fonseca, A. C., Simones, A., Rebelo, J. A., Ferreira, J. A., Cardoso, F., & Temudo, P. (1995). Hyperactivity and conduct disorder among Portugese children and adolescents: Data from parent's and teacher's reports. In J. Sergeant (Ed.), *Eunethydis: European approaches to hyperkinetic disorder* (pp. 115–129). Amsterdam: University of Amsterdam.

Forehand, R. & McMahon, R. (1981). *Helping the noncompliant child.* New York: Guilford Press.

Freibergs, V. (1965). *Concept learning in hyperactive and normal children.* Unpublished doctoral dissertation, McGill University, Montreal.

Freibergs, V., & Douglas, V. I. (1969). Concept learning in hyperactive and normal children. *Journal of Abnormal Psychology, 74,* 388–395.

Gelernter, J. O., O'Malley, S., Risch, N., Kranzler, H. R., Krystal, J., Merikangas, K., Kennedy, J. L., et al. (1991). No association between an allele at the D2 dopamine receptor gene (DRD2) and alcoholism. *Journal of the American Medical Association, 266,* 1801–1807.

Giedd, J. N., Castellanos, F. X., Casey, B. J., Kozuch, P., King, A. C., Hamburger, S. D., & Rapoport, J. L. (1994). Quantitative morphology of the corpus callosum in attention deficit hyperactivity disorder. *American Journal of Psychiatry, 151,* 665–669.

Gilger, J. W., Pennington, B. F., & DeFries, J. C. (1992). A twin study of the etiology of comorbidity: Attention-deficit hyperactivity disorder and dyslexia. *Journal of American Academy of Child and Adolescent Psychiatry, 31,* 343–348.

Gittelman, R. (1988). The assessment of hyperactivity: The DSM-III approach. In L. Bloomingdale & J. Sergeant (Eds.), *Attention deficit disorder: Criteria, cognition, and intervention* (pp. 9–28). New York: Pergamon Press.

Gittelman, R., & Abikoff, H. (1989). The role of psychostimulants and psychosocial treatments in hyperkinesis. In T. Sagvolden & T. Archer (Eds.), *Attention deficit disorder: Clinical and basic research* (pp. 167–180). Hillsdale, NJ: Erlbaum.

Gittelman, R., Abikoff, H., Pollack, E., Klein, D., Katz, S., & Mattes, J. (1980). A controlled trial of behavior modification and methylphenidate in hyperactive children. In C. Whalen & B. Henker (Eds.), *Hyperactive children: The social ecology of identification and treatment* (pp. 221–246). New York: Academic Press.

Gittelman-Klein, R., Klein, D. F., Abikoff, H., Katz, S., Gloisten, C., & Kates, W. (1976). Relative efficacy of methylphenidate and behavior modification in hyperkinetic children: An interim report. *Journal of Abnormal Child Psychology, 4,* 261–279.

Gittelman, R., Mannuzza, S., Shenker, R., & Bonagura, N. (1985). Hyperactive boys almost grown up: I. Psychiatric status. *Archives of General Psychiatry, 42,* 937–947.

Gjone, H., Stevenson, J., & Sundet, J. M. (1996). Genetic influence on parent-reported attention-related problems in a Norwegian general population twin sample. *Journal of the American Academy of Child and Adolescent Psychiatry, 35,* 588–596.

Gjone, H., Stevenson, J., Sundet, J. M., & Eilertsen, D. E. (1996). Changes in heritability across increasing levels of behavior problems in young twins. *Behavior Genetics, 26,* 419–426.

Glow, P. H., & Glow, R. A. (1979). Hyperkinetic impulse disorder: A developmental defect of motivation. *Genetic Psychological Monographs, 100,* 159–231.

Goldstein, S. (1997). *Managing attention and learning disorders in late adolescence and adulthood.* New York: Wiley.

Gomez, R. L., Janowsky, D., Zetin, M., Huey, L., & Clopton, P. L. (1981). Adult psychiatric diagnosis and symptoms compatible with the hyperactive syndrome: A retrospective study. *Journal of Clinical Psychiatry, 42,* 389–394.

Goodman, J. R., & Stevenson, J. (1989). A twin study of hyperactivity: II. The aetiological role of genes, family relationships, and perinatal adversity. *Journal of Child Psychology and Psychiatry, 30,* 691–709.

Goodyear, P., & Hynd, G. (1992). Attention deficit disorder with (ADD/H) and without (ADD/WO) hyperactivity: Behavioral and neuropsychological differentiation. *Journal of Clinical Child Psychology, 21,* 273–304.

Gordon, M. (1979). The assessment of impulsivity and mediating behaviors in hyperactive and nonhyperactive children. *Journal of Abnormal Child Psychology, 7,* 317–326.

Gordon, M. (1983). *The Gordon Diagnostic System.* DeWitt, NY: Gordon Systems.

Gordon, M. (1997). ADHD in cyberspace. *ADHD Report, 5*(4), 4–6.

Gordon, M., & Mettelman, B. B. (1988). The assessment of attention: I. standardization and reliability of a behavior based measure. *Journal of Clinical Psychology, 44,* 682–690.

Gray, J. A. (1982). *The neuropsychology of anxiety.* New York: Oxford Press.

Gray, J. A. (1987). *The psychology of fear and stress* (2nd ed.). Cambridge: Cambridge University Press.

Gray, J. A. (1994). Three fundamental emotional systems. In P. Ekman & R. J. Davidson (Eds.), *The nature of emotion: Fundamental questions* (pp. 243–247). New York: Oxford University Press.

Greenberg, L. M., & Waldman, I. D. (1992). *Developmental normative data on the Test of Variables of Attention (T.O.V.A.).* Minneapolis: Department of Psychiatry, University of Minnesota Medical School.

Haenlein, M., & Caul, W. F. (1987). Attention deficit disorder with hyperactivity: A specific hypothesis of reward dysfunction. *Journal of American Academy of Child and Adolescent Psychiatry, 26,* 356–362.

Hallowell, E. M., & Ratey, J. J. (1994). *Driven to distraction.* New York: Pantheon.

Halperin, J. M., & Gittelman, R., Klein, D. F., & Rudel, R. G. (1984). Reading-disabled hyperactive children: A distinct subgroup of Attention Deficit Disorder with hyperactivity? *Journal of Abnormal Child Psychology, 12,* 1–14.

Harticollis, P. (1968). The syndrome of minimal brain dysfunction in young adult patients. *Bulletin of the Menninger Clinic, 32,* 102–114.

Hastings, J., & Barkley, R. A. (1978). A review of psychophysiological research with hyperactive children. *Journal of Abnormal Child Psychology, 7,* 413–337.

Henig, R. M. (1988, March 15). Courts enter the hyperactivity fray: The drug Ritalin helps control behavior, but is it prescribed needlessly? *Washington Post,* p. 8.

Henker, B. & Whalen, C. (1980). The changing faces of hyperacivity; Retrospect and prospect. In C. Whalen & B. Henker (Eds.), *Hyperactive children: The social ecology of identification and treatment* (pp. 321–364). New York: Academic Press.

Herbert, M. (1964). The concept and testing of brain damage in children: A review. *Journal of Child Psychology and Psychiatry, 5,* 197–217.

Hertzig, M. E., Bortner, M., & Birch, H. G. (1969). Neurologic findings in children educationally designated as "brain damaged." *American Journal of Orthopsychiatry, 39,* 437–447.

Hinshaw, S. P. (1987). On the distinction between attentional deficits/hyperactivity and conduct problems/aggression in child psychopathology. *Psychological Bulletin, 101,* 443–447.

Hinshaw, S. P., Henker, B., & Whalen, C. K. (1984). Cognitive-behavioral and pharmacologic interventions for hyperactive boys: Comparative and combined effects. *Journal of Consulting and Clinical Psychology, 52,* 739–749.

Hoffman, H. (1865). Die Geschichte vom Zappel-Philipp. *Der Struwwelpeter.* Germany: Pestalozzi-Verlag.

Huessy, H. J. (1974). The adult hyperkinetic. *American Journal of Psychiatry, 131,* 724–725.

Humphries, T., Kinsbourne, M., & Swanson, J. (1978). Stimulant effects on cooperation and social interaction between hyperactive children and their mothers. *Journal of Child Psychology and Psychiatry, 19,* 13–22.

Hunt, R. D., Caper, L., & O'Connell, P. (1990). Clonidine in child and adolescent psychiatry. *Journal of Child and Adolescent Psychopharmacology, 1,* 87–102.

Hunt, R. D., Cohen, D. J., Anderson, G., & Minderaa, R. B. (1988). Noradrengergic mechanisms in ADDH. In L. Bloomingdale (Ed.), *Attention deficit disorder. Vol. 3: New research in attention, treatment, and psychopharmacology* (pp. 129–148). New York: Pergamon Press.

Hunt, R.D., Minderaa, R., & Cohen, D. J. (1985). Clonidine benefits children with attention deficit disorder and hyperactivity: Report of a double-blind placebo crossover therapeutic trial. *Journal of the American Academy of Child and Adolescent Psychiatry, 24,* 617–629.

Hynd, G. W., Hern, K. L., Novey, E. S., Eliopulos, D., Marshall, R., Gonzalez, J. J., & Voeller, K. K. (1993). Attention-deficit hyperactivity disorder and asymmetry of the caudate nucleus. *Journal of Child Neurology, 8,* 339–347.

Hynd, G. W., Semrud-Clikeman, M., Lorys, A. R., Novey, E. S., & Eliopulos, D. (1990). Brain morphology in developmental dyslexia and attention deficit disorder/hyperactivity. *Archives of Neurology, 47,* 919–926.

Hynd, G. W., Semrud-Clikeman, M., Lorys, A. R., Novey, E. S., Eliopulos, D., & Lyytinen, H. (1991). Corpus callosum morphology in attention deficit-hyperactivity disorder: morphometric analysis of MRI. *Journal of Learning Disabilities, 24,* 141–146.

James, W. (1890). *The principles of psychology.* London: Dover.

Kahn, E., & Cohen, L. H. (1934). Organic driveness: A brain stem syndrome and an experience. *New England Journal of Medicine, 210,* 748–756.

Kalverboer, A. F. (1988). Hyperactivity and observational studies. In L. Bloomingdale & J. Sergeant (Eds.), *Attention deficit disorder: Criteria, cognition, and intervention* (pp. 29–42). New York: Pergamon Press.

Kelly, K., & Ramundo, P. (1992). *You mean I'm not lazy, stupid, or crazy?* Cincinnati: Tyrell & Jerem.

Kelsoe, J. R., Ginns, E. I., Egeland, J. A., Gerhard, D. S., Goldstein, A. M., Bale, S. J., Pauls, D. L., et al. (1989). Re-evaluation of the linkage relationship between chromosome 11p loci and the gene for bipolar affective disorder in the Old Order Amish. *Nature, 342,* 238–243.

Kendall, P. C., & Braswell, L. (1985). *Cognitive-behavioral therapy for impulsive children.* New York: Guilford Press.

Kessler, J. W. (1980). history of minimal brain dysfunction. In H. Rie & E. Rie (Eds.), *Handbook of minimal brain dysfunctions: A critical view* (pp. 18–52). New York: Wiley.

Kinsbourne, M. (1977). The mechanism of hyperactivity. In M. Blau, I. Rapin, & M. Kinsbourne (Eds.), *Topics in child neurology* (pp. 289–306). New York: Spectrum.

Kirk, S. A. (1963). Behavioral diagnoses and remediation of learning disabilities. In *Proceedings of the annual meeting: Conference on exploration into the problems of the perceptually handicapped child* (Vol. 1, pp. 1–7). Evanston, IL.

Klorman, R. (1992). Cognitive event-related potentials in attention deficit disorder. In S. E. Shaywitz & B. A. Shaywitz (1992). *Attention deficit disorder comes of age: Toward the twenty-first century* (pp. 221–244). Austin, TX: Pro-Ed.

Knights, R. M., & Bakker, D. (Eds.). (1976). *The neuropsychology of learning disorders.* Baltimore: University Park Press.

Knights, R. M., & Bakker, D. (Eds.). (1980). *Treatment of hyperactive and learning disordered children.* Baltimore: University Park Press.

Knobel, M., Wolman, M. B., & Mason, E. (1959). Hyperkinesis and organicity in children. *Archives of General Psychiatry, 1,* 310–321.

Laccetti, S. (1988, August 13). Parents who blame son's suicide on Ritalin use will join protest. *Atlanta Journal,* pp. B1, B7.

Lahey, B. B., & Carlson, C. L. (1992). Validity of the diagnostic category of attention deficit disorder without hyperactivity: A review of the literature. In S. E. Shaywitz & B. A. Shaywitz (1992). *At-*

tention deficit disorder comes of age: Toward the twenty-first century (pp. 119–144). Austin, TX: Pro-Ed.

Lahey, B. B., Pelham, W. E., Schaughency, E. A., Atkins, M. S., Murphy, H. A., Hynd, G. W., Russo, M., Hartdagen, S., & Lorys-Vernon, A. (1988). Dimensions and types of attention deficit disorder with hyperactivity in children: A factor and cluster-analytic approach. *Journal of the American Academy of Child and Adolescent Psychiatry, 27*, 330–335.

Lahoste, G. J., Swanson, J. M., Wigal, S. B., Glabe, C., Wigal, T., King, N., & Kennedy, J. L. (1996). Dopamine D4 receptor gene polymorphism is associated with attention deficit hyperactivity disorder. *Molecular Psychiatry, 1*, 121–124.

Lambert, N. M. (1988). Adolesent outcomes for hyperactive children. *American Psychologist, 43*, 786–799.

Laufer, M., & Denhoff, E. (1957). Hyperkinetic behavior syndrome in children. *Journal of Pediatrics, 50*, 463–474.

Laufer, M., Denhoff, E., & Solomons, G. (1957). Hyperkinetic impulse disorder in children's behavior problems. *Psychosomatic Medicine, 19*, 38–49.

Levin, P. M. (1938). Restlessness in children. *Archives of Neurology and Psychiatry, 39*, 764–770.

Levy, F., & Hay, D. (1992, February). *ADHD in twins and their siblings.* Paper presented at the meeting of the Society for Research in Child and Adolescent Psychopathology, Sarasota, FL.

Loeber, R. (1990). Development and risk factors of juvenile antisocial behavior and delinquency. *Clinical Psychology Review, 10*, 1–42.

Loney, J. (1983). Research diagnostic criteria for childhood hyperactivity. In S. B. Guze, F. J. Earls, & J. E. Barrett (Eds.), *Childhood psychopathology and development* (pp. 109–137). New York: Raven.

Loney, J., Langhorne, J., & Peternite, C. (1978). An empirical basis for subgrouping the hyperkinetic/minimal brain dysfunction syndrome. *Journal of Abnormal Psychology, 87*, 431–444.

Loney, J., & Milich, R. (1982). Hyperactivity, inattention, and aggression in clinical practice. In D. Routh & M. Wolraich (Eds.), *Advances in developmental and behavioral pediatrics* (Vol. 3, pp. 113–147). Greenwich, CT: JAI Press.

Lou, H. C., Henriksen, L., & Bruhn, P. (1984). Focal cerebral hypoperfusion in children with dysphasia and/or attention deficit disorder. *Archives of Neurology, 41*, 825–829.

Lou, H. C., Henriksen, L., Bruhn, P., Borner, H., & Nielsen, J. B. (1989). Striatal dysfunction in attention deficit and hyperkinetic disorder. *Archives of Neurology, 46*, 48–52.

Mann, H. B., & Greenspan, S. I. (1976). The identification and treatment of adult brain dysfunction. *American Journal of Psychiatry, 133*, 1013–1017.

Mannuzza, S., Gittelman-Klein, R., Bessler, A., Malloy, P., & LaPadula, M. (1993). Adult outcome of hyperactive boys: Educational achievement, occupational rank, and psychiatric status. *Archives of General Psychiatry, 50*, 565–576.

Marwitt, S. J., & Stenner, A. J. (1972). Hyperkinesis: Delineation of two patterns. *Exceptional Children, 38*, 401–406.

Mash, E. J., & Johnston, C. (1982). A comparison of motherchild interactions of younger and older hyperactive and normal children. *Child Development, 53*, 1371–1381.

Mash, E. J., & Johnston, C. (1983). Sibling interactions of hyperactive and normal children and their relationship to reports of maternal stress and self-esteem. *Journal of Clinical Child Psychology, 12*, 91–99.

Mattes, J. A. (1980). The role of frontal lobe dysfunction in childhood hyperkinesis. *Comprehensive Psychiatry, 21*, 358–369.

Maynard, R. (1970, June 29). Omaha pupils given "behavior" drugs. *Washington Post.*

McGee, R., Williams, S., & Silva, P. A. (1984a). Behavioral and developmental characteristics of aggressive, hyperactive, and aggressive–hyperactive boys. *Journal of the American Academy of Child Psychiatry, 23*, 270–279.

McGee, R., Williams, S., & Silva, P. A. (1984b). Background characteristics of aggressive, hyperactive, and aggressive–hyperactive boys. *Journal of the American Academy of Child and Adolescent Psychiatry, 23*, 280–284.

McGee, R., Williams, S., Moffitt, T., & Anderson, J. (1989). A comparison of 13-year old boys with attention deficit and/or reading disorder on neuropsychological measures. *Journal of Abnormal Child Psychology, 17*, 37–53.

Meichenbaum, D. (1977). *Cognitive behavior modification: An integrative approach.* New York: Plenum.

Meichenbaum, D. (1988). Cognitive behavioral modification with attention deficit hyperactive children. In L. Bloomingdale & J. Sergeant (Eds.), *Attention deficit disorder: Criteria, cognition, and intervention* (pp. 127–140). New York: Pergamon Press.

Meichenbaum, D., & Goodman, J. (1971). Training impulsive children to talk to themselves: A means of developing self-control. *Journal of Abnormal Psyhology, 77,* 115–126.

Mendelson, W., Johnson, N., & Stewart, M. A. (1971). Hyperactive children as teenagers: A follow-up study. *Journal of Nervous and Mental Disease, 153,* 273–279.

Menkes, M., Rowe, J., & Menkes, J. (1967). A five-year follow-up study on the hyperactive child with minimal brain dysfunction. *Pediatrics, 39,* 393–399.

Meyer, E. & Byers, R. K. (1952). Measles encephalitis: A follow-up study of sixteen patients. *American Journal of Diseases of Children, 84,* 543–579.

Milich, R., Hartung, C. M., Matrin, C. A., & Haigler, E. D. (1994). Behavioral disinhibition and underlying processes in adolescents with disruptive behavior disorders. In D. K. Routh (Ed.), *Disruptive behavior disorders in childhood* (pp.109–138). New York: Plenum.

Milich, R., & Loney, J. (1979). The role of hyperactive and aggressive symptomatology in predicting adolescent outcome among hyperactive children. *Journal of Pediatric Psychology, 4,* 93–112.

Milich, R., Pelham, W., & Hinshaw, S. (1985). Issues in the diagnosis of attention deficit disorder: A cautionary note. *Psychopharmacology Bulletin, 22,* 1101–1104.

Milich, R. , Wolraich, M. , & Lindgren, S. (1986). Sugar and hyperactivity: A critical review of empirical findings. *Clinical Psyhology Review, 6,* 493–513.

Molitch, M., & Eccles, A. K. (1937). Effect of benzedrine sulphate on intelligence scores of children. *American Journal of Psychiatry, 94,* 587–590.

Morrison, J. R., & Minkoff, K. (1975). Explosive personality as a sequel to the hyperactive child syndrome. *Comprehensive Psychiatry, 16,* 343–348.

Morrison, J. R., & Stewart, M. (1973). The psychiatric status of the legal families of adopted hyperactive children. *Archives of General Psychiatry, 28,* 888–891.

Murphy, K., & Barkley, R. A. (1996). Attention deficit hyperactivity disorder in adults. *Comprehensive Psychiatry, 37,* 393–401.

Murphy, K. R., & LeVert, S. (1994). *Out of the fog.* New York: Hyperion.

Nadeau, K. (1995). *A comprehensive guide to adults with attention deficit hyperactivity disorder.* New York: Brunner/Mazel.

National Advisory Committee on Hyperkinesis and Food Additives. (1980). [Report]. New York: Nutrition Foundation.

Nightline. (1988). [Segment on Ritalin controversy]. New York: American Broadcasting Company.

Offord, D. R., Boyle, M. H., Szatmari, P., Rae-Grant, N., Links, P. S., Cadman, D. T., Byles, J. A., Crawford, J. W., Munroe-Blum, H., Byrne C., Thomas H., & Woodward, C. (1987). Ontario child health study: Six month prevalence of disorder and rates of service utilization. *Archives of General Psychiatry, 44,* 832–836.

O'Leary, K. D. (1981). Assessment of hyperactivity: Observational and rating scale methodologies. In S. A. Miller (Ed.), *Nutrition and behavior* (pp. 291–298). Philadelphia: Franklin Institute Press.

O'Leary, K. D., Pelham, W. E., Rosenbaum., A., &, Price, G. H. (1976). Behavioral treatment of hyperkinetic children: An experimental evaluation of its usefulness. *Clinical Pediatrics, 15,* 510–515.

Ounsted, C. (1955). The hyperkinetic syndrome in epileptic children. *Lancet, 53,* 303–311.

Packer, S. (1978). Treatment of minimal brain dysfunction in a young adult. *Canadian Psychiatric Association Journal, 23,* 501–502.

Parry, P. A., & Douglas, V. I. (1976). *The effects of reward on the performance of hyperactive children.* Unpublished doctoral dissertation, McGill University, Montreal.

Parry, P. A., & Douglas, V. I. (1983). Effects of reinforcement on concept identification in hyperactive children. *Journal of Abnormal Child Psychology, 11,* 327–340.

Pasamanick, B., Rogers, M., & Lilienfeld, A. M. (1956). Pregnancy experience and the development of behavior disorder in children. *American Journal of Psychiatry, 112,* 613–617.

Paternite, C., & Loney, J. (1980). Childhood hyperkinesis: Relationships between symptomatology and home environment. In C. K. Whalen & B. Henker (Eds.), *Hyperactive children: The social ecology of identification and treatment* (pp. 105–141). New York: Academic Press.

Patterson, G. R. (1982). *Coercive family process.* Eugene, OR: Castalia.

Patterson, G. R. (1986). Performance models for antisocial boys. *American Psychologist, 41,* 432–444.

Pauls, D. L. (1991). Genetic factors in the expression of attention-deficit hyperactivity disorder. *Journal of Child and Adolescent Psychopharmacology, 1,* 353–360.

Pelham, W. E. (1977). Withdrawal of a stimulant drug and concurrent behavior intervention in the treatment of a hyperactive child. *Behavior Therapy, 8,* 473–479.

Pelham, W. E., Schnedler, R., Bologna, N., & Contreras, A. (1980). Behavioral and stimulant treatment of hyperactive children: A therapy study with methylphenidate probes in a within subject design. *Journal of Applied Behavior Analysis, 13,* 221–236.

Pennington, B. F., & Ozonoff, S. (1996). Executive functions and developmental psychopathology. *Journal of Child Psychology and Psychiatry, 37,* 51–87.

Pfiffner, L. J., & McBurnett, K. (1997). Social skills training with parent generalization: Treatment effects for children with attention deficit disorder. *Journal of Consulting and Clinical Psychology, 65,* 749–757.

Pfiffner, L. J., & O'Leary, S. G. (1987). The efficacy of all-positive management as a function of the prior use of negative consequences. *Journal of Applied Behavior Analysis, 20,* 265–271.

Pliszka, S. R. (1987). Tricyclic antidepressants in the treatment of children with attention deficit disorder. *Journal of the American Academy of Child and Adolescent Psychiatry, 26,* 127–132.

Pontius, A. A. (1973). Dysfunction patterns analogous to frontal lobe system and caudate nucleus syndromes in some groups of minimal brain dysfunction. *Journal of the American Medical Women's Association, 26,* 285–292.

Prechtl, H., & Stemmer, C. (1962). The choreiform syndrome in children. *Developmental Medicine and Child Neurology, 8,* 149–159.

Psychiatrist sued over attention span drug. (1987, November 10). *Investors' Daily,* p. 26.

Quay, H. C. (1987). The behavioral reward and inhibition systems in childhood behavior disorder. In L. M. Bloomingdale (Ed.), *Attention deficit disorder: III. New research in treatment, psychopharmacology, and attention* (pp. 176–186). New York: Pergamon Press.

Quay, H. C. (1988). Attention deficit disorder and the behavioral inhibition system: The relevance of the neuropsychological theory of Jeffrey A. Gray. In L. M. Bloomingdale & J. Sergeant (Eds.), *Attention deficit disorder: Criteria, cognition, intervention* (pp. 117–126). New York: Pergamon Press.

Quay, H. F. (1997). Inhibition and attention deficit hyperactivity disorder. *Journal of Abnormal Child Psychology, 25,* 7–14.

Quitkin, F., & Klein, D. F. (1969). Two behavioral syndroms in young adults related to possible minimal brain dysfunction. *Journal of Psychiatric Research, 7,* 131–142.

Rapin, I., (1964). Brain damage in children. In J. Brennemann (Ed.), *Practice of pediatrics* (Vol. 4). Hagerstown, MD: Prior.

Rapoport, J. L., & Zametkin, A. (1988). Drug treatment of attention deficit disorder. In L. Bloomingdale & J. Sergeant (Eds.), *Attention deficit disorder: Criteria, cognition, and intervention* (pp. 161–182). New York: Pergamon Press.

Rhee, S. H., Waldman, I. D., Hay, D. A., & Levy, F. (1995). Sex differences in genetic and environmental influences on DSM-III-R attention-deficit hyperactivity disorder (ADHD). *Behavior Genetics, 25,* 285.

Rie, H. E., & Rie, E. D. (Eds.). (1980). *Handbook of minimal brain dysfunction: A critical review.* New York: Wiley.

Rise in Ritalin use could mean drug abuse. (1987, December 6). *Worcester Telegram and Gazette.*

Ritalin linked to bludgeoning death of teenager. (1988, March 8). *The Call,* p. 3.

Roberts, M. A. (1979). *A manual for the Restricted Academic Playroom Situation.* Iowa City, IA: Author.

Robin, A., & Foster, S. (1989). *Negotiating parent–adolescent conflict.* New York: Guilford Press.

Rosenthal, R. H., & Allen, T. W. (1978). An examination of attention, arousal, and learning dysfunctions of hyperkinetic children. *Psychological Bulletin, 85,* 689–715.

Ross, D. M., & Ross, S. A. (1976). *Hyperactivity: Research, theory, and action.* New York: Wiley.

Ross, D. M., & Ross, S. A. (1982). *Hyperactivity: Current issues, research, and theory.* New York: Wiley.

Routh, D. K. (1978). Hyperactivity. In P. Magrab (Eds.), *Psychological management of pediatric problems* (pp. 3–48). Baltimore: University Park Press.

Routh, D. K., & Schroeder, C. S. (1976). Standardized playroom measures as indices of hypercativity. *Journal of Abnormal Child Psychology, 4*, 199–207.

Rutter, M. (1977). Brain damage syndromes in childhood: Concepts and findings. *Journal of Child Psychology and Psychiatry, 18*, 1–21.

Rutter, M. (1982). Syndromes attributable to "minimal brain dysfunction" in childhood. *American Journal of Psychiatry, 139*, 21–33.

Rutter, M. (1983). Introduction: Concepts of brain dysfunction syndromes. In M. Rutter (Ed.), *Developmental neuropsychiatry* (pp. 1–14). New York: Guilford Press.

Rutter, M. (1988). DSM-III-R: A postscript. In M. Rutter, A. H. Tuma, & I. S. Lann (Eds.), *Assessment and diagnosis in child psychopathology* (pp. 453–464). New York: Guilford Press.

Rutter, M. (1989). Attention deficit disorder/hyperkinetic syndrome: Conceptual and research issues regarding diagnosis and classification. In T. Sagvolden & T. Archer (Eds.), *Attention deficit disorder: Clinical and basic research* (pp. 1–24). Hillsdale, NJ: Erlbaum.

Ryan, N. D. (1990). Heterocyclic antidepressants in children and adolescents. *Journal of Child and Adolescent Psychopharmacology, 1*, 21–32.

Rybak, W. S. (1977). More adult minimal brain dysfunction. *American Journal of Psychiatry, 134*, 96–97.

Safer, D. J. , & Allen, R. (1976). *Hyperactive children.* Baltimore: University Park Press.

Sagvolden, T., Wultz, B., Moser, E. I., Moser, M., & Morkrid, L. (1989). Results from a comparative neuropsychological research program indicate altered reinforcement mechanisms in children with ADD. In T. Sagvolden & T. Archer (Eds.), *Attention deficit disorder: Clinical and basic research* (pp. 261–286). Hillsdale, NJ: Erlbaum.

Satterfield, J. H., Satterfield, B. T., & Cantwell, D. P. (1981). Three-year multimodality treatment study of 100 hyperactive boys. *Journal of Pediatrics, 98*, 650–655.

Schachar, R. J. (1986). Hyperkinetic syndrome: Historical development of the concept. In E. Taylor (Ed.), *The overactive child* (pp. 19–40). Philadelphia: Lippincott.

Schachar, R., Rutter, M., & Smith, A. (1981). The characteristics of situationally and pervasively hyperactive children: Implications for syndrome definition. *Journal of Child Psychology and Psychiatry, 22*, 375–392.

Schachar, R. J., Tannock, R., & Logan, G. (1993). Inhibitory control, impulsiveness, and attention deficit hyperactivity disorder. *Clinical Psychology Review, 13*, 721–739.

Schrag, P., & Divoky, D. (1975). *The myth of the hyperactive child.* New York: Pantheon.

Semrud-Clikeman, M., Filipek, P. A., Biederman, J., Steingard, R., Kennedy, D., Renshaw, P., & Bekken, K. (1994). Attention-deficit hyperactivity disorder: Magnetic resonance imaging morphometric analysis of the corpus callosum. *Journal of the American Academy of Child and Adolescent Psychiatry, 33*, 875–881.

Sergeant, J. (1988). From DSM-III attentional deficit disorder to functional defects. In L. Bloomingdale & J. Sergeant (Eds.), *Attention deficit disorder: Criteria, cognition, and intervention* (pp. 183–198). New York: Pergamon.

Sergeant, J., & van der Meere, J. J. (1989). The diagnostic significance of attentional processing: Its significance for ADDH classification—A future DSM. In T. Sagvolden & T. Archer (Eds.), *Attention deficit disorder: Clinical and basic research* (pp. 151–166). Hillsdale, NJ: Erlbaum.

Sergeant, J., & van der Meere, J. J. (1994). Toward an empirical child psychopathology. In D. K. Routh (Ed.), *Disruptive behavior disorders in children* (pp. 59–86). New York: Plenum.

Shaffer, D. (1994). Attention deficit hyperactivity disorder in adults. *American Journal of Psychiatry, 151*, 633–638.

Shalev, R. S., Hartman, C. A., Stavsky, M., & Sergeant, J. A. (1995). Conners Rating Scales of Israeli children. In J. Sergeant (Ed.), *Eunethydis: European approaches to hyperkinetic disorder* (pp. 131–147). Amsterdam: University of Amsterdam.

Shaywitz, S. E., Shaywitz, B. A., Cohen, D. J., & Young, J. G. (1983). Monoaminergic mechanisms in hyperactivity. In M. Rutter (Ed.), *Developmental neuropsychiatry* (pp. 330–347). New York: Guilford Press.

Shekim, W. O., Asarnow, R. F., Hess, E., Zaucha, K., & Wheeler, N. (1990). A clinical and demographic profile of a sample of adults with attention deficit hyperactivity disorder, residual state. *Comprehensive Psychiatry, 31*, 416–425.

Shekim, W. O., Glaser, E., Horwitz, E., Javaid, J., & Dylund, D. B. (1987). Psychoeducational correlates of catecholamine metabolites in hyperactive children. In L. Bloomingdale (Ed.), *Attention deficit disorder: New research in attention, treatment, and psychopharmacology* (Vol. 3, pp. 149–150). New York: Pergamon Press.

Shelley, E. M., & Riester, A. (1972). Syndrome of minimal brain damage in young adults. *Diseases of the Nervous System, 33,* 335–339.

Shelton, T. L., Barkley, R. A., Crosswait, C., Moorehouse, M., Fletcher, K., Barrett, S., Jenkins, L., & Metevia, L. (1997). *Early psychiatric and psychological morbidity in preschool children with high levels of aggressive and hyperactive-impulsive behavior.* Manuscript submitted for publication.

Shirley, M. (1939). A behavior syndrome characterizing prematurely born children. *Child Development, 10,* 115–128.

Silberg, J., Rutter, M., Meyer, J., Maes, H., Hewitt, J., Simonoff, E., Pickles, A., Loeber, R., & Eaves, L. (1996). Genetic and environmental influences on the covariation between hyperactivity and conduct disturbance in juvenile twins. *Journal of Child Psychology and Psychiatry, 37,* 803–816.

Skinner, N. (1988, June 22). Dyslexic boy's parents sue school. *Roanoke Gazette.*

Solomons, G. (1965). The hyperactive child. *Journal of the Iowa Medical Society, 55,* 464–469.

Spencer, T., Biederman, J., Wilens, T., & Faraone, S. V. (1994). Is attention-deficit hyperactivity disorder in adults a valid disorder? *Harvard Review of Psychiatry, 1,* 326–335.

Spencer, T., Wilens, T., Biederman, J., Faraone, S. V., Ablon, S., & Lapey, K. (1995). A double-blind, crossover comparison of methylphenidate and placebo in adults with childhood onset attention-deficit hyperactivity disorder. *Archives of General Psychiatry, 52,* 434–443.

Spitzer, R. L., Davies, M., & Barkley, R. A. (1990). The DSM-III-R field trial for the Disruptive Behavior Disorders. *Journal of the American Academy of Child and Adolescent Psychiatry, 29,* 690–697.

Sprague, R. L., Barnes, K. R., & Werry, J. S. (1970). Methylphenidate and thioridazine: Learning, activity, and behavior in emotionally disturbed boys. *American Journal of Orthopsychiatry, 40,* 613–628.

Sroufe, L. A. (1975). Drug treatment of children with behavior problems. In F. Horowitz (Ed.), *Review of child development research* (Vol. 4, pp. 347–408). Chicago: University of Chicago Press.

Stevenson, J. (1994, June). *Genetics of ADHD.* Paper presented at the Professional Group for ADD and Related Disorders, London.

Stewart, M. A., deBlois, S., & Cummings, C. (1980). Psychiatric disorder in the parents of hyperactive boys and those with conduct disorder. *Journal of Child Psychology and Psychiatry, 21,* 283–292.

Stewart, M. A. (1970). Hyperactive children. *Scientific American, 222,* 94–98.

Still, G. F. (1902). Some abnormal psychical conditions in children. *Lancet, 1,* 1008–1012, 1077–1082, 1163–1168.

Strauss, A. A., & Lehtinen, L. E. (1947). *Psychopathology and education of the brain-injured child.* New York: Grune & Stratton.

Strecker, E., & Ebaugh, F. (1924). Neuropsychiatric sequelae of cerebral trauma in children. *Archives of Neurology and Psychiatry, 12,* 443–453.

Stryker, S. (1925). Encephalitis lethargica—The behavior residuals. *Training School Bulletin, 22,* 152–157.

Swanson, J. M., McBurnett, K., Christian, D. L., & Wigal, T. (1995). Stimulant medications and the treatment of children with ADHD. In T. H. Ollendick & R. J. Prinz (Eds.), *Advances in clinical child psychology* (Vol. 17, pp. 265–322). New York: Plenum.

Swanson, J. M., Wigal, S., Greenhill, L., Browne, R., Waslick, B., Lerner, M., Williams, L., Flynn, D., Agler, D., Crowley, K., Feinberg, E., Baren, M., & Cantwell, D. P. (1997). *Adderall in children with ADHD: Time-response and dose-reponse effects.* Manuscript submitted for publication.

Tannock, R. (in press). Attention deficit disorders with anxiety disorders. In T. E. Brown (Ed.), *Subtypes of attention deficit disorders in children, adolescents, and adults.* Washington, DC: American Psychiatric Press.

Taylor, E. A. (1983). Drug response and diagnostic validation. In M. Rutter (Ed.), *Developmental neuropsychiatry* (pp. 348–368). New York: Guilford Press.

Taylor, E. A. (1986). *The overactive child.* Philadelphia: Lippincott.

Taylor, E. A. (1988). Diagnosis of hyperactivity—A British perspective. In L. Bloomingdale & J. Sergeant (Eds.), *Attention deficit disorder: Criteria, cognition, and intervention* (pp. 141–160). New York: Pergamon Press.

Taylor, E. A. (1989). On the epidemiology of hyperactivity. In T. Sagvolden & T. Archer (Eds.), *Attention deficit disorder: Clinical and basic research* (pp. 31–52). Hillsdale, NJ: Erlbaum.

Thapar, A., Hervas, A., & McGuffin, P. (1995). Childhood hyperactivity scores are highly heritable and show sibling competition effects: Twin study evidence. *Behavior Genetics, 25,* 537–544.

Toone, B. K., & van der Linden, J. H. (1997). Attention deficit hyperactivity disorder or hyperkinetic disorder in adults. *British Journal of Psychiatry, 170,* 489–491.

Toufexis, A. (1989, January 16). Worries about overactive kids: Are too many youngsters being misdiagnosed and medicated? *Time,* p. 65.

Tredgold, A. F. (1908). *Mental deficiency (amentia).* New York: W. Wood.

Trites, R. L. (1979). *Hyperactivity in children: Etiology, measurement, and treatment implications.* Baltimore: University Park Press.

Twyman, A. S. (1988, May 4). Use of drug prompts suit. *Newton Graphic,* p. 28.

Ullmann, R. K., Sleator, E. K., & Sprague, R. (1984). A new rating scale for daignosis and monitoring of ADD children. *Psychopharmacology Bulletin, 20,* 160–164.

van den Oord, E. J. C. G. Verhulst, F. C., & Boomsma, D. I. (1996). A genetic study of maternal and paternal ratings of problem behaviors in 3-year-old twins. *Journal of Abnormal Psychology, 105,* 349–357.

van der Meere, J. (in press). The role of attention. In S. Sandberg (Ed.), *Monographs on child and adolesent psychiatry: Hyperactivity disorders* (pp. 109–146). London: Cambridge University Press.

van der Meere, J., & Sergeant, J. (1988a). Focused attention in pervasively hyperactive children. *Journal of Abnormal Child Psychology, 16,* 627–640.

van der Meere, J., & Sergeant, J. (1988b). Controlled processing and vigilance in hyperctivity: Time will tell. *Journal of Abnormal Child Psychology, 16,* 641–656.

Vermeerschm S., & Fombonne, E. (1995). Attention and aggressive problems among French school-aged children. In J. Sergeant (Ed.), *Eunethydis: European approaches to hyperkinetic disorder* (pp. 37–49). Amsterdam: University of Amsterdam.

Voelker, S. L., Lachar, D., & Gdowski, C. L. (1983). The Personality Inventory for Children and response to methylphenidate: Preliminary evidence for predictive validity. *Journal of Pediatric Psychology, 8,* 161–169.

Weiner, J. (1988, May 14). Dignosis, treatment of ADHD requires skill. *Worcester Telegram and Gazette,* p. 14.

Weiss, G., & Hechtman, L. (1979). The hyperactive child syndrome. *Science, 205,* 1348–1354.

Weiss, G., & Hechtman, L. (1986). *Hyperactive children grown up.* New York: Guilford Press.

Weiss, G., & Hechtman, L. (1993). *Hyperactive children grown up* (2nd ed.). New York: Guilford Press.

Weiss, L. (1992). *ADD in adults.* Dallas, TX: Taylor.

Welner, Z., Welner, A., Stewart, M., Palkes, H., & Wish, E. (1977). A controlled study of siblings of hyperactive children. *Journal of Nervous and Mental Disease, 165,* 110–117.

Wender, P. (1971). *Minimal brain dysfunction.* New York: Wiley.

Wender, P. (1973). Minimal brain dysfunction in children. *Pediatric Clinics of North America, 20,* 187–202.

Wender, P. (1995). *Attention-deficit hyperactivity disorder in adults.* New York: Oxford University Press.

Wender, P. H., Reimherr, F. W., & Wood, D. R. (1981). Attention deficit disorder ("minimal brain dysfunction") in adults. *Archives of General Psychiatry, 38,* 449–456.

Wender, P. H., Reimherr, F. W., Wood, D. R., & Ward, M. (1985). A controlled study of methylphenidate in the treatment of attention deficit disorder, residual type, in adults. *American Journal of Psychiatry, 142,* 547–552.

Werner, H., & Strauss, A. A. (1941). Pathology of figure-ground relation in the child. *Journal of Abnormal and Social Psychology, 36,* 236–248.

Werry, J. S. (1988). Differential diagnosis of attention deficits and conduct disorders. In. L. M. Bloomingdale & J. A. Sergeant (Eds.), *Attention deficit disorder: Criteria, cognition, intervention* (pp. 83–96). London: Pergamon Press.

Werry, J. S. (1992). History, terminology, and manifestations at different ages. In G. Weiss (Ed.), *Child and Adolescent Psychiatry Clinics of North America: Attention deficit disorder* (pp. 297–310). Philadelphia: Saunders.

Werry, J. S., & Sprague, R. (1970). Hyperactivity. In C. G. Costello (Ed.), *Symptoms of psychopathology* (pp. 397–417). New York: Wiley.

Whalen, C. K., & Henker, B. (1980). *Hyperactive children: The social ecology of identification and treatment.* New York: Academic Press.

Whalen, C. K., Henker, B., & Dotemoto, S. (1980). Methylphenidate and hyperactivity: Effects on teacher behaviors. *Science, 208,* 1280–1282.

Whalen, C. K., Henker, B., & Dotemoto, S. (1981). Teacher response to methylphenidate (Ritalin) versus placebo status of hyperactive boys in the classroom. *Child Development, 52,* 1005–1014.

Whalen, C. K., Henker, B., & Hinshaw, S. (1985). Cognitive behavioral therapies for hyperactive children: Premises, problems, and prospects. *Journal of Abnormal Child Psychology, 13,* 391–410.

Wilens, T., Biederman, J., Prince, J., Spencer, T. J., Faraone, S. V., Warburton, R., Schleifer, D., Harding, M., Linehan, C., & Geller, D. (1996). Six-week, double-blind, placebo-controlled study of desipramine for adult attention deficit hyperactivity disorder. *American Journal of Psychiatry, 153,* 1147–1153.

Williams, L. (1988, January 15). Parents and doctors fear growing misuse of drug used to treat hyperactive kids. *Wall Street Journal,* p. 10.

Willis, T. J., & Lovaas, I. (1977). A behavioral approach to treating hyperactive children: The parent's role. In J. B. Millichap (Ed.), *Learning disabilities and related disorders* (pp. 119–140). Chicago: Yearbook Medical Publications.

Wolraich, M. L., Wilson, D. B., & White, J. W. (1995). The effect of sugar on behavior or cognition in children: A meta-analysis. *Journal of the American Medical Association, 274,* 1617–1621.

Wood, D. R., Reimherr, F. W., Wender, P. W., & Johnson, G. E. (1976). Diagnosis and treatment of minimal brain dysfunction in adults: A preliminary report. *Archives of General Psychiatry, 33,* 1453–1460.

World Health Organization. (1978). *International classification of diseases* (9th ed.). Geneva, Switzerland: Author.

Zametkin, A. J., Nordahl, T. E., Gross, M., King, A. C., Semple, W. E., Rumsey, J., Hamburger, S., & Cohen, R. M. (1990). Cerebral glucose metabolism in adults with hyperactivity of childhood onset. *New England Journal of Medicine, 323,* 1361–1366.

Zametkin, A., & Rapoport, J. L. (1986). The pathophysiology of attention deficit disorder with hyperactivity: A review. In B. Lahey & A. Kazdin (Eds.), *Advances in clinical child psychology* (Vol. 9, pp. 177–216). New York: Plenum.

Chapter 2

PRIMARY SYMPTOMS, DIAGNOSTIC CRITERIA, PREVALENCE, AND GENDER DIFFERENCES

ॐ

A tremendous amount of research has been published on children with Attention-Deficit/Hyperactivity Disorder (ADHD) and their primary characteristics and related problems, as well as on the situational variability of these problems, their prevalence, and their etiologies. It was estimated by 1979 that more than 2,000 studies existed on this disorder (Weiss & Hechtman, 1979) and this figure has surely doubled or even tripled in the past 19 years. In this volume, I have attempted to cull from a substantial fund of research that information I believe is most useful for clinical work with these children and adults. Yet it is surely not the intent of this chapter, or of this book, to provide a critical review of the scientific literature. Instead, it is to glean from that literature that which has a direct bearing on the clinical diagnosis, assessment, and management of ADHD. This chapter reviews the clinically useful findings on the primary symptoms of this condition as they occur in both children and adults, along with those pertaining to situational variability, pervasiveness, prevalence, and gender differences.

Throughout this chapter, and the remainder of this book, the term "ADHD" is used, although the research on which this discussion is based may have employed the related diagnoses of hyperactivity, hyperactive child syndrome, hyperkinetic reaction of childhood, minimal brain dysfunction, or Attention-Deficit Disorder with Hyperactivity. I realize that these terms and the diagnostic criteria used for them in this research are not necessarily equivalent. However, I believe that the clinical description of the children studied under these terms and the criteria used to select them for study are sufficiently similar to argue that researchers were evaluating sufficiently similar groups of children to permit some clinical generalities to be drawn about them. This does not mean that the results across these rather diverse studies should be combined for any mathematical analysis as some have recently done (Hill & Schoener, 1996), as there are numerous methodological reasons why the results would not lend themselves to such an analysis (Barkley, 1997d). To gain a general impression of the disorder and for the clinical purposes of this text, the minor differences that may exist among these groups because of these somewhat different terms and selection criteria do not seem, at least to me, sufficiently important to justify qualifying each finding to be discussed by the manner in which the particularly subjects were selected and diagnosed. But I fully appreciate that for research purposes, such differences among sample selection criteria are quite significant for both qualifying and interpreting one's findings.

PRIMARY SYMPTOMS

ADHD children and adults are commonly described as having chronic difficulties with inattention and/or impulsivity–hyperactivity—the "holy trinity" of ADHD. They are believed to display these characteristics early, to a degree that is inappropriate for their age or developmental level and across a variety of situations that tax their capacity to pay attention, restrain their movement, inhibit their impulses, and regulate their own behavior relative to rules, time, and the future. As noted in Chapter 1, definitions varied considerably throughout the history of this disorder as did the recommended criteria for obtaining a diagnosis. The currently recommended criteria are set forth later in this chapter. For now, I review the nature of the major symptom constructs believed to form the essence of this disorder as they are expressed in children and adults.

Inattention

By definition, children who have ADHD display difficulties with attention relative to normal children of the same age and gender. However, attention is a multidimensional construct that can refer to alertness, arousal, selectivity, sustained attention, distractibility, or span of apprehension, among others (Barkley, 1988, 1994; Hale & Lewis, 1979; Mirsky, 1996). Research to date suggests that ADHD children have their greatest difficulties with persistence of effort, or sustaining their attention (responding) to tasks (or vigilance) (Douglas, 1983). These difficulties are sometimes apparent in free-play settings, as evidenced by shorter durations of play with each toy and frequent shifts in play across various toys (Barkley & Ullman, 1975; Routh & Schroeder, 1976; Zentall, 1985). However, they are seen most dramatically in situations requiring the child to sustain attention to dull, boring, repetitive tasks (Barkley, Dupaul, & McMurray, 1990; Luk, 1985; Shelton et al., 1997, for a review; Milich, Landau, Kilby, & Whitten, 1982; Ullman, Barkley, & Brown, 1978; Zentall, 1985, for a review) such as independent schoolwork, homework, or chore performance.

The problem is not so much one of heightened distractibility, or the ease with which a child is drawn off task by extraneous stimulation, though this can be a problem under some circumstances. Research on the distractibility of ADHD children is somewhat contradictory on this issue but in general finds these children to be no more distractible than normal children to extratask stimulation (Campbell, Douglas, & Morgenstern, 1971; Cohen, Weiss, & Minde, 1972; Rosenthal & Allen, 1980; Steinkamp, 1980). Instead, the problem appears consistently to be one of diminished persistence of effort or sustained responding to tasks that have little intrinsic appeal or minimal immediate consequences for completion (Barkley, 1989a, 1997a).The findings for irrelevant stimulation provided within the task are more conflicting, however. Some studies find that such stimulation worsens the performance of ADHD children (Barkley, Koplowitz, Anderson, & McMurray, 1997; Rosenthal & Allen, 1980) whereas others find no such effect (Fischer, Barkley, Edelbrock, & Smallish, 1993), or even sometimes an enhancing effect on attention (Zentall, Falkenberg, & Smith, 1985).

The clinical picture may be different, however, when alternate, competing activities are available that promise immediate reinforcement or gratification in contrast to the weaker reinforcement or consequences associated with the assigned task. In such cases, the ADHD child may appear distracted and in fact is likely to shift "off task" to engage in the highly rewarding competing activity. For example, Landau, Lorch, and Milich (1992) show that ADHD children spend significantly less time observing a television program when toys are available for play than do normal children. It is not clear whether this shift represents true distraction, as described previously (orients to extraneous stimuli), or behavioral disinhibition (fails to follow rules or instructions when provided with competing, highly rewarding activities). It is my view that the latter is more likely to account for this attentional shift than is a more generalized problem with orienting to extraneous stimuli (Barkley, 1997a).

Parents and teachers often describe these attentional problems in terms such as "Doesn't seem to listen," "Fails to finish assigned tasks," "Daydreams," "Often loses things," "Can't concentrate," "Easily distracted," "Can't work independently of supervision," "Requires more redirection," "Shifts from one uncompleted activity to another," and "Confused or seems to be in a fog" (Barkley, DuPaul, & McMurray, 1990; Stewart, Pitts, Craig, & Dieruf, 1966). Many of these terms are the most frequently endorsed items from rating scales completed by the caregivers of these ADHD children. Studies using direct observations of child behavior find that off-task behavior or not paying attention to work is recorded substantially more often for ADHD children and adolescents than for learning-disabled or normal children (Abikoff, Gittelman-Klein, & Klein, 1977; Barkley, DuPaul, & McMurray, 1990; Luk, 1985; Fischer, Barkley, Edelbrock, & Smallish, 1990; Ullman et al., 1978). What is not so clear in these studies is whether this deficit in paying attention reflects a primary deficit in sustained attention or is secondary to the problem of behavioral disinhibition described later.

No data currently exist using direct behavioral observations of inattention with adults with ADHD that parallel the previously cited research in children. Nevertheless, some studies document greater difficulties with attention on continuous performance or vigilance tests (Barkley, Murphy, & Kwasnik, 1996a; Epstein, Conners, Sitarenios, & Erhardt, 1997; Seidman, Biederman, Faraone, Weber, & Ouellette, 1997), though one did not (Holdnack, Moberg, Arnold, Gur, & Gur, 1995). Yet even the latter study found adults with ADHD to have slower reaction times, which previously has been interpreted by others as reflecting lapses in attention to the task (Barkley, 1988). These adults are also highly likely to self-report many of the same symptoms of inattention from the DSM symptom list as are reported by parents of ADHD children. Murphy and Barkley (1996a) found that 83% of adults diagnosed with ADHD reported having difficulties with sustaining attention (vs. 68% of a clinical control group and 10% of a normal sample); 94% reported being easily distracted (vs. 86% and 19%, respectively); 90% claimed to often not listen to others (vs. 57% and 6%, respectively); 91% reported that they often failed to follow through on tasks or activities (vs. 78% and 6%, respectively); and 86% reported that they frequently shift from one uncompleted activity to another (vs. 75% and 12%, respectively). These self-reports are corroborated by others who know the subjects well, such as spouses ($r = .64$) or parents ($r = .75$), as is the recall of these adults of similar symptoms during their childhood years ($r = .74$ with parent reports) (Murphy & Barkley, 1996a). Thus, there is ample justification to believe that adults with ADHD suffer from many of the same attentional problems as do children who have the disorder.

Impulsiveness or Behavioral Disinhibition

ADHD is frequently associated with a deficiency in inhibiting behavior in response to situational demands, or what may be called impulsivity, again relative to others of the same mental age and gender. Like attention, impulsivity is also multidimensional in nature (Kindlon, Mezzacappa, & Earls, 1995; Milich & Kramer, 1985). Those forms of impulsivity often associated with undercontrol of behavior and the inability to delay a response or defer gratification or to inhibit dominant or prepotent responses are the ones most frequently identified in children having ADHD (Barkley, 1997a). Clinically, these children are often noted to respond quickly to situations without waiting for instructions to be completed or adequately appreciating what is required in the setting. Heedless or careless errors are often the result. These children may also fail to consider the potentially negative, destructive, or even dangerous consequences that may be associated with particular situations or behaviors. Thus they seem to engage in frequent, unnecessary risk taking. Taking chances on a dare or whim, especially from a peer, may occur more often than is normal. Consequently, accidental poisonings and injuries are not uncommon (see Chapter 3, this volume), and ADHD children may carelessly damage or destroy others' property considerably more frequently than do normal children. Waiting one's turn in a game or in a group lineup before going to an activity is often problematic for them. When faced with tasks or situations in which they are encouraged to delay seeking gratification and to work toward a longer-term goal and larger reward, they often opt for the immediate, smaller reward that requires less work to achieve. They are notorious for taking "shortcuts" in their work performance, applying the least amount of effort and taking the least amount of time in performing tasks they find boring or aversive. When they desire something to which others control access and they must wait a while to obtain it, as in a parent's promise to eventually take them shopping or to a movie, they may badger the parent excessively during the waiting interval, appearing to others as incessantly demanding and self-centered. Situations or games that involve sharing, cooperation, and restraint with peers are particularly problematic for these impulsive children. Verbally, they often say things indiscreetly without regard for the feelings of others or for the social consequences to themselves. Blurting out answers to questions prematurely and interrupting the conversations of others are commonplace. The layman's impression of these children, therefore, is often one of poor self-control, irresponsibility, immaturity or childishness, laziness, and outright rudeness. Little wonder that these children experience more punishment, criticism, censure, and ostracism by adults and their peers than do normal children.

The problem of impulsivity is sometimes scientifically defined as a pattern of rapid, inaccurate responding to tasks (Brown & Quay, 1977), such as the Matching Familiar Figures Test (MFFT; Kagan, 1966). In this task, a child is shown a picture below which are six similar pictures. The child must select among the six the one that is identical to the sample. ADHD children are noted to respond more quickly than others and to make more mistakes. Most often, it is their number of errors rather than their rapidity of responding that sets them apart from normal children (Brown & Quay, 1977), but even here findings are conflicting with this task (Fischer et al., 1990; Barkley, DuPaul, & McMurray, 1990; Milich & Kramer, 1985). Impulsivity may also refer to poor sustained inhibition of responding (Barkley, 1997a; Gordon, 1979), poor delay of gratification (Campbell, 1987; Rapport, Tucker, DuPaul, Merlo, & Stoner, 1986), or impaired adherence to commands to regulate or inhibit behavior in social contexts (Barkley, 1985; Kendall & Wilcox, 1979; Kindlon et al., 1995). Furthermore, studies that have factor-analyzed ratings of impulsive behavior mixed in with ratings of inattention and overactivity (Achenbach & Edelbrock, 1983; DuPaul, 1991; DuPaul, Anastopoulos, et al., 1997; Lahey et al., 1994; Milich & Kramer, 1985) have failed to differentiate an impulsivity dimension from that measuring hyperactivity—that is, overactive children are also impulsive children and vice versa. This finding calls into serious question the existence of overactivity as a separate dimension of behavioral impairment apart from poor inhibition in these children. It also strongly implies that the more global problem of behavioral disinhibition unites these two symptoms (Barkley, 1997a).

Evidence that behavioral disinhibition, or poor regulation and inhibition of behavior, is in fact the hallmark of this disorder is so substantial that it can be considered fact (see

Barkley, 1997a; Pennington & Ozonoff, 1996, for reviews). First, studies typically show that it is not inattention that distinguishes ADHD children from other clinical disorders or from normal children as much as it is their hyperactive, impulsive, and disinhibited behavior (Barkley, Grodzinsky, & DuPaul, 1992; Halperin, Matier, Bedi, Sharma, & Newcorn, 1992). Second, when objective measures of the three symptoms of ADHD are subjected to a disciminant function analysis (a statistical method of examining the variables that most contribute to group discrimination), it is routinely the symptoms of impulsive errors, typically on vigilance tasks or those assessing response inhibition, and excessive activity level that best discriminate and classify ADHD children from non-ADHD children (Barkley, Dupaul, & McMurray, 1990; Corkum & Siegel, 1993; Grodzinsky & Diamond, 1992; Losier, McGrath, & Klein, 1996). A third source of evidence derived from the field trial (Spitzer, Davies, & Barkley, 1990) that tested the sensitivity and specificity of the 14 descriptors that comprise the DSM-III-R diagnostic criteria for ADHD (see Chapter 1, Table 1.2, this volume). These descriptors were rank-ordered by their discriminating power and presented in DSM-III-R in that descending order. Careful inspection of this rank ordering revealed that, again, symptoms characteristic of disinhibition, such as poorly regulated activity and impulsivity, are more likely to discriminate ADHD from other psychiatric disorders and normal children. For these reasons, I believe that the evidence available is sufficient to conclude that it is not inattention as much as behavioral disinhibition that is the hallmark of ADHD. In fact, it is this disinhibition or poor inhibitory regulation of behavior that may result in the attention problems often noted in these children. That is, the attention problems may be secondary to a disorder of behavioral regulation and inhibition rather than being a primary and distinct deficit apart from such disinhibition. The theory of ADHD presented in Chapter 7 (this volume) further develops this idea.

In adults with ADHD, several studies using CPTs demonstrated more errors of commission or impulsiveness (Barkley et al., 1996a; Epstein et al., 1997) although others did not (Holdnack et al., 1995; Seidman et al., 1997). Even so, adults diagnosed with ADHD, in comparison to clinical and normal control groups, often self-report symptoms of poor impulse control, such as difficulty awaiting turns (67% vs. 39% of a control group and 18% of a normal sample), blurting out answers (57% vs. 46% vs. 16%, respectively), and interrupting or intruding on others (57% vs. 39% vs. 9%, respectively) (Murphy & Barkley, 1996a). These symptoms are often thought of as the hallmarks of the poor impulse control seen in clinically diagnosed children with ADHD. These adults are also highly likely to report difficulties with their driving associated with poor impulse control (e.g., excessive speeding) and to make more impulsive errors on a driving simulator (Barkley, Murphy, & Kwasnik, 1996b). Impulsive comments to others, difficulties in inhibiting the impulsive spending of money, and poor inhibition in their emotional reactions to others are often described by these patients in our clinic for adults with ADHD. Thus, once again it appears that the symptoms characterizing childhood ADHD are likely to be associated with its adult equivalent.

Hyperactivity

The third primary characteristic of those with ADHD is their excessive or developmentally inappropriate levels of activity, whether motor or vocal. Restlessness, fidgeting, and generally unnecessary gross bodily movements are commonplace (Barkley & Cunningham, 1979; Luk, 1985; Stewart et al., 1966; Still, 1902). These movements are often irrelevant to the task or situation and at times seem purposeless. Parents often describe these children as "always up and on the go," "acts as if driven by a motor," "climbs excessively," "can't sit still," "talks excessively," "often hums or makes odd noises," and is "squirmy." Observations of such children at school or while working on independent tasks find them out of their seats, moving about the class without permission, restlessly moving their arms and legs while working, playing with objects not related to the task, talking out of turn to others, and making unusual vocal noises (Abikoff et al., 1977; Barkley, DuPaul, & McMurray, 1990; Cammann & Miehlke, 1989; Fischer et al., 1990; Luk, 1985). Making running commentaries on the activities around them or about others' behavior is not unusual. Direct observations of their social interactions with others as well as their self-speech during play and work performance also indicate generally excessive speech and commentary (Barkley, Cunningham, & Karlsson, 1983; Berk & Potts, 1991; Copeland, 1979; Zentall, 1988).

Numerous scientific studies attest to complaints that ADHD children are more active, restless, and fidgety than normal children throughout the day and even during sleep (Barkley & Cunningham, 1979; Porrino et al., 1983; Teicher, Ito, Glod, & Barber, 1996). As with poor sustained attention, however, there are many different types of activity (Barkley & Ullman, 1975; Cromwell, Baumeister, & Hawkins, 1963), and it is not always clear exactly which types are the most deviant for ADHD children. Measures of ankle movement and locomotion seem to most reliably differentiate them from normal (Barkley & Cunningham, 1979), but even some studies of wrist activity and total body motion found them to be different as well (Barkley & Ullman, 1975; Porrino et al., 1983; Teicher et al., 1996). There are also significant situational fluctuations in this symptom (Jacob, O'Leary, & Rosenblad, 1978; Luk, 1985; Porrino et al., 1983) implying that it may be the failure to regulate activity level to setting or task demands that is so socially problematic in ADHD (Routh, 1978) in addition to just a greater-than-normal absolute level of movement. However, it has not been convincingly shown that excessive activity level distinguishes ADHD from other clinic-referred groups of children (Firestone & Martin, 1979; Sandberg, Kutler, & Taylor, 1978; Shaffer, McNamara, & Pincus, 1974), even though ADHD children are clearly more active than is normal.

Some research suggests that it may be the pervasiveness of the hyperactivity across settings (home and school) that separates ADHD from these other diagnostic categories (Taylor, 1986). Indeed, some have gone so far as to advocate that the clinical syndrome or disorder be restricted only to those children having such pervasiveness of symptoms (Schachar, Rutter, & Smith, 1981). As discussed later, this distinction may have more to do with the sources of information (parents vs. teachers) than with real differences in the nature of ADHD children with situational versus pervasive ADHD (Costello, Loeber, & Stouthamer-Loeber, 1991; Rapoport, Donnelly, Zametkin, & Carrougher, 1986).

As noted previously for impulsivity, it is difficult in studies of objective measures or behavior ratings of hyperactivity to find that hyperactivity forms a separate factor or dimension apart from impulsivity. Typically, studies that factor-analyze behavioral ratings often find that items of restlessness may load on a factor composed of primarily poor attention and organization whereas other types of overactivity load on a factor constituting impulsive or disinhibited behavior. It is this latter factor, and not so much inattention, that best distinguishes ADHD from other clinical conditions and from normal, as noted earlier. Hence, in ranking the importance of these primary symptoms, greater weight should be given to the behavioral class of impulsive–hyperactive characteristics than to inattention in conceptualizing this disorder and in its clinical delineation. Again, it is the poor self-regulation and inhibition of behavior that seem to be so distinctive in this disorder.

In adults with ADHD, symptoms of hyperactive or restless behavior are often present but appear to involve more difficulties with fidgeting, a more subjective sense of restlessness, and excessive speech than in the more gross motor overactivity characteristic of young ADHD children. Murphy and Barkley (1996a) found that nearly 74% of adults with ADHD reported often fidgeting with their hands or feet versus 57% of a clinical control group and only 20% of a normal sample of adults. Nearly 66% of adults clinically diagnosed with ADHD complained of often having difficulties remaining seated versus 32% of a clinical control group and only 6% of a normal sample. Like ADHD children, adults with ADHD often verbalize more than others, with nearly 60% complaining that they often talk excessively. Although this complaint did not distinguish them from a clinical control group, 60% of whom also reported excessive speech, both of these groups report speaking more often than does a normal sample of adults, only 22% of whom reported such a difficulty. Again, research into the symptoms of ADHD in adults is still in its infancy and no direct observational studies of these adults have been conducted to corroborate these self-reports of symptoms of hyperactivity.

CONSENSUS DIAGNOSTIC CRITERIA FOR ADHD

At present, the primary characteristics of ADHD and the diagnostic criteria officially developed for clinical use are set forth in the fourth edition of the *Diagnostic and Statistical Manual of Mental Disorders* (DSM-IV; American Psychiatric Association, 1994), which is used primarily in the United States. It is similar, though not identical to, the definition for the disorder in the tenth edition of *International Classification of Diseases* (ICD-10; World Health Organization, 1994), which is used mainly in Europe. Table 2.1 presents the DSM-IV criteria.

The criteria stipulate that individuals have their symptoms of ADHD for at least 6 months, that these symptoms be to a degree that is developmentally deviant, and that the symptoms have developed by 7 years of age. From the Inattention item list, six of nine items must be endorsed as developmentally inappropriate. From the Hyperactive–Impulsive item lists, six of nine items, total, must be endorsed as deviant. The type of ADHD to be diagnosed depends on whether criteria are met for either or both symptom lists: Predominantly Inattentive, Predominantly Hyperactive–Impulsive, and Combined Type.

Merits of DSM-IV

These diagnostic criteria are some of the most rigorous and most empirically derived criteria ever available in the history of clinical diagnosis for this disorder. They were derived from a committee of some of the leading experts in the field, a literature review of ADHD, an informal survey of rating scales assessing the behavioral dimensions related to ADHD by the committee, and statistical analyses of the results of a field trial of the items using 380 children from 10 different sites in North America (Lahey et al., 1994). The criteria are a considerable improvement over those provided in the earlier versions of DSM (American Psychiatric Association, 1968, 1980, 1987) in many respects:

1. The items used to make the diagnosis were selected primarily from factor analyses of items from parent and teacher rating scales in which the items already showed high intercorrelation with each other and validity in distinguishing ADHD from other groups of children (Spitzer et al., 1990).

2. The DSM-IV clusters items underneath a given construct (e.g., inattention and hyperactivity) based on a factor analysis of the items (Lahey et al., 1994) and consistent with the two dimensions often found in other studies of parent and teacher ratings having similar item content (DuPaul, 1991; DuPaul, Anastopoulos, et al., 1997; Goyette, Conners, & Ulrich, 1978).

3. Unlike the first three versions of DSM and earlier versions of ICD, the cutoff points for the number of symptoms necessary for a diagnosis were determined in a field trial (Lahey et al., 1994) and thus have some empirical basis for their selection and the clustering of the items into categories (e.g., inattention and hyperactive–impulsive). Although the DSM-III-R also used a field trial for much the same purpose (Spitzer et al., 1990), it was not of the same degree of rigor or magnitude as the DSM-IV field trial.

TABLE 2.1. DSM-IV Criteria for ADHD

A. Either (1) or (2):

    (1) six (or more) of the following symptoms of **inattention** have persisted for at least 6 months to a degree that is maladaptive and inconsistent with developmental level:

    Inattention
      (a) often fails to give close attention to details or makes careless mistakes in schoolwork, work, or other activities
      (b) often has difficulty sustaining attention in tasks or play activities
      (c) often does not seem to listen when spoken to directly
      (d) often does not follow through on instructions and fails to finish schoolwork, chores, or duties in the workplace (not due to oppositional behavior or failure to understand instructions)
      (e) often has difficulty organizing tasks and activities
      (f) often avoids, dislikes, or is reluctant to engage in tasks that require sustained mental effort (such as school work or homework)
      (g) often loses things necessary for tasks or activities (e.g., toys, school assignments, pencils, books, or tools)
      (h) is often easily distracted by extraneous stimuli
      (i) is often forgetful in daily activities

    (2) six (or more) of the following symptoms of **hyperactivity–impulsivity** have persisted for at least 6 months to a degree that is maladaptive and inconsistent with developmental level:

    Hyperactivity
      (a) often fidgets with hands or feet or squirms in seat
      (b) often leaves seat in classroom or in other situations in which remaining seated is expected
      (c) often runs about or climbs excessively in situations in which it is inappropriate (in adolescents or adults, may be limited to subjective feelings of restlessness)
      (d) often has difficulty playing or engaging in leisure activities quietly
      (e) is often "on the go" or often acts as if "driven by a motor"
      (f) often talks excessively

    Impulsivity
      (g) often blurts out answers before the questions have been completed
      (h) often has difficulty awaiting turn
      (i) often interrupts or intrudes on others (e.g., butts into conversations or games)

B. Some hyperactive–impulsive or inattentive symptoms that caused impairment were present before age 7 years.

C. Some impairment from the symptoms is present in two or more settings (e.g., at school [or work] and at home).

D. There must be clear evidence of clinically significant impairment in social, academic, or occupational functioning.

E. The symptoms do not occur exclusively during the course of a Pervasive Developmental Disorder, Schizophrenia, or other Psychotic Disorder, and are not better accounted for by another mental disorder (e.g., Mood Disorder, Anxiety Disorder, Dissociative Disorder, or a Personality Disorder).

Code based on type:
    314.01 Attention-Deficit/Hyperactivity Disorder, Combined Type: if both Criteria A1 and A2 are met for the past 6 months.
    314.00 Attention-Deficit/Hyperactivity Disorder, Predominantly Inattentive Type: if Criterion A1 is met but Criterion A2 is not met for the past 6 months
    314.01 Attention-Deficit/Hyperactivity Disorder, Predominantly Hyperactive–Impulsive Type: if Criterion A2 is met but Criterion A1 is not met for the past 6 months.

    Coding note: For individuals (especially adolescents and adults) who currently have symptoms that no longer meet full criteria, "In Partial Remission" should be specified.

Note. From American Psychiatric Association (1994). Copyright 1994 by American Psychiatric Association. Reprinted by permission.

4. The specification of guidelines in DSM-IV for establishing the degree of situational pervasiveness of the symptoms seems important to many researchers in the field in view of findings that pervasiveness of symptoms across home and school settings may be an important marker for at least the more severe cases of disorder if not for the clinical syndrome itself (Goodman & Stevenson, 1989; Schachar et al., 1981). Nevertheless, clinicians should keep in mind that this means of determining pervasiveness may confound the source of information (parent vs. teacher) with the settings across which one is attempting to determine pervasiveness. Thus any differences between these groups may simply be an artifact of the source (Costello et al., 1991; Rapoport et al., 1986). Perhaps it would be more useful or clinically prudent to establish that a history of symptoms exists across the home and school settings rather than requiring current parent–teacher agreement on symptoms to establish the presence of the disorder. Research suggests that when agreement across parent, teacher, and clinician is a requirement for diagnosis, it severely restricts the diagnosis to approximately 1% or less of the childhood population (Lambert, Sandoval, & Sassone, 1978; Szatmari, Offord, & Boyle, 1989).

5. DSM-IV has returned to the subtyping of Attention-Deficit Disorder with and without Hyperactivity as first presented in DSM-III, except in this case, ADD without Hyperactivity is now ADHD Predominantly Inattentive Type and the symptoms of impulsiveness are no longer included. This subtyping certainly permits clinicians the opportunity to diagnose clinic-referred children who have significant attentional dysfunction but no significant disinhibition. Yet, as noted later, it has not been established in research that this subtype is actually a true subtype of ADHD having the same problems with inattention as the Combined Type of ADHD or whether, as suggested in Chapter 3 (this volume), the Predominantly Inattentive Type is a qualitatively different disorder entirely, with a different attention disturbance from that seen in ADHD Combined Type.

6. The addition of a requirement of impairment as a criterion for diagnosis of a mental disorder is crucial, and its importance cannot be overemphasized. Efforts to define the nature of a mental disorder typically incorporate such a requirement to distinguish a mental disorder from the wide range of normal human behavior that does not necessarily lead to a harmful dysfunction or impairment (Wakefield, 1997). Thus, simply because a child or adult may show a higher frequency or severity of symptoms related to ADHD than is typical of others does not, by itself, warrant a diagnosis of ADHD (a mental disorder). This more extreme degree of symptoms must also lead to interference or disruption in one or more of the major domains of life activities associated with that age group (typically home, school, or work).

Issues Requiring Further Consideration in the DSM-IV View of ADHD

This discussion of the merits of DSM-IV does not imply that its criteria cannot be improved. Recent research on the disorder suggests that the following may need to be considered to further improve the rigor or sensitivity of these criteria in distinguishing ADHD from normal and from other clinical disorders.

1. *It is not clear that the Predominantly Inattentive Type of ADHD (ADHD-PI) is actually a subtype of ADHD,* sharing a common attention deficit with the other types. This issue is discussed further in Chapter 3. Suffice it to say here that a number of qualitative differences between this subtype and those with hyperactive–impulsive behavior are emerging in research that suggest that it is unlikely that these subtypes have the same impairment in attention. The Predominantly Inattentive Type seems to be associated more with problems in focused/selective attention and sluggish information processing, whereas the Combined Type

of ADHD is associated more with problems of persistence of effort and distractibility. Should these group differences continue to be confirmed in additional research, it would indicate that the Predominantly Inattentive Type (or ADD without Hyperactivity) should be made a separate, distinct, and independent disorder from ADHD. It would also mean that clinicians and researchers need to take greater care in their classification of cases of ADHD in adolescents and adults into these subtypes. These problems arise because the hyperactivity symptoms in DSM-IV decline more steeply over development than do the symptoms of inattention. Thus there will be many cases of ADHD Hyperactive–Impulsive Type or the later Combined Type who, by adolescence or young adulthood no longer have sufficient symptoms of hyperactivity to remain in the Combined Type. If DSM-IV criteria were strictly followed, these individuals might now be reclassified in the Predominantly Inattentive Type. Yet conceptually they would not be similar to that subgroup of patients who had been in the Inattentive Type since childhood and who never had significant symptoms of hyperactivity or disinhibition. It is my view that clinicians and researchers would do well to continue to conceptualize the former group as still classically ADHD Combined Type even though they no longer have sufficient hyperactive symptoms to do so. This is because the *sine qua non* of the Combined Type is actually disinhibition and as long as this group presents clinically with inhibitory difficulties despite a decline in gross motor overactivity, group members should remain conceptualized as falling in the disinhibitory form of the disorder. As noted above, those adolescents or adults who have always been in the Inattentive Type since childhood and who present clinically with no significant difficulties with disinhibition, both currently and in childhood, should be thought of as having a qualitatively different condition.

2. *It is also unclear whether the Predominantly Hyperactive–Impulsive Type (ADHD–PHI) is really a separate type from the Combined Type (ADHD–C) or simply an earlier developmental stage of it.* The field trial found that ADHD–PHI primarily consisted of preschool age children whereas ADHD–C primarily consisted of school-age children. As noted earlier, this is what one would expect to find given that research previously found hyperactive–impulsive symptoms to appear first in development, followed within a few years by those of inattention (Hart, Lahey, Loeber, Applegate, & Frick, 1995; Loeber, Green, Lahey, Christ, & Frick, 1992). If inattention symptoms are required to be part of the diagnostic criteria, the age of onset for such symptoms will necessitate that ADHD–C have a later age of onset than ADHD–PHI, which seems to be the case (Applegate et al., 1997). Thus, it seems that these two types may actually be different developmental stages of the same type of ADHD.

3. *Thus the issue is raised whether the requirement for significant inattention to diagnose ADHD is even necessary* given that ADHD–PHI children are likely to eventually move into ADHD–C. Does the added requirement of significant inattention for the hyperactive–impulsive group add any greater power in predicting additional impairments not already achieved by the hyperactive–impulsive symptoms? Apparently not much, according to the results of the field trial (Lahey et al., 1994). Significant levels of inattention mainly predicted additional problems with completing homework that were not as well predicted by the hyperactive–impulsive behavior. Otherwise, the latter predicted most of the other areas of impairment studied in this field trial. This study is consistent with follow-up studies that found that childhood symptoms of hyperactivity are related to adolescent negative outcomes whereas those of inattention are much less so, if at all, and, if predictive of outcome, are mainly limited to academic outcome (Fischer, Barkley, Fletcher, & Smallish, 1993; Fergusson, Lynskey, & Horwood, 1997; Weiss & Hechtman, 1993).

4. *How well the diagnostic thresholds set for the two symptom lists apply to age groups outside those used in the field trial* (ages 4–16 years, chiefly) is another critical issue. This concern arises out of the well-known findings that the behavioral items comprising these lists decline significantly with age, particularly the hyperactive–impulsive list (Hart et al., 1995).

Applying the same threshold across such a declining developmental slope could produce a diminishing sensitivity to disorder: a situation in which a larger percentage of young pre–school-age children (ages 2–3) would be inappropriately diagnosed as ADHD (false positives) while a smaller-than-expected percentage of adults would meet the criteria (false negatives). A recent study (Murphy & Barkley, 1996b) that collected norms for the DSM-IV item lists on a large sample of adults ages 17 to 84 years found just such a problem with using these criteria for adults. The threshold needed to place an individual at the 93rd percentile for his or her age group declined to four of nine inattention items and five of nine hyperactive–impulsive items for ages 17–29 years, then to four of nine on each list for the 30- to 49-year age group, then to three of nine on each list for those 50 years and older. Studies of the applicability of the diagnostic thresholds to preschool children remain to be done. Until then, it seems prudent to utilize the recommended thresholds on each symptom list only for children ages 5–16 years, being more liberal than with the diagnostic thresholds used for adults.

5. These developmental changes in symptom thresholds raise another critical issue for developing diagnostic criteria for ADHD: *the appropriateness of the item set for different developmental periods.* Inspection of the item lists suggests that the items for inattention may have a wider developmental applicability across school-age ranges of childhood and even into adolescence and young adulthood. Those for hyperactivity, in contrast, seem much more applicable to young children and less appropriate or not at all to older teens and adults. The items for impulsivity are few and may or may not be as applicable to teens and adults as much as to children. Yet, as in the theoretical model discussed later, disinhibition may be the central feature of the disorder. Recall the observations found in recent research (Hart et al., 1995) that the symptoms of inattention remain stable across middle childhood into early adolescence while those for hyperactive–impulsive behavior decline significantly over this same course. Although this may represent a true developmental decline in the severity of the latter symptoms with maturation, and possibly in the severity and prevalence of ADHD itself, it could also represent an illusory developmental trend. That is, it might be an artifact of the developmental restrictedness of some items (hyperactivity) more than others (inattention) and the minimal sampling of impulsive behavior appropriate for the various developmental periods.

An analogy using mental retardation illustrates the issue. Consider the following items that might be chosen to assess developmental level in preschool-age children: being toilet-trained, recognizing primary colors, counting to 10, repeating 5 digits, buttons snaps on clothing, recognizing and drawing simple geometric shapes, and using a vocabulary repertoire of at least 100 words. This is a fixed item set, like DSM. Evaluating whether or not a child is able to do these things may prove to be very useful in distinguishing mentally retarded from nonretarded preschoolers. However, if we continued to use this same item set to assess retarded children as they grew older, we would find a decline in the severity of the retardation in such children as they achieved progressively more items with age. We would also find that the prevalence of retardation declined with age as many formerly retarded children outgrew this problem. But we know these findings are illusory because mental retardation represents a *developmentally relative deficit* in the achievement of these and other mental and adaptive milestones. All that is happening with age is that the symptom list is increasingly less sensitive to disorder and retarded children are simply outgrowing the symptom list and not the disorder.

Returning to the diagnosis of ADHD, if we apply the same fixed item sets throughout development with no attempt to adjust either the thresholds or, more important, the types of items developmentally appropriate for different periods, we might see the same results as with the analogy to mental retardation. The fact that similar results to this analogy do occur with ADHD (e.g., sensitivity to disorder does seem to diminish with age) should give us pause before we interpret the observed decline in symptom severity (and even the observed decline in apparent prevalence) as being accurate. If the theoretical model developed in Chapter 7 (this volume) is at all accurate, then developmentally sensitive sets of items for disinhibition need to be created and tested for use in this disorder to more accurately capture its nature and the fact that it, like mental retardation, probably represents a developmentally relative deficit. As it now stands, ADHD is defined mainly by one of its earliest developmental manifestations (hyperactivity) and one of its later (school-age) yet secondary sequelae (inattention or goal-directed impersistence) and only minimally by its central feature (disinhibition).

The issue is not just speculative. My colleagues and I involved in follow-up research with ADHD children into their adulthood have been impressed at the chronicity of impairments created by the disorder despite an *apparent* decline in the percentage of cases continuing to meet diagnostic criteria and an *apparent* decline in the severity of the symptoms used in these criteria (Barkley, Fischer, Edelbrock, & Smallish, 1990; Fischer, Barkley, Edelbrock, & Smallish, 1993). Making developmentally referenced adjustments to the diagnostic thresholds at their adolescent follow-up resulted in a larger number continuing to meet criteria for the disorder (71% to 84%). Such adjustments, however, did not correct for the potentially increasing inappropriateness of the item sets for this aging sample; thus it is difficult to say how many of those not meeting these adjusted criteria may still have had the disorder. More important, we found few differences in our measures of impairment between those no longer meeting diagnostic criteria for ADHD and those still doing so (Fischer et al., 1990).

6. A somewhat different critical issue concerning the diagnostic criteria for ADHD in Table 2.1 pertains to *whether or not the criteria should be adjusted for the gender of the child being diagnosed.* Research evaluating these and similar item sets demonstrates that male children in the general population display more of these items and to a more severe degree than do females (Achenbach & Edelbrock, 1983; DuPaul, 1991; Goyette et al., 1978). If so, should the same threshold for diagnosis be applied to both genders? Doing so would seem to result in females having to meet a higher threshold relative to other females to be diagnosed as ADHD than do males relative to other males. The problem is further accentuated by the fact that the majority of individuals in the DSM field trial were males making the DSM criteria primarily male-referenced. Adjusting the cutoff scores for each gender separately might well result in nullifying the finding that ADHD is more common in males than females by a ratio of roughly 3:1 (see later). A conference held at the National Institute of Mental Health in November 1994 to discuss gender differences in ADHD did not recommend that this be done as yet (Arnold, 1997). But a consensus emerged that sufficient evidence existed warranting further study to determine whether females with ADHD not meeting current diagnostic thresholds were actually impaired. If so, gender-based thresholds for diagnosis would be necessary.

7. *The requirement of an age of onset for ADHD symptoms (7 years) in the diagnostic criteria has also come under recent challenge* from its own field trial (Applegate et al., 1997) as well as from other longitudinal studies (McGee, Williams, & Feehan, 1992). Such a criterion for age of onset suggests that there may be qualitative differences between those who meet the criterion (early onset) and those who do not (late onset). Some results do suggest that those with an onset before age 6 may have more severe and persistent conditions and more problems with reading and school performance more generally (McGee et al., 1992). But these were matters of degree and not of kind in this study. The DSM-IV field trial also was not able to show any clear discontinuities in degree of ADHD or in the types of impairments it examined between those meeting and not meeting the 7-year age of onset. It remains unclear at this time just how specific an age of onset may need to be for distinguishing ADHD from other disorders. Meanwhile, I and Joseph Biederman cogently argued (Barkley & Biederman, 1997) that the age-of-onset criterion be generously broadened to include onset

of symptoms during childhood, in keeping with the conceptualization of this disorder as having a childhood onset while not restricting it with a wholly indefensible and highly specific onset of 7 years of age. This argument would have the added advantage of making the DSM-IV criteria more suitable for use with adults, who would have less difficulty recalling an onset of their symptoms sometime in childhood versus one prior to 7 years of age.

8. A related potential problem for these criteria occurs in their *failure to stipulate a lower bound age group for giving the diagnosis below which no diagnosis should be made*. This is important because research on preschool children shows that a separate dimension of hyperactive–impulsive behavior is not distinguishable from one of aggression or defiant behavior until about 3 years of age (Achenbach & Edelbrock, 1987; Campbell, 1990). Below this age, these behaviors cluster together to form "behavioral immaturity," or an under-controlled pattern of temperament or conduct. All this implies that the symptoms of ADHD may be difficult to distinguish from other early behavioral disorders until at least 3 years of age; thus, this age might serve as a lower bound for diagnostic applications.

9. Similarly, research discussed later implies that *a lower bound of IQ might also be important* below which the nature of ADHD may be quite different. For instance, Rutter and colleagues (Rutter, Bolton, et al., 1990; Rutter, Macdonald, et al., 1990) concluded that children who fall below an IQ of 50 may have a qualitatively different form of mental retardation. This conclusion is inferred from findings that this group is overrepresented for its position along a normal distribution and from findings that genetic defects contribute more heavily to this subgroup. Given this shift in the prevalence and causes of mental retardation below this level of IQ, a similar state of affairs might exist for the form of ADHD associated with it, necessitating its distinction from the type of ADHD that occurs in individuals above this IQ level. Consistent with such a view are findings that the percentage of positive responders to stimulant medication in those with ADHD falls off sharply below this threshold of IQ (Demb, 1991).

10. Another pertinent issue is *the problem of the duration requirement being set at 6 months.* This number was chosen mainly in keeping with earlier DSMs, with little or no research support for selecting this particular length of time for symptom presence. It is undoubtedly important that the symptoms be relatively persistent if we are to view this disorder as within the individual rather than arising purely from context or out of a transient, normal developmental stage. Yet specifying a precise duration is difficult in the absence of much research to guide the issue. Research on preschool age children might prove helpful here, however. Such research shows that many children ages 3 years (or younger) may have parent or preschool teachers who report concerns about the activity level or attention of the children, yet these concerns have a high likelihood of remission within 12 months (Beitchman, Wekerle, & Hood, 1987; Campbell, 1990; Lerner, Inui, Trupin, & Douglas, 1985; Palfrey, Levine, Walker, & Sullivan, 1985). It would seem for preschoolers, then, that the 6-month duration specified in DSM-IV may be too brief, resulting in overidentification of ADHD children at this age (false positives). However, this same body of research found that for those children whose problems lasted at least 12 months or beyond age 4 years, a persistent pattern of behavior was established that was highly predictive of its continuance into the school-age range. The finding suggests that a duration of symptoms of at least 12 months might prove more rigorous.

11. The DSM requirement that *the symptoms be demonstrated in at least two of three environments to establish pervasiveness of symptoms is new to this edition and problematic.* By stipulating that the symptoms must be present in at least two of three contexts (home, school, work, in the case of DSM-IV; home, school, clinic, in the case of ICD-10), the criteria now confound settings with sources of information (parent, teacher, employer, clinician), as noted earlier. Research shows that the degree of agreement between parents and teacher, for in-

stance, is modest, often ranging between .30 and .50 depending on the behavioral dimension being rated (Achenbach, McConaughy, & Howell, 1987). This degree of agreement sets an upper limit on the extent to which parents and teachers are going to agree on the severity of ADHD symptoms and, thus, on whether or not the child has the disorder in that setting. Whereas such disagreements among sources certainly reflect differences in the child's behavior as a function of true differential demands of these settings, they also reflect differences in the attitudes and judgments between different people.

Insisting on such agreement on diagnostic criteria may reduce the application of the diagnosis to some children unfairly simply as a result of such well-established differences between parents' and teachers' opinions. It may also create a confounding of the disorder with issues of comorbidity with Oppositional Defiant Disorder (ODD; Costello et al., 1991). Parent-only-identified ADHD children may have predominantly ODD with relatively milder ADHD while teacher-only-identified ADHD children may have chiefly ADHD and minimal or no ODD symptoms. Children identified by both parents and teachers as ADHD may, therefore, carry a higher likelihood of ODD. They may also simply reflect a more severe condition of ADHD than do the home- or school-only cases, being different in degree rather than in kind (Tripp & Luk, 1997). Research is clearly conflicting on the matter of whether pervasiveness of symptoms defines a valid syndrome (Cohen & Minde, 1983; Rapoport et al., 1986; Schachar et al., 1981; Taylor, Sandberg, Thorley, & Giles, 1991; Tripp & Luk, 1997). Considering that teacher information on children is not always obtainable or convenient to obtain and that diagnosis based on parents' reports will lead to a diagnosis based on teacher reports 90% of the time (Biederman, Keenan, & Faraone, 1990), parent reports may suffice for diagnostic purposes for now. Until more research is done to address this issue, the requirement of pervasiveness should probably be interpreted to mean a history of symptoms in multiple settings rather than current parent–teacher agreement on number and severity of symptoms.

12. The findings discussed in this chapter indicate that behavioral disinhibition or poor regulation and inhibition of behavior are the hallmarks of ADHD (Barkley, 1997a, 1997d; Pennington & Ozonoff, 1997b; Quay, 1988, 1997); thus *greater emphasis should be placed on the hyperactive–impulsive symptoms rather than the inattention symptoms in describing the disorder* for clinicians. Behavioral disinhibition is more discriminating of ADHD from other disorders and thus meeting a cutoff score for these items should be a first requirement in the diagnostic criteria.

13. A final point of improvement pertains to the stipulation in DSM-IV that symptoms must be developmentally inappropriate. Yet, *the diagnostic criteria do not specify precisely how developmental inappropriateness is to be established.* Borrowing again from the disorder of mental retardation, a specific degree of general cognitive delay is specified in the criteria: an IQ score below 70. In contrast, for ADHD, no guidance is given as to just what constitutes developmental inappropriateness or how to assess it. The ubiquity of well-normed behavior rating scales assessing ADHD symptoms generally, and now DSM-IV ADHD symptoms specifically, argues for the use of such instruments to determine the extent of developmental deviance in a particular case (see Chapter 8, this volume, for such scales). Although not wholly objective, such instruments do provide a means of quantifying parent and teacher opinion in the case of children and adult self-report and other-reports of symptoms in the case of adults evaluated for ADHD. Moreover, national norms are now available for the parent and teacher versions of these instruments (DuPaul et al., 1997; DuPaul et al., in press), and some local norms (Massachusetts) are available for adults (Murphy & Barkley, 1996b) with national norms now being collected. The use of such scales automatically provides for the establishment of deviance relative to both age and gender membership of the individual, as discussed earlier, given that norms are provided separately for males and females by age

groups. It also would seem prudent to establish a cutoff score on these scales of at least the 90th percentile and, preferably the 93rd percentile, as the demarcation for clinical significance given that the 93rd percentile (+1.5 standard deviations above the mean) is a traditionally employed cut point for this purpose (Achenbach, 1991). Although I previously suggested that mental age (Barkley, 1990) be taken into consideration in the use of such norms given the low but significant negative correlation between symptoms of ADHD and IQ (see Barkley, 1997a), research in the interim suggests that using a chronological-age comparison group is sufficient for making determinations of developmental inappropriateness of symptoms and that adjusting for mental age is actually unnecessary (Pearson & Aman, 1994).

Despite these numerous problematic issues for the DSM approach to diagnosis, the criteria are actually some of the best ever advanced for the disorder and represent a vast improvement over the state of affairs that existed prior to 1980. The various editions of DSM also spawned a large amount of research into ADHD, its symptoms, subtypes, criteria, and even etiologies that likely would not have occurred had such criteria not been set forth for professional consumption and criticism. The most recent criteria provide clinicians with a set of guidelines more specific, reliable, empirically based or justifiable, and closer to the scientific literature on ADHD than earlier editions and thus deserve to be adopted in clinical practice. Yet, the issues raised here suggest that such adoption not become diagnostic dogma but instead warrant the criteria being applied with some adjustments for particular instances and, as always, with some clinical judgment.

IS ADHD A MENTAL DISORDER?

Social critics (Kohn, 1989; McGinnis, 1997; Schrag & Divoky, 1975) charge that professionals have been too quick to label energetic and exuberant children as having a mental disorder and that educators also may be using these labels as an excuse for simply poor educational environments. In other words, children who are hyperactive or ADHD are actually normal but are being labeled mentally disordered because of parent and teacher intolerance (Kohn, 1989). If this were actually true, we should find no differences of any cognitive, behavioral, or social significance between children so labeled and normal children. We should also find that being labeled ADHD is not associated with any significant later risks in development for maladjustment within any domains of adaptive functioning or social or school performance. Furthermore, research on potential etiologies for the disorder should, likewise, come up empty-handed. This is hardly the case. Differences between ADHD and normal children are numerous, as noted earlier and in Chapter 3 (this volume) (see also Barkley, 1997a). And, as shown later, numerous developmental risks await the child meeting clinical diagnostic criteria for the disorder. Moreover, certain potential etiological factors are becoming consistently noted in the research literature as being associated with ADHD.

Conceding all this, however, does not automatically entitle ADHD to be placed within the realm of mental disorders. Wakefield (1992) argued that mental disorders must meet several criteria to be viewed as such: (1) they must engender substantial harm to the individual or those around him or her and (2) they must incur dysfunction of natural mental mechanisms that have been selected in an evolutionary sense (have survival value). It should become clear from the totality of information on ADHD presented here, in Chapter 3, and elsewhere (Barkley, 1990, 1997a; Hinshaw, 1994) that the disorder handily meets both criteria. Those with ADHD, as described previously, have significant deficits in behavioral inhibition and, as shown in Chapters 3 and 7 (this volume), in the executive functions dependent on it that are critical for effective self-regulation. It has been argued that these executive functions are selected for in evolution to assist individuals with organizing their behavior relative to time and the future and thereby helping them maximize long-term over short-term consequences (Barkley, 1997a, 1997c). And those with ADHD experience significant and numerous risks for harm to themselves over development. Thus, we can safely conclude, at least by Wakefield's standards, that ADHD is a mental disorder because it produces a harmful dysfunction in a set of mental mechanisms evolved to have a survival advantage.

IS ADHD A CLINICAL SYNDROME?

A troublesome issue for attempts to define a disorder or syndrome is the frequent finding that objective measures of ADHD symptoms do not correlate well with each other (Barkley, 1991; Barkley & Ullman, 1975; Routh & Roberts, 1972; Ullman et al., 1978). Typically, for a disorder to be viewed as a syndrome its major features should be related—the more deviant an individual is on one symptom the more the individual should be on the other major symptoms. The relatively weak or insignificant correlations among laboratory measures of activity, attention, and impulsivity are often used as evidence against the existence of ADHD as a disorder or syndrome by both scientists (Shaffer & Greenhill, 1979) and social critics alike (Kohn, 1989; Shrag & Divoky, 1975). However, these weak relationships may have more to do with the manner in which we define the attention deficit or overactivity problems in ADHD children (Rutter, 1989) and, more likely, with the measures we choose to assess these behaviors (Barkley, 1991). How long a child looks at a classroom lecture may be a very different type of attentional process than that required to perform a vigilance test or to search out important from unimportant features in a picture (Barkley, 1988; Ullman et al., 1978). Similarly, taking adequate time to examine a picture before choosing one identical to it from a number of similar pictures (as in Kagan's MFFT, discussed earlier) may be a different type of impulsivity from that seen when a child is asked to draw a line slowly or whether he or she wishes to work a little for a small reward now or do more work for a large reward later (Milich & Kramer, 1985; Rapport et al., 1986). It is a small wonder then that these types of measures correlate at all with each other.

In contrast, studies that factor-analyze parent or teacher ratings of ADHD symptoms often find that they are highly interrelated (Achenbach & Edelbrock, 1981; Barkley, 1988; DuPaul, 1991; Hinshaw, 1987; Lahey et al., 1994) and can be combined into a single dimension (Hyperactivity) or at most two dimensions (Inattention–Restless and Impulsive–Hyperactive). Similarly, when measures of attention and impulsivity are taken within the same task, as in scores for omission and commission errors on a continuous performance test, they are highly related to each other (Barkley, 1991; Gordon, 1983). This finding suggests that the frequent failure to find relationships among various lab measures of ADHD symptoms has more to do with the source or types of measures chosen, their highly limited sampling of behavior (typically 20 minutes or less per task), and their sampling of quite diverse aspects of attention, impulsivity, or activity than to a lack of relationships among the natural behaviors of these children.

Furthermore, even if the symptoms may not occur to a uniform degree in the same children does not rule out the value of considering ADHD a syndrome. As Rutter (1977, 1989) has noted, a disorder need not show such uniform variation to still be clinically useful as a syndrome. If such children show a relatively similar course and outcome, their symptoms predict differential responses to certain treatments relative to other disorders, or they tend to share a common etiology or set of etiologies, it may still be valuable to consider children with such characteristics as having a syndrome of ADHD. I and others (Douglas, 1983; Rutter, 1989; Taylor, 1986; Taylor et al., 1991) believe the evidence supports such an interpretation of ADHD.

More problematic for the concept of a syndrome, however, is whether the defining features of ADHD can discriminate ADHD from other types of psychiatric disturbance in children. The evidence here was certainly conflicting and less compelling (Reeves, Werry, Elkind, & Zamethin, 1987; Werry, Elkind, & Reeves, 1987) until the end of the 1980s. Mentally retarded, autistic, psychotic, depressed, conduct-disordered, anxious, and learning-disabled children were thought to show deficits in attention, suggesting that inattention was a rather nonspecific symptom. When early studies compared such groups, they often found few differences among them on measures of ADHD characteristics (see Werry, 1988, for a review). However, such studies often did not take into account the comorbidity of many of these disorders with each other. Comorbidity means that children with one disorder may have a high likelihood of having a second. Some children may have only one of the disorders, some may have the other, and many have both. This is often noted with ADHD, ODD, Conduct Disorder, and the learning disabilities. Many studies on this issue have not taken care to choose subjects that have only one of these disorders to compare against those who have "pure" cases of the other disorders. As a result, they compare mixed cases of ADHD with mixed cases of other disorders, which greatly weakens the likelihood that differences among the groups will emerge. When this was done, differences between pure ADHD and other disorders are more significant and numerous (August & Stewart, 1983; Barkley, DuPaul, & McMurray, 1990; Barkley, DuPaul, & McMurray, 1991; Barkley, Fischer, et al., 1990; McGee, Williams, & Silva, 1984a, 1984b; Pennington & Ozonoff, 1996). Moreover, it appears that deficits in response inhibition are quite specific to ADHD (Barkley, 1997a; Pennington & Ozonoff, 1996).

Certainly, differences in the approaches that were previously taken to define ADHD also contributed to the difficulties in evaluating ADHD as a distinct clinical syndrome. Research in the 1960s and 1970s was characterized by poorly specified and often subjective criteria for deciding on which subjects would be called hyperactive, or ADHD, with tremendous discrepancies across studies in these selection criteria (Barkley, 1982). Such criteria guaranteed not only that the studies would differ greatly in their findings but also that many employed subjects of mixed comorbidity ensured a conflicting pattern of results across the literature. With the development of consensus criteria for clinical diagnosis, as in DSM-III-R and the more recent DSM-IV, or for research diagnoses (Barkley, 1982; Sergeant, 1988), and with greater attention to the study of pure cases of the disorder, better, more critical tests of the notion of ADHD as a distinct disorder can now be undertaken. For now, it seems that the symptoms of ADHD, particularly those pertaining to poor behavioral inhibition, appear to be quite specific to this disorder, are not typically shared by other child psychiatric disorders, and thus provide further evidence that ADHD can be considered a developmental or mental disorder distinct from many others.

IS ADHD A DIMENSION OR A CATEGORY?

One debate in the scientific literature occurring over the last decade was whether or not ADHD represented a category or a dimension of behavior. The notion of applying categories for psychopathologies of children seems to derive from the medical model where such categories constitute disease states (Edelbrock & Costello, 1984). From this perspective, an individual either has the disorder or does not. The DSM, in one sense, uses this categorical approach (all or none) by requiring that certain thresholds be met to be placed within the category of ADHD. The view of psychopathologies as representing dimensions of behavior, or even typologies (profiles) of these dimensions, arises from the perspective of developmental psychopathology (Achenbach & Edelbrock, 1983). In this view, ADHD constitutes the extreme end of a dimension, or dimensions, of behavior that falls along a continuum with normal children. The dimensional view (more or less) does not necessarily see ADHD as a disease entity but as a matter of degree in what is otherwise a characteristic of normal children.

The debate as it pertains to ADHD seems to have lessened recently for several reasons, some of which relate to the construction of DSM-III-R and now DSM-IV. First, and not widely known, is the fact that the DSM-III-R committee relied on several of the most commonly used behavior rating scales (Conners scales, Child Behavior Checklist, Behavior Problem Checklist) as one source in selecting items to be included in the symptom list(s) and to be tested out in the field trials (Spitzer et al., 1990). Second, the casting of these symptoms into lists along which a threshold of severity is placed for granting a diagnosis tacitly represents the disorder as a dimension. Third, the ICD-10 criteria for this disorder formally recommend the use of standardized dimensional measures to assess the degree of deviancy of the individual in determining the presence of the disorder—a further acknowledgment of the dimensional nature of the disorder. Texts on the clinical diagnosis of ADHD in North America (Barkley, 1990; Goldstein & Goldstein, 1990; Hinshaw, 1994), likewise, recommend the addition of child behavior rating scales to the clinical assessment procedures for ADHD children, lending further endorsement to the dimensional view of ADHD. A fourth line of evidence supporting the dimensional view comes from demonstrations that the majority of subjects placed at extreme ends of dimensions of behavior related to ADHD on rating scales will receive the diagnosis when structured interviews using the diagnostic criteria are given (Chen, Faraone, Biederman, & Tsuang, 1994; Edelbrock & Costello, 1984). Of course, this is not surprising given the previous three points bearing on this issue. Finally, recent genetic studies support the notion that ADHD represents a dimensional trait rather than a pathological category (Levy, Hay, McStephen, Wood, & Waldman, 1997; Sherman, McGee, & Iacono, 1997). The debate must ultimately be settled by whether or not qualitative differences exist between individuals who achieve the diagnostic threshold versus those who are subthreshold. Until such discontinuities are demonstrated, the dimensional approach to ADHD seems most consistent with the available evidence whereas the categorical approach remains one of convenience, parsimony, and tradition (Hinshaw, 1994) rather than one with empirical validation.

SITUATIONAL AND TEMPORAL VARIATION

As already noted, all the primary symptoms of ADHD show significant fluctuations across various settings and caregivers (Barkley, 1981b; Zentall, 1985). Play alone, washing and bathing, and when father is at home are a few of the situations that are less troublesome for ADHD children, whereas instances when children are asked to do chores, when parents are on the telephone, when visitors are in the home, or when children are in public places may be times of peak severity of their disorder (Barkley, 1990). Figures 2.1 and 2.2 show the mean activity level for 12 hyperactive and 12 normal children monitored during school hours and after school activities on school days, respectively (Porrino et al., 1983). Again, significant fluctuations in activity are evident across these different contexts for both ADHD and normal children, with the differences between them becoming most evident during school classes in reading and math. Despite these situational fluctuations, ADHD children appear to be more deviant in their primary symptoms than normal children in most settings, yet these differences can be exaggerated greatly as a function of several factors related to the settings and tasks given to children to perform in them (Luk, 1985; Zentall, 1985).

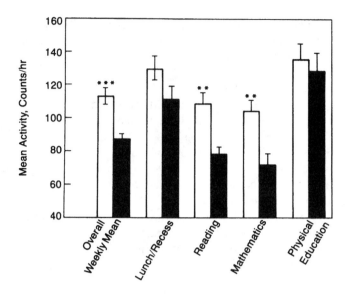

FIGURE 2.1. Mean hourly activity scores (with standard errors of measurement) over a period of 4 days for 12 hyperactive children (open bars) and 12 control children (solid bars) during school hours. Asterisks indicate significant differences on two-tailed *t* tests: triple asterisk, $p < .001$; double asterisk, $p < .01$. From Porrino et al. (1983). Copyright 1983 by the American Medical Association. Reprinted by permission.

Degree of Environmental Demands for Inhibition

Some of the factors determining this variation have been delineated. One of these, the extent to which caregivers make demands on ADHD children to restrict behavior, appears to affect the degree of deviance of the child's behavior from normal children. In free-play or low-demand settings, ADHD children are less distinguishable from normal children than in highly restrictive ones (Barkley, 1985; Jacob et al., 1978; Luk, 1985; Routh & Schroeder, 1976). Related to this issue of setting demands is the effect of task complexity on ADHD children. The more complicated the task and hence its greater demand for planning, organization, and executive regulation of behavior, the greater the likelihood that ADHD children will perform more poorly on the task than normal children (Douglas, 1983; Luk, 1985). Clearly, the symptoms of ADHD are only handicapping when the demands of the environment or task exceed the child's capacity to sustain attention, regulate activity, and restrain impulses. In environments that place little or no demands on these behavioral faculties, ADHD children will appear less deviant and certainly be viewed by others as less troublesome than in settings or tasks that place high demands on these abilities. As Zentall (1985) rightly noted in her comprehensive review of setting factors in the expression of ADHD symptoms, we must look closely at the nature of the stimuli in the task and setting to which the child is being required to respond to gain a better understanding of why these children have so much trouble in some settings and with some tasks than others.

Behavior toward Fathers Compared to Mothers

ADHD children appear to be more compliant and less disruptive with their fathers than mothers (Tallmadge & Barkley, 1983). There are several possible reasons for this. For one, mothers are still the primary custodians of children within the family, even when they are employed outside the home, and may therefore be the ones who are most likely to tax or exceed the children's limitations in the areas of persistence of attention, activity regulation, impulse control, and rule-governed behavior. Getting children to do chores and schoolwork, perform self-care routines, and control their behavior in public remain predominantly maternal responsibilities; thus mothers may be more likely to witness ADHD symptoms than are fathers. It would be interesting to examine families of ADHD children in which these roles were reversed to see whether fathers were the ones reporting more deviance of the children's behavior. Another reason may be that mothers and fathers tend to respond to inappropriate child behavior somewhat differently. Mothers may be more likely to reason with children, repeat their instructions, and use affection as a means of governing child compliance. Fathers seem to repeat their commands less, to reason less, and to be quicker to discipline children for misconduct or noncompliance. The larger size of fathers and their consequently greater strength, among other characteristics, may also be perceived as more threatening by children and hence more likely to elicit compliance to commands given by fathers. For whatever reason, the greater obedience of ADHD children to their fathers than mothers is now well established. It should not be construed as either a sign that the child is not actually ADHD or necessarily that the child's problems are entirely the result of maternal mismanagement.

Repetition of Instructions

On tasks in which instructions are repeated frequently to the ADHD child, problems with sustained responding are lessened (Douglas, 1980, 1983). Research has shown that when directions for a laboratory task or psychological test are repeated by the examiner, better performance is derived from ADHD children. However, it is not clear whether this is specific to these laboratory tasks and the novel examiner or can be generalized to activities done

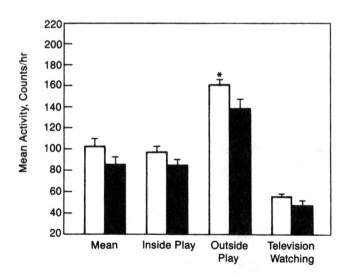

FIGURE 2.2. Mean hourly activity scores (with standard errors of measurement) over a period of 4 days for 12 hyperactive children (open bars) and 12 control children (solid bars), calculated for specific situations during after-school hours. Asterisk indicates significant difference on two-tailed *t* tests at $p < .05$. From Porrino et al. (1983). Copyright 1983 by the American Medical Association. Reprinted by permission.

with routine caregivers. I raise this doubt because, as noted earlier, it is not uncommon to find that parents and teachers frequently complain that repeating their commands and instructions to ADHD children produces little change in compliance.

Novelty and Task Stimulation

ADHD children display fewer behavioral problems in novel or unfamiliar surroundings or when tasks are unusually novel but increase their level of deviant behavior as familiarity with the setting increases (Barkley, 1977; Zentall, 1985). It would not be unexpected to find that ADHD children are rated as far better in their behavior at the beginning of the academic year when they are presented with new teachers, classmates, classrooms, and even school facilities. Their behavioral control, however, would deteriorate over the initial weeks of school. Similarly, when ADHD children visit with grandparents whom they have not seen frequently, who are likely to provide them with considerable one-to-one attention, and who are unlikely to make numerous demands of their self-control, it seems likely that ADHD children would be at their best levels of behavioral control.

The degree of stimulation in the task also seems to be a factor in the performance of ADHD children. Research suggests that colorful or highly stimulating educational materials are likely to improve the attention of these children to such materials than relatively low stimulation or uncolored materials (Zentall, 1985). Interestingly, such differences may not affect the attention of normal children as much or may even worsen it. One would think that video games or television offer ADHD children more stimulation than would many other activities. This leads many to suggest that children with ADHD should show few or no difficulties with attention or hyperactivity during these activities. Yet, studies do show that ADHD children look away from these activities more than do normal children and, in the case of video games, may have more problems with their performance than do normal children (Barkley & Ullman, 1975; Landau, Lorch, & Milich, 1992; Tannock, 1997).

Magnitude of Consequences

Settings or tasks that involve a high rate of immediate reinforcement or punishment for compliance to instructions result in significant reductions in, or in some cases amelioration of, attentional deficits (Barkley, 1997b; Barkley, Copeland, & Sivage, 1980; Douglas, 1983; Douglas & Parry, 1983). Few ADHD children seem to demonstrate attention deficits to popular video games, such as Nintendo, or when large amounts of money or salient rewards are promised them immediately on completion of a task. Differences in activity level between hyperactives and normals while watching television may be less than in other activities whereas such differences are substantially evident during reading and math classes at school (Porrino et al., 1983). It seems that when ADHD children are engaged in highly reinforcing activities, they may even perform at normal or near-normal levels. However, when the schedule and magnitude of reinforcement are decreased, the behavior of ADHD children may become readily distinguishable from normal (Barkley et al., 1980). Such dramatic changes in the degree of deviance of behavior as a function of motivational parameters in the setting led several scientists to question the notion that ADHD is actually a deficit in attention at all. Instead, they suggest it may be more of a problem in the manner in which behavior is regulated by rules and by motivational factors in the task (Barkley, 1989a, 1997c; Draeger, Prior, & Sanson, 1986; Glow & Glow, 1979; Haenlein & Caul, 1987; Prior, Wallace, & Milton, 1984).

A situational factor related to motivation appears to involve the degree of individualized attention being provided to the ADHD child. During one-to-one situations, ADHD children may appear less active, inattentive, and impulsive, whereas in group situations, where their is little such attention, ADHD children may appear at their worst. Some studies, for instance, found that whether the experimenter sits in the room with the child or not greatly determines whether differences between ADHD children on visual or auditory attention tasks or on attention to arithmetic work are found (Draeger et al., 1986; Steinkamp, 1980).

Fatigue

Fatigue or time of day (or both) may have an impact on the degree of deviance of ADHD symptoms. I am aware of only one study that has investigated this issue (Zagar & Bowers, 1983). The authors observed the behavior of ADHD children in their classrooms and during various problem-solving tasks and found that they performed significantly better on these tasks in the mornings, whereas their classroom behavior was significantly worse in the afternoons. These changes in behavior with time of day did not appear to be a function of boredom or fatigue with the task as efforts were made to counterbalance the order of administration of the tests across mornings and afternoons. Performance in the afternoon was routinely worse whether it was the first or second administration of the task. However, the possibility that general fatigue defined simply as time since the last resting or sleeping period may still explain these results. Similar effects of time of day were noted in the study by Porrino et al. (1983), which monitored 24-hour activity levels across school days and weekends separately. These findings are shown in Figure 2.3 for school days and indicate that the hours of 1 P.M. to 5 P.M. to be the peak times of activity for ADHD children.

This is not to say that differences between hyperactive and normal children do not exist in early mornings but emerge only as time of day advances, for this is not the case (Porrino et al., 1983). Normal children show similar effects of time of day on their behavior and thus hyperactive children appear to be more active and inattentive than normal children regardless of time of day. It is to say, however, that relatively better performances on tasks and in

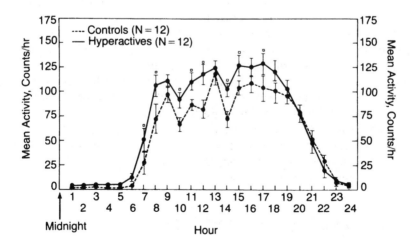

FIGURE 2.3. Mean hourly activity scores (with standard errors of measurement) over a period of 3 to 5 days for 12 hyperactive children and 12 control children, calculated for a typical weekday. Small squares indicate significant differences between groups at the *p* < .05 level. From Porrino et al. (1983). Copyright 1983 by the American Medical Association. Reprinted by permission.

classrooms by ADHD children may be obtained at some times of the day more than others. The findings so far suggest that educators would do well to schedule overlearned, repetitive, or difficult tasks that require the greatest powers of attention and behavioral restraint for morning periods while placing recreational, entertaining, or physical activities in the afternoons (Zagar & Bowers, 1983). Such findings certainly raise serious doubts about the adequacy of the practice of scheduling homework periods for ADHD children in late afternoons or early evenings.

IMPLICATIONS FOR DIAGNOSIS AND MANAGEMENT

These situational fluctuations in symptom levels have significant implications for clinical diagnosis of ADHD. It is clear that the disorder is not completely pervasive across all settings. As a result, the previous and common clinical practice of establishing places where the ADHD child could behave normally and then ruling out the diagnosis is no longer tenable. Many clinicians have interrogated parents as to how their ADHD children behave while watching television, playing video games, and interacting with their fathers, grandparents, or baby-sitters. After learning that the children were much better behaved or normal in these settings, the clinician proceeded to conclude that such children could not be ADHD because the symptoms were neither persistent nor pervasive. Some even went as far as to state that because the children were better for their fathers (and often better during the office exam with the clinician), the problem must rest with the mothers' inept management of their children. Such a prejudice against mothers, in fact, is still rather pervasive among laymen and even some professionals. It is now quite clear that ADHD children show a tremendous variability in their symptom severity across settings, tasks, and time. And although they are typically more deviant than normal children in their levels of activity and inattention in most settings, the factors within the setting and especially in the demands of the task are highly related to the level of deviance noted (Zentall, 1985). It therefore seems best in searching for information to assist with the diagnosis to focus clinical attention more on the ability of ADHD children to sustain attention, regulate activity, control impulses, and follow rules under conditions of tedium, especially boring, repetitive, or protracted work assignments, or under social conditions demanding restraint.

As already noted, these situational changes in behavior and performance can also have some impact on the management of ADHD children. An awareness of the situational or task factors that can enhance performance may greatly empower a parent or teacher to devise methods or schedules of work that best fit with the ADHD child's limited capacities for sustaining attention and regulating activity level. Difficult, complex, or tedious work can be organized into smaller units, provided with greater clarity, and enhanced by providing more immediate and salient reinforcers for task completion. Scheduling such activities during morning hours, as suggested earlier, may further enhance task performance. Permitting some motion and talking during task completion and interspersing periods of restraint with periods of exercise or movement may also help.

PREVALENCE AND GENDER RATIO

Because ADHD cannot be strictly defined and precisely and objectively measured, its true prevalence cannot be accurately determined. Some social critics have used this point to challenge whether a disorder of ADHD exists at all (Kohn, 1989; Shrag & Divoky, 1975). But this challenge reflects a startling naiveté about the nature of mental disorders because this same problem surely plagues efforts to define and establish the prevalence of all psychiatric disorders and even many medical conditions (Alzheimer's disease, Reye's syndrome, etc.). Yet this problem hardly makes them clinically useless or fictitious disorders. The consensus of expert opinion seems to be that approximately 3–5% of the childhood population has ADHD (American Psychiatric Association, 1994). This number greatly hinges, however, on how one chooses to define and measure ADHD, the population studied, the geographic locale of the survey, and even the degree of agreement required between parents, teachers, and professionals (Lambert, Sandoval, & Sassone, 1978). Early estimates varied between 1% and 20% (DuPaul, 1991; Ross & Ross, 1982; Szatmari et al., 1989).

The individual symptoms of ADHD can be found in a large percentage of normal children. For instance, in 1958, Rema Lapouse and Mary Monk had teachers evaluate a large sample of school-age children as to the presence of various behavior problems. Their findings revealed that 57% of the boys and 42% of the girls were rated as overactive. Similarly, John Werry and Herbert Quay (1971) also surveyed a large population of schoolchildren and found that teachers rated 30% of the boys and 12% of the girls as overactive, 49% of the boys and 27% of the girls as restless, and 43% of the boys and 25% of the girls as having a short attention span.

Critics of the concept of ADHD as a disorder have used such figures to argue that if so many normal children have these features, how can one choose to label some of them as having a clinical or psychiatric disorder (Kohn, 1989; Schrag & Divoky, 1975). These critics ignore the requirement that both the number and the degree of these behavioral characteristics must be developmentally inappropriate for that child's age and gender before it can be considered a clinical disorder (American Psychiatric Association, 1994; Barkley, 1981a, 1982, 1990). In other words, a statistical criterion is applied in which the referred child is compared to his or her peers in their level of these problematic behaviors to determine how deviant they are from same-age, same-gender children. The further the children are from their peers in these behaviors, the greater the odds that they will be impaired in their educational and social adjustment and will eventually be diagnosed as ADHD.

For instance, DSM-IV requires that each symptom be described as occurring at least "Often" before it can be counted as a symptom (as developmentally inappropriate). How often do normal children show any of these symptoms as occurring "Often"? Critics contend that many normal children show such symptoms and so would qualify as ADHD. But this simply is not so. Research indicates that only 7–23% of normal boys have any particular DSM-IV symptom described as occurring to this extent ("Often") and only 4–19% of normal girls, depending on the particular symptom (Gadow & Sprafkin, 1997). And the fact is that no single symptom qualifies a child for the disorder. Instead, the child must have at least six or more such symptoms rated as "Often" occurring to meet the symptom threshold for any subtype of ADHD. Moreover, lost on such social critics is the requirement that these symptoms must demonstrate an early onset in childhood and a persistence over time and lead to significant impairment in one or more domains of major life activities for the child, such as home, school, community, adaptive, and peer functioning. When all these requirements for a mental disorder are taken into account, ADHD appears to be far less prevalent than both the social critics and the early studies of prevalence would have one believe.

Defining Deviance

A problem here, admittedly, is deciding what cutoff point is needed to determine that the child is "developmentally inappropriate" in his or her behavior. Some have used the criterion of 1.5 standard deviations above the normal mean on parent or teacher rating scales of these ADHD symptoms. However, surveys of large samples of children, such as that done by Ronald Trites and colleagues in 1979 using 14,083 schoolchildren, find that this cutoff score can identify an average of 14% of the population as hyperactive (Trites, Dugas, Lynch, & Ferguson, 1979). In other studies (see Szatmari et al., 1989; Taylor, 1986), estimates can range from less than 1% to more than 22% using cutoff scores ranging from 1 to 2 standard deviations above the mean on structured psychiatric diagnostic interviews. However, when others have applied the cutoff of 2 standard deviations above the mean using DSM-III-R symptoms, a more acceptable range of 2–9% would be labeled hyperactive or ADHD (DuPaul, 1991). Applying a more stringent statistical criterion, such as 2 standard deviations from the mean, is obviously somewhat arbitrary but in keeping with tradition in defining other conditions, such as learning disabilities and mental retardation, as deviant. It also ensures that an excessive number of children are not being given a psychiatric diagnosis and reserves the diagnosis for the most severely afflicted. When such a stringent criteria as the 97th percentile is applied (2 standard deviations above the mean), it does appear to identify a group of children whose ADHD symptoms are not only seriously deviant but are also stable over as long a time as 8 to 10 years and highly predictive of later maladjustment, particularly in academic adjustment and attainment (Barkley, Fischer, et al., 1990). Yet such a cutoff point can be overly stringent, excluding children who are both relatively deviant and impaired by their symptoms. Given that one should err in clinical practice on the side of over- rather than underidentification, it would seem prudent to employ a cutoff criterion somewhat below that of the 97th percentile, or 2 standard deviations; that of 1.5 standard deviations (the 93rd percentile) would seem to serve this purpose adequately and has been suggested by others as a useful demarcation of clinical significance (Achenbach & Edelbrock, 1983).

Prevalence Determined by Rating Scales

A rather common approach to establishing the prevalence of ADHD has been to employ a parent or teacher rating scale of the symptoms of the disorder and then to survey large populations of children. For instance, using samples in the United States, Pelham, Nagy, Greenslade, and Milich (1992) found a prevalence of 7.1% among 931 boys (Pittsburgh area) between grades K–8 using teacher ratings of DSM-III-R symptoms. Similarly, Wolraich, Hannah, Pinnock, Baumgaertel, and Brown (1996) reported a prevalence of 7.3% of 8,258 children (Tennessee area) between grades K–5 also using teacher ratings of DSM-III-R symptoms. Gadow and Sprafkin (1997), using samples of children from New York, Missouri, and Wisconsin for a total of 1,441 children, reported a prevalence of 7.7% for the Inattentive Type, 2% for the Hyperactive–Impulsive Type, and 2.9% for the Combined Type using DSM-IV items and recommended symptom thresholds. These results are all quite similar to the much smaller community survey using DSM-III-R symptoms conducted by DuPaul (1991) in Worcester, Massachusetts. Wolraich et al. (1996) also used teacher ratings of the DSM-IV symptom list in their Tennessee study and found a prevalence of 6% when the Predominantly Inattentive Type was excluded; a figure not too different from the 4.9% found by Gadow and Sprafkin (1997) and the 7% found by Pelham et al. (1992) and Wolraich et al. (1996). The rate for the Inattentive Type was 5.4% which is only slightly lower than that found by Gadow and Sprafkin (1997).

In Canada, Szatmari et al. (1989) reported the results of a survey of the entire province of Ontario, Canada, in which they found the prevalence of ADHD to be 9% in boys and 3.3% in girls. These rates varied somewhat by age for boys, with a prevalence of slightly more than 10% in the 4- to 11-year age group dropping to 7.3% in the 12- to 16-year age group. The prevalence for girls, however, did not vary significantly across these age groupings (3.3 vs.

3.4%, respectively). The study is difficult to compare with those in the United States because DSM symptom lists for ADHD were not used.

A study in a different country (Germany) finds an even higher rate of prevalence. Using teacher ratings of DSM-III-R symptoms with 1,077 German schoolchildren, Baumgaertel, Wolraich, and Dietrich (1995) found a prevalence of 10.9%, which rose to 17.8% if DSM-IV symptoms and cutoff scores were employed and all three subtypes were considered. However, more than half of this prevalence figure (9%) was the result of including children who were in the Predominantly Inattentive subtype of ADHD, a group not typically considered in earlier studies of prevalence using rating scales. Excluding this group left a prevalence of 8.7%.

In Japan, Kanbayashi, Nakata, Fujii, Kita, and Wada (1994) employed parent ratings of DSM-III-R symptoms of ADHD with 1,022 children ages 4–12 and found a prevalence of 7.7%. The findings of this study are very close to those for the United States discussed previously when DSM III-R symptoms are employed. Overall, then, a prevalence of approximately 7–17% of children between 4 and 16 years of age are likely to have ADHD if only rating scales are used to establish prevalence. If the Predominantly Inattentive subtype of ADHD is considered separately, the rates of ADHD for the two remaining types are roughly 4–10%. The prevalence of this Inattentive subtype of ADHD appears to be between 5% and 9% when rating scales of inattentive symptoms are employed.

Prevalence Using Clinical Diagnostic Criteria

As noted earlier, the diagnostic criteria for a mental disorder should and do consist of more than simply establishing a level of statistical deviance on a rating scale. DSM also requires an early onset of symptoms (before age 7), pervasiveness across settings, the exclusion of several other disorders, and, most important, impairment in one or more major domains of life functioning. A number of studies now exist that employed complete DSM diagnostic criteria through interviews with parents, children, and/or teachers instead of merely teacher or parent ratings. Table 2.2 shows the results for 15 such studies.

As this table indicates, the prevalence of ADHD ranges from 2% to 9.5% of children when DSM-III criteria are utilized. The exception to this is the extraordinarily high rate of disorder (29%) found in the oldest age group (11- to 12-year-olds) in the study of Indian children by Bhatia, Nigam, Bohra, and Malik (1991). The average prevalence across these studies using DSM-III is 4.9% if the results of the Bhatia et al. (1991) study are excluded as being a statistical outlier.

When DSM-III-R criteria are utilized, the prevalence ranges from 1.4% to 13.3% with an average of 5.9% based on adult reports. One of the highest prevalence rates (12.2%) occurs among the study by Jensen et al. (1995) employing children of military personnel, suggesting that this group of children may be at increased risk for ADHD. Likewise, the study by Velez, Johnson, and Cohen (1989) of children in upstate New York also found a higher-than-average prevalence of 13.3%. It is not possible to determine from the published studies why these rates are so far above those found in the remaining studies using DSM-III-R criteria, which ranged from 1.4% to 8.9%.

As Table 2.2 suggests, the use of an impairment criterion as a necessity in the diagnosis of the disorder reduces the prevalence of the disorder to some extent. The prevalence is also affected by age, with adolescent samples being more likely to have a lower prevalence rate than younger ones. And it appears that DSM-III-R results in the identification of somewhat more children as having ADHD than does DSM-III, whether rating scales (Baumgaertel et al., 1995) or interviews using DSM diagnostic criteria are applied (Leung et al., 1996). Al-

TABLE 2.2. Summary of Prevalence Studies of ADHD Employing DSM/ICD Criteria and Diagnostic Interviews

Study and country	Sample	Age (years)	Criteria[a]	Prevalence	Comments
Kashani, Orvaschel, Ronsenberg, & Reid (1989), United States	4,810	8, 12, and 17	DSM-III	3.3%	7.2% at age 8; 2.9% at age 12; 0.0% at age 17
Costello et al. (1988), United States	785	7–11	DSM-III	2.2%	Criteria employed were more severe than DSM requires
McGee et al (1990), New Zealand	943	15	DSM-III	2.0%	1% girls; 3% boys; male:female ratio of 2.5:1
Anderson, Williams, McGee, & Silva (1987), New Zealand	792	11	DSM-III	6.7%	Male:female ratio of 5.1:1
Bird et al. (1988), Puerto Rico	777	4–17	DSM-III	9.5%	With impairment
Esser, Schmidt, & Woerner (1990), Germany	216	8	ICD-9	4.2%	All diagnosed subjects were boys
Bhatia et al. (1991), India	1,000	3–12	DSM-III	5.2–29%	Ages 3–4 to ages 11–12
Leung et al. (1996), China	3,069	School age	DSM-III DSM-III-R	6.1% 8.9%	
Velez et al. (1989), United States	776	9–18	DSM-III-R	13.3%	Average prevalence across ages 12–18
Lewinsohn, Hops, Roberts, Seeley, & Andrews (1993), United States	1,710	High school	DSM-III-R	3.1%	1.8% girls; 4.5% boys
Siminoff et al. (1997), United States	2,762 twins	8–16	DSM-III-R	2.4% 1.4%	Without impairment With impairment
August, Realmuto, Macdonald, Nugent, & Crosby (1996), United States	7,231	Grades 1–4	DSM-III-R	2.8%	
Jensen et al. (1995), U.S. military	294	6–17	DSM-III-R	11.9% 12.2% 2.4%	With impairment Without impairment Requiring services
Fergusson, Horwood, & Lynskey (1993), New Zealand	986	15	DSM-III-R	3.0% 2.8%	Parent report Self-report
Verhulst, van der Ende, Ferdinand, & Vasios (1996), The Netherlands	780	13–18	DSM-III-R	1.8% 1.3%	Parent report Self-report

[a]DSM-III, *Diagnostic and Statistical Manual of Mental Disorders* (3rd ed.); DSM-III-R, *Diagnostic and Statistical Manual of Mental Disorders* (3rd ed., rev.); ICD-9, *International Classification of Diseases* (9th ed.).

though this might suggest that the DSM-III criteria are preferable so as not to diagnose too many children with a mental disorder, it should be recalled from Chapter 1 that DSM-III criteria were not based on any field trial or empirical information. In contrast, DSM-III-R was so evaluated, making the DSM-III-R criteria somewhat more rigorously developed and empirically defensible and hence preferable over the criteria of DSM-III. Based on the research of Baumgaertel et al. (1995) in Germany and Wolraich et al. (1996) in Tennessee using ratings of DSM-III, DSM-III-R, and DSM-IV criteria, the DSM-IV criteria result in the identification of an even larger percentage of children as ADHD than do previous DSMs. This is due largely to DSM-IV's inclusion of the new subtype of Predominantly Inattentive ADHD which was not included in DSM-III-R and was poorly and unempirically defined in DSM-III.

There is no doubt that ADHD is a worldwide phenomenon, found in every country in which it has been studied. Comparing rates of disorder across countries, it appears that India has the highest prevalence of ADHD among its 11- to 12-year-old children, reporting a rate of 29%. India is followed in order by the rate of disorder of 13.3% among children in up-state New York (Velez et al., 1989), then the rate of 11.9–12.2% among children of military personnel, and then by the prevalence among Puerto Rican children (9.5%). Excluding the two outlier studies of U.S. mainland samples by Velez et al. (1989) and Jensen et al. (1995), the prevalence of disorder ranges from 1.8% to 3.3% in the United States. Rates in New Zealand range from 2% to 6.7% whereas the lowest prevalence for disorder is among adolescents in The Netherlands (1.8%).

Prevalence of Adult ADHD

Three studies could be located that attempted to determine the prevalence of ADHD in an adult sample. Murphy and Barkley (1996a) surveyed a sample of 720 adults renewing their driver's licenses in the region of central Massachusetts using a rating scale of DSM-IV symptoms (both current and childhood symptoms). They found a prevalence of 4.7% for all subtypes of ADHD. The prevalence of ADHD was 0.9% Combined Type, 2.5% Hyperactive–Impulsive Type, and 1.3% for the Predominantly Inattentive subtype. In a sample of 700 college students from three geographically diverse cites around the United States, DuPaul, Weyandt, Schaughency, and Ota (1997) found almost precisely these same prevalence rates using DSM-IV symptom lists and diagnostic thresholds: 0.6% for Combined Type, 2.6% for Hyperactive–Impulsive Type, and 1.3% for the Inattentive Type. Similarly, Heiligenstein, Conyers, Beurns, and Smith (1997) collected self-reports of DSM-IV symptoms from 468 college students in Madison, Wisconsin. They reported a 4% prevalence for all subtypes, just slightly lower than the 4.5% found by DuPaul, Weyandt, et al. (1997) and the 4.7% found by Murphy and Barkley (1996b) for adults, ages 17–83. The prevalence for each subtype in the Heiligenstein et al. study was 0.9% for the Combined Type, 0.9% for the Hyperactive–Impulsive Type, and 2.2% for the Inattentive Type. Although neither of these two studies of college students required that subjects meet symptom thresholds for childhood symptoms (assessed by recall of the subjects) as did Murphy and Barkley (1996b), the estimates of both overall and subtype prevalence across these studies are strikingly similar.

Factors Affecting Prevalence

Szatmari (1992; Szatmari et al., 1989) found that the prevalence of ADHD in a large sample of children from Ontario, Canada, also varied as a function of young age, male gender, chronic health problems, family dysfunction, low socioeconomic status, presence of a developmental impairment, and urban living. Others found similar conditions associated with the risk for ADHD (Velez et al., 1989). Important, however, was the additional finding in the Szatmari et al. (1989) study that when comorbidity with other disorders was statistically controlled in the analyses, gender, family dysfunction, and low socioeconomic status were no longer significantly associated with occurrence of the disorder. Health problems, developmental impairment, young age, and urban living remained significantly associated with the occurrence of the disorder.

As noted previously in discussing the DSM criteria, it may be that the declining prevalence of ADHD with age is partly or wholly artifactual. This result could possibly come from the use of items in the diagnostic symptom lists which are chiefly applicable to young children. These items may reflect the underlying construct(s) of ADHD very well at younger ages but may be increasingly less applicable to ever older age groups. This could create a situation where individuals remain impaired in the construct(s) comprising ADHD as they mature while outgrowing the symptom list for the disorder, resulting in an illusory decline in prevalence as was noted in the earlier example using mental retardation. Until more age-appropriate symptoms are studied for adolescent and adult populations, this issue remains unresolved.

Few studies examined the relation of ADHD to social class, and those that did are not especially consistent. Lambert et al. (1978) found only slight differences in the prevalence of hyperactivity across social class when parent, teacher, and physician all agreed on the diagnosis. However, social class differences in prevalence did arise when only two of these three sources had to agree, with there generally being more ADHD children in lower than higher social classes. For instance, when parent and teacher agreement (but not physician) was required, 18% of children identified as hyperactive were in the high social class, 36% in the middle, and 45% in the low social class. When only the teacher's opinion was used, the percentages were 17, 41, and 41, respectively. Likewise, Trites (1979) also found the prevalence of hyperactivity, as defined by a threshold on a teacher rating scale, to vary as a function of neighborhood and social class. As noted earlier, Szatmari (1992) found in his review that rates of ADHD tended to increase with lower socioeconomic status. However, his own study (Szatmari et al., 1989) found that psychosocial variables, such as low socioeconomic status (SES), were no longer associated with rates of ADHD when other comorbid conditions, such as conduct disorder, were controlled. For now, it is clear that ADHD occurs across all socioeconomic levels. When differences in prevalence rates are found across levels of social class, they may be artifacts of the source used to define the disorder or of the comorbidity of ADHD with other disorders known to be related to social class, such as aggression and conduct disorder. Certainly, no one has made the argument that the nature or qualitative aspects of ADHD differ across social classes.

The Problem of Agreement among Caregivers

Social critics often make much of the fact that the prevalence of ADHD appears to differ significantly as a function of how many people must agree on the diagnosis (Kohn, 1989). The study by Lambert et al. (1978) on this issue is the one most often cited in which parents, teachers, and physicians of 5,000 children in elementary school were asked to identify the children they considered to be hyperactive. Approximately 5% of these children were defined as hyperactive when the opinion of only one of these caregivers (parent, teacher, physician) was required—a prevalence figure close to that found by both Szatmari et al. (1989) in their Canadian survey and DuPaul (1991) in the United States. However, this prevalence figure dropped to about 1% when agreement among all three was required. This finding should hardly be surprising considering that no effort was made to provide these "social definers" with any criteria for making their judgments or any training in the actual symptoms believed to constitute this disorder. Research routinely finds agreements between people to be low to modest when judging the behavior of another unless more specific and operational definitions of the behavior being judged and training in the application of the definitions are provided.

It is well established, for instance, that parent and teacher ratings of many different types of child behavioral problems are likely to have interrater agreement coefficients of less than .50 (Achenbach et al., 1987). Even fathers and mothers may have agreements of little more than .60 to .70. Certainly, the fact that children behave differently in different situations and with different adults can be a major factor contributing to this lack of agreement. The often subjective judgments required in determining whether a child's behavior occurs "often" or is "deviant" can be another. Undoubtedly, the fleeting or ephemeral nature of behavior and the constant stream of new behaviors or actions of children can create further confusion as to which of these actions should be considered in the judgment. Finally, the use of adult opinions to determine the diagnosis of hyperactivity will always be somewhat confounded by the characteristics and mental status of the adult informant in addition to the child's actual behavior. As discussed in more detail in Chapter 8 (this volume) on behavior rating scales, psychological distress, depression, family discord, and social biases can affect the judgments adults make about children and can therefore add to the lack of agreement among adults about the presence and degree of a child's ADHD. Hence, the lack of agreement across caregivers and the variations in the prevalence of ADHD which may arise as a result of it are hardly indictments of the concept of ADHD as a disorder but apply to many other types of human behavior and virtually all mental disorders.

Gender Differences in Prevalence

The prevalence of ADHD is also known to vary significantly as a function of gender of the children being studied. The proportion of males versus females manifesting the disorder varies considerably across studies, from 2:1 to 10:1 (Ross & Ross, 1982) with an average of 6:1 most often cited for clinic-referred samples of children. However, epidemiological studies, as shown in Table 2.2, find the proportion ranging from 2.5:1 to 5.1:1 with an average of approximately 3.4:1 among nonreferred children (Szatmari et al., 1989; Trites et al., 1979). The considerably higher rate of males among clinic samples of children compared to community surveys seems to be due to referral bias in that males are more likely than females to be aggressive and antisocial and such behavior is more likely to get a child referred to a psychiatric center. Hence, more males than females with ADHD will get referred to such centers. In support of this explanation are the findings that aggression occurs far more frequently in clinic-referred ADHD children than in those identified through epidemiological sampling (community surveys), that hyperactive girls identified in community surveys are often less aggressive than hyperactive boys (see the section "Gender Differences in the Nature of ADHD," later), but that girls who are seen in psychiatric clinics are likely to be as aggressive as boys with ADHD (Befera & Barkley, 1984; Breen & Barkley, 1988). Even so, males remain more likely to manifest ADHD than girls even in community-based samples, suggesting that there may be some gender-linked mechanism involved in the expression of the disorder.

Has ADHD Increased in Incidence?

A related issue is whether the incidence of ADHD has increased within the past few decades. The question is difficult to address as no community surveys of ADHD were repeated in the same populations or geographic areas over sufficiently long periods to evaluate for such trends. Some writers (Block, 1977; Ross & Ross, 1982) believe that it may be as a result of increasing cultural tempo or the rate of stimulation and change in a culture. Such speculations based on "tempo," however, are quite difficult to prove scientifically. Others intimate that the more sophisticated and successful life-saving efforts of the medical profession as seen in neonatal intensive care units may be increasing the incidence of ADHD by saving babies that would otherwise have died or been more severely developmentally handicapped. Such logic suggests that a higher-than-normal incidence of ADHD should be seen in long-term survivors of such intensive care units, and this does appear to be the case. However, this research can be faulted for failing to account for the higher-than-normal association of low SES with babies in these medical units such that it may be the variable of lower SES and not the presence of perinatal complications that accounts for the higher incidence of ADHD. Finally, the actual occurrence of ADHD may not be increasing although its detection may well be, which may partly stem from a greater awareness on the part of the public about the nature of the disorder. It could also be due to the trend toward earlier enrollment in preschool for many children such that their difficulties with attention, overactivity, and impulsivity will be noticed earlier as well.

GENDER DIFFERENCES IN THE NATURE OF ADHD

As already noted, boys are three times more likely to have ADHD than girls and six to nine times more likely than girls to be seen with ADHD among clinic-referred children. Given these differences in prevalence, one might wonder if there are differences in the expression of the disorder or its related features between boys and girls. One study (Brown, Abramowitz, Dadan-Swain, Eckstrand, & Dulcan, 1989) evaluated a sample of clinic-referred children diagnosed as having ADHD. They found that girls ($N = 18$) were more socially withdrawn and had more internalizing symptoms (anxiety, depression) than did boys ($N = 38$). Other studies based on school-identified hyperactive children tended to find that hyperactive girls are rated as having fewer behavioral and conduct problems, such as aggressiveness, than hyperactive boys but usually are not different on any laboratory measures of their symptoms (deHaas, 1986; deHaas & Young, 1984; Nolan, Gadow, Sprafkin, & Volpe, 1997; Pascaulvaca, Wolf, Healey, Tweedy, & Halperin, 1988). In contrast, two early studies using children referred to pediatric learning and developmental disability clinics suggested that hyperactive girls had lower verbal IQ scores, were more likely to have language disabilities, had a greater prevalence of problems with mood and enuresis, and had a lower prevalence of conduct problems (Berry, Shaywitz, & Shaywitz, 1985). These studies may be biased toward finding greater cognitive and developmental problems in their samples because of the source of referrals (learning-disorder clinics). Subsequent studies that used referrals to psychology or psychiatry clinics found virtually no differences between ADHD boys and girls on measures of intelligence, academic achievement, peer relations, emotional problems, or behavioral disorders (Breen, 1989; Horn, Wagner, & Ialongo, 1989; McGee, Williams, & Silva, 1987; Sharp et al., 1997). The exception to this were the data reported by Taylor (1986, pp. 141–143) that girls referred to a child psychiatry service at Maudsley Hospital in London had a greater degree of intellectual deficits than boys but were otherwise equivalent in the onset and severity of their hyperactive symptoms. Sharp et al. (1997) also found girls with ADHD to be more impaired in reading ability.

Recently, Gaub and Carlson (1997) conducted a meta-analysis of past research on gender differences in samples of ADHD children. They concluded that there were no gender differences in levels of impulsiveness, academic performance, social functioning, fine motor control, or family factors such as parental education level or parental depression. Girls were found to be more impaired in their intelligence, less hyperactive, and less likely to demonstrate other externalizing symptoms (i.e., aggression, defiance, and conduct problems). These gender differences appeared to be related to whether the samples under investigation were derived from clinical or community-based samples. Within clinical samples, there were likely to be few gender differences apparent, but in community-derived samples, girls were likely to be less aggressive and to show less internalizing symptoms than males.

Problematic in this review is the fact that many of the studies it incorporated used very small samples of girls. In a more recent study of gender differences in children with ADHD that employed the largest sample of girls to date, Biederman (1997) and colleagues (Faraone, 1997; Millberger, 1997) compared 130 girls with ADHD ages 6–17 with 120 normal control girls. In terms of their risk for comorbid psychiatric disorders, the ADHD girls showed comparably elevated rates of major depression (17%), anxiety disorder (32%), and bipolar disorder (10%) as were found in past studies of boys by these same investigators. The only findings that differed from their earlier studies of boys were the rates of ODD and Conduct Disorder, which were found to be about half the level as that found in boys with ADHD. Approximately 33% of the ADHD girls had ODD and 10% had Conduct Disorder. Although these ADHD girls had somewhat lower intelligence, reading, and math scores than the control girls, they still fell within the normal range on these measures and were comparable in this respect to boys with ADHD studied by this same research team. The same findings held true for the types of services these girls required, such as tutoring for school, special education, counseling, and medication treatment, all of which were elevated above the control girls but were in the same range of frequency as that seen for ADHD boys. The levels of psychiatric disorders among the relatives and specifically the siblings of the ADHD girls were likewise similar to those seen in ADHD boys (Mick, 1997). Interestingly, the risks of comorbid disorders to siblings were entirely mediated by whether or not the sibling also had ADHD. Thus, it would seem that the most reliable difference between girls and boys with ADHD is the lowered risk of girls for ODD and Conduct Disorder relative to boys.

Slight differences have been found in mothers' treatment of their ADHD boys compared to mothers' treatment of ADHD girls such that boys receive greater praise and direction from their mothers but boys were less compliant than girls with their mothers' commands (Barkley, 1989b; Befera & Barkley, 1984). No gender differences were noted in the effects of stimulant medication on these interactions (Barkley, 1989b) or in the clinical response of girls to stimulants more generally (Pelham, Walker, Sturgis, & Hoza, 1989; Sharp et al., 1997).

SUMMARY

This chapter described in detail the primary symptoms of ADHD and concluded that it is behavioral disinhibition that is the *sine qua non* of this disorder, excluding, of course, the recently developed subtype of Predominantly Inattentive ADHD, which is discussed further in Chapter 3. Such disinhibition creates difficulties with maintaining attention to tasks, especially in settings in which other activities offer competing immediate consequences of a higher magnitude than those inherent in the task assigned to the children. The diagnostic criteria set forth in DSM-IV for ADHD were reviewed and their merits discussed. Nevertheless, a number of areas were discussed for possible improvement in these criteria.

This chapter also discussed the manner in which the ADHD symptoms may be affected by situational variations and possible contributors to this variation. A review of epidemiological studies suggests that the prevalence of the disorder is approximately 5% and that it occurs in boys approximately three times as often as in girls. Despite this gender difference in prevalence, clinical studies suggest that girls and boys referred to clinics are quite similar in their presenting symptoms. However, epidemiological studies imply that in community samples, girls are considerably less likely to manifest aggressive behavior or conduct problems. Evidence suggests that ADHD clearly qualifies as a mental disorder under the conditions specified by Wakefield (1997) in that it comprises a dysfunction in a cognitive ability that leads to a harmful dysfunction for the individual. This chapter briefly reviewed the evidence for a syndrome of ADHD and concluded that although such evidence is not always consistent, it is sufficiently compelling and clinically useful to view the disorder as a syndrome.

REFERENCES

Abikoff, H., Gittelman-Klein, R., & Klein, D. (1977). Validation of a classroom observation code for hyperactive children. *Journal of Consulting and Clinical Psychology, 45*, 772–783.

Achenbach, T. M. (1991). *Child Behavior Checklist and Child Behavior Profile—Cross-Informant Version.* Burlington, VT: Author.

Achenbach, T. M., & Edelbrock, C. S. (1981). Behavioral problems and competencies reported by parents of normal and disturbed children aged four through sixteen. *Monographs of the Society for Research in Child Development, 46*(1), 1–82.

Achenbach, T. M., & Edelbrock, C. S. (1983). *Manual for the Child Behavior Profile and Child Behavior Checklist.* Burlington, VT: Author.

Achenbach, T. M., Edelbrock, C. S. (1987). Empirically based assessment of the behavioral/emotional problems of 2- and 3-year-old children. *Journal of Abnormal Child Psychology, 15*, 629–650.

Achenbach, T. M., McConaughy, S. H., & Howell, C. T. (1987). Child/adolescent behavioral and emotional problems: Implications of cross informant correlations for situational specificity. *Psychological Bulletin, 101*, 213–232.

American Psychiatric Association. (1968). *Diagnostic and statistical manual of mental disorders* (2nd ed.). Washington, DC: Author.

American Psychiatric Association. (1980). *Diagnostic and statistical manual of mental disorders* (3rd ed.). Washington, DC: Author.

American Psychiatric Association. (1987). *Diagnostic and statistical manual of mental disorders* (3rd ed., rev.). Washington, DC: Author.

American Psychiatric Association. (1994). *Diagnostic and statistical manual of mental disorders* (4th ed.). Washington, DC: Author.

Anderson, J. C., Williams, S., McGee, R., & Silva, P. A. (1987). DSM-III disorders in preadolescent children: Prevalence in a large sample from the general population. *Archives of General Psychiatry, 44*, 69–76.

Applegate, B., Lahey, B. B., Hart, E. L., Waldman, I., Biederman, J., Hynd, G. W., Barkley, R. A., Ollendick, T., Frick, P. J., Greenhill, L., McBurnett, K., Newcorn, J., Kerdyk, L., Garfinkel, B., & Shaffer, D. (1997) . Validity of the age of onset criterion for ADHD: A report from the DSM-IV field trials. *Journal of the American Academy of Child and Adolescent Psychiatry, 36*, 1211–1221.

Arnold, L. E. (1997). Sex differences in ADHD: Conference summary. *Journal of Abnormal Child Psychology, 24*, 555–569.

August, G. J., Realmuto, G. M., MacDonald, A. W., Nugent, S. M., & Crosby, R. (1996). Prevalence of ADHD and comorbid disorders among elementary school children screened for disruptive behavior. *Journal of Abnormal Child Psychology, 24*, 571–595.

August, G. J., & Stewart, M. A. (1983). Family subtypes of childhood hyperactivity. *Journal of Nervous and Mental Disease, 171*, 362–368.

Barkley, R. (1977). The effects of methylphenidate on various measures of activity level and attention in hyperkinetic children. *Journal of Abnormal Child Psychology, 5*, 351–369.

Barkley, R. A. (1981a). *Hyperactive children: A handbook for diagnosis and treatment.* New York: Guilford Press.

Barkley, R. A. (1981b). Hyperactivity. In E. J. Mash & L. G. Terdal (Eds.), *Behavioral assessment of childhood disorders* (pp. 127–184). New York: Guilford Press.

Barkley, R. A. (1982). Guidelines for defining hyperactivity in children (attention-deficit disorder with hyperactivity). In B. Lahey & A. Kazdin (Eds.), *Advances in clinical child psychology* (Vol. 5, pp. 137–180). New York: Plenum.

Barkley, R. A. (1985). The social interactions of hyperactive children: Developmental changes, drug effects, and situational variation. In R. McMahon & R. Peters (Eds.), *Childhood disorders: Behavioral–developmental approaches* (pp. 218–243). New York: Brunner/Mazel.

Barkley, R. A. (1988). Attention. In M. Tramontana & S. Hooper (Eds.), *Assessment issues in child neuropsychology* (pp. 145–176). New York: Plenum.

Barkley, R. A. (1989a). The problem of stimulus control and rule-governed behavior in children with attention deficit disorder with hyperactivity. In J. Swanson & L. Bloomingdale (Eds.), *Attention deficit disorders* (pp. 203–234). New York: Pergamon Press.

Barkley, R. A. (1989b). Hyperactive girls and boys: Stimulant drug effects on mother–child interactions. *Journal of Child Psychology and Psychiatry, 30,* 379–390.

Barkley, R. A. (1990). *Attention-deficit hyperactivity disorder: A handbook for diagnosis and treatment.* New York: Guilford Press.

Barkley, R. A. (1991). The ecological validity of laboratory and analogue assessments of ADHD symptoms. *Journal of Abnormal Child Psychology, 19,* 149–178.

Barkley, R. A. (1994). Impaired delayed responding: A unified theory of attention deficit hyperactivity disorder. In D. K. Routh (Ed.), *Disruptive Behavior Disorders: Essays in honor of Herbert Quay* (pp. 11–57). New York: Plenum.

Barkley, R. A. (1997a). *ADHD and the nature of self-control.* New York: Guilford Press.

Barkley, R. A. (1997b). ADHD, self-regulation, and time: Towards a more comprehensive theory of ADHD. *Journal of Developmental and Behavioral Pediatrics, 18,* 271–279.

Barkley, R. A. (1997c). Age dependent decline in ADHD: True recovery or statistical illusion? *ADHD Report, 5*(1), 1–5.

Barkley, R. A. (1997d). Behavioral inhibition, sustained attention, and executive functions: Constructing a unifying theory of ADHD. *Psychological Bulletin, 121,* 65–94.

Barkley, R. A., & Biederman, J. (1997). Towards a broader definition of the age of onset criterion for attention deficit hyperactivity disorder. *Journal of the American Academy of Child and Adolescent Psychiatry, 36,* 1204–1210.

Barkley, R. A., Copeland, A., & Sivage, C. (1980). A self-control classroom for hyperactive children. *Journal of Autism and Developmental Disorders, 10,* 75–89.

Barkley, R. A., & Cunningham, C. E. (1979). The effects of methylphenidate on the mother–child interactions of hyperactive children. *Archives of General Psychiatry, 36,* 201–208.

Barkley, R. A., Cunningham, C., & Karlsson, J. (1983). The speech of hyperactive children and their mothers: Comparisons with normal children and stimulant drug effects. *Journal of Learning Disabilities, 16,* 105–110.

Barkley, R. A., DuPaul, G. J., & McMurray, M. B. (1990). A comprehensive evaluation of attention deficit disorder with and without hyperactivity. *Journal of Consulting and Clinical Psychology, 58,* 775–789.

Barkley, R. A., DuPaul, G. J., & McMurray, M. B. (1991). Attention deficit disorder with and without hyperactivity: Clinical response to three doses of methylphenidate. *Pediatrics, 87,* 519–531.

Barkley, R. A., Fischer, M., Edelbrock, C. S., & Smallish, L. (1990). The adolescent outcome of hyperactive children diagnosed by research criteria: I. An 8 year prospective follow-up study. *Journal of the American Academy of Child and Adolescent Psychiatry, 29,* 546–557.

Barkley, R. A., Grodzinsky, G., & DuPaul, G. (1992). Frontal lobe functions in attention deficit disorder with and without hyperactivity: A review and research report. *Journal of Abnormal Child Psychology, 20,* 163–188.

Barkley, R. A., Koplowitz, S., Anderson, T., & McMurray, M. B. (1997). Sense of time in children with ADHD: Effects of duration, distraction, and stimulant medication. *Journal of the International Neuropsychological Society, 3,* 359–369.

Barkley, R. A., Murphy, K. R., & Kwasnik, D. (1996a). Psychological adjustment and adaptive impairments in young adults with ADHD. *Journal of Attention Disorders, 1,* 41–54.

Barkley, R. A., Murphy, K. R., & Kwasnik, D. (1996b). Motor vehicle driving competencies and risks in teens and young adults with ADHD. *Pediatrics, 98,* 1089–1095.

Barkley, R. A., & Ullman, D. G. (1975). A comparison of objective measures of activity level and distractibility in hyperactive and nonhyperactive children. *Journal of Abnormal Child Psychology, 3,* 213–244.

Baumgaertel, A., Wolraich, M. L., & Dietrich, M. (1995). Comparison of diagnostic criteria for attention deficit disorders in a German elementary school sample. *Journal of the American Academy
   of Child and Adolescent Psychiatry, 34,* 629–638.

Befera, M., & Barkley, R. A. (1984). Hyperactive and normal girls and boys: Mother–child interactions,
   parent psychiatric status, and child psychopathology. *Journal of Child Psychology and Psychiatry, 26,* 439–452.

Beitchman, J. H., Wekerle, C., & Hood, J. (1987). Diagnostic continuity from preschool to middle
   childhood. *Journal of the American Academy of Child and Adolescent Psychiatry, 26,* 694–699.

Berk, L. E., & Potts, M. K. (1991). Development and functional significance of private speech among
   attention-deficit hyperactivity disorder and normal boys. *Journal of Abnormal Child Psychology,
   19,* 357–377.

Berry, C. A., Shaywitz, S. E., & Shawitz, B. A. (1985). Girls with attention deficit disorder: A silent
   majority? A report on behavioral and cognitive characteristics. *Pediatrics, 76,* 801–809.

Bhatia, M. S., Nigam, V. R., Bohra, N., & Malik, S. C. (1991). Attention deficit disorder with hyperactivity among paedritic outpatients. *Journal of Child Psychology and Psychiatry, 32,* 297–306.

Biederman, J. (1997, October). *Comorbidity in girls with with ADHD.* Paper presented at the American Academy of Child and Adolescent Psychiatry, Toronto, Canada.

Biederman, J., Keenan, K., & Faraone, S. V. (1990). Parent-based diagnosis of attention deficit disorder predicts a diagnosis based on teacher report. *American Journal of Child and Adolescent Psychiatry, 29,* 698–701.

Bird, H. R., Canino, G., Rubio-Stipec, M., et al. (1988). Estimates of the prevalence of childhood maladjustment in a community survey in Puerto Rico. *Archives of General Psychiatry, 45,* 1120–1126.

Block, G. H. (1977). Hyperactivity: a cultural perspective. *Journal of Learning Disabilities, 110,* 236–240.

Breen, M. J. (1989). ADHD girls and boys: An analysis of attentional, emotional, cognitive, and family variables. *Journal of Child Psychology and Psychiatry, 30,* 711–716.

Breen, M. J., & Barkley, R.A. (1988). Parenting stress with ADDH girls and boys. *Journal of Pediatric
   Psychology, 13,* 265–280.

Brown, R. T. Abramowitz, A. J., Madan-Swain, A., Eckstrand, D., & Dulcan, M. (1989, October).
   ADHD gender differences in a clinic-referred sample. Paper presented at the annual meeting of the
   American Academy of Child and Adolescent Psychiatry, New York.

Brown, R. T., & Quay, H. C. (1977). Reflection–impulsivity of normal and behavior-disordered children. *Journal of Abnormal Child Psychology, 5,* 457–462.

Cammann, R., & Miehlke, A. (1989). Differentiation of motor activity of normally active and hyperactive boys in schools: Some preliminary results. *Journal of Child Psychology and Psychiatry, 30,*
   899–906.

Campbell, S. B. (1987). Parent-referred problem three-year-olds: Developmental changes in symptoms. *Journal of Child Psychology and Psychiatry, 28,* 835–846.

Campbell, S. B. (1990). *Behavior problems in preschool children.* New York: Guilford Press.

Campbell, S. B., Douglas, V. I., & Morganstern, G. (1971). Cognitive styles in hyperactive children and
   the effect of methylphenidate. *Journal of Child Psychology and Psychiatry, 12,* 55–67.

Chen, W. J., Faraone, S. V., Biederman, J., & Tsuang, M. T. (1994). Diagnostic accuracy of the Child
   Behavior Checklist Scales for attention-deficit hyperactivity disorder: A receiver-operating characteristic analysis. *Journal of Consulting and Clinical Psychology, 62,* 1017–1025.

Cohen, N. J., & Minde, K. (1983). The "hyperactive syndrome" in kindergarten children: Comparison of children with pervasive and situational symptoms. *Journal of Child Psychology and Psychiatry, 24,* 443–455.

Cohen, N. J., Weiss, G., & Minde, K. (1972). Cognitive styles in adolescents previously diagnosed as
   hyperactive. *Journal of Child Psychology and Psychiatry, 13,* 203–209.

Copeland, A. P. (1979). Types of private speech produced by hyperactive and nonhyperactive boys.
   Journal of Abnormal Child Psychology, 7, 169–177.

Corkum, P. V., & Siegel, L. S. (1993). Is the continuous performance task a valuable research tool for
   use with children with attention-deficit-hyperactivity disorder? *Journal of Child Psychology and
   Psychiatry, 34,* 1217–1239.

Costello, E. J., Costello, A. J., & Edelbrock, C. S. (1988). Psychiatric disorders in pediatric primary care.
   Archives of General Psychiatry, 45, 1107–1116.

Costello, E. J., Loeber, R., & Stouthamer-Loeber, M. (1991). Pervasive and situational hyperactivity—Confounding effect of informant: A research note. *Journal of Child Psychology and Psychiatry, 32,* 367–376.

Cromwell, R. L., Baumeister, A., & Hawkins, W. F. (1963). Research in activity level. In N. R. Ellis (Ed.), *Handbook of mental deficiency.* New York: McGraw-Hill.

deHaas, P. A. (1986). Attention styles and peer relationships of hyperactive and normal boys and girls. *Journal of Abnormal Child Psychology, 14,* 457–467.

deHaas, P. A., & Young, R. D. (1984). Attention styles of hyperactive and normal girls. *Journal of Abnormal Child Psychology, 12,* 531–546.

Demb, H. B. (1991). Use of Ritalin in the treatment of children with mental retardation. In L. Greenhill & B. Osmon (Eds.), *Ritalin: Theory and patient management* (pp. 155–170. New York: Mary Ann Liebert.

Douglas, V. I. (1980). Higher mental processes in hyperactive children: Implications for training. In R. Knights & D. Bakker (Eds.), *Treatment of hyperactive and learning disordered children* (pp. 65–92). Baltimore: University Park Press.

Douglas, V. I. (1983). Attention and cognitive problems. In M. Rutter (Ed.), *Developmental neuropsychiatry* (pp. 280–329). New York: Guilford Press.

Douglas, V. I., & Parry, P. A. (1983). Effects of reward on delayed reaction time task performance of hyperactive children. *Journal of Abnormal Child Psychology, 11,* 313–326.

Draeger, S., Prior, M., & Sanson, A. (1986). Visual and auditory attention performance in hyperactive children: competence or compliance. *Journal of Abnormal Child Psychology, 14,* 411–424.

DuPaul, G. R. (1991). Parent and teacher ratings of ADHD symptoms: Psychometric properties in a community-based sample. *Journal of Clinical Child Psychology, 20,* 242–253.

DuPaul, G. J., Anastopoulos, A. D., Power, T. J., Reid, R., Ikeda, M. J., & McGoey, K. E. (1997). *Parent ratings of attention-deficit/hyperactivity disorder symptoms: Factor structure, normative data, and psychometric properties.* Manuscript submitted for publication.

DuPaul, G. J., Power, T. J., Anastopoulos, A. D., Reid, R., McGoey, K. E., & Ikeda, M. J. (1997). Teacher ratings of attention-deficit/hyperactivity disorder symptoms: Factor structure, normative data, and psychometric properties. *Psychological Assessment, 9,* 436–444.

DuPaul, G. J., Weyandt, L., Schaughency, L., & Ota, K. (1997). *Self-report of ADHD symptoms in U.S. college students: Factor structure and symptom prevalence.* Manuscript submitted for publication.

Edelbrock, C. S., & Costello, A. (1984). Structured psychiatric interviews for children and adolescents. In G. Goldstein & M. Hersen (Eds.), *Handbook of psychological assessment* (pp. 276–290). New York: Pergamon Press.

Epstein, J. N., Conners, C. K., Sitarenios, G., & Erhardt, D. (1997). *Use of the continuous performance test for use with adults with attention deficit/hyperactivity disorder (ADHD).* Manuscript submitted for publication.

Esser, G., Schmidt, M. H., & Woerner, W. (1990). Epidemiology and course of psychiatric disorders in school-age children—Results of a longitudinal study. *Journal of Child Psychology and Psychiatry, 31,* 243–263.

Faraone, S. V. (1997, October). *Familial aggregation of ADHD in families of girls with ADHD.* Paper presented at the American Academy of Child and Adolescent Psychiatry, Toronto, Canada.

Fergusson, D. M., Horwood, L. J., & Lynskey, M. T. (1993). Prevalence and comorbidity of DSM-III-R diagnoses in a birth cohort of 15 year olds. *Journal of the American Academy of Child and Adolescent Psychiatry, 32,* 1127–1134.

Fergusson, D. M., Lynskey, M. T., & Horwood, L. J. (1997). Attentional difficulties in middle childhood and psychosocial outcomes in young adulthood. *Journal of Child Psychology and Psychiatry, 38,* 633–644.

Firestone, P., & Martin, J. E. (1979). An analysis of the hyperactive syndrome: A comparison of hyperactive, behavior problem, asthmatic, and normal children. *Journal of Abnormal Child Psychology, 7,* 261–273.

Fischer, M., Barkley, R. A., Edelbrock, K., & Smallish, L. (1990). The adolescent outcome of hyperactive children diagnosed by research criteria: II. Academic, attentional, and neuropsychological status. *Journal of Consulting and Clinical Psychology, 58,* 580–588.

Fischer, M., Barkley, R. A., Edelbrock, C. S., & Smallish, L. (1993). The stability of dimensions of behavior in ADHD and normal children over an 8-year follow-up. *Journal of Abnormal Child Psychology, 21*, 315–337.

Fischer, M., Barkley, R. A., Fletcher, K., & Smallish, L. (1993). The adolescent outcome of hyperactive children diagnosed by research criteria: V. Predictors of outcome. *Journal of the American Academy of Child and Adolescent Psychiatry, 32*, 324–332.

Gadow, K. D., & Sprafkin, J. (1997). *Child symptom inventory 4: Norms manual.* Stony Brook, NY: Checkmate Plus.

Gaub, M., & Carlson, C. L. (1997). Gender differences in ADHD: A meta-analysis and critical review. *Journal of the American Academy of Child and Adolescent Psychiatry, 36*, 1036–1045.

Glow, P. H., & Glow, R. A. (1979). Hyperkinetic impulse disorder: A developmental defect of motivation. *Genetic Psychology Monographs, 100*, 159–231.

Goldstein, S., & Goldstein, M. (1990). *Managing attention disorders in children.* New York: Wiley.

Goodman, J. R., & Stevenson, J. (1989). A twin study of hyperactivity: II. The aetiological role of genes, family relationships, and perinatal adversity. *Journal of Child Psychology and Psychiatry, 30*, 691–709.

Gordon, M. (1979). The assessment of impulsivity and mediating behaviors in hyperctive and nonhyperactive children. *Journal of Abnormal Child Psychology, 7*, 317–326.

Gordon, M. (1983). *The Gordon Diagnostic System.* DeWitt, NY: Gordon Systems.

Goyette, C. H., Conners, C. K., & Ulrich, R. F. (1978). Normative data on revised Conners parent and Teacher Rating Scales. *Journal of Abnormal Child Psychology, 6*, 221–236.

Grodzinsky, G. M., & Diamond, R. (1992). Frontal lobe functioning in boys with attention-deficit hyperactivity disorder. *Developmental Neuropsychology, 8*, 427–445.

Haenlein, M., & Caul, W. F. (1987). Attention deficit disorder with hyperactivity: A specific hypothesis of reward dysfunction. *Journal of the American Academy of Child and Adolescent Psychiatry, 26*, 356–362.

Hale, G. A., & Lewis, M. (1979). *Attention and cognitive development.* New York: Plenum.

Halperin, J. M., Matier, K., Bedi, G., Sharma, V., & Newcorn, J. H. (1992). Specificity of inattention, impulsivity, and hyperactivity to the diagnosis of attention-deficit hyperactivity disorder. *Journal of the American Academy of Child and Adolescent Psychiatry, 31*, 190–196.

Hart, E. L., Lahey, B. B., Loeber, R., Applegate, B., & Frick, P. J. (1995). Developmental changes in attention-deficit hyperactivity disorder in boys: A four-year longitudinal study. *Journal of Abnormal Child Psychology, 23*, 729–750.

Heiligenstein, E., Conyers, L. M., Berns, A. R., & Smith, M. A. (1997). *Preliminary normative data on DSM-IV attention deficit hyperactivity disorder in college students.* Manuscript submitted for publication.

Hill, J. C., & Schoener, E. P. (1996). Age-dependent decline of attention deficit hyperactivity disorder. *American Journal of Psychiatry, 153*, 1143–1146.

Hinshaw, S. P. (1987). On the distinction between attentional deficits/hyperactivity and conduct problems/aggression in child psychopathology. *Psychological Bulletin, 101*, 443–447.

Hinshaw, S. P. (1994). *Attention deficits and hyperactivity in children.* Thousand Oaks, CA: Sage.

Holdnack, J. A., Moberg, P. J., Arnold, S. E., Gur, R. C., & Gur, R. E. (1995). Speed of processing and verbal learning deficits in adults diagnosed with attention deficit disorder. *Neuropsychiatry, Neuropsychology, and Behavioral Neurology, 8*, 282–292.

Horn, W. F., Wagner, A. E., & Ialongo, N. (1989). Sex differences in school-aged children with pervasive attention deficit hyperactivity disorder. *Journal of Abnormal Child Psychology, 17*, 109–125.

Jacob, R. G., O'Leary, K. D., & Rosenblad, C. (1978). Formal and informal classroom settings: Effects on hyperactivity. *Journal of Abnormal Child Psychology, 6*, 47–59.

Jensen, P. S., Watanabe, H. K., Richters, J. E., Cortes, R., Roper, M., & Liu, S. (1995). Prevalence of mental disorder in military children and adolescents: Findings from a two-stage community survey. *Journal of the American Academy of Child and Adolescent Psychiatry, 34*, 1514–1524.

Kagan, J. (1966). Reflection–impulsivity: The generality and dynamics of conceptual tempo. *Journal of Abnormal Psychology, 71*, 17–24.

Kanbayashi, Y., Nakata, Y., Fujii, K., Kita, M., & Wada, K. (1994). ADHD-related behavior among non-referred children: Parents' ratings of DSM-III-R symptoms. *Child Psychiatry and Human Development, 25*, 13–29.

Kashani, J. H., Orvaschel, H., Ronsenberg, T. K., & Reid, J. C. (1989). Psychopathology in a community sample of children and adolescents: A developmental perspective. *Journal of the American Academy of Child and Adolescent Psychiatry, 28,* 701–706.

Kendall, P. C., & Wilcox, L. E. (1979). Self-control in children: Development of a rating scale. *Journal of Consulting and Clinical Psychology, 47,* 1020–1029.

Kindlon, D., Mezzacappa, E., & Earls, F. (1995). Psychometric properties of impulsivity measures: Temporal stability, validity and factor structure. *Journal of Child Psychology and Psychiatry, 36,* 645–661.

Kohn, A. (1989). Suffer the restless children. *Atlantic Monthly,* pp. 90–100.

Lahey, B. B., Applegate, B., McBurnett, K., Biederman, J., Greenhill, L., Hynd, G. W., Barkley R. A., Newcorn, J., Jensen, P., Richters, J., Garfinkel, B., Kerdyk, L., Frick, P. J., Ollendick, T., Perez, D., Hart, E. L., Waldman, I., & Shaffer, D. (1994). DSM-IV field trials for attention deficit/hyperactivity disorder in children and adolescents. *Journal of the American Academy of Child and Adolescent Psychiatry, 151,* 1673–1685.

Lambert, N. M., Sandoval, J., & Sassone, D. (1978). Prevalence of hyperactivity in elementary school children as a function of social system definers. *American Journal of Orthopsychiatry, 48,* 446–463.

Landau, S., Lorch, E. P., & Milich, R. (1992). Visual attention to and comprehension of television in attention deficit hyperactivity disordered and normal boys. *Child Development, 63,* 928–937.

Lapouse, R., & Monk, M. (1958). An epidemiological study of behavior characteristics in children. *American Journal of Public Health, 48,* 1134–1144.

Lerner, J. A., Inui, T. S., Trupin, E. W., & Douglas, E. (1985). Preschool behavior can predict future psychiatric disorders. *Journal of the American Academy of Child Psychiatry, 24,* 42–48.

Leung, P. W. L., Luk, S. L., Ho, T. P., Taylor, E., Mak, F. L., & Bacon-Shone, J. (1996). The diagnosis and prevalence of hyperactivity in Chinese schoolboys. *British Journal of Psychiatry, 168,* 486–496.

Levy, F., Hay, D. A., McStephen, M., Wood, C., & Waldman, I. (1997). Attention-deficit hyperactivity disorder: A category or a continuum? Genetic analysis of a large-scale twin study. *Journal of the American Academy of Child and Adolescent Psychiatry, 36,* 737–744.

Lewinsohn, P. M., Hops, H., Roberts, R. E., Seeley, J. R., & Andrews, J. A. (1993). Adolescent psychopathology: I. Prevalence and incidence of depression and other DSM-III-R disorders in high school students. *Journal of Abnormal Psychology, 102,* 133–144.

Loeber, R., Green, S. M., Lahey, B. B., Christ, M. A. G., & Frick, P. J. (1992). Developmental sequences in the age of onset of disruptive child behaviors. *Journal of Child and Family Studies, 1,* 21–41.

Losier, B. J., McGrath, P. J., & Klein, R. M. (1996). Error patterns on the continuous performance test in non-medication and medicated samples of children with and without ADHD: A meta-analysis. *Journal of Child Psychology and Psychiatry, 37,* 971–987.

Luk, S. (1985). Direct observations studies of hyperactive behaviors. *Journal of the American Academy of Child and Adolescent Psychiatry, 24,* 338–344.

McGee, R., Feehan, M., Williams, S., Partridge, F., Silva, P. A., & Kelly, J. (1990). DSM-III disorders in a large sample of adolescents. *Journal of the American Academy of Child and Adolescent Psychiatry, 29,* 611–619.

McGee, R., Williams, S., & Feehan, M. (1992). Attention deficit disorder and age of onset of problem behaviors. *Journal of Abnormal Child Psychology, 20,* 487–502.

McGee, R., Williams, S., & Silva, P. A. (1984a). Behavioral and developmental characteristics of aggressive, hyperactive, and aggressive–hyperactive boys. *Journal of the American Academy of Child Psychiatry, 23,* 270–279.

McGee, R., Williams, S., & Silva, P. A. (1984b). Background characteristics of aggressive, hyperactive, and aggressive–hyperactive boys. *Journal of the American Academy of Child and Adolescent Psychiatry, 23,* 280–284.

McGee, R., Williams, S., & Silva, P. A. (1987). A comparison of girls and boys with teacher-identified problems of attention. *Journal of the American Academy of Child and Adolescent Psychiatry, 26,* 711–717.

McGinnis, J. (1997, September). Attention deficit disaster. *Wall Street Journal.*

Mick, E. J. (1997, October). *Psychiatric and social functioning in siblings of girls with ADHD.* Paper presented at the annual meeting of the American Academy of Child and Adolescent Psychiatry, Toronto.

Milberger, S. (1997, October). *Impact of adversity on functioning and comorbidity of girls with ADHD.* Paper presented at the American Academy of Child and Adolescent Psychiatry, Toronto, Canada.

Milich, R., & Kramer, J. (1985). Reflections on impulsivity: An empirical investigation of impulsivity as a construct. In K. Gadow & I. Bialer (Eds.), *Advances in learning and behavioral disabilities* (Vol. 3, pp. 57–94). Greenwich, CT: JAI Press.

Milich, R., Landau, S., Kilby, G., & Whitten, P. (1982). Preschool peer perceptions of the behavior of hyperactive and aggressive children. *Journal of Abnormal Child Psychology, 10,* 497–510.

Mirsky, A. F. (1996). Disorders of attention: A neuropsychological perspective. In R. G. Lyon & N. A. Krasnegor (Eds.), *Attention, memory, and executive function* (pp. 71–96). Baltimore: Paul H. Brookes.

Murphy, K., & Barkley, R. A. (1996a). Attention deficit hyperactivity disorder in adults. *Comprehensive Psychiatry, 37,* 393–401.

Murphy, K., & Barkley, R. A. (1996b). Prevalence of DSM-IV symptoms of ADHD in adult licensed drivers: Implications for clinical diagnosis. *Journal of Attention Disorders, 1,* 147–161.

Palfrey, J. S., Levine, M. D., Walker, D. K., & Sullivan, M. (1985). The emergence of attention deficits in early childhood: A prospective study. *Developmental and Behavioral Pediatrics, 6,* 339–348.

Pascaulvaca, D. M., Wolf, L. E., Healey, J. M., Tweedy, J. R., & Halperin, J. M. (1988, January). *Sex differences in attention and behavior in school-aged children.* Paper presented at the 16th annual meeting of the International Neuropsychological Society, New Orleans.

Pearson, D. A., & Aman, M. G. (1994). Ratings of hyperactivity and developmental indices: Should clinicians correct for developmental level? *Journal of Autism and Developmental Disorders, 24,* 395–411.

Pelham, W. E., Gnagy, E. M., Greenslade, K. E., & Milich, R. (1992). Teacher ratings of DSM-III-R symptoms for the disruptive behavior disorders. *Journal of the American Academy of Child and Adolescent Psychiatry, 31,* 210–218.

Pelham, W., Walker, J. L., Sturgis, J., & Hoza, J. (1989). Comparative effects of methylphenidate on ADD girls and ADD boys. *Journal of the American Academy of Child and Adolescent Psychiatry, 28,* 773–776.

Pennington, B. F., & Ozonoff, S. (1996). Executive functions and developmental psychopathology. *Journal of Child Psychology and Psychiatry, 37,* 51–87.

Porrino, L. J., Rapoport, J. L., Behar, D., Sceery, W., Ismond, D. R., & Bunney, W. E., Jr. (1983). A naturalistic assessment of the motor activity of hyperactive boys. *Archives of General Psychiatry, 40,* 681–687.

Prior, M., Wallace, M., & Milton, I. (1984). Schedule-induced behavior in hyperactive children. *Journal of Abnormal Child Psychology, 12,* 227–244.

Quay, H. C. (1988). The behavioral reward and inhibition systems in childhood behavior disorder. In L. M. Bloomingdale (Ed.), *Attention deficit disorder: III. New research in treatment, psychopharmacology, and attention* (pp. 176–186). New York: Pergamon Press.

Quay, H. C. (1997). Inhibition and attention deficit hyperactivity disorder. *Journal of Abnormal Child Psychology, 25,* 7–14.

Rapoport, J. L., Donnelly, M., Zametkin, A., & Carrougher, J. (1986). Situational hyperactivity" in a U.S. clinical setting. *Journal of Child Psychology and Psychiatry, 27,* 639–646.

Rapport, M. D., Tucker, S. B., DuPaul, G. J., Merlo, M., & Stoner, G. (1986). Hyperactivity and frustration: The influence of control over and size of rewards in delaying gratification. *Journal of Abnormal Child Psychology, 14,* 181–204.

Reeves, J. C., Werry, J., Elkind, G. S., & Zametkin, A. (1987). Attention deficit, conduct, oppositional, and anxiety disorders in children: II. Clinical characteristics. *Journal of the American Academy of Child and Adolescent Psychiatry, 26,* 133–143.

Rosenthal, R. H., & Allen, T. W. (1980). Intratask distractibility in hyperkinetic and nonhyperkinetic children. *Journal of Abnormal Child Psychology, 8,* 175–187.

Ross, D. M., & Ross, S. A. (1982). *Hyperactivity: Research, theory and action.* New York: Wiley.

Routh, D. K. (1978). Hyperactivity. In P. Magrab (Eds.), *Psychological management of pediatric problems* (pp. 3–48). Baltimore: University Park Press.

Routh, D. K., & Roberts, R. D. (1972). Minimal brain dysfunction in children: Failure to find evidence for a behavioral syndrome. *Psychological Reports, 31,* 307–314.

Routh, D. K., & Schroeder, C. S. (1976). Standardized playroom measures as indices of hyperactivity. *Journal of Abnormal Child Psychology, 4,* 199–207.

Rutter, M. (1977). Brain damage syndromes in childhood: Concepts and findings. *Journal of Child Psychology and Psychiatry, 18,* 1–21.

Rutter, M. (1989). Attention deficit disorder/hyperkinetic syndrome: Conceptual and research issues regarding diagnosis and classification. In T. Sagvolden & T. Archer (Eds.), *Attention deficit disorder: Clinical and basic research* (pp. 1–24). Hillsdale, NJ: Erlbaum.

Rutter, M., Bolten, P., Harrington, R., LeCouteur, A., Macdonald, H., & Simonoff, E. (1990). Genetic factors in child psychiatric disorders—I. A review of research strategies. *Journal of Child Psychology and Psychiatry, 31,* 3–37.

Rutter, M., Macdonald, H., LeCouteur, A., Harrington, R., Bolton, P., & Bailey, P. (1990). Genetic factors in child psychiatric disorders—II. Empirical findings. *Journal of Child Psychology and Psychiatry, 31,* 39–83.

Sandberg, S. T., Rutter, M., & Taylor, E. (1978). Hyperkinetic disorder in psychiatric clinic attenders. *Developmental Medicine and Child Neurology, 20,* 279–299.

Schachar, R., Rutter, M., & Smith, A. (1981). The characteristics of situationally and pervasively hyperactive children: Implications for syndrome definition. *Journal of Child Psychology and Psychiatry, 22,* 375–392.

Schrag, P., & Divoky, D. (1975). *The myth of the hyperactive child.* New York: Pantheon.

Seidman, L. J., Biederman, J., Faraone, S. V., Weber, W., & Ouellette, C. (1997). Toward defining a neuropsychology of attention deficit–hyperactivity disorder: Performance of children and adolescence from a large clinically referred sample. *Journal of Consulting and Clinical Psychology, 65,* 150–160.

Sergeant, J. (1988). From DSM-III attentional deficit disorder to functional defects. In L. Bloomingdale & J. Sergeant (Eds.), *Attention deficit disorder: Criteria, cognition, and intervention* (pp. 183–198). New York: Pergamon.

Shaffer, D., & Greenhill, L. (1979). A critical note on the predictive validity of "the hyperkinetic syndrome." *Journal of Child Psychology and Psychiatry, 20,* 61–72.

Shaffer, D., McNamara, N., & Pincus, J. H. (1974). Controlled observations on patterns of activity, attention, and impulsivity in brain-damaged and psychiatrically disturbed boys. *Psychological Medicine, 4,* 4–18.

Sharp, W. S., Walter, J. M., Hamburger, S. D., Marsh, W. L., Rapoport, J. L., & Castellanos, F. X. (1997, October). *Comparison between girls and boys with ADHD: A controlled study.* Paper presented at the annual meeting of the American Acdemy of Child and Adolescent Psychiatry, Toronto, Canada.

Shelton, T. L., Barkley, R. A., Crosswait, C., Moorehouse, M., Fletcher, K., Barrett, S., Jenkins, L., & Metevia, L. (1997). *Early psychiatric and psychological morbidity in preschool children with high levels of aggressive and hyperactive-impulsive behavior.* Manuscript submitted for publication.

Sherman, D. K., McGeue, M. K., & Iacono, W. G. (1997). Twin concordance for attention deficit hyperactivity disorder: A comparison of teachers' and mothers' reports. *American Journal of Psychiatry, 154,* 532–535.

Siminoff, E., Pickles, A., Meyer, J. M., Silberg, J. L., Maes, H. H., Loeber, R., Rutter, M., Hewitt, J. K., & Eaves, L. J. (1997). The Virginia Twin Study of adolescent behavioral development. *Archives of General Psychiatry, 54,* 801–808.

Spitzer, R. L., Davies, M., & Barkley, R. A. (1990). The DSM-III-R field trial for the Disruptive Behavior Disorders. *Journal of the American Academy of Child and Adolescent Psychiatry, 29,* 690–697.

Steinkamp, M. W. (1980). Relationships between environmental distractions and task performance of hyperactive and normal children. *Journal of Learning Disabilities, 13,* 40–45.

Stewart, M. A., Pitts, F. N., Craig, A. G., & Dieruf, W. (1966). The hyperactive child syndrome. *American Journal of Orthopsychiatry, 36,* 861–867.

Still, G. F. (1902). Some abnormal psychical conditions in children. *Lancet, 1,* 1008–1012, 1077–1082, 1163–1168.

Szatmari, P. (1992). The epidemiology of attention-deficit hyperactivity disorders. In G. Weiss (Ed.), *Child and Adolescent Psychiatry Clinics of North America: Attention deficit disorder* (pp. 361–372). Philadelphia: Saunders.

Szatmari, P., Offord, D. R., & Boyle, M. H. (1989). Correlates, associated impairments, and patterns of service utilization of children with attention deficit disorders: Findings from the Ontario Child Health Study. *Journal of Child Psychology and Psychiatry, 30*, 205–217.

Tallmadge, J., & Barkley, R. A. (1983). The interactions of hyperactive and normal boys with their mothers and fathers. *Journal of Abnormal Child Psychology, 11*, 565–579.

Tannock, R. (1997). Television, video games, and ADHD: Challenging a popular belief. *ADHD Report, 5*(3), 3–7.

Taylor, E. (1986). *The overactive child.* Philadelphia: Lippincott.

Taylor, E., Sandberg, S., Thorley, G., & Giles, S. (1991). *The epidemiology of childhood hyperactivity.* London: Oxford University Press.

Teicher, M. H., Ito, Y, Glod, C. A., & Barber, N. I. (1996). Objective measurement of hyperactivity and attentional problems in ADHD. *Journal of the American Academy of Child and Adolescent Psychiatry, 35*, 334–342.

Tripp, G., & Luk, S. L. (1997). The identification of pervasive hyperactivity: Is clinic observation necessary? *Journal of Child Psychology and Psychiatry, 38*, 219–234.

Trites, R. L. (1979). *Hyperactivity in children: Etiology, measurement, and treatment implications.* Baltimore: University Park Press.

Trites, R. L., Dugas, F., Lynch, G., & Ferguson, B. (1979). Incidence of hyperactivity. *Journal of Pediatric Psychology, 4*, 179–188.

Ullman, D. G., Barkley, R. A., & Brown, H. W. (1978). The behavioral symptoms of hyperkinetic children who successfully responded to stimulant drug treatment. *American Journal of Orthopsychiatry, 48*, 425–437.

Velez, C. N., Johnson, J., & Cohen, P. (1989). A longitudinal analysis of selected risk factors for childhood psychopathology. *Journal of the American Academy of Child and Adolescent Psychiatry, 28*, 861–864.

Verhulst, F. C., van der Ende, J., Ferdinand, R. F., & Kasius, M. C. (1997). The prevalence of DSM-III-R diagnoses in a national sample of Dutch adolescents. *Archives of General Psychiatry, 54*, 329–336.

Wakefield, J. C. (1992). The concept of mental disorder: On the boundary between biological facts and social values. *American Psychologist, 47*, 373–388.

Wakefield, J. C. (1997). Normal inability versus pathological disability: Why Ossorio's definition of mental disorder is not sufficient. *Clinical Psychology: Science and Practice, 4*, 249–258.

Weiss, G., & Hechtman, L. (1979). The hyperactive child syndrome. *Science, 205*, 1348–1354.

Weiss, G., & Hechtman, L. (1993). *Hyperactive children grown up* (2nd ed.). New York: Guilford Press.

Werry, J. S. (1988). Differential diagnosis of attention deficits and conduct disorders. In. L. M. Bloomingdale & J. A. Sergeant (Eds.), *Attention deficit disorder: Criteria, cognition, intervention* (pp. 83–96). London: Pergamon.

Werry, J. S., Elkind, G. S., & Reeves, J. S. (1987). Attention deficit, conduct, oppositional, and anxiety disorders in children: III. Laboratory differences. *Journal of Abnormal Child Psychology, 15*, 409–428.

Werry, J. S., & Quay, H. C. (1971). The prevalence of behavior symptoms in younger elementary school children. *American Journal of Orthopsychiatry, 41*, 136–143.

Wolraich, M . L., Hannah, J. N., Pinnock, T. Y., Baumgaertel, A., & Brown, J. (1996). Comparison *of diagnostic criteria for attention-deficit hyperactivity disorder in a country-wide sample. Journal of the American Academy of Child and Adolescent Psychiatry, 35*, 319–324.

World Health Organization. (1994). *International classification of diseases* (10th ed.). Geneva, Switzerland: Author.

Zagar, R., & Bowers, N. D. (1983). The effect of time of day on problem-solving and classroom behavior. *Psychology in the Schools, 20*, 337–345.

Zentall, S. S. (1984). Context effects in the behavioral ratings of hyperactivity. *Journal of Abnormal Child Psychology, 12*, 345–352.

Zentall, S. S. (1985). A context for hyperactivity. In K. D. Gadow & I. Bialer (Eds.), *Advances in learning and behavioral disabilities* (Vol. 4, pp. 273–343). Greenwich, CT: JAI Press.

Zentall, S. S. (1988). Production deficiencies in elicited language but not in the spontaneous verbalizations of hyperactive children. *Journal of Abnormal Child Psychology, 16*, 657–673.

Zentall, S. S., Falkenberg, S. D., & Smith, L. B. (1985). Effects of color stimulation and information on the copying performance of attention-problem adolescents. *Journal of Abnormal Child Psychology, 13*, 501–511.

Chapter 3

ASSOCIATED PROBLEMS

Besides their primary problems with inattention, impulsivity, and overactivity, children with Attention-Deficit/Hyperactivity Disorder (ADHD) may have a variety of other difficulties. Such children have a higher likelihood of having other cognitive, developmental, behavioral, emotional, academic, and even medical difficulties. Not all ADHD children display all these problems, but many display them to a degree that is greater than expected in normal children. They are therefore considered associated features as they are not diagnostic of the disorder when present, nor do they rule out the diagnosis when absent. This chapter describes these frequently coexisting problems seen in ADHD children and adolescents. Chapter 4 reviews those comorbid psychiatric disorders often seen in clinic-referred children, while Chapter 6 describes those seen in adults with ADHD. Chapter 4 also presents some of the more promising subtyping approaches being proposed in an effort to reduce the heterogeneity of this disorder. Chapter 5 addresses the developmental course and adult outcome of ADHD.

INTELLECTUAL DEVELOPMENT

Children with ADHD are more likely to be behind in their intellectual development than either normal children or the siblings of the ADHD children manifesting an average of 7 to 15 points below the control groups on standardized intelligence tests (Faraone et al., 1993; Fischer, Barkley, Fletcher, & Smallish, 1990; McGee, Williams, Moffitt, & Anderson, 1989; Prior, Leonard, & Wood, 1983; Tarver-Behring, Barkley, & Karlsson, 1985; Werry, Elkind, & Reeves, 1987). It is not clear whether these differences in scores represent real differences in intelligence or just differences in test-taking behavior in that ADHD children perform more poorly due to their inattentive–impulsive response style. It is also possible that because these studies often used mixed groups of children having both ADHD and learning disability (LD), the lower intelligence scores in the ADHD groups could be related to the coexisting learning disorders and not to the ADHD per se, as some have suggested (Bohline, 1985). However, in a study of ADHD and LD children in our clinic, the LD children who were not ADHD actually had IQ estimates even lower than those found in the mixed ADHD/LD group whose IQ estimates were still lower than the normal control group (Barkley, DuPaul, &

McMurray, 1990). In any case, ADHD children are likely to represent the entire spectrum of intellectual development, with some being gifted while others are normal, slow learners, or even mildly intellectually retarded.

As discussed in Chapter 7, impairment in behavioral inhibition and the executive functions dependent on it as is seen in children with ADHD could be expected to result in a small but significant and negative relationship between ADHD and IQ, particularly verbal IQ. This is because the latter is likely to be related to working memory, internalized speech and the eventual development of verbal thought. Studies using both normal samples (Hinshaw, Morrison, Carte, & Cornsweet, 1987; McGee, Williams, & Silva, 1984) and behavioral problem samples (Sonuga-Barke, Lamparelli, Stevenson, Thompson, & Henry, 1994) found significant negative associations between degree of rated hyperactive–impulsive behavior and measures of intelligence. In contrast, associations between ratings of conduct problems and intelligence in children are often much smaller or even nonsignificant, particularly when hyperactive–impulsive behavior is partialed out of the relationship (Hinshaw et al., 1987; Lynam, Moffitt, & Stouthamer-Loeber, 1993; Sonuga-Barke et al., 1994), implying that the relationship between IQ and disruptive behavior in children is relatively specific to the hyperactive–impulsive element of the disruptive behavior disorders (see Hinshaw, 1992, for a review).

When samples of hyperactive or ADHD children are selected for study without specifically equating groups for IQ, such studies often find these children to differ significantly from control groups in their intelligence, particularly verbal intelligence (Barkley, Karlsson, & Pollard, 1985; Faraone et al., 1993; Mariani & Barkley, 1997; McGee, Williams, & Feehan, 1992; Moffitt, 1990; Stewart, Pitts, Craig, & Dieruf, 1966; Werry et al., 1987). Given that several of the subtests from intelligence tests (e.g., those on the Wechsler Intelligence Scale for Children, third edition) are partly assessing working memory (mental arithmetic, digit span, etc.), it should not be surprising in view of the theoretical model advanced in Chapter 7 that ADHD is associated with decreased performance on these particular subtests (Anastopoulos, Spisto, & Maher, 1994; Lufi, Cohen, & Parrish-Plass, 1990). Differences in IQ have also been found in hyperactive boys and their normal siblings (Halperin & Gittelman, 1982; Tarver-Behring et al., 1985; Welner, Welner, Stewart, Palkes, & Wish, 1977), suggesting that impulsive–hyperactive behavior generally, and ADHD specifically, has an inherent association with diminished IQ, particularly verbal IQ, (Halperin & Gittelman, 1982; Hinshaw, 1992; McGee et al., 1992; Sonuga-Barke et al., 1994; Werry et al., 1987). This small but significant relationship implies that between 3% and 10% of the variance in IQ may be a function of symptoms of ADHD (hyperactive–impulsive behavior). It also implies that when differences between ADHD and control groups in IQ are found in a study, they should probably not be statistically controlled out in the analyses as this may remove some of the variation in the measures under study that is due to ADHD itself.

ADAPTIVE FUNCTIONING

Adaptive functioning is frequently used to refer to the child's development of age-appropriate motor skills, self-help abilities (i.e., dressing, bathing, and feeding), personal responsibility and independence (chore performance, trustworthy, use of money, etiquette), and peer relationships. Since the last edition of this book, several studies have consistently documented diminished overall adaptive functioning in children with ADHD relative to normal or control groups of children (Barkley, Fischer, Edelbrock, & Smallish, 1990; Greene et al., 1996; Roizen, Blondis, Irwin, & Stein, 1994; Stein, Szumowski, Blondis, & Roizen, 1995). These studies find that children with ADHD often function in the low average to borderline range of adaptive functioning despite having generally normal intelligence. And although other psychiatric and developmental disorders often demonstrate low adaptive functioning, the discrepancy between adaptive functioning and IQ is often greater in children with ADHD than these other groups (Stein et al., 1995). This discrepancy suggests that, apart from lower levels of intelligence that may be associated with ADHD (see earlier), ADHD takes a specific toll on adaptive functioning. The greater this discrepancy between IQ and adaptive functioning, the greater the impairment the ADHD child is likely to experience and the more likely he or she is to experience comorbid psychiatric disorders (Greene et al., 1996). Moreover, the greater the degree of social or adaptive impairment, the greater is the risk at a 4-year follow-up that the ADHD children will have comorbid psychiatric disorders and substance use (Greene, Biederman, Faraone, Sienna, & Garcia-Jetton, 1997).

ACADEMIC PERFORMANCE

One area of tremendous difficulty for ADHD children is in their academic performance (work productivity in the classroom) and achievement (the level of difficulty of the material the child has mastered). Almost all clinic-referred ADHD children are doing poorly at school, typically underperforming relative to their known levels of ability as determined by intelligence and academic achievement tests. Such performance is believed to be the result of their inattentive, impulsive, and restless behavior in the classroom. Evidence supporting this interpretation comes from numerous studies of stimulant medication with ADHD children that demonstrate significant improvements in academic productivity and sometimes accuracy when the children are on their medication (Barkley, 1977; Pelham, Bender, Caddell, Booth, & Moorer, 1985; Rapport, DuPaul, Stoner, & Jones, 1986). Even so, ADHD children are also likely to show performances on standardized achievement tests that are considerably lower than their classmates' by as much as 10 to 30 standard score points on various achievement tests, including reading, spelling, math, and reading comprehension (Barkley, Dupaul, & McMurray, 1990; Brock & Knapp, 1996; Cantwell & Satterfield, 1978; Casey, Rourke, & Del Dotto, 1996; Dykman & Ackerman, 1992; Fischer et al., 1990; Semrud-Clikeman et al., 1992). This suggests that they are not simply underperforming in school relative to their ability but that they may have less academic ability than normal classmates. Consequently, it is not surprising to find that as many as 56% of ADHD children may require academic tutoring, approximately 30% may repeat a grade in school, and 30–40% may be placed in one or more special education programs. As many as 46% may be suspended from school and 10 to 35% may drop out entirely and fail to complete high school (Barkley, Fischer et al., 1990; Barkley, DuPaul & McMurray, 1990; Brown & Borden, 1986; Faraone et al., 1993; Munir, Biederman, & Knee, 1987; Stewart et al., 1966; Szatmari, Offord, & Boyle, 1989; Weiss & Hechtman, 1993).

LEARNING DISABILITIES

It is presumed that ADHD children are also more likely than normal children to have learning disabilities (Safer & Allen, 1976). An LD, however, is not simply failing to do one's work in school but is typically defined as a significant discrepancy between one's intelligence, or general mental abilities, and academic achievement, such as reading, math, spelling, handwriting, or language. Both intelligence and achievement must be assessed by well-standardized tests. The prevalence rates of LD can vary greatly as a function of how this "significant discrepancy" is defined.

Several different formulas can be applied to define an LD. For a review of the previous literature on LD in ADHD children using a variety of approaches, see the report by Semrud-Clikeman et al. (1992). One such formula used in past research with ADD children (Lambert & Sandoval, 1980) compared scores on intelligence tests with those on achievement tests for reading and math. An LD is defined as a significant discrepancy between these standard scores. Such a discrepancy can be based on an absolute amount, say 20 points, or on the standard deviation (*SD*) or error of the tests, say 15 points or one *SD*, where both tests have a mean of 100 and *SD* of 15. A problem with this IQ–achievement discrepancy approach is that it tends to overestimate the prevalence of learning disorders, especially in children performing normally in school and those who are intellectually above average or gifted. For instance, when Dykman and Ackerman (1992) defined a reading disorder as a discrepancy between IQ and achievement of only 10 points, as well as a standard score on the reading test below 90, they found that 45% were so disordered. Likewise, when Semrud-Clikeman et al. (1992) required only a 10-point discrepancy between IQ and achievement, 38% of their ADHD children could be considered reading disabled and 55% math disabled (the rates for normal children were 8% and 33%, respectively). Yet, such children may be performing perfectly adequately in school and on achievement tests but, because of higher than normal levels of intelligence, may have a significant discrepancy between their IQ and achievement test scores (i.e., IQ = 130 whereas Reading Standard Score = 100). In the previous edition of this text (Barkley, 1990), I reported on the prevalence of ADHD children who had an LD by this relatively simple criterion (15 point IQ–achievement discrepancy) using the results of one of my studies (Barkley, DuPaul, & McMurry, 1990). The rates were 40% in reading, nearly 60% in spelling, and nearly 60% in math. However, the rates in the normal control group were 20, 38, and 35%, respectively, being defined as LD. Clearly this is not a rigorous approach to defining LD.

Using a somewhat larger discrepancy (20 points), Frick et al. (1991) estimated that 16% of ADHD children had a reading disability whereas 21% had a math disability. The corresponding prevalence in their normal control group was 5% and 7%, respectively. Likewise, when Semrud-Clikeman et al. (1992) increased the required discrepancy to 20 points, 23% of the ADHD children could be considered reading disabled and 30% math disabled, versus 2% and 22% of normal children, respectively.

A second approach is to define LD as a score falling below 1.5 *SD*s from the normal mean on an achievement test (7th percentile), regardless of the child's IQ. This approach is far less likely to diagnose normal children as LD. But, it may diagnose borderline mildly retarded children as such because their achievement test scores would be consistent with their low IQ scores and place them below this LD cutoff point. Using this approach (Barkley, 1990), I found the following prevalence of LD in ADHD children: 21% in reading, 26% in spelling, and over 28% in math. For the normal children, these rates were 0%, 2.9%, and 2.9%, respectively. None of the children in this particular study were in the borderline range of IQ or lower (mental retardation), and thus the rate of misclassifying ADHD children with so low an IQ score cannot be determined from this study.

A more intricate approach to calculating a discrepancy formula involves first converting the standard scores on the IQ and achievement tests to *Z* scores and then estimating the expected achievement score with a regression equation that takes into consideration both the correlation between the IQ and achievement test and the standard error of estimate for the achievement test. To be LD, the child must have a discrepancy that exceeds a *Z* score of -1.65 (the $p < .05$ confidence level). Using this approach, Frick et al. (1991) reported a prevalence of 13% for reading disability and 14% for math disability (23% for either). Using this same approach, Faraone et al. (1993) found that 18% of their ADHD group had a reading disability and 21% had a math disability.

A different approach being used in research is to combine several of the previously discussed methods. In this case, LD is defined as both a score below some level on an achievement test, say 1 *SD* or even 1.5 *SD*s (7th percentile) on an achievement test *and* a significant discrepancy between IQ and achievement on that test, say 20 points or 1.5 *SD*s (15 points). Requiring that children be at the 7th percentile on their achievement test and have at least a 15-point discrepancy between their IQ and achievement test resulted in the following rates of LD in my sample of ADHD children: 19% in reading, nearly 24% in spelling, and over 26% in math (Barkley, 1990). The rates among the normal control group were 0%, 0%, and nearly 3%, respectively. Similarly, August and Garfinkel (1990) defined an LD as a 15-point IQ–achievement discrepancy and a standard score below 85 (1 *SD*) on a reading test and found that 39% of their ADHD children were reading disabled. Using the same formula, Semrud-Clikeman et al. (1992) found that 15% were reading disabled and 33% were math disabled (compared to none of the normal control group). Again, using this same formula, Casey et al. (1996) found that nearly 31% children with Attention-Deficit Disorder with Hyperactivity had a reading disorder, 27% had a spelling disorder, and nearly 13% had a math disorder. When Frick et al. (1991) required their children to have both a 20-point IQ–achievement discrepancy and to be below a standard score of 1 *SD* below the mean (84) on the achievement test, they found that 8% had a reading disability and 12% had a math disability (normal control group rates were 2 and 2%, respectively).

In conclusion, if the more rigorous approaches to defining LD are employed (i.e., Frick et al.'s regression equation or the combined approach discussed previously), then approximately 8–39% of ADHD children are likely to have a reading disability, 12–30% have a math disability, and approximately 12–27% may have a spelling disorder. It is worth noting here that Frick et al. (1991) found similar rates of learning disabilities in a sample of children with Conduct Disorder (CD), but this was entirely due to the presence of comorbid ADHD in those children. This finding underscores the point made earlier by Hinshaw (1987, 1992) that ADHD is more often associated with cognitive and achievement deficits rather than CD and thus the possible presence of ADHD needs to be evaluated in children diagnosed as CD as it is more likely to account for their cognitive deficits than is their diagnosis of CD.

An important clinical issue is whether the presence of early learning difficulties or disabilities can lead to the development of ADHD or vice versa. The available evidence on the issue is rather paltry. When initially reviewed by McGee and Share (1988), the conclusion, albeit very tentative, was that longitudinal research did not indicate that ADHD could lead to later learning disabilities but that early learning difficulties might be associated with a rise in ADHD symptoms over development, even though this was not consistently shown across the studies reviewed. In their longitudinal study of children, Fergusson and Horwood (1992) reached the opposite conclusion, finding that early attention problems increased the risk for later reading difficulties whereas reading difficulties did not increase the later risk for attentional problems. Thus the causal relationship of learning difficulties to ADHD and vice versa remains unsettled at the moment.

SPEECH AND LANGUAGE DEVELOPMENT

Although ADHD children do not appear to have a high rate of serious or generalized language delays, they are more likely to have more specific problems in their speech development than do normal children. Using community-based samples, many studies found them to be somewhat more likely to be delayed in the onset of talking in early childhood than were normal children (6 to 35% vs. 2 to 5.5%) (Hartsough & Lambert, 1985; Stewart et al., 1966; Szatmari et al., 1989) whereas other studies using clinic-referred children found no differences in the risk for delayed speech development (Barkley, DuPaul, & McMurray, 1990). However, whether speech onset is delayed or not, studies do show that ADHD children are more likely to have problems with expressive language but not in receptive language, with 10% to 54% having speech problems compared to 2% to 25% of normal children (Barkley, DuPaul, & McMurray, 1990; Hartsough & Lambert, 1985; Munir et al., 1987; Szatmari et al., 1989). However, other studies have not found this relationship (Humphries, Koltun, Malone, & Roberts, 1994) when evaluating children who have simply higher than normal levels of inattention. Nevertheless, such inattentive children did have more difficulties with the organization and conversational pragmatics of their speech than did learning disabled or normal children. Conversely, between 16% and 37% of children with speech and language disorders are likely to have ADHD (Baker & Cantwell, 1987).

As already noted, ADHD children are likely to talk more than normal children, especially during spontaneous conversation (Barkley, Cunningham, & Karlsson, 1983; Zentall, 1988). However, when confronted with tasks in which they must organize and generate speech in response to specific task demands, they are likely to talk less, to be more dysfluent (e.g., use pauses, fillers such as "uh," "er," and "um," and misarticulations), and be less proficient in their organization of speech (Hamlett, Pelligrini, & Conners, 1987; Purvis & Tannock, 1997; Zentall, 1985). Because confrontational speech tasks or explanatory speech is more difficult and requires more careful thought and organization than does spontaneous or descriptive speech, these speech difficulties of ADHD children suggest that their problems are not so much in speech and language per se but in the higher-order cognitive processes involved in organizing and monitoring thinking and behavior, known as executive processing.

Children with ADHD have been noted to perform more poorly on tests of simple verbal fluency (Carte, Nigg, & Hinshaw, 1996; Grodzinsky & Diamond, 1992; Reader, Harris, Schuerholz, & Denchla, 1994), although others have not documented such differences (Fischer et al., 1990; Loge, Staton, & Beatty, 1990; McGee et al., 1989; Weyandt & Willis, 1994). The discrepancy in findings may pertain, in part, to the type of fluency test used. Tests in which subjects generate words within semantic categories (Weyandt & Willis, 1994), such as names for animals or fruits, are easier and thus not as likely to discriminate ADHD and control children as those using more subtle organizing cues, such as letters (Grodzinsky & Diamond, 1992; Reader et al., 1994). Age may also be a factor given that older ADHD children may have far fewer difficulties on such tests than younger ADHD children (Grodzinsky & Diamond, 1992; Fischer et al., 1990). Low statistical power and the use of nonclinical samples (Loge et al., 1990; McGee et al., 1989), as discussed previously, could also contribute to failures to find differences between ADHD and control groups in these studies. It appears, then, that simple word fluency, particularly on tasks using letters as the generative rule, may be diminished in young children with ADHD, although the finding is not always evident in research. This deficit may dissipate with age, although it does not necessarily mean that a problem with reconstitution or behavioral diversity is dissipating (see Chapter 7).

Studies of more complex language fluency and discourse organization are much more likely to reveal problems in this domain in children with ADHD. As noted previously, ADHD children appear to produce less speech in response to confrontational questioning than do normal children (Tannock, 1996; Ludlow, Rapoport, Brown, & Mikkelson, 1979). They are also less competent in verbal problem-solving tasks (Douglas, 1983; Hamlett et al., 1987) and less capable of communicating task-essential information to peers in cooperative tasks (Whalen, Henker, Collins, McAuliffe, & Vaux, 1979). They also produce less information and less organized information in their story narratives (Tannock, 1996; Tannock, Purvis, & Schachar, 1992; Zentall, 1988) or in describing their own strategies used during task performance (Hamlett et al., 1987). When no goal or task is specified, the verbal discourse of ADHD children does not appear to differ from that of normal children (Barkley et al., 1983; Zentall, 1988).

The relationship of ADHD to the language processing problem known as central auditory processing disorder (CAPD) is uncertain as of this writing. Some imply that they may not be separate disorders at all given that teacher ratings of inattention in ADHD children were significantly related to several tests of auditory processing (Gascon, Johnson, & Burd, 1986). The problem here is largely though not entirely due to definition problems. CAPD has been generously defined as deficits in the processing of audible signals that cannot be ascribed to peripheral hearing sensitivity or intellectual impairment. The nub of the issue is that CAPD may involve distractibility and inattentiveness as well as difficulties with memory, reading, spelling, and written language. As Riccio, Hynd, Cohen, Hall, and Molt (1994) note, it is this inclusion of inattention, albeit in the auditory domain, in the conceptualization of CAPD that is so problematic. It creates an automatic overlap with ADHD symptoms, the inattention of which is thought to be generalized or transsensory rather than limited to a single modality. Children with ADHD often have difficulties with auditory vigilance or attention (Gascon et al., 1986; Keith & Engineer, 1991) and so may automatically qualify for a diagnosis of CAPD. Some (Moss & Sheiffe, 1994) have restricted the definition of CAPD to deficits in processing speech and language specifically, which would greatly assist with determining the degree of overlap with ADHD and would likely restrict it.

To study the overlap of these disorders, Riccio et al. (1994) studied children referred to a speech and language clinic and to a neuropsychology clinic who met diagnostic criteria for CAPD. These criteria included evidence of impairment on at least two of four auditory processing tasks involving both speech and nonspeech information. Of 30 children with CAPD, 50% met criteria for a diagnosis of ADHD using the third revised edition of the *Diagnostic and Statistical Manual of Mental Disorders* (DSM-III-R; American Psychiatric Association, 1987). The authors also utilized the older DSM-III criteria, which permitted subtyping of the subjects into those having ADD with and without hyperactivity. In this case, 33.3% of the subjects had ADHD, half of whom fell into each subtype. Although the prevalence of ADHD among children referred for and meeting diagnostic criteria for CAPD is higher than that expected of a normal population (i.e., 3–5%), it is similar to the rate of ADHD found among children referred to a speech and language clinic and diagnosed with such speech and language difficulties up to 37% of whom have ADHD using DSM-III criteria (Baker & Cantwell, 1987). To what extent this overlap of ADHD with CAPD represents a referral bias, then, is not clear given that ADHD tends to be overrepresented among clinic-referred children in general. What is clear from this study is that CAPD and ADHD are not identical disorders if rigorous criteria are used to determine the presence of CAPD apart from merely clinical complaints of auditory inattentiveness. It is interesting to note that among ADHD children with evidence of CAPD, their auditory processing deficits improve significantly with stimulant medication (Gascon et al., 1986; Keith & Engineer, 1991). This raises questions about whether additional intervention would be needed for this comorbid group beyond the customary medication treatment employed for their ADHD. Others, however, have not found such improvements in auditory processing with medication (Dalebout, Nelson, Hleto, & Frentheway, 1991)

DEFICIENT RULE-GOVERNED BEHAVIOR

Although it is not yet widely accepted, some investigators suggest that poor rule-governed behavior, or difficulties with adherence to rules and instructions, may also be a primary deficit or at least an associated condition of ADHD in children (American Psychiatric Association, 1987, 1994; Barkley, 1981, 1989, 1990; Kendall & Braswell, 1984). Care is taken here to exclude poor compliance that may stem from sensory handicaps (i.e., deafness), impaired language development, or defiance or Oppositional Defiant Disorder (ODD).

Rules are contingency-specifying stimuli; they specify a relationship among an event, a response, and the consequences likely to occur for that response. Language provides a substantial amount of such stimuli. Skinner (1953) hypothesized that this influence of language over behavior occurs in three stages: (1) the control of behavior by the language of others; (2) the progressive control of behavior by self-directed and eventually private speech, as discussed earlier; and (3) the creation of new rules by the individual, which came about through the use of self-directed questions (second-order rules). Rule-governed behavior appears to provide a means of sustaining behavior across large gaps in time among the units of a behavioral contingency (event–response–outcome). By formulating rules, the individual can construct novel, complex (hierarchically organized), and prolonged behavioral chains. These rules can then provide the template for reading off the appropriate sequences of behavioral chains, guiding behavior toward the attainment of a future goal (Cerutti, 1989; Hayes, 1989; Skinner, 1969). By this process, the individual's behavior is no longer under the total control of the immediate surrounding context. Behavior is now shifted to control by internally represented information (in this case, covert verbal behavior and the rules it generates).

Some Specific Characteristics of Rule-Governed Behavior

Hayes (1989) and Cerutti (1989) stipulated a number of specific effects on behavior which rule governance produces. These could be considered predictions about the deficits that might be expected in ADHD if they were deficient in rule governance. Behavior that is rule governed rather than contingency shaped is likely to have the following characteristics: (1) the variability of responses to a task is more reduced when rule-governed behavior is in effect than when behavior is contingency shaped (developed and maintained by the environmental contingencies alone); (2) behavior that is rule governed may be less affected or entirely unaffected by the immediate contingencies operating in a situation or by momentary and potentially spurious changes in those contingencies; (3) when rules and immediate contingencies compete in a given situation, the rule is more likely to gain control over behavior, and progressively more so as the individual matures; (4) rule-governed responding under some conditions may be rigid or inflexible even if the rule being followed is eventually shown to be incorrect; and (5) self-directed rules permit individuals to persist in responding under conditions of very low levels of immediate reinforcement or even the absence of reward as well as during extreme delays in the consequences for responding. Some of the additional characteristics of rule-governed behavior cited by Skinner (1969) might be added to the list): (6) rule-governed behavior is likely to be associated with less emotion or passion, given that the individual has not been exposed to the actual contingencies in the setting that would give rise to greater affect associated with responding; and (7) it is likely to appear more conscious, intentional, deliberate, and purposive rather than impulsive, reactive, and ill-considered.

In short, rules assist with bridging temporal gaps in behavioral contingencies and thus contribute to the cross-temporal organization of behavior. The motor execution of such verbal rules appears to be partially dependent on the capacity to retain the rules in working memory (to restate the rule) and to inhibit prepotent or irrelevant responses that compete with the rule (Zelazo, Reznick, & Pinon, 1995).

Stages of Rule-Governed Behavior

Hayes, Gifford, and Ruckstuhl (1996) described three levels of functions within a hierarchy of the development of rule-governed behavior which they hypothesize may reflect corresponding stages of moral development: pliance, tracking, and augmenting.

Pliance

This level represents responding to rules on the basis of being previously socially rewarded for doing so. It represents compliance to directions, instructions, commands, and other forms of rules on the basis of socially mediated reinforcement for rule following and is believed to represent the most rudimentary form of rule-governed behavior.

Tracking

At this level, rules are followed because of a history of agreement or correspondence between those rules and the actual contingencies to which they pertain. In other words, such behavior reflects the success of the rules in predicting the actual contingencies and the individual's prior history of being rewarded by the contingencies when following such rules. If one has been told to do something so that some outcome will happen and when they do so the predicted outcome occurs, the next time a similar rule is given it is likely to be followed: This is a form of tracking.

Augmenting

This form of rule-governed behavior is the result of rules that alter the capacity of particular events to function as consequences. Some augmentals are motivative; such rules increase or decrease the degree to which previously established consequences serve as rewards and punishments. Other augmentals are formative; they establish new consequences as being rewarding or punitive. Hayes et al. (1996) gives the example of "if 'being good' has developed reinforcing functions over a period of time, and 'sharing' is identified as being good, then 'sharing' may function as a formative augmental, as it has now acquired some of the functions of 'being good'" (p. 292). It is possible that the capacity to generate or create one's own rules and to adhere to them may represent a fourth level of the development of rule-governed behavior within this developmental hierarchy, as Skinner (1953) suggested.

Deficits in Rule-Governed Behavior in ADHD

Do ADHD children manifest a delay in rule-governed behavior or the ability to comply with or complete verbal instructions? ADHD children have been observed to be less compliant with directions and commands given by their mothers than are normal children (see Danforth, Barkley, & Stokes, 1991, for a review). The problem seems most acute, however, in that subgroup having ODD. In addition, ADHD children appear to be less able to restrict their behavior in accordance with experimenter instructions during lab playroom observations when rewarding activities are available; the latter findings are not always consistently observed, however (see Luk, 1985, for a review). And studies, discussed in Chapter 2 (this volume), have found ADHD children to be much less able to resist forbidden temptations than same-age normal peers. Such rule following seems to be particularly difficult for ADHD children when the rules compete with rewards available for committing rule violations (Hinshaw, Heller, & McHale, 1992; Hinshaw, Simmel, & Heller, 1995). These results might indicate problems with the manner in which rules and instructions control behavior in children with ADHD.

Further evidence consistent with a development delay in rule-governed behavior comes from studies showing that ADHD children are less adequate at problem solving (Douglas, 1983; Hamlett et al., 1987; Tant & Douglas, 1982), and are also less likely to use organizational rules and strategies in their performance of memory tasks (August, 1987; Butterbaugh et al., 1989; Douglas & Benezra, 1990; Voelker, Carter, Sprague, Gdowski, & Lachar, 1989). Problem solving and the discovery of strategies may be a direct function of rule-governed behavior and the self-questioning associated with it (Cerutti, 1989).

As noted previously, Hayes (1989) set forth a number of features that would characterize rule-governed behavior. The features could be considered predictions about the types of deficiencies that might be evident in children with ADHD if their behavior were less rule-governed. Some evidence does seem to exist for these predicted deficiencies in that ADHD children (1) demonstrate significantly greater variability in patterns of responding to laboratory tasks, such as those involving reaction time or continuous performance tests (see Corkum & Siegel, 1993; Douglas, 1983; Douglas & Peters, 1978, for reviews; van der Meere & Sergeant, 1988a, 1988b; Zahn, Krusei, & Rapoport, 1991); (2) perform better under conditions of immediate versus delayed rewards; (3) have significantly greater problems with task performance when delays are imposed within the task and as these delays increase in duration; (4) display a greater and more rapid decline in task performance as contingencies of reinforcement move from being continuous to intermittent; (5) show a greater disruption in task performance when noncontingent consequences occur during the task (see Barkley, 1989; Douglas, 1983; Haenlein & Caul, 1987; Sagvolden, Wultz, Moser, Moser, & Morkrid, 1989, for reviews; also Douglas & Parry, 1994; Freibergs & Douglas, 1969; Parry & Douglas, 1983; Schweitzer & Sulzer-Azaroff, 1995; Sonuga-Barke, Taylor, & Heppinstall, 1992; Sonuga-Barke, Taylor, Sembi, & Smith, 1992; Zahn et al., 1991); and (6) are less able to work for delayed rewards in delay of gratification tasks (Rapport et al., 1986).

However, others have not found evidence for item (4), that partial reinforcement schedules are necessarily detrimental to the task performances of ADHD children relative to their performance under continuous reinforcement. Instead, the schedule of reinforcement appears to interact with task difficulty in determining the effect of reinforcement on performance by ADHD children (Barber & Milich, 1989). It is also possible that differences in the delay periods between reinforcement contribute to these inconsistent findings; if delay intervals are sufficiently brief, no differences between ADHD and normal children under partial reinforcement should be noted. Thus studies of reinforcement schedules and children with ADHD cannot be interpreted in any straightforward fashion as supportive of the view that poor rule-governed behavior underlies any problem ADHD children may have with partial reinforcement schedules. As already noted, Barber, Milich, and Welsh (1996) recently suggested that an inability to sustain effort over time may better explain these findings. Thus these results seem more suggestive of poor self-regulation of motivation.

The problems with rule-governed behavior suggested here indicate that those with ADHD seem to have more trouble doing what they know, rather than in knowing what to do. Such a problem was evident in the study by Greve, Williams, and Dickens (1996) in which ADHD children displayed deficiencies in sorting cards by a rule on a task similar to the Wisconsin Card Sort Task even when the examiner gave them the rule they needed to do so. Children with ADHD have been shown to have more difficulty not only spontaneously developing a strategy to organize material to be memorized (August, 1987) but also following that rule over time (August, 1987). Conte and Regehr (1991) also found that hyperactive children were less likely to transfer the rules they had acquired on a prior task to a new task, consistent with this hypothesis.

Other evidence, albeit less direct, suggests a problem with extant knowledge poorly governing behavioral performance in those with ADHD. Past studies found that hyperactive–impulsive children are more prone to accidents than are normal children (Bijur, Golding, Haslem, & Kurzon, 1988; Methany & Fisher, 1984; Taylor, Sandberg, Thorley, & Giles, 1991), yet they are not deficient in their knowledge of safety or accident prevention (Mori & Peterson, 1995). Barkley, Murphy, and Kwasnik (1996) also found that teens and young adults with ADHD have significantly more motor vehicle accidents and other driving risks (speeding) but demonstrated no deficiencies in their knowledge of driving, safety, and accident prevention.

In any case, it is quite common clinically to hear these children described as not listening, failing to initiate compliance to instructions, unable to maintain compliance to an instruction over time, and poor at adhering to directions associated with a task. All these descriptors are problems in the regulation and inhibition of behavior, especially by rules, and their failure to adequately develop in ADHD children speaks to serious problems with behavioral disinhibition in this disorder.

DELAYED INTERNALIZATION OF LANGUAGE

The origin of the difficulties with rule-governed behavior in children with ADHD may actually reside in the delayed internalization of language consistently demonstrated in ADHD children to date.

The Internalization of Language

Vygotsky's theory on the development of private speech remains the most accepted view on the topic at this time (Berk, 1992, 1994; Diaz & Berk, 1992; Vygotsky 1978, 1987). Such speech is defined as "speech uttered aloud by children that is addressed either to the self or to no one in particular" (Berk & Potts, 1991, p. 358). In its earliest stages, it is thought spoken out loud which accompanies ongoing action. As it matures, it functions as a form of self-guidance and direction by assisting with the formulation of a plan that will eventually assist the child in controlling his or her own actions (Berk & Potts, 1991). Gradually, as speech becomes progressively more private or internalized and behavior comes increasingly under its control, such speech is now internal, verbal thought that can exert a substantial controlling influence over behavior. This internalization of speech proceeds in an orderly fashion. It seems to evolve from more conversational, task-irrelevant, and possibly self-stimulating forms of speech to more descriptive, task-relevant forms, and then on to more prescriptive and self-guiding speech. It then progresses to more private, inaudible speech and finally to fully private, subvocal speech (Berk, 1992, 1994; Berk & Garvin, 1984; Berk & Potts, 1991; Bivens & Berk, 1990; Frauenglas & Diaz, 1985; Kohlberg, Yaeger, & Hjertholm, 1968). Ample research exists to show that overt private speech increases with the difficulty of the task being done (Diaz & Berk, 1992). This finding is further evidence that such private speech serves a self-regulatory function helping to facilitate problem solving, as noted earlier. Its greater impact, however, may be more on the later performance of similar tasks than on the task with which the self-speech is concurrent (Berk, 1992).

Delays in the Internalization of Speech in ADHD

Studies using hyperactive children or those with ADHD have consistently found that ADHD children are less mature in their self-speech and seem to be developmentally delayed in this process (Rosenbaum & Baker, 1984; Berk & Potts, 1991; Copeland, 1979; Gordon, 1979). The most elegant and rigorous of these studies is the research of Berk and her colleagues (Berk & Potts, 1991; Berk & Landau, 1993; Landau, Berk, & Mangione, 1996). In the initial study of ADHD children by Berk and Potts (1991), ADHD and normal children were observed in their natural classroom settings and the occurrences of private (self-directed but publicly observable) speech were recorded while the children were engaged in math work at their desks. The observations were classified into one of three levels of private speech believed to reflect the maturational progression of such private speech as originally proposed by Vygotsky. Level I speech consisted of task-irrelevant utterances. Level II consisted of task-relevant externalized private speech such as describing one's own actions and giving self-guiding comments, task-relevant, self-answered questions, reading aloud and sounding out words, and task-relevant affect expression. Level III was considered task-relevant external manifestations of inner speech. The latter included inaudible muttering but mouthing of clear words related to the task and lip and tongue movements associated with the task.

The results indicated that the overall amount of private speech was not significantly different between groups but differences were observed in the levels of private speech employed by each group. ADHD children were found to use significantly more Level II and significantly less Level III speech than did their matched control counterparts. In contrast, to the findings of Copeland (1979), the two groups did not differ in their use of Level I (task-irrelevant) speech. Berk and Potts (1991) analyzed their results as a function of age of the children in these groups and found significant differences in the developmental patterns (see Figure 3.1). No significant effects related to age were evident in Level I speech or total private speech and so are not shown in the figure. As Figure 3.1 illustrates, however, ADHD children at all ages engaged in more Level II speech than did control children. Both groups declined significantly in their use of this level of private speech with age. Regarding Level III speech, ADHD children were found to increase markedly in this level of speech between ages 6–7 and 8–9, leveling off at the 10- to 11-year age group. Control subjects, in contrast, remained high in their use of this form of speech across the two youngest ages (6–7, 8–9 years) and then declined in their use of this level of speech by the oldest age group (10–11 years). This decline in Level III speech was interpreted by the authors as being consistent with Vygotsky's theoretical position that speech by this age is moving to being fully internalized

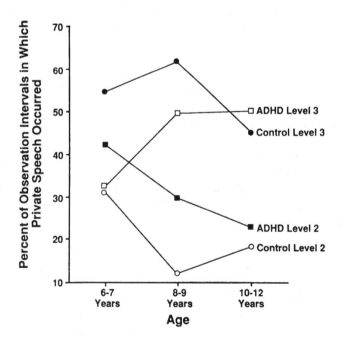

FIGURE 3.1. Development trends in Levels 2 and 3 private speech for ADHD and control children. From Berk & Potts (1991). Copyright 1991 by Plenum Publishing Corporation. Reprinted by permission.

(covert) and so less observable. The conclusion of this study was that ADHD and normal children show a similar pattern of development of private speech but that those with ADHD are considerably delayed in this process relative to control children.

It is important to demonstrate in such a study that the private speech of children serves a controlling or governing function over behavior. Berk and Potts (1991) correlated the private speech categories of these children with observations of the motor behavior associated with the task as well as with their attention to the task. Children in both groups who were more likely to have difficulty sustaining attention were found to display more Level II forms of private speech. Both Level I and Level II speech were also negatively correlated with focused attention and were positively correlated with diversions from seatwork. Level II speech was also significantly and positively associated with the amount of task-facilitating behavior shown by the child. Greater degrees of Level III speech, thought to reflect greater maturity, were significantly correlated with degree of focused attention and were negatively associated with amount of task diversion (off-task behavior). Interestingly, only the ADHD boys showed a significant positive association between Level III speech and self-stimulating forms of behavior. The authors interpret such findings as indicative of a delay in the controlling effects of speech in gaining control over behavior as it proceeds to internalization.

Two additional studies further support the conclusion of this initial study that children with ADHD are delayed in the internalization of speech. Berk and Landau (1993) observed 56 LD children and 56 normal children in grades 3 through 6 while they performed their daily math and language assignments at their desks in their natural classroom settings. The LD children were further subdivided into those without ADHD ($N = 47$) and those with ADHD ($N = 9$) on the basis of teacher ratings on a behavior rating scale of ADHD symptoms. Note that the sample size for the LD/ADHD group was exceptionally small and thus severely limited the statistical power of this study to detect effects due to ADHD beyond those resulting from the presence of learning disabilities. Consistent with the earlier study, rates of private speech (self-directed yet public speech) during work were exceptionally high. Level of cognitive development (IQ) was significantly and negatively related to amounts of Level II speech ($r = -.25$). Again, this finding suggests that the greater the mental maturity of children, the faster their rate of progression through the stages of internalization of speech. Both the LD and normal children showed a developmental (age-related) pattern similar to that found by Berk and Potts (1991): Level II speech declined linearly with increasing grade level while Level III speech demonstrated a quadratic effect. That is, Level III speech was found to increase from grades 3 to 4 and then decline from grades 4 to 5 after which it stabilized from grades 5 to 6. LD children engaged in more than twice as much private, task-relevant (Level II) speech as the normal children. However, there were no significant differences between LD and control children in Level III speech, nor did the LD children show more task-irrelevant (Level I) speech. When the LD/ADHD children were separated and contrasted with the other two groups (pure LD and control), the results showed that the ADD group displayed more than three times as much task-relevant, externalized (Level II) speech as did the pure LD group and about four times as much as the control children. The ADHD children also demonstrated significantly less Level III speech, which is the most mature stage of internalization measured in this study, than did the pure LD or control children. Such significant group differences despite low statistical power in the ADHD subgroup suggest that this finding of delayed speech is rather robust. These findings also suggest that ADHD more than LD contributes to a delay in the internalization of speech. Such findings for the ADHD group are quite consistent with the findings of Berk and Potts (1991), discussed earlier.

In a more recent study, Landau et al. (1996) compared the self-speech of impulsive and nonimpulsive children during their performance of math problems. These children were not clinically diagnosed as ADHD but represented 55 regular school students in first through third grades who were rated as either most or least impulsive by their teachers. Impulsive children were found to be significantly more dependent on externalized private speech for problem solving an their instructional level in math than were the nonimpulsive children. However, as the level of difficulty of the problems rose to becoming very challenging, the private speech of nonimpulsive children increased, as predicted by Vygotsky and shown in other research (Berk, 1992), while it decreased for impulsive children. In general, impulsive children used more task-irrelevant, less mature speech as the math problems became more challenging while the nonimpulsives did not use task-irrelevant speech at any level of difficulty but increased their task-relevant speech as problem difficulty increased. The results were interpreted as reflecting a more adaptive use of private speech by the nonimpulsive children. All these studies provide considerable support for the conclusion that ADHD and impulsiveness generally are associated with a significant delay in the internalization of speech.

GREATER VARIABILITY OF TASK PERFORMANCE

Another characteristic which some believe to be a primary deficit in ADHD children is their excessive variability of task or work performance over time. Douglas (1972) described this problem in observing ADHD children performing reaction-time tasks or serial problem solving and many others have reported it since. It is a finding repeatedly noted on other tasks as well. One often finds that their standard deviation of performance on multitrial tasks is considerably larger than that seen in normal children. Both the number of problems or items completed as well as their accuracy of performance change substantially from moment to moment, trial to trial, or day to day in the same setting. Teachers often report much greater variability in homework and test grades as well as in-class performance than is seen in normal children. An inspection of the teacher's grade book for this child often reveals this pattern of performance. Similarly, parents may find that their children perform certain chores swiftly and accurately on some occasions yet sloppily if at all on other days.

MEMORY AND PLANNING DIFFICULTIES

Deficits in children with ADHD have not typically been found on traditional measures of memory, such as recall, long-term storage, and long-term retrieval (Barkley, DuPaul, & McMurray, 1990; Douglas, 1983). However, on tasks thought to assess working memory, a number of studies documented deficits in this type of executive function (Barkley, 1997a, 1997b). Working memory has been defined as the capacity to hold information in mind that will be used to guide a subsequent response (Fuster, 1989; Goldman-Rakic, 1995). The construct has been assessed in neuropsychological research using a variety of tasks. Nonverbal working memory has been less studied than verbal working memory (see Becker, 1994, for reviews). Tasks assessing nonverbal working memory typically involve memory for objects and particularly for their spatial location. Measures assessing nonverbal planning ability as well as sense of time are also considered to fall within this domain (Barkley, 1997b), though such measures rarely reflect pure assessments of nonverbal abilities. I review evidence relating to nonverbal working memory deficits associated with ADHD first, sparse as it is, before turning to the evidence pertaining to verbal working memory, which is far more substantial.

Nonverbal Working Memory

Evidence for impaired nonverbal working memory associated with ADHD is limited. Some evidence for deficits in this form of working memory in ADHD comes from findings of impaired memory for spatial location (Mariani & Barkley, 1997). However, Weyandt and Willis (1994) were unable to find deficits associated with ADHD in an apparently related task requiring visual search of a display for a target item.

The use of nonverbal working memory might seem to be involved in the organization and reproduction of complex designs, such as in the Rey–Osterrieth Complex Figure Drawing Test. A number of studies of ADHD identify organizational deficits in these children on this task (Douglas & Benezra, 1990; Grodzinsky & Diamond, 1992; Sadeh, Ariel, & Inbar, 1996; Seidman, Benedict, et al., 1995). Two studies did not find such group differences (Moffitt & Silva, 1988; Reader et al., 1994), and another found deficits only in ADHD children with reading disorders (McGee et al., 1989). Two of the three studies that found nonsignificant results for ADHD children employed samples drawn from community screenings of children, whereas most of those studies that found differences used clinic-referred samples. Community-derived samples may not be as severe in their symptoms of ADHD as those referred to clinics, perhaps explaining these inconsistent results.

The capacity to hold information in mind that comprises working memory would seem to be involved in the ability to imitate the complex and lengthy behavioral sequences performed by others that may be novel to the subject. No studies of ADHD were found that expressly tested this ability to see if it might be impaired in those with the disorder. However, several studies employed more rudimentary imitation tasks that could be taken to suggest a deficit in imitative behavior. These studies found that children with ADHD are less proficient at imitating increasingly lengthy and novel sequences of simple motor gestures than are normal children, such as those required on the K-ABC Hand Movements Test (Breen, 1989; Grodzinsky & Diamond, 1992; Mariani & Barkley, 1997). Adults with ADHD have also been shown to be less able to replicate increasingly longer sequences involving pointing to locations than are non-ADHD adults (Barkley, Murphy, & Kwasnik, 1996b).

Verbal Working Memory

Verbal working memory tasks typically involve the retention and oral repetition of digit spans (especially in reverse order), mental computation or arithmetic, such as serial addition, and memory tasks that require the retention of verbal material across delay intervals. Often the latter tasks impose a demand for organizing the material in some way to more easily restate the material when called on to do so. Children with ADHD have been found to be significantly less proficient in speed of mental computation (Ackerman, Anhalt, & Dykman, 1986; Barkley, DuPaul, & McMurray, 1990; Mariani & Barkley, 1997; Zentall & Smith, 1993; Zentall, Smith, Lee, & Wieczorek, 1994). More recently, adolescents with ADHD have been shown to have a similar deficiency (MacLeod & Prior, 1996). Both children and adults with ADHD have also shown more difficulties with digit span (particularly backwards) (Barkley, Murphy, & Kwasnik, 1996b; Mariani & Barkley, 1997). The Freedom-from-Distractibility factor of the Wechsler Intelligence Scale for Children—Revised (WISC-III) comprises tests of digit span, mental arithmetic, and coding (digit symbol) and thus has been interpreted as reflecting executive processes, such as verbal working memory and resistance to distraction (Ownby & Matthews, 1985). ADHD children have been found to perform more poorly on this factor than do normal children (Anastopoulos et al., 1994; Golden, 1996; Lufi et al., 1990; Milich & Loney, 1979; van der Meere, Gunning, & Stemerdink, 1996). A recent study of adults with ADHD documented similar deficiencies in the performance of these same tests on the Wechsler Adult Intelligence Scale (Matochik, Rumsey, Zametkin, Hamburger, & Cohen, 1996). By themselves, such findings might suggest a variety of problems besides working memory (deficient arithmetic knowledge, slow motor speed, etc.). However, Zentall and Smith (1993) were able to rule out some of these potential confounding factors in their study of mental computation in ADHD children, thus giving greater weight to deficient verbal working memory as being associated with ADHD. The high comorbidity of learning disorders with ADHD, nevertheless, argues for some caution in interpreting these findings until more studies are able to distinguish to what extent those disorders may have contributed to such findings of group differences between ADHD and control subjects.

As noted previously, the storage and recall of simple information using verbal memory tests has not been found to be impaired in those with ADHD (Barkley, DuPaul, & McMurray, 1990; Cahn & Marcotte, 1995; Douglas, 1983, 1988). Instead, it seems that when larger, and more complex amounts of verbal information must be held in mind, especially over a lengthy delay period, such deficits become evident (Douglas, 1983, 1988; Seidman, Biederman, et al., 1995; Seidman, Biederman, Faraone, Weber, & Oullette, 1997). Also, when strategies are required that assist with organizing material to respond to it or to remember it more effectively, those with ADHD are less proficient than control groups (Amin, Douglas, Mendelson, & Dufresne, 1993; August, 1987; Benezra & Douglas, 1988; Borcherding et al., 1988; Douglas, 1983; Douglas & Benezra, 1990; Felton, Wood, Brown, Campbell, & Harter, 1987; Frost, Moffitt, & McGee, 1989; Shapiro, Hughes, August, & Bloomquist, 1993). Not only is this true of ADHD children, but it has more recently been demonstrated in adults with ADHD (Holdnack, Morberg, Arnold, Gur, & Gur, 1995). Thus there seems to be ample evidence that ADHD is associated with deficits in verbal working memory.

HINDSIGHT, FORETHOUGHT, AND PLANNING

Working memory, or the capacity to hold information in mind across a delay in time to guide a subsequent response, has been thought to be composed of two temporally symmetrical functions: the retrospective and prospective functions. Both Fuster (1989) and Goldman-Rakic (1995) described these functions; they have also been called hindsight and forethought (Bronowski, 1977). These constructs have not been well-studied in those with ADHD except as they are likely to pertain to measures of planning (e.g., in such tasks as the Tower of London or Tower of Hanoi tests and maze performances, discussed later). But if in its most elementary form hindsight can be taken to mean the ability to alter subsequent responses based on immediately past mistakes, then research findings imply a deficit in hindsight in ADHD. ADHD children, like adults with prefrontal lobe injuries, are less likely to adjust their subsequent responses based on an immediately past incorrect response in an information-processing task (Sergeant & van der Meere, 1988). The findings of perseveration on the Wisconsin Card Sort Test, as noted later, also suggest such a problem.

Research using complex reaction-time tasks with warning stimuli and preparation intervals may be relevant to the construct of forethought. In such research, ADHD children often fail to use the warning stimulus to prepare for the upcoming response trial (Douglas, 1983), with longer preparatory intervals making the performance of ADHD children worse than in control children (Chee, Logan, Schachar, Lindsay, & Wachsmuth, 1989; van der Meere, Vreeling, & Sergeant, 1992; Zahn et al., 1991). The capacity to create and maintain anticipatory set for an impending event also has been shown to be impaired by ADHD (van der Meere et al., 1992).

The Tower of London (TOL) task places heavy emphasis on working memory, and on the nonverbal form in particular though not exclusively. This task requires the subject to construct a design using colored disks of different sizes and three upright pegs, employing the least moves possible and with several constraints. Forethought and planning are felt to be instrumental to performance of this task. This task requires that individuals be able to mentally represent and test out various ways of removing and replacing disks on a set of pegs or spindles to match the design presented by the experimenter. This task involves substantial mental planning that must occur before and while undertaking the actual motor execution of the rearrangement. Studies of ADHD using the TOL and a related task, the Tower of Hanoi (TOH), consistently found ADHD children to perform more poorly than normal children (Brady & Denckla, 1994; Pennington, Grossier, & Welsh, 1993; Weyandt & Willis, 1994).

Like the TOL/TOH, maze performance probably reflects aspects of planning ability as well, though perhaps not as much. After all, the solution to the maze is obviously within the maze design that sits before the child but simply must be discovered, whereas the solution to the TOL design problem is not as readily apparent. Perhaps this explains why some studies found ADHD children to perform poorly on maze tasks (Weyandt & Willis, 1994) but many others did not (Barkley, Grodzinsky, & DuPaul, 1992; Grodzinsky & Diamond, 1992; Mariani & Barkley, 1997; McGee et al., 1989; Milich & Kramer, 1985; Moffit & Silva, 1988). The young age of the subjects may be a factor in some of the negative findings (Mariani & Barkley, 1997), as may be the low power associated with the use of small samples ($N < 20$ per group) (Barkley et al., 1992; McGee et al., 1989; Moffit & Silva, 1988). As already noted, the TOH and TOL tasks may better reflect the capacity to plan or "look ahead" (Pennington et al., 1993), and children with ADHD perform poorly on these tasks. The findings reviewed here are at least suggestive of deficiencies in hindsight, forethought, and planning ability that depend on working memory.

SENSE OF TIME AND CROSS-TEMPORAL BEHAVIOR

Nonverbal working memory is described as being integral to the development of psychological awareness of time and the organization of behavior relative to time (Fuster, 1989; Michon, 1985). This description led me to predict that those with ADHD should have an impairment in their sense of time as a consequence of their poor inhibition and working memory difficulties (Barkley, 1997a, 1997b). Several studies have documented such an impairment (Cappella, Gentile, & Juliano, 1977; Dooling-Litfin, 1997; Grskovic, Zentall, & Stormont-Spurgin, 1995; Senior, Town, & Huessy, 1979; Walker, 1982; White, Barratt, & Adams, 1979).

In a recent series of studies, my colleagues and I evaluated the sense of time in children with ADHD (Barkley, Koplowitz, Anderson, & McMurray, 1997). First, we surveyed parents of ADHD children using a questionnaire about their child's sense of time and the child's ability to organize behavior relative to time. Substantial differences were noted between the ADHD and normal children. Dooling-Litfin (1997) later corroborated these results in her sample of ADHD children. Then we tested the ability of ADHD children to reproduce prospectively presented time intervals. In time reproduction, the subject is presented with a sample duration but not told its length. The subject then uses some device (say, a flashlight) to signal the beginning and end of an interval to demonstrate that duration.

In a preliminary study of 32 ADHD and 32 control children, we had the children reproduce 6- and 10-second durations with no distraction present. We then had them reproduce intervals of 10 and 16 seconds with distractions present. We found that the ADHD subjects made significantly larger reproduction errors than the controls during the 6- and 10-second trials as well as during the 10- and 16-second trials with distraction. Both groups made larger errors of reproduction as the duration to be reproduced increased in size; findings comparable to those of Cappella et al. (1977). However, we did not find that the ADHD subjects showed greater such increases than the control group.

In the second study, 12 children with ADHD were compared to 26 normal children in their ability to reproduce durations of 12, 24, 36, 48, and 60 seconds. On half the trials presented at each duration, a distraction was created. Figure 3.2 shows some of the results. These results are for the measure of the absolute discrepancies in the time reproductions (magnitude of the error above or below the sample duration expressed as an absolute number). They indicate that the ADHD subjects made greater errors of time reproductions than the control subjects across these time intervals. Both groups made increasingly larger errors as the durations to be reproduced increased. The distractions affected the ADHD subjects rather than the control subjects, particularly at the 12- and 36-second durations.

These results can be recast as coefficients of accuracy to determine whether the errors made by the subjects tended to be in one direction more than another. That is, did the ADHD subjects tend to overreproduce or underreproduce the sample intervals. This score is created by dividing the subject's raw score for the duration of the reproduction by the actual duration of the sample interval. A score greater than 1.00 reflects a tendency to overreproduce the interval; a score less than 1.00 indicates the opposite. Figure 3.3 shows these results. As this figure illustrates, control subjects tended to slightly underreproduce the intervals. They also tended to increase the magnitude of their underreproductions as the sample intervals increased in duration. The presence of the distractor had no impact on their reproductions. In contrast, the ADHD subjects significantly overreproduced the shorter time durations (12 and 24 seconds). But, like the normal subjects, they moved toward a progressively greater likelihood of underreproducing the intervals as the sample durations increased in size. The effect of distraction was to increase the likelihood of overreproducing the interval, primarily at the 12- and 36-second intervals.

The totality of the results indicate that children with ADHD are less accurate in their sense of time than are control subjects, as measured by this time-reproduction method. These results have been subsequently replicated by Dooling-Litfin (1997), who also found that ADHD children were less accurate in their time reproductions than were normal control children.

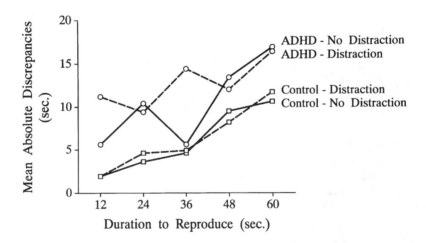

FIGURE 3.2. The mean absolute magnitude of errors in the time productions of ADHD and control children at five different durations with and without distraction. From Barkley, Koplowitz, Anderson, & McMurray (1997). Copyright 1997 by Cambridge University Press. Reprinted by permission.

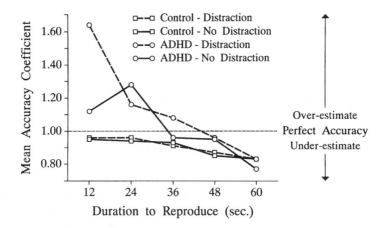

FIGURE 3.3. The mean coefficient of accuracy scores for the time productions of ADHD and control children at five different durations with and without distraction. From Barkley et al. (1997). Copyright 1997 by Cambridge University Press. Reprinted by permission.

All these studies on sense of time and ADHD/hyperactivity had a number of significant methodological flaws, making attempts at replication imperative. Their general consistency, however, tentatively suggests that sense of time is probably impaired in those with ADHD.

Perhaps related to these studies, numerous studies found that both temporal delays interposed within tasks as well as temporal uncertainties result in poorer performances in children with ADHD relative to control groups (Chee et al., 1989; Gordon, 1979; Sonuga-Barke, Taylor, & Hepinstall, 1992; Sonuga-Barke, Taylor, Sembi, & Smith, 1992; van der Meere, Shalev, Borger, & Gross-Tsur, 1995; van der Meere et al., 1992; Zahn et al., 1991). These results intimate some sort of problem with time, the timing of responses, and the cross-temporal organization of behavior more generally in those with ADHD.

SELF-REGULATION OF EMOTION

Irritability, hostility, excitability, and a general emotional hyperresponsiveness toward others have been frequently described in the clinical literature on ADHD (see Barkley, 1990; Still, 1902). Douglas (1983, 1988) anecdotally observed and later objectively documented the tendency of ADHD children to become overaroused and excitable in response to rewards and to be more visibly frustrated when past rates of reinforcement declined (Douglas & Parry, 1994; Wigal et al., 1993). Rosenbaum and Baker (1984) also reported finding greater negative affect expressed by ADHD children during a concept learning task involving noncontingent negative feedback. And Cole, Zahn-Waxler, and Smith (1994) found that levels of negative affect were significantly and positively correlated with symptoms of and risk for ADHD, but only in boys. The opposite proved true for girls. These clinical observations and research studies intimate that emotional self-control may be problematic for children with ADHD.

Greater emotional reactivity has been reported as well in the social interactions of ADHD children. Mash (personal communication, February 1993) found that children with ADHD displayed greater emotional intonation in their verbal interactions with their mothers. Studies of peer interactions also found ADHD children to be more negative and emotional in their social communications with peers. This greater level of expressed negative emotion in children with ADHD is most salient in the subgroup that has high levels of comorbid aggression (Hinshaw & Melnick, 1995). Consistent with such findings, Keltner, Moffitt, and Stouthamer-Loeber (1995) recorded the facial expressions of adolescent boys during a structured social interaction. Four groups of boys were created; one was rated as having high levels of externalizing symptoms (hyperactive–impulsive–inattentive–aggressive behavior), a second consisted of boys rated as having more internalizing symptoms (anxiety, depression, etc.), a third group consisted of boys having elevations on ratings of both types of symptoms, and the fourth group was composed of nondisordered adolescent boys. Boys showing high levels of externalizing symptoms were found to demonstrate significantly more facial expressions of anger than the other groups, which were low in externalizing symptoms. These results suggest the possibility that the commonly noted association of ADHD with defiant and hostile behavior (see Hinshaw, 1987, for a review) may, at least in part, stem from a deficiency in emotional self-regulation in those with ADHD. Again, however, these findings merely suggest rather than confirm a link between ADHD and emotional self-regulation and tend to imply that the poorest emotion modulation may be within the aggressive subgroup of ADHD children.

Despite these apparent difficulties with emotional self-control, ADHD children have not been found to have any difficulties with the perception or recognition of others' emotions (Shapiro et al., 1993); children with ADHD were not observed to be significantly different in their processing of emotional information compared to normal children, except on two auditory tests that appeared to make demands on auditory–verbal working memory.

CREATIVITY

Elsewhere I (Barkley, 1997a, 1997b; also Chapter 7, this volume) suggested that behavioral or verbal creativity (flexibility and originality) in ADHD may be impaired in those with ADHD as a consequence of their poor behavioral inhibition. Few studies have actually examined the issue. They are plagued, as is the field of creativity research itself, by problems in the very definition of creativity (Boden, 1994; Brown, 1989; Sternberg & Lubart, 1996). Creativity during free play (Alessandri, 1992) and performance of nonverbal, figural creativity tasks (Funk, Chessare, Weaver, & Exley, 1993) have been noted to be significantly below normal in children with ADHD. This would seem to support the earlier prediction of such deficits being associated with ADHD. However, Shaw and Brown (1990) did not find a deficit in creativity in a small sample of high-IQ ADHD children. They did find that those with ADHD gathered and used more diverse, nonverbal, and poorly focused information and displayed higher figural creativity. Using so small a sample and only bright ADHD children, however, hardly poses a reasonable test of this prediction. More research on creativity in ADHD is clearly needed in testing this prediction of the model.

MOTIVATIONAL DIFFICULTIES

Clinical descriptions of children and adults with ADHD are often rife with references to poor motivation and impaired persistence of effort. Researchers have also frequently commented on such difficulties in tasks requiring repetitive responding that involve little or no reinforcement (Barber et al., 1996; Barkley, 1990; Douglas, 1972, 1983, 1989). Written productivity in arithmetic tasks, in particular, may be taken as a measure of persistence; those with ADHD have been found to be less productive on such tasks than control children (Barkley, DuPaul, & McMurray, 1990). Multiple studies also have documented an impairment in persistence of effort in laboratory tasks with ADHD children (August, 1987; August & Garfinkel, 1990; Barber et al., 1996; Borcherding et al., 1988; Douglas & Benezra, 1990; Milich, in press; Ott & Lyman, 1993; Solanto, Wender, & Bartell, 1997; van der Meere et al., 1995; Wilkison, Kircher, McMahon, & Sloane, 1995). Thus, the evidence for difficulties in the self-regulation of motivation (particularly persistence of effort) in ADHD is impressive.

It is possible that this evidence explains the apparent insensitivity to reinforcement reported in some studies of children with ADHD (see Barkley, 1989; Douglas, 1989; Haenlein & Caul, 1987; Sagvolden et al., 1989, for reviews). Studies using varying schedules of reinforcement typically find that ADHD and normal children do not differ in their task performances under immediate and continuous reward (Barber et al., 1996; Cunningham & Knights, 1978; Douglas & Parry, 1983, 1994; Parry & Douglas, 1983). In contrast, when partial reinforcement is introduced, the performance of ADHD children may decline relative to that of normal children (Parry & Douglas, 1983; Freibergs & Douglas, 1969). Just as many studies, however, have not found this decline (Barber et al., 1996; Pelham, Milich, & Walker, 1986) or have found that the difficulty of the task moderates the effect (Barber & Milich, 1989). In a similar vein, the performance of ADHD children during relatively tedious tasks involving little or no reward is often enhanced by the addition of reinforcement; yet, so is the performance of normal children (Carlson & Alexander, 1993; Iaboni, Douglas, & Baker, 1995; Kupietz, Camp, & Weissman, 1976; Pelham et al., 1986; Solanto, 1990; van der Meere, Hughes, Borger, & Sallee, 1995). And the addition of reinforcement to the task does not alter the significant deterioration in effort over time that is seen in ADHD children on such tasks (Solanto et al., 1997). Although some interpreted the early findings in this area as suggesting that ADHD children have a reduced sensitivity to reinforcement (Haenlein & Caul, 1987) or are dominated by immediate reinforcement (Douglas, 1983; Sagvolden et al., 1989), the similar enhancement of the performance of normal children by reward in the studies noted above challenged this interpretation (Pelham et al., 1986; Solanto, 1990). Moreover, Douglas and her colleagues (Iaboni et al., 1995) did not find the reward dominance effect that she earlier hypothesized might be associated with ADHD (Douglas, 1989). And Solanto et al. (1997) found that the impact of stimulant medication on the task performance and persistence of effort of ADHD children does not appear to be entirely mediated by the enhancement of brain reward systems, as some earlier speculated (Haenlein & Caul, 1987).

Elsewhere I suggested a possible explanation for these results (Barkley, 1997b). It focuses on the observations that the performance of normal children is superior to that of ADHD children under conditions of little or no reward and may be less affected by reductions in schedules of reinforcement, depending on the task duration and its difficulty level. This effect may result from normal children developing the capacity to bridge temporal delays between the elements of behavioral contingencies via their better-developed working memory abilities and internalized language. Combined with working memory as well as self-directed speech and the rule-governed behavior it permits, the self-regulation of motivation may allow normal children not only to retain the goal of their performance in mind and subvocally encourage themselves in their persistence but in so doing to create the drive necessary for such persistence, as has been suggested by others (Berkowitz, 1982; Mischel, Shoda, & Peake, 1988). This line of reasoning would suggest that, across development, the behavior of those with ADHD remains more contingency shaped, or under the control of the immediate and external sources of reward, than it does in normal children. Therefore, it is not that ADHD children are either less sensitive to reinforcement or conversely dominated by a tendency to seek immediate rewards. They instead have a diminished capacity to bridge delays in reinforcement and permit the persistence of goal-directed acts.

PROBLEMS WITH AROUSAL

Some evidence does exist for possible problems in the regulation of central and autonomic nervous system arousal to meet task demands in those with ADHD. Multiple reviews of the psychophysiological (Hastings & Barkley, 1978; Brand & van der Glugt, 1989; Klorman et al., 1988; Rosenthal & Allen, 1978; Rothenberger, 1995) and cognitive literatures (Douglas, 1983, 1988) have concluded that ADHD children show greater variability in central and autonomic arousal patterns. They also seem to be underreactive to stimulation in evoked-response paradigms, particularly in the later P300 features of the evoked response (Klorman et al., 1988; Klorman, 1992). These P300 characteristics have been shown to be associated with frontal lobe activation (Klorman et al., 1988; Klorman, 1992; Knights, Grabowecky, & Sabini, 1995). ADHD children have also been shown to display less anticipatory activation on electroencephalograph in response to impending events within tasks (known as the CNV [contingent negative variation] or "expectancy" wave) (Hastings & Barkley, 1978) and to have less recruiting of psychophysiological activity over the frontal regions when necessary for appropriate task performance relative to control groups (Brand & van der Glugt, 1989; Rothenberger, 1995).

More recently, studies using positron emission tomography (PET) as a means of measuring brain activity also found diminished brain activity in adults as well as adolescent females with ADHD (Ernst et al., 1994; Zametkin et al., 1990). Results have not been as reliably obtained with adolescent males (Zametkin et al., 1993). Similarly, studies using cerebral blood flow as a means of measuring brain activity have found decreased perfusion of the frontal regions and striatum in those with ADHD (Lou, Henriksen, & Bruhn, 1984; Lou, Henriksen, Bruhn, Borner, & Neilsen, 1989; Sieg, Gaffney, Preston, & Hellings, 1995). All this implies that ADHD is associated with difficulties with phasic or reactive arousal and activation, particularly in response to environmental events.

SENSORY PROBLEMS

No evidence indicates that ADHD children are any more likely than normal children to have difficulties in the development of their peripheral hearing, although they may have more otitis media or middle-ear infections than normal (Mitchell, Aman, Turbott, & Manku, 1987). Recently, some research suggests that ADHD children may be more sensitive to auditory loudness, preferring lower levels of speech when asked to define what sound level is most comfortable and tolerable for themselves (Lucker, Geffner, & Koch, 1996). The precise meaning of this research is unclear at the moment, though it could imply a hypersensitivity to speech loudness associated with ADHD. Other research has also shown that ADHD children have difficulties with the accurate discrimination of the speech of others when both speech or nonspeech noise occurs in the background (Geffner, Lucker, & Koch, 1996). If replicated, these results would suggest that teachers and parents make an effort to reduce background noise when attempting to teach, instruct, or otherwise direct ADHD children through verbal means.

Some have noted greater difficulties in vision for ADHD children, particularly with strabismus (Hartsough & Lambert, 1985; Stewart et al., 1966). Even so, the percentage with such visual problems is quite low (19% to 21%). However, others (Barkley, DuPaul, & McMurray, 1990) have not found any history of visual problems in ADHD children.

PROBLEMS WITH MOTOR DEVELOPMENT

Results are conflicting as to whether ADHD children experience a greater risk of delays in walking, with some not finding any higher prevalence of this problem (Hartsough & Lambert, 1985) and others finding so (Mitchell et al., 1987; Szatmari et al., 1989). Some studies (Hartsough & Lambert, 1985) found children with ADHD to be somewhat more likely to have delays in the onset of crawling (6.5%) compared to normal children (1.6%). Others found no greater risk for delays in any areas of motor development (Barkley, DuPaul, & McMurray, 1990). Nevertheless, as a group, as much as 52% of ADHD compared to up to 35% of normal children are characterized as having poor motor coordination (Barkley, DuPaul, & McMurray, 1990; Hartsough & Lambert, 1985; Stewart et al., 1966; Szatmari et al., 1989).

Neurological examinations for "soft" signs related to motor coordination and motor overflow movements find ADHD children to demonstrate more such signs as well as generally sluggish gross motor movements than control children, including those with purely learning disabilities (Carte et al., 1996; Denckla & Rudel, 1978; Denckla, Rudel, Chapman, & Krieger, 1985; McMahon & Greenberg, 1977; Shaywitz & Shaywitz, 1984; Werry et al., 1972). These overflow movements have been interpreted as indicators of delayed development of motor inhibition (Denckla et al., 1985).

Studies using tests of fine motor coordination, such as balance, fine motor gestures, electronic or paper-and-pencil mazes, and pursuit tracking often find children with ADHD to be less coordinated in these actions (Hoy, Weiss, Minde, & Cohen, 1978; Mariani & Barkley, 1997; McMahon & Greenberg, 1977; Moffitt, 1990; Shaywitz & Shaywitz, 1984; Ullman, Barkley, & Brown, 1978). Simple motor speed, as measured by finger-tapping rate or grooved pegboard tests, does not seem to be as affected in ADHD as is the execution of complex, coordinated sequences of motor movements (Barkley et al., 1996; Breen, 1989; Grodzinsky & Diamond, 1992; Mariani & Barkley, 1997; Seidman, Biederman, et al., 1995; Seidman et al., 1997). The bulk of the available evidence, therefore, supports the existence of deficits in motor control, particularly when motor sequences must be performed, in those with ADHD.

Compelling evidence for a motor-control deficit in ADHD also comes from the substantial programmatic research of Sergeant and van der Meere (1990) and colleagues in Holland. Employing an information-processing paradigm, these studies isolated the cognitive deficit in those with ADHD to the motor-control stage rather than to an attentional or information-processing stage. Specifically, their research suggests that the deficit is not at the response choice stage but at the motor presetting stage involved in motor preparedness to act (Oosterlaan & Sergeant, 1995; van der Meere et al., 1996). Both a greater sluggishness and greater variability in motor preparation seem evident. This program of research also identified an insensitivity to errors in the motor performance of children with ADHD (Oosterlaan & Sergeant, 1995; Sergeant & van der Meere, 1988). In agreement with these results, other investigators (Hall, Halperin, Schwartz, & Newcorn, 1997) have also shown that ADHD is associated with deficits in response decision making and response organization, particularly those who may have comorbid reading disorders.

Complex motor sequencing and generating complex, novel motor responses as well as their syntax have not received much attention in research on ADHD. Handwriting, however, is just such a complex sequencing of simpler motor movements built into complex, novel patterns of new arrangements of letters, words, and sentences requiring great flexibility and fluency of fine motor movement. Handwriting has often been noted in the clinical literature to be less mature in those with ADHD (Sleator & Pelham, 1986) and was recently shown by more objective means to be significantly impaired in both the Combined and Inattentive subtypes of ADHD, though more so in the former than the latter (Marcotte & Stern, 1997). Difficulties with drawing have likewise been found in children with ADHD (Hoy et al., 1978; McGee et al., 1992). And speech certainly represents the ability to assemble complex fine motor sequences to articulate language. As noted earlier, those with ADHD have been found more likely to have speech problems relative to control groups (Barkley, DuPaul, & McMurray, 1990; Hartsough & Lambert, 1985; Munir et al., 1987; Szatmari et al., 1989; Taylor et al., 1991). All this might imply problems with the programming and rapid execution of complex, fine motor sequences in those with ADHD.

One test which seems to capture a simpler form of motor sequencing is the Hand Movements Test from the Kaufman Assessment Battery for Children (Kaufman & Kaufman, 1983). Three studies used this task in ADHD and all found the ADHD group to be significantly less proficient (Breen, 1989; Grodzinsky & Diamond, 1992; Mariani & Barkley, 1997), suggesting a problem with temporal ordering of motor sequences (Kesner, Hopkins, & Fineman, 1994). The developers of the test battery also commented that hyperactive children performed poorly on this task during the clinical validation trials of the battery (Kaufman & Kaufman, 1983).

REDUCED RESPONSE FLEXIBILITY AND GREATER PERSEVERATION

Clinical descriptions of children with ADHD often suggest that they are more likely to respond with more overlearned and automatic responses when faced with problem-solving situations or contexts that demand the thoughtful formation of novel responses. Such response flexibility may be measured using certain scores from the Wisconsin Card Sort Test (WCST). A large number of studies have used the WCST with samples of ADHD children. I reviewed a total of 20 studies using the WCST with subjects having ADHD (Barkley, 1997b). Focusing on studies using children and adolescents, a box score tally finds that 13 of the 20 studies showed ADHD subjects to be deficient in their performance of the WCST. The score most often found to be deficient was perseverative errors; the score for number of categories achieved correctly was also occasionally found to be deficient. Three more studies of adults with ADHD exist that used the WCST, and they did not find group differences on this measure.

Perseverative responding on the WCST may be reflecting the capacity to use rules to govern behavior and to inhibit automatic forms of behavior when new rules become operative. The score of number of categories correctly achieved, however, may be more reflective of concept formation or the capacity to derive rules from relatively ambiguous information about performance (Barkley, 1997b). If this distinction is correct, the weight of the evidence from the WCST supports a problem primarily with rule following/inhibition of automatic responding (perseverative responding) in ADHD. Less consistent though still evident in some studies is also a difficulty that ADHD children have with rule formulation or concept formation given feedback about errors.

A recent study by Greve et al. (1996) attempted to disentangle this issue by using a test similar to the WCST, known as the California Card Sorting Test (CCST) with ADHD and control children. Although subjects must sort cards based on rules, the test involves three different forms of administration. One includes telling the subject the rule to be used for sorting (Cued Sort), another includes the examiner sorting the cards but the child stating the rule from the sorting pattern (Structured Sort), and the third involves the subject both sorting the cards and stating the rule they are using (Free Sort). It was hypothesized that if ADHD children have problems with concept formation, they will have difficulties with Free Sort and Structured Sort, both of which require the child to identify or formulate the rule in effect. They will have no difficulty on Cued Sort because they have been explicitly told the rule to use for sorting. Conversely, if ADHD children have difficulty with rule-governed behavior (the control of the rule over motor responding), then deficits will be apparent in Cued Sort as well as in the other sorting routines. In the other two sort procedures, however, they will be able to accurately describe the rule in use when they are correctly sorting. Their errors, then, in the latter two sorts are evidence of poor rule execution not of rule formulation.

The results of this study indicated that ADHD children differed on scores that implied a problem with rule execution. These results might indicate that the difficulties ADHD children have with the WCST in their number of correct categories achieved is not so much that they cannot formulate the new sorting rule as much as that they cannot adhere to it in response execution. However, because of the relatively small sample sizes (24 ADHD and 39 control), the statistical power of this study may be limited. The failure to find group differences may not necessarily be interpreted as a failure to find evidence of poor concept formation in children with ADHD. Still, the results are intriguing and are worthy of replication with larger sample sizes.

MINOR PHYSICAL ANOMALIES

It has been repeatedly shown that ADHD children have more minor physical anomalies than do normal children (Firestone, Lewy, & Douglas, 1976; Lerer, 1977; Quinn & Rapoport, 1974; Still, 1902). Minor physical anomalies refer to slight deviations in the outward appearance of the child. Such things as an index finger longer than the middle finger, a curved fifth finger, a third toe as long or longer than the second toe, adherent ear lobes, a single transverse palmer crease, furrowed tongue, greater than normal head circumference, low seated or soft, fleshy ears, electric fine hair, two whorls of hair on back of head, eyes placed slightly further apart than normal, and greater skin on nasal side of eyelid, among others, are considered minor anomalies in these studies. Studies of infants have shown that a higher number of minor anomalies in infancy may be significantly related to the development of behavioral problems and specifically hyperactivity at age 3 (Waldrop, Bell, McLaughlin, & Halverson, 1978). Others, however, have been unable to replicate these findings (Burg, Hart, Quinn, & Rapoport, 1978; Quinn, Renfield, Berg, & Rapoport, 1977; Rapoport, Pandoni, Renfield, Lake, & Ziegler, 1977). Other studies have noted that minor anomalies are related to hyperactivity in boys, but to overly inhibited and hypoactive behavior in girls (Waldrop, Bell, & Goering, 1976). However, these findings were contradicted by a later study (Jacklin, Maccoby, & Halverson, 1980) and others found no relationship whatsoever between number of anomalies and behavior (LaVeck, Hammond, & Laveck, 1980). Thus, although ADHD children may display more of these anomalies, there is little if any consistent relationship between high numbers of minor anomalies and hyperactive behavior (Firestone et al., 1976; Krouse & Kauffman, 1982).

HEALTH AND ACCIDENTAL INJURIES

Some studies noted a greater incidence of *maternal health and pre- and perinatal complications,* such as toxemia, preclampsia, postmaturity, and fetal distress, in the pregnancies of ADHD children compared to normal children (Hartsough & Lambert, 1985). However, as many or more studies did not find this to be the case (Barkley, DuPaul, & McMurray, 1990; Stewart et al., 1966).

Several studies have found ADHD children to have more problems with general health than normal children. Hartsough and Lambert (1985) found that 50.9% of hyperactive children were described as in *poor health during infancy* whereas Stewart et al. (1966) found a prevalence of 24% of their sample to be so described. The figures for control children were 29.2 and 2.7%, respectively. The presence of chronic health problems, such as recurring *upper respiratory infections and allergies*, were also noted more often in hyperactive than in normal children (39–44% vs. 8–25%) (Hartsough & Lambert, 1985; Mitchell et al., 1987; Szatmari et al., 1989). Trites, Tryphonas, and Ferguson (1980) also noted more allergies among hyperactive than normal children, and others have noted the inverse; that is, more ADHD symptoms among children with atopic (allergic) disorders (Roth, Beyreiss, Schlenzka, & Beyer, 1991). One study found that only children with hyperactivity not associated with conduct problems were more likely to have allergies (Blank & Remschmidt, 1993). But others have not found an association between ADHD and allergies (McGee, Stanton, & Sears, 1993; Mitchell et al., 1987) or any association between the specific allergy of atopic rhinitis (hay fever) and ADHD (Hart, Lahey, Hynd, Loeber, & McBurnett, 1995). Thus the nature of an association between ADHD and allergies remains unclear at the moment.

Several studies have examined whether ADHD children are more likely to suffer from *asthma*. An initial report by Hartsough and Lambert (1985) suggested such an increased risk for asthma among children considered hyperactive. Yet several subsequent studies using large samples of children ($N = 140$) have not found this to be the case when clinical diagnostic criteria for ADHD were used to identify the children (Biederman, Milberger, Faraone, Guite, & Warburton, 1994; Biederman et al., 1995).

One study examined a large sample of 124 ADHD children and adolescents for the presence of growth deficits in height and weight (Spencer et al., 1996). The investigators found no evidence of weight deficits in ADHD children, even though 89% of the sample had been treated with stimulant medications that were previously thought to create reductions in weight. There were small but significant deficits in height in ADHD children compared to the control group but not between ADHD adolescents and their control group. These deficits were not related to treatment with stimulant medications. The authors concluded that ADHD may be associated with temporary deficits in growth in childhood through mid-adolescence that may no longer be evident by late adolescence.

Enuresis, particularly nighttime bedwetting, has been noted to occur in as many as 43% of ADHD children compared to normal children (28%) (Stewart et al., 1966), although two more recent studies did not find this to be the case (Barkley, DuPaul, & McMurray, 1990; Kaplan, McNichol, Conte, & Moghadam, 1988). Hartsough and Lambert (1985) reported that ADHD children were more likely to have difficulties with *bowel training* compared to normal children (10.1% vs. 4.5%) whereas Munir et al. (1987) found that 18% had functional *encopresis*. We were unable to replicate either of these findings, however (Barkley, DuPaul, & McMurray, 1990). Thus, it is not clear whether ADHD children are more likely to have problems with enuresis or encopresis, but the evidence seems far from convincing to date.

Children with ADHD are considerably more likely to experience *injuries due to accidents* than are normal children, with up to 57% being described as accident prone and 15% having had at least four or more serious accidental injuries, such as broken bones, lacerations, head injuries, severe bruises, lost teeth, or accidental poisonings (Hartsough & Lambert, 1985; Mitchell et al., 1987; Reebye, 1997; Stewart et al., 1966). Results for the comparison or normal groups of children in these studies were 11% and 4.8%, respectively. Stewart, Thach, and Friedin (1970) found that 21% of hyperactive children had experienced at least one accidental poisoning compared to 7.7% for normal children. In a much larger study of more than 2,600 children, Szatmari et al. (1989) found that 7.3% of ADHD children had an accidental poisoning whereas 23.2% suffered bone fractures compared to prevalence of 2.6% and 15.1%, respectively, in the control group. However, retrospective and prospective studies generally find a relationship between degree of aggressiveness, not the degree of overactivity, and the likelihood of accidental injury in preschoolers (Davidson, Hughes, & O'Connor, 1988; Langley, McGee, Silva, & Williams, 1983). Because ADHD children are more likely to be aggressive or oppositional, it may be this characteristic that increases their accident proneness rather than their higher rates of activity level or impulsivity (Langley et al., 1983; Mannheimer & Mellinger, 1967). Moreover, accident proneness is moderated by certain parental characteristics such as degree of monitoring of child behavior and maternal neuroticism (Davidson et al., 1988; Davidson, Taylor, Sandberg, & Thorley, 1992). Yet, a large population study of 10,394 British children found that both overactivity and aggression contributed independently to the prediction of accidents (Bijur et al., 1988). Thus, it may be that both ADHD and aggression are linked to accident proneness.

Research on children experiencing accidents suggests they are more likely to be overactive, impulsive, and defiant (Cataldo et al., 1992; Rosen & Peterson, 1990; Stewart et al., 1970). Pless, Taylor, and Arsenault (1995) found that children injured as pedestrians or bicycle riders in traffic accidents performed more poorly on tests of vigilance and impulse control and received higher parent and teacher ratings of hyperactive–aggressive behavior. This study suggests that among those experiencing such serious accidents, a higher percentage may have ADHD or greater-than-normal ADHD symptoms.

In the Canadian follow-up research of hyperactive children into adulthood, evidence emerged suggesting that such children, as young adults, may have *a higher risk for traffic accidents* (Weiss & Hechtman, 1993). Our Milwaukee follow-up study, similarly, suggested that adolescents with ADHD were more likely to drive illegally before obtaining a permit. Group differences in auto accident rates were not significant, most likely because fewer than 20% had drivers' licenses at this follow-up point. A subsequent 3- to 5-year follow-up study of adolescents with ADHD into their early driving years was able to document an increased risk for traffic accidents and speeding tickets than in a control group followed contemporaneously (Barkley, Guevremont, Anastopoulos, DuPaul, & Shelton, 1993). More recently, we corroborated these same risks with a somewhat older sample of young adults with ADHD with more driving experience (Barkley, Murphy, & Kwasnik, 1996a). And these results have since been replicated in New Zealand (Nada-Raja et al., 1997), where a study of 916 adolescents found that ADHD symptoms, as well as those of conduct disorder, were significantly associated with increased driving offenses and vehicular crashes.

The relationships between ADHD and increased (1) accident proneness in childhood, (2) speeding and auto accidents in adolescence and young adulthood, (3) crime (Satterfield, Hoppe, & Schell, 1982), (4) suicide attempts (Weiss & Hechtman, 1993), (5) substance use and abuse (alcohol and tobacco primarily) in adolescence and adulthood (Biederman et al., 1996), and (6) a general pattern of risk-taking behavior all intimate that ADHD might be expected to be associated with a *reduced life expectancy*. The diminished regard for the future consequences of one's behavior that characterizes many adolescents and adults with ADHD would also predict a reduced concern for health-conscious behavior, such as exercise, proper diet, and moderation in using legal substances (caffeine, tobacco, and alcohol) throughout life (Barkley, Fischer, et al., 1990; Milberger, Biederman, Faraone, Chen, & Jones, 1996a).

No follow-up studies of hyperactive or ADHD children have lasted long enough to document such a reduction in life expectancy; the oldest subjects now appear to be entering their 40s (Weiss & Hechtman, 1993). Yet concern over life expectancy in ADHD is not unfounded given the findings from the follow-up study of Terman's original sample of highly intelligent children. Most of those subjects are now in their 70s or older and half of them are deceased (Friedman et al., 1995). The follow-up study of that group indicated that the most significant childhood personality characteristic predictive of reduced life expectancy by all causes was related to impulsive, undercontrolled personality characteristics. Individuals classified as having this set of characteristics lived an average of 8 years less than those who did not (73 vs. 81 years). Subjects in this study were defined as impulsive by virtue of falling within the lowest 25% of the sample in impulse control. Given that subjects defined as ADHD typically fall well below this threshold, in the lowest 5–7%, the risk for reduced longevity in those with ADHD would seem to be even greater than was found among Terman's subjects. That conclusion would seem to be further supported by the fact that Terman's subjects were intellectually gifted and came from families of above-average or higher economic backgrounds. Both of these factors probably would have conveyed a greater advantage toward longer life expectancy than would be the case for intellectually normal ADHD children who tend to come from middle or lower economic backgrounds. Thus, there is some reason to suspect that the implications of this model for reduced reproductive advantage and life expectancy as a function of ADHD are not without some merit, at least as issues deserving of future research if not as well-supported conclusions at the moment.

ADHD children have not been found to have any more hospitalizations, length of hospital stays, or surgeries than normal children (Barkley, DuPaul, & McMurray, 1990; Hartsough & Lambert, 1985; Stewart et al., 1966).

SLEEP PROBLEMS

Several studies found children with ADHD to have a higher likelihood of sleeping problems than normal children. Difficulties with time taken to fall asleep may be seen in as many as 56% of ADHD children compared to 23% of normal children, and up to 39% of ADHD children may show problems with frequent night waking (Greenhill, Anich, Goetz, Hanton, & Davies, 1983; Kaplan et al., 1987; Stewart et al., 1966; Trommer, Hoeppner, Rosenberg, Armstrong, & Rothstein, 1988). More than 55% of ADHD children have been described by parents as tired on awakening compared to 27% of normal children (Trommer et al., 1988). Ball, Tiernan, Janusz, and Furr (1997) found that 53–64% of their ADHD subjects had sleep problems as reported by parents, and that whether or not the children were taking stimulant medication did not seem to influence these results. This higher incidence of sleep difficulties may appear as early as infancy in ADHD children (Stewart et al., 1966; Trommer et al., 1988), with as many as 52% of ADHD children described as such in infancy compared to 21% of normal children. Resistance to going to bed and fewer total sleep hours may be the most important sleep difficulties that ADHD children experience (Wilens, Biederman, & Spencer, 1994). Importantly, it appears that much of these behavioral difficulties surrounding children's bedtime are more a function of the disorders often comorbid with ADHD (ODD, anxiety disorders) than to ADHD (Corkum, Beig, Tannock, & Moldofsky, 1997). Despite this well-documented risk for sleep problems in children with ADHD, studies using polysomnograms of overnight sleep have not documented any difficulties in the nature of sleeping itself associated with this disorder (Ball & Koloian, 1995).

SUMMARY

This chapter reviewed the myriad cognitive, academic, social, emotional, health, and developmental problems associated with ADHD. These problems are summarized in Table 3.1.

TABLE 3.1. **Summary of Impairments Likely to Be Associated with ADHD**

Cognitive

Mild deficits in intelligence (approximately 7–10 points)
Deficient academic achievement skills (range of 10–30 standard score points)
Learning disabilities: reading (8–39%), spelling (12–26%), math (12–33), and handwriting
    (common but unstudied)
Poor sense of time, inaccurate time estimation and reproduction
Decreased nonverbal and verbal working memory
Impaired planning ability
Reduced sensitivity to errors
Possible impairment in goal-directed behavioral creativity

Language

Delayed onset of language (up to 35% but not consistent)
Speech impairments (10–54%)
Excessive conversational speech (commonplace), reduced speech to confrontation
Poor organization and inefficient expression of ideas
Impaired verbal problem solving
Coexistence of central auditory processing disorder (minority but still uncertain)
Poor rule-governed behavior
Delayed internalization of speech ($\geq$ 30% delay)
Diminished development of moral reasoning

Adaptive functioning: 10–30 standard score points behind normal

Motor development

Delayed motor coordination (up to 52%)
More neurological "soft" signs related to motor coordination and overflow movements
Sluggish gross motor movements

Emotion

Poor self-regulation of emotion
Greater problems with frustration tolerance
Underreactive arousal system

School performance

Disruptive classroom behavior (commonplace)
Underperforming in school relative to ability (commonplace)
Academic tutoring (up to 56%)
Repeat a grade (30% or more)
Placed in one or more special education programs (30–40%)
School suspensions (up to 46%)
School expulsions (10–20%)
Failure to graduate high school (10–35%)

Task performance

Poor persistence of effort/motivation
Greater variability in responding
Decreased performance/productivity under delayed rewards
Greater problems when delays are imposed within the task and as they increase in duration
Decline in performance as reinforcement changes from being continuous to intermittent
Greater disruption when noncontingent consequences occur during the task

Medical/health risks

Greater proneness to accidental injuries (up to 57%)
Possible delay in growth during childhood
Difficulties surrounding sleeping (up to 30–60%)
Greater driving risks: vehicular crashes and speeding tickets

They are clearly substantial and serious. At the very least, such findings ought to give considerable pause to anyone who would contend that ADHD is a phantom disease (Kohn, 1989; McGinnis, 1997), that it is simply a label being used to give a psychiatric diagnosis to otherwise normally exuberant children who do not want to take responsibility for their own behavior, that it merely reflects parental or teacher intolerance for such childhood exuberance, or that is an otherwise benign condition with little or no developmental, psychiatric, educational, or social consequences. Henceforth, such claims ought to be dismissed as the scientifically illiterate statements they represent rather than considered to reflect a true scientific debate over the validity and worth of the diagnosis of ADHD. That validity and utility have been well established by nearly a century of research and thousands of published studies on the distinguishing symptoms, associated impairments, and developmental risks that befall those children and adolescents unfortunate enough to receive a clinical diagnosis of this condition. Even more than the evidence presented in Chapter 2 (this volume), the evidence reviewed here overwhelmingly demonstrates that ADHD comprises a harmful dysfunction (Wakefield, 1992, 1997) and is therefore deserving of the status of a true mental disorder as much as or more than any other child psychiatric disorder currently known.

REFERENCES

Ackerman, P. T., Anhalt, J. M., & Dykman, R. A. (1986). Arithmetic automatization failure in children with attention and reading disorders: Associations and sequela. *Journal of Learning Disabilities, 19*, 222–232.

Alessandri, S. M. (1992). Attention, play, and social behavior in ADHD preschoolers. *Journal of Abnormal Child Psychology, 20*, 289–302.

American Psychiatric Association. (1987). *Diagnostic and statistical manual of mental disorders* (3rd ed., rev.). Washington, DC: Author.

American Psychiatric Association. (1994). *Diagnostic and statistical manual of mental disorders* (4th ed.). Washington, DC: Author.

Amin, K., Douglas, V. I., Mendelson, M. J., & Dufresne, J. (1993). Separable/integral classification by hyperactive and normal children. *Development and Psychopathology, 5*, 415–431.

Anastopoulos, A. D., Spisto, M. A., & Maher, M. C. (1994). The WISC-III Freedom from Distractibility Factor: Its utility in identifying children with attention deficit hyperactivity disorder. *Psychological Assessment, 6*, 368–371.

August, G. J. (1987). Production deficiencies in free recall: A comparison of hyperactive, learning-disabled, and normal children. *Journal of Abnormal Child Psychology, 15*, 429–440.

August, G. J., & Garfinkel, B. D. (1990). Comorbidity of ADHD and reading disability among clinic-referred children. *Journal of Abnormal Child Psychology, 18*, 29–45.

Baker, L., & Cantwell, D. P. (1987). A prospective psychiatric follow-up of children with speech/language disorders. *Journal of the American Academy of Child and Adolescent Psychiatry, 26*, 545–553.

Ball, J. D., & Koloian, B. (1995). Sleep patterns among ADHD children. *Clinical Psychology Review, 15*, 681–691.

Ball, J. D., Tiernan, M., Janusz, J., & Furr, A. (1997). Sleep patterns among children with attention-deficit hyperactivity disorder: A reexamination of parent perceptions. *Journal of Pediatric Psychology, 22*, 389–398.

Barber, M. A., & Milich, R. (1989, February). *The effects of reinforcement schedule and task characteristics on the behavior of attention-deficit hyperactivity disordered boys.* Paper presented at the annual meeting of the Society for Research in Child and Adolescent Psychopathology, Miami, FL.

Barber, M. A., Milich, R., & Welsh, R. (1996). Effects of reinforcement schedule and task difficulty on the performance of attention deficit hyperactivity disordered and control boys. *Journal of Clinical Child Psychology, 25*, 66–76.

Barkley, R. A. (1977). A review of stimulant drug research with hyperactive children. *Journal of Child Psychology and Psychiatry, 18*, 137–165.

Barkley, R. A. (1981). *Hyperactive children: A handbook for diagnosis and treatment.* New York: Guilford Press.

Barkley, R. A. (1989). The problem of stimulus control and rule-governed behavior in children with attention deficit disorder with hyperactivity. In J. Swanson & L. Bloomingdale (Eds.), *Attention deficit disorders* (pp. 203–234). New York: Pergamon Press.

Barkley, R. A. (1990). *Attention-Deficit Hyperactivity Disorder: A handbook for diagnosis and treatment.* New York: Guilford Press.

Barkley, R. A. (1997a). Behavioral inhibition, sustained attention, and executive functions: Constructing a unifying theory of ADHD. *Psychological Bulletin, 121,* 65–94.

Barkley, R. A. (1997b). *ADHD and the nature of self-control.* New York: Guilford Press.

Barkley, R., Cunningham, C., & Karlsson, J. (1983). The speech of hyperactive children and their mothers: Comparisons with normal children and stimulant drug effects. *Journal of Learning Disabilities, 16,* 105–110.

Barkley, R. A., DuPaul, G. J., & McMurray, M. B. (1990). A comprehensive evaluation of attention deficit disorder with and without hyperactivity. *Journal of Consulting and Clinical Psychology, 58,* 775–789.

Barkley, R. A., Fischer, M., Edelbrock, C. S., & Smallish, L. (1990). The adolescent outcome of hyperactive children diagnosed by research criteria: I. An 8 year prospective follow-up study. *Journal of the American Academy of Child and Adolescent Psychiatry, 29,* 546–557.

Barkley, R. A., Grodzinsky, G., & DuPaul, G. (1992). Frontal lobe functions in attention deficit disorder with and without hyperactivity: A review and research report. *Journal of Abnormal Child Psychology, 20,* 163–188.

Barkley, R. A., Guevremont, D. C., Anastopoulos, A. D., DuPaul, G. J., & Shelton, T. L. (1993). Driving-related risks and outcomes of attention deficit hyperactivity disorder in adolescents and young adults: A 3–5-year follow-up survey. *Pediatrics, 92,* 212–218.

Barkley, R. A., Karlsson, J., & Pollard, S. (1985). Effects of age on the mother–child interactions of hyperactive children. *Journal of Abnormal Child Psychology, 13,* 631–38.

Barkley, R. A., Koplowicz, S., Anderson, T., & McMurray, M.B. (1997). Sense of time in children with ADHD: Effects of duration, distraction, and stimulant medication. *Journal of the International Neuropsychological Society.*

Barkley, R. A., Murphy, K. R., & Kwasnik, D. (1996). Motor vehicle driving competencies and risks in teens and young adults with ADHD. *Pediatrics, 98,* 1089–1095.

Becker, J. T. (1994). Special section: Working memory. *Neuropsychology, 8,* 483–562.

Benezra, E., & Douglas, V. I. (1988). Short-term serial recall in ADDH, normal, and reading-disabled boys. *Journal of Abnormal Child Psychology, 16,* 511–525.

Berk, L. E. (1992). Children's private speech: An overview of theory and the status of research. In R. M. Diaz & L. E. Berk (Eds.), *Private speech: From social interaction to self-regulation* (pp. 17–54). Mahwah, NJ: Erlbaum.

Berk, L. E. (1994, November). Why children talk to themselves. *Scientific American,* 78–83.

Berk, L. E., & Garvin, R. A. (1984). Development of private speech among low-income appalachian children. *Developmental Psychology, 20,* 271–286.

Berk, L. E., & Landau, S. (1993). Private speech of learning disabled and normally achieving children in classroom academic and laboratory contexts. *Child Development, 64,* 556–571.

Berk, L. E., & Potts, M. K. (1991). Development and functional significance of private speech among attention-deficit hyperactivity disorder and normal boys. *Journal of Abnormal Child Psychology, 19,* 357–377.

Berkowitz, M. W. (1982). Self-control development and relation to prosocial behavior: A response to Peterson. *Merrill-Palmer Quarterly, 28,* 223–236.

Biederman, J., Milberger, S., Faraone, S. V., Guite, J., & Warburton, R. (1994). Associations between childhood asthma and ADHD: Issues of psychiatric comorbidity and familiality. *Journal of the American Academy of Child and Adolescent Psychiatry, 33,* 842–848.

Biederman, J., Milberger, S., Faraone, S. V., Lapey, K. A., Reed, E. D., & Seidman, L. J. (1995). No confirmation of Geschwind's hypothesis of associations between reading disability, immune disorders, and motor preference in ADHD. *Journal of Abnormal Child Psychology, 23,* 545–552.

Biederman, J., Wilens, T., Mick, E., Faraone, S. V., Weber, W., Curtis, S., Thornell, A., Pfister, K., Jetton, J. G., & Soriano, J. (1996). Is ADHD a risk factor for psychoactive substance use disorders? Findings from a four-year prospective follow-up study. *Journal of the American Academy of Child and Adolescent Psychiatry, 36,* 21–29.

Bijur, P., Golding, J., Haslum, M., & Kurzon, M. (1988). Behavioral predictors of injury in school-age children. *American Journal of Diseases of Children, 142,* 1307–1312.

Bivens, J. A., & Berk, L. E. (1990). A longitudinal study of the development of elementary school children's private speech. *Merrill-Palmer Quarterly, 36,* 443–463.

Blank, R., & Remschmidt, H. (1993). *Hyperkinetic syndrome: The role of allergy among psychological and neurological factors.* Unpublished manuscript, Kinderzentrum Munchen, Germany.

Boden, M. A. (1994). Precis of *The creative mind: Myths and mechanisms. Behavioral and Brain Sciences, 17,* 519–570.

Bohline, D. S. (1985). Intellectual and effective characteristics of attention deficit disordered children. *Journal of Learning Disabilities, 18,* 604–608.

Borcherding, B., Thompson, K., Krusei, M., Bartko, J., Rapoport, J. L., & Weingartner, H. (1988). Automatic and effortful processing in attention deficit/hyperactivity disorder. *Journal of Abnormal Child Psychology, 16,* 333–345.

Brady, K. D., & Denckla, M. B. (1994). *Performance of children with attention deficit hyperactivity disorder on the Tower of Hanoi task.* Unpublished manuscript, Johns Hopkins University School of Medicine, Baltimore.

Brand, E., & van der Vlugt, H. (1989). Activation: Base-level and responsivity—A search for subtypes of ADDH children by means of electrocardiac, dermal, and respiratory measures. In T. Sagvolden & T. Archer (Eds.), *Attention deficit disorder: Clinical and basic research* (pp. 137–150). Hillsdale, NJ: Erlbaum.

Breen, M. J. (1989). ADHD girls and boys: An analysis of attentional, emotional, cognitive, and family variables. *Journal of Child Psychology and Psychiatry, 30,* 711–716.

Brock, S. W., & Knapp, P. K. (1996). Reading comprehension abilities of children with attention-deficit/hyperactivity disorder. *Journal of Attention Disorders, 1,* 173–186.

Bronowski, J. (1977). Human and animal languages. *A sense of the future* (pp. 104–131). Cambridge, MA: MIT Press.

Brown, R. T. (1989). Creativity: What are we to measure? In J. A. Glover, R. R. Ronning, & C. R. Reynolds (Eds.), *Handbook of creativity* (pp. 3–32). New York: Plenum.

Brown, R. T., & Borden, K. A. (1986). Hyperactivity at adolescence: Some misconceptions and new directions. *Journal of Clinical Child Psychology, 15,* 194–209.

Burg, C., Hart, D., Quinn, P. O., & Rapoport, J. L. (1978). Clinical evaluation of one-year old infants: Possible predictors of risk for the "hyperactivity syndrome." *Journal of Pediatric Psychology, 3,* 164–167.

Butterbaugh, G., Giordani, B., Dillon, J., Alessi, N., Breen, M., & Berent, S. (1989, October). *Effortful learning in children with hyperactivity and/or depressive disorders.* Paper presented at the American Academy of Child and Adolescent Psychiatry, New York.

Cahn, D. A., & Marcotte, A. C. (1995). Rates of forgetting in attention deficit hyperactivity disorder. *Child Neuropsychology, 1,* 158–163.

Cantwell, D. P., & Satterfield, J. H. (1978). The prevalence of acdemic underachievement in hyperactive children. *Journal of Pediatric Psychology, 3,* 168–171.

Cappella, B., Gentile, J. R., & Juliano, D. B. (1977). Time estimation by hyperactive and normal children. *Perceptual and Motor Skills, 44,* 787–790.

Carlson, C. L., & Alexander, D. K. (1993, February). *Effects of variations in reinforcement and feedback strategies on the performance and intrinsic motivation of ADHD children.* Paper presented at the Society for Research in Child and Adolescent Psychopathology, Sante Fe, NM.

Carte, E. T., Nigg, J. T., & Hinshaw, S. P. (1996). Neuropsychological functioning, motor speed, and language processing in boys with and without ADHD. *Journal of Abnormal Child Psychology, 24,* 481–498.

Casey, J. E., Rourke, B. P., & Del Dotto, J. E. (1996). Learning disabilities in children with attention deficit disorder with and without hyperactivity. *Child Neuropsychology, 2,* 83–98.

Cataldo, M. F., Finney, J. W., Richman, G. S., Riley, A. W., Hook, R. J., Brophy, C. J., & Nau, P. A. (1992). Behavior of injured and uninjured children and their parents in a simulated hazardous setting. *Journal of Pediatric Psychology, 17,* 73–80.

Cerutti, D. T. (1989). Discrimination theory of rule-governed behavior. *Journal of the Experimental Analysis of Behavior, 51,* 259–276.

Chee, P., Logan, G., Schachar, R., Lindsay, P., & Wachsmuth, R. (1989). Effects of event rate and display time on sustained attention in hyperactive, normal, and control children. *Journal of Abnormal Child Psychology, 17,* 371–391.

Cole, P. M., Zahn-Waxler, C., & Smith, D. (1994). Expressive control during a disappointment: Variations related to preschoolers behavior problems. *Developmental Psychology, 30,* 835–846.

Conte, R., & Regehr, S. M. (1991). Learning and transfer of inductive reasoning rules in overactive children. *Cognitive Therapy and Research, 15,* 129–139.

Copeland, A. P. (1979). Types of private speech produced by hyperactive and nonhyperactive boys. *Journal of Abnormal Child Psychology, 7,* 169–177.

Corkum, P. V., Beig, S., Tannock, R., & Moldofsky, H. (1997, October). *Comorbidity: The potential link between attention-deficit/hyperactivity disorder and sleep problems.* Paper presented at the annual meeting of the American Academy of Child and Adolescent Psychiatry, Toronto, Canada.

Corkum, P. V., & Siegel, L. S. (1993). Is the continuous performance task a valuable research tool for use with children with attention-deficit–hyperactivity disorder? *Journal of Child Psychology and Psychiatry, 34,* 1217–1239.

Cunningham, S. J., & Knights, R. M. (1978). The performance of hyperactive and normal boys under differing reward and punishment schedules. *Journal of Pediatric Psychology, 3,* 195–201.

Dalebout, S. D., Nelson, N. W., Hleto, P. J., & Frentheway, B. (1991). Slective auditory attention and children with attention-deficit hyperactivity disorder: Effects of repeated measurement with and without methylphenidate. *Language, Speech, and Hearing Services in Schools, 22,* 219–227.

Danforth, J. S., Barkley, R. A., & Stokes, T. F. (1991). Observations of parent–child interactions with hyperactive children: Research and clinical implications. *Clinical Psychology Review, 11,* 703–727.

Davidson, L. L., Hughes, S. J., & O'Connor, P. A. (1988). Preschool behavior problems and subsequent risk of injury. *Pediatrics, 82,* 644–651.

Davidson, L. L., Taylor, E. A., Sandberg, S. T., & Thorley, G. (1992). Hyperactivity in school-age boys and subsequent risk of injury. *Pediatrics, 90,* 697–702.

Denckla, M. B., & Rudel, R. G. (1978). Anomalies of motor development in hyperactive boys. *Annals of Neurology, 3,* 231–233.

Denckla, M. B., Rudel, R. G., Chapman, C., & Krieger, J. (1985). Motor proficiency in dyslexic children with and without attentional disorders. *Archives of Neurology, 42,* 228–231.

Diaz, R. M., & Berk, L. E. (1992). *Private speech: From social interaction to self-regulation.* Mahwah, NJ: Erlbaum.

Dooling-Litfin, J. (1997). Time perception in children with ADHD. *ADHD Report, 5*(5), 13–16.

Douglas, V. I. (1972). Stop, look, and listen: The problem of sustained attention and impulse control in hyperactive and normal children. *Canadian Journal of Behavioural Science, 4,* 259–282.

Douglas, V. I. (1983). Attention and cognitive problems. In M. Rutter (Ed.), *Developmental neuropsychiatry* (pp. 280–329). New York: Guilford Press.

Douglas, V. I. (1988). Cognitive deficits in children with attention deficit disorder with hyperactivity. In L. M. Bloomingdale & J. A. Sergeant (Eds.), *Attention deficit disorder: Criteria, cognition, intervention* (pp. 65–82). London: Pergamon Press.

Douglas, V. I. (1989). Can Skinnerian psychology account for the deficits in attention deficit disorder?: A reply to Barkley. In L. Bloomingdale & J. Sergeant (Eds.), *Attention deficit disorders* (Vol. 4, pp. 235–254). New York: Pergamon Press.

Douglas, V. I., & Benezra, E. (1990). Supraspan verbal memory in attention deficit disorder with hyperactivity, normal, and reading disabled boys. *Journal of Abnormal Child Psychology, 18,* 617–638.

Douglas, V. I., & Parry, P. A. (1983). Effects of reward on delayed reaction time task performance of hyperactive children. *Journal of Abnormal Child Psychology, 11,* 313–326.

Douglas, V. I., & Parry, P. A. (1994). Effects of reward and non-reward on attention and frustration in attention deficit disorder. *Journal of Abnormal Child Psychology, 22,* 281–302.

Douglas, V. I., & Peters, K. G. (1978). Toward a clearer definition of the attentional deficit of hyperactive children. In G. A. Hale & M. Lewis (Eds.), *Attention and the developmente of cognitive skills* (pp. 173–248). New York: Plenum.

Dykman, R. A., & Ackerman, P. T. (1992). Attention deficit disorder and specific reading disability: Separate but often overlapping disorders. In. S. Shaywitz, & B. A. Shaywitz (Eds.), *Attention deficit disorder comes of age: Toward the twenty-first century* (pp. 165–184). Austin, TX: Pro-Ed.

Ernst, M., Liebenauer, L. L., King, A. C., Fitzgerald, G. A., Cohen, R. M., & Zametkin, A. J. (1994). Reduced brain metabolism in hyperactive girls. *Journal of the American Academy of Child and Adolescent Psychiatry, 33*, 858–868.

Faraone, S. V., Biederman, J., Lehman, B., Keenan, K., Norman, D., Seidman, L. J., Kolodny, R., Kraus, I., Perrin, J., & Chen, W. (1993). Evidence for the independent familial transmission of attention deficit hyperactivity disorder and learning disabilities: Results from a family genetic study. *American Journal of Psychiatry, 150*, 891–895.

Felton, R. H., Wood, F. B., Brown, I.S., Campbell, S. K., & Harter, M. R. (1987). Separate verbal memory and naming deficits in attention deficit disorder and reading disability. *Brain and Language, 31*, 171–184.

Fergusson, D. M., & Horwood, L. J. (1992). Attention deficit and reading achievement. *Journal of Child Psychology and Psychiatry, 33*, 375–385.

Firestone, P., Lewy, F., & Douglas, V. I. (1976). Hyperactivity and physical anomalies. *Canadian Psychiatric Association Journal, 21*, 23–26.

Fischer, M., Barkley, R., Fletcher, K., & Smallish, L. (1990). The adolescent outcome of hyperactive children diagnosed by research criteria, II: Academic, attentional, and neuropsychological status. *Journal of Consulting and Clinical Psychology, 58*, 580–588.

Frauenglass, M. H., & Diaz, R. M. (1985). Self-regulatory functions of children's private speech: A critical analysis and recent challenges to Vygotsky's theory. *Developmental Psychology, 21*, 3537–364.

Freibergs, V., & Douglas, V. I. (1969). Concept learning in hyperactive and normal children. *Journal of Abnormal Psychology, 74*, 388–395.

Frick, P. J., Kamphaus, R. W., Lahey, B. B., Loeber, R., Christ, M. A. G., Hart, E. L., & Tannenbaum, L. E. (1991). Academic underachievement and the disruptive behavior disorders. *Journal of Consulting and Clinical Psychology, 59*, 289–294.

Friedman, H. S., Tucker, J. S., Schwartz, J. E., Tomlinson-Keasey, C., Martin, L. R., Wingard, D. L., & Criqui, M. H. (1995). Psychosocial and behavioral predictors of longevity: The aging and death of the "Termites." *American Psychologist, 50*, 69–78.

Frost, L. A., Moffitt, T. E., & McGee, R. (1989). Neuropsychological correlates of psychopathology in an unselected cohort of young adolescents. *Journal of Abnormal Psychology, 98*, 307–313.

Funk, J. B., Chessare, J. B., Weaver, M. T., & Exley, A. R. (1993). Attention deficit hyperactivity disorder, creativity, and the effects of methylphenidate. *Pediatrics, 91*, 816–819.

Fuster, J. M. (1989). *The prefrontal cortex.* New York: Raven.

Gascon, G. G., Johnson, R., & Burd, L. (1986). Central auditory processing and attention deficit disorders. *Journal of Child Neurology, 1*, 27–33.

Geffner, D., Lucker, J. R., & Koch, W. (1996). Evaluation of auditory discrimination in children with ADD and without ADD. *Child Psychiatry and Human Development, 26*, 169–180.

Golden, J. (1996). Are tests of working memory and inattention diagnostically useful in children with ADHD? *ADHD Report, 4*(5), 6–8.

Goldman-Rakic, P. S. (1995). Architecture of the prefrontal cortex and the central executive. In J. Grafman, K. J. Holyoak, & F. Boller (Eds.), *Annals of the New York Academy of Sciences: Vol. 769. Structure and functions of the human prefrontal cortex* (pp. 71–83). New York: New York Academy of Sciences.

Gordon, M. (1979). The assessment of impulsivity and mediating behaviors in hyperctive and nonhyperactive children. *Journal of Abnormal Child Psychology, 7*, 317–326.

Greene, R. W., Biederman, J., Faraone, S. V., Ouellette, C. A., Penn, C., & Griffin, S. M. (1996). Toward a new psychometric definition of social disability in children with attention-deficit hyperactivity disorder. *Journal of the American Academy of Child and Adolescent Psychiatry, 35*, 571–578.

Greene, R. W., Biederman, J., Faraone, S. V., Sienna, M., & Garcia-Jetton, J. (1997). Adolescent outcome of boys with attention-deficit/hyperactivity disorder and social disability: Results from a 4-year longitudinal follow-up study. *Journal of Consulting and Clinical Psychology, 65,* 758–767.

Greenhill, L., Anich, J. P., Goetz, R., Hanton, C., & Davies, M. (1983). Sleep architecture and REM sleep measures in prepubertal children with attention deficit disorder with hyperactivity. *Sleep, 6,* 91–101.

Greve, K. W., Williams, M. C., & Dickens, T. J., Jr. (1996, February). *Concept formation in attention disordered children.* Poster presented at the meeting of the International Neuropsychological Society, Chicago.

Grodzinsky, G. M., & Diamond, R. (1992). Frontal lobe functioning in boys with attention-deficit hyperactivity disorder. *Developmental Neuropsychology, 8,* 427–445.

Grskovic, J. A., Zentall, S. S., & Stormont-Spurgin, M. (1995). Time estimation and planning abilities: Students with and without mild disabilities. *Behavioral Disorders, 20,* 197–203.

Gualtieri, C. T., & Hicks, R. E. (1985). Neuropharmacology of methylphenidate and a neural substrate for childhood hyperactivity. *Psychiatric Clinics of North America, 8,* 875–892.

Haenlein, M., & Caul, W. F. (1987). Attention deficit disorder with hyperactivity: A specific hypothesis of reward dysfunction. *Journal of the American Academy of Child and Adolescent Psychiatry, 26,* 356–362.

Hall, S. J., Halperin, J. M., Schwartz, S. T., & Newcorn, J. H. (1997). Behavioral and executive functions in children with attention-deficit hyperactivity disorder and reading disability. *Journal of Attention Disorders, 1,* 235–247.

Halperin, J. M., & Gittelman, R. (1982). Do hyperactive children and their siblings differ in IQ and academic achievement? *Psychiatry Research, 6,* 253–258.

Hamlett, K. W., Pellegrini, D. S., & Conners, C. K. (1987). An investigation of executive processes in the problem-solving of attention deficit disorder–hyperactive children. *Journal of Pediatric Psychology, 12,* 227–240.

Hart, E. L., Lahey, B. B., Hynd, G. W., Loeber, R., & McBurnett, K. (1995). Association of chronic overanxious disorder with atopic rhinitis in boys: A four-year longitudinal study. *Journal of Clinical Child Psychology, 24,* 332–337.

Hartsough, C. S., & Lambert, N. M. (1985). Medical factors in hyperactive and normal children: Prenatal, developmental, and health history findings. *American Journal of Orthopsychiatry, 55,* 190–210.

Hastings, J., & Barkley, R. A. (1978). A review of psychophysiological research with hyperactive children. *Journal of Abnormal Child Psychology, 7,* 413–337.

Hayes, S. (1989). *Rule-governed behavior.* New York: Plenum.

Hayes, S. C., Gifford, E. V., & Ruckstuhl, Jr. (1996). Relational frame theory and executive function: A behavioral analysis. In G. R. Lyon & N. A. Krasnegor (Eds.), *Attention, memory, and executive function* (pp. 279–306). Baltimore: Paul H. Brookes.

Hinshaw, S. P. (1987). On the distinction between attentional deficits/hyperactivity and conduct problems/aggression in child psychopathology. *Psychological Bulletin, 101,* 443–447.

Hinshaw, S. P. (1992). Externalizing behavior problems and academic underachievement in childhood and adolescence: Causal relationships and underlying mechanisms. *Psychological Bulletin, 111,* 127–155.

Hinshaw, S. P., Heller, T., & McHale, J. P. (1992). Covert antisocial behavior in boys with attention-deficit hyperactivity disorder: External validation and effects of methylphenidate. *Journal of Consulting and Clinical Psychology, 60,* 274–281.

Hinshaw, S. P., & Melnick, S. M. (1995). Peer relationships in boys with attention-deficit hyperactivity disorder with and without comorbid aggression. *Development and Psychopathology, 7,* 627–647.

Hinshaw, S. P., Morrison, D. C., Carte, E. T., & Cornsweet, C. (1987). Factorial dimensions of the Revised Behavior Problem Checklist: Replication and validation within a kindergarten sample. *Journal of Abnormal Child Psychology, 15,* 309–327.

Hinshaw, S. P., Simmel, C., & Heller, T. L. (1995). Multimethod assessment of covert antisocial behavior in children: Laboratory observations, adult ratings, and child self-report. *Psychological Assessment, 7,* 209–219.

Holdnack, J. A., Moberg, P. J., Arnold, S. E., Gur, R. C., & Gur, R. E. (1995). Speed of processing and verbal learning deficits in adults diagnosed with attention deficit disorder. *Neuropsychiatry, Neuropsychology, and Behavioral Neurology, 8,* 282–292.

Hoy, E., Weiss, G., Minde, K., & Cohen, N. (1978). The hyperactive child at adolescence: Cognitive, emotional, and social functioning. *Journal of Abnormal Child Psychology, 6,* 311–324.

Humphries, T., Koltun, H., Malone, M., & Roberts, W. (1994). Teacher-identified oral langauage difficulties among boys with attention problems. *Developmental and Behavioral Pediatrics, 15,* 92–98.

Iaboni, F., Douglas, V. I., & Baker, A. G. (1995). Effects of reward and response costs on inhibition in ADHD children. *Journal of Abnormal Psychology, 104,* 232–240.

Jacklin, C. G., Maccoby, E. E., & Halverson, C. F. Jr. (1980). Minor anomalies and preschool behavior. *Journal of Pediatric Psychology, 5,* 199–205.

Kaplan, B. J., McNichol, J., Conte, R. A., & Moghadam, H. K. (1987). Sleep disturbance in preschool-aged hyperactive and nonhyperactive children. *Pediatrics, 80,* 839–844.

Kaufman, A. S., & Kaufman, N. L. (1983). *Kaufman Assessment Battery for Children.* Circle Pines, MN: American Guidance Services.

Keith, R. W., & Engineer, P. (1991). Effects of methylphenidate on the auditory processing abilities of children with attention deficit-hyperactivity disorder. *Journal of Learning Disabilities, 24,* 630–636.

Keltner, D., Moffitt, T. E., & Stouthamer-Loeber, M. (1995). Facial expressions of emotion and psychopathology in adolescent boys. *Journal of Abnormal Psychology, 104,* 644–652.

Kendall, P., & Braswell, L. (1984). *Cognitive-behavioral therapy for impulsive children.* New York: Guilford Press.

Kesner, R. P., Hopkins, R. O., & Fineman, B. (1994). Item and order dissociation in humans with prefrontal cortex damage. *Neuropsychologia, 32,* 881–891.

Klorman, R. (1992). Cognitive event-related potentials in attention deficit disorder. In S. E. Shaywitz & B. A. Shaywitz (1992). *Attention deficit disorder comes of age: Toward the twenty-first century* (pp. 221–244). Austin, TX: Pro-Ed.

Klorman, R., Brumaghim, J. T., Coons, H. W., Peloquin, L., Strauss, J., Lewine, J. D., Borgstedt, A. D., & Goldstein, M. G. (1988). The contributions of event-related potentials to understanding effects of stimulants on information processing in attention deficit disorder. In L. M. Bloomingdale & J. A. Sergeant (Eds.), *Attention deficit disorder: Criteria, cognition, intervention* (pp. 199–218). London: Pergamon Press.

Kohlberg, L., Yaeger, J., & Hjertholm, E. (1968). Private speech: Four studies and a review of theories. *Child Development, 39,* 691–736.

Kohn, A. (1989, November). Suffer the restless children. *Atlantic Monthly,* pp. 90–100.

Krouse, J. P., & Kaufman, J. M. (1982). Minor physical anomalies in exceptional children: A review and critique of research. *Journal of Abnormal Child Psychology, 10,* 247–264.

Kupietz, S. S., Camp, J. A., & Weissman, A. D. (1976). Reaction time performance of behaviorally deviant children: Effects of prior preparatory interval and reinforcement. *Journal of Child Psychology and Psychiatry, 17,* 123–131.

Lambert, N. M., & Sandoval, J. (1980). The prevalence of learning disabilities in a sample of children considered hyperactive. *Journal of Abnormal Child Psychology, 8,* 33–50.

Lambert, N. M., Sandoval, J., & Sassone, D. (1978). Prevalence of hyperactivity in elementary school children as a function of social system definers. *American Journal of Orthopsychiatry, 48,* 446–463.

Landau, S., Berk, L. E., & Mangione, C. (1996, March). *Private speech as a problem-solving strategy in the face of academic challenge: The failure of impulsive children to get their act together.* Paper presented at the meeting of the National Association of School Psychologists, Atlanta.

Langley, J., McGee, R., Silva, P., & Williams, S. (1983). Child behavior and accidents. *Journal of Pediatric Psychology, 8,* 181–189.

LaVeck, B., Hammond, M. A., & LaVeck, G. D. (1980). Minor congenital anomalies and behavior in different home environments. *Journal of Pediatrics, 97,* 940–941.

Lerer, R. J. (1977). Do hyperactive children tend to have abnormal palmer creases? Report of a suggestive association. *Clinical Pediatrics, 16,* 645–647.

Loge, D. V., Staton, D., & Beatty, W. W. (1990). Performance of children with ADHD on tests sensitive to frontal lobe dysfunction. *Journal of the American Academy of Child and Adolescent Psychiatry, 29,* 540–545.

Lou, H. C., Henriksen, L., & Bruhn, P. (1984). Focal cerebral hypoperfusion in children with dysphasia and/or attention deficit disorder. *Archives of Neurology, 41*, 825–829.

Lou, H. C., Henriksen, L., Bruhn, P., Borner, H., & Nielsen, J. B. (1989). Striatal dysfunction in attention deficit and hyperkinetic disorder. *Archives of Neurology, 46*, 48–52.

Lucker, J. R., Geffner, D., & Koch, W. (1996). Perception of loudness in children with ADD and without ADD. *Child Psychiatry and Human Development, 26*, 181–190.

Ludlow, C., Rapoport, J., Brown, G., & Mikkelson, E. (1979). The differential effects of dextroamphetamine on the language and communication skills of hyperactive and normal children. In R. Knights & D. Bakker (Eds.), *Rehabilitation, treatment, and management of learning disorders.* Baltimore: University Park Press.

Lufi, D., Cohen, A., & Parish-Plass, J. (1990). Identifying ADHD with the WISC-R and the Stroop Color and Word Test. *Psychology in the Schools, 27*, 28–34.

Luk, S. (1985). Direct observations studies of hyperactive behaviors. *Journal of the American Academy of Child and Adolescent Psychiatry, 24*, 338–344.

Lynam, D., Moffitt, T., & Stouthamer-Loeber, M. (1993). Explaining the relation between IQ and delinquency: Class, race, test motivation, school failure, or self-control? *Journal of Abnormal Psychology, 102*, 187–196.

MacLeod, D., & Prior, M. (1996). Attention deficits in adolescents with ADHD and other clinical groups. *Child Neuropsychology, 2*, 1–10.

Manheimer, D. I., & Mellinger, G. D. (1967). Personality characteristics of the child accident repeater. *Child Development, 38*, 491–513.

Marcotte, A. C., & Stern, C. (1997). Qualitative analysis of graphomotor output in children with attentional disorders. *Child Neuropsychology, 3*, 147–153.

Mariani, M., & Barkley, R. A. (1997). Neuropsychological and academic functioning in preschool children with attention deficit hyperactivity disorder. *Developmental Neuropsychology, 13*, 111–129.

Matochik, J. A., Rumsey, J. M., Zametkin, A. J., Hamburger, S. D., & Cohen, R. M. (1996). Neuropsychological correlates of familial attention-deficit hyperactivity disorder in adults. *Neuropsychiatry, Neuropsychology, and Behavioral Neurology, 9*, 186–191.

McGee, R., & Share, D. L. (1988). Attention deficit disorder–hyperactivity and academic failure: Which comes first and what should be treated? *Journal of the American Academy of Child and Adolescent Psychiatry, 27*, 318–327.

McGee, R., Stanton, W. R., & Sears, M. R. (1993). Allergic disorders and attention deficit disorder in children. *Journal of Abnormal Child Psychology, 21*, 79–88.

McGee, R., Williams, S., & Feehan, M. (1992). Attention deficit disorder and age of onset of problem behaviors. *Journal of Abnormal Child Psychology, 20*, 487–502.

McGee, R., Williams, S., Moffitt, T., & Anderson, J. (1989). A comparison of 13–year old boys with attention deficit and/or reading disorder on neuropsychological measures. *Journal of Abnormal Child Psychology, 17*, 37–53.

McGee, R., Williams, S., & Silva, P. A. (1984). Behavioral and developmental characteristics of aggressive, hyperactive, and aggressive–hyperactive boys. *Journal of the American Academy of Child Psychiatry, 23*, 270–279.

McGinnis, J. (1997, September). Attention deficit disaster. *Wall Street Journal.*

McMahon, S. A., & Greenberg, L. M. (1977). Serial neurologic examination of hyperactive children. *Pediatrics, 59*, 584–587.

Methany, A. P., Jr., & Fisher, J. E. (1984). Behavioral perspectives on children's accidents. In M. Wolraich & D. K. Routh (Eds.), *Advances in behavioral pediatrics* (Vol. V, pp. 221–263). Greenwich, CT: JAI Press.

Michon, J. A. (1985). Introduction. In J. Michon & T. Jackson (Eds.), *Time, mind, and behavior.* Berlin, Germany: Springer-Verlag.

Milberger, S., Biederman, J., Faraone, S. V., Chen, L., & Jones, J. (1996). ADHD is associated with early initiation of cigarette smoking in children and adolescents. *Journal of the American Academy of Child and Adolescent Psychiatry, 36*, 37–44.

Milich, R. (in press). The response of children with ADHD to failure: If at first you don't succeed, do you try, try again? *School Psychology Review.*

Milich, R., & Kramer, J. (1985). Reflections on impulsivity: An empirical investigation of impulsivity as a construct. In K. Gadow & I. Bialer (Eds.), *Advances in learning and behavioral disabilities* (Vol. 3, pp. 57–94). Greenwich, CT: JAI Press.

Milich, R., & Loney, J. (1979). The factor composition of the WISC for hyperkinetic/MBD males. *Journal of Learning Disabilities, 12*, 67.

Mischel, W., Shoda, Y., & Peake, P. K. (1988). The nature of adolescent competencies predicted by preschool delay of gratification. *Journal of Personality and Social Psychology, 54*, 687–696.

Mitchell, E. A., Aman, M. G., Turbott, S. H., & Manku, M. (1987). Clinical characteristics and serum essential fatty acid levels in hyperactive children. *Clinical Pediatrics, 26*, 406–411.

Moffitt, T. E. (1990). Juvenile delinquency and attention deficit disorder: Boys' developmental trajectories from age 3 to 15. *Child Development, 61*, 893–910.

Moffitt, T. E., & Silva, P. A. (1988). Self-reported delinquency, neuropsychological deficit, and history of attention deficit disorder. *Journal of Abnormal Child Psychology, 16*, 553–569.

Mori, L., & Peterson, L. (1995). Knowledge of safety of high and low active–impulsive boys: Implications for child injury prevention. *Journal of Clinical Child Psychology, 24*, 370–376.

Moss, W. L., & Sheiffe, W. A. (1994). Can we differentially diagnose an attention deficit disorder without hyperactivity from a central auditory processsing problem? *Child Psychiatry and Human Development, 25*, 85–96.

Munir, K., Biederman, J., & Knee, D. (1987). Psychiatric comorbidity in patients with attention deficit disorder: A controlled study. *Journal of the American Academy of Child and Adolescent Psychiatry, 26*, 844–848.

Nada-Raja, S., Langley, J. D., McGee, R., Williams, S. M., Begg, D. J., & Reeder, A. I. (1997). Inattentive and hyperactive behaviors and driving offenses in adolescence. *Journal of the American Academy of Child and Adolescent Psychiatry, 36*, 515–522.

Oosterlaan, J., & Sergeant, J. A. (1995). Response choice and inhibition in ADHD, anxious, and aggressive children: The relationship between S–R compatibility and stop signal task. In J. A. Sergeant (Ed.), *Eunethydis: European approaches to hyperkinetic disorder* (pp. 225–240). Amsterdam: University of Amsterdam.

Ott, D. A., & Lyman, R. D. (1993). Automatic and effortful memory in children exhibiting attention deficit hyperactivity disorder. *Journal of Clinical Child Psychology, 22*, 420–427.

Ownby, R. L., & Matthews, C. G. (1985). On the meaning of the WISC-R third factor: Relations to selected neuropsychological measures. *Journal of Consulting and Clinical Psychology, 53*, 531–534.

Parry, P. A., & Douglas, V. I. (1983). Effects of reinforcement on concept identification in hyperactive children. *Journal of Abnormal Child Psychology, 11*, 327–340.

Pelham, W. E., Bender, M. E., Caddell, J., Booth, S., & Moorer, S. H. (1985). Methylphenidate and children with attention deficit disorder. *Archives of General Psychiatry, 42*, 948–952.

Pelham, W. E., Milich, R., & Walker, J. L. (1986). Effects of continuous and partial reinforcement and methylphenidate on learning in children with attention deficit disorder. *Journal of Abnormal Psychology, 95*, 319–325.

Pennington, B. F., Grossier, D., & Welsh, M. C. (1993). Contrasting cognitive deficits in attention deficit disorder versus reading disability. *Developmental Psychology, 29*, 511–523.

Pless, I. B., Taylor, H. G., & Arsenault, L. (1995). The relationship between vigilance deficits and traffic injuries involving children. *Pediatrics, 95*, 219–224.

Prior, M., Leonard, A., & Wood, G. (1983). A comparison study of preschool children diagnosed as hyperactive. *Journal of Pediatric Psychology, 8*, 191–207.

Purvis, K. L., & Tannock, R. (1997). Language abilities in children with attention deficit hyperactivity disorder, reading disabilities, and normal controls. *Journal of Abnormal Child Psychology, 25*, 133–144.

Quinn, P. O., & Rapoport, J. L. (1974). Minor physical anomalies and neurological status in hyperactive boys. *Pediatrics, 53*, 742–747.

Quinn, P. O., Renfield, M., Burg, C., & Rapoport, J. L. (1977). Minor physical anomalies: A newborn screening and 1-year follow-up. *Journal of the American Academy of Child Psychiatry, 16*, 662–669.

Rapoport, J. L., Pandoni, C., Renfield, M., Lake, C. R., & Ziegler, M. G. (1977). Newborn dopamine beta hydroxylase, minor physical anomalies, and infant temperament. *American Journal of Psychiatry, 134*, 676–679.

Rapport, M. D., DuPaul, G. J., Stoner, G., & Jones, J. T. (1986). Comparing classroom and clinic measures of attention deficit disorder: Differential, idiosyncratic, and dose–response effects of methylphenidate. *Journal of Consulting and Clinical Psychology, 54*, 334–341.

Rapport, M. D., Tucker, S. B., DuPaul, G. J., Merlo, M., & Stoner, G. (1986). Hyperactivity and frustration: The influence of control over and size of rewards in delaying gratification. *Journal of Abnormal Child Psychology, 14*, 181–204.

Reader, M. J., Harris, E. L., Schuerholz, L. J., & Denckla, M. B. (1994). Attention deficit hyperactivity disorder and executive dysfunction. *Developmental Neuropsychology, 10*, 493–512.

Reebye, P. N. (1997, October). *Diagnosis and treatment of ADHD in preschoolers.* Paper presented at the annual meeting of the American Academy of Child and Adolescent Psychiatry, Toronto, Canada.

Riccio, C. A., Hynd, G. W. Cohen, M. J., Hall, J., Molt, L. (1994). Comorbidity of central auditory processing disorder and attention-deficit hyperactivity disorder. *Journal of the American Academy of Child Psychiatry, 33*, 849–857.

Roizen, N. J., Blondis, T. A., Irwin, M., & Stein, M. (1994). Adaptive functioning in children with attention-deficit hyperactivity disorder. *Archives of Pediatric and Adolescent Medicine, 148*, 1137–1142.

Rosen, B. N., & Peterson, L. (1990). Gender differences in children's outdoor play injuries: A review and an integration. *Clinical Psychology Review, 10*, 187–205.

Rosenbaum, M. & Baker, E. (1984). Self-control behavior in hyperactive and nonhyperactive children. *Journal of Abnormal Child Psychology, 12*, 303–318.

Rosenthal, R. H., & Allen, T. W. (1978). An examination of attention, arousal, and learning dysfunctions of hyperkinetic children. *Psychological Bulletin, 85*, 689–715.

Roth, N., Beyreiss, J., Schlenzka, K., & Beyer, H. (1991). Coincidence of attention deficit disorder and atopic disorders in children: Empirical findings and hypothetical background. *Journal of Abnormal Child Psychology, 19*, 1–13.

Rothenberger, A. (1995). Electrical brain activity in children with hyperkinetic syndrome: Evidence of a frontal cortical dysfunction. In J. A. Sergeant (Ed.), *Eunethydis: European approaches to hyperkinetic disorder* (pp. 255–270). Amsterdam: University of Amsterdam.

Sadeh, M., Ariel, R., & Inbar, D. (1996). Rey–Osterrieth and Taylor Complex Figures: Equivalent measures of visual organization and visual memory in ADHD and normal children. *Child Neuropsychology, 2*, 63–71.

Safer, D., & Allen, R. (1976). *Hyperactive children.* New York: Wiley.

Sagvolden, T., Wultz, B., Moser, E. I., Moser, M., & Morkrid, L. (1989). Results from a comparative neuropsychological research program indicate altered reinforcement mechanisms in children with ADD. In T. Sagvolden & T. Archer (Eds.), *Attention deficit disorder: Clinical and basic research* (pp. 261–286). Hillsdale, NJ: Erlbaum.

Satterfield, J. H., Hoppe, C. M., & Schell, A. M. (1982). A prospective study of delinquency in 110 adolescent boys with attention deficit disorder and 88 normal adolescent boys. *American Journal of Psychiatry, 139*, 795–798.

Schweitzer, J. B., & Sulzer-Azaroff, B. (1995). Self-control in boys with attention-deficit hyperactivity disorder: Effects of added stimulation and time. *Journal of Child Psychology and Psychiatry, 36*, 671–686.

Seidman, L. J., Benedict, K. B., Biederman, J., Bernstein, J. H., Seiverd, K., Milberger, S., Norman, D., Mick, E., & Faraone, S. V. (1995). Performance of children with ADHD on the Rey–Osterrieth Complex Figure: A pilot neuropsychological study. *Journal of Child Psychology and Psychiatry, 36*, 1459–1473.

Seidman, L. J., Biederman, J., Faraone, S. V., Milberger, S., Norman, D., Seiverd, K., Benedict, K., Guite, J., Mick, E., & Kiely, K. (1995). Effects of family history and comorbidity on the neuropsychological performance of children with ADHD: Preliminary findings. *Journal of the American Academy of Child and Adolescent Psychiatry, 34*, 1015–1024.

Seidman, L. J., Biederman, J., Faraone, S. V., Weber, W., & Ouellette, C. (1997). Toward defining a neuropsychology of attention deficit–hyperactivity disorder: Performance of children and adolescence from a large clinically referred sample. *Journal of Consulting and Clinical Psychology, 65*, 150–160.

Semrud-Clikeman, M., Biederman, J., Sprich-Buckminster, S., Lehman, B. K., Faraone, S. V., & Norman, D. (1992). Comorbidity between ADDH and learning disability: A review and report in a clinically referred sample. *Journal of the American Academy of Child and Adolescent Psychiatry, 31*, 439–448.

Senior, N., Towne, D., & Huessy, D. (1979). Time estimation and hyperactivity, a replication. *Perceptual and Motor Skills, 49*, 289–290.

Sergeant, J. A., & van der Meere, J. (1988). What happens when the hyperactive child commits an error? *Psychiatry Research, 24*, 157–164.

Sergeant, J., & van der Meere, J. J. (1990). Convergence of approaches in localizing the hyperactivity deficit. In B. B. Lahey & A. E. Kazdin (Eds.), *Advances in clinical child psychology* (Vol. 13, pp. 207–245). New York: Plenum.

Shapiro, E. G., Hughes, S. J., August, G. J., & Bloomquist, M. L. (1993). Processing emotional information in children with attention deficit hyperactivity disorder. *Developmental Neuropsychology, 9*, 207–224.

Shaw, G. A., & Brown, G. (1990). Laterality and creativity concomitants of attention problems. *Developmental Neuropsychology, 6*, 39–57.

Shaywitz, S. E., & Shaywitz, B. A. (1984). Diagnosis and management of attention deficit disorder: A pediatric perspective. *Pediatric Clinics of North America, 31*, 429–457.

Sieg, K. G., Gaffney, G. R., Preston, D. F., & Hellings, J. A. (1995). SPECT brain imaging abnormalities in attention deficit hyperactivity disorder. *Clinical Nuclear Medicine, 20*, 55–60.

Skinner, B. F. (1953). *Science and human behavior.* New York: Macmillan.

Skinner, B. F. (1969). *Contingencies of reinforcement: A theoretical analysis.* New York: Appleton-Century-Crofts.

Sleator, E. K., & Pelham, W. E. (1986). *Attention deficit disorder.* Norwalk, CT: Appleton-Century-Crofts.

Solanto, M. V. (1990). The effects of reinforcement and response-cost on a delayed response task in children with attention deficit hyperactivity disorder: A research note. *Journal of Child Psychology and Psychiatry, 31*, 803–808.

Solanto, M. V., Wender, E. H., & Bartell, S. S. (1997). Effects of methylphenidate and behavioral contingencies on sustained attention in attention-deficit hyperactivity disorder: A test of the reward dysfunction hypothesis. *Journal of Child and Adolescent Psychopharmacology, 7*, 123–136.

Sonuga-Barke, E. J., Lamparelli, M., Stevenson, J., Thompson, M., & Henry, A. (1994). Behaviour problems and pre-school intellectual attainment: The associations of hyperactivity and conduct problems. *Journal of Child Psychology and Psychiatry, 35*, 949–960.

Sonuga-Barke, E. J. S., Taylor, E., & Hepinstall, E. (1992). Hyperactivity and delay aversion: II. The effect of self versus externally imposed stimulus presentation periods on memory. *Journal of Child Psychology and Psychiatry, 33*, 399–409.

Sonuga-Barke, E. J. S., Taylor, E., Sembi, S., & Smith, J. (1992). Hyperactivity and delay aversion: I. The effect of delay on choice. *Journal of Child Psychology and Psychiatry, 33*, 387–398.

Spencer, T. J., Biederman, J., Harding, M., O'Donnell, D., Faraone, S. V., & Wilens, T. E. (1996). Growth deficits in ADHD children revisited: Evidence for disorder-associated growth delays? *Journal of the American Academy of Child and Adolescent Psychiatry, 35*, 1460–1469.

Stein, M. A., Szumowski, E., Blondis, T. A., & Roizen, N. J. (1995). Adaptive skills dysfunction in ADD and ADHD children. *Journal of Child Psychology and Psychiatry, 36*, 663–670.

Sternberg, R. J., & Lubart, T. I. (1996). Investing in creativity. *American Psychologist, 51*, 677–688.

Stewart, M. A., Pitts, F. N., Craig, A. G., & Dieruf, W. (1966). The hyperactive child syndrome. *American Journal of Orthopsychiatry, 36*, 861–867.

Stewart, M. A., Thach, B. T., & Friedin, M. R. (1970). Accidental poisoning and the hyperactive child syndrome. *Disease of the Nervous System, 31*, 403–407.

Still, G. F. (1902). Some abnormal psychical conditions in children. *Lancet, 1*, 1008–1012, 1077–1082, 1163–1168.

Szatmari, P., Offord, D. R., & Boyle, M. H. (1989). Correlates, associated impairments, and patterns of service utilization of children with attention deficit disorders: Findings from the Ontario Child Health Study. *Journal of Child Psychology and Psychiatry, 30*, 205–217.

Tannock, R. (1996, January). *Discourse deficits in ADHD: Executive dysfunction as an underlying mechanism?* Paper presented at the annual meeting of the International Society for Research in Child and Adolescent Psychopathology, Santa Monica, CA.

Tannock, R., Purvis, K. L., & Schachar, R. J. (1992). Narrative abilities in children with attention deficit hyperactivity disorder and normal peers. *Journal of Abnormal Child Psychology, 21*, 103–117.

Tant, J. L., & Douglas, V. I. (1982). Problem-solving in hyperactive, normal, and reading-disabled boys. *Journal of Abnormal Child Psychology, 10*, 285–306.

Tarver-Behring, S., Barkley, R. A., & Karlsson, J. (1985). The mother–child interactions of hyperactive boys and their normal siblings. *American Journal of Orthopsychiatry, 55*, 202–209.

Taylor, E., Sandberg, S., Thorley, G., & Giles, S. (1991). *The epidemiology of childhood hyperactivity.* London: Oxford University Press.

Trites, R. L., Tryphonas, H., & Ferguson, H. B. (1980). Diet treatment for hyperactive children with food allergies. In R. M. Knight & D. Bakker (Eds.), *Treatment of hyperactive and learning disordered children* (pp. 151–166). Baltimore: University Park Press.

Trommer, B. L., Hoeppner, J. B., Rosenberg, R. S., Armstrong, K. J., & Rothstein, J. A. (1988). Sleep disturbances in children with attention deficit disorder. *Annals of Neurology, 24*, 325.

Ullman, D. G., Barkley, R. A., & Brown, H. W. (1978). The behavioral symptoms of hyperkinetic children who successfully responded to stimulant drug treatment. *American Journal of Orthopsychiatry, 48*, 425–437.

van der Meere, J., Gunning, W. B., & Stemerdink, N. (1996). Changing response set in normal development and in ADHD children with and without tics. *Journal of Abnormal Child Psychology, 24*, 767–786.

van der Meere, J., Hughes, K. A., Borger, N., & Sallee, F. R. (1995). The effect of reward on sustained attention in ADHD children with and without CD. In J. A. Sergeant (Ed.), *Eunethydis: European approaches to hyperkinetic disorder* (pp. 241–253). Amsterdam: University of Amsterdam.

van der Meere, J., & Sergeant, J. (1988a). Focused attention in pervasively hyperactive children. *Journal of Abnormal Child Psychology, 16*, 627–640.

van der Meere, J., & Sergeant, J. (1988b). Controlled processing and vigilance in hyperctivity: Time will tell. *Journal of Abnormal Child Psychology, 16*, 641–656.

van der Meere, J., Shalev, R., Borger, N., & Gross-Tsur, V. (1995). Sustained attention, activation and MPH in ADHD: A research note. *Journal of Child Psychology and Psychiatry, 36*, 697–703.

van der Meere, J., Vreeling, H. J., & Sergeant, J. (1992). A motor presetting study in hyperactive, learning disabled and control children. *Journal of Child Psychology and Psychiatry, 33*, 1347–1354.

Voelker, S. L., Carter, R. A., Sprague, D. J., Gdowski, C. L., & Lachar, D. (1989). Developmental trends in memory and metamemory in children with attention deficit disorder. *Journal of Pediatric Psychology, 14*, 75–88.

Vygotsky, L. S. (1978). *Mind in society.* Cambridge, MA: Harvard University Press.

Vygotsky, L. S. (1987). Thinking and speech. In *The collected works of L. S. Vygotsky: Vol. 1. Problems in general psychology* (N. Minick, Trans.). New York: Plenum.

Wakefield, J. C. (1992). The concept of mental disorder: On the boundary between biological facts and social values. *American Psychologist, 47*, 373–388.

Wakefield, J. C. (1997). Normal inability versus pathological disability; Why Ossorio's definition of mental disorder is not sufficient. *Clinical Psychology: Science and Practice, 4*, 249–258.

Waldrop, M. F., Bell, R. Q., & Goering, J. D. (1976). Minor physical anomalies and inhibited behavior in elementary school girls. *Journal of Child Psychology and Psychiatry, 17*, 113–122.

Waldrop, M. F., Bell, R. Q., McLaughlin, B., & Halverson, C. F., Jr. (1978). Newborn minor physical anomalies predict short attention span, peer aggression, and impulsivity at age 3. *Science, 199*, 563–564.

Walker, N. W. (1982). Comparison of cognitive tempo and time estimation by young boys. *Perceptual and Motor Skills, 54*, 715–722.

Weiss, G., & Hechtman, L. (1993). *Hyperactive children grown up* (2nd ed.). New York: Guilford Press.

Welner, Z., Welner, A., Stewart, M., Palkes, H., & Wish, E. (1977). A controlled study of siblings of hyperactive children. *Journal of Nervous and Mental Disease, 165*, 110–117.

Werry, J. S., Elkind, G. S., & Reeves, J. S. (1987). Attention deficit, conduct, oppositional, and anxiety disorders in children: III. Laboratory differences. *Journal of Abnormal Child Psychology, 15,* 409–428.

Werry, J. S., Minde, K., Guzman, A., Weiss, G., Dogan, K., & Hoy, E. (1972). Studies on the hyperactive child: VII. Neurological status compared with neurotic and normal children. *American Journal of Orthopsychiatry, 42,* 441–451.

Weyandt, L. L., & Willis, W. G. (1994). Executive functions in school-aged children: Potential efficacy of tasks in discriminating clinical groups. *Developmental Neuropsychology, 19,* 27–38.

Whalen, C. K., Henker, B., Collins, B. E., McAuliffe, S., & Vaux, A. (1979). Peer interaction in structured communication task: Comparisons of normal and hyperactive boys and of methylphenidate (Ritalin) and placebo effects. *Child Development, 50,* 388–401.

White, J., Barratt, E., & Adams, P. (1979). The hyperactive child in adolescence: A comparative study of physiological and behavioral patterns. *Journal of the American Academy of Child Psychiatry, 18,* 154–169.

Wigal, T., Swanson, J. M., Douglas, V. I., Wigal, S. B., Stoiber, C. M., & Fulbright, K. K. (1993). *Reinforcement effects on frustration and persistence in children with attention-deficit hyperactivity disorder.* Manuscript submitted for publication.

Wilens, T. E., Biederman, J., & Spencer, T. (1994). Clonidine for sleep disturbances associated with attention-deficit hyperactivity disorder. *Journal of the American Academy of Child and Adolescent Psychiatry, 33,* 424–426.

Wilkison, P. C., Kircher, J. C., McMahon, W. M., & Sloane, H. N. (1995). Effects of methylphenidate on reward strength in boys with attention-deficit hyperactivity disorder. *Journal of the American Academy of Child and Adolescent Psychiatry, 34,* 877–885.

Zahn, T. P., Krusei, M. J. P., & Rapoport, J. L. (1991). Reaction time indices of attention deficits in boys with disruptive behavior disorders. *Journal of Abnormal Child Psychology, 19,* 233–252.

Zametkin, A. J., Liebenauer, L. L., Fitzgerald, G. A., King, A. C., Minkunas, D. V., Herscovitch, P., Yamada, E. M., & Cohen, R. M. (1993). Brain metabolism in teenagers with attention-deficit hyperactivity disorder. *Archives of General Psychiatry, 50,* 333–340.

Zametkin, A. J., Nordahl, T. E., Gross, M., King, A. C., Semple, W. E., rumsey, J., Hamburger, S., & Cohen, R. M. (1990). Cerebral glucose metabolism in adults with hyperactivity of childhood onset. *The New England Journal of Medicine, 323,* 1361–1366.

Zelazo, P. R., Reznick, J. S., & Pinon, D. E. (1995). Response control and the execution of verbal rules. *Developmental Psychology, 31,* 508–517.

Zentall, S. S. (1985). A context for hyperactivity. In K. D. Gadow & I. Bialer (Eds.), *Advances in learning and behavioral disabilities* (Vol. 4, pp. 273–343). Greenwich, CT: JAI Press.

Zentall, S. S. (1988). Production deficiencies in elicited language but not in the spontaneous verbalizations of hyperactive children. *Journal of Abnormal Child Psychology, 16,* 657–673.

Zentall, S. S., & Smith, Y. S. (1993). Mathematical performance and behavior of children with hyperactivity with and without coexisting aggression. *Behaviour Research and Therapy, 31,* 701–710.

Zentall, S. S., Smith, Y. N., Lee, Y. B., & Wieczorek, C. (1994). Mathematical outcomes of attention-deficit hyperactivity disorder. *Journal of Learning Disabilities, 27,* 510–519.

Chapter 4

COMORBID DISORDERS, SOCIAL RELATIONS, AND SUBTYPING

This chapter discusses those additional problems often associated with Attention-Deficit/ Hyperactivity Disorder (ADHD) in the realm of coexisting psychiatric disorders and social relationship difficulties. In addition, it explores the critical issue of subtyping approaches that may be clinically useful in subdividing the quite heterogeneous population of those diagnosed as ADHD.

PSYCHIATRIC DISORDERS

The diagnosis of ADHD conveys a significant risk for other coexisting psychiatric disorders. Up to 44% of ADHD children may have at least one other psychiatric disorder, 32% have two others, and 11% have at least three other disorders (Szatmari, Offord, & Boyle, 1989a). As a group, ADHD children are rated as having more symptoms of anxiety, depression or dysthymia, and low self-esteem than normal children or children with learning disabilities who do not have ADHD (Biederman, Faraone, Mick, Moore, & Lelon, 1996; Bohline, 1985; Breen & Barkley, 1983, 1984; Jensen, Burke, & Garfinkel, 1988; Jensen, Shervette, Xenakis, & Richters, 1993; Margalit & Arieli, 1984; Weiss, Hechtman, & Perlman, 1978). This risk for associated emotional and conduct problems is indicated in Figure 4.1, which shows the typical profile for 26 hyperactive and 26 normal children on the Personality Inventory for Children (Breen & Barkley, 1983).

Anxiety and Mood Disorders

Given this higher occurrence of emotional symptoms in ADHD children, are they more likely to meet full criteria for a diagnosis of other affective or mood disorders? Definitely. Studies at Massachusetts General Hospital suggest that 20–36% of children with ADHD have a major

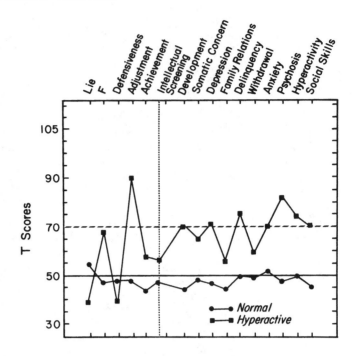

FIGURE 4.1. The profile of *T* scores for 26 hyperactive and 26 normal boys on the Personality Inventory for Children. From Breen & Barkley (1983). Copyright 1983 by Plenum Publishing Corporation. Reprinted by permission.

affective disorder and 27–30% meet criteria for an anxiety disorder, such as overanxious disorder (Biederman, Newcorn, & Sprich, 1991; Munir, Biederman, & Knee, 1987). Szatmari et al. (1989a), in their large epidemiological survey, found that 17% of girls and 21% of boys with ADHD between 4 and 11 years of age had at least one of these neurotic disorders, while this figure rose to 24% for boys and 50% for girls during the adolescent years. Jensen et al. (1993) found that nearly 49% of their sample of ADHD children had an anxiety disorder, depression, or both. Other studies also found that between 13% and 30% of ADHD children have a comorbid anxiety or mood disorder (Anderson, Williams, McGee, & Silva, 1987; Bird, Canino, Rubio-Stipec, et al., 1988; Jensen et al., 1988; P. Cohen, Velez, Brook, & Smith, 1989). Reviews of the literature on the overlap of ADHD with anxiety disorders reported a range of 10% to 40% and suggested that about 25% of ADHD children, on average, were likely to have such a disorder (Biederman, Newcorn, & Sprich, 1991; Tannock, in press). The presence of anxiety with ADHD seems also to significantly reduce the level of impulsiveness in these children below that seen in ADHD children without anxiety, though the latter remain more impulsive than normal children (Epstein, Goldberg, Conners, & March, 1997; Gordon, Mettelman, & Irwin, 1990; Pliszka, 1989, 1992; Tannock, in press). A review of the literature on the comorbidity of major depression or mood disorder (dysthymia) found a range between 15% and 75%. However, most studies reported rates of 9–32% with major depression (Biederman et al., 1991). The comorbidity of anxiety or mood disorder along with ADHD is often associated with a history of greater family and personal stress, greater parental symptoms of anxiety and mood disturbance, and reduced responsiveness to stimulant medication (see Jensen, Martin, & Cantwell, 1997, for a review). Though not well established, this group of comorbid children may respond better to tricyclic antidepressants than do those ADHD children without comorbidity for anxiety disorder or other internalizing symptoms (Biederman, Baldessarini, Wright, Keenan, & Faraone, 1993; Jensen et al., 1997). Research does suggest that the anxiety disorders in families with ADHD children are transmitted independently within these families with the higher rate of anxiety disorders representing an artifact of referral bias to mental health clinics (Biederman, Faraone, & Lapey, 1992; Biederman & Faraone, 1997). However, major depression does demonstrate a linkage with ADHD in these families such that risk for one disorder in a child predisposes to risk for the other disorder among family members and vice versa (Biederman, Faraone, & Lapey, 1992; Biederman & Faraone, 1997).

Bipolar disorder occurs in approximately 1% of children (Lewinsohn, Klein, & Seeley, 1995). It is a serious, severe, and potentially life-threatening mental disorder (G. A. Carlson, 1990; Geller & Luby, 1997). The relationship of ADHD to Bipolar Disorder (BPD), or manic depression, has been controversial and has received considerable attention since the last edition of this text was published. Milberger, Biederman, Faraone, Murphy, and Tsuang (1995) found that 11% of their ADHD children had BPD; the figure was 10% among girls with ADHD (Biederman, 1997). In a separate study by Biederman et al. (1992), they found BPD in 13% of ADHD children seen at a child psychiatry clinic and 10% of children seen in a health maintenance organization. In a 4-year follow-up involving many of these children, 12% of the ADHD adolescents now met criteria for BPD (Biederman, Faraone, Mick, Wozniak, et al., 1996). Another study reported a rate of 20% of ADHD children having BPD (Wozniak et al., 1995). The subjects with BPD were considerably more impaired in their functioning than were those with ADHD alone, experiencing a greater risk for hospitalization and for additional forms of psychopathology (Biederman, Faraone, Mick, Wozniak, et al., 1996; Biederman et al., 1995; Wozniak et al., 1995). Children with bipolar disorder who have ADHD also appear to experience an earlier onset to their BPD than do those without ADHD (Faraone, Biederman, Wozniak, et al., 1997). Faraone and colleagues (Faraone, Biederman, Wozniak, et al., 1997) suggest that ADHD with bipolar disorder is a distinct subtype of ADHD. When ADHD children are subdivided by those who do or do not have BPD, both groups demonstrate a higher rate of ADHD among their relatives. However, only that subgroup of ADHD children who have BPD have a higher rate of BPD as well as major depression with severe impairment among their relatives. This research group has also suggested that this subtype (ADHD + BPD) may overlap genetically with that subgroup of ADHD who have Conduct Disorder (Faraone & Biederman, 1997). Thus, children with ADHD appear to have a small but significant risk for BPD (6–20%) whereas children with childhood-onset BPD have a very high probability of having ADHD (98%) (Wozniak et al., 1995). Yet, adolescents with BPD have a substantially lower rate of ADHD (11%) (Lewinsohn et al., 1995). However, the symptom list for BPD in editions of the *Diagnostic and Statistical Manual of Mental Disorders* (DSM; see, e.g., American Psychiatric Association, 1980, 1994) includes items that overlap with ADHD. Thus it may be that this overlap between disorders in children with ADHD is entirely a function of this overlap in diagnostic criteria. Milberger et al. (1995) used a subtraction method to remove the symptom overlap and found that 47% of the ADHD children with BPD retained the latter diagnosis. This suggests that about 6% of ADHD children may have a legitimate comorbidity for BPD that is not an artifact of merely having more severe ADHD symptoms.

Greater somatic complaints have also been noted in ADHD compared to normal children (Barkley, DuPaul, & McMurray, 1990). Complaints of headaches and stomachaches and vague somatic complaints, as well as complaints related to the aforementioned physical problems (i.e., colds, otitis media, and allergies), appear to be more common among ADHD children. Szatmari, Boyle, and Offord (1989) found that as many as 24% of ADHD boys and 35% of ADHD girls between 12 and 16 years met criteria for a somatization disorder.

Oppositional and Conduct Disorder

It is widely accepted by scientists studying ADHD children that they display a greater degree of difficulties with oppositional and defiant behavior, aggressiveness and conduct problems, and even antisocial behavior relative to normal children (see Figure 4.1). Over 65% of clinic-referred samples may show significant problems with stubbornness, defiance or refusal to obey, temper tantrums, and verbal hostility toward others (Loney & Milich, 1982; Stewart, Pitts, Craig, & Dieruf, 1966). Studies suggest that 54% to 67% of ADHD children and adolescents will meet full diagnostic criteria for Oppositional Defiant Disorder (Barkley, DuPaul, & McMurray, 1990; Barkley & Biederman, 1997; Biederman et al., 1992; Faraone & Biederman, 1997; Fischer, Barkley, Edelbrock, & Smallish, 1990; P. Cohen et al., 1989) with an average across studies of at least 35% (Biederman et al., 1991). These same studies also indicate that as many as 20% to 56% of ADHD children and 44% to 50% of adolescents will be diagnosed as having the more serious problem of Conduct Disorder (see also Szatmari, Boyle, & Offord, 1989). Studies of Puerto Rican children indicate considerably higher rates of comorbidity than the previous studies suggest. Bird and colleagues (Bird, Gould, & Staghezza, 1993) found that 93% of the Puerto Rican children having ADHD also had either Oppositional Defiant or Conduct Disorder. The most common types of conduct problems found in these studies are lying, stealing, truancy, and, to a lesser degree, physical aggression.

Earlier, some investigators had expressed the belief that ADHD and conduct problems were the same or quite similar disorders (Shapiro & Garfinkel, 1986; Stewart, deBlois & Cummings 1981), but more recent research indicates that relatively pure cases of both can be found and that these disorders are likely to have different correlates and outcomes (see Hinshaw, 1987; Jensen et al., 1997; Werry, 1988, for reviews). Children with conduct disorders usually come from backgrounds with greater social adversity and have a higher prevalence of psychiatric disorders, particularly Antisocial Personality Disorder, substance dependence and abuse, major depression, and Conduct Disorder, among their parents and relatives than ADHD children without significant conduct problems (Faraone, Biederman, Jetton, & Tsuang, 1997; Jensen et al., 1997; McGee, Williams, & Silva, 1984b; Reeves, Werry, Elkind, & Zametkin, 1987; Szatmari, Boyle, & Offord, 1989). In contrast, ADHD children are more likely to have developmental delays and cognitive deficits than are those with Conduct Disorder (McGee, Williams, & Silva, 1984a; Szatmari, Boyle, & Offord, 1989). When children have both disorders, they often display the mixture of both the cognitive and attentional/inhibitory deficits typical of ADHD as well as a greater likelihood of factors associated with social adversity, family psychiatric problems, and family conflict (Barkley et al., 1991; Jensen et al., 1997). They are also more likely to have an earlier onset to their antisocial activities, greater persistence of those activities, more school disciplinary consequences, greater substance use and abuse, more traffic offenses and vehicular crashes, and generally a worse overall outcome than those ADHD children who do not have Conduct Disorder (Barkley, Fischer, Edelbrock, & Smallish, 1990; Barkley et al., 1991; Jensen et al., 1997; Moffitt, 1990).

SOCIAL RELATIONSHIPS

This section examines the difficulties ADHD children often have in their family and peer relationships.

Parent–Child Interactions

ADHD is classified in DSM-IV (American Psychiatric Association, 1994) as a Disruptive Behavior Disorder because of the significant difficulties it creates for children in disrupting their social conduct and general social adjustment. The interpersonal behaviors of those with ADHD, as noted earlier, are often characterized as more impulsive, intrusive, excessive, disorganized, engaging, aggressive, intense, and emotional. And so they are "disruptive" of the smoothness of the ongoing stream of social interactions, reciprocity, and cooperation that may constitute the children's daily life with others (Whalen & Henker, 1992). This makes sense given the theoretical model presented later; ADHD is associated with an impairment in self-regulation and this impairment must radiate into the social ecology of these children, affecting others and the manner in which they may reciprocate.

Research finds that ADHD affects the interactions of children with their parents and, hence, the manner in which parents may respond to these children. Those with ADHD are more talkative, negative and defiant, less compliant and cooperative, more demanding of assistance from others, and less able to play and work independently of their mothers (Barkley, 1985; Danforth, Barkley, & Stokes, 1991; Gomez & Sanson, 1994; Mash & Johnston, 1982). Their mothers are less responsive to their questions, more negative and directive, and less rewarding of their behavior (Danforth et al., 1991). Mothers of ADHD children have been shown to give both more commands and more rewards to their ADHD sons than to their ADHD daughters (Barkley, 1989; Befera & Barkley, 1984) but also to be more emotional and acrimonious in their interactions with their sons (Buhrmester, Camparo, Christensen, Gonzalez, & Hinshaw, 1992; Taylor, Sandberg, Thorley, & Giles, 1991). ADHD children seem to be somewhat less problematic for their fathers than for their mothers (Buhrmester et al., 1992; Tallmadge & Barkley, 1983), but even the latter interactions are different from those of normal father–child dyads. Research demonstrates that these mother–child conflicts may result in increased father–child conflict when mothers and fathers interact jointly (triadically) with their hyperactive children, especially hyperactive boys (Buhrmester et al., 1992). Such increased maternal negativity and acrimony toward sons in these interactions has been shown to predict greater noncompliance in classroom and play settings and greater covert stealing away from home, even when the level of the child's own negativity and parental psychopathology are statistically controlled in the analyses (Anderson, Hinshaw, & Simmel, 1994). These negative parent–child interaction patterns occur in the preschool age group (Cohen, Sullivan, Minde, Novak, & Keens, 1983) and may be at their most negative and stressful (to the parent) in this age range (Mash & Johnston, 1982, 1990). With increasing age, the degree of conflict in these interactions lessens but remains deviant from normal into later childhood (Barkley, Karlsson, & Pollard, 1985; Mash & Johnston, 1982) and adolescence (Barkley, Anastopoulos, Guevremont, & Fletcher, 1992; Barkley, Fischer, Edelbrock, & Smallish, 1991). Negative parent–child interactions in childhood have been observed to be significantly predictive of continuing parent–child conflicts 8 to 10 years later in adolescence in families with ADHD children (Barkley et al., 1991). Few differences are noted between the interactions of mothers of ADHD children with those children as compared to their interactions with the siblings of the ADHD children (Tarver-Behring, Barkley, & Karlsson, 1985).

Important in this line of family research has been the discovery that *it is the presence of comorbid Oppositional Defiant Disorder (ODD) that is associated with most of the conflicts* noted in the mother–child interactions of ADHD children and adolescents (Barkley, Anastopoulos, et al., 1992; Barkley et al., 1991). In a sequential analysis of these parent–teen interaction sequences, investigators have noted that it is the immediate or first lag in the sequence that is most important in determining the behavior of the other member of the dyad

(Fletcher, Fischer, Barkley, & Smallish, 1996). That is, the behavior of each member is determined mainly by the immediately preceding behavior of the other member and not by earlier behaviors of either member in the chain of interactions. The interactions of the comorbid ADHD/ODD group reflected a strategy best characterized as "tit for tat" in that the type of behavior (positive, neutral, or negative) of each member was most influenced by the same type of behavior emitted immediately preceding it. Mothers of ADHD only and normal teens were more likely to utilize positive and neutral behaviors regardless of the immediately preceding behavior of their teens, characterized as a "be nice and forgive" strategy that is thought to be more mature and more socially successful for both parties in the long run (Fletcher, Fischer, Barkley, & Smallish, 1996). Even so, those with ADHD alone are still found to be deviant from normal in these interaction patterns even though less so than the comorbid ADHD/ODD group. The presence of comorbid ODD has also been shown to be associated with greater maternal stress and psychopathology as well as marital difficulties (Barkley, Anastopoulos, et al., 1992; Barkley et al., 1991). Yet parents of ADHD children, more than parents of normal children, appear to sense that the disruptive behavior of their children is internally rather than externally caused, less controllable by the child, and more stable over development (Johnston & Freeman, 1997). In contrast, they evaluate the prosocial behavior of their ADHD children as less internal and less stable than do control parents.

The interaction conflicts in families with ADHD children are not limited only to parent–child interactions. Increased conflicts have been observed between ADHD children and their siblings relative to normal child–sibling dyads (Mash & Johnston, 1983; Taylor et al., 1991). Research on the larger domain of family functioning has also shown that families of ADHD children experience more parenting stress and decreased sense of parenting competence and self-esteem (Anastopoulos, Guevremont, Shelton, & DuPaul, 1992; Breen & Barkley, 1988; Fischer, 1990; Johnston, 1996; Mash & Johnston, 1990), increased alcohol consumption in parents (Cunningham, Benness, & Siegel, 1988; Pelham & Lang, 1993), decreased extended family contacts (Cunningham et al., 1988), and increased marital conflict, separations, and divorce as well as maternal depression in parents of ADHD children (Befera & Barkley, 1984; Cunningham et al., 1988; Barkley, Fischer, et al., 1990; Lahey et al., 1988; Taylor et al., 1991). Again, the comorbid association of ADHD with ODD, or its later stage of Conduct Disorder (CD), is linked to even greater degrees of parenting stress, parental psychopathology, marital discord, and divorce than in ADHD-only children (Barkley, Fischer, et al., 1990; Barkley et al., 1991; Johnston, 1996; Lahey et al., 1988; Taylor et al., 1991). Interestingly, Pelham and Lang (1993) have shown that the increased alcohol consumption in these parents is, in part, directly a function of the stressful interactions they have with their ADHD children.

Research has demonstrated that the primary direction of effects within these interactions is from child to parent (Fischer, 1990; Mash & Johnston, 1990) rather than the reverse. That is, much of the disturbance in the interaction seems to stem from the effects of the child's excessive, impulsive, unruly, noncompliant, and emotional behavior on the parent rather than from the effects of the parent's behavior on the child. This finding was documented primarily through studies that evaluated the effects of stimulant medication on the behavior of the children and their interaction patterns with their mothers. Such research found that medication improves the compliance of those with ADHD and reduces their negative, talkative, and generally excessive behavior such that their parents reduce their levels of directive and negative behavior as well (Barkley & Cunningham, 1979; Barkley, Cunningham, & Karlsson, 1983; Danforth et al., 1991; Humphries, Kinsbourne, & Swanson, 1978). These medication effects are noted even in the preschool age group of children with ADHD (Barkley, 1988) as well as in those in late childhood (Barkley, Karlsson, Pollard, & Murphy, 1985) and in both sexes of ADHD children (Barkley, 1989). Besides a general reduction in the negative, disruptive, and conflictual interaction patterns of these children with parents resulting from stimulant medication, general family functioning also seems to improve when ADHD children are treated with stimulant medication (Schachar, Taylor, Wieselberg, Thorley, & Rutter, 1987).

These patterns of disruptive, intrusive, excessive, negative, and emotional social interactions of ADHD children have been found to occur in their interactions with teachers (Whalen, Henker, & Dotemoto, 1980). Like the interactions of ADHD children with their parents, the interactions of these children with their teacher have also been shown to be significantly improved by administration of stimulant medication (Whalen et al., 1980).

Peer Relations

Pelham and Bender (1982) once estimated that more than 50% of ADHD children have significant problems in social relationships with other children. Mothers (Campbell & Paulauskas, 1979), teachers (Barkley, DuPaul, & McMurray, 1990), and peers (Johnston, Pelham, & Murphy, 1985; Pope, Bierman, & Mumma, 1989) find hyperactive children to be significantly more aggressive, disruptive, domineering, intrusive, noisy, and socially rejected in their social relations than normal children, especially if they are male hyperactives and particularly if they are aggressive (Hinshaw & Melnick, 1995; Milich, Landau, Kilby, & Whitten, 1982; Pelham & Bender, 1982).

Studies that have directly observed these peer interactions suggest that the inattentive, disruptive, off-task, immature, provocative, aggressive, and noncompliant behaviors of ADHD children quickly elicit a pattern of controlling and directive behavior from their peers when they must work together (Clark, Cheyne, Cunningham, & Siegel, 1988; Cunningham & Siegel, 1987; Hinshaw, 1992; Hinshaw & Melnick, 1995; Whalen, Henker, Collins, Finck, & Dotemoto, 1979; Whalen, Henker, Collins, McAuliffe, & Vaux, 1979). There also seems to be a tendency for ADHD children to accept other ADHD children as playmates more than do normal children (Hinshaw & Melnick, 1995). In their communication patterns, ADHD children in these studies have been found to talk more but to be less efficient in organizing and communicating information to peers with whom they are asked to work. Moreover, despite talking more, the ADHD children are less likely to respond to the questions or verbal interactions of their peers. Hence, there is clearly less reciprocity in the social exchanges of hyperactive children with their peers (Cunningham & Siegel, 1987; Landau & Milich, 1988). ADHD children have also been shown to have less knowledge about social skills and appropriate behavior with others (Grenell, Glass, & Katz, 1987). Among ADHD children, those who are the most sensation seeking, emotionally reactive, aggressive, and noncompliant received the greatest disapproval from their peers (Hinshaw & Melnick, 1995)

Some research suggests that ADHD children tend to have a more external locus of control than do normal children (Linn & Hodge, 1982). That is, they are more likely to view the events that happen to them as outside their personal control or due to "fate." They also tend to have more inflated perceptions of themselves, their likelihood of success in tasks, and the extent to which others like them than do normal children (Diener & Milich, 1997; Milich & Greenwell, 1991; Milich & Okazaki, 1991; O'Neill & Douglas, 1991). Although this finding may indicate an immaturity in the development of self-awareness and perceptions, given that younger children tend to overestimate their own abilities, a recent study suggests that this inflated self-assessment may be a form of self-protection (Diener & Milich, 1997; Milich, 1994), an effort to present themselves in the best possible light to protect their self-esteem and mask their self-perceived incompetence.

Those ADHD children who are also aggressive may display an additional tendency to overinterpret the actions of others toward them as actually having hostile intentions and are therefore more likely to respond with aggressive counterattacks over minimal if any provocation (Milich & Dodge, 1984). Such communication problems, skills deficits, attribution biases, and interaction conflicts could easily lead to the ADHD children, especially those who are aggressive, being rejected as playmates by their classmates and neighborhood peers in very short order. Many have noted that it takes few social exchanges over a period of only 20 to 30 minutes between ADHD and normal children for normal children to find the ADHD children disruptive, unpredictable, and aggressive and hence to react to them with aversion, criticism, and rejection, and sometimes even counteraggression. Certainly they are likely to withdraw from the ADHD child when opportunities to do so arise (Milich et al., 1982; Pelham & Bender, 1982; Pelham & Milich, 1984).

PARENTAL PSYCHIATRIC DISORDERS

Almost 20 years ago, reports were appearing that biological parents and extended relatives of hyperactive children were more likely to have had hyperactivity themselves in childhood (Morrison & Stewart, 1973), with 5% of the mothers and 15% of the fathers reporting this problem (vs. 2% in the control group). More recent studies have corroborated these earlier and less methodologically sophisticated studies and indicate that biological parents of ADHD children are themselves more likely to have ADHD, or at least some of the residual characteristics of the disorder (Alberts-Corush, Firestone, & Goodman, 1986; Deutsch et al., 1982; Singer, Stewart, & Pulaski, 1981). However, the prevalence of ADHD in the parents in these later studies is even higher than originally suspected. In general, it seems that 15–20% of the mothers and 20–30% of the fathers of ADHD children may also have ADHD themselves. For instance, Faraone and Biederman (1997) reported that 13% of fathers of ADHD girls and 21% of their mothers had ADHD. This greater risk of ADHD is also seen among the biological siblings of ADHD children: approximately 17–37% may have the disorder (Faraone & Biederman, 1997; Welner, Welner, Stewart, Palkes, & Wish, 1977). In general, the average risk of ADHD among the first-degree biological relatives of ADHD children is between 25% and 37% (Biederman, Gastfriend, & Jellinek, 1986; Biederman, Baldessarini, Wright, Knee, & Harmatz, 1989; Biederman, Munir, & Knee, 1987), or five to seven times the risk in the general population.

Parents of ADHD children are also more likely to experience a variety of other psychiatric disorders, the most common of which appear to be conduct problems and antisocial behavior (25–28%), alcoholism (14–25%), hysteria or affective disorder (10–27%), and learning disabilities (Cantwell, 1972; Faraone & Biederman, 1997; Morrison & Stewart, 1973; Singer et al., 1981). Even if they are not abusing alcohol, parents of ADHD children consume more alcohol than do those of normal children (Cunningham et al., 1988). Biederman and colleagues (Biederman, 1997; Biederman et al., 1987, 1989; Faraone & Biederman, 1997) also reported a higher prevalence of affective disorders, particularly major depression, among the parents and siblings of ADHD children (27–32%), whether boys or girls, as compared to control children (6%).

Family Psychiatric Disturbance and Child Conduct Disorder

In 1983, August and Stewart suggested that the greater incidence of antisocial behavior and alcoholism among these first-degree relatives of ADHD children was primarily associated with ADHD children who also had conduct problems and antisocial behavior. ADHD children free of these comorbid conduct problems often had only a greater history of ADHD and learning disorders among their relatives. Hence, the greater family histories of alcoholism and antisocial behavior is associated only with antisocial behavior in children, not with ADHD (Stewart et al., 1980). These findings have been replicated in more recent studies (Biederman et al., 1987; Faraone & Biederman, 1997) in which up to 46% of the first-degree relatives of ADHD children with comorbid ODD/CD also had ODD, CD, or antisocial personality as compared to only 5–13% of the relatives of pure ADHD children. Sex of the ADHD child did not appear to result in any differences in this risk to family members if the child had comorbid CD (Faraone & Biederman, 1997). A study by Lahey, Piacentini, et al. (1988) likewise demonstrated this clear relationship between familial antisocial behavior and affective disorders in relatives with that of antisocial behavior in ADHD children. All these studies taken together suggest a somewhat linear relationship between the severity of aggressive and oppositional behavior in ADHD children and the degree of antisocial behavior, alcoholism, and affective disorders among their parents and extended relatives. In other words, ADHD children with little or no aggressive behavior are likely to have considerably fewer of these psychiatric disorders among their parents than those with ADHD and ODD. However, children in the latter group are likely to have fewer of these problems in their parents than do children with ADHD and CD (a more severe form of ODD) who have the highest rates of these disorders among all the ADHD subgroups.

SUBTYPING OF ADHD

As can be seen from the foregoing review, ADHD comprises a heterogeneous group of children believed to have in common the characteristics of developmentally inappropriate levels of inattention, impulsivity, and in some cases overactivity. Despite these apparent commonalities, children so diagnosed are acknowledged to present with a diversity of related psychiatric symptoms, family backgrounds, developmental courses, and responses to treatments. Given this diversity, increasing scientific attention has been paid to identifying approaches to subtyping this disorder into more homogeneous, clinically meaningful subgroups. Such subtyping approaches are clinically useful if they provide important differential predictions about etiologies, developmental courses, outcomes, or responses to therapies between the subtypes. In short, they must show some value beyond the differences that would be expected on the measures on which the subtyping occurred or those measures known to be related to them. Many ways of subtyping ADHD children have been employed, some without much clinical merit, such as sorting ADHD children on the presence or absence of reading disorders (Halperin, Gittelman, Klein, & Rudel, 1984). Three approaches to subtyping, however, have proven promising or have established themselves as clinically useful.

Subtyping on Hyperactivity

One subtyping approach introduced in DSM-III (American Psychiatric Association, 1980) is based on the presence or absence of significant degrees of overactivity. Children with ADHD were sorted into those having ADD (Attention Deficit Disorder) with Hyperactivity or those without Hyperactivity. This method of creating subtypes was later deemphasized in the DSM-III-R (American Psychiatric Association, 1987) given the lack of research at that time on the utility of this approach. But it has returned in DSM-IV (see Chapter 2) with the label Predominantly Inattentive and with the inclusion now of impulsiveness with hyperactivity as the feature that is either ruled in or out to create the subtypes. Since the last edition of this text, little new research has focused on distinctions between these subtypes. More thorough reviews of this literature can be found elsewhere (Barkley, Grodzinsky, & DuPaul, 1992; Lahey & Carlson, 1992; Goodyear & Hynd, 1992)

Several of the early studies on this issue found little if any important differences between ADD children with hyperactivity (+H) as compared to those without it (–H) (Maurer & Stewart, 1980; Rubinstein & Brown, 1984). Later ones, however, indicated that +H children were more oppositional and aggressive, more rejected by peers, had lower self-esteem, were more depressed, and may be more impaired in cognitive and motor test performance than –H children (Barkley, DuPaul, & McMurray, 1990; Berry, Shaywitz, & Shaywitz, 1985; Cantwell & Baker, 1992; Carlson, Lahey, Frame, Walker, & Hynd, 1987; Hern & Hynd, 1992; Hynd et al., 1991; Lahey, Schaughency, Hynd, Carlson, & Nieves, 1987; King & Young, 1982; Morgan, Hynd, Riccio, & Hall, 1996; Wheeler & Carlson, 1994). Our own study of these subtypes found that more than twice as many ADD+H children than –H children are diagnosed as ODD (41% vs. 19%), using DSM-III-R criteria, and more than three times as many as having Conduct Disorder (21% vs. 6%) (Barkley, DuPaul, & McMurray, 1990). The +H children are also more likely to have more speech and language problems, greater marital discord between their parents, and more maternal psychiatric disorders (Cantwell & Baker, 1992). In contrast, –H children with ADD were characterized as more anxious, daydreamy, lethargic, and sluggish than +H children when using teacher ratings of classroom adjustment (Edelbrock, Costello, & Kessler, 1984; Lahey, Shaughency, Strauss, & Frame, 1984; Lahey et al., 1987).

Some studies have compared these subtypes on more objective tests and measures with mixed results. When measures of academic achievement and neuropsychological functions were used, most studies found no important differences between the groups (Carlson, Lahey, & Neeper, 1986; Casey, Rourke, & Del Dotto, 1996; Lamminmaki, Aohen, Narhi, Lyytinen, & de Barra, 1995)—both groups were found to be more impaired in academic skills and in some cognitive areas than normal control children. However, Hynd and colleagues (Hynd et al., 1991; Morgan et al., 1996) found greater academic underachievement, particularly in math, and a higher percentage of learning disabilities (60%) in their samples of ADD–H children compared to ADD+H children. Using considerably larger samples, my colleagues and I were not able to find any differences between the subtypes on measures of achievement or in rates of learning disability (LD) (Barkley, DuPaul, & McMurray, 1990). Nor were Casey et al. (1996) able to find such differences in achievement or rates of LD using the same means to define the subtypes of ADD and to classify children as LD. These two studies found both groups of ADD children to be impaired in their academic achievement. Our own study also found both subtypes to have been retained in grade (32% in each group) and placed in special education considerably more than our normal control children (45% vs. 53%). Alternatively, we found that +H children were more likely to have been placed in special classes for behavior-disordered children (emotionally disturbed) than the –H children (12% vs. 0%), whereas the latter children were more likely to be in classes for learning-disabled children than the +H children (34% for +H and 53% for –H). These differences in class placement do not appear to be the result of actual differences in the rates of LD between these disorders, as we found no such differences when using commonly accepted definitions of LD applied to achievement an intelligence tests as discussed later. Instead, both groups of children have equivalent rates of LD, but it is the additional problems with conduct and antisocial behavior that are likely to result in the ADD+H children being assigned to the behaviorally disturbed programs rather than the LD programs.

We determined the prevalence of learning disabilities in each subtype as defined by three separate empirical definitions of LD (see the "Learning Disabilities" section in Chapter 3 for these definitions). Regardless of the manner in which LD was defined, the two ADD groups did not differ in their percentage of LD children, ranging from 19% to 40% in reading, 22%

to 59% in spelling, and 22% to 59% in math. The best definition of LD, that combining the IQ–Achievement Discrepancy formula with the Low Achievement formula, indicates that approximately 20% of both groups of ADD children have a learning disability in reading, spelling, or math. Casey et al. (1996) also reported comparable rates of LD among these two subtypes of ADHD who were not found to differ significantly from each other (reading = 31% for ADD+H vs. 18% for –H, spelling = 27% for +H vs. 18% for –H, and math = 13% for +H and 14% for –H).

Only one study examined handwriting problems among subtypes of ADHD children (Marcotte & Stern, 1997). This study of 40 ADHD children with Combined Type and 40 with Predominantly Inattentive Type found that both groups were more impaired in graphomotor output than normal children but that the Combined Type was even further impaired than the Predominantly Inattentive Type.

Unfortunately, none of these studies directly addressed whether ADD–H and ADD+H are subtypes of the same type of attentional disorder or whether they represent qualitatively different disorders despite having similar levels of deviance on teacher rating scales of inattention. Such an examination would require a more comprehensive and objective assessment of different components of attention in both groups. In the one study that used four different types of reaction time tasks to study neurocognitive processing, few meaningful differences between the subtypes were obtained (Hynd et al., 1989). However, these reaction time tasks do not necessarily evaluate the different components of attention as viewed from neuropsychological models (Mirsky, 1996; Posner, 1987); thus the question whether these subtypes have the same type of attentional disturbance remains unanswered.

But the results of our own study of these subtypes implies that their attentional disturbances are not identical. We (Barkley, DuPaul, & McMurray, 1990) found that the –H children performed considerably worse on the coding subtest of the Wechsler Intelligence Scale for Children—Revised and on a measure of consistent retrieval of verbal information from memory. The +H children did not differ from normal subjects on either of these measures. These findings intimate that –H children may have more of a problem with memory, perceptual–motor speed, or even more central cognitive processing speed, whereas +H children manifest more problems with behavioral disinhibition and poor attention to tasks in addition to their overactivity.

We examined a smaller subset of these same subject groups on neuropsychological measures of frontal lobe functions (Barkley et al., 1992). The +H children performed considerably worse than –H children on both the Stroop Color Test and the Hand Movements subtest of the Kaufman Assessment Battery for Children, whereas –H children were not different from the normal or LD groups on any frontal lobe measures. The totality of these findings, when placed in the context of neuropsychological (Mirsky, 1996) or information-processing (Sergeant & van der Meere, 1989) models of attention, suggest that –H children may have more trouble with focused attention or speed of information processing (input analysis and retrieval of stored information). In contrast, +H children have greater difficulty with sustained attention and impulse control, or motivational parameters involved in the task (resource allocation or maintaining effort). Later reviews of this same literature reached similar conclusions (Lahey & Carlson, 1992; Goodyear & Hynd, 1992).

Our own study (Barkley, DuPaul, & McMurray, 1990) produced findings for the developmental and medical histories of these groups of subjects that were somewhat discrepant from those reported by Frank and Ben-Nun (1988). We did not find an increased incidence of perinatal and neonatal abnormalities in the ADD+H group as compared to the –H group. We did find a greater history of ADD among the paternal relatives and of substance abuse among the maternal relatives in the +H children than –H children, whereas Frank and Ben-Nun (1988) did not find such differences in family histories. Moreover, we noted a significantly greater prevalence of anxiety disorders among the maternal relatives of the –H than the +H children that was not reported by the Frank and Ben-Nun study. Our finding, however, was also not replicated in another study of family history (Lahey & Carlson, 1992), suggesting that anxiety disorders may not be more common among the relatives of ADD–H children. Consistent with our findings, though, were the reports by Frank and Ben-Nun (1988) of no differences between these ADD subgroups in abnormal medical histories and developmental delays.

Unlike several prior studies (Befera & Barkley, 1984; Cantwell & Baker, 1992; Cunningham et al., 1988), we did not find mothers of our ADD+H children to report themselves as more depressed or to have more marital conflict than our ADD–H, LD, or normal control children. Mothers in all three of our clinical groups reported greater levels of interpersonal sensitivity and hostility as well as general psychological distress than did mothers of the normal children.

Such differences in the types of attention affected in these groups of ADD children would be expected to have different neuroanatomical loci (Mirsky, 1996; Posner, 1987). ADD+H might be a problem in the functional level of prefrontal–limbic pathways, particularly the striatum (Lou, Henriksen, & Bruhn, 1984; Lou, Henriksen, Bruhn, Borner, & Nielsen, 1989), whereas ADD–H may involve more posterior associative cortical areas and/or cortical–subcortical feedback loops perhaps involving the hippocampal system (Heilman, Voeller, & Nadeau, 1991; Hynd et al., 1991; Posner, 1987). Consistent with this notion of different neurological mechanisms underlying these disorders were the preliminary findings of Shaywitz et al. (1986) that small samples of ADD+H children show a different response than do –H children in growth hormone and prolactin levels in blood plasma when placed on methylphenidate. The authors imply that ADD+H may involve a problem with dopamine whereas ADD–H may selectively involve norepinephrine. These neuropsychological and neurochemical hypotheses regarding ADD–H are quite conjectural at present. Nevertheless, they hint at the possibility of eventually identifying two distinctive attentional disorders in children that corroborate distinctions already being made in the study of normal attentional processes in the basic neurosciences (Mirsky, 1996; Posner, 1987).

These differences between the ADD subtypes in behavior and cognitive test performance are quite consistent with some previous studies (Berry et al., 1985; Carlson et al., 1987; Lahey et al., 1987) in finding +H children to be more disinhibited and impulsive, conduct disordered, and socially rejected whereas –H children are more cognitively sluggish, daydreamy, and socially withdrawn. Furthermore, our inspection of the types of inattention items rated by teachers as problematic for these subtypes revealed a different pattern of attentional problems and cognitive styles for each, similar to those found in prior research (Edelbrock et al., 1984; Lahey, Schaughency, Frame, & Strauss, 1985). The ADD+H children were described as more noisy, disruptive, messy, irresponsible, and immature whereas the ADD–H children were rated as more confused, daydreamy or lost in thought, and apathetic and lethargic.

In general, these results suggest that ADD+H children have considerably different patterns of psychiatric comorbidity than do ADD–H children, being at significantly greater risk for other Disruptive Behavior Disorders, academic placement in programs for behaviorally disturbed children, school suspensions, and receiving psychotherapeutic interventions than are ADD–H children. These patterns of comorbidity along with the findings of different family psychiatric histories suggest that these are dissimilar psychiatric disorders rather than subtypes of a shared disturbance in attentional processes. The research also appears to indicate that children with ADD–H can be distinguished in a number of domains of adjustment and cognitive performance from those with ADD+H. Not only do they present as having different levels of activity, but they also have quite distinct differences in the kinds of attentional problems they manifest. And, although both groups are equally academically at risk, they are quite different in their social morbidity with ADD+H children evidencing considerably greater levels of aggression, oppositional–defiant behavior, and conduct disorders.

Based on the evidence available to date, I believe we should begin considering these two subtypes as actually separate and unique childhood psychiatric disorders and not as subtypes of an identical attention disturbance. In our own clinic, we have come to label the ADD+H group as ADHD Combined Type, following the currently recommended guidelines in the DSM-IV, and as being conceptualized as chiefly a problem with behavioral disinhibition. We also see it as belonging to the larger category of Disruptive Behavior Disorders given the high rate of comorbidity among these disorders (ADHD, ODD, CD). In contrast, we consider the ADD–H group, or the Predominantly Inattentive Type of ADHD in DSM-IV, as a *Focused or Selective Attention Disorder* involving poor focus of attention/awareness and deficient speed of cognitive processing of information.

A survey (Szatmari et al., 1989a) indicates that the prevalence of these two disorders within the population are quite different, especially in the childhood years (6 to 11 years of age). The –H disorder appears to be considerably less prevalent than the +H group in this epidemiological study. Only 1.4% of boys and 1.3% of girls have ADD–H whereas 9.4% of boys and 2.8% of girls have the ADD+H. These figures change considerably in the adolescent age groups, in which 1.4% of males and 1% of females have ADD–H and 2.9% of males and 1.4% of females have ADD+H. In other words, the rates of –H remain relatively stable across these developmental age groupings whereas +H, especially in males, shows a considerable decline in prevalence with age. Among all children with either type ADD, about 78% of boys and 63% of girls will have the +H type of disorder. Baumgaertel, Wolraich, and Dietrich (1995) found a considerably higher prevalence rate for ADD–H among German schoolchildren. Using the DSM-III definitions for these subtypes, 3.2% had the –H type whereas 6.4% had the +H type. In contrast, when the more recent DSM-IV criteria for subtyping was employed, 9% of the children met criteria for the Predominantly Inattentive Type (–H) whereas 8.8% fell into the Hyperactive–Impulsive and Combined Types (+H). The differences in these studies are difficult to reconcile as both employed rating scales to define their subtypes. However, the Szatmari et al. (1989a) study did not use DSM symptom lists but constructed their subtypes based on ratings of items related to inattention and to hyperactive–impulsive behavior whereas Baumgaertel et al. (1995) employed symptom lists from the past three versions of the DSM.

It remains to be seen just how stable the ADD–H disorder is over development. One recent developmental study of a large sample of clinic-referred children suggests that its stability is quite poor, with none of the children originally diagnosed as having ADD–H receiving that same diagnosis 4 years later (Cantwell & Baker, 1992). The sample of ADD–H children in this study was also quite small ($N = 9$) making the results of the study questionable as to how representative they are of ADD–H children. Consequently, this research can hardly be considered a definitive longitudinal study on the outcome of this disorder. More research on the long-term outcome of ADD–H is to be encouraged.

Unfortunately, at present, little is known about which types of treatment may be more effective with the ADD–H group while much is known about the treatment of the ADHD group (see Part III of this volume). Five studies exist on the response of these two types of ADD to different doses of stimulant medication. They suggest that both groups generally respond positively to medication but that a lower dose of medication is sufficient to manage the problems of ADD–H children while higher doses appear to be more effective for the ADD+H children (Barkley, DuPaul, & McMurray, 1990; Famularo & Fenton, 1987; Saul & Ashby, 1986; Sebrechts et al., 1986; Ullmann & Sleator, 1985). More research is to be encouraged on the response of these different disorders to other types of behavioral, educational, and pharmacological interventions.

Subtyping on Aggression

Another, more accepted subtyping approach that has already demonstrated considerable clinical significance is based on aggression (Loney, Kramer, & Milich, 1981; Loney & Milich, 1982). Aggression refers to behaviors such as oppositional, defiant, stubborn, explosive, hostile, verbally aggressive, and fighting. Current diagnostic nomenclature refers to children with these symptoms as having ODD (American Psychiatric Association, 1994). This disorder is believed to be highly related to later CD and antisocial behavior (Barkley, Fischer, et al., 1990; Loeber, 1990; Reeves et al., 1987) and is viewed by some as an earlier developmental precursor of it. Although these ODD symptoms can certainly occur independently of ADHD, many studies show they are highly interrelated (Hinshaw, 1987; Shapiro & Garfinkel, 1986), especially in clinic- referred samples. Hence, the two disorders appear to overlap considerably (as noted earlier in the section "Psychiatric Disorders"), in that children who have one disorder often manifest the other. Yet, as already noted, much evidence has accumulated that shows important differences between children having either disorder alone and those having both ADHD and aggression (ODD/CD) (Hinshaw, 1987; Jensen et al., 1997; McGee, Williams, & Silva, 1984a, 1984b; Werry, 1988).

In general, children with ADHD and aggression display significantly greater levels of physical aggression, lying, and stealing, as well as more rejection by peers than either purely ADD or purely aggressive children (Loney, Langhorne, & Paternite, 1978; Milich et al., 1982; Walker, Lahey, Hynd, & Frame, 1987). These children also display different patterns of social attribution (Milich & Dodge, 1984), often viewing others' actions as intentionally aggressive against them. They are typically rated as more severely maladjusted (McGee, Williams, & Silva, 1984b; Moffitt, 1990), and have a poorer adolescent and young adult outcome (Barkley, Fischer, et al., 1990; Milich & Loney, 1979; Weiss & Hechtman, 1993) than do children having ADHD alone. Finally, children who have both disorders have greater levels of parental and family psychopathology, particularly antisocial conduct, major depressive disorders, and substance use disorders as well as greater social adversity than do children with either disorder alone (Barkley, Fischer, et al., 1990; Biederman, 1997; Faraone & Biederman, 1997; Biederman et al., 1987; Lahey, Piacentini, McBurnett, Stone, Hartdagan, & Hynd, 1988; Reeves et al., 1987; Szatmari, Offord, & Boyle, 1989b). Indeed, some have argued that ADHD with Conduct Disorder may represent a distinct familial subtype of ADHD (Biederman, Faraone, Keenan, et al., 1992). Clearly, the use of aggression, or ODD/CD, for subtyping of children with ADHD has been of great scientific and clinical utility.

Subtyping on Internalizing Symptoms

Another approach to subtyping ADHD, considerably less studied than the others cited previously, is based on the presence and degree of anxiety and depression in ADD children (often referred to as internalizing symptoms) (see Jensen et al., 1997, for a review). This subtyping model is based on several studies that showed that children who had relatively high ratings of internalizing symptoms were more likely to have poor or adverse responses to stimulant medication (DuPaul, Barkley, & McMurray, 1994; Pliszka, 1989; Taylor, 1983; Voelker, Lachar, & Gdowsky, 1983) and may be more appropriate for antidepressant medications (Biederman et al., 1993; Pliszka, 1989). Results of other studies suggest the possibility that, within the broader population of ADHD children, those with greater internalizing symptoms as children may have the greater likelihood of mood and affective disorders in adolescence. Research shows that some anxiety disorders and depressive symptoms in childhood may evolve into other types of anxiety or mood disorders or even major depressive disorders in later childhood or adolescence (Cantwell & Baker, 1989; Strauss et al., 1988).

However, no studies have specifically examined the stability and differential course of ADHD children with and without significant internalizing symptoms; thus the actual clinical predictive value of this subtyping approach remains unstudied.

SUMMARY

This chapter indicates that beyond the myriad cognitive, academic, developmental, and medical risks that exist in children with ADHD, a high probability of having comorbid psychiatric disorders also exists. Table 4.1 summarizes these psychiatric and social risks. Chief among them are ODD and CD; thus it is with good reason that DSM-IV classes ADHD with these other two disorders under the supracategory Disruptive Behavior Disorders. Up to half or more of children diagnosed with ADHD are destined to have at least one of these additional disorders. The co-occurrence of mood and anxiety disorders with ADHD is only somewhat less than for ODD and CD, with at least 25% or more of ADHD children experiencing these internalizing forms of psychopathology. Although BPD occurs with considerably less frequency with ADHD than do these other disorders, its occurrence is still 6 to 10 times greater than would be expected in a normal population and is probably one of the most serious and impairing of the comorbidities that may exist with ADHD.

Besides these comorbid disorders, children with ADHD are significantly more likely to experience problems in their relationships with family members, peers, and teachers, particularly if they fall into that subgroup of ADHD children who have significant levels of aggression, ODD, or CD. The family members of children with ADHD are also more likely to experience ADHD, among other disorders; once again, these risks to family members are highest in the group with comorbid ODD and CD.

From this increasing wealth of research on the families of ADHD children, a number of implications for clinical practice seem evident.

1. The clinical assessment of ADHD children must incorporate measures that assess not only child behavior and adjustment but also parent–child interactions, parental psychological status, and marital functioning if a thorough picture of the social-ecological fabric of ADHD children is to be more fully appreciated.

2. Reference must be made to the developmental context in which the findings from this assessment were obtained. The manner in which these levels of the social ecological system have interacted to result in the family as it now presents must be appreciated. Fault find-

---

TABLE 4.1. Summary of Comorbid Psychiatric Disorders and Social Impairments

Psychiatric disorders

Anxiety Disorders (10–40%, average 25%)
Major Depression (9–32%, average 25%)
Bipolar Disorder (6–20%; most likely 6–10% after subtracting overlapping symptoms)
Somatization Disorder (24–35% of adolescents)
Oppositional Defiant Disorder (20–67%, average 35%)
Conduct Disorder (20–56%)

Social impairments

Poor peer relationships, low social acceptance/status, increased aggression to peers, misattribution of intentions of others
Less compliance to parental requests, poor sustained compliance, and greater requests for assistance; receive more commands, reprimands, and punishment

ing within such reciprocal systems is often difficult to prove and needlessly judgmental. One can identify those problems within the family that seem primarily attributable to separate child and parent characteristics without the witch-hunt atmosphere that sometimes occurs in such clinical assessments. Great compassion and empathy are far more useful in both discovering these sources of maladjustment and in understanding their direction of effects.

3. In counseling the parents of ADHD children, it is necessary to separate the causes and mechanisms for the children's ADHD from that of hostile–defiant behavior or ODD/CD. The former is clearly a developmental disorder of behavioral disinhibition associated with neuromaturational immaturity and having a strong hereditary predisposition. Parents therefore cannot be held liable for this developmental disorder. The ODD/CD however is likely to arise within and be maintained by family characteristics, particularly parental psychiatric factors and conditions of social adversity. These characteristics permit both the modeling of aggressive social exchanges with others as well as the success of garden-variety aggression in escaping these attacks and unwanted task demands made by others. Consequently, parents can and should be held accountable (not blamed) for many, though not all, of these circumstances and should be strongly encouraged to accept this responsibility and seek mental health services to change them. The treatments for ADHD and ODD/CD are clearly distinct.

4. The clinical treatment of ADHD when it coexists with ODD/CD must involve more comprehensive interventions which focus, as needed, on parental beliefs and attitudes, psychological distress, communication and conflict resolution skills, and family systems rather than simply using medication or training parents in child management skills alone. Training in child management, when provided, must concentrate on the inconsistent and often noncontingent use of social consequences within these families and on increasing the availability of rewards and incentives for prosocial conduct. It must also strive to increase parental involvement and particularly monitoring of child behavior both at home and in the neighborhood if it is to prevent the escalation to more serious stages of antisocial behavior. My coauthors describe exemplar programs for each of these approaches in the sections of this text dealing with treatment.

5. The families of both ADHD and ODD/CD are likely to require more frequent and periodic monitoring via follow-up visits and periodic reintervention as the case dictates than other types of childhood psychological disorders if a significant impact is to be made on the long-term outcome of these children.

Finally, this chapter examined various approaches to the subtyping of ADHD. Results suggest that subtyping on the basis of presence of hyperactive–impulsive behavior, as DSM-IV currently does, may actually be distinguishing two separate disorders rather than two subtypes having the same attentional disturbance and risks for comorbid conditions. Certainly, the Predominantly Inattentive Type appears to be the more benign of the two and possibly less developmentally stable than are the other types of ADHD. Subtyping ADHD children on the basis of comorbid ODD/CD distinguishes a group that carries considerably greater family problems, social adversity, and parental psychopathology as well as a greater risk for later academic maladjustment, social rejection, early substance experimentation and abuse, and more persistent antisocial/criminal activities. This approach to subtyping may be exceptionally useful for identifying those ADHD children having one of the highest risks for long-term maladjustment, perhaps second only to those ADHD children who may experience comorbid BPD. ADHD children with comorbid anxiety disorder form a somewhat less risk-prone subtyping approach but one that may still be clinically useful for identifying children who are somewhat less impulsive than their nonanxious ADHD counterparts but who also may respond less well to stimulant medications and possibly better to antidepressants.

Over the past decade, then, there has been a considerably advance in our understanding of ADHD and how it may best be subgrouped to yield clinically valuable information.

REFERENCES

Alberts-Corush, J., Firestone, P., & Goodman, J. T. (1986). Attention and impulsivity characteristics of the biological and adoptive parents of hyperactive and normal children. *American Journal of Orthopsychiatry, 56*, 413–423.

American Psychiatric Association. (1980). *Diagnostic and statistical manual of mental disorders* (3rd ed.). Washington, DC: Author.

American Psychiatric Association. (1987). *Diagnostic and statistical manual of mental disorders* (3rd ed., rev.). Washington, DC: Author.

American Psychiatric Association. (1994). *Diagnostic and statistical manual of mental disorders* (4th ed.). Washington, DC: Author.

Anastopoulos, A. D., Guevremont, D. C., Shelton, T. L., & DuPaul, G. J. (1992). Parenting stress among families of children with attention deficit hyperactivity disorder. *Journal of Abnormal Child Psychology, 20*, 503–520.

Anderson, C. A., Hinshaw, S. P., & Simmel, C. (1994). Mother–child interactions in ADHD and comparison boys: Relationships with overt and covert externalizing behavior. *Journal of Abnormal Child Psychology, 22*, 247–265.

Anderson, J. C., Williams, S., McGee, R., & Silva, P. A. (1987). DSM-III disorders in preadolescent children. *Archives of General Psychiatry, 44*, 69–76.

August, G. J., & Stewart, M. A. (1983). Family subtypes of childhood hyperactivity. *Journal of Nervous and Mental Disease, 171*, 362–368.

Barkley, R. A. (1985). The social interactions of hyperactive children: Developmental changes, drug effects, and situational variation. In R. McMahon & R. Peters (Eds.), *Childhood disorders: Behavioral-developmental approaches* (pp. 218-243). New York: Brunner/Mazel.

Barkley, R.A. (1988). The effects of methylphenidate on the interactions of preschool ADHD children with their mothers. *Journal of the American Academy of Child and Adolescent Psychiatry, 27*, 336–341.

Barkley, R. A. (1989). Hyperactive girls and boys: Stimulant drug effects on mother–child interactions. *Journal of Child Psychology and Psychiatry, 30*, 379-390.

Barkley, R. A., Anastopoulos, A. D., Guevremont, D. G., & Fletcher, K. F. (1992). Adolescents with attention deficit hyperactivity disorder: Mother–adolescent interactions, family beliefs and conflicts, and maternal psychopathology. *Journal of Abnormal Child Psychology, 20*, 263–288.

Barkley, R. A., & Biederman, J. (1997). Towards a broader definition of the age of onset criterion for attention deficit hyperactivity disorder. *Journal of the American Academy of Child and Adolescent Psychiatry, 36*, 1204–1210.

Barkley, R. A., & Cunningham, C. E. (1979). The effects of methylphenidate on the mother–child interactions of hyperactive children. *Archives of General Psychiatry, 36*, 201-208.

Barkley, R., Cunningham, C., & Karlsson, J. (1983). The speech of hyperactive children and their mothers: Comparisons with normal children and stimulant drug effects. *Journal of Learning Disabilities, 16*, 105-110.

Barkley, R. A., DuPaul, G. J., & McMurray, M.B. (1990). A comprehensive evaluation of attention deficit disorder with and without hyperactivity. *Journal of Consulting and Clinical Psychology, 58*, 775–789.

Barkley, R. A., Fischer, M., Edelbrock, C. S., & Smallish, L. (1990). The adolescent outcome of hyperactive children diagnosed by research criteria: I. An 8-year prospective follow-up study. *Journal of the American Academy of Child and Adolescent Psychiatry, 29*, 546–557.

Barkley, R. A., Fischer, M., Edelbrock, C. S., & Smallish, L. (1991). The adolescent outcome of hyperactive children diagnosed by research criteria: III. Mother–child interactions, family conflicts, and maternal psychopathology. *Journal of Child Psychology and Psychiatry, 32*, 233–256.

Barkley, R. A., Grodzinsky, G., & DuPaul, G. (1992). Frontal lobe functions in attention deficit disorder with and without hyperactivity: A review and research report. *Journal of Abnormal Child Psychology, 20*, 163–188.

Barkley, R. A., Karlsson, J. & Pollard, S. (1985). Effects of age on the mother–child interactions of hyperactive children. *Journal of Abnormal Child Psychology, 13,* 631–38.

Barkley, R.A., Karlsson, J., Pollard, S., & Murphy, J.V. (1985). Developmental changes in the mother–child interactions of hyperactive boys: Effects of two dose levels of Ritalin. *Journal of Child Psychology and Psychiatry and Allied Disciplines, 26,* 705–715.

Baumgaertel, A., Wolraich, M. L., & Dietrich, M. (1995). Comparison of diagnostic criteria for attention deficit disorders in a German elementary school sample. *Journal of the American Academy of Child and Adolescent Psychiatry, 34,* 629–638.

Befera, M., & Barkley, R. A. (1984). Hyperactive and normal girls and boys: Mother–child interactions, parent psychiatric status, and child psychopathology. *Journal of Child Psychology and Psychiatry, 26,* 439–452.

Berry, C. A., Shaywitz, S. E., & Shaywitz, B. A. (1985). Girls with attention deficit disorder: A silent majority? A report on behavioral and cognitive characteristics. *Pediatrics, 75,* 801–809.

Biederman, J. (1997, October). *Returns of comorbidity in girls with ADHD.* Paper presented at the annual meeting of the American Academy of Child and Adolescent Psychiatry, Toronto, Canada.

Biederman, J., Baldessarini, R. J., Wright, V., Keenan, K., & Faraone, S. V. (1993). A double-blind placebo controlled study of desipramine in the treatment of ADD: III. Lack of impact of comorbidity and family history factors on clinical response. *Journal of the American Academy of Child and Adolescent Psychiatry, 32,* 199–204.

Biederman, J., Baldessarini, R. J., Wright, V., Knee, D., & Harmatz, J. S. (1989). A double-blind placebo controlled study of desimpramine in the treatment of ADD: I. Efficacy. *Journal of the American Academy of Child and Adolescent Psychiatry, 28,* 777–784.

Biederman, J., & Faraone, S. V. (1997, October). *Patterns of comorbidity in girls with ADHD.* Paper presented at the annual meeting of the American Academy of Child and Adolescent Psychiatry, Toronto.

Biederman, J., Faraone, S. V., & Lapey, K. (1992). Comorbidity of diagnosis in attention-deficit hyperactivity disorder. In G. Weiss (Ed.), *Child and adolescent psychiatry clinics in North America: Attention deficit disorder* (pp. 335–360). Philadelphia: W. B. Saunders.

Biederman, J., Faraone, S., Mick, E., Moore, P., & Lelon, E. (1996). Child Behavior Checklist findings further support comorbidity between ADHD and major depression in a referred sample. *Journal of the American Academy of Child and Adolescent Psychiatry, 35,* 734–742.

Biederman, J., Faraone, S., Mick, E., Wozniak, J., Chen, L., Ouellette, C., Marrs, A., Moore, P., Garcia, J., Mennin, D., & Lelon, E. (1996). Attention-deficit hyperactivity disorder and juvenile mania: An overlooked comorbidity? *Journal of the American Academy of Child and Adolescent Psychiatry, 35,* 997–1008.

Biederman, J., Gastfriend, D. R., & Jellinek, M. S. (1986). Desipramine in the treatment of children with attention deficit disorder. *Journal of Clinical Psychopharmacology, 6,* 359–363.

Biederman, J., Munir, K., & Knee, D. (1987). Conduct and oppositional disorder in clinically referred children with attention deficit disorder: A controlled family study. *Journal of the American Academy of Child and Adolescent Psychiatry, 26,* 724–727.

Biederman, J., Newcorn, J., & Sprich, S. (1991). Comorbidity of attention deficit hyperactivity disorder with conduct, depressive, anxiety, and other disorders. *American Journal of Psychiatry, 148,* 564–577.

Biederman, J., Wozniak, J., Kiely, K., Ablon, S., Faraone, S., Mick, E., Mundy, E., & Kraus, I. (1995). CBCL clinical scales discriminate prepubertal children with structured-interview-derived diagnosis of mania from those with ADHD. *Journal of the American Academy of Child and Adolescent Psychiatry, 34,* 464–471.

Bird, H. R., Canino, G., Rubio-Stipec, M., et al. (1988). Estimates of the prevalence of childhood maladjustment in a community survey in Puerto Rico. *Archives of General Psychiatry, 45,* 1120–1126.

Bird, H., Gould, M. S., & Staghezza, B. M. (1993). Patterns of diagnostic comorbidity in a community sample of children aged 9 through 16 years. *Journal of the American Academy of Child and Adolescent Psychiatry, 32,* 361–368.

Bohline, D. S. (1985). Intellectual and effective characteristics of attention deficit disordered children. *Journal of Learning Disabilities, 18,* 604–608.

Breen, M., & Barkley, R. (1983). The Personality Inventory for Children (PIC): Its clinical utility with hyperactive children. *Journal of Pediatric Psychology*, 359–366.

Breen, M., & Barkley, R. (1984). Psychological adjustment in learning disabled, hyperactive, and hyperactive/learning disabled children using the Personality Inventory for Children. *Journal of Clinical Child Psychology, 13*, 232–236.

Breen, M., & Barkley, R.A. (1988). Parenting stress with ADDH girls and boys. *Journal of Pediatric Psychology, 13*, 265–280.

Buhrmeister, D., Camparo, L., Christensen, A., Gonzalez, L. S., & Hinshaw, S. P. (1992). Mothers and fathers interacting in dyads and triads with normal and hyperactive sons. *Developmental Psychology, 28*, 500–509.

Campbell, S. B., & Paulauskas, S. (1979). Peer relations in hyperactive children. *Journal of Child Psychology and Psychiatry, 20*, 233–246.

Cantwell, D. P. (1972). Psychiatric illness in the families of hyperactive children. *Archives of General Psychiatry, 27*, 414–427.

Cantwell, D. P., & Baker, L. (1989). Stability and natural history of DSM-III childhood diagnoses. *Journal of the American Acdemy of Child and Adolescent Psychiatry, 28*, 691–700.

Cantwell, D. P., & Baker, L. (1992). Association between attention deficit-hyperactivity disorder and learning disorders. In S. E. Shaywitz & B. A. Shaywitz (Eds.), *Attention deficit disorder comes of age: Toward the twenty-first century* (pp. 145–164). Austin, TX: Pro-Ed.

Carlson, C. L., Lahey, B. B., Frame, C. L., Walker, J., & Hynd, G. W. (1987). Sociometric status of clinic-referred children with attention deficit disorders with and without hyperactivity. *Journal of Abnormal Child Psychology, 15*, 537–547.

Carlson, C. L., Lahey, B. B., & Neeper, R. (1986). Direct assessment of the cognitive correlates of attention deficit disorders with and without hyperactivity. *Journal of Behavioral Assessment and Psychopathology, 8*, 69–86.

Carlson, G. A. (1990). Child and adolescent mania—Diagnostic considerations. *Journal of Child Psychology and Psychiatry, 31*, 331–342.

Casey, J. E., Rourke, B. P., & Del Dotto, J. E. (1996). Learning disabilities in children with attention deficit disorder with and without hyperactivity. *Child Neuropsychology, 2*, 83–98.

Clark, M. L., Cheyne, J. A., Cunningham, C. E., & Siegel, L. S. (1988). Dyadic peer interaction and task orientation in attention-deficit-disordered children. *Journal of Abnormal Child Psychology, 16*, 1–15.

Cohen, N. J., Sullivan, J., Minde, K., Novak, C., & Keens, S. (1983). Mother–child interaction in hyperactive and normal kindergarten-aged children and the effect of treatment. *Child Psychiary and Human Development, 13*, 213–224.

Cohen, P., Velez, C. N., Brook, J., & Smith, J. (1989). Mechanisms of the relation between perinatal problems, early childhood illness, and psychopathology in late childhood and adolescence. *Child Development, 60*, 701–709.

Cunningham, C. E., Benness, B. B., & Siegel, L. S. (1988). Family functioning, time allocation, and parental depression in the families of normal and ADDH children. *Journal of Clinical Child Psychology, 17*, 169–177.

Cunningham, C. E., & Siegel, L. S. (1987). Peer interactions of normal and attention-deficit disordered boys during free-play, cooperative task, and simulated classroom situations. *Journal of Abnormal Child Psychology, 15*, 247–268.

Danforth, J. S., Barkley, R. A., & Stokes, T. F. (1991). Observations of parent–child interactions with hyperactive children: Research and clinical implications. *Clinical Psychology Review, 11*, 703–727.

Deutsch, C. K., Swanson, J. M., Bruell, J. H., Cantwell, D. P., Weinberg, F., & Baren, M. (1982). Overrepresentation of adoptees in children with the attention deficit disorder. *Behavioral Genetics, 12*, 231–238.

Diener, M. B., & Milich, R. (1997). Effects of positive feedback on the social interactions of boys with attention deficit hyperactivity disorder: A test of the self-protective hypothesis. *Journal of Clinical Child Psychology, 26*, 256–265.

DuPaul, G. J., Barkley, R. A., McMurray, M. B. (1994). Response of children with ADHD to methylphenidate: Interaction with internalizing symptoms. *Journal of the American Academy of Child and Adolescent Psychiatry, 33*, 894–903.

Edelbrock, C. S., Costello, A., & Kessler, M. D. (1984). Empirical corroboration of attention deficit disorder. *Journal of the American Academy of Child and Adolescent Psychiatry, 23,* 285–290.

Epstein, J. N., Goldberg, N. A., Conners, C. K., & March, J. S. (1997). The effects of anxiety on continuous performance test functioning in an ADHD clinic sample. *Journal of Attention Disorders, 2,* 45–52.

Famularo, R., & Fenton, T. (1987). The effect of methylphenidate on school grades in children with attention deficit disorder without hyperactivity: A preliminary report. *Journal of Clinical Psychiatry, 48,* 112–114.

Faraone, S. V., & Biederman, J. (1997, October). *Familial transmission of attention-deficit/hyperactivity disorder and comorbid disorders.* Paper presented at the annual meeting of the American Academy of Child and Adolescent Psychiatry, Toronto, Canada.

Faraone, S. V., Biederman, J., Jetton, J. G., & Tsuang, M. T. (1997). Attention deficit disorder and conduct disorder: Longitudinal evidence for a familial subtype. *Psychological Medicine, 27,* 291–300.

Faraone, S. V., Biederman, J., Wozniak, J., Mundy, E., Mennin, D., & O'Donnell, D. (1997). Is comorbidity with ADHD a marker for juvenile-onset mania? *Journal of the American Academy of Child and Adolescent Psychiatry, 36,* 1046–1055.

Fischer, M. (1990). Parenting stress and the child with attention deficit hyperactivity disorder. *Journal of Clinical Child Psychology, 19,* 337–346.

Fischer, M., Barkley, R. A., Edelbrock, C.S., & Smallish, L. (1990). The adolescent outcome of hyperactive children diagnosed by research criteria: II. Academic, attentional, and neuropsychological status. *Journal of Consulting and Clinical Psychology, 58,* 580–588.

Fletcher, K., Fischer, M., Barkley, R. A., & Smallish, L. (1996). A sequential analysis of the mother–adolescent interactions of ADHD, ADHD/ODD, and normal teenagers during neutral and conflict discussions. *Journal of Abnormal Child Psychology, 24,* 271–297.

Frank, Y., & Ben-Nun, Y. (1988). Toward a clinical subgrouping of hyperactive and nonhyperactive attention deficit disorder: Results of a comprehensive neurological and neuropsychological assessment. *American Journal of Diseases of Children, 142,* 153–155.

Geller, B., & Luby, J. (1997). Child and adolescent bipolar disorder: A review of the past 10 years. *Journal of the American Academy of Child and Adolescent Psychiatry, 36,* 1168–1176.

Gomez, R., & Sanson, A. V. (1994). Mother–child interactions and noncompliance in hyperactive boys with and without conduct problems. *Journal of Child Psychology and Psychiatry, 35,* 477–490.

Goodyear, P., & Hynd, G. (1992). Attention deficit disorder with (ADDH) and without (ADDWO) hyperactivity: Behavioral and neuropsychological differentiation. *Journal of Clinical Child Psychology, 21,* 273–304.

Gordon, M., Mettelmman, B. B., & Irwin, M. (1990, August). *The impact of comorbidity on ADHD laboratory measures.* Paper presented at the annual meeting of the American Psychological Association, Boston.

Grenell, M. M., Glass, C. R., & Katz, K. S. (1987). Hyperactive children and peer interaction: Knowledge and performance of social skills. *Journal of Abnormal Child Psychology, 15,* 1–13.

Halperin, J. M., Gittelman, R., Klein, D. F., & Rudel, R. G. (1984). Reading-disabled hyperactive children: A distinct subgroup of attention deficit disorder with hyperactivity? *Journal of Abnormal Child Psychology, 12,* 1–14.

Heilman, K. M., Voeller, K. K. S., & Nadeau, S. E. (1991). A possible pathophysiological substrate of attention deficit hyperactivity disorder. *Journal of Child Neurology, 6,* 74–79.

Hern, K. L., & Hynd, G. W. (1992). Clinical differentiation of the attention deficit disorder subtypes: Do sensorimotor deficits characterize children with ADDWO? *Archives of Clinical Neuropsychology, 7,* 77–83.

Hinshaw, S. P. (1987). On the distinction between attentional deficits/hyperactivity and conduct problems/aggression in child psychopathology. *Psychological Bulletin, 101,* 443–447.

Hinshaw, S. P. (1992). Externalizing behavior problems and academic underachievement in childhood and adolescence: Causal relationships and underlying mechanisms. *Psychological Bulletin, 111,* 127–155.

Hinshaw, S. P., & Nelnick, S. M. (1995). Peer relationship in boys with attention deficit hyperactivity disorder with and without comorbid aggression. *Developmental Psychopathology, 7,* 627–647.

Humphries, T., Kinsbourne, M., & Swanson, J. (1978). Stimulant effects on cooperation and social interaction between hyperactive children and their mothers. *Journal of Child Psychology and Psychiatry, 19,* 13–22.

Hynd, G. W., Lorys, A. R., Semrud-Clikeman, M., Nieves, N., Huettner, M. I. S., & Lahey, B. B. (1991). Attention deficit disorder without hyperactivity: A distinct behavioral and neurocognitive syndrome. *Journal of Child Neurology, 6,* S37–S43.

Hynd, G. W., Nieves, N., Conner, R., Stone, P., Town, P., Becker, M. G., Lahey, B. B., & Lorys-Vernon, A. R. (1989). Speed of neurocognitive processing in children with attention deficit disorder with and without hyperactivity. *Journal of Learning Disabilities, 22,* 573–580.

Jensen, J. B., Burke, N., & Garfinkel, B. D. (1988). Depression and symptoms of attention deficit disorder with hyperactivity. *Journal of the American Academy of Child and Adolescent Psychiatry, 27,* 742–747.

Jensen, P. S., Martin, D., & Cantwell, D. P. (1997). Comorbidity in ADHD: Implications for research, practice, and DSM-V. *Journal of the American Academy of Child and Adolescent Psychiatry, 36,* 1065–1079.

Jensen, P. S., Shervette, R. E. III, Xenakis, S. N., & Richters, J. (1993). Anxiety and depressive disorders in attention deficit disorder with hyperactivity: New findings. *American Journal of Psychiatry, 150,* 1203–1209.

Johnston, C. (1996). Parent characteristics and parent–child interactions in families of nonproblem children and ADHD children with higher and lower levels of oppositional–defiant disorder. *Journal of Abnormal Child Psychology, 24,* 85–104.

Johnston, C., & Freeman, W. (1997). Attributions of child behavior in parents of children with behavior disorders and children with attention deficit–hyperactivity disorder. *Journal of Consulting and Clinical Psychology, 65,* 636–645.

Johnston, C., Pelham, W. E., & Murphy, H. A. (1985). Peer relationships in ADDH and normal children: A developmental analysis of peer and teacher ratings. *Journal of Abnormal Child Psychology, 13,* 89–100.

King, C., & Young, R. (1982). Attentional deficits with and without hyperactivity: Teacher and peer perceptions. *Journal of Abnormal Child Psychology, 10,* 483–496.

Lahey, B. B., & Carlson, C. L. (1992). Validity of the diagnostic category of attention deficit disorder without hyperactivity: A review of the literature. In S. E. Shaywitz & B. A. Shaywitz (Eds.), *Attention deficit disorder comes of age: Toward the twenty-first century* (pp. 119–144). Austin, TX: Pro-Ed.

Lahey, B. B., Pelham, W. E., Schaughency, E. A., Atkins, M. S., Murphy, H. A., Hynd, G. W., Russo, M., Hartdagen, S., & Lorys-Vernon, A. (1988). Dimensions and types of attention deficit disorder with hyperactivity in children: A factor and cluster-analytic approach. *Journal of the American Academy of Child and Adolescent Psychiatry, 27,* 330–335.

Lahey, B. B., Piacentini, J. C., McBurnett, K., Stone, P., Hartdagen, S., & Hynd, G. (1988). Psychopathology in the parents of children with conduct disorder and hyperactivity. *Journal of the American Academy of Child and Adolescent Psychiatry, 27,* 163–170.

Lahey, B. B., Schaughency, E., Frame, C. L., & Strauss, C. C. (1985). Teacher ratings of attention problems in children experimentally classified as exhibiting attention deficit disorders with and without hyperactivity. *Journal of the American Academy of Child Psychiatry, 24,* 613–616.

Lahey, B. B., Schaughency, E., Hynd, G., Carlson, C., & Nieves, N. (1987). Attention deficit disorder with and without hyperactivity: Comparison of behavioral characteristics of clinic-referred children. *Journal of the American Academy of Child Psychiatry, 26,* 718–723.

Lahey, B. B., Schaughency, E., Strauss, C., & Frame, C. (1984). Are attention deficit disorders with and without hyperactivity similar or dissimilar disorders? *Journal of the American Academy of Child Psychiatry, 23,* 302–309.

Lamminmaki, T., Ahonen, T., Narhi, V., Lyytinent, H., & de Barra, H. T. (1995). Attention deficit hyperactivity disorder subtypes: Are there differences in academic problems? *Developmental Neuropsychology, 11,* 297–310.

Landau, S., & Milich, R. (1988). Social communication patterns of attention deficit-disordered boys. *Journal of Abnormal Child Psychology, 16*, 69–81.

Lewinsohn, P. M., Klein, D. N., & Seeley, J. R. (1995). Bipolar disorders in a community sample of older adolescents: Prevalence, phenomenology, comorbidity, and course. *Journal of the American Academy of Child and Adolescent Psychiatry, 34*, 454–463.

Linn, R. T., & Hodge, G. K. (1982). Locus of control in childhood hyperactivity. *Journal of Consulting and Clinical Psychology, 50*, 592–593.

Loeber, R. (1990). Development and risk factors of juvenile antisocial behavior and delinquency. *Clinical Psychology Review, 10*, 1–42.

Loney, J., Kramer, J., & Milich, R. (1981). The hyperkinetic child grows up: predictors of symptoms, delinquency, and achievement at follow-up. In K. Gadow & J. Loney (Eds.), *Psychosocial aspects of drug treatment for hyperactivity*. Boulder, CO: Westview Press.

Loney, J., Langhorne, J., & Paternite, C. (1978). An empirical basis for subgrouping the hyperkinetic/minimal brain dysfunction syndrome. *Journal of Abnormal Psychology, 87*, 431–444.

Loney, J., & Milich, R. (1982). Hyperactivity, inattention, and aggression in clinical practice. In D. Routh & M. Wolraich (Eds.), *Advances in developmental and behavioral pediatrics* (Vol. 3, pp. 113– 147). Greenwich, CT: JAI Press.

Lou, H. C., Henriksen, L., & Bruhn, P. (1984). Focal cerebral hypoperfusion in children with dysphasia and/or attention deficit disorder. *Archives of Neurology, 41*, 825–829.

Lou, H. C., Henriksen, L., Bruhn, P., Borner, H., & Nielsen, J. B. (1989). Striatal dysfunction in attention deficit and hyperkinetic disorder. *Archives of Neurology, 46*, 48–52.

Marcotte, A. C., & Stern, C. (1997). Qualitative analysis of graphomotor output in children with attentional disorders. *Child Neuropsychology, 3*, 147–153.

Margalit, M., & Arieli, N. (1984). Emotional and behavioral aspects of hyperactivity. *Journal of Learning Disabilities, 17*, 374–376.

Mash, E. J., & Johnston, C. (1982). A comparison of mother–child interactions of younger and older hyperactive and normal children. *Child Development, 53*, 1371–1381.

Mash, E. J., & Johnston, C. (1983). Sibling interactions of hyperactive and normal children and their relationship to reports of maternal stress and self-esteem. *Journal of Clinical Child Psychology, 12*, 91–99.

Mash, E. J., & Johnston, C. (1990). Determinants of parenting stress: Illustrations from families of hyperactive children and families of physically abused children. *Journal of Clinical Child Psychology, 19*, 313–328.

Maurer, R. G., & Stewart, M. (1980) Attention deficit disorder without hyperactivity in a child psychiatric clinic. *Journal of Clinical Psychiatry, 41*, 232–233.

McGee, R., Williams, S., & Silva, P. A. (1984a). Behavioral and developmental characteristics of aggressive, hyperactive, and aggressive–hyperactive boys. *Journal of the American Academy of Child Psychiatry, 23*, 270–279.

McGee, R., Williams, S., & Silva, P. A. (1984b). Background characteristics of aggressive, hyperactive, and aggressive–hyperactive boys. *Journal of the American Academy of Child and Adolescent Psychiatry, 23*, 280–284.

Milberger, S., Biederman, J., Faraone, S. V., Murphy, J., & Tsuang, M. T. (1995). Attention deficit hyperactivity disorder and comorbid disorders: Issues of overlapping symptoms. *American Journal of Psychiatry, 152*, 1783–1800.

Milich, R. (1994). The response of children with ADHD to failure: If at first you don't succeed, do you try, try again? *School Psychology Review, 23*, 11–18.

Milich, R., & Dodge, K. A. (1984). Social information processing in child psychiatric populations. *Journal of Abnormal Child Psychology, 12*, 471–490.

Milich, R., & Greenwell, L. (1991, December). *An examination of learned helplessness among attention-deficit hyperactivity disordered boys.* Paper presented at the annual meeting of the Association for Advancement of Behavior Therapy, New York.

Milich, R., S., Landau, S., Kilby, G., & Whitten, P. (1982). Preschool peer perceptions of the behavior of hyperactive and aggressive children. *Journal of Abnormal Child Psychology, 10*, 497–510.

Milich, R., & Loney, J. (1979). The role of hyperactive and aggressive symptomatology in predicting adolescent outcome among hyperactive children. *Journal of Pediatric Psychology, 4*, 93–112.

Milich, R., & Okazaki, M. (1991). An examination of learned helplessness among attention-deficit hyperactivity disordered boys. *Journal of Abnormal Child Psychology, 19,* 607–623.

Mirsky, A. F. (1996). Disorders of attention: A neuropsychological perspective. In R. G. Lyon & N. A. Krasnegor (Eds.), *Attention, memory, and executive function* (pp. 71–96). Baltimore, MD: Paul H. Brookes.

Moffitt, T. E. (1990). Juvenile delinquency and attention deficit disorder: Boys' developmental trajectories from age 3 to 15. *Child Development, 61,* 893–910.

Morgan, A. E., Hynd, G. W., Riccio, C. A., & Hall, J. (1996). Validity of DSM-IV ADHD Predominantly Inattentive and Combined Types: Relationship to previous DSM diagnoses/ subtype differences. *Journal of the American Academy of Child and Adolescent Psychiatry, 35,* 325–333.

Morrison, J., & Stewart, M. (1973). The psychiatric status of the legal families of adopted hyperactive children. *Archives of General Psychiatry, 28,* 888–891.

Munir, K., Biederman, J., & Knee, D. (1987). Psychiatric comorbidity in patients with attention deficit disorder: A controlled study. *Journal of the American Academy of Child and Adolescent Psychiatry, 26,* 844–848.

O'Neill, M. E., & Douglas, V. I. (1991). Study strategies and story recall in attention-deficit hyperactivity disorder and reading disability. *Journal of Abnormal Child Psychology, 19,* 671–692.

Pelham, W. E., & Bender, M. E. (1982). Peer relationships in hyperactive children: Description and treatment. In K. D. Gadow & I. Bialer (Eds.), *Advances in learning and behavioral disabilities* (Vol. 1, pp. 365–436). Greenwich, CT: JAI Press.

Pelham, W. E., & Lang, A. R. (1993). Parental alcohol consumption and deviant child behavior: Laboratory studies of reciprocal effects. *Clinical Psychology Review, 13,* 763–784.

Pelham, W. E., & Milich, R. (1984). Peer relationships in children with hyperactivity/attention deficit disorder. *Journal of Learning Disabilities, 17,* 560–567.

Pliszka, S. R. (1989). Effect of anxiety on cognition, behavior, and stimulant responding in ADHD. *Journal of the American Academy of Child and Adolescent Psychiatry, 28,* 882–887

Pliszka, S. R. (1992). Comorbidity of attention-deficit hyperactivity disorder and overanxious disorder. *Journal of the American Academy of Child and Adolescent Psychiatry, 31,* 197–203.

Pope, A. W., Bierman, K. L., & Mumma, G. H. (1989). Relations between hyperactive and aggressive behavior and peer relations at three elementary grade levels. *Journal of Abnormal Child Psychology, 17,* 253–267.

Posner, M. (1987). *Structures and functions of selection attention.* Washington, DC: American Psychological Association.

Reeves, J. C., Werry, J., Elkind, G. S., & Zametkin, A. (1987). Attention deficit, conduct, oppositional, and anxiety disorders in children: II. Clinical characteristics. *Journal of the American Academy of Child and Adolescent Psychiatry, 26,* 133–143.

Rubinstein, R. S., & Brown, R. T. (1984). An evaluation of the validity of the diagnostic category of attention deficit disorder. *American Journal of Orthopsychiatry, 54,* 398–414.

Saul, R. C., & Ashby, C. D. (1986). Measurement of whole blood serotinin as a guide for prescribing psychostimulant medication for children with attention deficits. *Clinical Neuropharmacology, 9,* 189–195.

Schacher, R., Taylor, E., Weiselberg, M., Thorley, G., & Rutter, M. (1987). Changes in family function and relationships in children who respond to methylphenidate. *Journal of the American Academy of Child and Adolescent Psychiatry, 26,* 728–732.

Sebrechts, M. M., Shaywitz, S. E., Shaywitz, B. A., Jatlow, P., Anderson, G. M., & Cohen D. J. (1986). Components of attention, methylphenidate dosage, and blood levels in children with attention deficit disorder. *Pediatrics, 77,* 222–228.

Sergeant, J., & van der Meere, J. (1989). The diagnostic significance of attentional processing: Its significance for ADDH classification—A future DSM. In T. Sagvolden & T. Archer (Eds.), *Attention deficit disorder: Clinical and basic research* (pp. 151–166). Hillsdale, NJ: Erlbaum.

Shapiro, S., & Garfinkel, B. (1986). The occurrence of behavior disorders in children: The interdependence of attention deficit disorder and conduct disorder. *Journal of the American Acdaemy of Child Psychiatry, 25,* 809–919.

Shaywitz, S. E., Shaywitz, B. A., Jatlow, P. R., Sebrechts, M., Anderson, G. M., & Cohen, D. T. (1986). Biological differentiation of attention deficit disorder with and without hyperactivity: A preliminary report. *Annals of Neurology, 21,* 363.

Singer, S. M., Stewart, M. A., & Pulaski, L. (1981). Minimal brain dysfunction: Differences in cognitive organization in two groups of index cases and their relatives. *Journal of Learning Disabilities, 14,* 470–473.

Stewart, M., deBlois, S., & Cummings, C. (1980). Psychiatric disorder in the parents of hyperactive boys and those with conduct disorder. *Journal of Child Psychology and Psychiatry, 21,* 283–292.

Stewart, M. A., Pitts, F. N., Craig, A. G., & Dieruf, W. (1966). The hyperactive child syndrome. *American Journal of Orthopsychiatry, 36,* 861–867.

Szatmari, P., Boyle, M., & Offord, D. R. (1989). ADDH and conduct disorder: Degree of diagnostic overlap and differences among correlates. *Journal of the American Academy of Child and Adolescent Psychiatry, 28,* 865–872.

Szatmari, P., Offord, D. R., & Boyle, M. H. (1989a). Ontario Child Health Study: Prevalence of attention deficit disorder with hyperactivity. *Journal of Child Psychology and Psychiatry, 30,* 219–230.

Szatmari, P., Offord, D. R., & Boyle, M. H. (1989b). Correlates, associated impairments, and patterns of service utilization of children with attention deficit disorders: Findings from the Ontario Child Health Study. *Journal of Child Psychology and Psychiatry, 30,* 205–217.

Tallmadge, J., & Barkley, R. A. (1983). The interactions of hyperactive and normal boys with their mothers and fathers. *Journal of Abnormal Child Psychology, 11,* 565–579.

Tannock, R. (in press). Attention deficit disorders with anxiety disorders. In T. E. Brown (Ed.), *Subtypes of attention deficit disorders in children, adolescents, and adults.* Washington, DC: American Psychiatric Press.

Tarver-Behring, S., Barkley, R. A., & Karlsson, J. (1985). The mother–child interactions of hyperactive boys and their normal siblings. *American Journal of Orthopsychiatry, 55,* 202–209.

Taylor, E. A. (1983). Drug response and diagnostic validation. In M. Rutter (Ed.), *Developmental neuropsychiatry* (pp. 348–368). New York: Guilford Press.

Taylor, E., Sandberg, S., Thorley, G., & Giles, S. (1991). *The epidemiology of childhood hyperactivity.* London: Oxford University Press.

Ullmann, R. K., & Sleator, E. K. (1985). Attention deficit disorder children with and without hyperactivity: Which behaviors are helped by stimulants? *Clinical Pediatrics, 24,* 547–551.

Voelker, S. L., Lachar, D., & Gdowski, C. L. (1983). The Personality Inventory for Children and response to methylphenidate: Preliminary evidence for predictive validity. *Journal of Pediatric Psychology, 8,* 161–169.

Walker, J. L., Lahey, B. B., Hynd, G. W., & Frame, C. (1987). Comparison of specific patterns of antisocial behavior in children with conduct disorder with and without coexisting hyperactivity. *Journal of Consulting and Clinical Psychology, 55,* 910–913.

Weiss, G., & Hechtman, L. (1993). *Hyperactive children grown up* (2nd ed.). New York: Guilford Press.

Weiss, G., Hechtman, L., & Perlman, T. (1978). Psychiatric status of hyperactives as adults: School, emploer, and self-rating scales obtained during ten-year follow-up evaluation. *American Journal of Orthopsychiatry, 48,* 438–445.

Welner, Z., Welner, A., Stewart, M., Palkes, H., & Wish, E. (1977). A controlled study of siblings of hyperactive children. *Journal of Nervous and Mental Disease, 165,* 110–117.

Werry, J. S. (1988). Differential diagnosis of attention deficits and conduct disorders. In L. Bloomingdale & J. Sergeant (Eds.), *Attention deficit disorder: Criteria, cognition, and intervention* (pp. 83–96). New York: Pergamon Press.

Whalen, C. K., & Henker, B. (1992). The social profile of attention-deficit hyperactivity disorder: Five fundamental facets. In G. Weiss (Ed.), *Child and adolescent psychiatric clinics of North America: Attention-deficit hyperactivity disorder* (pp. 395–410). Philadelphia: Saunders.

Whalen, C. K., Henker, B., Collins, B. E., Finck, D., & Dotemoto, S. (1979). A social ecology of hyperactive boys: Medication effects in systematically structured classroom environments. *Journal of Applied Behavior Analysis, 12,* 65–81.

Whalen, C. K., Henker, B., & Dotemoto, S. (1980). Methylphenidate and hyperactivity: Effects on teacher behaviors. *Science, 208,* 1280–1282.

Wheeler, J., & Carlson, C. L. (1994). The social functioning of children with ADD with hyperactivity and ADD without hyperactivity: A comparison of their peer relations and social deficits. *Journal of Emotional and Behavioral Disorders, 2,* 2–12.

Wozniak, J., Biederman, J., Kiely, K., Ablon, S., Faraone, S. V., Mundy, E., & Mennin, D. (1995). Mania-like symptoms suggestive of childhood-onset bipolar disorder in clinically referred children. *Journal of the American Academy of Child and Adolescent Psychiatry, 34,* 867–876.

Chapter 5

ETIOLOGIES

20

Since the first edition of this text was published, considerable research has accumulated on various etiologies for ADHD. Even so, this research continues to be methodologically difficult and at times inconsistent in its results. Yet there is even less doubt now among senior investigators in this field than there was at the time of the last edition that although multiple etiologies may lead to Attention-Deficit/Hyperactivity Disorder (ADHD), evidence points to neurological and genetic factors as the greatest contributors to this disorder. Our knowledge of the final common neurological pathway through which these factors produce their effects on behavior is significantly increased by converging lines of evidence from cerebral blood flow studies, studies of brain electrical activity using computer-averaging techniques, studies using neuropsychological tests sensitive to frontal lobe dysfunction, and neuroimaging studies using positron emission tomography (PET) and magnetic resonance imaging (MRI). Neurochemical abnormalities that may underlie this disorder have still proven extremely difficult to document with any certainty. Over the past decade, evidence is converging on a probable neurological site or network for ADHD. Nevertheless, most findings on etiologies are correlational in nature and do not permit direct evidence of immediate and primary causality. For instance, even though parents of ADHD children may smoke tobacco more during their pregnancies and pregnant women who smoke are more likely to have ADHD children, this does not directly prove that smoking causes the ADHD. It is possible that parents of ADHD children, themselves likely to have some manifestations of the disorder, may smoke more than parents of normal children. It is the genetic relationship between the parents and children that may be important here rather than the smoking itself. For this reason, great care needs to be taken in interpreting the correlational results of much of the research on etiologies of ADHD.

NEUROLOGICAL FACTORS

A variety of etiologies have been proposed for ADHD. Brain damage was initially proposed as a chief cause of ADHD symptoms (see Chapter 1, this volume), resulting from known brain infections, trauma, or other injuries or complications occurring during pregnancy or at the time of delivery. Several studies show that brain damage, particularly hypoxic/anoxic types of insults, are associated with greater attention deficits and hyperactivity (Cruikshank, Eliason, & Merrifield, 1988; O'Dougherty, Nuechterlein, & Drew, 1984). ADHD symptoms also occur more in children with seizure disorders (Holdsworth & Whitmore, 1974). However, most ADHD children have no history of significant brain injuries and such injuries are unlikely to account for the majority of children with this condition (Rutter, 1977).

Throughout the century, investigators have repeatedly noted the similarities between symptoms of ADHD and those produced by *lesions or injuries to the frontal lobes more generally and the prefrontal cortex specifically* (Benton, 1991; Heilman, Voeller, & Nadeau, 1991; Levin, 1938; Mattes, 1980). Both children and adults suffering injuries to the prefrontal region demonstrate deficits in sustained attention, inhibition, regulation of emotion and motivation, and the capacity to organize behavior across time (Fuster, 1989; Grattan & Eslinger, 1991; Stuss & Benson, 1986).

Neuropsychological Studies

Much of the neuropsychological evidence pertaining to ADHD was reviewed in the previous chapter under the particular form of cognitive impairment to which it pertains. A large number of studies have used neuropsychological tests of frontal lobe functions and have detected deficits on these tests, albeit inconsistently (Conners & Wells, 1986; Chelune, Ferguson, Koon, & Dickey, 1986; Epstein, Conners, Erhardt, March, & Swanson, 1997; Fischer, Barkley, Fletcher, & Smallish, 1990; Grodzinsky & Diamond, 1992, Heilman et al., 1991; Mariani & Barkley, 1997; for a recent and thorough review of this extensive literature, see Barkley, 1997). When consistent, the results suggest that it is disinhibition of behavioral responses that is evident from these tests in addition to difficulties with working memory, planning, verbal fluency, perseveration, motor sequencing, and other frontal lobe functions. Adults with ADHD also display similar deficits on neuropsychological tests of executive functions (Seidman, 1997). Moreover, recent research shows that not only do siblings of ADHD children who have ADHD show similar executive function deficits but even those siblings of ADHD children who do not actually manifest ADHD appear to have milder yet significant impairments in these same executive functions (Seidman, 1997; Seidman, Biederman, Faraone, Weber, & Ouellette, 1997). Such findings imply a possible genetically linked risk for executive function deficits in families that have ADHD children, even if symptoms of ADHD are not fully manifest in those family members. The totality of findings in this area is impressive in further suggesting that dysfunction of the prefrontal lobes (inhibition and executive function deficits) is a likely basis for explaining ADHD (Barkley, 1997).

Neurological Studies

It is only within the past 10–15 years that more direct research findings pertaining to neurological integrity in ADHD have increasingly supported the view of a neurodevelopmental origin to the disorder. Studies using *psychophysiological measures* of nervous system (central and autonomic) electrical activity, variously measured (electroencephalograms, galvanic skin responses, heart rate deceleration, etc.), have been inconsistent in demonstrating group differences between ADHD and control children. But when differences from normal are found, they are consistently in the direction of *diminished arousal or arousability* in those with ADHD (see Ferguson & Pappas, 1979; Hastings & Barkley, 1978; Rosenthal & Allen, 1978; Ross & Ross, 1982, for reviews).

Far more consistent are the results of *quantitative electroencephalograph (QEEG) and evoked response potential (ERP)* measures taken in conjunction with performance of vigilance tests (Frank, Lazar, & Seiden, 1992; Klorman et al., 1988). Although results have varied substantially across these studies (see Tannock, 1998, for a review), the most consistent pattern for QEEG research is increased slow wave, or theta, activity, particularly in the frontal lobe, and excess beta activity (Chabot & Serfontein, 1996; Kuperman, Johnson, Arndt, Lindgren, & Wolraich, 1996; Mann, Lubar, Zimmerman, Miller, & Muenchen, 1992; Matsuura et al., 1993). ADHD children have been found to have smaller amplitudes in the late positive components of their ERPs. These late components are believed to be a function of the prefrontal regions of the brain, are related to poorer performances on vigilance tests, and are corrected by stimulant medication (Klorman et al., 1988; Kuperman et al., 1996). Thus, although the evidence is far from conclusive, evoked response patterns related to sustained attention and inhibition suggest an underresponsiveness of ADHD children to stimulation that is corrected by stimulant medication.

Several studies have also examined *cerebral blood flow* in ADHD and normal children. They consistently show decreased blood flow to the prefrontal regions and pathways connecting these regions to the limbic system via the striatum and specifically its anterior region (the caudate) (Lou, Henriksen, & Bruhn, 1984, 1990; Lou, Henriksen, Bruhn, Borner, & Nielsen, 1984; Sieg, Gaffney, Preston, & Hellings, 1995).

More recently, studies using PET to assess cerebral glucose metabolism found diminished metabolism in adults (Zametkin et al., 1990) and adolescent females with ADHD (Ernst et al., 1994) but proved negative in adolescent males with ADHD (Zametkin et al., 1993). An attempt to replicate the finding with adolescent females who have ADHD in younger female ADHD children failed to find such diminished metabolism (Ernst, Cohen, Liebenauer, Jons, & Zametkin, 1997). Such studies are often plagued by their exceptionally small sample sizes, which results in low power to detect group differences and considerable unreliability in replicating previous findings. However, significant correlations have been noted between diminished metabolic activity in the left anterior frontal region and severity of ADHD symptoms in adolescents with ADHD (Zametkin et al., 1993). This demonstration of an association between the metabolic activity of certain brain regions and symptoms of ADHD is critical to proving a connection between the findings pertaining to brain activation and the behavior comprising ADHD.

The gross structure of the brain as portrayed by coaxial tomographic (CT) scan has not shown differences between ADHD and normal children (B. A. Shaywitz, Shaywitz, Byrne, Cohen, & Rothman, 1983) but greater brain atrophy was found in adults with ADHD who had a history of substance abuse (Nasrallah et al., 1986). The latter, however, seems more likely to account for these results than does the ADHD.

More fine-grained analysis of brain structures using the higher resolution MRI devices have begun to suggest differences in some brain regions in those with ADHD relative to control groups. Much of this work has been done by Hynd and his colleagues (see Tannock, 1998, for a review). Initial studies from this group examined the region of the left and right temporal lobes associated with auditory detection and analysis (planum temporale) in ADHD, learning-disabled (reading), and normal children. For some time, researchers studying reading disorders have focused on these brain regions given their connection to the analysis of speech sounds. Both the ADHD and learning-disabled children were found to have smaller right hemisphere plana temporale than the control group, whereas only the learning-disabled subjects had a smaller left plana temporale (Hynd, Semrud-Clikeman, Lorys, Novey, & Eliopulos, 1990). In the next study, the corpus callosum was examined in those with ADHD. This structure assists with the interhemispheric transfer of information. Those with ADHD were found to have a smaller callosum, particularly in the area of the genu and splenium and that region just anterior to the splenium (Hynd, Semrud-Clikeman, Lorys, Novey, & Eliopulos, 1991). An attempt to replicate this finding, however, failed to show any differences between ADHD and control children in the size or shape of the entire corpus callosum with the exception of the region of the splenium (posterior portion), which again was significantly smaller in subjects with ADHD (Semrud-Clikeman et al., 1994).

The various brain regions often described in MRI research are illustrated in Figure 5.1. Here the right hemisphere of the brain is shown but the left hemisphere has been cut away to expose the location of the striatum in relation to the prefrontal regions controlling movement specifically and behavior generally.

Because of the earlier research by Lou et al. (1984) demonstrating decreased blood flow in the striatal regions, a subsequent study concentrated on the morphology of this region in children with ADHD. Lesions of this region have been associated with symptoms very similar to ADHD. Results of this study indicated that children with ADHD had a significantly smaller left caudate nucleus creating a reversal of the normal pattern of left > right asymmetry of the caudate (Hynd et al., 1993). This finding is consistent with the earlier blood flow studies of decreased activity in this brain region.

Important to understand here is the problem of very small sample sizes employed in many of these studies. Such small samples typically fall well below levels needed for adequate statistical power and thus may obscure minor differences in brain structure/function that would be significant with larger samples. These small samples also tend to contribute to a high probability of failures by others, using similarly small samples, to replicate the original findings. The variability across studies using small samples has the potential to be quite large.

Fortunately, several more recent studies had larger samples of ADHD and control subjects using quantitative MRI technology. These studies indicated significantly smaller ante-

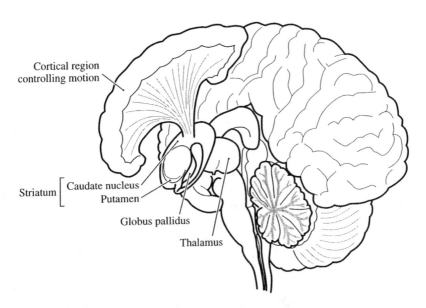

FIGURE 5.1. Diagram of the human brain showing the right hemisphere, and particularly the location of the striatum, globus pallidus, and thalamus. Most of the left hemisphere has been cut away up to the prefrontal lobes to reveal the striatum and other midbrain structures. Adapted with permission from an illustration by Carol Donner from page 53 of the article by M. B. H. Youdin & P. Riederer (1997). Understanding Parkinson's disease. *Scientific American, 276* (January), pp. 52–59. Copyright by *Scientific American*, 415 Madison Avenue, New York, NY 10017-1111.

rior right frontal regions, smaller size of the caudate nucleus, and smaller globus pallidus regions in children with ADHD compared to control subjects (Aylward et al., 1996; Castellanos et al., 1994; Castellanos et al., 1996; Filipek et al., 1997; Singer et al., 1993). The putamen, however, has not been found to be smaller in children with ADHD (Aylward et al., 1996; Castellanos et al., 1996; Singer et al., 1993). Interestingly, Castellanos et al. (1996) also found smaller cerebellar volume in those with ADHD, possibly consistent with recent views that the cerebellum may have some role in the motor presetting aspects of sensory perception that derive from planning and other executive functions (Akshoomoff, & Courchesne, 1992; Houk & Wise, 1995). No differences between groups were found in the regions of the corpus callosum in either of the studies by Castellanos et al. (1994, 1996) as was suggested in the small studies discussed earlier or as was found in a prior study by this same research team (Giedd et al., 1994). However, the study by Filipek et al. (1997) did find smaller posterior volumes of white matter in both hemispheres in the regions of the parietal and occipital lobes that might be consistent with the earlier studies showing smaller volumes of the corpus callosum in this same area. Castellanos et al. (1996) suggest that such differences in corpus callosal volume, particularly in the posterior regions, may be more related to learning disabilities which are often found in a large minority of ADHD children than to ADHD itself.

The results for the smaller size of the caudate nucleus are quite consistent across studies but are inconsistent in indicating which side of the caudate may be smaller. The work by Hynd and colleagues (Hynd et al., 1993) discussed earlier found the left caudate to be smaller than normal in their ADHD subjects. The more recent study by Filipek et al. (1997) found the same result. However, Castellanos et al. (1996) also reported a smaller caudate but found this to be on the right side. The normal human brain demonstrates a relatively consistent asymmetry in volume in favor of the right frontal cortical region being larger than the left (Giedd et al., 1996). This led Castellanos et al. (1996) to conclude that a lack of frontal asymmetry (a smaller than normal right frontal region) probably mediates the expression of ADHD. However, whether this asymmetry of the caudate of right side > left side is true in normal subjects is debatable as other studies found the opposite pattern in their normal subjects (Filipek et al., 1997; Hynd et al., 1993). As Filipek and colleagues noted, many of these differences in the findings of studies regarding which side of the caudate is more affected in subjects with ADHD could readily be explained by subject and procedural differences as well as differences in defining the boundaries of the caudate. More consistent across these studies are the findings of smaller right prefrontal cortical regions and smaller caudate volume, whether it be more on the right than left side.

Others reviewing this literature over the last two decades have reached similar conclusions—that abnormalities in the development of the frontal–striatal regions probably underlie the development of ADHD (Arnsten, Steere, & Hunt, 1996; Benton, 1991; Gualtieri & Hicks, 1985; Mattes, 1980; Mercugliano, 1995; Pontius, 1973; Tannock, 1998).

Important here is the fact that none of the neuroimaging studies found evidence of brain damage in any of these structures in those with ADHD. The regions identified as related to ADHD are simply smaller than normal, typically resulting in no asymmetry in size between the right and left frontal regions (or those of the caudate and globus pallidus) when such asymmetries are normal (right larger than left regions). This is consistent with past reviews of the literature suggesting that brain damage was probably a contributor to less than 5% of those with hyperactivity (Rutter, 1977, 1983). When differences in brain structures are found, they are likely the result of abnormalities in brain development within these particular regions, the causes of which are unknown but are probably under genetic control. After all, genes control in large part the developmental construction of the brain.

Neurotransmitter Deficiencies

Possible neurotransmitter dysfunction or imbalances have been proposed, resting chiefly on the responses of ADHD children to differing drugs. Given the findings that normal children show a positive, albeit lesser, response to stimulants (Rapoport et al., 1978), evidence from drug responding by itself cannot be used to support a neurochemical abnormality in ADHD. However, some direct evidence from studies of cerebral spinal fluid in ADHD and normal children indicates decreased brain dopamine in ADHD children (Raskin, Shaywitz, Shaywitz, Anderson, & Cohen, 1984). Evidence from other studies using blood and urinary metabolites of brain neurotransmitters have proven conflicting in their results (S. E. Shaywitz, Shaywitz, Cohen, & Young, 1983; S. E. Shaywitz et al., 1986; Zametkin & Rapoport, 1986). What evidence there is seems to point to a selective deficiency in the availability of both dopamine and norepinephrine, but this evidence cannot be considered conclusive at this time.

Pregnancy and Birth Complications

Some studies have not found a greater incidence of pregnancy or birth complications in ADHD compared to normal children (Barkley, DuPaul, & McMurray, 1990) whereas others have found a slightly higher prevalence of unusually short or long labor, fetal distress, low forceps delivery, and toxemia or eclampsia (Hartsough & Lambert, 1985; Minde, Webb, & Sykes, 1968). Nichols and Chen (1981) found that low birthweight was associated with an increased risk of hyperactivity, inattention, disruptive behavior, and poor school adjustment. These results have been replicated more recently (Breslau et al., 1996; Schothorst & van Engeland, 1996; Sykes et al., 1997; Szatmari, Saigal, Rosenbaum, & Campbell, 1993). It is not merely low birthweight that seems to pose the risk for symptoms of ADHD or the disorder itself, among other psychiatric disorders, but the extent of white matter abnormalities due to birth injuries, such as parenchymal lesions and/or ventricular enlargement (Whittaker et al., 1997).

Several studies suggest that mothers of ADHD children conceive these children at an age younger than that of mothers of control children and that such pregnancies may have a greater risk of adversity (Denson, Nanson, & McWatters, 1975; Hartsough & Lambert, 1985; Minde et al., 1968). Because pregnancy complications are more likely to occur among young mothers, mothers of ADHD children may have a higher risk for such complications which may act neurologically to predispose their children toward ADHD. However, the complications that have been noted to date are rather mild and hardly compelling evidence of pre- or perinatal brain damage as a cause of ADHD. Furthermore, large-scale epidemiological studies have generally not found a strong association between pre- or perinatal adversity and symptoms of ADHD once other factors are taken into account, such as maternal smoking and alcohol use (see later) as well as socioeconomic disadvantage, all of which may predispose to perinatal adversity and hyperactivity (Goodman & Stevenson, 1989; Nichols & Chen, 1981; Werner et al., 1971).

One study found that the season of a child's birth was significantly associated with risk for ADHD, at least among those subgroups that also either had learning disability or did not have any psychiatric comorbidity (Mick, Biederman, & Faraone, 1996). Birth in September was overrepresented in this subgroup of ADHD children. The authors conjecture that the season of birth may serve as a proxy for the timing of seasonally mediated viral infections to which these mothers and their fetuses may have been exposed and that this may account for approximately 10% of cases of ADHD.

GENETIC FACTORS

No evidence exists to show that ADHD is the result of abnormal chromosomal structures, as in Down syndrome, their fragility (as in fragile X) or transmutations, or extra chromosomal material, as in XXY syndrome. Children with such chromosomal abnormalities may show greater problems with attention, but such abnormalities are very uncommon in children with ADHD. By far, the greatest research evidence suggests that ADHD is highly hereditary in nature, making heredity one of the most well-substantiated etiologies for ADHD.

Family Aggregation Studies

Multiple lines of research support such a conclusion. For years, researchers have noted the higher prevalence of psychopathology in the parents and other relatives of children with ADHD. In particular, higher rates of ADHD, conduct problems, substance abuse, and depression have been repeatedly observed in these studies (Barkley et al., 1990; Biederman et al., 1992; Pauls, 1991). By separating the group of ADHD children into those with and without Conduct Disorder (CD), it has been shown that the conduct problems, substance abuse, and depression in the parents is related more to the presence of CD in the ADHD children than to ADHD itself (August & Stewart, 1983; Barkley, Fischer, Edelbrock, & Smallish, 1991; Biederman et al., 1992; Lahey et al., 1988). Yet rates of hyperactivity or ADHD remain high even in relatives of the group of ADHD children without CD (Biederman et al., 1992). Research shows that between 10% to 35% of the immediate family members of children with ADHD are also likely to have the disorder with the risk to siblings of the ADHD children being approximately 32% (Biederman et al., 1992; Biederman, Keenan, & Faraone, 1990; Pauls, 1991; Welner, Welner, Stewart, Palkes, & Wish, 1977). Rates of family aggregation of the disorder have been found in African-American families similar to rates reported in families of Caucasian children (Samuel et al., 1997). Even more striking, recent research shows that if a parent has ADHD, the risk to the offspring is 57% (Biederman et al., 1995). Thus, ADHD clusters among biological relatives of children or adults with the disorder, strongly implying an hereditary basis to this condition. Interestingly, research by Faraone and Biederman (1997) at Massachusetts General Hospital suggests that depression among family members of children with ADHD may be a nonspecific expression of the same genetic contribution hat is related to ADHD. This is based on their findings that family members of children with ADHD are at increased risk for Major Depression whereas individuals who have Major Depression have first-degree relatives at increased risk for ADHD.

Adoption Research

Another line of evidence for genetic involvement in ADHD has emerged from studies of adopted children. Cantwell (1975) and Morrison and Stewart (1973) both reported higher rates of hyperactivity in the biological parents of hyperactive children than in adoptive parents who have such children. Both studies suggest that hyperactive children are more likely to resemble their biological parents than their adoptive parents in their levels of hyperactivity. Yet, both studies were retrospective and both failed to study the biological parents of the adopted hyperactive children as a comparison group (Pauls, 1991). Cadoret and Stewart (1991) studied 283 male adoptees and found that if one of the biological parents had been judged delinquent or to have an adult criminal conviction, the adopted-away sons had a higher likelihood of having ADHD. A later study (van den Oord, Boomsma, & Verhulst, 1994) using biologically related and unrelated pairs of international adoptees identified a strong genetic component (47% of the variance) for the Attention Problems dimension of the Child Behavior Checklist, a rating scale commonly used in research in child psychopathology. This particular scale has a strong association with a diagnosis of ADHD (Biederman, Milbverger, Faraone, Guite, & Warburton, 1994) and is often used in research in selecting subjects with the disorder. Thus, like the family association studies discussed earlier, results of adoption studies point to a strong possibility of a significant hereditary contribution to hyperactivity.

Twin Studies

Studies of twins provide a third avenue of evidence for a genetic contribution to ADHD. Early studies demonstrated a greater agreement (concordance) for symptoms of hyperactivity and inattention between monozygotic (MZ) compared to dizygotic twins (DZ) (O'Connor, Foch, Sherry, & Plomin, 1980; Willerman, 1973). Studies of very small samples of twins (Heffron, Martin, & Welsh, 1984; Lopez, 1965) found complete (100%) concordance for MZ twins for hyperactivity and far less agreement for DZ twins. A later study of a much larger sample of twins (570) found that approximately 50% of the variance in hyperactivity and inattention in this sample was due to heredity whereas 0–30% may have been environmental (Goodman & Stevenson, 1989). Examining only those twins with clinically significant degrees of ADHD within this sample revealed a heritability of 64% for hyperactivity and inattention. This finding implies that the more deviant or clinically serious the degree of symptoms of ADHD, the more genetic factors may be contributing to it. Other large-scale twin studies are also quite consistent with these findings (Edelbrock, Rende, Plomin, & Thompson, 1995; Gillis, Gilger, Pennington, & DeFries, 1992; Levy & Hay, 1992). For instance, Gilger, Pennington, and DeFries (1992) found that if one twin was diagnosed as ADHD, the concordance for the disorder was 81% in MZ twins and 29% in DZ twins. Sherman, McGue, and Iacono (1997) found that the concordance for MZ twins having ADHD (mother identified) was 67% versus 0% for DZ twins. Stevenson (1994) summarized the status of twin studies on symptoms of ADHD up to that time by stating that the average heritability is .80 for symptoms of this disorder (range .50–.98). Subsequent and numerous large-scale twin studies have been remarkably consistent with this conclusion, demonstrating that the majority of variance (70–91%) in the trait of hyperactivity–impulsivity is a result of genetic factors (averaging approximately 80%) and that such a genetic contribution may increase the more extreme the scores along this trait happen to be, although this latter point is debatable (Faraone, 1996; Gjone, Stevenson, & Sundet, 1996; Gjone, Stevenson, Sundet, & Eilertsen, 1996; Hudziak, 1997; Levy, Hay, McStephen, Wood, & Waldman, 1997; Rhee, Waldman, Hay, & Levy, 1995; Sherman, Iacono, & McGue, 1997; Sherman, McGue, & Iacono, 1997; Silberg et al., 1996; Thapar, Hervas, & McGuffin, 1995; van den Oord, Verhulst, & Boomsma, 1996). Thus, twin studies indicate that the average heritability of ADHD is at least 0.80 and is often higher than this when clinical diagnostic criteria serve as the basis for determining ADHD. This research adds substantially more evidence to that already found in family and adoption studies supporting a strong genetic basis to ADHD and its behavioral symptoms.

But twin studies can also tell us as much about environmental contributions as they do about genetic factors affecting the expression of a trait (Faraone, 1996; Pike & Plomin, 1996; Plomin, 1995). Across the twin studies conducted to date, the results have been reasonably consistent in demonstrating that the shared environment contributes little, if any, explanation to individual differences in the trait underlying ADHD (hyperactive–impulsive–inattentive), accounting for typically 0–13% of the variance among individuals (Levy et al., 1997; Sherman, Iacono, & McGue, 1997; Silberg et al., 1996). Similar findings have been noted for other forms of child psychopathology (Pike & Plomin, 1996). Such shared environmental factors include social class and family educational/occupational status, the general home environment, family nutrition, toxins that may be present in the home environment (i.e., lead), parental and childrearing characteristics that are common or shared across children in the family, and other such nongenetic factors that are common to the twins under investigation in these studies. In their totality, such shared environmental factors seem to account for 0–6% of individual differences in the behavioral trait(s) related to ADHD. It is for this reason that little attention will be given here to discussing purely environmental or social factors as involved in the causation of ADHD. The large number of twin studies to date have not been able to support such common environmental factors as contributing much of significance to individual differences in symptoms of ADHD.

The twin studies cited earlier have also been able to indicate the extent to which individual differences in ADHD symptoms are the result of nonshared environmental factors. Such factors include not only those typically thought of as involving the social environment but also all biological factors that are nongenetic in origin. Factors in the nonshared environment are those events or conditions that will have uniquely affected only one twin and not the other. Besides biological hazards or neurologically injurious events that may have befallen only one member of a twin pair, the nonshared environment also includes those differences in the manner in which parents may have treated each child. Parents do not interact with all their children in an identical fashion and such unique parent–child interactions are believed to make more of a contribution to individual differences among siblings than do those factors about the home and child rearing that are common to all children in the family. Twin studies to date have suggested that approximately 9–20% of the variance in hyperactive–impulsive–inattentive behavior or ADHD symptoms can be attributed to such nonshared environmental (nongenetic) factors (Levy et al., 1997; Sherman, Iacono, & McGue, 1997; Silberg et al., 1996). Research suggests that the nonshared environmental factors also contribute disproportionately more to individual differences in other forms of child psychopathology than do factors in the shared environment (Pike & Plomin, 1996). Thus, if researchers were interested in identifying environmental contributors to ADHD, these twin studies suggest that such research should focus on those biological, interactional, and social experiences that are specific and unique to the individual and are not part of the common environment to which other siblings have been exposed.

Molecular Genetic Research

Quantitative genetic analyses of the large sample of families studied in Boston by Biederman and his colleagues suggest that a single gene may account for the expression of the disorder (Faraone et al., 1992). The focus of research initially was on the dopamine type 2 gene given findings of its increased association with alcoholism, Tourette syndrome, and ADHD (Blum, Cull, Braverman, & Comings, 1996; Comings et al., 1991) but others have failed to replicate this finding (Gelernter et al., 1991; Kelsoe et al., 1989). More recently, the dopamine transporter gene (DAT1) has been implicated in two studies of ADHD children (Cook et al., 1995; Cook, Stein, & Leventhal, 1997; Gill, Daly, Heron, Hawi, & Fitzgerald, 1997). However, here again other laboratories have not been able to replicate this association (Swanson et al., 1997).

Another gene related to dopamine, the DRD4 (repeater gene), was recently found to be overrepresented in the 7-repetition form of the gene in children with ADHD (Lahoste et al., 1996). Such a finding is quite interesting because this gene was previously associated with the personality trait of high novelty-seeking behavior, this variant of the gene affects pharmacological responsiveness, and the gene's impact on postsynaptic sensitivity is primarily found in frontal and prefrontal cortical regions believed to be associated with executive functions and attention (Swanson et al., 1997). The finding of an overrepresentation of the DRD4 gene at 7 repetitions has now been replicated in four subsequent studies using not only children with ADHD but also adolescents and adults with the disorder (Joseph Biederman, personal communication, December 6, 1997; Swanson et al., 1997; Sonuhara et al., 1997). Approximately 29% of these ADHD samples seem to have the 7-repeat allele, which may indicate a more homogeneous phenotypical subgroup within the ADHD population. This is one of the few genes identified so far that has been reliably associated with a sizable subgroup of individuals with ADHD. Clearly, research into the genetic mechanisms involved in the transmission of ADHD across generations promises to be an exciting and fruitful area of research endeavor over the next decade as the human genome is mapped and better understood.

Thyroid Disorder

Resistance to thyroid hormone (RTH) represents a variable tissue hyposensitivity to thyroid hormone and is known to be inherited as an autosomal dominant characteristic in most cases. It has been associated with mutations in the thyroid hormone beta receptor gene; thus, a single gene for the disorder has been identified. One study (Hauser et al., 1993) found that 70% of individuals with RTH had ADHD. Other research has suggested that 64% of patients with RTH display hyperactivity or learning disabilities (Refetoff, Weiss, & Usala, 1993). A later study was not able to corroborate a link between RTH and ADHD (Weiss et al., 1993). In a later study, Stein, Weiss, and Refetoff (1995) did find that half of their children with RTH met clinical diagnostic criteria for ADHD. Even so, the degree of ADHD in RTH patients is believed to be milder than that seen in clinic-referred and -diagnosed cases of ADHD. The RTH patients often have more learning difficulties and cognitive impairments than do the ADHD children without RTH. Given that RTH is exceptionally rare in children with ADHD (prevalence of 1 in 2,500) (Elia, Gullotta, Rose, Morin, & Rapoport, 1994), thyroid dysfunction is unlikely to be a major cause of ADHD in the population. An interesting recent finding is that RTH children having ADHD may show a positive behavioral response to liothyronine, with decreased impulsiveness, than do ADHD children who do not have RTH (Weiss, Stein, & Refetoff, 1997).

ENVIRONMENTAL TOXINS

As the twin and quantitative genetic studies suggest, the environment may play some role in individual differences in symptoms of ADHD, but these involve biological events, not just family influences or those influences within the psychosocial realm. As noted previously, variance in the expression of ADHD that may be a result of environmental sources means all nongenetic sources more generally. These include pre-, peri-, and postnatal complications and malnutrition, diseases, trauma, and other neurologically compromising events that may occur during the development of the nervous system before and after birth. Among these various biologically compromising events, several have been repeatedly linked to risks for inattention and hyperactive behavior.

One such event is exposure to environmental toxins and specifically lead. *Elevated body lead* burden has been shown to have a small but consistent and statistically significant relationship to the symptoms comprising ADHD (Baloh, Sturm, Green, & Gleser, 1975; David, 1974; de la Burde & Choate, 1972, 1974; Needleman et al., 1979; Needleman, Schell, Bellinger, Leviton, & Alfred, 1990). However, even at relatively high levels of lead, less than 38% of children are rated as having the behavior of hyperactivity on a teacher rating scale (Needleman et al., 1979), implying that most lead-poisoned children do not develop symptoms of ADHD. And most ADHD children, likewise, do not have significantly elevated lead burdens, although one study indicates that their lead levels may be higher than in control subjects (Gittelman & Eskinazi, 1983). Studies that have controlled for the presence of potentially confounding factors in this relationship found the association between body lead (in blood or dentition) and symptoms of ADHD to be .10–.19 with the more factors controlled, the more likely the relationship falls below .10 (Fergusson, Fergusson, Horwood, & Kinzett, 1988; Silva, Hughes, Williams, & Faed, 1988; Thomson et al., 1989). This finding suggests that no more than 4% (at best) of the variance in the expression of these symptoms in children with elevated lead is explained by their lead levels. Moreover, two serious methodological issues plague even the better conducted studies in this area:

1. None of the studies used clinical criteria for a diagnosis of ADHD to determine precisely what percentage of lead-burdened children actually have the disorder—all simply used behavior ratings comprising only a small number of items of inattention or hyperactivity.
2. None of the studies assessed for the presence of ADHD in the parents and controlled its contribution to the relationship. Given the high heritability of ADHD, this factor alone could attenuate the already small correlation between lead and symptoms of ADHD by as much as a third to a half its present levels.

Other types of environmental toxins found to have some relationship to inattention and hyperactivity are *prenatal exposure to alcohol and tobacco smoke* (Bennett, Wolin, & Reiss, 1988; Denson et al., 1975; Milberger, Biederman, Faraone, Chen, & Jones, 1996; Nichols & Chen, 1981; S. E. Shaywitz, Cohen, & Shaywitz, 1980; Streissguth et al., 1984; Streissguth, Bookstein, Sampson, & Barr, 1995). It has also been shown that parents of children with ADHD do consume more alcohol and smoke more tobacco than those in control groups even when not pregnant (Cunningham, Benness, & Siegel, 1988; Denson et al., 1975). Thus, it is reasonable for research to continue to pursue the possibility that these environmental toxins may be causally related to ADHD. However, as in the lead studies discussed earlier, most research in this area suffers from the same two serious methodological limitations: the failure to utilize clinical diagnostic criteria to determine rates of ADHD in exposed children and the failure to evaluate and control for the presence of ADHD in the parents. Until these steps are taken in future research, the relationships demonstrated so far between these toxins and ADHD must be viewed with some caution. In the area of maternal smoking during pregnancy, at least, such improvements in methodology were used in a recent study that found the relationship between maternal smoking during pregnancy and ADHD to remain significant after controlling for symptoms of ADHD in the parent (Milberger et al., 1996).

SIDE EFFECTS OF MEDICATIONS

Some evidence indicates that the medications used to treat seizure disorders, particularly phenobarbital and dilantin, are likely to result in increased problems with inattention and hyperactivity in children taking these medications (Committee on Drugs, 1985). Between 9% and 75% of children given phenobarbital are likely to develop hyperactivity or to have any preexisting ADHD symptoms worsened by this drug (Committee on Drugs, 1985; Wolf & Forsythe, 1978). However, a more recent study suggests that although such symptoms are more common in children treated with phenobarbital, few if any of these children meet full clinical criteria for ADHD (Brent, Crumrine, Varma, Allen, & Allman, 1987). Instead, more of the children treated with this medication were likely to be diagnosed as depressed or irritable. Considering that few ADHD children are taking these medications, such drugs cannot be considered to be a major cause of ADHD in the population. It would still be advisable, however, for clinicians working with ADHD children with epilepsy to be cautious about the possibility that certain types of anticonvulsants could worsen such a preexisting condition.

Some clinical anecdotal evidence suggests that methylxanthines, such as theophylline, a medication often used in treating asthma, and caffeine may cause such side effects as inattention and hyperactivity. It is not that these effects reach degrees that could be considered to warrant a diagnosis ADHD but that they may sufficiently predispose a child on these medications to be somewhat poorer at paying attention in school or that they may exacerbate the symptoms of an already ADHD child. A meta-analysis of the research literature (Stein, Krasowski, Leventhal, Phillips, & Bender, 1996) found no evidence of significant deleterious effects of either theophylline or caffeine on behavioral or cognitive functioning.

PSYCHOSOCIAL FACTORS

A few environmental theories of ADHD have been proposed (Block, 1977; Willis & Lovaas, 1977) but have not received much support in the available literature. Willis and Lovaas (1977) claimed that hyperactive behavior was the result of poor stimulus control by maternal commands and that this poor regulation of behavior arose from poor parental management of the children. Others have also conjectured that ADHD results from difficulties in the parents' overstimulating approach to caring for and managing the child as well as parental psychological problems (Carlson, Jacobvitz, & Sroufe, 1995; Jacobvitz & Sroufe, 1987; Silverman & Ragusa, 1992). But these theories have not been clear in articulating just how deficits in behavioral inhibition and other cognitive deficits commonly associated with clinically diagnosed ADHD as described in Chapters 2 and 3 (this volume) could arise from such social factors. Moreover, many of these studies proclaiming to have evidence of parental characteristics as potentially causative of ADHD did not use clinical diagnostic criteria to identify their children as ADHD; instead, they relied merely on elevated parental ratings of hyperactivity or laboratory demonstrations of distractibility to classify the children as ADHD (Carlson et al., 1995; Silverman & Ragusa, 1992). Nor have these theories received much support in the available literature that has studied clinically diagnosed children with ADHD (see Danforth, Barkley, & Stokes, 1991, concerning child management issues).

In view of the twin studies discussed previously that show minimal or nonsignificant contributions of the common or shared environment to the expression of symptoms of ADHD, theories based entirely on social explanations of the origins of ADHD are difficult to take seriously any longer. Despite the large role heredity seems to play in ADHD symptoms, they remain malleable to unique environmental influences and nonshared social learning. The actual severity of the symptoms, the continuity of those symptoms over development, the types of secondary symptoms, and the outcome of the disorder are related in varying degrees to environmental factors (Biederman et al., 1996; Milberger, 1997; van den Oord & Rowe, 1997; Weiss & Hechtman, 1993). Yet even here care must be taken in interpreting these findings as evidence of a pure environmental contribution to ADHD because many measures of family function and adversity also show a strong heritable contribution to them, largely owing to the presence of symptoms and disorders in the parents similar to those evident in the child (Pike & Plomin, 1996; Plomin, 1995). Thus, there is a genetic contribution to the family environment, a fact that often goes overlooked in studies of family and social factors involved in ADHD.

Moreover, as noted in the last chapter, several investigators attempted to evaluate the direction of effects within parent–child interactions. They did so by investigating the effects of stimulant medication and placebo on these mother–child interactions. The studies consistently found that the medications resulted in significant improvements in child hyperactivity and compliance. There was a corresponding reduction in mothers' use of commands, direction, and negative behavior when the children were on medication, indicating that much of the negative behavior of the mothers appeared to be in response to the difficult behavior of these children (Barkley & Cunningham, 1979; Barkley, Karlsson, Strzelecki, & Murphy, 1984; Barkley, Karlsson, Pollard, & Murphy, 1985; Cunningham & Barkley, 1979; Humphries, Kinsbourne, & Swanson, 1978). Further supporting this view were the findings from the large study of hyperactivity in twins by Goodman and Stevenson (1989). They also found that mothers' use of criticism and their general malaise in parenting were associated to a small but significant degree with ADHD symptoms. But these factors accounted for less than 10% of the variance in these symptoms in this population. The finding is consistent with other twin studies in suggesting that the shared environment, of which general parental psychological characteristics and caretaking ability are a part, accounts for only 0–6% of the variance in ADHD symptoms, on average. Thus, common parenting factors are not viewed as a major contributor to the occurrence of ADHD symptoms or the disorder in children.

Taken together, these findings suggest that the overly critical, commanding, and negative behavior of mothers of hyperactive children is most likely a reaction to the difficult, disruptive, and noncompliant behavior of these children rather than being a cause of it. This is not to say that the manner in which parents attempt to manage their children's ADHD behavior cannot exacerbate it or maintain higher levels of conflict between mother and child over time. Studies have shown that the continuation of hyperactive behavior over development and especially the maintenance of oppositional behavior in these children are related in part to parents' use of commands and criticism and an overcontrolling and intrusive style of management (Barkley et al., 1991; Campbell, 1987, 1989; Campbell & Ewing, 1990). But it is to say that theories of the causation of ADHD can no longer be based solely or even primarily on social factors, such as parental characteristics, caregiving abilities, child management, or other family environmental factors.

As discussed in Chapter 1 (this volume), Block (1977) proposed that an increase in "cultural tempo" in Western civilization may account for the prevalence of hyperactivity in these countries. Precisely what is meant by cultural tempo is not operationally defined, nor is evidence presented to suggest that underdeveloped or Eastern cultures have less hyperactivity than do more developed cultures. Although intriguing, this theory and its modification by Ross and Ross (1982) remain speculative and would seem to be almost scientifically untestable. Moreover, such theories once again conflict with a wealth of information on genetics and heritability of this behavior pattern and disorder that would argue against those theories as explanations for the occurrence of most ADHD in children.

SUMMARY

It should be evident from the research reviewed here that neurological and genetic factors make a substantial contribution to symptoms of ADHD and the occurrence of the disorder. A variety of genetic and neurological etiologies (e.g., pregnancy and birth complications, acquired brain damage, toxins, infections, and genetic effects) can give rise to the disorder through some disturbance in a final common pathway in the nervous system. That final common pathway appears to be the integrity of the prefrontal cortical–striatal network. It now appears that hereditary factors play the largest role in the occurrence of ADHD symptoms in children. It may be that what is transmitted genetically is a tendency toward a smaller and less active prefrontal–striatal network. The condition can also be caused or exacerbated by pregnancy complications, exposure to toxins, or neurological disease. Social factors alone cannot be supported as causal of this disorder, but such factors may exacerbate the condition, contribute to its persistence, and, more likely, contribute to the forms of comorbid disorders associated with ADHD. Cases of ADHD can also arise without a genetic predisposition to the disorder provided the child is exposed to significant disruption or neurological injury to this final common neurological pathway, but this would seem to account for only a small minority of ADHD children. In general, then, research conducted since the last edition of this text has further strengthened the evidence for genetic and developmental neurological factors as likely causal of this disorder while greatly reducing the support for purely social or environmental factors as having a role in the causation of this disorder. Even so, environmental factors involving family and social adversity may still serve as exacerbating factors, determinants of comorbidity, and contributors to persistence of disorder over development.

REFERENCES

Akshoomoff, N. A., & Courchesne, E. (1992). A new role for the cerebellum in cognitive operations. *Behavioral Neurosciences, 106,* 731–738.

Arnsten, A. F. T., Steere, J. C., & Hunt, R. D. (1996). The contribution of alpha$_2$ noradrenergic mechanism to prefrontal cortical cognitive function. *Archives of General Psychiatry, 53,* 448–455.

August, G. J., & Stewart, M. A. (1983). Family subtype of childhood hyperactivity. *Journal of Nervous and Mental Disease, 171,* 362–368.

Aylward, E. H., Reiss, A. L., Reader, M. J., Singer, H. S., Brown, J. E., & Denckla, M. B. (1996). Basal ganglia volumes in c hildren with attention-deficit hyperactivity disorder. *Journal of Child Neurology, 11,* 112–115.

Baloh, R., Sturm, R., Green, B., & Gleser, G. (1975). Neuropsychological effects of chronic asymptomatic increased lead absorption. *Archives of Neurology, 32,* 326–330.

Barkley, R. A. (1997). *ADHD and the nature of self-control.* New York: Guilford Press.

Barkley, R. A., & Cunningham, C. E. (1979). The effects of methylphenidate on the mother child interactions of hyperactive children. *Archives of General Psychiatry, 36,* 201–208.

Barkley, R. A., DuPaul, G. J., & McMurray, M.B. (1990). A comprehensive evaluation of attention deficit disorder with and without hyperactivity. *Journal of Consulting and Clinical Psychology, 58,* 775–789.

Barkley, R. A., Fischer, M., Edelbrock, C. S., & Smallish, L. (1991). The adolescent outcome of hyperactive children diagnosed by research criteria: III. Mother–child interactions, family conflicts, and maternal psychopathology. *Journal of Child Psychology and Psychiatry, 32,* 233–256.

Barkley, R. A., Karlsson, J., Pollard, S., & Murphy, J. V. (1985). Developmental changes in the mother–child interactions of hyperactive boys: Effects of two dose levels of Ritalin. *Journal of Child Psychology and Psychiatry and Allied Disciplines, 26,* 705–715.

Barkley, R., Karlsson, J., Strzelecki, E. & Murphy, J. (1984). The effects of age and Ritalin dosage on the mother-child interactions of hyperactive children. *Journal of Consulting and Clinical Psychology, 52,* 750–758.

Bennett, L. A., Wolin, S. J., & Reiss, D. (1988). Cognitive, behavioral, and emotional problems among school-age children of alcoholic parents. *American Journal of Psychiatry, 145,* 185–190.

Benton, A. (1991). Prefrontal injury and behavior in children. *Developmental Neuropsychology, 7,* 275–282.

Biederman, J., Faraone, S. V., Keenan, K., Benjamin, J., Krifcher, B., Moore, C., Sprich-Buckminster, S., Ugaglia, K., Jellinek, M. S., Steingard, R., Spencer, T., Norman, D., Kolodny, R., Kraus, I., Perrin, J., Keller, M. B., & Tsuang, M. T. (1992). Further evidence for family-genetic risk factors in attention deficit hyperactivity disorder; Patterns of comorbidity in probands and relatives in psychiatrically and pediatrically referred samples. *Archives of General Psychiatry, 49,* 728–738.

Biederman, J., Faraone, S. V., Mick, E., Spencer, T., Wilens, T., Kiely, K., Guite, J., Ablon, J. S., Reed, E., Warburton, R. (1995). High risk for attention deficit hyperactivity disorder among children of parents with childhood onset of the disorder: A pilot study. *American Journal of Psychiatry, 152,* 431–435.

Biederman, J., Faraone, S., Milberger, S., Curtis, S., Chen, L., Marrs, A., Ouellette, C., Moore, P., & Spencer, T. (1996). Predictors of persistence and remission of ADHD into adolescence: Results from a four-year prospective follow-up study. *Journal of the American Academy of Child and Adolescent Psychiatry, 35,* 343–351.

Biederman, J., Keenan, K., & Faraone, S. V. (1990). Parent-based diagnosis of attention deficit disorder predicts a diagnosis based on teacher report. *American Journal of Child and Adolescent Psychiatry, 29,* 698–701.

Biederman, J., Milberger, S., Faraone, S. V., Guite, J., & Warburton, R. (1994). Associations between childhood asthma and ADHD: Issues of psychiatric comorbidity and familiality. *Journal of the American Academy of Child and Adolescent Psychiatry, 33,* 842–848.

Block, G. H. (1977). Hyperactivity: A cultural perspective. *Journal of Learning Disabilities, 110,* 236–240.

Blum, K., Cull, J. G., Braverman, E. R., & Comings, D. E. (1996). Reward deficiency syndrome. *American Scientist, 84,* 132–145.

Brent, D. A., Crumrine, P. K., Varma, R. R., Allan, M., & Allman, C. (1987). Phenobarbital treatment and major depressive disorder in children with epilepsy. *Pediatrics, 80,* 909–917.

Breslau, N., Brown, G. G., DelDotto, J. E., Kumar, S., Exhuthachan, S., Andreski, P., & Hufnagle, K. G. (1996). Psychiatric sequelae of low birth weight at 6 years of age. *Journal of Abnormal Child Psychology, 24,* 385–400.

Cadoret, R. J., & Stewart, M. A. (1991). An adoption study of attention deficit/hyperactivity/aggression and their relationship to adult antisocial personality. *Comprehensive Psychiatry, 32,* 73–82.

Campbell, S. B. (1987). Parent-referred problem three-year-olds: Developmental changes in symptoms. *Journal of Child Psychology and Psychiatry, 28,* 835–846.

Campbell, S. B. (1990). *Behavior problems in preschool children.* New York: Guilford Press.

Campbell, S. B., & Ewing, L. J. (1990). Follow-up of hard-to-manage preschoolers: Adjustment at age nine years and predictors of continuing symptoms. *Journal of Child Psychology and Psychiatry, 31,* 891–910.

Cantwell, D. (1975). *The hyperactive child.* New York: Spectrum.

Carlson, E. A., Jacobvitz, D., & Sroufe, L. A. (1995). A developmental investigation of inattentiveness and hyperactivity. *Child Development, 66,* 37–54.

Castellanos, F. X., Giedd, J. N., Eckburg, P., Marsh, W. L., Vaituzis, C., Kaysen, D., Hamburger, S. D., & Rapoport, J. L. (1994). Quantitative morphology of the caudate nucleus in attention deficit hyperactivity disorder. *American Journal of Psychiatry, 151,* 1791–1796.

Castellanos, F. X., Giedd, J. N., Marsh, W. L., Hamburger, S. D., Vaituzis, A. C., Dickstein, D. P., Sarfatti, S. E., Vauss, Y. C., Snell, J. W., Lange, N., Kaysen, D., Krain, A. L., Ritchhie, G. F., Rajapakse, J. C., & Rapoport, J. L. (1996). Quantitative brain magnetic resonance imaging in attention-deficit hyperactivity disorder. *Archives of General Psychiatry, 53,* 607–616.

Chabot, R. J., & Serfontein, G. (1996). Quantitative electroencephalographic profiles of children with attention deficit disorder. *Biological Psychiatry, 40,* 951–963.

Chelune, G. J., Ferguson, W., Koon, R., & Dickey, T. O. (1986). Frontal lobe disinhibition in attention deficit disorder. *Child Psychiatry and Human Development, 16,* 221–234.

Comings, D. E., Comings, B. G., Muhleman, D., Dietz, G., Shahbahrami, B., Tast, D., Knell, E., Kocsis, P., Baumgarten, R., Kovacs, B. W., Levy, D. L., Smith, M., Borison, R. L., Evans, D. D., Klein, D. N., MacMurray, J., Tosk, J. M., Sverd, J., Gysin, R., & Flanagan, S. D. (1991). The dopamine D2 receptor locus as a modifying gene in neuropsychiatric disorders. *Journal of the American Medical Association, 266,* 1793–1800.

Committee on Drugs, American Academy of Pediatrics. (1985). Behavioral and cognitive effects of anticonvulsant threapy. *Pediatrics, 76,* 644–647.

Conners, C. K., & Wells, K. (1986). *Hyperactive children: A neuropsychological approach.* Beverly Hills, CA: Sage.

Cook, E. H., Stein, M. A., Krasowski, M. D., Cox, N. J., Olkon, D. M., Kieffer, J. E., & Leventhal, B. L. (1995). Association of attention deficit disorder and the dopamine transporter gene. *American Journal of Human Genetics, 56,* 993–998..

Cook, E. H., Stein, M. A., & Leventhal, D. L. (1997). Family-based association of attention-deficit/ hyperactivity disorder and the dopamine transporter. In K. Blum (Ed.), *Handbook of psychiatric genetics* (pp. 297–310). New York: CRC Press.

Cruickshank, B. M., Eliason, M., & Merrifield, B. (1988). Long-term sequelae of water near-drowning. *Journal of Pediatric Psychology, 13,* 379–388.

Cunningham, C. E., & Barkley, R. A. (1979). The interactions of hyperactive and normal children with their mothers during free play and structured task. *Child Development, 50,* 217–224.

Cunningham, C. E., Benness, B. B., & Siegel, L. S. (1988). Family functioning, time allocation, and parental depression in the families of normal and ADDH children. *Journal of Clinical Child Psychology, 17,* 169–177.

Danforth, J. S., Barkley, R. A., & Stokes, T. F. (1991). Observations of parent–child interactions with hyperactive children: Research and clinical implications. *Clinical Psychology Review, 11,* 703–727.

David, O. J. (1974). Association between lower level lead concentrations and hyperactivity. *Environmental Health Perspective, 7,* 17–25.

de la Burde, B., & Choate, M. (1972). Does asymptomatic lead exposure in children have latent sequelae? *Journal of Pediatrics, 81,* 1088–1091.

de la Burde, B., & Choate, M. (1974). Early asymptomatic lead exposure and development at school age. *Journal of Pediatrics, 87,* 638–642.

Denson, R., Nanson, J. L., & McWatters, M. A. (1975). Hyperkinesis and maternal smoking. *Canadian Psychiatric Association Journal, 20,* 183–187.

Edelbrock, C. S., Rende, R., Plomin, R., & Thompson, L. (1995). A twin study of competence and problem behavior in childhood and early adolescence. *Journal of Child Psychology and Psychiatry, 36,* 775–786.

Elia, J., Gullotta, C., Rose, J. R., Marin, G., & Rapoport, J. L. (1994). Thyroid function in attention deficit hyperactivity disorder. *Journal of the American Academy of Child and Adolescent Psychiatry, 33,* 169–172.

Epstein, J. N., Conners, C. K., Erhardt, D., March, J. S., & Swanson, J. M. (1997). Assymetrical hemispheric control of visual–spatial attention in adults with attention deficit hyperactivity disorder. *Neuropsychology, 11,* 467–473.

Ernst, M., Cohen, R. M., Liebenauer, L. L., Jons, P. H. & Zametkin, A. J. (1997). Cerebral glucose metabolism in adolescent girls with attention-deficit/hyperactivity disorder. *Journal of the American Acdemy of Child and Adolescent Psychiatry, 36,* 1399–1406.

Ernst, M., Liebenauer, L. L., King, A. C., Fitzgerald, G. A., Cohen, R. M., & Zametkin, A. J. (1994). Reduced brain metabolism in hyperactive girls. *Journal of the American Academy of Child and Adolescent Psychiatry, 33,* 858–868.

Faraone, S. V. (1996). Discussion of: "Genetic influence on parent-reported attention-related problems in a Norwegian general population twin sample." *Journal of the American Academy of Child and Adolescent Psychiatry, 35,* 596–598.

Faraone, S. V., Biederman, J., Chen, W. J., Krifcher, B., Keenan, K., Moore, C., Sprich, S., & Tsuang, M. T. (1992). Segregation analysis of attention deficit hyperactivity disorder. *Psychiatric Genetics, 2,* 257–275.

Ferguson, H. B., & Pappas, B. A. (1979). Evaluation of psychophysiological, neurochemical, and animal models of hyperactivity. In R. L. Trites (Eds.), *Hyperactivity in children.* Baltimore: University Park Press.

Fergusson, D. M., Fergusson, I. E., Horwood, L. J. & Kinzett, N. G. (1988). A longitudinal study of dentine lead levels, intelligence, school performance, and behaviour. *Journal of Child Psychology and Psychiatry, 29,* 811–824.

Filipek, P. A., Semrud-Clikeman, M., Steingard, R. J., Renshaw, P. F., Kennedy, D. N., & Biederman, J. (1997). Volumetric MRI analysis comparing subjects having attention-deficit hyperactivity disorder with normal controls. *Neurology, 48,* 589–601.

Fischer, M., Barkley, R., Fletcher, K. & Smallish, L. (1990). The adolescent outcome of hyperactive children diagnosed by research criteria: II. Academic, attentional, and neuropsychological status. *Journal of Consulting and Clinical Psychology, 58,* 580–588.

Frank, Y., Lazar, J. W., & Seiden, J. A. (1992). Cognitive event-related potentials in learning-disabled children with or without attention-deficit hyperactivity disorder [Abstract]. *Annals of Neurology, 32,* 478.

Fuster, J. M. (1989). *The prefrontal cortex.* New York: Raven.

Gelernter, J. O., O'Malley, S., Risch, N., Kranzler, H. R., Krystal, J., Merikangas, K., Kennedy, J. L., et al. (1991). No association between an allele at the D2 dopamine receptor gene (DRD2) and alcoholism. *Journal of the American Medical Association, 266,* 1801–1807.

Giedd, J. N., Castellanos, F. X., Casey, B. J., Kozuch, P., King, A. C., Hamburger, S. D., & Rapoport, J. L. (1994). Quantitative morphology of the corpus callosum in attention deficit hyperactivity disorder. *American Journal of Psychiatry, 151,* 665–669.

Giedd, J. N., Snell, J. W., Lange, N., Rajapakse, J. C., Casey, B. J., Kozuch, P. L., Vaituzis, A. C., Vauss, Y. C., Hamburger, S. D., Kaysen, D., & Rapoport, J. L. (1996). Quantitative magnetic resonance imaging of human brain development: Ages 4–18. *Cerebral Cortex, 6,* 551–560.

Gilger, J. W., Pennington, B. F., & DeFries, J. C. (1992). A twin study of the etiology of comorbidity: Attention-deficit hyperactivity disorder and dyslexia. *Journal of the American Academy of Child and Adolescent Psychiatry, 31,* 343–348.

Gill, M., Daly, G., Heron, S., Hawi, Z., & Fitzgerald, M. (1997). Confirmation of association between attention deficit hyperactivity disorder and a dopamine transporter polymorphism. *Molecular Psychiatry, 2,* 311–313.

Gillis, J. J., Gilger, J. W., Pennington, B. F., & Defries, J. C. (1992). Attention deficit disorder in reading-disabled twins: Evidence for a genetic etiology. *Journal of Abnormal Child Psychology, 20,* 303–315.

Gittelman, R., & Eskinazi, B. (1983). Lead and hyperactivity revisited. *Archives of General Psychiatry, 40,* 827–833.

Gjone, H., Stevenson, J., & Sundet, J. M. (1996). Genetic influence on parent-reported attention-related problems in a Norwegian general population twin sample. *Journal of the American Academy of Child and Adolescent Psychiatry, 35,* 588–596.

Gjone, H., Stevenson, J., Sundet, J. M., & Eilertsen, D. E. (1996). Changes in heritability across increasing levels of behavior problems in young twins. *Behavior Genetics, 26,* 419–426.

Goodman, R., & Stevenson, J. (1989). A twin study of hyperactivity: II. The aetiological role of genes, family relationships, and perinatal adversity. *Journal of Child Psychology and Psychiatry, 30,* 691–709.

Grattan, L. M., & Eslinger, P. J. (1991). Frontal lobe damage in children and adults: A comparative review. *Developmental Neuropsychology, 7,* 283–326.

Grodzinsky, G. M., & Diamond, R. (1992). Frontal lobe functioning in boys with attention-deficit hyperactivity disorder. *Developmental Neuropsychology, 8,* 427–445.

Gualtieri, C. T., & Hicks, R. E. (1985). Neuropharmacology of methylphenidate and a neural substrate for childhood hyperactivity. *Psychiatric Clinics of North America, 8,* 875–892.

Hartsough, C. S., & Lambert, N. M. (1985). Medical factors in hyperactive and normal children: Prenatal, developmental, and health history findings. *American Journal of Orthopsychiatry, 55,* 190–210.

Hastings, J., & Barkley, R. A. (1978). A review of psychophysiological research with hyperactive children. *Journal of Abnormal Child Psychology, 7,* 413–337.

Hauser, P., Zametkin, A. J., Martinez, P., et al. (1993). Attention deficit hyperactivity disorder in people with generalized resistance to thyroid hormone. *New England Journal of Medicine, 328,* 997–1001.

Heffron, W. A., Martin, C. A., & Welsh, R. J. (1984). Attention deficit disorder in three pairs of monozygotic twins: A case report. *Journal of the American Academy of Child Psychiatry, 23,* 299–301.

Heilman, K. M., Voeller, K. K. S., & Nadeau, S. E. (1991). A possible pathophysiological substrate of attention deficit hyperactivity disorder. *Journal of Child Neurology, 6,* 74–79.

Holdsworth, L., & Whitmore, K. (1974). A study of children with epilepsy attending ordinary schools: I. Their seizure patterns, progress, and behaviour in school. *Developmental Medicine and Child Neurology, 16,* 746–758.

Houk, J. C., & Wise, S. P. (1995). Distributed modular architectures linking basal ganglia, cerebellum, and cerebral cortex: Their role in planning and controlling action. *Cerebral Cortex, 2,* 95–110.

Hudziak, J. (1997, October). *The genetics of attention deficit hyperactivity disorder.* Paper presented at the annual meeting of the American Academy of Child and Adolescent Psychiatry, Toronto, Canada.

Humphries, T., Kinsbourne, M., & Swanson, J. (1978). Stimulant effects on cooperation and social interaction between hyperactive children and their mothers. *Journal of Child Psychology and Psychiatry, 19,* 13–22.

Hynd, G. W., Hern, K. L., Novey, E. S., Eliopulos, D., Marshall, R., Gonzalez, J. J., & Voeller, K. K. (1993). Attention-deficit hyperactivity disorder and asymmetry of the caudate nucleus. *Journal of Child Neurology, 8,* 339–347.

Hynd, G. W., Semrud-Clikeman, M., Lorys, A. R., Novey, E. S., & Eliopulos, D. (1990). Brain morphology in developmental dyslexia and attention deficit disorder/hyperactivity. *Archives of Neurology, 47,* 919–926.

Hynd, G. W., Semrud-Clikeman, M., Lorys, A. R., Novey, E. S., Eliopulos, D., & Lyytinen, H. (1991). Corpus callosum morphology in attention deficit-hyperactivity disorder: morphometric analysis of MRI. *Journal of Learning Disabilities, 24,* 141–146.

Jacobvitz, D., & Sroufe, L. A. (1987). The early caregiver–child relationship and attention-deficit disorder with hyperactivity in kindergarten: A prospective study. *Child Development, 58,* 1488–1495.

Kelsoe, J. R., Ginns, E. I., Egeland, J. A., Gerhard, D. S., Goldstein, A. M., Bale, S. J., Pauls, D. L., et al. (1989). Re-evaluation of the linkage relationship between chromosome 11p loci and the gene for bipolar affective disorder in the Old Order Amish. *Nature, 342,* 238–243.

Klorman, R., Brumaghim, J. T., Coons, H. W., Peloquin, L., Strauss, J., Lewine, J. D., Borgstedt, A. D., & Goldstein, M. G. (1988). The contributions of event-related potentials to understanding effects of stimulants on information processing in attention deficit disorder. In L. M. Bloomingdale & J. A. Sergeant (Eds.), *Attention deficit disorder: Criteria, cognition, intervention* (pp. 199–218). London: Pergamon Press.

Kuperman, S., Johnson, B., Arndt, S., Lindgren, S., & Wolraich, M. (1996). Quantitative EEG differences in a nonclinical sample of children with ADHD and undifferentiated ADD. *Journal of the American Academy of Child and Adolescent Psychiatry, 35,* 1009–1017.

Lahey, B. B., Pelham, W. E., Schaughency, E. A., Atkins, M. S., Murphy, H. A., Hynd, G. W., Russo, M., Hartdagen, S., & Lorys-Vernon, A. (1988). Dimensions and types of attention deficit disorder with hyperactivity in children: A factor and cluster-analytic approach. *Journal of the American Academy of Child and Adolescent Psychiatry, 27,* 330–335.

Lahoste, G. J., Swanson, J. M., Wigal, S. B., Glabe, C., Wigal, T., King, N., & Kennedy, J. L. (1996). Dopamine D4 receptor gene polymorphism is associated with attention deficit hyperactivity disorder. *Molecular Psychiatry, 1,* 121–124.

Levin, P. M. (1938). Restlessness in children. *Archives of Neurology and Psychiatry, 39,* 764–770.

Levy, F., & Hay, D. (1992, February). *ADHD in twins and their siblings.* Paper presented at the International Society for Research in Child and Adolescent Psychopathology, Sarasota, FL.

Levy, F., Hay, D. A., McStephen, M., Wood, C., & Waldman, I. (1997). Attention-deficit hyperactivity disorder: A category or a continuum? Genetic analysis of a large-scale twin study. *Journal of the American Academy of Child and Adolescent Psychiatry, 36,* 737–744.

Lopez, R. (1965). Hyperactivity in twins. *Canadian Psychiatric Association Journal, 10,* 421.

Lou, H. C., Henriksen, L., & Bruhn, P. (1984). Focal cerebral hypoperfusion in children with dysphasia and/or attention deficit disorder. *Archives of Neurology, 41,* 825–829.

Lou, H. C., Henriksen, L., & Bruhn, P. (1990). Focal cerebral dysfunction in developmental learning disabilities. *Lancet, 335,* 8–11.

Lou, H. C., Henriksen, L., Bruhn, P., Borner, H., & Nielsen, J. B. (1989). Striatal dysfunction in attention deficit and hyperkinetic disorder. *Archives of Neurology, 46,* 48–52.

Mann, C., Lubar, J. F., Zimmerman, A. W., Miller, C. A., & Muenchen, R. A. (1992). Quantitative analysis of EEG in boys with attention-deficit hyperactivity disorder: Controlled study with clinical implications. *Pediatric Neurology, 8,* 30–36.

Mariani, M., & Barkley, R. A. (1997). Neuropsychological and academic functioning in preschool children with attention deficit hyperactivity disorder. *Developmental Neuropsychology, 13,* 111–129.

Matsuura, M., Okuba, Y. Toru, M., Kojima, T., He, Y., Hou, Y., Shen, Y., & Lee, C. K. (1993). A cross-national EEG study of children with emotional and behavioral problems: A WHO collaborative study in the Western Pacific region. *Biological Psychiatry, 34,* 59–65.

Mattes, J. A. (1980). The role of frontal lobe dysfunction in childhood hyperkinesis. *Comprehensive Psychiatry, 21,* 358–369.

Mercugliano, M. (1995). Neurotransmitter alterations in attention-deficit/hyperactivity disorder. *Mental Retardation and Developmental Disabilities Research Reviews, 1,* 220–226.

Mick, E., Biederman, J., & Faraone, S. V. (1996). Is season of birth a risk factor for attention-deficit hyperactivity disorder? *Journal of the American Academy of Child and Adolescent Psychiatry, 35,* 1470–1476.

Milberger, S. (1997, October). *Impact of adversity on functioning and comorbidity in girls with ADHD.* Paper presented at the annual meeting of the American Academy of Child and Adolescent Psychiatry, Toronto, Canada.

Milberger, S., Biederman, J., Faraone, S. V., Chen, L., & Jones, J. (1996). Is maternal smoking during pregnancy a risk factor for attention deficit hyperactivity disorder in children? *American Journal of Psychiatry, 153,* 1138–1142.

Minde, K., Webb, G., & Sykes, D. (1968). Studies on the hyperactive child: VI. Prenatal and perinatal factors associated with hyperactivity. *Developmental Medicine and Child Neurology, 10,* 355–363.

Morrison, J., & Stewart, M. (1973). The psychiatric status of the legal families of adopted hyperactive children. *Archives of General Psychiatry, 28,* 888–891.

Nasrallah, H. A., Loney, J., Olson, S. C., McCalley-Whitters, M., Kramer, J., & Jacoby, C. G. (1986). Cortical atrophy in young adults with a history of hyperactivity in childhood. *Psychiatry Research, 17,* 241–246.

Needleman, H. L., Gunnoe, C., Leviton, A., Reed, R., Peresie, H., Maher, C., & Barrett, P. (1979). Deficits in psychologic and classroom performance of children with elevated dentine lead levels. *New England Journal of Medicine, 300,* 689–695.

Needleman, H. L., Schell, A. Bellinger, D. C., Leviton, L., & Alfred, E. D. (1990). The long-term effcts of exposure to low doses of lead in c hildhood: An 11–year follow-up report. *New England Journal of Medicine, 322,* 83–88.

Nichols, P. L., & Chen, T. C. (1981). *Minimal brain dysfunction: A prospective study.* Hillsdale, NJ: Erlbaum.

O'Connor, M., Foch, T., Sherry, T., & Plomin, R. (1980). A twin study of specific behavioral problems of socialization as viewed by parents. *Journal of Abnormal Child Psychology, 8,* 189–199.

O'Dougherty, M., Nuechterlein, K. H., & Drew, B. (1984). Hyperactive and hypoxic children: Signal detection, sustained attention, and behavior. *Journal of Abnormal Psychology, 93,* 178–191.

Pauls, D. L. (1991). Genetic factors in the expression of attention-deficit hyperactivity disorder. *Journal of Child and Adolescent Psychopharmacology, 1,* 353–360.

Pike, A., & Plomin, R. (1996). Importance of nonshared environmental factors for childhood and adolescent psychopathology. *Journal of the American Academy of Child and Adolescent Psychiatry, 35,* 560–570.

Plomin, R. (1995). Genetics and children's experiences in the family. *Journal of Child Psychology and Psychiatry, 36,* 33–68.

Pontius, A. A. (1973). Dysfunction patterns analogous to frontal lobe system and caudate nucleus sundromes in some groups of minimal brain dysfunction. *Journal of the American Medical Women's Association, 26,* 285–292.

Rapoport, J. L., Buchsbaum, M. S., Zahn, T. P., Weingarten, H., Ludlow, C., & Mikkelsen, E. J. (1978). Destroamphetamine: Cognitive and behavioral effects in normal prepubertal boys. *Science, 199,* 560–563.

Raskin, L. A. Shaywitz, S. E., Shaywitz, B. A., Anderson, G. M., & Cohen, D. J. (1984). Neurochemical correlates of attention deficit disorder. *Pediatric Clinics of North America, 31,* 387–396.

Refetoff, S., Weiss, R. W., & Usala, S. J. (1993). The syndromes of resistance to thyroid hormone. *Endocrine Research, 14,* 348–399.

Rhee, S. H., Waldman, I. D., Hay, D. A., & Levy, F. (1995). Sex differences in genetic and environmental influences on DSM-III-R attention-deficit hyperactivity disorder (ADHD). *Behavior Genetics, 25,* 285.

Rosenthal, R. H., & Allen, T. W. (1978). An examination of attention, arousal, and learning dysfunctions of hyperkinetic children. *Psychological Bulletin, 85,* 689–715.

Ross, D. M., & Ross, S. A. (1982). *Hyperactivity: Research, theory and action.* New York: Wiley.

Rutter, M. (1977). Brain damage syndromes in childhood: Concepts and findings. *Journal of Child Psychology and Psychiatry, 18,* 1–21.

Rutter, M. (1983). Introduction: Concepts of brain dysfunction syndromes. In M. Rutter (Ed.), *Developmental neuropsychiatry* (pp. 1–14). New York: Guilford Press.

Samuel, V., George, P., Thornell, A., Curtis, S., Taylor, A., Brome, D., Mick, E., Faraone, S., & Biederman, J. (1997, October). *A pilot controlled family study of ADHD in African-American children.* Paper presented at the annual meeting of the American Academy of Child and Adolescent Psychiatry, Toronto, Canada.

Schothorst, P. F., & van Engeland, H. (1996). Long-term behavioral sequelae of prematurity. *Journal of the American Academy of Child and Adolescent Psychiatry, 35,* 175–183.

Seidman, L. J. (1997, October). *Neuropsychological findings in ADHD children: Findings from a sample of high-risk siblings.* Paper presented at the annual meeting of the American Academy of Child and Adolescent Psychiatry, Toronto, Canada.

Seidman, L. J., Biederman, J., Faraone, S. V., Weber, W., & Ouellette, C. (1997). Toward defining a neuropsychology of attention deficit-hyperactivity disorder: Performance of children and adolescence from a large clinically referred sample. *Journal of Consulting and Clinical Psychology, 65,* 150–160.

Semrud-Clikeman, M., Filipek, P. A., Biederman, J., Steingard, R., Kennedy, D., Renshaw, P., & Bekken, K. (1994). Attention-deficit hyperactivity disorder: Magnetic resonance imaging morphometric analysis of the corpus callosum. *Journal of the American Academy of Child and Adolescent Psychiatry, 33,* 875–881.

Shaywitz, B. A., Shaywitz, S. E., Byrne, T., Cohen, D. J., & Rothman, S. (1983). Attention deficit disorder: Quantitative analysis of CT. *Neurology, 33,* 1500–1503.

Shaywitz, S. E., Cohen, D. J., & Shaywitz, B. E. (1980). Behavior and learning difficulties in children of normal intelligence born to alcoholic mothers. *Journal of Pediatrics, 96,* 978–982.

Shaywitz, S. E., Shaywitz, B. A., Cohen, D. J., & Young, J. G. (1983). Monoaminergic mechanisms in hyperactivity. In M. Rutter (Ed.), *Developmental neuropsychiatry* (pp. 330–347). New York: Guilford Press.

Shaywitz, S. E., Shaywitz, B. A., Jatlow, P. R., Sebrechts, M., Anderson, G. M., & Cohen, D. J. (1986). Biological differentiation of attention deficit disorder with and without hyperactivity. A preliminary report. *Annals of Neurology, 21,* 363.

Sherman, D. K., Iacono, W. G., & McGue M. K. (1997). Attention-deficit hyperactivity disorder dimensions: A twin study of inattention and impulsivity–hyperactivity. *Journal of the American Academy of Child and Adolescent Psychiatry, 36,* 745–753.

Sherman, D. K., McGue, M. K., & Iacono, W. G. (1997). Twin concordance for attention deficit hyperactivity disorder: A comparison of teachers' and mothers' reports. *American Journal of Psychiatry, 154,* 532–535.

Sieg, K. G., Gaffney, G. R., Preston, D. F., & Hellings, J. A. (1995). SPECT brain imaging abnormalities in attention deficit hyperactivity disorder. *Clinical Nuclear Medicine, 20,* 55–60.

Silberg, J., Rutter, M., Meyer, J., Maes, H., Hewitt, J., Simonoff, E., Pickles, A., Loeber, R., & Eaves, L. (1996). Genetic and environmental influences on the covariation between hyperactivity and conduct disturbance in juvenile twins. *Journal of Child Psychology and Psychiatry, 37,* 803–816.

Silva, P. A., Hughes, P., Williams, S., & Faed, J. M. (1988). Blood lead, intelligence, reading attainment, and behaviour in eleven year old children in Dunedin, New Zealand. *Journal of Child Psychology and Psychiatry, 29,* 43–52.

Silverman, I. W., & Ragusa, D. M. (1992). A short-term longitudinal study of the early development of self-regulation. *Journal of Abnormal Child Psychology, 20,* 415–435.

Singer, H. S., Reiss, A. L., Brown, J. E., Aylward, E. H., Shih, B., Chee, E., Harris, E. L., Reader, M. J., Chase, G. A., Bryan, R. N., & Denckla, M. B. (1993). Volumetric MRI changes in basal ganglia of children with Tourette's syndrome. *Neurology, 43,* 950–956.

Sonuhara, G. A., Barr, C., Schachar, R. J., Tannock, R., Roberts, W., Malone, M. A., Jain, U. R., & Kennedy, J. L. (1997, October). *Association study of the dopamine D4 receptor gene in children and adolescents with ADHD.* Paper presented at the annual meeting of the American Academy of Child and Adolescent Psychiatry, Toronto, Canada.

Stein, M. A., Krasowski, M., Leventhal, B. L., Phillips, W., & Bender, B. G. (1996). Behavioral and cognitive effects of methylxanthines: A meta-analysis of theophylline and caffeine. *Archives of Pediatric and Adolescent Medicine, 150,* 284–288.

Stein, M. A., Weiss, R. E., & Refetoff, S. (1995). Neurocognitive characteristics of individuals with resistance to thyroid hormone: Comparisons with individuals with attention-deficit hyperactivity disorder. *Journal of Developmental and Behavioral Pediatrics, 16*, 406–411.

Stevenson, J. (1994, June). *Genetics of ADHD.* Paper presented at the Professional Group for ADD and Related Disorders, London.

Streissguth, A. P., Bookstein, F. L., Sampson, P. D., & Barr, H. M. (1995). Attention: Prenatal alcohol and continuities of vigilance and attentional problems from 4 through 14 years. *Development and Psychopathology, 7*, 419–446.

Streissguth, A. P., Martin, D. C., Barr, H. M., Sandman, B. M., Kirchner, G. L., & Darby, B. L. (1984). Intrauterine alcohol and nicotine exposure: Attention and reaction time in 4-year-old children. *Developmental Psychology, 20*, 533–541.

Stuss, D. T., & Benson, D. F. (1986). *The frontal lobes.* New York: Raven.

Swanson, J. M., Sunohara, G. A., Kennedy, J. L., Regino, R., Fineberg, E., Wigal, E., LaHoste, G. J., & Wigal, S. (1997). *Association of the dopamine receptor D4 (DRD4) gene with a refined phenotype of attention deficit hyperactivity disorder (ADHD): A family-based approach.* Manuscript submitted for publication.

Sykes, D. H., Hoy, E. A., Bill, J. M., McClure, B. G., Halloiday, H. L., & Reid, M. M. (1997). Behavioral adjustment in school of very low birthweight children. *Journal of Child Psychology and Psychiatry, 38*, 315–325.

Szatmari, P., Saigal, S., Rosenbaum, P., & Campbell, D. (1993). Psychopathology and adaptive functioning among extremely low birthweight children at eight years of age. *Development and Psychopathology, 5*, 345–357.

Tannock, R. (1998). Attention deficit hyperactivity disorder: Advances in cognitive, neurobiological, and genetic research. *Journal of Child Psychology and Psychiatry, 39*, 65–100.

Thapar, A., Hervas, A., & McGuffin, P. (1995). Childhood hyperactivity scores are highly heritable and show sibling competition effects: Twin study evidence. *Behavior Genetics, 25*, 537–544.

Thomson, G. O. B., Raab, G. M., Hepburn, W. S., Hunter, R., Fulton, M., & Laxen, D. P. H., (1989). Blood-lead levels and children's behaviour—Results from the Edinburgh lead study. *Journal of Child Psychology and Psychiatry, 30*, 515–528.

van den Oord, E. J. C., Boomsma, D. I., & Verhulst, F. C. (1994). A study of problem behaviors in 10- to 15-year-old biololgically related and unrelated international adoptees. *Behavior Genetics, 24*, 193–205.

van den Oord, E. J. C., & Rowe, D. C. (1997). Continuity and change in children's social maladjustment: A developmental behavior genetic study. *Developmental Psychology, 33*, 319–332.

van den Oord, E. J. C., Verhulst, F. C., & Boomsma, D. I. (1996). A genetic study of maternal and paternal ratings of problem behaviors in 3-year-old twins. *Journal of Abnormal Psychology, 105*, 349–357.

Weiss, G., & Hechtman, L. (1993). *Hyperactive children grown up* (2nd ed.). New York: Guilford Press.

Weiss, R. E., Stein, M. A., & Refetoff, S. (1997). Behavioral effects of liothyronine (L_3-T_3) in children with attention deficit hyperactivity disorder in the presence and absence of resistance to thyroid hormone. *Thyroid, 7*, 389–393.

Weiss, R. E., Stein, M. A., Trommer, B., et al. (1993). Attention-deficit hyperactivity disorder and thyroid function. *Journal of Pediatrics, 123*, 539–545.

Welner, Z., Welner, A., Stewart, M., Palkes, H., & Wish, E. (1977). A controlled study of siblings of hyperactive children. *Journal of Nervous and Mental Disease, 165*, 110–117.

Werner, E. E., Bierman, J. M., French, F. W., Simonian, K., Connor, A., Smith, R. S., & Campbell, M. (1968). Reproductive and environmental casualties: A report on the 10-year follow-up of the children of the Kauai pregnancy study. *Pediatrics, 42*, 112–127.

Whittaker, A. H., Van Rossem, R., Feldman, J. F., Schonfeld, I. S., Pinto-Martin, J. A., Torre, C., Shaffer, D., & Paneth, N. (1997). Psychiatric outcomes in low-birth-weight children at age 6 years: Relation to neonatal cranial ultrasound abnormalities. *Archives of General Psychiatry, 54*, 847–856.

Willerman, L. (1973). Activity level and hyperactivity in twins. *Child Development, 44*, 288–293.

Willis, T. J., & Lovaas, I. (1977). A behavioral approach to treating hyperactive children: The parent's role. In J. B. Millichap (Ed.), *Learning disabilities and related disorders* (pp. 119–140). Chicago: Yearbook Medical Publications.

Wolf, S. M., & Forsythe, A. (1978). Behavior disturbance, phenobarbital, and febrile seizures. *Pediatrics, 61*, 728–731.

Youdin, M. B. H., & Riederer, P. (1997). Understanding Parkinson's disease. *Scientific American, 276*, 52–59.

Zametkin, A. J., Liebenauer, L. L., Fitzgerald, G. A., King, A. C., Minkunas, D. V., Herscovitch, P., Yamada, E. M., & Cohen, R. M. (1993). Brainmetabolism in teenagers with attention-deficit hyperactivity disorder. *Archives of General Psychiatry, 50*, 333–340.

Zametkin, A. J., Nordahl, T. E., Gross, M., King, A. C., Semple, W. E., Rumsey, J., Hamburger, S., & Cohen, R. M. (1990). Cerebral glucose metabolism in adults with hyperactivity of childhood onset. *New England Journal of Medicine, 323*, 1361– 1366.

Zametkin, A. J., & Rapoport, J. L. (1986). The pathophysiology of attention deficit disorder with hyperactivity: A review. In B. B. Lahey & A. E. Kazdin (Eds.), *Advances in clinical child psychology* (Vol. 9, pp. 177–216). New York: Plenum.

Chapter 6

DEVELOPMENTAL COURSE, ADULT OUTCOME, AND CLINIC-REFERRED ADHD ADULTS

さ

As discussed in Chapter 2 (this volume), the symptoms of Attention-Deficit/Hyperactivity Disorder (ADHD) appear to arise relatively early in childhood, with the mean age of onset being between 3 and 4 years old (Barkley, Fischer, Edelbrock, & Smallish, 1990; Barkley, Fischer, Newby, & Breen, 1988) and ranging between infancy and as late as 11 years of age (Applegate et al., 1997; Barkley & Biederman, 1997). Although most cases may develop before age 7 years, in a sizable minority of cases the children may have had their ADHD characteristics for quite some time but they did not interfere with their academic or social functioning until later childhood. Thus, the onset of impairment may succeed the onset of symptoms by several years or more. The latter seems to occur in very bright or gifted ADHD children whose superior intellect appears to allow them to pass through the early grades of school without difficulty because they do not need to apply much effort to be successful. As the work at home and school increases in length and complexity and greater demands for responsibility and self-control are made in later childhood, such ADHD children are now handicapped by their deficits. This interface between environmental demands and child capabilities seems important in determining the degree to which a child's ADHD characteristics will prove socially disabling throughout their development.

This chapter discusses the developmental course and adult outcome of ADHD children as revealed by many different follow-up studies, including my own research in this area. The discussion begins with factors that appear to be associated with a risk for and early emergence of the disorder and may eventually prove to be early predictors of ADHD.

FACTORS ASSOCIATED WITH RISK FOR DEVELOPING ADHD

Certain parental characteristics have been noted to be associated with ADHD in children, as described previously. Early studies in this area implied that parents with depression, alcoholism, Conduct Disorder, and antisocial personality may be more likely to have children with ADHD (Cantwell, 1975; Morrison & Stewart, 1973). However, these disorders may be more likely associated with subsequent risk in their children for aggression and antisocial behavior than for ADHD. Certainly, ADHD in the parents and relatives of children would appear to be an important marker for increased risk of the disorder (Barkley, DuPaul, & McMurray, 1990; Deutsch et al., 1982). For instance, if a parent has ADHD, the risk of disorder to the offspring of that parent has been found to be as high as 54% (Biederman et al., 1995). Having a hyperactive sibling may also be a predictor of higher risk of hyperactivity among other children in the family (Nichols & Chen, 1981). Goodman and Stevenson (1989) estimate this risk to be approximately 13–17% for female siblings and 27–30% for male siblings regardless of whether the hyperactive proband is male or female. Welner, Welner, Stewart, Palkes, and Wish (1977) found a 35% risk of hyperactivity in siblings of diagnosed hyperactive children. In short, families with an existing history of ADHD among their relatives, especially the immediate parents and siblings, are more likely to have hyperactive or ADHD children than those families without such familial disorders. Other family risk factors associated with the early emergence and persistence of ADHD symptoms are low maternal education and socioeconomic status and single parenthood or father desertion (Nichols & Chen, 1981; Palfrey, Levine, Walker, & Sullivan, 1985).

Several studies showed that pregnancy complications and problems at time of delivery are more likely to be associated with ADHD children than with normal children (Hartsough & Lambert, 1985; Minde, Webb, & Sykes, 1968; Nichols & Chen, 1981), although others did not find such an association (Barkley, DuPaul, & McMurray, 1990; Reebye, 1997). This is not to say that such factors are the cause of the children's hyperactivity but that when such factors exist, they may at least be a marker for later development of the disorder. In their large epidemiological study, Nichols and Chen (1981) found that the following pregnancy factors, in decreasing order of importance, were predictive of later hyperactivity in children: number of cigarettes smoked per day, maternal convulsions, maternal hospitalizations, fetal distress, and placental weight. Hartsough and Lambert (1985) found an association between young motherhood as well as poor maternal health and hyperactivity in the children. Alcohol consumption during pregnancy is also associated with later attention deficits in children, as discussed in Chapter 5 (this volume). For whatever reason, these factors appear to be associated with a higher risk for ADHD among the children born of such pregnancies.

Certain neonatal and infancy variables have been studied for their association with ADHD. Nichols and Chen (1981) found delayed motor development, smaller head circumference at birth and at 12 months of age, meconium staining, neonatal nerve damage, primary apnea, and low birthweight, among others, to be predictive of later hyperactivity to a low but significant degree (regression weights below .19). Prematurity of delivery was also noted by some (see Chapter 5, this volume) to be associated with a greater risk for later ADHD in childhood, particularly in children with evidence of parenchymal injuries or ventricular enlargement (Whittaker et al., 1997). Greater health problems and delayed motor development were also found by others to be associated with a higher risk for early and persistent ADHD symptoms (Hartsough & Lambert, 1985; Palfrey et al., 1985). The early emergence of excessive activity level, short durations of responding to objects, low persistence of pursuing objects with which to play, strong intensity of response, and demandingness in infancy are more often found in ADHD than in normal or other clinical control groups of children (Barkley, Dupaul, & McMurray, 1990; Hartsough & Lambert, 1985). These factors also predict the persistence of these behavioral problems into the preschool years (Campbell, 1990; McInerny & Chamberlin, 1978; Palfrey et al., 1985).

The appearance of early and persistent problems with social interaction with parents and peers, excessive activity, inattention, and emotional difficulties such as aggression or fearfulness and social withdrawal was associated with ADHD in the preschool years (ages

2 to 5) (Carlson, Jacobvitz, & Sroufe, 1995; Jacobvitz & Sroufe, 1987; Palfrey et al., 1985; Prior, Leonard, & Wood, 1983). In particular, negative temperament appears to be an important risk factor. Temperament refers to early and relatively persistent personality characteristics of children, such as activity level, intensity or degree of energy in a response, persistence or attention span, demandingness of others, quality of mood (i.e., irritability or quickness to anger or display emotion), adaptability or capacity to adjust to change, and rhythmicity or the regularity of sleep/waking periods, eating, and elimination. These temperamental variables were noted earlier in discussing infant predictors of ADHD and appear to be equally significant as predictors in the preschool years. These characteristics, especially overactivity, high intensity, inattention, negative mood, and low adaptability, also predicted a continuation of both ADHD symptoms and aggression or conduct problems on entry into formal schooling (Buss, Block, & Block, 1980; Campbell, 1990; Earls & Joung, 1987; Fagot, 1984; Fischer, Rolf, Hasazi, & Cummings, 1984; Garrison, Earls, & Kindlon, 1984; Halverson & Waldrop, 1976; Palfrey et al., 1985) and greater reading and academic achievement delays and greater use of special educational services by second grade (Palfrey et al., 1985). This same set of variables further predicts a significantly greater risk for psychiatric diagnosis, particularly for Disruptive Behavior Disorders, by adolescence (Lerner, Inui, Trupin, & Douglas, 1985). Certainly, children whose inattentive–hyperactive symptoms are sufficiently severe to warrant a diagnosis of ADHD in childhood are quite likely to continue to receive this diagnosis up to 5–8 years later (Barkley, Fischer, et al., 1990; Beitchman, Wekerle, & Hood, 1987).

However, several studies also indicate that although early negative temperament may continue to predict ongoing negative temperament, by itself, it is a relatively weak predictor of later clinically significant levels of psychological or behavioral problems in children (Cameron, 1978; Carey & McDevitt, 1978; Chamberlin, 1977). Greater power of prediction in such studies is achieved by combining these temperamental variables with knowledge of parental characteristics, especially psychiatric ones and those related to management of the child. Campbell (1990) found that the existence of a negative, critical, and commanding style of child management by mothers of children with preschool hyperactivity was also associated with the persistence of hyperactivity by ages 4, 6, and 9 years. Others (Cameron, 1978; Earls & Jung, 1987) also found that prediction of behavioral problems in childhood was greatly enhanced by considering parent psychiatric distress, hostility, and marital discord in addition to preschool temperament. Thus, it appears that child temperament, although an important early risk factor, can be moderated or exacerbated by a particular caregiver environment and that knowledge of the caregiver and home environment can enhance prediction of later behavioral problems such as ADHD.

Taken together, these findings suggest that it is possible to identify children at risk for developing an early and persistent pattern ADHD symptoms prior to their entrance into kindergarten and perhaps even as early as 4 years of age. A combination of both child and parental variables seems the most useful. The following factors would appear to be useful as potential predictors of the early emergence and persistence of ADHD in children: (1) family, especially parental, history of ADHD; (2) maternal smoking and alcohol consumption and poor maternal health during pregnancy; (3) single parenthood and low educational attainment; (4) poor infant health and developmental delays; (5) the early emergence of high activity level and demandingness in infancy; and (6) critical/directive maternal behavior in early childhood. Some studies have examined factors that may be protective against the development of ADHD or its persistence from early childhood to school age are (1) higher maternal education; (2) better infant health; (3) higher cognitive ability, and perhaps language skills particularly, in the child; and (4) greater family stability (see Campbell, 1987, 1990; Palfrey et al., 1985; Weithorn & Kagan, 1985).

PRESCHOOL ADHD CHILDREN

Many studies indicate that preschool-age children are likely to be rated inattentive and over-active by their parents. In their follow-up study of children from birth to second grade, Palfrey et al. (1985) found that up to 40% of these children by age 4 years had sufficient problems with inattention to be of concern to their parents and teachers. Yet this and other studies (Campbell, 1990; Campbell & Ewing, 1990) show that the vast majority of these concerns remit within 3 to 6 months. Even among those children whose problems may be severe enough to receive a clinical diagnosis of ADHD, only 48% will have this same diagnosis by later childhood or early adolescence. This finding suggests that the appearance of significantly inattentive and overactive behavior by age 3 to 4 years, by itself, is not indicative of a persistent pattern of ADHD into later childhood or adolescence in at least 50–90% of those children so characterized. Palfrey et al. (1985) noted that approximately 5% of their total sample of children, or about 10% of those with concerns about inattention, eventually developed a pattern of persistent inattention to be predictive of behavior problems, low academic achievement, and need for special educational services by second grade. Campbell (1990) also showed that among difficult-to-manage 3-year-olds, those whose problems still existed by age 4 years were much more likely to be considered clinically hyperactive and to have difficulties with their hyperactivity as well as conduct problems by ages 6 and 9 years. Therefore, both the degree of ADHD symptoms *and* their duration determine which children are likely to show a chronic course of their ADHD symptoms throughout later development.

Parents of children with this durable pattern of ADHD in this age group described them as restless, always up and on the go, acting as if driven by a motor, and frequently climbing on and getting into things. They are more likely to encounter accidental injuries as a result of their overactive, inattentive, impulsive, and often fearless pattern of behavior. "Child-proofing" the home at this age becomes essential to reduce the risk of such injury or poisoning as well as to protect family valuables from the often vigorous and destructive pattern of play that many of these children show. Persistent in their wants, demanding of parental attention, and often insatiable in their curiosity of their environment, ADHD preschoolers pose a definite challenge to the child-rearing skills of their parents. Such children require far more frequent and closer monitoring of their ongoing conduct than do normal preschoolers, at times having to be tethered to allow parents to complete necessary household functions that require their undivided attention. That group of ADHD children with excessive moodiness, quickness to anger, and low adaptability and rhythmicity as described earlier are likely to prove the most distressing to their mothers. Noncompliance is common, and at least 30–60% are actively defiant or oppositional, especially if they are boys. Although temper tantrums may be common instances even for normal preschoolers, their frequency and intensity are often exacerbated in ADHD children. Mothers of these children are likely to find themselves giving far more commands, directions, criticism, supervision, and punishment than do mothers of normal preschoolers (Barkley, 1988; Battle & Lacey, 1972; Campbell, 1990; Cohen & Minde, 1981). Although the mothers of ADHD preschoolers are likely to report feeling competent in their sense of knowing how to manage children, this finding will progressively decline as these children grow older and parents find that the typical techniques used to manage normal children are less effective with ADHD children (Mash & Johnston, 1983). The coexistence of additional difficulties such as sleep problems, toilet training difficulties, and/or motor and speech delays in a small percentage of ADHD children is likely to further tax the patience and competence of many of their parents. No wonder then that parents of preschool ADHD children report their lives to be much more stressful in their parental roles than do mothers of normal preschoolers *or mothers of older ADHD children* (Fischer, 1990; Mash & Johnston, 1982, 1983).

Should such a child happen to have a mother whose own mental health is compromised by psychiatric problems, such as depression, anxiety, or hysteria, or whose marriage is in trouble, the combination of negative child temperament with a psychologically distressed caregiver could be potentially explosive and increase the risk of physical abuse to the child. This same situation may also arise when the father of this child is alcoholic, antisocial, or highly aggressive within the family. Research indicates that this combination of parent and child characteristics is a strong predictor of those children who go on to develop significant aggressive behavior and Oppositional Defiant Disorder (see Chapter 4, this volume).

Placement of these children in day care, a progressively increasing practice for preschool children in our society, is likely to bring additional distress as day-care personnel begin to complain about the child's disruptive behavior, aggression toward others in many cases, and difficulties in being managed. Such children are often noted to be out of their seats, wandering the classroom inappropriately, disrupting the play activities of other children, excessively demanding during peer interactions, and especially vocally noisy and talkative (Campbell, Endman, & Bernfield, 1977; Campbell, Schleifer, Weiss, 1978; Schleifer et al., 1975). It is not uncommon to find the more active and aggressive among these ADHD children to actually be "kicked out" of preschool (Reebye, 1997)—so begins the course of school adjustment problems that afflict many of these children throughout their compulsory educational careers. Other ADHD children, especially those who are not oppositional or aggressive, who are milder in their level of ADHD, or who are intellectually brighter may have little or no difficulties with the demands of a typical day-care or preschool program. This is especially so if it is only for a half-day program a few days each week.

Difficulties in obtaining babysitters for their ADHD children, especially the more severely ADHD and oppositional among them, is reported by mothers of children at this age during clinical interviews. This difficulty may result in a greater restriction of both socializing with other adults and the ability to carry out the typical and necessary errands within the community needed to care for a household. For single parents of ADHD children, these limitations may prove more frequent and distressing as there is no other adult with whom to share the burden of raising such children.

As ADHD preschool children approach entry into formal schooling, research suggests they are already at high risk for academic failure. Not only does their symptom picture predispose them to be less ready to learn in school, but they are also more likely to be behind in basic academic readiness skills (e.g., pre–reading abilities, simple math concepts, and fine motor skills) (Mariani & Barkley, 1997; Shelton et al., 1997). And, as noted in Chapter 3 (this volume), they may be somewhat less intelligent than their peers and significantly delayed in their adaptive functioning.

THE ADHD CHILD IN MIDDLE CHILDHOOD

Once ADHD children enter school, a major social burden is placed on them that will last at least the next 12 years of their lives—that burden is formal, compulsory education. Studies suggest that it is the area of greatest impact on the children's ADHD (Barkley, Fischer, et al., 1990; Biederman, 1997) and will create the greatest source of distress for many of them and their parents. The ability to sit still, attend, listen, obey, inhibit impulsive behavior, cooperate, organize actions, and follow through on instructions as well as share, play well, and interact pleasantly with other children is essential to negotiating a successful academic career beyond those cognitive and achievement skills needed to master the curriculum itself. It is not surprising that the vast majority of ADHD children will have been identified as deviant in their behavior by entry into formal schooling, particularly first grade. Parents not only have to contend with the ongoing behavioral problems at home noted during the preschool years but now have the additional burden of helping their children adjust to the academic and social demands of school. Regrettably, these parents must also tolerate the complaints of some teachers who see the child's problems at school as stemming entirely from home problems or poor child-rearing abilities in the parents.

Often at this age, parents must confront decisions about whether to retain the children in kindergarten because of "immature" behavior and/or slow academic achievement. The fact that many schools now assign homework, even to first-graders, adds an additional demand on both the parent and the child to accomplish these tasks together. It is not surprising to see that homework time at home becomes another area in which conflict now arises in the family. For those 20–35% of ADHD children likely to have a reading disorder, it will be soon noted as the child tries to master the early reading tasks at school. Such children are doubly handicapped in their academic performance by the combinations of these disabilities. Among those who will develop math and writing disorders, these problems often go undetected until several years into elementary school. Even for those without comorbid learning disabilities, almost all ADHD children are haunted by their highly erratic educational performance over time, some days performing at or near normal levels of ability and accomplishing all assignments, other days failing quizzes and tests and not completing assigned work. Disorganized desks, lockers, coat closet spaces, and even notebooks are highly characteristic of these children, forcing others to step in periodically and reorganize their materials to try to facilitate better academic performance.

At home, parents often complain that their ADHD children do not accept household chores and responsibilities as well as do other children their age. Greater supervision of and assistance with these daily chores and self-help activities, (dressing, bathing, etc.) are common and lead to the perception that these children are quite immature. Although temper tantrums are likely to decline, as they do in normal children, ADHD children are still more likely to emit such behavior when frustrated than do normal children. Relations with siblings may be tense as the siblings grow tired and exasperated at trying to understand and live with so disruptive a force as their ADHD brother or sister. Some siblings develop resentment over the greater burden of work they often carry compared to their hyperactive siblings. Certainly, siblings are often jealous of the greater amount of time these ADHD children receive from their parents, especially those siblings who are younger than the ADHD children. At an age when other children are entering extracurricular community and social activities, such as clubs, music lessons, sports, and scouts, ADHD children are likely to find themselves barely tolerated in these group activities or outright ejected from them in some cases. Parents frequently find that they must intervene in these activities on behalf of their children to explain and apologize for their behavior and transgressions to others, to try to aid the children in coping better with the social demands, or to defend their children against sanctions that may be applied for their unacceptable conduct.

An emerging pattern of social rejection will have appeared by now, if not earlier, in over half of all ADHD children because of their poor social skills, as described in Chapter 3 (this volume). Even when the ADHD child displays appropriate or prosocial behavior toward others, it may be at such a high rate or intensity that it elicits rejection by and avoidance of the child in subsequent situations or even punitive responses from his or her peers (Hinshaw, 1992; Ross & Ross, 1982). This rejection can present a confusing picture to the ADHD child attempting to learn appropriate social skills. This high rate of behavior, vocal noisiness, and tendency to touch and manipulate objects more than is normal for age combine to make the ADHD child overwhelming, intrusive, and even aversive to others. By late childhood, and for obvious and varied reasons, many ADHD children commonly develop feelings of depression and a sense of inadequate competence (Diener & Milich, 1997). Yet many place the blame for these difficulties on their parents, teachers, or peers because of their limited self-awareness.

By later childhood and preadolescence, these patterns of academic, familial, and social conflicts have become well established for many ADHD children. At least 40–60% have developed Oppositional Defiant Disorder (ODD) (see Chapter 4, this volume) and as many as 25–40% are likely to develop symptoms of Conduct Disorder (CD) and antisocial behavior between 7 and 10 years of age (Barkley, Fischer, et al., 1990; Biederman et al., 1997; see also Chapter 4, this volume). The most common among these symptoms are lying, petty thievery, and resistance to the authority of others. At least 25% or more may have problems with fighting with other children. For the socially aggressive subgroup, bragging or boasting about fictitious accomplishments, cheating others at games or in schoolwork, and in some cases truancy from school may also be seen. It is the minority of ADHD children who have not developed some comorbid psychiatric (ODD/CD), academic (learning disability and underachievement), or social disorder by this time. Those who remain purely ADHD whose attention problems are most prominent are likely to have the best adolescent outcomes, experiencing problems primarily with academic performance and eventual attainment (Fergusson, Lynskey, & Horwood, 1997; G. Weiss & Hechtman, 1993). For others, an increasing pattern of familial conflict and antisocial behavior in the community may begin to appear or worsen where it already existed. Such family conflicts often prove particularly recalcitrant to treatment (Barkley, Guevremont, Anastopoulos, & Fletcher, 1992). The majority of ADHD children (60–80%) by this time have been placed on a trial of stimulant medication, and over half have participated in some type of individual and family therapy (Barkley, DuPaul, & McMurray, 1990; Barkley, Fischer, et al., 1990a; Faraone et al., 1993; Munir, Biederman, & Knee, 1987; Semrud-Clikeman et al., 1992). Approximately 30–45% will also be receiving formal special educational assistance for their academic difficulties by the time they enter adolescence.

ADOLESCENT OUTCOME OF ADHD CHILDREN

Despite a decline in their levels of hyperactivity and an improvement in their attention span and impulse control (Hart, Lahey, Loeber, Applegate, & Frick, 1995), 70–80% of ADHD children are likely to continue to display these symptoms into adolescence to an extent inappropriate for their age group (Barkley, Fischer, et al., 1990; Barkley, Anastopoulos, Guevremont, & Fletcher, 1991). As Ross and Ross (1976) have indicated, the adolescent years of ADHD individuals may be some of the most difficult because of the increasing demands for independent, responsible conduct as well as the emerging social and physical changes inherent in puberty. Issues of identity, peer group acceptance, dating and courtship, and physical development and appearance erupt as a second source of demands and distress with which the ADHD adolescent must now cope. Sadness, major depression in as many as 25% of cases, poor self-confidence, diminished hopes of future success, and concerns about school completion may develop.

Follow-up studies published during the past 17 years have done much to dispel the notion that the disorder is typically outgrown by the adolescent years. These studies have consistently demonstrated that up to 80% of children diagnosed as hyperactive in childhood continue to display their symptoms to a significant degree in adolescence and young adulthood (August, Stewart, & Holmes, 1983; Barkley, Fischer, et al., 1990; Biederman, Faraone, Milberger, Curtis, et al., 1996; Brown & Borden, 1986; Cantwell & Baker, 1989; Claude &

Firestone, 1995; Thorley, 1984; G. Weiss & Hechtman, 1993). In general, these studies indicate that between 30 and 80% of these children continue to be impaired by their symptoms in adolescence or to meet current diagnostic criteria for ADHD (Gittelman, Mannuzza, Shenker, & Bonagura, 1985; Lambert, Hartsough, Sassone, & Sandoval, 1987). More recent studies using more contemporary and rigorous diagnostic criteria consistently find higher rates of persistence of symptoms of disorder than earlier, less methodologically rigorous studies. As many as 25–45% of the adolescents display oppositional or antisocial behavior or CD (Biederman, Faraone, Milberger, Curtis, 1996; Biederman et al., 1997), and 30–58% have failed at least one grade in school (Barkley, Anastopoulos, et al., 1991; Barkley, Fischer, et al., 1990; Brown & Borden, 1986). Other studies clearly show these children to be significantly behind matched control groups in academic performance at follow-up (Fischer, Barkley, Edelbrock, & Smallish, 1990; Lambert et al., 1987; G. Weiss & Hechtman, 1993). Research has been less consistent in documenting whether hyperactive children are at greater risk for substance abuse than normal children upon reaching adolescence, with some finding a greater occurrence of alcohol or drug use (Blouin, Bornstein, & Trites, 1978; Hoy, Weiss, Minde, & Cohen, 1978; Loney, Kramer, & Milich, 1981) and others finding it only for drug use (Gittelman et al., 1985; Minde et al., 1971; G. Weiss & Hechtman, 1993). Most of these studies followed groups of clinically diagnosed hyperactive children. When epidemiologically derived samples were used, rates of antisocial behavior, academic failure, and continuation of the symptoms of ADHD remained higher than in matched normal samples but less than half that reported in the clinical samples (Lambert et al., 1987).

A significant limitation of many of these studies, particularly those initiated in the early 1970s, was the lack of consensus criteria for the diagnosis of hyperactivity. Many of these early studies relied exclusively on the referral of the child based on parental or teacher complaints of hyperactivity and clinical diagnosis as the primary inclusion criteria. None of these studies used standardized child behavior rating scales to establish a cutoff score for the degree of deviance of their subjects in ADHD symptoms. Considering that many normal children may have parent or teacher complaints of inattentiveness, hyperactivity, or impulsivity (Achenbach & Edelbrock, 1983), it is likely that previous studies have been overly inclusive, permitting many children with borderline or marginal ADHD characteristics to be included in their samples. The result could be a considerably more positive outcome of the hyperactive sample and a sample with much higher remission rates than if more rigorous research selection criteria were employed, as is now customary in more recent studies. All these studies were begun, and many completed, prior to the publication of consensus diagnostic criteria for ADHD in the third edition of the *Diagnostic and Statistical Manual of Mental Disorders* (DSM-III; American Psychiatric Association, 1980) or DSM-III-R (American Psychiatric Association, 1987), leading to tremendous variation across studies in their selection criteria.

A more detailed picture of the adolescent outcome of ADHD children has emerged in several more recent outcome studies (Barkley, Fischer, et al., 1990; Biederman, Faraone, Milberger, Curtis, et al. 1996; Fischer et al., 1990). The following results are from my own study (Barkley, Fischer, et al., 1990) of a large sample of ADHD and normal children followed prospectively 8 years after their initial evaluation. Unlike past studies, the clinic-referred children diagnosed as hyperactive in the present study fulfilled a set of rigorous research criteria designed to select a sample of children who were truly developmentally deviant in their symptoms relative to same-age normal children.

The initial sample consisted of 158 hyperactive children and 81 normal children between 4 and 12 years of age. A total of 123 hyperactive children and 66 normal children were located and agreed to be interviewed and complete our questionnaires either in person or by telephone (interview) and mail (rating scales). This number represents a total of 78% of the original sample for hyperactive children and 81% for the normal group. These recruitment rates compare favorably to the prospective follow-up studies by Lambert et al. (1987) and Gittelman et al. (1985) in which the average recruitment rate was between 72% and 85% and are considerably higher than those in most of the earlier follow-up studies (see Brown & Borden, 1986, for a review). In the hyperactive group, 12 of the subjects (9.7%) were female and 111 were male, whereas in the normal group 4 of the subjects (6.1%) were female and 62 were male.

Comorbidity for Other Disruptive Behavior Disorders

We examined the rates of the occurrence of the Disruptive Behavior Disorders diagnoses in both groups of children. We also calculated the number of symptoms within each disorder that represented two standard deviations above the mean (97th percentile) for the normal adolescents. We did so because the DSM-III-R cutoff scores for these disorders were based on field trials of primarily elementary-age children in whom one would expect a greater occurrence of the ADHD characteristics and a lesser degree of CD symptoms within the normal population at that age range. Because these symptoms are known to vary considerably with age, it is likely that the cutoff scores may be overinclusive for some age groups and underinclusive for others.

We found that the vast majority of our hyperactive subjects (71.5%) met the DSM-III-R criteria for ADHD, with a mean number of nine symptoms versus only one and a half in the control group. Furthermore, when the cutoff of two standard deviations above the normal mean was used to make the diagnosis for ADHD, the cutoff score must be adjusted downward to 6 rather than 8 of 14 symptoms. Using this norm-referenced cutoff score resulted in a larger percentage of the hyperactive group (83.3%) being eligible for a diagnosis of ADHD in adolescence. The mean age of onset for the subjects ADHD symptoms was 3.7 years. More than 59% of the hyperactive group met DSM-III-R criteria for a diagnosis of ODD as compared to 11% of the control group, and this rate did not change appreciably when the cutoff score of two standard deviations from the normal mean was substituted as the diagnostic cutoff point (five or more symptoms). Approximately 43% of the hyperactive group qualified for a diagnosis of CD using DSM-III-R criteria as compared to only 1.6% of the control group. Again, readjusting the symptom cutoff score based on the two-standard-deviations mark for the normal control group results in a lowering of the cutoff score from three symptoms to two and leads to a much larger percentage of the hyperactive group being diagnosed as CD (60%). The mean age of onset for ODD was 6.7 and for CD was 6 years.

Table 6.1 reports the relative rates of occurrence for each of the DSM symptoms within each of the three Disruptive Behavior Disorders. Among the ADHD symptoms, it seems that difficulties with attention and instruction following are the most problematic for this group at outcome. Among the ODD symptoms, arguing and irritable or touchy manner are the most frequent. As one might expect, the occurrence for each symptom of CD was considerably less than for these other two disorders, but in all but four of these symptoms the rate in the hyperactive group was still significantly greater than that seen in the normal adolescents. Only running away, sexual assault, and theft involving confronting a victim were not significantly different.

Auto Accidents

Prior research (G. Weiss & Hechtman, 1993) suggests that hyperactive adolescents have a higher incidence of automobile accidents than do normal adolescents. Our study of a sample of ADHD teens followed prospectively for 3 to 5 years found that they were significantly more likely to have had an auto crash, to have had more such crashes, to have more bodily inju-

TABLE 6.1. Prevalence of Disruptive Behavior Disorders and Symptoms at Outcome

Diagnosis/symptom	Hyperactives (%)	Normals (%)	*p*
Attention-Deficit/Hyperactivity Disorder			
Fidgets	73.2	10.6	<.01
Difficulty remaining seated	60.2	3.0	<.01
Easily distracted	82.1	15.2	<.01
Difficulty waiting turn	48.0	4.5	<.01
Blurts out answers	65.0	10.6	<.01
Difficulty following instructions	83.7	12.1	<.01
Difficulty sustaining attention	79.7	16.7	<.01
Shifts from one uncompleted task to another	77.2	16.7	<.01
Difficulty playing quietly	39.8	7.6	NS
Talks excessively	43.9	6.1	<.01
Interrupts others	65.9	10.6	<.01
Doesn't seem to listen	80.5	15.2	<.01
Loses things needed for tasks	62.6	12.1	<.01
Engages in physically dangerous behavior	37.4	3.0	<.01
Oppositional Defiant Disorder			
Argues with adults	72.4	21.1	<.01
Defies adult requests	55.3	9.1	<.01
Deliberately annoys others	51.2	13.6	<.01
Blames others for own mistakes	65.9	16.7	<.01
Acts touchy or easily annoyed by others	70.7	19.7	<.01
Angry or resentful	50.4	10.6	<.01
Spiteful or vindictive	21.1	0.0	NS
Swears	40.7	6.1	<.01
Conduct Disorder			
Stolen without confrontation	49.6	7.6	<.01
Runs away from home overnight (2+ times)	4.9	3.0	NS
Lies	48.8	4.5	<.01
Deliberately engaged in fire setting	27.6	0.0	<.01
Truant	21.1	3.0	<.01
Broken in home, building, or car	9.8	1.5	NS
Deliberately destroyed others property	21.1	4.5	<.01
Physically cruel to animals	15.4	0.0	<.01
Forced someone into sexual activity	5.7	0.0	NS
Used a weapon in a fight	7.3	0.0	NS
Physically fights	13.8	0.0	NS
Stolen with confrontation	0.8	0.0	NS
Physically cruel to people	14.6	0.0	<.01

Note. p values listed in last column are for chi-square or *t*-test results, as appropriate. NS means the statistical test was not significantly different between the groups. Age of onset for each disorder is not reported for the normal subjects given that the vast majority of these subjects did not have these disorders at outcome. From Barkley, Fischer, et al. (1990). Copyright 1990 by Williams & Wilkins. Reprinted by permission.

ries associated with such accidents, and to be at fault more often for such accidents. They were also more likely to receive traffic citations, particularly for speeding (Barkley, Guevremont, Anastopolous, DuPaul, & Shelton, 1993).

Substance Use and Abuse

Previous research has been equivocal concerning whether the rates of substance use and abuse among hyperactive adolescents differ from that of normal adolescents. Table 6.2

presents the rates of occurrence for eight specific categories of substance use. Cigarette and alcohol use are the only categories of substance use that significantly differentiate the hyperactive and normal teenagers, according to teens' self-reports. A previous follow-up study by Gittelman et al. (1985) found that the differences between clinically diagnosed hyperactive children and the control group in substance use at adolescent outcome were primarily accounted for by those hyperactive teens who received a diagnosis of CD. In agreement, a more recent study using an epidemiologically derived sample reported by Lynskey and Fergusson (1995) found that rates of adolescent substance use and abuse were elevated only in ADHD children having comorbid conduct problems as children. We separated our subjects into those who were purely hyperactive and, in agreement with the above studies, found that they had no greater use of cigarettes, alcohol, or marijuana than did normal subjects. However, the mixed hyperactive/CD subjects displayed two to five times the rate of use of these substances than the pure hyperactives or normals. Biederman et al. (1997) also found a higher percentage (40%) of their adolescents with ADHD qualified for a diagnosis of substance dependence or abuse compared to a control group, although 33% of their control group met such criteria as well.

TABLE 6.2. Illicit Substance Use at Outcome as Reported by Mother and Adolescent for Hyperactive and Normal Groups and for Hyperactive Subjects Subgrouped as to the Presence or Absence of Conduct Disorder

Substance	Entire sample (%)			Hyperactives (%)		
	Hyperactives	Normals	p	w/ CD	w/o CD	p
By mother's report						
Cigarettes	48.8	30.3	NS	65.2	32.2	<.01
Alcohol	41.5	22.7	NS	54.3	29.0	NS
Marijuana	15.4	7.6	NS	28.3	4.8	<.01
Hashish	0.0	1.5	NS	0.0	0.0	NS
Cocaine	0.8	0.0	NS	2.2	0.0	NS
Stimulants	1.6	0.0	NS	4.3	0.0	NS
Sedatives	0.8	0.0	NS	2.2	0.0	NS
Tranquilizers	1.6	0.0	NS	2.2	1.6	NS
Heroin	0.0	0.0	NS	0.0	0.0	NS
Hallucinogens	0.0	0.0	NS	0.0	0.0	NS
By adolescent's report						
Cigarettes	48.0	26.7	.02	63.6	35.7	<.01
Alcohol	40.0	21.7	NS	57.7	33.9	NS
Marijuana	17.0	5.0	NS	27.3	8.9	NS
Hashish	7.0	1.7	NS	11.4	3.6	NS
Cocaine	4.0	0.0	NS	9.1	0.0	NS
Stimulants	6.0	0.0	NS	4.5	7.1	NS
Sedatives	2.0	0.0	NS	4.5	0.0	NS
Tranquilizers	1.0	0.0	NS	2.3	0.0	NS
Heroin	0.0	0.0	NS	0.0	0.0	NS
Hallucinogens	2.0	1.7	NS	4.5	0.0	NS

Note. p values are the probability levels for the results of the chi-square analyses between the groups. NS means that the statistsical test results were not significant. w/ CD means with Conduct Disorder as diagnosed by DSM-III-R criteria, while w/o CD means without Conduct Disorder. From Barkley, Fischer, et al. (1990). Copyright 1990 by Williams & Wilkins. Reprinted by permission.

Academic Outcome

The academic outcome of the hyperactive adolescents was considerably poorer than that of the normal adolescents, with at least three times as many hyperactive subjects having failed a grade (29.3% vs. 10%), been suspended (46.3% vs. 15.2%), or been expelled (10.6% vs. 1.5%). Among another sample of clinic-referred teenagers with ADHD, we found a similar risk for school retention and suspension (Barkley, Anastopoulos, et al., 1991). Almost 10% of the hyperactive sample followed into adolescence had quit school at this follow-up point compared to none of the normal sample (Barkley, Fischer, et al., 1990). The mean number of grade retentions (0.33 vs. 0.11), suspensions (3.69 vs. 0.35), and expulsions (0.14 vs. 0.02) was also significantly greater within the hyperactive than the normal group. We also found that the levels of academic achievement on standard tests were significantly below normal on tests of math, reading, and spelling, falling toward the lower end of the normal range (standard scores between 90 and 95).

We again examined whether the presence of CD at follow-up within the hyperactive group accounted for these greater than normal rates of academic failure. The results indicated that although hyperactivity alone increases the risk of suspension (30.6% of pure hyperactives vs. 15.2% of controls) and dropping out of school (4.8% of pure hyperactives vs. 0% for controls), the additional diagnosis of CD greatly increases these risks (67.4% suspended and 13% dropped out). Moreover, the presence of CD accounts almost entirely for the increased risk of expulsion within the hyperactive group in that the pure hyperactive group does not differ from normal in expulsion rate (1.6 vs. 1.5%) whereas 21.7% of the mixed hyperactive/CD group had been expelled from school. In contrast, the increased risk of grade retention in the hyperactives is entirely accounted for by their hyperactivity with no further risk occurring among the mixed hyperactive/CD group.

Treatment Received

Table 6.3 shows the extent of various interventions received in the ensuing 8 years since initial evaluation and their durations for both groups. Not surprisingly, more ADHD children had received medication and individual and group therapy as well as special educational services than had normal children. Similar results were found in our later study of clinic-referred adolescents having ADHD (Barkley, Anastopoulos, et al., 1991). In terms of their duration of treatment among those receiving it, the hyperactive children had received a substantial period of stimulant medication treatment (mean of 36 months) and individual and family therapy (16 and 7 months, respectively), as well as special educational assistance for learning, behavioral, and speech disorders during the past 8 years (65, 59, and 40 months, respectively). This pattern is similar to that found in our study of clinic-referred ADHD teens (Barkley, Anastopoulos, et al., 1991) and by Lambert et al. (1987) in their follow-up of 58 hyperactives and controls.

Conclusions and Integration with Past Research

The results of this follow-up study are consistent with those of many other adolescent outcome studies in finding hyperactive children to be at substantially higher risk for negative outcomes in the domains of psychiatric, social, legal, academic, and family functioning than a control group of normal children followed concurrently (August et al., 1983; Biederman, Faraone, Milberger, Curtis, et al., 1996; Biederman, Faraone, Milberger, Guite, et al., 1996; Brown & Borden, 1986; Thorley, 1984; G. Weiss & Hechtman, 1993). In contrast to early studies that followed hyperactives into adolescence, however, the present research found a

TABLE 6.3. Treatment History of the Hyperactive and Normal Groups at Outcome

Type of treatment	Hyperactives	Normals	p
Medication			
Methylphenidate	80.5%	0.0	<.01
Duration	36.1 mo	0.0	<.01
D-Aphetamine	3.3%	0.0	NS
Duration	1.1 mo	0.0	NS
Pemoline	19.5%	0.0	<.01
Duration	2.6 mo	0.0	NS
Tranquilizers	1.6%	0.0	NS
Duration	0.1 mo	0.0	NS
Other psychotropic drugs	14.6%	3.0%	NS
Duration	0.4 mo	3.0 mo	NS
Individual psychotherapy	63.4%	13.6%	<.01
Duration	16.3 mo	2.0 mo	<.01
Group psychotherapy	17.9%	4.5%	<.02
Duration	1.8 mo	0.1 mo	NS
Family therapy	49.6%	24.2%	<.01
Duration	7.2 mo	1.4 mo	<.01
Inpatient psychiatric treatment	9.8%	1.5%	NS
Duration	0.3 mo	0.03 mo	NS
Residential psychiatric treatment	8.9%	0.0	NS
Duration	1.9 mo	0.0	NS
Foster care	4.9%	0.0	NS
Duration	1.7 mo	0.0	NS
Special educational services			
Learning disability classes	32.5%	3.0%	<.01
Duration	65.5 mo	48.0 mo	NS
Behavior disorder classes	35.8%	6.1%	<.01
Duration	59.1 mo	37.5 mo	NS
Speech therapy	16.3%	1.5%	<.01
Duration	40.2 mo	6.0 mo	<.01
Other			
Biological mother in therapy	46.3%	28.8%	NS
Biological father in therapy	21.1%	13.6%	NS
Biological mother and father received			
marital therapy	30.9%	19.7%	NS

Note. p values are the probability levels for the results of the chi-square analyses between the groups. NS means that the statistical test results were not significant. From Barkley, Fischer, et al. (1990). Copyright 1990 by Williams & Wilkins. Reprinted by permission.

substantially greater number of hyperactive children with negative outcomes in many of these domains of functioning than was previously demonstrated in studies using less rigorous entry criteria into the study. Our rates for continuing ADHD were very similar to the rate of 68% having ADHD at some time since age 13 years found in the Gittelman et al. (1985) adult outcome study and considerably higher than the 43% continuing to be hyperactive in the

Lambert et al. (1987) study. Nevertheless, the rates are equal to those found in the August et al. (1983) study as well as those found in Claude and Firestone (1995), Biederman, Faraone, Milberger, Curtis, et al. (1996); and Cantwell and Baker (1989). In any case, our findings make it clear that when a rigorous set of criteria is used to diagnose children as hyperactive or ADHD, (Barkley, 1981, 1982), these criteria select a group of children whose symptom deviance remains highly stable over time (8 years), with the vast majority of them (over 80%) continuing to have this disorder into adolescence.

Yet the research of G. Weiss and Hechtman (1993) suggests that although present, these primary ADHD symptoms are not the major concerns of either parents or the adolescents at outcome. Instead, poor schoolwork, social difficulties with peers, problems related to authority, especially at school, and low self-esteem are major concerns at this developmental stage. Our results, discussed later, lend considerable credence to these concerns. A review of the concerns of parents of children with ADHD, however, would likely indicate that the first three of these concerns are the primary reasons they also seek clinical services for their children. Social conflict within the family would likely be listed as the fourth concern of these childhood years. This finding suggests to me that at any stage in the course of development, the concerns of parents of ADHD children will stem primarily from the impact of the children's deficits on their functioning in the school, in the family, and within the peer group and not from the ADHD symptoms per se. Only later in development is one likely to see the impact of the ADHD symptoms on personal satisfaction and self-acceptance, and thus problems such as low self-esteem may then emerge as significant concerns of the adolescent or young adult with ADHD. Once again it appears that when the ADHD symptoms are not disabling to the individual, they are of considerably less concern to the caregivers of ADHD children than when they are proving especially handicapping in meeting environmental expectations.

The rates of antisocial behavior and CD in our study were also higher than those seen in most early follow-up studies but are consistent with more recent studies, such as those by Biederman and colleagues (Biederman, Faraone, Milberger, Guite, et al., 1996; Biederman et al., 1997). Most early studies of adolescent outcome found between 22% and 30% of their hyperactives engaging in antisocial acts (see Brown & Borden, 1986, for a review; Mendelson, Johnson, & Stewart, 1971; Zambelli, Stam, Maintinsky, & Loiselle, 1977). Gittelman et al. (1985) reported that 45% of their sample met criteria for CD using DSM-III guidelines at some time since age 13 years of age. Biederman et al. (1997) found that 42% of their adolescents had CD. Our results are similar to these two studies in finding that 43% of our hyperactives could be diagnosed as CD using the more recent DSM-III-R criteria. The most common antisocial acts were stealing, thefts outside the home, and fire setting. This subgroup of hyperactives is at substantial risk for later criminal activities in adulthood. Antisocial activities in adolescence seems to be highest among those hyperactive or ADHD children who had comorbid conduct problems or CD earlier in childhood (August et al., 1983; Biederman, Faraone, Milberger, Curtis, et al., 1996; Claude & Firestone, 1995; Fischer et al., 1990; Satterfield, Swanson, Schell, & Lee, 1994; G. Weiss & Hechtman, 1993). This does not mean that ADHD children without comorbid CD carry no higher risk for later antisocial activities as adolescence—for they do seem to show such an elevated risk over normal children (Satterfield et al., 1994; Taylor, Chadwick, Hepinstall, & Danckaerts, 1996)—but only that the risk is considerably increased should conduct problems or CD also be present during childhood.

Like many of the other follow-up studies discussed earlier (see also Wilson & Marcotte, 1996), we found a significantly higher rate of academic performance problems in our hyperactive as compared to control group. Our hyperactives were three times more likely to have failed a grade or been suspended and more than eight times as likely to have been expelled or dropped out of school compared to the normal controls at adolescent outcome. Our rates for truancy were comparable to those (17%) reported in other follow-up studies (Mendelson et al., 1971). The level of grade repetition was 20–49% in our studies of teenagers, falling somewhat below that found in previous follow-up studies (56 to 70%; Ackerman, Dykman, & Peters, 1977; Mendelson et al., 1971; Minde et al., 1971; Stewart, Mendelson, & Johnson, 1973; G. Weiss, Minde, Werry, Douglas, & Nemeth, 1971). Perhaps the availability of special educational services in the later 1970s has something to do with this diminution in rates of grade retention in later follow-up studies such as our own. In general, it appears that academic performance difficulties in adolescence are associated with having persistent ADHD since childhood, whereas school disciplinary actions such as suspensions and expulsions are more closely linked to comorbid conduct problems or CD than to ADHD alone (Barkley, Fischer, et al., 1990; Wilson & Marcotte, 1996). ADHD children with the lowest levels of adaptive functioning in childhood are also the most likely to have comorbid psychiatric disorders and academic impairments in adolescence (Greene, Biederman, Faraone, Sienna, & Garcia-Jetton, 1997; Wilson & Marcotte, 1996).

Our findings for substance use are consistent with several previous follow-up studies. We found a significantly greater number of hyperactives had smoked cigarettes or marijuana, whereas Hartsough and Lambert (1985) found only cigarette use to be greater in hyperactive than in normal adolescents. Borland and Heckman (1976) also found more of their hyperactives to be smoking cigarettes than their brothers at follow-up, all of which certainly points to a higher than normal risk for cigarette use among hyperactives in adolescence. Blouin, Bornstein, and Trites (1978), in a retrospective study, found that 57% of hyperactives versus 20% of the controls had used alcohol at least once per month. G. Weiss and Hechtman (1993) also found somewhat more of their hyperactives, as teenagers, to have used nonmedical substances, particularly alcohol, than did their control subjects. And Biederman et al. (1997) found that 40% of their teens had some form of substance dependence or abuse. With the exception of the study by Hartsough and Lambert (1985), there is some consistency across studies in finding hyperactives to be at somewhat higher risk for alcohol use in adolescence than normal children. Several of these studies concurred with our own in finding that the elevated risk for substance use and abuse in adolescence is to be found primarily among hyperactive or ADHD children who had conduct problems in childhood (August et al., 1983; Barkley, Fischer, et al., 1990a; Biederman et al., 1997; Claude & Firestone, 1995; Gittelman et al., 1985; Lynskey & Fergusson, 1995; Wilson & Marcotte, 1996).

Predictors of Adolescent Outcome

Several follow-up studies of hyperactive children examined the degree to which certain childhood and family characteristics at study entry predict the adolescent outcomes of hyperactive children (August et al., 1983; Biederman, Faraone, Milberger, Guite, et al., 1996; Fergusson, Lynskey, & Horwood, 1996; Fischer, Barkley, Fletcher, & Smallish, 1993b; Lambert et al., 1987; Paternite & Loney, 1980; Taylor et al., 1996; G. Weiss & Hechtman, 1993). No single predictor, by itself, seems especially useful in prophesizing the outcome of ADHD children. The combination of several factors is important in such an exercise, with the following predictors appearing to be useful. First, the socioeconomic status (SES) of the family and general level of intelligence of the child are positively related to outcome, especially to academic outcome, eventual educational attainment, and level of employment. Family SES is also related to the severity of ADHD symptoms at outcome with children from lower SES levels having significantly higher degrees of ADHD. Second, the degree to which children experienced peer relationship problems predicts the degree to which they will experience interpersonal problems in adulthood. Third, the degree of aggressiveness and conduct problems in childhood predicts a poorer outcome in many different domains of adjustment, including poorer educational adjustment and attainment, poorer social relationships, and increased risk for substance abuse. As expected, childhood aggression was also related to adolescent delinquency and antisocial offenses. Fourth, the degree to which parental psychopathology, particularly a family history of ADHD, was present in the families of ADHD children was associated with an increased risk of psychiatric and emotional problems in the ADHD children themselves by late adolescence. Families that also had comorbid conduct problems, antisocial behavior, and substance dependence and abuse are even more likely to have children with ADHD who experience greater difficulties in adolescence than those ADHD children without such a family history. Fifth, the degree of conflict and hostility in the interactions of parents with their ADHD children is significantly associated with the degree to which these conflicts as well as generally aggressive behavior are present in adolescence. And sixth, the degree of ADHD in childhood is related only to the degree of academic attainment in adolescence. To date, research has not found the type or extent of childhood intervention to have much impact on the adolescent or young adult outcome of ADHD children. Indeed, it seems to correlate negatively with outcome; that is, the more services the children received across their development, the worse their prognosis in some particular domain of outcome (Fischer, Barkley, Fletcher, & Smallish, 1993a). This finding, however, can be seen to be an artifact of the severity of disorder—more severe cases receive more treatment and are also likely to have worse outcomes, thus making duration or range of treatment a marker for the severity of disorder. Some hope for the success of interventions with ADHD is held out by the initial results of the multimodal treatment study of Satterfield, Satterfield, and Cantwell (1980, 1981). They found that a combination of medication, special education, parent counseling, and training in child management, classroom consultation, and individual counseling of the children may, if maintained over several years into early adolescence, alter the prognosis for ADHD children. The study has a number of methodological problems that keep it from being definitive on this point, thus the field now must await the more rigorous evaluation of multimodal treatment by the five-site treatment project initiated by the National Institute of Mental Health (Arnold et al., 1997).

ADULT OUTCOME

Only a few studies followed samples of hyperactive children into adulthood. Most of this research is nicely summarized in the excellent text by G. Weiss and Hechtman (1993) and in a review by Klein and Mannuzza (1991). When appropriate, the results from the more recent follow-up study of Mannuzza, Gittelman-Klein, Bessler, Malloy, and LaPadula (1993) and from my own follow-up study in Milwaukee with Mariellen Fischer and Kenneth Fletcher are noted (Barkley, Fischer, Fletcher, & Smallish, 1998).

Persistence of ADHD in Adulthood

The results of research to date, based largely on North American samples, suggest that problems with behavior in general and ADHD symptoms specifically continue for 50–65% of these children as they achieve adulthood (G. Weiss & Hechtman, 1993). A follow-up study in China (Wenwei, 1996) found that nearly 70% of 197 children diagnosed 15 years earlier as having minimal brain dysfunction persisted in having symptoms of ADHD into young adulthood (ages 20–33 years, mean 25.5 years).

The rate of persistence of the full disorder, however, varies as a function of the study and the methods used to determine presence of the diagnosis. For instance, in early adulthood, using the self-reports of the subjects, Gittelman et al. (1985; see also Mannuzza, Klein, & Addalli, 1991) found a persistence of 30–31% for ADHD (using DSM-III criteria) in their formerly hyperactive subjects which subsequently fell to a rather surprising level of 11% at a follow-up point just 5 years later when the subjects were 24–33 years of age (mean = 26 years) (Mannuzza et al., 1993). In the recently completed Milwaukee follow-up study, we found a rate of only 3% of our hyperactive subjects qualifying for a DSM-III-R diagnosis of ADHD when based on their self-report (Fischer, 1997). However, when we subsequently interviewed their parents about the presence of disorder using DSM-IV criteria, the rate rose to 42%. And if an empirical criterion for presence of disorder was employed with these same parent reports (e.g., above 1.5 standard deviations above the mean for the normal control group on DSM-IV symptom list), 68% of the hyperactive subjects exceeded this cutoff score and could be said to have retained the disorder. Thus, persistence of ADHD into adulthood is very much a matter of the source of information and the diagnostic criteria being employed (Fischer, 1997). If DSM criteria are applied to the subject's own self-reports, low rates of persistence of ADHD are found in this study. But if parent reports of the subjects continue to be used, as they were in the prior follow-up assessments (and in other studies of ADHD into adolescence), persistence of disorder is 14 times greater. And if an empirical criterion is established for disorder, rates are nearly 23 times greater. This and other information (see Chapter 1, this volume) suggests that the DSM criteria become increasingly less sensitive to the disorder with age. This information also implies that subjects with ADHD may be prone to seriously underreporting their symptoms of the disorder relative to what others may say about them; a problem we noted at the adolescent follow-up point as well (Fischer et al., 1993b).

Recently, Hill and Schoener (1996) attempted to predict the persistence of ADHD across childhood into adulthood. To do so, they developed an exponential function from nine data points taken from six follow-up projects using hyperactive or attention-deficit children discussed earlier in this chapter. The authors then extrapolated this statistical function into later adulthood to predict the likely prevalence of adult ADHD for these later decades of life. The general conclusion of this article was that ADHD declines by 50% approximately every 5 years from childhood throughout adulthood. At this rate of decline, the authors predicted a prevalence rate of ADHD of 0.21% (2 in 1,000) by age 30 years, 0.05% (5 in 10,000) in adults at age 40 years, and 0.01% (1 in 10,000) by age 50 years.

This conclusion is stunning. Indeed, if it were correct, it would imply that ADHD is a relatively benign condition resolving by young adulthood in the vast majority of cases. If only this were true. My concern here is not that outcome studies might show a more benign course than has been thought to occur for ADHD—a course one can only hope might be so. My concern is, however, that such flawed data as were combined and analyzed by Hill and Schoener create flawed conclusions. And such flawed conclusions will be echoed by others citing this article who may be unaware of its multiple, serious methodological shortcomings. Because this particular article has the capacity to greatly mislead others less sophisticated in research on ADHD about whether the disorder persists into adulthood, it receives more attention here than would otherwise be deemed appropriate for any single research report. The silver lining of this controversy, however, may be that by exposing the article's methodological flaws, they can be instructive as to the kinds of considerations that need to be given in both interpreting the results of follow-up studies concerning this issue of persistence of disorder and the performance of future research in this area. At least seven fatal flaws completely undermine the conclusions of Hill and Schoener (1996) and their predictions of infinitesimally low rates of ADHD into later life besides the improper use and interpretation of their statistical analysis for their purpose, as addressed by Sawilowsky and Musial (1998).

1. *Glossing over significant differences across studies.* An obvious problem with the article by Hill and Schoener (1996) is their combining studies as if they used comparably diagnosed subjects when those studies actually employed a diversity of samples, subject selection procedures, and definitions of ADHD. Three of the earliest studies included in the Hill and Schoener analysis studied "hyperactive" children, a diagnosis that is not quite the same as the current clinical diagnosis of ADHD using recent DSM criteria. Indeed, none of the studies analyzed by Hill and Schoener selected ADHD subjects as that disorder has come to be defined in the previous three DSMs (III, III-R, and IV, American Psychiatric Association, 1994). These early studies used such diverse and unsystematic selection criteria as to make any assumptions of similarities across these samples precarious at best. Hill and Schoener (1996) assume, as indeed they must for their analysis to proceed, that all the subjects across these six follow-up projects were diagnosed as ADHD (p. 1143). This is a key assumption. If it should be false, the statistical exercise in which they subsequently engage, no matter how elegant, essentially has little meaning. But even a cursory review of these early studies would reveal substantial differences in the manner in which subjects were selected and assessed at study entry and follow-up. Such differences also suggest just how unreliable the diagnosis of hyperactive was likely to have been in many of these studies. For instance, subjects in the 1971 study by Mendelson et al. were diagnosed as hyperactive using nothing but the investigators' subjective opinion. The likely unreliability of diagnosis in that study is underscored by the authors' own statement: "We were not able to use uniform criteria for selection because the symptoms associated with hyperactivity had not been recorded systematically in the charts" (p. 273).

Nor does it seem advisable to consider children labeled as having "attention disorders" or "minimal brain dysfunction," as was done in the study by Feldman et al. cited in the analysis by Hill and Schoener (1996), as being the same as or similar to those selected as hyperactive in this same era or to subjects defined as ADHD by more recent DSMs. Minimal brain dysfunction was believed at the time to have up to 99 symptoms (Clements, 1966) and to encompass the disorders today known as learning disabilities. It also had no systematic or reliable diagnostic criteria, eventually being jettisoned at the end of the 1970s because it was a speculative and virtually useless term (Rie & Rie, 1980).

The remaining three of the six follow-up projects used by Hill and Schoener were cited as employing DSM-II criteria for the diagnosis of hyperkinetic reaction of childhood as their selection criteria at study entry. But DSM-II criteria are substantially different and substantially deficient relative to later DSM criteria for ADD/ADHD. DSM-II provided only one sentence to describe the hyperkinetic disorder of childhood (American Psychiatric Association, 1968) and contained no symptom lists to help identify the disorder, no thresholds for establishing how many symptoms should be present, no criteria for duration of symptoms or age of onset, and no requirements for developmental inappropriateness of symptoms. Thus, DSM-II hardly constitutes reliable or credible diagnostic criteria for use in research on the persistence of ADHD, relying too much as it did on the subjective opinion of the investigator and nothing more. All this makes it extraordinarily difficult to conclude that the subjects in these various early studies have ADHD, as Hill and Schoener had to assume for their analysis. Without that assumption, the results of Hill and Schoener's analysis are a statistical illusion resulting from the forcing together of highly disparate studies that create the impression of a developmental pattern of remarkable recovery from ADHD.

2. *Reliability of measurement of disorder over time.* Hill and Schoener (1996) also failed to consider the important issue of the unreliability of measurement of symptoms of any disorder across development. This is a significant problem for any follow-up study even when the same instruments are used to assess subjects at their entry and subsequent follow-up points. It becomes an even larger problem for interpreting figures of persistence when dif-

ferent measures and symptom lists are employed across the different assessment occasions. Yet the latter is typical for most of the follow-up studies analyzed by Hill and Schoener. As others have noted in studying the developmental persistence of reading disability and childhood aggression/conduct problems (Fergusson, Horwood Caspi, Moffitt, & Silva, 1996; Fergusson, Horwood, & Lynskey, 1995), the failure to consider the (un)reliability of the measures used to assess the disorder results in a substantial underestimate of the persistence of disorder across development. Such analyses that control for unreliability of measurement have not yet been employed in follow-up studies with ADHD children, but they need to be if the true pattern of persistence of disorder is to be ascertained. There is every reason to believe that when such corrections are applied to follow-up data, rates of retention of ADHD will be considerably higher than past studies have suggested.

3. *The shift from parent to self-report measures at young adult follow-up.* Hill and Schoener (1996) also did not mention the highly significant change in methodology that occurred between the adolescent follow-up data points they employed in their analysis and the single data point they used for the young adult age range. With one exception, all the childhood and adolescent data points analyzed by Hill and Schoener used information about the subjects' symptoms that was obtained from others (parents, primarily, and teachers, in some cases). Only the New York City (NYC) project (Mannuzza, Klein, Bonagura, et al., 1991) used both subject and parent self-reports and only then at the late adolescent follow-up period (mean ages 17–18 years). At the young adult follow-up (mean age 25.5 years) in that project (Mannuzza et al., 1993), only self-reports of symptoms were used. Even then, not all subjects were interviewed about their hyperactive symptoms or about all ADHD symptoms represented in DSM-III-R.

This change from using the reports of others to exclusively relying on self-reports only for the young adult follow-up data point poses a substantial methodological problem for the conclusions that Hill and Schoener (1996) draw from their statistical analysis. The self-reports of ADHD adolescents and young adults may underestimate the degree to which symptoms of their disorder are present relative to what others say about the subjects. Mannuzza et al. (1993) discussed this issue, even acknowledging that they found such differences between source of reports at their late adolescent follow-up point. Those authors also gave evidence suggesting that the reports of others may be more accurate than are the self-reports of the subjects. And they rightly noted that this exclusive reliance on self-report at the young adult follow-up may have caused an underestimation of the persistence of the disorder at that follow-up point.

As noted earlier, the Milwaukee follow-up study showed that the source of the information was highly important in determining persistence of disorder. If only DSM-III-R criteria were used as reported by the subjects, then just 3% of the subjects met full criteria for the disorder. Using parent reports of these subjects, however, resulted in at least 42% of the subjects being classified as still having ADHD by DSM-IV criteria and 68% retaining the disorder if a more empirical diagnostic criterion were used. Therefore, there are several good reasons to question Hill and Schoener's use of a single study to represent the rate of retention of ADHD at the young adult age range.

4. *The reliance on a single project to create the late adolescent and young adult slope of the curve.* The foregoing discussion raises a further significant problem for the statistical analysis of Hill and Schoener: their use of the NYC project only to represent persistence into late adolescence (17–18 years) and young adulthood (25.5 years). As a consequence of doing so, this project exerts a profound influence over the nature of the exponential function at these later ages, basically permitting a single project to define this portion of the curve-fitting analysis. This single data point at adulthood creates a "bottleneck" through which this curve-fitting exercise must pass to extend the exponential function into this adult age group. The

rampant recovery from ADHD found by Hill and Schoener, therefore, is an illusion created by a statistical bottleneck that results from use of a sole data point in a curve-fitting procedure.

5. *The problem of curve extrapolation to later adulthood.* Hill and Schoener (1996) use their exponential function to speculate as to the probable rate of ADHD throughout later decades of adulthood in the general population. They predicted from this function that the prevalence of adult ADHD would be a mere 0.01% by age 50 (essentially 1 in 10,000). These figures, however, are unlikely to hold true for two good reasons. First, as noted previously, their analysis utilized but a single and probably underrepresentative data point to form the curve in young adulthood, thus creating the illusion of a vanishingly small persistence rate into later decades of life. Second, several lines of recent evidence clearly contradict the Hill and Schoener predictions. They simply are not true. As noted in Chapter 2 (this volume), Murphy and Barkley (1996a), using a large sample (*N* = 720) of adults ages 17–84 years, estimated the prevalence of ADHD using DSM-IV thresholds for the number of symptoms. The result was that 1.3% were found to have the Inattentive Type of ADHD, 2.5% the Hyperactive–Impulsive Type, and 0.9% the Combined Type, for a total of 4.7% across all subtypes. Several other groups of investigators (see Chapter 2, this volume) found very similar prevalence estimates among college students as well. Thus, the predicted prevalence rates of ADHD into later decades of adult life drawn from Hill and Schoener's exponential function are gross underestimates of true prevalence by as much as 100-fold or more.

6. *The developmental appropriateness of DSM criteria for adults.* This issue was debated in the committee meetings associated with the creation of the DSM-IV criteria but was not fully resolved. It was also discussed earlier in Chapter 2 (this volume). Most DSM items are still far more pertinent to childhood than to adult contexts. This fact poses a problem for the study of persistence of ADHD over the life span. To appreciate this point, it should be understood that ADHD is increasingly being conceptualized as primarily a deficit in behavioral inhibition that contributes to a larger impairment in self-regulation (Barkley, 1997a, 1997b; Pennington & Ozonoff, 1996). This deficiency in inhibition and self-regulation may remain across development yet give rise to age-specific symptoms. These symptoms may seem to improve or even resolve with time but be replaced by modified or even new forms of symptomatic behavior. If this were so, then the DSM item sets will become increasingly less sensitive to the disorder with age. Use of the DSM criteria across the life span would make it appear as if individuals with ADHD were outgrowing their disorder when in reality they were simply outgrowing the DSM item set (see Chapter 2, this volume, for further details on this point).

7. *The selective use of follow-up studies and their rates of retention.* Surprisingly, the results of another well-known follow-up study of hyperactive children were not analyzed by Hill and Schoener. This is the Montreal follow-up study (G. Weiss & Hechtman, 1993). That study as well as another by Borland and Heckman (1976) were excluded from the curve-fitting procedure. Both projects reported retention rates of symptoms and probably of disorder that were approximately two to four times that of the only study at adulthood that was analyzed by Hill and Schoener (the NYC study).

Four other follow-up studies also were not included in Hill and Schoener's analysis (August et al., 1983; Biederman, Faraone, Milberger, Curtis, et al., 1996; Cantwell & Baker, 1989; Claude & Firestone, 1995). All these studies used more rigorous diagnostic criteria than did many of the studies used by Hill and Schoener and all found rates of retention similar to my Milwaukee follow-up project (65–80% retain the disorder). All provide evidence that the results of the Hill and Schoener analysis misrepresent the rates of retention of disorder into adolescence, suggesting that when more rigorous diagnostic criteria are used that more closely approximate current diagnostic standards, ADHD is a highly persistent condition into adolescence. Granted, some of these studies were not available to Hill and Schoener at the time they conducted their analysis, but that is beside the point. The point is that the findings of these studies directly contradict Hill and Schoener's predictions.

Certainly all these additional studies have their methodological problems, but no more so than those of Hill and Schoener, in deriving their exponential function. Many of these overlooked studies, in fact, are more methodologically sound from the standpoint of definition of disorder. Had Hill and Schoener included these other follow-up studies, especially those from the Montreal and Borland and Heckman projects for age 30 years, a far different conclusion about the persistence of ADHD into adulthood would have resulted. But these additional follow-up studies should not be taken as just more grist for the curve-fitting mill of anyone so inclined to analyze follow-up studies of hyperactive children in this improper way. That exercise would not overcome the other serious limitations described previously that would plague any such statistical exercise.

As this critique indicates, the article by Hill and Schoener (1996) is fraught with serious problems. All these limitations seriously erode the confidence that can be placed in the conclusions drawn by Hill and Schoener about the persistence of ADHD across development or the prevalence of ADHD in later decades of adult life, as I indicated in a letter to the editor of the journal in which their article was published (Barkley, 1997c). These limitations are instructive of ways in which subsequent follow-up studies of those with ADHD can be improved to yield a more accurate evaluation of the persistence of disorder into adulthood. And they illustrate important issues to which clinicians should pay attention in reading journal articles concerning the persistence of ADHD in follow-up studies. These issues also will certainly require further attention in future efforts to improve on the diagnostic criteria used for ADHD as it may be found across the life span.

Other Psychiatric Diagnoses and Impairments

Antisocial behavior is likely to be troublesome for a sizable minority of ADHD children as adults, with at least 18–28% having Antisocial Personality Disorder (Gittelman et al., 1985; Mannuzza, Klein, Bonagura, et al., 1991; Mannuzza et al., 1993; G. Weiss & Hechtman, 1993)—a pattern of repetitive antisocial behavior beginning in early adolescence. The Milwaukee follow-up study found a rate of 22% for Antisocial Personality Disorder among its formerly hyperactive subjects. These cases of antisocial conduct overlap considerably with the 10–20% who are likely to be having a Substance Abuse Disorder (Gittelman et al., 1989; Mannuzza, Klein, Bonagura, et al., 1991; Mannuzza et al., 1993). However, in both the Canadian study of G. Weiss and Hechtman (1993) and the Milwaukee follow-up study, the rates of specific forms of substance abuse or dependence were not found to be significantly higher than those found in the control groups.

The Milwaukee follow-up study recently documented a significantly higher rate of Major Depression among the hyperactive subjects in young adulthood compared to the control subjects (28% vs. 12%). This has not been documented in the other follow-up studies that employed DSM criteria for assessing psychiatric disorders at adult outcome (Mannuzza et al., 1993). Personality disorders have also been documented to be more prevalent at this young adult follow-up point: Passive–aggressive (19% vs. 8 %), Histrionic (11% vs. 0%), Narcissistic (5% vs. 0%), Borderline (14% vs. 3%), and Antisocial (22% vs. 4%). No other psychiatric disorders were found to be significantly higher in the hyperactive than control group.

Up to 67% of ADHD children as adults are free of psychiatric diagnosis (Mannuzza, Klein, Bonagura, et al., 1991; Mannuzza et al., 1993). Still, some research shows that approximately 79% of ADHD children, as adults, complain of difficulties with neurotic symptoms, such as anxiety, sadness, somatic complaints, or other internalizing features, and 75% report interpersonal problems versus about 51% and 54%, respectively, of control subjects (G. Weiss & Hechtman, 1993). The incidence of psychotic disorders in ADHD children at adulthood is no greater than that for the normal control group. The results of the G. Weiss and Hechtman (1993) study suggest that almost 10% will have attempted suicide within the past 3 years and about 5% will die from either suicide or accidental injury. Both percentages are considerably greater than those seen in control groups, where none of the subjects experiences these events.

Antisocial Activities

As adults, individuals with a prior history of ADHD were found to have a greater likelihood of contacts with the police and courts, primarily for traffic offenses (18% vs. 5% for controls) (G. Weiss & Hechtman, 1993). However, problems with theft and nonprescription sale of drugs may occur in a significant minority of subjects. In the Canadian follow-up study, approximately 20% of ADHD children committed acts of physical aggression toward others in adulthood within the past 3 years compared to 5% of control children (G. Weiss & Hechtman, 1993). In the Milwaukee young adult follow-up study, several forms of antisocial activity were more common among the hyperactive than the control subjects: theft of property (85% vs. 66%), breaking and entering (20% vs. 8%), disorderly conduct (68% vs. 54%), assault with fists (74% vs. 53%), carrying a weapon (39% vs. 11%), assault with a weapon (22% vs. 7%), intentionally setting fires (16% vs. 5%), and ran away from home as a teenager (31% vs. 16%). Overall, 22% of the formerly hyperactive subjects had been arrested for a felony compared to only 3% of the control group. Satterfield et al. (1981) found that between 36% and 52% of their hyperactive subjects had been arrested at least once. Similarly, Mannuzza, Gittelman, Konig, and Giampino (1989) found that 39% of their hyperactive subjects had been arrested (vs. 20% in the control group) and 23% had been arrested more than once (vs. 8% of the control group). Consequently, rates of incarceration were also higher in the hyperactive group (9% vs. 1%). Only the G. Weiss and Hechtman (1993) study did not find higher rates of arrest among their sample of Canadian hyperactive children followed into adulthood. It is fair to say that the vast majority of ADHD individuals are not antisocial in adulthood but that a small number, perhaps 25%, are so and display a persistent pattern of such conduct over time. Klein and Mannuzza (1991) found in their study that the greater arrest and incarceraion rates were exclusively among those hyperactive subjects who had Antisocial Personality Disorder in adulthood.

Academic Attainment

The trends toward lower academic achievement and ability and greater grade retentions, suspensions, and expulsions evident in the adolescent years increase such that by adulthood, the percentage of ADHD children having difficulties in these areas is even greater than those percentages noted in adolescence and, of course, greater than those of control subjects. The Milwaukee study found that by 19–27 years of age (mean = 21 years), more than 60% of ADHD subjects reported having been suspended from school (vs. 18% of the control group) and more than 13% had been expelled (vs. 5% of the control group). Although many ADHD children who are now adults will be employed and self-supporting, their general level of educational attainment and socioeconomic status is less than that of control children or even their siblings (Mannuzza et al., 1993). Up to 30% will drop out and never complete high school as compared to less than 10% of control children (G. Weiss & Hechtman, 1993). In the Milwaukee follow-up study, the rate of failure to graduate from high school was 32%.

Inspection of high school transcripts obtained from these subjects indicated a significantly lower high school grade point average (1.69 vs. 2.56 out of a possible 4.0) and their average class ranking in high school was significantly lower (69th percentile vs. 49th percentile). In the Canadian follow-up study, approximately 20% attempted a college program yet only 5% completed a university degree program as compared to over 41% of control children (G. Weiss & Hechtman, 1993).

Employment Functioning

Results from past studies suggest that as adolescents, ADHD individuals are no different in their functioning in their jobs than are normal adolescents (G. Weiss & Hechtman, 1993). However, these findings need to be qualified by the fact that most jobs taken by adolescents are unskilled or only semiskilled and are usually part time. As ADHD children enter adulthood and take on full-time jobs that require skilled labor, independence of supervision, acceptance of responsibility, and periodic training in new knowledge or skills, their deficits in attention, impulse control, and regulating activity level as well as their poor organizational and self-control skills could begin to handicap them on the job. The findings from the few outcome studies that have examined job functioning suggest this may be the case. Although ADHD adults are likely to be employed full time, are completely self-sufficient of their families, and are upwardly mobile (increasing in economic status with time), the quality of their work adjustment differs significantly from that of normal control subjects in adulthood (G. Weiss & Hechtman, 1993). The Milwaukee follow-up study obtained employer ratings of work performance at the young adult assessment and found that hyperactive subjects are rated as performing significantly more poorly at work than are control subjects. ADHD adults are likely to have lower socioeconomic status' than their brothers or control subjects in these studies and to move and change jobs more often but to also have more part-time jobs outside their full-time employment. Employers have been found to rate ADHD adults as less adequate in fulfilling work demands, less likely to be working independently and to complete tasks, and less likely to be getting along well with supervisors. They also do more poorly at job interviews than do normal individuals. ADHD adults report that they are more likely find certain tasks at work too difficult for them. Finally, ADHD adults are more likely to have been fired from jobs as well as to be laid off from work relative to control subjects. In general, ADHD adults appear to have a poorer work record and lower job status than normal adults (G. Weiss & Hechtman, 1993). These findings were recently corroborated in our Milwaukee follow-up study as well.

Social Skills

G. Weiss and Hechtman (1993) are the only investigators to date to have studied the social skills of ADHD adults followed prospectively from childhood. Their findings indicate greater social skills and interaction problems for ADHD adults, particularly in the areas of heterosocial skills (male–female interactions) and assertion. It should not be surprising then that the greater self-esteem problems of ADHD children noted in adolescence continue and may even worsen as they reach adulthood.

Sexual Activity

In the Canadian follow-up study (G. Weiss & Hechtman, 1993), sexual adjustment problems were described by as many as 20% of the ADHD group in adulthood, a figure greater than that of the control group (i.e., 2.4%). For this reason, we chose to examine sexual activity in the ongoing Milwaukee follow-up study. We questioned subjects about their sexual activities as part of the evaluation at the young adult follow-up point. Preliminary results indicate that the hyperactive subjects began having sexual intercourse at an earlier age than the control group (15 vs. 16 years), have had more sexual partners in their lives (19 vs. 7), are more likely to have conceived a pregnancy (38% vs. 4%), are less likely to employ birth control methods, are more likely to have contracted a sexually transmitted disease (17% vs. 4%), and are more likely to have been tested for AIDS/HIV (54% vs. 21%). Such findings indicate a high-risk sexual lifestyle among the formerly hyperactive subjects on reaching young adulthood in comparison to the control subjects.

Driving

The study by G. Weiss and Hechtman (1993) found that significantly more of their hyperactive subjects as adults had been involved in motor vehicle crashes and had received speeding tickets compared to their control group. As noted earlier, we found similar results in ADHD adolescents followed over the first 3–5 years of their initial driving careers. In the Milwaukee outcome study, at their young adult assessment, we have not found a greater number of accidents or speeding tickets by self-report of the subjects. However, more hyperactive subjects than control subjects reported having had their licenses suspended or revoked (42% vs. 28%), been involved in accidents in which the vehicle was totaled (49% vs. 16%), and been involved in a hit-and-run accident (14% vs. 2%). Also, the number of total traffic citations and license suspensions/revocations was significantly greater in the hyperactive subjects as was the amount of damage done in their first vehicular crashes. During a behind-the-wheel driving evaluation, the hyperactive subjects were rated by a driving examiner as significantly more distractible and impulsive and were rated by themselves and their parents as using significantly poorer driving skills.

Predictors of Adult Outcome

G. Weiss and Hechtman (1993) reported on potential predictors of adult outcome in a prospectively followed group of hyperactive children. Their results suggest that those predictors of adolescent outcome may be useful in predicting adult outcome as well. The emotional adjustment of ADHD adults was related to the emotional climate of their homes, particularly the mental health of family members, in childhood and the emotional stability and intelligence of the ADHD subjects themselves. It is important to note here that emotional stability as measured in this study was highly related to childhood aggression, making these results consistent with those for predictors of adolescent outcome when childhood aggression was highly related to many aspects of adolescent adjustment. Friendships in ADHD adults were also related to the early emotional climate of the home. Academic attainment (grades completed) was best predicted by a combination of factors: childhood intelligence, hyperactivity, poor child-rearing practices, socioeconomic status of the parents, and the emotional climate of the home. The employment functioning of these ADHD adults was significantly related to their childhood intelligence estimates and their relationships with adults.

Earlier antisocial behavior was significantly associated with being fired from a greater number of jobs and, in combination with earlier hyperactivity and relationships with adults, with general work record as rated by current employers. The likelihood of committing criminal offenses in adulthood was most associated with childhood emotional instability (aggression) and to a lesser degree with intelligence, hyperactivity, socioeconomic status, mental health of family members, emotional climate in the home, and parental overprotectiveness in child rearing. Not surprisingly, these same factors were associated with the likelihood of later nonmedical drug use.

Despite the discovery of these significant predictors of outcome, the amount of variance accounted for by any one predictor in the outcome under study has been exceptionally small. In general, no single childhood factor is likely to be of much use in predicting the adult adjustment of ADHD individuals. As G. Weiss and Hechtman (1993) argued, the combination of child cognitive ability (intelligence) and emotional stability (aggression, low frustration tolerance, greater emotionality) with family environment (mental health of family members, socioeconomic status, emotional climate of home) and child-rearing practices provides a considerably more successful prediction of adult outcome.

In contrast, Loney et al. (1981) found that only IQ and the number of siblings in the family was predictive of outcome, in this case a diagnosis of Antisocial Personality Disorder, whereas only IQ was related to later alcoholism. No other childhood predictors were found to predict various outcomes in adulthood in this study. The NYC follow-up study, however, was not able to identify any significant predictors of outcome after controlling for chance associations among the large number of statistical tests often conducted in such research (Klein & Mannuzza, 1991).

CLINIC-REFERRED ADULTS DIAGNOSED WITH ADHD

Over the past decade, an as yet small but increasing body of scientific literature has begun to emerge on the nature of ADHD as it is likely to appear in adults who are self-referred to clinics specializing in the treatment of adults with ADHD. For now, far more clinical wisdom is being propounded than solid scientific studies that may support that wisdom. Popular books on the subject of adults with ADHD abound (Hallowell & Ratey, 1994; Kelly & Ramundo, 1992; Murphy & LeVert, 1994; Nadeau, 1995; Solden, 1995; L. Weiss, 1992) and a few clinical textbooks for professionals have also emerged (Goldstein, 1997; Gordon & McClure, 1996; Nadeau, 1995; Wender, 1995). But, for all their good intentions, many of the assertions made in popular books about the nature of clinic-referred adults diagnosed with ADHD have not been put to the empirical test of controlled scientific research. The information obtained from such clinical cases is fraught with various confounding variables not the least of which are referral bias and comorbid psychiatric disorders. Thus, useful as they may initially be when a vacuum exists in scientific information about a disorder, such case reports still remain purely anecdotal wisdom, for better or worse. A few studies of relatively large samples of clinic-referred adults with ADHD have been published in the past 8 years, however. Their results speak to both the legitimacy and the specificity of this diagnosis in adults, as if the follow-up studies of ADHD children reviewed earlier were not sufficient evidence.

Even without making the suggested modifications to the DSM diagnostic criteria for ADHD set forth in Chapter 2 (this volume), the DSM criteria as published can be used successfully in the clinical diagnosis of adult self-referrals. When this is done, the gender ratio found in adults diagnosed with ADHD ranges from 1.8:1 to 2.6:1, favoring males over females (Barkley, Murphy, & Kwasnik, 1996b; Biederman et al., 1993; Murphy & Barkley, 1996b; Roy-Byrne et al., 1997). This ratio is similar to that reported in community prevalence studies of ADHD in children using DSM criteria (see Chapter 2, this volume) but is well below the ratio of males:females often seen in samples of ADHD children referred to clinics. The latter, of course, is most likely driven by a referral bias given that boys are more aggressive than girls with ADHD and thus are more likely to get referred for evaluation and treatment. In any case, the DSM diagnostic criteria for ADHD do appear to identify a group of individuals who are impaired in their daily adaptive functioning and show patterns of deficits in both clinical interviews and psychological testing comparable to those patterns found in children diagnosed with ADHD.

Presenting Symptoms

In a review of the charts of more than 170 adults with ADHD who presented to our adult ADHD clinic during its first few years of operation, Kevin Murphy and I identified a number of symptoms about which these adults were complaining. Table 6.4 summarizes these symptoms. As this table suggests, the types of symptoms reported by adults with ADHD are similar to the difficulties described in ADHD children and adolescents by their parents and teachers, especially as they pertain to school functioning. It is as if the very same difficulties that ADHD teens experience in school were translated to the adult employment setting and now become the difficulties that adults with ADHD and their employers are likely to notice. And such difficulties are quite close to those described in the theoretical model of ADHD developed in the next chapter.

In general, the chief presenting complaints in adults with ADHD who refer themselves to clinics are quite consistent with conceptualizations of this disorder as involving impairments in attention, inhibition, and self-regulation.

Comorbid Psychiatric Disorders

Just as do children and adolescents diagnosed with ADHD, adults given a clinical diagnosis of ADHD have considerably higher amounts of comorbid ODD and CD than do both clinical control groups without a diagnosis of ADHD and normal, nonreferred adults. Approximately 24–35% of clinic-referred adults diagnosed with ADHD have ODD and 17–25% manifest CD, either currently or over the course of their earlier development (Barkley, Murphy, & Kwasnik, 1996a; Biederman et al., 1993; Murphy & Barkley, 1996b; Spencer, 1997). These figures are below those reported in studies of ADHD children, particularly studies of hyperactive children followed to adulthood, where levels of ODD and CD may be double these reported for adults diagnosed with ADHD (Barkley, Fischer, et al., 1990; G. Weiss & Hechtman, 1993; see also the section "Adolescent Outcome of ADHD Children"). Among adult relatives of children having ADHD who also meet criteria for ADHD, 53% have had ODD and 33% have had CD sometime in their lives (Biederman et al., 1993), figures closer to those seen in follow-up studies of hyperactive or ADHD children. Antisocial Personality Disorder is often an associated adult outcome in a large minority of those adolescents who have CD; thus it is not surprising to find that 7–18% of adults diagnosed with ADHD qualify for a diagnosis of this personality disorder (Biederman et al., 1993; Shekim, Asarnow, Hess, Zaucha, & Wheeler, 1990). Even among those who do not qualify for this diagnosis, many receive higher than normal ratings on those personality traits associated with this personality disorder (Tzelepis, Schubiner, & Warbase, 1995).

Given this relationship of adult ADHD to adult Antisocial Personality Disorder, one would not be surprised to find ADHD overrepresented in adult prison populations. I am aware of only one published study on the issue (Eyestone & Howell, 1994). A random sampling of 102 inmates in the Utah State Prison was employed in the study. Results indicated that 25.5% of those inmates evaluated qualified for a diagnosis of adult ADHD. This diagnosis required that they have self-reported significant symptoms of the disorder since childhood and meet DSM-III-R criteria for ADHD. Of interest in the study was its finding of a strong association of adult ADHD to major depression in this population, where the prevalence of disorder was also 25.5%. The overlap of the two disorders was 47% with evidence that increasing severity of ADHD symptoms was associated with increasing risk for major

TABLE 6.4. Frequent Presenting Complaints of Adults with ADHD Self-Referred to Clinics

Poor school/work performance related to

Deficient sustained attention to reading, paperwork, lectures, etc.
Poor reading comprehension
Easily bored by tedious material or tasks
Poor organization, planning, and preparation
Procrastination until deadlines are imminent
Subjectively restless; objectively fidgety
Less able to initiate and sustain effort to uninteresting tasks
Highly distractible when context demands concentration
Trouble staying in a confined space or context, such as dull meetings (not a phobia)
Impulsive decision making
Cannot work well independently of supervision
Does not listen carefully to directions
Less able to follow through on instructions or assignments
Frequent impulsive job changes; more often fired from employment
Poor academic grades for ability
Often late for work/appointments
Frequently misplace things
Forgetful of things that must be done
Poor sense of time; deficient time management
Trouble thinking clearly and using sound judgment, especially under stressful conditions
Generally poor self-discipline
Less able to pursue goals as well as others

Poor interpersonal skills

Difficulties making friendships; fewer friends than others
Significant marital problems; more likely to divorce
Impulsive comments to others
Quick to anger or frustrate
Verbally abusive to others when angered
Poor follow-through on commitments
Perceived by others as self-centered and immature
Often fail to see others' needs or activities as important
Poor listening skills
Trouble sustaining friendships or intimate relations

Emotional problems

Low self-esteem
Dysthymic
Quick-tempered
Proneness to emotional upset or hysteria
Demoralized over chronic failures, often since childhood
Generalized anxiety disorder
Poor regulation of emotions

Antisocial behavior

Full Antisocial Personality Disorder (10–15+%)
Substance dependence/abuse disorders (10–20%)
More frequent lying and stealing
History of physical aggression toward others
Greater likelihood of criminal activities and arrests

Adaptive behavior problems

Chronic employment difficulties
Generally less educated than others of their cognitive ability
Poor financial management, failure to pay bills on time, frequent impulse purchases, and excess debt
Poor driving habits, frequent traffic accidents, violations, and license suspensions
Perceive themselves as less adequate in child care/management if they have children
Trouble organizing/maintaining home; poor housekeeping
More chaotic personal and family routines
Less health conscious than others (poor exercise, diet, weight control, management of cholesterol; increased likelihood of smoking and alcohol consumption; riskier sexual lifestyle, less likely to employ birth control or disease protection during sex, more sexual partners than typical, and greater likelihood of having children at an early age)

depression. These authors also cited an unpublished master's thesis by Favarino which was reported to have found a similar prevalence rate for adult ADHD in a prison population. Given the problems with self-reports cited earlier, these figures are probably underestimates.

Substance dependence and abuse are known to occur to a more frequent degree among hyperactive or ADHD children who develop CD by adolescence or Antisocial Personality Disorder by adulthood. Adults clinically diagnosed with ADHD seem to be no exception to this rule. Studies have found lifetime rates of alcohol dependence or abuse disorders ranging between 32% and 53% of adults diagnosed with ADHD, whereas 8–32% may manifest some other form of substance dependence or abuse (Barkley et al., 1996b; Biederman et al., 1993; Murphy & Barkley, 1996b; Roy-Byrne et al., 1997; Shekim et al., 1990). Tzelepis et al. (1995) reported that 36% of their 114 adults with ADHD had experienced dependence on or abuse of alcohol, 21% for cannabis, 11% for cocaine or other stimulants, and 5% for polydrug dependence. Moreover, at the point of their initial evaluation, 13% met criteria for alcohol dependence or abuse within the past month.

Approximately 25% of children with ADHD have an anxiety disorder (Tannock, in press; see Chapter 4, this volume). The corresponding figure among adults is 24% to 43% for Generalized Anxiety Disorder and 52% for a history of Overanxious Disorder (Barkley et al., 1996a; Biederman et al., 1993; Murphy & Barkley, 1996b; Shekim et al., 1990). The figure is somewhat higher than that found in children and may likely reflect an artifact of referral bias, as has been found with clinic-referred children having ADHD (see Chapter 4, this volume). That is, ADHD seems to show little or no inherent association with anxiety disorders but may be found to be more common in those with ADHD seen in clinics by virtue of the fact that clinic-referred populations are likely to have multiple disorders. Indeed, both studies by Murphy and Barkley (1996b) and Roy-Byrne et al. (1997) found no higher degree of anxiety disorders among their adults with ADHD than occurred in a clinical control group of adults seen at the same clinic who were not diagnosed with ADHD. Consistent with this argument, the amount of anxiety disorders among adults with ADHD who are relatives of clinically diagnosed ADHD children is lower: 20% (Biederman et al., 1993). And we have not found a higher occurrence of anxiety disorders in our hyperactive children followed to adulthood in Milwaukee than occurred in our control group of nonreferred children.

As discussed in Chapter 4 (this volume), major depression does seem to have some inherent affinity with ADHD, unlike the anxiety disorders noted previously. Approximately 16% to 31% of adults meeting ADHD diagnostic criteria also have Major Depressive Disorder (Barkley et al., 1996b; Biederman et al., 1993; Murphy & Barkley, 1996b; Roy-Byrne et al., 1997; Tzelepis et al., 1995). Dysthymia, a milder form of depression, has been reported to occur in 19–37% of clinic-referred adults diagnosed with ADHD (Murphy & Barkley, 1996b; Roy-Byrne et al., 1997; Shekim et al., 1990; Tzelepis et al., 1995). Some follow-up studies have not been able to document an increased risk for depression among hyperactive children followed to adulthood (see earlier). However, my own Milwaukee follow-up study of a large sample of hyperactive children has recently found a prevalence of 28% for major depression by young adulthood—a finding quite consistent with the studies on adults diagnosed with ADHD. Even so, a few studies comparing clinic-referred ADHD adults to adults seen at the same clinic without ADHD have not found a higher incidence of depression among the ADHD adults (Murphy & Barkley, 1996b; Roy-Byrne et al., 1997), implying that, like the anxiety disorders, the elevated occurrence of depression and mood disorders among ADHD adults seen in clinics may reflect, in part, simply referral bias—that is, all adults seen in general psychiatric outpatient clinics have a higher than normal rate of these mood and anxiety disorders, and this rate is no higher in those with ADHD.

Obsessive–Compulsive Disorder (OCD) was initially reported to occur in 14% of clinically diagnosed adults with ADHD (Shekim et al., 1990). Tzelepis et al. (1995) were unable to replicate this finding and reported only 4% of their adults met diagnostic criteria for OCD.

Roy-Byrne et al. (1997) likewise reported a 4.3–6.5% prevalence rate, which was not significantly different from their clinical control group. Spencer (1997) recently reported that OCD was more common (12%) only among those adults with a comorbid tic disorder whereas the figure for those ADHD adults without tics was approximately 2%. Thus, OCD does not appear to be significantly associated with ADHD.

Therefore, it would seem that, with the exception of anxiety disorders, adults meeting diagnostic criteria for ADHD demonstrate both comparable levels and patterns of comorbid psychiatric disorders as do hyperactive or ADHD children followed to adolescence and adulthood.

Intelligence and Academic Functioning

Studies of ADHD children often find them to be significantly below those in control groups in their intellectual estimates, averaging about 7–10 IQ points difference (see Chapter 3, this volume). This does not seem to be the case for clinic-referred adults with ADHD, for whom intelligence estimates fall in the normal range and are comparable to control groups of clinic-referred adults (Barkley et al., 1996b; Murphy & Barkley, 1996b). Although Biederman et al. (1993) found that their adults diagnosed with ADHD had IQ scores significantly below their control groups, the IQ scores for the adults with ADHD were 107–110, nearly identical to the results of our own studies of adults with ADHD. The ADHD adults in the Biederman et al. (1993) study therefore seem to differ significantly from the control groups only by virtue of the control groups having above-average IQs (110–113).

Adults diagnosed with ADHD seem to share a similar likelihood of problems in academic functioning at some time during their schooling, as was found in children having ADHD followed over development. Between 16% and 40% of clinic-referred adults have repeated a grade, in keeping with the figures reported for ADHD children discussed earlier in this chapter (Barkley et al., 1996b; Biederman et al., 1993; Murphy & Barkley, 1996b). Up to 43% have also received some form of extra tutoring services in their academic histories to assist them with their schooling (Biederman et al., 1993). Barkley et al. (1996b) found that 28% of their young adult sample had received special educational services; a figure about half that found in hyperactive children followed to young adulthood but still higher than normal. Consistent with these studies, Roy-Byrne et al. (1997) also found clinic-referred adults with ADHD to have significantly greater frequency of achievement difficulties in school, grade retentions, and special educational services. A history of behavioral problems and school suspensions is also significantly more common in clinic-referred adults with ADHD than in clinical control groups (Murphy & Barkley, 1996b). Yet, young adults with ADHD seen in clinics are far more likely to have graduated high school (92%) and attended college (68%) than are clinic-referred children with ADHD followed to adulthood (Barkley et al., 1993), for whom the high school graduation rate is only about 64% (see earlier). Some studies indicate that clinic-referred adults with ADHD may have less education than non-ADHD adults seen at the same clinic (Roy-Byrne et al., 1997), a finding consistent with adult follow-up studies of ADHD children (Mannuzza et al., 1993). Others, in contrast, have not found this to be the case (Murphy & Barkley, 1996b).

Concerning actual academic achievement skills, adults diagnosed with ADHD have been found to perform significantly more poorly on tests of math than those in control groups (Biederman et al., 1993). Only those adults with ADHD who were relatives of ADHD children were found to be significantly lower on tests of reading in this study. Others have also found clinic-referred adults with ADHD to perform more poorly on reading achievement tests than do control groups from the same clinic (Roy-Byrne et al., 1997). Yet the mean scores on both achievement tests in these studies were still within the normal range for these adults with

ADHD. Still, these findings are in keeping with studies of children with ADHD, who are almost routinely found to be below normal in their academic achievement skills (see Chapter 3, this volume). The prevalence of learning disabilities in adults diagnosed with ADHD is well below that found in ADHD children, ranging from 0% to 12% (Barkley et al., 1996b; Biederman et al., 1993; Matochik, Rumsey, Zametkin, Hamburger, & Cohen, 1996).

All this suggests that although clinically diagnosed adults with ADHD share some of the same types of academic difficulties in their histories as do hyperactive or ADHD children followed over development, their intellectual levels are higher and their likelihood of having academic difficulties is considerably less in most respects than that level seen in children with ADHD followed to adulthood.

This higher level of intellectual and academic functioning in clinic-referred ADHD adults makes sense given that they are self-referred to clinics in comparison to ADHD children. This fact makes it much more likely that these adults have employment, health insurance, and a sufficient educational level to be so employed and insured, as well as a sufficient level of intellect and self-awareness to perceive themselves as being in need of assistance for their psychiatric problems and difficulties in adaptive functioning. Children with ADHD brought to clinics by their parents are less likely to have these attributes by the time they reach adulthood. They are not as educated, are having considerable problems sustaining employment, are more likely to have had a history of aggression and antisocial activities, and are not as self-aware of their symptoms as adults having ADHD who are self-referred to clinics. As already discussed, only 3% of hyperactive children followed to adulthood in our Milwaukee study endorsed sufficient symptoms to receive a clinical diagnosis of ADHD, whereas that figure was 48% if their parents' reports were employed. This suggests that ADHD children brought to clinics as children may have a more severe form of ADHD, or one that at least predisposes them to more severe impairments and a greater likelihood of comorbid oppositional, conduct, and antisocial disorders, than do adults self-referred to clinics and diagnosed then as having ADHD.

Neuropsychological Findings

A few studies have reported the neuropsychological test performances of adults diagnosed with ADHD using similar or even the same neuropsychological tests employed with children with ADHD (see Chapter 3, this volume). Matochik et al. (1996) compared 21 ADHD adults against the norms provided with the neuropsychological tests. They found that performance of mental arithmetic and digit span on the Wechsler Adult Intelligence Scale—Revised were significantly below normal, as they are often found to be in children with ADHD. Barkley et al. (1996b) and Kovner et al. (1997) also found adults with ADHD to perform more poorly on this digit span subtest, all of which implies difficulties with working memory in adults with ADHD (see Chapter 3, this volume). In contrast, tests of verbal learning and verbal memory have generally not been found to discriminate adults with ADHD from those in control groups (Holdnack, Moberg, Arnold, Gur, & Gur, 1995; Kovner et al., 1997).

Performance on the Wisconsin Card Sort Test (WCST) was found by Barkley et al. (1996b) to be within the normal range in their ADHD young adults. Others have also not found performance on the WCST to discriminate groups of ADHD adults from control groups (Holdnack et al., 1995; Seidman, 1997). Studies of childhood ADHD also found this task to be quite inconsistent in its results (see Chapter 3, this volume).

Barkley et al. (1996b) compared a small sample of young adults with ADHD ($N = 25$) to a control group ($N = 23$) on measures of creativity, verbal fluency, working memory, and a continuous performance test (CPT). No differences were found in creativity and verbal fluency; the latter finding is discrepant with some of the findings in the child ADHD literature (see Chapter 3, this volume), but even there results for fluency tests have not been consistent. Also, the Barkley et al. study has very low statistical power to detect group differences because of its small sample sizes; thus the absence of findings must go uninterpreted. Adults with ADHD were found to perform significantly worse on a working memory task involving the Simon Tone/Color Game in which increasing lengthy sequences of tone/color key presses must be imitated.

Studies of children with ADHD that employ CPTs frequently find them to perform these tasks more poorly than do control groups (Corkum & Siegel, 1993; see Chapter 2, this volume). Barkley et al. (1996a) found that their young adults with ADHD also demonstrated more omission and commission errors on the Conners CPT compared to the control group. So did two other recent studies (Epstein, Conners, Erhardt, March, & Swanson, 1997; Seidman, 1997). Roy-Byrne et al. (1997) compared adults diagnosed with ADHD (probable ADHD) to a group having current adult ADHD symptoms without persuasive childhood history (possible ADHD) and to a clinical control group using the Conners CPT. In contrast to the previous studies, they found that those adults who have possible ADHD were significantly poorer on a composite CPT score than those in the control group, with the probable ADHD adult group falling between these two groups. Holdnack et al. (1995) also found poorer CPT performance in adults with ADHD, though in this instance it was on the measure of reaction time only and not omission or commission errors. A study by Kovner et al. (1997) likewise found reaction times on a test measuring the ability to shift response sets in a task to be slower in adults with ADHD ($N = 19$) compared to a control group ($N = 10$).

For the most part, neuropsychological studies of adults with ADHD have employed very small sample sizes, often well below those necessary for adequate statistical power to detect small to moderate effect sizes (group differences) in such research. As a consequence, the failure to find group differences on some measures for which differences in the child ADHD literature have been found may simply be a result of low power. Clearly, future research on the cognitive deficits associated with ADHD in adults will need to employ more adequate sample sizes. Nevertheless, what group differences have been observed are quite consistent with those deficits found in children and adolescents having ADHD.

Adaptive Functioning

Few studies have examined the adaptive functioning of clinic-referred adults with ADHD in comparison to those in control groups. In one such study of 172 adults with ADHD, Murphy and Barkley (1996b) reported that ADHD adults were more likely to have divorced and remarried than control adults and tended to report less marital satisfaction in their current marriages ($p < .08$). More adults with ADHD had been fired from employment (53% vs. 31%), had impulsively quit a job (48% vs. 16%), and were more likely to report chronic employment difficulties (77% vs. 57%). The ADHD adults also had changed jobs significantly more often than those in the control group (6.9 vs. 4.6). Such findings for employment difficulties are in keeping with the outcomes of follow-up studies of hyperactive children (Mannuzza et al., 1993; G. Weiss & Hechtman, 1993).

As suggested earlier in this chapter, hyperactive or ADHD children followed into later adolescence are likely to have more negative driving outcomes than are control subjects followed over this same period. Several studies of adults with ADHD have inquired about their driving risks. In their driving of a motor vehicle, adults with ADHD were more likely to have received speeding tickets, to have received more of them, and to have had more motor vehicle accidents (Barkley et al., 1996a; Murphy & Barkley, 1996b). There was also a marginally significant finding for more of these ADHD adults to have had such crashes. Consistent across both of these studies is the observation that more adults with ADHD have had their licenses suspended or revoked than those in the control groups (24–32% vs. 4%). In the most thorough study of driving risks and behavior to date, Barkley et al. (1996a) also found that their young adults with ADHD were more likely to have been involved in crashes that resulted in bodily injuries and were rated by themselves and others as demonstrating significantly less sound driving practices during driving than did the control group. The authors obtained the official driving records of these subjects, which corroborated many of the above findings. Adults with ADHD had more driving violations on their official records, including speeding tickets and were indeed more likely to have had their licenses suspended or revoked (48% vs. 9%) and to experience such suspensions more often (mean of 1.5 vs. 0.1 episodes). The differences between groups for officially recorded crashes were marginally significant ($p < .08$) both for the percentage of subjects having crashes (80% vs. 52%) and for the total number of such crashes recorded on their record (means of 0.8 vs. 0.3). The problems with driving in these young adults could not be attributed to poor driving knowledge as no differences between the groups were found on an extensive assessment of such knowledge. Howeer, these young adults, when tested on a computer-simulated driving task, displayed more erratic steering of the vehicle and had more scrapes and crashes while operating this simulated vehicle than did subjects in the control group. Thus, it appears that like ADHD children followed into adolescence and young adulthood, adults with ADHD who self-refer to clinics are likely to have significantly poorer driving habits and a greater risk of various negative driving outcomes than are normal or clinical control groups of adults.

SUMMARY

This chapter described the developmental course and adolescent and adult outcomes of hyperactive or ADHD children with particular attention paid to both the adolescent and young adult status of these children. A number of promising early predictors of risk for ADHD in early childhood were noted. Chief among these seem to be a family history of ADHD and the emergence of difficult temperament in the preschool years. High activity levels combined with demandingness in the child, when coupled with maternal psychological distress and family dysfunction, are highly related to the persistence of ADHD into later childhood and to the development of oppositional behaviors. Throughout their development, ADHD children are at greatest risk for academic problems in both their skill development and behavioral adjustment. Their second greatest risk is for antisocial conduct, which itself becomes a strong predictor of adolescent substance use and abuse and later adult Antisocial Personality Disorder and criminality. As adults, they are likely to be less educated, to be underachieving in their occupational settings, and to be having problems with working independently of supervision. A small but significant minority, perhaps 15–20%, become persistent antisocial personalities in adulthood. Although most ADHD children continue to have symptoms of their disorder well into adolescence and adulthood, the majority no longer meet formal DSM diagnostic criteria for the disorder. This may reflect as much a problem with the increasing developmental insensitivity of these criteria to the disorder as it may the actual developmental recovery from the disorder itself. Identifying predictors of the adult outcome of hyperactive or ADHD children has not been easy. Some studies have identified such predictors, but others have not and even those predictors that have been identified account for only a small amount of variance in the outcome under study.

Research on clinic-referred adults with ADHD indicates that they have comparable educational and social histories, comorbid psychiatric diagnoses, and adaptive functioning impairments as do hyperactive or ADHD children followed into adulthood. These self-referred ADHD adults are also likely to have problems in the same areas of neuropsychological functioning as are children with ADHD, particularly on CPTs and tests of working memory (such as mental arithmetic and digit span). Differences between self-referred adults with ADHD and children with ADHD followed to adulthood are chiefly in their levels of anxiety disorders (somewhat higher in self-referred adults); in oppositional, conduct, or antisocial disorders (somewhat lower in self-referred adults), and in intellectual and academic functioning (self-referred adults may be more intelligent, have better achievement skills, and be better educated). Nevertheless, the general pattern of these findings is consistent between the two literatures (clinically diagnosed adults with ADHD and children with ADHD followed to adulthood) and is sufficient to conclude that ADHD among clinic-referred adults is a valid adult psychiatric disorder—a conclusion reached by others independently reviewing this body of literature as well (Spencer, Biederman, Wilens, & Faraone, 1994).

REFERENCES

Achenbach, T. M., & Edelbrock, C. S. (1983). *Manual for the Child Behavior Profile and Child Behavior Checklist.* Burlington, VT: Author.

Ackerman, P., Dykman, R., & Peters, J. E. (1977). Teenage status of hyperactive and nonhyperactive learning disabled boys. *American Journal of Orthopsychiatry, 47,* 577–596.

American Psychiatric Association. (1968). *Diagnostic and statistical manual of mental disorders* (2nd ed.). Washington, DC: Author.

American Psychiatric Association. (1980). *Diagnostic and statistical manual of mental disorders* (3rd ed.). Washington, DC: Author.

American Psychiatric Association. (1987). *Diagnostic and statistical manual of mental disorders* (3rd ed., rev.). Washington, DC: Author.

American Psychiatric Association. (1994). *Diagnostic and statistical manual of mental disorders* (4th ed.). Washington, DC: Author.

Applegate, B., Lahey, B. B., Hart, E. L., Waldman, I., Biederman, J., Hynd, G. W., Barkley, R. A., Ollendick, T., Frick, P. J., Greenhill, L., McBurnett, K., Newcorn, J., Kerdyk, L. , Garfinkel, B., & Shaffer, D. (1997) . Validity of the age of onset criterion for ADHD: A report from the DSM-IV field trials. *Journal of the American Academy of Child and Adolescent Psychiatry, 36,* 1211–1221.

Arnold, L. E., Abikoff, H., Cantwell, D. P., Conners, C. K., Elliott, G., Greenhill, L. L., Hechtman, L., Hinshaw, S. P., Hoza, B., Jensen, P. S., Kraemer, H. C., March, J. S., Newcorn, J. H., Pelham, W. E., Richters, J. E., Schiller, E., Severe, J. B., Swanson, J. M., Vereen, D., & Wells, K. C. (1997). National Institute of Mental Health collaborative multimodal treatment study of children with ADHD (MTA). *Archives of General Psychiatry, 54,* 865–870.

August, G. J., Stewart, M. A., & Holmes, C. S. (1983). A four-year follow-up of hyperactive boys with and without conduct disorder. *British Journal of Psychiatry, 143,* 192–198

Barkley, R. A. (1981). *Hyperactive children: A handbook for diagnosis and treatment.* New York: Guilford Press.

Barkley, R. A. (1982). Specific guidelines for defining hyperactivity in children (attention deficit disorder with hyperactivity). In B. Lahey & A. Kazdin (Eds.), *Advances in clinical child psychology* (Vol. 5, pp. 137–180). New York: Plenum.

Barkley, R. A. (1988). The effects of methylphenidate on the interactions of preschool ADHD children with their mothers. *Journal of the American Academy of Child and Adolescent Psychiatry, 27,* 336_2D341.

Barkley, R. A. (1997a). Behavioral inhibition, sustained attention, and executive functions: Constructing a unifying theory of ADHD. *Psychological Bulletin, 121,* 65–94.

Barkley, R. A. (1997b). *ADHD and the nature of self-control.* New York: Guilford Press.

Barkley, R. A. (1997c). Advancing age, declining ADHD. *American Journal of Psychiatry, 154,* 1323–1324.

Barkley, R. A., Anastopoulos, A. D., Guevremont, D. G. & Fletcher, K. F. (1991). Adolescents with attention deficit hyperactivity disorder: Patterns of behavioral adjustment, academic functioning, and treatment utilization. *Journal of the American Academy of Child and Adolescent Psychiatry, 30,* 752–761.

Barkley, R. A., & Biederman, J. (1997). Towards a broader definition of the age of onset criterion for attention deficit hyperactivity disorder. *Journal of the American Academy of Child and Adolescent Psychiatry, 36,* 1204–1210.

Barkley, R. A., DuPaul, G. J., & McMurray, M. B. (1990). A comprehensive evaluation of attention deficit disorder with and without hyperactivity. *Journal of Consulting and Clinical Psychology, 58,* 775–789.

Barkley, R. A., Fischer, M., Edelbrock, C. S., & Smallish, L. (1990). The adolescent outcome of hyperactive children diagnosed by research criteria: I. An 8-year prospective follow-up study. *Journal of the American Academy of Child and Adolescent Psychiatry, 29,* 546–557.

Barkley, R. A., Fischer, M., Fletcher, K., & Smallish, L. (1998). [Young adult outcome of hyperactive children]. Unpublished raw data.

Barkley, R. A., Fischer, M., Newby, R., & Breen, M. (1988). Development of a multi-method clinical protocol for assessing stimulant drug responses in ADHD children. *Journal of Clinical Child Psychology, 17,* 14–24.

Barkley, R. A., Guevremont, D. G., Anastopoulos, A. D., DuPaul, G. J., & Shelton, T. L. (1993). Driving-Related risks and outcomes of attention deficit hyperactivity disorder in adolescents and young adults: A 3–5-year follow-up survey. *Pediatrics, 92,* 212–218.

Barkley, R. A., Guevremont, D. G., Anastopoulos, A. D., & Fletcher, K. (1992). A comparison of three family thereapy programs for treating family conflicts in adolescents with attention-deficit hyperactivity disorder. *Journal of Consulting and Clinical Psychology, 60,* 450–462.

Barkley, R. A., Murphy, K. R., & Kwasnik, D. (1996a). Psychological adjustment and adaptive impairments in young adults with ADHD. *Journal of Attention Disorders, 1,* 41–54.

Barkley, R. A., Murphy, K. R., & Kwasnik, D. (1996b). Motor vehicle driving competencies and risks in teens and young adults with ADHD. *Pediatrics, 98,* 1089–1095.

Battle, E. S., & Lacey, B. (1972). A context for hyperactivity in children, over time. *Child Development, 43,* 757–773.

Beitchman, J. H., Wekerle, C., & Hood, J. (1987). Diagnostic continuity from preschool to middle childhood. *Journal of the American Academy of Child and Adolescent Psychiatry, 26,* 694–699.

Biederman, J. (1997, October). *Returns of comorbidity in girls with ADHD.* Paper presented at the annual meeting of the American Academy of Child and Adolescent Psychiatry, Toronto, Canada.

Biederman, J., Faraone, S. V., Mick, E., Spencer, T., Wilens, T., Kiely, K., Guite, J., Ablon, J. S., Reed, E., Warburton, R. (1995). High risk for attention deficit hyperactivity disorder among children of parents with childhood onset of the disorder: A pilot study. *American Journal of Psychiatry, 152,* 431–435.

Biederman, J., Faraone, S. V., Milberger, S., Curtis, S., Chen, L., Marrs, A., Ouellette, C., Moore, P., & Spencer, T. (1996). Predictors of persistence and remission of ADHD into adolescence: Results from a four-year prospective follow-up study. *Journal of the American Academy of Child and Adolescent, 35,* 343–351.

Biederman, J., Faraone, S., Milberger, S, Guite, J., Mick, E., Chen, L., Mennin, D., Ouellette, C., Moore, P., Spencer, T., Norman, D., Wilens, T., Kraus, I., & Perrin, J. (1996). A prospective 4-year follow-up study of attention-deficit hyperactivity and related disorders. *Archives of General Psychiatry, 53,* 437–446.

Biederman, J., Faraone, S., Spencer, T., Wilens, T., Norman, D., Lapey, K. A., Mick, E., Lehman, B. K., & Doyle, A. (1993). Patterns of psychiatric comorbidity, cognition, and psychosocial functioning in adults with attention deficit hyperactivity disorder. *American Journal of Psychiatry, 150,* 1792–1798.

Biederman, J., Faraone, S. V., Taylor, A., Sienna, M., Williamson, S., & Fine, C. (1997, October). *Diagnostic continuity between child and adolescent ADHD: Findings from a longitudinal clinical sample.* Paper presented at the annual meeting of the American Academy of Child and Adolescent Psychiatry, Toronto, Canada.

Blouin, A. G., Bornstein, M. A., & Trites, R. L. (1978). Teenage alcohol abuse among hyperactive children: A five year follow-up study. *Journal of Pediatric Psychology, 3,* 188–194.

Borland, H. L., & Heckman, H. K. (1976). Hyperactive boys and their brothers: A 25-year follow-up study. *Archives of General Psychiatry, 33,* 669–675.

Brown, R. T., & Borden, K. A. (1986). Hyperactivity in adolescence: Some misconceptions and new directions. *Journal of Clinical Child Psychology, 15,* 194–209.

Buss, D. M., Block, J. H., & Block, J. (1980). Preschool activity level: Personality correlates and developmental implications. *Child Development, 51,* 401–408.

Cameron, J. R. (1978). Parental treatment, children's temperament, and the risk of childhood behavioral problems: II. Initial temperament, parental attitudes, and the incidence and form of behavioral problems. *American Journal of Orthopsychiatry, 48,* 140–147.

Campbell, S. B. (1987). Parent-referred problem three-year-olds: Developmental changes in symptoms. *Journal of Child Psychology and Psychiatry, 28,* 835–846.

Campbell, S. B. (1990). *Behavior problems in preschool children.* New York: Guilford Press.

Campbell, S. B., Endman, M., & Bernfield, G. (1977). A three-year follow-up of hyperactive preschoolers into elementary school. *Journal of Child Psychology and Psychiatry, 18,* 239–249.

Campbell, S. B., & Ewing, L. J. (1990). Follow-up of hard to manage preschoolers: Adjustment at age 9 and predictors of continuing symptoms. *Journal of Child Psychology and Psychiatry, 31,* 871–889.

Campbell, S. B., Schleifer, M., & Weiss, G. (1978). Continuities in maternal reports and child behaviors over time in hyperactive and comparison groups. *Journal of Abnormal Child Psychology, 6,* 33–45.

Cantwell, D. (1975). *The hyperactive child.* New York: Spectrum.

Cantwell, D. P., & Baker, L. (1989). Stability and natural history of DSM-III childhood diagnoses. *Journal of the American Academy of Child and Adolescent Psychiatry, 28,* 691–700.

Carey, W. B., & McDevitt, S. C. (1978). A revision of the Infant Temperament Questionnaire. *Pediatrics, 61,* 735–739.

Carlson, E. A., Jacobvitz, D., & Sroufe, L. A. (1995). A developmental investigation of inattentiveness and hyperactivity. *Child Development, 66,* 37–54.

Chamberlin, R. W. (1977). Can we identify a group of children at age two who are at risk for the development of behavioral or emotional problems in kindergarten or first grade? *Pediatrics, 59* (Suppl.), 971–981.

Claude, D., & Firestone, P. (1995). The development of ADHD boys: A 12-year follow-up. *Canadian Journal of Behavioral Science, 27,* 226–249.

Clements, S. D. (1966). *Task Force One: Minimal brain dysfunction in children* (Monograph No. 3). Washington, DC: National Institute of Neurological Diseases and Blindness, U.S. Department of Health, Education, and Welfare.

Cohen, N. J., & Minde, K. (1981). The "hyperactive syndrome" in kindergarten children: Comparison of children with pervasive and situational symptoms. *Journal of Child Psychology and Psychiatry, 24,* 443–455.

Corkum, P. V., & Siegel, L. S. (1993). Is the continuous performance task a valuable research tool for use with children with attention-deficit-hyperactivity disorder? *Journal of Child Psychology and Psychiatry, 34,* 1217–1239.

Deutsch, C. K., Swanson, J. M., Bruell, J. H., Cantwell, D. P. Weinberg, F., & Baren, M. (1982). Overrepresentation of adoptees in children with the attention deficit disorder. *Behavioral Genetics, 12,* 231–238.

Diener, M. B., & Milich, R. (1997). Effects of positive feedback on the social interactions of boys with attention deficit hyperactivity disorder: A test of the self-protective hypothesis. *Journal of Clinical Child Psychology, 26,* 256–265.

Earls, F., & Jung, K. G. (1987). Temperament and home environment characteristics as causal factors in the early development of childhood psychopathology. *Journal of the American Academy of Child and Adolesecnt Psychiatry, 26,* 491–498.

Epstein, J. N., Conners, C. K., Erhardt, D., March, J. S., & Swanson, J. M. (1997). Assymetrical hemispheric control of visual–spatial attention in adults with attention deficit hyperactivity disorder. *Neuropsychology, 11,* 467–473.

Eyestone, L. L., & Howell, R. J. (1994). An epidemiological study of attention-deficit hyperactivity disorders and major depression in a male prison population. *Bulletin of the American Academy of Psychiatry and Law, 22,* 181–193.

Fagot, B. (1984). The consequences of problem behavior in toddler children. *Journal of Abnormal Child Psychology, 12*, 385–396.

Faraone, S. V., Biederman, J., Lehman, B., Keenan, K., Norman, D., Seidman, L. J., et al. (1993). Evidence for the independent familial transmission of attention deficit hyperactivity disorder and learning disabilities: Results from a family genetic study. *American Journal of Psychiatry, 150*, 891–895.

Fergusson, D. M., Horwood, L. J., Caspi, A., Moffitt, T. E., & Silva, P. A. (1996). The (artefactual) remission of reading disability: Psychometric lessons in the study of stability and change in behavioral development. *Developmental Psychology, 32*, 132–140

Fergusson, D. M., Horwood, L. J., & Lynskey, M. T. (1995). The stability of disruptive childhood behaviors. *Journal of Abnormal Child Psychology, 23*, 379–396.

Fergusson, D. M., Lynskey, M. T., & Horwood, L. J. (1996). Factors associated with continuity and changes in disruptive behavior patterns between childhood and adolescence. *Journal of Abnormal Child Psychology, 24*, 533–553.

Fergusson, D. M., Lynskey, M. T., & Horwood, L. J. (1997). Attention difficulties in middle childhood and psychosocial outcomes in young adulthood. *Journal of Child Psychology and Psychiatry, 38*, 633–644.

Fischer, M. (1990). Parenting stress and the child with attention deficit hyperactivity disorder. *Journal of Clinical Child Psychology, 19*, 337–346.

Fischer, M. (1997). The persistence of ADHD into adulthood: It depends on whom you ask. *ADHD Report, 5*(4), 8–10.

Fischer, M., Barkley, R. A., Edelbrock, C. S., & Smallish, L. (1990). The adolescent outcome of hyperactive children diagnosed by research criteria, II: Academic, attentional, and neuropsychological status. *Journal of Consulting and Clinical Psychology, 58*, 580–588.

Fischer, M., Barkley, R. A., Fletcher, K. & Smallish, L. (1993a). The stability of dimensions of behavior in ADHD and normal children over an 8 year period. *Journal of Abnormal Child Psychology, 21*, 315–337.

Fischer, M., Barkley, R. A., Fletcher, K., & Smallish, L. (1993). The adolescent outcome of hyperactive children diagnosed by research criteria, V: Predictors of outcome. *Journal of the American Academy of Child and Adolescent Psychiatry, 32*, 324–332.

Fischer, M., Rolf, J. E., Hasazi, J. E., & Cummings, L. (1984). Follow-up of a preschool epidemiological sample: Cross-age continuities and predictions of later adjustment with internalizing and externalizing dimensions of behavior. *Child Development, 55*, 1317–1350.

Garrison, W., Earls, F., & Kindlon, D. (1984). Temperament characteristics in the third year of life and behavioral adjustment at school entry. *Journal of Clinical Child Psychology, 13*, 298–303.

Gittelman, R., Mannuzza, S., Shenker, R., & Bonagura, N. (1985). Hyperactive boys almost grown up: I. Psychiatric status. *Archives of General Psychiatry, 42*, 937–947.

Goldstein, S. (1997). *Managing attention and learning disorders in late adolescence and adulthood.* New York: Wiley.

Goodman, J. R., & Stevenson, J. (1989). A twin study of hyperactivity: II. The aetiological role of genes, family relationships, and perinatal adversity. *Journal of Child Psychology and Psychiatry, 30*, 691–709.

Gordon, M., & McClure, D. (1996). *The down and dirty guide to adult ADD.* DeWitt, NY: GSI Publications.

Greene, R. W., Biederman, J., Faraone, S. V., Sienna, M., & Garcia-Jetton, J. (1997). Adolescent outcome of boys with attention-deficit/hyperactivity disorder and social disability: Results from a 4-year longitudinal follow-up study. *Journal of Consulting and Clinical Psychology, 65*, 758–767.

Hallowell, E. M., & Ratey, J. J. (1994). *Driven to distraction.* New York: Pantheon.

Halverson, C. F., & Waldrop, M. F. (1976). Relations between preschool activity and aspects of intellectual and social behavior at age 7.5 years. *Developmental Psychology, 12*, 107–112.

Hart, E. L., Lahey, B. B., Loeber, R., Applegate, B., & Frick, P. J. (1995). Developmental changes in attention-deficit hyperactivity disorder in boys: A four-year longitudinal study. *Journal of Abnormal Child Psychology, 23*, 729–750.

Hartsough, C. S., & Lambert, N. M. (1985). Medical factors in hyperactive and normal children: Prenatal, developmental, and health history findings. *American Journal of Orthopsychiatry, 55*, 190–210.

Hill, J. C., & Schoener, E. P. (1996). Age-dependent decline of attention deficit hyperactivity disorder. *American Journal of Psychiatry, 153,* 1143–1146.

Hinshaw, S. P. (1992). Externalizing behavior problems and academic underachievement in childhood and adolescence: Causal relationships and underlying mechanisms. *Psychological Bulletin, 111,* 127–155.

Holdnack, J. A., Moberg, P. J., Arnold, S. E., Gur, R. C., & Gur, R. E. (1995). Speed of processing and verbal learning deficits in adults diagnosed with attention deficit disorder. *Neuropsychiatry, Neuropsychology, and Behavioral Neurology, 8,* 282–292.

Hoy, E., Weiss, G., Minde, K., & Cohen, N. (1978). The hyperactive child at adolescence: Cognitive, emotional, and social functioning. *Journal of Abnormal Child Psychology, 6,* 311–324.

Huessy, H. (1974). The adult hyperkinetic. *American Journal of Psychiatry, 131,* 724–725.

Jacobvitz, D., & Sroufe, L. A. (1987). The early caregiver–child relationship and attention-deficit disorder with hyperactivity in kindergarten: A prospective study. *Child Development, 58,* 1488–1495.

Kelly, K., & Ramundo, P. (1992). *You mean I'm not lazy, stupid, or crazy?* Cincinnati: Tyrell & Jerem.

Klein, R. G., & Mannuzza, S. (1991). Long-term outcome of hyperactive children: A review. *Journal of the American Academy of Child and Adolescent Psychiatry, 30,* 383–387.

Kovner, R., Budman, C., Frank, Y., Sison, C., Lesser, M., & Halperin, J. M. (1997). *Neuropsychological testing in adult attention deficit hyperactivity disorder: A pilot study.* Manuscript submitted for publication.

Lambert, N. M., Hartsough, C. S., Sassone, S., & Sandoval, J. (1987). Persistence of hyperactive symptoms from childhood to adolescence and associated outcomes. *American Journal of Orthopsychiatry, 57,* 22–32.

Lerner, J. A., Inui, T. S., Trupin, E. W., & Douglas, E. (1985). Preschool behavior can predict future psychiatric disorders. *Journal of the American Academy of Child Psychiatry, 24,* 42–48.

Loney, J., Kramer, J., & Milich, R. (1981). The hyperkinetic child grows up: predictors of symptoms, delinquency, and achievement at follow-up. In K. Gadow & J. Loney (Eds.), *Psychosocial aspects of drug treeatment for hyperactivity.* Boulder, CO: Westview Press.

Lynskey, M. T., & Fergusson, D. M. (1995). Childhood conduct problems, attention deficit behaviors, and adolescent alcohol, tobacco, and illicit drug use. *Journal of Abnormal Child Psychology, 23,* 281–302.

Mannuzza, S., Gittelman, R., Konig, P. H., & Giampino, T. L. (1989). Hyperactive boys almost grown up: VI. Criminality and its relationship to psychiatric status. *Archives of General Psychiatry, 46,* 1073–1079.

Mannuzza, S., Gittelman-Klein, R., Bessler, A., Malloy, P., & LaPadula, M. (1993). Adult outcome of hyperactive boys: Educational achievement, occupational rank, and psychiatric status. *Archives of General Psychiatry, 50,* 565–576.

Mannuzza, S., Klein, R. G., & Addalli, K. A. (1991). Young adult mental status of hyperactive boys and their brothers: A prospective follow-up study. *Journal of the American Academy of Child and Adolescent Psychiatry, 30,* 743–751.

Mannuzza, S., Klein, R. G., Bonagura, N., Malloy, P., Giampino, H., & Addalli, K. A. (1991). Hyperactive boys almost grown up: Replication of psychiatric status. *Archives of General Psychiatry, 48,* 77–83.

Mariani, M., & Barkley, R. A. (1997). Neuropsychological and academic functioning in preschool children with attention deficit hyperactivity disorder. *Developmental Neuropsychology, 13,* 111–129.

Mash, E. J., & Johnston, C. (1982). A comparison of mother–child interactions of younger and older hyperactive and normal children. *Child Development, 53,* 1371–1381.

Mash, E. J., & Johnston, C. (1983). Sibling interactions of hyperactive and normal children and their relationship to reports of maternal stress and self-esteem. *Journal of Clinical Child Psychology, 12,* 91–99.

Matochik, J. A., Rumsey, J. M., Zametkin, A. J., Hamburger, S. D., & Cohen, R. M. (1996). Neuropsychological correlates of familial attention-deficit hyperactivity disorder in adults. *Neuropsychiatry, Neuropsychology, and Behavioral Neurology, 9,* 186–191.

McInerny, T., & Chamberlin, R. W. (1978). Is it feasible to identify infants who are at risk for later behavioral problems?: The Carey Temperament Questionnaire as a prognostic tool. *Clinical Pediatrics, 17,* 233–238.

Mendelson, W., Johnson, N., & Stewart, M. A. (1971). Hyperactive children as teenagers: a follow-up study. *Journal of Nervous and Mental Disease, 153*, 273–279.

Minde, K., Lewin, D., Weiss, G., Lavigueur, H., Douglas, V., & Sykes, E. (1971). The hyperactive child in elementary school: A 5-year, controlled follow-up. *Exceptional Children, 38*, 215–221.

Minde, K., Webb, G., & Sykes, D. (1968). Studies on the hyperactive child, VI: Prenatal and perinatal factors associated with hyperactivity. *Developmental Medicine and Child Neurology, 10*, 355–363.

Morrison, J., & Stewart, M. (1973). The psychiatric status of the legal families of adopted hyperactive children. *Archives of General Psychiatry, 28*, 888–891.

Munir, K., Biederman, J., & Knee, D. (1987). Psychiatric comorbidity in patients with attention deficit disorder: A controlled study. *Journal of the American Academy of Child and Adolescent Psychiatry, 26*, 844–848.

Murphy, K., & Barkley, R. A. (1996a). Attention deficit hyperactivity disorder in adults. *Comprehensive Psychiatry, 37*, 393–401.

Murphy, K., & Barkley, R. A. (1996b). Prevalence of DSM-IV symptoms of ADHD in adult licensed drivers: Implications for clinical diagnosis. *Journal of Attention Disorders, 1*, 147–161.

Murphy, K. R., & LeVert, S. (1994). *Out of the fog.* New York: Hyperion.

Nadeau, K. (1995). *A comprehensive guide to adults with attention deficit hyperactivity disorder.* New York: Bruner/Mazel.

Nichols, P. L., & Chen, T. C. (1981). *Minimal brain dysfunction: A prospective study.* Hillsdale, NJ: Erlbaum.

Palfrey, J. S., Levine, M. D., Walker, D. K., & Sullivan, M. (1985). The emergence of attention deficits in early childhood: A prospective study. *Developmental and Behavioral Pediatrics, 6*, 339–348.

Paternite, C., & Loney, J. (1980). Childhood hyperkinesis: Relationships between symptomatology and home environment. In C. K. Whalen & B. Henker (Eds.), *Hyperactive children: The social ecology of identification and treatment* (pp. 105–141). New York: Academic Press.

Pennington, B. F., & Ozonoff, S. (1996). Executive functions and developmental psychopathology. *Journal of Child Psychology and Psychiatry, 37*, 51–87.

Prior, M., Leonard, A., & Wood, G. (1983). A comparison study of preschool children diagnosed as hyperactive. *Journal of Pediatric Psychology, 8*, 191–207.

Reebye, P. N. (1997, October). *Diagnosis and treatment of ADHD in preschoolers.* Paper presented at the annual meeting of the American Academy of Child and Adolescent Psychiatry, Toronto, Canada.

Rie, H. E., & Rie, E. D. (1980). *Handbook of minimal brain dysfunction.* New York: Wiley.

Ross, D. M., & Ross, S. A. (1976). *Hyperactivity: Research, theory, and action.* New York: Wiley.

Ross, D. M., & Ross, S. A. (1982). *Hyperactivity: Research, theory and action.* New York: Wiley.

Roy-Byrne, P., Scheele, L., Brinkley, J., Ward, N., Wiatrak, C., Russo, J., Townes, B., & Varley, C. (1997). Adult attention-deficit hyperactivity disorder: Assessment guidelines based on clinical presentation to a specialty clinic. *Comprehensive Psychiatry, 38*, 133–140.

Satterfield, J. H., Satterfield, B. T., & Cantwell, D. P. (1980). Multimodality treatment. *Archives of General Psychiatry, 37*, 9115–919.

Satterfield, J. H., Satterfield, B. T., & Cantwell, D. P. (1981). Three-year multimodality treatment study of 100 hyperactive boys. *Journal of Pediatrics, 98*, 650–655.

Satterfield, J. H., Swanson, J. M., Schell, A., & Lee, F. (1994). Prediction of antisocial behavior in attention-deficit hyperactivity disorder boys from aggression/defiance scores. *Journal of the American Academy of Child and Adolescent Psychiatry, 33*, 185–190.

Schleifer, M., Weiss, G., Cohen, N. J., Elman, M., Cvejic, H., & Kruger, E. (1975). Hyperactivity in preschoolers and the effect of methylphenidate. *American Journal of Orthopsychiatry, 45*, 38–50.

Seidman, L. J. (1997, October). *Neuropsychological findings in ADHD children: Findings from a sample of high-risk siblings.* Paper presented at the annual meeting of the American Academy of Child and Adolescent Psychiatry, Toronto, Canada.

Semrud-Clikeman, M., Biederman, J., Sprich-Buckminster, S., Lehman, B. K., Faraone, S. V., & Norman, D. (1992). Comorbidity between ADDH and learning disability: A review and report in a clinically referred sample. *Journal of the American Academy of Child and Adolescent Psychiatry, 31*, 439–448.

Shekim, W., Asarnow, R. F., Hess, E., Zaucha, K., & Wheeler, N. (1990). An evaluation of attention deficit disorder-residual type. *Comprehensive Psychiatry, 31*(5), 416–425.

Shelton, T. L., Barkley, R. A., Crosswait, C., Moorehouse, M., Fletcher, K., Barrett, S., Jenkins, L., &

Metevia, L. (1997). *Early psychiatric and psychological morbidity in preschool children with high levels of aggressive and hyperactive–impulsive behavior.* Manuscript submitted for publication.

Solden, S. (1995). *Women with attention deficit disorder.* Grass Valley, CA: Underwood.

Spencer, T. (1997, October). *Chronic tics in adults with ADHD.* Paper presented at the annual meeting of the American Academy of Child and Adolescent Psychiatry, Toronto, Canada.

Spencer, T., Biederman, J., Wilens, T., & Faraone, S. V. (1994). Is attention-deficit hyperactivity disorder in adults a valid disorder? *Harvard Review of Psychiatry, 1*, 326–335.

Stewart, M. A., Mendelson, W. B., & Johnson, N. E. (1973). Hyperactive children as adolescents: How they describe themselves. *Child Psychiatry and Human Development, 4*, 3–11.

Tannock, R. (in press). Attention deficit disorders with anxiety disorders. In T. E. Brown (Ed.), *Subtypes of attention deficit disorders in children, adolescents, and adults.* Washington, DC: American Psychiatric Press.

Taylor, E., Chadwick, O., Hepinstall, E., & Danckaerts, M. (1996). Hyperactivity and conduct problems as risk factors for adolescent development. *Journal of the American Academy of Child and Adolescent Psychiatry, 35*, 1213–1226.

Thorley, G. (1984). Review of follow-up and follow-back studies of childhood hyperactivity. *Psychological Bulletin, 96*, 116–132.

Tzelepis, A., Schubiner, H., & Warbasse, L. H., III (1995). Differential diagnosis and psychiatric comorbidity patterns in adult attention deficit disorder. In K. Nadeau (Ed.), *A comprehensive guide to attention deficit disorder in adults: Research, diagnosis, treatment* (pp. 35–57). New York: Bruner/Mazel.

Weiss, L. (1992). *ADD in Adults.* Dallas, TX: Taylor.

Weiss, G., & Hechtman, L. (1993). *Hyperactive children grown up* (2nd ed.). New York: Guilford Press.

Weiss, G., Minde, K., Werry, J., Douglas, V., & Nemeth, E. (1971). Studies on the hyperactive child: VIII. Five year follow-up. *Archives of General Psychiatry, 24*, 409–414.

Weithorn, C. J., & Kagan, E. (1978). Interaction of language development and activity level on performance of first graders. *American Journal of Orthopsychiatry, 48*, 148–159.

Welner, Z., Welner, A., Stewart, M., Palkes, H., & Wish, E. (1977). A controlled study of siblings of hyperactive children. *Journal of Nervous and Mental Disease, 165*, 110–117.

Wender, P. (1995). *Attention-deficit hyperactivity disorder in adults.* New York: Oxford University Press.

Wenwei, Y. (1996). An investigation of adult outcome of hyperactive children in Shanghai. *Chinese Medical Journal, 109*, 877–880.

Whittaker, A. H., Van Rossem, R., Feldman, J. F., Schonfeld, I. S., Pinto-Martin, J. A., Torre, C., Shaffer, D., & Paneth, N. (1997). Psychiatric outcomes in low-birth-weight children at age 6 years: Relation to neonatal cranial ultrasound abnormalities. *Archives of General Psychiatry, 54*, 847–856.

Wilson, J. M., & Marcotte, A. C. (1996). Psychosocial adjustment and educational outcome in adolescents with a childhood diagnosis of attention deficit disorder. *Journal of the American Academy of Child and Adolescent Psychiatry, 35*, 579–587.

Zambelli, A. J., Stam, J. S., Maintinsky, S., & Loiselle, D. L. (1977). Auditory evoked potential and selective attention in formerly hyperactive boys. *American Journal of Psychiatry, 134*, 742–747.

Chapter 7

A THEORY OF ADHD: INHIBITION, EXECUTIVE FUNCTIONS, SELF-CONTROL, AND TIME

It is the intent of this chapter to provide a conceptual model of the development of self-regulation that should be of some heuristic value in understanding the nature of Attention-Deficit/Hyperactivity Disorder (ADHD) and in explaining many of the myriad cognitive deficits associated with the disorder (see Chapter 3, this volume). The scientific basis for this model of self-regulation and the executive functions that provide for it have been reviewed in detail elsewhere (Barkley, 1997b) along with the scientific evidence for its applicability to ADHD. Those bodies of evidence are not repeated here. Suffice it to say that a growing body of evidence supports the appropriateness of this model for understanding ADHD, albeit more for some components of the theory than for others. The theory certainly offers a richer conceptualization of the nature of ADHD and provides a number of new, untested hypotheses about the nature of additional cognitive deficits likely to be seen in ADHD that have received little or no previous research attention.

It is fair to ask at this point why a new theory of ADHD is even necessary given the current clinical consensus view of ADHD, as proffered in the fourth edition of the *Diagnostic and Statistical Manual of Mental Disorders* (DSM-IV; American Psychiatric Association, 1994) and in many clinical and lay textbooks on the subject. This view, discussed in Chapter 1 (this volume) holds that ADHD represents a combination of deficits in two dimensions of cognitive and behavioral functioning: Inattention and hyperactive–impulsive behavior. Which of these are impaired determines to which subtype of ADHD the child or adult patient will be assigned. This view, or minor variations of it, has served the scientific and clinical field reasonably well for the past 18 years or longer. Thus, it is reasonable to ask why it is essential to undertake a new paradigm for understanding ADHD at this time.

This chapter is adapted from several chapters in the text by Barkley (1997b). Copyright 1997 by The Guilford Press. Adapted by permission.

THE NEED FOR A NEW THEORY OF ADHD

As I have stated elsewhere (Barkley, 1997a, 1997b), a new paradigm for understanding the nature of ADHD is needed for a number of reasons. First, current research on ADHD is nearly atheoretical, at least regarding its basic nature. Much of the research into the basic nature of ADHD has been mainly exploratory and descriptive, with three exceptions. One exception is Herbert Quay's use of Jeffrey Gray's neuropsychological model of anxiety to explain the origin of the poor inhibition seen in ADHD (Quay, 1988a, 1988b, 1997). This Quay/Gray model, noted in Chapter 1 (this volume), states that the impulsiveness characterizing ADHD arises from diminished activity in the brain's behavioral inhibition system (BIS). That system is said to be sensitive to signals of conditioned punishment that, when detected, result in increased activity in the BIS and a resulting inhibitory effect on behavior. This theory predicts that those with ADHD should prove less sensitive to such signals, particularly in passive avoidance paradigms (Quay, 1988a; Milich, Hartung, Martin, & Haigler, 1994).

The second exception to the mainly descriptive nature of research into the essence of ADHD is the work of Sergeant and van der Meere (1988; Sergeant, 1995a, 1995b, 1996; van der Meere, in press; van der Meere, van Baal, & Sergeant, 1989). These researchers have been successfully employing information-processing theory and its associated energetic model (arousal, activation, and effort) in the isolation of the central deficit(s) in ADHD as they might be delineated within that paradigm (Sergeant, 1995b). But this approach actually does not set forth a theory of ADHD.

The third exception is the work of Schachar, Tannock, and Logan (1993) on the inhibitory deficits associated with ADHD. This approach draws on the race model of Logan in which environmental stimuli are seen as initiating signals of both activation of responding and inhibition of responding. These signals race against each other to determine whether behavior toward the stimulus event will be initiated or inhibited. The first signal to reach the motor control system in essence wins the race and determines the nature of the eventual response (approach/responding or withdrawal/inhibition of responding). Using the stop-signal paradigm discussed in Chapter 2 (this volume), these investigators and others (Oosterlaan & Sergeant, 1995, 1996), show that the principal deficits in ADHD appear to be both in a slower initiation of response inhibition as well as an inability to disengage or shift responding when signaled to do so within this task.

Like the Quay/Gray hypothesis of ADHD, these research paradigms have generally reached the conclusion that ADHD involves a central deficiency in response inhibition, albeit qualified by some additional deficits depending on the paradigm. As noted in Chapter 2, I also reached the same conclusion based on the substantial body of research supporting it. All these research programs are concerned with the origin of this inhibitory deficit within their respective paradigms. They are to some extent complementary rather than contradictory approaches to understanding ADHD. Sergeant and van der Meere go further than Quay and Schachar, Tannock, and Logan in also concluding that the inhibitory deficit in ADHD is associated with additional deficiencies in motor presetting (response selection) and in effort or arousal. But all these researchers make no effort at large-scale theory construction to provide a unifying account of the various cognitive deficits associated with ADHD. I began my theory construction where these other paradigms leave off: with the premise that ADHD does indeed represent a developmental delay in response inhibition processes. I then went on to show how behavioral inhibition is essential to the effective execution of four executive functions (actions of self-regulation) that control the motor system in the initiation and performance of goal-directed, future-oriented behavior (Barkley, 1997b).

More recently, van der Meere (in press) attempted to reduce all these difficulties to a central deficiency in arousal. Although I accept that those with ADHD may have difficulties with the regulation of arousal and alertness, as Douglas (1983) has previously noted, I would not go so far as to stipulate that this is the origin of the inhibitory deficits in ADHD as van der Meere seems to do. As I show here, deficits in the regulation of arousal and alertness in the service of goal-directed actions can arise as a secondary consequence of difficulties in behavioral inhibition and the impairments this creates within the executive functions that depend on it.

The present theory, however, goes much further in arguing that ADHD, by virtue of its delay in inhibitory processes, disrupts the development and performance of self-regulation. This theory provides a needed definition of self-regulation, articulates the cognitive components (executive functions) that contribute to it, specifies the primacy of behavioral inhibition within the theory and the evidence for such a conclusion, and sets forth a motor control component to ADHD. Most important, the model reveals a diversity of new, untested, yet testable predictions about additional cognitive and behavioral deficits in ADHD deserving of further study than do these other paradigms of ADHD. The present paradigm, then, does not contradict these earlier attempts at a theory of the nature of ADHD but complements them and builds on them.

A second reason why a theory of ADHD is sorely needed is that the current clinical view of ADHD (i.e., DSM-IV) is purely descriptive, describing as it does the two behavioral deficits (inattention and hyperactivity–impulsivity) that are believed to comprise the disorder. This descriptive approach to ADHD, helpful as it has been for the purpose of clinical diagnosis, cannot readily account for the many cognitive and behavioral deficits that have emerged in studies of ADHD (see Chapter 3, this volume). To account for those associated findings, any theoretical model of ADHD must fulfill at least five key requirements:

1. It must explain why an actual deficit in attention in children with ADHD has not been found (Schachar et al., 1993; Sergeant, 1995a, 1995b; van der Meere, in press; van der Meere & Sergeant, 1988a, 1988b) even though research on parent and teacher ratings of ADHD repeatedly identifies a factor of "inattention." If attention is thought of as involving the perception, filtering, selecting, and processing of information—in other words, as involving "input" into the brain—then research on ADHD has not reliably documented such deficits. The work of Sergeant, van der Meere, and others nicely documents that the cognitive problems associated with ADHD are within the motor control or "output" side of the brain's information processing system. Although such a deficit may feed back to produce secondary impairments in the executive management of the sensory information-processing system for the purposes of goal-directed behavior (self-regulation), the origin of ADHD is not felt to reside within the sensory information and attentional processing functions of the brain. The current clinical description of ADHD (DSM-IV) makes no attempt at such delineations, important as they are for understanding the basic nature of the disorder.

2. A theory must explain the link that exists between poor behavioral inhibition (hyperactivity–impulsivity) and the sister impairment of inattention, or whatever this latter symptom turns out to be. These two dimensions are correlated to a moderate but significant degree $r = .49–.56$; Achenbach & Edelbrock, 1983; Hudziak, 1997). What does this dimension labeled inattention represent if not a deficit in attention? Why is it associated to a moderate degree with problems of behavioral inhibition in this disorder? Why do the apparent problems with "inattention" seem to arise later in the development of this disorder than do the problems with hyperactive–impulsive behavior as noted earlier in this text (Chapter 2)? Again, the current clinical consensus view of ADHD makes no attempt to address such questions.

3. Any credible theory of ADHD also must link the two dimensions of hyperactive–impulsive behavior and inattention that currently describe this disorder with the concept of

executive or metacognitive functions because most, if not all, of the additional cognitive deficits associated with ADHD (noted in Chapter 3) seem to fall within the realm of self-regulation or executive functions (Barkley, 1995, 1996, 1997a, 1997b; Denckla, 1994, 1996; Douglas, 1988; Douglas, Barr, Desilets, & Sherman, 1995; Grodzinsky & Diamond, 1992; Pennington & Ozonoff, 1996; Seidman et al., 1995; Torgesen, 1994; Welsh, Pennington, & Grossier, 1991; Weyandt & Willis, 1994). Why and how are the hyperactive–impulsive and inattention symptoms of ADHD linked to problems with executive functions and self-control? What are those executive functions exactly? Once more, the present clinical view of ADHD as mainly an attention deficit fails miserably in answering such important questions in psychological research on the disorder.

4. For a theory of ADHD to be persuasive, it must ultimately bridge the literature on ADHD with the larger literatures of developmental psychology and developmental neuropsychology as they pertain to self-regulation and executive functions. In most instances, past studies of ADHD have not been based on studies of normal developmental processes, nor have efforts been made to interpret their findings in the light of extant findings in the developmental psychological literature. Likewise, researchers in developmental psychology and developmental neuropsychology have typically failed to draw on the findings accruing in their respective literatures on self-regulation and executive functions, respectively, to enlighten each other's understanding of these processes, as Welsh and Pennington previously noted (1988). And rarely have researchers in these two disciplines drawn on the substantial scientific knowledge accumulated on ADHD to illuminate the study of these normal processes. But if it is to be argued that ADHD arises from a deviation from or a disruption in normal developmental processes, then those normal developmental processes must be specified in explaining ADHD. And bridges must be built from the findings on ADHD to the findings on those normal developmental processes. The current view of ADHD does not make such an attempt to link the understanding of the disorder with an understanding of normal child development in the areas of behavioral inhibition, self-control, and executive functions. The present theory does so (see Barkley, 1997b).

5. Any theory of ADHD must prove to be useful as a scientific tool. Not only must it better explain what is already known about ADHD, but it must make explicit predictions about new phenomena that were not previously considered in the literature on ADHD, or which may have received only cursory research attention. New theories often predict new relationships among constructs or elements that existing theories or descriptions did not predict. Those new predictions can serve as hypotheses that drive research initiatives. And such hypothesis testing can also provide a means for falsifying the theory. The present conceptualization of ADHD in the DSM provides no such utility as a scientific tool. This fact does not detract from the utility of the DSM view of ADHD as a clinical diagnostic tool, as noted in Chapter 2 (this volume), for that is a different enterprise than the one being discussed here. But as an instrument to advance the scientific understanding of ADHD, the current consensus view of the disorder is sorely wanting.

A third reason for a new model of ADHD is that the current view treats the subtypes of ADHD as sharing qualitatively identical deficits in attention while differing only in the presence of hyperactive–impulsive symptoms. As noted in Chapter 4 (this volume), it is doubtful that the problems with inattention associated with hyperactive–impulsive behavior lie in the realm of attention. However, those problems seen in the Predominantly Inattentive type appear to do so if current research findings on this subtype continue to support some initial findings on the matter.

CONSTRUCTING THE THEORY
OF SELF-REGULATION AND ADHD

Elsewhere (Barkley, 1997a, 1997b) I reviewed several previous models of the executive or prefrontal lobe functions developed by others in neuropsychology, noted their points of overlap and distinction, argued for their combination into a hybrid model, and discussed evidence from both neuropsychology and developmental psychology for the existence of behavioral inhibition and four separable executive functions. Research consistently shows these functions to be mediated by the prefrontal regions of the brain and to be disrupted by damage or injury to these various regions. The hybrid model presented in this chapter is therefore a theory of prefrontal lobe functions, or the executive function system. Consequently, it is also a developmental neuropsychological model of human self-regulation. This theory specifies that behavioral inhibition, representing the first and foundation component in the model, is critical to the proficient performance of the four executive functions. It permits them, supports their occurrence, and protects them from interference, just as it does for the generation and execution of the cross-temporal goal-directed behavioral structures developed from these executive functions. The four executive functions are non-verbal working memory, internalization of speech (verbal working memory), the self-regulation of affect/motivation/arousal, and reconstitution. These executive functions can shift behavior from control by the immediate environment to control by internally represented forms of information by their influence over the last component of the model, motor control. Before describing each component, it is necessary to first define the terms behavioral inhibition, self-regulation, and the executive functions as I use them here.

Behavioral Inhibition

Behavioral inhibition refers to three inter-related processes: (1) inhibiting the initial prepotent response to an event, (2) stopping an ongoing response or response pattern thereby permitting a delay in the decision to respond or continue responding, and (3) protecting this period of delay and the self-directed responses that occur within it from disruption by competing events and responses (interference control). It is not just the delay in responding that results from response inhibition or the self-directed actions within it that are protected but also the eventual execution of the goal-directed responses generated from those self-directed actions (Bronowski, 1977; Fuster, 1989).

The prepotent response is defined as that response for which immediate reinforcement (positive or negative) is available or has been previously associated with that response. Both forms of reinforcement need to be considered prepotent. Some prepotent responses do not function to gain an immediate positive reinforcer as much as to escape or avoid immediate aversive, punitive, or otherwise undesirable consequences (negative reinforcement). Both forms of prepotent response are difficult for those with ADHD to inhibit.

The initiation of self-regulation must begin with inhibiting the prepotent response from occurring or with the interruption of an ongoing response pattern that is proving ineffective. This inhibition or interruption creates a delay in responding during which the other executive functions can occur. Thus those other executive functions are dependent on this one for their effective execution and for their regulation over the motor programming and execution component of the model (motor control). Figure 7.1 shows this component of the model, where it exerts a direct influence over the behavioral programming and motor control system of the brain as indicated by the downward arrow between these two systems.

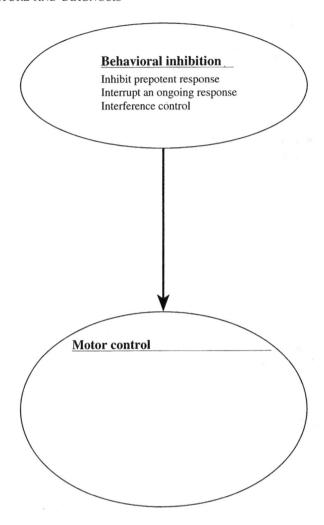

FIGURE 7.1. Diagram showing the influence of the behavioral inhibition system on the motor control system. From Barkley (1997b). Copyright 1997 by The Guilford Press. Reprinted by permission.

Behavioral inhibition does not directly cause the four executive functions (intermediate boxes) to occur but merely sets the occasion for their performance and protects that performance from interference. To visibly represent this crucial point, the lines I use to eventually connect the component of behavioral inhibition to those other four executive functions are blunted. But because these executive functions themselves produce direct and causal effects on the motor programming and execution system, lines that have arrowheads are placed between each of these executive functions and aimed at the motor control system to convey that direct, controlling influence.

Preventing a prepotent response from occurring is critical to self-control. The individual cannot engage in self-control to maximize later outcomes related to a particular event if he or she has already acted to maximize the immediate ones related to that event or context. This is particularly evident when there is a conflict between the valences of the immediate versus later outcomes (immediately rewarding outcomes that lead to later and larger punitive ones or immediately aversive ones that lead to later and larger rewarding ones). Such situations create a conflict for the individual between sources of behavioral control (typically external and temporally immediate information vs. internal, temporally distant information) and so impose a demand on the individual to utilize self-directed, private forms of behavior and information to successfully manage that situation.

The capacity to interrupt an ongoing sequence of behavior is likewise critical to self-regulation. If the individual is currently engaged in a pattern or series of responses and feedback for those responses is signaling their apparent ineffectiveness, such as a shift in the schedule of the consequences toward apparently greater punitiveness or errors, this sequence of behavior must be interrupted and the sooner the better. A flexibility in ongoing behavior must exist that allows it to be altered quickly as the exigencies of the situation change and the individual detects those changes. This presupposes a degree of self-monitoring and awareness of immediately past responses and their outcomes. That monitoring permits the individual to read the signs in the trail of past behavior for information that may signal the need to shift response patterns. This self-monitoring function is probably contributed by the nonverbal working memory component of the model. Thus the capacity to interrupt ongoing response patterns likely reflects an interaction of the BIS with working memory to achieve this end, creating both a sensitivity to errors and the appearance of flexibility in the individual's ongoing performance in a task or situation. Once interrupted, the delay in responding is, again, used for further self-directed action by the executive functions that will give rise to a new and ideally more effective pattern of responding toward the task or situation. The detection of the errors in the past and ongoing behavioral performance and the new pattern of behavior that will eventually be generated from analysis of that pattern of feedback both are believed to arise from the working memory component. However, the behavioral inhibition component must still become engaged to halt the current stream of responses to permit such analysis, synthesis, and midcourse correction to occur, thereby redirecting the motor programming and execution system onto this new tack of responding.

The third inhibitory process in this component of the model is interference control. Interference control is as important to self-regulation as are the other inhibitory processes, especially during the delay in responding when the other executive functions are at work. As Fuster (1980, 1989) noted, this is a time that is particularly vulnerable to both external and internal sources of interference. The world does not stop changing around an individual just because his or her responses to it have temporarily ceased and covert forms of self-directed behavior are engaged. New events playing out around the individual may be disruptive to those executive functions taking place during the delay; the more similar those events are to the information being generated by these executive functions (private behaviors), the more difficult it is to protect those functions from disruption, distortion, or perversion. Likewise, sources of internal interference may arise, such as other ideas that occur in association with the ones that are the focus of the executive actions yet are not relevant to the goal. And the immediate past contents of working memory must be cleansed or suppressed not to carry forward into the formulation of the new goal-directed behavioral structure and thereby disrupt its construction and performance. All this requires inhibition that protects the self-regulatory actions of the individual from interference. Figure 7.2 shows this aspect of the model. The schematic diagram of the model now shows the BIS having not only a direct influence over the motor control system but also a supportive and protective role in regard to the other four executive functions, the boxes for which have been left blank for the moment.

The inhibitory process involved in the third form of behavioral inhibition known as interference control may be separable from that involved in delaying a prepotent response or ceasing an ongoing response. Indeed, as others have argued (see Goldman-Rakic, 1995; Roberts & Pennington, 1996), it may be an inherent part of the executive function of working or representational memory. As noted previously, the second form of inhibition (ceas-

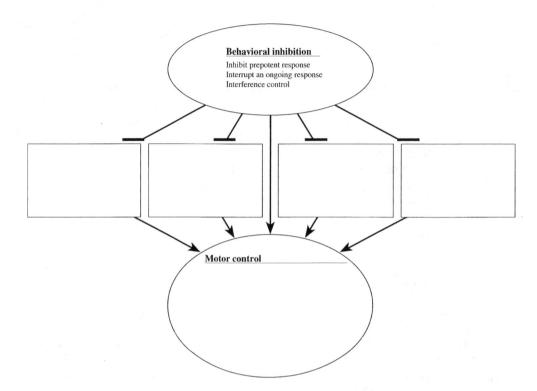

FIGURE 7.2. Diagram demonstrating the relationship of the behavioral inhibition system to four executive functions (boxes) and their relationship to the motor control system. From Barkley (1997b). Copyright 1997 by The Guilford Press. Reprinted by permission.

ing ongoing responses) may arise as an interaction of the working memory function (which retains information about outcomes of immediately past performance that feed forward to planning the next response) with the ability to inhibit prepotent responses (Fuster, 1989), thereby creating a sensitivity to errors. If so, this second form of inhibition also may be distinguishable from these other forms. Nevertheless, some of the previous neuropsychological models on which the present one was developed clustered them as forms of inhibition. That fact, along with research reviewed in Chapter 2 (this volume) suggesting that all three inhibitory activities are impaired in ADHD led to their treatment here as a single global construct for the time being.

Self-Regulation

Self-control (or self-regulation) is any response, or chain of responses, by the individual that alters the probability of their subsequent response to an event and, in so doing, functions to alter the probability of a later consequence related to that event. *Six key ingredients* implicit in this definition deserve notice, as I discuss in detail elsewhere (Barkley, 1997b):

1. Self-regulation means behavior by an individual that is directed at the individual rather than at the environmental event that may have initiated the self-regulation.
2. Such self-regulatory actions are designed to alter the probability of a subsequent response by the individual.

3. Behaviors that are classified as self-regulatory function to change a later rather than an immediate outcome. This process achieves a net maximization of beneficial consequences across both short- and long-term outcomes of a response for the individual, particularly when there is a discrepancy between the valences of the short- and long-term outcomes.

4. For self-control to occur, the individual must have developed a preference for the long-term over the short-term outcomes of behavior. There is an increasing preference for larger delayed rewards over smaller immediate ones across development until approximately the early 30s (Green, Fry, & Meyerson, 1994).

5. Self-regulatory actions by an individual have as an inherent property the bridging of time delays across the elements comprising behavioral contingencies. As long as there is little or no time between these event–response–outcome arrangements, there is less or even no need for self-regulation. However, when time delays are introduced among these elements, self-directed actions must be undertaken to bridge them successfully and maximize the longer-term outcomes. Thus, a capacity for the cross-temporal organization of behavioral contingencies is implicit in the definition of self-regulation.

6. For self-control to occur, some neuropsychological or mental faculty must exist that permits the capacity to sense time and the conjecturing of the future and to put them to use in the organization and execution of behavior. To conjecture the future, the past must be capable of recall and analysis for patterns among sequential chains of events and their behavioral contingencies, because it is from the recall of the past that such hypothetical futures can be constructed. This mental faculty is working memory (see below).

The Executive Functions

As noted previously, behavioral inhibition delays the decision to respond to an event. The self-directed actions occurring during the delay in the response constitute the executive functions. They are often not publicly observable, although it is likely that in early development many of them are. Over development, they may become progressively more private or covert in form. The development of internalized, self-directed speech (see Chapter 3, this volume), seems to exemplify this process. Although eventually "internalized," these self-directed actions remain essentially self-directed forms of behavior despite the fact that they have become disengaged from their more obvious and public motor manifestations (muscoloskeletal movements). Therefore, the term "executive function" refers here to those self-directed actions of the individual that are being used to self-regulate.

The four executive functions, despite having distinct labels, are believed to share a common purpose: to internalize or privatize behavior to anticipate change and the future. All this is done to maximize the long-term outcomes or benefits for the individual. I believe that these four executive functions share a common characteristic: all represent private, covert forms of behavior that at one time in early child development and/or in human evolution were entirely public and outer/other-directed in form. They have become turned on the self as a means to control one's own behavior and have become increasingly covert, privatized, or "internalized" in form over human evolution and child maturation. Nonverbal working memory is the privatization of sensory–motor activities (resensing to the self). Verbal working memory is the internalization of speech. The self-regulation of affect, motivation, and arousal occurs as a consequence of the privatization of emotion/motivation. Finally, reconstitution represents the internalization of play.

If, as I believe, the executive functions represent the privatization or internalization of behavior to anticipate change in the environment, that change represents essentially the concept of time. Thus, what the internalization of behavior achieves is the internalization of a sense of time that is then applied to the organization of behavior in anticipation of change in the environment—events that probably lie ahead in time. Such behavior is therefore future oriented and the individual who employs it can be said to be goal directed, purposive, and intentional in their actions. I predict that, like language and its internalization during child development, this developmental process of privatizing behavior and a sense of time is universal and instinctive; it is not merely a product of cultural training. It makes some sense, then, that behavioral inhibition should be so instrumentally related to this process for it is probably behavioral inhibition that assists with the suppression of those observable motor accompaniments associated with each form of executive function (internalized behavior).

Behavioral inhibition and at least three of the executive functions appear to be mediated by separate but surely interactive regions of the prefrontal lobes (see Barkley, 1997b). Behavioral inhibition and its component processes seem to be localized to the orbital–frontal regions and its interconnections to the striatum. Accumulating evidence demonstrates that persistent inhibition or resistance to distraction (interference control) may be somewhat more lateralized to the right anterior prefrontal region, but the capacity to inhibit prepotent responses to delay the decision to respond seems well situated in the orbitoprefrontal region. Working memory (both verbal and nonverbal) seems to be associated with the dorsolateral regions. And the regulation of affect/motivation/arousal has been attributed to the ventral-–medial regions.

Although I believe that each of these functions is capable of being dissociated from the others, all these functions are interactive and interreliant in their naturally occurring state. This is a critical point. It is the action of these functions in concert that permits and produces normal human self-regulation. Deficits in any particular executive function will produce a relatively distinct impairment in self-regulation, different from that impairment in self-control produced by deficits in the other functions.

Undoubtedly, these executive functions and the future-directed forms of behavior they permit do not all arise suddenly or simultaneously in human development. Phases or stages to their development are likely, arising as they probably do in some staggered sequence during maturation. I have conjectured that behavioral inhibition arises first, and quite likely in parallel with the nonverbal working memory functions, followed by the beginning of the internalization of affect and motivation, then closely followed by the progressive internalization of speech. Finally, the internalization of play, or the reconstitution component of the model, develops. The sequence of stages here may not be correct, though there is certainly evidence that inhibition and nonverbal working memory are the first to arise in child development (Barkley, 1997b). Nor is it clear that the internalization of affect/motivation necessarily precedes that of speech. Indeed, it may be that the former (internalized affect/motivation) actually depends on and is a mere result of the internalization of sensory–motor activities (nonverbal working memory) and speech. Far more research is surely needed on the development of these executive functions and their sequential staging; thus I only wish to emphasize here the prospect of stage-related sequencing in their development.

Behavioral inhibition and the four other executive functions it supports influence the motor system, wresting it from complete control by the immediate environment to bring behavior under the possible control of internal information, the concept of time (change) it represents, and the probable future and thus to make behavior goal directed. I labeled the motor component of the model "motor control/fluency/syntax." The latter component emphasizes not only the features of control or management of the motor system that these executive functions afford but also the synthetic capacity for generating a diversity of novel, complex, publicly observable motor responses and their sequences in a goal-directed manner. Such complex behavior requires an ideational syntax that is placed for now within the reconstitution component of the model yet which must be translated into actual motor responding. Thus, although the generation of ideational syntax is placed under the reconstitution component, its translation into the actual execution of motor sequences is placed within the motor control component.

As in constructing a model from Tinker Toys, I build the hybrid model one piece at a time. Although I represent the components of the model as geometric shapes (see Figures 7.1 to 7.7), I do not intend to represent them as stages in an information-processing model. I prefer, instead, to think of the rectangular boxes as representing simply different forms of private, self-directed, and often covert behavior. Nor is the particular configuration of these boxes intended to be a critical element of the model. It is the functions these boxes represent that I wish to emphasize here and their hierarchical configuration. The executive functions depend on behavioral inhibition. The motor control component depends on both inhibition and those executive functions if behavior is to be internally guided (self-regulated) in the service of a goal (the future). Beyond intending to convey this set of conditional relations, the exact arrangement of the boxes in the model is unimportant.

Nonverbal Working Memory: Covert Sensing to the Self

Nonverbal working memory is defined as the capacity to maintain internally represented information in mind or on line that will be used to control a subsequent response. It represents covert sensing to one's self. What is being resensed by this process is not just the event or its sensory representations but the entire behavioral contingency related to the event (event, response, and outcome). Figure 7.3. illustrates this component of the model. And although it includes all forms of sensory–motor behavior of which humans are capable, two of these are particularly important to human self-regulation: covert visual imagery (seeing to one's self) and covert audition (hearing to one's self). These two internalized, covert sensory–motor behaviors or actions, along with the other types of sensory behavior, comprise a form of internal information or stimuli that is then used to guide behavior across time toward a goal. Even though, in this discussion, I use the neuropsychological term "nonverbal working memory" to represent these self-directed forms of sensory–motor behavior, it is important to keep in mind the forms of private behavior the term represents—private sensing to the self.

The retention and reactivation of prior sensory representations are the means by which events or information is "held in mind." When we see to ourselves, we are covertly reactivating the images of the past, just as when we hear, or taste, or smell to ourselves we are reactivating and maintaining prior sensory representations within these modalities. The number and types of such past events that can be reactivated and held on line at any one time as well as the length or complexity of their temporal sequence likely increase with development. Eventually, individuals develop the capability not only to hold such events or series of events in mind (reactivate and maintain prior sensory events) but also to *manipulate or act on the events* as task demands may necessitate. As I note later, this ability to manipulate, analyze, and synthesize such sensory representations is likely to represent a later, more highly developed ability of the working memory systems that is discussed further under the reconstitution component of the model.

This executive ability probably underlies the power of individuals to *imitate complex sequences of behavior* demonstrated by others. Imitation is a powerful tool by which humans learn new behaviors. The power to imitate requires the capacity to retain a mental representation of the behavior to be imitated. In many cases, that representation will be through visual imagery or covert audition. The more lengthy and complex are the sequences of new behavior that individuals are expected to imitate, the greater will be the demand of such tasks on working memory systems.

The ability to reactivate past sensory events (such as the images and sounds of the past) and to prolong their existence during a delay in responding is the basis for *hindsight*. By this

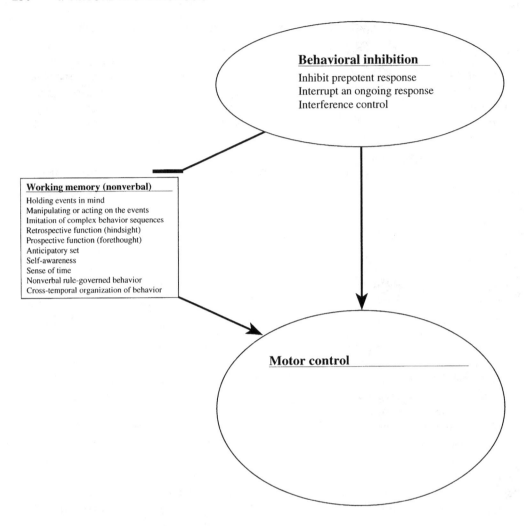

FIGURE 7.3. Diagram illustrating the functions of the nonverbal working memory system and its relationship to the behavioral inhibition and motor control systems. From Barkley (1997b). Copyright 1997 by The Guilford Press. Reprinted by permission.

function, the individual's pertinent past history is able to come forward into the moment to inform the selection of a response to an event and to aid in guiding that eventual response at some future point. A delay in responding is critical to engaging in hindsight. Over development, the individual builds up a progressively larger archive of such past sensory representations that can be reactivated during delay periods as they may be pertinent to the formulation of a response in the present situation. Important in such recall is the ability to keep the temporal sequence of these past events in a correct order to guide the correct sequence of responses that will be based on them. Therefore a syntax must exist for recall and ongoing representation of events within working memory (Butters, Kaszniak, Glisky, Eslinger, & Schachter, 1994; Fuster, 1989; Godbout & Doyon, 1995; Grafman, 1995; McAndrews & Milner, 1991; Milner, 1995; Sirigu et al., 1995).

A parallel or temporally symmetrical function arises out of hindsight, and that is *forethought*. The reactivation of prior sensory representations appears to simultaneously activate the motor response patterns associated with those prior events. In a sense, what is being reactivated is not just the individual's sensory experience of the past event but a relational network of that sensory information with the prior motor responses to it and their associated somatic markers (affective and motivational tones)—the entire behavioral contingency of which all these were a part. The reactivation and prolongation of past sensory events leads to a priming of those motor responses associated with those events should the somatic markers linked to those responses bias toward their selection rather than their inhibition. In this way, hindsight creates forethought and a preparation to act.

The recall of the past permits the anticipation of a hypothetical future, which acts to prepare or prime a set of motor responses directed toward that future, known as the *anticipatory set*. Hindsight represents the more sensory aspects of this process (the reactivation of past sensory experiences) whereas the forethought linked with it represents the more motor aspects of this process, or the presetting and priming of motor response patterns associated with those sensory events. To eventually initiate these primed or preset motor responses, an ongoing comparison of the sequence of events playing out in the external world with the sequence of sensory events being represented in working memory must be operating. Such a comparative process will instruct the timing of the release of the primed responses. Negative feedback or information about one's errors during task performance should be a particularly important source of self-regulating information. That feedback indicates a discrepancy between the actual current state (external situation) and the internally represented desired state of affairs (outcome) and the adequacy of the current plans for achieving that outcome. This feedback must be temporarily held in mind to assist with correcting and refining the internally represented plans which then feed forward to result in changes in behavior that may better achieve the desired state. Thus, a sensitivity to errors and a flexibility of behavioral responding should be a consequence of effective self-regulation.

The referencing of the past to inform and regulate the individual's present behavior and aim it toward the future events anticipated from such a process most likely contributes to *self-awareness*. Past events and behaviors involving one's self are being reactivated and prolonged (held in mind) to prepare for a future for oneself out of which likely arises an awareness of oneself.

The retention of a sequence of events in working memory appears to provide the basis for the human *sense of time*. By holding such sequences in mind and making comparisons among the events in the sequence, a sense of both time and temporal durations appears to arise (Brown, 1990; Michon & Jackson, 1984). It is fair to say that the human sense of time is actually based on the perception of change and may derive from the need to perceive and predict the motion of objects in space. To perceive such change, a prior event must be held in mind and compared against more immediate events in this perception sequence. The perception of events in a sequence permits the analysis of those sequences for patterns of recurrence. And these patterns of recurring events allow for the prediction of future such patterns when events found to exist early in the pattern are detected in the environment. The processing of events in a sequence, or what is essentially temporal information, is not automatic but requires effort. This effort reflects a form of "attention," and that attention is likely afforded through the working memory system. The judgment of temporal durations requires that attention to internal and external sources of temporal information (change) be increased and that paid to purely spatial information be decreased, suggesting that the sense of time, as a result of its dependence on working (sequential) memory, requires the protection from interference that is provided by the BIS. It also may help to explain why behavioral inhibition appears to be related to the capacity to accurately estimate and reproduce temporal durations.

Working memory and the hindsight, forethought, and sense of time it permits may contribute to or even underlie the development of an increasing preference for delayed over immediate rewards, as discussed previously. Such a preference would seem to be a prerequisite for the development of self-control given that the ultimate function of self-control is the maximization of future over immediate consequences.

In a way, the development of hindsight and forethought creates a window on time (past, present, future) of which the individual is aware. The opening of that temporal window probably increases across development, at least up to age 30 if the development of a preference for delayed over immediate rewards is any indication. Across child and adolescent development, the individual develops the capacity to organize and direct behavior toward events that lie increasingly distant in the future. By adulthood (ages 20–81), behavior is being organized typically to deal with events of the near future (8–12 weeks ahead). This time horizon can be extended to events even further in to the future if the consequences associated with those events are particularly salient (Fingerman & Perlmutter, 1994). This sequence then may represent, as Fuster suggested, the overarching function of the prefrontal cortex: *the cross-temporal organization of behavior*. Wheeler, Stuss, and Tulving (1997) recently referred to this same capacity to be aware of oneself across time as *autonoetic awareness*, a function they believe is localized more to the right than to the left prefrontal region. The temporal period over which such cross-temporal behavior can be organized could be expected to be considerably shorter in young children and to increase across development as this cortex matures. One means then of judging the maturity of one's time horizon at differing ages is to examine the average period prior to an event that typically results in the initiation of preparatory behaviors.

If the mental representation of past events in working memory ultimately initiates and guides motor responses associated with those events, then such mental representations take on the power of rules in governing behavior. Rule-governed behavior and its characteristics were discussed in Chapter 3 (this volume). Working memory, therefore, seems to afford the individual a capacity for *nonverbal rule-governed behavior*.

Internalization of Speech (Verbal Working Memory)

Developmental psychologists (Berk & Potts, 1991; Kopp, 1982) and developmental neuropsychologists (Vygotsky, 1978, 1987) have emphasized the importance of this process for the development of self-control. Yet the internalization of speech seems to have gone relatively unnoticed or been underemphasized. This is particularly so of its role in the governance of motor behavior in most modern neuropsychological models of the executive functions, despite Luria's (1961) emphasis of it in earlier conceptualizations of the executive functions. Berk and Potts (1991) argued that the influence of private speech on self-control certainly may be reciprocal—inhibitory control contributes to the internalization of speech, which contributes to even greater self-restraint and self-guidance. Despite this reciprocity, initial primacy within this bidirectional process is given here to behavioral (motor) inhibition.

Figure 7.4. demonstrates this component of the hybrid model. Although it is discussed here as representing the internalization of speech, it is believed to comprise what some neuropsychologists have considered verbal working memory, or the articulatory loop (Baddeley & Hitch, 1994). The capacity to converse with one's self in a quasi-dialogical fashion brings about a number of important features for self-regulation. Self-directed speech is believed to provide a means for *reflection and description* by which the individual covertly labels, describes, and verbally contemplates the nature of an event or situation prior to responding to that event. Private speech also provides a means for *self-questioning* through language, creating an important source of *problem-solving ability* as well as a means of formulating rules and plans. Eventually, rules about rules *(meta-rules)* can be generated into a hierarchically arranged system that resembles the concept of metacognition in developmental psychology (Flavell, Miller, & Miller, 1993). The interaction of self-speech (verbal working

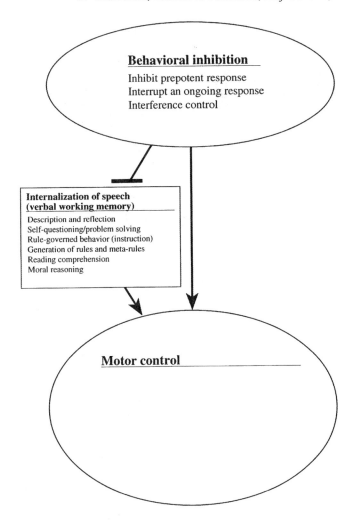

FIGURE 7.4. Diagram showing the functions of the verbal working memory system and its relationship to the behavioral inhibition and motor control systems. From Barkley (1997b). Copyright 1997 by The Guilford Press. Reprinted by permission.

memory) with nonverbal working memory may contribute to three other mental abilities: delayed performance of a current instruction containing a future reference for that performance (see "Deficient Rule-Governed Behavior," Chapter 3), *reading comprehension*, and *moral reasoning*.

Self-Regulation of Affect/Motivation/Arousal

We not only have the capacity to privately sense and behave to ourselves but also to emote to or motivate ourselves as an integral part of this process of private, self-directed actions. And it is this power that provides the drive, in the absence of external rewards, that fuels the individual's persistence in goal-directed action. This is how the delay to future outcomes is bridged (Fuster, 1989). Figure 7.5 shows this component of the hybrid model.

Everyone recognizes that external events elicit emotional reactions of varying degrees along with the motor responses to those events. But, as Damasio (1994, 1995) and others

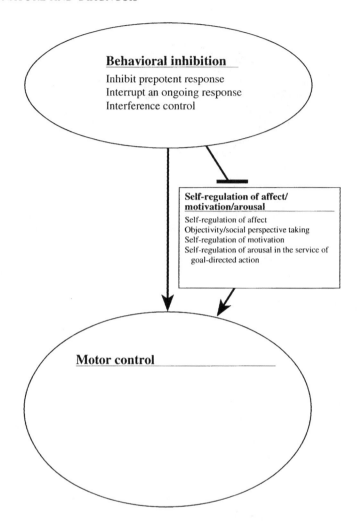

FIGURE 7.5. Diagram showing the functions of the self-regulation of affect/motivation/arousal system to the behavioral inhibition and motor control systems. From Barkley (1997b). Copyright 1997 by The Guilford Press. Reprinted by permission.

(Fuster, 1989) have noted, the internally generated events arising from nonverbal working memory and self-speech are also paired with affective and motivational tones, or somatic markers. Covert visual imagery and covert self-speech, among other forms of covert self-directed behavior, produce not only private images and verbalizations but also the private emotional charges associated with them.

The power to inhibit and delay prepotent responses to events brings with it this power to delay the expression of those emotional reactions that would have been elicited by the event and whose expression would have been a part of the performance of those prepotent responses. Just as the delaying of the prepotent response permits a period for self-regulation through the use of internally generated and self-directed behavior (e.g., imagery and private speech), so the delaying of the affective response to the emotional charge of that event permits it to likewise undergo a change as a function of self-directed, private action. The covert deliberations concerning the decision to respond not only result in a modification of the eventual response to the event but also affect the eventual emotional charge, if any, that is emitted in conjunction with that response. This modification of the initial emotional response prior to its public display could be achieved through private imagery, in which images that have a different emotional charge are used to offset that which may have been initially associated with the event. So, too, does private, self-directed speech have the ability to modulate emotional reactions by virtue of the contrasting emotions it can elicit relative to the prepotent emotional reaction. Such use of private action to countermand or counterbalance the initial emotional charge of external events contributes to the development of *emotional self-control* (Kopp, 1982).

Such self-directed emotions may become progressively more private or covert in form over development eventually being internalized and having little or no publicly observable manifestations. Among the variety of human emotions, the negative array of emotions may be most in need of such self-control (Kopp, 1982). This is because negative affect may prove more socially unacceptable, thereby producing more salient, long-term negative social consequences for the individual relative to such positive emotions as laughter or affection. For this reason, negative prepotent emotions are more likely to be in need of inhibition and self-regulation than are positive emotional reactions to events.

Such a process permits the original affective charge of an event to be separated and modified during the period of delayed responding. Thus, not only is the eventual response made by the individual more deliberate, conscious, and reasoned but so is the eventual emotional tone that is associated with it. Impulsive prepotent responses are often charged with far more emotion than those responses that are emitted after a delay and a period of self-regulation. That is, internally guided behavior, such as that being governed by rules, is often associated with significantly less emotion than behavior that is impulsive and contingency shaped (Skinner, 1969). The delay in the emotional response and the self-regulation of that response would seem to permit individuals the capacity for *objectivity* (Bronowski, 1977) and even the ability to consider the perspective of another in determining the eventual response to an event.

Also included in this component is the self-generation of drive or motivational and arousal states that support the execution of goal-directed actions and persistence toward the goal. This combination of emotional self-control with that of motivational self-control into a single component makes sense. Lang (1995) cogently argued that the array of human emotions can be reduced to a two-dimensional grid of which one dimension is *motivation* (reinforcement and punishment) and the other level of *arousal*. Other researchers in the field of emotion likewise associate it with motivational properties, even defining an emotion as a motivational state (see Ekman & Davidson, 1994, for reviews). Emotions are the result of continual appraisals that take place as the individual moves about and interacts with the external world, informing the individual about the significance of events for one's own concerns. The emotions have motivational or reinforcement significance; they motivate action in response to an event that elicits them and may induce adjustments to energy resources or level of activation as a consequence (Frijda, 1994). This would argue that the ability to self-regulate and even *induce* emotional states as needed in the service of goal-directed behavior also brings with it the ability to regulate and even induce motivation, drive, and arousal states in support of such behavior.

Reconstitution

Figure 7.6 illustrates this component of the hybrid model. It represents two important interrelated activities: *analysis and synthesis.* Analysis means the ability to take the units of behavioral sequences apart, as might be seen in the capacity to dismember a sentence into its component elements (words) and even to dismember words into their syllables or even those into their phonological units. Units of behavior are built into sequences, and these be-

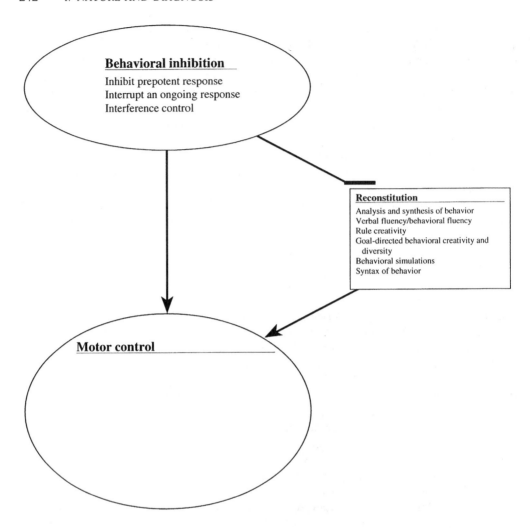

FIGURE 7.6. Diagram demonstrating the functions of the reconstitution system and its relationship to the behavioral inhibition and motor control systems. From Barkley (1997b). Copyright 1997 by The Guilford Press. Reprinted by permission.

havioral structures can be combined into more complex sequences which can be hierarchically organized into more complex sequences having subroutines of sequences within them, and so on, giving human behavior its complex and hierarchically organized nature. The subhierarchies of which such complex hierarchies are composed, as well as their own behavioral units and subunits, can be taken apart in this process of analysis. These behavioral units can then be recombined to create novel behaviors and sequences of behaviors out of previously learned responses in a process Bronowski called synthesis.

The analytical and synthetic functions are not just evident in human speech but in nonverbal forms of fine and gross motor behavior. For instance, consider the human capacity to play the piano. The rapid assembling of such fine motor gestures by an accomplished pianist into such extraordinarily complex sequences of the movements of digits on both hands simultaneously when playing a concerto is a marvel of human ability unduplicated in any other animal species. And although this nicely demonstrates the synthetic function of behavior of which I speak here, the capacity to break down these same gestures into their component parts illustrates the analytical function just as nicely. The recombination of these dismembered units (synthesis) once again results in a novel sequence of fine motor actions, not to mention a new melody from the sounds those gestures create on the keyboard. Many examples of other forms of complex human motor responses and their reconstitution to provide new behavioral structures could be used to illustrate this process (ballet, modern dance, gymnastics, drawing, handwriting, etc.), but the point here should be evident. Humans have a tremendous capacity to analyze their past behavioral repertoire and then to synthesize novel chains and hierarchies of response from that repertoire granting them a substantial generative power to behavior.

Verbal fluency is one manifestation of this reconstitutive function. It would be evident through the person's capacity to rapidly and effectively assemble the units of language to create a diversity of verbal responses. But it would also be evident in *nonverbal fluency*. Thus fine or gross motor fluency, written fluency, musical or vocal fluency, and even design fluency also ought to be manifestations of this process of reconstitution. Whenever a goal must be accomplished, regardless of the form of behavior that may be required to attain it, the reconstitutive function will be available to act on the archive of previously acquired structures of those forms of behavior to assist with generating a range of novel, complex structures that may be of value in the attainment of that goal. Reconstitution, then, is the source or generator of behavioral diversity and novelty not only in language and the rules that language can be used to formulate but in nonverbal behavior as well. In a sense then, the reconstitutive function contributes to *goal-directed behavioral flexibility and creativity*: the power to assemble multiple potential responses for the resolution of a problem or the attainment of a future goal. Such new response assemblies are, in a way, *simulations of behaviors* that can be covertly constructed and tested before one is eventually selected for performance.

A problem arises, however, when such analytical and synthetic functions are operative. The combination of units of behavior must be based on a syntax or set of rules governing the temporal sequencing of such units and especially their contingent "if–then" relations. Just as many recombinations of genes are harmful or even deadly, so too may be many potential recombinations of behavior, proving themselves to be utterly useless or even life threatening (e.g., squeezing the trigger *before* aiming the gun). A syntax for assembling units of behavior into potentially useful sequences undoubtedly exists just as one exists for the composition of words into sentences. Thus the *syntax of behavior* is placed within this component, little understood as it seems to be at the moment. Such a syntax probably has much to do with aspects of causality or event contingencies in the external world as the individual has previously encountered them.

Now it is likely that the reconstitution function identified here can be subdivided into both a verbal and nonverbal form, consistent with the separation of nonverbal from verbal working memory in the model, and from the more well-recognized distinction between verbal and nonverbal (visual–spatial–constructional) intelligence. For the time being, I set up this function as a single component within the hybrid model developed here because I am uncertain whether its processes are specific to either domain, even though the goals, problems, or tasks to which it is applied may well be domain or content specific. Thus, one may find that measures of verbal analysis, fluency, and synthesis comprise a separate factor from those that assess design analysis, fluency, and synthesis, for example. But the meta-process at work on both of these domains may turn out to be rather similar or even identical. They may operate as a relatively random process with some constraints in its parsing and reconstituting of units of behavioral information, much as meiosis may parse then recombine sequences of DNA. And so as Campbell (1960) has noted, new original ideas arise as a consequence of a form of cognitive natural selection, or ideational Darwinism.

Motor Control/Fluency/Syntax

Internal, covert forms of self-directed behavior that comprise the executive functions and the information they generate come to increasingly control the actions of the behavioral programming and execution systems across child development giving behavior not only an increasingly deliberate, reasoned, and dispassionate nature but also a more purposive, intentional, and future-oriented one as well. These executive functions produce observable effects on behavioral responding and motor control. Many of these effects were either directly mentioned or implied earlier in the discussion of each executive function. I reiterate those effects on motor control here to complete the model. Figure 7.7 shows that completed model of executive functioning.

As a result of this internal regulation of behavior, both sensory input and motor behavior that is unrelated to the goal and its internally represented behavioral structures become minimized or even suppressed during task- or goal-directed performances. This protective suppression occurs not only during the operation of these executive functions but also during the execution of the complex, goal-directed motor responses they generate. Once goal-directed actions are formulated and prepared for transfer to the motor execution system, the motivation or drive necessary to maintain this sequence of goal-directed behavioral structures must be recruited or self-induced. This induction may happen automatically as a result of the affective and motivational states that are associated with the internally represented information held in working memory and used to formulate the goal-directed behavior. Regardless of precisely how it arises, such a recruitment of motivation in the service of goal-directed behavior, when combined with working memory and interference control, drives that behavior toward its intended destination. The total process creates *goal-directed persistence*—a persistence that is characterized by willpower, self-discipline, determination, single-mindedness of purpose, and a drivenness or intentional quality.

Throughout the execution of goal-directed behaviors, working memory permits the feedback from the last response(s) to be held in mind (retrospective function) in order to feed forward (prospective function) in modifying subsequent responding, thereby creating *a sensitivity to errors*. Just as important, when interruptions in this chain of goal-directed behaviors occur, the individual is able to *disengage, respond to the interruption, and then reengage the original goal-directed sequence* because the plan for that goal-directed activity has been held in mind despite interruption. Thus, inhibition sets the occasion for the engagement of the four executive functions which then provide considerably greater control over behavior by the internally represented information they generate. This, in turn, provides for the cross-temporal organization of behavior—the organization of behavior relative to time and the future.

THE PLACE OF SUSTAINED
ATTENTION IN THE MODEL

If the current model of self-control and executive functions is to be at all applicable to ADHD, it must identify not only the nature of the inhibitory deficiencies known to be associated with this disorder, which I have done, but also the difficulties with inattention, particularly poor sustained attention, involved in this disorder. This relationship can now be readily understood as resulting from the interaction of the BIS with those executive functions that provide for the control of behavior by internally represented information (especially covert imagery, rules, and self-motivation). Interference control seems particularly critical to the persistence of goal-

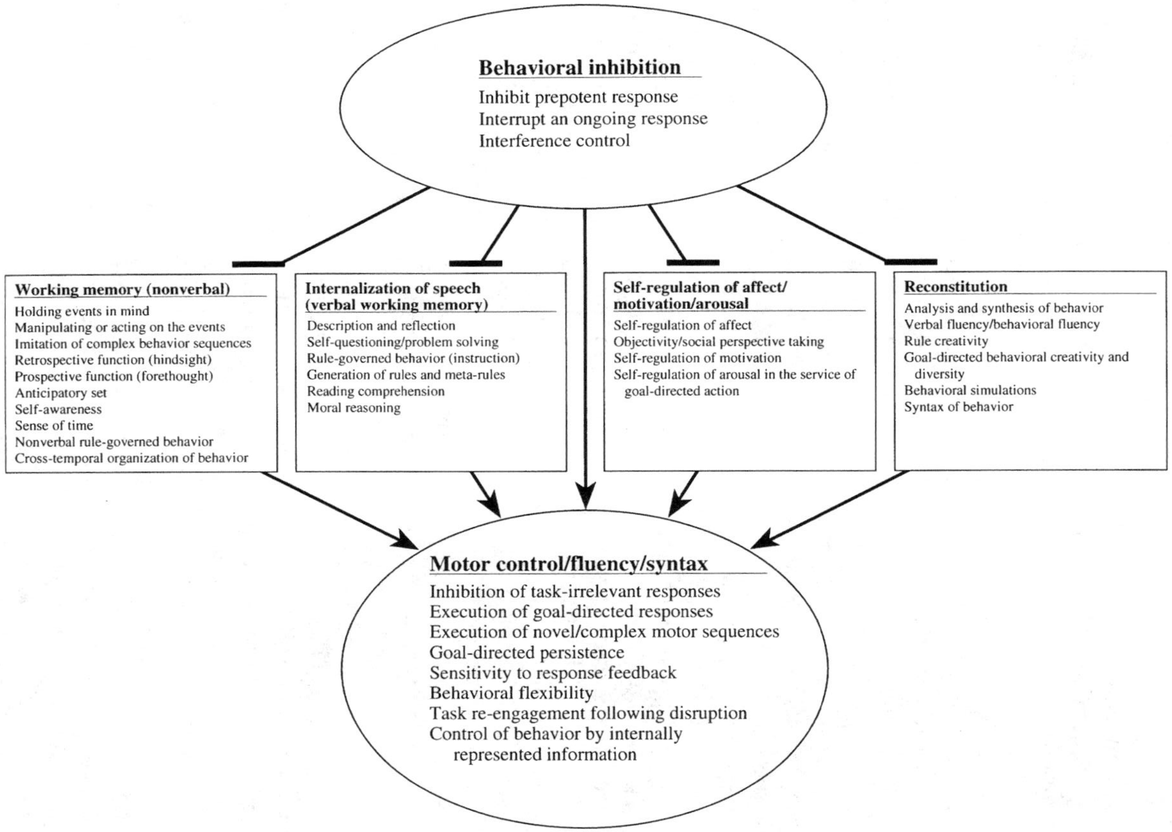
Behavioral inhibition
Inhibit prepotent response
Interrupt an ongoing response
Interference control
Working memory (nonverbal)
Holding events in mind
Manipulating or acting on the events
Imitation of complex behavior sequences
Retrospective function (hindsight)
Prospective function (forethought)
Anticipatory set
Self-awareness
Sense of time
Nonverbal rule-governed behavior
Cross-temporal organization of behavior
Internalization of speech (verbal working memory)
Description and reflection
Self-questioning/problem solving
Rule-governed behavior (instruction)
Generation of rules and meta-rules
Reading comprehension
Moral reasoning
Self-regulation of affect/ motivation/arousal
Self-regulation of affect
Objectivity/social perspective taking
Self-regulation of motivation
Self-regulation of arousal in the service of goal-directed action
Reconstitution
Analysis and synthesis of behavior
Verbal fluency/behavioral fluency
Rule creativity
Goal-directed behavioral creativity and diversity
Behavioral simulations
Syntax of behavior
Motor control/fluency/syntax
Inhibition of task-irrelevant responses
Execution of goal-directed responses
Execution of novel/complex motor sequences
Goal-directed persistence
Sensitivity to response feedback
Behavioral flexibility
Task re-engagement following disruption
Control of behavior by internally represented information

FIGURE 7.7. Diagram illustrating the complete hybrid model of executive functions (boxes) and the relationship of these four functions to the behavioral inhibition and motor control systems. From Barkley (1997b). Copyright 1997 by The Guilford Press. Reprinted by permission.

directed behavior, which I believe represents a special form of sustained attention. When responses that are under the control and guidance of internally represented information must be sustained over long periods, the individual must resist responding to distractions that may arise both internally and externally during task performance or pursuit of a goal. This resistance is provided by the interference control functions of the BIS. The individual must also formulate and hold in mind the goal of the task and the plan for attaining that goal so that it serves as a template for constructing the necessary behavioral structures to that end. Thus, the working memory functions may be involved in goal-directed persistence as well. But most important, the individual must also kindle, sustain, and renew internally represented sources of drive and motivation that continuously support behavior toward the goal in the absence of external sources of reinforcement or motivation for doing so.

These covert, self-controlling functions are not necessary in situations or tasks in which the individual's pattern of responding is simply being maintained by the prevailing schedule of immediate reinforcement. That form of sustained responding is not being internally guided but is a function of the motivational factors in the immediate task and context—it is, in a sense, externally maintained attention or sustained responding.

The former type of sustained attention that is internally guided is better termed "goal-directed persistence," and its origin lies in self-regulation and the interaction of the executive functions, especially self-regulation of motivation and effort. The other type of sustained attention is *contingency-shaped or context-dependent responding,* and its origins lie in the nature of those immediate contingencies operating within the task or setting and the individual's contact with them. Both of these forms of sustained attention appear as sustained responding to the casual observer. Their differences in origins and the variables maintaining them, however, can be readily detected by removing any source of immediate reinforcement that may be provided by the task or external context. This removal should have little or no effect on goal-directed persistence that is being internally (covertly) mediated or guided while resulting in a significant decline in or extinction of the sustained responding that was contingency shaped and maintained by the external consequences prevailing in the task. It is the former (goal directed, internally guided) type of persistence and not the latter form of sustained attention (contingency shaped, externally regulated) that is predicted here to be disrupted in ADHD.

Most measures of sustained attention in psychological and neuropsychological research on this construct are actually assessing goal-directed persistence rather than contingency-shaped sustained attention. Subjects are given an instruction as to how to perform the task, and this instruction becomes both a rule and a goal. Quite often, most of these tasks involve little, if any, reinforcement within the task, thus requiring that subjects sustain their responding toward the rule or goal in the absence of external reinforcement. Consequently, such tasks do not as much assess sustained attention of the contingency-shaped sort but goal-directed persistence of the internally guided form. Neuroimaging and other neuropsychological studies have found that the right prefrontal region is more likely to be involved in the performance of tasks that involve the type of behavioral or motor persistence I describe here (Goldberg & Podell, 1995; Kertesz, Nicholson, Cancelliere, Kassa, & Black, 1985; Knights, Grabowecky, & Scabini, 1995; Pardo, Fox, & Raichle, 1991; Rueckert & Grafman, 1996). Other neuroimaging research shows that this region seems to be smaller in those with ADHD (Castellanos et al., 1996; Filipek et al., 1997), perhaps explaining why those with ADHD may have difficulties on such tasks.

The involvement of the prefrontal cortex is probably not necessary for the contingency-shaped type of sustained attention. The goal-directed form, however, is dependent on the prefrontal cortex and the executive functions that cortex and its networks permit.

HUMAN VOLITION AND WILL

The hybrid model presented in this chapter is intended to capture those executive functions that provide for self-regulation. These functions provide for the transfer of behavior from external control by the immediate environment to internal control by mentally represented information and the goals it subserves; from control by the moment to control by the hypothetical future. Such a transfer in behavioral control results in a shift from the maximization of merely immediate consequences to a net maximization of long-term consequences relative to those immediate consequences.

As Bastian (1892) and James (1890/1992) both noted, behavior that is being internally guided, as described earlier, gives the appearance of a will being possessed by the organism. The same is often said of machines that have internal guidance systems, such as modern guided missiles. The organism could be said to have a free will. But that will is free only in the sense that behavior has been freed of its control by immediate, momentary, and external sources of control. It is still being controlled. The control in this instance is by other sources. Those other sources are the result of internal, self-directed actions and the information they yield. And that information contributes to decision making about response options.

Control over behavior has not been removed by such a process of internal self-regulation, nor has behavior become totally free. The control of behavior merely has been transferred. It has been shifted from the present to the hypothetical future, from the immediate consequence of a response to conjectures regarding its delayed or more distant ones, from the immediate three-dimensional spatial environment to a four-dimensional environment in which time is a more salient dimension in the control of behavior. The executive functions and the self-regulation they permit do not free up the individual's behavior from being controlled by the environment; far from it. They actually allow the person's behavior to be more effectively controlled by that environment—an environment in which time is a critical dimension.

Time is an integral, inseparable part of the physical world. To fail to be affected or controlled by this dimension of the physical world is analogous to failing to be affected or controlled by visuospatial information in the brain-injured patient who has a neglect syndrome. From this perspective, both prefrontal lobe lesions and ADHD create a form of temporal neglect, time blindness, or temporal myopia, which results not only in the most obvious shift in the control over behavior from internal to external guidance but in a more subtle yet socially devastating reduction in the control over behavior from four dimensions of the physical world to three in such individuals. It is no longer space within time, or space–time, that is effectively regulating the individual's behavior but space within the temporal moment that is doing so.

The irony in all this, of course, is that individuals who demonstrate greater self-regulation are far more under the control of their environment than are those with less self-regulation. Thus the former individual benefits far more in the long run than does the latter. *Self-regulation increases the effectiveness of control of the individual by the physical world, a world in which time is an inherent feature.*

This view of the functions of the prefrontal cortex and the executive functions it affords as an apparatus for regulating behavior relative to space–time has a significant implication for testing these functions. It suggests that the neuropsychological tests most likely to elicit the executive functions are those that set up competing sources of control between the immediate three-dimensional world and that world with time included as a factor in the task. The ultimate competition here is not as much between rules and other sources of behavioral control, as Hayes, Gifford, and Kuckstuhl (1996) suggested, though that is true in a sense. That competition is between space in the temporal moment and space–time in the regulation of behavior. Rules are simply one means through which time exerts its control over behavior. Thus, the conflict set up by a test of executive functions is between the future and the present, between time and the temporal now.

As is evident from this chapter and the previous two, this shift in control is directly attributable to the prefrontal cortex, making the prefrontal cortex of the human brain, in a sense, a time machine (Wheeler et al., 1997) More accurately, it is a space–time machine. It acts to perceive sequences of events and uses those sequences to regulate behavior. Thus time comes to control behavior. This perception of events in sequences makes the sense of time seem to flow or have a direction as a consequence. Patterns are discerned in those event sequences that will be used to make educated guesses concerning future events. As Fuster said, this brain region organizes behavior across time on the basis of internally conjectured future events. Such behavior appears intentional, purposive, future oriented, self-disciplined, and having a single-mindedness of purpose. But the future cannot actually control behavior because it has not yet happened to that individual. What controls behavior is an internal representation of the expected future—a hypothetical conjecture of the likely sequence of events that may unfold—which has been derived from a resensing of past event sequences and our experiences with them. In other words, the present elicits a past from which is conjectured a future, the anticipation of which controls our behavior.

EXTENDING THE MODEL
OF SELF-REGULATION TO ADHD

Increasing evidence (see Chapter 5, this volume) suggests that ADHD may arise from deficiencies in the development, structure, and function of the prefrontal cortex and its networks with other brain regions, especially with the striatum. Therefore, any model of prefrontal executive functions, such as that developed here, should also offer great promise as a model for understanding ADHD. Compelling evidence exists that ADHD comprises a deficit in the development of behavioral inhibition (Chapter 2, this volume). The hybrid model of executive functions developed in Figure 7.7 posits that behavioral inhibition makes a fundamental contribution to the effective performance of four other executive functions: nonverbal working memory, verbal working memory (internalized speech), the self-regulation of affect/motivation/arousal, and reconstitution. It does so because it permits the internalization of behavior that goes into the formation of these executive functions. The inhibitory deficit that characterizes ADHD disrupts the control of goal-directed motor behavior by its detrimental effects on these executive functions and the internally represented information they generate. In short, ADHD delays the internalization of behavior that forms the executive functions and thereby delays the self-regulation they afford to the individual.

Although I use the terms "deficit" or "deficiency" here interchangeably, it is worth noting that what I intend to mean is that they refer to relative delays in the development of the abilities under discussion. To some, the term "deficiency" implies that a function or ability once existed at its normal level and then was lost or impaired through some pathological process. This is not the meaning I wish to imply here for that term. Those with ADHD are behind in the proficiency of the executive abilities because they are behind their peers in their development of behavioral inhibition. But in using or implying the term "delay" here, I do not wish to connote either that the ability under discussion is expected eventually to catch up with that of the normal peer group, as in some temporary delay in a developmental process that will bloom later on. Just as mental retardation is taken to imply a chronic developmental delay in general cognitive ability which is not outgrown with time or maturation, so also do I wish to impart a similar meaning here when I state that ADHD represents a developmental delay in behavioral inhibition and the executive functions (self-regulation) dependent on it.

Given all this, those with ADHD could be said to have impairments in all of the executive functions and their subfunctions listed in Figure 7.7. Consequently, they would manifest the difficulties evident in the motor control component of that model as well. Here, then, is a relatively comprehensive theory of ADHD that links up the delay in behavioral inhibition ascribed to the disorder by myself and many others with the executive functions, self-regulation, and time, which means that ADHD is not just a deficit in behavioral inhibition but also a deficit in executive functioning and self-regulation as a consequence of that inhibitory impairment. This deficit results in a renegade motor control system that is not under the same degree of control by internally represented information, time, and the future as would be evident in the normal peer group of that ADHD individual.

IMPLICATIONS FOR UNDERSTANDING ADHD

Elsewhere I have gone into great detail regarding the implications of this theoretical model for understanding, diagnosing, assessing, and treating ADHD (Barkley, 1997b). Some of these points are sufficiently important to be reiterated here.

ADHD as a Disorder of Performance, Not of Skill

The totality of the deficits associated with ADHD cleave thought from action, knowledge from performance, past and future from the moment, and the dimension of time from the rest of the three-dimensional world more generally. This definition means that ADHD is not a disorder of knowing what to do but of doing what one knows. It produces a disorder of applied intelligence by partially dissociating the crystallized intelligence of prior knowledge from its application in the day-to-day stream of adaptive functioning. ADHD, then, is a disorder of performance more than a disorder of skill—a disability in the "when" and "where" and less in the "how" or "what" of behavior. Those with ADHD often know what they should do or should have done before, but knowing provides little consolation to them, little influence over their behavior, and often much irritation to others. Such knowledge seems to matter little when they are actually behaving at particular moments.

Events predicted to lie ahead in the distant future will elicit planning and anticipatory behaviors in others at a far greater future time horizon than is likely to be seen in those with ADHD. Those with ADHD, instead, may not begin to make preparations, if at all, until the event is far closer in time, imminent, or even immediately upon them. This pattern is a recipe for a life of chaos and crisis. Individuals with ADHD squander their energies dealing with the emergencies or urgencies of the more temporal now when a few moments forethought and planning could have eased the burden and likely avoided the crisis. ADHD greatly constricts the temporal window or time horizon over which those with the disorder consider the consequences of their actions, and it is through no fault of their own that they find themselves in this predicament.

ADHD and Personal Responsibility

I fully appreciate the conundrum such conclusions about ADHD pose for the notion of personal accountability and responsibility within society. The argument here could be used by some to seek a finding of "diminished capacity" in the mental status of those with ADHD, as that capacity was originally conceived to be in common law. That capacity was the power to consider one's actions in light of past experience and future consequences; too deliberate the outcomes of one's acts relative to time. In a way, those seeking to make such a case would be correct in this analysis—ADHD does create a diminished capacity to deliberate on the outcomes of one's actions.

It is clear that ADHD is disrupting the cross-temporal organization of behavior, loosening the binding of past and future consequences to the deliberations on current behavior, and lessening the capacity to bridge delays among the elements of a behavioral contingency. Given this circumstance, I submit that the required response of others to the poor self-control shown by those with ADHD, then, is not to eliminate the outcomes of their actions and to excuse them from personal accountability. It is to temporally tighten up those consequences, emphasizing more immediate accountability. Consequences must be made more immediate, increased in their frequency, made more "external" and salient, and provided more consistently than is likely to be the case for the natural consequences associated with one's conduct. More feedback, more often is the resulting conclusion; more accountability and holding to responsibility, not less, are the watchwords in helping those with ADHD. Their problem is not so much being held accountable for the outcomes of their actions but *the delays in that accountability* that are often inherent in those natural outcomes. The most salient natural outcomes of our behavior are often those that are delayed in time, such as eventually being retained in grade after several years of poor school performance, being suspended from school after years of repeated misconduct in that environment, and being arrested and jailed for years of impulsive criminal conduct. The provision of more proximal outcomes more often should preclude or minimize the likelihood of these more harmful, socially damaging, yet temporally distal natural outcomes of the conduct of those with ADHD.

ADHD is, therefore, not an excuse but an explanation, not a reason to dismiss outright the ultimate consequences of one's actions but a reason to increase accountability by making it more temporally contiguous with those actions. Time, not consequences, is the problem in life's behavioral contingencies for those with ADHD. Therefore, removing time, not removing outcomes, is the solution to their problem of "diminished capacity." Time and the future are the nemeses of those with ADHD, not outcomes and personal responsibility. And it is through no fault of their own that they find themselves in this temporal dilemma. Thus, society should not absolve those with ADHD of accountability or responsibility for their actions, but it should absolve them of the moral indignation of others that often accompanies this issue.

IMPLICATIONS FOR TREATMENT OF ADHD

There are numerous implications for the clinical treatment or management of ADHD that stem from the model of executive functions and self-regulation developed here and extrapolated to ADHD (see Barkley, 1997b). Space here permits a brief discussion of only the more important or obvious ones.

Time as the Ultimate Disability

This text takes as its premise that *time is the ultimate yet nearly invisible disability afflicting those with ADHD.* If one cannot see spatial distances very well, the solution is corrective lenses. If one neglects to respond to events at visuospatial distances as a consequence of brain injury, the prescription is cognitive rehabilitation. But what are the solutions to those with a myopia or blindness to time and a neglect of distances that lie ahead in time? And how can those individuals be expected to benefit from any corrective or rehabilitative treatments when the very cognitive mechanisms that subserve the use of these treatments—the self-regulatory or executive functions—are precisely where the damage caused by ADHD lies?

Teaching time awareness and management to a person who cannot *perform* time awareness or time management, no matter how much they may *know* about time and time management, is not going to prove especially fruitful. Given the information in this chapter, we should not be surprised to find that the person with ADHD often may not even show up for the appointments for such rehabilitation or show up on time given his or her disability in performing within time. Understanding time and how one comes to organize behavior within it and toward it, then, is a major key to the mystery of understanding ADHD.

Treating at the Point of Performance

An important implication of this model is that *the most useful treatments are those in place in natural settings at the point of performance, where the desired behavior is to occur.* Ingersoll and Goldstein (1993) say that this "point of performance" seems to be a key concept in the management of those with ADHD. The further away in space and time the location of the intervention from this point of performance is, the less effective it should prove to be for managing or treating those having ADHD. This implication immediately suggests that clinic-delivered treatments, such as play therapy, counseling of the child, neurofeedback, or other such therapies, are not as likely to produce clinically significant improvement in ADHD, if at all, in comparison to treatments undertaken by caregivers in natural settings at the places and times the performance of the desired behavior is to occur. The latter treatments would be programs such as behavior modification that undertake to restructure the natural setting and its contingencies to achieve a change in the desired behavior *and to maintain that desired behavior over time.*

Treatment Is Symptomatic

This perspective suggests an additional implication of the model for treating those with ADHD: Any such treatment will be purely symptomatic. That is, treatments that alter the natural environment to increase desired behavior at critical points of performance will result in changes in that behavior and its maintenance over time only insofar as the treatments are maintained in those places over time. Behavioral treatments or any other such method of management applied at the point of performance is not altering the underlying neuropsychological and largely genetic deficits in behavioral inhibition. It only provides immediate relief from these deficits by reducing or restructuring those environmental factors that appear to handicap the performance of the individual with ADHD in that setting. Eliminate the behavioral treatments and environmental structure created to sustain the behavior and, to a large degree, a reversal of the treatment effects should occur.

Behavior modification treatments may be highly successful in altering behavior in the contexts in which they are applied and in sustaining those treatment gains as long as they are applied. But the removal of the contingencies often spells the death knell for further maintenance of these treatment gains. Nor should we expect to find that such treatments, even when in place, produce generalization of treatment effects to other settings where no such treatments are in place. Thus, treatment of the individual with ADHD is not so much a "cure" that eliminates the underlying cause of the disorder. It is, instead, a means of providing temporary improvement in the symptoms of the disorder, and even then only in those settings in which such treatments are applied. Although this treatment may be initiated to reduce those future risks that are secondary consequences of having unmanaged ADHD, as yet, little or no evidence suggests that such benefits accrue from these short-term treatments unless they are sustained over the long term. Nevertheless, the management of behavior in the immediate environments in which it is problematic for those with ADHD is a laudable goal in and of itself, even if it is not shown to produce additional benefits for the individual in later years. After all, the reduction of immediate distress and improvement in immediate success is a legitimate treatment outcome for improving the immediate quality of life for the individual.

Inhibition and Stimulant Medications

This theory suggests a more specific implication for the management of ADHD. Only a treatment that can result in improvement or normalization of the underlying neuropsychological deficit in behavioral inhibition is likely to result in an improvement or normalization of the executive functions dependent on such inhibition. To date, the only treatment that exists that has any hope of achieving this end is stimulant medication or other psychopharmacological agents that improve or normalize the neural substrates in the prefrontal regions that likely underlie this disorder. Evidence to date suggests that this improvement or normalization in inhibition and some of the executive functions may occur as a temporary consequence of active treatment with stimulant medication, yet only during the time course the medication remains within the brain (see Chapter 19, this volume). Research shows that clinical improvement in behavior occurs in as many as 75–92% of those with the hyperactive–impulsive form of ADHD and results in normalization of behavior in approximately 50–60% of these cases, on average. The model of ADHD developed here, then, implies that stimulant medication is not only a useful treatment approach for the management of ADHD but the predominant treatment approach among those treatments currently available because it is the only treatment known to date to produce such improvement/normalization rates.

Society may view medication treatment of ADHD children as anathema largely as a result of a misunderstanding of both the nature of ADHD specifically and the nature of self-control more generally. In both instances, many in society wrongly believe the causes of both ADHD and poor self-control to be chiefly social in nature, with poor upbringing and child management by the parents of the poorly self-controlled child seen as the most likely culprit. The present model states that not only is this view of ADHD incorrect but so is this view of self-regulation. And this model also implies that using stimulant medication to help to temporarily improve or alleviate the underlying neuropsychological dysfunction is a commendable, ethically and professionally responsible, and humane way of proceeding with treatment for those with ADHD.

Externalize Information to Manage Behavior

Turning to more specific implications of this model of ADHD for treatment, it can be reasoned that if ADHD results in an undercontrol of behavior by internally represented forms of information, caregivers should get that information "externalized" as much as possible, whenever feasible. These internal forms of information, if they have been generated at all, appear to be extraordinarily weak in their ability to control and sustain behavior in its more futuristic and beneficial form for the individual with ADHD. Self-directed visual imagery, audition, and the other covert resensing activities that form nonverbal working memory as well as covert self-speech, if they are functional at all at certain times and contexts, are not yielding up information of sufficient power to control behavior. That behavior is remaining largely under the control of the salient aspects of the immediate three-dimensional context.

The solution to this problem is not to carp at ADHD individuals to simply try harder or to remember what they are supposed to be working on or toward. It is instead to take charge of that immediate context and fill it with forms of stimuli comparable to their internal counterparts that are proving so ineffective. In a sense, clinicians treating those with ADHD must beat the environment at its own game. Sources of high-appealing distracters that may serve to subvert, pervert, or disrupt task-directed behavior should be minimized whenever possible. In their place should be forms of stimuli and information that are just as salient and appealing yet are directly associated with or an inherent part of the task to be accomplished.

Specifically, parents or educators of children with ADHD may need to rely on external prompts, cues, reminders, or even physical props that supplement the internal forms of information that are proving ineffective. If the rules that are understood to be operative during classroom individual desk work, for instance, do not seem to be controlling the ADHD child's behavior, they should be externalized. The rules can be externalized by posting signs about the classroom that are related to these rules, or by creating a poster displayed at the front of the class or typed on a card taped to the child's desk that reminds the child of these rules. Having the child verbally self-state these rules aloud before and during these individual work performances may also be helpful. Tape-recording these reminders on a cassette tape which the child listens to through an earphone while working is another way to externalize the rules and put them at the points of performance. It is not the intention of this chapter to articulate the details of the many treatments that can be designed from this model. That is done in later chapters of this textbook. All I wish to do here is simply show that with the knowledge this model provides and a little ingenuity, many of these forms of internally represented information can be externalized for better management of the child or adult with ADHD.

Chief among these internally represented forms of information that either need to be externalized or removed entirely from the task are those related to time. As I have stated earlier, time and the future are the enemies of people with ADHD when it comes to task accomplishment or performance toward a goal. An obvious solution, then, is to reduce or eliminate these elements of a task when feasible. For instance, rather than assign a behavioral contingency that has large temporal gaps among its elements to someone with ADHD, those temporal gaps should be reduced whenever possible. In other words, the elements should be made more contiguous.

For example, let us consider a book report assigned to an ADHD student. That report is assigned today but stipulates that the report is due in 2 weeks after which it will be at least 1 week or more before the grade for it is returned to the student. There is a 2-week gap between the event (assignment) and response (report) in this contingency as well as a 1-week gap between the response and its consequence (the grade). Moreover, the grade is a rather weak source of motivation for someone with ADHD as it is symbolic, secondary, and a formative type of augmental in rule-governed behavior. This additional implication of the model, dealing with the requirement for more external sources of behavioral motivation to undergird task or goal-directed performances for those with ADHD, is discussed later. The important point here is that large gaps in time exist within this temporal contingency that are detrimental to the successful performance of this contingency by those with ADHD. This model suggests, instead, that instructions for the task be presented to the child with ADHD as follows: (1) Read five pages right now from your book, then (2) write two to three sentences based on what you read, after which (3) I will give you five tokens (or some other immediate privilege) that you have earned for following this rule. Although the example may seem simplistic, the concepts underlying it are not; those concepts are critical to developing effective management programs for those with ADHD according to this model. Gaps in time within behavioral contingencies must be reduced or eliminated whenever possible.

When they cannot be eliminated, the sense of time itself, or its passage, needs to be externalized in some way. If the individual's internal, cognitive clock is not working well, an external clock in the immediate context should become part of the task's performance. For instance, instead of telling a child with ADHD that he or she has 30 minutes to get some classwork or school homework or a chore done, caregivers should consider other, more helpful options. Not only does the rule of the assignment need to be more externalized, for example, by using of printed rules on chore, homework, or classwork cards, discussed previously, but the time interval itself should be as well. Caregivers can accomplish this goal by writing that number on the card to signify the time limit and also by setting a spring-loaded kitchen cooking timer to 30 minutes and placing it before the child while he or she performs the task. Then there is little need for the child to fall back on an internal sense of this temporal duration, inaccurate as I have shown that is likely to be (see Chapter 3, this volume). Time can be externalized within tasks or settings in many ways that might prove beneficial to those with ADHD and simply require some cleverness to construct. Likewise, other ways of "bridging" temporal delays may help those with ADHD—limited only by the creativity of the clinician or caregiver. The point I wish to emphasize here, once again, is not the method but the concept—externalize time and the bridges we use across it!

Externalize Sources of Motivation and Drive

Yet there is a major caveat to all these implications for externalizing forms of internally represented information. This caveat stems from the component of the model that deals with self-regulation of emotion, motivation, and arousal: No matter how much clinicians, educators, and caregivers externalize the internalized forms of information by which they desire the person with ADHD to be guided (stimuli, events, rules, images, sounds, etc.), it is likely to prove only partially successful, and even then only temporarily, if internal sources of motivation are not augmented with more powerful external forms as well. It is not simply the internally represented information that is weak in those with ADHD, it is the internally generated sources of motivation associated with them that are critical to driving goal-directed behavior toward tasks, the future, and the intended outcome in the absence of external motivation in the immediate context. Addressing one form of internalized information without addressing the other is a sure recipe for ineffectual treatment. Anyone wishing to treat or manage those with ADHD has to understand that sources of motivation must also be externalized in those contexts in which tasks are to be performed, rules followed, and goals accomplished. Complaining to ADHD individuals about their lack of motivation (laziness), drive, will power, or self-discipline will not suffice. Pulling back from assisting them to let the natural consequences occur, as if this will teach them a lesson that will correct their behavior, is likewise a recipe for disaster. Instead, artificial means of creating external sources of motivation must be arranged *at the point of performance* in the context in which the work or behavior is desired.

For example, token systems in the form of artificial reward programs for children 5 years of age and older are one of the best means to subserve the weak internal sources of motivation in ADHD children. Plastic poker chips can be given throughout and at the end of the work performance, as suggested earlier in the book report example. These chips can be exchanged for access to other more salient privileges, rewards, treats, and so on that the child with ADHD may desire. The point here is not as much the technique as the concepts. Rewards, in most cases artificial or socially arranged ones, must be instituted more immediately and more often throughout a performance context for those with ADHD and must be tied to more salient reinforcers that are available within relatively short periods if the behavior of those with ADHD is to be improved. This point applies as much to mild punishments for inappropriate behavior or poor work performance as it does to rewards. And, as I noted earlier, such artificial sources of motivation must be maintained over long periods or the gains in performance they initially induce will not be sustained.

The methods of behavior modification are particularly well suited to achieving these ends and many techniques exist within this form of treatment that can be applied to those with ADHD (see later chapters for such methods). What first needs to be recognized, as this model of ADHD stipulates, is that (1) internalized, self-generated forms of motivation are weak at initiating and sustaining goal directed behavior; (2) externalized sources of motivation, often artificial, must be arranged within the context at the point of performance; and (3) these compensatory, prosthetic forms of motivation must be sustained for long periods.

Concerning the latter recommendation, it is certainly likely that with neurological maturation, those with ADHD improve their ability to self-generate motivation, as is implied in the concept of a developmental delay. They merely lag behind their normal peers in this capacity at each age at which we examine them. Thus, like normal children, we can diminish their reliance on external sources of motivation and the intensity and frequency with which they are arranged as they mature and develop the capacity for self-motivation. This means that behavior modification programs using artificial rewards can be "thinned" or reduced in their frequency and immediacy over time as the ADHD child's maturation results in an increase in the ability to self-motivate. But this model also argues that at any age at which we work with an individual with ADHD, such external sources of motivation must still be relied on more than is normal for the individual's age even though with less rigor, immediacy, frequency, and consistency than at earlier ages.

Addressing Deficits in Reconstitution

Thus far, I have tried to address the treatment implications for the first three executive function deficits in the model of ADHD created here: working memory, internalized speech, and self-regulated motivation. How to deal with the problem of reconstitution predicted to be deficient in those with ADHD seems to me to be more difficult to address. If more were known about the process of analysis/synthesis and the behavioral creativity to which it gives rise, ways of externalizing this process might be more evident and useful to those with ADHD in this domain of their executive deficits. Perhaps taking the problem assigned to the ADHD individual and placing its parts on some externally represented material would help, along with prompting and guidance as to how to take apart and move about these forms of information to recombine them into more useful forms. Adults seem to do this when struggling with a difficult problem; they make their previous internal forms of problem-solving behavior external. For instance, we see this when people talk to themselves out loud when solving a difficult puzzle or acquisition of a complex procedure; begin to doodle on a pad, playing with certain designs; free associate publicly to the topic of the problem under discussion; or even reduce a number of words to slips of paper or pieces of magnets and then randomly reshuffle them to create new arrangements. (The game Magnetic Poetry does this with words on small magnetic strips, as Boggle, Scrabble, and anagrams do with letters.) Regardless, the point of this discussion is the same as for the other executive functions—by externalizing what should otherwise be internally represented information and even externalizing the process by which that information is being generated caregivers may be able to assist those with ADHD in compensating for their weak executive functions. Again, such structuring of tasks and contexts must be sustained over long periods if the gains it initially achieves are to be sustained as well.

Managing ADHD as a Chronic Disability

The foregoing leads to a much more general implication of this model of ADHD: The approach taken to its management must be the same as that taken in the management of other chronic medical or psychiatric disabilities. I frequently use diabetes as an analogous condition to ADHD in trying to assist parents and other professionals in grasping this point. At the time of diagnosis, all involved realize that no cure exists as yet for the condition. Still, multiple means can provide symptomatic relief from the deleterious effects of the condition, including taking daily doses of medication and changing settings, tasks, and lifestyles. Immediately following diagnosis, the clinician designs and brings to bear a treatment package on the condition. This package must be maintained over long periods to maintain the symptomatic relief that the treatments initially achieve. Ideally, the treatment package, so maintained, will reduce or eliminate the secondary consequences of leaving the condition unmanaged. However, each patient is different and so is each instance of the chronic condition being treated. As a result, symptom breakthrough and crises are likely to occur periodically over the period of treatment that may demand reintervention or the design and implementation of entirely new treatment packages. Throughout all this management, the goal of the clinician, family members, and patients themselves is to try to achieve an improvement in the quality of life and success for the individual, though it may never be totally normal.

CONCLUSION

In this chapter I attempted to construct out of prior theories a hybrid model of the nature of executive functions. The model developed here and shown in Figure 7.7 contains six components. The first component is behavioral inhibition, which is the foundation on which the other four executive functions depend. These four functions are nonverbal working memory, verbal working memory, the self-regulation of affect/motivation/arousal, and reconstitution. They are covert, self-directed forms of behavior which yield information that is internally represented and exert a controlling influence over the sixth component of the model: the motor control and execution system. Although I have resorted to the more common neuropsychological terms used for these four executive functions, they could be redefined in terms of their behavioral equivalents as (1) covert, self-directed sensing (nonverbal working memory); (2) covert, self-directed speech (verbal working memory); (3) covert, self-directed affect/motivation/arousal or emoting to one self; and (4) covert, self-directed behavioral manipulation, experimentation, and play (reconstitution). Each is believed to derive from its more public, outer-directed and observable counterparts in human behavior that have become turned on the self and made progressively more private, covert, or unobservable (internalized) in form.

These executive functions permit outer behavior to be guided by forms of inner behavior that effectively bridge cross-temporal contingencies and direct behavior toward hypothetical future events (outcomes, goals, etc.). They also give rise to a new form of sustained responding (attention), apart from that form controlled by the immediate prevailing contingencies, that arises out of such internally guided forms of behavior directed toward a goal.

Time, timing, and timeliness, then, become important concepts in understanding such goal-directed behavior and in determining it, making time, in a way, the "central executive." These forms of covert executive behaviors and the future-directed behavior they permit comprise the human will or volition. They provide a means for greater prediction and control over one's own behavior relative to the environment, which results in greater control over that environment and hence more effective control of behavior by that environment. That environment is not simply physical space but physical space–time. The ultimate utility function of these executive actions and the self-regulation relative to time they provide is the net maximization of long-term consequences or outcomes for the benefit of the individual's self-interests.

I fully recognize that I painted this model with large strokes and many of the finer details of each executive function and their linkages need to be specified. At this stage of theory development, however, I believe that all that can be achieved is a relatively crude approximation of what a theory of self-regulation and executive functions may eventually be. However, even that rough approximation of a theory created here brings with it a substantial number of implications, many profound, for the nature of ADHD.

This means that ADHD is far more than just a disorder of attention. Indeed, I have shown that the central problem to the disorder is inhibiting behavior, but I have also tried to show that ADHD is far more than just a deficit in behavioral inhibition. For it appears from research in both neuropsychology and developmental psychology that behavioral inhibition is instrumental to the development and effective performance of the brain's executive functions and the self-regulation they permit. Those with ADHD are left with a form of temporal nearsightedness or time blindness that produces substantial social, educational, and occupational devastation via its disruption of their day-to-day adaptive functioning relative to time and the future.

A number of treatment implications flow from this model for the management of ADHD. Chief among them seems to be the use of stimulant medications as a temporarily corrective treatment for the underlying neuropsychological deficit in behavioral inhibition. But the use of stimulant medications also needs to be accompanied by the externalization of sources of information aimed at controlling the individual's behavior, and along with it sources of behavioral motivation as well. These modifications to the environment will not correct the underlying difficulties with inhibition and self-regulation but will partially compensate for them. Such modifications must be sustained over long periods if they are to continue to benefit the individual with ADHD. Thus, a chronic disability perspective seems more appropriate to the management of ADHD, as it is for diabetes, than would be a short-term curative model, such as the treatment of infection with antibiotics.

REFERENCES

Achenbach, T. M., & Edelbrock, C. S. (1983). *Manual for the Child Behavior Profile and Child Behavior Checklist* Burlington, VT: Author.

American Psychiatric Association. (1994). *Diagnostic and statistical manual of mental disorders* (4th ed.). Washington, DC: Author.

Baddeley, A. D., & Hitch, G. J. (1994). Developments in the concept of working memory. *Neuropsychology, 8*, 1485–493.

Barkley, R. A. (1995). Linkages between attention and executive functions. In G. R. Lyon & N. A. Krasnegor (Eds.), *Attention, memory, and executive function* (pp. 307–326). Baltimore: Paul H. Brookes.

Barkley, R. A. (1996). Attention-deficit/hyperactivity disorder. In E. J. Mash & R. A. Barkley (Eds.), *Child psychopathology* (pp. 63–112). New York: Guilford Press.

Barkley, R. A. (1997a). Behavioral inhibition, sustained attention, and executive functions: Constructing a unifying theory of ADHD. *Psychological Bulletin, 121*, 65–94.

Barkley, R. A. (1997b). *ADHD and the nature of self-control.* New York: Guilford Press.

Bastian, H. C. (1892). On the neural processes underlying attention and volition. *Brain, 15*, 1–34.

Berk, L. E., & Potts, M. K. (1991). Development and functional significance of private speech among attention-deficit hyperactivity disorder and normal boys. *Journal of Abnormal Child Psychology, 19*, 357–377.

Bronowski, J. (1977). Human and animal languages. *A sense of the future* (pp. 104–131). Cambridge, MA: MIT Press.

Brown, J. W. (1990). Psychology of time awareness. *Brain and Cognition, 14,* 144–164

Butters, M. A., Kaszniak, A. W., Glisky, E. L., Eslinger, P. J., & Schacter, D. L. (1994). Recency discrimination deficits in frontal lobe patients. *Neuropsychology, 8,* 343–353.

Campbell, D.T. (1960). Blind variation and selective retention in creative though as in other knowledge processes. *Psychological Review, 67,* 380–400.

Castellanos, F. X., Giedd, J. N., Marsh, W. L., Hamburger, S. D., Vaituzis, A. C., Dickstein, D. P., Sarfatti, S. E., Vauss, Y. C., Snell, J. W., Lange, N., Kaysen, D., Krain, A. L., Ritchhie, G. F., Rajapakse, J. C., & Rapoport, J. L. (1996). Quantitative brain magnetic resonance imaging in attention-deficit hyperactivity disorder. *Archives of General Psychiatry, 53,* 607–616.

Damasio, A. R. (1994). Descartes' error: Emotion, reason, and the human brain. New York: Putnam & Sons.

Damasio, A. R. (1995). On some functions of the human prefrontal cortex. In J. Grafma, K. J. Holyoak, & F. Boller (Eds.), *Annals of the New York Academy of Sciences: Vol. 769. Structure and functions of the human prefrontal cortex* (pp. 241–251). New York: New York Academy of Sciences.

Denckla, M. B. (1994). Measurement of executive function. In G. R. Lyon (Ed.), *Frames of reference for the assessment of learning disabilities: New views on measurement issues* (pp. 117–142). Baltimore: Paul H. Brookes.

Denckla, M. B. (1996). A theory and model of executive function: A neuropsychological perspective. In G. R. Lyon & N. A. Krasnegor (Eds.), *Attention, memory, and executive function* (pp. 263–277). Baltimore: Paul H. Brookes.

Douglas, V. I. (1983). Attention and cognitive problems. In M. Rutter (Ed.), *Developmental neuropsychiatry* (pp. 280–329). New York: Guilford Press.

Douglas, V. I. (1988). Cognitive deficits in children with attention deficit disorder with hyperactivity. In. L. M. Bloomingdale & J. A. Sergeant (Eds.), *Attention deficit disorder: Criteria, cognition, intervention* (pp. 65–82). London: Pergamon Press.

Douglas, V. I., Barr, R. G., Desilets, J., & Sherman, E. (1995). Do high doses of stimulants impair flexible thinking in attention-deficit hyperactivity disorder? *Journal of the American Academy of Child and Adolescent Psychiatry, 34,* 877–885.

Ekman, P., & Davidson, R. J. (1994). *The nature of emotion: Fundamental questions.* New York: Oxford University Press.

Filipek, P. A., Semrud-Clikeman, M., Steingard, R. J., Renshaw, P. F., Kennedy, D. N., & Biederman, J. (1997). Volumetric MRI analysis comparing subjects having attention-deficit hyperactivity disorder with normal controls. *Neurology, 48,* 589–601.

Fingerman, K. L., & Perlmutter, M. (1994). Future time perspective and life events across adulthood. *Journal of General Psychology, 122,* 95–111.

Flavell, J. H., Miller, P. H., & Miller, S. A. (1993). *Cognitive development.* Englewood Cliffs, NJ: Prentice-Hall.

Frijda, N. H. (1994). Emotions are functional, most of the time. In P. Ekman & R. J. Davidson (Eds.), *The nature of emotion: Fundamental questions* (pp. 112–122). New York: Oxford University Press.

Fuster, J. M. (1989). *The prefrontal cortex.* New York: Raven.

Godbout, L., & Doyon, J. (1995). Mental representation of knowledge following frontal-lobe or postrolandic lesions. *Neuropsychologia, 33,* 1671–1696.

Goldberg, E., & Podell, K. (1995). Lateralization in the frontal lobes. In H. H. Jasper, S. Riggio, & P. S. Goldman-Rakic (Eds.), *Epilepsy and the functional anatomy of the frontal lobe* (pp. 85–96). New York: Raven.

Goldman-Rakic, P. S. (1995). Architecture of the prefrontal cortex and the central executive. In J. Grafman, K. J. Holyoak, & F. Boller (Eds.), *Annals of the New York Academy of Sciences: Vol. 769. Structure and functions of the human prefrontal cortex* (pp. 71–83). New York: New York Acdemy of Sciences.

Grafman, J. (1995). Similarities and distinctions among current models of prefrontal cortical functions. In J. Grafman, K. J. Holyoak, & F. Boller (Eds.), *Annals of the New York Academy of Sciences: Vol. 769. Structure and functions of the human prefrontal cortex* (pp. 337–368). New York: New York Academy of Sciences.

Green, L., Fry, A. F., & Meyerson, J. (1994). Discounting of delayed rewards: A life-span comparison. *Psychological Science, 5*, 33–36.

Grodzinsky, G. M., & Diamond, R. (1992). Frontal lobe functioning in boys with attention-deficit hyperactivity disorder. *Developmental Neuropsychology, 8*, 427–445.

Hayes, S. C., Gifford, E. V., & Ruckstuhl, Jr. (1996). Relational frame theory and executive function: A behavioral analysis. In G. R. Lyon & N. A. Krasnegor (Eds.), *Attention, memory, and executive function* (pp. 279–306). Baltimore: Paul H. Brookes.

Hudziak, J. (1997, October). *The genetics of attention deficit hyperactivity disorder.* Paper pressented at the annual meeting of the American Academy of Child and Adolescent Psychiatry, Toronto, Canada.

Ingersoll, B., & Goldstein, S. (1993). *Attention deficit disorder and learning disabilities: Realities, myths, and controversial treatments.* New York: Doubleday.

James, W. (1992). *Principles of psychology.* Chicago: Encyclopedia Brittanica. (Original work published 1890)

Kertesz, A., Nicholson, I., Cancelliere, A., Kassa, K., & Black, S. E. (1985). Motor impersistence: A right hemisphere syndrome. *Neurology, 35*, 662–666.

Knights, R. T., Grabowecky, & Scabini, D. (1995). Role of human prefrontal cortex in attention control. In H. H. Jasper, S. Riggio, & P. S. Goldman-Rakic (Eds.), *Epilepsy and the functional anatomy of the frontal lobe* (pp. 21–34). New York: Raven.

Kopp, C. B. (1982). Antecedents of self-regulation: A developmental perspective. *Developmental Psychology, 18*, 199–214.

Lang, P. J. (1995). The emotion probe: Studies of motivation and attention. *American Psychologist, 50*, 372–385.

Luria, A. R. (1961). *The role of speech in the regulation of normal and abnormal behavior* (J. Tizard, Ed.). New York: Liveright.

McAndrews, M. P., & Milner, B. (1991). The frontal cortex and memory for temporal order. *Neuropsychologia, 29*, 849–859.

Michon, J. A., & Jackson, J. L. (1984). Attentional effort and cognitive strategies in the processing of temporal information. In J. Gibbon & L. Allan (Eds.), *Annals of the New York Academy of Sciences: Vol. 423. Timing and time perception* (pp. 298–321). New York: New York Academy of Sciences.

Milich, R., Hartung, C. M., Matrin, C. A., & Haigler, E. D. (1994). Behavioral disinhibition and underlying processes in adolescents with disruptive behavior disorders. In D. K. Routh (Ed.), *Disruptive behavior disorders in childhood* (pp. 109–138). New York: Plenum.

Milner, B. (1995). Aspects of human frontal lobe function. In H. H. Jasper, S. Riggio, & P. S. Goldman-Rakic (Eds.), *Epilepsy and the functional anatomy of the frontal lobe* (pp. 67–81). New York: Raven.

Oosterlaan, J., & Sergeant, J. A. (1995). Response choice and inhibition in ADHD, anxious, and aggressive children: The relationship between S-R compatibility and stop signal task. In J. A. Sergeant (Ed.), *Eunethydis: European approaches to hyperkinetic disorder* (pp. 225–240). Amsterdam: University of Amsterdam.

Oosterlaan, J., & Sergeant, J. A. (1996). Inhibition in ADHD, anxious, and aggressive children: A biologically based model of child psychology. *Journal of Abnormal Child Psychology, 24*, 19–36.

Pardo, J. V., Fox, P. T., & Raichle, M. E. (1991). Localization of a human system for sustained attention by positron emission tomography. *Nature, 349*, 61–64.

Pennington, B. F., & Ozonoff, S. (1996). Executive functions and developmental psychopathology. *Journal of Child Psychology and Psychiatry, 37*, 51–87.

Quay, H. C. (1988a). The behavioral reward and inhibition systems in childhood behavior disorder. In L. M. Bloomingdale (Ed.), *Attention deficit disorder: III. New research in treatment, psychopharmacology, and attention* (pp. 176–186). New York: Pergamon Press.

Quay, H. C. (1988b). Attention deficit disorder and the behavioral inhibition system: The relevance of the neuropsychological theory of Jeffrey A. Gray. In L. M. Bloomingdale & J. Sergeant (Eds.), *Attention deficit disorder: Criteria, cognition, intervention* (pp. 117–126). New York: Pergamon Press.

Quay, H. F. (1997). Inhibition and attention deficit hyperactivity disorder. *Journal of Abnormal Child Psychology, 25*, 7–14.

Roberts, R. J., & Pennington, B. F. (1996). An integrative framework for examining prefrontal cognitive processes. *Developmental Neuropschology, 12,* 105–126.

Rueckert, L., & Grafman, J. (1996). Sustained attention deficits in patients with right frontal lesions. *Neuropsychologia, 34,* 953–963.

Schachar, R. J., Tannock, R., & Logan, G. (1993). Inhibitory control, impulsiveness, and attention deficit hyperactivity disorder. *Clinical Psychology Review, 13,* 721–739.

Seidman, L. J., Biederman, J., Faraone, S. V., Milberger, S., Norman, D., Seiverd, K., Benedict, K., Guite, J., Mick, E., & Kiely, K. (1995). Effects of family history and comorbidity on the neuropsychological performance of children with ADHD: Preliminary findings. *Journal of the American Academy of Child and Adolescent Psychiatry, 34,* 1015–1024.

Sergeant, J. A. (1995a). Hyperkinetic disorder revisited. In J. A. Sergeant (Ed.), *Eunethydis: European approaches to hyperkinetic disorder* (pp. 7–17). Amsterdam: University of Amsterdam.

Sergeant, J. A., (1995b). A theory of attention: An information processing perspective. In G. R. Lyon & N. A. Krasnegor (Eds.), *Attention, memory, and executive function* (pp. 57–69). Baltimore, Paul H. Brookes.

Sergeant, J. A. (1996, January). *The cognitive–energetic model of ADHD.* Paper presented at the annual meeting of the International Society for Research in Child and Adolescent Psychopathology, Los Angeles.

Sergeant, J. A., & van der Meere, J. (1988). What happens when the hyperactive child commits an error? *Psychiatry Research, 24,* 157–164.

Sirigu, A., Zalla, T., Pillon, B., Grafman, J., Bubois, B., & Agid, Y. (1995). Planning and script analysis following prefrontal lobe lesions. In J. Grafman, K. J. Holyoak, & F. Boller (Eds.), *Annals of the New York Academy of Sciences: Vol. 769. Structure and functions of the human prefrontal cortex:* (pp. 277–288). New York: New York Academy of Sciences.

Skinner, B. F. (1969). *Contingencies of reinforcement: A theoretical analysis.* New York: Appleton-Century-Crofts.

Torgesen, J. K. (1994). Issues in the assessment of of executive function: An information-processing perspective. In G. R. Lyon (Ed.), *Frames of reference for the assessment of learning disabilities: New views on measurement issues* (pp. 143–162). Baltimore, Paul H. Brookes.

van der Meere, J. (in press). The role of attention. In S. Sandberg (Ed.), *Mongraphs on child and adolesent psychiatry: Hyperactivity disorders* (pp. 109–146). London: Cambridge University Press.

van der Meere, J., & Sergeant, J. (1988a). Focused attention in pervasively hyperactive children. *Journal of Abnormal Child Psychology, 16,* 627–640.

van der Meere, J., & Sergeant, J. (1988b). Controlled processing and vigilance in hyperctivity: Time will tell. *Journal of Abnormal Child Psychology, 16,* 641–656.

van der Meere, J., van Baal, M., & Sergeant, J. (1989). The additive factor method: A differential diagnostic tool in hyperactivity and learning disability. *Journal of Abnormal Child Psychology, 17,* 409–422.

Vygotsky, L. S. (1978). *Mind in society.* Cambridge, MA: Harvard University Press.

Vygotsky, L. S. (1987). Thinking and speech. In *The collected works of L. S. Vygotsky: Vol. 1. Problems in general psychology* (N. Minick, Trans.). New York: Plenum.

Welsh, M. C., & Pennington, B. F. (1988). Assessing frontal lobe functioning in children: Views from developmental psychology. *Developmental Neuropsychology, 4,* 199–230.

Welsh, M. C., Pennington, B. F., & Grossier, D. B. (1991). A normative–developmental study of executive function: A window on prefrontal function in children. *Developmental Neuropsychology, 7,* 131–149.

Weyandt, L. L., & Willis, W. G. (1994). Executive functions in school-aged children: Potential efficacy of tasks in discriminating clinical groups. *Developmental Neuropsychology, 19,* 27–38.

Wheeler, M. A., Stuss, D. T., & Tulving, E. (1997). Toward a theory of episodic memory: The frontal lobes and autonoetic consciousness. *Psychological Bulletin, 121,* 331–354.

Part II

ASSESSMENT

Chapter 8

DIAGNOSTIC INTERVIEW, BEHAVIOR RATING SCALES, AND THE MEDICAL EXAMINATION

Russell A. Barkley
Gwenyth Edwards

Probably the three most important components to a comprehensive evaluation of the client with Attention-Deficit/Hyperactivity Disorder (ADHD) are the clinical interview, the medical examination, and the completion and scoring of behavior rating scales. This importance applies equally to adults presenting for evaluation of their own ADHD symptoms as well as to parents bringing their children or adolescents for evaluation of suspected ADHD. In this chapter, we describe the details of conducting clinical interviews with parents, teachers, and children/adolescents when it is the child or adolescent who is presenting for evaluation of ADHD. We also briefly discuss the essential features of the medical examination of ADHD children and issues that examination needs to address. This discussion is followed by an overview of some of the most useful behavior rating scales to incorporate in the clinical evaluation. When it is feasible, clinicians may wish to supplement these components of the evaluation with objective assessments of the ADHD symptoms, such as psychological tests of attention or direct behavioral observations. These tests are not essential to reaching a diagnosis, however, or to treatment planning, but they may yield further information about the presence and severity of cognitive impairments that could be associated with some cases of ADHD. Those methods of assessment are discussed in Chapter 9 (this volume). Eight case examples of evaluations can be found in Chapter 10 (this volume). Readers wishing to have many of the clinical tools referenced here can find them in a convenient format with limited permission granted by the publisher for photocopying in the clinical manual accompanying this textbook (Barkley & Murphy, 1998).

ASSESSMENT ISSUES

Clinicians should bear in mind several goals when evaluating children for ADHD. A major goal of such an assessment is the determination of the presence or absence of ADHD as well as the differential diagnosis of ADHD from other childhood psychiatric disorders. This differential diagnosis requires extensive clinical knowledge of these other psychiatric disorders, and readers are referred to a text on child psychopathology for a review of the major childhood disorders (see Mash & Barkley, 1996). In any child evaluation, it may be necessary to draw on measures that are normed for the individual's ethnic background, if such instruments are available, to preclude the overdiagnosis of minority children when diagnostic criteria developed on white American children are extrapolated to other ethnic groups.

A second purpose of the evaluation is to begin delineating the types of interventions needed to address the psychiatric disorders and psychological, academic, and social impairments identified in the course of assessment. As noted later, these may include individual counseling, parent training in behavior management, family therapy, classroom behavior modification, psychiatric medications, and formal special educational services, to name just a few. For a more thorough discussion of treatments for childhood disorders, readers are referred to a recent text on this subject (Mash & Barkley, 1998).

Another important purpose of the evaluation is to determine conditions that often coexist with ADHD and the manner in which these conditions may affect prognosis or treatment decision making. For instance, the presence of high levels of physically assaultive behavior by a child with ADHD may indicate that a parent training program (see, e.g., the one recommended later in this text, in Chapter 12) is contraindicated, at least for the time being, because such training in limit setting and behavior modification could temporarily increase child violence toward parents when limits on noncompliance with parental commands are established. Or, consider the presence of high levels of anxiety specifically and internalizing symptoms more generally in children with ADHD. Research shows such symptoms to be a predictor of poorer responses to stimulant medication (see Chapter 17, this volume). Similarly, the presence of high levels of irritable mood, severely hostile and defiant behavior, and periodic episodes of serious physical aggression and destructive behavior may be early markers for later Bipolar Disorder (Manic–Depression) in children. Oppositional behavior is almost universal in juvenile-onset Bipolar Disorder (Wozniak et al., 1995). Such a disorder is likely to require the use of several psychiatric medications in conjunction with a parent training program.

A further objective of the evaluation is to identify the pattern of the child's psychological strengths and weaknesses and to consider how these strengths and weaknesses may affect treatment planning. This identification may also include gaining some impression as to the parents' own abilities to carry out the treatment program as well as the family's social and economic circumstances and the treatment resources that may (or may not) be available within their community and cultural group. Some determination also must be made as to the child's eligibility for special educational services within his or her school district if eligible disorders, such as developmental delay, learning disabilities, or speech and language problems, are present.

As the foregoing discussion illustrates, the evaluation of a child for the presence of diagnosable ADHD is but one of many purposes of the clinical evaluation. A brief discussion now follows regarding the different methods of assessment that may be used in the evaluation of ADHD children.

INFORMATION OBTAINED
AT THE TIME OF REFERRAL

Surprisingly enough, the initial phase of a diagnostic interview might not be conducted by the clinician but by a support staff member. The initial phone intake provides invaluable information when conducted by a well-trained individual; otherwise, it is a lost opportunity. When a parent calls to request an evaluation, it is useful to collect the following information: What is the reason for the parent's request? Is it an open-ended question, such as "What's wrong with my child?", or a specific one, "Does my child have ADHD?" Who referred the family? Is the family self-referred because members recently read a newspaper article or saw a television program which raised their concerns? Is the family referred by the child's school because of school-related rather than parental concerns? Is the family referred by a pediatrician or another health or mental health professional who questions ADHD but wants diagnostic confirmation? Has the child been previously evaluated or tested by someone else? Is the family looking for a second opinion, or for a reevaluation of ADHD that was diagnosed when the child was younger? Does the child have any other diagnosed conditions, such as mood disorders, substance abuse, or other developmental delays? Has the child been tested and diagnosed by the school system to have learning disabilities or cognitive delays? Is the child already on medication? Are the parents seeking an evaluation of their child's response to medication rather than a diagnostic evaluation? If the child is on stimulant medication, would the parents consent to withhold the medication on the day of the evaluation? The content of the diagnostic interview is influenced by all these factors, and important information can be collected and reviewed ahead of time when the reason for the referral is clear.

Thus, once the child is referred for services, the clinician must glean some important details from the telephone interview. This information also allows the clinician to set in motion some initial procedures. In particular, it is important at this point to do the following: (1) obtain any releases of information to permit reports of previous professional evaluations to be sought, (2) contact the child's treating physician for further information on health status and medication treatment if any, (3) obtain the results of the most recent evaluation from the child's school or have the parent initiate one immediately if school performance concerns are part of the referral complaints, (4) mail out the packet of parent and teacher behavior rating forms to be completed and returned before the initial appointment, being sure to include the written release of information permission form with the school forms, and (5) obtain any information from social service agencies that may be involved in providing services to this child.

INFORMATION OBTAINED IN ADVANCE OF THE INTERVIEW

Clinicians may want to send out a packet of questionnaires to parents and teachers following the parents' call to their clinic but in advance of the scheduled appointment. In fact, the parents of children referred to our clinic are not given an appointment date until these packets of information are completed and returned to the clinic. This system ensures that the packets are completed reasonably promptly and that the information is available for review by the clinician prior to meeting with the family, making the evaluation process far more efficient in its collection of important information. In these days of increasing cost consciousness concerning mental health evaluations, particularly in managed care environments, efficiency of the evaluation is paramount and time spent directly with the family is often limited and at a premium. Besides a form cover letter from the professional asking the parents to complete the packet of information, and it also contains the General Instruction Sheet, a Child and Family Information Form, and a Developmental and Medical History Form, all of which can be obtained for limited photocopying purposes in the clinical manual accompanying this textbook (Barkley & Murphy, 1998). This packet also includes a reasonably comprehensive child behavior rating scale that covers the major dimensions of child psychopathology, such as the Child Behavior Checklist (CBCL; Achenbach, 1991) or the Behavior Assessment System for Children (BASC; Reynolds & Kamphaus, 1994). Also in this packet should be a copy of a rating scale that specifically assesses ADHD symptoms. Such a form can also be found in the clinical manual by Barkley and Murphy (1998). That scale permits the clinician to obtain information ahead of the appointment concerning the presence of symptoms of Oppositional Defiant Disorder (ODD) and Conduct Disorder (CD), as well as ADHD symptoms and their severity. ODD and CD are quite common among children referred for ADHD, and it is useful to know of their presence in advance of the appointment. Clinicians who wish to assess adaptive behavior via the use of a questionnaire might consider including the Normative Adaptive Behavior Checklist (NABC; Adams, 1984) in this packet. Finally, the Home Situations Questionnaire (HSQ) is included so that the clinician can gain a quick appreciation for the pervasiveness and severity of the child's disruptive behavior across a variety of home and public situations (see Barkley & Murphy, 1998, for this form and its norms). Such information is of clinical interest not only for indications of pervasiveness and severity of behavior problems but also for focusing discussions around these situations during the evaluation and subsequent parent training program. These rating scales are discussed later.

It is useful to collect and review previous records before the interview. They might include any one or combination of the following: report cards, standardized testing results, medical records (including neurology, audiology, optometry, speech, and occupational therapy), individual educational plans, psychoeducational testing, psychological testing, and psychotherapy summaries.

A similar packet of information is sent to the teachers of this child, with parental written permission obtained beforehand, of course. This packet does not contain the Medical and Developmental History Form or any adaptive behavior survey that may have been included for parents. This packet could contain the teacher version of the CBCL or BASC, the School Situations Questionnaire (SSQ), and the the same rating scale for assessing ADHD symptoms (see Barkley & Murphy, 1998, for the latter two scales and their norms). The Social Skills Rating Scale (Gresham & Elliott, 1990) might also be included if the clinician desires information about the child's social problems in school as well as his or her academic competence. The clinician can quickly see, for example, if the teacher feels the child is functioning at grade level in various subject areas, how the child has performed on group-administered achievement or aptitude tests, or subjective impressions of the child's general mood and behavioral functioning. If possible, it is quite useful to contact the child's teachers for a brief telephone interview prior to meeting with the family. Otherwise, a meeting can take place following the family's appointment.

Once the parent and teacher packets are returned, the family should be contacted by telephone and given their appointment date. It is our custom also to send out a letter confirming this appointment date with directions for driving to the clinic. With this letter, the clinician might send a short instruction sheet entitled "How to Prepare for Your Child's Evaluation." It is provided in the clinical manual accompanying this text (Barkley & Murphy, 1998). This instruction sheet gives the parents some information about what to expect on the day of the evaluation and what information to organize prior to this appointment. It also may set them at ease if having a mental health evaluation is disconcerting or anxiety inducing for them.

On the day of the appointment, the following still remains to be done: (1) parental and child interview, (2) completion of self-report rating scales by the parents, and (3) any psychological testing that may be indicated by the nature of the referral (intelligence and achievement testing, etc.).

PARENT INTERVIEW

The parent (often maternal) interview, although often criticized for its unreliability and sub-jectivity, is an indispensable part of the evaluation of children and adolescents present-ing with concerns about ADHD. No adult is likely to have the wealth of knowledge about, history of interactions with, or sheer time spent with a child than the parents.

Whether wholly accurate or not, parent reports provide the most ecologically valid and important source of information concerning the child's difficulties. It is the parents' com-plaints that often lead to the referral of the child, will affect the parents' perceptions of and reactions to the child, and will influence the parents' adherence to the treatment recommen-dations to be made. Moreover, the reliability and accuracy of the parental interview have much to do with the manner in which it is conducted and the specificity of the questions offered by the examiner. An interview that uses highly specific questions about symptoms of psychopathology that have been empirically demonstrated to have a high degree of asso-ciation with particular disorders greatly enhances diagnostic reliability.

The interview, particularly a semistructured interview, allows the clinician in a sense to become another instrument in the assessment process. Although scorable data are ob-tained, the small details and nuances of parent and child report resonates with clinician-acquired knowledge (from previous interviews, research, readings, workshops, etc.) in such a way as to flesh out and support final diagnostic conclusions. In other words, the interview provides the phenomenological data that rating scales cannot capture.The interview must also, however, focus on the specific complaints about the child's psychological adjustment and any functional parameters (eliciting and consequating events) associated with those prob-lems if psychosocial and educational treatment planning is to be based on the evaluation.

Purposes

The parental interview often serves several purposes.

1. It establishes a necessary rapport among the parents, the child, and the examiner that will prove invaluable in enlisting parental cooperation with later aspects of assessment and treatment.

2. The interview is an obvious source of highly descriptive information about the child and family, revealing the parents' particular views of the child's apparent problems and nar-rowing the focus of later stages and components of the evaluation.

3. It can readily reveal the degree of distress the child's problems are presenting to the family, especially the parent being interviewed, and well as the overall psychological integ-rity of the parent. Hypotheses as to the presence of parental personality or psychiatric prob-lems (depression, hostility, marital discord, etc.) may be revealed that will require further evaluation in subsequent components of the evaluation and consideration in formulating treatment recommendations.

Examiners must be cautious not to overinterpret any informal observations of the child's behavior during this clinic visit. The office behavior of ADHD children is often far better than that observed at home (Sleator & Ullman, 1981). Such observations merely raise hy-potheses about potential parent–child interaction problems that can be explored in more detail with parents toward the end of this interview as well as during later direct behavioral observations of parent and child during play and task performance together. At the end of this portion of the interview, the examiner should inquire how representative the child's immediate behavior is compared to that seen at home when the parent speaks with other adults in the child's presence.

We do not typically have the child in the same room when we conduct the parental interview. Other clinicians, however, may choose to do so. The presence of the child during the parental interview, however, raises thorny issues for the evaluation to which the examiner must be sensitive. Some parents are less forthcoming about their concerns and the details of the child's specific problems when the child is present, not wishing to sensitize or embarrass the child unnecessarily or to create another reason for arguments at home about the nature of the child's problems. Others are heedless of the potential problems posed for their child by this procedure, making it even more imperative that the examiner review these issues with them before beginning the evaluation. Still other parents may use the child's presence to further publicly humiliate the child about his or her deficiencies or the distress the child has created for the family by behaving the way he or she does. Suffice it to say here that before starting the interview, the examiner must discuss and review with each unique family whether the advantages of having the child present are outweighed by these potential negative effects.

4. The initial parent interview can help to focus the parent's perceptions of the child's problems on more important and more specific controlling events within the family. Parents often tend to emphasize historical or developmental causes of a global nature in discussing their children's problems, such as what they did or failed to do with the child earlier in development that has led to this problem (i.e., placing the child in infant daycare, an earlier divorce, the child's diet in earlier years, etc.). The interactional interview discussed later can serve to shift the parents' attention to more immediate antecedents and consequences surrounding child behaviors, thereby preparing the parents for the initial stages of parent training in child management skills.

5. The interview is designed to formulate a diagnosis and to develop treatment recommendations. Although diagnosis is not always considered necessary for treatment planning (a statement of the child's developmental and behavioral deficits is often adequate), the diagnosis of ADHD, however, does provide some utility in terms of predicting developmental course and prognosis for the child, determining eligibility for some special educational placements, and predicting potential response to a trial on stimulant medication. Many child behavior problems are believed to remit over short periods in as many as 75% of the cases. However, ADHD is a relatively chronic condition warranting much more cautious conclusions about eventual prognosis and preparation of the family for coping with these later problems.

6. A parental interview may serve as sheer catharsis, especially if this is the first professional evaluation of the child or when previous evaluations have proven highly conflicting in their results and recommendations. Ample time should be permitted to allow parents to ventilate this distress, hostility, or frustration. It may be helpful to note at this point that many parents of ADHD children have reported similarly distressing, confusing, or outright hostile previous encounters with professionals and educators about their child, as well as well-intentioned but overly enmeshed or misinformed relatives. Compassion and empathy for the plight of the parents at this point can often result in a substantial degree of rapport with and gratitude toward the examiner and a greater motivation to follow subsequent treatment recommendations. At the very least, parents are likely to feel that they have finally found someone who truly understands the nature of their child's problems and the distress they have experienced in trying to assist the child and has recommendations to do something about them.

The suggestions that follow for interviewing parents of ADHD children are not intended as rigid guidelines, only as areas that clinicians should consider. Each interview clearly differs according to individual child and family circumstances. Generally, those areas of importance to an evaluation include demographic information, child-related information, school-related information, and details about the parents, other family members, and community resources that may be available to the family.

Demographic Information

If not obtained in advance, the routine demographic data concerning the child and family (e.g., ages of child and family members; child's date of birth; parents' names, addresses, employers, and occupations; and the child's school, teachers, and physician) should be obtained at the outset of the appointment. We also use this initial introductory period to review with the family any legal constraints on the confidentiality of information obtained during the interview, such as the clinician's legal duty (as required by state law) to report to state authorities instances of suspected child abuse, threats the child (or parents) may make to cause physical harm to other specific individuals (the duty to inform), and threats the child (or parents) may make to harm themselves (e.g., suicide threats).

Major Parental Concerns

The interview then proceeds to the major referral concerns of the parents, and of the professional referring the child when appropriate. A parental interview form designed by Barkley and colleagues is available in the clinical manual accompanying this text (Barkley & Murphy, 1998). It can be very helpful in collecting the information discussed later. This form not only contains major sections for the important information discussed here but also contains the diagnostic criteria used for ADHD as well as the other childhood disorders most likely to be seen in conjunction with ADHD (ODD, CD, anxiety and mood disorders, Bipolar Disorder). Such a form allows clinicians to collect the essential information likely to be of greatest value to them in evaluating children using a convenient and standardized format across their client populations.

General descriptions of concerns by parents must be followed with specific questions by the examiner to elucidate the details of the problems and any apparent precipitants. Such an interview probes for the specific nature, frequency, age of onset, and chronicity of the problematic behaviors. It can also obtain information, as needed, on the situational and temporal variation in the behaviors and their consequences. If the problems are chronic, which they often are, determining what prompted the referral at this time reveals much about parental perceptions of the children's problems, current family circumstances related to the problems' severity, and parental motivation for treatment.

Review of Major Developmental Domains

Following this part of the interview, the examiner should review with the parents potential problems that might exist in the developmental domains of motor, language, intellectual, academic, emotional, and social functioning. Such information greatly aids in the differential diagnosis of the child's problems. To achieve this differential diagnosis requires that the examiner have an adequate knowledge of the diagnostic features of other childhood disorders, some of which may present as ADHD. For instance, many children with Atypical Pervasive Developmental Disorders, Asperger's Disorder, or early Bipolar Disorder may be viewed by their parents as ADHD as the parents are more likely to have heard about the latter disorder than the former ones and will recognize some of the qualities in their children. Questioning about inappropriate thinking, affect, social relations, and motor peculiarities may reveal a more seriously and pervasively disturbed child. If such symptoms seem to be present, the clinician might consider employing the Children's Atypical Development Scale (see Barkley, 1990) to obtain a more thorough review of these symptoms. Inquiry also must be made as to the presence or history of tics or Tourette syndrome in the child or the immediate biological family members. When noted, these disorders would result in a recommendation for the cautious use of stimulant drugs in the treatment of ADHD or, perhaps, lower doses of such medicine than typical to preclude the exacerbation of the child's tic disorder (see Chapter 17, this volume).

School, Family, and Treatment Histories

The examiner should also obtain information on the school and family histories. The family history must include a discussion of potential psychiatric difficulties in the parents and siblings, marital difficulties, and any family problems centered around chronic medical conditions, employment problems, or other potential stress events within the family. Of course, the examiner will want to obtain some information about prior treatments received by the child and his or her family for these presenting problems. When the history suggests potentially treatable medical or neurological conditions (allergies, seizures, Tourette syndrome, etc.), a referral to a physician is essential. Without evidence of such problems, however, referral to a physician for examination usually fails to reveal any further useful treatment information. But when the use of psychiatric medications is contemplated, a referral to a physician is clearly indicated.

Information about the child's family is essential for two reasons. First, ADHD is not caused by family stress or dysfunction. Therefore, the family history can help to clarify whether the child's attentional or behavioral problems are developmental or actually a reaction to stressful events that have taken place. Second, a history of certain psychiatric disorders in the extended family might influence diagnostic impressions or treatment recommendations. For example, because ADHD is hereditary, a strong family history of ADHD in biological relatives lends weight to the ADHD diagnosis, especially when other diagnostic factors are questionable. A family history of Bipolar Disorder in a child with severe behavioral problems might suggest particular medication choices that otherwise might not be considered.

The interviewer can organize this section by first asking about the child's siblings (whether there is anything significant about sibling relationships, whether siblings have any health or developmental problems). Then, questions about the parents may include how long they have been married, the overall stability of their marriage, whether each parent is in good physical health, whether either parent has ever been given a psychiatric diagnosis, and whether either parent has had a learning disability. The clinician should always be cautious of inquiring too much into the parents' personal concerns. The purpose is to rule out family stress as a cause for the child's difficulties and to determine what treatment recommendations may be appropriate.

In asking about extended family history, the interviewer should include maternal and paternal relatives (see clinical workbook by Barkley & Murphy, 1998).

Although it may seem tedious, it is *extremely* useful to go through the child's school history year by year, starting with preschool. The examiner should ask parents open-ended questions: "What did his teachers have to say about him?", "How did he do academically?", or "How did he get along socially?" The examiner should avoid pointed, leading questions (e.g., "Did the teacher think he had ADHD?"). Examiners should allow parents to tell them their child's story and listen for the red flags (e.g., the teacher thought he was immature, he had trouble with work completion, his organizational skills were terrible, he could not keep his hands to himself, or he would not do homework).

Gathering a reliable school history gives the clinician two crucial pieces of the diagnostic puzzle. First, is there evidence of symptoms or characteristics of ADHD in school previous to adolescence? Second, is there evidence of impairment in the child's academic functioning as a result of these characteristics?

Examiners should ask parents what strategies teachers may have attempted to help the child in class. They should also inquire about tutoring services, school counselors, study skills classes, or peer helpers. The examiner should find out when and why teachers referred the child for psychoeducational testing. If the child is not doing well in school, the examiner should ask whether school personnel have ever offered an explanation. As always, the examiner should listen for clues about possible problems with behavioral regulation, impulse control, or sustained attention. If the child has a diagnosed learning disability, are there problems in school that cannot be explained by that learning disability?

Review of Childhood Psychiatric Disorders

As part of the general interview of the parent, the examiner must cover the symptoms of the major child psychiatric disorders likely to be seen in ADHD children. A review of the major childhood disorders in the fourth edition of the *Diagnostic and Statistical Manual of Mental Disorders* (DSM-IV; American Psychiatric Association, 1994) in some semistructured or structured way is imperative if any semblance of a reliable and differential approach to diagnosis and the documentation of comorbid disorders is to occur (see interview in Barkley & Murphy, 1998). The examiner must exercise care in the evaluation of minority children to avoid over-diagnosing psychiatric disorders simply by virtue of ignoring differing cultural standards for child behavior. Chapter 2 (this volume) discusses insuring that the behaviors of children are statistically deviant as well as associated with evidence of impairment in adaptive functioning or some other "harmful dysfunction." Should the parent indicate that a symptom is present, one means of precluding overidentification of psychopathology in minority children is to ask the following question: "*Do you consider this to be a problem for your child compared to other children of the same ethnic or minority group?*" Only if the parent answers "yes" is the symptom to be considered present for purposes of psychiatric diagnosis.

Before proceeding, an explanation is in order as to why ODD and CD are queried first. Many parents arrive at the diagnostic evaluation overwhelmed by emotional stress, frustrations with home behaviors, or endless criticisms about the child from the school; thus they may be inclined to say yes to anything. Starting with ODD and CD questions allows these parents to get some of this frustration out of their system. Thus, when they are asked questions about ADHD, the answers are potentially more reliable and accurate.

In addition, unfortunately some parents actually "shop" for the ADHD diagnosis. They may have an agenda that involves obtaining a diagnosis for their child that is not entirely objective. Beginning the clinical interview with the reason for referral and then the ODD questions may assist the clinician in gaining important clinical impressions about the parents' agenda. This is also why it can be extremely useful for clinicians to *completely* eliminate the word "attention" from their vocabulary during the interview. When the clinician asks specific questions about ADHD symptoms, the questions should be phrased in such a way that they are concrete and descriptive.

As suggested in Chapter 2, adjustments may need to be made to the DSM-IV criteria for ADHD (see Table 2.1):

1. The cutoff scores on both symptom lists (6 of 9) were primarily based on children ages 4–16 years in the DSM-IV field trial (Lahey et al., 1994), making the extrapolation of these thresholds to age ranges outside those in the field trial of uncertain validity. ADHD behaviors tend to decline in frequency within the population over development,

again suggesting that a somewhat higher threshold may be needed for preschool children (ages 2–4).

2. The children used in the DSM-IV field trial were predominantly males. Studies reliably demonstrate that parents and teachers report lower levels of those behaviors associated with ADHD in girls than in boys (Achenbach & Edelbrock, 1983, 1986; DuPaul, 1991). It is possible, then, that the cutoff points on the DSM-IV symptom lists, based as they are mainly on males, are unfairly high for females. Some latitude should be granted to females who are close to but may fall short of the diagnostic criteria by a single symptom.

3. The specific age of onset of 7 years is not particularly critical for identifying ADHD children (Barkley & Biederman, 1997). The field trial for the DSM-IV found that ADHD children with various ages of onset were essentially similar in the nature and severity of impairments as long as their symptoms developed prior to ages 10–12 years (Applegate et al., 1997). Thus, so stipulating an onset of symptoms in childhood is probably sufficient for purposes of clinical diagnosis.

4. The criterion that duration of symptoms be at least 6 months was not specifically studied in the field trial and was held over from earlier DSMs primarily out of tradition. Some research on preschool children suggests that a large number of 2- to 3-year-olds may manifest the symptoms of ADHD as part of that developmental period and that they may remain present for periods of 3–6 months or longer (Campbell, 1990; Palfrey, Levine, Walker, & Sullivan, 1985). Children whose symptoms persisted for at least 1 year or more, however, were likely to remain deviant in their behavior pattern into the elementary school years (Campbell & Ewing, 1990; Palfrey et al., 1985). Adjusting the duration criterion to 12 months would seem to make good clinical sense.

5. The criterion that symptoms must be evident in at least two of three settings (home, school, work) essentially requires that children have sufficient symptoms of ADHD by both parent and teacher report before they can qualify for the diagnosis. This requirement bumps up against a methodological problem inherent in comparing parent and teacher reports. On average, the relationship of behavior ratings from these two sources tends to be fairly modest, averaging about 0.30 (Achenbach, McConaughy, & Howell, 1987). However, if parent and teacher ratings are unlikely to agree across the various behavioral domains being rated, the number of children qualifying for the diagnosis of ADHD is unnecessarily limited, due mainly to measurement artifact. Fortunately, some evidence demonstrates that children who meet DSM criteria (in this case, DSM-III-R; American Psychiatric Association, 1987) by parent reports have a high probability of meeting the criteria by teacher reports (Biederman, Keenan, & Faraone, 1990). Even so, stipulating that parents and teachers *must* agree on the diagnostic criteria before a diagnosis can be rendered is probably unwise and unnecessarily restrictive. For now, to grant the diagnosis, clinicians are advised to seek evidence that symptoms of the disorder existed at some time in the past or present of the child in several settings rather than insisting on the agreement of the parents with a current teacher.

The foregoing issues should be kept in mind when applying the DSM criteria to particular clinical cases. It helps to appreciate the fact that the DSM represents guidelines for diagnosis, not rules of law or dogmatic prescriptions. Some clinical judgment is always going to be needed in the application of such guidelines to individual cases in clinical practice. For instance, if a child meets all criteria for ADHD including both parent and teacher agreement on symptoms except that the age of onset for the symptoms and impairment is 9 years, should the diagnosis be withheld? Given the previous discussion concerning the lack of specificity for an age of onset of 7 years and ADHD, the wise clinician would grant the diagnosis anyway. Likewise, if an 8-year-old girl meets five of the nine ADHD Inattention or Hyperactive–Impulsive symptoms and all other conditions are met for ADHD, the diagnosis should likely be granted given the previous comments about gender bias within these criteria. Some flexibility (and common sense), then, must be incorporated into the clinical application of any DSM criteria.

To assist clinicians with the differential diagnosis of ADHD from other childhood mental disorders, we compiled a list of differential diagnostic tips (see Table 8.1). Under each disorder, we list those features that would distinguish this disorder, in its pure form, from ADHD. However, many ADHD children may have one or more of these disorders as comorbid conditions with their ADHD; thus the issue here is not which single or primary disorder the child has but what other disorders besides ADHD are present and how they affect treatment planning.

For years, some clinicians eschewed diagnosing children, viewing it as a mechanistic and dehumanizing practice that merely results in unnecessary labeling. Moreover, they felt that it got in the way of appreciating the clinical uniqueness of each case, unnecessarily homogenizing the heterogeneity of clinical cases. Some believed that labeling a child's condition with a diagnosis is unnecessary as it is far more important to articulate the child's pattern of behavioral and developmental excesses and deficits in planning behavioral treatments. Although there may have been some justification for these views in the past, particularly prior to the development of more empirically based diagnostic criteria, this is no longer the case in view of the wealth of research that went into creating the DSM-IV childhood disorders and their criteria. This is not to say that clinicians should not document patterns of behavioral deficits and excesses, as such documentation is important for treatment planning; only that this documentation should not be used as an excuse not to diagnose at all. Furthermore, given that the protection of rights and access to educational and other services may actually hinge on awarding or withholding the diagnosis of ADHD, dispensing with diagnosis altogether could well be considered professional negligence. For these reasons and others, clinicians, along with the parent of each child referred to them, must review in some systematic way the symptom lists and other diagnostic criteria for various childhood mental disorders.

The parental interview may also reveal that one parent, usually the mother, has more difficulty managing the ADHD child than does the other. Care should be taken to discuss differences in the parents' approaches to management and any marital problems these differences may have spawned. Such difficulties in child management can often lead to reduced leisure and recreational time for the parents and increased conflict within the marriage and often within the extended family should relatives live nearby. It is often helpful to inquire as to what the parents attribute the causes or origins of their child's behavioral difficulties, because such exploration may unveil areas of ignorance or misinformation that will require attention during the initial counseling of the family about the child's disorder(s) and their likely causes. The examiner also should briefly inquire about the nature of parental and family social activities to determine how isolated, or insular, the parents are from the usual social support networks in which many parents are involved. Research by Wahler (1980) shows that the degree of maternal insularity is significantly associated with failure in subsequent parent training programs. When present to a significant degree, such a finding might support addressing the isolation as an initial goal of treatment rather than progressing directly to child behavior management training with that family.

Psychosocial Functioning

The first topic in this portion of the interview involves peer relationships and recreational activities. A clinical diagnosis of ADHD requires impairment in the child's functioning in at least two important areas. This area could certainly be one of them. In addition, evidence of impaired peer relationships may lead to important treatment recommendations such as participation in a peer social skills training group or a peer support group.

TABLE 8.1. Differential Diagnostic Tips for Distinguishing Other Mental Disorders from ADHD

ADHD, Predominantly Inattentive Type

Lethargy, staring, and daydreaming more likely than in ADHD, Combined Type
Sluggish cognitive tempo/slow information processing
Lacks impulsive, disinhibited, or aggressive behavior
Possibly greater family history of anxiety disorders and learning disabilities
Makes significantly more errors in academic work
No elevated risk for Oppositional Defiant or Conduct Disorder

Oppositional Defiant Disorder and Conduct Disorder

Lacks impulsive, disinhibited behavior
Defiance primarily directed toward mother initially
Able to cooperate and complete tasks requested by others
Lacks poor sustained attention and marked restlessness
Resists initiating demands, whereas ADHD children may initiate but cannot stay on task
Often associated with parental child management deficits or family dysfunction
Lacks neuromaturational delays in motor abilities

Learning Disabilities

Has a significant IQ/achievement discrepancy (+1 standard deviation)
Places below the 10th percentile in an academic achievement skill
Lacks an early childhood history of hyperactivity
Attention problems arise in middle childhood and appear to be task or subject specific
Not socially aggressive or disruptive
Not impulsive or disinhibited

Anxiety/Affective Disorders

Likely to have a focused not sustained attention deficit
Not impulsive or aggressive; often overinhibited
Has a strong family history of anxiety disorders
Restlessness is more like fretful, worrisome behavior not the "driven," inquisitive, or overstimulated type
Lacks preschool history of hyperactive, impulsive behavior
Not socially disruptive; typically socially reticent

Thought Disorders

Show oddities/atypical patterns of thinking not seen in ADHD
Peculiar sensory reactions
Odd fascinations and strange aversions
Socially aloof, schizoid, disinterested
Lacks concern for personal hygiene/dress in adolescence
Atypical motor mannerisms, stereotypies, and postures
Labile, capricious, unpredictable moods not tied to reality
Poor empathy, cause–effect perception,
Poor perception of meaningfulness of events

Juvenile-Onset Mania or Bipolar I Disorder

Characterized by severe and persistent irritability
Depressed mood exists more days than not
Irritable/depressed mood typically punctuated by rage outbursts
Mood swings often unpredictable or related to minimal events
Severe temper outbursts and aggression with minimal provocation (thus, ODD is often present and severe)
Later onset of symptoms than ADHD (but comorbid early ADHD is commonplace)
Press of speech and flight of ideas often present
Psychotic-like symptoms often present during manic episodes
Family history of Bipolar I Disorder more common
Expansive mood, grandiosity of ideas, inflated self-esteem, and high productivity (goal-directed activity periods) often seen in adults with Bipolar Disorder are usually not present; children more often have the dysphoric type of disorder
Requires that sufficient symptoms of Bipolar Disorder be present after excluding distractibility and hyperactivity (motor agitation) from Bipolar symptom list in DSM-IV before granting Bipolar I diagnosis to a child with symptoms of ADHD
Suicidal ideation is more common in child (and suicide attempts more common in family history)

Parents are asked if the child has trouble making or keeping friends, how the child behaves around other children, and how well the child fits in at school. Parents are also asked if they have concerns about the friends with whom their child spends time (e.g., do parents view them as "troublemakers"). Finally, they are asked about recreational activities in which the child participates outside school and any problems that occurred during those activities.

Compliance with parental requests and parental use of compensatory or motivational strategies also can be explored, especially if the clinician anticipates conducting parent training in child management skills with this family. These questions also substantiate evidence of impairment in family functioning as well as possible treatment recommendations for parent management training. If the interview on parent–child interactions discussed later is not to be used, parents are asked to describe how quickly their child complies with parental requests, if there are discrepancies in the child's behavior with mother and father, and if parents generally agree on how to manage their child. They are also asked to describe the types of disciplinary strategies they use and whether or not they have tried incentive systems to encourage more appropriate behavior.

At a later appointment, perhaps even during the initial session of parent training, the examiner may wish to pursue more details about the nature of the parent–child interactions surrounding the following of rules by the child. Parents should be questioned about the child's ability to accomplish commands and requests in a satisfactory manner in various settings, to adhere to rules of conduct governing behavior in various situations, and to demonstrate self-control (rule following) appropriate to the child's age in the absence of adult supervision. We have found it useful to follow the format set forth in Table 8.2 in which parents are questioned about their interactions with their children in a variety of home and public situations. When problems are said to occur, the examiner follows up with the list of questions in Table 8.2. When time constraints are problematic, the HSQ rating scale can be used to provide similar types of information. After parents complete the scale, they can be

TABLE 8.2. Parental Interview Format for Assessing Child Behavior Problems at Home and in Public

Situation to be discussed	If a problem, follow-up questions to ask
Overall parent–child interactions	1. Is this a problem area? If so, then proceed with questions 2–9.
Playing alone	
Playing with other children	2. What does the child do in this situation that bothers you?
Mealtimes	
Getting dressed/undressed	3. What is your response likely to be?
Washing and bathing	4. What will the child do in response to you?
When parent is on telephone	5. If the problem continues, what will you do next?
Child is watching television	6. What is usually the outcome of this situation?
When visitors are in your home	7. How often do these problems occur in this situation?
When you are visiting someone else's home	8. How do you feel about these problems?
In public places (stores, restaurants, church, etc.)	9. On a scale of 1 (no problem) to 9 (severe), how severe is this problem for you?
When father is in the home	
When child is asked to do chores	
When child is asked to do school homework	
At bedtime	
When child is riding in the car	
When child is left with a baby-sitter	
Any other problem situations	

Note. From Barkley (1981). Copyright 1981 by The Guilford Press. Reprinted by permission.

questioned about one or two of the problem situations using the same follow-up questions as in Table 8.2. The HSQ scale is discussed later.

Such an approach yields a wealth of information on the nature of parent–child interactions across settings, the type of noncompliance shown by the child (stalling, starting the task but failing to finish it, outright opposition and defiance, etc.), the particular management style employed by parents to deal with noncompliance, and the particular types of coercive behaviors used by the child as part of the noncompliance.

The parental interview can then conclude with a discussion of the children's positive characteristics and attributes as well as potential rewards and reinforcers desired by the children that will prove useful in later parent training on contingency management methods. Some parents of ADHD children have had such chronic and pervasive management problems that upon initial questioning they may find it hard to report anything positive about their children. Getting them to begin thinking of such attributes is actually an initial step toward treatment as the early phases of parent training will teach parents to focus on and attend to desirable child behaviors (see Chapter 12, this volume).

CHILD INTERVIEW

Some time should always be spent directly interacting with the referred child. The length of this interview depends on the age, intellectual level, and language abilities of the children. For preschool children, the interview may serve merely as a time to become acquainted with the child, noting his or her appearance, behavior, developmental characteristics, and general demeanor. For older children and adolescents, this time can be fruitfully spent inquiring about the children's views of the reasons for the referral and evaluation, how they see the family functioning, any additional problems they feel they may have, how well they are performing at school, their degree of acceptance by peers and classmates, and what changes in the family they believe might make life for them happier at home. As with the parents, the children can be queried as to potential rewards and reinforcers they find desirable which will prove useful in later contingency management programs.

Children below the age of 9–12 years are not especially reliable in their reports of their own disruptive behavior. The problem is compounded by the frequently diminished self-awareness and impulse control typical of defiant children with ADHD (Hinshaw, 1994). Such ODD/ADHD children often show little reflection about the examiner's questions and may lie or distort information in a more socially pleasing direction. Some report that they have many friends, have no interaction problems at home with their parents, and are doing well at school, in direct contrast with the extensive parental and teacher complaints of inappropriate behavior by these children. Because of this tendency of ADHD children to underreport the seriousness of their behavior, particularly in the realm of disruptive or externalizing behaviors (Barkley, Fischer, Edelbrock, & Smallish, 1991; Fischer, Barkley, Fletcher, & Smallish, 1993), the diagnosis of ODD or ADHD is never based on the reports of the child. Nevertheless, children's reports of their internalizing symptoms, such as anxiety and depression, may be more reliable and thus should play some role in the diagnosis of comorbid anxiety or mood disorders in children with ADHD (Hinshaw, 1994).

Although notation of children's behavior, compliance, attention span, activity level, and impulse control in the clinic is useful, clinicians must guard against drawing any diagnostic conclusions when the children are not problematic in the clinic or office. Many ODD and ADHD children do not misbehave in the clinician's office; thus reliance on such observations would clearly lead to false negatives in the diagnosis (Sleator & Ullmann, 1981). In some instances, the behavior of the children with their parents in the waiting area prior to the appointment may be a better indication of the children's management problems at home than is the children's behavior toward the clinician, particularly when the interaction between child and examiner is one to one.

This is not to say that the office behavior of a child is entirely meaningless. When it is grossly inappropriate or extreme, it may well signal the likelihood of problems in the child's natural settings, particularly school. It is the presence of relatively normal conduct by the child that may be an unreliable indicator of the child's normalcy elsewhere. For instance, in an ongoing study of 205 4- to 6-year-old children, we have examined the relationship of office behavior to parent and teacher ratings. Of these children, 158 were identified at kindergarten registration as being 1.5 standard deviations above the mean (93rd percentile) on parent ratings of ADHD and ODD (aggressive) symptoms. These children were subsequently evaluated for nearly 4 hours in a clinic setting, after which the examiner completed a rating scale of the child's behavior in the clinic. We then classified the children as falling below or above the 93rd percentile on these clinic ratings using data from a normal control group. The children were also classified as falling above or below this threshold on parent ratings of home behavior and teacher ratings of school behavior using the CBCL. We have found to date that no significant relationship exists between the children's clinic behavior (normal or abnormal) and the ratings by their parents. However, a significant relationship exists between abnormal ratings in the clinic and abnormal ratings by the teacher: 70% of the children classified as abnormal in their clinic behavior were also classified as such by the teacher ratings of class behavior, particularly on the externalizing behavior dimension. Normal behavior, however, was not necessarily predictive of normal behavior in either parent or teacher ratings. This finding suggests that abnormal or significantly disruptive behavior during a lengthy clinical evaluation may be a marker for similar behavioral difficulties in a school setting. Nevertheless, the wise clinician wil contact the child's teacher directly to learn about the child's school adjustment rather than relying entirely on such inferences about school behavior from clinic office behavior.

TEACHER INTERVIEW

At some point before or soon after the initial evaluation session with the family, contact with the children's teachers may be helpful to further clarify the nature of the children's problems. This contact will most likely occur by telephone unless the clinician works within the child's school system. Interviews with teachers have all of the same merits as interviews with parents, providing a second ecologically valid source of indispensable information about the child's psychological adjustment, in this case in the school setting. Like parent reports, teacher reports are also subject to bias, and the integrity of the informant, be it parent or teacher, must always be weighed by judging the validity of the information itself.

Many ADHD children have problems with academic performance and classroom behavior and the details of these difficulties need to be obtained. Initially this information may be obtained by telephone; however, when time and resources permit, a visit to the classroom and direct observation and recording of the children's behavior can prove quite useful if further documentation of ADHD behaviors is necessary for planning later contingency management programs for the classroom. Although this scenario is unlikely to prove feasible for clinicians working outside school systems, particularly in the climate of increasing managed health care plans, which severely restrict the evaluation time that will be compensated, for those professionals working within school systems, direct behavioral observations can prove very fruitful for diagnosis, and especially for treatment planning (Atkins & Pelham, 1992; DuPaul & Stoner, 1994).

Teachers should also be sent the rating scales mentioned earlier. They can be sent as a packet prior to the actual evaluation so that the results are available for discussion with the parents during the interview, as well as with the teacher during the subsequent telephone contact or school visit.

The teacher interview also should focus on the specific nature of the children's problems in the school environment, again following a behavioral format. The settings, nature, frequency, consequating events, and eliciting events for the major behavioral problems also can be explored. The follow-up questions used in the parental interview on parent–child interactions (shown in Table 8.1) may prove useful here as well. Given the greater likelihood of the occurrence of learning disabilities in this population, teachers should be questioned about such potential disorders. When evidence suggests their existence, the evaluation of the children should be expanded to explore the nature and degree of such deficits as viewed by the teacher. Even when learning disabilities do not exist, children who have ADHD are more likely to have problems with sloppy handwriting, careless approaches to tasks, poor organization of their work materials, and academic underachievement relative to their tested abilities. Time should be taken with the teachers to explore the possibility of these problems.

CHILD BEHAVIOR RATING SCALES FOR PARENT AND TEACHER REPORTS

Child behavior checklists and rating scales have become an essential element in the evaluation and diagnosis of children with behavior problems. The availability of several scales with excellent reliable and valid normative data across a wide age range of children makes their incorporation into the assessment protocol quite convenient and extremely useful. Such information is invaluable in determining the statistical deviance of the children's problem behaviors and the degree to which other problems may be present. As a result, it is useful to mail out a packet of these scales to parents prior to the initial appointment asking that they be returned on or before the day of the evaluation, as described earlier. Thus the examiner can review and score the scales before interviewing the parents, allowing vague or significant answers to be elucidated in the subsequent interview and focusing the interview on those areas of abnormality highlighted in the responses to scale items.

Numerous child behavior rating scales exist, and readers are referred to other reviews (Barkley, 1988a, 1990; Hinshaw & Nigg, in press) for greater details on the more commonly used scales and for a discussion of the requirements and underlying assumptions of behavior rating scales—assumptions all too easily overlooked in the clinical use of these instruments. Despite their limitations, behavior rating scales offer a means of gathering information from informants who may have spent months or years with the child. Apart from interviews, there is no other means of obtaining such a wealth of information with so little investment of time. The fact that such scales provide a means to quantify the opinions of others, often along qualitative dimensions, and to compare these scores to norms collected on large groups of children is further affirmation of the merits of these instruments. Nevertheless, behavior rating scales are opinions and are subject to the oversights, prejudices, and limitations on reliability and validity that such opinions may have.

Initially, it is advisable to utilize a "broad band" rating scale that provides coverage of the major dimensions of child psychopathology known to exist, such as depression, anxiety, withdrawal, aggression, delinquent conduct, and, of course, inattentive and hyperactive–impulsive behavior. These scales should be completed by parents and teachers. Such scales would be the BASC (Reynolds & Kamphaus, 1994) and the CBCL (Achenbach, 1991), both of which have versions for parents and teachers and satisfactory normative information.

The Personality Inventory for Children (Lachar, 1982) may also serve this purpose provided that one of the shortened versions is employed for convenience and the more contemporary norms are used for scoring purposes. It is, however, only a scale for parents to complete, precluding the informative comparison that can (and should) be made between parent and teacher reports on the same scale. The Connors Parent and Teacher Rating Scales (available from Multi-Health Systems, Niagara Falls Boulevard, North Tonawanda, NY 14120-2060) can also be used for this initial screening for psychopathology, but they do not provide quite the same breadth of coverage across these dimensions of psychopathology as do the aforementioned scales—particularly the revised versions of the Connors scales.

Narrow-band scales should be employed in the initial screening of children that focus specifically on the assessment of symptoms of ADHD. For this purpose, parent and teacher versions of a Disruptive Behavior Rating Scale can be found in the clinical workbook accompanying this text (Barkley & Murphy, 1998). Those scales obtain ratings of the DSM-IV symptoms of ODD, ADHD, and CD (parent-form only), as described earlier. DuPaul and colleagues recently collected norms for another version of an ADHD rating scale (DuPaul et al., 1997; DuPaul et al., in press).

The Child Attention Profile (see Barkley, 1990) is yet another narrow-band scale specific to ADHD. It has the advantage of being drawn directly from the teacher version of the CBCL and thus benefits from the rigor of standardization and norming that went into that scale's development (Achenbach & Edelbrock, 1986). Its disadvantage, like that of many of the specialized scales noted previously, is that it does not employ the precise symptom lists for inattention and hyperactivity–impulsivity from the DSM-IV. Thus, high scores alone on any of these scales would not automatically indicate a diagnosis of ADHD. In fact, readers should remember that scores on rating scales, alone, are not sufficient to render a psychiatric diagnosis (e.g., ODD or ADHD) in a child. The clinician must combine this information with that obtained from the parent and teacher interviews, as well as with his or her specialized knowledge in differential diagnosis, before he or she renders specific diagnoses.

The clinician should also examine the pervasiveness of the child's behavior problems within the home and school settings as such measures of situational pervasiveness appear to have as much or more stability over time than do the aforementioned scales (Fischer et al., 1993). The HSQ (Barkley, 1987, 1990) provide a means for doing so, and normative information for these scales is available (Altepeter & Breen, 1992; Barkley, 1990; Barkley & Edelbrock, 1987; DuPaul & Barkley, 1992). The HSQ requires parents to rate their child's behavioral problems across 16 different home and public situations. The SSQ similarly obtains teacher reports of problems in 12 different school situations.

The more specialized or narrow-band scales focusing on symptoms of ODD and ADHD as well as the HSQ and SSQ can be used to monitor treatment response when given prior to, throughout, and at the end of parent training (see Chapter 12, this volume). They can also be used to monitor the behavioral effects of medication on children with ADHD. In that case, use of the Side Effects Rating Scale is encouraged (see Barkley, 1990; Barkley & Murphy, 1998).

One of the most common problem areas for ADHD children is their academic productivity. The amount of work that ADHD children typically accomplish at school is often substantially less than that done by their peers within the same period. Demonstrating such an impact on school functioning is often critical for ADHD children to be eligible for special educational services (DuPaul & Stoner, 1994). The Academic Performance Rating Scale (see Barkley, 1990) was developed to provide a means of screening quickly for this domain of school functioning. It is a teacher rating scale of academic productivity and accuracy in major subject areas with norms based on a sample of children from central Massachusetts (DuPaul, Rapport, & Perriello, 1991).

Self-Report Behavior Rating Scales for Children

Achenbach and Edelbrock (1986) developed a rating scale quite similar to the CBCL which is completed by children ages 11 to 18 years (Youth Self-Report Form). Most items are similar to those on the parent and teacher forms of the CBCL except that they are worded in the first person. A later revision of this scale (Cross-Informant Version; Achenbach, 1991) now permits direct comparisons of results among the parent, teacher, and youth self-report forms of this popular rating scale. Research suggests that although such self-reports of ADHD children and teens are more deviant than the self-reports of youth without ADHD, the self-reports of problems by the ADHD youth, whether by interview or the CBCL Self-Report Form, are often less severe than the reports provided by parents and teachers (Fischer et al., 1993; Loeber, Green, Lahey, & Stouthamer-Loeber, 1991). The BASC, noted earlier, also has a self-report form that may serve much the same purpose as that for the CBCL.

The reports of children about internalizing symptoms, such as anxiety and depression, are more reliable and likely to be more valid than the reports of parents and teachers about these symptoms in their children (Achenbach et al., 1987; Hinshaw, Han, Erhardt, & Huber, 1992). For this reason, the self-reports of defiant children and youth should still be collected as they may have more pertinence to the diagnosis of comorbid internalizing disorders in children than to the defiant behavior itself.

Adaptive Behavior Scales and Inventories

Research has begun to show that a major area of life functioning affected by ADHD is the realm of general adaptive behavior (Barkley, DuPaul & McMurray, 1990; Roizen, Blondis, Irwin, & Stein, 1994). Adaptive behavior often refers to the child's development of skills and abilities that will assist them in becoming more independent, responsible, and self-caring individuals. This domain often includes (1) self-help skills, such as dressing, bathing, feeding, and toileting requirements, as well as telling and using time and understanding and using money; (2) interpersonal skills, such as sharing, cooperation, and trust; (3) motor skills, such as fine motor (zipping, buttoning, drawing, printing, use of scissors, etc.) and gross motor abilities (walking, hopping, negotiating stairs, bike riding, etc.); (4) communication skills; and (5) social responsibility, such as degree of freedom permitted within and outside the home, running errands, performing chores, and so on. So substantial and prevalent is this area of impairment among children with ADHD that Roizen et al. (1994) have even argued that a significant discrepancy between IQ and adaptive behavior scores (expressed as standard scores) may be a hallmark of ADHD.

Several instruments are available for the assessment of this domain of functioning. The Vineland Adaptive Behavior Inventory (Sparrow, Baila, & Cicchetti, 1984) is probably the most commonly used measure for assessing adaptive functioning. It is an interview, however, and takes considerable time to administer. When time is of the essence, we use the NABC (Adams, 1984) to assess this domain because of its greater ease of administration. It can be included as part of the packet of rating scales sent to parents in advance of the child's appointment for more efficient use of clinical time. The CBCL and the BASC completed by parents also contains several short scales that provide a cursory screening of several areas of adaptive functioning (Activities, Social, and School) in children, but it is no substitute for the in-depth coverage provided by the Vineland or NABC scales.

Peer Relationship Measures

As noted earlier, children with ADHD often demonstrate significant difficulties in their interactions with peers, and such difficulties are associated with an increased likelihood of persistence of their disorder. A number of different methods for assessing peer relations have been employed in research with behavior problem children, such as direct observation and recording of social interactions, peer and subject completed sociometric ratings, and parent and teacher rating scales of children's social behavior. Most of these assessment methods have no norms and thus would not be appropriate for use in the clinical evaluation of children with ADHD. Reviews of the methods for obtaining peer sociometric ratings can be found elsewhere (Newcomb, Bukowski, & Pattee, 1993). For clinical purposes, rating scales may offer the most convenient and cost-effective means for evaluating this important domain of childhood functioning. The CBCL and BASC rating forms described earlier contain scales that evaluate children's social behavior. As discussed earlier, norms are available for these scales, permitting their use in clinical settings. Three other scales that focus specifically on social skills are the Matson Evaluation of Social Skills with Youngsters (MESSY; Matson, Rotatori, & Helsel, 1983), the Taxonomy of Problem Social Situations for Children (TOPS; Dodge, McClaskey, & Fledman, 1985), and the Social Skills Rating System (Gresham & Elliott, 1990). The latter also has norms and a software scoring system, making it useful in clinical contexts. We have used it extensively in our research and clinical evaluations.

Parent Self-Report Measures

It has become increasingly apparent that child behavioral disorders, their level of severity, and their response to interventions are, in part, a function of factors affecting parents and the family at large. As noted in the Chapter 4 (this volume), several types of psychiatric disorders are likely to occur more often among family members of a child with ADHD than in matched groups of control children. Numerous studies over the past 20 years have demonstrated the further influence of these disorders on the frequency and severity of behavioral problems in ADHD children. As discussed earlier, the extent of social isolation in mothers of behaviorally disturbed children influences the severity of the children's behavioral disorders as well as the outcomes of parent training. Separate and interactive contributions of parental psychopathology and marital discord affect the decision to refer children for clinical assistance, the degree of conflict in parent–child interactions, and child antisocial behavior (Barkley, 1990). The degree of parental resistance to training also depends on such factors. Assessing the psychological integrity of parents, therefore, is an essential part of the clinical evaluation of defiant children, the differential diagnosis of their prevailing disorders, and the planning of treatments stemming from such assessments. Thus, the evaluation of children for ADHD is often a family assessment rather than one of the child alone. Although space does not permit a thorough discussion of the clinical assessment of adults and their disorders, this section provides a brief mention of some assessment methods clinicians may find useful as a preliminary screening for certain variables of import to treatment in ADHD children.

The parents can complete these instruments in the waiting room, during the time their child is being interviewed. (To save time, some professionals may prefer to send these self-report scales out to parents in advance of their appointment, at the same time they send the child behavior questionnaires to the parents. If so, the clinician needs to prepare a cover letter sensitively explaining to parents the need for obtaining such information.) On the day of the interview, the clinician can indicate to parents that having a complete understanding of a child's behavior problems requires learning more about both the children and their parents. This process includes gaining more information about the parents' own psychological adjustment and how they view themselves as succeeding in their role as parents. The rating scales can then be introduced as one means of gaining such information. Few parents refuse to complete these scales after an introduction of this type.

Parental ADHD and ODD

Family studies of the aggregation of psychiatric disorders among the biological relatives of children with ADHD and ODD clearly demonstrate an increased prevalence of ADHD and ODD among the parents of these children (see Chapters 4 and 5, this volume). In general, there seems to be at least a 40–50% chance that one of the two parents of the defiant child with ADHD will also have adult ADHD (15–20% of mothers and 25–30% of fathers). The manner in which ADHD in a parent might influence the behavior of an ADHD child specifically and the family environment more generally has not been well studied. Adults with ADHD have been shown to be more likely to have problems with anxiety, depression, personality disorders, alcohol use and abuse, and marital difficulties; to change their employment and residence more often; and to have less education and socioeconomic status than adults without ADHD (see Chapter 6, this volume). Greater diversity and severity of psychopathology among parents is particularly apparent among the subgroup of ADHD children with comorbid ODD or CD. More severe ADHD seems to also be associated with younger age of parents (Murphy & Barkley, 1996), suggesting that pregnancy during their own teenage or young adult years is more characteristic of parents of ADHD than non-ADHD children. It is not difficult to see that these factors, as well as the primary symptoms of ADHD as well, could influence the manner in which child behavior is managed within the family as well as the quality of home life for such children more generally. Some research in our clinic suggests that when the parent has ADHD, the probability that the child with ADHD will also have ODD increases markedly. A recent clinical case (Evans, Vallano, & Pelham, 1994) suggests that ADHD in a parent may interfere with the ability of that parent to benefit from a typical behavioral parent training program. Treatment of the parent's ADHD (with medication) resulted in greater success in subsequent retraining of the parent. These preliminary findings suggest of the importance of determining the presence of ADHD and even ODD in the parents of children undergoing evaluation for the disorder.

Recently, the DSM-IV symptom list for ADHD and ODD has been cast in the form of two behavior rating scales, one for current behavior and the other for recall of behavior during childhood. Some limited regional norms on 720 adults ages 17–84 years were collected (Murphy & Barkley, 1996). These two rating scales for adults along with their norms are provided in the clinical manual accompanying this text (Barkley & Murphy, 1998). Again, clinically significant scores on these scales do not, by themselves, grant the diagnosis of ADHD or ODD to a parent, but they should raise suspicion in the clinician's mind about such a possibility. If so, consideration should be given to referral of the parent for further evaluation and, possibly, treatment of adult ADHD or ODD.

The use of such scales in screening parents of ADHD children would be a helpful first step in determining whether the parents have ADHD. If the child meets diagnostic criteria for ADHD and these screening scales for ADHD in the parents prove positive (clinically significant), referral of the parents for a more thorough evaluation and differential diagnosis might be in order. At the very least, positive findings from the screening would suggest the need to take them into account in treatment planning and parent training.

Marital Discord

Many instruments exist for evaluating marital discord in parents. The one most often used in research on childhood disorders has been the Locke–Wallace Marital Adjustment Scale (Locke & Wallace, 1959). As noted in Chapter 4 (this volume), marital discord, parental separation, and parental divorce are more common in parents of ADHD children. Parents with such marital difficulties may have children with more severe defiant and aggressive behavior and such parents may also be less successful in parent training programs. Screening parents for marital problems, therefore, provides important clinical information to therapists contemplating a parent training program for such parents. Clinicians are encouraged to incorporate a screening instrument for marital discord into their assessment battery for parents of children with defiant behavior.

Parental Depression and General Psychological Distress

Parents of ADHD children, especially those with comorbid ODD or CD, are frequently more depressed than those of normal children, which may affect their responsiveness to behavioral parent training programs. The Beck Depression Inventory (Beck, Steer, & Garbin, 1988) is often used to provide a quick assessment of parental depression. Greater levels of psychopathology generally and psychiatric disorders specifically also have been found in parents of children with ADHD, most of whom also have ADHD (Breen & Barkley, 1988; Lahey et al., 1988). One means of assessing this area of parental difficulties is through the use of the Symptom Checklist 90—Revised (Derogatis, 1986). This instrument not only has a scale assessing depression in adults but also has scales measuring other dimensions of adult psychopathology and psychological distress. Whether clinicians use this or some other scale, the assessment of parental psychological distress generally and psychiatric disorders particularly makes sense in view of their likely impact on the child's course and the implementation of the child's treatments typically delivered via the parents.

Parental Stress

Research over the past 15 years suggests that parents of children with behavior problems, especially those children with comorbid ODD and ADHD, report more stress in their families and their parental role than those of normal or clinic-referred non-ADHD children (see Chapter 4, this volume). One measure frequently used in such research to evaluate this construct has been the Parenting Stress Index (PSI; Abidin, 1986). The original PSI is a 150-item multiple-choice questionnaire which can yield six scores pertaining to child behavioral characteristics (distractibility, mood, etc.), eight scores pertaining to maternal characteristics (e.g. depression, sense of competence as a parent, etc.), and two scores pertaining to situational and life stress events. These scores can be summed to yield three domain or summary scores: Child Domain, Mother Domain, and Total Stress. A shorter version of this scale is now available (Abidin, 1986) and clinicians are encouraged to utilize it in evaluation parents of defiant children.

LEGAL AND ETHICAL ISSUES

Apart from the legal and ethical issues involved in the general practice of providing mental health services to children, several such issues may be somewhat more likely to occur in the evaluation of ADHD children. The first involves the issue of custody or guardianship of the child as it pertains to who can request the evaluation of the child who may have ADHD. Children with ODD, ADHD, or CD are more likely than average to come from families in which the parents have separated or divorced or in which significant marital discord may exist between the biological parents. As a result, the clinician must take care at the point of contact between the family and the clinic or professional to determine who has legal custody of the child and particularly the right to request mental health services on behalf of the minor. It must also be determined in cases of joint custody, an increasingly common status in divorce/custody situations, whether the nonresident parent has the right to dispute the referral for the evaluation, to consent to the evaluation, to attend on the day of appointment, and/or to have access to the final report. This right to review or dispute mental health services may also extend to the provision of treatment to the child. Failing to attend to these issues before the evaluation can lead to contentiousness, frustration, and even legal action among the parties to the evaluation that could have been avoided had greater care been taken to iron out these issues beforehand. Although these issues apply to all evaluations of children, they may be more likely to arise in families seeking assistance for ADHD children.

A second issue that also arises in all evaluations but may be more likely in cases involving ADHD is the duty of the clinician to disclose to state agencies any suspected physical or sexual abuse or neglect of the child. Clinicians should routinely forewarn parents of this duty to report when it applies in a particular state *before* starting the formal evaluation procedures. In view of the greater stress that ADHD or ODD children appear to pose for their parents, as well as the greater psychological distress their parents are likely to report, the risk for abuse of defiant children may be higher than average. The greater likelihood of parental ADHD or other psychiatric disorders may further contribute to this risk, resulting in a greater likelihood that evaluations of children with disruptive behavior disorders will involve suspicions of abuse. Understanding such legal duties as they apply in a given state or region and taking care to exercise them properly yet with sensitivity to the larger clinical issues are the responsibility of any clinician involved in providing mental health services to children.

Increasingly over the past decade, ADHD children have been gaining access to government entitlements, sometimes thought of as legal rights, which makes it necessary for clinicians to be well informed about the legal issues if they are to properly and correctly advise the parents and school staff. For instance, children with ADHD in the United States are now entitled to formal special educational services under the Other Health Impaired Category of the Individuals with Disabilities in Education Act (1975; Public Law 101-476), provided of course that their ADHD is sufficiently serious to interfere significantly with school performance. In addition, such children also have legal protections and entitlements under Section 504 of the Rehabilitation Act of 1973 (Public Law 93-112) or the more recent Americans with Disabilities Act of 1990 (Public Law 101-336) as it applies to the provision of an appropriate education for children with disabilities (see DuPaul & Stoner, 1994; Latham & Latham, 1992, for discussions of these entitlements). And should ADHD children have a sufficiently severe disorder and reside in a family of low economic means, they may also be eligible for financial assistance under the Social Security Act. Space precludes a more complete explication of these legal entitlements here. Readers are referred to the excellent text by attorneys Latham and Latham (1992) for a fuller account of these matters. Suffice it to say here that clinicians working with ADHD children need to familiarize themselves with these various rights and entitlements if they are to be effective advocates for the children they serve.

A final legal issue related to ADHD children pertains to legal accountability for their actions in view of the argument made elsewhere (Barkley, 1997) that their ADHD is a developmental disorder of self-control. Should children with ADHD be held legally responsible for the damage they may cause to property, the injury they may inflict on others, or the crimes they may commit? In short, is ADHD an excuse to behave irresponsibly without being held accountable for the consequences? The answer is unclear and deserves the attention of sharper legal minds than ours. It is our opinion, however, that ADHD explains why certain impulsive acts may have been committed but does not sufficiently disturb mental faculties to excuse legal accountability, as might occur, for example, under the insanity defense (Barkley, 1997b). Nor should ADHD be permitted to serve as an extenuating factor in the determination of guilt or the sentencing of an individual involved in criminal activities, particularly those involving violent crime. This opinion is predicated on the fact that the vast majority of children with ADHD, even those with comorbid ODD, do not become involved in violent crime as they grow up. Moreover, studies attempting to predict criminal conduct within samples of ADHD children followed to adulthood either have not been able to find adequate predictors of such outcomes or have found them to be so weak as to account for a paltry amount of variance in such outcomes. Moreover, those variables that may make a significant contribution to the prediction of criminal or delinquent behavior more often involve measures of parental and family dysfunction as well as social disadvantage and much less so, if at all, measures of ADHD symptoms. Until this matter receives greater legal scrutiny, it seems wise to view ADHD as one of several explanations for impulsive conduct but not a direct, primary, or immediate cause of criminal conduct for which the individual should not be held accountable.

THE PEDIATRIC MEDICAL EXAMINATION

It is essential that children being considered for a diagnosis of ADHD have a complete pediatric physical examination. However, traditionally such examinations are brief, relatively superficial, and as a result often unreliable and invalid for achieving a diagnosis of ADHD or identifying other comorbid behavioral, psychiatric, and educational conditions (Costello et al., 1988; Sleator & Ullmann, 1981). This is often the result of ignoring the other two essential features of the evaluation of ADHD children: a thorough clinical interview, reviewed earlier, and the use of behavior rating scales. To properly diagnose and treat these children and adolescents, it is imperative that adequate time be committed to the evaluation to complete these components. If this is not possible, the physician is compelled to conduct the appropriate medical examination but withhold the diagnosis until the other components can be accomplished by referral to another mental health professional.

The features of the pediatric examination and the issues that must be entertained therein are described next and are taken from previous reviews of this exam by our medical colleagues Bennett and Sally Shaywitz (1984) of Yale University Medical School and Mary McMurray at the University of Massachusetts Medical Center (McMurray & Barkley, 1997).

The Medical Interview

Most of the contents of an adequate medical interview are identical to those described previously for the parental interview. However, greater time will clearly be devoted to a more thorough review of the child's genetic background, pre- and peri- natal events, and developmental and medical history as well as the child's current health, nutritional status, and gross sensory–motor development. The time to listen to the parents' story and the child's feelings and to explain the nature of the disorder is one of the most important things a physician can offer a family. In this way, the evaluation process itself can often be therapeutic.

One major purpose of the medical interview that distinguishes it from the psychological interview noted previously is its focus on differential diagnosis of ADHD from other medical conditions, particularly those that may be treatable. In rare cases, the ADHD may have arisen secondary to a clear biologically compromising event, such as recovery from severe Reye's syndrome, surviving an hypoxic–anoxic event such as near drowning or severe smoke inhalation, significant head trauma, or recovery from an central nervous system infection or cerebral–vascular disease. The physician should obtain details of these surrounding events as well as the child's developmental, psychiatric, and educational status prior to the event and significant changes in these domains of adjustment since the event. The physician should also document ongoing treatments related to such events. In other cases, the

ADHD may be associated with significant lead or other metal or toxic poisonings, which will require treatment in their own right.

It is also necessary to determine whether the child's conduct or learning problems are related to the emergence of a seizure disorder or are secondary to the medication being used to treat the disorder. As many as 20% of epileptic children may have ADHD as a comorbid condition and up to 30% may develop ADHD or have it exacerbated by the use of phenobarbital or dilantin as anticonvulsants (Wolf & Forsythe, 1978). In such cases, changing to a different anticonvulsant may greatly reduce or even ameliorate the attentional deficits and hyperactivity of such children.

A second purpose of the medical exam is to thoroughly evaluate any coexisting conditions that may require medical management. In this case, the child's ADHD is not seen as arising from these other conditions but as being comorbid with it. As noted in Chapter 3 (this volume), ADHD is often associated with higher risks not only for other psychiatric or learning disorders but also for motor incoordination, enuresis, encopresis, allergies, otitis media, and greater somatic complaints in general. A pediatric evaluation is desirable or even required for many of these comorbid conditions. For instance, the eligibility of the child for physical or occupational therapy at school or in a rehabilitation center may require a physician's assessment and written recommendation of the need for such. And, although most cases of enuresis and encopresis are not due to underlying physiological disorders, all cases of these elimination problems should be evaluated by a physician before beginning nutritional and behavioral interventions. Even though many of these cases are "functional" in origin, medications may be prescribed to aid in their treatment, as in the use of oxybutinin or imipramine for bedwetting. Certainly children with significant allergies or asthma require frequent medical consultation and management of these conditions, often by specialists who appreciate the behavioral side effects of medications commonly used to treat them. Theophyline, for example, is increasingly recognized as affecting children's attention span and may exacerbate a preexisting case of ADHD. For these and other reasons, the role of the physician in the evaluation of ADHD should not be underestimated despite overwhelming evidence that by itself it is inadequate as the sole basis for a diagnosis of ADHD.

A third purpose of the medical examination is to determine whether physical conditions exist that are contraindications for treatment with medications. For instance, a history of high blood pressure or cardiac difficulties warrants careful consideration about a trial on a stimulant drug given the known presser effects of these drugs on the cardiovascular system. Some children may have a personal or family history of tic disorders or Tourette syndrome, which would dictate caution in prescribing stimulants in view of their greater likelihood of bringing out such movement disorders or increasing the occurrence of those that already exist. These examples merely illustrate the myriad medical and developmental factors that need to be carefully assessed in considering whether a particular ADHD child is an appropriate candidate for drug treatment.

Physical Examination

In the course of the physical examination, height, weight, and head circumference require measurement and comparison to standardized graphs. Hearing and vision, as well as blood pressure, should be screened. Findings suggestive of hyper- or hypothyroidism, lead poisoning, anemia, or other chronic illness clearly need to be documented, and further workup should be pursued. The formal neurological examination often includes testing of cranial nerves, gross and fine motor coordination, eye movements, finger sequencing, rapid alternating movements, impersistence, synkinesia, and motor overflow, testing for choreiform movements, and tandem gait tasks. The exam is often used to look for signs of previous central nervous system insult or of a progressive neurological condition, abnormalities of muscle tone, and a difference in strength, tone, or deep tendon reflex response between the two sides of the body. The existence of nystagmus, ataxia, tremor, decreased visual field, or fundal abnormalities should be determined and further investigation pursued when found. This evaluation should be followed by a careful neurodevelopmental exam covering the following areas: motor coordination, visual–perceptual skills, language skills, and cognitive functioning. Although these tests are certainly not intended to be comprehensive or even moderately in-depth evaluations of these functions, they are invaluable as quick screening methods for relatively gross deficiencies in these neuropsychological functions. When deficits are noted, follow-up with more careful and extensive neuropsychological, speech and language, motor, and academic evaluations may be necessary to more fully document their nature and extent.

Routine physical examinations of ADHD children are frequently normal and of little help in diagnosing the condition or suggesting its management. However, the physician certainly needs to rule out the rare possibility of visual or hearing deficits which may give rise to ADHD like symptoms. Also, on physical inspection, ADHD children may have a greater number of minor physical anomalies in outward appearance (e.g., an unusual palmer crease, two whirls of hair on the head, increased epicanthal fold, or hyperteliorism). However, studies conflict on whether such findings occur more often in ADHD, but certainly they are non-specific to it, being found in other psychiatric and developmental disorders. Shaywitz and Shaywitz (1984) state that examining for these minor congenital anomalies may only be beneficial when the physician suspects maternal alcohol abuse during pregnancy, to determine the presence of fetal alcohol syndrome. The existence of small palpebral fissures and midfacial hypoplasia with growth deficiency supports this diagnosis.

Finally, given the considerably greater distress ADHD children present to their caregivers, their risk of being physically abused would seem to be higher than normal. Greater attention by physicians to physical or other signs of abuse during the examination is therefore required.

The routine examination for growth in height and weight is also often normal, although one study reported a younger bone age in children with minimal brain dysfunction, including hyperactivity. Nevertheless, when the physician contemplates a trial on a stimulant drug, accurate baseline data on physical growth, heart rate, and blood pressure are necessary against which to compare subsequent repeat exams during the drug trial or during long-term maintenance on these medications.

Similarly, the routine neurological examination is frequently normal in ADHD children. These children may display a greater prevalence of soft neurological signs suggestive of immature neuromaturational development, but again these are nonspecific for ADHD and can often be found in learning-disabled, psychotic, autistic, and retarded children, not to mention a small minority of normal children. Such findings are therefore not diagnostic of ADHD, nor does their absence rule out the condition (Reeves, Werry, Elkind & Zametkin, 1987). Instead, findings of choreiform movements, delayed laterality development, fine or gross motor incoordination, dysdiadochokinesis, or other soft signs may suggest that the child requires more thorough testing by occupational or physical therapists and may be in need of some assistance in school with fine motor tasks or adaptive physical education.

ADHD children may also have a somewhat higher number of abnormal findings on brief mental status examinations or screening tests of higher cortical functions, especially those related to frontal lobe functions (e.g., sequential hand movement tests, spontaneous verbal fluency tests, and go–no-go tests of impulse control). When these are found, more thorough neuropsychological testing may be useful in further delineating the nature of these deficits and providing useful information to educators for making curriculum adjustments for these children. In some cases, findings on brief mental status exams may have more to do with a coexisting learning disability in a particular case than with the child's ADHD. When problems with visual–spatial–constructional skills or simple language abilities are noted, they are most likely signs of a comorbid learning disorder as they are not typical of ADHD children generally. It is often the case that these brief mental status examinations are normal. This does not necessarily imply that all higher cortical functions are intact as these screening exams are often relatively brief and crude methods of assessing neuropsychological functions. More sensitive, and lengthier, neuropsychological tests may often reveal deficits not detected during a brief neurological screening or mental status exam. Even so, the routine assessment of ADHD children with extensive neuropsychological test batteries is also likely to have a low yield. It should be undertaken only when there is a question of coexisting learning or processing deficits that require further clarification, and even then tests should be selected carefully to address these specific hypotheses.

Laboratory Tests

A number of studies of ADHD children have used a variety of physical, physiological, and psychophysiological measures to assess potential differences between ADHD and other clinical or control groups of children. Although some of these studies have demonstrated such differences, as in reduced cerebral blood flow to the striatum or diminished orienting galvanic skin responses (see Chapter 5, this volume), none of these laboratory measures are of value in the diagnostic process as yet. Parents, teachers, or even other mental health professionals are sometimes mislead by reports of such findings or by the conclusion that ADHD is a biologically based disorder, and they frequently ask for their children to be tested medically to confirm the diagnosis. At this moment, no such tests exist. Consequently, laboratory studies, such as blood work, urinalysis, chromosome studies, electroencephalograms, averaged evoked responses, magnetic resonance imaging, or computerized axial tomograms (CT scans) should not be used routinely in the evaluation of ADHD children. Only when the medical and developmental history or physical exam suggests that a treatable medical problem exists, such as a seizure disorder, or that a genetic syndrome is a possibility, would these laboratory procedures be recommended, and yet such cases are quite rare.

   When ADHD children are being placed on the stimulant drug Cylert (pemoline), routine liver function studies need to be done at baseline and again periodically during the use of this drug because of an apparently greater risk of hepatic complications from this medication. This is not the case for the more popular stimulants, Ritalin (methylphenidate), Dexedrine (D-amphetamine), or Adderall. Blood assays of levels of stimulant medication have so far proven unhelpful in determining appropriate dosage and therefore are not recommended as part of routine clinical titration and long-term management of these medications. The use of the tricyclic antidepressants for treating ADHD children, especially those with greater anxiety or depressive symptoms, requires that a baseline routine electrocardiogram be done and then repeated several weeks after beginning drug treatment given the greater potential for changes in cardiac rhythm and cardiotoxicity of these drugs. Whether blood levels of the tricyclics are useful in titrating them for maximum clinical response is debatable at this time as there is little standardized information to serve as a guide in the matter.

THE FEEDBACK SESSION

The feedback session with parents concludes the diagnostic evaluation. This session should take place after all the direct testing with the child is completed and scored and after the clinician has reviewed all the data and drawn diagnostic conclusions (the family may need to wait while the clinician makes any necessary collateral phone calls to the school, current therapist, etc.). As with the parent interview, children under the age of 16 are not generally included in the feedback session, but they may be invited in at the end of the session to be given diagnostic conclusions at a level appropriate to their age and cognitive development.

The first step in the feedback session is to give parents some information about ADHD. We generally explain to parents that ADHD is defined as a developmental disorder, not mental illness or the result of stress in families. The developmental delay affects the child's ability to regulate behavior, control activity level, inhibit impulsive responding, or sustain attention. In other words, the child with ADHD will be more active, impulsive, and less attentive than other children of the same age.

We then explain that there is no direct test for ADHD—no lab test, X-ray, or psychological test that definitely tells us that a child has ADHD. What we have to do instead is collect a lot of information and analyze it statistically. Therefore, everything that has been learned about their child has been scored, and these scores are compared with the scores that have been collected on hundreds if not thousands of children of the same age. If their child's scores are consistently placing him or her at or above the 95th percentile in the areas of activity level, impulse control, or attention span, that suggests ADHD because it suggests that the child is having more difficulty than 95 of 100 children of the same age. This is the level of "developmental deviance" that must be established.

The second step is to establish a history consistent with the notion of a "developmental" problem. Do these symptoms have a long-standing history that stretches back over time, for at least the past year or since before the age of 7—not something that cropped up last week or last month, or something that only came about after a trauma occurred in the child's life.

The third step is to rule out any other logical explanation for the problem. Is there anything else going on that would overrule ADHD as a diagnosis or be a better explanation than ADHD for the problems the child is having.

We then walk parents through the data obtained about their child, step by step, so they can see clearly how the diagnostic conclusion was reached. These steps include the following:

Explanation and results of the ADHD Rating Scale
    Parent interview responses
    Parent ADHD Rating Scale
    Teacher ADHD Rating Scale
Broad-band scale results
    Parent versions, especially Attention Problems Scale
       and/or Hyperactivity Scale
    Teacher version
Teacher rating scales (such as the Connors Rating Scales or Child Attention
    Profile)
Parenting Stress Inventory
Social Skills Rating Scale
Academic Performance Rating Scale
Clinic-based testing results (such as the Continuous Performance Test)

Before any discussion of a treatment plan occurs, parents are asked if they have any questions about the diagnostic process or any comments about the conclusions that were drawn. Parents are always asked if they are surprised that their child was (or was not) diagnosed with ADHD.

By walking parents through the data this way, any confusion can be quickly clarified. Parents should leave the diagnostic interview with the impression that the clinician was comprehensive and competent. This sense of security will help them cope with the grief and disappointment they may experience at being told that their child has a developmental disability, as well as the confidence to follow any treatment recommendations that are made.

CONCLUSION

It should be clear from the foregoing that the assessment of ADHD children is a complex and serious endeavor requiring adequate time (approximately 3 hours, exclusive of medical exam and psychological testing), knowledge of the relevant research and clinical literature as well as differential diagnosis, skillful clinical judgment in sorting out the pertinent issues, and sufficient resources to obtain multiple types of information from multiple sources (parents, child, teacher) using a variety of assessment methods. When time and resources permit, direct observations of defiant and ADHD behaviors in the classroom could also be made by school personnel. At the very least, telephone contact with a child's teacher should be made to follow-up on his or her responses to the child behavior rating scales and to obtain greater detail about the classroom behavior problems of the defiant child. To this list of assessment methods would be added others necessary to address any comorbid problems often found in conjunction with ADHD in children.

REFERENCES

Abidin, R. R. (1986). *The Parenting Stress Index.* Charlottesville, VA: Pediatric Psychology Press.

Achenbach, T. M. (1991). *Child Behavior Checklist—Cross-Informant Version.* (Available from Thomas Achenbach, PhD, Child and Adolescent Psychiatry, Department of Psychiatry University of Vermont, 5 South Prospect Street, Burlington, VT 05401)

Achenbach, T. M., & Edelbrock, C. S. (1983). *Manual for the Child Behavior Profile and Child Behavior Checklist.* Burlington, VT: Author.

Achenbach, T. M., & Edelbrock, C. (1986). *Manual for the Teacher Report Form and the Child Behavior Profile.* Burlington, VT: Thomas Achenbach.

Achenbach, T. M., McConaughy, S. H., & Howell, C. T. (1987). Child/adolescent behavioral and emotional problems: Implications of cross informant correlations for situational specificity. *Psychological Bulletin, 101,* 213–232.

Adams, G. L. (1984). *Normative Adaptive Behavior Checklist.* San Antonio, TX: The Psychological Corporation.

Applegate, B., Lahey, B. B., Hart, E. L., Waldman, I., Biederman, J., Hynd, G. W., Barkley, R. A., Ollendick, T., Frick, P. J., Greenhill, L., McBurnett, K., Newcorn, J., Kerdyk, L., Garfinkel, B., & Shaffer, D. (1997). Validity of the age of onset criterion for ADHD: A report from the DSM-IV field trials. *Journal of the American Academy of Child and Adolescent Psychiatry, 36,* 1211–1221.

Altepeter, T. S., & Breen, M. J. (1992). Situational variation in problem behavior at home and school in attention deficit disorder with hyperactivity: A factor analytic study. *Journal of Child Psychology and Psychiatry, 33,* 741–748.

American Psychiatric Association. (1949). *Diagnostic and statistical manual of mental disorders* (4th ed.). Washington, DC: Author.

Atkins, M. S., & Pelham, W. E. (1992). School-based assessment of attention deficit-hyperactivity disorder. In S. E. Shaywitz & B. A. Shaywitz (Eds.), *Attention deficit disorder comes of age: Toward the twenty-first century* (pp. 69–88). Austin, TX: Pro-Ed.

Barkley, R. A. (1981). *Hyperactive children: A handbook for diagnosis and treatment.* New York: Guilford Press.

Barkley, R. A. (1987). *Defiant children: A clinician's manual for parent training.* New York: Guilford Press.

Barkley, R. A. (1988). Child behavior rating scales and checklists. In M. Rutter, H. Tuma, & I. Lann (Eds.), *Assessment and diagnosis in child psychopathology.* (pp. 113–155). New York: Guilford Press.

Barkley, R. A. (1990). *Attention-deficit hyperactivity disorder: A handbook for diagnosis and treatment.* New York: Guilford Press.

Barkley, R. A. (1997). *ADHD and the nature of self-control.* New York: Guilford Press.

Barkley, R. A., & Biederman, J. (1997). Towards a broader definition of the age of onset criterion for attention deficit hyperactivity disorder. *Journal of the American Academy of Child and Adolescent Psychiatry, 36,* 1204–1210.

Barkley, R. A., DuPaul, G. J., & McMurray, M. B. (1990). A comprehensive evaluation of attention deficit disorder with and without hyperactivity. *Journal of Consulting and Clinical Psychology, 58,* 775–789.

Barkley, R. A., & Edelbrock, C. S. (1987). Assessing situational variation in children's behavior problems: The Home and School Situations Questionnaires. In R. Prinz (Ed.), *Advances in behavioral assessment of children and families* (Vol. 3, pp. 157–176). Greenwich, CT: JAI Press.

Barkley, R. A., Fischer, M., Edelbrock, C. S., & Smallish, L. (1991). The adolescent outcome of hyperactive children diagnosed by research criteria: III. Mother–child interactions, family conflicts, and maternal psychopathology. *Journal of Child Psychology and Psychiatry, 32,* 233–256.

Barkley, R. A., & Murphy, K. R. (1998). *Attention-deficit hyperactivity disorder: A clinical workbook* (2nd ed.). New York: Guilford Press

Beck, A. T., Steer, R. A., & Garbin, M. G. (1988). Psychometric properties of the Beck Depression Inventory: Twenty-five years of evaluation. *Clinical Psychology Review, 8,* 77–100.

Biederman, J., Keenan, K., & Faraone, S. V. (1990). Parent-based diagnosis of attention deficit disorder predicts a diagnosis based on teacher report. *American Journal of Child and Adolescent Psychiatry, 29,* 698–701.

Breen, M. J., & Barkley, R. A. (1988). Child psychopathology and parenting stress in girls and boys having attention deficit disorder with hyperactivity. *Journal of Pediatric Psychology, 13,* 265–280.

Campbell, S. B. (1990). *Behavior problems in preschool children: Clinical and developmental issues.* New York: Guilford Press.

Campbell, S. B., & Ewing, L. J. (1990). Follow-up of hard to manage preschoolers: Adjustment at age 9 and predictors of continuing symptoms. *Journal of Child Psychology and Psychiatry, 31,* 871–889.

Costello, E. J., Edelbrock, C. S., Costello, A. J., Dulcan, M. K., Burns, B. J., & Brent, D. (1988). Psychopathology in pediatric primary care: The new hidden morbidity. *Pediatrics, 82,* 415–424.

Derogatis, L. R. (1985). *Manual for the Symptom Checklist 90—Revised (SCL-90-R).* Baltimore, Author.

Dodge, K. A., McClaskey, C. L., & Feldman, E. (1985). A situational approach to the assessment of social competence in children. *Journal of Consulting and Clinical Psychology, 53,* 344–353.

DuPaul, G. R. (1991). Parent and teacher ratings of ADHD symptoms: Psychometric properties in a community-based sample. *Journal of Clinical Child Psychology, 20,* 2425–2453.

DuPaul, G. J., Anastopoulos, A. D., Power, T. J., Reid, R., Ikeda, M. J., & McGoey, K. E. (1997). *Parent ratings of attention-deficit/hyperactivity disorder symptoms: Factor structure, normative data, and psychometric properties.* Manuscript submitted for publication.

DuPaul, G. J., & Barkley, R. A. (1992). Situational variability of attention problems: Psychometric properties of the Revised Home and School Situations Questionnaires. *Journal of Clinical Child Psychology, 21,* 178–188.

DuPaul, G. J., Power, T. J., Anastopoulos, A. D., Reid, R., McGoey, K. E., & Ikeda, M. J. (in press). Teacher ratings of attention-deficit/hyperactivity disorder symptoms: Factor structure, normative data, and psychometric properties. *Psychological Assessment.*

DuPaul, G. J., Rapport, M. D., & Perriello, L. M. (1991). Teacher ratings of academic skills: The development of the Academic Performance Rating Scale. School *Psychology Review, 20,* 284–300.

DuPaul, G. J., & Stoner, G. (1994). *ADHD in the schools: Assessment and intervention strategies.* New York: Guilford Press.

Evans, S. W., Vallano, G., & Pelham, W. (1994). Treatment of parenting behavior with a psychostimulant: A case study of an adult with attention-deficit hyperactivity disorder. *Journal of Child and Adolescent Psychopharmacology, 4,* 63–69.

Fischer, M., Barkley, R. A., Fletcher, K., & Smallish, L. (1993). The stability of dimensions of behavior in ADHD and normal children over an 8 year period. *Journal of Abnormal Child Psychology, 21,* 315–337.

Gresham, F., & Elliott, S. (1990). *Social Skills Rating System.* Circle Pines, MN: American Guidance Service.

Hinshaw, S. P. (1994). *Attention deficits and hyperactivity in children.* Thousand Oaks, CA: Sage.

Hinshaw, S. P., Han, S. S., Erhardt, D., & Huber, A. (1992). Internalizing and externalizing behavior problems in preschool children: Correspondence among parent and teacher ratings and behavior observations. *Journal of Clinical Child Psychology, 21,* 143–150.

Hinshaw, S. P., & Nigg, J. (in press). Behavioral rating scales in the assessment of disruptive behavior disorders in childhood. In D. Shaffer & J. Richters (Eds.), *Assessment in child psychopathology.* New York: Plenum.

Lachar, D. (1982). *Personality Inventory for Children (PIC): Revised Format Manual Supplement.* Los Angeles: Western Psychological Services. (Available from Western Psychological Services, 12031 Wilshire Boulevard, Los Angeles, CA 90027-1261)

Lahey, B. B., Applegate, B., McBurnett, K., Biederman, J., Greenhill, L., Hynd, G. W., Barkley, R. A., Newcorn, J., Jensen, P., Richters, J., Garfinkel, B., Kerdyk, L., Frick, P. J., Ollendick, T., Perez, D., Hart, E. L., Waldman, I., & Shaffer, D. (1994). DSM-IV field trials for attention deficit/hyperactivity disorder in children and adolescents. *Journal of the American Academy of Child and Adolescent Psychiatry, 151,* 1673–1685.

Lahey, B. B., Pelham, W. E., Schaughency, E. A., Atkins, M. S., Murphy, H. A., Hynd, G. W., Russo, M., Hartdagen, S., & Lorys-Vernon, A. (1988). Dimensions and types of attention deficit disorder with hyperactivity in children: A factor and cluster-analytic approach. *Journal of the American Academy of Child and Adolescent Psychiatry, 27,* 330–335.

Latham, P., & Latham, R. (1992). *ADD and the law.* Washington, DC: JKL Communications.

Locke, H. J., & Wallace, K. M. (1959). Short marital adjustment and prediction tests: Their reliability and validity. *Journal of Marriage and Family Living, 21,* 251–255.

Loeber, R., Green, S., Lahey, B. B., & Stouthamer-Loeber, M. (1991). Differences and similarities between children, mothers, and teachers as informants on disruptive behavior disorders. *Journal of Abnormal Child Psychology, 19,* 75–95.

Mash, E. J., & Barkley, R. A. (Eds.). (1996). *Child psychopathology.* New York: Guilford Press.

Mash, E. J., & Barkley, R. A. (Eds.). (1998). *Treatment of childhood disorders* (2nd ed.). New York: Guilford Press.

Matson, J. L., Rotatori, A. F., & Helsel, W. J. (1983). Development of a rating scale to measure social skills in children: The Matson Evaluation of Social Skills with Youngsters (MESSY). *Behavior Research and Therapy, 21,* 335–340.

McMurray, M. B., & Barkley, R. A. (1997). The hyperactive child. In R. B. David (Ed.), *Child and adolescent neurology* (2nd ed., pp. 561–571). St. Louis: Mosby.

Murphy, K., & Barkley, R. A. (1996). Prevalence of DSM-IV symptoms of ADHD in adult licensed drivers: Implications for clinical diagnosis. *Journal of Attention Disorders, 1,* 147–161.

Newcomb, A. F., Bukowski, W. M., & Pattee, L. (1993). Children's peer relations: A meta-analytic review of popular, rejected, neglected, controversial, and average sociometric status. *Psychological Bulletin, 113,* 99–128.

Palfrey, J. S., Levine, M. D., Walker, D. K., & Sullivan, M. (1985). The emergence of attention deficits in early childhood: A prospective study. *Developmental and Behavioral Pediatrics, 6,* 339–348.

Reeves, J. C., Werry, J., Elkind, G. S., & Zametkin, A. (1987). Attention deficit, conduct, oppositional, and anxiety disorders in children: II. Clinical characteristics. *Journal of the American Academy of Child and Adolescent Psychiatry, 26,* 133–143.

Reynolds, C., & Kamphaus, R. (1994). *Behavioral Assessment System for Children.* (Available from American Guidance Service, 4201 Woodland Road, Circle Pines, MN 55014)

Roizen, N. J., Blondis, T. A., Irwin, M., & Stein, M. (1994). Adaptive functioning in children with attention-deficit hyperactivity disorder. *Archives of Pediatric and Adolescent Medicine, 148,* 1137–1142.

Shaywitz, S. E., & Shaywitz, B. A. (1984). Diagnosis and management of attention deficit disorder: A pediatric perspective. *Pediatric Clinics of North America, 31*, 429–457.

Sleator, E. K., & Ullmann, R. K. (1981). Can the physician diagnose hyperactivity in the office? *Pediatrics, 67*, 13–17.

Sparrow, S. S., Baila, D. A., & Cicchetti, D. V. (1984). *Vineland Adaptive Behavior Scales* (Available from American Guidance Service, 4201 Woodland Road, Circle Pines, MN 55014)

Wahler, R. G. (1980). The insular mother: Her problems in parent–child treatment. *Journal of Applied Behavior Analysis, 13*, 207–219.

Wolf, S. M., & Forsythe, A. (1978). Behavior disturbance, phenobarbital, and febrile seizures. *Pediatrics, 61*, 728–731.

Wozniak, J., Biederman, J., Kiely, K., Ablon, S., Faraone, S. V., Mundy, E., & Mennin, D. (1995). Mania-like symptoms suggestive of childhood-onset bipolar disorder in clinically referred children. *Journal of the American Academy of Child and Adolescent Psychiatry, 34*, 867–876.

Chapter 9

TESTS AND OBSERVATIONAL MEASURES

Michael Gordon
Russell A. Barkley

Over the past decade, researchers have made substantial progress developing objective tools for assessing Attention-Deficit/Hyperactivity Disorder (ADHD) symptoms in children. Several of the most popular tests now boast robust normative data and more detailed psychometrics. Despite ongoing debate, a rough consensus is also emerging about the proper role of such tests within the diagnostic process. Our review attempts to place psychological testing in context and to provide a general road map for making decisions regarding their inclusion and interpretation.

Incorporating information based on a child's actual behavior still has strong intuitive appeal, especially for a diagnostic process so heavily founded upon perception and opinion. The essential attraction of objective measures is that they seem to provide a beacon of reality when the diagnostic seas are cluttered by inconsistent reports and unreliable information. Indeed, research regarding the nature of subjective reports (whether formatted through a rating scale or gathered from semistructured interviews) discourages supreme confidence in their reliability. Although they represent the heart of the diagnostic process, they nonetheless are subject to a full spectrum of distorting influences of the sort detailed in the previous edition of this book (Barkley, 1990).

Despite advances in our knowledge about the role of psychological testing and the allure of numbers over perception, the search for accurate and reliable measures of ADHD symptoms has not yielded a litmus test. The absence of a gold standard for the diagnosis as well as the heterogeneity of the disorder itself precludes any one test (and, for that matter, rating scale or interview format) from claiming pinpoint accuracy. At best, research in this arena has produced techniques that can have some clinical utility but cannot supplant other sources of information. Perhaps their strongest contributions are in identifying comorbid conditions or in substantiating alternative diagnoses.

THE POTENTIAL CONTRIBUTIONS
OF PSYCHOLOGICAL TESTING

In our view, psychological testing can help the clinician address the three fundamental questions that lie at the heart of all evaluations for ADHD:

1. *Is the diagnosis of ADHD justified?* Clinicians often seek psychological testing for help in ruling ADHD in or out. Because no one source of information is free from potential error, inclusion of additional data may be indicated, especially when disagreements among other sources are wide or there are concerns about the credibility of other clinical information. Also, clinicians hope to gather information that will refine the diagnosis by providing evidence regarding severity, potential responsiveness to therapy, and outcome.

2. *If the diagnosis of ADHD is not justified, are there alternative explanations that better account for the symptoms?* A competent evaluation for ADHD works hard to rule out the possibility that presenting complaints are either variants of normality or are better tied to other diagnostic entities. Psychological testing can play an important role in this process because it can compare one child's functioning to nonreferred children with similar demographic characteristics. Therefore, it can place a youngster at points along population distributions for multiple traits and abilities. Such a profiling of scores for a particular patient often becomes indispensable for determining the potential role of intellectual and socioemotional factors.

3. *If the ADHD diagnosis is justified, are there comorbid conditions that should be identified and treated?* Because of the high rates of comorbidity (see Chapter 4, this volume), it is likely that a child with ADHD will exhibit other problems. Psychological testing is typically regarded as key in documenting such coexisting disorders. Clinicians hope that this information will put them in a better position to develop a comprehensive treatment program that best addresses the child's full mosaic of needs.

Our review of psychological testing is organized around these three domains: identifying ADHD, exploring alternate diagnoses, and documenting comorbidity. By way of overview, we make the following points:

- Psychological testing is usually most productive when the goals of the assessment are clearly established from the beginning. Is testing necessary primarily to document ADHD, to rule out alternative explanations, or to identify comorbid conditions? Or is it some combination of all three domains? Psychodiagnostic fishing expeditions often are inefficient and counterproductive.
- The goals of testing (and its potential contribution) vary widely depending on the nature of the clinical setting. In an ADHD subspecialty clinic, testing aimed at documenting the disorder may be less useful because the likelihood of identifying a youngster as ADHD is already high. Testing might be more important for establishing levels of severity or for identifying comorbid conditions. In most clinic settings, a test's ability to discriminate normal from abnormal children will also be less relevant because most referred children are not normal; they do have some disorder. For example, at the University of Massachusetts Medical Center ADHD Clinic, fewer than 6% of referred children are without any disorder (i.e., are not probably normal). Therefore, the greatest need in this type of setting is for a test that aids in differential diagnosis. Unfortunately, none of the specific tests reviewed in this chapter have been thoroughly evaluated from this perspective. A study by Matier-Sharma, Perachio, Newcorn, Sharma, and Halperin (1995) did evaluate a research version of the continuous performance test (discussed later in this chapter). Although they found that the test accurately classified children with abnormal scores as having ADHD in comparison to normal children (90–96%!), it accurately classified those same children with abnormal scores as having ADHD or some other psychiatric disorder at a level of only 50–60%. The accuracy of the test in predicting children with normal scores as not having ADHD in that same comparison (ADHD vs. other psychiatric disorders) was 62–73%. If these data replicated across a variety of clinic settings and populations, it may be that psychological or neuropsychological

testing is at its most limited utility in the domain that many clinicians would find it most relevant. In other settings with lower base rates of abnormality, for example in speech and languages clinics or schools, a test's ability to discriminate normal from abnormal may be more germane.

• Although data generated by psychological testing might contribute to the diagnostic process, *they cannot be considered in isolation.* Data from such testing are never conclusive (although, to be fair, no source of information has a lock on reality). With the possible exception of retardation, testing data alone cannot point directly to a psychiatric or learning disorder. In our view, problems with psychological tests derive not from their use, per se, but from their potential for overinterpretation. Testing is most abused when scores are judged out of the context of a child's history and current functioning. A diagnosis based entirely on test scores is a diagnosis to doubt.

• Psychological testing is at its weakest in determining etiology. To the best of our knowledge, no index from a psychological test can determine why a particular child suffers from a particular disorder or set of disorders. Proclamations of causality are especially risky in the ADHD arena because of the disorder's high degree of heritability. Clinicians should be especially careful about making assumptions about the presence of some specific neurological syndrome based on psychological testing.

• The patina of scientific credibility afforded by the standardization and, at times, computerization of tests does not obviate the need for credible psychometric data (Gordon, 1987). Advertising claims, testimonials, or justifications based on clinical experience or theoretical speculation cannot substitute for scientific information. The administration of psychological testing should enhance diagnostic rigor, not cloud matters further. At the same time, evaluating the validity of psychological testing for ADHD is inherently daunting because the field lacks a gold standard for diagnosis. Unfortunately, most studies purporting to explore test validity draw conclusions as if such a benchmark existed. But, in essence, it is hard to establish whether an arrow hits the mark when the mark's location is itself uncertain. Nonetheless, any measure employed should offer credible information regarding its psychometric properties. Specifically, a test or battery of tests should boast the following characteristics based on published research:

Ample standardization
Reliability of administration
Test–retest reliability
Evidence that it can discriminate among diagnostic groups (ADHD vs. normal, ADHD vs. other clinical entities, or other clinical entities from normal or other clinical entities)
Proof that it enhances diagnostic accuracy and treatment planning (even if it does not have high predictive value)
Demonstrated practicality

The last two points on our list warrant some elaboration. Much of the scientific focus on psychological testing falls, appropriately, on the capacity of a test to predict group status. Most studies explore the degree of agreement among various clinical measures, often with a selected combination established as the benchmark. However, a psychological test can be of significant value even if it does not wholly agree with other measures. For example, a test may provide unique information regarding the severity of pathology or the amenability of a child to certain treatments. A test might also have value in predicting outcome or confirming a diagnosis in unique populations or age groups. Therefore, a single-minded focus on discriminative power may overlook other possible contributions of testing (Fischer, Newby, & Gordon, 1995). Nevertheless, when test developers argue for the value of their tests in making diagnostic classifications, data must be provided from peer-reviewed scientific studies that the test, in fact, achieves those aims.

The requirement that tests should be practical to administer and interpret reflects the realities of modern clinical practice. As demands for cost efficiency mount, practitioners cannot afford to use measures that are unwieldy, time-consuming, or complicated. The ever-increasing focus on practicality has influenced our recommendations for psychological testing and observational techniques. Simply put, it makes little sense to consider approaches that are impractical, even if they might offer meaningful information.

A REVIEW OF PSYCHOLOGICAL TESTS

Our review of commonly administered psychological tests would be enhanced if we actually knew from current survey data which tests were commonly administered by clinicians who conduct ADHD evaluations. Aside from one survey of practitioners who use a particular continuous performance test (Gordon, 1994), this information is unavailable. However, our impression is that many clinicians, especially psychologists, administer a wide variety of psychological and neuropsychological tests, from IQ screening measures to inkblots. The various tests incorporated into ADHD-related evaluations tend to fall into four categories: (1) cognitive/achievement tests, (2) general neuropsychological batteries, (3) individual neuropsychological tests, and (4) projective/personality tests. We review measures in each category for the extent to which they have been documented as valid and useful for clinical determinations.

Intelligence/Achievement Tests

Information from intelligence and achievement testing is often considered central to differential diagnosis. Most clinicians routinely request prior evaluations from the school so that such information can be incorporated into the ADHD assessment. If such testing is not available, practitioners usually suggest that it be pursued. Indeed, some form of psychoeducational testing is often administered as a matter of course within a comprehensive ADHD evaluation, even if previous testing is available.

Are intelligence/achievement tests useful in the identification of ADHD? To date, these tests have not been shown to be of value in detecting ADHD characteristics. In other words, no subtest or configuration of subtests is sensitive or specific to the disorder. We arrive at this conclusion based largely on studies investigating the Freedom from Distractibility Factor of the Wechsler scales. This factor has been widely touted as a measure of attention and distractibility in children and has been adopted by many as a clinical measure of ADHD. It consists of the scores on the Arithmetic, Digit Span, and Coding subtests and was called Freedom from Distractibility "because of research with hyperactive children showing that drug therapy leads to decreased distractibility and improved memory and arithmetic skills in these youngsters" (Kaufman, 1980, p. 179). Scores on this factor have been found to correlate to a low but significant degree with other tests of attention (Klee & Garfinkel, 1983).

Evidence is conflicting, however, as to whether the tests forming this factor can adequately discriminate groups of ADHD from normal or reading-disabled children (Brown & Wynne, 1982; Milich & Loney, 1979). A recent large-scale study of Wechsler Intelligence Scale for Children (WISC) profiles of 465 Dutch children suggested that both mood disorders and ADHD in children may be associated with lower scores on this factor than for children with other psychiatric disorders (Rispens et al., 1997). Yet several other studies found that this factor was unable to distinguish ADD children with hyperactivity from those without hyperactivity or from learning-disabled and normal children (Anastopoulos, Spisto, & Maher, 1994; Barkley, Dupaul, & McMurray, 1990; Golden, 1996). Others, however, found group differences on these tests (see Chapter 3, this volume). These subtests appear to assess short-term or verbal working memory, facility with numbers, perceptual–motor speed, visual–spatial skills, and arithmetic calculation. Consequently, poor performances on this factor do not indicate in any straightforward way that deficits in attention account for them. Moreover, a number of investigators urged caution in interpreting these subtests as measures of distractibility, believing its label to be an oversimplification and misleading (Ownby & Matthews, 1985; Stewart & Moely, 1983; Wielkiewicz, 1990; Wielkiewicz & Palmer, 1996). Studies using the WISC-III version to assess depressed third factor scores have not found them to be reliably associated with the diagnosis of ADHD. Very poor rates of classification were noted, such that between 48% and 77% of ADHD children would be classified as normal (false negatives) if this factor were used for diagnostic purposes (Anastopoulos et al., 1994; Golden, 1996). Indeed, Greenblatt, Mattes, and Trad (1991), in a study of 526 clinic-referred children, found that although 11% had depressed third factor scores, this fact was relatively nonspecific to any disorder. Only 4.8% of the children with a diagnosis of ADHD according to the third edition of the *Diagnostic and Statistical Manual of Mental Disorders* (DSM-III; American Psychiatric Association, 1980) had depressed third factor scores. For all these reasons, we do not recommend that this factor be used in assessing attention or in establishing evidence for or against a diagnosis of ADHD.

IQ and achievement data can contribute to establishing the ADHD diagnosis in more indirect ways because the determination hinges, in part, on documenting severity of impairment. The argument that a youngster's deficits are significant and meaningful can be bolstered by evidence of serious problems acquiring age-appropriate skills. Well-normed tests can provide evidence of impairment relative both to the general population and also to the child's innate abilities. The argument is, of course, most compelling if evidence also exists from teacher reports that skill attainment has been heavily affected by ADHD-type symptoms.

Such tests also contribute to the diagnosis of ADHD by generating information that may help to rule in or out other possible explanations for presenting complaints. Consider the following scenario: A girl is referred because of inattention, poor concentration, and underachievement. The teachers report that she is especially unfocused during assignments that involve reading and creative thinking. Furthermore, although the parents indicate that their daughter can be somewhat fidgety and avoidant when frustrated by school demands, they do not paint a picture of severe impulsiveness across most settings. Because the symptoms of inattention and poor concentration are relatively circumscribed, the clinician becomes suspicious that learning problems may be more at the heart of this girl's difficulties than ADHD, per se. In this instance, administration of IQ and achievement testing might be instrumental in ruling out the possibility that the girl's inattention was secondary to problems handling grade-appropriate academic tasks.

More generally, IQ/achievement data help the clinician determine cognitive factors that might contribute to a youngster's inattention and academic underachievement. As we have indicated, they are especially valuable in ensuring that the child's symptoms are not largely a reaction to being overwhelmed by academic demands. Because specific learning disabilities so commonly coexist with ADHD (see Chapter 3, this volume), cognitively oriented testing also can play a key role in their identification.

Should IQ/achievement testing be conducted in every case? Our opinion is that clinicians should routinely have access to some estimate of overall intellectual functioning, whether the information is gleaned from past records or from current administration of a screening measure. Without some documentation that the youngster's abilities fall with a normal range, the possibility that youngster is either unusually limited or gifted cannot be eliminated. Because parent and teacher estimation of a child's intellectual level is not always accurate, some formal assessment may be necessary even when all involved are convinced that the youngster's abilities are average.

Although clinicians should have at least a rough estimate of the child's intellectual abilities, we do not feel that comprehensive psychoeducational assessment should necessarily be a routine component of all ADHD evaluations. If sufficient information is not often already available in the child's record, the testing can usually be administered by the school at no cost to the family. In the least, we feel that parents should be advised that they can have their child tested free of charge through their local school district.

If evidence from parent and teacher reports indicate that the youngster may suffer from some specific learning weakness (beyond the general academic underachievement common to all ADHD children), a comprehensive psychoeducational evaluation may be warranted. Data from such an evaluation might identify specific learning disabilities as either the primary condition or as comorbid to ADHD symptomatolgy. Of course, it may also rule out learning disabilities altogether. In any of these scenarios, data from testing would ultimately affect not only the diagnosis but also treatment planning.

Although complete psychoeducational testing may be justified in certain cases, clinicians often find it hard to interpret the data, especially for youngsters who have a highly impulsive style. The meaning of low test scores can be unclear if a youngster spent much of the session grabbing test materials, hiding under the table, and running to the bathroom. For highly distractible and active children, the gulf between competence and performance looms large. A recent study by Aylward, Gordon, and Verhulst (1997), for example, demonstrated that subtest scores from pschoeducational testing (including IQ and achievement scores) are pervasively, albeit moderately, correlated with measures of attention and self-control. Similar findings were reported by Billings (1996) and Gordon, Thomason, and Cooper (1990). Thus, for children with ADHD symptoms, testing for cognitive abilities and achievement may more accurately reflect actual competence if it is administered while the child is on a therapeutic dose of medication.

General Neuropsychological Batteries

Evaluations for ADHD may include administration of formal neuropsychological test batteries, such as the Halstead–Reitan (H-R) and the Luria–Nebraska Neuropsychological Battery (LNNB). These core batteries consist of various subtests that assess a broad range of neuropsychological functions. Their inclusion is typically justified by the compelling evidence of a strong neurobiological basis for ADHD symptomatolgy. The rationale is as follows: If neurobiological factors, particularly frontal lobe dysfunction, heavily contribute to ADHD symptom formation, neuropsychological testing should be useful in testing for the presence and strength of those factors.

Unfortunately, the fact that a series of tests is characterized as neuropsychological does not guarantee that it actually taps into relevant neuropsychological processes. In our review of the literature, we can establish no basis for suggesting routine administration of neuropsychological batteries within an ADHD evaluation (we cover individual tests in the next section). As for identification purposes, no single subtest or combination of subtests within the LNNB or the H-R demonstrated predictive value. For example, an article by Shaughency et al. (1989) showed that none of the subtests on the LNNB were related in any meaningful way to ADHD symptoms.

We have also been unable to justify core neuropsychological testing for highlighting alternative explanations for symptoms or for identifying comorbid conditions. Convincing data simply have not be presented demonstrating that neuropsychological testing of children contributes to the understanding of a child's functioning in a manner that is more predictive or prescriptive than a standard psychoeducational assessment. Although general neuropsychological testing may indicate significant and relevant weaknesses (especially if the battery includes IQ and achievement measures), those deficits will often either be clear from the child's academic functioning or reflected on IQ or academic testing itself without the need to pursue further neuropsychological testing.

We are concerned about two other issues related to routine administration of extensive, multitest batteries. First, the inclusion of many measures raises the possibility of false positive–type errors. Because of sequential error, the probability is high that at least several test scores from an array of 70 or 80 will be abnormal. The likelihood of overidentification of problems increases further because the psychometric properties for these tests have not been well established for child populations. Therefore, the scatter-shot quality of comprehensive neuropsychological testing almost guarantees some indication of abnormality.

Our other concern is tied more to economics than to methodology: If one accepts the proposition that most if not all the tests administered in a neuropsychological battery are of dubious diagnostic benefit for ADHD-related decisions, routine testing could fairly be judged by third-party payers as frivolous. Given the nature of our health system, it is not unlikely that psychological testing in general will be unfairly painted with the same brush. Because psychodiagnostic assessment certainly has a legitimate role in the diagnosis of other childhood disorders, we are concerned that the entire enterprise will be tarnished because of overtesting for ADHD. The exception may be in those instances in which evidence from history and imaging studies are suggestive of brain injury.

Individual Neuropsychological Measures

Although routine administration of core neuropsychological batteries is hard to justify, certain individual tests may have a role in the evaluation process. Before we actually review the most common of these techniques, we want to discuss the current state of the testing art: With the exception of certain computerized tests, remarkably little is actually known about many of the tests developed or adapted for the assessment of ADHD. For most, the totality of relevant published data might involve 50 clinic-referred children selected by somewhat idiosyncratic criteria. The scientific literature is often so sparse regarding a given measure that we are hesitant to comment either way about the test's utility. One or two studies should not be the basis on which a test is praised or damned, especially in light of the well-documented vagaries of clinical research. Therefore, the real conclusion to be drawn from an overview of this literature is that entirely too little empirical study has been conducted for a clinical activity that is so common, time-consuming, and costly. With these sentiments as a backdrop, we review the oft-cited individual measures.

Wisconsin Card Sort Test

The Wisconsin Card Sort Test (WCST; Grant & Berg, 1948) is one of the most commonly used measures of adult frontal lobe dysfunction (Lezak, 1983). An examiner presents a series of cards with various colored geometric shapes and numbers of shapes on them. The subject is to sort these cards based on a categorizing rule known only to the examiner (color, number, shape). The examiner gives the subject feedback after each effort to sort a card indicating whether the sort is correct or incorrect. From this feedback, subjects must deduce the categorizing rule as quickly as possible to limit their number of sorting errors. After a certain number of such trials, the examiner shifts the sorting rule to a different category and the subject must again deduce the rule from the limited feedback provided. Norms for children were reported by Chelune and Baer (1986). Test–retest reliability appears to be satisfactory (Lezak, 1983). Chelune Ferguson, Koon, and Dickey (1986) reported significant differences between ADHD and normal children on this particular test. However, subsequent efforts have failed to replicate these findings or have produced highly inconsistent results (Fischer, Barkley, Edelbrock, & Smallish, 1990; Grodzinsky & Diamond, 1992; see also Chapter 3, this volume). For instance, Barkley and Grodzinsky (1994) found that this test accurately predicted the presence of ADHD in only 50–71% of true cases while accurately predicting the absence of the disorder in only 49–56% of cases. False-negative rates were 61–89% and overall accuracy of classification ranged from 49% to 58%, depending on which score from the WCST was used. *Such findings do not encourage the diagnostic use of this test for ADHD.*

Stroop Word–Color Test

The Stroop Word–Color Test (Stroop, 1935) is a timed test measuring the ability to suppress or inhibit automatic responses. Children must read the names of colors although the names are printed in a different colored ink from the color specified in the name (e.g., the word "red" is printed in blue ink). Test–retest reliability is well established as is sensitivity to frontal lobe functions in adults (Lezak, 1983). Almost all studies employing this test have found groups of ADHD children to perform more poorly than control groups of children (see Chapter 2, this volume). Barkley and Grodzinsky (1994) found that this test accurately predicted presence of disorder in 88% of diagnosed cases but predicted the absence of disorder with only 43% accuracy and thus produced a false-negative rate of 53%. Its overall classification accuracy was only 68%. This finding clearly indicates that *this test cannot be used to accurately diagnose children as having ADHD.*

Hand Movements Test

The Hand Movements Test (Kaufman & Kaufman, 1983) is a well-standardized and normed test for children based on a traditional measure of frontal lobe function in adults. Children are presented with progressively longer sequences of three hand movements which they must imitate. The test has acceptable reliability and normative data and three studies have shown it to differentiate groups of ADHD from groups of normal children (Grodzinsky & Diamond, 1992; Mariani & Barkley, 1997) and from ADD children who are not hyperactive (Barkley, Grodzinsky, & Dupaul, 1992). Its sensitivity to ADHD may rest in the well-known fine motor coordination difficulties often seen in these children as well as in their inattention to the task itself, especially as sequences of movements become progressively longer. Yet, once again, when subjected to appropriate analysis of its classification accuracy, this test suffers from many of the same problems as those mentioned earlier. Among children with abnormal scores, 88% were found to have ADHD. However, it had a 66% rate of classifying children without the disorder, a false-negative rate of 63%, and an overall classification accuracy of only 70%. Thus, as with the other neuropsychological tests reviewed here, its major problem is in misclassifying children as normal who actually have the disorder (false negatives). *Again, we must caution against the use of this test for the diagnosis of ADHD.*

Rey–Osterrieth Complex Figure Drawing

This test (see Lezak, 1995) is a paper-and-pencil task requiring planning and visual–spatial–constructional abilities and is sensitive to deficits from frontal lobe injuries. The task requires the subject to copy a complex geometric shape. The Waber and Holmes (1985) scoring procedure is often used, yielding scores for organization age (five levels) and style (four categories). Several studies of groups of ADHD children have shown that they perform this test more poorly on average than do normal children (see Chapter 3, this volume). However, once again, Barkley and Grodzinsky (1994) found that although abnormal test scores accurately predicted the presence of ADHD 100% of the time, normal test scores accurately predicted the absence of disorder only 50% of the time, and the false-negative rate was a stunning 96%. Overall, the test accurately classified only 52% of the children. *Therefore, we urge clinicians not to employ this test for diagnostic purposes concerning ADHD.*

Trail Making Test (Parts A and B)

The Intermediate version is frequently used with children. It comprises two parts: A and B (Reitan & Wolfson, 1985). In Part A, the subject connects a series of numbered circles distributed arbitrarily on a page. Part B comprises circles that contain letters or numbers scattered randomly across the page. The subject is to alternate connecting numbers and letters in ascending order until the end of the sequences. The scores are the time taken to complete each part by the subject. Few studies have found this test to be useful for differentiating groups of ADHD children from control groups (Barkley et al., 1992). Barkley and Grodzinsky (1994) found that the tests accurately predicted presence of disorder 68–71% of the time, accurately predicted absence of disorder just 51% of the time, and had false negative rates of 80–82%. Overall classification accuracy was just 54%. Here, then is another test which *we must recommend against its use for diagnosing ADHD in children.*

Continuous Performance Tests

The most popular and widely studied form of testing for use in ADHD evaluations is based on a paradigm called the continuous performance test (CPT; Rosvold, Mirsky, Sarason, Bransome, & Beck, 1956). Although the CPT has been administered with many variations (e.g., visual, auditory, numbers, and characters), the most common one requires the youngster to observe a screen while individual letters or numbers are projected onto it at rapid pace (typically at one per second). The child is told to respond (e.g., press a button) when a certain stimulus or pair of stimuli in sequence appears. The scores derived from the CPT are the number of correct responses, number of target stimuli missed (omission errors), and number of responses following nontarget or incorrect stimuli (commission errors). The latter score is presumed to tap both sustained attention and impulse control whereas the two former measures are believed to assess sustained attention only (Sostek, Buchsbaum, & Rapoport, 1980).

Researchers have been examining versions of the CPT paradigm for almost 40 years. A wide-ranging literature has shown it to be the most reliable of psychological tests for discriminating groups of ADHD from normal children (Corkum & Siegel, 1993). It also is sensitive to stimulant drug effects among ADHD children and adolescents (Coons, Klorman, & Borgstedt, 1987; Fischer, 1996; Garfinkel et al., 1986). Although concerns abound about its actual discriminative ability and ecological validity (Barkley, 1991), the CPT nonetheless is the only psychological measure that seems to directly assess the core symptoms of the disorder, namely, impulsiveness and inattention. Moreover, the CPT assesses these dimensions without undue contamination from other cognitive factors, such as conceptual ability, visual scanning, and so on. In all its embodiments, the CPT places relatively little demand on subjects other than to sustain attention and to refrain from responding except in special circumstances.

The CPT serves as the paradigm for several commercially available performance measures including Conners's (1995) Continuous Performance Test, the Gordon Diagnostic System (GDS; Gordon, 1983), the Test of Variables of Attention (TOVA; Greenberg & Kindschi, 1996), and the Intermediate Visual and Auditory Continuous Performance Test (IVA; Sandford, Fine, & Goldman, 1995). Each format requires the child to respond to certain signals embedded in a series of irrelevant targets. Whereas each administers a CPT, the tasks vary considerably along what would seem to represent important dimensions, including the length of the task, the type of stimulus, and the instructions to the subject. For example, one version requires the child to respond based on the position of a certain graphic for 23 minutes, another presents numbers on a screen for 9 minutes, and still another presents a combination of numbers both visually and auditorally. The CPT that most differs from the traditional paradigm was developed by Conners (1995). In this test, the child is told to press a button until the target appears, at which time the child to inhibit responding, thereby requiring a different form of response inhibition.

Which CPT should a clinician choose? Because no data have been published on head-to-head comparisons for reliability, validity, or clinical utility, we cannot offer an empirically based opinion. It is therefore unclear whether these measures would differ from one another in their contributions to accurate identification, ruling out alternate explanations, or confirming comorbid conditions. It also is uncertain whether diagnosis would be more accurate or productive if some combination of these tests were administered. For example, some investigators say that attention should be assessed both in visual and in auditory modalities. Although some data suggest that children generally find auditory versions more difficult than visual ones (Aylward & Gordon, 1997), no one has presented data that show a superiority of one format over the other. Parenthetically, based on Barkley's theory of ADHD (see Chapter 7, this volume), it would be unlikely that a child would suffer problems with response inhibition in just one sensory modality.

In the absence of *Consumer Reports*-type comparisons, decisions must be based on the sort of parameters mentioned earlier in this chapter: practicality, robustness of standardization, reliability of administration, and the extent to which the technique has been scrutinized scientifically for its potential contributions (or lack thereof). Unfortunately, here again we are constrained by a literature that is limited in scope and depth. At the time of this writing, the TOVA, Conners CPT, and IVA have a combined total of only five published articles on issues related to standardization and discriminative ability. An additional article in a newsletter (Golden, 1996) did examine the predictive accuracy of the Conners CPT and found that it accurately predicted the presence of the disorder in only 57% of the cases. However, the study involved only 23 children and therefore can hardly be considered a definitive study of the classification accuracy of this test.

The only measure that has published information available on all these relevant dimensions was developed by the first author (M.G.). The GDS has been used extensively in research and clinical practice. This is a portable, solid-state, child-proofed computerized device that administers a 9-minute vigilance task wherein the child must press a button each time a specified, randomly presented numerical sequence (e.g., 1 followed by a 9) occurs. Another version of this task presents random distracters on either side of the center target. Normative data are available based on more than 1,000 children on the mainland United States ages 3 to 16 years (Gordon & Mettelman, 1988) and for Puerto Rican children (Bauermeister, Berrios, Jiminez, Acevedo, & Gordon, 1990). Norms are also available for an auditory version of this task (Gordon, Lewandowski, Clonan, & Malone, 1996). Gordon's CPT has been found to have satisfactory test–retest reliability (Gordon & Mettelman, 1988), to correlate modestly but significantly with other laboratory measures of attention (Barkley, 1991), to discriminate groups of ADHD from normal children (Barkley, DuPaul, & McMurray, 1991; Gordon, 1987; Grodzinsky & Diamond, 1992; Mariani & Barkley, 1997), and to be sensitive to moderate to high doses of stimulant medication (Barkley, Fischer, Newby, & Breen, 1988; Barkley, DuPaul, & McMurray, 1990; Fischer & Newby, 1991; Fischer, 1996; Rapport, Tucker, DuPaul, Merlo, Stoner, 1986). The GDS is useful in the assessment of children with hearing impairment (Mitchell & Quittner, 1996). A body of literature also suggests that poor GDS performance is tied to other neuropsychological measures (Grant, Ilai, Nussbaum, & Bigler, 1990) and to general academic underachievement (Aylward et al., 1997; Billings, 1996; Gordon, Mettelman, & Irwin, 1994).

As with the interpretation of any psychological test for the diagnosis of ADHD, interpreting the data from traditional validity studies of CPTs can be vexing because no gold standard is available to use for comparison with these tests (Gordon, 1993). Nonetheless, if we use either high scores on ADHD-related behavior rating scales and/or DSM clinical diagnoses as benchmarks, the GDS appears to accurately classify 83–90% of children with abnormal scores as ADHD (Barkley & Grodzinsky, 1994). Its classification accuracy for children with normal scores as being without the disorder (e.g., normal) is, however, 59–61%. Moreover, a range of 15% to 52% has been found for its false-negative rate (i.e., children rated by parents or teachers as having ADHD scoring normal on the test) (Gordon, Mettelman, & DiNiro 1989; Barkley & Grodzinsky, 1994; Trommer, Hoeppner, Lorber, & Armstrong, 1988). Therefore, as with all the neuropsychological tests discussed here, if a child performs well on this measure, it does not indicate that the child is normal or without ADHD. But it may have some diagnostic significance when a child otherwise considered ADHD performs normally on the GDS. Recent research by Fischer et al. (1995) shows that these children are typically rated as less impaired, more likely to show comorbid internalizing problems, and less likely to be prescribed stimulant medications. Data such as these suggest that, if anything, GDS performance might represent an indication of severity.

The false-positive rate of the instrument is good to excellent, with 2–17% of normal children being classified as ADHD (Gordon et al., 1989; Barkley & Grodzinsky, 1994). These kinds of data may be helpful in cases for which objective confirmation of the diagnosis is important. But even here the GDS cannot be used for objective *disconfirmation* of the disorder given the rate of false negatives found in some studies. Once again, the presence of an abnormal score probably (but not necessarily) indicates the presence of disorder whereas the presence of a normal score must go uninterpreted as it may not indicate the absence of disorder. As with rating scales, the test provides one source of information to be integrated with other sources in reaching a final diagnostic decision.

Cancellation Tasks

Several paper-and-pencil versions of CPT tasks have been used as methods of assessing attention. These tasks typically involve having the child scan a series of symbols (letters, numbers, shapes) presented in rows on sheets of paper. The child is typically required to draw a line through or under the target stimulus using a pencil. One such task which has shown promise in discriminating ADHD from normal children is the Children's Checking Task (CCT; Margolis, 1972). The CCT consists of seven pages with a series of 15 numerals per row printed in 16 rows on a page. A tape recorder reads off the numbers in each row, and the child is required to draw a line through each number as it is read. Discrepancies between the tape and printed page are to be circled by the child. There are seven discrepancies between the tape and printed pages. The CCT takes about 30 minutes to complete. Scores are derived for errors of omission (missed discrepancies) and errors of commission (numbers circled that were not discrepancies). Brown and Wynne (1982) found that the task discriminated groups of ADHD and reading-disabled children. The CCT correlates modestly but significantly with other measures of attention (Keogh & Margolis, 1976), often to a larger degree than any of the other laboratory measures (see Barkley, 1991). Perhaps this is because it is somewhat similar to academic accuracy demands made during work that children must do in the classroom. Nevertheless, its sensitivity to ADHD symptoms requires more research and replication of these initially promising results before it can be recommended for clinical practice.

Matching Familiar Figures Test

This Matching Familiar Figures Test (MFFT; Kagan, 1966) has a lengthy history of use in research studies investigating impulse control in normal and disturbed children and adolescents. This match-to-sample test involves the examiner presenting a picture of a recognizable object to the youngster who must choose the identical matching picture from among an array of six similar variants. The test includes 12 trials with scores derived for the mean time taken to the initial response (latency) and the total number of errors (incorrectly identified pictures). A longer version of the MFFT employing 20 stimulus trials (MFFT-20) has been developed (Cairns & Cammock, 1978). It is purported to achieve greater reliability among older children and adolescents (Messer & Brodzinsky, 1981). Unfortunately, more recent research on the original test often failed to find significant differences between ADHD and normal children (Barkley, et al., 1991; Fischer et al., 1990; Milich & Kramer, 1984). The MFFT has also shown conflicting and often negative results in detecting stimulant drug effects in ADHD children (Barkley, 1977; Barkley et al., 1991). Furthermore, norms for the adolescent population are not currently available for either version of this measure, thus limiting their use as diagnostic measures. Consequently, we do not endorse this instrument for use in clinical practice in making diagnostic decisions about ADHD children.

GDS Delay Task

This test, a part of the Gordon Diagnostic System discussed above, is a measure of response inhibition. It utilizes a paradigm of direct reinforcement of low rates. The child sits before the portable, computerized GDS device and is told to wait awhile before pressing a large blue button on the front panel of the device. Children are told that if they have waited long enough, they will earn a point when they push the button. If they press it too early, they must wait awhile before pushing the button again. Cumulative points are scored on a digital counter on the face of the device. The child is not informed of the actual delay required to earn reinforcement (6 seconds). The test lasts 8 minutes and has normative data for more than 1,000 children. Initial evidence (Gordon, 1979; Gordon & McClure, 1983; McClure & Gordon, 1984) indicated that the test discriminated groups of ADHD from non-ADHD and normal children, correlated significantly with parent and teacher ratings of hyperactivity and other lab measures of impulsivity, and had adequate test–retest reliability (Gordon & Mettelman, 1988). However, others (Barkley et al., 1988) have not found the task to be sensitive to stimulant drug effects in ADHD children and to correlate poorly if at all with ratings of hyperactivity by parents and teachers (Barkley, 1991). One benefit of such measures is that it allows a clinician to observe youngster in situation requiring inhibition and sustained attention. But the test has not been examined for its classification accuracy with regard to either discriminating ADHD from normal or ADHD from other psychiatric disorders and so its role in a diagnostic evaluation remains uncertain.

Measures of Activity

The measurement of activity level was discussed in the previous edition of this chapter (Barkley, 1990). Given that there have been no clinically meaningful advances in this field of study since that time, no further comment about such measures is made here. Although advances have been made in various technologies for the measurement of activity levels in children with ADHD (see Matier-Sharma et al., 1995; Teicher, Ito, Glod, & Barber, 1996), such improvements are most useful to research investigations of activity level rather than to making clinically accurate diagnoses. For instance, Matier-Sharma et al. (1995) examined the classification accuracy of a solid-state activity recording device (the actigraph) in judging children as either ADHD or normal and then as either ADHD or as having another psychiatric disorder. In the comparison of ADHD to normal, the activity measure accurately classified 91% of children with high activity scores as having ADHD. But it accurately classified children with low activity scores as being normal at a level of just 36%. The situation for the comparison of ADHD to other psychiatric disorders was worse. The presence of a high activity level predicted the presence of ADHD in this case with only 77% accuracy; the presence of a normal score predicted the presence of a non-ADHD disorder with an accuracy of just 63%. Such figures do not support a recommendation to use the activity measurement in the differential diagnosis of children with ADHD from either normal or children with other disorders. A parent and teacher rating scale of hyperactive–impulsive behavior would be a more economical and ecologically valid means of assessing this dimension of behavior than would the use of laboratory activity recording devices.

Projective Measures

No published studies demonstrate the predictive validity of projective tests (such as drawings, inkblots, or story-telling techniques) for the identification of ADHD. However, there is some indication of differences between ADHD and normals on the Rorschach Inkblots (Bartell & Solanto, 1995; Gordon & Oshman, 1981; Cotungo, 1995) and that indices of impulsiveness on the Rorschach may correlate with an objective measure of impulsiveness (Ebner & Hynan, 1994). Some evidence is also available that ADHD and normal children may differ on the Thematic Apperception Test (Costantino, Collin-Malgady, Malgady, & Perez, 1991). But the data do not support use of either test for judging whether a child suffers from this disorder. The gist of these studies is that ADHD children are indeed more impulsive and easily frustrated than controls. ADHD groups also demonstrate more intense feelings of loneliness and dependence and come across as more avoidant and socially uncomfortable. Yet much of this information could have been more economically obtained from the broad-band parent and teacher rating scales discussed in Chapter 8 (this volume) and likely with greater ecological validity.

    Projective measures might be justified when questions are raised about the possibility of serious thought or emotional disturbance. In our opinion, most of the best diagnostic indicators for ADHD are only valid for children who do not otherwise display the more devastating forms of psychiatric impairment. This holds especially true for judging the quality and onset of socially impulsive behavior, because deeply disturbed children (i.e., those suffering from pervasive developmental disorder, schizophrenia, another psychotic disorder, or an acute trauma) are also likely to act out with some consistency. Yet even here, poor inhibition seems to be relatively specific to ADHD (Pennington & Ozonoff, 1996). In these cases, administration of a reliable and valid test of cognitive coping skills may steer the clinician in the right diagnostic direction. For children and adolescents, the Rorschach Inkblots administered and scored according to the comprehensive system (Exner, 1993) can provide meaningful data regarding levels of psychopathology and stress. Yet it is also possible that this information could have been gleaned more economically from a structured psychiatric interview that reviews the major child psychiatric disorders with parents in combination with parent and teacher behavior rating scales, as recommended in Chapter 8 (this volume). Thus the utility of projective tests in the routine clinical evaluation of children with ADHD remains open to debate and in need of further research.

Observational Measures

Early editions of this book (Barkley, 1981, 1990) presented detailed protocols for conducting structured child observations. Over the years, it has become clear that, for the overwhelming majority of clinicians, formal behavior coding is wholly impractical. Although a number of studies support techniques such as direct observations in the classroom, they are not enough to justify the considerable cost and effort they involve for the sake of a clinical evaluation. Thus, we do not review them again here. Readers who want to consider instituting an informal observational protocol should refer to Gordon (1995). A more formal approach to behavior coding is available in the previous edition of this book (Barkley, 1990).

CONCLUSION

Our review places psychological testing somewhere in a middle ground of clinical utility. Although no evidence exists to support performance measures as pristinely diagnostic, data do justify their use under certain conditions and within a context of respect for their limitations. We therefore disagree with the extreme position that such measures are so inaccurate as to be always irrelevant to clinical evaluations of children with ADHD. Because markers for the disorder have been elusive, assessment and identification continue to rest on the integration of data derived from multiple yet inherently imperfect sources. Therefore, any meaningful information that can help a clinician judge the nature and severity of a child's deficits can be of potential benefit. As we have indicated, psychological test data may be of particular help when information from parents or teachers is unavailable or of questionable credibility.

Although we disagree with positions that completely reject psychological testing within ADHD evaluations, we are equally uncomfortable with the opposite stance. Psychological test data should not be oversold either as a basis for diagnosis or as a unitary standard for assessing treatment effects. The empirical basis for championing that level of confidence is far from solid. In our view, the most sensible advice is to target psychological testing to discrete diagnostic issues.

REFERENCES

American Psychiatric Association. (1980). *Diagnostic and statistical manual of mental disorders* (3rd ed.). Washington, DC: Author.

Anastopoulos, A. D., Spisto, M. A., & Maher, M. C. (1994). The WISC-III Freedom from Distractibility factor: Its utility in identifying children with attention deficit hyperactivity disorder. *Psychological Assessment, 6*, 368–371.

Aylward, G. P., & Gordon, M. (1997). Visual and auditory CPTs: Comparisons across clinical and nonclinical samples. *ADHD Newsletter, 24*, 2–4.

Aylward, G. P., Gordon, M., & Verhulst, S. J. (1997). Relationships between continuous performance task scores and other cognitive measures: causality or commonality? Assessment, 4(4), 313–324.

Barkley, R. A. (1977). A review of stimulant drug research with hyperactive children. *Journal of Child Psychology and Psychiatry, 18*, 137–165.

Barkley, R. A. (1981). *Hyperactive children: A handbook for diagnosis and treatment.* New York: Guilford Press.

Barkley, R. A. (1990). *Attention-Deficit Hyperactivity Disorder: A handbook for diagnosis and treatment.* New York: Guilford Press.

Barkley, R. A. (1991). The ecological validity of laboratory and analogue assessment methods of ADHD symptoms. *Journal of Abnormal Child Psychology, 19*, 149–178.

Barkley, R. A., DuPaul, G. J., & McMurray, M. B. (1990). A comprehensive evaluation of attention deficit disorder with and without hyperactivity. *Journal of Consulting and Clinical Psychology, 58*, 775–789.

Barkley, R. A., DuPaul, D. G., & McMurray, M. B. (1991). Attention deficit disorder with and without hyperactivity: Clinical response to three dose levels of methylphenidate. *Pediatrics, 87*, 519–531.

Barkley, R. A., Fischer, M., Newby, R., & Breen, M. (1988). Development of a multi-method clinical protocol for assessing stimulant drug responses in ADHD children. *Journal of Clinical Child Psychology, 17*, 14–24.

Barkley, R. A, & Grodzinsky, G. (1994). Are tests of frontal lobe functions useful in the diagnosis of attention deficit disorders? *Clinical Neuropsychologist, 8*, 121–139.

Barkley, R. A., Grodzinsky, G., & DuPaul, G. J. (1992). Frontal lobe functions in attention deficit disorder with and without hyperactivity: A review and research report. *Journal of Abnormal Child Psychology, 20*, 163–188.

Bartell, S. S., & Solanto, M. V. (1995). Usefulness of the Rorschach inkblot test in the assessment of attention deficit hyperactivity disorder. *Perceptual and Motor Skills, 80*(2), 531–541.

Bauermeister, J. J., Berrios, V., Jimenez, A. L., Acevedo, L., & Gordon, M. (1990). Some issues and instruments for the assessment of attention-deficit hyperactivity disorder in Puerto Rican children. *Journal of Clinical Child Psychology, 19*, 9–16.

Billings, R. (1996). *The relationship between the Gordon Diagnostic System and measures of intelligences and achievement.* Poster presented at the eighth national convention of CHADD, Chicago.

Brown, R. T., & Wynne, M. E. (1982). Correlates of teacher ratings, sustained attention, and impulsivity in hyperactive and normal boys. *Journal of Clinical Child Psychology, 11*, 262–267.

Cairns, E., & Cammock, T. (1978). Development of a more reliable version of the Matching Familiar Figures Test. *Developmental Psychology, 11*, 244–248.

Chelune, G. J., & Baer, R. A. (1986). Developmental norms for the Wisconsin Card Sort Test. *Journal of Clinical and Experimental Neuropsychology, 8*, 219–228.

Chelune, G. J., Ferguson, W., Koon, R., & Dickey, T. O. (1986). Frontal lobe disinhibition in attention deficit disorder. *Child Psychiatry and Human Development, 16*, 221–234.

Conners, C. K. (1995). *The Conners Continuous Performance Test.* North Tonawanda, NY: MultiHealth Systems.

Coons, H. W., Klorman, R., & Borgstedt, A. D. (1987). Effects of methylphenidate on adolescents with a childhood history of ADD: II. Information processing. *Journal of the American Academy of Child and Adolescent Psychiatry, 26*, 368–374.

Corkum, P. V., & Siegel, L. S. (1993). Is the continuous performance task a valuable research tool for use with children with attention-deficit-hyperactivity disorder? *Journal of Child Psychology and Psychiatry, 34*, 1217–1239.

Costantino, G., Collin-Malgady, G., Malgady, R. G., & Perez, A. (1991). Assessment of attention deficit disorder using a thematic apperception technique. *Journal of Personality Assessment, 57*, 87–95.

Cotungo, A. (1995). Personality attributes of ADHD using a Rorschach Inkblot Test. *Journal of Clinical Psychology, 5*, 554–562.

Ebner, D. L., & Hynan, L. S. (1994). The Rorschach and the assessment of impulsivity. *Journal of Clinical Psychology, 50*, 633–638.

Exner, J. E. (1993). *The Rorschach: A comprehensive system* (Vol. 1). New York: Wiley.

Fischer, M. (1996). Erratum regarding medication response of the Gordon Diagnostic System. *Journal of Clinical Child Psychology, 25*(1), 121.

Fischer, M., Barkley, R. A., Edelbrock, C. S., & Smallish, L. (1990). The adolescent outcome of hyperactive children diagnosed by research criteria: II. Academic, attentional, and neuropsychological status. *Journal of Consulting and Clinical Psychology, 58*, 580–588.

Fischer, M., & Newby, R. (1991). Assessment of stimulant response in ADHD children using a refined multimethod clinical protocol. *Journal of Clinical Child Psychology, 20*, 232–244.

Fischer, M., Newby, R. F., & Gordon. M. (1995). Who are the false negatives on continuous performance tests? *Journal of Clinical Child Psychology, 24*, 427–433.

Garfinkel, B. D., Brown, W. A., Klee, S. H., Braden, W., Beauchesne, H., & Shapiro, S. L. (1986). Neuroendocrine and cognitive responses to amphetamine in adolescents with a history of attention deficit disorder. *Journal of the American Academy of Child Psychiatry, 25*, 503–508.

Golden, J. (1996). Are tests of working memory and inattention diagnostically useful in children with ADHD? *ADHD Report, 4*(5), 6–8.

Gordon, M. (1979). The assessment of impulsivity and mediating behaviors in hyperactive and non-hyperactive children. *Journal of Abnormal Child Psychology, 7*, 317–326.

Gordon, M. (1983). *The Gordon Diagnostic System.* DeWitt, NY: Gordon Systems.

Gordon, M. (1987). How is a computerized attention test used in the diagnosis of attention deficit disorder? In J. Loney (Ed.), *The young hyperactive child: Answers to questions about diagnosis, prognosis, and treatment* (pp. 53–64). New York: Haworth Press.

Gordon, M. (1993). Do computerized measures of attention have a legitimate role in ADHD evaluations? *ADHD Report, 1*(6), 5–6.

Gordon, M. (1994). A survey of GDS users. *ADHD Hyperactivity Newsletter, 20*, 4.

Gordon, M. (1995). *How to operate an ADHD clinic or subspecialty practice.* Syracuse, NY: GSI Publications.

Gordon, M., Lewandowski, L., Clonan, S., & Malone, K. (1996). *Standardization of the Auditory Vigilance Task.* Paper presented at the eighth annual international conference of CHADD, Chicago.

Gordon, M., & McClure, F. D. (1983, August). *The objective assessment of attention deficit disorders.* Paper presented at the 91st annual convention of the American Psychological Association, Anaheim, CA.

Gordon, M., & Mettelman, B. B. (1988). The assessment of attention: I. Standardization and reliability of a behavior based measure. *Journal of Clinical Psychology, 44*, 682–690.

Gordon, M., Mettelman, B. B., & DeNiro, D. (1989, August). *Are continuous performance tests valid in the diagnosis of ADHD/hyperactivity?* Paper presented at the 97th annual convention of the American Psychological Association, New Orleans.

Gordon, M., Mettelman, B. B., & Irwin, M. (1994). Sustained attention and grade retention. *Perceptual and Motor Skills, 78*, 555–560.

Gordon, M., & Oshman, H. (1981). Rorschach indices of children classified as hyperactive. *Perceptual and Motor Skills, 52*, 703–707.

Gordon, M., Thomason, D., & Cooper, S. (1990). To what extent does attention affect K-ABC scores? *Psychology in the Schools, 27*, 144–147.

Grant, D. A., & Berg, E.A. (1948). *The Wisconsin Card Sort Test: Directions for administration and scoring.* Odessa, FL: Psychological Assessment.

Greenberg, L. M., & Kindschi, C. L. (1996). *T.O.V.A. Test of Variables of Attention: Clinical guide.* St. Paul, MN: TOVA Research Foundation.

Greenblatt, E., Mattis, S., & Trad, P. V. (1991). The ACID pattern and the Freedom from Distractibility factor in a child psychiatric population. *Developmental Neuropsychology, 7*, 121–130.

Grodzinsky, G. M., & Diamond, R. (1992). Frontal lobe functioning in boys with attention-deficit hyperactivity disorder. *Developmental Neuropsychology, 8*, 427–445.

Kagan, J. (1966). Reflection–impulsivity: The generality and dynamics of conceptual tempo. *Journal of Abnormal Psychology, 71*, 17–24.

Kaufman, A. S. (1980). Issues in psychological assessment: Interpreting the WISC-R intelligently. In B. B. Lahey & A. E. Kazdin (Eds.), *Advances in clinical child psychology* (Vol. 3, pp. 177–214). New York: Plenum.

Kaufman, A. S., & Kaufman, N. L. (1983). *Kaufman Assessment Battery for Children*. Circle Pines, MN: American Guidance Services.

Keogh, B. K., & Margolis, J. S. (1976). A component analysis of attentional problems of educationally handicapped boys. *Journal of Abnormal Child Psychology, 4*, 349–359.

Klee, S. H., & Garfinkel, B. D. (1983). The computerized continuous performance task: A new measure of attention. *Journal of the American Academy of Child Psychiatry, 11*, 487–496.

Lezak, M. D. (1983). *Neuropsychological assessment* (2nd ed.). New York: Oxford University Press.

Lezak, M. D. (1995). *Neuropsychological assessment* (3rd ed.). New York: Oxford

Mariani, M., & Barkley, R. A. (1997). Neuropsychological and academic functioning in preschool children with attention deficit hyperactivity disorder. *Developmental Neuropsychology, 13*, 111–129.

Margolis, J. S. (1972). *Academic correlates of sustained attention*. Unpublished doctoral dissertation, University of California–Los Angeles.

Matier-Sharma, K., Perachio, N., Newcorn, J. H., Sharma, V., & Halperin, J. M. (1995). Differential diagnosis of ADHD: Are objective measures of attention, impulsivity, and activity level helpful? *Child Neuropsychology, 1*, 118–127.

McClure, F. D., & Gordon, M. (1984). Performance of disturbed hyperactive and nonhyperactive children on an objective measure of hyperactivity. *Journal of Abnormal Child Psychology, 12*, 561–572.

Messer, S., & Brodzinsky, D. M. (1981). Three year stability of reflection–impulsivity in young adoloscents. *Developmental Psychology, 17*, 848–850.

Milich, R., & Kramer, J. (1984). Reflections on impulsivity: An empirical investigation of impulsivity as a construct. In K. Gadow & I. Bialer (Eds.), *Advances in learning and behavioral disabilities* (Vol. 3, pp. 57–94). Greenwich, CT: JAI.

Milich, R., & Loney, J. (1979). The role of hyperactive and aggressive symptomatology in predicting adolescent outcome among hyperactive children. *Journal of Pediatric Psychology, 4*, 93–112.

Mitchell, T. V., & Quittner, A. L. (1996). Multimethod study of attention and behavior problems in hearing-impaired children. *Journal of Clinical Child Psychology, 25*(1), 83–96.

Ownby, R. L., & Matthews, C. G. (1985). On the meaning of the WISC-R third factor: Relations to selected neuropsychological measures. *Journal of Consulting and Clinical Psychology, 53*, 531–534.

Pennington, B. F., & Ozonoff, S. (1996). Executive functions and developmental psychopathology. *Journal of Child Psychology and Psychiatry, 37*, 51–87.

Rapport, M. D., Tucker, S. B., DuPaul, G. J., Merlo, M., & Stoner, G. (1986). Hyperactivity and frustration: The influence of control over and size of rewards in delaying gratification. *Journal of Abnormal Child Psychology, 14*, 181–204.

Reitan, R. M., & Wolfson, D. (1985). *The Halstead–Reitan Neuropsychological 1 Test Battery*. Tucson, AZ: Neuropsychological Press.

Rispens, J., Swaab, H., van den Oord, E. J. C. C., Cohen-Kettenis, P., van Engeland, H., & van Yperen, T. (1997). WISC profiles in child psychiatric diagnosis: Sense or nonsense? *Journal of the American Academy of Child and Adolescent Psychiatry, 36*, 1587–1594.

Rosvold, H. E., Mirsky, A. F., Sarason, I., Bransome, E. D., & Beck, L. H. (1956). A continuous performance test of brain damage. *Journal of Consulting Psychology, 20*, 343–350.

Sandford, J. A., Fine, A. H., & Goldman, L. (1995). *Validity study of IVA: A visual and auditory CPT*. Paper presented at the annual convention of the American Psychological Association, New York.

Schaughency, E. A., Lahey, B. B., Hynd, G. W., Stone, P. A., Piacineini, J. C., & Frick, P. J. (1989). Neuropsychological test performance and the attention deficit disorders: Clinical utility of the Luria–Nebraska Neuropsychological Battery—Children's Revision. *Journal of Consulting and Clinical Psychology, 57*, 112–116.

Sostek, A. J., Buchsbaum, M. S., & Rapoport, J. L. (1980). Effects of amphetamine on vigilance performance in normal and hyperactive children. *Journal of Abnormal Child Psychology, 8*, 491–500.

Stewart, K. J., & Moely, B. E. (1983). The WISC-R third factor: What does it mean? *Journal of Consulting and Clinical Psychology, 51*, 940–941.

Stroop, J. R. (1935). Studies of interference in serial verbal reactions. *Journal of Experimental Psychology, 18*, 643–662.

Teicher, M. H., Ito, Y., Glod, C. A., & Barber, N. I. (1996). Objective measurement of hyperactivity and attentional problems in ADHD. *Journal of the American Academy of Child and Adolescent Psychiatry, 35*, 334–342.

Trommer, B. L., Hoeppner, J. B., Lorber, R., & Armstrong, K. (1988). Pitfalls in the use of a continuous performance test as a diagnostic tool in attention deficit disorder. *Developmental and Behavioral Pediatrics, 9,* 339–346.

Waber, D., & Holmes, J. M. (1985). Assessing children's copy productions of the Rey–Osterrieth Complex Figure. *Journal of Clinical and Experimental Neuropsychology, 7,* 264–280.

Wielkiewicz, R. M. (1990). Interpreting low scores on the WISC-R third factor: It's more than distractibility. *Psychological Assessment, 2,* 91–97.

Wielkiewicz, R. M., & Palmer, C. M. (1996). Can the WISC-R/WISC-III third factor help in understanding ADHD? *ADHD Report, 4*(3), 4–6.

Chapter 10

INTEGRATING THE RESULTS OF AN EVALUATION: EIGHT CLINICAL CASES

William Hathaway
Jodi K. Dooling-Litfin
Gwenyth Edwards

ॐ

This chapter contains the results of eight actual clinical cases seen at the Attention-Deficit/ Hyperactivity Disorder (ADHD) Clinic at the University of Massachusetts Medical Center. Five of the examples represent the most common types of cases seen the clinic: "pure" ADHD; ADHD with Oppositional Defiant Disorder (ODD); ADHD with Conduct Disorder (CD); ADHD, Predominantly Inattentive Type; and ADHD, Purely Inattentive. Three "negative" cases are also presented to illustrate the types of clinical problems sometimes mistakenly conceptualized as a result of ADHD: Anxiety Disorder; Dysthymia; and a case of possible atypical Pervasive Developmental Disorder (PDD). The case examples reflect the evaluation process at the clinic: the type of information gathered, the tests administered, some of the diagnostic issues considered in conceptualizing the clients, and the sorts of recommendations generated.

The ADHD clinic utilizes a multimethod, multi-informant assessment approach like that outlined in the foregoing chapters on assessment. First, it incorporates a diagnostic interview with the parents and a brief interview with the child. Telephone interviews with teachers or other key informants are pursued when needed. Parents and teachers complete the ADHD Rating Scale, which is a rating of the symptoms of ADHD according to the fourth edition of the *Diagnostic and Statistical Manual of Mental Disorders* (DSM-IV; American Psychiatric Association, 1994): either the Child Behavior Checklist (CBCL) or Behavior Assessment System for Children (BASC), which are general measures of social competence and child psychopathology; the Social Skills Rating Scale (SSRS), which assesses several facets of peer functioning; and the Disruptive Behavior Rating Scale (DBRS), which is a rating scale of the symptoms of ODD. A short questionnaire on the child's medical history is mailed to the child's pediatrician prior to the evaluation.

Several additional scales or forms are also completed by the parents and teachers. Parents complete the Parenting Stress Index—Short Form (PSI-SF), which is a measure of the stress arising from parenting the child, and the Symptom Checklist 90—Revised (SCL-90-R), which is a screening scale for parental personal distress and psychopathology. Prior to the evaluation, parents are given a developmental and health history information form to complete which briefly reviews the child's developmental and medical history. The teachers also complete the Child Attention Problems Scale (CAP), which is an additional rating of inattentiveness and overactivity, and the Academic Performance Rating Scale (APRS), which is a measure of the some key aspects of academic functioning.

A brief battery of direct testing is administered to each child at the clinic. Unless intelligence testing has recently been completed elsewhere, each child is given a Vocabulary subtest from either the Wechsler Intelligence Scale for Children (WISC-III) or Stanford–Binet Intelligence Test (4th ed.; SB-IV). This subtest is given as a brief screening of verbal intelligence. In younger children, the Peabody Picture Vocabulary Test—III (PPVT-III) is sometimes used for this purpose. The Conners Continuous Performance Test (CPT) is routinely administered to assess attentional skills and response inhibition.

ADHD, COMBINED TYPE, NO COMORBID CONDITIONS

Jimmy's parents, Mr. and Mrs. N., thought they had a busy job raising Jimmy's "rambunctious" older brother. By comparison, Jimmy made his brother look calm and controlled. Mr. and Mrs. N. emphasized that Jimmy was not a "bad" child. He was not oppositional, aggressive, or stubborn and ill tempered. Rather, he was difficult to keep up with because Jimmy was "always in motion." Mrs. N. recalled that "as soon as Jimmy learned to walk, he seemed to be wandering off and getting into things." Jimmy's active style was particularly problematic because he often made poor choices with seemingly little forethought (e.g., running out into the road without looking or putting keys in an electric outlet).

Jimmy seemed eager to please his parents, but he frequently did not follow through on things they asked of him (e.g., picking up his toys or making his bed). His parents explained that Jimmy was easily "sidetracked" by more interesting things and consequently failed to complete requested tasks. They did not feel this was due to a deliberate refusal to comply. For example, when they remind Jimmy about uncompleted tasks, he seems surprised and says, "Oh, I forgot." He quickly restarts uncompleted tasks when reminded but again becomes distracted if left to his own devices. Mr. and Mrs. N. have developed a very active parenting style to get Jimmy to finish tasks more consistently. They find it necessary to give short commands and always to be ready to check up on Jimmy's progress in carrying out instructions. They use immediate consequences, such as praise for compliance and privilege removal or time out for noncompliance, to motivate Jimmy. Even with this added structure, they find it necessary to give frequent prompts and reminders to keep Jimmy directed to assigned tasks.

Although Jimmy's inattentive, impulsive, and overactive behaviors required his parents to be very active in his management, it was not until Jimmy entered preschool that Mr. and Mrs. N. became aware of the magnitude of these behaviors. Jimmy briefly attended two different preschools but had great difficulty in these programs. When Jimmy was 3 years old his parents placed him in a Montessori preschool program. This program met for 2–3 hours 5 days a week and involved many structured, developmentally appropriate learning activities. Jimmy was unable to adjust to the "structure" of the program. For instance, he frequently talked out during quiet times, quickly lost interest in group activities and did not persist with preacademic tasks. His parents switched Jimmy to another preschool program after 3 months but similar problems arose in this setting. Jimmy was asked to leave the second preschool program after 1 month of attendance because he "engaged in too much imagination play," would not participate adequately in directed activities, and consequently distracted other students. Jimmy spent the remainder of his preschool time with a home day-care provider who was trained as an education consultant for children with special needs. The home day-care provider used a variety of behavioral strategies, such as a token system, to manage Jimmy's behavior.

Jimmy's kindergarten teacher noted problems with Jimmy "not being focused," being unable to work independently, and being too "active." These problems became disruptive to the class unless the teacher gave Jimmy a great deal of individualized attention: redirecting him back to school activities and reminding him about appropriate behavior when he was blurting out comments or interrupting others. Jimmy also had some difficulty with academic tasks that required attention to detail, such as letter writing. Although Jimmy did not fall "far below grade level" in his academics, his teacher expressed concerns that Jimmy seemed to be performing "beneath his potential." Because of his difficulties in kindergarten, Jimmy's parents requested an evaluation to determine whether Jimmy was eligible for government-mandated individualized education services. The school psychologist administered a WISC-III and a Woodcock–Johnson Psychoeducational Battery (WJ-R). He obtained a WISC-III Full Scale intelligence quotient of 111 (77th percentile), which fell in the high average range of overall intellectual functioning. His achievement scores on the WJ-R were somewhat mixed, ranging from the low average to high average range. The school psychologist stated that Jimmy had the intellectual ability to do better in school but "attentional factors seemed to be a key factor contributing to underachievement for Jimmy." Although Jimmy was not found eligible for government-mandated services based on his psychoeducational testing, the school psychologist recommended further evaluation of Jimmy's attentional problems.

Jimmy's impulsivity created problems in his social functioning that became increasingly evident as he transitioned into middle childhood. Jimmy was described as often "immature" or "silly" in his interpersonal style. By first grade, his peers were frequently complaining that Jimmy "bothered them" by "grabbing," "pulling," or otherwise "touching them." Jimmy's difficulties regulating his social behavior did not stand out as a problem in earlier years because few of his peers acted differently. As his peers started to develop greater restraint, Jimmy's social progress lagged further and further behind. Although Jimmy was typically engaging or "friendly," he was unable to maintain friendships. He also had difficulty in organized activities such as seasonal sports. His coaches frequently complained that Jimmy was "too off task" and his "silly" behavior sometimes led to conflicts with teammates.

Jimmy's first-grade teacher continued to note many of the problems that had surfaced in preschool and kindergarten: Jimmy frequently failed to follow through on instructions, did not complete work within an appropriate amount of time, and was often disruptive due to his "constant activity and noise making." By the end of the first grade Jimmy had fallen behind in his reading and writing skills because of his difficulty persisting on these tasks. His teacher frequently had to prompt Jimmy to return to assigned tasks and to cease off-task behaviors, such as playing with his pencil or "drumming" on his desk. Although Jimmy's teacher used a behavior management plan to reduce Jimmy's off-task behavior and increase his productivity, she stated that he continued to complete only a "minimum" of the required work. During a parent–teacher conference, his teacher reiterated the school psychologist's recommendation to have Jimmy evaluated for his attentional difficulties.

Jimmy's parents discussed the school's recommendation to have Jimmy evaluated with his pediatrician during a physical examination in the spring of his first-grade school year. The pediatrician referred Jimmy to our clinic for evaluation. Table 10.1 summarizes the results of the testing. Mr. and Mrs. N. reported a significant number of both the inattentive

TABLE 10.1. Assessment Results for a Case of ADHD in a 6-Year-Old Boy

Mother	Father	Teacher
Interview report of ADHD symptoms	**Interview report of ADHD symptoms**	**CAP** (Percentile)
Inattention 9	Inattention 9	Inattention 98*
Hyperactivity/Impulsivity 7	Hyperactivity/Impulsivity 8	Overactivity 98*

ADHD Rating Scale (Symptoms rated >2)	**ADHD Rating Scale** (Symptoms rated >2)	**ADHD Rating Scale** (Symptoms rated >2)
Inattention 9	Inattention 7	Inattention 8
Hyperactivity/Impulsivity 6	Hyperactivity/Impulsivity 6	Hyperactivity/Impulsivity 9

BASC		**BASC**		**BASC**	
Subscale	Percentile	Subscale	Percentile	Subscale	Percentile
Hyperactivity	95*	Hyperactivity	95*	Hyperactivity	96*
Aggression	58	Aggression	58	Aggression	72
Conduct Problems	78	Conduct Problems	67	Conduct Problems	72
Anxiety	82	Anxiety	64	Anxiety	80
Depression	89	Depression	74	Depression	73
Somatization	45	Somatization	9	Somatization	84
Atypicality	90	Atypicality	79	Atypicality	92
Withdrawal	44	Withdrawal	44	Withdrawal	53
Attention Problems	97*	Attention Problems	95*	Attention Problems	96*
Social Skills	3*	Social Skills	39	Social Skills	30
				Learning Problems	90

PSI-SF	**DBRS**	**SSRS**
Total Stress 85	Number of Defiant Behaviors 1	Total Score 26 (below average)

APRS

Productivity Score 38
(low average)

	Testing data		
Test	Raw score	Standard/scaled score	Percentile
WISC-III Vocabulary		15	95*
Conners CPT			
Hits	279 (86%)		91
Omissions	51 (16%)		72
Commissions	21 (58%)	44	28
Hit Rate	508	43	27
Hit Rate Standard Error	22	67	96*
Variability of *SE*	28	50	50

Note. An asterisk indicates a clinically significant elevation (>95th percentile or <5th percentile).

and impulsive/overactive symptoms of ADHD for Jimmy during an interview and on rating scales. His first-grade teacher also reported significant levels of both inattentiveness and impulsivity/overactivity on rating scales. Both Jimmy's parents and his first-grade teacher rated him as having significantly fewer than average social skills. Despite being described as a very "bright" boy, Jimmy's teacher rated him as "low average" in productivity compared to other first-grade boys on the APRS. No evidence of other psychiatric difficulties, such as depression or anxiety, was obtained from the evaluation results. During the interview, Jimmy's parents explained that their son's ADHD characteristics had caught them "off guard." They denied any previous family history of ADHD, learning disabilities, or other psychiatric problems. Although Jimmy's brother was also very active, they pointed out that Jimmy's difficulties seemed to be substantially greater.

Jimmy participated willingly in the interview and testing but shifted in his seat and fidgeted a great deal. He mentioned that he often "daydreams" in school and finds reading very boring. He also reported having great difficulty listening to the teacher when she is talking. He often makes noises in the classroom, "for no particular reason." Jimmy's performance on the Conners CPT provided some evidence of problems with attention. Although Jimmy only infrequently responded to inappropriate test items (commissions), he frequently failed to respond to appropriate items (omissions) and was highly variable in his speed of response. This pattern suggested difficulties with sustaining his level of attention.

The clinical impression of Jimmy that emerged from the evaluation was of a 6-year, 9-month-old boy of above-average intelligence who has a significant, chronic, and pervasive history of the inattentive and impulsive/overactive symptoms of ADHD. These features were evident since Jimmy's early childhood years and significantly impaired his school behavior and social functioning. No other psychiatric difficulties were detected for Jimmy. Consequently, Jimmy was diagnosed as ADHD, Combined Type.

We made a number of recommendations to Jimmy's parents:

1. We emphasized parent education about ADHD through follow-up consultation, suggested readings, and participation in a support group.
2. We suggested a trial of stimulant medication.
3. We developed a variety of beneficial environmental modifications such as those described in Chapters 12 and 15 (this volume).
4. We advised the development of a home-based reinforcement program to increase appropriate school behavior and academic productivity. This program made use of the daily school behavior report card (see Chapter 15, this volume).

Jimmy's case highlights a number of important observations about individuals who have ADHD, Combined Type, but who do not have comorbid conditions. Because of the high comorbidity of ADHD and ODD, it is common for individuals to confuse the two disorders. Jimmy was not viewed as an oppositional child either at home or at school. Although Jimmy required a more active, structured, and deliberate management style in both of these settings, he was not viewed as a "conduct problem" by his parents or his teachers. Adults generally regarded Jimmy as a well-meaning boy who too often allowed his impulses to "get the better of him." Jimmy's inappropriate and disruptive behavior appeared to stem from disinhibition rather than from the intentional misbehavior, coercive defiance cycles, or deliberate aggression associated with ODD.

Jimmy's case also illustrates the pervasive and chronic nature of the ADHD features required for the diagnosis. Jimmy's ADHD characteristics were present since his preschool years. However, they did not create a substantial problem in his functioning until Jimmy entered a setting that taxed his weak self-regulation skills. Jimmy's ADHD created problems primarily in his social functioning and school behavior. Although his ADHD appeared to be interfering with his educational functioning, Jimmy's academic performance was not substantially impaired by his ADHD relative to that typical for same-age peers. Whereas Jimmy may have been underachieving in school relative to his intellectual ability, it was his inappropriate school behavior that first raised concerns about him. Although intelligence cannot completely buffer the impact of ADHD, it is likely that Jimmy would have displayed greater academic difficulties due to his ADHD if his level of intellectual functioning was significantly lower.

ADHD WITH OPPOSITIONAL DEFIANT DISORDER

Sam was difficult-tempered from birth. Although he displayed no developmental problems as an infant or toddler, he was overactive, stubborn, and colicky. It seemed impossible to maintain Sam on a consistent eating and sleeping schedule. Sam always had a "mind of his own" and consequently everything was a battle: If he did not want to be dressed as a toddler he would take off his shoes immediately after his parents dressed him and hide them. Once Sam began to speak, he incessantly demanded things from his parents and forcefully shouted "No!" when he did not want to comply with their requests. When Sam's parents, Mr. and Mrs. G., pushed him to finish a task, such as eating his dinner or picking up after himself, Sam often displayed intense outbursts of anger. His parents dreaded taking him to public locations, such as grocery stores or malls, because Sam typically threw a tantrum during the outings.

By early childhood, Sam's behavior had become increasingly aggressive. His defiance escalated to include hitting his mother, throwing objects, and screaming "I hate you!" at his parents. On some occasions, his outbursts turned destructive. For instance, he impulsively threw a wrench through his mother's windshield and smashed a toy through a glass coffee table when he was upset. Sam always seemed to be in an irritable mood. However, even when he was not being aggressive he was difficult to manage. Once Sam learned to walk, he was "always on the go." He was constantly climbing and running in inappropriate places, such as through the clothing racks at department stores. If Sam was around, it seemed impossible to carry on a conversation because of his frequent interrupting and noisy play. Although he was difficult for both parents to manage, he seemed to be much more challenging for his mother. His parents often argued over how to handle Sam. His mother tried to be much more appeasing while his father was stern. Despite their disagreement over how to handle Sam, neither parent felt they knew how to manage him well.

Sam was placed in a day-care program when he was 9 months of age. Even at this early age, his teachers often made comments about Sam being obstinate, overactive, and disruptive. As Sam entered the toddler years, he was often aggressive with his peers. He rarely shared toys with other children but often grabbed toys away from his peers. Although new children at the day-care center often played with Sam, they soon learned to avoid him because of his "bossy" and physically aggressive style. Sam was very short-tempered at the day-care program; he was easily provoked and would hit, push, or bite when upset. Consequently, Sam was typically rejected by his peers. By the time Sam was 5 years old, Mr. and Mrs. G. had attempted to involve Sam in several organized recreational activities such as baseball or skating. However, he was asked to stop participating in these activities because he "unable to wait his turn."

Halfway through Sam's 4th year, he started attending an integrated preschool program run by the public school system in his community. Sam attended the preschool for 2–3 hours, 3 days a week. All the children in this program had special needs or were viewed as "at risk" for educational problems. Sam stood out from his preschool classmates as a much more "moody," "argumentative," and "angry" child. Sam seemed unable to persist with preacademic tasks and frequently displayed inappropriate behaviors in the classroom, such as running around the desks, yelling out, interrupting, not staying seated during group time, and grabbing other people or their things.

Sam responded to teacher cues to behave appropriately but required many such cues to maintain a minimal level of acceptable behavior throughout the day. When corrected for misbehavior, Sam typically talked back or covered his ears in defiance. Sam's inappropriate behavior improved somewhat after being in the program for several months secondary to an intense behavior management plan initiated by his teacher. The plan involved clearly delineated rules for specific activities, such as circle time or using the rest room. The class would often recite the rules. Consequences for breaking the rules, including time out, were described in advance. Engaging in desired activities, such as using the computer or doing crafts, was used as an incentive for compliance. In addition to this general management plan, Sam's teacher seated Sam immediately next to her, frequently prompted Sam to behave appropriately, and gave him abundant praise for efforts at appropriate behavior. During special events or anticipated blocks of unstructured time, such as performing a school play, Sam's teacher often asked his father to attend the class to provide additional support in managing Sam. Sam's teacher observed that Sam was able to behave in a modestly appropriate manner with this amount of management but that it was very taxing for him. At a parent–teacher conference, she expressed concerns about Sam's ability to engage in the level of "academic listening" that would be required in elementary school. For instance, she noted that during the "language circle," all of Sam's efforts seemed to be invested in trying to behave appropriately. Consequently, his performance seemed to be far below his conversational language skills displayed at other times. His teacher questioned whether Sam should be placed in a regular kindergarten program the following year and recommended that his parents have Sam evaluated for ADHD.

Mr. and Mrs. G. brought Sam to the ADHD clinic for an assessment of his impulsive, restless, and aggressive behavior. His parents requested assistance in identifying any disorder that might be contributing to Sam's problems and advice on how to better manage Sam both at home and at school. Table 10.2 summarizes the results of this evaluation. Both Sam's parents and preschool teacher reported all of the impulsive/overactive features of ADHD either on rating scales or during an interview. His mother also reported significant levels of the inattentive features of ADHD. Both Sam's mother and his teacher rated him as having significantly below-average levels of social skills. Although his teacher also rated Sam as displaying significant levels of "depression" on the BASC, the significant elevation seemed to be due to items reflecting his "irritable," "moody," or "negative" demeanor. In terms of his oppositional behaviors, Sam's parents reported all eight of the defiant behaviors required for a diagnosis of ODD as frequently displayed by Sam. His mother described very high levels of stress arising from parenting Sam.

During the interview, Sam's parents stated that they had hoped Sam would "grow out of his problems but they only seemed to get worse." They had some experience dealing with "psychiatric problems" in the past: Mr. G. had been treated for both alcohol abuse and depression. He had been sober for 5 years by the time of the evaluation but continued to attend Alcoholics Anonymous. Sam's paternal grandfather also had chronic difficulties with alcohol abuse and had been diagnosed with a bipolar mood disorder. His grandfather had been hospitalized on several occasions due to his mood disability and had been on a "full disability" pension since he was 50.

Sam separated easily from his parents and was spontaneously engaging during the interview. His speech appeared to be normal in tone, rate, and volume. However, he talked constantly throughout the interview. Sam appeared to understand directions to testing tasks but was able to complete these tasks only with frequent prompting and encouragement. He frequently fidgeted and appeared to be very restless. His affect and thought process appeared within normal limits. Table 10.2 summarizes direct testing results obtained during the evaluation. Because psychoeducational testing had never been performed with Sam, he was given a PPVT-III to obtain a brief estimate of his verbal intelligence. On the PPVT-III, Sam obtained a raw score of 78, which corresponded to a scaled score of 110 and fell at the 75th

TABLE 10.2. Results for a Case of Mixed ADHD and ODD in a 5-Year-Old Boy

Mother		Father		Teacher	
Interview report of ADHD symptoms		Interview report of ADHD symptoms		ADHD Rating Scale (Symptoms rated <2)	
Inattention	7	Inattention	5	Inattention	2
Hyperactivity/Impulsivity	9	Hyperactivity/Impulsivity	9	Hyperactivity/Impulsivity	9

ADHD Rating Scale

(Symptoms rated >2)

Inattention	7
Hyperactivity/Impulsivity	9

BASC		BASC	
Subscale	Percentile	Subscale	Percentile
Hyperactivity	97*	Hyperactivity	96*
Aggression	97*	Aggression	95*
Anxiety	85	Anxiety	80
Depression	80	Depression	95*
Somatization	20	Somatization	14
Atypicality	68	Atypicality	54
Withdrawal	30	Withdrawal	59
Attention Problems	97*	Attention Problems	90
Social Skills	5*	Social Skills	41

PSI-SF		SSRS	
Total Stress	98*	Total Score 25 (below average)	

Testing data			
Test	Raw score	Standard/scaled score	Percentile
PPVT-III	78	110	75
Conners CPT			
Hits	273 (84%)		
Omissions	51 (16%)		72
Commissions	29 (81%)	54	69
Hit Rate	453	59	82
Hit Rate Standard Error	33	71	98*
Variability of *SE*	64	66	95*

Note. An asterisk indicates a clinically significant elevation (>95th percentile or <5th percentile).

percentile. His performance on this receptive vocabulary test suggests that Sam has a high average level of verbal intelligence. Although he did not fail to respond to appropriate items (omissions) or mistakenly respond to inappropriate items (commissions) to an unusually degree on the Conners CPT, he was very inconsistent in his speed and pattern of response. This response pattern provided evidence of difficulties with sustained attention.

Based on the results of the evaluation, Sam was viewed as a 5-year, 1-month-old boy of presumably above-average intelligence who had chronic and pervasive difficulties with noncompliance, excessive inappropriate activity, aggression, and poor sustained attention. A significant level of the impulsive/overactive features of ADHD was reported both at home and at school. Although only Sam's mother rated him as displaying significant levels of the inattentive features of ADHD, his teacher also described many problems with inattention in written comments about Sam. Sam was given the diagnosis of ADHD, Combined Type (314.01). Sam's ADHD was complicated by a significant pattern of defiant behavior, both at home and at school, that met the criteria for ODD (313.81). Sam's combination of ADHD and ODD substantially impaired his social functioning, school adjustment, and family relationships.

Following the evaluation, we made a number of recommendations to Sam's family:

1. We emphasized parent education about the nature of both ADD and ODD through follow-up consultation, suggested readings, and participation in a support group. The importance of implementing an adequate treatment plan to reduce the chances of negative outcomes, such as school failure or conduct disorder, was stressed.
2. We advised parent participation in a 9-week course of behavior management training, identical to that described in Chapter 12.
3. We suggested a trial of stimulant medication.
4. We gave Sam's parents information about legal rights relevant to the education of children with ADHD. We encouraged Sam's parents to request an evaluation by Sam's school to determine whether an individualized education plan should be established for Sam.
5. We suggested a variety of environmental modifications/accommodations for implementation during Sam's kindergarten year.

Sam's case illustrates the characteristics of an ADHD subgroup researchers have described as an early-onset "aggressive type" (Hinshaw, 1987). This group is discussed in Chapter 4 (this volume). The ADHD–aggressive subgroup tends to have an irritable temperament, poor sustained attention, and high activity level, which is quite evident by an early age. Sam's difficult temperament was recognized from birth and concerns about his ADHD symptoms have been recognized since his toddler years. Also common for the aggressive subtype of ADHD, Sam has been rated as significantly below average in his social functioning both at home and at school. His aggressive and overly impulsive behavior frequently resulted in Sam's being rejected by his peers.

There has been some discussion in recent years about a higher rate of Bipolar Mood Disorder in ADHD children (see Chapter 4, this volume). Biederman (1995) and his associates (Faraone et al., 1997; Wozniak et al., 1995) have argued that the early-onset aggressive subgroup of individuals with ADHD are often suffering from a bipolar mood disorder. A chief difficulty in evaluating this claim is the equivocation of persistent irritable moods with the manic or hypomanic phase of the disorder. DSM-IV lists criterion A for a manic episode as "a distinct period of abnormally and persistently elevated, expansive or irritable mood, lasting at least 1 week." However, a number of the diagnostic indicators for ODD reflect frequent or persistent patterns of irritability such as "often loses temper," "is often touchy or easily annoyed by others," and "is often angry and resentful." The primary difference between the expressions of irritability in the two disorders may be historical. Manic irritability is characterized in DSM-IV as tied to a "distinct period" or phase. The irritability characteristic of the aggressive–ADHD subgroup reflects a general temperament and is less tied to distinct periods. It is possible that an individual may meet the criteria for both ADHD and a bipolar mood disorder. In Sam's case, there is a positive family history of a bipolar mood disorder in a paternal grandfather. However, his temperamental difficulties have not been expressed in a phasic manner. Furthermore, he does not meet criterion B for a manic episode. Although he may be at increased risk for a bipolar mood disorder, he did not meet the criteria for this condition at the time of the evaluation.

ADHD WITH CONDUCT DISORDER

Jesse was born into a rather chaotic family. His mother had been married once before, when she was very young, and had two children from that marriage. She met his father in a bar following the dissolution of her first marriage, and they were married soon after. Theirs was not an easy union. In the early years of their marriage, both parents were practicing alcoholics. Jesse's father was also a very impulsive, hot-tempered man. They had two children in quick succession soon after their marriage. Jesse was the youngest.

From the time of Jesse's birth, people commented on how like his father he was. He was born with a very "difficult" temperament and was an extremely active toddler. After the children were born, Jesse's father decided to quit drinking and take his life more seriously. He found work as a mechanic and joined Alcoholics Anonymous. Jesse's mother also attempted to quit drinking for a while.

Although Jesse had always been stubborn, as he entered school he became more defiant and argumentative. He learned that he could get away with things when his father was not home. His mother found it difficult to set limits, and Jesse learned that a tantrum would almost always get him his way. His behavior began to escalate, and his parents found him increasingly difficult to manage. His father would often come onto the scene and impose extremely harsh punishments, such as telling him he could not go outside for a week, but Jesse knew that as soon as his father went to work, he would get his way. His parents often argued about disciplining him.

Around this time, Jesse's mother began drinking again. She had taken a job as a cocktail waitress to pay off her credit card debts. She began staying at work well into the early morning hours, drinking with her friends. Jesse's father often forced the children to stay up with him, waiting for her to return. There was a great deal of arguing in the house. Frequently, Jesse's father got into fights with his mother's male coworkers and then left for a few days, and Jesse's teenage brothers would be left to care for him when their mother was out.

Concerns were raised about Jesse's school behavior from the time he entered kindergarten. He was very aggressive toward other children and was seen as extremely active and impulsive. He also had some language delays. He began receiving speech and language therapy in kindergarten. In first grade, he had difficulty learning to read. He began to receive special educational services to help with his reading, but he remained in the regular classroom. His teachers urged his parents to have him evaluated for possible attentional problems, even obtaining rating scales for them, but the parents never followed through.

As the family conflict increased and Jesse was left to fend for himself more often, he began to look to his brothers for guidance. They were all substance abusers at a young age and were frequently involved in the juvenile court system for offenses such as shoplifting, underage drinking, and marijuana possession. Jesse began to run with a "tough" and aggressive neighborhood crowd. His behaviors progressed to more serious violations of others' rights. He himself engaged in shoplifting and frequent fighting, and he even tortured animals.

By this time, Jesse was in the fourth grade. School personnel called a meeting because of their serious concerns about Jesse's behavior, and his parents agreed to bring him into our clinic for the assessment of problems related to inattentive, impulsive, and restless behaviors.

At the time of the evaluation, Jesse had recently undergone a physical examination and was found to be in very good health. IQ and achievement testing conducted recently by the school indicated that his overall cognitive abilities were average, with no evidence of any specific learning disabilities, other than a moderate language delay.

During a review of childhood psychiatric symptoms, Jesse's parents endorsed eight to nine of nine symptoms of inattentiveness, as well as six to nine of nine symptoms of impulsivity/overactivity, as being characteristic of Jesse. They also reported that Jesse displayed six of eight symptoms of ODD to a significant degree for his age: argumentativeness with adults, frequent temper outbursts, spitefulness, defying adult requests, annoying others, and blaming others for his own mistakes. Jesse also reportedly displayed four behaviors associated with CD: frequently initiating physical fights, starting fires, lying, and physical cruelty toward animals. Jesse did not meet criteria for any other childhood psychiatric condition.

A review of the family psychiatric history revealed significant pathology on the maternal side. One maternal uncle had been diagnosed with schizophrenia, and another experienced epilepsy. Many biological relatives on both sides of the family had significant problems with alcohol abuse. Jesse's parents admitted to their past alcohol abuse, and the mother acknowledged that she "probably still drank too much." Jesse's father acknowledged that he displayed attention problems and impulsivity not unlike the behaviors he observed in Jesse. One of Jesse's half brothers was being treated for depression and ADHD and had attempted suicide in the months prior to the evaluation by ingesting his mother's sleeping pills. Jesse's parents acknowledged their marital conflict and frequent separations. Such a family history of psychiatric problems, parental antisocial behavior and substance abuse, family conflict, inconsistent discipline, and poor monitoring is not uncommon in ADHD children manifesting CD. It would not be surprising if Jesse progressed into substance abuse of his own, particularly if he becomes involved in a peer group who abuses alcohol and/or drugs.

Table 10.3 shows the results of the rating scales completed by Jesse's parents. On the BASC, significant clinical elevations were noted from both parents on the Attention Problems, Aggression, and Conduct Problems subscales. Jesse's father also noted hyperactivity. Jesse's mother noted depression, difficulty adapting to new situations, and poor social skills. On the ADHD Rating Scale, Jesse was rated as displaying seven or eight of nine symptoms of inattentiveness, as well as four to eight of nine symptoms of impulsivity/overactivity occurring on a frequent basis within the home setting. The PSI-SF results for both parents were significantly elevated, suggesting greater than would be expected levels of parenting stress. Such stress would seem to stem not only from interactions between Jesse and his parents but also from characteristics he reportedly possesses that make it difficult for them to parent him in traditional ways. However, it is necessary to view the degree of deviance on these ratings with some caution, as both parents rated themselves as mildly depressed on the SCL-90-R. Depressed parents are more likely to endorse symptoms of psychopathology in their children.

Jesse's fourth-grade teacher and his school counselor completed a number of behavior rating scales as well. Table 10.3 also shows these results. Their ratings were based on observations of Jesse in a classroom with 24 students, one teacher, and an occasional aide, as well as in one-to-one counseling situations. Their ADHD Rating Scale results revealed all symptoms of inattentiveness, as well as five or six of nine symptoms of impulsivity/overactivity occurring on a frequent basis within the school. Results of the BASC revealed significant elevations in the areas of attention problems, hyperactivity, aggression, depression, difficulty adapting to new situations, poor study skills, conduct problems, learning problems, and anxiety. Results of the CAP fell at the 99th percentile with respect to both inattentiveness and impulsivity/overactivity. SSRS results revealed below-average peer socialization skills. Results of the APRS revealed that Jesse's overall academic productivity fell below the average range when compared with other fourth-grade boys.

Jesse was administered a number of psychological tests, the results of which appear in Table 10.3 as well. The Vocabulary subtest of the WISC-III revealed a scaled score of 6, suggesting that Jesse's verbal abilities fall below the average range when compared with same-age peers. This test is given to determine whether comparisons with same-age peers are appropriate. Although Jesse scored below average, previous testing results indicated that he was of average intelligence with a language delay. It was determined that comparisons of his be-

TABLE 10.3. A Case of ADHD and CD in a 10-Year-Old Male

Mother		Father		School counselor	
Interview report of ADHD symptoms		Interview report of ADHD symptoms		CAP (Percentile)	
Inattention	8	Inattention	9	Inattention	99*
Hyperactivity/Impulsivity	6	Hyperactivity/Impulsivity	9	Overactivity	99*
ADHD Rating Scale (Symptoms rated >2)		ADHD Rating Scale (Symptoms rated >2)		ADHD Rating Scale (Symptoms rated >2)	
Inattention	8	Inattention	7	Inattention	9
Hyperactivity/Impulsivity	8	Hyperactivity/Impulsivity	4	Hyperactivity/Impulsivity	6
BASC		BASC		SSRS	
Subscale	Percentile	Subscale	Percentile	Raw Score 14 (below average)	
Hyperactivity	89	Hyperactivity	99*		
Aggression	99*	Aggression	99*	**Teacher**	
Conduct Problems	99*	Conduct Problems	99*		
Anxiety	48	Anxiety	15	CAP (Percentile)	
Depression	94	Depression	92		
Somatization	19	Somatization	77	Inattention	99*
Atypicality	85	Atypicality	90	Overactivity	99*
Withdrawal	58	Withdrawal	69		
Attention Problems	89	Attention Problems	92	ADHD Rating Scale (Symptoms rated >2)	
				Inattention	9
				Hyperactivity	5
				SSRS	
				Raw Score 16 (below average)	
				APRS	
				Productivity 25 (below average)	

	Testing data		
Test	Raw score	Standard/scaled score	Percentile
WISC-III Vocabulary	20	6	
Conners CPT			
Hits	295 (91%)		99*
Omissions	29 (9%)		99*
Commissions	32 (89%)	61	87
Hit Rate	473	30	3*
Hit Rate Standard Error	22	84	99*
Variability of *SE*	47	68	97*

Note. An asterisk indicates a clinically significant elevation (>95th percentile or <5th percentile).

havior with same-age peers were appropriate despite the lower Vocabulary score obtained during the current evaluation. Results of the CPT provided strong evidence of attentional difficulties and impulsivity. This is a lab test comparing a child's attention and impulsivity on this 14-minute task with that of other children of the same age. Although a normal score on this task does not rule out ADHD, an abnormal score suggests that there is some kind of problem affecting an individual's performance on a task of this kind. Jesse displayed the slow and inconsistent response style and the elevated number of omission errors suggestive of inattentiveness, as well as the elevated number of commission errors suggestive of impulsivity.

In general, it was our opinion that although Jesse's language delays might explain inattentive behavior, they would not explain his impulsivity and overactivity. In the absence of an alternative explanation, the evaluation results indicated that he met DSM-IV criteria for a diagnosis of Attention-Deficit/Hyperactivity Disorder, Combined Type. Evidence of impairment was found in his parent- and teacher-reported below-average peer socialization skills and academic productivity. In addition, his parents, teacher, and school counselor reported that he displayed a pattern of behavior in which major age-appropriate societal norms and rules were violated. This behavior was of sufficient frequency and severity to warrant an additional DSM-IV diagnosis of Conduct Disorder. Given the parental alcohol abuse and severe marital discord, Jesse was considered to be at risk for developing more serious delinquent behaviors and possible substance abuse. We made the following recommendations to the parents:

1. We recommended selected readings to educate the parents about ADHD and its associated features. During our feedback session, we explained which of Jesse's behaviors were symptoms of ADHD and which were symptoms of CD, so that his parents would not attribute conduct problems to the developmental disorder. We also recommended that Jesse's parents consider participating in a support group for parents of ADHD children.

2. We recommended that Jesse's mother receive treatment for her alcohol abuse, and that the parents pursue marital therapy to attempt to address their extreme marital conflict. We pointed out to them that it would be difficult to help Jesse improve his behavior while they were experiencing their current level of stress.

3. To reduce the level of parenting stress, and to gain greater control over Jesse's ADHD/CD behaviors in the home setting, we recommended detailed instruction in the use of specialized behavior management strategies. Jesse's parents did contact the clinic and begin attending a behavioral parent training group. However, they dropped out after only two sessions. It is not unusual for parents who are experiencing severe personal stress to have poor outcomes in such a parent training group.

4. We suggested several classroom accommodations for ADHD and behavior problems, such as those discussed in Chapter 15, this volume. Following the implementation of such accommodations for a reasonable length of time, it was recommended that school personnel meet with Jesse's parents to discuss whether Jesse had made sufficient improvement in his behavior and academic performance. If his aggressive behavior continued, he might need to be considered for placement in a separate classroom for children with behavior disorders.

5. We recommended that Jesse's poor social skills be addressed in a school-based program. Although he was likely receiving some benefit from his individual counseling with the school counselor, it was unlikely that such counseling would result in improvements in his classroom behavior or peer socialization skills. Such skills would be better taught in the context of a peer social skills training group, which would

afford him the opportunity for receiving supervised practice in a relatively realistic context.

6. We also recommended a trial on stimulant medication. Jesse's parents contacted his pediatrician, who initiated such a trial and reported that it resulted in improvements in his impulsivity and attention.

This case was included as an example of childhood-onset CD in combination with ADHD. Jesse's story is, unfortunately, not atypical of children from chaotic homes with parental psychopathology and poor monitoring. This case emphasizes the importance of looking beyond ADHD at family functioning when making treatment recommendations. Jesse's ADHD was clearly a problem, but his conduct problems warranted immediate attention.

ADHD, PSEUDO-PREDOMINANTLY INATTENTIVE TYPE, IN AN OLDER ADOLESCENT

Daniel was raised in an intact family. He was the youngest of three children. His parents had a stable marriage. Daniel's father had a high school education and owned a limousine service. His mother had an associate's degree and worked as an occupational therapy assistant.

Daniel was a healthy infant who was difficult to put on a schedule. Subsequent major developmental milestones were achieved at normal ages. As a toddler, he was very stubborn and always quite active. Because the family was a very busy and active family, these traits were not identified as deviant. Daniel attended the public schools. He was seen as very active beginning in kindergarten. Throughout his elementary school years, his teachers commented on his distractibility, inattention, overactivity, impulsivity, and failure to complete assignments. When he completed his work it was usually of high quality, but he frequently forgot to turn in his assignments, rushed through them, or simply did not complete them. Thus, his grades averaged C's, with his poor work habits partially compensated for by his excellent test performance. He was always seen as a happy child, with no behavioral or emotional concerns. However, because he appeared so inattentive and distractible and was not putting forth the expected amount of effort in school, school personnel conducted a psychoeducational evaluation in the fifth grade. The results of the evaluation indicated that Daniel was of above-average intelligence and had no specific learning disabilities. School personnel determined that he was ineligible for any special services.

As Daniel entered middle school, his behavior at home became more difficult to manage. He was frequently argumentative with his parents and refused to comply with their requests. He also threw tantrums when he did not get his way. His parents found that the traditional parenting techniques they had used successfully with their older children did not work with Daniel. They found themselves engaged in increasingly negative interactions with him and giving in when they got tired of arguing. Finally, they consulted a behavior therapist for parenting suggestions. The use of these resulted in some improvement in Daniel's behavior in the home setting.

In school, however, Daniel was experiencing difficulty as the workload and responsibilities increased. His grades began to drop. His teachers, aware of his cognitive abilities, reprimanded him frequently for being "lazy" and "unmotivated." Finally, Daniel failed the eighth grade. His parents took Daniel to see a counselor to determine why he was not working up to his potential. Daniel did not want to go to therapy, and his parents finally gave up the struggle to make him attend, as they did not see any improvement. Daniel appeared to stop trying in school after failing, and his mood became more noticeably subdued. Although he continued to enjoy spending time with a few close friends, he appeared sad or irritable at home. He appeared to worry about school and continued to perform poorly. He also began experimenting with marijuana and alcohol around this time. He failed the 10th grade. After repeating the 10th grade, Daniel failed all but one of his courses in the first semester of 11th grade. Art classes were the only courses in which he consistently performed well. He rarely completed the work in any other courses.

School personnel conducted another psychoeducational evaluation after Daniel failed the first semester of 11th grade. Results of a Wechsler Adult Intelligence Scale—Revised (WAIS-R) revealed a Full Scale IQ of 129. Behavior rating scales completed by his parents and teachers noted the presence of inattentiveness. A self-report measure completed by Daniel noted the presence of depressive symptomatology. Despite a clear history of academic underachievement dating back to the first grade, and no evidence of depressive symptomatology prior to Daniel's junior high school years, the school psychologist attributed Daniel's school failure to depression and recommended a medication evaluation. Daniel's parents were not convinced that this was the root of Daniel's problems and brought him into our clinic for an evaluation.

At the time of the evaluation, Daniel was 17 years, 10 months old. He was in the 11th grade. His health was very good, although he was nearsighted and had poor handwriting skills. His most recent medical examination had been completely normal. A review of family psychiatric history indicated that one of Daniel's paternal uncles had experienced school difficulties, alcohol abuse, and depression. There was no history of any other psychiatric or learning difficulties on either side of the family.

Throughout the interview, Daniel was quite fidgety and active. He tapped his feet throughout the evaluation and shifted in his chair frequently. He occasionally got up and walked around the room. This activity did not appear to be motivated by anxiety, as Daniel appeared very comfortable during the evaluation. His answers were clear and informative. He reported having no problems at home but did indicate that he did not enjoy spending time with his family. He reported that he preferred to spend time with his friends skateboarding and playing music. He admitted to occasional marijuana and alcohol use in the past 2 or 3 years. He reported that he did not enjoy school, because he did not like the rules and found most of the work boring. He did enjoy his art classes. He reported some worries about his school performance but denied that these symptoms interfered with his life. Daniel indicated that he had been depressed in the past but denied any current depressive symptoms or suicidal ideation. He indicated that he felt he had been depressed because he was not doing well in school, despite trying. He viewed many of his difficulties as being the result of distractibility and inattentiveness. Daniel reported that he displayed nine of nine symptoms of inattentiveness and four of nine symptoms of impulsivity/overactivity on a frequent basis.

Similarly, Daniel's parents endorsed nine of nine symptoms of inattentiveness, as well as three or four of nine symptoms of impulsivity/overactivity as being typical of Daniel. They also reported Daniel to display five of eight behaviors associated with ODD to a significant degree for his age, including irritability and noncompliance with adult requests. No symptoms of CD were endorsed, nor did Daniel currently meet criteria for any other psychiatric condition.

Table 10.4 shows the results of the parent and teacher rating scales and psychological testing. Daniel's mother completed the CBCL, which indicated clinically significant problems on the Attention Problems, Withdrawal, Social Problems, Delinquent, and Anxious/ Depressed factors. On the ADHD Rating Scale, Daniel was rated as having all symptoms of inattentiveness occurring on a frequent basis within the home setting. Results of the DBRS revealed significant symptoms of ODD occurring on a frequent basis within the home setting. SSRS results revealed below-average peer socialization skills.

TABLE 10.4. Results for a Case of ADHD, Predominantly Inattentive Type, in a 17-Year-Old Adolescent

Mother		Father		Teachers	
Interview report of ADHD symptoms		Interview report of ADHD symptoms		ADHD Rating Scale (Symptoms rated <2)	
Inattention	9	Inattention	9	Inattention	6 and 7
Hyperactivity/Impulsivity	4	Hyperactivity/Impulsivity	4	Hyperactivity/Impulsivity	2 and 4
ADHD Rating Scale (Symptoms rated >2)					
Inattention	9				
Hyperactivity/Impulsivity	1				

CBCL			CBCL	
Subscale	T score		Subscale	T score
Withdrawn	82*		Withdrawn	63
Somatic Complaints	59		Somatic Complaints	50
Anxious/Depressed	70*		Anxious/Depressed	53
Social Problems	73*		Social Problems	56
Thought Problems	57		Thought Problems	58
Attention Problems	75*		Attention Problems	67*
Delinquent Behavior	72*		Delinquent Behavior	61
Aggressive Behavior	62		Aggressive Behavior	50

DBRS			SSRS	
(Symptoms rated >2)	5		Standard Score 70 (below average)	

Testing data			
Test	Raw score	Standard/scaled score	Percentile
Stanford–Binet			
Vocabulary	36	108	
Conners CPT			
Hits	324 (100%)		18
Omissions	0 (0%)		18
Commissions	8 (22%)	40	15
Hit Rate	525	18	1*
Hit Rate Standard Error	9	63	91
Variability of *SE*	10	53	65

Note. An asterisk indicates a clinically significant elevation (>95th percentile or <5th percentile).

Teacher ratings also revealed significant attention problems. These rating scales were completed by Daniel's English and algebra teachers, based on their observations of him in 45-minute classes with 30 other students, over the course of a semester. On the CBCL-TRF, Daniel obtained scores in the clinically significant range on the Attention Problems scale. His teachers' ADHD Rating Scale results revealed six or seven of nine symptoms of inattentiveness, and two to four of nine symptoms of impulsivity/overactivity occurring on a frequent basis within the classroom setting. These ratings of ADHD behaviors in the classroom are quite high for high school teachers to report. Because their interactions with students are much more limited than those of elementary or even middle school teachers, they are less likely to notice and report significant symptoms of ADHD. Results of the Defiant Behavior Rating Scale revealed that in the classroom, zero or one of eight behaviors associated with ODD occurred on a frequent basis. SSRS results revealed below average peer socialization skills in the areas of cooperation, assertiveness, and self-control.

Daniel was administered psychological tests, the results of which appear in Table 10.4 as well. Daniel's SB-IV Vocabulary test performance yielded a total score of 36 and a corresponding standardized score of 108, which is within the average range. Although Daniel's CPT performance was slow and inconsistent, this test did not provide strong evidence of attentional difficulties.

The results of this evaluation supported a diagnosis of ADHD and ODD. According to both Daniel and his parents, he did not meet DSM-IV criteria for any other psychiatric disorder. His marijuana and alcohol use was more experimental at this time rather than indicative of a substance abuse disorder. Daniel's depressive symptomatology was subclinical, based on his report and that of his parents. Furthermore, it appeared to be secondary to the years of school failure, rather than primary, as the school psychologist had believed. The chronological onset of the depression was much later than the onset of ADHD symptoms. Daniel's ODD behaviors were much more significant in the home than in school. In fact, his teachers did not see him as defiant.

Evidence of impairment was found in Daniel's history of academic underachievement and school failure, as well as his parent- and teacher-reported peer socialization difficulties.

We made several recommendations to the family:

1. We emphasized education about ADHD and its associated features for Daniel, his parents, and his teachers.
2. We recommended a course of family therapy, focused on problem-solving and communication training for Daniel and his parents. The therapy described in Chapter 14 (this volume) would be ideal.
3. We referred Daniel to a psychiatrist for consideration of a trial of stimulant medication.
4. We made a number of educational modifications for Daniel's ADHD difficulties in the school setting, including a guidance counselor or other school personnel to play a coaching role, a modified homework load, and additional time to complete assigned tasks.
5. We suggested supportive counseling for Daniel to help him adjust to his ADHD diagnosis and plan for his future, considering his ADHD as part of his pattern of strengths and weaknesses.

Daniel refused to participate in any form of family therapy but readily agreed to the other interventions.

This case illustrates a number of issues in assessing ADHD in older adolescents. First of all, because ADHD is a developmental disorder, there must be a history of preadolescent onset of ADHD characteristics. This history is often difficult to ascertain in an older adolescent. In Daniel's case, school report cards from his entire academic career were available and clearly confirmed his mother's report of early ADHD symptomatology. It is important to attempt to obtain such objective data. Second, it is interesting to note that other mental health professionals had attributed Daniel's difficulties to depression. Although he did display depressive symptomatology and had possibly been clinically depressed at the time of the previous evaluation, a diagnosis of depression or dysthymia does not necessarily rule out comorbid ADHD. In Daniel's case, careful interviewing revealed that the ADHD symptoms predated the onset of the depression by at least 5 years. Third, this case illustrates some points about the developmental course of ADHD. Although Daniel was given the diagnosis of

ADHD, Predominantly Inattentive Type, this type must be discriminated from *pure inattention*. If evaluated as a child, it is quite possible that Daniel might have met diagnostic criteria for ADHD, Combined Type. He had a history of impulsivity and continues to be fidgety and impulsive even now. However, in the course of development, symptoms of hyperactivity are likely to decline, whereas the inattentiveness and impulsivity may continue. The DSM-IV items were normed on children, and the items do not necessarily apply as well to the manifestation of ADHD in adolescents or adults. Thus, it is entirely possible for an older adolescent or an adult to meet DSM-IV criteria for ADHD, Predominantly Inattentive Type when they actually display a pattern of symptoms that is characteristic of ADHD, Combined Type: namely, difficulties with response inhibition.

ADHD, PREDOMINANTLY INATTENTIVE TYPE

Tim was a quiet and somewhat introverted child who readily "faded into the crowd." Apart from his quiet demeanor, his early development was unremarkable. He reached the developmental milestones at appropriate times and was not a behavior problem for his mother who had raised Tim and his younger brother alone. Tim's father and mother had split up before Tim was born and Tim had no contact with his father.

Tim attended a parochial elementary school where he performed "adequately" both academically and behaviorally. However, he never volunteered information and often seemed to be "off in a daze." His teachers frequently had to repeat questions when they called on him because he did not seem to catch what they asked. Although Tim did not have problems with reading decoding, he had some difficulty staying with a train of thought when he began to read passages. This pattern created problems in his ability to comprehend what he read, and consequently Tim received some individual assistance from his teachers for his weak reading skills. Tim's family moved prior to his entering the third grade, resulting in a transfer to another parochial school. About this time, Tim began to display greater difficulties in school because of the increased amount of independent work expected of him. Tim typically failed to complete his work in an appropriate amount of time and had trouble finishing assigned readings. His teachers often made comments that Tim seemed unable to "focus" on his work and consequently made very inefficient use of his time.

Because of these difficulties, Ms. P. requested that the local public school system evaluate Tim to determine whether he was eligible for government-mandated individualized education services prior to his entering fourth grade. The school evaluation team detected some weaknesses in reading skills, but Tim was not found eligible for such services. Tim's problems with "attentional lapses," "poor focusing," and low productivity continued to be problems as he transitioned into middle school in fifth grade. His grades became much more inconsistent in middle school ranging from B's to D's. Although Tim was on a rotating schedule in middle school and consequently had much briefer contact with his teachers, school personnel continued to comment about Tim's "spacy" demeanor and frequent tendency to get lost in "daydreams." Tim's productivity continued to decline in seventh and eighth grade as a result of uncompleted homework, inadequate preparation, and slow completion of classroom work. Tim obtained passing grades, but his greatest difficulties were in reading-intensive subjects, such as English and history.

Tim's social adjustment was generally uneventful. He had no problems forming or maintaining friendships and was typically well received by his peers. Tim's interpersonal style was often described as "reserved" or "somewhat withdrawn." Tim never showed an interest in organized recreational activities and did not usually initiate social contacts with his peers. Yet he often was included by his friends in informal activities such as playing basketball or going to the mall. Despite Tim's tendency to "keep to himself," his friends seem to enjoy having him around.

During his freshman year at high school, Tim's attentional problems and poor study habits had a more significant impact on his academic performance. He failed three classes because of low test scores and uncompleted work. He was able to pass on to the 10th grade because he retook the failed classes in summer school. Tim's academic difficulties became a larger point of contention between him and his mother at about this time. They frequently argued about Tim's poor performance, and his mother often accused Tim of "not trying hard enough." Tim expressed frustration over these accusations and typically retorted that he was doing his best. Despite the increased pressure from his mother, Tim failed his 10th-grade English class and had to take the class over in summer school to enter the 11th grade. Although his 10th-grade teachers did not view Tim as a conduct problem, they frequently complained about his failure to complete work, weak ability to focus, distractibility, and disorganization. Because of Tim's persistent difficulty displaying appropriate study skills in academic subjects, his mother and school officials decided to transfer him to a vocational high school for 11th grade. Although he still faced academic demands, they were interspersed with more applied activities. He spent every other week in an auto mechanic program. Despite this alternative school placement, Tim was clearly failing a literature course 3 months into the school year and his teachers commented about his frequent "zoning out in class."

Ms. P. decided to take Tim to a psychiatrist for an evaluation of his "attentional problems" halfway through his 11th-grade year. Based on an interview with Tim and his mother, the psychiatrist diagnosed Tim with a "provisional" ADHD. He placed Tim on a trial of Cylert (pemoline), which produced some subjective improvement in Tim's ability to focus, but his teachers noted no objective improvement. Consequently, the medication was stopped until a more extensive evaluation could be accomplished. Tim's psychiatrist referred him to the ADHD clinic for further evaluation and consultation. Table 10.5 presents the results of this evaluation. Tim's mother and two teachers all reported a significant number of the inattentive features of ADHD. However, none of the impulsive/overactive symptoms of ADHD were reported for Tim. Although Tim's teachers rated him as displaying an average number of social skills, his mother also rated Tim as significantly "withdrawn."

During the interview, Ms. P. described Tim as a frequently "sullen" youth. Yet she pointed out that Tim had never displayed any prolonged periods of depression or excessive anxiety. She stated that their relationship had become tense and periodically conflictual over the few years prior to the evaluation, with the focus of their disagreements being on Tim's inconsistent academic performance. Ms. P. indicated that Tim is often irritable around her, often blames others for his mistakes, and frequently "talks back." However, she denied any substantial problems with Tim complying with her wishes in other areas. For example, she indicated that Tim typically completes chores around the house when asked or expected to do so.

Tim appeared very calm during the interview and readily cooperated with the examiner. Table 10.5 summarizes Tim's test results. Because no recent cognitive testing had been completed with Tim, he was given the SB-IV Vocabulary subtest to obtain a brief estimate of his verbal intelligence. Tim obtained a raw score of 32 and a corresponding verbal reasoning standard score of 96 on this subtest. His performance fell at the 39th percentile and in the average range, suggesting that Tim has at least an average level of verbal intelligence. Consequently, comparison of test results with chronological age norms were deemed appropriate. Tim displayed a good performance on the CPT. Tim responded to target items with an average level of accuracy (omissions) and only infrequently responded to inappropriate test items (commissions), indicating a normal performance on this measure of inattention and impulsivity.

TABLE 10.5. Results for a Case of Purely Inattentive ADHD in a 17-Year-Old Male

Mother	English teacher	Math teacher

Interview report of ADHD symptoms		ADHD Rating Scale (Symptoms rated >2)		ADHD Rating Scale (Symptoms rated >2)	
Inattention	6	Inattention	9	Inattention	7
Hyperactivity/Impulsivity	0	Hyperactivity/Impulsivity	0	Hyperactivity/Impulsivity	0

ADHD Rating Scale
(Symptoms rated >2)

Inattention	5
Hyperactivity/Impulsivity	0

CBCL		CBCL		CBCL	
Subscale	Percentile	Subscale	Percentile	Subscale	Percentile
Withdrawn	95*	Withdrawn	84	Withdrawn	50
Somatic Complaints	50	Somatic Complaints	76	Somatic Complaints	50
Anxious	93	Anxious	55	Anxious	73
Social Problems	50	Social Problems	84	Social Problems	63
Thought Problems	50	Thought Problems	50	Thought Problems	50
Attention Problems	95*	Attention Problems	95*	Attention Problems	88
Delinquent Behavior	86	Delinquent Behavior	61	Delinquent Behavior	60
Aggressive Behavior	84	Aggressive Behavior	70	Aggressive Behavior	50

SSRS		SSRS		SSRS	
Standard Score 85	16	Standard Score 105	63	Standard Score 96	39

DBRS
Number of ODD Symptoms 3

	Testing data		
Test	Raw score	Standard/scaled score	Percentile
SB-IV Verbal Reasoning (prorated from Vocabulary score)	32	96	39
Conners CPT			
Hits	324 (100%)		18
Omissions	0 (0%)		18
Commissions	13 (36%)	46	35
Hit Rate	348	47	38
Hit Rate Standard Error	4	43	25
Variability of *SE*	4	43	26

Note. An asterisk indicates a clinically significant elevation (>95th percentile or <5th percentile).

Tim acknowledged seven inattentive symptoms of ADHD but denied any impulsive or overactive symptoms. He mentioned that his attentional problems are most significant on reading tasks. Tim explained that he has problems "focusing" on what he is reading. He described his focusing problems as being unable to tune out distractions. Tim often has had to read and reread literature in a very quiet area to comprehend what he is reading. Although his inattentive difficulties have been present since his elementary school years, Tim felt that they have been most intense since high school.

Based on the evaluation, an impression was formed of Tim as a 17-year, 9-month-old young man of presumably average intelligence who has displayed a chronic history of inattentiveness, distractibility, and underachievement on academic tasks since kindergarten. A significant number of the inattentive symptoms of ADHD were consistently reported for Tim, but he had no history of any of the impulsive/overactive symptoms of this condition. Based on the DSM-IV criteria, Tim's pattern of symptoms and associated difficulties supported a diagnosis of ADHD, Predominantly Inattentive Type (314.00). No other clinical diagnoses emerged from the evaluation. The pattern of conflict between Tim and Ms. P. was classified as Parent–Child Relational Problem (V61.20). Tim's difficulties were complicated by a history of weaknesses on reading-related tasks. Psychoeducational testing completed by the school had reportedly ruled out any substantial specific learning disabilities, which would account for his reading-related weaknesses. Yet it was unclear whether subtle processing problems, such as a central auditory processing deficit, had been fully ruled out as a contributing factor in Tim's inconsistent academic performance.

We made several recommendations to Ms. P. and Tim following the evaluation:

1. Parent and patient education about ADHD through directed readings, follow-up consultation, and participation in a support group were suggested. However, the purely inattentive type of ADHD was distinguished from the more common form of ADHD.
2. A neuropsychological evaluation was recommended to more definitively rule out the possibility that a language-related learning disability may have been contributing to Tim's academic difficulties.
3. Vocational assessment to help establish appropriate career goals for Tim was emphasized.
4. Participation in family counseling by Tim and his mother was stressed.
5. A variety of organizational and compensatory behavior strategies for Tim were discussed, such as those described in Chapter 15 (this volume).
6. The option of treatment with stimulant medication was discussed. The lower efficacy of medication for the treatment of the purely inattentive form of ADHD was noted.

Tim's case illustrates the differences between the more common form of ADHD, which seems to be primarily a problem of response control, and a *purely inattentive* type of the condition. No DSM-IV category explicitly outlines the *purely inattentive type* of the condition. The most related DSM-IV classification for this group is ADHD, *Predominantly Inattentive Type*. Yet although many individuals may not display a significant number of the impulsive/overactive symptoms of ADHD, particularly by adolescence, problems with impulsivity or self-regulation are often present. The *purely inattentive subtype*, discussed in Chapter 4 (this volume), is a much rarer group that appears to have distinct attentional problems and associated difficulties. This subgroup is characterized by a history of inattentive problems devoid of any significant difficulties with impulsivity or overactivity. Such individuals tend to be described as "daydreamy," "spacy," or "in a fog." They tend to be viewed more as lethargic and slow. Both the purely inattentive and combined type of ADHD individuals tend to have academic problems such as failing to complete work. Yet such problems are often due to different reasons for these subtypes. Individuals with purely inattentive ADHD typically have trouble completing work because they struggle to process competing sources of information. Individuals with ADHD, Combined Type tend to either impulsively rush through their work or to have difficulty holding themselves to the task. Although individuals suffering from purely inattentive ADHD, are more frequently anxious, depressed, and withdrawn, they typically have fewer social problems than do ADHD children.

Tim's case illustrated many of these differences. There was no evidence of the substantial problems with response control characteristic of ADHD, Combined Type. Although some difficulty in his interactions with his mother was reported, no significant behavioral disorder was evident at home. Tim had been rated as significantly "withdrawn" but no substantial problems in his social functioning were reported. His academic difficulties appeared to be due to his problems in focusing attention, particularly on reading tasks, rather than due to problems with sustaining attention. It is possible that a neurocognitive problem, such as a subtle learning disability or a "central auditory processing" deficit, may be the source of Tim's *purely inattentive* form of ADHD.

ANXIETY DISORDER WITHOUT ADHD

Fifteen-year-old Vanessa was the eldest of two sisters. Her mother had been treated for "nerves" early in her marriage to Vanessa's father. From the time Vanessa was born, she was difficult to comfort and appeared to display greater difficulty adjusting to new situations than Vanessa's mother had seen her friends' children display. However, her early development was normal.

In addition to her own history of probable anxiety, Vanessa's mother was somewhat anxious and protective with Vanessa. She discouraged exploration and risk taking. Vanessa's father was much more impulsive, and Vanessa's mother did what she could to make certain Vanessa did not take after him. When Vanessa was 3, her sister was born. It was clear early on that the two girls had very different temperaments. People often said that Vanessa was the image of her mother, and her sister took after her father.

Vanessa had a great deal of difficulty separating from her mother when she began school. She would cling to her mother and cry each day when her mother left her at kindergarten. After a few weeks, Vanessa was able to tolerate the separation, but she was a very shy child who hung back and did not initiate interactions with the other children. Academically, however, Vanessa did extremely well. She was an A student throughout her school years, and the only concerns teachers ever expressed had to do with her social reticence.

Vanessa's parents, however, noticed that she was a "worrier." Although she consistently performed well in school, she spent a great deal of time on her school work and expressed anxiety regarding tests and her academic performance. She also worried about making friends, and any number of possible things that might go wrong with her family members. She complained of frequent headaches and stomachaches when tests were coming up or when she had to give a presentation in class.

When Vanessa entered middle school in the sixth grade, she moved to a bigger school and did not have classes with many of her friends. She appeared very sad, and withdrew from activities in which she had been interested. Her mother noted that she seemed easily fatigued and somewhat distracted. She saw a counselor, and her mood seemed to improve by the time she entered seventh grade. Soon thereafter Vanessa's father went to see a psychologist after he was fired from a job because he could not keep up with his paperwork. He was diagnosed with ADHD and successfully treated with a stimulant. As Vanessa's mother began reading about ADHD, she wondered if Vanessa's symptoms of inattentiveness and distractibility might be explained by this disorder. She learned that it was hereditary and felt that Vanessa might meet the "Inattentive Type" profile.

Vanessa was in the 10th grade at the time of the evaluation. Her health was reported to be very good. She did experience environmental allergies. She also had difficulty falling asleep at night, which had been true for much of her life. She experienced related difficulty waking in the morning. Her appetite was normal. Her speech, hearing, vision, and motor coordination skills were also within normal limits.

The review of childhood and adolescent psychiatric symptoms with Vanessa's mother indicated that Vanessa displayed four of nine symptoms of inattentiveness and no symptoms of impulsivity/overactivity. She frequently failed to pay close attention to details, was easily distracted, and appeared forgetful in her daily activities. No ODD or CD behaviors were endorsed. Her mood was described as typically worried or sad, and many symptoms of Generalized Anxiety Disorder and Dysthymic Disorder were endorsed. She was reported to have a withdrawn peer interaction style and difficulty making friends. Vanessa had done well academically throughout her school years, and no teacher had ever reported any behavioral problems or difficulty with inattentiveness or distractibility. A review of the family psychiatric history revealed depression and anxiety on the maternal side. Vanessa's sister had recently been diagnosed with ODD.

The interview with Vanessa revealed a neatly groomed adolescent who participated willingly in the interview and testing but appeared reserved and bit her nails throughout the session. No obvious signs of ADHD were observed. Vanessa responded to interview questioning in a clear and informative manner. She was generally aware of the reasons for her being evaluated. She reported that she liked school overall, especially seeing her friends and going to gym class. She reported that did not like some of her peers and did not enjoy much of the schoolwork. She admitted that she was somewhat shy but reported that she did have a group of friends with whom she went to the mall and to see movies. She described a variety of additional recreational activities she enjoyed, such as playing with the computer and playing pool. Vanessa reported positive family relationships. She indicated that she was generally worried about a lot of things and had been at least since late elementary school. She stated that she was worried more days than not, and her worries interfered with her social life as well as with her schoolwork. She had difficulty controlling the worry. Vanessa endorsed five of the nine symptoms associated with inattentiveness in the DSM-IV ADHD symptom list but reported that those symptoms were primarily present when she was worried about something.

Table 10.6 shows the behavior rating scales and results of psychological testing. The results of the parent rating scales revealed normal scores on all scales except the BASC subscale pertaining to social withdrawal. Results of the parent version of the ADHD Rating Scale revealed borderline significant symptoms of inattentiveness occurring on a frequent basis within the home setting and no symptoms of impulsivity/overactivity. None of the scores on the various teacher rating scales were clinically elevated. The teacher endorsed no symptoms of either inattentiveness or impulsivity/overactivity on the ADHD Rating Scale.

Vanessa's WISC-III Vocabulary scaled score of 11 suggested that her overall verbal abilities were within the average range. The CPT provided no evidence for problems with inattention or impulsivity.

The results of this evaluation did not support a diagnosis of ADHD. The only significant ratings of ADHD symptoms came from Vanessa's mother, and even those were merely in the borderline range or even lower on most of the rating scales. In addition, there was no evidence of any impairment due to her inattention in any domain of Vanessa's life. She has performed very well in school. Vanessa's difficulties lay more clearly in the emotional domain. She and her mother both reported that she had been experiencing, at least since late elementary school, a pattern of excessive anxiety of sufficient frequency and severity to warrant a DSM-IV diagnosis of Generalized Anxiety Disorder. Given the paternal history of ADHD, it is understandable that Vanessa's parents identified her attentional difficulties as possibly being related to ADHD. However, the distractibility and difficulty concentrating can also be symptoms of anxiety, and in this case, the evidence pointed much more clearly in

TABLE 10.6. Results for a Case of Generalized Anxiety Disorder in a 15-Year-Old Female

Mother		Math teacher	
Interview report of ADHD symptoms		ADHD Rating Scale	
		(Symptoms rated >2)	
Inattention	4	Inattention	0
Hyperactivity/Impulsivity	0	Hyperactivity/Impulsivity	0
ADHD Rating Scale			
(Symptoms rated >2)			
Inattention	6		
Hyperactivity/Impulsivity	0		

CBCL		CBCL	
Subscale	Percentile	Subscale	Percentile
Withdrawn	50	Withdrawn	55
Somatic Complaints	74	Somatic Complaints	78
Anxious	50	Anxious	78
Social Problems	50	Social Problems	50
Thought Problems	50	Thought Problems	50
Attention Problems	87	Attention Problems	50
Delinquent Behavior	50	Delinquent Behavior	50
Aggressive Behavior	50	Aggressive Behavior	50

DBRS		DBRS	
Number of ODD Symptoms	0	Number of ODD Symptoms	0

Testing data			
Test	Raw score	Standard/scaled score	Percentile
WISC-III Vocabulary	46	11	
Conners CPT			
Hits	324 (100%)		14
Omissions	0 (0%)		14
Commissions	28 (78%)	73	99*
Hit Rate	287	64	92
Hit Rate Standard Error	4	39	15
Variability of *SE*	5	42	22

Note. An asterisk indicates a clinically significant elevation (>95th percentile or <5th percentile).

that direction as an explanation for Vanessa's difficulties. We made the following recommendations to the family:

1. We stressed cognitive-behavioral therapy and relaxation training for Vanessa aimed at ameliorating her emotional difficulties, as well as social skills training.
2. We emphasized the development of organizational strategies for Vanessa as well as coping strategies to help manage anxiety regarding school projects.
3. We referred the family to a therapist in the family's home community.

The family planned to follow through on the recommendations.

In this case, Vanessa's symptom of inattentiveness had a different flavor to it than does the inattentiveness typically found in ADHD. For instance, she was distracted by her own intrusive thoughts rather than being impulsively drawn off task, as someone with ADHD would experience. Her inattentiveness cut across all activities, whereas someone with ADHD would not display attention problems when the task at hand was interesting. She was more preoccupied, easily fatigued, and had difficulty *focusing* on tasks, whereas the ADHD adolescent would display more problems with *vigilance* or *sustained* attention.

This case illustrates the importance of viewing inattentiveness as a symptom, rather than a disorder in and of itself. Inattentiveness and distractibility can be symptoms of many things, from anxiety to ADHD to learning disabilities to a hearing impairment. It is important for the evaluating clinician to consider all possible explanations for the symptom of inattention rather than simply assuming that inattention in and of itself is evidence of ADHD.

DYSTHYMIA WITHOUT ADHD

Eric's early life gave little indication of the depression that would characterize his adolescence. He was described as an "alert, cheerful, and affectionate infant" who was "easy to comfort" and generally "easy tempered." Eric's mother reported a very close relationship with her son as an infant and toddler. When his younger siblings were born, 4-year-old Eric greatly enjoyed playing with them and helping to care for them. The only unusual thing about Eric during these early years was his tendency to be "insecure" in new situations. His mother took him to preschool for about 1 month when he was 4 years old. It was a daily battle to leave Eric at the preschool as he would cling to his mother and cry loudly. She decided to take him out of the preschool. At home, Eric seemed to be active and happy. He spent his days playing with his toys, siblings, or neighborhood peers.

When Eric entered kindergarten, he continued to display uneasiness over separating from his mother to go to school. After a period of adjusting to being at school each day, Eric settled in and participated in the class. He was an "artistic" kindergarten student who liked to do crafts and painting. Eric became active in seasonal sports at this time. He was a gifted soccer player and also did quite well with other sports, such as baseball. By the time Eric entered first grade, his reservations about attending school were behind him. However, he remained somewhat quiet or "reserved" in group situations apart from athletics. Academically, Eric did very well throughout elementary school. He had no problems learning new material and readily completed classwork. Eric attended a small public school that included all grades through eight in one building. By the time he entered sixth grade, Eric felt very comfortable with the school and his classmates. He had developed a number of friendships and seemed eager to go to school. Eric made the honor role in seventh and eighth grades. Outside school, Eric was involved in a number of different activities. He continued to be very active in sports. He also participated in scouting. He always seemed to look forward to campouts and was invested in earning merit badges and advancing to higher scout ranks.

Everything seemed to change when Eric entered high school. Eric switched to a new school that was much larger, incorporating students from several smaller schools. Although Eric had old friends at the school, he complained about the change and developed a negative attitude toward school. His grades began to decline and teachers complained about a lack of studying, failure to complete homework, and general lack of concern about his academic performance. During the summer after ninth grade, Eric began to smoke marijuana (cannabis). By the end of the summer, Eric was smoking marijuana on a daily basis. Eric lost interest in many things he had always enjoyed: He dropped out of scouts, stopped playing sports, and became less active with his friends. He seemed to always be in a "sad" or "irritable" mood. In 10th and 11th grades, some mild behavioral problems arose in school. Eric began to "talk back" to his parents and teachers and frequently lied to get out of trouble. Because of uncompleted work and lack of studying, Eric began to fail classes in 11th grade.

Midway through his junior year, Eric's parents requested an evaluation from the school to determine whether Eric was qualified for a government-mandated individualized education plan. The school administered psychoeducational testing, including the WAIS-R and the WJ-R Achievement battery. Eric obtained a WAIS-R Full Scale IQ score of 108, which fell in the average range of overall intellectual functioning. Some problems in "reading comprehension" were noted for Eric on the WJ-R, but his scores were not significantly discrepant from his estimated aptitude on the WAIS-R. Although Eric did not qualify for government-mandated individualized educational services, the school decided to place him in a resource room for one period a day to receive help with his studies. A school counselor also met with Eric on a few occasions because of concerns about Eric's "depressed mood." However, Eric would not open up with the counselor and no further contact was pursued. By the time Eric entered 12th grade, he seemed to have completely given up on school. He frequently cut classes, rarely completed independent work, and made no effort to prepare for tests. When confronted about his poor grades, he typically found somebody else to blame for his problems. His parents attempted to address these problems in family counseling on two separate occasions during the fall of his Eric's senior year. The counseling was discontinued because Eric refused to cooperate in the sessions and would not return after the initial session.

During the spring of Eric's senior year, his parents learned about the ADHD clinic through a friend whose child had been diagnosed with ADHD. Because Eric's failure to complete work, lack of preparation, and oppositional behavior were all problems shared with the friend's child, Eric's parents decided to have him tested for ADHD. Table 10.7 presents the results of the evaluation. Although there were a few significant parent and teacher ratings of the inattentive symptoms of ADHD, most ratings of Eric's ADHD symptoms were not significant. There were no significant ratings of the impulsive/overactive features of ADHD. Furthermore, Eric's parents indicated that the symptoms of inattentiveness they acknowledged for Eric had only been present since 9th or 10th grade. Eric was rated as displaying an average level of social skills by his teachers. Although some defiant behaviors were reported in written teacher comments, his teachers did not report a significant number of ODD symptoms on the DBRS.

Eric was very reserved and disengaged during the portion of the interview in which his parents were present. He became more engaged during the individual interview. He adopted a relaxed demeanor and readily discussed his difficulties. Eric was aware of the reasons for being evaluated. He reported frequently feeling bored in school and indicated that he consequently has trouble "paying attention." Eric indicated that he often felt "drained" and did not seem to have the energy or desire to invest himself in his schoolwork. If he tried to concentrate, he felt like everything was "just too big of an effort." When asked specifically about ADHD symptoms, his self-report did not reveal a significant number of such symptoms. Eric described his current mood as depressed. He said he had been frequently depressed since 13–14 years of age. This dysphoria worsened after the summer of his sophomore year to the point where he had suicidal ideation. He reported that he had used marijuana on a nearly daily basis during that summer. The depression lessened somewhat but had been present more days than not since that time. He denied any further suicidal ideation, plans, or intent. He found it difficult to enjoy things that typically interested him in the past and felt that he had greater concentration problems than before feeling depressed. He denied awareness of any precipitants for the depression. He stated that he continued to use cannabis periodically from his sophomore year until the end of his junior year. He decided to stop using cannabis because he felt it was "bringing him down" and keeping him from being productive. In terms of his family life, Eric described his parents as helpful. He indicated that he "got along well" with his peers but only had a few long-term friendships. Leisure activities included "hanging out with friends" and playing pool and basketball. Eric mentioned that he was no longer

TABLE 10.7. **Results for a Case of Dysthymia, No ADHD, in a 17-Year-Old Male**

Mother		Father		Math teacher	
Interview report of ADHD symptoms		Interview report of ADHD symptoms		CAP (Percentile)	
Inattention	5	Inattention	5	Inattention	NS
Hyperactivity/Impulsivity	1	Hyperactivity/Impulsivity	1	Overactivity	NS
ADHD Rating Scale (Symptoms rated >2)		ADHD Rating Scale (Symptoms rated >2)		ADHD Rating Scale (Symptoms rated >2)	
Inattention	5	Inattention	6	Inattention	6
Hyperactivity/Impulsivity	2	Hyperactivity/Impulsivity	0	Hyperactivity/Impulsivity	3
CBCL		CBCL		SSRS	
Subscale	Percentile	Subscale	Percentile	Standard Score 89	23
Withdrawn	81	Withdrawn	50	DBRS	
Somatic Complaints	50	Somatic Complaints	50	Number of Defiant Behaviors	0
Anxious	61	Anxious	50		
Social Problems	50	Social Problems	50		
Thought Problems	50	Thought Problems	76	Chemistry teacher	
Attention Problems	83	Attention Problems	76		
Delinquent Behavior	79	Delinquent Behavior	66	CAP (Percentile)	
Aggressive Behavior	50	Aggressive Behavior	50		
DBRS		DBRS		Inattention	93
				Overactivity	NS
Number of Defiant Behaviors	4	Number of Defiant Behaviors	3	ADHD Rating Scale (Symptoms rated >2)	
				Inattention	5
				Hyperactivity/Impulsivity	4
				SSRS	
				Standard Score 94	34
				DBRS	
				Number of Defiant Behaviors	1

Testing data			
Test	Raw score	Standard/scaled score	Percentile
Conners CPT			
Hits	321 (99%)		63
Omissions	3 (1%)		63
Commissions	10 (28%)	42	22
Hit Rate	309	56	74
Hit Rate Standard Error	8	58	81
Variability of *SE*	12	55	73

Note. An asterisk indicates a clinically significant elevation (>95th percentile or <5th percentile).

involved in organized extracurricular activities although they had been a big part of his lie when younger. He expressed no regrets over this. When asked about his own future plans, Eric was ambivalent. He did not have any specific career goals. He indicated that might "work and travel" for a year and then go to college.

Eric's performance on Conners CPT was normal and did not suggest problems with either inattention or impulsivity (see Table 10.7). Eric displayed an average response rate, responded to target items with an average level of accuracy (omissions), and only infrequently responded to inappropriate test items (commissions), indicating a good performance on measures of inattention and impulsivity.

The clinical impression of this 17-year, 1-month-old young man that emerged from the evaluation did not fit the diagnostic picture required for ADHD. There was no evidence of Eric having displayed significant ADHD symptoms until well into adolescence. Furthermore, there was no consistent report of a significant number of ADHD symptoms during the 6-month period prior to the evaluation assessed by the rating scales. Eric's difficulties in completing work and focusing in class appeared to be readily explained by his chronic depressive features, which had been present since the onset of his academic difficulties. These depressive features were sufficient to meet the criteria for Dysthymic Disorder (300.4). Because Eric did not display a significant, pervasive or chronic pattern of the symptoms of ADHD, and because his difficulties can be accounted for by other factors, he was not given the diagnosis of ADHD.

We made treatment recommendations to Eric and his parents that were appropriate for Eric's combination of Dysthymia and past abuse of marijuana:

1. We advised being familiar with how to activate emergency mental health services and being aware of when such services may be needed.
2. We emphasized obtaining appropriate treatment for Eric's dysthymic disorder. In particular, we described cognitive and psychosocial treatments for this condition. We also pointed out that the prognosis for Eric recovering from his Dysthymia without further difficulties was relatively poor if he did not cooperate with such treatment.
3. We also discussed medication management options. We mentioned the possibility of treating Eric with a medication, such as Wellbutrin (bupropion hydrochloride), that could address both his depressive difficulties and attentional problems. We advised follow-up consultation with a psychiatrist, should Eric or his family wish to pursue this option.
4. We strongly recommended continued abstinence from cannabis use. This abstinence could also be monitored/addressed in the context of counseling.

We also generated a few recommendations for Eric's school, including continuing to address his learning difficulties with an individualized education plan and attempting to reduce his discouragement about school through careful management of his behavior. Although Eric's depression does not excuse misbehavior, it is not unusual for such conditions to have an adverse impacted on behavior. Eric's sporadic class cutting and failure to complete work may be motivated in part by his depression. Consequently, appropriate discipline/management of his behavior should proceed in a manner sensitive to these issues. A harsh management style at school may only further discourage Eric and increase his desire to avoid school.

Eric's case demonstrates the importance of carefully identifying the specific types of difficulties lumped together under descriptions of "poor attention." Psychoemotional conditions, such as the depressive disorders, can interfere with a student's academic productivity, concentration, and motivation. Because the more obvious neurovegetative symptoms of depression that characterize acute conditions such as Major Depression are often absent in Dysthymia, it is easier for this condition to go undetected or be misidentified. A prolonged, moderate depressive condition such as Dysthymia often leads to reduced productivity, increased apathy, and a subjective loss of mental efficiency without being clearly attributable to a specific depressogenic event. Eric's case was further complicated by his substance use. He reported a period of 1–2 years during which he regularly smoked marijuana. Although some controversy exists in the marijuana research, a pattern of increased apathy and reduced motivation has long been suggested as an outcome of recurrent marijuana use.

LANGUAGE DELAY AND POSSIBLE ATYPICAL PERVASIVE DEVELOPMENTAL DISORDER WITHOUT ADHD

Mark, age 6, was the youngest of three children. His parents were well educated. His father was an orthodontist, and his mother was a former social worker who stayed home with the children. The parents had a stable marriage, and the older two children were healthy and developed normally. Mark, however, had always experienced health problems. He was a somewhat sickly baby, but his parents did not notice any major problems initially. However, when Mark was approximately 1 year old, he developed a persistent cough that never seemed to get better. His breathing became labored, and his parents took him to see a number of specialists. Finally he was diagnosed with severe asthma and was treated with steroids intermittently from that point on.

Perhaps because of his health problems, Mark's parents did not notice any developmental abnormalities right away. They thought he was developing a bit more slowly than their other two children but were not very concerned. After all, his motor development and self-care skills were age appropriate. However, when Mark entered preschool at age 3, his teachers noticed problems with his language immediately. He was evaluated by a speech and language pathologist, who found severe delays in both expressive and receptive language, particularly in the area of pragmatics. At that time he began receiving speech and language therapy. That same year, an audiologist did further evaluation. Findings indicated the presence of auditory processing difficulties.

Mark displayed a number of peculiarities that concerned his parents and teachers and led to peer relationship difficulties. He would often become preoccupied for months at a time with a topic, memorizing facts about it and talking about it constantly. One such topic was hurricanes, and Mark's knowledge in this area was striking. He also displayed echolalic speech. When upset, Mark would hit his head or sometimes bite himself.

When Mark was 4, a team consisting of a psychologist, psychiatrist, audiologist, and speech/language pathologist diagnosed Mark's delays as characteristic of Pervasive Developmental Disorder. An evaluation by a second team of professionals 1 month later resulted in a diagnosis of a severe auditory processing disorder, a moderate to severe expressive language delay, and severely reduced social pragmatic language skills. A subsequent evaluation by a pediatric psychologist resulted in a diagnosis of Pervasive Developmental Disorder, Not Otherwise Specified (PDD-NOS). PDD-NOS is a DSM-IV diagnostic category used to describe children who show symptoms of autism but do not fully meet critiera for Autistic Disorder (Klinger & Dawson, 1996). Rather than having impairments in all three areas required for a diagnosis of autism (communication, social interaction, and stereotyped behavior or restricted range of interests), they may exhibit subthreshold symptomatology or impairments in only two of the three areas.

Mark attended the public schools. Lobbying by his parents had led to the placement of a 1:1 aide in his classroom to keep him on task, and he continued to receive speech and language therapy. He completed very little work at school and had little positive interaction with peers. A speech and language review by school personnel in the first grade indicated low average overall language abilities with particular difficulty in the area of pragmatic skills. A reevaluation regarding the question of PDD was inconclusive. Mark's parents sought another opinion from a pediatric neurologist, who ruled out PDD, and attributed Mark's difficulties to ADHD. He prescribed 5 mg of Ritalin (methylphenidate) twice a day. Mark's parents were not certain whether the medication was helpful and sought a second opinion from our clinic.

At the time of evaluation, Mark was in the first grade. His motor development was age appropriate, and his hearing, vision, and self-care skills were also age-appropriate. His patterns of eating and sleeping were normal. Both parents were physically healthy, and neither reported a history of psychiatric or learning difficulties. No psychosocial stressors had affected the immediate family over the previous year. Among the extended biological relatives, there was a reported history of learning disabilities on the paternal side of the family.

During the portion of the interview concerning child psychiatric symptoms, Mark's parents described Mark as displaying five or six of nine symptoms of inattentiveness, and two or three of nine symptoms of impulsivity/overactivity and noted that these had been present since he was at least 3 years old. Mark was reported to display no symptoms of ODD or CD. For the most part, Mark was a happy boy. He continued to be, however, relatively unsuccessful in making and maintaining satisfactory peer relationships, probably due to his immature and somewhat odd peer interaction style. He continued to display preoccupations with tornadoes, echolalic speech, and occasional self-injurious behavior. He did not display any rituals, stereotypical movements, self-stimulatory behavior, or extreme social withdrawal. At no time had he displayed any prolonged episodes of clinically significant depression, anxiety, compulsions, or tics. There was no reported or suspected evidence of either physical or sexual abuse.

Mark displayed no difficulty separating from his parents for the interview and testing. He was observed to have a somewhat awkward cadence and accent to his speech. He appeared to have difficulty understanding or to be ignoring some questions. His interactive conversational skills were observed to be poor; sometimes he would answer a question but at other times he would follow his own agenda. His speech was perseverative and one instance of echolalic speech was noted. He made infrequent eye contact, and his affect was somewhat flat. No obvious ADHD symptomatology was noted.

Mark stated that he was aware of the reasons for his being evaluated but was unable to or refused to elaborate on those reasons. He indicated that he generally enjoyed school, particularly art and music classes. He indicated that one peer teased him but said he had many friends. He had generally positive comments regarding his family. Mark reported enjoying a number of recreational activities, including watching movies and playing with a hula hoop. The general impression was of a child with peculiarities in speech and interactional style. He refused to complete one of the tests.

The parents and teacher completed the standard battery of child behavior rating scales, the results of which are shown in Table 10.8, along with findings from psychological testing. Results from the parent-completed BASC revealed normal scores from his father and significantly elevated scores from his mother on the subscales pertaining to attention problems, withdrawal, and social skills difficulties. The parents' ADHD Rating Scale results revealed between five and seven of nine symptoms of inattentiveness, as well as two of nine symptoms of impulsivity/overactivity occurring on a frequent basis within the home setting.

Teacher ratings on the BASC indicated clinical elevations on the scales pertaining to attention problems, atypical behaviors, withdrawal, learning problems, and poor social skills. Her ADHD Rating Scale results revealed nine of nine symptoms of inattentiveness but only

TABLE 10.8. Assessment Results for a Case of Language Delay and Possible Atypical PDD without ADHD in a 6-Year-Old Boy

Mother		Father		Teacher	
Interview report of ADHD symptoms		Interview report of ADHD symptoms		CAP (Percentile)	
Inattention	6	Inattention	5	Inattention	95*
Hyperactivity/Impulsivity	3	Hyperactivity/Impulsivity	2	Overactivity	84
ADHD Rating Scale (Symptoms rated >2)		ADHD Rating Scale (Symptoms rated >2)		ADHD Rating Scale (Symptoms rated >2)	
Inattention	5	Inattention	7	Inattention	9
Hyperactivity/Impulsivity	2	Hyperactivity/Impulsivity	2	Hyperactivity/Impulsivity	3
BASC		BASC		BASC	
Subscale	Percentile	Subscale	Percentile	Subscale	Percentile
Hyperactivity	71	Hyperactivity	32	Hyperactivity	73
Aggression	37	Aggression	6	Aggression	83
Conduct Problems	15	Conduct Problems	15	Conduct Problems	81
Anxiety	24	Anxiety	11	Anxiety	69
Depression	18	Depression	49	Depression	55
Somatization	32	Somatization	32	Somatization	48
Atypicality	33	Atypicality	88	Atypicality	99*
Withdrawal	69	Withdrawal	99*	Withdrawal	99*
Attention Problems	86	Attention Problems	97*	Attention Problems	99*
Social Skills	50	Social Skills	7*	Learning Problems	98*
				Social Skills	2*
PSI-SF		PSI-SF		SSRS	
Total Stress	69	Total Stress	76	Total Score 15 (below average)	
				APRS	
				Productivity Score 32 (low average)	

Testing data			
Test	Raw score	Standard/scaled score	Percentile
WISC-III Vocabulary		11	
WISC-III Block Design		12	

Note. An asterisk indicates a clinically significant elevation (>95th percentile or <5th percentile).

three of nine symptoms of impulsivity/overactivity occurring on a frequent basis within the classroom setting. Results of the CAP revealed inattentiveness elevated to the 95th percentile, whereas the impulsivity/overactivity scale was not significantly elevated. The SSRS revealed below-average peer socialization skills overall when compared with same-age peers. The APRS could not be compared with available norms because Mark was not asked to complete the same amount of work independently that other peers were asked to complete.

On the Vocabulary subtest of the WISC-III, Mark obtained a raw score of 13 and a corresponding scaled score of 11. These scores would suggest that his overall verbal abilities are within the average range when compared with same-age peers. Likewise, on the Block Design subtest of the WISC-III, Mark obtained a raw score of 17 and a corresponding scaled score of 12, suggesting that his nonverbal abilities are well within the average range when compared with those of same-age peers. Mark refused to complete the CPT, rendering the results of that test invalid.

Mark's parents completed the SCL-90-R, the results of which were within the normal range. Thus, there was no evidence of significant psychological distress in either parent. Likewise, the PSI-SF revealed that any parenting stress they experienced was within normal limits.

It was our impression that Mark was a child of presumably average intelligence with significant delays in his language abilities as well as social peculiarities that were possibly related to an atypical pervasive developmental disorder. In addition, he had been displaying difficulties with inattentiveness since he entered preschool. Although Mark's IQ and motor development appeared normal, he had delays and/or peculiarities in a number of domains of development: social, language, and attentional. Although these delays were not pervasive across *all* domains, he was delayed in a number of areas that could provide alternative explanations for his attentional difficulties. Because Mark's delays were more pervasive than the typical presentation of ADHD, we determined that a diagnosis of ADHD was not warranted. We made the following recommendations to the parents:

1. We recommended that the parents consult with the staff of a school that specialized in working with children with language disabilities, as they might be better able to provide Mark with the intensive focus on language that he would likely require to make gains. We advised the parents to have personnel from such a school observe their son and give their impressions regarding whether that school would be an appropriate environment for him, both academically and socially.
2. We advised the parents to continue to consult with speech and language specialists regarding the nature of Mark's condition and to obtain recommendations for remediation.
3. We advised the parents to evaluate the effectiveness of Mark's current stimulant medication regimen, using a double-blind medication trial design.

This case illustrates an increasingly common problem facing practitioners today. When a child presents with symptoms of inattention yet other developmental delays and/or peculiarities are also present, is the diagnosis of ADHD warranted? The DSM-IV criteria clearly state that a diagnosis of PDD rules out the ADHD diagnosis. Yet controversy remains regarding this point, and the diagnosis is frequently given in clinical settings to children with autism or other pervasive developmental disorders. When a child like Mark does not clearly meet criteria for a pervasive developmental disorder, the picture becomes even murkier. Another sad fact is that the ADHD diagnosis is much more palatable to parents than a diagnosis of autism or PDD. Thus, they may be looking for a professional to give an alternative, less stigmatizing, explanation for their child's difficulties. Although these are all difficult issues that require more research, a practitioner can sort through them by carefully examining the entire picture of presenting problems. If there are clear alternative explanations for ADHD-like symptoms, the additional diagnosis is probably not warranted. In Mark's case, for instance, either a pervasive developmental disorder or severe language delay might explain his attentional difficulties. However, if additional difficulties with impulse control relative to peers remain that cannot be explained by the other delays and/or psychiatric conditions, and these difficulties are consistent with a typical presentation of ADHD, comorbid diagnoses may be warranted. For instance, if a language-delayed child was very inattentive *and* impulsive, the clinician should not rule out ADHD on the basis of the language delay because language delay would not be a logical explanation for the impulsivity. Although a language delay may cause a child to look inattentive, there is no clear reason why it would make him more likely to have difficulty regulating his behavior.

Another point to keep in mind is that the ADHD diagnosis is given when difficulties in impulse control are noted *relative to peers.* This means that when determining whether an individual has ADHD, the clinician needs to compare the individual's behavior to that of peers of the same mental age. Therefore, if an individual experiences developmental delays, he or she would need to display impulse control problems *greater than would be expected for peers with similar developmental delays* to warrant the diagnosis of ADHD.

The important question to ask is what the diagnosis of ADHD would add to the picture in terms of understanding and treatment recommendations. If ADHD would aid in conceptualizing the child's difficulties and would lead to a useful treatment plan, it may make sense to give the diagnosis after careful examination of the history. However, if a diagnosis of ADHD would just "muddy the waters" by adding another label that does not really add anything to (or even confuses) the understanding of the child, it is probably better to simplify the diagnostic picture rather than to use the "cookbook" approach to DSM-IV diagnosis. Giving a child three or four diagnoses simply because symptoms can be checked off on a list is not generally helpful. It is best to spend time exploring the core difficulties that the child is having and determining which DSM diagnosis actually fits the nature of his or her difficulties.

REFERENCES

American Psychiatric Association. (1994). *Diagnostic and statistical manual of mental disorders* (4th ed.). Washington, DC: Author.

Biederman, J. (1995). Developmental subtypes of juvenile bipolar disorder. *Sexual and Marital Therapy*, 3(4), 227–230.

Hinshaw, S. P. (1987). On the distinction between attentional deficits/hyperactivity and conduct problems/aggression in child psychopatholoy. *Psychological Bulletin, 101,* 443–463.

Faraone, S. V., Biederman, J., Wozniak, J., Mundy, E., Mennin, D., & O'Connell, D. (1997). Is comorbidity with ADHD a marker for juvenile-onset mania? *Journal of the American Academy of Child and Adolescent Psychiatry, 36*(8), 1046–1055.

Klinger, L. G., & Dawson, G. (1996). Autistic disorder. In E. J. Mash & R. A. Barkley (Eds.), *Child psychopathology* (pp. 311–339), New York: Guilford Press.

Wozniak, J., Biederman, J., Kiely, K., Ablon, J., Faraone, S., Mundy, E., & Mennin, D. (1995). Mania-like symptoms suggestive of childhood-onset bipolar disorder in clinically referred children. *Journal of the American Academy of Child and Adolescent Psychiatry, 34*(7), 867–876.

Chapter 11

ASSESSMENT OF ADULTS WITH ADHD

Kevin R. Murphy
Michael Gordon

ᶓᶓ

The idea that the core symptoms of Attention-Deficit/Hyperactivity Disorder (ADHD) might persist into adulthood is relatively new on the clinical scene. In fact, the first edition of this handbook focused largely on childhood variants and contained very little information on adult manifestations. This focus reflected the state of the art at that time. Until the late 1980s, ADHD was generally considered a childhood disorder that was typically outgrown by adolescence and always by adulthood (see Chapter 1, this volume). Clinicians routinely told parents that if they survived their hyperactive child's elementary school years, the future would be rosy.

We now have clear evidence that ADHD symptoms do not usually diminish with the onset of puberty. Numerous prospective and retrospective studies of children diagnosed with ADHD followed into adulthood have demonstrated that from 50% to 80% continue to experience significant ADHD symptoms and associated impairment into their adult lives (see Chapter 6, this volume; also Barkley, Fischer, Edelbrock, & Smallish, 1990; Weiss, Minde, Werry, Douglas, & Nemeth, 1971; Mendelson, Johnson, & Stewart, 1971; Menkes, Rowe, & Menkes, 1967; Borland & Hechtman, 1976; Feldman, Denhoff, & Denhoff, 1979; Loney, Whaley-Klahn, Kosier, & Conboy, 1981; Weiss, Hechtman, Perlman, Hopkins, & Wener, 1979; Hechtman, Weiss, & Perlman, 1978, 1980; Hechtman, Weiss, Perlman, & Tuck, 1985; Weiss, Hechtman, Milroy, & Perlman, 1985; Satterfield, Hoppe, & Schell, 1982; Gittelman, Mannuzza, Shenker, & Bonagura, 1985; Mannuzza, Gittelman-Klein, Bessler, Malloy, & LaPadula, 1993; Wender, 1995; Weiss & Hechtman, 1993). Although there is some question about the actual percentage of ADHD children who will still suffer from the disorder when they become adults, little doubt remains that it is a substantial number (see Chapter 6, this volume).

Why did it take so long for researchers and clinicians to realize that ADHD is a disorder that, more often than not, endures across the life span? Much of the blame can be assigned to the natural life history of the disorder itself. ADHD's most visible and disruptive feature, physical overactivity, often diminishes with age. Research has established that most

ADHD children are somewhat less motoric by the time they reach adolescence (Hart et al., 1995). Although they may still suffer from profound problems associated with the more cognitive manifestations of impulsiveness, these symptoms are often more subtle and more difficult to detect. Poor planning, self-regulation, time management, and disorganization are not quite as obvious a set of symptoms as ill-conceived flights from the tops of trees or head-long bursts into traffic.

The other reason for the delayed emergence of recognition of adult ADHD relates to the time and expense involved in the conduct of longitudinal research. The most empirically sophisticated studies are just now evaluating the life circumstances and clinical functioning of once hyperactive children who are now entering young adulthood. At least another decade will pass until data are available regarding the nature of ADHD in individuals who are squarely into adulthood. Complicating matters is that criteria for the disorder change (sometimes often) over the years that subjects are slowly aging. Therefore, conclusions are often based on subject selection criteria that have long since been supplanted.

Although the concept of ADHD in adulthood was late in arriving, it has certainly gained visibility with lightning speed. What was unheard of just a decade ago has now become a popular topic within the conversations of our society. Hardly a week passes that a story or editorial about the disorder fails to appear in the media. Bookstore shelves are filling with volumes for both professionals and for the lay public. Even the cartoon pages are apt to carry references to ADHD in adults, so thoroughly has the label found its way into everyday parlance.

In our view, the explosion of interest in adult ADHD has been the most mixed of blessings. On the positive side, the widespread exposure has resulted in scores of adults benefiting from accurate diagnosis and treatment, for many after years of failure and frustration. The quality of life for these adults has surely improved markedly as they find it easier to lead more productive and satisfying lives. In the least, they can take comfort from knowing that their struggles have a legitimate explanation that rests more on neurogenetics than on attributions to poor character. The popularity of this disorder has therefore heightened awareness of its existence, forced clinicians to take adult variants of symptoms seriously, and promoted the beginnings of scientific exploration.

Although the benefits of the widespread publicity about the disorder are tangible, so too are the downsides. Simply put, the public interest in ADHD and the attendant pressures for services have completely outstripped the pace and volume of scientific inquiry. We cannot emphasize enough how extraordinarily little sound empirical data are available to guide clinical management. From a scientific standpoint, the field of ADHD in adults is in its infancy at best. For the most part, what many purvey as common knowledge is based on clinical impression, anecdote, and extrapolations from the more robust child literature. One of the unfortunate by-products of limited scientific information is that myths become entrenched, speculations and impressions pass for "truths," and diagnostic conclusions emerge based on hunches and pet theories rather than on well-established evidence.

The fervor that has accompanied the adult ADHD movement seems to have given rise to more folklore than fact. For example, many popular books and speakers claim as truth that adults with ADHD are often more creative, intelligent, or entrepreneurial than others. In reality, not a particle of data supports these contentions. The gulf between speculation and what is actually known about ADHD in adults is wide. Therefore, we advise clinicians to hold a sincere and healthy respect for the paucity of sound scientific information.

All the intense focus on ADHD in adults and even the meager body of scientific literature would, of course, be far more manageable if this were a less elusive disorder to identify. If clinicians could point to a unique set of symptoms, a configuration of test scores, or a specific etiological event and, with some certainty, identify the disorder, we would not be nearly as concerned about the current frenzy. But the length of this book alone serves as testament to the challenges inherent in identifying and treating ADHD across the life span.

Why is ADHD at any age so difficult to diagnose? The answer goes directly to the very nature of the disorder itself (see, e.g., Gordon, 1995; Gordon & Irwin, 1996). First, the core symptoms of the disorder are also core symptoms of human nature. All of us are prone toward inattention and impulsiveness at one time or another, especially if we are under some physical or mental distress. The mere fact that an individual might be inattentive or impulsive is of little diagnostic value because these are such ubiquitous human proclivities. Whereas some symptoms of mental illness (e.g., hallucinations) are pathognomonic, the same cannot be said for the characteristics of ADHD. The symptoms alone do not necessarily demarcate abnormal functioning. To be fair, of course, ADHD is not unique in this regard because almost all mental illnesses, from depression to mania, represent normal human tendencies gone awry.

Parenthetically, the nonspecific nature of some ADHD symptoms accounts for much of its current popularity as a presenting complaint. Metaphorically, these symptoms fashion a suit of clothes that most of us can fit ourselves (or our children) into, especially if we are experiencing a setback or if we have the sense that we are somehow underperforming. The ease with which individuals can don the ADHD label is further promoted by a culture that often seeks psychiatric explanations for failures that might better be accounted for in other terms.

The second barrier to easy identification is that some ADHD symptoms are typical not only of normal behavior but also of the full range of psychiatric abnormalities. Nearly every listing of criteria in the fourth edition of the *Diagnostic and Statistical Manual of Mental Disorders* (DSM-IV; American Psychiatric Association, 1994) contains at least one symptom associated with poor concentration and disorganization. In fact, inattention is so universal a symptom of mental illness that, in isolation, it provides little diagnostic direction. If anything, it is a global marker for distress, regardless of origin.

The third characteristic of ADHD that ensures a degree of diagnostic complexity is its dimensionality. As already mentioned in this textbook (Chapter 2, this volume) and elsewhere (Gordon & Murphy, 1998), ADHD is not an all-or-nothing condition like pregnancy. Instead, it represents the extreme end of a continuum or normal curve. Because it is defined by a point along a continuum, its identification inherently involves some degree of subjectivity and even arbitrariness in establishing cut points. How inattentive or impulsive one has to be to qualify for a diagnosis is therefore a matter of some judgment, especially when the intensity of problems falls within those gray zones between normal and abnormal. Whenever opinion forms the basis for important aspects of diagnostic decision making, the door is left open for a measure of uncertainty and inconsistency. Beyond these three elemental features of ADHD at any age, the diagnosis is especially difficult in adulthood for the following reasons:

- The diagnosis of ADHD in adulthood hinges primarily on reports of functioning during childhood. Most patients provide this historical information more from memory than from actual records. Such retrospective data, of course, are notoriously vulnerable to historical inaccuracy, incompleteness, or distortion.
- Although ADHD is often joined by other disorders at all ages, adults are especially prone to suffer from a wide range of comorbid conditions, some of which are likely secondary to the years of ADHD-related frustration and failure. Outcome studies have established that individuals diagnosed with ADHD in childhood are at risk for developing comorbid conditions, including anxiety and affective disorders, substance abuse, antisocial personality, and intermittent explosive disorder as adults (Biederman et al., 1987; Weiss and Hechtman, 1993;

see also Chapter 6, this volume). Therefore, adults referred for ADHD commonly display a complex interweaving of psychiatric disorders. Ironically, although some comorbid conditions represent fallout from years of ADHD-type functioning, they can often develop a life of their own and can actually come to predominate the clinical picture.

• Many psychiatric disorders have their typical onset in late adolescence or young adulthood. Thus, clinicians evaluating adults have a broader range of disorders to rule out than those working with children. Furthermore, many of these later-onset disorders have symptoms that can, at least in part, mimic ADHD characteristics. Patients with Borderline or other personality disorders, Bipolar Disorder, Hypomania, Cyclothymia, depression, Obsessive Compulsive Disorder, Generalized Anxiety Disorder, Schizophrenia, substance abuse, chronic pain, pre-Alzheimer's disease, or head injury may all endorse many DSM-IV symptoms of ADHD.

• Adults are more prone to suffer from medical conditions that can produce ADHD-like symptoms. Hypo- or hyperthyroidism, malnutrition, diabetes, certain heart problems, and other adult physical disorders can all affect attentional performance. The heightened possibility that ADHD symptoms in adults can have a medical cause underscores the importance of ruling out medical conditions before arriving at a final diagnostic determination. This may require a comprehensive physical exam in some cases.

• A longer life also means more opportunities to suffer from stressful or traumatic life events. Divorce, grief, financial problems, health concerns, or other major lifestyle changes can affect an individual's ability to concentrate. The performance-impairing effects of stress are therefore important to rule out prior to assigning an ADHD diagnosis.

• It can be more difficult to determine degree of impairment in adults as compared to children. Because all children are in classrooms, teacher input and ratings are not especially difficult to obtain. Adult jobs vary in demands for attention, planning, listening, structure, or attention to detail. Obtaining supervisor input or ratings is much more difficult and potentially risky.

• A growing problem in the diagnosis of ADHD in adults is informant bias. With the bounty of publicity, patients are savvy about formal characterizations of the disorder. Consciously or otherwise, this knowledge can affect the accuracy of information that patients present to clinicians.

With this onslaught of cautions and caveats about ADHD in adults, are we suggesting that the assessment process is hopelessly difficult or that the diagnosis itself should even be abandoned? Not at all. All the potential pitfalls notwithstanding, ADHD is not a phantom disorder that defies proper diagnosis. Clear evidence exists that this is a legitimate diagnostic entity which trained clinicians can identify in ways that are efficient and accurate. But it absolutely requires a comprehensive and thoughtful assessment that fairly considers critical aspects of past history and current functioning, the degree of impairment, and the possible validity of alternative explanations.

We presented this litany of warnings about the diagnostic process simply to encourage a careful and conservative approach to diagnosis. Our sense is that many clinicians are overly enthusiastic about encouraging individuals to seek a label of ADHD. This observation stems in part from watching changing trends in our own clinics. Five years or so ago, upwards of 85% of adults referred for evaluations (usually from mental health practitioners or primary care physicians) ultimately received the diagnosis of ADHD. That percentage has plummeted to 50% or lower, even though at least as many patients are referred by other professionals. Nowadays it is far more likely that a patient will leave our respective clinics either with no diagnosis at all or with a diagnosis other than ADHD.

Our concern about the potential for misdiagnosis or overdiagnosis is more than an exercise in academic handwringing. Beyond lost opportunities for appropriate treatment (or for staying free of treatment), inaccurate identification diminishes the credibility of the disorder itself. If individuals receive a diagnosis even though they do not meet criteria, skepticism about ADHD will quickly mount. Those who truly suffer from the disorder will not benefit from the serious consideration they deserve. The ADHD label should be assigned only to those individuals with a lifelong history of serious inattention and poor self-control. It should not be diluted to cover what amounts to normal manifestations of personality.

The emphasis on careful adherence to diagnostic standards is also heightened by the impact of antidiscrimination laws, such as the Americans with Disabilities Act of 1990 (Public Law 101-336). This body of legislation is intended to level the playing field for those individuals with substantial disabilities (see Gordon & Keiser, 1998; Murphy & Gordon, 1996; Gordon, Barkley, & Murphy, 1997). According to federal regulations and case law, ADHD is considered a legitimate disability. Employers, educational institutions, and testing organizations are therefore required to provide reasonable accommodations to those who suffer from this disorder. If clinicians are overly liberal in assigning the diagnosis, people who actually function within a normal range will receive benefits and advantages that are not warranted.

CORE CONSIDERATIONS IN DETERMINING THE DIAGNOSIS OF ADHD

Before plunging into the intricacies of the assessment of ADHD, we want to outline a general strategy for the diagnostic process. Our focus here is on those concepts that underlie formal criteria for the disorder. We discuss clinical interviews, rating scales, psychological testing, and other methods for gathering information, but we begin by highlighting our diagnostic quarry.

The evaluation for ADHD should be designed to answer four fundamental questions:

1. Is there credible evidence that the patient experienced ADHD-type symptoms in early childhood that, at least by the middle school years, led to substantial and chronic impairment across settings?
2. Is there credible evidence that ADHD-type symptoms currently cause the patient substantial and consistent impairment across settings?
3. Are there explanations other than ADHD that better account for the clinical picture?
4. For patients who meet criteria for ADHD, is there evidence for the existence of comorbid conditions?

In questions 1 and 2, by credible we mean evidence that is capable of corroboration by some other means than just the patient's verbal self-report.

Of the four questions, the first one concerning a childhood history of ADHD is the most critical and, unfortunately, the most often overlooked or sidestepped. *To qualify for the diagnosis of adult ADHD, the patient must have suffered from ADHD as a child.* This does not mean that the individual must have been formally diagnosed in childhood; only that sufficient symptoms were present that make it plausible that the condition existed at that stage of development. Although some debate exists concerning the specific age by which symptoms must appear (Barkley & Biederman, 1997), the consensus is that the symptoms must cause meaningful impairment no later than the early teenage years. The only exceptions come in rare instances in which an adult acquires ADHD symptoms because of brain injury or other medical condition. Therefore, any credible evaluation for ADHD in adults must provide compelling evidence of early-appearing and long-standing problems with attention and self-control. Without such evidence, the diagnosis of ADHD is likely inappropriate even in the face of other clinical information that might appear consistent. For example, abnormal scores on psychological testing are never diagnostic unless they coincide with a childhood history of ADHD-type impairment, and possibly not even then if other comorbid disorders better account for the test results.

Although documentation of a childhood history is essential, we recognize that it is no easy task. Parents may be unavailable or deceased, school report cards may be hard to obtain, and many adults attended school at a time when ADHD was not commonly identified. Nevertheless, every effort should be made to gather as much hard historical data as possible. Hard data help to substantiate self-reported recollections, improve reliability, and elevate the degree of confidence clinicians have in rendering the diagnosis.

As we indicated, a diagnosis of ADHD requires evidence of early onset. It is important to make a distinction between ADHD symptoms and impairment. The DSM-IV states that symptoms producing impairment must be present by age 7. In other words, the patient must show some traits or characteristics of the disorder from early in life that led to impairment. However, in some cases those characteristics do not produce tangible impairment in functioning until sometime after age 7. An individual can therefore show signs (or symptoms) of the disorder before age 7 years without necessarily exhibiting actual impairment before that age. It has been argued that at this time, clinicians should focus on the onset of symptoms sometime during childhood, broadly construed, as the criterion for diagnosis and not insist on an onset of impairment before age 7 (Barkley & Biederman, 1997). Certainly, signs of impairment from the symptoms must be evident for the diagnosis to be granted, but that impairment need not predate 7 years of age. Yet, it also is extraordinarily rare for someone with bona fide ADHD not to show signs of impairment by at least the middle school years. Those who display no observable signs of disruption until college, graduate school, or later may have valid symptoms and impairment, but it is highly unlikely that their current problems stem from having ADHD. Again, the basic premise is that those suffering from ADHD virtually always leave a trail of evidence in their wake as they go through life. Because ADHD is defined by impairment, there should be markers (some sort of paper trail) along the way that reflect impairment. The only exceptions are those in which the individual operated within a family or educational environment that was extraordinarily unusual for the extent of supervision and support it provided.

In the absence of a convincing early history of impairment, clinicians often offer a series of explanations which too often beg credibility. The most common is that high intelligence masked symptoms and allowed for successful compensation throughout childhood and even adolescence. Accordingly, the individual was able to hide deficits because he or she was so swift at managing the material and devising ways to compensate. Although this argument may make intuitive sense, in reality no evidence supports it. Although IQ is related to academic achievement, it is not associated in a meaningful way with ADHD symptom presentation; if anything, the presence of ADHD appears to diminish intellectual functioning by as much as 7 to 10 points and certainly diminishes executive functioning substantially (see Chapter 3, this volume). Those with high IQs can still exhibit the full range of ADHD symptoms, and, of course, people with normal or low IQs can be normally attentive. High intelligence may reduce the level of academic impairment, but it does not serve as a protective factor that shuts down the expression of ADHD symptoms across settings. For instance, Fischer, Barkley, Fletcher, and Smallish (1993) found that IQ in childhood in ADHD children was significantly predictive of levels of academic achievement skills in adolescence but accounted for less than 14% of the variance in that outcome. Moreover, IQ was unrelated to any other domain of functioning at outcome, including the extent to which the subjects may have repeated a grade, been suspended or expelled, suffered from other disorders, committed antisocial acts, or experienced peer rejection. All this suggests that IQ is not as protective a factor from the developmental risks of impairments associated with ADHD as some have believed. If an individual meets criteria for ADHD, those symptoms will become manifest throughout childhood even in the context of high intelligence. In essence, no amount of intellectual power can overcome the impact of ADHD-level disinhibition. Cognitive capacity may allow for quicker learning, but it does not guarantee efficient self-control, organization, time management, or the exercise of good judgment.

Another common explanation for the absence of a childhood history is based on the notion of compensation. The argument is made that a patient showed no symptoms because he was able to compensate sufficiently to graduate high school without any discernible impairment. In our view, the capacity to compensate successfully reflects healthy functioning and belies clinically significant impairment. We base this view on the notion that all children have a profile of relative strengths and weaknesses. One of the tasks of childhood is to learn ways to compensate for abilities that are less well developed. Children who are able to master all the challenges of schooling without any meaningful problems have adequately adapted to any weaknesses. Their ability to manage the many demands of school, home, and neighborhood reflect intact psychological functioning. If problems first surface after secondary school, they are more likely the result of circumstance, inappropriate career choice, other psychiatric disorder, or factors not related to the core features of ADHD. Indeed, the disorder is defined by poor compensation during the childhood years.

Having stated a firm rule, we acknowledge the possibility of exceptions. As we already mentioned, some may have been enrolled in remarkably unique educational environments that entailed so much supervision and structure that only the most desperately impulsive would experience problems. Others may have gone to school in extraordinarily chaotic environments in which grossly impulsive behavior was the norm. And still others may have been able to compensate but only with massive amounts of special educational services, tutoring, extraordinary time and effort, and psychological support. It may be that the person also paid a high psychological price for compensation to the extent that a formal psychiatric disorder emerged (as opposed to common reactions to daily stress). In other words, a particular patient may have compensated generally, but at such great personal strain that formal symptoms of depression or anxiety were documented.

The second fundamental question that lies at the heart of an evaluation concerns the degree of current impairment. Are the patient's ADHD symptoms still present and sufficiently disruptive to warrant a current diagnosis of ADHD? This question may seem easy or obvious, but it often is not. Who among the general population would not like to be more attentive, organized, efficient, focused, or productive? It is part of the human condition to be fallible, and there is always room for improvement. How does the clinician differentiate the threshold of impairment necessary to justify a clinical diagnosis from symptoms or behavior falling within the "normal" range?

As we have stressed, the diagnosis of ADHD in adulthood requires a body of evidence that establishes a long-standing pattern of serious life disruption because of impulsive and inattentive behavior. Isolated instances of minor setbacks of the "welcome to the human race" variety do not constitute the kind of impairment that should qualify for a diagnosis. Bona fide ADHD is a serious disorder that affects daily adaptive functioning and causes a chronic and pervasive pattern of impairment in academic, vocational, and social arenas. Individuals with ADHD can provide evidence of poor adjustment with rather serious consequences: loss of jobs due to ADHD-related problems, a history of severe academic underachievement relative to ability, unsatisfactory interpersonal or marital relationships, disruption of employment and daily adaptive functioning due to impulsiveness, forgetfulness, disorganization, and generally inadequate day to day adjustment.

Does this mean that a patient has to fail miserably in all academic or vocational settings to qualify for a diagnosis? No. However, the nature and degree of impairment in our view need to be robust and documented by objective records attesting to lifetime struggles—not transient ones such as failing a particular exam or having problems in a course of study. These objective records could be in the form of elementary, junior high, and high school report cards; college or graduate school transcripts; performance reviews from prior jobs held; past psychological/educational test reports; notes or letters from past treatment providers and/ or tutors; evidence of being granted academic accommodations in prior schooling; copies of prior individualized education plans; standardized test scores; or any documented academic or behavioral problems from earlier functioning. These kinds of supporting documents can be extraordinarily helpful in understanding the nature, chronicity, and degree of disruption the symptoms caused. They can also serve either to validate or to refute self-reported recollections of prior symptoms.

What about those who report or complain about a subjective sense of never achieving the goals of which they believe they are capable? Their "internal barometer" tells them they should be doing better, and they may feel an inner sense of dissatisfaction and/or frustration around not meeting all their aspirations. Is this enough "impairment" to qualify for a diagnosis? We feel that, in most instances, self-perceptions of underattainment are not the basis for declaring psychiatric abnormality. "Perceived" impairment is not always synonymous with "real" impairment. We have encountered countless patients who come in completely convinced that having ADHD is responsible for their perceived underachievement—despite an almost complete absence of a childhood history of symptoms, current impairment that is nowhere near clinically significant, and a failure and/or unwillingness to consider other possible reasons for their difficulties.

A multitude of reasons besides ADHD account for why people do not achieve as much as they would like. Many are quick to conclude that ADHD may be the culprit, despite much evidence to the contrary. In fact, we have our most difficult and contentious feedback sessions when we inform people they do not have the diagnosis. Patients are often angry and defensive because they feel we have dismissed the seriousness of their problems. However, once they hear our rationale for why they do not meet the criteria, they usually have a better understanding and acceptance of our diagnostic conclusion.

We understand that in the heat of clinical battle, making these kinds of diagnostic judgments and distinctions can be difficult. A significant number of cases may fall along the margins and can be particularly hard calls to make. Clinicians need to determine their own thresholds for what constitutes clinically significant impairment and make every attempt to apply their decision-making paradigm in an objective and consistent manner across cases. To assist in making diagnostic judgments it may be helpful for diagnosticians to picture themselves on the stand being cross-examined by an opposing attorney regarding what evidence substantiates the ADHD diagnosis. If diagnosticians sense they are on thin ice regarding the quality, quantity, and credibility of the data, we would recommend against rendering the diagnosis—at least at that time. If additional objective historical information that sufficiently substantiates an ADHD-like pattern is provided at a later time, the diagnostic conclusion could be changed.

To determine the degree to which someone is impaired, the clinician must establish the benchmark for comparison. For example, if a person functions well enough to gain entry to law school but fails several courses, is impairment indicated? Some clinicians may argue that relative to other law students, the patient demonstrated relatively poor functioning. But comparison to an educational cohort can lead to the slippery slope. That person may have at least average or even above-average abilities across the board but be declared abnormal simply because of failure to perform as well as others in a chosen (or perhaps ill-chosen) training program. We believe that an individual is not necessarily psychiatrically impaired simply because he or she achieves less well than others who are high achievers.

The retort to this position is that disability can be defined by the relative discrepancy between what someone should be able to achieve (usually defined by IQ) and what someone actually manages to attain. The flaw in this argument is that IQ, although it may predict academic achievement through high school, is a poor indicator of overall occupational, social, or psychiatric adjustment. The extent to which an individual achieves, even in college or graduate settings, is determined by far more than intellectual factors. IQ is therefore not a birthright that guarantees that an individual should be able to achieve a certain academic level. Put another way, it is not a reliable indicator of what an individual should be able to attain because so many other psychological, motivational, and environmental factors are involved. Anxiety, inadequate social skills, personality style, unrealistic goals, a mismatch between demands and abilities, socioeconomic status, accessibility to educational/vocational opportunities, cultural issues, motivation, substance abuse, or having a relative weakness in a selected area are just some of the possible reasons that could explain discrepancies between measured intelligence and real-world performance. Our inclination then is to use the population mean as the basis for determining discrepancies in important dimensions of functioning, consistent with the interpretation of the Americans with Disabilities Act (ADA) by the Equal Opportunity Employment Commission.

For determinations of disability under antidiscrimination laws such as the ADA, the "average person" basis comparison has been well established. An individual can only be qualified as disabled if he or she is functionally impaired relative to the general population. Under the ADA, for example, a person is not disabled if he or she functions at least as well or better than most people. Clinicians who evaluate patients seeking legally sanctioned accommodations, such as those required by the ADA, must keep this standard in mind.

An obvious but again often neglected aspect of an adult ADHD evaluation is to review the official DSM-IV criteria for ADHD with the patient (and parent, spouse, or significant other if possible) both currently and retrospectively to determine whether diagnostic thresholds are met. Strictly speaking, without reviewing the formal criteria with the patient to see if the criteria are met, there is no way to rule in or rule out the disorder. We highly recommend using the DSM-IV symptom list because it is considered to be the "gold standard" in our current conceptualization of this disorder. Although other symptom lists/rating scales are often used, most notably the Wender Utah Rating Scale and the Brown Attention–Activation Disorder Scale, the DSM-IV items should be included because they remain the most commonly recognized, accepted, and scientifically verified set of criteria.

The third key area in the assessment of adult ADHD has already been alluded to several times but bears repeating. It is to make sure that the presenting symptoms are not better explained by some other psychiatric diagnosis, personality disorder, learning problem, or situational stressor. Documenting an attempt in the written report of the evaluation to rule out other conditions as being responsible for the ADHD-like symptoms is another critical but often overlooked component of an evaluation. The rationale for arriving at the ADHD diagnosis should be clearly spelled out, and a discussion or statement as to why other possible diagnoses do not fit should be included in the report. It seems many clinicians get caught up trying to "make ADHD fit" when they should be considering the range of alternative hypotheses that could account for the symptoms. Administering the Structured Clinical Interview for DSM-IV (SCID), which surveys all the major Axis I diagnoses, can be helpful in both ruling out other reasons for the symptoms and establishing comorbid conditions.

The last goal of the evaluation is to identify any conditions that might be joining ADHD as part of the clinical picture. Adult patients often have comorbid psychiatric diagnoses which in some cases may be far more problematic and impairing than their ADHD. Clinicians need to prioritize any comorbid conditions by their degree of impact on functioning. For example, it is more important to treat and stabilize a current major depression, manic episode, or alcohol dependence before treating the ADHD component. Patient outcomes can be seriously compromised if clinicians look only for ADHD and fail to consider or treat other potentially more serious conditions first.

In summary, the major aim of the evaluation process is to garner enough data and evidence to reliably answer the four core considerations we have been discussing. Figure 11.1 offers a pictorial diagram summarizing what we believe are the essential steps in the assessment of ADHD in adults.

How clinicians gather their data in support of these four key questions and the methods they use in the process are in our view not as important as ensuring that at the end of the evaluation these questions can be answered in as valid and reliable way as possible. It may be helpful to view the four prongs as the "process" or the "thinking/judgment/intellectual" part that underlies a credible assessment. The methodology employed is more the mechani-

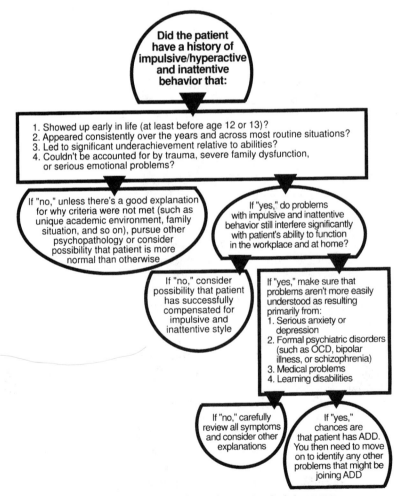

FIGURE 11.1. The road to a diagnosis of adult ADHD.

cal or "content" part of the evaluation and should be considered tools in service to helping answer these four core questions. The methods or tools used can be considered data-gathering mechanisms that help to enhance the reliability and validity of the diagnostic conclusions drawn. There are many ways to pursue this information and no one right way.

UNIVERSITY OF MASSACHUSETTS MEDICAL CENTER PROTOCOL

The assessment protocol currently used at the Adult ADHD Clinic at the University of Massachusetts Medical Center is one way to conduct a comprehensive evaluation (although not necessarily the best and certainly not the only way). Clinicians need to tailor their methods depending on the time and resources available to them. But all evaluations should attempt to address the four questions at the heart of an adult ADHD evaluation. Interviews and rating scales that readers may wish to use in this evaluation are provided in the workbook accompanying this text (see Barkley & Murphy, 1998).

When patients call the clinic, the administrative assistant conducts a brief intake interview over the phone; gathers demographic and insurance information, reason for the referral, and referral source; and asks a set of questions to ensure that it is an appropriate referral. A packet of rating scales and questionnaires (described later) are then mailed out to the patient and spouse/parent if appropriate. These questionnaires and rating scales are completed at home and are returned to the clinic in a self-addressed, stamped envelope. At this point an appointment date is scheduled. We strongly encourage a spouse, parent, or significant other who knows the patient well to participate in the evaluation. Also, patients are emphatically asked to search for and bring with them (or mail) any and all kinds of objective records that attest to their prior history and behavior. These records include report cards, past testing evaluations, individualized education plans, performance evaluations from prior jobs, college transcripts, and the like. Our typical adult evaluation lasts approximately 3 to 3½ hours. It consists of a comprehensive interview with the patient, spouse, and/or parent, an intellectual assessment, and a detailed feedback session. In most cases, we also administer a continuous performance test, and in some cases a Wide Range Achievement Test—3 (Wilkinson, 1993) to screen for the presence of learning disabilities.

Patient Rating Scales

DSM-IV ADHD Symptom Rating Scale

As previously discussed, it is crucial to determine the number of DSM-IV symptoms of ADHD endorsed both currently and retrospectively during childhood. Therefore, we ask the patient, spouse, and parent/significant other to complete the ADHD portion of the Adult Interview (see Barkley & Murphy, 1998), which lists the DSM-IV criteria for current functioning. The parent and patient also complete the retrospective version for childhood (ages 5 to 12). Each item is rated on a scale from 0 to 3 (rarely or never, sometimes, often, or very often, respectively). Items endorsed as "often" or "very often" indicate presence of the symptom.

Developmental History Questionnaire

The patient also completes a developmental history questionnaire which asks about neonatal and birth complications, mood and temperament difficulties, early peer relationships, whether developmental milestones were reached at age-appropriate times, and whether significant developmental or behavioral problems occurred early on. Again, during the evaluation we attempt to gather as much data as possible beginning from neonatal development and continuing up to the present. Parents sometimes describe their sense of knowing that this child was different from other siblings and indicate early concerns about behavior, temperament, mood, or activity level. However, because many children diagnosed with ADHD experience relatively normal early developmental histories, clinicians should not overinterpret or place too much emphasis on developmental history as being necessarily diagnostic or not diagnostic of ADHD.

Health History Questionnaire

The health history questionnaire asks about current and past medical problems, current and past medications, prior head injuries, allergies to any medications, or the presence of any other serious conditions such as epilepsy, high blood pressure, thyroid problems, chronic pain, and heart conditions. This information can help to rule out possible medical reasons for ADHD-like symptoms and may also have implications in treatment decisions, especially regarding medication choices.

Employment History Questionnaire

The employment history questionnaire asks about current employment status, job title, the number of past jobs held, the types of difficulties encountered in past jobs, the number and reasons for prior terminations, military experience and any problems encountered in the service, and the kinds of coping strategies patients have employed to manage their symptoms in the past. Employment history is pursued in more depth during the interview in an effort to determine the exact nature of the symptoms and difficulties the patient has experienced, the types of work that have been most successful, and what current and future vocational goals might be. A major goal is to shed light on the nature and degree of vocational impairment (and success) experienced historically over the course of the patient's life. Probing for specific examples regarding strengths and weaknesses can help to illuminate the nature and degree of impairment stemming from a patient's symptoms. This is an often overlooked area of assessment that can also have important implications for treatment—regarding optimal job choices in the future.

Social History Questionnaire

The social history questionnaire inquires about the ability to make and maintain friendships, typical moods, temper problems, and perceived reasons for any social skills difficulties during childhood and currently. Two additional open-ended questions are included on this questionnaire: (1) In what ways do your ADHD symptoms interfere in your life? (2) In what ways have you tried to compensate for or cope with your deficits? How patients answer these questions can offer valuable clues regarding the nature of their most troublesome symptoms, scope of impairment, and prior attempts to manage symptoms. The clinical interview can explore the realm of social functioning in greater detail if necessary.

Locke–Wallace Marital Adjustment Scale

The Locke–Wallace Marital Adjustment Scale is a brief 15-item rating scale to assess degree of marital satisfaction which is routinely administered to the patient and his or her spouse (see Chapter 8, this volume). It is often used for research purposes and is not essential for assessing ADHD but does offer a valid and reliable way of measuring degree of marital satisfaction/discord.

Michigan Alcohol Screening Test

The Michigan Alcohol Screening Test is a screen for assessing substance abuse problems that previous research has shown to be reliable and valid. It consists of 27 yes–no questions about substance use behavior and can be used in conjunction with the clinical interview to explore past and present substance use/abuse behavior. This test is also given to the spouse and parent when possible to determine degree of agreement with the patient's views.

Symptom Checklist 90—Revised

The Symptom Checklist 90—Revised (Derogatis, 1986), a self-report scale, assesses a variety of symptoms of psychological maladjustment using 90 items, each rated on a 5-point scale. It is a screening instrument that provides a measure of current psychological distress. Scores for nine subscales are obtained (Anxious, Phobic, Paranoia, Depression, Somatization, Obsessive–Compulsive, Interpersonal Sensitivity, Psychoticism, Hostility) as well as a global severity index.

Spouse or Significant Other Forms

Spouses are mailed the DSM-IV ADHD symptom scale for current functioning, the Locke–Wallace Marital Adjustment Scale, and the Michigan Alcohol Screening Test. They are asked to mail their completed forms back to the clinic. Spouses are strongly encouraged to participate in the diagnostic interview as well, preferably in person or via a telephone interview.

Parent or Sibling Rating Scales

Parents are mailed the DSM-IV ADHD Symptom Scale for current functioning and retrospective childhood functioning, the Michigan Alcohol Screening Test, and the Retrospective Attention Profile (RAP). The RAP was derived from the Children's Attention Profile and asks parents to rate the adult patient on typical ADHD symptomatology on a 3-point scale (not true, sometimes true, often true). It also asks an open-ended question inviting parents to describe any relevant history, behavior, or concerns they have that would assist the clinician in better understanding their son or daughter. There is no standard way of scoring this questionnaire. Its primary purpose is to elicit parental input and recollections regarding the patient's symptom history.

The Clinical Interview

A comprehensive clinical interview should be conducted that surveys past and present ADHD symptomatology: developmental and medical history; school history; work history; psychiatric history including any medications prescribed, dosages, and responses; social adjustment; family history of ADHD or any psychiatric or medical conditions that are evident in the family bloodlines; any arrests or trouble with the law; and general day-to-day adaptive functioning (i.e., how the patient is doing in meeting the demands of daily life). In our view, this is the most crucial component of the assessment. It should not simply be a brief, cursory, surface-level exam. To accomplish the appropriate rule-outs and to truly understand the patient's life history in all the necessary domains, the interview usually requires a minimum of 1 to 2 hours. Ideally, the interview should rely on several informants (a parent and spouse if possible) and survey behavior over time and across multiple settings (work, school, social, home). In most cases, interviews with the patient, parent, and/or spouse are conducted jointly. Only in rare cases (severe animosity or defensiveness between patient and/or parent/spouse) have we found it necessary to do separate interviews. However, we also find it valuable to offer some private time to each party participating in the assessment to elicit any data that the individual may have been reluctant to share in the presence of others. It is also during the clinical interview that the clinician must attempt to rule in or rule out other psychiatric diagnoses that may be a more accurate explanation for the presenting symptoms. We use the SCID, which asks standardized questions surveying criteria for all Axis I diagnoses. This instrument not only helps in the differential diagnosis of ADHD but may also help to establish the existence of comorbid conditions that may accompany ADHD.

Psychological Testing

Our views on the role of psychological testing for adult evaluations are consistent with those expressed for children and adolescents in Chapter 10 (this volume). Psychological testing can play a meaningful role in clinical assessment, but practitioners should be highly circumspect when interpreting such data. Such caution is especially justified when dealing with adults because the scientific literature on this subject is wafer thin. Prior research has demonstrated that no single test or battery of tests has adequate predictive validity or specificity to reliably make an ADHD diagnosis.

Unfortunately, we have often seen evaluations that consist almost entirely of psychological testing, usually incorporating measures of marginal relevance or validity to the identification of this disorder. *Under no conditions should psychological testing be offered as a sole basis for the diagnosis of ADHD.* We particularly discourage evaluations that focus too broadly on neuropsychological test performance in the absence of other clinical data. In the adult arena, psychological testing is most helpful when it is used to support conclusions derived from childhood history, rating scales, and a careful analysis of current functioning.

Beyond the sentiments expressed in Chapter 10 (this volume), we offer the following observations:

• We routinely administer a brief IQ screening measure such as the Shipley Institute of Living Scale or the Kaufman Brief Intelligence Test. In this way we can screen for any gross cognitive weaknesses. We can also get a sense of a discrepancy between measured intelligence and academic performance. For example, it is quite common (but not diagnostic) for an adult with ADHD to score in the average to above-average or even superior range of intelligence and yet have a school history of extreme grade variability with mostly C's, D's, and F's.

• Routine administration of a complete IQ test, such as the Wechsler Adult Intelligence Scale—Revised (WAIS-R; Wechsler, 1981) is in our view not necessary unless there are specific questions about the possibility of specific cognitive deficits. In most cases, a brief screening measure is sufficient.

• Significant splits between Verbal and Performance subscales on the WAIS-R are often offered as evidence of ADHD. No evidence exists that such discrepancies are at all meaningful for this diagnosis. The same conclusion holds for specific patterns of subtest scores or for disparities between IQ test scores and indices of achievement.

• We usually administer a computerized measure of sustained attention and distractibility such as the Conners Continuous Performance Test (CPT; Conners, 1995), the Test of Variables of Attention (Greenberg & Kindschi, 1996), or the Gordon Diagnostic System

(Gordon, 1983). Although the latter offers published normative data (Saykin et al., 1995) and some validity data (Rasile, Burg, Burright, and Donovick, 1995) none of the measures yet boasts data sufficient to justify much reliance. (Part of the reason for the absence of good data is because criteria for subject inclusion in the adult arena are still highly uncertain.) So, why do we administer them? Simply because these tests provide the opportunity to observe the patient cope with a task that requires sustained attention and impulse control. We have noticed that many who ultimately receive the diagnosis struggle with these tasks. For example, it is not uncommon for some ADHD patients to develop a headache or to appear worn or tired after just a few minutes of testing even if their scores ultimately fall in the average range. These observations, although never unilaterally diagnostic, can be informative. Also, when an adult fares poorly on a CPT, we have found that it often confirms other clinical data supportive of the ADHD diagnosis.

ASSESSMENT DILEMMAS

In clinical practice, assessment data are not always consistent across sources. Significant discrepancies may exist between patient/parent/spouse reports on symptom rating scales or on perceptions of severity of impairment. For example, in our experience it is not uncommon for parents of adult ADHD patients to endorse far fewer DSM-IV ADHD symptoms (current and retrospective) than their son or daughter does. Why might this be so? A number of reasons are possible, ranging from simply forgetting behavior that occurred long ago to parental psychopathology (my parents had their own problems and were unable or unwilling to tune into mine). Other possible explanations for lack of symptom endorsement by parents include cultural factors, guilt (maybe I should have sought help during childhood but because I did not, the behavior must not have been that bad), relative impairment compared to other siblings (he was not nearly as bad as his brother), or simply a general reluctance to view one's offspring as not normal. Whose version is the most reliable or valid? How do clinicians resolve these apparent discrepancies? Assessing the credibility of each source is crucial. Although not always, we have found the patient is often the most credible reporter. If the preponderance of the assessment data point to a robust history of ADHD and the only piece that does not seem to fit is the parents' or spouse's endorsement of fewer DSM-IV symptoms, the clinician may want to weigh this piece less and consider potential explanations for the differing viewpoints.

For example, is it a contentious marriage? Has the parent been absent for many years? How mentally healthy is the parent and how involved has the parent been? Is there a cultural or generational barrier against psychiatric labels that lowers the probability of positive symptom endorsement? In other cases it may go in the opposite direction. For example, sometimes adolescents and younger adults tend to deny their ADHD symptoms and their parents' report may be more accurate. Clinicians need to carefully consider these types of issues and exercise sound clinical judgment in their attempts to resolve these discrepancies.

ADHD, Predominantly Inattentive Type

Patients who present primarily with complaints of inattention and distractibility but who do not offer a history of poor self-control and overactivity are often the most difficult to evaluate. Although early-appearing, chronic, and pervasive disinhibition is associated almost uniquely with ADHD, the same cannot be said about inattention when it presents outside the context of poor self-control. As we have indicated, inattention is an omnipresent member of symptoms lists for most psychiatric and many medical conditions. It can also be a result of situational or environmental stressors. It is therefore hard to justify a diagnosis of ADHD, Predominantly Inattentive Type unless convincing evidence is presented to rule out the full range of other psychiatric and medical possibilities.

We generally approach the diagnosis of ADHD, Predominantly Inattentive Type as a process of elimination. If a patient presents with symptoms that fall almost entirely in a cognitive realm (inattention, poor concentration, lack of focus, distractibility), we first rule out the possibility that other psychiatric problems are at play, especially those related to anxiety, depression, Obsessive Compulsive Disorder, and Schizophrenia. If those explanations prove inappropriate, we next consider learning problems, such as intellectual limitations, specific learning disabilities, or a poor match between abilities and the patient's educational program or occupation. If learning problems fail to account for the patient's presenting complaints, the diagnosis of ADHD, Predominantly Inattentive Type may be indicated. However, this diagnosis still requires evidence that the patient's ability to attend is limited to such a degree that it causes clinically significant impairment. We again remind the reader that inattention is a common outcropping of human nature. Pathological inattention therefore requires an uncommon degree of underperformance and poor adjustment.

In our experience, the inattentive-only variant of ADHD is a relatively rare phenomenon. Most of the patients referred to us who have already been assigned this diagnosis exit our evaluation either with a different diagnosis or none at all. In many cases, our impression is that other clinicians, hearing complaints of inattention, jumped quickly to the ADHD, Predominantly Inattentive Type diagnosis without exploring other possibilities. We suggest that this diagnosis be applied judiciously and only after all other diagnostic avenues have been pursued.

Substance Abuse/Dependence and ADHD

The high degree of comorbidity between substance abuse and ADHD can offer another set of challenges to the clinician. The most frequent drugs of choice in our clinic populations are alcohol, marijuana, and, to a lesser extent, cocaine. The kinds of questions that routinely arise include the following: Are the ADHD symptoms due to substance abuse, ADHD, or both? Is it appropriate to prescribe a stimulant to someone who is a substance abuser? Does the patient need to completely stop using before beginning medication treatment for ADHD? If so, how long must the patient remain sober before attempting a medication trial? Will medication for ADHD jeopardize the patient's sobriety or make the patient worse?

In the case of alcohol abuse, when attempting to make a differential diagnosis, it is important to consider the following: When did alcohol abuse begin? Was there clear evidence of ADHD symptomatology during childhood before the onset of the alcohol abuse? How would the patient's life be different if he or she was able to maintain sobriety for a significant length of time? Would the ADHD symptoms then remit? Or, is there evidence of ongoing ADHD symptomatology even after a period of sustained sobriety of at least several months? Answering questions such as these will give valuable clues in differentiating ADHD from substance abuse.

What about the issue of substance abuse versus substance dependence? In our view, those who meet criteria for substance dependence should always be referred to primary substance abuse treatment to stabilize their addiction before any ADHD medication treatment is attempted. Even if ADHD is present in the substance-dependent patient, we believe the first step in his or her ADHD treatment is to get the substance problem under control. Once this is accomplished, assessment of any residual ADHD symptomatology can be more reliably made. In our experience, we usually require at least 1 to 2 months of sobriety before prescribing any stimulant medication to treat comorbid ADHD symptomatology.

In the case of episodic substance abuse, where the patient is not addicted or out of control, we sometimes take a more liberal stance. If the assessment yields a clear history of ADHD with comorbid substance abuse, we do not routinely disqualify these patients from a medication trial for their ADHD. In some of our cases, concurrent treatment for ADHD (with stimulant medication) and substance abuse has resulted in significant improvement of both the substance abuse and the underlying ADHD symptomatology. In other individuals, this has not been the case. All instances of ADHD and comorbid substance abuse require close vigilance and monitoring to ensure safety and optimal treatment outcome. In most cases, a reasonable course to follow in differentiating ADHD from substance dependence is to (1) determine the age of onset of the substance abuse, (2) determine whether there was a childhood history of ADHD predating the substance abuse, and (3) require a significant period of sobriety with reassessment of any residual ADHD symptomatology before assigning the ADHD diagnosis.

Differential Diagnosis from Other Psychiatric Disorders

As we have repeatedly emphasized, it is critical to make sure the ADHD assessment attempts to rule out other psychiatric conditions before assigning the ADHD diagnosis. In addition to substance abuse, other conditions that can mimic ADHD that need to be ruled out include mood disorders, anxiety disorders, head injury, Borderline Personality Disorder, Schizophrenia, Obsessive Compulsive Disorder, and Bipolar Disorder. The SCID can help determine whether criteria are met for these other disorders. Generally speaking, most other psychiatric disorders have a later onset of symptoms (after age 7); a childhood school history that does not indicate disruptive behavior or teacher complaints concerning inattentive, hyperactive, or impulsive behavior; and a different symptom profile and course. Again, paying close attention to age of onset, whether or not there is clear evidence of ADHD symptoms from early childhood, and the qualitative description and nature of the presenting symptoms/impairment offer important clues in differentiating ADHD from other psychiatric conditions.

ADHD versus Bipolar Disorder

The differential diagnosis between ADHD and Bipolar Disorder can be a tricky and sometimes difficult task. Impulsivity, hyperactivity, distractibility, increased talkativeness, agitation, and emotional lability can be characteristic of both ADHD and Bipolar Disorder. Further, the DSM-IV criteria for ADHD and for Major Depressive Disorder both have symptoms related to concentration and agitation. Given this significant symptom overlap, it is not surprising that these two disorders can be commonly confused.

In our view, it is not particularly difficult to differentiate ADHD from Bipolar I. True mania, with its associated symptoms of severe emotional lability, the perception of possessing special powers or abilities, insomnia for long periods, and in some cases psychotic symptoms, is clearly different from ADHD. However, it can be far more difficult to distinguish a severe form of ADHD from Bipolar II, Hypomania, or Cyclothymia. A hyperactive child or adult with pronounced impulsivity, disinhibition, hyperactivity, and emotional overreactivity can be very difficult to distinguish from one of these lower-magnitude forms of Bipolar Disorder.

The following guidelines may assist in distinguishing the two types of disorders:

1. The age of onset is typically earlier in ADHD than in Bipolar Disorder. In our clinical experience, it is quite rare for a child to be diagnosed with Bipolar Disorder, which typically tends to have an onset in the late teenage or early adult years. However, recent research

(Wozniak & Biederman, 1994; Wozniak et al., 1995) has challenged the view that childhood-onset Bipolar Disorder is rare. Further research may shed additional light on this issue in the future.

2. ADHD results in a chronic and pervasive pattern of impairment over time and across situations. Bipolar Disorder tends to be characterized by more of an episodic and cyclical nature with wide mood swings and grandiosity. The person with Bipolar Disorder is clearly not his or her normal self and may engage in reckless behavior such as spending sprees, excessive speeding, or other dangerous and uncharacteristic behavior. Such people may believe they have special powers or abilities and exhibit enormous energy. Bipolar Disorder may be characterized by bursts of productivity, where the person accomplishes a great deal in a short amount of time and sleeps very little over the course of several days. ADHD is relatively free from these bursts of productivity and tends to have a more chronic and consistent presentation with less variability in behavior, mood, energy, and productivity.

3. There is an absence of psychotic features and abnormally expansive or elevated mood in ADHD, whereas these features can be evident in Bipolar Disorder. Further, Bipolar Disorder I requires meeting criteria for both a major depression and a manic episode, which is not the case for ADHD.

4. An examination of the extended family bloodlines for psychiatric illness may offer important clues. For example, if several first-degree relatives have a history of Bipolar Disorder and ADHD is absent from the family bloodlines, this could be considered supportive evidence for an affective disorder. Conversely, if there is a family pattern of ADHD and no mood or affective disorders in the extended family, the possibility of ADHD is stronger.

5. Evaluating responses to prior medication trials may offer clues as to whether the patient has ADHD or a mood disorder. For example, those with ADHD (and not Bipolar Disorder) typically respond rather poorly to lithium but rather well to a stimulant. Conversely, those with a mood disorder may describe a history of positive responses to antidepressant medication or lithium and would typically not respond as well to a stimulant.

Part of the difficulty in differentiating these two disorders is also related to the possibility that both disorders can occur together. Hence, it is not always an either–or proposition. A thorough and careful assessment is essential to adequately address this potential comorbidity. Although both disorders can occur together, in our population this has proven to be quite rare.

THE PHENOMENOLOGY OF ADULT ADHD

Another aspect of the evaluation is to pay attention to how the person behaves, responds, or comes across over the course of the evaluation. How a person responds to certain questions may offer important clues in determining whether this person has lived with or experienced true ADHD. Rating scales, testing, and parental and/or significant other input and inspection of past records are all important parts of the evaluation, but it is also important to consider the overall behavior of the person throughout the course of the evaluation. Although not scientific, these subjective impressions can be invaluable in helping to make diagnostic decisions and bolstering one's confidence in those decisions. As a result of listening to many hundreds of adult ADHD patients share their lifetime struggles, we have developed a "sixth sense" of sorts regarding how someone who has lived with clinically significant ADHD all their life behaves in the context of an evaluation.

The clinician should be aware of the "tone" of the interview. Those who have lived with ADHD almost always communicate a sense of long-standing pain, frustration, and underachievement, and they display a certain emotional "heaviness" regarding the type and degree of impairment they have experienced historically. Often these patients display episodic tears and express despair, intense frustration, anger, a sense of lost opportunities, regret, low self-esteem, defensiveness, and sometimes a sense of learned helplessness. However, some patients (especially since the media explosion on adult ADHD) display a relative lack of pain and come across simply desiring to do better in a particular life domain. They are reasonably satisfied with their lives, are experiencing no obvious impairment, and seem to be seeking performance enhancement—not help for a disability. The tone of the evaluation for someone who turns out not to have ADHD is often lighter and relatively free from significant frustration or impairment. These patients may laugh about their foibles and imply that their behavior is seen as cute or funny instead of causing bona fide problems. When the overall tone is lighthearted, nonserious, and full of laughter and the degree of disruption/pain/impairment seems minimal, the patient is not likely to be describing ADHD. This is not to say that a heavy pall must be cast over the entire course of the evaluation and that patient cannot display a sense of humor. It simply means that ADHD is defined by significant impairment, which by definition is disruptive to one's life. People who seek evaluations for ADHD are usually in some pain or distress. If this is not evident during the evaluation, the person is unlikely to have ADHD. Put another way, if the diagnostician has to struggle with the question, "Where's the impairment?", chances are he or she is not dealing with ADHD.

Semantics

During the course of the evaluation, we take note of both qualitative and quantitative responses offered to certain key questions. For example, at the outset of an evaluation we routinely ask the question, "What are some of the symptoms you have experienced that make you think you have ADD?" How the person responds to this question can be telling and may yield valuable information. Often, those who truly have the disorder respond to that question in a robust and compelling way. They are usually not at a loss for words and have no difficulty answering this question. They frequently express a litany of symptoms, with an overall tone of intense exasperation or frustration. They may well describe numerous examples of not finishing tasks, of frustrations and failures in school, of social/interpersonal difficulties, and of problems in the workplace. The quality of their response to this question may assist clinicians to better determine if this person has "walked the walk" and knows firsthand what it is like to live with ADHD day in and day out. Those who do not have the disorder or who may have another psychiatric problem instead of ADHD, often provide a response to this question that comes across as more hollow and far less compelling and robust with respect to capturing the experience of living with ADHD. Often, those who turn out to receive the diagnosis of ADHD need to be interrupted or redirected as they go on and on in describing their symptoms and associated impairment.

Another useful question in follow-up to the previous question is to ask, "And how long have these symptoms been going on for you?" Again, those who truly have the disorder often answer this question with such statements as "as long as I can remember," "ever since school started," "forever," or "it has never been any different for me." Their answer clearly suggests that their symptoms have been longstanding and have been present over time and across situations throughout their life. Those who turn out not to have ADHD may answer this question by describing an onset of problems at some point in their adult life and identifying a situational stressor such as a divorce or death in the family, job termination or change, lifestyle change such as a new baby, onset of a major depression, or onset that coincides with beginnings of a substance abuse problem.

Another question we frequently ask toward the end of an evaluation is, "If I had a magic wand and could make two or three things much better for you, what would you want me to fix or help you improve upon?" The purpose of this question is to determine whether the patient's response is consistent with or magnifies/reinforces the "impairment themes" that emerged over the course of the evaluation. Does the patient immediately and unflinchingly come back to themes that are reflective of typical ADHD disruption? Or is the patient confused by the question or having a difficult time coming up with an answer? More often than not, those with bona fide ADHD respond with a variation of the following: "I just want to be able to focus and concentrate"; "I just want to finish something"; "I want to be able to sustain my effort and motivation long enough to complete something"; "I want to be less impulsive or be able to think before I act"; "I want to have better control of my temper"; "I just want to slow down and relax"; "I want to be able to do the routine things in life more efficiently"; or "I want to be able to read, study, and remember more effectively." The person who turns out not to have ADHD usually answers this question in a qualitatively different way, which gives the diagnostician the sense that his or her core problems have little to do with attention, concentration, distractibility, hyperactivity, or impulse control.

Because underachievement in school relative to native potential is so common in those with ADHD, we often ask and take note of the response to the following question: "What is your best guess as to why you did not perform as well as you should have in school?" Those with ADHD frequently pause, make a halfhearted attempt at an explanation, and finally may express frustration and exasperation and impatiently say, "I just don't know." They usually do not have a good answer for this question and may say something like, "I was not interested in school"; "I was lazy"; or "It was too boring." Sometimes they may even express or imply cynically that if they knew the answer to that question they would not be sitting there in the office.

Another question we routinely ask the patient (and spouse or parent) at the end of the evaluation is, "On an impairment scale ranging from 1 to 10 (1 being extremely mild and 10 being severe impairment), how would you rate yourself in terms of how impairing your symptoms are to you in your overall life and why?" The rating and reasoning for their choices can help to illuminate the degree of perceived impairment and add another piece of data in determining whether the data are sufficient to meet the threshold for a clinical diagnosis of ADHD.

Recognition Responses

Being cognizant of both verbal and affective responses to certain symptom items is another nonscientific but potentially useful piece of information to consider. We have noticed some fairly common behavioral and affective reactions (recognition responses) in many of our bona fide adult ADHD cases. For example, when asked about the symptom of losing things frequently, the person with ADHD (and usually his or her spouse) often rolls his or her eyes and disgustedly recites a litany of examples that clearly indicate that person's degree of forgetfulness and losing items is far different from that of the "average person" in the population. It often has a "you wouldn't believe how bad it is" quality, and the person or his or her spouse may display a sense of humor about it as well. When this information is followed up by asking what specifically the person loses, those who turn out to have ADHD may well offer a series of items—keys, wallet, license, credit cards, bills, clothes, books—and then, with obvious exasperation, say, "Everything!" Clearly, none of these examples alone is sufficient to substantiate the diagnosis, but in combination with other objective and reliable historical information, they can add additional support for the diagnosis.

The patient or the parent may also relate childhood nicknames of the patient that reflected his or her behavioral/symptom pattern (Calamity Jane, space cadet, absent-minded professor, Dennis the Menace, dream girl). Parents may also relate childhood stories that are legendary in the family circles detailing instances of impulse control problems or hyperactivity. There is often a rich cache of stories and events attesting to the patient's consistently annoying or disruptive behavior. These memories or stories are not simply isolated instances of misbehavior; they represent a consistent pattern that clearly makes the point that "Johnny has always been Johnny" over time and across situations. Conversely, as evidence for ADHD, some of our adult patients offer recollections of an isolated example of ADHD-like behavior that may have occurred once or twice in third grade. They may offer such statements as "I remember when my fourth-grade teacher said I looked out the window too much" or "I remember that time when Mr. Smith gave me a detention for not handing in my homework." What is important to remember is that in most cases of bona fide ADHD, this behavioral pattern is quite evident to teachers and parents and not difficult to identify. Such persons usually leave a trail of evidence in their wake as they move on in school/life.

Related questions we routinely ask include, "Did your parents ever take you to see anyone about these problems when you were a child?"; "How old were you when you first sought any treatment or professional help? For what reasons?" Those with clinically significant ADHD usually (although by no means always) either sought help or were referred for assistance relatively early on in life. In our experience it is relatively rare (although not impossible) for an adult who never sought or received any prior treatment to be diagnosed with ADHD.

Another useful question to ask is, "Did you have any trouble doing homework?" Both the content and the affect inherent in the response are important to consider. If the student with ADHD has one universal Achilles heel, most would agree it is in consistently doing homework. Almost all adults with ADHD (and children for that matter) report histories of problems completing homework. Many of our adult patients scoff and say one of the following: "I never did homework"; "I always copied someone else's"; "I did it five minutes before class"; "I only did it when I had to"; "I never took books home"; "I could never sit still and focus long enough to get it done"; "There was always something better or more fun/interesting to do"; "I was great at pulling a rabbit out of my hat at the last minute"; "I was a good schmoozer and was always able to get teachers to cut me some slack"; or "I was in the lower group and was never given homework." Careful questioning on this issue often uncovers that their choice not to do homework was not usually deliberate. What may be more accurate is that despite their best efforts, these patients had been unable to focus, concentrate, or sustain their effort/motivation long enough to get it done. Homework is so often a frustrating and emotionally charged issue for both parents and children. If an adult reported no history of homework difficulty or did not remember if it was a problem, we would seriously question an ADHD diagnosis.

In summary, taking into account not just what the patient says in response to assessment questions but how they say it in terms of tone, affect, and robustness can offer useful clues in making diagnostic decisions regarding ADHD.

A WORD ABOUT ADHD AS A BASIS FOR DISABILITY

Over the past few years, increasing numbers of students and employees have been pursuing ADHD evaluations to document requests for accommodations under the ADA. This law is designed to prevent discrimination against individuals with physical, mental, or learning disabilities. Under ADA-related regulations and case law, ADHD is considered a legitimate disability.

Providing documentation for ADA requests is a complicated undertaking which requires special knowledge about the law. A recent book on this general topic (Gordon & Keiser, 1998) contains a chapter specifically on legal documentation for the ADHD diagnosis (Gordon & Murphy, 1998). We have also summarized the essential steps in this process in two articles (Murphy & Gordon, 1996; Gordon, Barkley, & Murphy, 1997). Table 11.1 summarizes the gist of these articles.

Although a full discussion about disability determination falls outside the scope of this book, we offer the following comment: The burden of proof for these legal determinations is greater than for everyday clinical diagnosis. Institutions and employers have the right to request that individuals supply full and convincing documentation of disability. These reports are often reviewed by other professionals who pay close attention to evidence that the individual is truly impaired. According to the bulk of case law, the standard for judging impairment is the functioning of the average American. Therefore, to be qualified as disabled under the ADA requires evidence that, in a major life activity, the individual demonstrates substantial impairment relative to most people (and not, for example, a cohort of other students in a professional program). In the case of ADHD, the clinician has to supply evidence that the patient fully meets DSM-IV criteria for both early and current impairment. Also

TABLE 11.1. Documenting Requests for Accommodations under the Americans with Disabilities Act

1. Show that DSM-IV symptoms occur to a degree that is significantly greater than the normal population (state that DSM-IV was employed; report number of symptoms endorsed for current functioning).

2. Show that DSM-IV symptoms arose in childhood (state that DSM-IV was employed retrospectively; report number of symptoms endorsed for childhood; report approximate age of onset of symptoms [onset before age 12 is acceptable—cite Barkley & Biederman, 1997, to support his adjustment to age of onset if need be]).

3. Present evidence of impairment since childhood. Indicate how disorder has significantly interfered with the individual's social, educational, or occupational functioning.

4. Present evidence of cross-setting symptoms/impairment. Provide history of symptoms producing impairment in home and school settings in childhood.

5. Demonstrate corroboration of symptoms in childhood from someone who knew the patient well (parents, siblings, longtime friend, etc.).

6. Demonstrate corroboration of current symptoms of ADHD from someone who knows the patient well (spouse, dating partner, parent, sibling, or employer, etc.).

7. Show evidence of current impairment in a major life activity (education, occupation, social, etc.). Impairment has been defined in the ADA as being relative to the average person or the majority of the population—*not* relative to a high achieving, highly intelligent, or high-functioning peer group (graduate, professional, or medical students, college students, etc.). State the evidence and how it has reduced the person's functioning well below that of the average person.

8. State a differential diagnosis was conducted and other disorders were ruled out that might have better accounted for this person's performance problems or current symptoms and impairment.

9. Describe the history of prior treatment and its success.

10. Describe any history of prior accommodations for the disorder and their success. If no prior accommodations were ever provided for disorder, explain why not.

11. State accommodations being recommended *and* why; what is the rationale for each and why are they reasonable for this disorder in this person.

12. If the diagnostician does not hold a terminal degree in clinical psychology or psychiatry, indicate what training qualifies the professional to conduct a differential diagnosis of mental illness.

required is a clear rationale for why the accommodations requested are in keeping with both the nature of the disorder and the circumstances in which the person functions.

CONCLUSION

It should be quite clear by now that the assessment of adult ADHD is a formidable challenge. Our current state of scientific knowledge and the maturity of our technology and assessment measures are still quite primitive. Further, the relative lack of well-normed rating scales for adults, the fact that everyone experiences the symptoms of ADHD to some degree, the high degree of comorbidity, the myths and confusion perpetuated in part by widespread media exposure, and the lack of a "litmus test" for diagnosing the disorder all contribute to making this a most difficult disorder to diagnose accurately. The major goals of this chapter have been (1) to communicate the complexities of this disorder, (2) to show that the diagnosis should be reserved only for those who meet full clinical criteria (early onset, current and historical evidence of clinically significant impairment in major life domains, and not better explained by another condition), (3) to show that having ADHD is disruptive and impairing to lives and is not advantageous, and (4) to show that ADHD is not simply the identification of certain personality characteristics or a simple matter of symptom endorsement. It is our hope that this "tighter" conceptualization of ADHD will help to uphold the legitimacy and integrity of the disorder, help to reduce some of the current confusion and skepticism surrounding ADHD in adults, and assist clinicians in better understanding and diagnosing this often misunderstood disorder.

REFERENCES

American Psychiatric Association. (1994). *Diagnostic and statistical manual of mental disorders* (4th ed.). Washington, DC: Author.

Barkley, R. A., & Biederman, J. (1997). Toward a broader definition of the age-of-onset criterion for attention-deficit hyperactivity disorder. *Journal of the American Academy of Child and Adolescent Psychiatry, 36*(9), 1204–1210.

Barkley, R. A., Fischer, M., Edelbrock, C. S., & Smallish, L. (1990). The adolescent outcome of hyperactive children diagnosed by research criteria: I. An 8-year prospective follow-up study. *Journal of the American Academy of Child and Adolescent Psychiatry, 29,* 546–555.

Barkley, R. A., & Murphy, K. R. (1998). *Attention-Deficit/Hyperactivity Disorder: A clinical workbook.* New York: Guilford Press.

Biederman, J., Munir, K., Knee, D., Armentano, M., Autor, S., Waternaux, C., & Tsuang, M. (1987). High rate of affective disorders in probands with attention deficit disorders and their relatives: A controlled family study. *American Journal of Psychiatry, 144,* 330–333.

Borland, B. L., & Heckman, H. K. (1976). Hyperactive boys and their brothers: A 25-year follow-up study. *Archives of General Psychiatry, 33,* 669–675.

Conners, C. K. (1995). *The Conners Continuous Performance Test.* North Tonawanda, NY: Multi-Health Systems.

Derogatis, L. R. (1986). *Manual for the Symptom Checklist 90—Revised (SCL-90-R).* Baltimore: Author.

Feldman, S. A., Denhoff, E., & Denhoff, J. I. (1979). The attention disorders and related syndromes: Outcome in adolescence and young adult life. In L. Stern & E. Denhoff (Eds.), *Minimal brain dysfunction: A developmental approach.* New York: Masson.

Fischer, M., Barkley, R. A., Fletcher, K. E., & Smallish, L. (1993). The adolescent outcome of hyperactive children: Predictors of psychiatric, academic, social, and emotional adjustment. *Journal of the American Academy of Child and Adolescent Psychiatry, 32,* 324–332.

Gittelman, R., Mannuzza, S., Shenker, R., & Bonagura, N. (1985). Hyperactive boys almost grown-up. *Archives of General Psychiatry, 42,* 937–947.

Gordon, M. (1983). *The Gordon Diagnostic System.* DeWitt, NY: Gordon Systems.

Gordon, M. (1995). *How to operate an ADHD clinic or subspecialty practice.* Syracuse, NY: GSI Publications.

Gordon, M., Barkley, R. A., & Murphy, K. (1997). ADHD on trial. *ADHD Report, 5*(4), 1–4.

Gordon, M., & Irwin, M. (1996). ADD/ADHD: *A no-nonsense guide for the primary care physician.* Syracuse, NY: GSI Publications.

Gordon, M., & Keiser, S. (Eds.). (1998). *Accommodations in higher education under the Americans with Disabilities Act (ADA): A no-nonsense guide for clinicians, educators, administrators, and lawyers.* New York: Guilford Press.

Gordon, M., & McClure, D. (1995). *The down and dirty guide to adult ADD.* Syracuse, NY: GSI Publications.

Gordon, M., & Murphy, K. R. (1998). Attention-deficit/hyperactivity disorder. In M. Gordon & S. Keiser (Eds.), *Accommodations in higher education under the Americans with disabilities act: A no-nonsense guide for clinicians, educators, administrators, and lawyers* (pp. 98–129). New York: Guilford Press.

Greenberg, L. M., & Kindschi, C. L. (1996). *T.O.V.A. Test of Variables of Attention: Clinical guide.* St. Paul, MN: TOVA Research Foundation.

Hechtman, L., Weiss, G., & Perlman, T. (1978). Growth and cardiovascular measures in hyperactive individuals as young adults and in matched normal controls. *Canadian Medical Association Journal, 118,* 1247–1250.

Hechtman, L., Weiss, G., & Perlman, T. (1980). Hyperactives as young adults: Self-esteem and social skills. *Canadian Journal of Psychiatry, 25,* 478–483.

Hechtman, L., Weiss, G., Perlman, T., & Tuck, D. (1985). Hyperactives as young adults: various clinical outcomes. *Adolescent Psychiatry, 9,* 295–306.

Loney, J., Whaley-Klahn, M. H., Kosier, T., & Conboy, J. (1981). *Hyperactive boys and their brothers at 21: Predictors of aggressive and antisocial outcomes.* Paper presented at the meeting of the Society for Life History Research, Monterey, CA.

Mannuzza, S., Gittelman-Klein, R. G., Bessler, A. A., Malloy, P., & LaPadula, M. (1993). Adult outcome of hyperactive boys: Education achievement, occupational rank, and psychiatric status. *Archives of General Psychiatry, 50,* 565–576.

Mendelson, W. B., Johnson, N. E., & Stewart, M. A. (1971). Hyperactive children as teenagers: A follow-up study. *Journal of Nervous and Mental Disease, 153,* 273–279.

Menkes, M. M., Rowe, J. S., & Menkes, J. H. (1967). A twenty-five-year follow-up study on the hyperkinetic child with minimal brain dysfunction. *Pediatrics, 39,* 393–399.

Murphy, K., & Gordon, M. (1996). ADHD as a basis for test accommodations: A primer for clinicians. *ADHD Report, 4*(6), 10–11.

Rasile, D. A., Berg, J. S., Burright, R. G., & Donovick, P. J. (1995). The relationship between performance on the Gordon Diagnostic System and other measures of attention. *International Journal of Psychology, 30*(1), 35–45.

Satterfield, J. H., Hoppe, C. M., & Schell, A. M. (1982). A prospective study of delinquency in 110 adolescent boys with attention deficit disorder and 88 normal adolescent boys. *American Journal of Psychiatry, 139,* 795–798.

Saykin, A. J., Gur, R. C., Gur, R. E., Shtasel, D. L., Flannery, K. A., Mozley, L. H., Mailamut, B. L., Watson, B., & Mozley, P. D. (1995). Normative neuropsychological test performance: Effects of age, education, gender, and ethnicity. *Applied Neuropsychology, 2*(2), 79–88.

Wechsler, D. (1981). *Wechsler Adult Intelligence Scale—Revised.* New York: Psychological Corporation.

Weiss, G., & Hechtman, L. T. (1993). *Hyperactive children grown up* (2nd ed.). New York: Guilford Press.

Weiss, G., Hechtman, L., Milroy, T., & Perlman, T. (1985). Psychiatric status of hyperactives as adults: A controlled 15-year follow-up of 63 hyperactive children. *Journal of the American Academy of Child Psychiatry, 24,* 211–220.

Weiss, G., Hechtman, L., Perlman, T., Hopkins, J., & Wener, A. (1979). Hyperactive children as young adults: A controlled prospective 10-year follow-up of the psychiatric status of 75 children. *Archives of General Psychiatry, 36,* 675–681.

Weiss, G., Minde, K., Werry, J. S., Douglas, V. I., & Nemeth, E. (1971). Studies on the hyperactive child: VIII. Five year follow-up. *Archives of General Psychiatry, 24,* 409–414.

Wender, P. (1995). *Attention deficit–hyperactivity disorder in adults.* New York: Oxford University Press.

Wilkinson, G. S. (1993). *Wide Range Achievement Test—3.* Wilmington, DE: Wide Range, Inc.

Wozniak, J., & Biederman, J. (1994). Prepubertal mania exists and co-exists with ADHD. *ADHD Report, 2,* 5–6.

Wozniak, J., Biederman, J., Kiely, K., Ablon, S., Faraone, S. V., Mundy, E., & Mennin, D. (1995). Mania-like symptoms suggestive of childhood-onset bipolar disorder in clinically referred children. *Journal of the American Academy of Child and Adolescent Psychiatry, 34,* 867–876.

Part III

TREATMENT

&

Chapter 12

COUNSELING AND TRAINING PARENTS

Arthur D. Anastopoulos
Julianne M. Smith
Emily E. Wien

As discussed in previous chapters (e.g., Chapter 2), the behavioral problems of children with Attention-Deficit/Hyperactivity Disorder (ADHD) are by no means limited to the school setting. Another place in which there is great potential for encountering ADHD difficulties is in the home. Because of their inattention difficulties, many children with ADHD do not listen carefully to parental instructions, thereby missing information critical to completing assigned tasks. Even if they start off on the right foot, many of these same children do not sustain their attention long enough to complete even the most routine household chores. The tendency of children with ADHD to be hyperactive–impulsive can also complicate home life a great deal. This behavior may be seen in terms of their not being able to sit still through dinner, jumping up and down on furniture, interrupting parental conversations, or blurting out inappropriate comments.

Although most parents consider such behaviors unacceptable, few have the specialized parenting knowledge and skills necessary for bringing them under better control. As they become increasingly more aware of their inability to resolve these child management problems, many parents begin to experience secondary personal difficulties, including sadness, frustration, guilt, stress, and marital strains. Such conditions are often the impetus for seeking out professional advice.

It is with these sorts of circumstances in mind that we now begin discussing the role that parent training and counseling can serve in the overall clinical management of children with ADHD. The original description of this approach appeared in Barkley (1981). Subsequent modifications were described in Barkley (1987) and in Anastopoulos and Barkley (1990). Additional changes to this program were outlined recently in Barkley (1997a).

What follows is a detailed description of the parent training and counseling program that we currently employ with clinic-referred children who have ADHD. We begin this discussion by presenting our rationale for utilizing this particular combination of treatment strategies. Thereafter, we provide a detailed account of the specific steps by which this intervention program is routinely implemented.

RATIONALE

As with any other type of treatment, it is first necessary to address the question: On what basis is there justification for incorporating parent training (PT) and counseling in the clinical management of children with ADHD? Although by no means complete, part of the answer to this question comes from a consideration of the following clinical, theoretical, and empirical points.

Clinical Considerations

Although stimulant medication therapy is by far the most commonly used treatment in the clinical management of children with ADHD (Barkley, 1990), 10–20% of those who take such medication do not show clinically significant improvements in their primary ADHD symptomatology (Taylor, 1986). Even when a favorable response is obtained, some children experience side effects that are of sufficient frequency and severity to preclude continued use of stimulant medication. Independent of these issues, many parents prefer not to use any form of medication in treating their child. To the extent that there are children with ADHD for whom stimulant medication therapy, as well as other medications, is not a viable treatment option, alternative treatments must be used. Among these, PT is certainly worthy of further consideration.

PT can also be helpful to children with ADHD who are stimulant medication responders. For example, in an effort to reduce the risks for insomnia and various other side effects, most physicians limit their stimulant prescriptions to twice and thrice daily dosages. For similar reasons, some physicians further limit the child's medication regimen to school days only. What this means from a practical standpoint is that for substantial portions of any given day, usually in the late afternoons and early evening, children are not deriving any therapeutic benefits from stimulant medication. For parents and other caretakers, this necessitates finding other means for handling their child's behavioral difficulties in the home. Here again, PT can play a useful role.

Additional justification for utilizing PT stems from a consideration of the potential for comorbidity. As was noted earlier (Chapter 4), children with ADHD often display oppositional–defiant behavior, aggression, conduct difficulties, and other externalizing problems. Because such secondary features cannot be fully addressed through the use of medication, alternative treatment approaches need to be considered. In view of its highly successful track record with noncompliant and conduct-disordered populations (Forehand & McMahon, 1981; Kazdin, 1997; Patterson, 1982; Webster-Stratton, 1994), PT is well suited to this purpose.

Of additional clinical importance is that raising a child with ADHD can place enormous strains on family functioning. Research has shown, for example, that parents of children with ADHD often become overly directive and negative in their parenting style (Cunningham & Barkley, 1979). In addition to viewing themselves as less skilled and less knowledgeable in their parenting roles (Mash & Johnston, 1990), they may also experience considerable stress in their parenting roles, especially when comorbid oppositional–defiant features are present (Anastopoulos, Guevremont, Shelton, & DuPaul, 1992). Such problems are not usually due to faulty parenting. On the contrary, many parents of children with ADHD use parenting strategies that work just fine for normal siblings in the family. Alerting parents to this reality begins the process of alleviating their distress. Teaching them more effective ways of dealing with their difficult child, through the use of PT, can also facilitate their personal adjustment.

Of additional clinical significance is that parents of children with ADHD are at increased risk for depression, anxiety, and marital discord (Lahey et al., 1988). The extent to which these complications result directly from the child's ADHD is not entirely clear at present. Clinical experience would suggest that they probably do result from the child's ADHD, at least in part, given the increased caretaking demands that such children impose on their parents. These demands include more frequent displays of noncompliance, related to difficulties in following through on parental instructions (Cunningham & Barkley, 1979). In addition, parents of these children often find themselves involved in resolving various school, peer, and sibling difficulties, which occur throughout childhood (Barkley, 1990) and into adolescence as well (Barkley, Anastopoulos, Guevremont, & Fletcher, 1991). Although successful implementation of PT may alleviate some of these concerns, it is often necessary to consider other intervention strategies. One such option is to use the counseling portion of the program to deal with these issues. Cognitive restructuring and various other cognitive therapy techniques are particularly well suited for this purpose given that so many of these parental problems stem from faulty perceptions of themselves, of their child's future, and so forth.

What should be readily apparent from the preceding discussion is that many commonly encountered clinical situations provide a basis for using PT and counseling in the overall management of children with ADHD. Additional justification for implementing these treatments comes from a consideration of several theoretical matters.

Theoretical Considerations

As noted earlier in this volume (e.g., Chapter 7), there has been a recent shift in the way that ADHD is conceptualized as a disorder. Specifically, many experts in the field today have begun to view ADHD as a condition characterized by neurologically based deficits in behavioral inhibition (Barkley, 1997b; Quay, 1997; Schachar, Tannock, & Logan, 1993). To the extent that deficits in behavioral inhibition are central to understanding this disorder, it suggests that children with ADHD are not very adept at thinking through the consequences of their actions. Working from this assumption, it would then seem reasonable to consider increasing the child's awareness of the connection between his or her behavior and the consequences that follow. More so than many other forms of treatment, PT lends itself especially well to meeting this therapeutic objective.

Further theoretical justification stems from a consideration of the apparent relationship that exists among ADHD, Oppositional Defiant Disorder (ODD), and Conduct Disorder (CD). Specifically, recent findings from the field of developmental psychopathology implicate the possibility of a developmental pathway leading from ADHD to these comorbid conditions (Loeber, Keenan, Lahey, Green, & Thomas, 1993). If having ADHD greatly increases the risk for developing ODD or CD at a later point in time, it would seem to be of utmost clinical importance to begin treatment as soon as possible to reduce this risk among children not yet affected by these comorbid conditions. Although research of this sort has yet to be conducted, the fact that PT has worked so well with noncompliant and conduct-disordered populations (Forehand & McMahon, 1981; Kazdin, 1997; Patterson, 1982; Webster-Stratton, 1994) provides some basis for considering its use in such a preventive role.

Family systems theory (Minuchin, 1974) also seems to have bearing on this topic. According to this viewpoint, having a child with ADHD places the family at increased risk for disruptions in normal family relations. This might include, for example, strained alliances between mothers and fathers and brothers and sisters who treat the sibling affected by ADHD as an outcast, and so forth. When such circumstances arise, family systems theory would propose that changes in the structure of the family need to occur to normalize family functioning. To this end, PT may strengthen the alliance between parents by teaching them common ways to parent the child with ADHD. Similarly, cognitive therapy strategies may be used to alter the way that other family members view the child with ADHD, thereby making them more accepting and tolerant, which are necessary conditions for interacting in a more normalized fashion.

Empirical Findings

Despite the plethora of research on PT in behavior modification (Kazdin, 1997), few studies have examined the efficacy of this approach with children specifically identified as having ADHD. What few studies exist can be interpreted with cautious optimism as supporting the use of PT with such children (Anastopoulos, Shelton, DuPaul, & Guevremont, 1993; Erhardt & Baker, 1990; Pisterman, McGrath, Firestone, & Goodman, 1989; Pisterman, Firestone, McGrath, & Goodman, 1992). Most of these interventions utilized weekly therapy sessions in either group or individual formats that were short term in nature, spanning 6 to 12 weeks in length. By and large, most of these programs trained parents in the use of specialized contingency management techniques, such as positive reinforcement, response cost, and/or time-out strategies. Some, however, combined contingency management training with didactic counseling, aimed at increasing parental knowledge and understanding of ADHD (Anastopoulos et al., 1993; Pisterman et al., 1992). In addition to producing changes in child behavior, PT interventions have also led to improvements in various aspects of parental and family functioning, including decreased parenting stress and increased parenting self-esteem (Anastopoulos et al., 1993; Erhardt & Baker, 1990; Pisterman et al., 1989).

Information about the efficacy of PT also comes from studies in which this form of treatment was combined with other interventions, such as pharmacotherapy (Abikoff & Hechtman, 1996; Pollard, Ward, & Barkley, 1983) and self-control therapy (Horn, Ialongo, Pascoe, & Greenberg, 1991; Ialongo, Horn, Pascoe, & Greenberg, 1993). In contrast to what is found when PT is used alone, many of these multimodal intervention studies, especially those involving medication, have noted that PT contributes very little to outcome above and beyond that accounted for by the other treatment. Because so few of these studies have been conducted to date, it would seem premature to discount the potential therapeutic benefits of PT in a multimodal intervention package. Fortunately, further clarification of this matter is forthcoming (Richters, Arnold, Jensen, & Abikoff, 1995).

PARENT TRAINING PROGRAM

Although there are many ways to conduct PT programs (Forehand & McMahon, 1981; Patterson, 1982; Webster-Stratton, 1994), little is known about their relative efficacy in regards to the treatment of children with ADHD. Thus, it would not be unreasonable to present any one of them to illustrate how PT is applied in clinical practice. For the purposes of this chapter, we present the one that was recently described in Barkley (1997a). In addition to outlining the basic steps of this program, we discuss commonly employed variations of these procedures.

Client Selection Criteria

One of the most frequently misunderstood aspects of PT is that it is not appropriate for all children who receive an ADHD diagnosis. Additional child, parent, and/or family characteristics must be taken into account as part of the clinical decision-making process.

One of the simplest criteria to assess is the chronological age of the identified child. In most cases, children must be between 3 and 11 years of age for their parents to be considered for the program. Such age guidelines presume a relatively close correspondence between a child's chronological age and mental age. When a significant discrepancy exists, the discrepancy can affect the referral process. For instance, when a child with ADHD has a mental age that falls below 3 years, it is not likely that his or her parents would benefit a great deal from participation in the program. In contrast, participation in PT may be of some therapeutic value to parents of an adolescent with ADHD whose mental age falls below 12 years.

In addition to these chronological and mental age considerations, the identified child's diagnostic status must be taken into account. In particular, the severity of the ADHD diagnosis needs to be considered, as well as the presence and severity of various co-occurring conditions. In our experience, the complete treatment program is often ideally suited to meeting the clinical management needs of children with ADHD who also display significant oppositional–defiant behavior or conduct problems. Even when these associated behavioral complications are absent, the program may still be beneficial to children whose ADHD is moderate to severe in intensity. In cases in which the ADHD may be extremely severe, it may first be necessary to place the children on a trial of stimulant medication. To avoid confounding the outcome of such therapeutic trials, participation in the parent training/counseling program is temporarily postponed. Once it has been determined that a child will or will not continue to receive stimulant medication therapy, parent training/counseling services may then be employed. When children show a favorable response to stimulants, continued use of such medication generally makes their behavior easier to manage, thereby facilitating parental efforts to employ recommended PT skills.

For those children whose ADHD difficulties are mild and who do not exhibit oppositional–defiant behavior or related problems, implementation of the complete treatment program may not be the most efficient means of meeting their clinical management needs. Nevertheless, their psychosocial circumstances may still be enhanced either by the parent counseling portion of the program or by parental acquisition of select contingency management skills (e.g., a home token system) that address their deficits. Other ADHD children for whom the complete program may initially be inappropriate are those who are also experiencing significant depression, anxiety, or other sorts of emotional difficulties. In many cases like these, the child's emotional complications are independent of the ADHD and clearly of greater clinical concern. For this latter reason in particular, they must often be addressed first. Once such difficulties are resolved, it may then be appropriate to initiate parent training/counseling services.

Referral to the program is by no means just a function of the child's status. Numerous parent characteristics enter into the clinical decision-making process as well. Perhaps the most important of these is the parents' ability to tolerate the child's deviant behavior. Whereas some parents are able to cope satisfactorily with even the most severe child behavior problems, others are highly distressed by much milder child difficulties. For this reason their referral for parent training/counseling depends a great deal on their perceived need for such services. There are times that parents do not perceive such a need, and yet it is our professional opinion that they might benefit from the program. This occurs most often among parents who, although they have control over their child's behavior, are experiencing a great deal of stress in maintaining such control. In such situations, we frequently advise parents to participate in the program. By doing so, parents gain access to more efficient child management techniques and coping strategies, which in turn reduces the stress they experience in their parenting role.

Another basis for referral arises when parental differences of opinion exist with respect to various child management issues. For example, a husband and wife may differ a great deal in their interpretation of their child's ADHD, or they may seriously disagree over how to manage their child's behavior. Joint participation in the treatment program affords them an opportunity for acquiring a common base of ADHD knowledge, from which they may also employ more consistent child management strategies. Joint participation can increase the parenting alliance, reduce marital tensions related to child management, and facilitate parental efforts to gain control over their child's problem behaviors.

When marital tensions stem from areas other than child management issues, referral to the program may not be appropriate at first for several reasons. Some parents may be so preoccupied with their troubled marital circumstances that they are unable to commit the time and energy necessary for meeting the increased parenting responsibilities required by the treatment program. Or, as sometimes happens, parents are so unwilling to compromise with each other that they are unlikely to agree on using recommended PT strategies. When such serious complications exist, parents are advised to begin receiving marriage counseling, either prior to or concurrent with their participation in the parent training/counseling program. As might be expected, failure to do so greatly jeopardizes the outcome of any subsequent treatment that may be rendered on behalf of the child.

Marital difficulties are not the only circumstance affecting the timing of parental participation in the program. One or both parents may have adult ADHD difficulties or be depressed, anxious, or affected by other types of medical or psychological difficulties, the primary cause of which is not their child with ADHD. Because coping with such personal distress may necessarily divert parental attention from meeting routine parenting responsibilities, many parents may find it difficult to put forth the effort necessary to benefit from participation in the parent training/counseling program. For this reason it is often necessary to direct them to appropriate medical and/or mental health professionals to begin addressing their own concerns. Such assistance can occur either prior to or during their participation in PT.

In addition to these personal and marital issues, parents of children with ADHD may face external stresses and strains that are not readily under their control, including sudden financial strains resulting from a recent job loss or ongoing stresses pertaining to the daily care of a chronically ill relative. Although such complications may not require ongoing professional assistance, they too may still affect the timing of when parents decide to become involved in the treatment program.

As a rule, parental levels of education and intelligence are not major factors in deciding whether to refer a family for PT. In extreme cases, however, they may need to be taken into account. For example, parents with borderline to mildly delayed intellectual functioning may not be able to implement recommended child management strategies or to understand fully the counseling objectives of the program. Although this can happen, professionals should not automatically assume it to be the case. Instead, the clinician should generally try to implement the program at a pace commensurate with the parents' learning style. If after a few sessions it becomes clear that this is not working, it may be necessary to ask parents to have a close friend or relative accompany them during subsequent treatment sessions. Once properly informed, such individuals frequently are in an excellent position to communicate important therapeutic information and to ensure that recommended treatment strategies are used correctly within the home setting.

Another commonly encountered clinical situation that affects referral decisions occur when the child with ADHD and/or other members of the family are already receiving mental health services. Before starting PT, we generally contact the professional providing treatment (with the family's consent, of course). Once the therapeutic nature and intent of such services are clarified, a decision is made as to whether participation in PT is at cross-purposes with the existing treatment. If it is, we generally advise against doing both treatments simultaneously, leaving it up to the parents to decide which type of therapeutic assistance they will pursue. If no apparent conflict exists, we initiate the program but thereafter monitor the situation periodically to ensure that no conflict arises.

Although it is not an exclusionary factor, the number of parents likely to be attending treatment sessions may also enter into the referral decision-making process. In two-parent families, the presence of both parents is highly desirable but not always feasible, due to job schedule conflicts, child caretaking responsibilities, and so forth. Instead of automatically restricting such families from the program, we generally allow for one-parent participation. In many cases this can be an acceptable arrangement as long as the parent who is not in attendance is understanding, cooperative, and supportive of the treatment process. An additional reason for allowing one-parent participation is that several methods exist for getting around this sort of problem. For example, the parent in attendance may take detailed session notes or audiotape the session. Such recorded information may then be shared and discussed with the absent parent later at home.

What should be evident by now is that the referral process for parent training and counseling is not a simple or straightforward matter. On the contrary, numerous psychosocial circumstances must be taken into account to ensure that this form of treatment is clinically appropriate for referred children with ADHD and their families.

Therapist Qualifications

At face value, delivering PT to parents of children with ADHD might seem to be a relatively easy task. If all that is done is didactic in nature—that is, simply presenting a packaged program (Barkley, 1997a) to an attentive and cooperative parent—it may be possible to implement it in a "cookbook" fashion. More often than not, however, this is not the case. Thus, its delivery typically requires the skills of a qualified therapist.

The therapist's professional degree is perhaps the least important of these qualifications. What is of utmost relevance is the therapist's familiarity with and expertise in using behavior management strategies. Having these skills is especially critical to the success of the program because a one-size-fits-all approach just does not work. Finding ways to tailor PT to fit the needs of individual parents requires a great deal of flexibility and creativity. Thus, extensive experience in using various child behavior therapy strategies, especially contingency management techniques, is highly desirable. This experience is especially critical when delivering the program in a group format.

Being well versed in current ADHD research findings is another important qualification in light of the increasing number of talks, magazine articles, newspaper stories, and television presentations on the Ritalin (methylphenidate) controversy, as well as other aspects of ADHD. Clinicians lacking such knowledge are likely to encounter parents who themselves possess a great deal of ADHD knowledge. If by chance such a clinician were to respond to sophisticated parent questioning in an unsatisfactory manner, parental confidence in his or her expertise might diminish significantly, which in turn might interfere with future therapeutic efforts.

Because the counseling portion of the treatment program routinely incorporates cognitive therapy strategies, we also recommend experience in using these techniques. This is not to suggest that clinicians of other theoretical orientations should refrain from using the program. On the contrary, they are encouraged to do so, provided they become relatively familiar with the behavioral and cognitive principles of the program. As is the case with other treatment approaches, the more skilled clinicians might be in using cognitive-behavioral strategies, the more likely it is that they will be able to overcome parental difficulties in utilizing recommended PT strategies, to help parents in their adjustment to having a child with ADHD, and so on. Familiarity with cognitive techniques can also serve as a basis for dealing with parental depression and other types of parental psychopathology that might be present.

Clinical and Stylistic Considerations

Being cognitive-behavioral in nature, the treatment program routinely and systematically incorporates the use of highly specific between-session assignments, which are generally carried out within the home setting. Such assignments in part facilitate parents' acquisition of various observational and monitoring techniques pertinent to their child's behavior. Of additional clinical significance is that they increase the likelihood that acquired parenting skills will generalize from the clinic, where they are learned, to the home setting. Between-session assignments may also serve as a vehicle for indirectly accessing clinically relevant thoughts and feelings, which parents may experience in the process of employing recommended child management tactics. Such information may then be used for cognitive restructuring purposes or for any other aspect of the counseling that is conducted.

Because satisfactory completion of between-session assignments is a critical factor in the outcome of the program, clinicians must take steps to ensure that it occurs. One such step is to send parents home with written handouts, which summarize important in-session and between-session information. At times it may also be appropriate to have them audiotape treatment sessions. Such recorded information may then be reviewed as often as necessary to clarify clinical points pertinent to the between-session assignment. Should insurmountable problems arise in implementing a particular assignment, parents can also contact therapists by telephone to solve problems prior to their next regularly scheduled treatment session.

At the start of every session, time is set aside for reviewing parental efforts to carry out between-session assignments. Special attention is typically focused on those assignments related to parental implementation of recommended child management strategies. Refinements in the parents' application of such strategies are made as necessary. When clinicians begin to sense that parents have acquired a certain level of skill mastery, they shift therapeutic attention to the next treatment step. In this regard the PT portion of the program follows a building-block model, with each step dependent on successful completion and mastery of the preceding step. Use of such a model affords clinicians ample flexibility in proceeding with treatment at a pace meeting the needs of individual children and their parents.

Successful passage through the treatment program also requires close collaboration and cooperation between parents and clinicians. Several clinical and stylistic considerations must be taken into account in achieving this goal. As should be the case in other treatment approaches, clinicians must convey to parents a sense of genuine understanding, caring, respect, and support. At the same time they must present therapeutic information in ways that are clear and easy to understand. Everyday language should be employed, rather than professional jargon, which may be confusing to many parents. For similar reasons, daily life experiences, commonly encountered by children with ADHD and their families, should be used as a context for illustrating clinical points that need to be made. Given that parenting children with ADHD can be a very trying and stressful experience, it is sometimes helpful as well to incorporate humor into the sessions. Not only does humor allow parents a welcome moment of relief, it can also help them understand and remember clinical information more effectively.

A Socratic style of questioning is also routinely used throughout treatment to foster close collaboration and cooperation. Such questioning generally makes it easier for clinicians to avoided succumbing to professional lecturing, which some parents may find disrespectful and condescending. It also forces parents to become more actively involved in the treatment process. By responding to questions that lead to therapeutically desirable solutions, parents gain a sense of having reached such solutions on their own. This sense in turn increases parenting self-esteem and decreases parental dependence on clinicians. Such decreased dependence increases the likelihood that treatment gains will generalize across situations, even when they have not specifically been covered in treatment. Decreased dependence on the therapist can also increase the chances that treatment gains will remain stable after the active portion of the PT program is completed.

Although implementation of these clinical and stylistic considerations can facilitate the therapy process, it does not necessarily guarantee a successful outcome. Even with ongoing clinical supervision, some parents may continue to experience child management difficulties. Such difficulties frequently stem from complications that parents encounter in practicing recommended treatment strategies. These complications might include family illnesses or job schedule changes that arise unexpectedly and interfere with parent training efforts. As long as these sorts of complications are not chronic in nature, their impact on the treatment program is minimal and therefore they do not need to be addressed as a clinical issue. If, on the other hand, they occur more regularly, it may become necessary to postpone completion of the treatment program until after such complications have been resolved.

Forgetfulness, procrastination, and even adult ADHD symptoms can contribute to parental difficulties in practicing recommended parenting skills. When these sorts of problems arise, clinicians may wish to impose appropriate contingencies upon parents as a way of increasing their motivation to incorporate prescribed child management tactics. Withholding treatment sessions until greater compliance is achieved is one method for dealing with this kind of difficulty. Another useful method of promoting greater parental compliance is a breakage-fee system (Patterson, 1982). In this system parents leave a predetermined, fixed sum of money with the therapist. Specified amounts are then returned to parents when satisfactory compliance with between-session assignment occurs. Whenever noncompliance occurs, money is mailed to a political group or an organization intensely disliked by the parents. Generally speaking, this approach works quite well in motivating parents who agree to its use.

As noted earlier in this chapter, parents who maintain negative perceptions of themselves and of their children with ADHD may also find it difficult to employ recommended treatment strategies. To the extent that this occurs, counseling should be initiated to help them identify the basis of their faulty thinking. Once they do so, alternative perceptions should be generated and put to the test. Presumably, this will lead parents to more accurate appraisals of themselves and of their children, which eventually should facilitate their implementation of prescribed home management strategies.

There are times, of course, when parental difficulties in utilizing specialized child management techniques are not related to improper motivation or to faulty perceptions. Instead, they may be the result of parenting skill deficiencies. An especially effective way of pinpointing such deficiencies is through clinic-based observations of parent–child interactions. Specifically, parents may be asked to implement the intervention strategy in question while being observed through a one-way mirror. This observation allows the clinician to identify any problems that parents may be having in using a particular technique. Feedback about such problems may then be given to parents after the session is completed. Or the clinician may choose to demonstrate the proper application of the strategy with the child and then ask the parents to try it once again before they depart. In an extension of this approach, parents may be asked to wear a "bug-in-the-ear" device while being observed. This device allows clinicians to provide discreet feedback, which parents may then use immediately to facilitate their management of their child. As might be expected, such close clinical supervision is usually highly effective in bringing about desired improvements in targeted parenting skills.

Use of these supervisory tactics does not have to be limited to problem situations. In some cases they may be employed throughout all phases of treatment to enhance parental acquisition of all child management techniques that are part of the program. For many clinicians, this may not be a feasible option because they do not have access to one-way mirrors or bug-in-the-ear devices. If these resources are not available, other therapeutic strategies may be utilized to enhance parental learning of new child management procedures. For example, clinicians may include in-session modeling and role-playing exercises as part of their therapeutic contact with parents. In addition, they may choose to amplify clinical points by representing them pictorially or graphically, either on a chalkboard or on a piece of paper; the latter may then be taken home for review.

Treatment Objectives

One of the program's most important goals is to provide parents with ongoing clinical supervision in the use of specialized contingency management techniques to address the noncompliance and other behavioral problems displayed by children with ADHD. A second objective is to facilitate parental adjustment to having a child with ADHD, primarily through the use of cognitive therapy strategies. Cognitive therapy strategies may also be used to achieve a third goal, which is increasing parental compliance with the prescribed treatment regimen. Finally, it is the overall purpose of this treatment program to provide parents with coping skills that will lead to happier and less stressful lives both for themselves and for their children.

Specific Training Steps

Before describing the specific steps of the program, it is necessary to mention two important qualifications. First, although this treatment approach can be used either with individual families or with several families in a group therapy format, our description of it here pertains primarily to its application with individual families. Second, because many features of the current program have been discussed in great deal elsewhere (Barkley, 1997a), it is not our intent to provide the equivalent of a clinician's manual. Instead, we limit our discussion to summary descriptions of these procedures. By presenting information in this way, it is our hope that readers will gain a better understanding of the framework that guides us in our clinical application of this program.

Although the PT program typically can be completed in 8 to 12 sessions, it does not confine clinicians to a specific number of treatment sessions that must be followed inflexibly. Instead, it allows them to guide parents through treatment in a step-by-step fashion, taking as many sessions as is necessary to bring about desired therapeutic change. With this in mind, we now turned to the 10 steps that make up the intervention program. Readers interested in a more detailed account of this program are encouraged to see Barkley (1997a).

Step 1: Why Children Misbehave

This session typically starts with parents providing a brief update of their status since the completion of the diagnostic evaluation. If necessary, we do additional assessments to evaluate the emergence of any new child behavioral problems and to provide a more accurate baseline against which future therapeutic changes may be gauged. After completing the updating process, we discuss the rationale, purpose, and content of the training program. Also covered at this time are the boundaries of confidentiality and relevant billing matters.

The therapeutic objectives of this session are (1) to educate parents about the causes of children's defiant behavior, (2) to urge parents to identify those causes of or contributors to defiant behavior that may exist in their families, and (3) to encourage parents to begin to remedy those causes of defiance that can be rectified within their families.

As the first step in meeting these objectives, clinicians provide parents with a conceptual framework for understanding deviant parent–child interactions and their therapeutic management. In particular, the theoretical views of Bell (Bell & Harper, 1977) and Patterson (1982) are introduced in general terms. In this context, parents are alerted to four major factors which, in various combinations, can contribute to the emergence and/or maintenance of children's behavioral difficulties.

The first of these involves the child's characteristics. Prominent among them is the youngster's inborn temperamental style, which encompasses general activity level, attention span, emotionality, sociability, responsiveness to stimulation, and habit regularity. Along with child's characteristics, a like number and variety of parent characteristics are cited as circumstances that can place children at risk for conflict with their parents. Additional attention is directed to the goodness of fit between various child and parent characteristics. Stresses impinging upon the family are recognized as well. In particular, parents are taught several ways in which family stress can contribute to the emergence and/or maintenance of behavioral difficulties by altering parental perceptions of the child, by altering the child's emotional well-being directly, and/or by preoccupying parents to the point that they become highly variable and inconsistent in their disciplinary approach. The way that parents respond to child behavior is also discussed. In particular, attention is directed to explaining how certain situational consequences or parenting styles (e.g., excessive or harsh criticism, inconsistency), although not the cause of ADHD, nevertheless can complicate the management of this disorder and its associated features. Against this background, attention is called to the fact that the model predicts that altering any of the four factors should lead to reductions in parent–child conflict. By noting that parenting style is by far the one most amenable to change, clinicians are thus able to provide parents with a clear rationale for conducting the remainder of the program.

At the end of the session, parents are asked to conduct two homework assignments prior to the next visit. The first of these is to complete an inventory of family problems, which is used to explore other possible areas of difficulty. If it has not been done already, the second assignment involves having parents childproof their home to reduce the risk for personal injury or physical damage, which often times occurs among children with ADHD features.

Step 2: Pay Attention!

This step begins with a clarification of carryover concerns and a review of how the between-session assignments went. Once these issues are addressed, the primary objective of the session is to teach parents positive attending and ignoring skills in the context of special time. This lesson begins with a discussion of the importance of attending positively to individuals of any age. An especially useful way to make this point is through an adult analogy. In particular, parents are asked to participate in the "favorite supervisor–least favorite supervisor" exercise, which involves listing the characteristics of someone they know who fits these descriptions. Next, parents are asked to comment on how each type of attending affected their own behavior and performance. Against this background, parents are then asked to describe how their children might perceive adults in their life—as "favorite" or "least favorite" supervisors. Such a connection highlights the need for attending more positively to children.

Another important point is that it is not uncommon for parents to shy away from interacting with their child because children with ADHD frequently engage in behaviors that can be rather aversive. When parent–child interactions do occur, parents often assume that negative child behavior will arise and therefore adopt a parenting style that is overly directive, corrective, coercive, or unpleasant in nature. This style in turn contributes to children becoming even less willing to behave in a compliant manner.

For reasons such as these, we present the "special time" assignment. Unlike other types of special time, which simply involve setting aside time with the child, special time in this program requires that parents must remain as nondirective and as noncorrective as possible. Doing so allows them to see their child's behavior in a different light, in particular allowing them the opportunity to "catch 'em being good." This special time then leads to opportunities to attend positively to the child, which in turn helps to rebuild positive parent–child relations, which is accomplished in the following manner.

Parents first set aside a daily period, usually 15 to 20 minutes on average, for interacting with their child. Ideally this period should be scheduled in the absence of major time pressures or other types of interference. During special time the child is allowed to decide what to do, within broad limits, of course. Parents must refrain from asking too many questions and avoid the temptation to suggest alternative play or interaction approaches. While continuing to observe their child in this manner, they must try to narrate the ongoing play activities in positive terms, ignoring any mildly inappropriate behavior that may arise.

Those who have ever tried special time are well aware of how difficult it is to do. This difficulty, along with various other complications (e.g., busy daily schedules), is called to the attention of parents for the purpose of setting realistic expectations for its implementation. To be sure that parents get sufficient practice, they are encouraged to catch their children being good, not just during special time but throughout the day as well. Such spontaneous opportunities can be used for increasing the amount of positive attention that children receive.

To assist parents in their efforts to practice these techniques between sessions, they are given a written handout summarizing the procedure. Should unforeseen problems arise in their efforts to practice, parents are encouraged to telephone the therapist for assistance.

Step 3: Increasing Compliance and Independent Play

As always, this session begins with a clarification of carryover concerns and a review of the between-session homework assignment. Before introducing any new material, suggestions are made for fine tuning special time, which parents continue to implement throughout the remainder of the program.

Next, the objectives of this step are presented in terms of (1) training parents to use attending skills to increase child compliance with parental commands; (2) increasing the effectiveness of parental commands; (3) increasing parental use of effective attending skills for independent, nondisruptive compliance by children; and (4) increasing parental monitoring of child behavior inside and outside the home. Readers familiar with any of the earlier versions of this program likely recognize that the components of this step were previously spread out across two sessions. Because recent experience has suggested that such a delay is not necessary, the content of these two sessions was condensed into one.

Once it is clear that parents have become sufficiently adept at using positive attending strategies in the context of special time, it becomes possible to extend these skills to other situations. Many children, especially those with ADHD who have difficulty waiting for things, become disruptive when parents are engaged in home activities, such as talking on the telephone, preparing dinner, or visiting with company. After calling attention to the fact that parents generally do not hesitate to interrupt an ongoing activity to address disruptions, the following questions are posed: Should parents stop what they are doing to attend positively to children when they are engaged in independent play that is not disruptive? Most parents do not think so, citing the "let sleeping dogs lie" philosophy as their rationale. This assumption is first examined from a cognitive therapy perspective—specifically, in terms of the fact that it is an example of jumping to conclusions (in this case, a negative future outcome). Parents are then asked how certain they are that dispensing positive attention in this manner will be disruptive. Most often they state that they are pretty sure, but not 100%. While acknowledging that parents might in fact be correct in their prediction, clinicians also point out that they may not be. Until their "sleeping dogs" philosophy is put to an empirical test against an alternative hypothesis, neither can be confirmed or disconfirmed. Additional justification for putting these competing assumptions to test may be inferred from a consideration of general behavior management principles. Specifically, parents are reminded that when any behavior—in this case, appropriate independent play—is ignored, this decreases its probability of occurring. This in turn increases the likelihood that various disruptive behaviors will develop inadvertently. If attended to positively, however, such independent play is much more likely to reappear in the future. Recognizing that initial parental attempts to reinforce appropriate independent play may at first be disruptive, parents are reminded that children eventually become accustomed to this change in parental response. This then leads to gradual improvements in their tendency to behave appropriately while their parents are busy.

Positive attending skills may also be applied to parental command situations. Although most parents have little trouble pointing out the various ways in which children with ADHD do not comply with their requests, it is much harder for them to identify request situations that elicit compliance. Some even get to the point of believing that their child "does nothing that I ask him (or her) to do." Although it is certainly true that children with ADHD are frequently noncompliant, it is equally important for parents to recognize an unintentional tendency on their part to ignore instances of compliance when they occur. In cognitive therapy terms, parents are selectively attending to the negative aspects of their child's responses to their requests. In behavior therapy terms, they are discouraging compliance through their ignoring, and encouraging noncompliance through their attention to it. Against this background, clinicians point out the importance of paying positive attention to children whenever they are compliant. In addition, parents are advised to set the stage for practicing their use of such positive attending skills by issuing brief sequences of simple household commands that have a high probability of eliciting compliance from their child. Over time this should lead to a gradual increase in the child's overall compliance with parental requests, including those of relatively low probability.

The next topic for this step is the manner in which commands are given. Verbal and nonverbal parameters of how parents communicate commands to children are examined. We generally make the following recommendations: that parents only issue commands they intend to follow through on; that commands take the form of direct statements rather than questions; that commands be relatively simple; that they be issued in the absence of outside distractions, and only when direct eye contact is being made with the child, to increase the likelihood of the child's attending to such instructions; and that commands be repeated back to the parents to give them an opportunity to clarify any misunderstanding before the child responds.

Finally, parental attention is directed to the importance of monitoring children's activities. In particular, parents are told of the apparent connection that exists between low levels of parental monitoring and various conduct problems (stealing, vandalism, etc.). By no means does this mean that parents are encouraged to watch their children like hawks. They are, however, advised that periodic checks of ongoing child activities will reduce the likelihood of conduct problems arising, especially when accompanied by frequently dispensed positive attention for good behavior or immediate punishments for whatever rule violations might arise.

Like all other steps in this training program, this session ends with a specific request for parents to practice these techniques prior to the next session. To assist the parents in doing so, they receive written reminder handouts summarizing all that was covered in this session. Parents are additionally reminded to continue practicing special time and spontaneous positive attending. In anticipation of the next step, clinicians have the option of asking parents to begin developing lists of requests and privileges, which will be used in the home-based token system.

Step 4: When Praise Is Not Enough: Poker Chips and Points

Setting up a reward-oriented home token system is the major focus of this step. Such a system serves to provide children with ADHD the external motivation they need to complete parent-requested activities that may be of little intrinsic interest and/or a trigger for their defiance. Another reason for using such a system is that positive attending and ignoring strategies are often insufficient for managing children with ADHD, who generally require more concrete and meaningful rewards.

Following review and refinement of the therapeutic skills taught in Step 3, clinicians embark on a somewhat philosophical, yet practical, discussion of what children's rights are and what their privileges are. Such a discussion often alerts parents to how they have inadvertently been treating many of their child's privileges as if they were rights. This alert in turn makes it easier to set up the home-based poker chip or point system described next.

First, parents are asked to generate two lists: one list of daily, weekly, and long-range privileges that are likely to be interesting and motivating to the child; the other list pertains to regular chores and/or household rules that parents would like done better. Such target behaviors should include not only instances of noncompliance and defiance but also those situations in which a child does not follow through because of loss of interest, distractions, and other ADHD problems. Later, at home, parents may wish to incorporate input from the child as to any other items that should be included in these lists.

Point values are then assigned to each list. For children 9 years old and under, plastic poker chips are used as tokens. Earned poker chips are collected and stored in a home "bank" that the child sets aside specifically for that purpose. For 9- to 11-year-old children, points are used in place of chips and are monitored in a checkbook register or some other type of notebook of interest to a youngster. Generally speaking, children can earn predetermined numbers of poker chips or points for complying with initial parent requests and for completing assigned tasks, which previously may have been left incomplete because of lack of interest or motivation in doing them. In addition, parents can dispense bonus chips or points for especially well-done chores or independent displays of appropriate behavior. At no time, however, should chips or points be taken away for noncompliance in this phase of the training program. Instead, any noncompliance parents encounter should be handled in the same way they dealt with such situations previously.

Parental motivation, which may have been quite high up until now, may begin to waver for several reasons. Some parents may announce, for example, "I've done this before and it doesn't work." As described earlier, cognitive therapy strategies may be used to correct this type of faulty thinking, which has the potential to interfere with parental efforts to institute a home token system. Another potentially self-defeating assumption that parents may express is "I don't think my child will go along with this." When parents make such a statement, it becomes necessary to discuss the issue of who is in charge: parent or child? In the context of such a discussion, parental control is framed as a constructive responsibility, one that children may not like or appreciate immediately but nevertheless one that is ultimately in their best interests. When they look at it in this light, most parents are at the very least willing to give the home token system a try.

Having made sure that parents fully understand the working mechanics of this token system, clinicians provide them with a detailed handout summarizing this phase of the program. This handout serves as a useful reminder of what to do as the parents practice this technique at home prior to the next session. Parents are also reminded to continue practicing all other facets of the program and to call immediately for consultation should problems arise.

Step 5: Time Out! and Other Disciplinary Methods

This session begins with a careful review of parental efforts to implement the home token system. Because problems inevitably arise, it is not uncommon for a big portion of this session to be spent on clarifying confusion and making suggestions for increasing the effectiveness of this system.

Following this discussion, the response-cost technique is introduced, which represents the first time in the treatment program that a penalty or punishment approach is considered for use. Specifically, parents are instructed to begin deducting poker chips or points for noncompliance with one or two particularly troublesome requests on the list. Similar penalties may be used for one or two "don't behaviors"—that is, don't hit, don't talk back, and so on—that may be added to the program. At this stage, not only does the child with ADHD fail to earn chips or points that would have resulted from compliance, but also previously earned chips or points are now removed from the bank for displays of noncompliance. The number of chips or points lost is equal to the number of chips or points that would have been gained had compliance occurred. For many children with ADHD, who over the past week may have learned how to expend minimal effort to get the privileges they desire, adding a response-cost component to their token system often increases their overall level of compliance with parental requests because they now have the additional incentive of trying not to lose what they already earned. Clinicians also routinely caution parents to avoid getting into punishment spirals whereby so many chips are taken away that a debt is incurred. As a rule, parents should not employ response-cost more than twice in a row for the same noncompliant behavior. If needed, backup penalties, such as time out, can be employed instead. Furthermore, parents need to take steps to ensure that a child's token reserves do not approach a zero balance, which might diminish interest in the program. If the balance gets low, parents must dispense bonus tokens for any display of appropriate child behavior, whether or not it happens to be on the list.

Clinicians also begin discussing "time out from reinforcement," or simply time out. Although most types of noncompliance will continue to be handled via response cost, parents are encouraged to identify one or two especially resistant or serious types of noncompliance or rule violations (e.g., hitting a sibling) that may become the targets of time out. Once these are identified, attention is then focused on teaching the mechanics of implementing the time out procedure. Like the token system, time out is a rather difficult technique to employ. Its use must be explained very carefully before asking parents to practice it at home.

Critical to the success of this technique is that three conditions must be met prior to releasing the youngster from time out. First, the child must serve a minimum amount of time, generally equal in minutes to the number of years in his or her age. Once this condition is met, parents may approach the time-out area only when the child has been quiet for a brief period. This avoids the problem of inadvertently dispensing parental attention for inappropriate behavior. Next, and perhaps most important, parents must reissue the request or command that initially led the youngster to be placed into time out. When the child does not comply with the reissued directive, the entire three-step time-out cycle is repeated as many times as is necessary until compliance is achieved. Thus, under no circumstances does the child avoid doing what was asked. Once compliance is achieved, parents thank the child in a neutral manner for doing what was asked but no tokens are dispensed. A few moments later, however, parents should look for an opportunity to reinforce the child with poker chips or points, thereby balancing out their use of punishment.

In addition to covering these facets of time out, clinicians routinely address other aspects of this procedure, including how to select a location for serving time out and what to do if the child defiantly leaves the time out area. In regards to this latter point, various backup penalty strategies may be employed, such as response cost, privilege removal, grounding, and/or physical restraint. Although a mild spanking procedure was offered as another type of backup strategy in earlier descriptions of this program (Barkley, 1987), its use is no longer recommended.

More so than any of the other procedures in this program, time out is a strategy that usually has been tried previously in one form or another. Thus, many parents have firm beliefs about its potential for success, or lack thereof. Such biases need to be addressed via cognitive restructuring techniques. Failure to do so runs the risk that parents will not be properly motivated to incorporate this treatment strategy in the manner in which it was intended, which in turn may increase parental frustration and diminish any further interest in participation in the program.

As always, parents leave with a written handout on these punishment strategies and are reminded to call for assistance as needed prior to the next session.

Step 6: Extending Time Out to Other Misbehavior

Unlike all other steps in this program, this session does not introduce any new material. Instead, its purpose is to troubleshoot and to resolve any problems that parents may have encountered in using response-cost and time-out strategies. When parents were highly successful in using these techniques over the past week, we recommend extending their use to other parental commands or rule situations that elicit noncompliance.

Step 7: Anticipating Problems: Managing Children in Public Places

Initially, parental efforts to incorporate time-out strategies are reviewed and refined as needed. All other facets of the program are reviewed and refined as well. If the home-based program is judged to be running relatively smoothly, attention is directed to a discussion of settings outside the home in which problem behaviors arise. Among the many settings that are often identified by parents as problematic are grocery stores, department stores, malls, movie theaters, restaurants, churches, and synagogues. Disciplinary strategies previously employed in such settings are reviewed and analyzed in terms of their overall ineffectiveness.

Against this background, the importance of anticipating such problems in public is discussed. In particular, parents are advised to have a plan of action before entering a predictably problematic public situation. This plan may be accomplished using the following "think aloud–think ahead" procedure. First, parents must review their expectations for behavior in the setting. Next, they must establish some incentive for compliance with these rules. Finally, they must specify what types of punishment they will apply should noncompliance with these rules ensue. For this strategy to work most effectively, parents should ask the child to state their understanding of these rules and consequences prior to entering the public situation. Such a statement allows parents an opportunity to clarify any misunderstanding on the part of the child that may result from confusion or from inattentiveness.

Generally speaking, modified versions of the strategies used successfully within the home are incorporated into this plan. These versions may include dispensing poker chips for on-going compliance with parental requests, such as "stay close, don't touch, don't beg," or removal of poker chips for noncompliance with these same requests. Modified versions of time out may also be employed by parents, using quiet, out-of-the-way public areas for this purpose.

In contrast with their eagerness to try out various home management techniques, many parents are much less enthusiastic about experimenting with these techniques in public places. The perceived threat of public embarrassment is often cited. After all, "what will people think?" The mind-reading aspects of this particular situation are highlighted as the basis for the parents jumping to such a conclusion. Alternative viewpoints of what people might think, and the relative importance of what others think when it pertains to their child's welfare, are discussed. Addressing parental perceptions of this situation in this manner generally makes it possible to reduce the parent's uneasiness and to increase their motivation for trying such a new and challenging approach.

Parents are then asked to practice these procedures on at least two separate occasions prior to the next session. To facilitate these efforts, a written handout on the topic is distributed.

Step 8: Improving School Behavior from Home:
The Daily School Behavior Report Card

In addition to reviewing and fine tuning parental efforts to deal with problem behavior in public places, clinicians discuss and refine all other aspects of the training program.

Thereafter, they direct attention to various school issues, often beginning with a discussion of the legal rights of children with ADHD within the school system. In the context of this discussion, emphasis is placed on the child being in the least restrictive educational environment. How and when to consider special education accommodations is covered as well.

Independent of placement issues, parents receive numerous suggestions for modifying their child's classroom environment to accommodate the child's ADHD. Particular attention is directed to the mechanics of setting up a daily school behavior report card system. In this system teachers monitor specific classroom behaviors (e.g., finishes assigned tasks) by providing ratings on an index card, which is sent home on a daily basis. These teacher ratings, often ranging from 1 (excellent) to 5 (very unacceptable), are then converted into either token gains or token losses, proportional to the quality of behavior and performance displayed by the child that day. One major advantage to using home-based consequences in this system is that they are consistently more meaningful and effective than stickers, extra recess, or other types of consequences typically available in school. Another significant advantage is that it imposes very little burden on classroom teachers, who must also direct their time and energy to meeting the needs of other students in the class. Of more general importance is that the daily school behavior report card system incorporates many of the behavior management principles specific to children with ADHD. For example, implicit in its use is an attempt to provide extremely specific, immediate, and frequent feedback, all of which should facilitate classroom performance.

Although much of what is discussed with parents might suggest an insensitivity to the needs of the teacher or the other students in the class, nothing could be further from the truth. On the contrary, parents are made aware of the various budgetary constraints, personnel limitations, and so forth that might make it most difficult to implement all of what they might like for their child. In light of this possibility, they are strongly encouraged to work with school personnel in as collaborative and cooperative manner as possible.

Step 9: Handling Future Behavior Problems

After reviewing and fine tuning all aspects of the program, clinicians ask parents to discuss what they believe might be problematic for them in the future and how they might handle such problematic situations. Attention is then directed to the various ways in which many parents slip away from adherence to this program. Some degree of slippage or departure from the protocol is acceptable, and in fact encouraged, but too much may lead to increased behavioral difficulties. For this reason parents are informed about how to run a check on themselves to ascertain where fine tuning of their specialized child management skills is required. A written handout summarizing this self-check system is distributed at this time.

The final portion of this session is used to address termination and/or disposition issues. In addition to agreeing on an appropriate booster session date, efforts are made to determine whether any other types of clinical services are needed. These services might include adding a medication component or scheduling school consultation visits to address classroom management concerns directly with school personnel.

Step 10: Booster Session and Follow-Up Meetings

Although any length of time may be deemed acceptable, it is customary to meet with parents for a booster session approximately 1 month after conducting Step 9. One objective of this session is to readminister pertinent child behavior and parent self-report rating scales and questionnaires, which serve as indices of any posttreatment changes that may have occurred. Further review and refinement of previously learned intervention strategies are conducted as well. Also established at this time is a mutually agreed-upon final clinical disposition. If desired, this may include scheduling of additional booster sessions.

PROCEDURAL VARIATIONS

Throughout the preceding discussion it was noted that the PT program is flexible in its nature, thereby allowing clinicians to tailor its application to the needs of individual children and their families. In addition to the possible modifications mentioned earlier in this chapter, variations in the program's implementation can occur in many other ways.

For example, it is not uncommon for clinicians to include an extra session in which an overview of ADHD is provided. When such a session is added to the program, more often than not it appears on the front end of the sequence as Step 1. The rationale for doing so is to provide a conceptual framework for understanding and accepting ADHD, which for many parents is a necessary step before embarking on the PT program.

Included in this overview of ADHD is a review of its history, its numerous label changes, its core symptoms, its currently accepted diagnostic criteria, and its prevalence rates. Also covered are many of the commonly encountered associated features of ADHD, including oppositional–defiant behavior, aggressiveness, academic underachievement, social skills deficits, and emotional immaturity. This discussion is generally followed by a discussion of what is known about the immediate and extended families of children with ADHD. Up-to-date information about the developmental course of this disorder is presented as well. Attention is then directed to etiological concerns. In the context of this discussion, emphasis is placed on the view that, for most children, ADHD is a biologically based inborn temperamental style that predisposes them to be inattentive, impulsive, and physically restless. Special efforts are also made to clarify the confusion surrounding the situational variability of this disorder's primary symptoms. Against this background, the importance of using a multimethod assessment and intervention approach is discussed and emphasized.

Presentation of this information should be as brief as possible to allow parents to focus more attentively on the main points that need to be made. It is also helpful for clinicians to limit their references to summary statistics and percentages obtained from the ADHD population as a whole. As so many parents have so frankly stated, they are not interested in facts and figures that have little to do with their child. The more that the presentation relates to the parents' particular child, the more likely it is that the parents will grasp the clinical and theoretical points that need to be made. Another precaution for clinicians to bear in mind as they describe the general ADHD population is that some parents will incorrectly infer that their child is doomed to a life filled with comorbidity, failure, and misery. For this reason, clinicians must be sure to clarify that (1) what applies to the ADHD population as a whole does not necessarily apply to any one individual, and (2) outcome is determined by a large number and variety of factors, of which ADHD is just one influence, albeit an important one.

Although it is certainly possible to conduct this session in a lecture format, most clinicians would agree that its therapeutic impact is much greater when parents have an opportunity to ask questions, to voice their emotional reactions to what they just heard, and to discuss expectations for the program. Should parents feel overwhelmed by the sheer volume of new ADHD information, they are reminded that processing such information will occur gradually over time. Should they wish to facilitate their acquisition of such knowledge, they are also alerted to the availability of pertinent texts and encouraged to review videotaped presentations on the topic. To the extent that parental feelings of shock, guilt, sadness, or anger arise, therapeutic attention must be directed to addressing such negative emotional reactions. In this situation cognitive restructuring and other cognitive therapy techniques are especially helpful.

Another place where the basic program may be modified is in Step 1. Based on the assumption that knowledge of behavior management principles facilitates parental acquisition of contingency management techniques, clinicians can include behavior management principles as an additional topic of discussion. This overview may be introduced with a description of how antecedent events, as well as consequences, can be altered to modify children's behavior. Included as part of this discussion are different types of positive reinforcement, ignoring, and punishment strategies; the need for using such consequences in combination; and the advantages of dispensing them in a specific, immediate, and consistent fashion. In this portion of the session, special attention is also directed to the role played by negative reinforcement. In particular, parents are first taught that children often misbehave or exhibit noncompliance either to gain positive consequences or to avoid unpleasant or boring situations. An especially useful way to illustrate this latter situation is to describe the request–noncompliance cycle—that is, the cycle of multiple parental requests, following multiple instances of child noncompliance, that generally leads to escalating emotions and coercive interactions, not to mention an increased likelihood of further noncompliance from the child. Throughout this entire discussion, parents are reminded that the behavior management needs of children with ADHD can be somewhat different from those of other children at times. For example, because children with ADHD become bored rather easily and quickly, parents must be sure to use consequences that are particularly salient and meaningful and to change such consequences periodically to keep them interesting and motivating.

For parents of children who do not display ODD or CD symptoms in conjunction with their ADHD, it may not be necessary to spend two full sessions on the use of response-cost and time-out strategies. When one session covering these topics suffices, clinicians have the option of spending an extra session refining parental implementation of the home poker chip or point systems. Alternatively, they may choose not to incorporate any substitution, thereby reducing the overall length of the program by one session.

CONCLUSION

What should be readily apparent from the preceding discussion is that PT seems to have a place in the overall clinical management of children with ADHD. One of the major advantages to using PT is that it can be used to target not only the child's primary ADHD symptomatology but also many of the comorbid features, including oppositional–defiant behavior and conduct problems. Moreover, because PT interventions often utilize parents as co-therapists, many parents themselves derive indirect therapeutic benefits from their involvement in treatment. Although it remains to be seen what the long-term impact of PT interventions might be, preliminary evidence seems to suggest that treatment-induced improvements in psychosocial functioning can be maintained in the absence of ongoing therapist contact, at least in the short run.

As noted earlier, much of the research to date has focused on the clinical efficacy of PT interventions when used alone. One benefit of pursuing this type of research is that it allows for a better understanding of the unique impact that this form of treatment can have on outcome within an ADHD population. Moreover, examining PT by itself provides important insight into its therapeutic limitations, including the fact that not everyone benefits from PT. Of additional concern is that in multimodal interventions, PT thus far has not added a great deal to treatment outcome above and beyond that accounted for by other treatments, such as medication. Although some individuals might view such limitations as contraindications for using PT, they could also view them as an impetus for conducting further research. For example, such information could be used to guide research that addresses the following questions: (1) With which treatments might PT be combined to maximize therapeutic outcome? (2) For which children and their families is the combination of PT with other treatments a viable intervention approach?

REFERENCES

Abikoff, H. B., & Hechtman, L. (1996). Multimodal therapy and stimulants in the treatment of children with attention-deficit hyperactivity disorder. In E. D. Hibbs & P. S. Jensen (Eds.), *Psychosocial treatments for child and adolescent disorders: Empirically based strategies for clinical practice* (pp. 341–369). Washington, DC: American Psychological Association.

Anastopoulos, A. D., & Barkley, R. A. (1990). Counseling and training parents. In R. A. Barkley, *Attention-deficit hyperactivity disorder: A handbook for diagnosis and treatment* (pp. 397–431). New York: Guilford Press.

Anastopoulos, A. D., Guevremont, D. C., Shelton, T. L., & DuPaul, G. J. (1992). Parenting stress among families of children with attention deficit hyperactivity disorder. *Journal of Abnormal Child Psychology, 20,* 503–520.

Anastopoulos, A. D., Shelton, T. DuPaul, G. J., & Guevremont, D. C. (1993). Parent training for attention deficit hyperactivity disorder: Its impact on parent functioning. *Abnormal Child Psychology, 21,* 581–596.

Barkley, R. A. (1981). *Hyperactive children: A handbook for diagnosis and treatment.* New York: Guilford Press.

Barkley, R. A. (1987). *Defiant children: A clinician's manual for parent training.* New York: Guilford Press.

Barkley, R. A. (1990). *Attention-deficit hyperactivity disorder: A handbook for diagnosis and treatment.* New York: Guilford Press.

Barkley, R. A. (1997a). *Defiant children* (2nd ed.): *A clinician's manual for assessment and parent training.* New York: Guilford Press.

Barkley, R. A. (1997b). Behavioral inhibition and executive functions: Constructing a unified theory of ADHD. *Psychological Bulletin, 121,* 65–94.

Barkley, R. A., Anastopoulos, A. D., Guevremont, D. C., & Fletcher, K. E. (1991). Adolescents with ADHD: Patterns of behavioral adjustment, academic functioning, and treatment utilization. *Journal of the American Academy of Child and Adolescent Psychiatry, 30,* 752–761.

Bell, R. Q., & Harper, L. (1977). *Child effects on adults.* New York: Wiley.

Cunningham, C. E., & Barkley, R. A. (1979). The interactions of hyperactive and normal children with their mothers during free play and structured task. *Child Development, 50,* 217–224.

Erhardt, D., & Baker, B. L. (1990). The effects of behavioral parent training on families with young hyperactive children. *Journal of Behavior Therapy and Experimental Psychiatry, 21,* 121–132.

Forehand, R. L., & McMahon, R. J. (1981). *Helping the noncompliant child: A clinician's guide to parent training.* New York: Guilford Press.

Horn, W. F., Ialongo, N., Pascoe, J. M., & Greenberg, G. (1991). Additive effects of psychostimulants, parent training, and self-control therapy with ADHD children. *Journal of the American Academy of Child and Adolescent Psychiatry, 30,* 233–240.

Ialongo, N. S., Horn, W. F., Pascoe, J. M., & Greenberg, G. (1993). The effects of multimodal intervention with attention-deficit hyperactivity disorder children: A 9-month follow-up. *Journal of the American Academy of Child and Adolescent Psychiatry, 32,* 182–189.

Kazdin, A. E. (1997). Parent management training: Evidence, outcomes, and issues. *Journal of the American Academy of Child and Adolescent Psychiatry, 36,* 1349–1356.

Lahey, B. B., Piacentini, J., McBurnett, K., Stone, P., Hatdagen, S., & Hynd, G. (1988). Psychopathology in the parents of children with conduct disorder and hyperactivity. *Journal of the American Academy of Child and Adolescent Psychology, 27,* 163–170.

Loeber, R., Meenan, K., Lahey, B. B., Green, S. M., & Thomas, C. (1993). Evidence for developmentally based diagnoses of oppositional defiant disorder and conduct disorder. *Journal of Abnormal Child Psychology, 21,* 377–410.

Mash, E. J., & Johnston, C. (1990). Determinants of parenting stress: Illustrations from families of hyperactive children and families of physically abused children. *Journal of Clinical Child Psychology, 19,* 313–328.

Minuchin, S. (1974). *Families and family therapy.* Cambridge, MA: Harvard University Press.

Patterson, G. R. (1982). *Coercive family process.* Eugene, OR: Castalia.

Pisterman, S., Firestone, P., McGrath, P., & Goodman, J. T. (1992). The role of parent training in treatment of preschoolers with ADDH. *American Journal of Orthopsychiatry, 62,* 397–408.

Pisterman, S., McGrath, P., Firestone, P., & Goodman, J. T. (1989). Outcome of parent-mediated treatment of preschoolers with attention deficit disorder with hyperactivity. *Journal of Consulting and Clinical Psychology, 57,* 636–643.

Pollard, S., Ward, E. M., & Barkley, R. A. (1983). The effects of parent training and Ritalin on the parent–child interactions of hyperactive boys. *Child and Family Therapy, 5,* 51–69.

Quay, H. C. (1997). Inhibition and attention deficit hyperactivity disorder. *Journal of Abnormal Child Psychology, 25,* 7–13.

Richters, J. E., Arnold, L. E., Jensen, P. S., Abikoff, H. (1995). NIMH collaborative multisite multimodal treatment study of children with ADHD: I. Background and rationale. *Journal of the American Academy of Child and Adolescent Psychiatry, 34,* 987–1000.

Schachar, R. J., Tannock, R., & Logan, G. (1993). Inhibitory control, impulsiveness, and attention deficit hyperactivity disorder. *Clinical Psychology Review, 13,* 721–739.

Taylor, E. (1986). *The overactive child.* Philadelphia: Lippincott.

Webster-Stratton, C. (1994). Advancing videotape parent training: A comparison study. *Journal of Consulting and Clinical Psychology, 62,* 585–593.

Chapter 13

A LARGE-GROUP, COMMUNITY-BASED, FAMILY SYSTEMS APPROACH TO PARENT TRAINING

Charles E. Cunningham

The diagnosis of Attention-Deficit/Hyperactivity Disorder (ADHD) emphasizes the child's problems with sustained attention, activity level, and impulse control, but it is the impact of these difficulties on the child's social relationships that often prompts parents to seek professional assistance. The difficulties experienced by children with ADHD may adversely affect their relationships with parents (Cunningham & Barkley, 1979; Mash & Johnston, 1982), peers (Cunningham, Siegel, & Offord, 1985, 1991; Cunningham & Siegel, 1987; Clark, Cheyne, Cunningham, & Siegel, 1988), and teachers (Campbell, Endman, & Bernfield, 1977; Whalen, Henker, & Dotemoto, 1980). With their parents, children with ADHD are more active, less cooperative, and less likely to sustain their attention to play or task-related activities (Cunningham & Barkley, 1979; Mash & Johnston, 1982), difficulties that contribute to problems in virtually all daily activities (Barkley & Edelbrock, 1987). Parents of children with ADHD report low self-esteem (Mash & Johnston, 1983), a limited sense of control over the child's difficulties (Sobol, Ashbourne, Earn, & Cunningham, 1989), and higher depression scores (Cunningham, Benness, & Siegel, 1988). The active, poorly regulated, behavior of children with ADHD elicits a more controlling, less positive approach to child management (Barkley, Karlsson, Pollard, & Murphy, 1985; Barkley & Cunningham, 1979; Cunningham & Barkley, 1978, Cunningham & Barkley, 1979; Mash & Johnston, 1982; Humphries, Kinsbourne, & Swanson, 1978), which may compound the child's difficulties (Patterson, 1982; Patterson, Ried, & Dishion, 1992) and adversely influence longer-term adjustment (Barkley, 1990; Campbell, 1990; Earls & Jung, 1987; Weiss & Hechtman, 1986).

Parent training programs of the type described in Chapter 12, (this volume) have emerged as an important component in the management of children with ADHD. Parent training improves child management skills (Pisterman et al., 1989), enhances parental confidence (Anastopoulos, Shelton, DuPaul, & Guevremont, 1993; Pisterman et al., 1992), reduces stress (Anastopoulos et al., 1993; Pisterman et al., 1992) and improves family relationships (Anastopoulos et al., 1993). Improvements in parenting skills are accompanied by a reduction in inattention, overactivity (Anastopoulos et al., 1993; Dubey, O'Leary, & Kaufman, 1983; Freeman, Phillips, & Johnston, 1992), noncompliance (Pisterman et al., 1989; Pollard, Ward, & Barkley, 1983), aggression (Anastopoulos et al., 1993; Freeman et al., 1992), and general management problems (Cunningham, Bremner, & Boyle, 1995). The gains established in parent training programs are maintained at both short-term (Anastopoulos et al., 1993; Cunningham et al., 1995; Dubey et al., 1983; Freeman et al., 1992; Pisterman et al., 1989;) and longer-term follow-ups (McMahon, 1994).

There is an emerging consensus that parent training is most effective conducted with reference to a wider family and community framework. This "systems" perspective implies that parent–child relationships will influence and be affected by structural and transactional relationships within the child's nuclear family, extended family, and community. Several lines of evidence suggest that a more systemic approach might be particularly useful with families of children with ADHD. First, during the course of the child's development, families of children with ADHD confront a substantially larger number of behavioral, developmental, and educational problems than those of children without ADHD. The time, logistical demands, and energy required to cope with these difficulties place an enormous burden of stress on all aspects of marital and family functioning (Emery, 1982; Epstein, Bishop, & Levine, 1978).

Second, although referrals to parent training programs are often prompted by child management difficulties, parents of children with ADHD frequently report problems in related areas of individual, marital, and family functioning. These include lack of confidence in parenting skills (Mash & Johnston, 1983), depression (Cunningham et al., 1988; Befera & Barkley, 1985; Breen & Barkley, 1988), and less frequent, less helpful contacts with extended family members (Cunningham et al., 1988). Social isolation (Wahler, 1980), marital conflict, family dysfunction, and parental depression may negatively bias parental perceptions of child behavior (Greist, Wells, & Forehand, 1979; Webster-Stratton & Hammond, 1988), adversely effect parental management (Mash & Johnston, 1983; Panaccione & Wahler, 1986), and reduce the effectiveness of parenting programs (McMahon, Forehand, Greist, & Wells, 1981).

Third, from 40% to 60% of ADHD children also evidence significant oppositional or conduct problems (Szatmari, Offord, & Boyle, 1989a, 1989b). Children with ADHD and Oppositional Defiant Disorder (ODD) or conduct problems confront parents with more management difficulties (Barkley, Fischer, Edelbrock, & Smallish, 1990) and are at greater long-term risk than children with either disorder alone (Taylor, Chadwick, Heptinstall, & Danckaerts, 1996). Whereas epidemiological evidence suggests that ADHD is correlated with developmental variables, conduct problems are associated with increased odds of marital conflict and family dysfunction (Szatmari, Boyle, & Offord, 1989).

REDESIGNING PARENT TRAINING PROGRAMS

In a previous edition of this text, I described a systems-oriented parent training program for couples of children with ADHD (Cunningham, 1990). Although our own experience and accumulating evidence (Webster-Stratton, 1994) support a combined emphasis on parenting and family functioning, limitations to this clinic-based approach to individual families have prompted a major revision in our program.

First, ADHD is among the most prevalent childhood psychiatric disorders (Offord et al., 1987) and the most common referrals to outpatient clinics. Utilization studies in both Canada (Boyle, 1991) and the United States (Tuma, 1989; Zahner, Pawelkiewicz, DeFrancesco, & Adnopoz, 1992), however, suggest that a significant majority of children with psychiatric difficulties do not receive professional assistance. To extend the availability of parent training programs for families of children with ADHD, we have developed a large group version of our individual family programs (Barkley, 1990), a model we call the Community Parent Education (COPE) program (Cunningham, Bremner, & Secord-Gilbert, 1997).

Second, clinic-based parent training programs may pose barriers that prevent potentially interested parents from participating. Work schedules that do not allow daytime attendance, extracurricular activities, travel time, or transportation costs may prevent parents from enrolling in or consistently attending parent training programs (Cunningham et al., 1995; Kazdin, Holland, & Crowley, 1997; Prinz & Miller, 1994). These factors may pose particular difficulties to families whose children are at higher risk. Thus, younger, economically disadvantaged, socially isolated, or depressed parents of children with the most severe problems are least likely to enroll in or complete intervention programs (Firestone & Witt, 1982; Kazdin, 1990; Kazdin, Mazurick, & Bass, 1993; Kazdin, Mazurick, & Siegel, 1994). To reduce barriers and increase accessibility, COPE courses are conducted in convenient neighborhood schools throught the community. According to consumer demand, most COPE courses are conducted in the evening.

Families interested in a parent training program may also have difficulty securing reliable child care. Child care may may pose a special problem to socially isolated or economicaly disadvantaged families that might benefit most from a parenting course. The COPE program's on-site children's social skills activity group, therefore, allows parents who are unable to obtain child care to participate.

The psychological or cultural implications of seeking professional mental health assistance may represent barriers to other families (McMiller & Wesz, 1996). Immigrant families or parents using English as a second language, for example, are less likely to enroll in parent training programs conducted at children's mental health centers (Cunningham et al., 1995). Whereas parents from different cultural backgrounds are more likely to use community-based parenting courses (Cunningham et al., 1995), COPE's leader training workshops encourage the adoption of this program by professionals from different cultural, ethnic, and linquistic groups.

Families of children with ADHD move more frequently (Barkley et al., 1990), consider extended family members less helpful, and report fewer contacts with relatives who may provide an important source of child-care assistance, childrearing information, and social support (Cunningham et al., 1988). Social isolation may compromise parenting and limit the effectiveness of parent training programs (Wahler, 1980). COPE's large-group, community-based model encourages the development of supportive personal contacts and the exchange of knowledge regarding local resources useful to parents of children with ADHD.

Access to mental health resources is increasingly limited by financial constraints (Boyle & Offord, 1988). The availability of parent training is restricted by locating programs in expensive clinic or hospital settings, devoting a disproportionate percentage of the professional resources available to extensive preprogram diagnostic assessments (see Chapter 10, this volume), and a preference for programs dealing with individual families. The COPE program is designed to reduce costs and increase availability by offering parent training in large groups, relying on a single-leader model, and scheduling courses in community settings that are underutilized (e.g., school libraries in the evening). In addition to increasing the cost of parent training, the waiting lists and assessment requirements encountered in clinic-based programs may delay access and reduce readiness for participation (Cunningham, 1997). To accelerate access, COPE programs may be conducted as a skill-building continuing adult educational service.

STRUCTURE AND PROCESS
OF THE LARGE-GROUP PROGRAM

The structure and processes of this large-group program are based on an integration of principles, techniques, and goals from social learning-based parenting programs, social-cognitive psychology, family systems theory, small-group interventions, and larger-support-group models.

Social Learning Contributions to Large-Group Process

The parenting component of this program is based on the social learning approach developed by Connie Hanf (Hanf & Kling, 1973) at the University of Oregon Health Sciences Center and is similar to the program presented in Chapter 12 of this volume (see also Barkley, 1997a). Many of the child management strategies addressed in the program are based on social learning principles common to related parenting programs (Barkley, 1997a; Forehand & McMahon, 1981; Webster-Stratton, 1994). Social learning models also contribute to the COPE program's large-group process. Leaders use modeling, role playing, goal setting, and self-monitored homework strategies to introduce new skills.

Cognitive and Social Psychological Contributions

Because successful parent training often requires a shift in firmly established expectations and beliefs regarding child behavior, discipline, and family relationships, this program incorporates a number of principles from cognitive and social psychological models of attitude change (Leary & Miller, 1986). Social psychological research suggests that optimal shifts in attitudes and behavior will be obtained when parents devise their own solutions and rationales (Leary & Miller, 1986; Meichenbaum & Turk, 1987). Indeed, more didactic instructional strategies may increase resistance to skill acquisition (Cunningham, Davis, Bremner, Dunn, & Rzasa, 1993; Patterson & Forgatch, 1985). This program incorporates a coping-modeling problem-solving approach in which participants collaborate in the formulation of solutions to common problems (Cunningham, Davis, et al., 1993). The course leader presents videotaped vignettes depicting exaggerated versions of common child management errors. Participants identify errors, discuss their consequences, develop alternative strategies, and formulate supporting rationales. Leaders model the solutions and parents rehearse the strategy in role-playing exercises and daily homework assignments.

    This large-group coping-modeling approach has several advantages. First, the exaggerated videotaped model simplifies complex child management problems, highlights errors, and depicts longer-term consequences that may be less evident in daily interaction. Exploring the consequences of both positive and negative approaches to management enhances comprehension of complex child behavior problems.

    Second, formulating alternative strategies and devising supporting rationales in the program's small- and large-group discussions enhances adherence and committment (Greenwald & Albert, 1968; Janis & King, 1954; King & Janis, 1956; Meichenbaum & Turk, 1987). Developing solutions to complex problems promotes a sense of personal accomplishment, encourages a sense of ownership, and enhances commitment to the success of homework goals (Cunningham, Davis, et al., 1993).

    Third, a coping-modeling approach to problem solving elicits less resistance and yields a more positive large-group process than more didactic instructional strategies (Cunningham, Davis, et al., 1993; Patterson & Forgatch, 1985). Group leaders adopt a neutral facilitative approach to group discussions which encourages participants to take an active role in resolving disagreements by exploring the potential advantages and disadvantages of alternative approaches.

Fourth, although the COPE program described here is designed for families of children with ADHD, there is considerable heterogeneity in the age, severity, and comorbid characteristics of their children. Moreover, the cultural, ethnic, and sociodemographic composition of groups may vary considerably. Coping-modeling problem solving yields solutions with greater validity to individual members.

Fifth, in coping-modeling discussions, participants break complex problems into smaller components, discuss potential errors, generate alternative strategies, consider the relative advantages and disadantages of different approaches, select promising alternatives, and evaluate the efficacy of potential solutions in modeling, role playing, and homework exercises. The large-group coping-modeling process, therefore, builds collaborative problem-solving skills, an important goal of this systems-oriented parenting program.

To facilitate the group's discussion of the relative advantages of different child management skills, the course leaders pose a series of attributional questions. *Social learning* attributional questions, for example, encourage parents to consider the lessons that different strategies teach. *Relational/communicative* attributional questions invite the group to explore the "messages" that different management strategies communicate. *Long-term outcome* attributional questions anticipate the long-term effects of alternative strategies.

In addition to contributions to the design of the large group's process, cognitive and social psychological models suggest a number of targets for the training program. Attributional research, for example, suggests that parental explanations regarding the causes of children's behavior exert an important impact on their emotional and disciplinary responses (Baden & Howe, 1992; Johnston & Freeman, 1997). The COPE program's large- and small-group discussions encourage participants to collaborate in the fomulation of cognitive strategies that promote an accurate interpretation of the child's behavior, a longer-term perspective on change, and a sense of personal control.

As the problems of many children with ADHD reflect deficits in self-regulation (Barkley, 1997b, 1997c), COPE's social skills activity group teaches simple self-control strategies. The parenting course, in turn, includes strategies to prompt and reinforce the ADHD child's planning and self regulatory efforts.

Contributions from Family Systems Theory

This program's systemic goals are derived from the McMaster Model of Family Functioning (Epstein et al., 1978). Although many families of children with ADHD do not evidence major deficits in family functioning (Cunningham et al., 1988; Szatmari et al., 1989a, 1989b), the long-term task of managing a child with ADHD may erode the family's coping skills. Although this program does not represent a comprehensive approach to intervention with families of children with ADHD, formulating, mastering, implementing, and maintaining parenting skills provide an opportunity to develop an effective approach to the solution of child management problems, a more balanced distribution of child management responsibilities, and more supportive communication among family members.

Contributions from Group Theory

The processes occurring in both small subgroups and the larger group make a considerable contribution to the outcome of the parenting program (MacKenzie, 1990). Groups provide a sense of universal parenting experiences that place the problems facing individual families in greater perspective. Other participants provide child management suggestions, coping strategies, and information regarding children's development which can assist in the solution of complex problems and provide the emotional support needed to confront child management difficulties. Indeed, the opportunity to support and assist other parents is a source of considerable altruistic satisfaction (MacKenzie, 1990). In addition to the skill building, cognitive, and systemic dimensions of the program, leaders must facilitate the development of a cohesive working group, capitalize on the contributions of different membership roles, and encourage completion of the tasks critical to each stage of the group's development (MacKenzie, 1990).

ORGANIZATION OF THE LARGE-GROUP PARENTING PROGRAM

Table 13.1 summarizes the organization of the parent training program.

Advertising and Recruiting Participants

To realize the service delivery potential of large-group COPE courses, catch parents during critical windows when interest in parent training emerges and family schedules permit participation, and increase utilization among families less likely to use existing mental health services, COPE conducts a continuous community wide advertising program. Because schools are a point of virtually universal contact with families of children with ADHD, COPE advertises upcoming courses in school newsletters, places posters on parent information boards, and encourages educators to speak directly to parents who might benefit.

Community physicians provide an alternative contact with families that might benefit from parent training. Using general practice, family medicine, or pediatric office visits to contact parents allows more preventive programs during the child's preschool years when parent training may be more effective (Dishion & Patterson, 1992). Although the COPE program notifies community physicians of upcoming courses, child management concerns rarely manifest themselves in office settings (Sleator & Ullman, 1981) and may not be the focus of the consultation. The program, therefore, advertises directly to parents by placing

---

TABLE 13.1. Curriculum of a 12-Week Large-Group Course for Parents of 4- to 12-Year-Old Children with ADHD

  I. Advertise and recruit participants
 II. Information contracting session
III. Parent training curriculum
    Session 1: Introduction to ADHD
    Session 2: Attending and balancing attending among siblings
    Session 3: Rewards
    Session 4: Planned ignoring
    Session 5: Transitional warnings and when–then
    Session 6: Point systems I
    Session 7: Point systems II (response cost)
    Session 8: Planning ahead
    Session 9: Time out from positive reinforcement I
    Session 10: Time out from positive reinforcement II
    Session 11: Problem solving
    Session 12: Closing session
IV. Monthly booster group

---

posters announcing COPE courses in the waiting rooms of local physicians. Finally, COPE advertises via local ADHD parent support groups (such as CHADD), children's mental health centers, and the local media's community service opportunities.

Information Night

Parents considering enrolling in COPE programs attend a 2-hour information session. The leader introduces participants, outlines the goals of the program, discusses the format of individual sessions, and presents the time and location of different COPE courses. As many parents anticipate the short-term resolution of chronic child management difficulties, the leader provides a more realistic estimate of the changes that might be expected as a result of parenting courses. Leaders encourage participants to consider the potential benefits of consistent attendance, active participation, and conscientious completion of homework projects. Finally, because transportation difficulties, babysitting problems, or work schedules prevent many parents from enrolling, parents consider solutions to obstacles that might limit participation.

The decision to participate in parent training requires accurate information regarding the etiology of ADHD, factors influencing the course of the disorder, and the relative benefits of different interventions. Andrews, Swank, Foorman, and Fletcher (1995), for example, demonstrated that videotaped information (Barkley, 1992a, 1992b) regarding ADHD increased service utilization and improved outcome. Information night sessions, therefore, feature a videotaped introduction to ADHD (Barkley, 1992a, 1992b). These very popular videotapes provide a common theoretical and empirical framework which informs the program's large-group discussions.

Readiness-for-change research (Cunningham, 1997; Prochaska, DiClemente, & Norcross, 1992) suggests that parents attending information night will be at different stages in the process of change. Some, attending on the advice of health or educational professionals, may be at a contemplative stage: simply exploring the possibility of change. Others will be at a preparatory or action stage: ready to initiate a change in child management skills. Research in this area suggests that a shift to the preparatory or action stage occurs when the anticipated benefits of change outweigh the logistical costs of change (Prochaska et al., 1994). To enhance readiness, participants are encouraged to share their goals for the course and discuss the benefits participation might provide parents, children, and families. Accurate information regarding the long-term course of ADHD, familiarity with the format of the program, and large-group discussions regarding the many potential benefits of participation enhances readiness for change and increases the proportion of information night attendees who enroll and attend subsequent sessions.

Parenting Course

The parenting course is organized into a curriculum of from 8 to 16 2-hour weekly sessions. Shorter courses may be achieved by combining sessions addressing similar issues (e.g., attending and balanced attending), deleting advanced topics, or breaking the program into a series of three to four session modules. Table 13.1 presents the curriculum of a 12-session course on COPE-ing with ADHD.

Children's Social Skills Activity Group

Children have the option of participating in a social skills activity group scheduled during the parenting course. The children's group introduces a weekly curriculum of social skills.

Children have an opportunity to observe adult models and rehearse new skills in role-playing exercises. Leaders prompt children to apply skills during in-session activities, reward follow-through, and help plan homework projects (Cunningham, Clark, Heaven, Durrant, & Cunningham, 1989). This group builds social and self-regulatory skills, familiarizes children with strategies that will be used by their parents (e.g., planning ahead and point systems), and allows parents to rehearse new strategies during brief activities with their children.

Supporting Gains: COPE Booster Groups

To sustain the gains accomplished in the course, participants are encouraged to join a monthly discussion group available to graduates of all COPE courses. This allows parents to renew acquaintances, meet parents from other courses, share useful strategies, reinstate previously successful approaches, refine skills, formulate solutions to new problems, explore community resources, and invite speakers with expertise on topics of interest. The COPE program is part of a larger community educational service providing lectures, workshops, and skill-building courses on a wide range of topics. Parents are encouraged to formulate an educational plan providing the knowledge, skills, and support needed at different stages in the child's development.

STRUCTURE OF LARGE-GROUP SESSIONS

Table 13.2 outlines the structure the COPE program's large-group sessions.

Social Networking and Community Resources

Each session begins with a social phase encouraging supportive interaction among parents. Groups develop a resource table with refreshments, information regarding local resources, extracurricular activities, books, and videotapes of interest. Parents are encouraged to add resources, request information on topics of special interest, and borrow materials.

Subgrouping

To allow active participation in groups that average 25 members, parents are divided into five- to seven-member subgroups and seated around separate tables. Each table identifies

TABLE 13.2. Structure of Large-Group Sessions

Phase 1:	Informal social activities
Phase 2:	Leader outlines session plan
Phase 3:	Subgroups review homework successes
Phase 4:	Large-group discussion of homework projects
Phase 5:	Subgroups formulate solutions to videotaped coping model
Phase 6:	Large-group discussion of proposed solutions
Phase 7:	Leader models group's solution
Phase 8:	Subgroups brainstorm application
Phase 9:	Dyads rehearse strategies
Phase 10:	Homework planning
Phase 11:	Leader closes session

a subgroup leader responsible for keeping members on task, encouraging participation, recording the subgroup's discussions, and sharing the subgroup's conclusions with the larger group. To accelerate the emergence of cohesive working relationships (MacKenzie, 1990), members are grouped according to important shared characteristics (age, diagnostic subgroup, family status, etc.) and encouraged to work together for the duration of the program.

Subgroup Homework Reviews

Each subgroup member presents a situation in which the preceding session's strategies were applied successfully. To minimize unrealistic short-term outcome expectations and build self-efficacy (Mash & Johnston, 1983), parents are encouraged to focus on successful application, small gains, and the longer-term impact of strategies on parent–child relationships, self-regulation, or social conduct. The course leader prompts participants to give supportive feedback regarding homework efforts to partners or subgroup members. Following homework discussions, subgroup leaders give the larger group an example of each member's homework project. The leader sumarizes these examples and encourages a larger-group attributional discussion (e.g., the lessons different strategies might teach, the messages they communicate, or their longer-term impact).

Troubleshooting Videotaped Parenting Errors

In this phase, participants formulate solutions to common child management problems. Leaders play a videotape depicting errors in the management of problems to which that session's strategies might be applied. According to the program's coping-modeling problem-solving protocol, parents formulate solutions by identifying mistakes and discussing potential consequences using the attributional model noted here (Cunningham, Davis, et al., 1993; Cunningham et al., 1995). Subgroup leaders summarize these discussions for the larger group. Next, each subgroup formulates alternative strategies, considers their relative merits, and presents their subgroup's conclusions to the larger group. Leaders complete this phase by summarizing and integrating the conclusions of the respective subgroups and prompting a large group attributional discussion.

Modeling Proposed Strategies

To facilitate the solution of problems relevant to participants, the larger group suggests several common problems to which the session's strategy might be applied (e.g., sibling relationships, chores, and homework). The group selects one problem and develops a concrete plan as to how the session's strategy might be applied. The course leader summarizes the plan proposed by the group, models the solution with a member of the group playing the role of a child, and prompts an attributional discussion. This process is repeated for each of three problems.

Brainstorming Application

To encourage a more generalized application of the strategies formulated during coping-modeling problem-solving discussions and modeling exercises, each subgroup lists a range of different situations, behaviors, or problems to which the session's strategy might be applied. Subgroup leaders present their subgroups suggestions to the larger group.

Rehearsing

To strengthen skills, build confidence, and prepare for the application of new skills at home, participants divide into dyads, find a comfortable location in the room, and develop a plan as to how the session's strategy might be applied to a homework problem of interest. With one participant playing a child, parents rehearse the session's strategy. After each exercise, role-playing partners give positive feedback regarding the effective use of new skills. Parents whose children are enrolled in the social skills activity group may be given an opportunity to rehearse these strategies in a series of structured interactions with their child.

Planning Homework

Parents set goals to apply new strategies at home, post visual reminders of the session's plan, and monitor daily follow-through. Parents whose children are in the social skills activity group review the skills introduced during the session and discuss how strategies developed in the course might be used to encourage the application of new social skills at home.

Closing the Session

To enhance participation and strengthen social networks, the course leader closes sessions by prompting members to contact participants who were unable to attend the session. The larger group discusses solutions to obstacles (e.g., car pooling) that might prevent members from attending the next session.

STRENGTHENING FAMILY FUNCTIONING

COPE courses provide an opportunity for participants to build the systems, levels, and skills needed to manage children with ADHD effectively. Large-group sessions prompt positive shifts in the way many parents approach the solution of common problems, share child management responsibilities, and communicate supportively. Behavioral and social psychological models suggest a number of strategies via which the course leader may enhance commitment to these changes.

During homework reviews and problem-solving, brainstorming, and role-playing exercises, participants are encouraged to give supportive feedback to either their partner or another member of their subgroup. Once this type of positive feedback is exchanged comfortably, the leader *fades prompts* by gradually reducing the amount of detail provided in each instruction. Over the course of the large-group sessions, the amount of spontaneous supportive feedback increases dramatically. Leaders point out in-session examples of problem solving, shared management responsibility, and supportive communication and prompt a large-group attributional discussion exploring lessons learned, messages communicated by, or longer-term impact of these approaches to family relationships.

Troubleshooting videotaped examples of common errors in problem solving, distribution of child management responsibilities, or communication represents an alternative approach to building the systems skills. On session 12 of the course outlined in Table 13.1, for example, participants identify videotaped problem-solving errors, discuss their consequences, generate an alternative approach, formulate supporting rationales, and plan problem-solving homework projects.

Most parenting strategies are applicable to interactions with other members of the family, extended family, or community. Conversational skills, strategies for balancing time and attention, avoiding escalating arguments, compliments, and planning solutions to potential problems may prove useful in a variety of contexts. Leaders prompt the group to consider whether child management strategies discussed in the session are applicable to interactions with older children or adults, a strategy we term "prompting generational transfer."

As the group's committment to new approaches to problem solving, communication, and role allocation emerges, these systemic goals are included in weekly homework assignments. Participants formulate a detailed plan as to how specific changes might be introduced, anticipate obstacles, develop reminders, and monitor implementation at home. These projects are included in each session's homework review.

CURRICULUM OF THE PROGRAM

The curriculum of a 12-session course for families of children with ADHD is outlined below. Each session is conducted within the general framework discussed earlier.

Encouraging Positive Behavior and Improving Parent–Child Relationships

Although children with ADHD seem to respond favorably to more immediate, frequent, and salient reinforcement (Barkley, 1990; Haenlein & Caul, 1987), their poorly regulated oppositional behavior elicits a less positive parental response (Cunningham & Barkley, 1979; Mash & Johnston, 1982; Barkley et al., 1985; Patterson, 1982). In early sessions, therefore, participants expand their repertoire of attending and reward strategies, identify situations to which attending skills might be applied, and target behaviors to reinforce. These strategies strengthen positive behavior, reduce coercive interactions, and contribute to the development of language, conversational skills, and social competence. Attending strategies foster parent–child relationships that support the solution of more complex problems and are critical components of the strategies developed in later sessions.

Balancing Family Relationships

Difficult children often demand a disproportionate amount of attention; thus siblings are often upset by unequal allocations of parental time. In session 2, therefore, parents develop strategies for balancing time and attention among siblings and attending to several children simultaneously (e.g., "You've both been very helpful this morning"). This general principle is used to examine balance in dimensions of family life that may effect child management and coping skills (e.g., time for children vs. spouse or time for family vs. self).

Avoiding Conflicts

The behavior of children with ADHD may be irritating or provocative. In session 4, therefore, parents formulate strategies for ignoring minor disruptions, disengaging from escalating conflicts, and controlling thoughts which intensify anger ("No child is going to speak to me in that tone of voice."). Homework assignments encourage parents to agree on behaviors that are best ignored, identify potentially explosive encounters, and rehearse the application of new cognitive coping strategies.

Managing Transitions

Children with ADHD often fail to anticipate transitions, have difficulty modulating their reaction to the termination of reinforcing activities, or resist the start of more effortful tasks. Session 5 focuses on the development of more effective transitional strategies. Parents shift the child's attention by reinforcing positive behaviors, present a transitional prompt ("At the end of this game it will be bath time."), discourage arguments by ignoring protests, and reward follow-through. When–then strategies encourage compliance via the application of the Premack principle, where low-probability behaviors (e.g., homework completion) are rewarded by access to higher-probability behaviors (television). During brainstorming and homework exercises, parents organize daily activities into a series of when–then sequences in which completion of a task is followed by a rewarding activity. Consumer feedback consistently supports the utility of this strategy, which includes both self-regulatory (specifying a task and anticipating positive consequences) and immediately rewarding motivational components.

Point Systems

In session 6, parents develop a home-based token economy. Participants identify target behaviors, construct a menu of reinforcers, assign costs, and select tokens. A response-cost system in which points are lost for agreed-on infractions is introduced on session 7. To enhance the impact of the program on problems at school, parents develop a daily report card in which points earned at school are exchanged for home-based rewards. Point systems bridge intervals between positive behavior and more distant rewards and allow parents to use response-cost contingencies (e.g., losing points when prenegotiated rules are broken).

Improving Self-Regulation

Because children with ADHD often fail to anticipate problematic situations, review relevant rules, consider alternative strategies, or anticipate the consequences of their behavior, they approach social and academic activities in a poorly planned impulsive manner (Barkley, 1997b). Because short-term programs may not realize generalized improvements (Abikoff, 1991), COPE integrates planning and self-regulatory strategies (e.g., transitional warnings, when–then, and planning ahead) into daily interactions with the child. Session 8 focuses on planning-ahead strategies in which parents (1) identify a potentially problematic situation ("I'm expecting an important phone call."), (2) prompt the child to develop a plan ("What could you do to help out?"), and (3) negotiate incentives. To encourage the application of well-intentioned but easily forgotten plans, parents prompt the child to review plans immediately prior to the situation ("Before we go, tell me your plan for riding in the car."), ignore minor errors, reward follow-through, and prompt the child to review plans as necessary.

Dealing with More Serious Problems

The positive strategies developed during the first several sessions of this program encourage prosocial behavior, but parents of many children with ADHD require effective responses to defiant aggressive behaviors. Groups typically formulate a time-out-from-positive-reinforcement strategy which includes (1) the presentation of firm emotionally neutral commands; (2) a quick neutral warning if noncompliance occurs; and if necessary (3) the application of an effective consequence (e.g., time in a chair or room, loss of privileges, or loss of points earned in a token incentive program). Groups explore the negative consequences of harsh physical discipline, which may increase aggression and adversely effect social development (Weiss, Dodge, Bates, & Petit, 1992)

Problem Solving

Although a significant number of problems have been solved by this point, most participants need an opportunity to address unresolved difficulties. In session 11, parents formulate a general approach to the solution of child management problems (PASTE-ing problems). This typically includes scheduling problem solving at a time when discussion can proceed without serious interruption, (P) picking one soluble problem, (A) analyzing the advantages and disadvantages of alternative solutions, (S) selecting the most promising alternative, (T) trying it out, and (E) evaluating outcome. This general approach to problem solving is then applied to the solution of selected management difficulties.

BENEFITS OF LARGE-GROUP COMMUNITY-BASED COURSES

Service Utilization

Community-based courses appear to reduce the barriers clinic-based programs may pose. Cunningham et al. (1995), for example, demonstrated that parents from economically disadvantaged backgrounds, immigrants, parents using English as a second language, and families of children with more severe problems were more likely to utilize parenting courses conducted in neighborhood schools. Several factors linked to poor treatment adherence in clinic-based trials (Kazdin et al., 1993, 1994; Webster-Stratton & Hammond, 1990) are less likely to influence the utilization of this school-based program. Economic disadvantage, family dysfunction, and parental depression, for example, do not predict participation in large-group community-based programs (Cunningham et al., 1995, 1997). Together, these studies suggest large-group parenting courses conducted in neighborhood school settings place fewer demands on psychological adjustment and family functioning than individual programs conducted in outpatient clinics.

Large-Group Process

Social psychological research suggests that formulating solutions, devising supporting rationales, and setting personal goals in a group context should improve commitment and adherence to new strategies (Janis, 1983; Leary & Miller, 1986; Meichenbaum & Turk, 1987). Cunningham, Davis, et al. (1993) demonstrated that participants in coping-modeling conditions, in which strategies were formulated by the group, attended significantly more training sessions, arrived late to fewer sessions, completed significantly more homework assignments, interacted more positively during training sessions, reported a significantly higher personal accomplishment scores, and rated the program more favorably than those who were introduced to new skills in a more didactic mastery modeling condition.

Informal interactions, subgroup exercises, and larger-group discussions allow a valuable exchange of information regarding normal child development and behavior, problems common at different stages in the child's development, and potentially useful management strategies. Data from our own trials, for example, suggest that larger groups generate more potential solutions to child management problems than do individual parenting programs (Cunningham et al., 1995).

A problem-based model in which parents explore a wider range of child management strategies emphasizes a flexible approach that may better meet the diverse temperamental and developmental needs of this population (Grusec & Goodnow, 1994). In addition, encouraging participants to formulate their own solutions and generate their own rationales is more likely to yield strategies that respect differing cultural backgrounds of the participants enrolling in these community-based programs (Cunningham et al., 1995).

Parents of children with ADHD often find themselves isolated from potentially important extended family supports (Cunningham et al., 1988). Formal feedback suggests that large neighborhood school-based COPE courses provide an important sense of membership in a group sharing common problems, provide a perspective regarding the severity of child management problems, and normalize the experience of parent training. Informal interactions, discussions regarding local resources, car pooling, and the opportunity to collaborate in the solution of common problems encourage the supportive contacts that parents need to cope with the stress of managing a difficult child (Cochran & Brassard, 1979). Indeed, helping other parents solve shared problems may provide participants with an important source of altruistic satisfaction (MacKenzie, 1990).

Although COPE sessions focus on a relatively standard curriculum of child management skills, informal interactions, subgroup discussions, and issues raised by the larger group provide parents with a forum to discuss related concerns, an opportunity that appears to enhance the efficacy of parent training (Prinz & Miller, 1994).

The large-group format of the COPE program yields a process with several advantages. Videotapes of exaggerated examples of common child management errors provide a focus to group discussions that promotes a more cohesive integration of the program's large- and small-group discussions. Larger groups appear less vulnerable than smaller groups to the potentially disruptive effects of drop-outs (MacKenzie, 1990), while the consensus-building capabilities of large groups allow participants to resolve disagreements.

Cost Efficacy

Cunningham et al. (1995) compared the cost of large-group, community-based COPE programs with clinic-based services for individual famlies. Large-group, community-based COPE courses were more than six times as cost-effective as clinic-based programs. Community-based courses reduced the time and travel costs incurred by participants and did not increase the secondary costs resulting from contacts with other medical, mental health, or educational professionals.

Many of the participants enrolling in community-based COPE courses are families of children with less severe problems. Providing service to lower-risk cases in expensive clinic-based programs may increase costs and limit access by families of higher-risk children. Including parents of lower-risk children in large groups, in contrast, results in very small incremental costs (Cunningham et al., 1995). In addition to the potential preventive advantages of including families of lower-risk children, these parents often represent a valuable resource to the group.

Outcome

To examine the effectiveness of this larger group COPE model, we prospectively screened a community sample of 4-year-olds entering junior kindergarten programs, identifed children more than 1.5 standard deviations above the mean on a measure of behavior problems at home (Barkley & Edelbrock, 1987), and randomly assigned a sample of 150 participants to a large neighborhood school-based COPE course, an individual family clinic-based parent training program, or a waiting-list control group (Cunningham et al., 1995). Larger groups yielded greater improvements in objectively measured problem-solving skills, greater reductions in reported child management problems, and improved maintenance at 6–month follow-up.

REFERENCES

Abikoff, H. (1991). Cognitive training in ADHD children: Less to it than meets the eye. *Journal of Learning Disabilities, 24*, 205–209.

Anastopoulos, A. D., Shelton, T. L., DuPaul, G. J., & Guevremont, D. C. (1993). PT for attention deficit hyperactivity disorder: Its impact on child and parent functioning. *Journal of Abnormal Child Psychology, 21*, 581–596.

Andrews, J. A., Swank, P. R., Foorman, B., & Fletcher, J. M. (1995). Effects of educating parents about ADHD. *ADHD Report, 3*, 12–13.

Baden, A. & Howe, G. W. (1992). Mothers' attributions and expectancies regarding their conduct-disordered children. *Journal of Abnormal Child Psychology, 20*, 467–485.

Barkley, R. A. (1990). *Attention-deficit hyperactivity disorder: A handbook for diagnosis and treatment.* New York: Guilford Press.

Barkley, R. A. (1992a). *ADHD: What do we know?* [Videotape]. New York: Guilford Press.

Barkley, R. A. (1992b). *ADHD: What can we do?* [Videotape]. New York: Guilford Press.

Barkley, R. A. (1997a). *Defiant children* (2nd ed.): *A clinician's guide to assessment and parent training.* New York: Guilford Press.

Barkley, R. A. (1997b). Behavioral inhibition, sustained attention, and executive functions: Constructing a unifying theory of ADHD. *Psychological Bulletin, 121*, 65–94.

Barkley, R. A. (1997c). *ADHD and the nature of self-control.* New York: Guilford Press.

Barkley, R. A., & Cunningham, C. E. (1979). The effects of methylphenidate on the mother child interactions of hyperactive children. *Archives of General Psychiatry, 36*, 201–208.

Barkley, R. A., & Edelbrock, C. (1987). Assessing situational variation in children's problem behaviours: The Home and School Situations Questionnaires. In R. J. Prinz (Ed.), *Advances in behavioural assessment of children and families* (Vol. 3, pp. 157–176). New York: JAI Press.

Barkley, R. A., Fischer, M., Edelbrock, C. S., & Smallish, L. (1990). The adolescent outcome of hyperactive children diagnosed by research criteria: I. An 8-year prospective follow-up study. *Journal of the American Academy of Child and Adolescent Psychiatry, 29*, 546–557.

Barkley, R. A., Karlsson, J., Pollard, S., & Murphy, K. (1985). Developmental changes in the mother–child interactions of hyperactive children: Effects of two doses of Ritalin. *Journal of Child Psychology and Psychiatry, 13*, 631–638.

Befera, M., & Barkley, R. (1985). Hyperactive and normal boys and girls: Mother–child interaction, parent psychiatric status, and child psychopathology. *Journal of Child Psychology and Psychiatry, 26*, 439–452.

Boyle, M. H. (1991). Children's mental health issues: Prevention and treatment. In L. C. Johnson & D. Barnhorst (Eds.), *Children, families and public policy in the 90's* (pp. 73–104). Toronto: Thompson Educational Publishing.

Boyle, M. H., & Offord, D. R. (1988). Prevalence of childhood disorder, perceived need for help, family dysfunction, and resource allocation for child welfare and children's mental health services in Ontario. *Canadian Journal of Behavioural Science, 20*, 374–388.

Breen, M., & Barkley, R. A. (1988). Parenting stress and child psychopathology in ADHD boys and girls. *Journal of Pediatric Psychology, 13*, 265–280.

Campbell, S. B. (1990). *Behavior problems in preschool children.* New York: Guilford Press.

Campbell, S. B., Endman, M., & Bernfield, G. (1977). A three year follow-up of hyperactive preschoolers into elementary school. *Journal of Child Psychology and Psychiatry, 18*, 239–249.

Campbell, S. B., & Ewing, L. J. (1990). Follow-up of hard to manage preschoolers: Adjustment at age 9 and predictors of continuing symptoms. *Journal of Child Psychology and Psychiatry, 31*, 871–890.

Clark, M. L., Cheyne, A. J., Cunningham, C. E., & Siegel, L. S. (1988). Dyadic peer interaction and task orientation in attention-deficit disordered children. *Journal of Abnormal Child Psychology*, 16, 1–15.

Cochran, M., & Brassard, J. A. (1979). Child development and personal social networks. *Child Development*, 50, 601–615.

Cunningham, C. E. (1990). A family systems approach to PT. In R. A. Barkley, *Attention-deficit hyperactivity disorder: A handbook for diagnosis and treatment* (pp. 432–461). New York: Guilford Press.

Cunningham, C. E. (1997). Readiness for change: Applications to the management of ADHD. *ADHD Report*, 5, 6–9.

Cunningham, C. E., & Barkley, R. A. (1978). The effects of Ritalin on the mother child interactions of hyperactive identical twins. *Developmental Medicine and Child Neurology*, 20, 634–642.

Cunningham, C. E., & Barkley, R. A. (1979). The interactions of hyperactive and normal children with their mothers during free play and structured tasks. *Child Development*, 50, 217–224.

Cunningham, C. E., Benness, B., & Siegel, L. S. (1988). Family functioning, time allocation, and parental depression in the families of normal and ADHD Children. *Journal of Clinical Child Psychology*, 17, 169–178.

Cunningham, C. E., Boyle, M., Offord, D., Racine, Y., & Hundert, J., Secord, M. & McDonald, J. (1997). *Tri Ministry Project: Diagnostic and demographic correlates of school-based parenting course utilization.* Unpublished manuscript.

Cunningham, C. E., Bremner, R. B., & Boyle, M. (1995). Large group community-based parenting programs for families of preschoolers at risk for disruptive behaviour disorders: Utilization, cost effectiveness, and outcome. *Journal of Child Psychology and Psychiatry*, 36, 1141–1159.

Cunningham, C. E., Bremner, R. B. & Secord-Gilbert, M. (1997). *COPE (The Community Parent Education Program): A school based family systems oriented workshop for parents of children with disruptive behavior disorders (leader's manual).* Hamilton, Ontario: COPE Works.

Cunningham, C. E., Clark, M. L., Heaven, R. K., Durrant, J., & Cunningham, L. J. (1989). The effects of group problem solving and contingency management procedures on the positive and negative interactions of learning disabled and attention deficit disordered children with an autistic peer. *Child and Family Behavior Therapy*, 11, 89–106.

Cunningham, C. E., Cunningham, L. J., Martorelli, V., & Bohaychuk, D. (1996c). *Student mediated conflict resolution programs: A provincial survey.* Unpublished manuscript.

Cunningham, C. E., Davis, J. R., Bremner, R., Dunn, K., & Rzasa, T. (1993). Coping modelling problem solving versus mastery modelling: Effects on adherence, in-session process, and skill acquisition in a residential PT program. *Journal of Consulting and Clinical Psychology*, 61, 871–877.

Cunningham, C. E., & Siegel, L. S. (1987). Peer interactions of normal and attention-deficit disordered boys during free-play, cooperative task, and simulated classroom situations. *Journal of Abnormal Child Psychology*, 15, 247–268.

Cunningham, C. E., Siegel, C. S., & Offord, D. R. (1985). A developmental dose–response analysis of the efforts of methylphenidate on the peer interactions of attention deficit disordered boys. *Journal of Child Psychology and Psychiatry*, 26, 955–971.

Cunningham, C. E., Siegel, L. S., & Offord, D. R. (1991). A dose–response analysis of the effects of methylphenidate on the peer interactions and simulated classroom performance of ADD children with and without conduct problems. *Journal of Child Psychology and Psychiatry*, 32, 439–452.

Dishion, T. J., & Patterson, G. R. (1992). Age effects in parent training outcome. *Behavior Therapy*, 23, 719–729.

Dubey, D. R., O'Leary, S., & Kaufman, K. F. (1983). Training parents of hyperactive children in child management: A comparative outcome study. *Journal of Abnormal Child Psychology*, 11, 229–246.

Earls, F., & Jung, K. G. (1987). Temperament and home environment characteristics as causal factors in the early development of childhood psychopathology. *Journal of the American Academy of Child and Adolescent Psychiatry*, 26, 491–498.

Emery, R. E. (1982). Interparental conflict and the children of discord and divorce. *Psychological Bulletin*, 92, 310–330.

Epstein, N. B., Bishop, D. S., & Levine, S. (1978, October). The McMaster Model of Family Functioning. *Journal of Marriage and Family Counseling*, pp. 19–31.

Firestone, P., & Witt, J. (1982). Characteristics of families completing and prematurely discontinuing a behavioural PT program. *Journal of Pediatric Psychology, 7*, 209–221.

Forehand, R. L., & McMahon, R. J. (1981). *Helping the noncompliant child: A clinician's guide to parent training.* New York: Guilford Press.

Freeman, W., Phillips, J., & Johnston, C. (1992, June). *Treatment effects on hyperactive and aggressive behaviours in ADHD children.* Paper presented at the meeting of the Canadian Psychological Association, Quebec City.

Greenwald, A. G., & Albert, R. D. (1968). Acceptance and recall of improvised arguments. *Journal of Personality and Social Psychology, 8*, 31–35.

Greist, D. L., Wells, K. C., & Forehand, R. (1979). An examination of predictors of maternal perceptions of maladjustment in clinical-referred children. *Journal of Abnormal Psychology, 88*, 277–281.

Grusec, J., E. & Goodnow, J. (1994). Impact of parental discipline methods on the child's internalization of values: A reconceptualization of current point of view. *Developmental Psychology, 30*, 40–19.

Haenlein, M., & Caul, W. F. (1987). Attention deficit disorder with hyperactivity: A specific hypothesis of reward dysfunction. *Journal of the American Academy of Child and Adolescent Psychiatry, 26*, 356–362.

Hanf, C., & Kling, J. (1973). *Facilitating parent–child interactions: A two stage training model.* Unpublished manuscript, University of Oregon Medical School.

Humphries, T., Kinsbourne, M., & Swanson, J. (1978). Stimulant effects on cooperation and social interaction between hyperactive children and their mothers. *Journal of Child Psychology and Psychiatry, 19*, 13–22.

Janis, I. (1983). The role of social support in adherence to stressful decisions. *American Psychologist, 38*, 143–160.

Janis, I. L., & King, B. T. (1954). The influence of role-playing on opinion change. *Journal of Abnormal and Social Psychology, 49*, 211–218.

Johnston, C., & Freeman, W. (1997). Attributions for child behavior in parents of children without behavior disorders and children with attention deficit-hyperactivity disorder. *Journal of Consulting and Clinical Psychology, 65*, 636–645.

Kazdin, A. E. (1990). Premature termination from treatment among children referred for antisocial behavior. *Journal of Child Psychology and Psychiatry, 31*, 415–425.

Kazdin, A. E., Holland, L., & Crowley, M. (1997). Family experience of barriers to treatment and premature termination from child therapy. *Journal of Consulting and Clinical Psychology, 65*, 453–463.

Kazdin, A. E., Mazurick, J. L., & Bass, D. (1993). Risk for attrition in treatment of antisocial children and families. *Journal of Clinical Child Psychology, 22*, 2–16.

Kazdin, A. E., Mazurick, J. L., & Siegel, T. C. (1994). Treatment outcome among children with externalizing disorder who terminate prematurely versus those who complete psychotherapy. *Journal of the American Academy of Child and Adolescent Psychiatry, 33*, 549–557.

King, B. T., & Janis, I. L. (1956). Comparison of the effectiveness of improvised versus nonimprovised role-playing in producing opinion changes. *Human Relations, 9*, 1778–186.

Leary, M. R., & Miller, R. S. (1986). *Social psychology and dysfunctional behavior.* New York: Springer-Verlag.

MacKenzie, K. R. (1990). *Introduction to time limited group psychotherapy.* Washington, DC: American Psychiatric Press.

Mash, E. J., & Johnston, C. (1982). A comparison of the mother–child interactions of younger and older hyperactive and normal children. *Child Development, 53*, 1371–1381.

Mash, E. J., & Johnston, C. (1983). Parental perceptions of child behavior problems, parenting self-esteem, and mothers' reported stress in younger and older hyperactive and normal children. *Journal of Consulting and Clinical Psychology, 51*, 68–99.

McMahon, R. J. (1994). Diagnosis, assessment, and treatment of externalizing problems in children: The role of longitudinal data. *Journal of Consulting and Clinical Psychology, 62*, 901–917.

McMahon, R. J., Forehand, R. L., Greist, D. L., & Wells, K. C. (1981). Who drops out of treatment during parent behavioral training? *Behavioral Counseling Quarterly, 1*, 79–85.

McMiller, W. P., & Weisz, J. R. (1996). Help-seeking preceding mental health clinic intake among

African-American, Latino, and Caucasian youths. *Journal of the American Academy of Child and Adolescent Psychiatry, 35,* 1086–1097.

Meichenbaum, D., & Turk, D. C. (1987). *Facilitating treatment adherence: A practitioner's guidebook.* New York: Plenum.

Offord, D. R., Boyle, M. H., Szatmari, P., Rae-Grant, N., Links, P. S., Cadman, D., Byles, J. A., Crawford, J. W., Munroe-Blum, H., Byrne, C., Thomas, H., & Woodward, C. (1987). Ontario Child Health Study: II. Six month prevalence of disorder and rates of service utilization. *Archives of General Psychiatry, 44,* 832–836.

Panaccione, V. F., & Wahler, R. G. (1986). Child behavior, maternal depression, and social coercion as factors in the quality of child care. *Journal of Abnormal Child Psychology, 14,* 263–278.

Patterson, G. R. (1982). *Coercive family process.* Eugene, OR: Castalia.

Patterson, G. R., & Forgatch, M. S. (1985). Therapist behavior as a determinant for client noncompliance: A paradox for behaviour modification. *Journal of Consulting and Clinical Psychology, 53,* 846–851.

Patterson, G. R., Reid, J. B., & Dishion, T. J. (1992). *Antisocial boys.* Eugene, OR: Castalia.

Pisterman, S., McGrath, P. J., Firestone, P., Goodman, J. T., Webster, I., & Mallory, R. (1989). Outcome of parent-mediated treatment of preschoolers with attention deficit disorder with hyperactivity. *Journal of Consulting and Clinical Psychology, 57,* 636–643.

Pisterman, S., McGrath, P., Firestone, P., Goodman, J.T., Webster, I., Mallory, R., & Goffin B. (1992). The effects of parent training parenting stress and sense of competence. *Canadian Journal of Behavioural Science, 24,* 41–58.

Pollard, S., Ward, E. M., & Barkley, R. A. (1983). The effects of PT and Ritalin on the parent–child interactions of hyperactive boys. *Child and Family Therapy, 5,* 51–69.

Prinz, R. J., & Miller, G. E. (1994). Family-based treatment for childhood antisocial behavior: Experimental influences on dropout and engagement. *Journal of Consulting and Clinical Psychology, 62,* 645–650.

Prochaska, J. O., DiClemente, C. C., & Norcross, J. C. (1992). In search of how people change: Applications to addictive behaviors. *American Psychologist, 47,* 1102–1114.

Prochaska, J. O., Velicer, W. R., Rossi, J. S., Goldstein, M. G., Marcus, B. H., Rakowski, W., Fiore, C., Harlow, L. L., Redding, C. A., Rosenbloom, D., & Rossi, S. R. (1994). Stages of change and decisional balance for 12 problem behaviors. *Health Psychology, 13,* 39–46.

Sleator, E. K., & Ullman, R. L. (1981). Can the physician diagnose hyperactivity in the office? *Pediatrics, 67,* 13–17.

Sobol, M. P., Ashbourne, D. T., Earn, B. M., & Cunningham C. E. (1989). Parents' attributions for achieving compliance from attention-deficit disordered children. *Journal of Abnormal Child Psychology, 17,* 359–369.

Szatmari, P., Boyle, M. H., & Offord, D. R. (1989). ADDH and conduct disorder: Degree of diagnostic overlap and differences among correlates. *Journal of the American Academy of Child and Adolescent Psychiatry, 28,* 865–872.

Szatmari, P., Offord, D. R., & Boyle, M. H. (1989a). Ontario Child Health Study: Prevalence of attention deficit disorder with hyperactivity. *Journal of Child Psychology and Psychiatry, 30,* 219–230.

Szatmari, P., Offord, D. R., & Boyle, M. H. (1989b). Correlates, associated impairments and patterns of service utilization of children with attention deficit disorder: Findings from the Ontario Child Health Study. *Journal of Child Psychology and Psychiatry, 30,* 205–217.

Taylor, E., Chadwick, O., Heptinstall, E., & Danckaerts, M. (1996). Hyperactivity and conduct problems as risk factors for adolescent development. *Journal of the American Academy of Child and Adolescent Psychiatry, 35,* 1213–1226.

Tuma, J. M. (1989). Mental health services for children: The state of the art. *American Psychologist, 44* 188–199.

Wahler, R. G. (1980). The insular mother: Her problems in parent–child treatment. *Journal of Applied Behavior Analysis, 13,* 207–219.

Webster-Stratton, C. W. (1994). Advancing videotape parent training: A comparison study. *Journal of Consulting and Clinical Psychology, 62,* 583–593.

Webster-Stratton, C. W., & Hammond, M. (1988). Maternal depression and its relationship to life stress, perceptions of child behavior problems, parenting behaviors, and child conduct problems. *Journal of Abnormal Child Psychology, 16,* 299–315.

Webster-Stratton, C. W., & Hammond, M. (1990). Predictors of treatment outcome in parent training for families with conduct problem children. *Behavior Therapy, 21,* 319–337.

Weiss, B., Dodge, K. A., Bates, J. E., & Pettit, G. S. (1992). Some consequences of early harsh discipline: Child aggression and a maladapted social information processing style. *Child Development, 63,* 6, 1321–1335.

Weiss, G., & Hechtman, L. T. (1986). *Hyperactive children grown up:. Empirical findings and theoretical considerations.* New York: Guilford Press.

Whalen, C. K., Henker, B., & Dotemoto, S. (1980). Methylphenidate and hyperactivity: Effects on teacher behaviors. *Science, 208,* 1280–1282.

Zahner, G. E. P., Pawelkiewicz, J., Defrancesco, J. J., & Adnopoz, J. (1992). Children's mental health service needs and utilization patterns in an urban community: An epidemiological assessment. *Journal of the American Academy of Child and Adolescent Psychiatry, 31,* 951–960.

Chapter 14

TRAINING FAMILIES
WITH ADHD ADOLESCENTS

Arthur L. Robin

ও

Adolescence is a challenging developmental period for families because children are undergoing exponential physiological, cognitive, behavioral, and emotional changes. The normal problems of adolescence are magnified exponentially for the individual with Attention-Deficit/Hyperactivity Disorder (ADHD) and the family because the core symptoms and associated features of ADHD interfere with successfully mastering the developmental tasks of adolescence. As a result, ADHD teens suffer academic failure, social isolation, depression, and low self-esteem and become embroiled in many unpleasant conflicts with their families.

Parents encounter a variety of home management problems with their ADHD adolescents, including noncompliance with rules; conflicts over issues such as chores, curfew, friends, driving, and general attitude; and school-related issues such as homework. These conflicts usually reflect independence-related themes; for example, the adolescent desires to make his or her own decisions about chores, homework, or whatever the issue may be, and the parents desire to retain decision-making authority. Such conflicts take the form of unpleasant verbal exchanges characterized by shouting, yelling, name calling, and other hurtful and coercive communication styles.

THEORY

A comprehensive biobehavioral family systems model is helpful in understanding the factors that determine the degree of conflict concerning home management issues experienced by the family with an ADHD adolescent. Within this model, we postulate that the biological/genetic factors underlying ADHD interact with the developmental tasks of adolescence and environmental/family contingencies to influence the frequency and intensity of home management problems. Teenagers are expected to accomplish five major developmental tasks: (1) individuate from their parents, (2) adjust to sexual maturation, (3) develop new and deeper peer relationships, (4) form a self-identity, and (5) plan for a career. Parent–teen relations undergo radical restructuring punctuated by periodic perturbation and conflict as adolescents become more independent, necessitating a shift from a more authoritarian to a more democratic parental decision-making structure and communication process.

I (Robin, in press; Robin & Foster, 1989) have outlined three major dimensions of family relations that determine the degree of clinically significant conflict likely to occur as teenagers individuate from their parents: (1) problem-solving communication skill deficits, (2) cognitive distortions, and (3) family structure problems. Families that are unable to problem-solve through a process of mutual problem definition, brainstorming alternative solutions, solution evaluation and negotiation, and careful implementation planning are likely to develop excessive independence-related disputes. When a family also communicates in an accusatory, defensive, or sarcastic manner, members become enraged and act based on hot emotions rather than cool logic, precluding rational problem solving.

Cognitive distortions refer to unreasonable expectations and malicious attributions that elicit angry affect and sidetrack solution-oriented communication. A parent, for example, may fear the ruinous consequences of giving too much freedom to an adolescent, demand unflinching loyalty or obedience, or incorrectly attribute innocent adolescent behavior to malicious, purposeful motives. An adolescent may jump to the conclusion that the parents' rules are intrinsically unfair and likely to ruin any chance of having fun in peer relations, and that teenagers should have as much autonomy in decision making as they desire. In crisis situations, unreasonable beliefs color judgment and add emotional overtones to behavioral reactions. A father who demands obedience, is concerned about ruination, and believes the adolescent is purposely misbehaving will have a difficult time, for example, remaining rational at 2:00 A.M. when his daughter comes home 2 hours past the agreed-upon curfew. If the daughter thinks her father's midnight curfew is unfair because it prevents her from ever having any fun with her friends, and that her father has no right to dictate her curfew, she will also be less than rational. Such unrealistic cognitive reactions mediate emotional over-reactions, which spur continued conflict.

Family structure problems refer to difficulties in the organization of the family. All families have a hierarchy or "pecking order," and in Western civilization parents are typically in charge of children. Adolescence is a transitional period when parents are supposed to be upgrading the children's status in the hierarchy, culminating in an egalitarian relationship between adult children and their parents. It is easy for the coercive child to overwhelm the parents, and by adolescence the child may have too much power in the family, a situation we call hierarchy reversal. In the last edition (Barkley, 1990), Patterson's (1982) coercion theory was integrated with Barkley's research findings on family interaction between ADHD children and their parents to illustrate how the oppositional behavior of school-age ADHD children may develop into a pattern of severe hierarchy reversal meeting criteria according to the fourth edition of the *Diagnostic and Statistical Manual of Mental Disorders* (DSM-IV; American Psychiatric Association, 1994) for Oppositional Defiant Disorder (ODD) or Conduct Disorder (CD) by adolescence. Sometimes, one parent and the adolescent may also take sides against the other parent, forming a cross-generational coalition. Two family members may place the third in the middle of a conflict, forcing the third to take sides. This pattern, called triangulation, often occurs with ADHD adolescents when father comes home to find that mother and son have had a major battle earlier that afternoon. Mother and son both turn to father, presenting their sides of the argument and appealing for support, and father is triangulated or caught in the middle. Sometimes father sides with his wife, other times with his son. Each of these structural problems may result in a "divide and conquer" situation, where the adolescent can continue to engage in some antisocial or inappropriate behavior because the parents are not able to work well as an executive team setting and enforcing limits. Finally, the extent to which parents monitor their adolescent's whereabouts, also known as the degree of involvement or cohesion between family members, influences parent–

adolescent relations. Parents need to know where the adolescent is and what he or she is doing, but they need to obtain this knowledge without excessive intrusiveness (e.g., enmeshment) or excessive disengagement (e.g., too much distance).

We must also consider the impact on family relations of deficits in the four executive functions that follow from poor behavioral inhibition (as Barkley, 1997a, has reconceptualized the core characteristic of ADHD). Poor nonverbal working memory, or prolongation, may make it difficult for the ADHD adolescent to stay on task and problem-solve in a planful way when resolving conflicts during family discussions, to carry out agreements with parents, and to complete schoolwork, chores, or other responsibilities. The distorted sense of time associated with poor nonverbal working memory may spur increased conflict because impatient adolescents badger their parents to meet their demands right away, however unreasonable or inappropriate those demands may be (e.g., "Buy me a car," "Take me to my friend's house right now," "Let me get my license today").

Poor internalization of language (verbal working memory) may impede learning from past parental consequences and following parental rules, which frustrates parents tremendously and often leads them to form excessively malicious attributions that the adolescent is purposely failing to meet their expectations. Poor self-regulation of affect/motivaton/ arousal may account for the emotional overreactivity, poor frustration tolerance, poor intrinsic motivation, and explosiveness of many adolescents with ADHD, fueling family conflict. Poor reconstitution may contribute to poor interpersonal problem solving and the tendency to select the first solution that comes to mind rather than dissembling the problem into its component parts and attempting to creatively reassemble the parts into a new solution.

Individual psychopathology in the parents such as depression, substance abuse, anxiety, personality disorders, or schizophrenia adds even more complexity and stress to the home-based problems of the ADHD adolescent. As the genetic basis for ADHD is becoming more widely known and accepted, therapists are diagnosing many of the parents of the ADHD children as having ADHD. The stress of having two or more distractible, hottempered, impulsive, restless members in a single family exponentially raises the probability of clinically significant conflict. Finally, extrafamilial factors such as the school and peer environments have an impact on the overall family relationships.

Figure 14.1 summarizes this biobehavioral family systems model. Prior to the adolescence of its children, a family has developed a homeostatic pattern or system of "checks and balances" regulating its members' interactions. The developmental changes of adolescence disrupt homeostatic patterns, spurring an acute period of "normal parent–teen conflict" between ages 12 and 14. Most families emerge from this stage with new homeostatic patterns and methods of resolving home-based conflicts. Deficits in problem solving, communication skills, cognitive distortions, family structure problems, and individual/marital pathology promote clinically significant conflict during early adolescence. These five factors interact with the executive functions rendered less efficient by impaired behavioral inhibition to create a clinical presentation of severe, moderate, or mild ADHD with or without associated ODD or CD.

INTERVENTION

At the point of diagnosis and/or referral, most adolescents with ADHD are (1) experiencing difficulty completing their schoolwork and making satisfactory academic progress, and (2) getting into frequent conflict with their parents not only about their poor school performance but also about a variety of compliance-related issues such as chores, curfew, dating, bedtime,

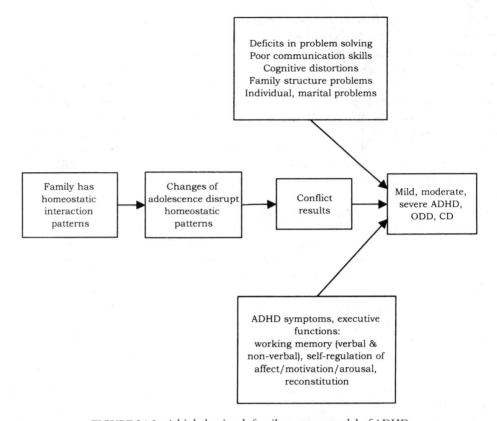

FIGURE 14.1. A biobehavioral–family systems model of ADHD.

fighting with siblings, negative voice tone, and general disrespect. Some are also having significant difficulties with peer relationships and behavior in the community, as well as low self-esteem, depression, anxiety, and other comorbid conditions. A minority are actively antisocial, aggressive, in trouble with the legal authorities, and/or abusing marijuana, alcohol, or other substances. To make matters worse, many of the younger adolescents, ages 12 to 15, vehemently deny that there is anything wrong with them and strongly resist taking medication or participating in any other interventions.

A multidimensional intervention approach is therefore essential to address these complex issues. Because ADHD is a lifelong disorder, we need to teach adolescents coping strategies they can use across time, but in this era of managed care, we need to adopt a short-term treatment philosophy. The majority of ADHD adolescents and their parents benefit from an intensive burst of 10–20 sessions of a flexible combination of family and individual therapy spaced over several months. Afterwards, the patient needs regular follow-up several times per year to help maintain new routines and environmental changes. Periodically, at major developmental transition points, the adolescent and the family may need another short-term burst of therapy.

Prioritizing Treatment Goals

Figure 14.2 provides a comprehensive flow chart for decision making and prioritizing treatment goals for this initial burst of therapy. The practitioner first needs to decide whether the adolescent is out of control in an antisocial, aggressive, and/or substance-abusing manner (e.g., comorbid diagnosis of CD or Substance Abuse Disorder). If either or both of these conditions apply, they become the highest-priority treatment goals. In the case of substance abuse, one decides whether the severity of the problem merits immediate referral to a substance abuse specialist or whether to proceed with the treatment program while monitoring substance use through, for example, random urine or breathalyzer testing. If the adolescent is using marijuana or alcohol on a recreational basis on weekends or even once or twice a week and he or she makes a genuine commitment to work toward curtailing drug use, I usually keep the case but arrange for urine or breathalyzer testing. More frequent marijuana or alcohol use, or any use of cocaine, heroine, hallucinogens, or other drugs, is cause for an immediate referral to a substance abuse specialist, who triages the patient to either an inpatient or outpatient substance abuse program.

In the case of conduct-disordered, out-of-control behavior, the practitioner should undertake an intensive outpatient family intervention designed to restore reasonable parental controls through the use of strategic/structural family interventions. If several months of intensive outpatient family therapy fail to restore parental controls, the practitioner should consider out-of-home placements for the adolescent. Such placements might include inpatient psychiatric hospitalization, therapeutic foster care, residential treatment, or even military school in certain cases.

In the majority of cases, the practitioner will proceed down the left-hand column of the flow chart in Figure 14.2. The adolescent and his or her family is next provided with comprehensive ADHD education, designed to instill the coping attitudes and expectations necessary to benefit from the remainder of the interventions. Because the natural developmental changes of adolescents render many youngsters highly resistant to acceptance of chronic conditions such as ADHD and their treatments, ADHD education assumes a very important role. Such education takes place over several weeks through direct discussions in family and individual sessions, bibliotherapy, videotapes, referrals to local and national support groups, and putting the adolescent in touch with peers who have ADHD who can serve as positive role models. Of course, like many facets of a comprehensive intervention, ADHD education continues for a long time beyond the initial efforts made by the practitioner.

Getting medication started is the next phase of intervention. If medication is to be prescribed, it is important to begin it early in the overall intervention, to help break the cycle of past failure and conflict abruptly and to have time to adequately titrate the dose and maximize the synergistic potential of medication plus educational and behavioral/psychological interventions. However, it is crucial to start medication after family ADHD education; a common error is to start medication immediately upon diagnosis, without taking adequate time to make sure the adolescent understands and accepts medication. Such an error is likely to result in premature rejection of medication, sometimes leading the adolescent to feel that the practitioner is not truly interested in him or her as a person but rather only interested in pleasing the parents by drugging the adolescent into compliance.

Whether to target school performance or home conflict next is the next decision point. If the family initially contacted me because of school performance problems, I usually target school problems first; if the family initially contacted me because of home conflict, I target this area first. Most times, both school and home issues were presenting problems, and I make a decision together with the family to prioritize targets. Most families choose school problems as higher priority than home conflict, and other things being equal, this is the preferred sequence. In cases of pure ADHD without comorbid ODD, most home-based conflicts are related to school issues such as homework or low grades. Targeting school performance first is a parsimonious approach because improvement in this area typically results in amelioration of home conflict, reducing the need for lengthy interventions focused on parent–teen

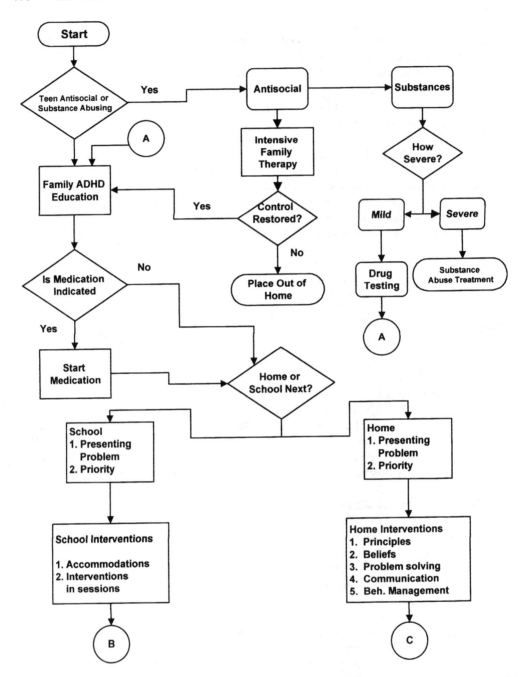

FIGURE 14.2. Prioritizing treatment goals.

conflict. More important, failure at school may have more devastating short-term consequences for the adolescent than continued home conflict.

School- and home-based interventions comprise the real meat of the initial burst of
treatment for adolescents with ADHD and often take 75% of the therapy sessions to complete. In cases of comorbid ODD, the parenting/home conflict interventions may take additional time. As the adolescent begins to experience success at school and the family begins

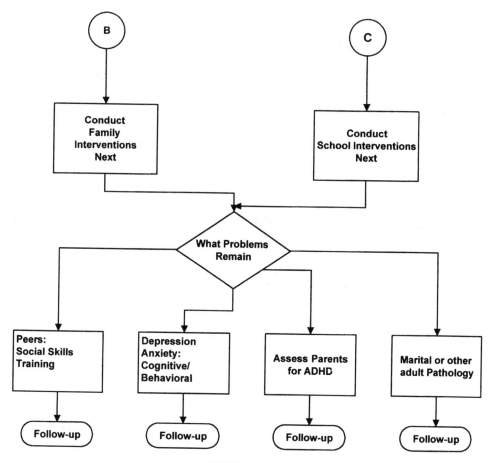

FIGURE 14.2. (*cont.*)

to integrate solution-oriented communication and effective parenting principles into their natural response styles, the therapist assesses the need to address any residual problems. Such residual problems often include peer relationship issues, anxiety or depression, possible ADHD in the parents or siblings, or parental marital and/or personal problems. Individual cognitive-behavioral and supportive interventions are helpful for addressing adolescent or parent anxiety, depression, or related issues. Social skills group interventions may be used for peer relationship problems, as long as the practitioner keeps in mind the lack of evidence for the generalizability and builds in procedures to spur generalization. Conjoint marital therapy is sometimes needed for the parents' marital conflicts.

In the last few sessions of the initial burst of intervention, the therapist lengthens the interval between sessions to 3 and then 4 weeks, helps the family consolidate the gains they have made, and shifts into the "dental checkup" model of follow-up care. Most families enthusiastically appreciate the idea of periodic ADHD checkups several times per year.

Typically, the 20 sessions are divided as follows: sessions 1–2 cover family ADHD education, session 3 covers medication issues, sessions 4–9 cover school success interventions, sessions 10–17 cover home/parenting/family interventions, sessions 18–20 focus on other issues, gradually fading out to the dental checkup follow-up mode. In the following sections of the chapter, each "module" of this multidimensional intervention is reviewed. Restoring parental control for the severely behavior disordered adolescent is discussed after family/home interventions, even though the therapist may need to implement this intervention earlier.

Family ADHD Education

The goal of family ADHD education is to deal with the full spectrum of reactions to the ADHD diagnosis, spur understanding and acceptance of the ADHD diagnosis, and develop in the adolescent and his or her family the kind of coping, positive attitudes compatible with active participation in the multifaceted treatments discussed in this book. Typically, this is more challenging with the adolescent than with the parent. The practitioner begins this process at the feedback session, where the results of the diagnostic evaluation are conveyed to the adolescent and the parents, and continues it over the course of the first few therapy sessions. Of course, emotional acceptance takes time; thus ADHD education becomes an ongoing issue throughout the entire course of therapy.

We find it helpful to conceptualize family ADHD education process as having four, broad and somewhat overlapping stages: (1) give the facts about ADHD and state the treatment options; (2) listen to the reactions to the presentations of the facts and the treatment options; (3) apply cognitive restructuring and reattributional techniques to correct myths and false beliefs and instill positive, coping attitudes toward ADHD; and (4) collaboratively establish the specific treatment goals and tailor the treatment options to the particular adolescent and his or her family. It is usually better to go through these steps separately with the adolescent and the parents because: (1) parents and adolescents have very different reactions and issues to be dealt with, and some steps are more applicable to parents whereas others are more applicable to adolescents; (2) separate meetings signals to the adolescent that the practitioner respects him or her as an individual whose opinions and ideas are important and worthwhile apart from the parents' ideas; (3) family interaction problems are removed as a source of variance from ADHD education; and (4) the adolescent may open up more in the absence of the parents. We usually need to spend a great deal more time on outlining the treatment options and tailoring them to the family with the parents, and a great deal more time on listening to the reactions and using cognitive restructuring to correct myths and instill positive attitudes with the adolescents.

Give the Facts

We usually start by making a clear statement that ADHD applies to the adolescent, giving a brief definition of ADHD, discussing its neurobiological/genetic etiology with the aide of concrete information such as a photograph of the positron emission tomography (PET) scans from Zametkin's classic study (Zametkin et al., 1990) and highlighting how it impairs the quality of their life in practical ways to which teenagers can relate. We talk in short, simple sentences which teenagers can understand, incorporate things the teenagers previously told us into our explanations, and pause often to check for understanding and questions. If the adolescent does not spontaneously bring up the most common myths about ADHD and its treatment, we bring them up and debunk them.

The following points, illustrated here in the language used with teenagers, need to be covered throughout this presentation, although not necessarily all in one meeting or in the order given here:

1. ADHD is a disorder involving difficulty paying attention, controlling the urge to act before thinking, and feeling or acting restless.
2. You are not crazy or sick if you have ADHD. It is an invisible disability that represents the extremes of traits or characteristics that all people exhibit to a more or lesser degree.
3. ADHD usually lasts a lifetime but changes as you mature and grow older. In par-

ticular, the restlessness changes from more physical to more mental, but the inattention and impulsivity remain.

4. ADHD affects all areas of your life, not just school. It may influence how you get along with other people, how you relate in intimate interpersonal situations, how organized you are at home, how you do in sports and hobbies, how easily you fall asleep and wake up, how you feel about yourself, and how you do on the job in the future.

5. ADHD is not your fault, your parents' fault, or anyone's fault. It is a physical disorder, usually inherited, and is caused by a mild chemical imbalance in the brain.

6. Chemicals called neurotransmitting chemicals which pass signals for self-control throughout the brain aren't operating efficiently in ADHD people. It would be like having too little brake fluid in your car; when you press the brake pedal, you can't stop. When an idea to do something pops into the ADHD person's mind, they can't stop and think whether it is good or bad before they do it, because the chemicals which help the brain stop and think aren't working properly.

7. Because ADHD usually is inherited, it is possible that your parents, brothers or sisters, or other relatives also have ADHD, even if they don't know it. If you have kids some day, they may also have ADHD. This could make family life like a real rollercoaster!

8. ADHD is also influenced by your environment, for example, your parents, your school, your friends. A good family, a good school, and good friends can make life a lot easier for the person with ADHD.

9. ADHD is a challenge, not an excuse. You are still responsible for your actions, even though you have a physical disorder which makes it harder for you to control your actions.

10. ADHD is influenced by your physical health. It will be easier to deal with ADHD if you take proper care of yourself, for example, get enough sleep, maintain good nutrition, don't smoke or put drugs or alcohol in your body, and exercise regularly.

11. Because ADHD is inherited and physical, we can't totally cure or eliminate it. Instead, we can help you learn to cope so life goes well for you. There are three general methods for learning to cope: (1) medical, (2) behavioral/psychological, and (3) educational. We will talk about these in detail as time goes on.

Listen to the Reactions to the Presentation

After presenting the facts, the practitioner listens carefully to the adolescent's reactions, using active listening to clarify how he or she is feeling but not challenging or being confrontational. It is very important for adolescents to feel that they have been listened to and understood, and their opinions have been taken seriously, as in the past their ideas may have often been discounted by adults. Let us look at an example of 15-year-old Bill, voicing his concerns about the diagnosis of ADHD:

BILL: So if I have ADHD, does this mean I am dumb and have a bad brain?

DR. ROBIN: You're feeling like having ADHD means you're stupid.

BILL: All the retards on the special education bus go to the office to get their pills at lunch. The whole football team whips their butts at gym.

DR. ROBIN: You would be very embarrassed if you had to go to the office and take a pill at lunch. It would make you feel like a retard, and you think your friends on the football team would give you a hard time about it.

BILL: Yeah, this is the kiss of death for me. My parents are going to freak out and take me to a million doctors, tutors, and shrinks. I'll probably miss football practice and get kicked off the team! And they will make me take medicine that will make me weird.

DR. ROBIN: So ADHD is going to mess up your whole life, take away all your free time and fun, and make you into a zombie?

BILL: Yeah, and just when Jennifer was starting to like me too. Now Mike will get her for sure.

DR. ROBIN: You will also strike out with girls? This all sounds like a nightmare.

BILL: Yeah.

As Bill voices his fears and anxieties about peer ridicule, feeling stupid, having to go to a lot of doctors, getting kicked off the football team, losing his freedom and never having a girlfriend, I empathetically clarify them but do not yet deal with them. Many adolescents might be thinking what Bill verbalized, but it could take many sessions before they become comfortable confiding their worries in the therapist, although an advantage of being impulsive is that they often blurt out their worries despite their desire to hide them.

Dealing with Reactions: Application of Cognitive Restructuring

Cognitive restructuring and reattributional techniques, two of the mainstays of cognitive-behavioral therapy (Braswell & Bloomquist, 1991), are applicable techniques for dealing with adolescents' negative reactions to the ADHD diagnosis. Typically, one or more of the following types of distorted beliefs underlies the negative reaction:

1. ADHD is a life sentence; my life is over. I'll never amount to anything.
2. This means I am really dumb, stupid, crazy, or a bad person. All the bad things my parents and teachers have said about me are really true.
3. I'll never have any friends anymore; they will all think I'm a total nerd.
4. I'll never have any fun because I will have to spend all my time with tutors, doctors, and therapists.
5. Medication will change my personality in bad ways. I like being wild, loud, and crazy. This is me, who I am, and no one is going to change me.
6. I'm different from my friends and I'll never be normal.
7. I've really messed up now. It's all my fault.
8. This whole ADHD thing is bull; it's just one more way my parents are trying to control my life.

These beliefs are really variations on the underlying extreme belief themes of ruination, autonomy, and perfectionism, to which adolescents commonly adhere (Robin & Foster, 1989): (1) ruination—this ADHD diagnosis is going to ruin my life, fun, and friends; (2) autonomy—having ADHD will take away or limit my freedom; or (3) perfectionism—now the world will know I'm less than a perfect person and that's terrible. We will revisit these beliefs later within the context of parenting and family conflict.

In cognitive restructuring with adolescents, the therapist tactfully collaborates with the patient to (1) identify the distorted belief, (2) provide a logical challenge to it, (3) suggest a more reasonable belief, and (4) help the patient discover based on collection of evidence that the reasonable belief is more valid than the unreasonable belief (Robin & Foster, 1989). Often, reframing negatively valenced ideas or thoughts to more positive motives or connotations is used along with cognitive restructuring.

Let us see how cognitive restructuring might proceed with Bill:

DR. ROBIN: I understand how you feel that ADHD will mess up your whole life, but before we jump to any quick conclusions, let's look at the evidence.

BILL: What evidence? I'm done, finished, all washed up!

DR. ROBIN: Start with the idea that you are dumb. On the IQ test I just gave you, you received a score of one hundred fifteen, which is above average. You may feel like you are dumb, but in fact you are smart. ADHD has nothing to do with being smart or dumb.

BILL: If I'm so smart, why do I do dumb things like spray paint on the garage?

DR. ROBIN: Good question. Your brain is like an expensive sports car without any brake fluid. We all get crazy ideas popping into our minds. People without ADHD press the brake pedal and it works; they don't act on their crazy ideas. People with ADHD press the brake pedal and nothing happens. They just keep on acting. This has nothing to do with IQ. You have a high IQ, just as the sports car has a great engine. But without brake fluid, the car won't stop, no matter how good the engine is. Let's take your worry about having to go to the office to take pills and your friends teasing you. First of all, not everyone with ADHD takes medication. You would only take medication if you agree to, after you fully understand it. But let's say you did agree. We now have medicines which you take once in the morning and they last all day, so the only way your friends will know about it is if you tell them.

BILL: Great! Those drugs would make me into a weird zombie all day then.

DR. ROBIN: The truth is, most people don't feel any different on medicine for ADD, except they are not as hungry while it is in their body. Are any of your good friends on medicine for ADHD?

BILL: You wouldn't catch me hanging out with those retards.

DR. ROBIN: Do you know a kid named Danny Jones?

BILL: Danny Jones? Sure. The whole school knows him. He is captain of the football team, Mr. Cool. Every girl in school goes nuts over him. But he is really a great guy.

DR. ROBIN: He has ADHD and takes medicine for it every morning.

BILL: No way. Not Danny. He's too cool. Doc, you're kidding, right?

DR. ROBIN: Nope. Don't take my word for it. Ask him. He is glad to talk about it privately, and he gave me permission to tell other teens with ADHD about it, but he has no reason to announce it on the overhead speaker system in school. And don't forget to ask him whether medicine makes him feel weird.

The steps of cognitive restructuring flowed together in this case example. The discussion of the IQ test illustrates challenging a distorted belief with the introduction of a more reasonable alternative and clear-cut evidence to back it up. The introduction of the highly regarded positive peer model who happens to have ADHD is the most potent type of evidence for changing beliefs about ADHD in teenagers because peers are such an important part of their lives. It behooves clinicians who work with adolescents to develop a referral list of such positive ADHD peer models in the local areas in which they work. Of course, the peers must consent in writing to have their names released. Clinical experience strongly suggests that adolescents will be more convinced to accept and cope with ADHD by their peers than by adults.

The use of books and audiovisual materials on ADHD written by adolescents for adolescents and the orchestration of teen forum group sessions directed by adolescents are additional techniques for fostering understanding and acceptance of ADHD. Several such books and videos are commercially available (Amen & Amen, 1995; Gordon, 1993; Quinn, 1995; Schubiner, 1995). In addition, organizations such as Children and Adults with Attention Deficit Disorder (CHADD) and the National Attention Deficit Disorder Association (ADDA) schedule teen-directed sessions for adolescents at their national conferences and through their regional chapters.

Collaborative Treatment Planning

The last phase of the family ADHD education process with the adolescent is collaborative treatment planning. Let us return to Bill as I directly approach him about participating in treatment.

Dr. Robin: We have one last thing to talk about— exactly what you are going to do and how your parents, teachers, and I am going to help you deal with ADHD. For one, are you now willing to consider medication as one way to deal with ADHD?

Bill: I guess so.

Dr. Robin: I'm not asking you to take it for sure, but just to go talk to a friend of mine, Dr. Jones, who specializes in medicine for ADHD teens. Agreed?

Bill: OK. What else?

Dr. Robin: Do you want your parents off your case at home? And your teachers off your case at school?

Bill: Sure. How?

Dr. Robin: You got to be willing to learn some new habits. I am willing to be like a coach and give you ideas and guide you, if you will come in several times, but you will have to do the work.

Bill: Will I have to come at this time? I'm missing one of my favorite TV shows?

Dr. Robin: Absolutely not. We can find another time.

Bill: I'll try.

The therapist continues to discuss and formulate the treatment goals with the adolescent, interacting in this informal manner. Now that the therapist has taken the time to listen to and deal with the adolescent's reactions, the teenager is more cooperative. Most of the time, this strategy works. But the practitioner needs to be prepared to be patient in those minority of cases in which the adolescent's resistance lasts a longer time. With some 12- to 14-year-old adolescents, it is very difficult to enlist them collaboratively in the treatment process. Occasionally, the only reasonable strategy to follow is to decide to treat the case as if the young teenager were an 8- or 9-year-old and work with the parents on a management approach, without regularly involving the adolescent. Clearly the less preferred approach, this is nonetheless sometimes necessary.

Getting Medication Started

Whether or not medication will be prescribed is determined in the next session. If medication is to be prescribed, it is important to begin it early in the overall therapy to have time to titrate the dose and maximize the synergistic potential of medication plus behavioral skill training. The clinical use of stimulant medication is discussed in detail in Chapter 17(this volume). When prescribing medication with adolescents, the physician must pay particular attention to ensure an adequate dose level, careful titration of morning and afternoon doses to particular academic activities, clear-cut criteria for evaluating outcome, careful attention to minimizing side effects, and adjustment of timing to provide adequate length of medication coverage throughout the day. I have all too commonly been asked to evaluate ADHD adolescents who are reportedly "medication nonresponders," only to find that the physician prescribed 5 mg of Ritalin (methylphenidate) to a 150-pound adolescent at 7:00 A.M. and 3:00 P.M. When the mother returns to the physician 3 months later to complain that there has been no improvement in her son's report card and no decrease in conflict at home, it is concluded that Ritalin "doesn't work!" Physicians working with adolescents need to use long-acting medications liberally, especially dextroamphetamine spansules, which do in fact last 7–8 hours and eliminate the need for a noon dose in school. In this chapter, the focus is not on the basic technical skills of using medication with teenagers but rather on how to present the use of medication to an adolescent.

Virtually all ADHD adolescents resist taking stimulant medication, whether or not they had positive experiences with it throughout their younger years. During a time of identity exploration marked by a fierce desire to be different from their parents but carbon copies of their peers, adolescents do not want to do anything that makes them feel different from their friends. Nor do they wish to follow regimens they perceive as imposed by adults—parents or physicians. They believe they know what is best for themselves and look on medication as a source of "external control" from which they need to "individuate." Teenagers who took Ritalin as younger children often complain that the medication calms them down too much, or as one athletic youngster said, "Ritalin takes away my killer instinct." What they mean is that they enjoy being wild and impulsive, which medication curbs. They also often attribute a variety of extraneous somatic complaints to Ritalin, even though most of these bear little relation to the psychostimulant. Thus, their resistance stems from basic developmental needs, as well as a history of poor parent–child relations.

A sensitive professional must present the use of stimulant medication to an adolescent within a context that takes these developmental factors into account. The traditional "doctor knows best" authoritarian presentation often backfires. A Socratic approach, which treats the adolescent as an independent decision maker who needs to perceive the advantages of stimulant medication before agreeing to take it, is preferable. The following excerpt from a session with an adolescent illustrates this approach:

DR. JONES: I understand that things are pretty rotten at school. Tell me about it.

BILL: Yeah. I'm getting lousy grades. And the teachers get on my case about talking out.

DR. JONES: How would you like your grades to be?

BILL: C's, B's, but at least passing.

DR. JONES: From all our past talks, it seems like keeping your mind on the work in school and at homework time has been tough, right?

BILL: Sure has. School's so boring. I can't make myself study, even if I want to. And all the noise in class bugs me.

DR. JONES: This is all part of the ADHD thing we've talked about before. Your body won't let your mind stay with things, through no fault of yours. Say, I've got an idea I'd like to run by you. You and I both wear glasses. When we take our glasses off, what happens?

BILL: Things look foggy.

DR. JONES: Right! We need glasses to see clearly. We didn't choose to need glasses. That's the way our bodies and eyes are, right?

BILL: I guess so.

DR. JONES: ADHD is similar. You didn't choose to have trouble with concentrating and thinking before acting. You body is just that way. I don't have any glasses for concentration, but I do know of a medication called Ritalin which acts on your concentration like glasses do on your eyes.

BILL: What do you mean? I'm not taking any smart pills! Only retards need that.

DR. JONES: You feel like I think you're a retard because I'm suggesting medication?

BILL: All my friends make fun of those special ed kids on the bus who take pills at lunch.

DR. JONES: Bill, you have plenty of smarts. Remember, how I explained that you got a high score on the IQ tests?

BILL: Yeah

DR. JONES: And as for kids making fun of you, no one is going to know about the pills unless you tell. By the way, does wearing glasses make you or I retards?

BILL: I guess not.

DR. JONES: OK, fact is I can't drive a car without my glasses because I might get in an accident. People with ADHD concentration problems might get in accidents unless they do something to pay attention better.

BILL: You think mom might let me take driver's ed if I take this Ritalin stuff?

DR. JONES: I don't know. But I honestly can make a stronger case with your parents for anything that requires concentration—driver's ed, a new school, et cetera, if I know you are dealing with this ADHD thing.

BILL: Won't I get hooked on this stuff? Like dope. And won't I feel weird? There was some guy on TV who said Ritalin takes away your sex drive.

DR. JONES: Good questions. Not at all. You don't get addicted to Ritalin. You don't feel much different; in fact, your teachers and parents may see more change than you. And believe me, Ritalin does nothing to your sex drive. That's bull.

BILL: When do I start these pills? Can we talk to my mom about driving today?

Dr. Jones first established that Bill wished to improve his school performance and that increased concentration was essential. Then, he used the analogy of visual impairment to provide a rationale for stimulant medication. When Bill objected, he empathized with Bill's concerns but provided accurate information about Ritalin. By linking concentration to driving, he suggested a possible reinforcer for compliance with a medication regimen. Bill reached a decision that the advantages outweighed the disadvantages, particularly as he realized that good concentration might result in privileges such as driving. Professionals must help the adolescent decide on a goal for change linked to the use of medication, take the time to listen to the adolescent's concerns about stimulant medication, create an empathetic context for the provision of accurate information, and then help the adolescent weigh the advantages versus the disadvantages of the medication. In the course of providing information about medication, it is often helpful to cite anecdotal and quantitative data about past experiences of other adolescents with stimulant medication. For example, when adolescents express concern about the side effects of Ritalin, we often report the following data concerning the percentage of 52 successively referred ADHD adolescents at the Children's Hospital of Michigan ADD Clinic who reported side effects at the first return visit after starting Ritalin (mean daily dose = 25.8 mg; range = 10 to 60 mg): (1) decrease in appetite, 34%; (2) trouble falling asleep, 23%; (3) stomachache, 23%; (4) headache, 10%; (5) sadness, 8%; (6) getting more hyper, 8%; and (7) motor tics/twitches, 2%. Such data suggest a relatively low percentage of overall side effects.

If the adolescent persists in refusing to take medication, other interventions should be explored. Imposing medication upon a teenager without informed consent is not only ineffective but also unethical. The physician might try making a contract with the adolescent that if school grades improve, medication will not be mentioned again, but if other interventions prove insufficient to improve school grades, the adolescent would be willing to reconsider medication at the end of the next marking period.

Enhancing Academic Success

Adolescents with ADHD commonly present with one or more of the following school difficulties: (1) failure to complete their homework, (2) poor understanding of material, (3) poor study habits, (4) low test grades, (5) coming to classes unprepared, (6) failing report card grades, (7) poor classroom participation and failure to ask teachers for needed help, (8) sloppy or illegible handwriting, (9) disrupting the classroom, (9) arguing with teachers, (10) getting in fights with peers, and (11) truancy. Many adolescents with ADHD also have associated learning problems with input, organization, memory, or output, which have resulted in learning disabilities in reading, written or oral expression, and mathematics. In sessions 4–9 the therapist identifies which of these difficulties applies to a given adolescent, decides which areas can be remedied through the therapy sessions and which areas require accommodations by the school, intervenes in the area targeted for therapy, and approaches the school to make accommodations in the other areas. Many of the suggestions in this section of the chapter are based on ideas developed in more detail by Davis, Sirotowitz, and Parker (1996), Markel and Greenbaum (1996), and Robin (in press).

The therapist begins by reviewing the checklist in Figure 14.3 with the adolescent and the parents to pinpoint specific school problems. Each item is rated on a 1 to 5 Likert scale, with higher numbers representing more positive ratings. Any items rated 3 or less are considered potential targets for change. All such items are highlighted and discussed with the family, also taking into consideration recent report cards, ability and achievement testing, recent teacher conferences, current special education or Section 504 services offered to the student by the school, teacher rating scales, and the adolescent's perceptions of which classes are difficult or easy. Over the course of sessions 4–9, the therapist develops and implements a flexible plan for remediating the areas found deficient in Figure 14.3. This plan clearly delineates the responsibilities of the student, the parents, the teachers, and the therapist, working as a collaborative team to enhance the student's academic success. I discuss strategies for

Name of student_____ School_____ Grade_____

Date_____ Name of therapist_____

The therapist should review each item on this checklist with the parents and adolescent, deter-mining whether it applies. Most of the items refer to the behavior of the adolescent; some refer to the actions of the teachers and school personnel. Rate each item on a 1–5 scale:

1 = Never   2 = A little   3 = Sometimes   4 = Often   5 = Always

HOMEWORK

_____ 1. Uses an assignment book
_____ 2. Does homework in nondistracting, quiet environment
_____ 3. Has an planful approach to the order for doing homework
_____ 4. Completes homework on time
_____ 5. Hands in homework on time
_____ 6. Spends sufficient time on homework
_____ 7. Keeps and follows a written plan with calendar for long-term assignments
_____ 8. Is currently up-to-date on homework

ORGANIZATION

_____ 9. Comes to class prepared with materials
_____ 10. Keeps notebooks, papers, study area organized and accessible
_____ 11. Uses calendar, schedule, planner to manage time
_____ 12. Keeps track of grades regularly/knows grading criteria
_____ 13. Brings home materials needed for homework
_____ 14. Keeps locker organized

TEST PREPARATION AND TEST TAKING

_____ 15. Spends sufficient time studying (e.g., doesn't cram at last minute)
_____ 16. Matches study to the type of questions on exam
_____ 17. Uses old tests to help prepare for upcoming exams
_____ 18. Has an organized approach to studying (e.g., SQ4R)
_____ 19. Has an organized approach to taking tests
_____ 20. Reads and follows directions carefully and doesn't respond impulsively
_____ 21. Writes legibly or uses word processor
_____ 22. Pays attention adequately during tests
_____ 23. Receives passing or higher grades on tests
_____ 24. Does not cheat
_____ 25. Remembers information during the test
_____ 26. Finishes the test within the allotted time
_____ 27. Manages anxiety effectively during tests

NOTE TAKING

_____ 28. Takes notes during lectures
_____ 29. Gets main points in notes
_____ 30. Notes are legible
_____ 31. Uses notes for studying
_____ 32. Notes are accurate

READING COMPREHENSION

_____ 33. Uses organized method such as SQ4R
_____ 34. Can identify topics, main ideas, and details
_____ 35. Understands what has been read
_____ 36. Underlines text effectively
_____ 37. Can answer questions about text
_____ 38. Can summarize what was read
_____ 39. Has method for learning new vocabulary in readings
_____ 40. Can pay attention while reading

FIGURE 14.3. Diagnostic Checklist for School Success.

MEMORIZING

_____ 41. Plans strategies for memorization
_____ 42. Selects facts to memorize accurately from notes, books, handouts
_____ 43. Knows own learning style (auditory, visual, kinesthetic, combined)
_____ 44. Matches memorization techniques to learning style
_____ 45. Rehearses sufficiently to memorize material
_____ 46. Distributes rehearsal over time (e.g., doesn't cram)
_____ 47. Uses acrastrics (silly sentences)
_____ 48. Uses acronyms
_____ 49. Uses charting, graphing
_____ 50. Uses visualization
_____ 51. Uses word, sentence association techniques
_____ 52. Recalls information when needed

CLASSROOM PARTICIPATION AND CONDUCT

_____ 53. Attends all classes
_____ 54. Gets to class on time
_____ 55. Participates in discussion
_____ 56. Volunteers answers to questions
_____ 57. Is with the class when called on by the teacher
_____ 58. Cooperates with teacher
_____ 59. Raises hand and doesn't call out of turn
_____ 60. Follows classroom rules
_____ 61. Talks respectfully to teachers
_____ 62. Relates positively to peers
_____ 63. Asks for help when needed

UNDERSTANDING/PROCESSING PROBLEMS

_____ 64. Student understands material
_____ 65. Student decodes accurately
_____ 66. Student comprehends what is read
_____ 67. Handwriting is legible
_____ 68. Student can express thoughts in writing
_____ 69. Student can express thoughts orally
_____ 70. Student understands mathematical concepts
_____ 71. Mathematical calculation is accurate

SCHOOL RESPONSIBILITIES

_____ 72. Individual education program or 504 plan exists in writing
_____ 73. Written plan meets needs outlined above
_____ 74. Written plan is adequately implemented
_____ 75. Content area teachers are familiar with plan
_____ 76. Case manager appointed to monitor plan
_____ 77. Teachers are accountable for providing accommodations
_____ 78. Informal accommodations (not in writing)
_____ 79. School keeps parents informed of student progress

SOCIAL SCENE

_____ 80. Adolescent has close friends at school
_____ 81. Friends encourage academic success and prosocial behavior
_____ 82. Student is satisfied with his or her social life

FIGURE 14.3. (*cont.*)

enhancing completion of homework and test preparation and test taking in detail here because they are the most common therapeutic targets. Readers interested in more details about interventions for the other areas in the checklist should consult Markel and Greenbaum (1996) and Robin (in press).

Homework

The therapist conducts a logical analysis of where in the homework process there is a breakdown and aims the interventions at these weak links. The logical analysis is translated directly into a homework contract specifying how these points of breakdown will be overcome. Each of the following questions leads directly to components of this contract. Does the adolescent reliably and accurately write down the homework assignments in an assignment book, sheet, or some other organized medium? Are certain classes more of a problem than others in this regard, and if so, why? Does the adolescent bring home from school the assignment book, textbooks, notebooks, and other materials needed to complete homework? Do the parents monitor the assignment book? Is there a backup plan for getting the assignment if the adolescent forgets to bring it home? Does the adolescent have a quiet, nondistracting, well-lit, and comfortable place in which to do the homework? Are pens, pads, index cards, a computer, and other needed resources easily accessible and neatly organized in the room? Is there an agreed-upon time for starting homework, and does the adolescent have difficulty getting started at the agreed-upon time? Is there consistency in time and location for doing homework over days and weeks? Will a parent be in the house when the adolescent is supposed to be doing homework, to monitor and "keep the adolescent honest"? Does the adolescent have an organized plan of attack to sequence multiple homework assignments in one evening? To what extent does the adolescent become easily distracted and unable to concentrate and persist for the time it takes to get homework done? To what extent can the adolescent keep track of and manage time while doing his or her homework? Is it taking inordinate amounts of time despite good concentration because of a slow cognitive tempo or reading/writing difficulties? Is a calendar used to track long-term projects and upcoming tests, and does the adolescent break these larger tasks down into smaller units, working gradually through these units?

Are the parents actively involved in tracking completion of homework, and have they learned to achieve the delicate balance between confrontational intrusiveness and disengagement? How does the adolescent divide the time between the next day's assignments versus working on long-term projects? What steps does he or she take after completing the assignment to make sure that it will get to school and be handed in on time? How severe are the conflicts between the parent and adolescent about homework, and has homework become a battleground for adolescent independence seeking? If homework has become a battleground for independence, have the parents hired a tutor or other neutral party to work with the adolescent, separating parent–adolescent relationship issues from homework issues?

The homework contract clearly delineates the adolescent's, parents', teachers', and therapist's own role in the homework process (Markel & Greenbaum, 1996). The teacher's role is to give the student a rationale for doing homework, base homework on skills that have already been learned and need reinforcement or practice (not to ask students to learn new skills on their own or to ask parents to teach new skills), clearly give the assignment and outline expectations for its completion, grade the completed assignment and give feedback to the students about their homework in a timely manner, and keep parents informed when students fall behind on homework for more than 2 or 3 days. In addition, secondary education teachers need to keep in mind that there is life after school and to make the amount of homework realistic. When there is an accommodation plan, the teachers are also expected to implement the accommodations relevant to homework. The student's role is certainly to complete the homework, but it goes beyond this. Students are expected to keep track of what homework is assigned, develop a homework plan with assistance from their parents, decide when and where to do their homework with input from their parents, follow the homework plan without needing to be nagged, ask for help when they need it, complete their homework to the best of their ability, check it over for mistakes and legibility, and hand it in on time.

The parents' role is to stay involved in the structuring of their youngster's homework. (Even though most teenagers should take full responsibility for their own homework, it is not usually possible for teenagers who have ADHD.) Specifically, parental involvement includes helping the student develop a homework plan; providing the student with a nondistracting, comfortable location for doing homework; providing the student with the basic materials; being in the house to monitor compliance with the homework plan when they expect homework to be done; helping the student analyze homework problems when the student asks for help; expecting the adolescent to adhere to the plan; administering any agreed-upon positive or negative consequences for doing or not doing homework; and communicating regularly with the teachers to track whether homework has been completed and discuss any homework problems that arise. The therapist's role is to guide the adolescent and family in determining where the breakdown in the homework process is, to provide guidance and direct instruction for fixing the breakdown, and to help coordinate efforts between the school and family around homework issues.

Figure 14.4 illustrates such a very detailed homework contract for Michael Adams. Michael's contract includes sections related to keeping track of assignments, bringing home materials, setting and scheduling homework, prioritizing, medication, turning in assignments, feedback, and consequences. All of the homework problems outlined earlier are addressed in this contract. Many students require much shorter contracts, targeting only one or two of these areas. The therapist helps the family enlist the teachers in carrying out their part of the contract, assigns the family the task of carrying out its part, and over several sessions, follows up to see whether everyone complies with his or her roles in the contract, fine tuning the details and dealing with implementation problems and resistance.

Test Preparation and Test Taking

Adolescents with ADHD may do poorly on tests and examinations for a variety of reasons, including (1) difficulty understanding the material covered; (2) insufficient time studying or cramming at the last minute; (3) not knowing how to study for different types of tests; (4) poor use of memorization techniques; (5) reading and writing deficiencies which interfere with understanding and responding to the test questions; (6) difficulty remembering and organizing the information and writing it down during the test; (7) slow reading rate or lethargic cognitive tempo, resulting in inability to complete the test within the allotted time period; (8) difficulty maintaining attention during the test; (9) impulsive tendency to rush through the objective tests and pick the first answer read without thinking carefully; (10) careless mistakes resulting from failure to read the directions or overlooking important details such as responding in the correct box on scantron sheets; and (11) test anxiety. Students can be helped to overcome these difficulties with test preparation and test taking through a combination of direct instruction and accommodations.

A therapist external to the school can teach the adolescent how to prepare for different types of tests, how to take different types of tests efficiently, and how to manage test anxiety and can help the parents structure the study situation effectively for the adolescent. The teachers and school administrators need to be willing to make the accommodations that may be

I, Michael Adams, and my parents, my teachers, my guidance counselor, and Dr. Jones agree to carry out to the best of our ability the following homework plan:

I. Keeping track of assignments

    A. My teachers will write the assignments on the board every day. They will also give a copy of all the assignments for the week to Mrs. Smith, my guidance counselor, each Monday. She will keep a copy and mail a copy home to my parents.

    B. I will write down the assignment from the board every day before I leave each class. I will write it in the section of my assignment book for that subject. I will read over what I have written down to make sure I understand it. I will ask the teacher to explain any assignment I do not understand.

    C. During my last-period study hall, I will read over each assignment I have written down and make sure I understand what I am being asked to do. I will make a list of all of the materials I need to bring home and gather them from my locker. My study hall teacher agrees to give me a hall pass to go to my locker and find any materials I need during last period.

II. Bringing home materials

    A. I will bring home all the materials I have gathered and my assignment book.

    B. My mother agrees to ask me nicely one time without nagging to see my list of assignments. I agree to show it to her without a big hassle or an attitude.

    C. As a backup in case I forget to write the assignment down, I will pick a study buddy in each of my classes, get that person's phone number, and post those phone numbers on the refrigerator door.

III. Schedule and setting for doing homework

    A. From Sunday through Thursday, I agree to work on homework from 6:00 P.M. to 8:00 P.M. If I finish early, I will show my completed work to a parent, and if he or she agrees that it is completed, I can do whatever I want.

    B. I will do my homework at the big desk in the den. I can listen to soft music with headphones but no loud rock. If I find myself getting distracted, I will take a short break, do something physical (not telephone), and start working again.

    C. My mother will remind me once without nagging to start on my homework at 6:00 P.M. I will start without an attitude.

IV. Daily plan for organizing homework completion

    A. With help from my mother, I will make an organized plan for each night's homework. This plan will guide me in what subject I will do first, second, etc. It will also divide up homework time between assignments due tomorrow and long-term assignments. My mother agrees to permit me to determine the order of doing homework.

    B. In my plan, I will estimate the time needed to complete each assignment, as well as how I will check each assignment over for accuracy, completeness, and legibility.

    C. The plan will specify how often I will take breaks during homework time, how long the breaks will be, and how large assignments will be divided into smaller units.

    D. The plan will specify where I will put the completed assignments and how I will make sure I turn the work in.

V. Medication. I agree to take a dose of Ritalin at 5:00 P.M. on Sunday through Thursday, to help me concentrate on homework.

VI. Turning in assignments

    A. As I finish an assignment, I will put it in the section of my binder for that class

    B. I will do my best to remember to hand in each assignment.

VII. Feedback. My teachers agree to tell me how I did within 2 days after I hand in an assignment. They also agree to mail my parents feedback about how many of the last week's assignments were turned in on time when they send the next week's assignment list. The guidance counselor will collect these materials from the teachers and mail them out.

VIII. Rewards. My parents agree to let me make 20 minutes of long-distance phone calls to my girlfriend each night that I do my homework. If I do my homework for 5 nights in a row, they agree to let me make 45 minutes of long-distance phone calls on the weekend.

Signed,   *Michael Adams   Robert Adams   Barbara Adams   Bill Jones, Principal*
                Brenda Smith, Guidance Counselor   Millie Broadbent, Algebra   Tom Jones, English
                Darla Breeze, French   William Sonoma, Chemistry   F.A.O. Schwartz, Gym
                Neiman Marcus, History

FIGURE 14.4. The homework plan for Michael Adams.

necessary (extended time for testing, alternative evaluation methods, word processor for essays, etc.) and help the student with understanding the material; the therapist can help the adolescent and the family obtain the needed accommodations and services from the school regarding test taking.

Careful analysis of the Diagnostic Checklist for School Success will help the practitioner determine which test preparation and test-taking problems apply to a particular adolescent. In addition, the practitioner needs to decide how receptive the adolescent is to receiving help in test taking and, in the case of adolescents in denial about their test-taking problems, whether anything can be done to overcome their denial. For adolescents at least willing to commit to making a genuine effort to improve test taking, we recommend that the therapist (1) teach the adolescent a flexible, generalized approach to preparing for tests such as the modified SQ4R method discussed by Markel and Greenbaum (1996); (2) teach the adolescent specific skills for taking objective and essay exams; (3) teach the adolescent how to identify his or her preferred learning style (auditory, visual, kinesthetic) and use effective memorization techniques (Davis et al., 1996); and (4) attempt to get the content-area teachers and school support staff to make selected accommodations and give direct instruction in test taking tailored to each class.

In the SQ4R method, for example, the student is taught to survey questions, read and reflect, recite, write, and review and edit. First, in preparing for the test, the student is asked to *survey* the topics to be covered on the test to determine what material to study. This includes surveying any written materials about the test, the relevant textbooks, other readings, previous homework assignments, and class notes, culminating in identifying and listing the key topics and terms likely to be on the test. Second, the student attempts to predict what the test *questions* will be on all of the topics surveyed, locating sample questions in the book or handouts and creating different types of possible questions for each topic. The student should determine whether the test will consist of multiple-choice, fill-in, matching, or essay questions by talking to the teacher, so that the remaining stages can be customized to the format of the test questions. The sample questions should be generated in the same format as the test questions. Third, the student *reads and reflects* to locate and understand the information necessary to answer the sample questions, including tests, notes, handouts, and so on. At this stage the student needs to sort out essential from nonessential facts, details, or examples. Fourth, the student memorizes the necessary information by *reciting the answers to the questions*, allowing sufficient time and distribution of practice to effectively learn the material. Some students may benefit from reciting the answers or facts into a tape recording and listening back to themselves talking; others may benefit from reciting the material to a parent or even a peer in a group study session. It is at this stage that the practitioner deals with time management (planning study over several days to avoid cramming, etc.). Closely aligned to reciting is *writing answers to the questions*. Here the student needs to write the responses in the format likely to occur on the test to be fully prepared. Taking old exams or making up quizzes is helpful here. Writing is especially important with essay exams: The student needs to practice outlining, organizing, and actually committing to paper sample essays. The student needs to learn how much recitation and writing are necessary to be fully prepared for each examination through experimentation and practice. Finally, the student *reviews and edits* his or her written answers to the questions (both study and sample test questions), practicing checking for accuracy and completeness, identifying topics in need of elaboration, and identifying areas to be studied further. Parents and/or study buddies can be helpful at this stage.

The therapist can also give the adolescent helpful general hints about taking tests. For example, many ADHD students perseverate on the first difficult test item they encounter, becoming frustrated and running out of time before they can complete the test. They can be taught to check their negative emotional reaction to difficult items through coping self-in-structions ("It's only one item; I am going to skip it and not worry; I'll come back to it later."), to move on to the easier items, and if they have time at the end, return to the difficult items.

Their parents may need to help them practice these behaviors at home in a "mock" test situations. Many teenagers do not consider whether they are studying for the type of items on the test. Multiple-choice items require study focused on recognition tasks, whereas essay items require study emphasizing practice writing paragraphs in response to hypothetical test questions.

As things begin to fall into place for the adolescent in school, the therapist devotes less time in the sessions to these issues, and begins to move on to parenting, discipline, and family relations.

Home-Based Interventions: Overview

Over the course of sessions 10–17, we target problems between the parents and the adolescent at home in four stages: (1) present a framework and set of principles for parenting the ADHD adolescent, (2) use cognitive restructuring to help parents and adolescents adhere to reasonable expectations about their relationship, (3) teach problem-solving communication skills for conflict resolution, and (4) use strategic/structural interventions to restore parental control when necessary.

In keeping with the developmental tasks of adolescence, parents need to shift their parenting style more in a democratic direction to foster responsible independence-seeking behavior. The extremes of authoritarian control or permissiveness are not effective with ADHD adolescents, and although parents need to continue to structure situations and maintain ultimate control, they need to increase the involvement of the adolescent in decision making whenever feasible. We introduce parents to a set of principles for raising the adolescent with ADHD and ask them to watch a video tape elaborating on many of these principles (Robin and Weiss, 1997). Table 14.1. summarizes these principles. Then, we translate these principles into specific techniques for parents to survive on a day-to-day basis with their ADHD teenager. As we go over specific issues, we frequently refer to the list of principles, teaching parents to deduce additional interventions from them.

"Barkley's Basic 10" (Barkley, 1995) form the first part of our list of principles:

1. *Give the adolescent more immediate feedback and consequences.* Adolescents with short attention spans and impaired behavioral inhibition are more likely to stay on task when given immediate positive feedback contingent upon performance of boring and tedious tasks, coupled with mild negative consequences for shifting off task. Punishments given long after the misbehavior was committed are ineffective.

2. *Give the adolescent more frequent feedback.* ADHD adolescents benefit from frequently hearing nice things said about their actions and appearances, as well as from receiving frequent feedback and corrections for their errors. There are so many negatives in the life of the average ADHD adolescent which pull down the adolescent's self-esteem, that he or she desperately needs to hear frequently what he or she did right. We may need to teach busy parents creative ways to remember to give their adolescents frequent feedback.

3. *Use more powerful consequences.* Because ADHD children satiate easily on any one stimulus and respond best to highly salient stimuli, effective parenting involves using a wide variety of highly salient consequences, ranging from physical affection to verbal praise to material reinforcers.

4. *Use incentives before punishments.* It is a knee-jerk reaction for parents to ground an adolescent until the end of the next marking period when the adolescent receives a bad

TABLE 14.1. Principles for Parenting the Adolescent with ADHD

Barkley's Basic 10

1. Give the adolescent more immediate feedback and consequences.
2. Give the adolescent more frequent feedback.
3. Use more powerful consequences.
4. Use incentives before punishments.
5. Strive for consistency.
6. Act, don't yak.
7. Plan ahead for problem situations.
8. Keep a disability perspective.
9. Don't personalize the adolescent's problems or disorder.
10. Practice forgiveness.

Robin's Rest

11. Actively encourage and shape responsible independence-related behavior.
12. Divide the world of issues into those that can be negotiated and those that cannot.
13. Give explanations for the stated rules regarding nonnegotiable issues.
14. Involve the adolescent in decision making regarding negotiable issues.
15. Maintain good communication.
16. Actively monitor the adolescent's behavior outside the home.
17. Maintain structure and supervision for longer than you think you should.
18. Be the adolescent's cheerleading squad.
19. Encourage the adolescent to build on his or her strengths.

report card. Parents commonly load on immense punishments until they have used up all their ammunition and the adolescent has little else to lose by misbehaving. When parents wish to modify a behavior, such as poor study behavior, we need to train them to ask first what positive behavior they wish to see the adolescent perform and next how can they reinforce that positive behavior. Only after taking this step should they select a punishment for the negative behavior.

5. *Strive for consistency.* ADHD parents often give up easily on behavior change interventions at the first sign of failure. ADHD adolescents incessantly bicker with their parents, sometimes warring them down to the point where the parents back off. We need to help parents to stick with their interventions and demands (e.g., maintain consistency over time). "Divide and conquer" is also a motto of many ADHD adolescents, who have learned that if they can get mom and dad to disagree, they can avoid unpleasant effort and/or discipline. The divide-and-conquer principle is particularly common in step-families and divorced families, where natural structural changes give the coercive adolescent a golden opportunity to manipulate the system. Therapists need to help mothers and fathers work as a team (e.g., consistency across parents).

6. *Act, don't yak.* Many parents repeat themselves incessantly when their adolescents fail to comply with their requests. Adolescents quickly learn that mom or dad are "all talk, no action." We need to help parents learn that the time to talk is during family meetings and when negotiating solutions to disagreements, but after the rules have been stated and the consequences decided, it is the time to act, not yak.

7. *Plan ahead for problem situations.* Because many conflicts between parents and adolescents are highly predictable, it behooves therapists to help parents learn to anticipate and plan in advance to handle these situations. In a family where curfew violations have been a frequent problem, for example, the therapist might prepare the parents in advance for how they will respond at 2:00 A.M. when Sally comes home 2 hours late. Without such planning,

parents and adolescents often react based on emotion and do a lot of damage to their relationships in the heat of the moment.

8. *Keep a disability perspective.* This principle has to do with expectations and beliefs, which will be considered in depth later. Briefly, therapists need to help parents remember that their adolescents with ADHD have a neurobiologically based disability and that there is a "can't do" as well as a "won't do" component to their unthinking actions. Thus, parents can keep from overreacting with anger when their adolescents inevitably make mistakes.

9. *Don't personalize the adolescent's problems or disorder.* Closely aligned to the last principle, this principle is designed to help parents keep from blaming themselves or losing their personal sense of self-worth over their adolescent's problems.

10. *Practice forgiveness.* Parents need to forgive themselves for the mistakes they will inevitably make raising an ADHD adolescent and to forgive their adolescent for his or her mistakes. Adolescents should, however, be held accountable for their actions, and consequences should be administered as planned, but afterwards, parents should not "hold a grudge."

Nine additional principles—which we call "Robin's Rest"—have been derived from adolescent development research and the biobehavioral family systems model summarized earlier in the chapter.

11. *Actively encourage and shape responsible independence-related behavior.* Because becoming independent from the family is the primary developmental task of adolescence, and because ADHD individuals need extra guidance and learning trials to acquire new behaviors, parents need to look for opportunities to gradually give their adolescents more freedom in return for demonstrating responsibility. A parent might break the terminal independence response into small units and shape each behavior, moving on to the next step after the teenager has demonstrated responsibility on the last step. For example, one terminal behavior might be staying alone in the house for a weekend and taking proper care of the house (nothing left unlocked, nothing missing, lawn watered and pets fed, no wild parties, etc.). The parent might break this terminal behavior down into smaller units (staying in the house for an evening, a night, two nights, etc.). As the adolescent successfully accomplishes each step, the parent moves onto the next step.

12. *Divide the world of issues into those that can be negotiated and those that cannot.* There is an important distinction between issues that can be handled democratically and those that cannot. Each parent has a small set of bottom-line issues that relate to basic rules for living in civilized society, values, morality, and legality, which are not subject to negotiation. Such issues usually include drugs, alcohol, aspects of sexuality, religion, and perhaps several others. The remainder of issues can be negotiated between parents and adolescents. Each parent needs to clearly list and present to the teenager those issues that are nonnegotiable.

13. *Give explanations for the stated rules regarding nonnegotiable issues.* As mentioned earlier in the chapter, adolescents are more likely to accept nonnegotiable rules if they are legitimized with a compelling rationale rather than presented through pure power assertion ("Do it because I'm your mother or because I told you to"). Teenagers are developing the ability to reason abstractly and are better able to understand rationales for rules than when they were younger. Even if they do not agree with a parental restriction, they are less likely to rebel against it if they understand the reason for it than if the parent simply orders them to follow it. Parents show respect for the adolescent's emerging identity as an independent being by taking the time to give them reasons for decisions; power assertion negates the adolescent's emerging independence and insults his or her intelligence.

14. *Involve the adolescent in decision making regarding negotiable issues.* This is the single most important principle of parenting an adolescent, and it is one of the primary methods

of shaping responsible independence behaviors. Teenagers are more likely to comply with rules and regulations they helped to create. Furthermore, they may have novel and creative perspectives on issues because of their youth and unique position in the family. Often, their perspectives lead them to suggest novel solutions. Problem-solving training, discussed later in the chapter, is the primary technique for involving adolescents in decision making. Parents need to remember, however, that involvement in decision making does not necessarily mean always being an equal partner with parents and certainly does not mean dictating to parents. In some cases, parents may retain the ultimate veto over decisions. In other cases, adolescents may be equal partners with parents. Parents need to gradually increase the degree of involvement they give teenagers in decision making, through a shaping process.

15. *Maintain good communication.* Parents need to make themselves available to listen when their adolescents wish to talk but not to expect their adolescent to confide regularly in them. Parents and adolescents need to learn effective skills for listening to each other and expressing their ideas and feelings assertively but without putting down or hurting each other.

16. *Actively monitor the adolescent's behavior outside the home.* Parents should always know the answer to four basic questions: (a) Whom are your adolescents with? (b) Where are they? (c) What are they doing? (d) When will they be home? Research has shown that parents who cannot consistently answer these four questions have adolescents who are at risk for drifting into deviant peer groups, substance abuse, and delinquency (Patterson & Forgatch, 1987). Parents should also develop clear-cut "street rules" or rules for how they expect their adolescents to conduct themselves in the community outside of the home.

17. *Maintain structure and supervision for longer than you think you should.* Parents often ask when they can relax the increased structure they have created to monitor their adolescent's academic performance and home behavior. ADHD individuals need to be more closely monitored for their entire lives, but we expect them to learn to do some of their own monitoring and/or enlist the help of spouses and significant others in monitoring their actions by adulthood. Ideally, parents need to facilitate the transfer of monitoring to the adolescent throughout adolescence, but the reality is that most parents will continue the extra structure until the adolescent graduates high school, and in some cases beyond that.

18. *Be the adolescent's cheerleading squad.* ADHD adolescents need unconditional positive regard from their parents and focused positive time with their parents. Follow-up studies (Weiss & Hechtman, 1993) have found that successful ADHD adults say that the single most important thing during their adolescence was having at least one parent, or in some cases, an adult outside the family, who truly believed in their ability to succeed. ADHD adolescents need their parents to believe in them, to applaud their every positive achievement, and generally to be their cheerleading squad. They also need their parents to spend focused time with them; busy parents may not have a great deal of focused time to give, but it is the quality rather than the quantity of focused time that really matters.

19. *Encourage the adolescent to build on his or her strengths.* Many ADHD adolescents receive so much criticism they actually begin to believe that they are lazy and unmotivated. We need to teach parents to help the teenager identify those interests, hobbies, artistic pursuits, sports, and activities that are pockets of strength and help them pursue and succeed at these pursuits to build on their strengths.

Fostering Realistic Beliefs and Expectations

After introducing the 19 principles, I then focus primarily on the beliefs, expectations, and attitudes of the parents and the adolescent. This focus typically begins in session 11 and continues as needed throughout the remainder of the therapy. I used to teach problem-solving communication skills and behavioral contracting before focusing on beliefs and cognitions but found from clinical experience that many families have unrealistic expectations which interfered with applying these techniques, and that these beliefs ought to be addressed first. In the first half of the session, I meet with the parents; in the second half, I meet with the adolescent.

The parents are given a "crash course" in the basics of adolescent development to help foster realistic expectations. From a cognitive restructuring point of view, the crash course also represents a normalizing or reframing with a positive intent of much of the negative behavior adolescents inevitably emit. By presenting this information within the context of adolescent development, the therapist makes it easier for the parents to accept it without activating any natural defensive reactions they might otherwise have. The therapist is helping the parents learn to apply Barkley's principle 9—don't personalize the adolescent's problems—by distancing from the constant barrage of strange teenage behavior, understanding it within a developmental framework, and learning to prioritize what to respond to and what to ignore. The sensitive therapist will be cognizant of this attitudinal portion of the agenda and will monitor the parents' level of defensiveness and reactivity during the crash course, pacing his or her statements to shape their responses in productive directions.

The therapist reviews the five developmental tasks of adolescence discussed earlier in the chapter and points out that becoming a productive, happy, and personally fulfilled adult depends on successful accomplishment of these tasks. The adolescent is supposed to accomplish these tasks while getting along with his or her family and doing his or her schoolwork. The therapist helps the parents to realize that the adolescent has a great deal of work to do.

The nature of independence seeking or individuation from parents is explored in more depth. We find it useful to present the metaphor of a nation establishing its independence:

> "Imagine a nation establishing its independence, going from a dictatorship to a democracy. What often happens? This process does not typically go smoothly. There may be a bloody revolution with a great deal of fighting. Or if there isn't physical fighting, there is certainly a lot of verbal rhetoric and power plays. Why should you expect your family to make it through the independence seeking of your adolescence without a disturbance of the peace? A certain amount of conflict is inevitable and even healthy. I worry more about adolescents who never do anything rebellious than those to do rebel. This rebellion typically happens in early adolescence, between ages 12 and 14. In order to become independent, teenagers need to push against something, and parents are the something that they push against. Usually, the teenagers typically rebel more strongly against their mothers than their fathers. Wise parents learn how to channel their conflicts into more innocuous areas that have no ultimate impact on life. It is much better, for example, to have conflicts with your adolescent over how clean the room is than over sexuality and drugs."

We go on to help parents understand that it is natural for adolescents to reject established parental and other adult societal values during this process of individuation and to be embarrassed about being seen with their parents. To begin to establish their own identity, adolescents need to experiment with a variety of alternative ideas and values, usually those of their peers, and decide what they are comfortable with. At the same time this is happening, their bodies are changing very rapidly and their minds are maturing to the point where they now can think more abstractly. The multiple influences of rapid physical maturation, cognitive development, and emotional change are very unsettling to adolescents, leading them to have a fragile self-image. One response to this fragile self-image is to project an air of omnipotence or, put another way, to shy away from anything or anyone who suggests they are less than perfect physically or mentally. Thus, it is natural for the developing adolescent to be less than enthusiastic about disabilities, psychiatric diagnoses, chronic physical illnesses, or any other condition that could be seen as a further insult to an already fragile self-image. We help parents to understand that this is the basis for resistance to accepting the diagnosis of ADHD and its treatments.

The therapist then turns to the question of how ADHD interacts with these natural developmental tendencies during adolescence. Adolescents with ADHD undergo the same physical changes and face the same developmental challenges as other teenagers. They may experience the same desires for independence and freedom as other teenagers. Yet their social and emotional maturity may lag behind that of other teenagers. They may be less ready to assume the responsibilities that accompany more independence.

Specifically, teenagers with ADHD may lag behind other teenagers in the overall development of self-control and organization. Because of inefficient verbal and nonverbal working memory, they may be less able to exercise hindsight, forethought, and planning and to engage in future-oriented, goal-oriented behavior. Given the difficulties with self-regulation of affect, they may remain more likely to be victims of the moment, acting on impulse, self-centered and insensitive to the needs of others. Poor attention and follow-through make it more difficult for them to stick to discussions with their parents, carry out agreements with their parents, and finish homework. Impulsivity translates into increased moodiness (severe PMS for many teenage girls), hypersensitivity to criticism, emotional overreactivity, and poor judgment and low resistance to temptations. Hyperactivity often continues more as minor motor restlessness and mental restlessness than as overt physical overactivity. Such restless behavior is easily misinterpreted as "disrespect" by parents. Repeatedly badgering parents to get their way is another manifestation of hyperactivity in some adolescents with ADHD.

The ADHD symptoms become inextricably intertwined with the developmental changes of adolescence. Many parents ask the therapist whether a particular adolescent behavior is a result of ADHD or "just adolescence." They may be wondering whether to excuse or to punish the behavior. Did Stephanie really "forget" to put away the dishes, or was just she being "oppositional"? The answer usually is that the behavior is both an example of ADHD and the developmental changes of adolescence. We usually advise that the parent should hold the adolescent accountable for his or her actions and apply whatever consequence is warranted, but that the parent might temper his or her affective response and avoid attributing the adolescent's behavior to malicious motives. We often use the example of teenagers who get stopped by a policeman for going through a red light shortly after they get their license. The adolescent may tell the policeman that he failed to notice the red light because he has a disability and is protected under the Americans with Disabilities Act, but the policeman is not going to care. The adolescent will be held accountable for adherence to the traffic laws, regardless of his ADHD.

Next, I move on to address expectations and beliefs, reminding the parents of Barkley's principles 8 (keep a disability perspective), 9 (don't personalize the adolescent's problems or disorder), and 10 (practice forgiveness), and pointing out that we are now doing to discuss the beliefs and attitudes underlying these principles in more depth. Then, I might ask the parents to engage in the following mental imagery exercise, which vividly teaches people the connection between extreme thinking, negative affect, and behavioral overreactions:

> "Close your eyes, and imagine you are opening the mail and you find a progress report from your son's school. The progress report indicates that he is failing English and Math, and has fifteen late assignments in History. Suddenly you can feel your blood begin to boil and the tension mount throughout your body. Your son lied to you again! He said he was up to date on homework and passing all of his courses. This is one more example

of irresponsible behavior. He is always irresponsible. You told him to keep an assignment book. And get help from the teachers. He never does what he is told. He is so disobedient. If he keeps on going this way in school, he is going to fail out. He will never graduate, never go to college, and never get a good job. You will be supporting him until the day you die. And the thought of confronting him is not appealing at all. He will deny it all at first, then blame it all on the teachers, showing you total disrespect. He is just doing all of this to get you mad and upset. He has no consideration for your feelings. Now open your eyes, and tell me how you feel and what you are thinking. And also, tell me how you would react if your son walked through the door at this very moment?"

Through a Socratic discussion, the therapist helps the parents to realize how the extreme thinking evokes extreme affect and how difficult it would be to deal with the adolescent rationally, as a principle-centered parent is advised to do, in such a strong state of negative affect. Afterwards, we suggest to the parents that they need to strive toward adherence to the following overall coping expectation: "We will encourage our adolescent with ADHD to go for the stars, to do his or her best, but we will accept that it is not a catastrophe when he or she fails to achieve perfection, and it does not mean that he or she is headed for certain ruination or that he or she is purposely trying to anger us."

After discussing this rationale and the more positive coping attitude, we then distribute a copy of Table 14.2, Expectations and Beliefs, to each parent, and review the most common unreasonable beliefs. As we go through each unreasonable belief, we ask the parents to rate their own adherence to this belief and ask them for examples of particular situations that activated the belief. We look at the reasonable alternative beliefs and expectations in the right-hand column and ask the parents whether they find them credible. If they do find the reasonable beliefs credible, we continue; otherwise, we review the evidence for the unreasonable versus the reasonable belief and suggest experiments the parents can do to test out this evidence on their own after the session is over. The therapist does not usually have time to review every belief; he or she may quickly survey the table and concentrate on the beliefs that seem most salient for a particular family.

Most teenagers with ADHD feel that their parents are unfair and restrictive of their freedom, and that the restrictions are interfering with their life. In the portion of the session with the adolescent, the therapist's goals are (1) to assess the rigidity of these beliefs, (2) to determine how the amount of freedom given to the adolescent compares to the local norms for other adolescents of a similar age in the same schools and neighborhood, and (3) to correct any wildly unrealistic expectations which the adolescent may have. The therapist should distribute Table 14.3 to the adolescent and use it as a springboard for discussion. He or she should carry out the discussion in a lighthearted, tongue-in-cheek style, trying to remain animated and to keep the adolescent's attention. The therapist should make liberal use of exaggerations for effect. The therapist should abbreviate the session or shift gears if he or she senses that the adolescent is drifting. The therapist must not conduct a monologue and should not worry too much if the adolescent misses subtleties of his or her points. The extent to which the therapist will be able to accomplish the enumerated goals will vary greatly from adolescent to adolescent, depending on the adolescent's attention span, level of resistance, and general maturity.

Let us look in on Dr. Sam as he conducts the beliefs session with Abe, a 15-year-old recently diagnosed as having ADHD.

Dr. Sam: Look at the first thing on the list, the idea that your parents' rules are totally unfair and will mess up your life. Have you ever felt that way?

ABE: Yep. Just like the curfew one. They made me come home early from the homecoming dance. My friends probably thought I was a real nerd.

DR. SAM: If you keep thinking "my parents are unfair, my parents are unfair, they're going to mess me up, and so on," how are you going to feel?

ABE: Pissed off at them. I do feel that way.

DR. SAM: So if you are pissed as hell at them and go to try to get a later curfew, are you going to have a nice, calm discussion?

ABE: We always have a yelling match. And I get grounded.

DR. SAM: So maybe you can do something to keep from getting so pissed off at them that you lose your cool and then your privileges. If I were you, I'd try thinking to myself something like, "Yes, I don't like coming home early from the dance, but parents always worry too much about what could happen. Yes, it's unfair, but it's not the end of the world. My friends are loyal and will understand. There will be more dances, and maybe I can get a later curfew. I'm going to tell myself to stay cool and calm when I approach them to discuss this. I'm not going to blow it and get grounded again."

ABE: Do you really think I can convince them to change my curfew for the Halloween dance?

DR. SAM: I don't know, but if you stay calm and don't think the worst, you might. I'll help you and your parents to try to work it out to everyone's liking. What about the idea that you should have as much freedom as you want all the time. Do you ever feel that way?

ABE: Yes, it's like they are always bossing me around. Especially about homework. My mother keeps bugging me to start my homework.

DR. SAM: So your mom is the big bad slave driver on homework. Now I want you to be totally honest, and I will never tell, but do you really think you would get your homework done without your mother bugging you?

ABE: Well, I don't know. . . . Doc, probably you're right. Nope.

DR. SAM: ADHD people need structure to get things done. So how can we get you the structure around homework without you feeling like she is taking away your freedom? Any ideas?

ABE: I could set an alarm clock to go off when it's time to do homework.

DR. SAM: Great idea. We can talk that over with your parents.

ABE: Can we talk that over next week? How much longer till we stop?

DR. SAM: You've done a great job with this discussion. Let's stop right now.

Dr. Sam discussed unfairness/ruination and autonomy with Abe. The therapist used practical motivations, for examples, the possibility of a later curfew and getting his parents to stop nagging him about homework, to help reinforce the utility of considering more reasonable beliefs. Teenagers respond better to such tangible contingencies than to an abstract discussion such as why the world is intrinsically unfair or why unlimited autonomy is bad for adolescents. After a reasonable effort, when Abe indicated he was losing interest in the discussion, the therapist stopped the session. Covering one or two of the expectations and beliefs may be as much as it is reasonable to expect in a session with an inattentive adolescent.

TABLE 14.2. Parents' Expectations and Beliefs

Unreasonable beliefs	Reasonable beliefs
I. Perfection/obedience: Teens with ADHD should behave perfectly and obey their parents all the time without question.	I. It is unrealistic to expect teens with ADHD to behave perfectly or obey all of the time; we strive for high standards, but accept imperfections.
A. School	
1. He should always compete homework on time.	1. I will encourage him to complete homework all the time but recognize this won't always happen.
2. She should study 2 hours every night, even when she has no homework.	2. If your attention span is short, you are lucky to get your basic homework done. Extra study is just unrealistic. These kids need a break after all the effort it takes to do basic homework.
3. He should always come to class prepared.	3. He will sometimes come to class unprepared, but I will help him learn good organizational techniques.
4. She should do papers for the love of learning.	4. Research shows teens with ADHD need salient, external reinforcers to motivate their behavior. *C'est la vie.*
B. Driving	
1. He should never get any speeding tickets.	1. All teens with ADHD get at least one speeding ticket. He should be responsible for paying it and take his medicine.
2. She will never have an accident.	2. Research shows most teens with ADHD will get in at least one minor accident. She should take her medicine and do her best. She should drive an old car.
3. He shouldn't adjust the radio tuner while driving down the highway.	3. He should avoid tuning the radio while driving as much as possible, but this may occasionally happen.
4. She will always stop completely for stop signs.	4. I should stop completely at stop signs to model good behavior when my teen is in my car. Only expect my teen to do as well as I do.
C. Conduct	
1. He should be a perfect angel in church.	1. This is unrealistic. As long as there are no major disturbances, I'm satisfied. Perhaps I should find a youth group service of more interest for him anyway.
2. She will impress all the relatives with her love for family gatherings.	2. Give her space. Teens just don't want to be with their families that much. This is normal. She should attend some family functions, but that is all I can reasonably expect.
3. He should never treat us disrespectfully.	3. You can't become your own person without some rebellion. Some back-talk is natural. He shouldn't curse or ridicule severely and might be expected to apologize occasionally.
4. She should get out of a bad mood when we tell her to change her attitude.	4. People with ADHD are just moody and can't stop it. She should let us know when she is in a bad mood and wants to keep to herself. We should not make a lot of demands on her at such times.
D. Chores	
1. She should put away the dishes the first time I ask.	1. It won't always happen the first time, but after several reminders, I should act, not yak (e.g. apply consequences).
2. He should always get the room spotless.	2. He should get it generally neat. Spotless isn't realistic.

(cont.)

TABLE 14.2 (cont.)

Unreasonable beliefs	Reasonable beliefs
3. She should not waste electricity by leaving the lights on.	3. She is just forgetful. We could work out a reminder system. But this is the least of my worries with a teen with ADHD.
4. He shouldn't be on the telephone when I've sent him to his room to clean it up.	4. Teens with ADHD will get off task; I will redirect him back to the task, and if it happens too much, assume it is opposition and ground him from the telephone.
II. Ruination: If I give my teen too much freedom, she will mess up, made bad judgments, get in big trouble, and ruin her life.	II. She will sometimes mess up with too much freedom, but this is how teenagers learn responsibility: a bit of freedom and a bit of responsibility. If they backslide, no big deal. I just pull back on the freedom for a while, and then give her another chance.
A. Room incompletely cleaned: He will grow up to be a slovenly, unemployed, aimless welfare case.	A. The state of his room has little to do with how he turns out when he grows up.
B. Home late: She will have unprotected sex, get pregnant, dump the baby on us, take drugs, and drink alcohol.	B. I have no evidence that she would do all these things. She is just self-centered and focused on having fun.
C. Fighting with siblings: He will never learn to get along with others, have friends, have close relationships, or get married. He will end up a loser, and be severely depressed or commit suicide.	C. There is no scientific evidence that sibling fighting predicts later satisfaction in relationships. Siblings always fight. They will probably be closer when they grow up.
III. Malicious intent: My adolescent misbehaves on purpose to annoy me, or get even with me for restricting him.	III. Most of the time adolescents with ADHD just do things without thinking. They aren't planful enough to connive to upset parents on purpose.
A. Talking disrespectfully: She mouths off on purpose to get even with me for punishing her.	A. Impulsive teenagers just mouth off when frustrated. I'll try not to take it to heart.
B. Doesn't follow directions: He doesn't finish mowing the grass on purpose to get me angry.	B. Teens with ADHD are allergic to effort. They don't take the time to plan to upset parents.
C. Restless behavior: She shuffles her feet and plays with her hair to get on my nerves.	C. Teens with ADHD just can't contain themselves. I'll try not to attach meaning to her restlessness and ignore it.
D. Spending money impulsively: She bought $100 of CDs just to waste our money.	D. She probably just saw the CDs and had to have them. Poor delay of gratification is part of ADHD. She won't get any extra money for lunch or gas.
IV. Love/appreciation: My teen should love and appreciate all the great sacrifices I make: if she really loved me, she would confide in me more.	IV. Teens with ADHD are so self-centered they don't easily show appreciation until they grow up and have their own children with ADHD. Only then will they realize what you did for them.
A. Money: What do you mean you want more allowance? You should be grateful for all the money I spend on you now. Some kids are not so lucky.	A. You will have to earn more allowance. I'd appreciate a thank you even though I understand you don't really think about what I do for you.
B. Communication: She never tells me anything anymore; she must not love me.	B. It's natural as teens individuate to keep more to themselves. As long as I am available when she wants to talk that's all I can expect.
C. Spending time: If he really loved us, he wouldn't spend so much time alone in his room.	C. Spending time alone has nothing to do with love. It has to do with wanting privacy as he becomes more independent.

TABLE 14.3. Adolescents' Expectations and Beliefs

Unreasonable beliefs	Reasonable beliefs
I. Unfairness/ ruination: My parents' rules are totally unfair. I'll never have a good time or any friends. My parents are ruining my life with their unfair rules. They just don't understand me.	I. Yes, I don't like my parents' rules and maybe they are sometimes unfair. But who said life is supposed to be fair? And how many other teenagers have gone through the same thing. They turned out OK. So will I. I'll just have to put up with it the best I can.
A. Curfew: Why should I have to come home earlier than my friends? They will think I'm a baby. I'll lose all my friends.	A. My friends are loyal. They will understand that my parents are creeps about curfew. I won't lose any friends.
B. Chores: Why do I get stuck doing all of the work? Sam (brother) doesn't have to do anything. That's unfair!	B. Sam has some chores too. I'll count them up and if I have more, I'll talk nicely to my parents about it.
C. School: My teacher is unfair. She picks on me all the time. I always get stuck doing extra homework. I'll never have time for fun. Life is one big homework assignment.	C. Maybe she does pick on me. There could be a reason. I never am with the class or know the answer when she calls on me. Maybe if I kept up with the work she wouldn't call on me so much.
II. Autonomy: I ought to have complete and total freedom. My parents shouldn't boss me around or tell me what to do. I'm old enough for freedom now.	II. No teen has complete freedom. No adult really does either. Sometimes I need my parents, like for money or God forbid, even to talk to in times of trouble. I want a lot of freedom, but not total freedom.
A. Chores: I don't need any reminders. I can do it totally on my own.	A. I have not been getting them done on my own. I need to stop being an idiot and accept a little help.
B. Medicine: I don't need Ritalin anymore. I'm grown up now and can handle everything on my own.	B. Maybe I need to see whether I do better or worse on or off medicine. I'll keep an open mind about it.
C. Smoking: It's my body. I can do whatever I want with it. You have no right to tell me not to smoke.	C. It's my body. But do I really want to mess it up? My friends have gotten hooked on smoking. It costs a lot. And it tastes terrible when you kiss.
III. Love/appreciation: Getting material things is a sign that your parents love you. Getting your way is a sign that your parents really love you.	III. Material things don't tell you whether someone really cares about you. Sex doesn't make people really care about you either. It's how you are inside that makes the difference.
A. Clothes: If my parents really loved me, they would let me buy those designer clothes.	A. I would like designer clothes but that's not how I tell whether my parents love me. I can tell from how they act toward me and the affection they show.
B. Concert: If my parents really loved me, they would let me go to the rock concert with my friends.	B. If they really love me and think it is dangerous to go to the concert, they would try to stop me. I won't use this to judge how they feel.
C. Sexuality: If I have sex with my boyfriend, then he will really love me forever and marry me.	C. Love does not equal sex. I need to judge from how my boyfriend acts and expresses his feelings to me whether he love me. All boys want sex. So this tells me nothing about love.

Problem-Solving Communication Skill Training

In sessions 12 to 17 families are taught to follow the four-step model of problem solving in Table 14.4 when discussing parent–child disagreements over negotiable issues (Robin & Foster, 1989). First, each family member *defines the problem* by making a clear, short, non-accusatory "I statement," which pinpoints the others' problem actions and why. As each person gives his or her definition, the therapist teaches the others to verify their understanding of the definition by paraphrasing it to the speaker. This phase ends with a statement by the therapist acknowledging that there may be several different "problems" defined, but that if all agreed to the same definition, there would be no disagreement.

Second, the family members take turns *generating a variety of alternative solutions* to the problem. Three rules of brainstorming are enforced by the therapist to facilitate free exchange of ideas:

1. List as many ideas as possible—quantity breeds quality.
2. Don't evaluate the ideas as criticism stifles creativity.
3. Be creative, knowing that just because you say it doesn't mean you will have to do it.

The therapist has the family members take turns recording the ideas on a worksheet. At first, the adolescent may be asked to record the ideas, a strategy that helps maintain a minimal level of attention to the task. Usually, parents and adolescents begin by suggesting their original positions as solutions. Gradually, new ideas emerge. If the atmosphere is very tense or the family runs out of ideas, the therapist may suggest ideas too, but usually the therapist suggests outlandish ideas to lighten the atmosphere and spur creativity. When the therapist judges that there are one or two "workable" ideas (workable means ideas that may achieve mutual acceptance), the family is asked to move to the next phase of problem solving.

Third, the family is asked to *evaluate the ideas and decide on the best one.* They take turns evaluating each idea, projecting the consequences of implementing it and rating it "plus" or "minus." The therapist teaches family members to clarify each others' projections of the consequences of particular ideas but to refrain from critical crosstalk which could sidetrack the discussion. The ratings are recorded in separate columns for each member on the worksheet. Here the therapist prompts members to consider carefully whether the ideas address their perspectives on the original problem. When the ideas have all been rated, the family reviews the worksheet to determine whether a consensus was reached (all "plus") for any ideas. Surprisingly, a consensus is reached about 80% of the time. The family then selects one of the ideas rated positively by everyone, or combines several such ideas into the solution.

If a consensus was not reached on any idea, the therapist teaches the family negotiation skills. The therapist looks for the idea on which the family came closest to a consensus, and uses it as a catalyst for generating additional alternatives and conducting further evaluations, to spur agreement to a compromise position. A great deal of emphasis is placed on analyzing the factors impeding parent and child from reaching agreement and addressing them. Often, cognitive distortions underlie intransigence in reaching a consensus, and these factors must be addressed following suggestions later in this chapter before a consensus can be reached.

During the fourth phase of problem solving, the family *plans to implement the selected solution and establishes the consequences for compliance versus noncompliance.* Family members must decide who will do what, when, where, and with what monitoring, to make the solution work. With ADHD adolescents in particular, establishing clear-cut consequences for compliance versus noncompliance is very important because we know that performance

TABLE 14.4. Problem-Solving Outline for Families

I. Define the problem.
  A. Tell the others what they do that bothers you and why. "I get very angry when you come home 2 hours after the 11 P.M. curfew we agreed upon."
  B. Start your definition with an "I"; be short, clear, and don't accuse or put down the other person.
  C. Did you get your point across? Ask the others to paraphrase your problem definition to check whether they understood you. If they understood you, go on. If not, repeat your definition.

II. Generate a variety of alternative solutions.
  A. Take turns listing solutions.
  B. Follow three rules for listing solutions:
    1. List as many ideas as possible.
    2. Don't evaluate the ideas.
    3. Be creative; anything goes since you will not have to do everything you list.
  C. One person writes down the ideas on a worksheet (See Figure 14.5).

III. Evaluate the ideas and decide on the best one.
  A. Take turns evaluating each idea.
    1. Say what you think would happen if the family followed the idea.
    2. Vote "plus" or "minus" for the idea and record your vote on the worksheet next to the idea.
  B. Select the best idea.
    1. Look for ideas rated "plus" by everyone.
    2. Select one of these ideas.
    3. Combine several of these ideas.
  C. If none are rated plus by everyone, negotiate a compromise.
    1. Select an idea rated "plus" by one parent and the teen.
    2. List as many compromises as possible.
    3. Evaluate the compromises (repeat steps III.A and III.B).
    4. Reach a mutually acceptable solution.
    5. If you still cannot reach an agreement, wait for the next therapy session.

IV. Plan to implement the selected solution.
  A. Decide who will do what, where, how, and when.
  B. Decide who will monitor the solution implementation.
  C. Decide upon the consequences for compliance or noncompliance with the solution.
    1. Rewards for compliance: privileges, money, activities, praise.
    2. Punishments for noncompliance. loss of privileges, groundings, work detail.

---

deteriorates in the absence of regular structure and immediate consequences. It is important to provide prompts for performing behaviors related to the solution, reinforcement for successful task completion, and punishment for noncompliance. Occasionally, a home token economy may be useful if reinforcement is needed for a number of solutions. Common reinforcers have included extensions on bedtime or curfew, extra telephone privileges, video games and movies, money, or access to the family car. Common punishments have included work detail around the house, groundings, and loss of video games or other privileges. Prompts must be salient and timely because the natural distractibility and forgetfulness that are part of ADHD make it difficult for teenagers to remember effortful tasks; for example, if the adolescent needs to remember to take the trash out on Tuesday and Thursday evenings, the mother might post a bright sign as a reminder earlier those afternoons and give one verbal reminder as the evening begins. Figure 14.5 illustrates a completed worksheet for a problem with chores.

Problem-solving skills are taught through the use of instructions, modeling, behavior rehearsal, and feedback. The therapist briefly introduces problem solving at the beginning of this phase of treatment and helps the family select an issue of moderate intensity for discussion. Moderate-intensity issues are better than hot issues in the early stages of training because the family can concentrate on skill acquisition without excessive anger. The therapist gives instructions and models, then guides the family to rehearse each step of problem solving. As family members emit each problem-solving behavior, the therapist gives them feedback, successively approximating criterion responses by prompting them to restate their point in an improved fashion. To facilitate completion of the discussion, negative communication is interrupted and redirected rather than corrected.

At the end of the discussion, the family is asked to implement the solution at home and report back to the therapist during the next week. If the solution was effectively implemented, the therapist praises the family and begins a new problem-solving discussion. Otherwise, the reasons for failure are analyzed, and the problem is again discussed to reach a more effective agreement. Generalization of problem solving is programmed by having the family establish a regular meeting time, during which accumulated complaints are problem-solved or components of problem solving are practiced.

After two sessions of problem-solving practice, the therapist introduces communication training by distributing a copy of Figure 14.6 and reviewing these common negative

---

Name of family: <u>The Joneses</u>   Date: <u>11/25/97</u>

Topic: <u>Household Chores</u>

Definitions of the problem:

Mom: "I get upset when I have to tell Allen 10 times to take out the trash and clean up his room."
Dad: "It bothers me to come home and find the trash still in the house and Allen's records and books all over the family room, with my wife screaming at him."
Allen: "My parents tell me to take out the trash during my favorite TV show. They make me clean up my room when all my friends are out having fun."

Solutions and evaluations:

	Mom	Dad	Allen
1. Do chores the first time asked.	+	+	−
2. Don't have any chores.	−	−	+
3. Grounded for 1 month if not done	−	+	−
4. Hire a maid	+	−	+
5. Earn allowance for chores	+	+	+
6. Room cleaned once—by 8 P.M.	+	+	+
7. Parents clean the room	−	−	+
8. Close the door to room	+	−	−
9. Better timing when asking Allen	+	+	+
10. One reminder to do chores	+	+	+

Agreement: <u>Nos. 5, 6, 9, 10</u>

Implementation plan: By 9 P.M. each evening Allen agrees to clean up his room, meaning books and papers neatly stacked and clothes in hamper or drawers. Doesn't have to pass "white glove test." Will earn extra $1.00 per day on allowance if complies with no reminders or one reminder. By 8 P.M. on Tuesdays, Allen agrees to have trash collected and out by curb. Will earn $2.00 extra if complies. Punishment for noncompliance: grounding for the next day after school. Dad to monitor trash; Mom to monitor room.

FIGURE 14.5. Example of a completed problem-solving worksheet.

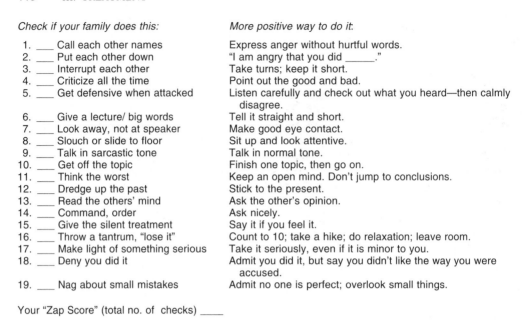

Check if your family does this:

1. ___ Call each other names
2. ___ Put each other down
3. ___ Interrupt each other
4. ___ Criticize all the time
5. ___ Get defensive when attacked

6. ___ Give a lecture/ big words
7. ___ Look away, not at speaker
8. ___ Slouch or slide to floor
9. ___ Talk in sarcastic tone
10. ___ Get off the topic
11. ___ Think the worst
12. ___ Dredge up the past
13. ___ Read the others' mind
14. ___ Command, order
15. ___ Give the silent treatment
16. ___ Throw a tantrum, "lose it"
17. ___ Make light of something serious
18. ___ Deny you did it

19. ___ Nag about small mistakes

More positive way to do it:

Express anger without hurtful words.
"I am angry that you did _____."
Take turns; keep it short.
Point out the good and bad.
Listen carefully and check out what you heard—then calmly disagree.

Tell it straight and short.
Make good eye contact.
Sit up and look attentive.
Talk in normal tone.
Finish one topic, then go on.
Keep an open mind. Don't jump to conclusions.
Stick to the present.
Ask the other's opinion.
Ask nicely.
Say it if you feel it.
Count to 10; take a hike; do relaxation; leave room.
Take it seriously, even if it is minor to you.
Admit you did it, but say you didn't like the way you were accused.

Admit no one is perfect; overlook small things.

Your "Zap Score" (total no. of checks) _____

FIGURE 14.6. Family handout on negative communication.

communication patterns with the family. The therapist asks the family to recall recent incidents of any negative communication habits that apply to them. The incidents are reviewed, identifying who said what to whom and what the impact was on the victim as well as the relationship between the perpetrator and the victim. The therapist is careful to note how negative communication not only produced bad feeling and a counterattack but also sidetracked the discussion away from effective problem solving. Thus, the hurtful effects of negative communication are identified and the reciprocal escalation of negative interchanges can be highlighted. Any examples that occur during the session become prime material for discussion. Next, the therapist points out alternative, more constructive methods for communicating negative affect, disagreement, criticism, and generally telling another person that their behavior is unacceptable. Family members are asked to rehearse specific positive communication interchanges that apply to them. The therapist is careful to emphasize that he or she is not urging family members to suppress their feelings and hide their anger but rather to express their legitimate affect with intensity but nonhurtful specificity.

Following this overview of communication skills, the therapist pinpoints one or two negative communication patterns per session and intervenes to change them. Whenever the negative pattern occurs, the therapist directly stops the session, gives feedback about the occurrence of the negative communication, and asks the family to "replay the scene" using more constructive communication methods. Such corrections are often frequent during this phase of intervention. To be effective, the therapist must wield a "velvet sledge hammer," coming down consistently on each instance of the inappropriate behavior but landing with aplomb. To program generalization, the family is assigned homework to practice positive communication skills in daily interchanges and at family meetings. Family members are taught how to correct each other's communication without spurring excessive antagonism, extending the "velvet sledge hammer" approach to the home.

Experience has suggested a number of special considerations when applying problem solving/communication training (PSCT) to ADHD adolescents and their parents. First, the therapist must maintain the adolescent's attention during crucial moments of each session, not a trivial task with many ADHD teens. Keeping comments brief, bringing the adolescent into the discussion at crucial moments and addressing the remainder of the comments to the parents, and talking in an animated manner are three useful hints for the therapist.

Second, some 12- to 14-year-old ADHD adolescents are not able to understand the concepts of problem solving or may not be ready emotionally and/or developmentally to assume responsibility for generating and negotiating solutions. Repeated difficulty in defining problems or generating solutions would be a sign of such a deficit, along with general silliness or social immaturity. In such cases, the therapist can rely more on behavioral contracting by having the parents take charge of establishing the contingencies, mainly consulting the adolescent about the reinforcers. Alternatively, the therapist can simplify the steps of problem solving to a level able to be processed by the immature adolescent; for example, the parents may generate a list of alternative solutions and through evaluation boil them down to three options, which are then presented to the adolescent for a "vote."

Third, ADHD family members may have such "short fuses" because of their deficits in behavioral inhibition that they often explode at each other during the sessions. The therapist should follow Robin and Foster's (1989, pp. 219–221) advice for maintaining session control—interrupting "runaway chains" as soon as they start, establishing nonverbal cues for "having the floor," teaching anger control and relaxation techniques, and being as directive as necessary to control the session.

Fourth, ADHD adolescents can be so impulsive and distractible that their parents feel the need to correct everything they do or say, creating an endless series of issues and negative communication patterns. Such adolescents are not typically aware of how their behavior "drives their parents up a tree," and they react strongly, spurring endless conflict. The therapist must build on the advice given during the earlier ADHD family education and beliefs/expectations phases of treatment; they must realize that the adolescent did not choose to be this way and cannot help some of the forgetful, counterintuitive behavior. Parents need to learn to "pick their issues wisely," deciding on what to take a stand and what to ignore. For example, fidgety/restless adolescent behavior during family discussions is best reframed as the result of a biological tendency and then ignored, rather than treated as "another sign of disrespect for authority." By contrast, impulsive name calling may be in part biologically based but cannot be ignored because it creates hurtful feelings and fuels coercive, escalating negative communication cycles.

The therapist usually sequences PSCT over six to seven sessions. The first two sessions typically involve problem-solving discussion followed by a communication training session. The fourth and fifth sessions involve continued problem-solving training with correction of negative communication habits. Intense issues are handled in these sessions. The sixth and seventh sessions include a great deal of emphasis on troubleshooting the use of the skills at home and preparing the family to continue their use without the therapist's guidance.

PSCT has been extensively evaluated and found to be more effective than wait-list controls and comparably effective as alternative, less structured family therapies with oppositional youth, but only a single study has specifically evaluated it with ADHD adolescents. Barkley, Guevremont, Anastopoulos, and Fletcher (1992) conducted a comparison of three family therapy programs for treating family conflicts in adolescents with ADHD. Sixty-one 12- to 18-year-olds were randomly assigned to 8 to 10 sessions of behavior management training (BMT), PSCT, or structural family therapy (SFT). To be eligible, the adolescents had to (1) be referred to the investigators' ADHD clinic, (2) meet DSM-III-R (American Psychiatric Association, 1987) criteria for ADHD and have parent or teacher complaints of inattention, impulsivity, and restlessness, (3) be willing to be off psychoactive medication for the duration of the study, and (4) have *T* scores greater than 65 on the hyperactivity scale of the Child Behavior Checklist. The treatments were conducted by two licensed clinical psychologists trained and supervised by senior clinicians expert in each treatment. The adolescent and at least one parent (usually the mother) participated in each SFT and PSCT session; the parent(s) participated in the BMT sessions without the adolescent.

The BMT approach followed Barkley's (1997b) manual with several modifications. The session on developing parental positive attention was modified slightly for adolescents, and the session on time out was changed such that brief groundings at home replaced the use of the time-out chair. Successive sessions focused on the use of positive parent attention, point systems or token reinforcement, daily home-school report cards linked with the home token system, groundings for unacceptable behavior, and instructions for parents on how to anticipate impending problem situations and establish plans in advance to deal with them. Regular homework was assigned following Barkley's (1997b) protocol.

The PSCT approach followed the guidelines outlined throughout this chapter and included three main activities: (1) problem-solving training, (2) communication training, and (3) cognitive restructuring of extreme beliefs and unreasonable expectations. Homework assignments were given in later sessions; these involved applications and practice of problem solving and communication skills. There was no systematic inclusion of ADHD family education, childrearing frameworks, or principles of parenting.

The SFT approach helped families identify and alter maladaptive family systems or interaction patterns, such as transgenerational coalitions, scapegoating, and triangulation. The therapists focused on creating transactions, joining with the family's transactions, and helping to restructure maladaptive transactions, relying on analysis and targeting of family boundaries, alignments, and power. Homework assignments typically involved instructions to replace ineffective transactions with novel strategies.

Each family was assessed before and after treatment and at a 3-month follow-up on the following dependent measures: (1) the Child Behavior Checklist (CBC), Parent and Youth Self-Report versions, social competence scales, and broad-band Internalizing and Externalizing psychopathology scales; (2) the Conflict Behavior Questionnaire (CBQ); (3) the Issues Checklist (IC); (4) the Locke–Wallace Marital Adjustment Test; (5) the Beck Depression Inventory; and (6) videotaped interactions during a neutral and a conflict topic discussion coded with the Parent Adolescent Interaction Coding System—Revised (PAICS-R). The PAICS yields summary scores for the frequency of two negative communication categories (Put-downs/Commands, Defends/Complains), and four positive communication categories (Problem-Solves, Defines/Evaluates, Facilitates, and Talks). The Family Beliefs Inventory (FBI) was given at pre- and postassessment, and a five-item consumer satisfaction survey was given at the end of treatment. The therapists rated family cooperation on a five-item scale at the end of each session.

In general, analyses revealed that all three treatments resulted in significant improvements on most measures from before to after treatment, with further gains in many cases from postassessment to follow-up. There were few differences between treatments. Specifically, parents and adolescents reported improvement on the Internalizing and Externalizing scales of the CBC, with further improvement during the follow-up interval on the Internalizing scale. Parents also reported significant improvement on school adjustment after treatment. For the parent adjustment measures, improvements showed up after treatment on the Beck Depression Inventory but not on the Locke–Wallace Marital Assessment Test.

On self-reported family conflict, mothers and adolescents consistently reported significant gains in their interactions and levels of specific disputes on the CBQ and the IC, and teens reported some improvements in their relationships with their fathers during the follow-up interval. These results were clear-cut and indicative of amelioration of parent–adolescent conflict as seen by both the teenager and the mother, and by follow-up generalizing to the teenager's perception of the father–adolescent relationship, even though the fathers were not typically involved in the treatments.

The results were more variable and difficult to interpret on the observed family inter-actions. I would have predicted that the negative categories should decrease and the posi-tive categories should increase following treatment, but this did not consistently occur. Dur-ing the neutral topic discussion, mothers displayed decreases in Problem-Solves and increases in Talks from pre- to postassessment, along with increases in Facilitates and decreases in Define/Evaluates from postassessment to follow-up. Teenagers displayed increases in De-fends/Commands and Define/Evaluates and decreases in Problem-Solves and Facilitates from pre- to postassessment; Talk increased from postassessment to follow-up. During the con-flict discussion, there was no change for the teenagers; however, there were differences be-tween treatment for mothers. Only SFT mothers decreased on Facilitates, but they had dif-fered from the other two groups at preassessment. For Talks, the BMT and PSCT groups decreased between postassessment and follow-up. At follow-up, the PSCT group showed more Talks than the BMT or the SFT groups. The decreases in categories such as Defines/Evaluates, Facilitates, and Problem-Solves and the increases in Defends/Commands are con-trary to predictions and suggestive of a deterioration of interactions; however, Barkley et al. (1992) did not comment on this finding.

The FBI showed surprising results, counter to predictions. There were no overall de-creases in adherence to rigid, unrealistic ideas for either parents or adolescents after treat-ment. However, there were significant differences between treatment conditions. Parental adherence to beliefs about perfection and obedience increased from pre- to postassessment for the PSCT group but stayed the same for the BMT and SFT groups. There were, however, no significant differences between the three groups either before or after treatment. The PSCT was the only treatment to target unreasonable beliefs; we would have predicted an improve-ment rather than a deterioration on the FBI for this group. Several interpretations are plau-sible: (1) an initial emphasis on negative attributions without more time to deal with them may have exacerbated rather than improved these beliefs, or (2) the parents may have been unaware of such beliefs until the therapist brought them up in the PSCT group, leading to increased reports on the postassessment FBI. At least one other investigation with PSCT treat-ing volunteer families with parent–adolescent conflict found reductions in extreme beliefs on the FBI (Nayar, 1985). Further research is needed to determine the robustness of this find-ing and, if it replicates, what it means.

Barkley determined the clinical significance of the results following Jacobson and Truax's (1991) recommendations by computing the index of Reliable Change (magnitude of the improvement) and the Recovery Index (is client within the normal range?), using the IC quantity and weighted anger/intensity scores. For the number of conflicts, the percentages of subjects showing a reliable change were 10% for BMT, 24% for PSCT, and 10% for SFT; none showed deterioration. For the Recovery Index, the percentages of subjects who moved into the normal range were 5% for BMT, 19% for PSCT, and 10% for SFT. Comparable percentages were obtained for the weighted anger/intensity score. There were no significant differences between treatments on these indices.

Consumer satisfaction ratings were high and did not vary significantly across the three treat-ments. However, therapist ratings of family cooperation did differ significantly. The therapists rated the PSCT families as significantly less cooperative than either the BMT or the SFT fami-lies. Perhaps the greater amount of effort required of the PSCT group influenced these ratings.

The lack of either a no-treatment or an attention-placebo control leaves ambiguous the question whether the positive gains were due to the treatments or other factors such as the passing of time, therapist attention, or measurement artifact, and the relatively small sample sizes limits the power to obtain significant subtle differences between treatments.

The results of this study were promising in that they did indicate that all three treat-ment approaches resulted in statistically significant amelioration of self-reported parent–

adolescent conflicts and negative communication, decreases in externalizing and internalizing behavioral problems and maternal depression, and a high degree of consumer satisfaction with the treatments. At the same time, the results are very sobering when the stringent criteria of reliable change and movement into the normal range were applied: 80–95% of the families with ADHD adolescents did not make any clinically significant improvements through any of these family-based interventions. Nonetheless, the high degree of parental satisfaction suggests that even if clinically significant results were not obtained for the majority of families on the dependent measures, the families felt they benefited. Barkley et al. (1992) speculated that perhaps the parents felt better prepared to cope with the problems inherent in raising adolescents with ADHD, even if they continued to have conflicts with their adolescents.

Restoring Parental Control

We return here to the strategies for the therapist to use when ADHD adolescents present to the therapist with such severe oppositional and/or conduct-disordered behavior that they will successfully resist or sabotage all the other components of treatment until their acting-out behavior is modified. These are the adolescents with histories of aggressive behavior since early childhood or extreme hyperactivity persisting even into adolescence. At the time they arrive for therapy, their parents have very little real control over any of their behaviors. Often, other adults do not have any control over them either. They tell the therapist that they do not plan to cooperate and have outsmarted many previous therapists. These teenagers have acquired powerful repertoires of coercive behavior which reliably function to cause their parents and teachers to back down in discipline and/or limit-setting situations. In terms of family structure problems, the hierarchy of "parent in charge of child" is completely reversed, with the adolescents dictating to their parents, as well as to teachers and other adults.

The therapist must relate to these adolescents in an extremely assertive manner, making it clear that although their opinions will be valued and listened to, there will be certain ground rules for decent interpersonal conduct. Such ground rules usually include no physical violence during the session or at home, no vile language during the session, and all present taking a turn to express their opinion but only one person at a time talks. The therapist helps model control for the parents by enforcing these ground rules strictly during the sessions. The therapist moves to reestablish parental control by strengthening the parental coalition and teaching the parents to work as a team in setting limits and enforcing consequences. The power of extrafamilial sources of control such as the juvenile justice system, the police, and the inpatient mental health system can be used to back up parental authority. A "bottom line" for antisocial, illegal, and aggressive behavior must be set, with a clear specification of extrafamilial consequences if the adolescent crosses this line. For example, in a family where the adolescent physically assaults the parents, the therapist and parents may agree that the police will be called, charges will be brought, and the adolescent will spend some time in a juvenile lockup if assaultive behavior occurs. In a family where the adolescent chronically and repeatedly violates all of the household rules concerning curfew, smoking, participation in chores, and so on, the parents may decide that at a certain point the teenager must leave home and go to a foster home for a period of time.

When the bottom line is set, the therapist meets individually with the adolescent, then the couple. In the session with the adolescent, the therapist has the adolescent project the positive and negative consequences of "crossing the bottom line" and being removed from the house. Graphic descriptions of juvenile settings and foster homes, with careful comparison of the material advantages and disadvantages of the adolescent's own home versus the extrafamilial setting, are given. The therapist is careful not to preach to the adolescent but rather to develop a Socratic discussion of these points. It is important for the therapist to indicate that the adolescent must choose what is best for him or her, not the therapist and not the parents.

In the meeting with the couple, the therapist begins the process of asking the parents to reach an agreement about appropriate limits and consequences for severe acting-out behavior. Usually, the couple needs a lot of support and direction from the therapist to accomplish this task as they have been unable to reach effective agreements in the past and feel extremely "burned out" by the time of this session. The spouses often have different styles of relating to the adolescent—one overinvolved and emotional; the other disengaged and harsh—and the adolescent has often been able to take advantage of these differences to "divide and conquer," transforming disciplinary efforts into marital disputes. The therapist should break down the severe antisocial behaviors into small components and help the parents reach agreements to work as a team in exercising effective control over one component at a time. As each component is targeted for change, the parents are helped to anticipate all the adolescent's possible "escape routes" to avoid compliance and close them off.

When a plan of action for controlling antisocial behavior has been reached, the therapist asks the parents to present it assertively to the adolescent in a family session, empathizing with the adolescent's anger but insisting on the necessity for implementing the plan. At the next session, the therapist reviews the effectiveness of the plan, helps the parents make adjustments, responds to reasonable suggestions from the adolescent for modifications, and then moves onto additional components of antisocial behavior in a similar fashion.

Case Examples of Restoring Parental Control

I will use two cases to contrast a successful versus an unsuccessful effort to restore parental control. In the Nordon family, 14-year-old Andrew was having impulsive temper tantrums at home, during which he engaged in destructive behavior toward his father's property or aggressive behavior toward his mother and sister. Seemingly minor provocations set off Andrew's tantrums. When his father refused to take him to the store to purchase a Halloween costume, Andrew squirted a bottle of mustard on his father's $400 suit, ruining it. When his mother refused to give him his favorite desert, he threw a bottle of pop at her, making a hole in the wall. He terrorized his sister constantly, randomly punching her, pulling her hair, and stealing her money and possessions. Mr. and Mrs. Nordon disagreed vehemently with each other about how to handle their son. Mr. Nordon favored physical punishments ("the belt") while his wife was afraid that Andrew and his dad would hurt each other if her husband used too many spankings. She tried to "reason" with her son, and in fact stood between her husband and son to prevent physical confrontations. Aside from reasoning, she did nothing to consequate tantrums. The couple argued constantly about Andrew's tantrums, which occurred four to five times per week.

When the therapist met with the couple, they agreed that the bottom line would be to call the police and press charges in the event of assaultive behavior and to require financial restitution in the case of destruction of property. They had a very difficult time, though, reaching an agreement about how to respond at the time of each impulsive episode. Mr. Nordon insisted on the necessity for physical punishment, and his wife insisted on doing nothing except for having a quiet discussion with her son at a later time. Each parent rigidly accused the other of perpetuating Andrew's tantrums. Andrew minimized the intensity of his tantrums and claimed he could control them at any time. He objected to his parent's "stupid" rules and perceived his destructive behavior as "getting even." Mrs. Nordon also punished her husband for hitting her son by withdrawing sexually from him for a week following each episode. However, she did this subtlety, developing headaches or other somatic symptoms rather than directing refusing to have sexual relations. By the end of the week, he would move out of their bedroom and sleep on the couch in the living room.

The therapist pushed the parents to reach a number of agreements for controlling components of Andrew's tantrums. First, the father agreed to refrain from physical violence toward his son if his wife would be verbally assertive in telling Andrew to get in control or go to his room for 30 minutes until he calmed down during a tantrum. The implementation of this agreement was fraught with perils because Mrs. Nordon either "forgot" to be assertive or despite prior rehearsal responded to her son in a "mousy manner." Mr. Nordon at first exercised restraint, but by the third time his wife refused to assert herself, he resorted to physical punishment. Only when her husband actually stood by and coached her every statement was Mrs. Nordon able to begin to respond to her son assertively. After a month of pushing the parents to refine and implement their agreement, Mrs. Nordon began to assert herself. An episode where Andrew hit and taunted his sister so intensely that she huddled in the corner sucking her thumb and crying hysterically was the turning point for Mrs. Nordon. She "realized" how tyrannical her son was and began to crack down. Mr. Nordon was incredulous but strongly supported his wife. Within 3 more weeks, the tantrums had diminished from four or five to one or two per week. Andrew attributed the change in his behavior to his own "will power," a fantasy the therapist did not challenge. The couple was again having regular intimate relations, a change that strengthened their general resolve to work as a team. Strategic family therapists might wonder about the role of Andrew's tantrums in helping the couple avoid sexual relations, but whatever this connection, from a behavioral family systems viewpoint, therapy needed to focus directly on Andrew's behavior and his parents' responses to it.

In the second case, 17-year-old Jimmy Selby had a history of drug and alcohol use, stealing radar detectors to support his drug habit, aggression toward his parents and peers, extreme hyperactivity, school expulsion and failure, and destruction of property. The symptom of hyperactivity had not diminished as he entered adolescence, and his parents had little control over him at the time of therapy. He was taking 20 mg of Ritalin twice a day on school days; this was the highest dose he would agree to take, and as his mother said, "At least he can stop moving long enough for me to talk to him on medication." As with the Nordons, Mrs. Selby was more lenient than her husband. She tried to give her son every chance to improve, attributing much of his severe misbehavior to his ADHD. Mr. Selby basically concluded "Jimmy is a bad kid" and screamed, hit, or withdrew.

The couple agreed that the bottom line would be declaring Jimmy ungovernable and turning him over to the juvenile authorities for placement in a foster home or a residential treatment center. The first concrete issue around which the therapist pushed the couple to agree on consequences was Jimmy's habit of stealing his father's tools, which then turned up in local pawn shops. After much debate, they agreed that if any tool was missing, Jimmy would be assumed to be responsible and would lose the use of the family car for one weekend. The agreement was enforced for 2 weeks; then it broke down when the father lost his temper and struck his son over a missing tool. The father avoided the next two therapy sessions with "out-of-town business trips." The mother felt sorry for Jimmy when he was expelled from school for making lewd remarks to the principal's daughter on school grounds, and she let him use the car.

When the father returned for several sessions, the therapist again pushed the parents to reach agreements concerning consequences for oppositional behavior. They concurred that Jimmy should not bring a "beeper" to school, should only use the car for transportation to and from school, and should pay his father back for the missing tools out of his paycheck from a part-time job. The therapist attempted to get Mr. Selby to take an active role in the enforcement of these agreements, but most of the load fell on Mrs. Selby's shoulders. Meanwhile, she "hid" another series of Jimmy's misbehaviors from her husband (and the therapist), including chronic curfew violations, failing grades in school, and repeated in-school detentions for verbally abusing teachers. She was afraid that her husband would be "too hard on the boy." Eventually, her husband happened to answer a phone call from school and discovered what was happening. He was furious at his wife and again failed to attend therapy sessions.

By this time, Mrs. Selby was completely "burned out." Jimmy continued to protest that he was "innocent" and everyone was "framing him." The mother told the therapist she did not have the strength to continue and would seriously consider placement out of the home for Jimmy. Since therapy terminated, however, she has been unable to summon the courage to file for placement, and the drama continues unabated. She appears to fear that her son will pay his drug-pusher friends to burn down the family home and murder her if she contacts the police. Her husband comes and goes from the house as if Jimmy did not exist, and Jimmy does whatever he wants.

In the Selby case, the therapist was unable to maintain the involvement of the father in support of his wife in dealing with a difficult adolescent. The adolescent had the stamina to "wear down" both parents, who entered therapy already "burned out." The therapist could not convince the parents to exercise the bottom line of invoking external authorities. Jimmy had little or no remorse or conscience about his antisocial behavior. By contrast, Andrew felt badly about the effect of his tantrums on his family, even though he was unable to control them. The Nordons expressed a lot of affection for each other, whereas the Selbys related with cold hatred, clearly decreasing their motivation to change. Both adolescents had been diagnosed as having ADHD since age 7, and both were on Ritalin during the course of therapy. The differences between family members' overall degree of warmth/caring and their abilities to experience empathy and understanding of another's social perspective seemed to be the variables that facilitated or detracted from their responsivity to the therapist's attempts to restore parental control.

Individual Therapy

Although most of the goals of a home-management–oriented intervention for the ADHD adolescent are best accomplished through family-oriented sessions, there are times when individual sessions with the adolescent are helpful. Issues related to self-esteem, depression, and sexuality are often handled best in individual sessions, where the adolescent may feel free to share his or her feelings more openly than in the parents' presence. The therapist can also teach anger control techniques efficiently in individual sessions (Feindler & Ecton, 1987), and a variety of behavioral self-control techniques may also prove useful for ADHD adolescents to change their own study skills and social behaviors (Braswell & Bloomquist, 1991).

Concluding Phase of Therapy

The initial burst of home-management–oriented family intervention with the average ADHD adolescent and his or her parents comes to a conclusion after 10–20 sessions. By this time, parental control has been restored, the adolescent's school performance has improved, the family has acquired positive communication and effective problem-solving skills, and many of their extreme cognitions have begun to change. Crises continue to occur, but ideally the family is able to weather these storms with their newfound skills and attitudes. Typically, there has been little long-term personality change in family members but, rather, behavioral and attitudinal change in their interactions and interpretations of each other's behaviors. Either the family hints that they no longer need to attend therapy regularly or the therapist notices that they do not have many issues to bring up.

Therapy is gradually faded out by increasing the intervals between the last few sessions to 3, 4, and 6 weeks. In these final sessions, the therapist reviews previously acquired problem-solving skills, checks up on the continued success of solutions implemented throughout therapy, and helps the family to anticipate and plan to cope with upcoming events. When therapy ends, the family is left with an open invitation to return as needed. They are asked to contact the therapist for a 12-month follow-up and advised that with further developmental changes, new ADHD-related problems are likely to recur, necessitating "booster sessions."

CONCLUSION

In this chapter we have tried to give the practitioner a feel for the type of biobehavioral family systems intervention needed to address the issues of the ADHD adolescent. The intervention integrates PSCT, a family-based program originally developed for parent–teen conflict regardless of formal diagnosis (Robin & Foster, 1989), with medication, family ADHD education, and school-related interventions to enhance academic success. Modification in each of these programs to deal with the special considerations of ADHD in adolescence have been incorporated into the overall protocol presented here. Recent research has begun to delineate the family relationship problems of the ADHD adolescent (see Chapter 5, this volume) and examine the effectiveness of at least the PSCT portions of the treatment program with an ADHD population (Barkley et al., 1992). Clearly, much additional research evaluating the entire treatment package outlined here is needed.

The interventions outlined in this chapter should be regarded as a starting point for such research as well as clinical practice. As the practitioner experiments with clinical variations on the strategies presented here, it is suggested that he or she keep in mind the major developmental differences between adolescents and younger children. ADHD adolescents, like all adolescents, think they know all the answers and do not typically wish to have help. The democratically oriented, problem-solving based interventions that have been discussed are based on the notion of developing a collaborative relationship with the adolescent rather than a dictatorial, authoritarian approach, which is more appropriate for younger ADHD children.

REFERENCES

Amen, D. G., & Amen, A. J. (1995). *Teenager's guide to ADD: understanding and treating Attention Deficit Disorder through the teenager years audio cassette tapes.* Fairfield, CA: MindWorks Press.

American Psychiatric Association. (1987). *Diagnostic and statistical manual of mental disorders* (3rd ed., rev.). Washington, DC: Author.

American Psychiatric Association. (1994). *Diagnostic and statistical manual of mental disorders* (4th ed.). Washington, DC: Author.

Barkley, R. A. (1990). *Attention-deficit hyperactivity disorder: A handbook for diagnosis and treatment.* New York: Guilford Press.

Barkley, R. A. (1995). *Taking charge of ADHD: The complete, authoritative guide for parents.* New York: Guilford Press.

Barkley, R. A. (1997a). *ADHD and the nature of self-control.* New York: Guilford Press.

Barkley, R. A. (1997b). *Defiant children* (2nd ed.): *A clinician's manual for assessment and parent training.* New York: Guilford Press.

Barkley, R. A., Guevremont, D. G., Anastopoulous, A. D., & Fletcher, K. E. (1992). A comparison of three family therapy programs for treating family conflict in adolescents with attention-deficit hyperactivity disorder. *Journal of Consulting and Clinical Psychology, 60,* 450–462.

Braswell, L., & Bloomquist, M. L. (1991). *Cognitive-behavioral therapy with ADHD children.* New York: Guilford Press.

Davis, L., Sirotowitz, S., & Parker, H. G. (1996). *Study strategies made easy.* Plantation, FL: Specialty Press.

Feindler, E. L., & Ecton, R. B. (1987). *Adolescent anger control: Cognitive-behavioral strategies.* New York: Pergamon Press.

Gordon, M. (1993). *I would if I could: A teenager's guide to ADHD/hyperactivity.* DeWitt, NY: Gordon Systems.

Jacobson, N. S., & Truax, P. (1991). Clinical significance: A statistical approach to defining meaningful change in psychotherapy research. *Journal of Consulting and Clinical Psychology, 59,* 12–19.

Markel, G., & Greenbaum, J. (1996). *Performance breakthroughs for adolescents with learning disabilities or ADD.* Champaign, IL: Research Press.

Nayar, M. (1985). *Cognitive factors in the treatment of parent-adolescent conflict.* Unpublished doctoral dissertation, Wayne State University, Detroit.

Patterson, G. R. (1982). *Coercive family process.* Eugene, OR: Castalia.

Patterson, G. R., & Forgatch, M. (1987). *Parents and adolescent living together: Part I. The basics.* Eugene, OR: Castalia.

Quinn, P. O. (1995). *Adolescents and ADD.* New York: Magination Press.

Robin, A. L. (in press). *ADHD in adolescents: Diagnosis and treatment.* New York: Guilford Press.

Robin, A. L., & Foster, S. L. (1989). *Negotiating parent–adolescent conflict: A behavioral–family systems approach.* New York: Guilford Press.

Robin, A. L., and Weiss, S. (1997). *Managing oppositional youth* [Videotape]. Plantation, FL: Specialty Press.

Schubiner, H. (1995). *ADHD in adolescence: Our point of view* [Videotape]. Detroit: Children's Hospital of Michigan Department of Educational Services.

Weiss, G., & Hechtman, L. T. (1993). *Hyperactive children grown up* (2nd ed.): *ADHD in children, adolescents, and adults.* New York: Guilford Press.

Zametkin, A. J., Nordahl, T. E., Gross, M., King, A. C., Semple, W. E., Rumsey, J., Hamburger, S., & Cohen, R. M. (1990). Cerebral glucose metabolism in adults with hyperactivity of childhood onset. *New England Journal of Medicine, 323,* 1361–1366.

Chapter 15

TREATMENT OF ADHD IN SCHOOL SETTINGS

Linda J. Pfiffner
Russell A. Barkley

The purpose of this chapter is to summarize contemporary school-based interventions for assisting students with Attention-Deficit/Hyperactivity Disorder (ADHD). The behavioral technologies described here are much the same as those described in the prior version of this chapter. Recent advances lie more in the innovative application of the technology, rather than changes in the technology per se. The last several years have witnessed an unprecedented national response to the educational needs of children with ADHD. These include the following:

 • In 1991, the U.S. Department of Education recognized for the first time that ADHD may qualify a student for special assistance in general education under Section 504 of the Rehabilitation Act of 1973 (Public Law 93-112) and could be considered a disabling condition under the Individuals with Disabilities Education Act (IDEA; 1991, Public Law 101-476), thereby facilitating eligibility for special education services (Davila, William, & MacDonald, 1991).
 • The Office of Special Education Programs of the U.S. Department of Education funded five national centers to identify the needs of children with ADHD, assessment strategies, and effective interventions for working with the children in school settings (Burcham, Carlson, & Milich, 1993; Dykman & Ackerman, 1993; Fiore, Becker, & Nero, 1993; McKinney, Montague, & Hocutt, 1993; Swanson et al., 1993). Information gathered from the centers has been compiled and disseminated to schools around the country as part of an information kit distributed by the Office of Special Education Programs (U.S. Department of Education).
 • The U.S. Department of Education has funded a number of additional projects to disseminate information and to train school personnel to work more effectively with ADHD students. Among these are the Attention Deficit Disorders Telecourse Network (ADDNET), a teleconference on ADHD produced at the University of Georgia (McLaughlin & Bender, 1994), the ADD Training Program for Teachers, including an instruction manual and videotape, produced at the University of Kentucky (Welsh, Burcham, DeMoss, Martin, & Milich,

1997), and a consulting center/training institute on attention-deficit disorders in early adolescents, developed at Lehigh University (Shapiro, DuPaul, Bradley, & Bailey, 1996).

• The National Institute of Mental Health has funded a number of studies examining the efficacy of school-based programs with ADHD (Barkley et al., 1996; Arnold et al., 1997).

This national response is encouraging. However, much work remains to be done to meet the educational needs of children with ADHD.

TEACHER TRAINING AND SUPPORT

The educational success of children with ADHD involves not only a well-documented behavioral technology (reviewed later) but also the presence of teachers actively and willingly engaged in the process of working with ADHD students and an administration that supports identification and intervention for ADHD. The teacher's knowledge of and attitude about ADHD is critical. When teachers have a poor grasp of the nature, course, outcome, and causes of this disorder and misperceptions about appropriate therapies, little will be gained from attempting to establish behavior management programs within that classroom. On the other hand, a positive teacher–student relationship, based on teacher understanding of the student and the disorder, may improve academic and social functioning. Teachers should be aware of the following:

• ADHD is considered to be a biologically based, educational disability that is treatable but not curable. Interventions can have a powerful and positive impact because the severity of symptoms and comorbid conditions are very sensitive to environmental variables. However, the refractory nature of ADHD symptomatology makes it likely that these children will continue to experience at least some difficulty in their academic and social endeavors.

• ADHD is not the result of a lack of skill or knowledge but a problem of sustaining attention, effort, and motivation and inhibiting behavior in a consistent manner over time, especially when consequences are delayed, weak, or absent. Thus it is a disorder of performing what one knows, not of knowing what to do.

• It is harder for students with ADHD to do the same academic work and exhibit the social behavior expected of other students. Consider the student to be 30% or more behind in social skills and organization. The student with ADHD needs more structure, more frequent and salient positive consequences, more consistent negative consequences, and accommodations to assigned work.

• The most effective interventions for improving school performance are those applied consistently *within* the school setting and at the point of performance. Family therapy, individual therapy, and parent training, although often beneficial at home, rarely prove to be helpful in improving the academic and behavioral functioning of ADHD children (Abramowitz & O'Leary, 1991).

Education about ADHD can be imparted through inservice presentations and by providing brief reading materials or videotapes similar to those mentioned in Chapters 12 (this volume).

General education teachers also require training to implement behavioral programs because such training is rarely provided in their education credential programs. One-day inservices, although useful for imparting information about the disorder, are usually not sufficient for training teachers to implement behavior modification programs. Such school-sponsored training can be effective, however, if followed up by ongoing consultation or technical support. In recent years, many schools have adopted collaborative consultation models whereby a behavioral consultant (or school psychologist) works with educators in general and special education in a systematic manner to assess student needs and to plan and implement interventions (Dunson, Hughes, & Jackson, 1994; Shapiro et al., 1996).

One such program was developed at Lehigh University to serve students in middle school (Shapiro et al., 1996). The program begins with a 2-day inservice training focused on ADHD and school-based assessment and intervention. Following this basic training, intensive on-site consultation is provided for approximately 2 hours per day over a 60-day period. Consultation includes such activities as developing and implementing individual programs with students having difficulty (e.g., daily report card and self-management training), establishing methods of identifying and monitoring ADHD students, and assisting in communicating and interacting with physicians. Advanced training in ADHD is also provided. The program substantially improves the knowledge base and service to middle school students with ADHD and represents a very promising approach for systematizing training efforts within school districts.

Special education teachers with small classes may have little difficulty implementing behavioral programs for ADHD students. On the other hand, teachers of up to 30 to 40 students may find the recordkeeping, close monitoring of the child, and administration of a range of rewards and/or negative consequences to be very time-consuming and impractical. To help with this common situation, (1) the addition of a behavioral aide in the classroom can be invaluable, even when the aide must rotate across multiple classrooms because of budget limitations; (2) teachers should be provided with ongoing consultation to help plan and troubleshoot behavioral programs; and (3) teachers should be supported in their efforts to work with ADHD students. Support may include verbal recognition for their efforts, financial compensation for special materials and books, and planning and development time. Schools with effective practices for ADHD invariably have an administration that recognizes ADHD as a condition in need of specialized accommodations or interventions and provides training and resources necessary to adequately serve the special needs of these students.

Unfortunately, even with adequate resources, some teachers may still be averse to working with ADHD students or to using behavior modification procedures on theoretical grounds. In such cases of poor teacher motivation, or when teacher philosophy greatly conflicts with the necessary interventions for an ADHD child, parents are to be encouraged to be assertive in pressing the school administrators for either greater teacher accountability or a transfer to another classroom or school.

COLLABORATION BETWEEN HOME AND SCHOOL

An important consideration for enhancing the effectiveness of school interventions is the relationship between home and school. When both teacher and parents are knowledgeable about ADHD, have realistic goals, and are motivated to work with ADHD, effective collaborations develop easily. In other cases, home–school conflicts can be significant and ultimately compromise the student's progress. Parents may blame their child's difficulties on the school or may feel that the school system is failing to adequately address their child's needs. Teachers may believe that family problems are causing the child's symptoms or that medication should be considered in lieu of accommodations in the classroom. During recent years, conflict between home and school has escalated as demonstrated by increased involvement of child advocates and the legal system to sort out educational placement issues. Some of the conflict is the result of misinformation and can be addressed through education about ADHD. Parents and teachers need to dispel notions of blame and to work toward improving the fit between the child's characteristics and the environments at school and at home. A behavioral consultant/clinician with expertise in ADHD and behavior modification can help mediate these problems by providing information regarding the nature of ADHD and its causes as well as information regarding the role of behavioral interventions (including their strengths and limitations) in the treatment of ADHD. The need to establish interventions in all settings in which problems occur should be stressed to parents and school personnel as changes in one setting rarely generalize without intervention to other settings. Many collaborative teams within schools routinely include parents so that complementary programs can be designed at school and at home (Burcham et al., 1993; Kotkin, 1995).

To develop effective collaborations, clinicians should meet weekly or biweekly with the teacher and/or parent to provide instruction and coaching in behavioral management as well as continual monitoring and evaluation of the program. Older children should be included during some of these meetings to help set goals and determine appropriate and valuable rewards as involving the children in this way often enhances their motivation to participate and be successful in the program. For example, written contracts for a daily report card system (described in a later section) which indicate the different roles of teacher, parent and child (e.g., the teacher's role in monitoring child behavior, the parent's role in dispensing rewards, and the child's role in engaging in appropriate target behaviors) is a concrete method of ensuring consistent adherence to the plan over time. It is also important that parents understand that implementing behavior modification programs in the classroom is not an easy task for most teachers. We routinely encourage parents to be actively involved in their child's educational program, to follow through, and to use positive reinforcement liberally with their child's teacher, just as the clinician should use positive reinforcement liberally with the parent and teacher.

GENERAL BEHAVIORAL GUIDELINES

Selecting Target Behaviors

Effective management programs directly target the areas in which change is desired (e.g., deportment, academic problems, and social skills). Target behaviors should do the following:

- Focus on teaching children a set of skills and adaptive behaviors to replace the problems (DuPaul & Stoner, 1994). For example, a target behavior to address organizational problems may involve teaching the student to use and store materials in their desk or locker properly; an aggressive child may be taught to increase good sportsmanship skills. If positive alternative behaviors are not taught and only problem behavior is targeted for intervention, children may simply replace one problem behavior with another.
- Include academic performance (e.g., amount of work completed accurately) rather than just on-task behavior because improvement in classroom deportment is often not paralleled by improvement in academic functioning (e.g., children who are sitting quietly may not be any better at completing their work). Increased attention to the development of academic skills (reading, writing, spelling, etc.) in ADHD students has also been stressed to prevent deficits in academic achievement commonly experienced by ADHD students in their later elementary years.
- Include common problem situations such as transitions between classes and activities, recess and lunch. Teachers should consider very simple programs targeting these brief periods during the day.

More recently, investigators (DuPaul & Ervin, 1996; Ervin, DuPaul, Kern, & Friman, 1997) have studied methods to better link the selection of target behaviors with intervention for ADHD through use of functional assessment. A functional assessment covers several areas:

1. Carefully defining the target behavior in question so that the teacher is able to reliably monitor the behavior.

2. Identifying antecedents and consequences to the behavior in the natural environment through interviews with teachers, parents, and students and direct observation.

3. Generating hypotheses about the function of the problem behavior in terms of antecedent events that set the occasion for the behavior and/or consequences that maintain it. Potential antecedents include difficult or challenging work, a teacher direction or negative consequence, or disruption from another child. Potential consequences include teacher or peer attention or withdrawal of a task or teacher request. Antecedent events need not immediately precede the problem behavior to be important in this analysis. Distal events, or those occurring minutes to hours before the target behavior, may have some role to play in increasing the probability of disruptive behaviors. For instance, arguments or fights with other family members at home or with other children on the bus ride to school may alter certain affective states (e.g., anger and frustration), which may make the occurrence of aggressive or defiant behavior upon arrival at school more probable.

4. Systematically manipulating antecedents and consequences (those that can be) to test hypotheses about their functional relationship to the target behavior. DuPaul and Ervin (1996) summarize a number of possible functions of ADHD behaviors. The most common may be to avoid or escape effortful or challenging tasks (e.g., repetitive paper–pencil tasks). Others include obtaining teacher or peer attention, gaining access to an activity that is more reinforcing or interested to the child (e.g., fiddling with toys rather than completing work), or accessing pleasant sensory experiences (e.g., daydreaming).

5. Implementing interventions that alter the functional antecedents or consequences so that problem behavior is replaced with appropriate behavior. For example, a child who is easily distracted by small toys or objects in his or her desk, may be allowed access to those objects only after a specific amount of assigned work is completed.

Functional assessment provides a useful mechanism for tailoring interventions to individual children, one that goes well beyond a diagnosis of ADHD. This approach should help the clinician predict which of many behavioral interventions will have the greatest impact on changing specific problematic behaviors.

Intervention Principles

Behavioral interventions for ADHD in the classroom include a range of in-class consequences, home-based programs, self-management interventions, and modification of academic tasks and the classroom environment. Before discussing specific approaches, we review a number of general principles that apply to the classroom management of ADHD children stemming from the model presented earlier (Chapter 7, this volume) that ADHD is likely an impairment in the self-regulation of behavior by internal information, by rules, and by distal consequences. These principles apply as much to classroom management as they did to parent training in child management at home (Chapters 12 and 13, this volume). This conceptualization of ADHD requires the following:

1. Rules and instructions provided to ADHD children must be clear, brief, and often delivered through more visible and external modes of presentation than is required for the management of normal children. Stating directions clearly, having the child repeat them out loud, having the child utter them softly to themselves while following through on the instruction, and displaying sets of rules or rule-prompts (e.g., stop signs, big eyes, and big ears for "stop, look, and listen" reminders) prominently throughout the classroom are essential to

proper management of ADHD children. Relying on the child's recollection of the rules as well as on purely verbal reminders is often ineffective.

2. Consequences used to manage the behavior of ADHD children must be delivered swiftly and more immediately than is necessary for normal children. Delays in consequences greatly degrade their efficacy with ADHD children. As noted throughout this chapter, the timing and strategic application of consequences with ADHD children must be more systematic and is far more crucial to their management than it is for normal children.

3. Consequences must be delivered more frequently, not just more immediately, to ADHD children in view of their motivational deficits. Behavioral tracking, or the ongoing adherence to rules after the rule has been stated and compliance initiated, appears to be problematic for ADHD children. Frequent feedback or consequences for rule adherence seem helpful in maintaining appropriate degrees of tracking to rules over time.

4. The types of consequences used with ADHD children must often be of a higher magnitude, or more powerful, than these needed to manage the behavior of normal children. The relative insensitivity of ADHD children to response consequences dictates that those chosen for inclusion in a behavior management program must have sufficient reinforcement value or magnitude to motivate ADHD children to perform the desired behaviors. Mere occasional praise or reprimands are simply not enough to effectively manage ADHD children.

5. An appropriate and often richer degree of incentives or motivational parameters must be provided within a setting or task to reinforce appropriate behavior before punishment can be implemented. This means that punishment must remain within a relative balance with rewards or it is unlikely to succeed. It is therefore imperative that powerful reinforcement programs be established first and instituted over 1 to 2 weeks before implementing punishment for the punishment, sparingly used, to be maximally effective. Often ADHD children do not improve with the use of response cost or time out if the availability of reinforcement is low in the classroom and hence removal from it is unlikely to be punitive. "Positives before negatives" is the order of the day with ADHD children. When punishment fails, this is the first area clinicians, consultants, or educators should explore for problems before instituting higher-magnitude or more frequent punishment programs.

6. Those reinforcers or, particularly, rewards that are employed must be changed or rotated more frequently with ADHD than normal children given the penchant of the former for more rapid habituation or satiation to response consequences. This means that even though a particular reinforcer seems to be effective for the moment in motivating child compliance, it is likely that it will lose its reinforcement value more rapidly than normal over time. Therefore, reward menus in classes, such as those used to back up token systems, must be changed periodically, say every 2 to 3 weeks, to maintain the power of efficacy of the program in motivating appropriate child behavior. Failure to do so is likely to result in the loss of power of the reward program and the premature abandonment of token technologies based on the false assumption that they simply will not work any longer. Token systems can be maintained over an entire school year with minimal loss of power in the program provided that the reinforcers are changed frequently to accommodate to this problem of habituation. Such rewards can be returned later to the program once they have been set aside for a while, often with the result that their reinforcement value appears to improve.

7. Anticipation is the key with ADHD children. This means that teachers must be more mindful of planning ahead in managing ADHD children, particularly during phases of transition across activities or classes, to ensure that the children are cognizant of the shift in rules (and consequences) that is about to occur. It is useful for teachers to take a moment to prompt a child to recall the rules of conduct in the upcoming situation, repeat them orally, and recall what the rewards and punishments will be in the impending situation *before* en-

tering that activity or situation. *Think aloud, think ahead* is the important message to educators here. Following a three-step procedure similar to that used in parental management of ADHD children in public places (see Chapter 12, this volume) can be effective in reducing the likelihood of inappropriate behavior. As noted later, by themselves such cognitive self-instructions are unlikely to be of lasting benefit, but when combined with contingency management procedures they can be of considerable aid to the classroom management of ADHD children.

Parallel Teaching

A variety of effective management programs can be developed with the previously discussed principles in mind; the challenge lies in designing programs that can be easily integrated with classroom instruction and are practical to use. In an approach referred to as parallel teaching (Pfiffner, 1996), social behavior and academic material are taught "in parallel" throughout the day; ongoing instruction is blended with behavior management in the context of a structured classroom environment to facilitate a high state of learning readiness. This blending occurs by scanning the classroom every 1 to 2 minutes and inserting very brief interventions while simultaneously delivering the lesson plan or otherwise interacting with students. Interventions might be statements of praise to students who are on-task, redirections to those off-task, or questions about the lesson with the intention of involving students in the learning process. Managing student behavior in this manner better allows the teacher to issue consequences immediately, consistently, and frequently than if consequences are only administered only after behavior is out of control or only for exceptional behavior. The efficacy of embedding the teacher's managerial statements into ongoing teaching was recently studied by (Martens & Hiralall, 1997) with preschool children. They demonstrated that small changes (in this case, greater use of praise in scripted sequences) could be easily incorporated into ongoing teaching interactions with dramatic improvement in the student's behavior. In addition, once the skills are learned, it generally does not require any more time or resources than procedures the teacher is currently using. Often, teachers of hyperactive children are spending a great deal of time attending to negative behavior. This approach simply involves having the teacher alter his or her pattern of interaction from attending to negative to attending to positive behaviors; to help, the teacher can try the motivator. Again, it is the timing of the attention that is so important to its success in managing behavior. A range of behavioral interventions, reviewed later, can be embedded during teaching activities; these interventions should be considered a critical part of effective teaching rather than a time-consuming adjunct. However, behavioral aids in the classroom are likely to be necessary to implement interventions for students with more severe symptoms.

TEACHER-ADMINISTERED INTERVENTION STRATEGIES

Teacher-administered consequences continue to be the most commonly used behavioral interventions with ADHD students. A combination of positive consequences (praise, tangible rewards, token economies) and negative consequences (reprimands, response cost, time out) has been shown to be optimal. However, as noted earlier, their success with ADHD students is highly dependent on how and when they are administered. Consequences that are immediate, brief, consistent, salient, and, in the case of positive consequences, delivered frequently seem to be most effective.

Strategic Teacher Attention

Strategic teacher attention refers to the practice of purposely using attention to help students remain on-task and redirect those who are not. Praise and other forms of positive teacher attention (smiles, nods, pats on the back) have documented positive effects on ADHD students. Withdrawal of positive teacher attention contingent upon undesirable behavior (i.e., active ignoring) can decrease inappropriate behavior.

Although these procedures may seem unusually simplistic, the systematic and effective use of teacher attention in this manner requires great skill. In general, praise appears to be most effective when it specifies the appropriate behavior being reinforced and when it is delivered in a genuine fashion—with a warm tone of voice and varied content appropriate to the developmental level of the child (O'Leary & O'Leary, 1977). Praise is also more effective when it is delivered as soon as possible following the desired behavior, such as getting started on work, raising a hand to talk, and working quietly. It is this *strategic* timing in the application of teacher attention contingent upon appropriate child conduct and attention to behaviors that are normally expected that is so crucial to its effective as a behavior change agent.

Active ignoring requires the complete and contingent withdrawal of teacher attention—an approach most suitable for nondisruptive minor motor and nonattending behaviors intended to gain teacher attention. Because ignored behavior often increases at first, active ignoring is generally not effective in modifying problem behavior that is not maintained by teacher attention and should not be used aggressive or destructive behavior. Most behavioral problems of ADHD children are not purely bids for teacher attention; thus this strategy alone is unlikely to result in dramatic changes in the behavior of these children. However, the simultaneous use of praise and ignoring can be quite effective. Therefore, appropriate behavior (e.g., sitting in seat) that is incompatible with ignored behavior (e.g., wandering around the class) should be consistently praised. In addition, one of the most powerful uses of teacher attention for modifying problem behavior capitalizes on the positive spillover effects of positive attention. In this procedure, the teacher ignores the disruptive student and praises the student(s) who are working quietly. The behavior of the problem student often improves as a result, presumably due to the vicarious learning that has occurred through this modeling procedure and the child's desire for teacher attention.

To assist teachers with remembering to attend to and reinforce ongoing appropriate child conduct, several cue or prompt systems can be recommended.

One such system involves placing large smiley face stickers about the classroom in places where the teacher may frequently glance (e.g., toward the clock on the wall). When these are viewed, they cue the teacher to remember to check out what the ADHD student is doing and to attend to it if it is at all positive.

A second system relies on tape-recorded cues. A soft tone can be taped onto a 90- or 120-minute cassette such that it occurs at random intervals. This tape is then played during class—either openly to the class or with a small, portable, pocket-size tape player, with an earpiece for private monitoring by the teacher. Whenever the tone is emitted, the teacher is to briefly note what the ADHD child is doing and provide a consequence to the child (praise, token, or response cost) for the behavior at that time. We recommend that the tape contain relatively frequent tone prompts for the first 1 to 2 weeks, which can then be faded to less frequent schedules of prompts over the next several weeks. Such a system can then be converted to a self-monitoring program for second-grade level or older students by providing the children with two small white file cards on their desk. One card has a plus sign (+) or smiley face and is taped to the left side of the desk; the other has a minus sign (–) or frown face and is taped to the right side of the desk. The teacher then instructs the children that whenever they hear the tone, if they are doing as instructed for that activity, they can award themselves a hash mark on the plus card. If they were not obeying instructions or were off-task, they must place a hash mark on the negative card. The teacher's job at the sound of the tone is to rapidly scan the classroom and note the ADHD child's behavior, then note whether the child is delivering the appropriate consequence to him- or herself. The program can be made more effective by having an easel at the front of the classroom with a list of five or so rules that should be followed during that class period (the five rules for desk work might be stay in seat, stay on-task, don't space out, don't bug others, do your work). The teacher can then refer to the set of rules in force at that particular class period or activity when the activity begins and, flipping to the appropriate chart at that time, call the children's attention to these rules. A controlled, within-subject experiment supports the efficacy of this procedure (Edwards, Salant, Howard, Brougher, & McLaughlin, 1995).

A third system for prompting strategic teacher attending and monitoring is to have the teacher place 10 bingo chips in his or her left pocket that must be moved to the right pocket whenever positive attention has been given appropriately to the ADHD child. The goal is to eventually move all 10 chips to the right pocket by the end of that class period.

Tangible Rewards and Token Programs

Becuse of their decreased sensitivity to reward and their failure to sustain effort when reinforcement is inconsistent and weak, ADHD students usually require more frequent and more powerful reinforcement, often in the form of special privileges or activities, to modify classroom performance (Pfiffner, Rosen, & O'Leary, 1985). Special privileges or activities may be provided based on certain target goals. For example, a student may earn extra free time for completing assigned classwork promptly and accurately. In other cases, a token economy may be used. In this system, students earn tokens (points, numbers, hash marks for older children and tangible poker chips, stars, or tickets for younger children) throughout the day and then later exchange their earnings for "backup" rewards (privileges, activities). Backup rewards are typically assigned a purchase value so that rewards can be matched to the number of tokens or points earned. As described later, some programs also include a response-cost component where children lose points for inappropriate behavior. Some tangible or backup rewards are distributed on a daily basis, whereas longer periods (e.g., weekly) of appropriate behavior or academic functioning may be required for more valuable rewards.

The identification of powerful rewards and backup consequences is critical for program success and may be achieved through interviews with children regarding the kinds of activities or other rewards they would like to earn and observations of the high rate of activities normally engaged in by the children. Access to these activities can then be used as reinforcement. For instance, legos may be an effective reward for a child who spends much of his or her free time playing with legos. That is, the child will likely improve his or her behavior if lego play is made available only as a reward for appropriate behavior. Monitoring the manner in which the child spends free time activities over a week or so may suggest what privileges or activities are especially rewarding to that particular child. We have found homework passes, removing lowest grade or making up missing grade, grab bag with small toys or school supplies, free time, computer (e.g., Nintendo) time, stickers/stamps, running errands, helping the teacher, earning extra recess, playing special games, and art projects to be effective reinforcers.

In some cases, rewards available at school may not be sufficiently powerful to alter a child's behavior. Home-based reward programs, discussed in a subsequent section, may be considered in those cases. It is also possible to have parents provide a favorite toy or piece of play equipment from home to the teacher for contingent use in the classroom as part of a classroom token or reward system. By providing presentations to local civic club on the seriousness of classroom behavioral problems and the critical need for such reinforcers in the management of disruptive (and normal) children, we have been successful in getting them to donate reinforcement equipment to a particular classroom or at least partially to off-set its expense. Otherwise, soliciting each parent of a child in that classroom to donate a few dollars or so is often adequate to purchase these systems for reinforcement of child behavior.

Reward programs can be designed for individual children or for the entire class. Individual programs or classwide programs wherein students earn rewards for their own behavior are often best for the ADHD student. Involving the entire class may be particularly effective when peer contingencies are competing with teacher contingencies (e.g., when peers reinforce disruptive students by laughter or joining in on their off-task pursuits). Some sample programs (see Pfiffner, 1996) include the following:

- *"Big Deals."* In this group contingency, stickers called Big Deals are earned individually and/or as a group for exhibiting target behavior/social skills (e.g., following directions, sharing, using an assertive tone of voice). Stickers are posted on a Big Deal Chart. Once the class earns a predetermined number of stickers, the class earns a group party ("Big Deal fiesta").
- *"Peg system."* In this system for younger children, the teacher sets a timer for a brief period (2–5 minutes). If the student follows all class rules until the timer goes off, he or she earns a peg kept in a cup. Whenever the child breaks a rule, the teacher earns a peg and resets the timer. At the end of the period, if the child has more pegs than the teacher, the child selects an activity for the class to do. Otherwise, the teacher selects the activity and the child does not participate.
- *Visual aids* (cards) taped to students' desktops serve as a way to conveniently keep track of progress toward established goals. The cards may be divided into columns as described previously, or they may depict colorful pictures to correspond with progress. For example, a thermometer, with higher readings corresponding to greater on-task behavior may be used with younger students. Tangible rewards are earned at the end of the day for those with high readings.
- *Lotteries and auctions.* In this popular program, students earn tickets or "bucks" for a variety of target behaviors throughout the day and exchange them for chances in the lottery or items during class auctions offered at least once a week (daily at the beginning of the program).
- *Team contingencies.* In this variation of group programs, children are divided into competing teams and earn or lose points for their respective team depending on their behavior. The team with the greatest number of positive points or fewest negative points earns the group privileges. For example, teams may be divided by tables or rows. Points would be given to a team for behaviors of the individual members, such as getting along, keeping area clean, and so on. The team with the most points or all teams that meet a specified criteria earn the reward.
- *Class movies and theme parties.* To make it interesting, we have found that posters depicting the activity to be earned and a record of class progress toward earning the activity are helpful. In one example, for every 15 minutes class members are on-task, the children in the picture are moved an inch closer to a picture of a theater. When they reached the theater, they earn the movie.
- *The Good Behavior Game* (Barrish, Saunders, & Wolf, 1969). In this approach, the class is divided into two teams. Each team receives marks for rule violations of individual team members. After a specified period, both teams earn a reward if their marks do not exceed a certain number; otherwise the team with the fewest marks wins. This game has been effective in improving student behavior and has also been well accepted by teachers (Tingstrom, 1994).

Group programs targeting all students' behavior have the advantage of not singling out the ADHD child. Given the concern that some teachers have about possible stigmatization or undue attention to problem children receiving treatment, this approach may be preferable. Group programs may also be the treatment of choice when there is concern that children not involved in treatment will increase their misbehavior to be a part of the program and receive reinforcement. It should be noted, however, that concerns of stigmatization and escalation of problem behavior have not been substantiated in research studies. When using group contingencies, however, care should be taken to minimize possible peer pressure and subversion of the program by one or more children. Powerful reward-only programs may be effective in this regard.

The success of token programs in numerous studies and their utility with a wide range of problem behaviors have led to their widespread use in school settings. Tokens are portable; thus they can be administered in any situation and can usually be distributed immediately following desirable behavior. Token programs also tend to be very powerful because a wide range of backup rewards can be used to avoid satiation of any one reward. However, appropriate and realistic treatment goals are critical for the success of the program. In many typical classrooms, rewards are often reserved for exemplary performance. Although this practice may be sufficient for some children, it is unlikely to improve the performance of children exhibiting severe attentional and behavioral problems. Regardless of how motivated such a child may be initially, if the criteria for a reward is set too high, the child will rarely achieve the reward and will likely give up trying. To prevent this occurrence, rewards should initially be provided for approximations to the terminal response and should be set at a level that ensures the child's success. For instance, a child who has a long history of failing to complete work should be required to complete only part of his or her work to earn a reward. Similarly, a child who is often disruptive throughout the day may initially earn a reward for exhibiting quiet, on-task behavior for only a small segment of the day. As performance improves, more appropriate behavior can be shaped by gradually increasing the behavioral criteria for rewards.

It is important to point out that ADHD students typically lose interest if the same reward is used for too long. Rewards are much more effective if they are novel and change regularly. We recommend using a "reward menu" (a list of varied activities, privileges, or objects) and having the child select his or her own rewards. The "packaging" of the reward is especially important. We strongly recommend that teachers make the reward fun and interesting by using colorful posters, creative tokens, special words to describe the treat (e.g., "bonus" and "challenges") and by being enthusiastic.

Negative Consequences

Whereas use of positive approaches should be emphasized when working with ADHD students, negative consequences are usually necessary. In fact, some studies show that brief reprimands may be more important than praise for maintaining appropriate behavior (Acker & O'Leary, 1987). However, the effectiveness of negative consequences, particularly with ADHD students, is highly dependent on several stylistic features.

Reprimands

Reprimands and corrective statements are the most commonly used negative consequence. As is the case with praise, the effectiveness of reprimands is a function of how and when they are delivered. A number of studies (Pfiffner & O'Leary, 1993) indicate that reprimands that are immediate, unemotional, brief, and consistently backed up with time out or a loss of a privilege for repeated noncompliance are far superior to those that are delayed, long, or inconsistent. Proximity also seems to make a difference; reprimands that are issued in close proximity to the child have an edge over those yelled from across the room. Mixing positive and negative feedback for inappropriate behavior appears to be particularly deleterious. For example, children who are sometimes reprimanded for calling out but other times responded to as if they had raised their hands are apt to continue, if not increase, their calling out. In addition, children respond better to teachers who deliver consistently strong reprimands at the outset of the school year (immediate, brief, firm, and in close proximity to the child) than to teachers who gradually increase the severity of their discipline over time. Finally, the practice of using encouragement ("I know you can do it.") in attempt to coax a student into good behavior is not as effective as clear direct reprimands (Abramowitz & O'Leary, 1991).

Response Cost

Response cost involves the loss of a reinforcer contingent upon inappropriate behavior. Lost reinforcers can include a wide range of privileges and activities. Response cost has often been used to manage the disruptive behavior of ADHD children in the context of a token program. This procedure involves the child losing tokens for inappropriate behavior in addition to earning them for appropriate behavior. It is convenient, easy to use, and readily adapted to a variety of target behaviors and situations. Furthermore, response cost has been shown to be more effective than reprimands with ADHD children and can also increase the effectiveness of reward programs.

The classic study of response cost conducted by (Rapport, Murphy, and Bailey (1980) compared the effects of response cost with stimulant medication on the behavior and academic performance of two hyperactive children. In the response-cost procedure, the teacher deducted one point every time she saw a child not working. Each point loss translated into a loss of 1 minute of free time. An apparatus was placed at each child's desk to keep track of point totals. One child's apparatus consisted of numbered cards that could be changed to a lesser value each time a point was lost. The teacher had an identical apparatus on her desk where she kept track of point losses. The child was instructed to match the number value on his apparatus with that of the teacher's on a continual basis. The second child had a battery-operated electronic "counter" with a number display. The teacher decreased point values on the display via a remote transmitter. Both response-cost procedures resulted in increases in both on-task and academic performance, which compared favorably with the effects of stimulant medication. The immediacy with which consequences could be delivered in either procedure (the teacher was able to administer a consequence even when she was a distance away from the child) likely contributed to their efficacy.

The device used in this study, called the Attention Trainer®, was originally designed by Mark Rapport and later revised and marketed by Michael Gordon (available from Gordon Systems, DeWitt, NY). It continues to receive strong empirical support (DuPaul, Guevremont, & Barkley, 1992; Evans, Ferre, Ford, & Green, 1995; Gordon, Thomason, Cooper, & Ivers, 1990). Although some teachers initially believe that such a device may result in negative social stigma or excessive peer attention, we have not found this to be the case. The device can be faded out for use over 4 to 6 weeks and replaced by a less intensive class token system or self-monitoring program like the tone-prompt system described earlier or by a home–school report card described later.

Response cost has also been used in a variety of other formats: Color-coded response-cost programs have been implemented in several programs across the country (Barkley et al., 1996; Kotkin, 1995). In these programs, students' behavior is reviewed every 30 minutes and they receive a color card corresponding to how well they did. For example, each student starts the period with a red (the color representing optimal behavior). Following a minor infraction, the color changes to a yellow; following a major infraction the color changes to a blue. Color strips are either attached with Velcro or inserted in paper pockets to a board containing the students' names down one side and the period listed across the top. Color earnings are totaled one or two times per day (twice for younger children, once for older children). Earnings are exchanged for graduated activities and privileges (e.g., red earns choice of most desirable activities; blue earns fewest choices). Weekly rewards based on daily earnings are also provided.

Response cost has also been implemented in a group format. In one procedure, a self-contained class was given 30 tokens (poker chips) each day at the beginning of a 90-minute period. A token was removed contingent upon each occurrence of an interruption by any student. Tokens were counted at the end of the period; remaining tokens were exchanged for 1 minute of reading time by the teacher. Significant reduction in interruptions occurred and most of the students rated the program very favorably (Sprute, Williams, & McLaughlin, 1990).

A response-cost raffle was also successful in reducing mild disruptive behavior of junior high school students (Proctor & Morgan, 1991). In this system, five tickets were distributed to students at the beginning of each class period. Students lost one ticket for each instance of disruptive behavior. Remaining slips were collected at the end of the period. Two tickets were labeled with the word "group." One ticket was then randomly selected. The winning student chose from a list of potential rewards including free candy, gum, soda, chips, and so on. If a ticket labeled "group" was chosen, a class reward was selected (e.g., free talking, candy, or movie day).

As with other punishment procedures, response cost is most effective when it is applied immediately, unemotionally, and consistently. When delivered in this way, response cost is as effective as token reward programs. In addition, teachers and children's attitudes about response-cost programs appear to be as positive as they are for reward programs. However, special effort should be taken to continue monitoring and praising appropriate behavior when cost programs are in effect to avoid excessive attention to negative behavior. It is also advisable that when using rewards and response cost together, the opportunity to earn tokens be greater than the possibility of losing them to avoid negative earnings (i.e., below zero). Care should also be taken to avoid the use of unreasonably stringent standards which lead to excessive point or privilege losses. In the case of aggressive or very coercive behavior, teachers may be reluctant to administer the procedure right away due to a fear of the behavior escalating. However, response cost needs to be implemented consistently and immediately to be effective. Escalation may be minimized by reducing the amount of the "cost" when the student does not lose control.

Time Out

Time out from positive reinforcement (i.e., "time out") is often effective for hyperactive children who are particularly aggressive or disruptive. This procedure involves the withdrawal of positive reinforcement contingent upon inappropriate behavior. Several variations of time out are used in the classroom:

• Removal of the student from the classroom situation, referred to as social isolation, to a small empty room (i.e., "time-out room") for short periods (e.g., 2 to 10 minutes). Isolation time out has been increasingly criticized over the years due to ethical concerns and difficulty in implementing the procedure correctly.

- Removal of adult or peer attention by removing the child from the area of reinforcement or the opportunity to earn reinforcement. This may involve having the child sit in a three-sided cubicle or sit facing a dull area (e.g., a blank wall) in the classroom.
- Removal of materials, as in the case of having children put their work away (which eliminates the opportunity to earn reinforcement for academic performance) and their head down (which reduces the opportunity for reinforcing interaction with others) for brief periods.
- Using a "good behavior clock," as implemented by Kubany, Weiss, and Slogett (1971). In this procedure, rewards (e.g., penny trinkets or candy) are earned for a target child and the class contingent upon the child's behaving appropriately for a specified period. A clock runs whenever the child is on-task and behaving appropriately but is stopped for a short time when the child is disruptive or off-task.

Most time out programs set specific criteria that must be fulfilled prior to release from time out. Typically, these criteria involve the child being quiet and cooperative for a specified period during time out. In some cases, extremely disruptive hyperactive children may fail to comply with the standard procedure, either by refusing to go to time out or by not remaining in the time out area for the required duration. To reduce noncompliance in these cases (1) children can earn time off for complying with the procedure (i.e., the length of original time out is reduced); (2) the length of time out can be increased for each infraction; (3) the child may be removed from the class to serve the time out elsewhere (e.g., in another class, or in the principal's office); (4) a response cost procedure can be used wherein activities, privileges, or tokens are lost for uncooperative behavior in time out; (5) work tasks such as simple copying or marking tasks contingent upon failure to follow time-out rules, can be used; and (6) the child can stay after school to serve time-out for not cooperating in following time-out rules during school hours. The use of this procedure, however, depends on the availability of personnel to supervise the child after school.

Overall, time out appears to be an effective procedure for reducing aggressive and disruptive actions in the classroom, especially when they are maintained by peer or teacher attention. Time out may not be effective when inappropriate behavior is due to a desire to avoid work or be alone, because in these cases time out may actually be reinforcing. It is important that time out be implemented with minimal attention from teacher and peers. When a child's problem behavior consistently escalates during time out and requires teacher intervention (e.g., restraint) to prevent harm to self, others, or property, alternative procedures to time out may be indicated. Overall, procedural safeguards and appropriate reviews are important to ensure that time out is used in an ethical and legal way (Gast & Nelson, 1977).

Suspension

Suspension from school is sometimes used as punishment for severe problem behavior but may not be effective with students who have ADHD. The use of suspension violates several critical features of effective punishment: It is not immediate, it is not brief, and it may not remove rewarding activities (many children may find staying at home or full-day day care more enjoyable than being in school). Suspension should not be used when parents do not have the appropriate management skills needed for enforcement or when parents may be overly punitive or abusive.

In-school suspension programs, on the other hand, may be appropriate for particularly chronic, severe, intentional infractions (serious aggressive or destructive behavior) for which response cost, time out, and reward programs have been ineffective. For example, in-school suspension may be effective as a backup consequence when a student fails to take time-outs or accept a "cost" and becomes violent or seriously disruptive. If in-school suspension is used, the suspensions should be short-term (usually not more than a day or two) and have clear entry criteria, clear rules, and structured educational assignments for the student to do while they are away from the classroom.

Minimizing Adverse Side Effects

Despite the overall effectiveness of negative consequences, adverse side effects may occur if they are used improperly. Guidelines presented in the previous version of this chapter and taken from O'Leary and O'Leary (1977) are still timely and are reviewed here as well:

• Punishment should be used sparingly. Teachers who frequently use punishment to the exclusion of positive consequences may be less effective in managing children's behavior because of a loss in their reinforcing value and/or the child's having satiated or adapted to the punishment. Excessive criticism or other forms of punishment may also cause the classroom situation to become aversive. As a result, the child may begin to avoid certain academic subjects by skipping classes or to avoid school in general by becoming truant. Frequent harsh punishment may even accelerate a child's overt defiance, especially when a teacher inadvertently serves as an aggressive model.

• When teachers use negative consequences, they should teach and reinforce children for alternative appropriate behaviors. This practice will aid in teaching appropriate skills as well as decreasing the potential for the occurrence of other problem behaviors.

• Punishment involving the removal of a positive reinforcer (e.g., response cost) is usually preferable to punishment involving the presentation of an aversive stimulus. Use of the latter method, as exemplified by corporal punishment, is often limited for ethical and legal reasons.

Maintenance and Generalization

Maintaining treatment gains after withdrawing treatment continues to be a challenge, as does generalizing improvement made in one setting or class to another. Unfortunately, generalization does not occur automatically. The most effective approach for promoting improvement in behavior in all classes and periods (recess, lunch) is to implement behavioral programs in all the settings in which behavioral change is desired.

Technologies have also been developed to improve the probability that treatment gains will maintain over time. The most effective seems to be withdrawing the classroom contingency programs gradually. For example, a study conducted by (Pfiffner & O'Leary, 1987) found that the abrupt removal of negative consequences, even in the context of a powerful token program, led to dramatic deterioration in class behavior. However, when negative consequences were gradually removed, high on-task rates were maintained. Likewise, token economies should not be removed abruptly. Gradual withdrawal of token programs may be accomplished by reducing the frequency of feedback (e.g., fading from daily to weekly rewards) and substituting natural reinforcers (e.g., praise and regular activities) for token rewards. One particularly effective procedure for fading management programs involves varying the range of conditions or situations in which contingencies are administered to reduce the child's ability to discriminate when contingencies are in effect. The less the discriminability of the changes in contingencies when fading a program, the more successful the fading appears to be. When transitioning a student to a new class, it is wise to initially implement the same or similar program in the new class and then fade it once behavior is stable.

Self-management skills such as self-monitoring and self-reinforcement (to be described in a subsequent section) have also been taught in order to improve maintenance of gains from behavioral programs and to help prompt appropriate behavior in nontreated settings. These procedures have been found to improve maintenance following withdrawal of token programs. However, they are not effective in the absence of teacher supervision and little evidence exists to suggest that they facilitate generalization across settings.

The need to develop programs to enhance maintenance and generalization of teacher-administered interventions continues to be critical. At this time, specially arranged interventions for ADHD children should be required across school settings and for extended periods over the course of their education given the developmentally handicapping nature of their disorder.

PEER INTERVENTIONS

Efforts to involve peers in modifying the disruptive and intrusive behavior of ADHD children have focused on strategies to discourage peers from reinforcing their classmate's inappropriate behavior and instead to encourage their attention to positive, prosocial behavior. These strategies can vary considerably. For example, group contingencies, discussed earlier, indirectly motivate peers to encourage appropriate behavior and discourage misbehavior in their classmates.

In another scenario, teachers can have peers assume roles as "behavior modifiers," which involves their ignoring the disruptive, inappropriate behavior of their peers and praising or giving tokens for positive behavior such as being a good sport, getting a high grade on an exam (or accepting a low grade without tantruming), contributing to a class discussion, or helping another student. To promote peer use of reinforcement and ignoring, teachers must reward their efforts with praise, tangible rewards, or tokens in a token economy. Serving as a peer monitor or dispenser of reinforcers appears to be a particularly powerful reward, and children often purchase the privilege of distributing rewards with tokens they have earned. This approach may be useful for several reasons. Because teachers are unable continually to observe every student's behavior, peers may be to monitor their classmates' behavior and therefore to provide accurate, immediate, and consistent reinforcement. Also, training children to alter their interactions with peers not only improves peer behavior but also directly improves the behavior of the children implementing the intervention. This would seem particularly beneficial for ADHD children who are at such a great risk for poor peer relations. Moreover, peer reinforcement systems may facilitate generalization because peers may function as cues for appropriate behavior in multiple settings. In addition, peer-mediated programs may be more practical and require less time than traditional teacher-mediated programs. Despite these advantages, several cautions are in order. Peer-mediated programs are successful only to the extent that peers have the ability and motivation to learn and accurately implement the program. Peers may be overly lenient and reward too liberally due to peer pressure, fear of peer rejection, or more lenient definitions of misbehavior. On the other hand, children may use the program in a coercive or punitive fashion. Also, recent evidence shows that involving peers by having them correct only negative behavior of ADHD students (e.g., by using comments such as "you need to be working") can exacerbate the problem (Northup et al., 1997), presumably due to the reinforcing value of peer attention. Because of these concerns, it is advisable that peers not be involved in implementing any punishment programs. In addition, when peers are utilized as change agents, they should be carefully trained and supervised and contingencies should be provided for accurate ratings.

Peer tutoring represents the most recent advance in the utilization of peers as a part of the intervention process for ADHD children. Peer tutoring focuses specifically on improving academic skills (a target that has been relatively unaffected by traditional contingency management programs) and provides a learning environment well-suited to the needs of ADHD students (i.e., involves immediate, frequent feedback and active responding at the student's pace (DuPaul & Stoner, 1994). Classwide peer tutoring programs, tapping the "natural" resources of the classroom, have been developed in which each student is paired for tutoring with a classmate. Students are first trained in the rules and procedures for tutoring their peers in an academic area (e.g., math, spelling, and reading). Sitting in adjacent, separate seats, the tutor reads a script of problems to the tutee and awards points to the tutee for correct responses. The tutor corrects incorrect responses and the tutee can practice the correct response for an additional point. The script (problem list) is read as many times as possible for 10 minutes and then the students switch roles, with the tutee becoming the tutor and the tutor becoming the tutee. During the tutoring periods, the teacher monitors the tutoring process and provides assistance if needed. Bonus points are awarded to pairs following all the rules. At the end of the session, points are totaled and those with the most points are declared the "winners." Recent studies support the use of this approach with ADHD students (DuPaul & Henningson, 1993) with positive effects on both classroom behavior and academic performance. Both teachers and students have rated peer tutoring favorably. Peer tutoring is probably most effective for ADHD students when they are paired with well-behaved and conscientious classmates.

HOME-BASED CONTINGENCIES

Home-based contingency programs continue to be among the most commonly recommended interventions. Following the first edition of this chapter, Kelley (1990) has written a comprehensive book about school notes, which includes many examples and strategies for effective use. Briefly, these programs involve the provision of contingencies in the home based on the teacher's report of the child's performance at school. Teacher reports, often referred to as a "report card," list the target behavior(s) and a quantifiable rating for each behavior. Teacher reports should be sent home on a daily basis at first. As children's behavior improves, the daily reports may be faded to weekly, biweekly, monthly, and in some cases to the reporting intervals typically used in the school—although for many ADHD children, report cards should be used throughout the year on a weekly basis.

The following points should be considered when tailoring report cards for students:

1. *Select important target behaviors.* In-class behavior (sharing, playing well with peers, following rules) and academic performance (completing math or reading assignments) may be targeted along with homework, a common problem for ADHD students, who often have difficulty remembering to bring home assignments, completing the work, and then returning the completed work to school the next day. We recommend including at least one or two positive behaviors that the child is currently displaying reliably so that the child will be able to earn some points during the beginning of the program.

2. *The number of target behaviors may vary from as few as one to as many as seven or eight.* Targeting few behaviors is suggested when first implementing a program (to maximize the child's likelihood of success), when few behaviors require modification, or when teachers have difficulty monitoring many behaviors.

3. *The daily ratings of each target behavior should be quantifiable.* Ratings may be descriptive (e.g., "poor," "fair," and "good"), with each descriptor being clearly defined (e.g.,

"poor" = more than three rule violations), or more specific and objective, such as frequency counts of each behavior (e.g., interrupted less than three times) or the number of points earned or lost for each behavior.

4. *Children should be monitored and given feedback during each period, subject, or class throughout the school day.* In this way, a student's difficulty early on can be modified later in the day. To achieve success with a particularly high number of problem behaviors, children may initially be rated for only a portion of the day. As behavior improves, ratings may gradually include more periods/subjects until the child is being monitored throughout the day. When children attend several different classes taught by different teachers, programs may involve some or all of the teachers, depending on the need for intervention in each of the classes. When more than one teacher is included in the program, a single report card may include space for all teachers to sign, or different report cards may be used for each class and organized in a notebook for children to carry between classes.

5. *The success of the program requires a clear, consistent system for translating teacher reports into consequences at home.* The student may take a new card to school each day, or the cards can be kept at school and given to the student each morning, depending on the reliability of the parents to give the card out each day. When the child returns home, the parent immediately inspects the card and discusses the positive ratings with the child. The parent may ask about any negative ratings, but the discussion should be very brief, neutral, and business-like (not angry!). The child is then asked to formulate a plan for how to continue earning positive marks and avoid getting negative marks the next day (parents are to remind the child of this plan the next morning before the child departs for school). The parent then provides the child with a reward dependent on his or her earnings. Some programs involve rewards alone; others incorporate both positive and negative consequences. However, when parents tend to be overly coercive or abusive, reward-only programs are preferable. At a minimum, praise and positive attention should be provided whenever a child's goals are met; however, tangible rewards or token programs are usually necessary. For example, a positive note home may translate into TV time, a special snack, or a later bedtime or into points as part of a token economy. Both daily rewards (time with parent, special dessert, TV time) and weekly rewards (movie, dinner at a restaurant, special outing) are recommended, although parents should understand that it is the daily rewards that will be most important for motivating children with ADHD. Parents should be strongly encouraged to use rewards that are basic privileges and activities that the child enjoys—not elaborate or expensive items.

The following figures illustrate several types of home-based reward programs that rely on daily school behavior ratings. Figure 15.1 shows a card that contains four areas of potentially problematic behavior with ADHD children. Columns are provided for up to six different teachers to rate the child in these areas of behavior or for one teacher to rate the child multiple times across the school day. The teacher initials the bottom of the column after rating the child's performance during that class period and checking for the accuracy of the copied homework, to ensure against forgery. For particularly negative ratings, we also encourage teachers to provide a brief explanation to the parent as to what caused that negative mark. The teachers rate the children using a 3-point system.

The parent then awards the child points for each rating on the card (0 = no points, 1 = one point, 2 = two points). The child may then spend these points on activities from a home-reward menu.

A similar card system may be used when a child is having problems with peers during school recess periods. This card, shown in Figure 15.2, can be completed by the recess monitor during each recess period, inspected by the class teacher when the child returns to the classroom, and then sent home for use in a home-point system. The class teacher can also in-

Name: _____ Date: _____

Please rate child in areas below according to this scale:
2 = Very good
1 = OK
0 = Needs improvement

CLASS PERIOD/SUBJECT

TARGET BEHAVIOR	1	2	3	4	5	6
Participation						
Classwork						
Handed in homework						
Interaction with peers						
Teacher's initials						

Total points earned:

Homework for tonight (list class period by assignment):

Comments:

FIGURE 15.1. Classroom challenge.

struct the child to use a "think aloud, think ahead" procedure just prior to the child's leaving the class for recess. In this procedure, the teacher reviews the rules for proper recess behavior with the child, notes their existence on the card, and directs the child to give the card immediately to the recess monitor.

Overall, home-based reward programs can be an effective adjunct to classroom-based programs for ADHD children:

- They offer more frequent feedback than usually provided at school.
- They afford parents more frequent feedback regarding their child's performance than would normally be provided and can prompt parents when to reinforce a child's behavior as well as when behavior is becoming problematic and requires more intensive intervention.
- The type and quality of reinforcers available in the home are typically far more extensive than those available in the classroom (a factor which may be critical with children having ADHD as reviewed earlier).
- Virtually any child behavior can be targeted for intervention with these programs.
- Note-home programs can require somewhat less teacher time and effort than a classroom-based intervention and may be particularly popular with teachers who are concerned that use of classroom rewards for only some students is unfair.

However, as pointed out by Abramowitz and O'Leary (1991), effective implementation of daily report cards is not a simple procedure. All the behavioral skills needed for developing and implementing classroom contingency programs are also needed for use of report cards; in addition, teachers need to work effectively with parents. Both teacher and parents need to understand basic behavior modification, how to select and rotate rewards, and the concept of consistency (teachers need to implement the program every day and parents need to provide rewards exactly as specified). In addition, plans should be established for handling cases in which children attempt to subvert the system by failing to bring home a report, forging a teacher signature, or failing to get certain teacher signatures. To discourage this practice, missing notes or signatures should be treated the same way as a "bad" report (e.g., child fails to earn points or loses privileges or points). When parents are overly punitive or lack skills to follow through with consequences, their implementation of appropriate consequences should be closely supervised (possibly by a therapist), or other adults (e.g., school counselors or principal) may implement the program.

SELF-MANAGEMENT INTERVENTIONS

Self-management interventions, which include self-monitoring, self-reinforcement, and more comprehensive self-instruction and problem-solving approaches, were originally developed to directly treat the impulsive, disorganized, and nonreflective manner in which hyperactive children approach academic tasks and social interactions. Because of their emphasis on the development of self-control, investigators thought that these interventions would reduce the need for extrinsic rewards and would result in better maintenance and generalization of gains made by ADHD children than achieved by contingency management programs.

   Unfortunately, these programs have fallen short of initial expectations (Abikoff & Gittelman, 1985; Bloomquist, August, & Ostrander, 1991; Braswell et al., 1997). However, self-monitoring and self-reinforcement strategies have had some success with ADHD students. These approaches involve children monitoring and evaluating their own academic and social behavior and rewarding themselves (often with tokens or points) based on those evaluations. Training typically involves teaching children how to observe and record their own behavior and how to evaluate their behavior to determine whether they deserve a reward. Children may be prompted to observe their own behavior by a periodic auditory signal (tone) or visual cue (teacher's hand gesture) and trained to record instances of appropriate behavior. Accuracy of child ratings is usually assessed by comparing these ratings against the teacher's records.

Name: _____ Date: _____

Please rate this child in the following areas during recess and lunch. Use a rating of 3 = excellent, 2 = good, 1 = fair, 0 = poor.

	Recess or lunch			
	1	2	3	4
Keeps hands and feet to self—doesn't fight, push, kick, wrongly touch or take others' belongings				
Follows rules				
Tries to get along well with others				
Recess/lunch monitor's initials				

Total points earned:

Comments:

FIGURE 15.2. Recess/lunch challenge.

Research has developed several applications of self-management interventions.

Barkley, Copeland, and Sivage (1980) taught hyperactive 7- to 10-year-olds to monitor their behavior during individual seat work. If children had been following the rules when a tone sounded, they recorded a checkmark on an index card kept at their desk. Initially, the tone sounded on a variable 1-minute schedule but was faded to a variable-interval 5-minute schedule. Accurate reports, defined as matching an observer's report, were rewarded with token(s) which could be exchanged for privileges. Using this procedure, on-task behavior improved during individual seat work, particularly with older children, but improvements made during individual seat work did not generalize to the regular classroom. Thus, the effectiveness of self-monitoring and self-reinforcement seemed to be limited to the context in which they were taught and where contingencies were in effect for their use. More recently, Edwards et al. (1995) implemented a similar self-monitoring procedure with ADHD students and also found improved on-task behavior and reading comprehension among the students.

Hinshaw, Henker, and Whalen (1984) extended the use of self-monitoring and self-reinforcement to children's peer interactions in a training program called "Match Game," designed to teach children to self-evaluate and self-reward their cooperative interactions with peers. In this procedure, trainers first taught children behavioral criteria for a range of ratings by modeling various behavior (paying attention, doing work, cooperative behavior) and assigning the behavior from 1 to 5 points (e.g., 1 = pretty bad and 5 = great!). Thereafter, children participated in role-plays followed by naturalistic playground games in which trainers rated each child's behavior on the 1–5 scale and instructed children to monitor and rate their own behavior using the same scale. Children were encouraged to try to match the trainer's ratings. Initially, children were given extra points for accurate self-evaluations regardless of the actual point value. However, once children learned the procedure, they were rewarded only when their behavior was desirable *and* matched the trainers' ratings. Results of this study revealed that reinforced self-evaluation was more effective than externally administered reinforcement in reducing negative and increasing cooperative peer contacts on the playground.

The combination of self-monitoring and self-reinforcement has also been used with success to maintain gains from a token economy with secondary-level students, for whom contingency management procedures are often not viewed favorably by teachers or students (DuPaul & Stoner, 1994). Students are trained in evaluating their own behavior using a 6-point set of criteria (unacceptable to excellent) after they have achieved success in a standard teacher-administered token economy. They earn points for positive teacher ratings and bonus points if their ratings match the teacher's ratings. Over time, teacher ratings are gradually faded to random matching checks for accuracy; students earn points for their own ratings. The "matching challenges" are increased if student's ratings become inaccurate. Although teacher involvement can be faded quite a bit with this procedure, the continued checking of student ratings and backup reinforcers appears to be important in sustaining improvement.

Several recent studies have incorporated goal setting in addition to the self-monitoring and self-reinforcement strategies. In one study, six students were invited to participate in a tutoring class as "employees" and follow weekly employment contracts (Ajibola & Clement, 1995). Students set goals for the number of reading problems they would complete and signed a performance contract to this effect. Thereafter, they would give themselves one point on a wrist counter each time they answered a reading question. At the end of tutoring class each day, students received stamps based on the points earned. Stamps were later exchanged for backup reinforcers. Self-reinforcement resulted in significant improvement in academic performance compared to noncontingent reinforcement and also appeared to add to the benefits of a low dose of stimulant medication. In a variant of this approach, correspondence training, students are trained to match their verbal behavior (promises to inhibit hyperactive behavior and conduct problems) with their later nonverbal actions. In a simulated classroom, students were reinforced with small toys when their promise to inhibit a behavior was associated with their actual inhibition of that behavior over a 10-minute period. Preliminary results show a positive impact on child behavior (Paniagua & Black, 1992)

Many cognitive training programs involve teaching children self-instructional and problem-solving strategies in addition to self-monitoring and self-reinforcement (Meichenbaum & Goodman, 1971). The prototypical program involves teaching children a set of self-directed instructions to follow when performing a task. Self-instructions include defining and understanding the task or problem, planning a general strategy to approach the problem, focusing attention on the task, selecting an answer or solution, and evaluating performance. In the case of a successful performance, self-reinforcement (usually in the form of a positive self-statement such as "I really did a good job.") is provided. In the case of an unsuccessful performance, a coping statement is made (e.g., "Next time I'll do better if I slow down.") and errors are corrected. At first, an adult trainer typically models the self-instructions while performing a task. The child then performs the same task while the trainer provides the self-instructions. Next, the child performs the task while self-instructing aloud. These overt verbalizations are then faded to covert self-instructions. Reinforcement (e.g., praise, tokens, and toys) is typically provided to the child for following the procedure as well as selecting correct solutions.

Unfortunately, these programs have failed to show positive results with ADHD children (Abikoff & Gittelman, 1985; Diaz & Berk, 1995; Bloomquist et al., 1991; Braswell et al., 1997). When improvement does occur, it is when external or self-reinforcement is provided for accurate and positive self-evaluations in conjunction with self-instructional training. In fact, when programs are effective, it may be more a result of reinforcement rather than self-instructions.

In sum, self-monitoring and self-reinforcement strategies are the most promising of the self-management interventions, although the effects of these interventions are not as strong, as durable, or as generalizable as was once expected and are not superior to traditional behavioral programs. Complete transfer of management of the program from teacher to student is unrealistic; continued teacher monitoring of the ratings is necessary to ensure honest reporting. Self-instruction and problem solving show fewer positive effects, perhaps because the treatment is generally not specific to the deficits of the child. Most gains are achieved from self-management programs when the training is of sufficient duration (not just a few hours) and when there is overlap between the skills taught during training and the requirements of the classroom or playground. Training is required in all settings in which self-control is desirable, both for children and for the adult supervisors (e.g., teacher and recess monitors) and adults need to encourage children's application of the skills in day-to-day activities in each setting. As a result, these interventions frequently require an excessive amount of time and resources to implement properly. Because of inconsistent effects and the time necessary for training, the value of the widespread use of these procedures with ADHD children still remains to be seen. However, self-monitoring and self-reinforcement seem to facilitate partial fading of token programs. Also, there may be some value in using self-management, particularly with older students, because these procedures may be more acceptable to teachers than token programs and therefore more likely to be used consistently (DuPaul & Stoner, 1994). In any case, children must be adequately reinforced for displaying self-control skills to maintain this type of behavior—the training alone is insufficient.

CLASSROOM STRUCTURE AND TASK DEMANDS

In recent years, somewhat more attention has been paid to the importance of the structure of the classroom environment, classroom rules, and the nature of task assignments for improving hyperactive children's school functioning. Several specific features of the classroom environment may warrant modification when working with hyperactive children. Probably one of the most common classroom interventions involves moving the hyperactive child's desk away from other children to an area closer to the teacher. This procedure not only reduces the child's access to peer reinforcement of his or her disruptive behavior but also allows the teacher to better monitor the child's behavior. As a result, the teacher can provide more frequent feedback which, as discussed earlier, is necessary with many ADHD children. It may also be beneficial for ADHD children to have individual and separated desks. When children sit very near one another, attention to task often decreases due to disruptions that occur between children. Altering seating arrangements in this manner may sometimes be as effective as a reinforcement program in increasing appropriate classroom behavior.

Physically enclosed classrooms (with four walls and a door) are often recommended for hyperactive children over classrooms that do not have these physical barriers (i.e., "open" classrooms). An open classroom is usually noisier and contains more visual distractions because children can often see and hear the ongoing activities in nearby classes. In light of research showing that noisy environments are associated with less task attention and higher rates of negative verbalizations among hyperactive children (Whalen, Henker, Collins, Finck, & Dotemoto, 1979), open classrooms appear to be less appropriate for ADHD children.

The classroom should be well-organized, structured, and predictable, with the posting of a daily schedule and classroom rules. Visual aids are often recommended for ADHD children. Hand signals and brightly colored posters can reduce the need for frequent verbal repetitions of rules. Posted feedback charts regarding children's adherence to the classroom rules may also facilitate program success.

The following additional changes to classroom structure and curriculum are likely to prove beneficial to the management of ADHD children:

1. As with all children, academic tasks should be well-matched to the child's abilities. In the case of ADHD children, increasing the novelty and interest level of the tasks through use of increased stimulation (e.g., color, shape, and texture) seems to reduce activity level, enhance attention, and improve overall performance (Zentall, 1993).

2. Varying the presentation format and task materials (e.g., through use of different modalities) also seems to help maintain interest and motivation. When low-interest or passive tasks are assigned, they should be interspersed with high-interest or active tasks to optimize performance. Tasks requiring an active (e.g., motoric) as opposed to passive response may also allow hyperactive children to better channel their disruptive behaviors into constructive responses (Zentall, 1993).

3. Academic assignments should be brief (i.e., accommodated to the child's attention span) and presented one at a time rather than all at once in a packet or group (Abramowitz, Reid, & O'Toole, 1994). Short time limits for task completion should also be specified and may be enforced with the use of such external aids as timers. For example, a timer may be set for several minutes during which time the student is to complete a task. The goal for the student is to complete the task before the timer goes off. Feedback regarding accuracy of assignments should be immediate (i.e., as it is completed).

4. Children's attention during group lessons may be enhanced by delivering the lesson in an enthusiastic yet task-focused style, keeping it brief, and allowing frequent and active child participation. Tape-recording lectures may also be helpful.

5. Interspersing classroom lecture of academic periods with brief moments of physical exercise may also be helpful to diminish the fatigue and monotony of extending academic work periods (jumping jacks by the desk, a quick trip outside the classroom for a brisk 2-minute run or walk, forming a line and walking about the classroom in a "conga line" fashion, etc.)

6. Teachers should attempt to schedule as many academic subjects in morning hours as possible, leaving the more active, nonacademic subjects and lunch to the afternoon periods. This is done in view of the progressively worsening of the ADHD children's activity levels and inattentiveness over the course of the day (see Chapter 2, this volume).

7. Whenever possible, classroom instructions should be supplemented with a direct-instruction (DISTAR) drill of important academic skills or, even better, with computer-assisted drill programs. ADHD children are considerably more attentive to these types of teaching methods than to lectures.

8. For children with specific skills deficits in addition to ADHD, specialized curricula are required. For children with academic skills deficits, remedial instruction in skill areas such as reading, writing, spelling, and math is recommended. (For a review of instructional strategies for remediation, see DuPaul & Stoner, 1994.) Instructional programs for children with social skills deficits were reviewed in the last edition (Guevremont, 1990). Many ADHD students also have difficulty with organizational and study skills. Instruction in time and materials management is required. Such training may include note-taking strategies (Evans, Pelham, & Grudberg, 1994), desk checks for neatness, and filing systems for organizing completed work (DuPaul & Stoner, 1994; Pfiffner, 1996).

9. Other classroom accommodations for written work may include reducing the length of the written assignment (particularly when it is repetitious), using word processors to type reports, and allotting extra time to complete work.

MANAGING ACADEMIC PROBLEMS
WITH ADHD ADOLESCENTS

All the previous recommendations apply as much to adolescents with ADHD as to children. However, implementing these recommendations becomes considerably more difficult with the increased number of teachers involved in high-school-age adolescents; the short duration of the class periods; the greater emphasis on individual self-control, organization, and responsibility for completing assignments; and the frequent changes that occur in class schedules across any given week. For all these reasons, a dramatic drop in educational performance is likely in many ADHD children entering high school. At this level of education, teachers and students have little or no accountability until the behavioral offenses of the child become sufficiently heinous to attract attention or unless the academic deficiencies are grossly apparent. It is very easy for the average ADHD adolescent to literally "fall through the cracks" at this stage of education unless they were involved with the special educational system before entering high school. Those that were will have been "flagged" as in need of continuing special attention. But most ADHD adolescents were not in special education and thus are likely to be viewed merely as lazy and irresponsible. It is at this age level that educational performance becomes the most common reason ADHD adolescents are referred for clinical services.

Dealing with large educational institutions at this age level can be frustrating for parent, clinician, and ADHD teenager alike. Even the most interested teacher may have difficulties mustering sufficient motivation among her colleagues to help an ADHD adolescent in trouble at school. Following are a number of steps that can be attempted to manage poor educational performance and behavioral adjustment problems in middle and high school. To the degree that other methods described earlier can also be implemented, so much the better.

1. The clinician should immediately initiate an IDEA or Section 504 evaluation of the adolescent if one has not been done before or has not been done within the past 3 years (federal law requires a reevaluation every 3 years that a child is in special education). Special educational services will not be forthcoming until this evaluation is completed, which can take up to 90 days or longer in some districts. The sooner it is initiated, the better.

2. ADHD adolescents invariably require counseling on the nature of their handicapping condition. Although many have certainly been previously told by parents and others that they are "hyperactive" or have ADHD, many of them still have not come to accept that they actually have a disability. In our opinion, this counseling is not intended to depress the individual over what he or she cannot do but to teach the individual to accept that he or she has certain limitations and to find ways to prevent his or her disability from creating significant problems. Such counseling is difficult, requiring a sensitivity to the adolescents' striving to be independent and to form their own opinions of themselves and their world. It often takes more than a single session to succeed in this endeavor, but patience and persistence can pay off. Our approach is to stress the concept of individual differences—that everyone has a unique profile of both strengths and weaknesses in their mental and physical abilities and that each of us must adjust to them. We often confide about our own liabilities and use humor to get the adolescent to see that he or she is not the only one who has weaknesses. It is how we accept and cope with our weaknesses that determines how much they limit our successes in life. And yet, we have personally sat at many school meetings at which parents, teachers, school psychologists, and private tutors had all gathered to offer assistance to an ADHD teenager only to have the teenager refuse the offers while promising that he could turn things around on his own. Until ADHD adolescents accept the nature of their disorder, they are unlikely to fully accept the help that may be offered them.

3. If the adolescent was on medication previously and responded successfully, he or she should be counseled on the advantages of returning to the medication as a means of both improving his or her school performance and obtaining those special privileges at home that may be granted as a result of such improved performance. See Chapter 14 (this volume) for an example of such counseling with a teenager about medication. Many adolescents are concerned about others learning that they are on medication. They can be reassured that only they, their parents, and the physician are aware of this and that no one at school need know unless the teenager exposes it. Be prepared in many cases, however, for the ADHD adolescent to want to "go it alone" without the medication, believing that with extra applied effort he or she can correct the problem.

4. It is often essential that a team meeting be scheduled at the beginning of each academic year, and more often as needed, at which the teachers, school psychologist, guidance counselor, principal, parents, *and ADHD adolescent* are to be present. The clinician should bring a handout describing ADHD to give to each participant (he or she can circulate the chapter on ADHD from the text by Mash & Barkley, 1998, as a condensed reading on the disorder and its treatments). The clinician should briefly review the nature of the adolescent's disorder and the need for close team work among the school, parents, and teen if the teen's academic performance is to be improved. Each teacher must describe the current strengths and problems of the teen in their classes and make suggestions as to how they think they can help with the problem (being available after school a few days each week for extra assistance; reducing the length of written homework assignments; allowing the teen to provide oral means of demonstrating that knowledge has been acquired rather than relying on just writ-

ten, timed test grades; developing a subtle cuing system to alert the teen as to when he or she is not paying attention in class without drawing the whole class's attention to the fact; etc.). At this conference the teen should be asked to make a public commitment as to what he or she is going to strive to do to make school performance better. Once plans are made, the team should agree to meet again in 1 month to evaluate the success of their plans and troubleshoot any problem areas. Future meetings may need to be scheduled depending on the success of the program to date. At the least, meetings twice a year are to be encouraged even for the successful programs to monitor progress and keep the school attentive to the needs of this teen. The adolescent always attends these meetings.

5. The clinician should introduce daily home–school report cards as described earlier. These are often critical for teens more than for any other age group to permit the teen and parents to have daily feedback on how well the teen is performing in each class. The back of the card can be used to record daily homework assignments, which are verified by each teacher before completing the ratings on the card and initialing the front of the card. In conjunction with this card, a home-point system should be set up that includes a variety of desired privileges the teen can purchase with the points earned at school. Such things as telephone time, use of the family car, time out of the home with friends, extra money, clothes, musical tapes and compact discs, special snacks kept in the house, and so on, can be placed on the program. Points can also be set aside in a savings book to work toward longer-term rewards. However, it is the daily, short-term accessible privileges and not these longer-term rewards that give the program its motivational power; thus the reward menu should not be overweighted with too many long-term rewards. Once the adolescent is able to go for 3 weeks or so with no negative ratings on the card, the card is faded to a once- or twice-a-week schedule of completion. After a month of satisfactory ratings, the card can either be faded out or reduced to a monthly rating. The adolescent is then told that if word is received that grades are slipping, the card system will be reinstated.

6. Ideally, the school will provide a second set of books to the family, even if a small deposit is required to do so, so that homework can still be accomplished even if the teen forgets a book required for homework.

7. One of the teen's teachers, a home room teacher, a guidance counselor, or even a learning disabilities teacher should serve as the "coach," "mentor," or "case manager." This person's role is to meet briefly with the teen three times a day for just a few minutes to help keep the teen organized. The teen can stop at this person's office at the start of school, at which time the manager checks to see that the teen has all the homework and books needed for the morning's classes. At lunch, the teen checks in again with this manager to see if he or she has copied all necessary assignments from the morning classes, to help the teen select the books he or she needs for the afternoon classes, and then to see that the teen has the assignments that are to be turned in for afternoon classes. At the end of school, the teen checks in again with the manager to see that he or she has all assignments and books needed for homework. Each visit takes no more than 3 to 5 minutes, but interspersed as they are throughout the school day, these visits can be of great assistance to organizing the teen's schoolwork.

8. Getting a private tutor for the teen may be beneficial. Many parents find it difficult to do homework with their teen or to tutor them in areas of academic weakness. The teen often resists these efforts as well and the tension or arguments that can arise may spill over into other areas of family functioning even after the homework period has passed. When this is the case and it is within the family's financial means, hiring a tutor to work with the teen even twice a week can be of considerable benefit to both improving the teen's academic weakness and "decompressing" the tension and hostility that arises around homework in the family.

9. Parents should set up a special time each week to do something alone with this teen that is mutually pleasurable to provide opportunities for parent–teen interactions that are

not task oriented, school related, and fraught with the tensions that work-oriented activities with ADHD teens often bring. This can often contribute to keeping parent–teen relations positive and counterbalance the conflicts that school performance demands frequently bring to such families.

EDUCATIONAL PLACEMENT AND MODEL PROGRAMS

Most ADHD children continue to be placed in mainstream or general education classroom settings despite the increased accessibility to special education. For the mild to moderate case of ADHD, accommodations to the general education classroom sometimes coupled with pharmacological treatment are sufficient; there is no need for formalized special services. There are many advantages for maintaining students in general education, including reduced social stigma and interaction with appropriate peer models. However, in more severe cases or those with accompanying problems of opposition, aggression, or learning disabilities, alternative placements should be explored. ADHD students with severe emotional problems or learning disabilities are likely to receive special assistance through placement in a resource program for a part of the day or in a full-day self-contained classroom. ADHD children with significant speech and language or motor development problems are likely to receive language interventions, occupational and physical therapy, and adaptive physical education provided that these developmental problems are sufficient to interfere with academic performance.

The need for special education for ADHD per se has been debated over the past decade. Although ADHD is now recognized as a potentially handicapping condition, it is important to know that a diagnosis of ADHD does not automatically entitle a student to special services, through either general education or special education. The educational guidelines for ADHD state that significant impairment in school performance in conjunction with a diagnosis of ADHD are necessary to qualify for special services. In the case of suspected ADHD, a number of accommodations are usually attempted in the general education classroom prior to referral for a formal evaluation. If prereferral accommodations are unsuccessful, systematic screening procedures are implemented to determine the need for specialized interventions. Currently there are two mechanisms for obtaining these services. One is through Section 504 of the Rehabilitation Act of 1973, a civil rights law prohibiting discrimination against anyone with a disability. Under Section 504, individuals who have a physical or mental impairment that substantially limits their school functioning are eligible for special accommodations. Usually these services include a number of accommodations to the general education classroom such as using behavior management techniques, modifying homework and test delivery, using tape recorders, and/or simplifying lesson instructions. The second mechanism is through the Individuals with Disabilities Act under the "Other Health Impaired" classification. When children are eligible under this mechanism, they receive an individual education plan (IEP) and may be placed in small, special education classrooms. It is important that clinicians are aware that traditional special education programs were not specifically designed to serve the needs of ADHD children. For example, "pullout" resource programs, where a child spends a part of the day in a classroom with specialized curricula, were designed for children with specific learning probles (e.g., reading). Children with ADHD typically have erratic functioning throughout the day, which sabotages the appropriateness of such a program to address their needs. Furthermore, children in full-day special education placements often have problems very different from those of an ADHD student, such as severe learning disabilities, speech and language problems, or severe emotional disturbance. To date, most interventions for ADHD have involved accommodations to general education classes.

The predominant practice of educating ADHD students in mainstream settings is consistent with the established educational principal of "least restrictive environment," and clinicians should understand this concept as it applies to decisions regarding special educational placement. In particular, IDEA makes it clear that special services are to be provided in such a way that handicapped children may interact with nonhandicapped peers as much as possible. Hence, school districts are likely to place ADHD children in the least restrictive environment necessary to manage their academic and behavioral problems (i.e., in the program that provides the greatest contact with normal students). Some teachers are not always in agreement with this, preferring that even the child with mild ADHD be removed to special educational settings rather than having to adjust their classroom curriculum and behavior management style to accommodate the maintenance of these children in regular education. Parents may be equally biased toward special education, believing that the smaller class sizes, better trained teachers, and greater teacher attention they provide is to be preferred over regular education. School districts are likely to resist these pressures so as not to violate the rights of the child to the least restrictive environment or to risk legal action for doing so. Moreover, many ADHD students with mild to moderate problems are likely to be best served in general education classrooms with accommodations to improve attention, work habits, and peer relations. It is those students with more serious problems that would likely require placement in special education classrooms designed to meet their needs.

A model program recently developed for serving ADHD students in the general education classroom is referred to as the Irvine Paraprofessional Program (IPP; Kotkin, 1995, in press). This program involves close collaboration between school psychologists and teachers and utilizes trained paraprofessionals who serve as behavioral classroom aides. The aide's role is to assist the teachers in implementing an in-class token system and to provide collateral training in social skills. Children identified as having ADHD are initially referred to the program through the student study team (SST). The school psychologist works with the classroom teacher to develop an initial intervention plan which includes a number of accommodations in the classroom. If this is unsuccessful, a paraprofessional is assigned to the class for a 12 week intervention designed by the SST. The intervention consists of a token economy implemented by the paraprofessional for up to 3 hours a day and by the teacher during times when the paraprofessional is not present. The school psychologist provides periodic supervision of the paraprofessional and consults with the teacher regarding implementation of the program (see Figure 15.3). The child receives tokens (stamps) for up to four target behaviors every 15 minutes when the paraprofessional is in the class. Periods are longer (45 minutes) when the teacher is implementing the program. Students are also given one to three reminders during each period to do the target behavior. At the end of the day, stamp totals are exchanged for a 20-minute activity (e.g., computer games) in a schoolwide reinforcement center. The program also includes a three-tier levels system where students earn privileges as they move up each of three levels by consistently reaching daily and weekly goals. The levels system also serves as a way to fade the program as feedback intervals are increased (e.g., from 15 minutes to 1 hour) and the frequency of reminders are reduced as students achieve higher levels. The goal is to fade the program t a point where the teacher can successfully take it over. Students also participate in a social skills training group led by the paraprofessionals twice per week. The IPP model has been implemented in a number of school districts and a modified version of the program was utilized as one of several psychosocial treatments in a government-sponsored (NIMH) multisite study of ADHD (Arnold et al., 1997). Initial results appear to be favorable.

Several programs are also available to serve ADHD students with more severe problems in self-contained full-day settings. A summer treatment program, initially developed by Pelham and his colleagues, (Pelham et al., 1996; Pelham & Hoza, 1996) has been implemented with

Morning Schedule 8:00-12:00

On-Task Behavior

Staying Seated: Receive one stamp every 15 minutes that you remain seated. Getting out of seat with teacher's permission is OK.

8:15	8:30	8:45	9:00	9:15	9:30	Snack
10:15	10:30	10:45	11:00	11:30	11:45	

Working Quietly: Receive one stamp every 15 minutes if you do not visit with your neighbor or make distracting noises or gestures. Visiting neighbor with the teacher's permission is OK.

8:15	8:30	8:45	9:00	9:15	9:30	Snack
10:15	10:30	10:45	11:00	11:30	11:45	

Academic Performance

Amount of Work Completed: Receive one stamp every 15 minutes, if you complete assigned work during that period. During class discussions, stamps will be awarded if you are paying attention to the activity.

8:15	8:30	8:45	9:00	9:15	9:30	Snack
10:15	10:30	10:45	11:00	11:30	11:45	

Accuracy of Work: If 90% or more of work is completed accurately and your work is neat you will receive one stamp every 15 minutes. During class discussions, stamps will be awarded if contributions are accurate or task-related.

8:15	8:30	8:45	9:00	9:15	9:30	Snack
10:15	10:30	10:45	11:00	11:30	11:45	

Afternoon Schedule 12:45-2:00

Staying Seated: Earn 4 stamps every half hour that you remain seated.

1:15   1:45

Working Quietly: Receive 4 stamps every half hour if you do not visit with your neighbor or make distracting noises.

1:15   1:45

Amount of Work Completed: If you complete all work assigned you will receive 4 stamps every half hour.

1:15   1:45

Accuracy of Work: If 90% or more of work is completed accurately and is neat, you will receive 4 stamps every hour.

1:15   1:45

Total stamps possible= 80   Total stamps earned: _____

Reward

72 or more stamps = 90% Computer games
64 to 71 stamps = 80%   Free reading
66 to 70 stamps = 70%   Study hall

FIGURE 15.3. Jason's classroom challenge. Top: Format when paraprofessional is in the class. Bottom: Format when the teacher implements the token system. From Pfiffner (1996). Copyright 1996 by Linda Pfiffner. Reprinted by permission of Scholastic, Inc.

success for a number of years. The program includes intensive behavioral methods (point system with daily and weekly rewards, time out, social skills training) implemented by special education teachers during computer, art and academic learning centers and by five counselors as children participate in recreational activities (soccer, swimming) (Hoza, Vallano, & Pelham, 1995). This program has been modified by clinicians and academicians around the country and was also recently implemented as a part of psychosocial treatment in the multisite study of ADHD. This program was expanded to a year-round day-treatment service by Swanson and his colleagues in 1986 (Swanson, 1992) and continues to be operational today. The comprehensive clinical program includes an intensive classroom behavior modification system (including a token economy, schoolwide daily and weekly reinforcement, self-management training, daily behavioral report cards, and levels system), parent training, and social skills training. Once students achieve stable behavioral gains (usually over the course of 1 or 2 years), they transition back to their home school. Versions of these programs should be considered models for serving students with ADHD in general and special education placements.

It is essential that clinicians stay up-to-date with both the federal guidelines for special education as well as with their own specific state guidelines and any peculiar local district guidelines to knowledgeably advocate for the children in their practice. The phrase "You are only as good as your Rolodex." is a truism in dealing with educational placements for ADHD children, as well as locating resources within the private sector, such as private schools, formal and informal tutoring programs, and special summer camps for behavioral problem children. In some cases, the clinician is contacted to perform a "second opinion" on the case because of conflict between parents and school staff over the nature and extent of the child's problems and his or her eligibility for services. In such cases clinicians must determine the precise nature of school district's eligibility criteria and select assessment methods for addressing these criteria that are acceptable within school district policies.

CONCLUSION

Recognition by the U.S. Department of Education that ADHD may be considered a handicapping condition has increased the educational options for students with ADHD. The behavioral technology for serving ADHD students is well documented, particularly in the area of teacher-administered interventions. Continued research efforts to match specific instructional materials and behavior management techniques to specific child characteristics and to improve maintenance and generalization of intervention effects are clearly needed. However, the major challenge lies in disseminating and applying the technology in a way that is cost-effective. More and more school districts are accessing information about ADHD and providing inservices to their teachers. In addition, some districts are starting to develop consultation models for serving ADHD which involve collaboration between school psychologists, related school personnel, general and special education teachers, and parents. Further development and study of integrated and cost-effective intervention models in both general and special education are critical for meeting the needs of this large and diverse group of children.

REFERENCES

Abikoff, M., & Gittelman, R. (1985). Hyperactive children treated with stimulants: Is cognitive training a useful adjunct? *Archives of General Psychiatry, 42*, 953–961.

Abramowitz, A. J., & O'Leary, S. G. (1991). Behavioral interventions for the classroom: Implications for students with ADHD. *School Psychology Review, 20*(2), 220–234.

Abramowitz, A. J., Reid, M. J., & O'Toole, K. (1994). *The role of task timing in the treatment of ADHD.* Paper presented at the Association for Advancement of Behavior Therapy, San Diego, CA.

Acker, M. M., & O'Leary, S. G. (1987). Effects of reprimands and praise on appropriate behavior in the classroom. *Journal of Abnormal Child Psychology, 15,* 549–557.

Ajibola, O., & Clement, P. W. (1995). Differential effects of methylphenidate and self-reinforcement on attention deficit hyperactivity disorder. *Behavior Modification, 19*(2), 211–233.

Arnold, L. E., Abikoff, H. B., Cantwell, D. P., Conners, C. K., Elliott, G., Greenhill, L. L., Hechtman, L., Hinshaw, S. P., Hoza, B., Jensen, P. S., Kraemer, H. C., March, J. S., Newcorn, J. H., Pelham, W. E., Richters, J. E., Schiller, E., Severe, J. B., Swanson, J. M., Vereen, D., & Wells, K. C. (1997). NIMH Collaborative multimodal treatment study of children with ADHD (the MTA): Design challenges and choices. *Archives of General Psychiatry, 54*(9), 865–870.

Barkley, R. A., Copeland, A., & Sivage, C. (1980). A self-control classroom for hyperactive children. *Journal of Autism and Developmental Disorders, 10,* 75–89.

Barkley, R. A., Shelton, T. L., Crosswait, C., Moorehouse, M., Fletcher, K., Barrett, S., Jenkins, L., & Metevia, L. (1996). Preliminary findings of an early intervention program for aggressive hyperactive children. In C. F. Ferns & T. Grisso (Eds.), *Annals of the New York Academy of Sciences: Vol. 794. Understanding aggressive behavior in children* (pp. 277–289). New York: New York Academy of Sciences.

Barrish, H. H., Saunders, M., & Wolf, M. M. (1969). Good behavior game: Effects of individual contingencies for group consequences on disruptive behavior in a classroom. *Journal of Applied Behavior Analysis, 2,* 119–124.

Bloomquist, M. L., August, G. J., & Ostrander, R. (1991). Effects of school-based cognitive-behavioral intervention for ADHD children. *Journal of Abnormal Child Psychology, 19,* 591–605.

Braswell, L., August, G. J., Bloomquist, M. L., Realmuto, G. M., Skare, S.S., & Crosby, R. D. (1997). School-based secondary prevention for children with disruptive behavior. *Journal of Abnormal Child Psychology, 25,* 197–208.

Burcham, B., Carlson, L., & Milich, R. (1993). Promising school-based practices for students with attention deficit disorder. *Exceptional Children, 60*(2), 174–180.

Davila, R. R., William, M. L., & MacDonald, J. T. (1991). *Memorandum of chief state school officers re: Clarification of policy to address the needs of children with attention deficit disorder within general or special education.* Washington, DC: U.S. Department of Education.

Diaz, R. M., & Bark, L. E. (1995). A Vygotskian critique of self-instructional training. *Development and Psychopathology, 7,* 369–392.

Dunson, R. M. III, Hughes, J. M., & Jackson, T. W. (1994). Effect of behavioral consultation on student and teacher behavior. *Journal of School Psychology, 32*(3), 247–266.

DuPaul, G. J., & Ervin, R. A. (1996). Functional assessment of behaviors related to attention deficit hyperactivity disorder: Linking assessment to intervention design. *Behavior Therapy, 27,* 601–622.

DuPaul, G. J., Guevremont, D. C., & Barkley, R. A. (1992). Behavioral treatment of attention deficit hyperactivity disorder in the classroom. *Behavior Modification, 16*(2), 204–225.

DuPaul, G. J., & Henningson, P. N. (1993). Peer tutoring effects on the classroom performance of children with attention deficit hyperactivity disorder. *School Psychology Review, 22,* 134–143.

DuPaul, G. J., & Stoner, G. (1994). *ADHD in the schools: Assessment and intervention Strategies.* New York: Guilford Press.

Dykman, R. A., & Ackerman, P. T. (1993). Behavioral subtypes of attention deficit disorder. *Exceptional Children, 60,* 132–141.

Edwards, L., Salant, V., Howard, V. F., Brougher, J., & McLaughlin, T. F. (1995). Effectiveness of self-management on attentional behavior and reading comprehension for children with attention deficit disorder. *Child and Family Behavior Therapy, 17*(2), 1–17.

Ervin, R. A., DuPaul, G. J., Kern, L., & Friman, P. C. (1997). *Classroom-based functional and adjunctive assessments: Proactive approaches to intervention selection for adolescents with attention deficit hyperactivity disorder.* Unpublished manuscript, Western Michigan University.

Evans, J. H., Ferre, L., Ford, L. A., & Green, J. L. (1995). Decreasing attention deficit hyperactivity disorder symptoms utilizing an automated classroom reinforcement device. *Psychology in the Schools, 32,* 210–219.

Evans, S. W., Pelham, W., & Grudberg, M. V. (1994). The efficacy of notetaking to improve behavior and comprehension of adolescents with attention deficit hyperactivity disorder. *Exceptionality, 5*(1), 1–17.

Fiore, T. A., Becker, E. A., & Nero, R. C. (1993). Educational interventions for students with attention deficit disorder. *Exceptional Children, 60*(2), 163–173.

Gast, D. C., & Nelson, C. M. (1977). Time-out in the classroom: Implications for special education. *Exceptional Children, 43,* 461–464.

Gordon, M., Thomason, D., Cooper, S., & Ivers, C. L. (1990). Nonmedical treatment of ADHD/ Hyperactivity: The attention training system. *Journal of School Psychology, 29,* 151–159.

Guevremont, D. (1990). Social skills and peer relationship training. In R. A. Barkley, *Attention-deficit hyperactivity disorder: A handbook for diagnosis and treatment* (pp. 540–572). New York: Guilford Press.

Hinshaw, S. P., Henker, B., & Whalen, C. K. (1984). Cognitive-behavioral and pharmacological interventions for hyperactive boys: Comparative and combined effects. *Journal of Consulting and Clinical Psychology, 52,* 739–749.

Hoza, B., Vallano, G., & Pelham, W. E. (1995). Attention-deficit/hyperactivity disorder. In R. T. Ammerman & M. Hersen (Eds.), *Handbook of child behavior therapy in the psychiatric setting* (pp. 181–198). New York: Wiley.

Kelley, M. L. (1990). *School–home notes: Promoting children's classroom success.* New York: Guilford Press.

Kotkin, R. A. (1995). The Irvine Paraprofessional Program: Using paraprofessionals in serving students with ADHD. *Intervention in School and Clinic, 30*(4), 235–240.

Kotkin, R. (in press). Irvine Paraprofessional Program (IPP): A promising practice for serving students with ADHD. *Journal of Learning Disabilities.*

Kubany, E. S., Weiss, L. E., & Slogett, B. B. (1971). The good behavior clock: A reinforcement/time-out procedure for reducing disruptive classroom behavior. *Journal of Behavior Therapy and Experimental Psychiatry, 2,* 173–179.

Martens, B. K., & Hiralall, A. S. (1997). Scripted sequences of teacher interaction. *Behavior Modification, 21*(3), 308–323.

Mash, E. J., & Barkley, R. A. (Eds.). (1998). *Treatment of childhood disorders* (2nd ed.). New York: Guilford Press.

McKinney, J. D., Montague, M., & Hocutt, A. M. (1993). Educational assessment of students with attention deficit disorder. *Exceptional Children, 60,* 125–131.

McLaughlin, P. J., & Bender, W. N. (1994). *Attention Deficit Disorders Telecourse Network.* Athens: Georgia Center for Continuing Education, University of Georgia.

Meichenbaum, D., & Goodman, J. (1971). Training impulsive children to talk to themselves: A means of developing self-control. *Journal of Abnormal Psychology, 77,* 115–126.

Northup, J., Jones, K., Broussard, C., DiGiovanni, G., Herring, M., Fusilier, I., & Hanchey, A. (1997). A preliminary analysis of interactive effects between common classroom contingencies and methylphenidate. *Journal of Applied Behavior Analysis, 30*(1), 121–125.

O'Leary, K. D., & O'Leary, S. G. (1977). *Classroom management: The successful use of behavior modification* (2nd ed.). New York: Pergamon Press.

Paniagua, F. A., & Black, S. (1992). Correspondence training and observational learning in the management of hyperactive children: A preliminary study. *Child and Family Behavior Therapy, 14*(3), 1–19.

Pelham, W. E., Gnagy, B., Greiner, A., Hoza, B., Sams, S., Martin, L., & Wilson, T. (1996). A summer treatment program for children with ADHD. In M. Roberts & A. LaGreca (Eds.), *Model programs for service delivery for child and family mental health* (pp. 193–213). Hillsdale, NJ: Erlbaum.

Pelham, W. E., & Hoza, B. (1996). Intensive treatment: A summer treatment program for children with ADHD. In E. D. Hibbs, & Jensen, P. S. (Eds.), *Psychosocial treatments for child and adolescent disorders: Empirically based strategies for clinical practice* (pp. 311–340). Washington, DC: American Psychological Association.

Pfiffner, L. J. (1996). *All about ADHD: The complete practical guide for classroom teachers.* New York: Scholastic.

Pfiffner, L. J., & O'Leary, S. G. (1987). The efficacy of all-positive management as a function of the prior use of negative consequences. *Journal of Applied Behavior Analysis, 20*(3), 265–271.

Pfiffner, L. J., & O'Leary, S. G. (1993). School-based psychological treatments. In J. L. Matson (Ed.), *Handbook of hyperactivity in children* (pp. 234–255). Boston: Allyn & Bacon.

Pfiffner, L. J., Rosen, L. A., & O'Leary, S. G. (1985). The efficacy of an all-positive approach to classroom management. *Journal of Applied Behavior Analysis, 18*, 257–261.

Proctor, M. A., & Morgan, D. (1991). Effectiveness of a response cost raffle procedure on the disruptive classroom behavior of adolescents with behavior problems. *School Psychology Review, 20*(1), 97–109.

Rapport, M. D., Murphy, A., & Bailey, J. S. (1980). The effects of a response cost treatment tactic on hyperactive children. *Journal of School Psychology, 18*, 98–111.

Shapiro, E. S., DuPaul, G. J., Bradley, K. L., & Bailey, L. T. (1996). A school-based consultation program for service delivery to middle school students with attention deficit hyperactivity disorder. *Journal of Emotional and Behavioral Disorders, 4*(2), 73–81.

Sprute, K. A., Williams, R. L., & McLaughlin, T. F. (1990). Effects of group response cost contingency procedure on the rate of classroom interruptions with emotionally disturbed secondary students. *Child and Family Behavior Therapy, 12*(2), 1–12.

Swanson, J. M. (1992). *School-based assessments and interventions for ADD students.* Irvine, CA: K.C.

Swanson, J. M., McBurnett, K., Wigal, T., Pfiffner, L. J., Lerner, M., Williams, L., Christian, D. L., Tamm, L., Willcutt, E., Crowley, K., Clevenger, W., Khouzam, N., Woo, C., Crinella, F., & Fisher, T. (1993). Effect of stimulant medication on children with attention deficit disorder: A "review of reviews." *Exceptional Children, 60*, 154–162.

Tingstrom, D. H. (1994). The good behavior game: An investigation of teachers' acceptance. *Psychology in the Schools, 31*, 57–65.

Welsh, R., Burcham, B., DeMoss, K., Martin, C., & Milich, R. (1997). Attention deficit hyperactivity disorder diagnosis and management: A training program for teachers. Frankfurt: Kentucky Department of Education.

Whalen, C. K., Henker, B., Collins, B. E., Finck, D., & Dotemoto, S. (1979). A social ecology of hyperactive boys: Medication effects in structured classroom environments. *Journal of Applied Behavior Analysis, 12*, 65–81.

Zentall, S. (1993). Research on the educational implications of attention deficit hyperactivity disorder. *Exceptional Children, 60*(2), 143–153.

Chapter 16

STUDENT-MEDIATED CONFLICT RESOLUTION PROGRAMS

Charles E. Cunningham
Lesley J. Cunningham

ॐ

The active, inattentive, poorly regulated behavior of children with Attention-Deficit/Hyperactivity Disorder (ADHD) exerts a major impact on their social relationships. During interactions with their peers, for example, children with ADHD engage in higher rates of social interaction (Pelham & Bender, 1982; Whalen, Henker, Collins, Finck, & Dotemoto, 1979), have more difficulty adjusting behavior to contextual demands (Landau & Milich, 1988; Whalen, Henker, Collins, McAuliffe, & Vaux, 1979), and disrupt conversational reciprocity (Clark, Cheyne, Cunningham, & Siegel, 1988). Children with ADHD tend to interpret the behavior of peers as intentionally aggressive (Milich & Dodge, 1984) and engage in more uncooperative, controlling interaction (Clark et al., 1988; Cunningham & Siegel, 1987; Cunningham, Siegel, & Offord, 1985, 1991). Peers evaluate the child with ADHD more negatively (Johnston, Pelham, & Murphy, 1985; Milich & Landau, 1982), withdraw from social interaction (Clark et al., 1988), and adopt a less positive, less cooperative, more controlling response (Cunningham & Siegel, 1987; Cunningham et al., 1985, 1991).

Epidemiological studies suggest that 40–50% of ADHD children evidence conduct problems which may compound relationship difficulties (Hinshaw, 1987; Offord et al., 1987). Conduct problems may manifest themselves at school as arguments, threats, and fights. A significant number of relationship difficulties, conflicts, bullying episodes, and aggressive incidents occur in recess and playground settings where adult surveillance is low (Olweus, 1994; Whitney & Smith, 1993; Rivers & Smith, 1994). Students report that adults intervene in fewer than 5% of the bullying episodes that occur on school playgrounds, data supported by videotaped observational studies (Craig & Pepler, 1995). Under normal circumstances, other students are hesitant to interrupt these types of playground conflicts. As a result, most conflicts are left unresolved or dealt with counterproductively when students avoid conflicts or resolve disagreemens coercively (DeCecco & Richards, 1974). On those occasions adults detect student conflicts, solutions are typically imposed (DeCecco & Richards, 1974).

LIMITS OF TRADITIONAL TREATMENT PROGRAMS

Clinic-based approaches to treatment have not addressed the ADHD child's school-based relationships with peers. Utilization studies suggest that a significant majority of aggressive children do not receive professional assistance (Offord et al., 1987). Indeed a significant percentage of the parents of aggressive children do not feel that professional assistance is needed (Boyle, 1991). Moreover, parents of those children who are at greatest risk are least likely to enroll in or complete programs that might reduce aggressive behavior (Cunningham, Bremner, & Boyle, 1995; Kazdin, Holland & Crowley, 1997). When families do enroll in parent training programs that reduce problems at home, these changes may not consistently generalize to school settings (McNeil, Eyberg, Eisenstadt, Newcomb, & Funderburk, 1991).

STUDENT-MEDIATED CONFLICT RESOLUTION PROGRAMS

Preventing, interrupting the progression, or reducing the severity of ADHD and the comorbid difficulties that accompany ADHD require interventions that address problems in home, school, and community settings (Coie, 1996) and are sustainable across the broad developmental period in which these problems emerge. Programs need to reach children whose families do not have access to or participate in existing services and be affordable in an era of economic restraint (Offord, 1996). School-based, student-mediated conflict resolution (Cunningham & Cunningham, 1995; Cunningham et al., in press) is a promising component in a more comprehensive effort to improve the social relationships of children with ADHD. This chapter provides an overview of student-mediated conflict resolution, discusses the potential contribution of these programs to the management of children with ADHD, and considers evidence supporting their efficacy.

TYPES OF MEDIATION PROGRAMS

In student mediation programs, teams of older children trained as mediators help peers solve conflicts. On-line mediation programs help students negotiate solutions to playground conflicts occurring during recess or lunch periods. Mediators intervene in interpersonal conflicts, bullying episodes, and fights; offer disputants the opportunity to resolve disputes; help students negotiate a resolution; and plan a strategy for preventing future problems (Cunningham, Cunningham, & Martorelli, 1998). On-line mediation is most widely used in elementary and middle school contexts.

In office mediation programs, conflict resolution is conducted by a team of two mediators in a more private setting. Teachers, principals, playground supervisors, or other students may encourage disputants to make an appointment for office mediation. Office mediation allows the time needed to deal with longer-standing disputes, more complex conflicts, or incidents involving groups of students. Office mediation is typically used in conjunction with on-line playground mediation in middle school settings and is the model of choice in secondary and postsecondary settings.

Office mediation may be available as an alternative to disciplinary actions. For example, mediators may help students solve conflicts that might have resulted in detentions, suspensions, or juvenile justice system contacts. This is a highly specialized form of mediation in which disputants negotiate a solution, sign a contract, and propose alternative consequences.

In schoolwide programs (Johnson, Johnson, Dudley, & Burnett, 1992) all students are trained in mediation, negotiation, and conflict resolution strategies. Students are encouraged to apply these strategies to the solution of interpersonal conflicts that occur at home or school. Older students may also serve as members of the school's online playground or office mediation teams.

PREPARING FOR A STUDENT MEDIATION PROGRAM

The development of an effective student mediation program requires support from parents, teachers, school administrators, and the students themselves. All these stakeholders must be informed and consulted prior to the implementation of the program. The readiness to implement student mediation may require time, but it is important that key stakeholder groups are committed to the program. Table 16.1 summarizes key preparatory steps, policy prerequisites, and program benchmarks.

The implementation of a mediation program begins with a presentation to school administrators. This presentation typically includes an overview of the program, a videotaped or role-played example of a typical mediation, evidence regarding the effectiveness of student mediation programs, and an opportunity for questions and discussions.

With administrative support, a presentation for staff from schools interested in implementing a student mediation program is scheduled. Representatives present an overview of student mediation and summarize evidence regarding the effectiveness and limitations of the program. Teachers from schools that have conducted successful student mediation programs provide a helpful perspective. Experienced mediators often simulate the mediation of disputes, discuss the benefits of participation, and answer staff questions (e.g., Was it worth the time?). Finally, potential problems are considered. Teachers are often concerned about the

---

TABLE 16.1. Benchmarks of Effective Student-Mediated Conflict Resolution Programs

Stakeholder committment

Administration policy supporting mediation
Majority teacher decision supporting mediation
Parent organization decision supporting mediation

Policy prerequisites

Targets of mediation identified
Consequences for harrassing mediators

The mediation team

12- to 15-hour skill-focused training program
Adequate team size (e.g., eight mediators per recess period)
Team captains

Supportive infrastructure

Assembly launching the program
Morning announcement
Centrally posted team bulletin board
Two active playground supervisors
Two mediation team champions
Weekly team meeting

---

time training will take away from other activities, the response of other students to mediators, and the demands the mediation program might make on staff. If schools elect to implement a student mediation program, administrators schedule a similar presentation for parents and interested community members.

POLICY PREREQUISITES

Successful student mediation programs require a series of organizational and policy prerequisites. Schools considering a mediation program, therefore, complete a detailed program planning process. This section summarizes a selection of prerequisite benchmarks.

- *Agreement on mediation targets.* Disagreements regarding the types of problems warranting mediation will confuse students and undermine the mediation team's effectiveness. For example, although primary and middle school mediation teams can reliably discriminate play fighting from more serious conflicts, there may be considerable disagreement as to whether these incidents warrant intervention (Costabile et al., 1991; Smith, Hunter, Carvalho, & Costabile, 1992). Teachers, parents, and students, therefore, must establish a consensus regarding the behaviors that should be the targets of the mediation program.
- *Students refusing mediation.* Before mediation begins, disputants must agree to work toward a resolution of the conflict. Although a considerable number of students generally agree to work with mediators, schools must determine how they will respond to disputants who choose not to resolve conflicts by mediation. Mediators, for example, might notify playground supervisors who respond according to the school's procedures for dealing with the conflict that has occurred.
- *Response to harrassment.* Student mediators are not immune to teasing by peers. Angry disputants may, on occasion, subject mediators to swearing, threats, or aggressive behavior. Mediators who do not feel active support in the face of harassment by peers are hesitant to intervene, more inclined to leave the team, and less likely to participate in next year's mediation program. The school's harassment policy must identify unacceptable behaviors (staging fake conflicts, calling mediators names, threats, etc.) and the consequences of harassing a member of the mediation team. Because playground supervisors may not detect harassment, mediators need to report these incidents immediately.

RECRUITING STUDENT MEDIATORS

The impact of primary and middle school mediation programs depends, to some extent, on the success of the school's recruiting drive. Our studies suggest that mediators resolve approximately 90% of the conflicts in which they intervene (Cunningham et al., in press). Because most interventions are successful, the impact of a playground mediation team will be a function of the proportion of conflicts mediators detect and respond to. A successful on-line program must deploy a team large enough to monitor all areas of the playground where conflicts occur, deal with simultaneous disputes, allow frequent rotation, and provide a reserve of backup mediators. Most schools require at least three teams of 8 to 10 mediators. Smaller teams intervene in fewer conflicts and reduce the impact of the program on playground aggression (Cunningham et al., in press).

Once parents and teachers decide to develop a student mediation program, once they negotiate contracts and complete a planning worksheet, they make a presentation to students.

This presentation introduces the program, reviews the types of situations in which mediators will offer assistance, demonstrates the conflict resolution process, and explains the school's policy regarding the harassment of mediators. Presentations to students often include experienced mediators from other schools, school administrators, and community representatives (e.g., police officers, judges, and religious leaders). At the conclusion of this presentation, students in eligible grades are invited to join the mediation team. Teacher, parent, and student nominations increase the pool of potential mediators; ensure that the team reflects the gender, ethnic, cultural, and social composition of the school; and identify students who might benefit from participation.

TRAINING STUDENT MEDIATORS

A team of skillful committed student mediators is critical to the success of the program. Before assuming the responsibilities of a mediator, students must understand the concepts of mediation, master the program's component skills, identify conflicts quickly, and intervene confidently.

Overview of the Training Process

Primary division mediation teams, which may be selected from the fourth and fifth grades, require approximately 12 hours to complete the program described here. With a well-trained mediation team in place, the time required to train the next generation of mediators can be reduced by apprenticing prospective students to experienced members of the team. Middle school mediation teams master these skills more quickly and capitalize on incoming students with experience as members of primary division teams.

To facilitate skill acquisition in fourth- and fifth-grade students and address the needs of mediators with attentional difficulties, the training process is based on a cognitive-behavioral model. This process has several key strategies.

• *Forward chaining.* This program builds mediation skills via "forward chaining." Complex strategies are acquired in a series of steps beginning with the first stage of the mediation process. Before proceeding to the next component skill, the first step in the mediation process is rehearsed or "overlearned." For example, after a demonstration by the training team, each mediator practices running quickly to its assigned position on the playground and adopting the ready stance. Once the first step has been mastered, the second step is added: detecting conflicts and approaching the disputants. At this training stage, students run to their assigned position, adopt the ready stance, and approach students simulating a conflict. Training continues until all steps have been added to the mediation sequence.

• *Errorless approximation.* Training begins with simple, easily recognized conflicts. As skill and confidence increase, role-playing exercises move toward more complex conflicts and commonly encountered mediation difficulties. Members of the training team model each step and give prompts which ensure that component skills are rehearsed correctly. This type of errorless learning accelerates acquisition, reduces frustration, builds the confidence needed to deal effectively with playground conflicts, and meets the needs of mediators with attentional difficulties.

• *Self-monitoring.* Throughout training, mediators carry a clipboard with a self-monitoring sheet listing the basic steps in the mediation process. Mediators make a check on this sheet as each step of the mediation process is completed. Forms provide students with reminders regarding the steps of mediation while monitoring reinforces accurate follow-through.

 • *Training in context.* Modeling and role-playing exercises for primary division mediators are typically conducted in context: Students rehearse the resolution of the types of conflicts they are most likely to encounter, work with the members of their teams, and master skills in playground field trials.

Phase I: Introductions

Training teams typically consist of workshop leaders, at least two teachers serving as the school's mediation program champions, experienced mediators, and interested parents. Training begins with an introduction of the coaching team and the school's mediation program champions. The principal discusses the importance of the student mediation program and the responsibilities of the mediators. Prospective mediators are introduced to one another via activities that allow students to share information regarding themselves.

Phase II: Overview of Mediation

Next, leaders present an overview of the mediation program and outline the steps of the mediation process. Table 16.2 summarizes the steps in a standard playground mediation.

Phase III: Component Skill Building

In this extended phase, prospective mediators master the component skills of the mediation program. Trainers discuss each skill, model its application, and provide prospective mediators with an opportunity to rehearse the skill in role playing exercises. Students complete this phase when they have demonstrated mastery of each component skill.

Phase IV: Mastering the Mediation Process

In this phase, students master the complete execution of all steps of the mediation process by rehearsing the resolution of disputes of increasing complexity.

Phase V: Solving Common Problems

Next, mediators formulate solutions to common problems. These might include responding to students who refuse mediation or fail to agree on a solution.

Phase VI: Building Communication Skills

Effective mediation requires sophisticated communication skills. At each step of the mediation process, mediators must maintain a neutral position, listen carefully, summarize the content of disputant statements, reflect feelings, and facilitate problem solving. Once mediators master the basic components of the mediation program trainers use discussions, demonstrations, exercises, and role-playing activities to strengthen their communication skills. Fundamental concepts (e.g., mediator neutrality) and attitudes are introduced as relevant skills are developed. Students formulate rationales supporting each component of the mediation process, key mediation constructs (win–win solutions), the overall benefits of

TABLE 16.2. Component Skill Checklist

Step	Component skill
1	Mediators in assigned playground position before students arrive.
2	Mediators in ready position, clip board in hand, watching all students with special attention to high-risk areas or groups.
4	Mediator approaches disputants, asks whether problem has occurred.
5	Mediator asks whether disputants want to solve the problem?
6	Mediator finds a quiet area, seats disputants, and sits between disputants.
7	Mediator introduces self and asks names of disputants.
8	Mediator states rules and secures agreement on each of the following: Disputants must remain with mediator. Mediator is neutral and won't take sides. Disputants must listen without interrupting. Disputants must tell the truth. Disputants treat each other respectfully. Disputants must solve the problem. Disputants must abide by their agreement.
9	Mediator asks disputant 1 to tell story.
10	Mediator summarizes disputant 1's story.
11	Mediator asks disputant 2 to tell story.
12	Mediator summarizes disputant 2's story.
13	Mediator asks disputants to suggest solutions.
14	Mediator summarizes each suggestion.
15	Disputants review pros and cons of each suggestion.
16	Disputants choose a solution.
17	Disputants plan when and how they will implement their solution.
18	Mediator asks if each disputant is satisfied.
19	Mediator closes mediation (students to shake hands).

mediation, and their participation in the program. The opportunity to formulate supporting rationales enhances understanding of the program, yields explanations which may be of more significance to students, and builds personal commitment.

Phase VIII: Building Detection Skills

During this phase, mediators practice detecting events that warrant mediation. Mediators must identify behavior that should be ignored, problems warranting mediation, and incidents that should be drawn to the attention of the playground supervisor (e.g., disputes involving weapons). Because playground conflicts may escalate rapidly, mediators need to make these decisions quickly and approach disputants confidently.

Phase X: Field Simulation

Next, students master the mediation of simulated disputes in field conditions, which includes detecting disputes in simulated playground settings, stopping the dispute, conducting mediation, and solving common problems.

Phase XI: Supervised Implementation

Implementation of the program is monitored and supervised by the mediation team coaching staff. Prospective mediators must demonstrate mastery of the mediation process under actual playground conditions. To complete this phase, students must successfully mediate at least three conflicts under the supervision of a mediation team coach.

LAUNCHING THE STUDENT MEDIATION PROGRAM

The launch of the mediation service demonstrates administrative and community support, ensures that students understand the program, creates momentum, and maximizes the success of the program.

- *Graduation ceremonies.* Schools schedule an assembly of students, teachers, parents of mediators, and key community members celebrating the graduation of the mediation team. Principals, senior school administrators, and community representatives discuss the importance of the mediation program, introduce the team, and award diplomas. Mediators present a skit illustrating the steps in the resolution of several typical playground conflicts. Finally, the principal summarizes guidelines regarding the types of conflicts that will be the subject of mediation, the option of refusing mediation, and the consequences of harassing members of the mediation team.
- *Team building.* Mediators are organized into teams of at least eight members balanced with respect to gender, grade, and ethnicity. Teams work together on playground duty and sit together during weekly meetings with the school's mediation champions. Each team selects a captain from its oldest, most experienced, or influential members. Captains assist program champions and playground supervisors in ensuring that team members arrive before the start of recess, are positioned in their assigned quadrant, and have needed equipment (clipboards, forms, pencils, and uniforms). In addition, captains secure replacements when team members are absent, notify playground supervisors if mediators need assistance, and reinforce the team's efforts.
- *Maximize number of mediators present.* A full complement of uniformed mediators is present on the playground at the introduction of the program. The team's hats and vests provide a visual reminder of the program's goals; a large team ensures that most incidents are detected before disputes escalate.
- *Members of the training team are present.* Coaches and school mediation champions should be present during the first several days of the program. On the first day, coaches review the targets of mediation, rehearse mediation strategies, prompt intervention, and provide supportive feedback. Over the next several days, coaches shift responsibility for these tasks to the playground supervisor and team captains, provide supportive feedback, fade their presence, and remain available as a resource.
- *Administrative support.* The presence of the principal at the launch of the mediation service reminds students, mediators, and playground supervisors of the program's importance. Visits by administrative representatives (superintendents or trustees) during the first several weeks emphasizes the board's commitment to the program and motivates successful implementation. The presence of representatives from local parent–teacher organizations creates a sense of shared responsibility for the success of the mediation program.

SUPPORTING A MEDIATION PROGRAM

The *active* support of administrators, teachers, champions, playground supervisors, and students contributes to the success of the mediation program. This section describes several components of the infrastructure needed to support an effective mediation program.

• *Playground supervision.* On-line mediation teams require the *active* support of at least two playground supervisors. Playground supervisors ensure that mediators arrive promptly, review mediation plans, assign mediatiors to locations where conflicts can be detected quickly, deal with students who refuse mediation or harass team members, provide supportive feedback, solve problems, and organize preventive playground activities.

• *Mediation program champions.* At least two teaching staff serve as the program's mediation champions. Champions ensure the success of the mediation program by participating in training and conducting weekly team meetings. Champions support the mediation team, solve problems, recruit mediators for the coming year's team, and conduct the school's training programs.

• *Daily announcements.* The school's morning announcement lists the mediators on duty for the day, reminds students of the program's rules, supports the teams efforts, and acknowledges successful conflict resolution. Announcements encourage students to seek the assistance playground mediators or schedule an appointment for office mediation.

• *Mediation team bulletin board.* A centrally located bulletin board features the program's logo, team pictures, student posters supporting the program, and newspaper articles illustrating the application of mediation (e.g., labor disputes or international negotiations). A graph plotting the number of successful mediations completed each week recognizes the team's accomplishments, encourages active intervention, and promotes the use of office mediation services.

• *Weekly mediation program meetings.* The school's champions meet once weekly with the mediation team. Champions encourage skill development, acknowledge the team's efforts, compliment members for successful mediations, reinforce key skills, and support the solution of problems. Champions award certificates recognizing milestones (10, 20, 30 mediations), challenging mediations, supportive interaction among team members, and organize the larger rewarding events which are important in maintaining motivation (pizza, tickets to a dance, etc.)

• *Area wide meetings.* Champions from schools conducting mediation programs meet several times during the year to share ideas, solve problems, celebrate accomplishments, and provide support. An annual day-long, areawide workshop for mediators includes team-building activities, program displays (hats, shirts, mottos, posters) skill-building seminars, talks by older mediators, presentations by key community members (police officers, lawyers, judges, labor relations mediators, etc.), and addresses by school administrators.

• *Curriculum and classroom links.* Teachers support the program by linking classroom discussions of history, literature, and current events to the goals of the mediation program. Teachers use mediation strategies to resolve classroom disputes or encourage students needing assistance to arrange an appointment with the office mediation team.

MONITORING A PEER MEDIATION PROGRAM

Mediation team coaches and champions actively monitor implementation of the program. Mediators may need additional training, implementation may drift as mediators adopt inappropriate conflict-resolution strategies (e.g., suggesting solutions), or schools may make modifications that inadvertently compromise the program's effectiveness (Cunningham et al., in press). Teachers see a small percentage of the aggressive behavior occurring on playgrounds and may not detect the impact of these changes. As aggressive behavior declines, mediators may become bored and distracted or playground supervisors may neglect their responsibility to support the program.

Mediators complete a monitoring sheet documenting the process and outcome of each intervention. These forms remind mediators of the steps of the dispute resolution process, encourage reliable implementation, and provide important information regarding the success of the program. Champions review their completion at weekly team meetings and help plot successful mediations on the team's bulletin board.

Mediation program coaches visit each site at least once weekly during the initial stages of the program's implementation, complete a benchmark monitoring form, and provide feedback to the teacher champions and mediators.

SUSTAINING A STUDENT MEDIATION PROGRAM

To achieve their potential long-term impact on conflict resolution skills, student attitudes, school norms, and the level of aggression occurring at school, mediation programs must be conducted consistently from September to June and sustained through the elementary, middle school, and secondary years.

- *Recruiting the next generation.* In the spring, the mediation team's "champions" recruit new members for the upcoming school year. The school's teacher champions conduct a training program with experienced members of the team assisting in modeling and role-playing exercises. Newly trained mediators are paired with experienced members of the team. Apprenticed mediators shadow competent mediators, monitor each step of the dispute resolution process, intervene in simple conflicts, and attend weekly team meetings.
- *Introducing the new mediation team.* A fall assembly launches the new year and introduces the mediation team to incoming students. During the course of the year, a member of the mediation team and a school administrator introduce new students to the program, explain the school's guidelines regarding acceptable playground behaviour, describe the process of mediation, and outline the consequences of refusing to resolve conflicts.
- *Transferring graduating team members.* Mediators graduating from primary division to middle schools, or from middle to secondary schools, have acquired considerable skill and experience. As a majority are interested in continued participation (Cunningham et al., in press), champions facilitate contact with the mediation programs in the schools to which they are transferring.

ENHANCING THE EFFECTIVENESS OF MEDIATION PROGRAMS

High-Risk Students

A small group of high-risk students may contribute to a considerable proportion of the conflict on school playgrounds. There are several strategies via which mediation teams can respond to this very challenging group of students. First, champions assign older, socially influential mediators to areas where more serious conflicts occur. Second, two members of the team conduct playground mediations involving more challenging students. Third, the individual behavioral contracts and daily report cards of high risk students may include goals that support successful participation in conflict resolution.

Office Mediation

Office mediation allows the team to resolve chronic playground difficulties, relationally complex disputes, problems requiring a cooling-off period, or conflicts involving groups of students. The success of office mediation may be enhanced by selecting the team's most experienced members; identifying mediators reflecting the gender, cultural, or ethnic background of the disputants; devoting more time to the conflict resolution process; applying advanced mediation strategies; and establishing contracts (e.g., among disputants, principals, and referring teachers). Contracts ensure that a mutually acceptable solution is reached, specify the steps needed to resolve the problem, and state the consequences if the agreement is violated.

High-Risk Mediators

Children with ADHD and related disruptive behavior disorders often join mediation teams. Indeed, some schools actively recruit a small number of high-risk students or negative leaders to their mediation teams. The successful inclusion of challenging mediators requires adjustments in training, monitoring, and support. During training, high-risk mediators should be grouped with influential team members, positioned in close proximity to the trainers, and involved actively via eye contact, prompts, questions, and reinforcers. During implementation, high-risk team members should be placed on teams with strong captains, paired with older more influential team members, positioned in close proximity to playground supervisors, and provided with more frequent prompts and reinforcers. Daily report cards (Barkley, 1997) with individually negotiated goals and incentives provide additional support and encouragement. In view of the potential benefits of participation on the mediation team, suspension from the team should be a last resort to disciplinary problems.

Training Parents as Mediators

Parents are invited to participate in a skill-building workshop designed to increase their understanding of the process of mediation, to help parents support student mediators, and to develop the skills needed to apply mediation to conflicts between siblings and peers at home. Table 16.3 outlines a sample 3-hour workshop based on the Community Parent Education Program or COPE model (Cunningham, Bremner, & Secord-Gilbert, 1997).

Related Interventions

To make a meaningful contribution to the management of children with ADHD, student mediation programs must be included as a component of a more comprehensive treatment plan. Schoolwide social skills training programs (Hundert, 1995), for example, may support the development of the skills needed to establish more effective relationships with peers and function effectively as a member of the mediation team. Parent training programs described in Chapters 13 and 14 (this volume) provide the strategies families need to encourage the application of newly acquired conflict resolution skills at home, promote improved sibling and peer relationships, and support the individualized contracts needed by some members of the mediation team. Finally, the effects of stimulant medication on sustained attention, self-regulation, and conflict with peers (Cunningham et al., 1985, 1991) may permit ADHD

TABLE 16.3. Mediation Strategies for Parents

Step	Activity
1	Introduce the workshop leaders.
2	Outline the goals and methods of the workshop.
3	Introduce workshop participants.
4	Outline the rationale for mediation programs.
5	Outline the process of mediation.
6	Model common errors in conflict resolution.
7	Prompt the group to discuss the problems with this approach.
8	Prompt the group to suggest alternative conflict resolution strategies.
9	Leader models mediation strategies.
10	Participants rehearse mediation strategies.
11	Participants plan application.
12	Participants provide feedback.

children with more significant difficulties to benefit from the assistance of playground mediators or capitalize on the opportunities provided by membership on the mediation team.

BENEFITS OF STUDENT MEDIATION PROGRAMS

Student-mediated conflict resolution programs have a number of potential benefits of special interest in the management of children with ADHD and related disruptive behavior disorders. First, on-line programs operate during recesses when surveillance and intervention by teachers is low and the risk of conflict, bullying, and aggressive behavior is high (Olweus, 1991; Craig & Pepler, 1995).

Craig and Pepler (1995) found that although teachers reported that they intervened in 70% of the bullying episodes occuring on playgrounds, they dealt with only 4% of the incidents recorded on videotaped observations. Teams of mediators positioned strategically on the playground can detect emerging conflicts, offer mediation at a point at which a successful resolution is easily reached, and prevent minor disputes from escalating to more serious aggressive incidents. Whereas antisocial behavior is more likely to be expressed as physical aggression among boys, conflict between girls often occurs at the relational level (Cairns , Cairns, Neckerman, Gest, & Gariepy, 1988; Crick & Dodge, 1994; Crick, Bigbee, & Howes, 1996; Crick & Grotpeter, 1995; Rivers & Smith, 1994). Like physical aggression, relational aggression (e.g., damaging or manipulating peer relationships) is motivated by both anger and the intent to harm (Crick et al., 1996), linked to peer rejection, and associated with poor adjustment (Crick & Grotpeter, 1995). Relational aggression is particularly damaging to goals valued by girls and is a greater source of distress for them (Crick et al., 1996). Our research (Kadar & Cunningham, 1997) suggests that ADHD children are particularly vulnerable to relational aggression. Although relational aggression is more difficult for adults to detect than physical aggression, girls on mediation teams seem particularly adept at recognizing and intervening in relationally aggressive incidents.

Conducting mediation in the playground and peer group contexts where conflicts are most likely to occur may deal with the generalization failures noted in many school-based interventions (Hundert, 1995; Pepler, Craig, & Roberts, 1995). Although self-regulatory difficulties may limit the likelihood that children with ADHD will spontaneously apply conflict resolution skills to their own disputes, playground mediators are highly visible reminders of the goals of the school's conflict resolution program. Moreover, because mediators intervene to support conflict resolution, the disputes inevitably encountered by children with ADHD are more likely to be resolved successfully.

Student mediation is a schoolwide or universal program benefiting all students. Student mediation programs are not affected by the low utilization and high dropout rates observed in programs that require parental participation (Cunningham et al., 1995; Kazdin et al., 1997). Universal programs eliminate the risk of false-positive or false-negative screening (Offord, 1996), prevent stigmatization (Harris, Milich, Corbitt, Hoover, & Brady, 1992), and avoid the risks of aggregating high-risk children in treatment groups (Dishion & Andrews, 1995). Although mediation is a universal program, mediators intervene in actual conflicts. Children with ADHD who have difficulty with playground conflict, therefore, inevitably receive additional dispute resolution practice. This combination of universal and targeted programming represents an ideal approach to both prevention and treatment (Coie, 1996; Offord, 1996).

Mediation teams deal with the conflicts of children at all grade levels. By conducting mediation programs in primary, middle school, and secondary settings, the impact of this program can be extended. This is critical to the management of ADHD and the related disruptive behavior disorders that emerge at different stages (Moffitt, 1993; Patterson, Reid, & Dishion, 1992) and persist for many years (Offord et al., 1992).

Because mediation programs are perceived by teachers to be logistically manageable, endorsed by administrators, and supported by parents (Cunningham et al., in press), the probability that these programs will be disseminated, adopted, and sustained is high (Offord, 1996). Finally, as a program conducted by students with the support of school staff, student mediation is affordable in an era of fiscal restraint (Yates, 1994).

Placing High-Risk Students on the Mediation Team

A particularly promising dimension of student-mediated conflict resolution is its potential impact on mediators who have difficulty with social relationships or interpersonal conflict. A percentage of the student mediators in most programs evidence a history of aggressive behavior. Indeed, a considerable number of programs actively recruit students who have difficulty with conflict. Trainers and school mediation champions suggest that, in small numbers, students with conduct problems contribute effectively to mediation teams. These observations are consistent with more descriptive accounts of these programs and a wider range of studies demonstrating the effective use of peer tutoring, social skills, and substance abuse prevention programs (Botvin, 1996; Hundert, 1995).

Several lines of evidence suggest that students with ADHD and related disruptive behavior disorders benefit from participation as mediators. First, membership on the team provides a significant amount of exposure: mediators participate in 12 to 15 hours of training, a 1-hour assembly, several class presentations, weekly 1-hour meetings with the mediation team and teacher champions, and intervene in approximately 60 playground conflicts per year.

Cunningham et al. (in press) found that most of the primary division mediators reported fewer conflicts as a result of participation. This finding was confirmed by 100% of the teachers in study schools. Interviews with parents yielded similar conclusions. These findings are consistent with evidence that training in mediation and conflict resolution strategies reduces conflict at home (Gentry & Benenson, 1993; Johnson, Johnson, Dudley, Ward, & Magnuson, 1995).

There are several mechanisms via which participation on the mediation team might benefit high-risk students. First, playground mediation responsibilities reduce opportunities for aggressive behavior during low-surveillance, high-risk times (Fowler, Dougherty, Kirby, & Kohler, 1986; Jones & Offord, 1989). Second, mediators acquire skills that may assist the resolution of conflicts with peers or improve responsiveness to parent or teacher interventions (Johnson et al., 1995).

Third, some children with ADHD evidence a hostile attributional bias which may contribute to conflict with peers (Dodge & Frame, 1982; Dodge, 1993; Milich & Dodge, 1984). Mediation training, weekly problem-solving discussions, and the dispute resolution process expose mediators to alternative explanations regarding the causes of aggressive interactions. Summarizing the stories of peers and reflecting the feelings of disputants may enhance self-awareness and perspective-taking skills.

Fourth, the skills, attitudes, and status mediators acquire via team membership may encourage affiliation with peer groups whose norms support less aggressive solutions to social conflict. Joining the team and helping peers resolve conflicts represent the types of public commitment that might change attitudes toward conflict (Leary & Miller, 1986).

Participation as a member of the mediation team may alter the child's reputation (Harris et al., 1992; Hymel, 1986; Hymel, Wagner, & Butler, 1990), reduce peer rejection (Dodge, 1983), and limit differential association with deviant peers (Cairns et al., 1988), a key mechanism in the emergence and maintenance of more stable patterns of antisocial behaviour (Coie, 1996; Elliot, Huizinga, & Ageton, 1985; Patterson et al., 1992). Finally, mediation is the type of school-based extracurricular program that establishes the social networks and connections to the school that reduce secondary-school dropout in high-risk students (Mahoney & Cairns, 1997).

The fifth to eighth grades, when most high-risk students join the mediation team, are an optimal time for this type of intervention. First, the presence of relatively stable patterns of aggressive behavior can be identified by this age (Coie, 1996: Loeber et al., 1993). Second, the early starters (Patterson et al., 1992; Moffitt, 1993) evidencing problems by this age are at greatest risk for long-term difficulty (Coie, 1996; White, Moffit, Earls, & Robins, 1990). Third, participation may prevent differential association with deviant peers which begins during the middle school years and contributes to antisocial behavior in late adolescence. Fourth, this precedes the stage at which antisocial behavior increases sharply (Moffitt, 1993).

Trials of Student Mediation Programs

Descriptive reports suggest that mediators reduce playground conflict (Cameron & Dupuis, 1991; Johnson et al., 1992; Koch, 1988; Lane & McWhirter, 1992; Welch, 1989), but there are few controlled studies of these programs (Hundert, 1995). Johnson et al. (1995) studied the impact of a student mediation program on 144 primary division students. Students reported on 209 personal conflicts at school and 574 at home. Students in the training program were more likely to report using an integrative negotiating procedure to resolve conflicts at school. Moreover, students reported that conflict resolution strategies acquired at school were applied to conflicts at home, observations consistent with the findings of Gentry and Benenson (1993), who noted that parents of children receiving mediation training reported a reduction in the frequency and intensity of their child's conflicts with siblings.

Cunningham et al. (in press) completed a controlled trial of the effectiveness of a primary division student-mediated conflict resolution program. Teams of fifth-grade students were trained to mediate conflicts during recess periods. A multiple baseline (Hersen & Barlow, 1978) design was used to determine the effects of student-mediated conflict resolution on direct observations of physically aggressive playground interactions. Mediators successfully resolved 90% of the more than 1,010 playground conflicts in which they intervened. Figure 16.1 shows that student-mediated conflict resolution reduced direct observations of physically aggressive play-

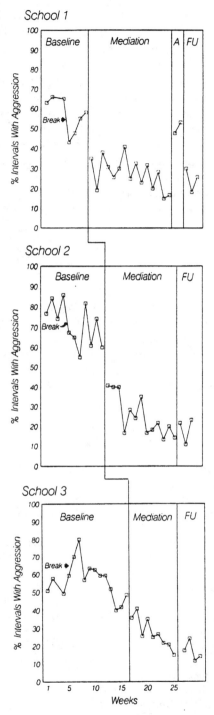

FIGURE 16.1. Percentage of 120 intervals in which physically aggressive behavior was observed each week during baseline, student mediation, and follow-up (FU) conditions at three primary division schools. "A" indicates an unplanned reversal when the mediation team was reduced from eight to two members. From Cunningham et al. (in press). Copyright 1998 by the *Journal of Child Psychology and Psychiatry*. Reprinted by permission.

ground behavior from 51% to approximately 65%. These effects were sustained at 1-year follow-up observations. Teacher and mediator satisfaction questionnaires provided strong support for social validity of this program, a particulary important issue in the development of interventions acceptable in community contexts (Coie, 1996; Hoagwood, Hibbs, Brent, & Jensen, 1995; Hundert, 1995; Kendall & Southam-Gerow, 1995; Offord, 1996).

Despite the potential benefits of joining mediation teams, their impact on students with ADHD requires further study. Moreover, the inclusion of children with ADHD as members of the mediation team poses several major challenges to coaches and champions. The ADHD child's attentional and self-regulatory deficits may impair the acquisition of complex mediation strategies. Poor sustained concentration might affect the detection of conflicts in highly distracting playground contexts. Finally, children with ADHD evidence social skills deficits (Cunningham & Siegel, 1987; Clark et al., 1988; Cunningham et al., 1991), which may adversely effect relationships with members of the mediation team or impair their performance as mediators.

CONCLUSION

Our studies suggest that student-mediated conflict resolution reduces the types of conflicts ADHD children encounter in playground settings. Converging evidence from teachers, parents, and mediators suggests that, in addition to the mediation program's primary effects on playground aggression, participation as a member of the mediation team may have a significant impact on high-risk students. In an era of unprecedented reductions in clinical resources, these programs deserve careful attention.

REFERENCES

Barkley, R. A. (1997). Behavioral inhibition, sustained attention, and executive functions: Constructing a unifying theory of ADHD. *Psychological Bulletin, 121,* 65–94.

Botvin, G. J. (1996). Substance abuse prevention through life skill training. In R. Peters & R. J. McMahon (Eds.), *Preventing childhood disorders, substance abuse, and delinquency* (pp. 215–240). Thousand Oaks, CA: Sage.

Boyle, M. H. (1991). Children's mental health issues: prevention and treatment. In L. C. Johnson & D. Barnhorst (Eds.), *Children, families and public policy in the 90's* (pp. 73–104). Toronto: Thompson Educational Publishing.

Cairns, R. B., Cairns, B. D., Neckerman, H. J., Gest, S. D., & Gariepy, J. L. (1988). Social networks and aggressive behavior: Peer support or peer rejection? *Developmental Psychology, 24,* 815–823.

Cameron, J., & Dupuis, A. (1991). The introduction of school mediation to New Zealand. *Journal of Research and Development in Education, 24,* 1–13.

Clark, M. L., Cheyne, A. J., Cunningham, C. E., & Siegel, L. S. (1988). Dyadic peer interaction and task orientation in attention-deficit disordered children. *Journal of Abnormal Child Psychology, 16,* 1–15.

Coie, J. D. (1996). Prevention of violence and antisocial behavior. In R. D. Peters & R. McMahon (Eds.), *Preventing childhood disorders, substance abuse and delinquency* (pp. 1–18). London: Sage.

Costabile, A., Smith, P. K., Matheson, L., Aston, J., Hunter, T., & Boulton, M. (1991). Cross-national comparison of how children distinguish serious and playful fighting. *Developmental Psychology, 27,* 881–887.

Craig, W. M., & Pepler, D. J. (1995). *Naturalistic observations of bullying and victimization in the school yard.* Manuscript submitted for publication.

Crick, N. R., Bigbee, M. A. & Howes, C. (1996). Gender differences in children's normative beliefs about aggression: How do I hurt thee? Let me count the ways. *Child Development, 67,* 1007–1014.

Crick, N. R., & Dodge, K. A. (1994). A review and reformulation of social information processing mechanisms in children's social development. *Psychological Bulletin, 115*, 47–101.

Crick, N. R., & Grotpeter, J. K. (1995). Relational aggression, gender, and social-psychological adjustment. *Child Development, 66*, 710–722.

Cunningham, C. E., Bremner, R. B., & Boyle, M. (1995). Large group school-based courses for parents of preschoolers at risk for disruptive behavior disorders: Utilization, outcome, and cost effectiveness. *Journal of Child Psychology and Psychiatry, 36*, 1141–1159.

Cunningham, C. E., Bremner, R. B., & Secord-Gilbert, M. (1997). *COPE: The Community Parent Education Program: A school-based family systems-oriented workshop for parents of children with disruptive behavior disorders.* Hamilton, Ontario: COPE Works.

Cunningham, C. E. & Cunningham, L. J. (1995). Reducing playground aggression: Student mediation programs. *ADHD Report*, 9–11.

Cunningham, C. E., Cunningham, L. J., & Martorelli, V. (1998). *Coping with conflict at school: The student-mediated conflict resolution program.* Hamilton, Ontario: COPE Works.

Cunningham, C. E., Cunningham, L. J., Martorelli, V., Tran, A., Young, J., & Zacharias, R. (in press). The effects of a primary division student mediation program on playground aggression. *Journal of Child Psychology and Psychiatry.*

Cunningham, C. E., & Siegel, L. S. (1987). Peer interactions of normal and attention-deficit disordered boys during free-play, cooperative task, and simulated classroom situations. *Journal of Abnormal Child Psychology, 15*, 247–268.

Cunningham, C. E., Siegel, C. S., & Offord, D. R. (1985). A developmental dose response analysis of the efforts of methylphenidate on the peer interactions of attention deficit disordered boys. *Journal of Child Psychology and Psychiatry, 26*, 955–971.

Cunningham, C. E., Siegel, L. S., & Offord, D. R. (1991). A dose–response analysis of the effects of methylphenidate on the peer interactions and simulated classroom performance of ADD children with and without conduct problems. *Journal of Child Psychology and Psychiatry, 32*, 439–452.

DeCecco, J., & Richards, A. (1974). *Growing pains: Uses of school conflict.* New York: Aberdeen.

Dishion, T. J., & Andrews, D. W. (1995). Preventing escalation in problem behaviors with high-risk young adolescents: Immediate and 1-year outcomes. *Journal of Consulting and Clinical Psychology, 63*, 538–548.

Dodge, K. A. (1983). Behavioral antecedents of peer social status. *Child Development, 54*, 1386–1399.

Dodge, K. A., & Frame, C. L. (1982). Social cognitive biases and deficits in aggressive boys. *Child Development, 55*, 163–173.

Elliot, D. S., Huizinga, D., & Ageton, S. S. (1985). *Explaining delinquency and drug use.* Beverly Hills, CA: Sage.

Fowler, S. A., Dougherty, B. S., Kirby, K. C., & Kohler, F. W. (1986). Role reversals: An analysis of therapeutic effects achieved with disruptive boys during their appointments as peer monitors. *Journal of Applied Behavior Analysis, 19*, 437–444.

Gentry, D. B., & Benenson, W. A. (1993). School-to-home transfer of conflict management skills among school-age children. *Families in Society: The Journal of Contemporary Human Services*, 67–73.

Harris, M. J., Milich, R., Corbitt, E. M., Hoover, D. W., & Brady, M. (1992). Self-fulfilling effects of stigmatizating information on children's social interactions. *Journal of Personality and Social Psychology 63*, 41–50.

Hersen, M., & Barlow, D. H. (1978). *Single case experimental design: Strategies for studying behavior change.* New York: Pergamon Press.

Hinshaw, S. P. (1987). On the distinction between attentional deficit/hyperactivity and conduct problems/aggression in child psychopathology. *Psychological Review, 101*, 443–463.

Hoagwood, K., Hibbs, E., Brent, D., & Jensen, P. (1995). Introduction to the special section: Efficacy and effectiveness in studies of child adolescent psychotherapy. *Journal of Consulting and Clinical Psychology, 63*, 683–687.

Hundert, J. (1995) *Enhancing social competence in young students.* Austin, TX: Pro-Ed.

Hymel, S. (1986). Interpretations of peer behavior: Affective bias in childhood and adolescence. *Child Development, 57*, 431–445.

Hymel, S., Wagner, E., & Butler, L. J. (1990). Reputational bias: View from the peer group. In S. R.

Asher & J. D. Coie (Eds.), *Peer rejection in childhood* (pp. 156–186). New York: Cambridge University Press.

Johnson, D. W., Johnson, R. T., Dudley, B., & Burnett, R. (1992). Teaching students to be peer mediators. *Educational Leadership, 50*, 10–13.

Johnson, D. W., Johnson, R., Dudley, B., Ward, M., & Magnuson, D. (1995). The impact of peer mediation training on the management of school and home conflicts. *American Educational Research Journal, 32*, 829–844.

Johnston, C., Pelham, W. E., & Murphy, A. (1985). Peer relationship in ADD-H and normal children: A developmental analysis of peer and teacher ratings. *Journal of Abnormal Child Psychology, 13*, 85–100.

Jones, M. G., & Offord, D. R. (1989). Reduction of antisocial behavior in poor children by non-school skill development. *Journal of Child Psychology and Psychiatry, 30*, 737–750.

Kadar, I., & Cunningham, C. E. (1997). *The Children's Relational Conflict Scale.* Unpublished manuscript, McMaster University.

Kazdin, A. E., Holland, L., & Crowley, M. (1997). Family experience of barriers to treatment and premature termination from child therapy. *Journal of Consulting and Clinical Psychology, 65*, 453–463.

Kendall, P. C., & Southam-Gerow, M. A. (1995). Issues in the transportability of treatment: The case of anxiety disorders in youths. *Journal of Consulting and Clinical Psychology, 63*, 702–708

Koch, M. S. (1988). Resolving disputes: Students can do it better. *NASSP Bulletin, 72*, 16–18.

Landau, S., & Milich, R. (1988). Social communication patterns of attention deficit-disordered boys. *Journal of Abnormal Child Psychology, 16*, 69–81.

Lane, P. S., & McWhirter, J. J. (1992). A peer mediation model: conflict resolution for elementary and middle school children. *Elementary School Guidance and Counselling, 27*, 15–23.

Leary, M. R., & Miller, R. S. (1986). *Social psychology and dysfunctional behaviour.* New York: Springer-Verlag.

Loeber, R., Wung, P., Keenan, K., Giroux, B., Stouthamer-Loeber, M., Van Kammen, W. B., & Maughan, B. (1993). Developmental pathways in disruptive child behavior. *Development and Psychopathology, 63*, 549–559.

Mahoney, J. L. & Cairns, R. B. (1997). Do extracurricular activities protect against early school dropout? *Developmental Psychology, 33*, 241–253.

McNeil, C. B., Eyberg, S. M., Eisenstadt, T. H., Newcomb, K., & Funderburk, B. (1991). Parent–child interaction therapy with behavior problem children: Generalization of treatment effects to the school setting. *Journal of Clinical Child Psychology, 55*, 169–182.

Milich, R., & Dodge, K. A. (1984). Social information processing in child psychiatric populations. *Journal of Abnormal Child Psychology, 12*, 471–490.

Milich, R., & Landau, S. (1982). Socialization and peer relations in hyperactive children. In K. D. Gadow & I. Bailer (Eds.), *Advances in learning and behavioral disabilities* (Vol. 1., pp. 283–339). Greenwich, CT: JAI Press.

Moffitt, T. E. (1993). Adolescence-limited and life-course persistent antisocial behavior: A developmental taxonomy. *Psychological Review, 100*, 674–701.

Offord, D. R. (1996). The state of prevention and early intervention. In R. Peters & R. McMahon (Eds.). *Preventing childhood disorders, substance, abuse, and delinquency intervention* (pp. 144–160). New York: Sage.

Offord, D. R., Boyle, M. H., Racine, Y. A., Fleming, J. E., Cadman, D. T., Munroe Blum, H., Byrne, C., Links, P. S., Lipman, E. L., MacMillan, H. L., Rae-Grant, N. I., Sanford, M. N., Szatmari, P., Thomas, H., & Woodward, C. (1992). Outcome, prognosis, and risk in a longitudinal follow-up study. *Journal of the American Academy of Child and Adolescent Psychiatry, 31*, 916–923.

Offord, D. R., Boyle, M. H., Szatmari, P., Rae-Grant, N., Links, P. S., Cadman, D., Byles, J. A., Crawford, J. W., Munroe-Blum, H., Byrne, C., Thomas, H., & Woodward, C. (1987). Ontario Child Health Study II: Six month prevalence of disorder and rates of service utilization. *Archives of General Psychiatry, 44*, 832–836.

Olweus, D. (1991). Bully/victim problems among school children: Basic facts and effects of a school-based intervention program. In D. J. Pepler & K. H. Rubin (Eds.), *The development and treatment of childhood aggression.* Hillsdale, NJ: Erlbaum.

Olweus, D. (1994). Annotation: Bullying at school: Basic facts and effects of a school based intervention program. *Journal of Child Psychology and Psychiatry, 35,* 1171–1190.

Patterson, G. R., Ried, J. B., & Dishion, T. J. (1992). *Antisocial boys.* Eugene, OR: Castalia.

Pelham, W. E., & Bender, M. E. (1982). Peer relationships in hyperactive children: Description and treatment. In K. D. Gadow & I. Bailer (Eds.), *Advances in learning and behavioral disabilities* (Vol. 1, pp. 365–436). Greenwich, CT: JAI Press.

Pepler, D. J., Craig, W., & Roberts, W. L. (1995). Social skills training and aggression in the peer group. In J. McCord (Ed.) *Coercion and punishment in long-term perspectives.* New York: Cambridge University Press.

Rivers, I., & Smith, P. K. (1994). Types of bullying behaviour and their correlates. *Aggressive Behavior, 20,* 359–368.

Smith, P. K., Hunter, T., Carvalho, A. M. A., & Costabile, A. (1992). Children's perceptions of playfighting, playchasing and real fighting: a cross-national interview study. *Social Development, 1,* 211–229.

Welch, G. (1989). How we keep our playground from becoming a battlefield. *Executive Educator, 11,* 23–31.

Whalen, C. K., Henker, B., Collins, B. E., Finck, D., & Dotemoto, S. (1979). A social ecology of hyperactive boys: Medication effects in structured classroom environments. *Journal of Applied Behavior Analysis, 12,* 65–81.

Whalen, C. K., Henker, B., Collins, B. E., McAuliffe, S., & Vaux, A. (1979). Peer interaction in a structured communication task: Comparison of normal and hyperactive boys and of methylphenidate (Ritalin) and placebo effects. *Child Development, 50,* 388–401.

White, J. H., Moffit, T., Earls, F., & Robins, L. (1990). Preschool predictors of persistent conduct disorder and delinquency. *Criminology, 28,* 443–453.

Whitney, I., & Smith, P. K. (1993). A survey of the nature and extent of bullying in junior/middle and secondary schools. *Educational Research, 35,* 3–25.

Yates, B. T. (1994). Toward the incorporation of costs, cost-effectiveness analysis, and cost-benefit analysis into clinical research. *Journal of Consulting and Clinical Psychology, 62,* 729–736.

Chapter 17

STIMULANTS

George J. DuPaul
Russell A. Barkley
Daniel F. Connor

Central nervous system (CNS) stimulant medications are the most commonly used psychotropic drugs to treat the symptoms of individuals with Attention-Deficit/Hyperactivity Disorder (ADHD). It has recently been estimated that 1.5 million children annually, or 2.8% of the school-age population, may be using stimulants for behavior management (Safer, Zito, & Fine, 1996). Historically, most of these children have been between 5 and 12 years of age. More recently, however, there has been a significant increase in the prescription of these medications for adolescents and adults with ADHD.

Substantial research has been conducted on the effects of stimulant medications on children. Empirical data consistently demonstrate the efficacy of the stimulants in improving behavioral, academic, and social functioning in about 50% to 95% of children treated, depending on the presence of comorbid psychiatric and/or developmental disorders. Despite the plethora of studies on their efficacy, the stimulants are no panacea for treating the behavioral and attentional difficulties associated with ADHD, nor should they be the sole form of therapy for individuals with this disorder. Having said this, however, we also recognize that the stimulants are the only treatment modality to date to demonstrate the normalization of inattentive, impulsive, and restless behavior in children. For most cases, though, one of the greatest benefits of stimulant therapy seems to be the theoretical possibility of maximizing the effects of concurrently applied psychosocial and educational treatments (e.g., behavior modification and academic tutoring).

Despite this tremendous body of scientific research, the use of stimulants with children continues to be controversial, both publicly and professionally. The inaccurate and, regrettably, successful media propaganda campaign conducted in the late 1980s by certain religious groups and pseudo-civil libertarian groups against the use of stimulants, particularly Ritalin (methylphenidate), with children (Barkley, 1990) may have been the basis for the dramatic decline in the prescribing of this medication that occurred between 1988 and 1990 (Daniel Safer, personal communication, September 1991). More recently, television reports of cases of stimulant abuse by adolescents, rare as they apparently turned out to be, may have another chilling effect on the prescribing of stimulants, particularly Ritalin, for ADHD. This latest wave of media attention to Ritalin, much of it sensationalized, may have been fueled in part by a dispute between the Drug Enforcement Agency and the national organization for Children and Adults with ADHD (CHADD) surrounding the efforts of CHADD to have Ritalin reclassified into the Schedule III category from its current placement with Schedule II drugs. Though eventually unsuccessful in that petition, the whirlwind of media stories concerning increasing rates of Ritalin prescribing and potential abuse once again contributed to a public atmosphere of concern and even alarm about this otherwise safe and effective form of treatment for children and adults with ADHD.

In this chapter, we summarize knowledge about the stimulant medications for the treatment of ADHD, suggest guidelines for their clinical use, and describe a protocol for evaluating the effects of these agents in treating individuals with this disorder.

PHARMACOLOGICAL ASPECTS OF STIMULANT MEDICATION: DEFINITION AND NOMENCLATURE

The term "CNS stimulants" refers to the ability of these medications to raise the level of activity, arousal, or alertness of the central nervous system. These drugs are structurally similar to brain catecholamines (i.e., dopamine and norepinephrine) and are called sympathomimetic compounds because they may mimic the actions of these brain neurotransmitters. The three most commonly employed stimulants are dextroamphetamine (Dexedrine), methylphenidate (Ritalin), and magnesium pemoline (Cylert). A new stimulant, Adderall (a combination of amphetamine and dextroamphetamine) has recently been approved for use with children and adults with ADHD. Methamphetamine (Desoxyn) has also been used in a small percentage of cases of ADHD. But in view of its greater abuse potential than other stimulants, the dearth of controlled research on its efficacy, and limited availability in some geographic regions, methamphetamine is not discussed here as a treatment option. Other (noncatecholaminergic) stimulant compounds (e.g., caffeine and deanol) are not discussed here because they have not been found to be nearly as effective as the CNS stimulants and cannot be recommended for clinical use.

Pharmacology

The primary mode of action of dextroamphetamine is believed to be that of enhancing catecholamine activity in the CNS, probably by increasing the availability of norepinephrine and/or dopamine at the synaptic cleft. The precise mechanism of this action is still poorly understood, and the increasing availability of molecular probes to investigate receptor sites, as well as other new investigational techniques, make this an area in which knowledge is likely to change rapidly in the next few years. Methylphenidate is a piperidine derivative structurally similar to dextroamphetamine. Its specific mode of action is even less clearly understood than that of dextroamphetamine. It may be that methylphenidate has a greater effect on dopamine activity than on other neurotransmitters, but that remains speculative at this time. Investigation of the pharmacology of Adderall is only now being completed but is highly likely to prove similar, if not identical, to that of the various amphetamines that make up this compound. Pemoline is similar in function to the other CNS stimulants, though it has minimal sympathomimetic effects and is structurally dissimilar. The specific mechanism of action of pemoline is poorly understood.

Catecholaminergic (especially noradrenergic) receptors are widely distributed throughout the brain. However, catecholaminergic neurons are few and localized to the brain stem.

Partly because of this wide receptor distribution, the actual site of action of the stimulants within the CNS also remains speculative. Early investigators conjectured that brain stem activation was the primary locus, but lately the midbrain or frontal cortex have been favored. Recent studies of cerebral blood flow have shown that activity in the area of the striatum and the connections between the orbital–frontal and limbic regions are enhanced during stimulant medication treatment (Lou, Henriksen, & Bruhn, 1984; Lou, Henriksen, Bruhn, Bomer, & Neilsen, 1989). Also, Redman and Zametkin (1991), using positron emission tomography (PET) scan, have demonstrated increased brain metabolic activity in the bilateral orbital–frontal area and in the left sensorimotor and parietal areas following a single dose of methylphenidate in seven adults with ADHD. Surprisingly, a *suppression* of activity was noted in the left temporal region following stimulant administration, but the brain is an exceedingly complex organ and changes in one area of the brain may be consequences of alterations in activity of other areas.

Gualtieri, Hicks, and Mayo (1983) hypothesized that the stimulants act to "canalize" or decrease fluctuation and variability in arousal, attention, and CNS reactivity thereby enhancing the persistence of responding and increasing cortical inhibition. Still others (e.g., Haenlein & Caul, 1987) propose that the stimulants decrease the threshold for reinforcement through enhancement of the arousal of the CNS behavioral activation (reward) system, thereby creating a persistence of responding to tasks or activities. Stated differently, activities in which the organism engages (particularly those that involve sustained effort) become more reinforcing, resulting in prolonged responding to them relative to nonmedication conditions.

Pharmacokinetics

CNS stimulants are almost always given orally, are quickly absorbed from the gastrointestinal tract, cross the bloodbrain barrier rapidly and easily, and are eliminated from the body within 24 hours (Diener, 1991). Dextroamphetamine achieves peak plasma levels in children within 2 to 3 hours with a plasma half-life between 4 to 6 hours that is subject to substantial *interindividual* variability. The breakdown of dextroamphetamine occurs primarily in the liver, where deamination and p-hydroxylation transform it to benzoic acid. A significant proportion is excreted in the urine, ranging from 2% in very alkaline urine to as high as 80% in very acidic urine, so that high gastric activity (which produces alkaline urine) and some treatments for urinary infections may affect concentration substantially (Brown et al., 1979). The behavioral effects of dextroamphetamine are noticeable within 30 to 60 minutes postingestion, appear to peak between 1 to 2 hours, and usually dissipate within 4 to 6 hours (Dulcan, 1990). Although data on Adderall have not yet been published, its pharmacokinetics are likely to be similar to those for dextroamphetamine and amphetamine given that these two drugs make up this hybrid stimulant compound.

Methylphenidate reaches peak plasma levels somewhat more quickly than dextroamphetamine, typically within 1.5 to 2.5 hours postingestion. The plasma half-life is usually shorter than dextroamphetamine, between 2 and 3 hours, and the drug is metabolized completely within 12 to 24 hours, with almost none of the drug appearing in the urine (Diener, 1991; Wargin et al., 1983). The metabolic pathway for the decomposition and elimination of methylphendiate appears to be via deesterification to ritalinic acid, to a lesser degree via hydroxylation to p-hydroxymethylphenidate, and the remainder to oxoritalinic acid and oxomethylphenidate, all of which are pharmacologically inactive (Cantwell & Carlson, 1978). As with dextroamphetamine, behavioral effects occur within 30 to 60 minutes, peak within 1 to 3 hours, and are dissipated within 3 to 6 hours after oral ingestion, creating an effective span of clinical improvement ranging from about 4 to 6 hours in most children. The plasma half-life of "sustained release" methylphenidate has been found to be nearly twice as long as that of the standard preparation (Birmaher, Greenhill, Cooper, Fried, & Maminski, 1989). Behavioral effects of sustained release methylphenidate appear to occur within 1 to 2 hours, peak within 3 to 5 hours, and slowly diminish until approximately 8 hours postingestion (Pelham et al., 1987, 1990). These effects are equivalent to those produced by the standard preparation for most children (Fitzpatrick, Klorman, Brumaghim, & Borgstedt, 1992). Significant interindividual variability exists with respect to these parameters; however, it necessitates clinical evaluation as to the frequency of dosage for individual children. The plasma level of the sustained release preparation does appear to be dose related (Patrick et al., 1987).

Pemoline appears to have a longer half-life than the other stimulants with peak plasma levels typically occurring approximately 2 to 4 hours postingestion. It is important to note, however, that this half-life is shorter with children (i.e., 7 to 8 hours) than with adults (i.e., 11 to 13 hours) (Sallee et al., 1985). Within 24 hours, 50% to 75% of the dose appears to be excreted in the urine. The time-course and response characteristics of its behavioral effects have not been well documented until recently. The behavioral effects of pemoline have been noted to develop approximately 2 hours after ingestion and are sustained through the seventh hour postingestion (Pelham, Swanson, Furman, & Schwindt, 1995) The half-life of this compound possibly increases with chronic use, which may lead to a buildup in plasma levels, thereby explaining the considerably delayed behavioral effects (up to 3 to 4 weeks after initial administration) of the medication (Dulcan, 1990).

Behavioral effects for the stimulants are not well predicted from peak or absolute blood levels compared to knowledge of dose alone (Kupietz, 1991; Swanson, 1988a). Peak behavioral changes often seem to lag behind peak blood levels by as much as an hour. Alternatively, changes in learning on laboratory learning tasks may correspond more closely to blood levels (Kupietz, 1991; Swanson, Kinsbourne, Roberts, & Zucker, 1978), although there are insufficient data to be sure. Consequently, when behavioral change is the goal of treatment, blood levels play little role in establishing the therapeutic range or response for any individual case beyond knowledge of the oral dose itself. Further data are necessary to determine whether changes in *learning performance* can be predicted reliably by blood levels, and, even so, such predictions are likely to be subject to considerable inter- and intraindividual variability (Kupietz, 1991). Thus, drawing blood to establish drug levels for guiding therapeutic adjustments to children's stimulant medication is not a recommended practice (Shaywitz & Shaywitz, 1991; Swanson, 1988a).

Tolerance to CNS stimulants has not been established in research; however, clinical anecdotes suggest decreased efficacy of the drugs, particularly pemoline, in some cases with chronic administration. Dulcan (1990) conjectured that this may stem from hepatic autoinduction, behavioral noncompliance with the prescribed regimen, weight gain, or environmental factors such as an intercurrent stress event (e.g., moves, parental divorce, and change in school classroom) or altered caregiver expectations for behavior. It also is possible, given the inherent complexity of dopamine receptors, that compensatory changes in the number of receptor sites may occur as a function of prolonged stimulant use.

SHORT-TERM CLINICAL EFFECTS

Substantial empirical data have been gathered to examine the effects of CNS stimulants on the behavior and learning of children with ADHD. Space does not permit reviewing these studies in any detail. Instead, this chapter focuses on those research findings that are most substantiated and/or have the greatest relevance for clinical practice. Most of these studies have been conducted with methylphenidate and considerably fewer with dextroamphetamine. Only a few have employed pemoline, but these suggest effects on learning and behavior that are consistent with the other two stimulants (e.g., Pelham et al., 1995). To date, no controlled studies of the clinical effects of Adderall have been published, but those recently completed by Swanson at the University of California Medical School at Irvine and by Greenhill at Columbia University in New York suggest that these effects are similar to those of the other stimulants.

General Behavioral Effects

Barkley's (1977) initial review of more than 120 studies up to 1977 indicated that between 73% and 77% of children treated with stimulants were seen as improved in their "behavior," variously measured. In contrast, the proportion responding to placebo was 39%. More recent studies (e.g., DuPaul & Rapport, 1993; Rapport, Denney, DuPaul, & Gardner, 1994) and reviews of this literature, including meta-analyses (Kavale, 1982), have reached similar conclusions concerning the response rates to the stimulants, although some found lower response rates to placebo than Barkley originally reported (Pelham, 1993; Spencer, Biederman, Wilens, et al., 1996; Swanson, McBurnett, Christian, & Wigal, 1995). CNS stimulants, therefore, have substantial empirical support for their efficacy relative to other types of child therapy.

Despite overwhelming evidence for the efficacy of stimulants at a group level of analysis, it should be noted that as many as 20% to 30% of children tried on stimulants may display no positive response to these medications or may display worsening in behavior in response to medication. Thus, it should not be assumed that all children with ADHD will either respond positively or in an identical fashion to these medications. Further complicating the clinical picture is the finding that children may respond well on one or a few measures of behavior and learning while showing no response or an adverse reaction on other types of measures. Moreover, when some children respond poorly to one type of stimulant, such as methylphenidate, it is possible that they might respond to a different one, such as dextroamphetamine (Elia & Rapoport, 1991) though this remains to be well established. All this suggests that the response of children to stimulants can be quite idiosyncratic and clinical evaluation of response across measures and doses (as well as possibly across medications) is essential. Finally, most empirical investigations of stimulant effects have been conducted on children between the ages of 6 and 12 years old. Despite more recent research examining stimulant response in young children, adolescents, and adults, caution must be employed when generalizing the results of medication studies to individuals younger or older than elementary school children.

Physical Effects

CNS stimulant effects on a variety of psychophysiological indices have been examined. Specifically, the impact of these medications has been investigated with respect to growth hormone release, height, weight, heart rate, and blood pressure, as well as autonomic and CNS functioning. As is the case for behavioral effects of these agents, considerable variation across individuals is the rule rather than the exception. Further, most medication-induced changes in physiological functioning do not have an impact on titration of dose or on behavioral response.

Methylphenidate and dextroamphetamine produce acute growth hormone release in both children and adults, which could lead to alterations in prolactin, cortisol, and beta-endorphins (Reeve & Garfinkel, 1991). Nevertheless, as Reeve and Garfinkel noted, long-term effects on the hypothalamic–pituitary–growth hormone axis have not been demonstrated. Despite some evidence of initial growth inhibition by these drugs, effects on eventual adult height or skeletal stature often are clinically insignificant (Klein & Mannuzza, 1988). Effects on weight are also frequently minimal, resulting in a loss of 0.5 to 1.0 kg during the initial year of treatment and often showing a rebound in growth by the second or later years of treatment (Dulcan, 1990; Gittelman, Landa, Mattes, & Klein, 1988; Reeve & Garfinkel, 1991). The effects on weight are likely to be the same for Adderall, although there is a report of a single case involving severe weight loss associated with this drug (Kalikow & Blumencranz, 1996). All the stimulants seem to reduce appetite to some degree, although it is temporary and mainly limited to the time of peak effects (Cantwell & Carlson, 1978).

Heart rate, as well as systolic and diastolic blood pressure, may be increased by methylphenidate; however, these effects appear to be small and moderated by a number of factors. For instance, higher dosages of methylphenidate are linearly related to increasing levels of heart rate, and these effects are dependent on both the initial (i.e., premedication) heart rate and the time course of the medication (Kelly, Rapport, & DuPaul, 1988). Those changes in cardiovascular functioning that do occur are often mild (range of increase is 6–15 beats per minute [bpm]; $M = 11$ bpm), are clearly dose dependent, and typically are outweighed by other normal daily physiological stresses (e.g., digestion) (Aman & Werry, 1975; Hastings & Barkley, 1978; Safer, 1992). Further, methylphenidate effects on heart rate may attenuate somewhat with chronic administration, and no electrocardiogram irregularities for any of the stimulants have been identified in the few studies examining this issue (Safer, 1992). Heart rate variability is reduced by methylphenidate, as is heart rate deceleration to a reaction time task. The latter result is consistent with changes in cognitive functions such as attention span and concentration. In all studies, cardiovascular effects of stimulants are subject to significant intra- and interindividual variability. Dexedrine and pemoline may be less likely than methylphenidate to produce effects on heart rate (Knights & Viets, 1975; Safer, 1992). Effects on blood pressure from all three stimulants are quite modest, when noted, and are not consistently found across studies (Safer, 1992). Clinicians should be aware, however, that African-American adolescents may have a greater risk than Caucasians for developing an increase in diastolic blood pressure, and this variable should be monitored closely in this population (Brown & Sexson, 1989).

A large, albeit inconclusive, literature exists on the effects of CNS stimulants on psychophysiological functioning (Hastings & Barkley, 1978; Rosenthal & Allen, 1978; Taylor, 1986). For example, stimulant effects on autonomic nervous system functioning have been noted in the literature for several decades. Skin conductance is often increased, primarily at doses of methylphenidate over 15 mg/day (Hastings & Barkley, 1978), whereas effects on both nonspecific and specific galvanic skin responses are equivocal (Barkley & Jackson, 1977; Satterfield & Dawson, 1971).

Background electrical activity of the CNS is sometimes increased by the stimulants, usually evidenced by reduced alpha or slow-wave activity, and CNS sensitivity to stimulation may also be heightened as measured by electroencephalograms (EEGs) and audio- and visual-evoked potentials (Hastings & Barkley, 1978; Coons, Klorman, & Borgstedt, 1987; Peloquin & Klorman, 1986). Consequently, cerebral blood flow and brain metabolic activity may be increased. These effects seem selective, however, as they are concentrated primarily in the anterior frontal regions bilaterally as documented in recent studies using cerebral blood flow and PET (Lou et al., 1989; Redman & Zametkin, 1991; Zametkin et al., 1990). Effects on the reticular activating system may also be noted, probably leading to the increases in heart rate, blood pressure, and, in a few cases, respiration. Effects on various aspects of sleep seem insignificant other than a mild delay to sleep onset, or insomnia, experienced by the majority of children on stimulants, (see section on side effects, below). Some evidence points to a temporary reduction in REM (rapid eye movement) sleep, which often returns to normal within several months (Hastings & Barkley, 1978).

In summary, the CNS stimulants appear to have minor effects on physical systems. The effects that are most commonly evidenced involve increases in aspects of both autonomic and CNS activity, but these changes typically are small and relatively insignificant in the context of clinical evaluation of drug response.

Effects on Behavior and Emotion

Empirical investigations consistently have demonstrated the positive effects of CNS stimulants on sustained attention and persistence of effort to assigned tasks while reducing task-irrelevant restlessness and motor activity (Barkley, 1977; Barkley & Cunningham, 1979; Bergman, Winters, & Cornblatt, 1991; Elia, Borcherding, Rapoport, & Keysor, 1991; Milich, Carlson, Pelham, & Licht, 1991). For most children treated with stimulants, attention to assigned classwork is improved to the extent that the child's behavior appears similar to his or her non-ADHD classmates (Abikoff & Gittelman, 1984; DuPaul & Rapport, 1993; Pelham & Milich, 1991; Rapport et al., 1994). Attention while playing sports may also improve in response to stimulant use (Pelham, McBurnett, et al., 1990). Other disruptive behaviors, such as aggression, impulsive behavior, noisiness, and noncompliance with authority figure commands, also have been shown to improve with these medications (Barkley, Fischer, Newby, & Breen, 1988; Hinshaw, 1991; Hinshaw, Henker, Whalen, Erhardt, & Dunnington, 1989; Murphy, Pelham, & Lang, 1992; Rapport, DuPaul, Stoner, & Jones, 1986; Rapport & Kelly, 1991).

The effects of CNS stimulants on antisocial behaviors associated with Conduct Disorder are less clear-cut; however, some recent investigations highlight possible therapeutic benefits in this domain. For example, Shah, Seese, Abikoff, and Klein (1994), using an open trial format, found that pemoline reduced symptoms of both ADHD and Conduct Disorder in a group of children who exhibited symptoms of both disorders. This report is consistent with a laboratory-based study showing that methylphenidate reduced covert antisocial behavior, such as stealing and property destruction, in boys with ADHD (Hinshaw, Heller, & McHale, 1992). It is possible that ADHD may amplify or increase conduct problem behaviors in some children and so the reduction in ADHD symptoms achieved by stimulant medication may lead to concomitant reductions in antisocial behavior.

Despite the finding that adults generally report elevations in mood and euphoria when taking stimulant medications, these effects are rarely reported in children or adolescents (Barkley, 1977; DuPaul, Anastopoulos, Kwasnik, Barkley, & McMurray, 1996; Rapoport et al., 1980). Some children do describe feeling "funny," "different," or dizzy as a function of medication. It may be that actual developmental differences in response to stimulant medication make adults more likely to experience temporary elevations in mood. It is also possible, however, that children are not as adept at labeling their feelings and thus underreport euphoria (e.g., referring to it as feeling "funny").

Some children may evidence various mild negative moods or emotions in reaction to the stimulants (Barkley, 1977), as described in the section on side effects. These mood changes occur later in the time course of the dose response, typically as the drugs are "washing out" of the body in late morning or late afternoon. These emotional reactions are frequently mild and are more prevalent among children treated with higher dosages of methylphenidate.

Effects on Cognition, Learning, and Academic Performance

The effects of CNS stimulants on measures of intellect, memory, vigilance, attention, concentration, and learning have been studied extensively. A plethora of studies found that these medications enhance performance on laboratory measures of vigilance, impulse control, fine-motor coordination, and reaction time (Knights & Viets, 1975; Rapport & Kelly, 1991). Further, positive though inconsistent drug effects have been obtained on measures of short-term memory and learning of paired verbal or nonverbal material (Bergman et al., 1991; Rapport, DuPaul, & Smith,1985; Solanto, 1991; Swanson & Kinsbourne, 1978). Performance on both simple and complex learning paradigms appears to be enhanced (Douglas, Barr, O'Neil, & Britton, 1988; Swanson, 1989; Vyse & Rapport, 1989) but not always consistently (Solanto, 1991). In addition, stimulant-related improvements are noted, albeit again not reliably, in perceptual efficiency and speed of symbolic or verbal retrieval (both short- and long-term) (Barkley, 1977; Sergeant & van der Meere, 1991; Swanson, 1988b). Alternatively, changes in functioning on more traditional measures of cognitive abilities (e.g., intelligence tests) have not been found (Barkley, 1977). The overall pattern of research findings indicates that the cognitive effects of CNS stimulants are most likely to be exhibited in situations that require children to restrict their behavior and concentrate on assigned tasks. As Werry (1978) has cogently noted, stimulant medications help children to show what they know but are unlikely to alter children's knowledge of what needs to be done.

Concern has arisen over whether CNS stimulants result in state-dependent learning (Swanson, 1989), wherein material children learn while on the medication may not be recalled as easily when they are off the medication, or vice versa. Empirical studies examining this phenomenon are contradictory, however, with the majority of studies failing to find evidence for state-dependent effects for stimulants (Becker-Mattes, Mattes, Abikoff, & Brandt, 1985; Stephens, Pelham, & Skinner, 1984). Furthermore, even when state-dependent effects have been obtained, these typically are of such small magnitude as to be clinically insignificant.

Over the short term (i.e., several weeks), stimulant medication treatment is associated with minimal improvement in academic achievement, as defined by the grade level of difficulty of the material children are asked to perform (Barkley, 1977; Barkley & Cunningham, 1978; Gittelman, Klein, & Feingold, 1983). Stimulant-induced improvements in academic productivity, teacher ratings of academic performance, and, to a less reliable degree, accuracy have been found in many studies (DuPaul, Barkley, & McMurray, 1994; Pelham & Milich, 1991; Rapport & Kelly, 1991). Further, a recent study showed that methylphenidate leads to reliable enhancement of academic performance using curriculum-based measurement probes (Stoner, Carey, Ikeda, & Shinn, 1994). Nevertheless, given that the evidence for positive effects on academic achievement is mixed, it remains to be seen whether short-term improvements in academic *performance* lead to greater scholastic *success* in the long run (Barkley & Cunningham, 1978; Weiss & Hechtman, 1993). Finally, as is the case for most clinical effects of stimulant medications, therapeutic changes in academic performance are subject to considerable intra- and interindividual variability (Rapport et al., 1994).

Effects on Social Interactions

The quality of social interactions between children with ADHD and their parents, peers, and teachers is significantly improved by CNS stimulant medication, along with concomitant reductions in the intensity of these interactions. Specifically, stimulants increase children's compliance with parental commands and enhance their responsiveness to the interactions of others (Barkley & Cunningham, 1979; Barkley, Karlsson, Pollard, & Murphy, 1985; Humphries, Kinsbourne, & Swanson, 1978). Negative and off-task behaviors are also reduced in compliance situations. As a result, both parents and teachers decrease their rate of commands and degree of supervision over these children, while increasing their praise and positive responsiveness to the children's behavior. These effects on interactions with parents do not differ as a function of sex of the child with ADHD (Barkley, 1990; Pelham, Walker, Sturges, & Hoza, 1989). Similar, positive medication effects are found with respect to the interactions of children with ADHD and their teachers (Whalen, Henker, & Dotemoto, 1980) and peers across a variety of situations. Alterations in social interactions are sometimes associated with improvements in the degree to which children with ADHD are accepted by their peers (Cunningham, Siegel, & Offord, 1985; Hinshaw, 1991; Whalen, Henker, Collins, Finck, & Dotemoto, 1979).

The primary change in peer social interactions that occurs as a function of stimulant medication is a reduction in negative and aggressive behavior. Typically, there are minimal alterations in the frequency of positive social behaviors as the latter occur at a rate similar to normal classmates even during placebo conditions (Whalen et al., 1987). In a minority of cases, rates of social disengagement can increase particularly at high doses (Mino & Ohara, 1991) and/or among younger children (Granger, Whalen, Henker, & Cantwell, 1996), possibly leading these children to be judged as passive or socially inhibited (Granger, Whalen, & Henker, 1993). It should also be noted that stimulant medications not only directly alter the behavior of children with ADHD but also indirectly affect the behaviors of important adults and peers toward those children. When the latter changes are obtained, these may contribute further to a positive drug response in the child.

Some concern has been raised that diminished self-esteem could be an emanative effect of methylphenidate as children may attribute the source of their success while on medication to external rather than internal factors (Whalen, Henker, Hinshaw, Heller, & Huber-Dressler, 1991). Alternatively, most studies examining the attributions of children with ADHD about their task performance and successes as well as their self-concept have not documented any deleterious effects of stimulants on their attributions or self-esteem (Carlson, Pelham, Milich, & Hoza, 1993; DuPaul et al., 1996; Ialongo, Lopez, Horn, Pascoe, & Greenberg, 1994). In fact, Pelham et al. (1992) found that boys treated with methylphenidate reported liking themselves to a significantly greater degree when receiving medication than during a placebo condition. It is important to note that all these studies examined changes in attribution and self-esteem over short periods (i.e., several weeks) of medication treatment. It is possible that more significant changes in self-concept (either deterioration or improvement) could occur with longer-term pharmacotherapy.

Dose Effects on Behavior and Learning

Early laboratory-based research appeared to demonstrate a differential effect of methylphenidate dose across variant domains of behavior and learning in children diagnosed as hyperactive (Sprague & Sleator, 1976, 1977). Specifically, it was purported that lower doses (0.3 mg/kg) produced maximum improvement in learning, whereas higher doses were more beneficial for social behavior while being detrimental to learning. Further, Sprague and Sleator's results implied that to the extent that physicians rely on parent and teacher report to titrate dosage, children with ADHD may be placed on higher than desirable doses if the true goal of treatment is improved classroom learning. Several other interpretations of these results are possible (e.g., teacher ratings are less sensitive to medication effects than are laboratory tasks); however, these conclusions have been the most popular ones. More recently, studies show that on a large number of learning and behavioral measures, performance is enhanced in a linear fashion across doses reaching a peak at 20 mg, or 1 mg/kg, when examined for a group of children (Barkley et al., 1988; Pelham et al., 1987; Rapport et al., 1994; Solanto, 1991). For example, Figure 17.1 shows the mean dose–reponse curves of 76 children with ADHD who were treated with four doses of methylphenidate ranging from 5 to 20 mg. Highly similar, linear dose–response effects were found for observations of on-task behavior during independent seat work, teacher ratings of disruptive behavior using the Abbreviated Conners Teacher Rating Scale (Goyette, Conners, & Ulrich, 1978), and accuracy on academic tasks. It should also be noted that no constriction of flexible thinking has

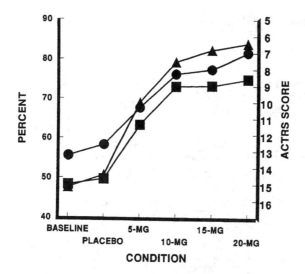

FIGURE 17.1. Mean group dose–response curves for a sample of 76 children with ADHD assessed across baseline, placebo, and four methylphenidate dosage conditions. Three classroom measures were used including observations of on-task behavior (●), academic efficiency score (■), and the Abbreviated Conners Teacher Rating Scale (ACTRS; ▲). Upward movement on the *y*-axis indicates improvement. From Rapport, Denney, DuPaul, & Gardner (1994). Copyright 1994 by the American Academy of Child and Adolescent Psychiatry. Reprinted by permission.

been found at a group level of analysis for doses up to 0.9 mg/kg of methylphenidate (Douglas, Barr, Desilets, & Sherman, 1995).

In contrast to group results, when dose–response effects are examined at the *individual level*, a significant degree of intersubject variability is evidenced. The response to methylphenidate of individual children could be categorized as (1) improvement related to stepwise or linear increases in dose, (2) subject to a "threshold" effect wherein no change is evidenced until a moderate or high dose is employed, (3) reaching a peak at a moderate dose with a decrement in performance at higher doses, or (4) inconsistent across doses (Rapport et al., 1987). These patterns have been found to be independent of a child's body weight and to vary across specific measures.

In addition to these individual differences in stimulant response, the degree to which clinical improvements are obtained with methylphenidate differs across doses and measures. Figure 17.2 displays rates of normalization, improvement, and deterioration as a function of four doses of methylphenidate ranging from 5 to 20 mg in a large sample of children with ADHD. Rates of normalization are highest for teacher ratings of disruptive behavior at the 15 and 20-mg doses, whereas accuracy on academic tasks is normalized for fewer children with minimal improvement in these rates beyond 10 mg. Thus, a high percentage of children can be expected to evidence improvement and/or normalization of classroom disruptive behavior as a function of stimulant treatment, whereas almost 50% of these children will not show either improvement or normalization in academic performance.

Research to date suggests that several factors moderate the dosage effects of the stimulants on the functioning of children: (1) results are highly variable across individual children and must be assessed at the latter level to be clinically useful; (2) dosage effects may vary across areas of functioning, but not necessarily in the systematic fashion suggested by Sprague and Sleator's (1977) study; (3) this task-specificity of dosage effects also appears to be subject to

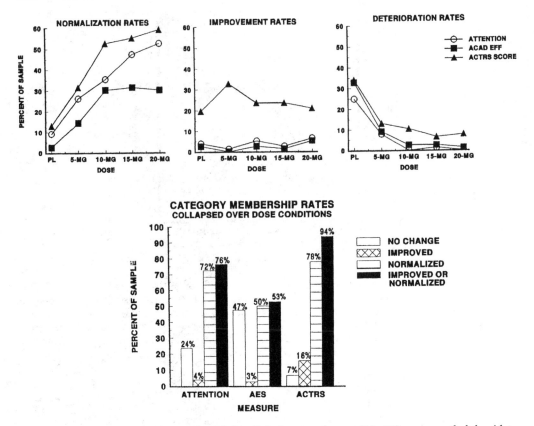

FIGURE 17.2. Upper three graphs display the clinical status of group ($N = 76$) across methylphenidate and placebo dose conditions for classroom attention, academic efficiency (Acad Eff), and teacher ratings of disruptive behavior (ACTRS Score). The bottom graph shows the clinical status of the group collapsed across methylphenidate dose conditions for the three classroom measures (AES = academic efficiency score; ACTRS = Abbreviated Conners Teacher Rating Scale). From Rapport, Denney, DuPaul, & Gardner (1994). Copyright 1994 by the American Academy of Child and Adolescent Psychiatry. Reprinted by permission.

individual differences; (4) dosages between 5 and 20 mg (i.e., 0.3 mg/kg and 1.0 mg/kg) have been found to optimize cognitive, academic, *and* behavioral performance at the group level, thus casting doubt on the notion of low doses being exclusively related to enhancement of learning; and (5) poor compliance to the prescribed regimen of taking the stimulant medication may also contribute to the apparent intraindividual variability of drug response (Kaufman, Smith-Wright, Reese, Simpson, & Jones, 1981). In addition, some caregivers, or even clinicians, expect far too much clinical improvement from the stimulants (i.e., view medication as a panacea) and, thus , may report dissatisfaction with the treatment regimen or dosage level when perfection in the eyes of the caregiver or clinician is not achieved.

To summarize, substantial evidence exists to show that the stimulants produce positive effects in many behavioral domains of children which translate into increased social acceptability. Effects on learning and academic performance are less clear-cut and are primarily limited to increases in work productivity and, less consistently, work accuracy. However, an improved ability to master increasingly difficult or higher-level academic material, such as that assessed in achievement tests, has not been demonstrated. These effects are highly variable across children and doses, again, mandating that individualization of drug, dosage, and titration occur in clinical practice.

LONG-TERM CLINICAL EFFECTS

Few studies employing rigorous methodology have evaluated the long-term efficacy of stimulant medications. Those that have examined the issue have generally found little advantage of medication over no medication when evaluated over extended periods (Pelham, 1985; Weiss & Hechtman, 1993). Children with ADHD who had been on drugs but were off at the time of follow-up were not found to differ in any important respect from those who had never recieved pharmacotherapy. Hence, no enduring effects of up to 5 years of medication treatment were observed in these studies. Many critical limitations of long-term outcome investigations have been identified and are not specifically reviewed here (Schachar & Tannock, 1993). Suffice it to say that there is abundant evidence of short-term benefit, particularly in classroom functioning (Schachar, Tannock, Cunningham, & Corkum, 1997), in studies of up to 7 months' duration which, if continued, would be expected to produce ongoing symptomatic relief from ADHD (Schachar & Tannock, 1993). Enduring effects of these medications after treatment termination seem unlikely, yet this issue must await more rigorous examination than has been possible to date. Further, the chronic and pervasive difficulties associated with more serious ADHD (i.e., among those most likely to receive medication) are probably not going to be permanently eradicated by any single treatment, even one with demonstrated short-term efficacy, such as stimulant medication (DuPaul & Barkley, 1990).

SIDE EFFECTS AND TOXICITY

Lethal Dose

No data were located on deaths that could be directly attributable to the use of acute toxic doses of stimulants in humans. Deaths and the need for liver transplants are noted as a rare secondary consequence of the hepatic dysfunction that can occur in some cases from prolonged use of pemoline. In rats, evidence suggests that doses over 100 mg/kg are lethal within 12 hours after ingestion. This dose in dogs did not produce mortality but did produce convulsions. Although simple extrapolation to humans is hazardous, the margin of safety, therefore, would seem to be at least 100:1 between a single dose representing the high end of the human clinical dose range (1.0 mg/kg) and lethal doses in small mammals (Diener, 1991).

Short-Term Side Effects

Typical Side Effects

Barkley, McMurray, Edelbrock, and Robbins (1990) conducted one of the most comprehensive studies of the prevalence of parent- and teacher-reported side effects to methylphenidate. A sample of 82 children received two doses (i.e., 0.3 mg/kg and 0.5 mg/kg) of methylphenidate, given twice daily, in the context of a double-blind, placebo-controlled medication trial. More than half the sample exhibited decreased appetite, insomnia, anxiety, irritability, or proneness to crying with both doses of methylphenidate. However, it should be noted that *many of these apparent side effects (especially those associated with mood) were present during the placebo condition* and may represent characteristics associated with the disorder rather than its treatment (Fine & Johnston, 1993). In most cases the severity of these side effects has been shown to be quite mild. Stomachaches and headaches were reported in about a third of the participants, but these were usually of mild severity as well. Thus, clinicians can expect some mild side effects such as insomnia or diminished appetite; however, care should be taken to assess their presence during nonmedication conditions to determine their "true" relation to stimulant use.

A similar profile of side effects has been obtained in more recent investigations with larger samples (Ahmann et al., 1993; Fine & Johnston, 1993). These studies have also found that some teacher-reported side effects on this same rating scale actually *declined* significantly during the drug trial, further supporting the notion that some "side effects" may actually be preexisting behavioral/emotional problems associated with ADHD. It also suggests that more side effects are associated with the "washout" phase of the time course rather than the peak phase.

DuPaul et al., (1996) investigated whether the number and severity of side effects of methylphenidate vary as a function of respondent (i.e., parent, teacher, or patient). A double-blind, placebo-controlled evaulation of three doses of methylphenidate was conducted for 24 children ranging in age from 9 to 15 years old ($M = 11.09$). The results indicated that, regardless of dose, children reported some side effects to be more severe than did parents and teachers (see Figure 17.3). As was the case for participants in the Ahmann et al. (1993) study, significant reductions in severity of side effects were reported by teachers during active methylphenidate versus placebo conditions. Thus, clinicians should be aware of potential differences in side effect profile across respondents and should include self-report of possible side effects at least when working with older children and adolescents.

As has been noted previously, stimulants typically are administered on a twice daily dosing schedule. Unfortunately, this schedule results in children being unmedicated during the evening hours, which may deleteriously affect their compliance with parental directives and timely completion of homework assignments. Clinical lore has held that adding a third dose in the late afternoon or early evening could increase the risk for appetite reduction at dinnertime or insomnia. The results of two recent studies contradict clinical wisdom by indicating that most children can tolerate a thrice-daily dosing regimen with no significant impact on sleep or appetite (Kent, Blader, Koplewicz, Abikoff, & Foley, 1995; Stein et al.,

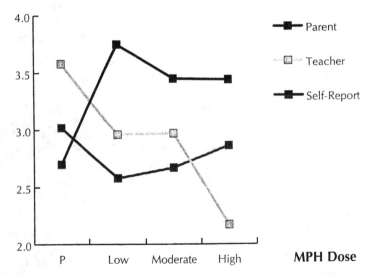

FIGURE 17.3. Mean severity of side effects across three doses of methylphenidate (MPH) as rated by parents, teachers, and children (self-report). From DuPaul, Anastopoulos, Kwasnik, Barkley, & McMurray (1996). Copyright 1996 by Multi-Health Systems, Inc. Reprinted by permission.

1996). Thus, a third daily dose of stimulant medication may be used safely in most instances when home behavior is of significant concern. Of course, clinicians must carefully assess whether changes in eating or sleeping patterns of individual children are deleteriously affected by using a three-times-a-day administration schedule.

Tics

One side effect that should receive serious attention from clinicians is the possible increase in motor or vocal tics produced by stimulant medications. A number of cases of irreversible Tourette's Disorder also have been reported as secondary to stimulant treatment, although these findings are somewhat controversial (Barkley, 1988a; Weiner, Nauseida, & Klawans, 1978). It has been estimated that fewer than 1% of children with ADHD who are treated with stimulants will develop a tic disorder and that in 13% of the cases, the medication may exacerbate preexisting tics (Caine, Ludlow, Polinsky, & Ebert, 1984). Although it is unclear whether stimulant medications cause Tourette's Disorder in previously unafflicted individuals, these compounds appear to exacerbate symptoms in patients who already exhibit this disorder (Erenberg, Cruse, & Rothner, 1984; Golden, 1988). The vast majority of such reactions typically subside once pharmacotherapy is discontinued, particularly with methylphenidate relative to dextroamphetamine (Castellanos et al., 1997); however, there are a few cases in the literature where the tics apparently did not diminish in frequency and severity following termination of stimulant medication (Barkley, 1988a). Alternatively, several recent studies suggested that the effects of stimulants on tics are less pronounced than was originally believed, resulting in minor increases in some motor tics and possible decreases in vocal tics (Gadow, Nolan, & Sverd, 1992; Gadow, Sverd, Sprafkin, Nolan, & Ezor, 1995). *It still seems prudent to screen children with ADHD adequately for a personal or family history of tics or Tourette's Disorder* prior to initiating stimulant therapy and to proceed cautiously with such treatment in those with positive histories.

When psychostimulants are used in the absence of apparent risk factors and tics develop, the dose can be lowered to see whether the tics subside or discontinued if the tics are significantly impairing. The tics will usually subside within 7 to 10 days. Treatment can then be resumed at a lower dose, if the child's behavioral adjustment has dramatically deteriorated, to determine whether a lower dose can be tolerated without production of tics. If not, trying an alternative stimulant medication or an antidepressant may prove successful. If these tactics are unsuccessful, the parents should be warned not to have their children treated with stimulants in the future without alerting the treating physician to this history of stimulant-induced tic reactions.

"Behavioral Rebound"

The behavioral rebound effect is defined as a deterioration in behavior (exceeding that which occurs during baseline or placebo conditions) that occurs in the late afternoon and evening following daytime administrations of stimulant medication. Johnston, Pelham, Hoza, and Sturges (1988) conducted a rigorous, placebo-controlled study of this phenomenon in a sample of 21 children with ADHD treated with two doses of methylphenidate and found that about a third of their sample exhibited rebound effects. The magnitude of these reactions varied considerably across days for individual children. Thus, the behavioral rebound effect is not as widespread as believed (once certain biases are controlled for) and, even when it does occur, its magnitude across days is highly variable. When observed, several options can be pursued that may diminish the severity of the rebound. Giving the child a lower dosage of medication in the late afternoon (provided that this does not lead to insomnia or loss of appetite at dinnertime) may help. The noontime dosage also may be reduced. In any case, one rarely has to resort to discontinuing the medication entirely because of rebound effects. Even so, it is a good idea to warn the parents about the possibility of a rebound effect or they may misinterpret this phenomenon as the medication worsening their child's behavior on a permanent basis.

Cognitive Toxicity

As noted earlier, the possibility exists that high doses of stimulants may produce an adverse impact on learning or other higher mental functions. High doses of stimulants conceivably may produce an overfocusing or constriction of attention (Safer, 1992; Solanto, 1991; Swanson, 1988b, 1989) and, perhaps, even a mental equivalent of motor stereotypies, such as perseverative responding or diminished flexibility in problem solving. Such findings have been demonstrated in only a few studies of small numbers of participants (Dyme, Sahakian, Golinko, & Rabe, 1982) or in subgroups of larger samples to date (Solanto & Wender, 1989), but not in the overall samples under study. These results imply that some children may have cognitively toxic effects on high doses of stimulants (above 0.6 mg/kg). However, a more recent study of the issue was unable to document any constriction of cognitive flexibility at doses up to 0.9 mg/kg of methylphenidate (Douglas et al., 1995). Equally as important, doses within the therapeutic range recommended here have typically not produced such effects, nor have they decreased mental creativity (Fiedler & Ullman, 1983). Although studies examining stimulant-induced cognitive toxicity have produced equivocal results, it is clear that some children who show a positive behavioral response to medication exhibit either no change or significant deterioration in academic performance (Rapport et al., 1994). Thus, possible iatrogenic effects on cognitive functioning cannot be inferred through behavioral measures (e.g., teacher ratings) and must be assessed through more direct means such as teacher report of academic performance, examination of academic products, or tests of cognitive skills.

Iatrogenic Effects on Social Behavior

There is some debate whether higher dosages of stimulants can reduce not only negative, aggressive interactions but prosocial behavior as well. Research indicates that low and moderate doses of methylphenidate do reduce the frequency of aggression and noncompliance in groups of children with ADHD but have no appreciable effect, in either direction, on prosocial or nonsocial behavior (Hinshaw, Buhrmester, & Heller, 1989). Nevertheless, isolated cases may arise in which parents note that a child is no longer "spontaneous" or childlike in his or her behavior and appears too controlled or socially aloof. In such cases, the dosage may need to be reduced or the medication discontinued.

Idiosyncratic Side Effects

Each of the stimulants may produce unique side effects. A few children may develop allergic skin rashes after a few weeks or more of treatment with pemoline. The rash typically disappears when the medication is discontinued and, in some cases, the practitioner may be able to return the child to the medication with no recurrence of the rash (Conners & Taylor, 1980). In animals, stimulants at higher doses can produce stereotyped behavior, and these are occasionally seen in children. All the stimulants may tend to increase choreiform movements (Sallee et al., 1989) and self-directed behavior, such as lip licking, lip biting, and light picking of the finger tips (not the nails). Dose reduction seems to eliminate these behaviors. Of greater concern, pemoline has been associated with chemical hepatitis (which may not always be reversible) in up to 3% of children taking this drug (Dulcan, 1990). As a consequence of 10 reports of acute liver failure in children in the United States, and additional reports of liver failure in children and adults in foreign countries, the company manufacturing this drug recently changed its package labeling to indicate that "Cylert should not ordinarily be considered as first-line drug therapy for Attention Deficit Hyperactivity Disorder (ADHD)" (Letter from Abbott Pharmaceutical Products Division, December 1996, Ref. 03-4735-R18). The earliest reported onset of hepatic abnormalities occurred 6 months after initiation of pemoline. The company recommends that the drug be discontinued at the first signs of clinically significant hepatic dysfunction during its use.

All the stimulants can produce temporary symptoms of psychosis (e.g., thought disorganization, press of speech, tactile hallucinations, and extreme anxiety) at very high doses, or even at smaller doses in a rare child. *Such reactions are quite uncommon* (Barkley, 1977; Dulcan, 1990). Rare cases of bone marrow suppression and neutropenia thrombocytopervia anemia also may be associated with stimulant use, leading some physicians to screen all children for complete blood count (CBC) during their initial drug trial. Yet the rarity of these cases may not justify the expense involved in screening all children for this side effect.

Summary of Short-Term Side Effects

Most of the short-term side effects of stimulants are clearly dose related and subject to individual differences. In many cases, side effects diminish within 1 to 2 weeks of beginning medication, and all, except possibly the occasional tic, disappear upon ceasing pharmacotherapy. When side effects persist beyond 1 to 2 weeks of treatment initiation, their severity typically can be reduced by a slight lowering of the dose. Alternatively, a trial of a different stimulant medication can be initiated, as some side effects may be unique to the specific stimulant employed. It has been estimated that 1% to 3% of children with ADHD cannot tolerate any dose of stimulant medication and need to be treated with alternative medications (Barkley, 1977).

Long-Term Side Effects

Potential iatrogenic effects of stimulant medications over several years have not been extensively studied as such investigations are fraught with practical limitations. Nevertheless, there are now a number of follow-up studies, some of quite substantial duration (Weiss & Hechtman, 1993), which have not found any significant disadvantages associated with long-term stimulant treatment.

Drug Dependence and Abuse

Parents are often understandably concerned about long-term stimulant use leading to possible addiction to these drugs or increased risk of abusing other drugs as teenagers. There are no reported individual cases of addiction or serious drug dependence to date with these medications. Several studies (as reviewed in Weiss & Hechtman, 1993) have sought to determine whether children treated with CNS stimulants are more likely to abuse illicit substances as teenagers than are their ADHD counterparts who have not received psychostimulant treatment. The results suggest that there is no increased risk for drug abuse associated with treatment, although more research is needed to rule this out conclusively.

Height and Weight Suppression

As noted earlier, one long-term side effect that has been of concern to many clinicians and scientists is the potential suppression of height and weight gain. Early reports indicated that both methylphenidate and dextroamphetamine produced this effect (Safer, Allen, & Barr, 1972; Safer & Allen, 1973). Later studies have found this to be a dose-related phenomenon, more prevalent with dextroamphetamine, and to occur primarily within the first year of treatment. The loss in weight is typically minimal (1 kg or less). Further, a rebound in growth or habituation to this effect seems to occur thereafter, and there is no appreciable effect on eventual adult height or weight (Mattes & Gittelman, 1983; Zeiner, 1995). Effects on growth are believed to be secondary to appetite suppression produced by stimulants, although several studies have indicated that these compounds may have some direct effects on growth hormone levels in the blood (Reeve & Garfinkel, 1991). Thus, any suppression in growth is typically minor, is a relatively transient side effect of the first year or so of treatment, and has no significant effect on eventual adult height or weight.

Recent evidence indicates that children with ADHD may be somewhat smaller than their normal counterparts prior to puberty and catch up with their peers during adolescence, yet such growth delay is associated with the disorder and not with stimulant treatment (Spencer, Biederman, Harding, et al., 1996). All these conclusions are based on the results of group studies, so it is possible that a few individuals within the group may experience more serious weight loss as a function of stimulant treatment, but, because there are so few cases, these individual results may be averaged out of the overall mean statistics. Consequently, it is important for clinicians to monitor weight and height periodically in children receiving stimulant medications and to alter dosage scheduling should clinically significant changes in these growth parameters occur as a function of stimulant treatment. For example, medication could be discontinued during the summer months and/or during school vacations to increase the probability of a growth rebound.

Cardiovascular Effects

Some parents may express concern as to the effects of chronic stimulant medication use on the development of the cardiovascular system in children. Unfortunately, there are few empirical investigations that can shed light on this issue. All the CNS stimulants have some effects on heart rate and blood pressure, albeit relatively mild. Those cardiovascular effects that do occur appear to diminish or even disappear with extended use of medication (i.e., as measured up to 1.75 years) (Zeiner, 1995). The primary concern, however, is that children taking stimulants over a number of years might be at an increased risk for cardiovascular problems in middle to late life. At present, other than the single report of acutely increased blood pressure in African-American males (Brown & Sexson, 1989), studies have not specifically addressed this important issue, but there is no reason from the extant data to suggest such long-term cardiovascular problems might arise.

THE CLINICAL USAGE OF STIMULANT MEDICATIONS

Diagnostic Considerations in Usage

CNS stimulant medications are routinely indicated when children and adolescents have significant problems with inattention, hyperactivity, and impulsivity associated with ADHD, Combined Type that lead to impairment in one or more areas of functioning (e.g., academic achievement or poor peer relations). Stimulants are also useful in children with ADHD, Inattentive Type, but the percentage of such children responding to medication may be somewhat lower (55% to 65%) than that seen in children with the Combined Type (70% to 90%), and the doses needed to achieve a therapeutic response may also be lower (Barkley, DuPaul, & McMurray, 1991; McBurnett, Lahey, & Swanson, 1991). No studies have specifically examined children who have the newest subtype of ADHD, Predominantly Hyperactive–Impulsive Type, but the latter is likely a preschool developmental precursor to the Combined Type and so these children may be just as likely to respond well to the medication as are children with the Combined Type, their young age notwithstanding.

When ADHD symptoms are associated with cognitive impairments such as mental retardation, the stimulants may also be useful for symptom management; however, clinical response may vary with the intellectual level of the child. One prominent researcher has argued that stimulants generally cause a focusing of attention and that some children who are mentally retarded (especially those with severe mental retardation) may already have overfocused attention (Aman, 1982). In one study, children with mental ages greater than 4½ years or IQs above 45 often had positive clinical responses whereas those with lower mental ages or IQs generally responded poorly (Aman, Marks, Turbotts, Wilsher, & Merry, 1991). It also appears that the closer the clinical picture of the patient with mental retardation approximates that of classical ADHD, the better may be the response to stimulant treatment (Aman et al., 1991). Alternatively, the results of at least one study indicate a higher rate of unacceptable side effects due to methylphenidate in children with mental retardation than is typically the case in children of normal IQ (Handen et al., 1991). In general, however, it appears that stimulants are useful in the management of ADHD symptoms in children with mental retardation (Aman, 1996; Aman et al., 1997).

ADHD has become increasingly recognized as likely to persist into the adult years of at least 8–66% of all diagnosed childhood cases, with more recent studies using more contemporary diagnostic criteria tending to favor the higher figure. The recognition of this disorder in adulthood led to several studies involving stimulant medication trials with adults having ADHD. The most recent of these using current diagnostic criteria shows that approximately 80% of adults with ADHD respond well to methylphenidate (Spencer et al., 1995). These results indicate that as children with ADHD become adults, stimulant medication treatment can be a relatively successful means of continuing to manage their symptoms should this treatment be necessary.

Predicting Behavioral Response to Stimulant Medication

It would be important for clinicians to be aware of empirically derived predictors of medication response when making treatment decisions for individual children. A variety of factors has been proposed to distinguish children with ADHD who would respond favorably to stimulant medications (responders) from those who would not (nonresponders), including psychophysiological factors, neurological variables, familial characteristics, demographic/sociological factors, diagnostic categories, rating scale scores, psychological profiles, and behavioral characteristics (Aman & Turbott, 1991; Barkley, 1976; Taylor, 1983). Those behavioral and psychophysiological measures related to attention span are typically the most reliable predictors of improvement during stimulant drug treatment. This is hardly surprising given that stimulants have their most consistent psychological effect on attention span. This conclusion is in keeping with related research that indicated that the behavioral effects of stimulants may be dependent on the drug-free rate of the behavior in question (i.e., rate dependent). In other words, the greater the inattention of children, the better their reaction to medication (i.e., the more pronounced effect on attention span). Further, it should be noted that the statistical magnitude of such rate-dependent effects has been found to exceed what would be predicted simply on the basis of regression to the mean (Rapport & DuPaul, 1986).

Some studies also found that the quality of the relationship between parent and child was a good predictor of drug response: The better the mother–child relationship, the greater the response to medication. This is related to the findings reported earlier that, for many children, the medication leads to positive changes in the behavior of both the children and their mothers. It may be that mothers who are more appreciative and rewarding of these initial positive changes in their children's behavior while on stimulants produce further gains associated with treatment. In support of this, Cunningham and Barkley (as cited in Barkley, 1981) have obtained results indicating that mothers who were more interactive with their children and more rewarding of child compliance prior to pharmacotherapy had children who exhibited greater positive changes in behavior as a result of treatment with medication.

Taylor (1986) found that higher levels of restless behavior (e.g., hyperactivity), poor motor coordination, younger age, and the absence of symptoms of overt emotional disorder predicted better stimulant response among a large sample of children with ADHD. Similar reports (Pliszka, 1989; Voelker, Lachar, & Gdowski, 1983) suggest that children who are more anxious or depressed according to parent and/or teacher ratings (e.g., Conners Rating Scales) have a poorer response to stimulant medications and are less likely to exhibit "normalized" behavior as a result of treatment than their noninternalizing counterparts (DuPaul et al., 1994).

Less research exists on the response to stimulants of developmentally delayed children who may also have ADHD (Aman, 1996). Empirical data gathered to date suggest that the percentage of cognitively delayed children responding to these medications may be somewhat less than in normal IQ children, particularly at IQ levels below 50 (Aman, 1996; Aman et al., 1997; Handen et al., 1992, 1994). Thus, the need for adjunctive interventions beyond medication is particularly acute in the cognitively delayed population.

At the current time, research would suggest that the younger (but still school-age), more inattentive, less coordinated, more hyperactive, less anxious, and less intellectually delayed a child may be, and the better the parental management and involvement in the care of the child, the better the response to psychostimulant treatment. Some clinicians have attempted to use neurometric tests as a means of predicting children's probable drug responses to the stimulants and to monitor such responses during their drug trial. To date, the authors are aware of no consistent body of research that would support this rather expensive and inconvenient practice.

Beyond a prediction of overall medication response, clinicians also are interested in predicting which dose will lead to optimal response for a given child with ADHD. Unfortunately, there are minimal, empirically derived guidelines for making such predictions. Factors such as body weight or body mass, as are assumed by dosing schemes based on mg/kg, are not related to dose-response effects of methylphenidate (Rapport & Denney, 1997; Rapport, DuPaul, & Kelly, 1989). Other variables such as symptom severity, age, and gender also are unrelated to dose response. Rapport et al. (1994) did find that a majority of children who fail to respond to lower doses of methylphenidate do eventually show a positive, behavioral response at higher doses, although this finding was not replicated for academic functioning. Thus, at present, the only reliable way to determine the best dose for a given individual is by assessing medication response across a range of doses wherein a lack of response to a low dose does not preclude assessing response to higher doses, except when clinically significant side effects occur.

Guidelines for Usage

Suggestions for ways in which to prescibe and monitor stimulant medications for children vary widely. We offer here an amalgamation of suggestions from our clinical practice and research on predictors of response, as well as the advice of other respected scientist-practitioners in this area (Cantwell & Carlson, 1978; Donnelly & Rapoport, 1985; Dulcan, 1990; Greenhill, 1991; Shaywitz & Shaywitz, 1991).

When to Use Medication

Despite the efficacy of stimulant medications and their relative safety with children, the decision to medicate individual patients must be made in the context of seriously considering a number of issues. As we have noted elsewhere (Barkley, 1981; Barkley, DuPaul, & Connor, in press; DuPaul & Barkley, 1990), *the diagnosis of ADHD does not automatically indicate the need to prescribe stimulant medication.* We suggest following several rules as aids in making this decision. These guidelines are intended only as rules of thumb, as clinicians should remain cognizant of the unique needs and circumstances of each case in making the decision to prescribe medication.

1. *Has the child had adequate physical and psychological evaluations?* Medications should never be prescribed if the child has not been directly examined in a thorough manner or if there is no other good evidence of physical health (e.g., pediatric or family physician assessment).

2. *How old is the child?* Pharmacotherapy is often less effective or leads to more severe side effects among children below the age of 4 and is therefore not usually recommended.

3. *Have other therapies been used?* If this is the family's initial contact with the professional, prescription of medication might be postponed until other interventions (e.g., parent training in child management skills) have been attempted. Alternatively, when the child's behavior presents a severe problem and the family cannot participate in child management training, medication may be the most viable initial treatment.

4. *How severe are the child's current symptoms?* In some cases, the child's behavior is so unmanageable or distressing to the family that medication may prove the fastest and most effective manner of dealing with the crisis until other forms of treatment can commence. Once progress is obtained with other therapies, some effort can be made to reduce or terminate the medication, although this is not always possible.

5. *Can the family afford the medication and associated costs (e.g., follow-up visits)?* Long-term compliance rates are typically poor and may be especially problematic among families of low socioeconomic status. Of course, their ability to afford and their compliance with alternative treatments would also be suspect.

6. *Are the parents sufficiently able to adequately supervise the use of the medications and guard against their abuse?* The cognitive capacity of the parents to accurately dispense the medication and report effects to the physician should be considered. If the parents are unable to complete these responsibilities, one possibility is for the school to dispense all doses of the medication, thus reducing the need for parental involvement.

7. *What is (are) the parents' attitude(s) toward pharmacotherapy?* Some parents are simply "antidrug" and should not be coerced into agreeing to this treatment as they will probably sabotage its efficacy. In such cases, it is advisable simply to offer accurate, verbal/written information about the advantages and disadvantages of stimulants and to let the parents decide when they want to pursue a trial of medication. It has been our experience that if the child's ADHD symptoms are sufficiently severe, the parents will eventually agree to at least a brief trial of the medication.

8. *Is there a substance-abusing sibling or drug-abusing parent in the household?* In this case, psychostimulant medication should not be prescribed because there is a high risk for its illicit use or sale. One might consider the use of pemoline, which seems to have little or no street value or potential for abuse, or alternative medications such as the tricyclic antidepressants or bupropion.

9. *Does the child have any history of tics, psychosis, or thought disorder?* If so, the stimulants are contraindicated as they may exacerbate such difficulties.

10. *Is the child highly anxious, fearful, or more likely to complain of psychosomatic disturbances?* Such children are less likely to respond positively to stimulant medications and may exhibit a better response to antidepressant medications.

11. *Does the physician have the time to monitor medication effects properly?* In addition to an initial assessment of drug efficacy and establishing the optimal dosage, periodic reassessment of drug response and effects on height and weight should be conducted throughout the year.

12. *How does the child feel about medication and its alternatives?* With older children and adolescents, it is important that the use of medication be discussed with them and its rationale fully explained. In cases where children are "antidrug" or oppositional, they may resist efforts to use it (e.g., refuse to swallow the pill).

13. *Is the child or adolescent involved in competitive sports in which urine screens for illicit drug use are routine?* If so, the clinician should discuss this issue with the parents as some children may be disqualified from participation in competitive sports as a result of taking methylphenidate immediately prior to or during such competitive events.

14. *Is the older adolescent being considered for medication treatment planning on entering the military?* A number of instances have been reported in the United States in which teenagers planning to enlist in the military have been denied admission because of a history of having ADHD and, in particular, of having been treated with stimulant medication within the past few years. Again, clinicians should discuss this issue with parents and the adolescent before initiating stimulant medication treatment.

Initial Medical Evaluation

Although the monitoring of physical, behavioral, cognitive, emotional, and social parameters in children undergoing medication trials has been dealt with earlier in this chapter, a few recommendations are pertinent. Height and weight should always be recorded and, if possible, earlier measurements obtained so that the child's current position and former trajectory on a growth velocity curve can be estimated. This makes it easier to evaluate any subsequent change in growth rate. Possible cardiological abnormality should be ruled out, and blood pressure and pulse should be taken. Before prescribing stimulants it is important to establish the child's previous eating and sleeping patterns. The pretreatment levels of potential behavioral side effects of stimulants should also be obtained by giving the Side Effects Rating Scale (see Figure 17.4) at this time as many clinic-referred children show such behavioral/emotional problems before beginning medication. Without such monitoring, these preexisting conditions might be misconstrued as treatment emergent effects during the subsequent trial. Finally, a careful history should be taken for evidence of possible seizure disorders and tics and follow-up investigation done if indicated. Other laboratory tests (CBC, liver function tests) are only needed as baseline data or as part of a routine physical evaluation and have no routine application in preparation for prescribing stimulants, unless pemoline is to be used. In view of the extraordinary rarity of reports of bone marrow suppression from stimulants, it is not clear that CBC screening of all medicated children would be sufficiently cost-effective to be recommended as standard care.

Prescribing and Titrating Stimulants

Very young children (i.e., under the age of 4) should not typically receive stimulant medication as a treatment of first choice given the lower probability of a positive response ($< 65\%$)

STIMULANT DRUG SIDE EFFECTS RATING SCALE

Name _____ Date _____

Person Completing This Form _____

Instructions: Please rate each behavior from 0 (absent) to 9 (serious). Circle only one number beside each item. A zero means that you have not seen the behavior in this child during the past week, and a 9 means that you have noticed it and believe it to be either very serious or to occur very frequently.

Behavior	Absent									Serious
Insomnia or trouble sleeping	0	1	2	3	4	5	6	7	8	9
Nightmares	0	1	2	3	4	5	6	7	8	9
Stares a lot or daydreams	0	1	2	3	4	5	6	7	8	9
Talks less with others	0	1	2	3	4	5	6	7	8	9
Uninterested in others	0	1	2	3	4	5	6	7	8	9
Decreased appetite	0	1	2	3	4	5	6	7	8	9
Irritable	0	1	2	3	4	5	6	7	8	9
Stomachaches	0	1	2	3	4	5	6	7	8	9
Headaches	0	1	2	3	4	5	6	7	8	9
Drowsiness	0	1	2	3	4	5	6	7	8	9
Sad/unhappy	0	1	2	3	4	5	6	7	8	9
Prone to crying	0	1	2	3	4	5	6	7	8	9
Anxious	0	1	2	3	4	5	6	7	8	9
Bites fingernails	0	1	2	3	4	5	6	7	8	9
Euphoric/unusually happy	0	1	2	3	4	5	6	7	8	9
Dizziness	0	1	2	3	4	5	6	7	8	9
Tics or nervous movements	0	1	2	3	4	5	6	7	8	9

FIGURE 17.4. The Side Effects Rating Scale. From Barkley (1981). Copyright 1981 by The Guilford Press. Reprinted by permission.

and a higher incidence of side effects relative to older children (Barkley, 1988b). Further, few well-controlled investigations of stimulant effects have been conducted with young children, thus warranting clinical prudence when a child in this age group presents with significant symptoms of ADHD and no contraindications to pharmacotherapy. Similarly, the percentage of clinic-referred adolescents with ADHD who respond to stimulant medication may be somewhat lower (approximately 50%) than the response rate seen in 5 to 12-year-olds with ADHD (i.e., 70–95%) (Pelham, Greenslade, et al., 1990). It is unclear whether this change in response rate has to do with true developmental alterations in the effects of these compounds or with differences in the extent of comorbid conditions associated with poorer drug response (or poorer compliance) that may be likely to be seen in clinic-referred adolescents relative to children. The risk of drug abuse of stimulants is clearly higher in adolescents than among children, especially those teens with comorbid conduct disorder who may abuse other substances.

Typically, methylphenidate is the medication of first choice because of its greater documentation in research, proven efficacy across a wide age range, and greater dose-response information. Because a child's failure to respond to one stimulant may not preclude a positive response to an alternate drug in the same class (Elia & Rapoport, 1991), we recommend a trial of dextroamphetamine as the next step. If a positive response to dextroamphetamine is not obtained, a trial of Adderall could be considered as clinical reports suggest that some patients may tolerate this combination better than dextroamphetamine, at least according to its manufacturer. If these medications are not effective, a trial of pemoline could be considered, though the risk of hepatic toxicity of this medication requires closer monitoring and periodic assessment of liver functioning, making it a less benign medication than the other stimulants. Alternatively, we suggest switching to an antidepressant, such as desipramine, imipramine, fluoxetine, or bupropion (see Chapter 10, this volume). If a positive response is not obtained with the antidepressants, pharmacotherapy may need to be discontinued for at least 1 year, if not altogether eliminated from consideration. It is important to note that children younger than the age of 6 who evidence a poor response to stimulants, may respond positively in later years (i.e., after the age of 6).

The stimulant medications, their available tablet sizes, and typical dose ranges are displayed in Table 17.1. Both fixed dose ranges and those based on body weight are shown, although body weight has not been shown to be related to drug response (e.g., Rapport & Denney, 1997). Idiosyncratic response is typically found among children of similar body weights and so the clinician must be prepared to titrate the dose to the individual responding of each case (which presumes careful monitoring). With methylphenidate, the usual practice is to start a child at a low dose such as 2.5 to 5 mg given once or twice daily, although children below age 5 years can be started on 2.5 mg given once daily to lessen the likelihood of an immediate adverse response. We recommend beginning with a twice-daily dose (morning and noon) for school-age children to assess dose response then progressing to a third dose for some children, as needed. Other practitioners with whom we are familiar prefer to start with a single morning dose only, as a few children may require a single dose per day to achieve a therapeutic response. Children who arise early or who have a more rapid elimination of the drug may require doses three times per day. Further, as mentioned previously, a third dose of methylphenidate in the late afternoon or evening may be beneficial to some children and typically does not increase latency to sleep onset or diminish sleep duration for most patients (Kent et al., 1995; Stein et al., 1996).

Methylphenidate dose typically is increased by 2.5- to 5-mg increments on a weekly basis until therapeutic effects are reported or significant side effects are exhibited. The dose needed

TABLE 17.1. Stimulant Medications, Available Doses, and Costs

Medication	Trade name	Manufacturer	Doses	Costs
Dextroamphetamine	Dexedrine	SmithKline Beecham	5-mg tablets (5-, 10-, and 15-mg spansules 5 mg/5ml elixir 5- and 10-mg tablets (generic)	$.13 $.29–.46 $.03–.04
			Recommended range: 2.5–20 mg	
Methylphenidate	Ritalin	CIBA	5-, 10-, and 20-mg tablets 20-mg sustained-release tablets 5-, 10-, and 20-mg tablets (generic)	$.23–.47 $.71 $.17–.36
			Recommended range: 2.5–60 mg	
Amphetamine/ dextroamphetamine	Adderall	Richwood	10- and 20-mg tablets	$.46–.67
			Recommended range: 2.5–40 mg	
Pemoline	Cylert	Abbott	18.75-, 37.5-, and 75-mg tablets 37.5-mg chewable tablets	$.36–.97
			Recommended range: 18.75–112.5 mg	

Note. Sources: Dulcan (1990) and Adderall product information sheet, Richwood Pharmaceuticals.

to achieve optimum behavior change typically does not need to exceed 20 mg per dose given two to three times daily because of a possible increase in the severity of side effects. Given the idiosyncratic nature of methylphenidate response, some children may benefit from somewhat higher doses than this recommended level. We rarely go beyond 40 to 60 mg per day in our clinic. Other clinicians have reported to us an average dose range of 5 to 15 mg per dose in the morning, tapering down to a half of the morning dose at noon, and then a third of the morning dose in the afternoon.

Administering medication at or immediately after mealtime may lessen the anorexia or stomachaches sometimes associated with stimulants. If these side effects are not present or are mild, it has been suggested that the medications be given 30 minutes before mealtimes to minimize excretion rates. The results of a study using a small sample suggests that the effect of meals on methylphenidate response is not statistically significant, but the trend of the data supported administration prior to meals (Chan et al., 1983). Although this may not typically be significant in individual cases, it may be worth adhering to this traditional advice in a child who is responding only marginally to medication despite adequate dosage.

As noted earlier, it is a matter of some controversy whether behavioral tolerance develops with chronic administration of stimulants. Extant research indicates that failure to maintain clinical response at a given dose is more likely to occur with higher dosages (i.e., 15 mg or 20 mg twice daily) after a period of 6 months or more of chronic use. This is, by no means, a universal phenomenon and each case must be evaluated individually. A reevaluation of a child's maintenance dose on an annual basis, as discussed later, is strongly recommended to determine the necessity of a dosage change.

As Table 17.1 indicates, dextroamphetamine is typically given in doses about half those of methylphenidate because of the greater potency of the former compound. Because the potency equivalence of these medications has not be properly established, a dose of dextroamphetamine that is one-fourth that of methylphenidate can also be used. Pemoline is prescribed and titrated quite differently given that it is a "steady-state" medication (i.e., requiring several days to develop a pharmacodynamic equilibrium). It is generally given only once a day, in the morning. The initial dose is usually 37.5 mg and is titrated upward in 18.75-mg increments every 3 to 5 days until a therapeutic effect is reported up to a maximum of 112.5 mg or 2.2 mg/kg for adolescents (Dulcan, 1990). On occasion, a second dose, often half that of the morning dose, may be given in midafternoon if the morning dose is proving ineffective during the afternoon. This, however, may increase the chances of insomnia occurring. Several investigations have indicated that pemoline is slower in achieving its peak effects and in "washing out" of the body than the other stimulants. Thus, its effects may last 2 to 3 days following its discontinuation.

Both methylphenidate and dextroamphetamine are available in short-acting and sustained release forms. The sustained release forms have several benefits such as making noontime medication administration at school unnecessary and affording greater confidentiality of treatment. At the peak of their time course, the sustained release forms of these medications appeared to be as effective as their standard preparations. However, there is both research and clinical evidence that sustained release methylphenidate may be less effective than the standard preparation during the first several hours postingestion (Pelham et al., 1987). In our experience, some patients may demonstrate a diminished efficacy, particularly during the morning hours, when switching from standard methylphenidate to the sustained release compound. For these reasons, the use of the shorter-acting forms of these medications may be more suitable except in situations in which in-school administration of the drugs is significantly problematic (e.g., no school nurse to dispense the medication or for teenagers who may be more sensitive to teasing or censure by peers).

Generic forms of the stimulants are now available and provide a less expensive alternative to their brand-name counterparts. Although no empirical investigations of differences in their efficacy have been reported, generic forms of these compounds may possibly vary in quality leading to complaints from parents or teachers of greater variability in the behavioral control achieved with the generic as compared to the trade name medication.

Methylphenidate and dextroamphetamine can be dispensed according to various schedules depending on the severity of the child's ADHD and associated difficulties. In a minority of cases, the medication may be used primarily for classroom management. If so, it is usually suggested that it be discontinued on weekends, holidays, and summer vacations. When reinitiation of the medication each Monday produces a renewal of side effects exhibited only at the start of each week, keeping the child on one-half or less of the regular dose during the weekend may promote habituation to side effects. Most children with ADHD, however, exhibit significant behavioral control difficulties at home and in the community as well as during school. Indeed, this might be considered almost a requirement of diagnosis if criteria according to the fourth edition of the *Diagnostic and Statistical Manual of Mental Disorders* (DSM-IV; American Psychiatric Association, 1994) for ADHD are to be strictly adhered to in clinical practice (i.e., the requirement of impairing symptoms in at least two settings). In these cases, it is recommended that the child receive medication 7 days a week with an attempt to discontinue pharmacotherapy during school vacations when possible or feasible. As noted previously, it may be necessary to recommend a three-times-a-day dose schedule with methylphenidate, primarily because effects may last 3–4 hours or less with some children. This problem is often discovered in contacts with the child's teachers, who may observe that the morning dose has essentially worn off by midmorning. In such cases, the following schedule may be employed: a breakfast dose at 7:00–8:00 A.M., a second dose at 10:30–11:00 A.M., and a final dose at 2:00–3:00 P.M.

In general, the dose should always be the lowest possible and should be given only as many times a day as necessary to achieve adequate management of the child's behavior. In many cases, pharmacotherapy need not be discontinued on holidays or summer vacations because of the benefits that accrue to increased self-control, social conduct, and task persistence from stimulants in settings other than school. Should a significant change in the child's growth trajectory be evident from such medication use, returning to the traditional drug holidays on weekends and school vacations may be necessary for some children to increase the probability of a growth rebound effect.

Titration of stimulant dosage should be based on an evaluation that includes multiple, objective assessment measures (as described later) and should start with the lowest possible increments. Sufficient time (e.g., 5 to 7 days) should be allowed to evaluate the efficacy of each dosage.

Parents should never be given permission to adjust the dosage of medication without consultation with the physician. Otherwise, parents may overmedicate the child, as the parents may increase the dose every time the child is temperamental, noncompliant, or obstinant. Instances of the latter behavior are usually better treated by the altering of parent management styles than by administration of medication on an as-needed basis.

Monitoring Response to Stimulant Medication

The methods used by practicing clinicians to monitor medication response vary widely in content and quality. Unfortunately, all too frequently, titration of dosage and long-term assessment of efficacy are based solely on the subjective reports of parents, thereby increasing the chances of erroneous decisions. Indeed, the most appropriate clinical dosage of a stimulant medication cannot be established adequately without school-based information, which can be obtained through standardized rating scales along with other measures (either directly or via the parent). In this section of the chapter, we describe methods to determine the initial dosage of medication as well as assessment procedures to determine whether medication treatment should be continued, altered in dosage, or discontinued altogether.

Assessing Initial Response to Stimulants

Objective data regarding changes in a child with ADHD behavior should always be collected across several doses given the frequently unique and idiosyncratic reactions of children to these medications. Under ideal circumstances, a patient's optimal dose should be established in the context of a double-blind, placebo- controlled assessment paradigm which includes multiple measures collected across several settings (i.e., home, school, and clinic). This type of evaluation allows for the aggregation of quantitative data regarding a child's treatment response as well as the use of a placebo control wherein teachers, parents, and children do not know the dosage being administered (Barkley et al., 1988; Chan et al., 1983).

Table 17.2 lists the measures that are most helpful in conducting an initial trial of medication, and includes behavior rating scales completed by parents and teachers, self-report questionnaires (for older children and adolescents), measures of academic performances, and, in some cases, clinic-based tests. Rather than administering a large number of teacher questionnaires, we recommend using two rating scales such that one measure assesses possible reductions in ADHD symptoms (e.g., ADHD Rating Scale-IV, Disruptive Behavior Disorders Rating Scale), and the other measure taps changes in the situational pervasiveness of ADHD symptoms (i.e., School Situations Questionnaire). In addition, it is often helpful for the parents and teachers to complete a weekly Side Effects Rating Scale (see Figure 17.4). Older children and adolescents should be asked about their perceptions of both symptom-

---

TABLE 17.2. **Possible Measures to Include in an Initial Stimulant Medication Trial**

Teacher rating scales
  Academic Performance Rating Scale
  ADDH Comprehensive Teacher Rating Scale
  ADHD Rating Scale-IV: School Version
  CAP Rating Scale
  Conners Teacher Rating Scale
  Disruptive Behavior Disorders Rating Scale
  School Situations Questionnaire
  Side Effects Rating Scale

Parent rating scales
  ADHD Rating Scale-IV: Home Version
  Conners Parent Rating Scale
  Home Situations Questionnaire
  Side Effects Rating Scale

Self-report rating scales
  ADHD Self-Report Scale
  Side Effects Rating Scale

Behavioral observations
  ADHD Behavior Coding System (restricted academic situation)

Academic performance
  Percentage of work completed correctly
  Curriculum-based measurement probes

Clinic-based tests
  Conners Continuous Performance Test

---

atic change and side effects as these ratings have been found to be drug sensitive (DuPaul et al., 1996).

Whenever possible, behavior ratings from parents, teachers, and patients should be supplemented with other measures that are sensitive to medication-induced changes in performance. Observations of attention and activity level (e.g, ADHD Behavior Coding System) can be conducted either in classroom or in clinic analog settings across dose levels. In particular, changes in on-task behavior while the child is completing academic work independently can be quite helpful in documenting stimulant response. For school-based practitioners, it may be possible to obtain direct measures of academic performance such as task accuracy rates and/or curriculum-based measurement data (see Stoner et al., 1994). When it is not possible to obtain direct measures of academic performance, teachers could be asked to complete the Academic Performance Rating Scale. Finally, clinic-based tests such as the Conners Continuous Performance Test allow the practitioner to document changes in attention span and impulse control as a function of dosage.

Clinicians should be aware of possible "practice effects" on behavior rating scales between their first and second, and possibly later, administrations. Many parent and teacher rating scales show significant declines in scores between their first and second administrations even when there has been no intervening treatment. Clinicians who give the scales once, begin pharmacotherapy, and then give them again a week or two later are likely to misinterpret practice effects, concluding that the medication or that dose of it was helpful when it may not have been. Clinicians using these scales should give them twice before using them in drug trials and use the second administration as the baseline against which to measure changes due to medication trials.

Determining the optimal dose of medication involves an analysis of the obtained data and clinical judgment. As Gadow (1986) has pointed out, the results of the evaluation should be used to determine the minimal effect dose which is defined as the lowest dose producing clinically significant behavior change with the least side effects. Recent attempts have been made to objectify the process of deciding which is the optimal dose for individual patients. For example, DuPaul and Barkley (1993) describe a method using a reliable change index (RCI; Jacobsen & Truax, 1991) to determine the degree to which medication-induced behavioral changes (relative to a placebo or nonmedication condition) are significant beyond chance levels. For each measure of medication response, the RCI statistic is calculated by taking the change score (i.e., mean score at a particular dosage of medication – mean placebo score) and dividing the remainder by the standard error of difference between the two scores. The latter is calculated directly from the standard error of measurement (S_E) as follows: $S_{diff} = \sqrt{2 \times (S_E)2}$. The S_{diff} is indicative of the spread of the distribution of change scores that is expected if no actual change had occurred. When the absolute value of an obtained RCI is greater than 1.96, it is considered to reflect stastically significant change in this measure (Jacobsen & Truax, 1991). In this fashion, a particular dose of medication is identified as leading to significant change on a measure when the RCI for the latter is greater than 1.96. Of course, RCIs can only be calculated for measures that have known test-retest reliability coefficients.

Table 17.3 presents an example of a medication evaluation for which RCI statistics were used to determine optimal dosage. The data are for an 8-year-old boy with ADHD who was evaluated using a clinic-based, double-blind, placebo-controlled protocol of three doses of methylphenidate (5, 10, and 15 mg). The numbers displayed in the table are the raw scores for weekly behavior ratings and for behavioral observations conducted in the clinic. Those scores that are associated with RCIs greater than 1.96 are highlighted by an asterisk. For example, the RCIs for the mean percentage of on-task behavior were calculated on the basis of an S_E of 8.42 and an S_{diff} of 11.91. Specifically, the RCI for mean on-task percentage at

TABLE 17.3. Sample Summary of Results for a Trial of Methylphenidate

Measure	Dose			
	Placebo	5 mg	10 mg	15 mg
Parent ratings				
HSQ-R				
No. of problems	11.0	12.0	12.0	4.0
Mean severity	7.0	8.0	6.3	3.5*
ADHD Rating Scale				
Total	32.0	38.0	30.0	14.0*
Inattention	22.0	26.0	21.0	9.0*
Impulsivity	19.0	21.0	16.0	8.0*
Side Effects Rating Scale				
Number	0.0	2.0	0.0	0.0
Mean severity	0.0	5.5	0.0	0.0
Teacher ratings				
SSQ-R				
No. of problems	8.0	0.0*	1.0*	0.0*
Mean severity	5.0	0.0*	1.0*	0.0*
ADHD Rating Scale				
Total	34.0	12.0*	13.0*	0.0*
Inattention	18.0	3.0*	7.0*	0.0*
Impulsivity	19.0	9.0*	8.0*	0.0*
Behavioral observation				
Restricted academic situation				
Mean percent on-task	57.5	76.0*	85.0*	89.5*
Mean percent ADHD	43.5	22.0*	15.0*	12.5*
Academic performance				
Mean percent complete	70.0	100.0	100.0	100.0
Mean percent correct	50.0	73.5	81.5	88.0

Note. HSQ-R, Home Situations Questionnaire—Revised; SSQ-R, School Situations Questionnaire—Revised. From DuPaul & Barkley (1993). Copyright 1993 by the Association for Advancement of Behavior Therapy. Reprinted by permission.
*Reliable change index > 1.96. Reliable change indices were not calculated for side effects ratings and academic performance measures as the test–retest reliabilities of these measures are unknown.

10 mg of methylphenidate was obtained as follows: RCI = (85.0 − 57.5)/11.91 = 2.31. Note that RCIs were not calculated for side effects ratings or for academic performance measures as the test–retest reliabilities of these measures are unknown. Overall, the 15–mg dose was found to lead to the most reliable change across settings and measures. Further, this dose was not reported by the boy's mother to lead to increases in the number or severity of side effects relative to the placebo condition. Thus, 15 mg was determined to be his optimal dose.

Assessing Long-Term Progress on Medication

Once a child's optimal dosage is established, then some, preferably all, of the measures listed in Table 17.2 should be collected periodically throughout the school year to evaluate the need for dosage adjustments or the onset of side effects. The vast majority of the questionnaires need only be readministered every several months or so; however, it is usually a good idea to review items from the Side Effects Questionnaire each month when the parents call to obtain another prescription. In addition, at each monthly contact (usually by telephone), a checklist of questions (see Figure 17.5) is reviewed with parents to assess continued drug efficacy.

Parents may call to complain about ineffective doses that were formerly effective. Physicians should employ caution before deciding to increase the level of medication. If no precipitating stressful events or family turmoil are present, it may indeed be true that the current dosage has become less effective. Careful questioning of the parent as to the ways in which the child's behavior is different or worse can be useful in making the decision. In addition, the child's teacher should be contacted to ascertain whether similar deterioration in functioning has occurred in the school setting. The parent and teacher questionnaires discussed previously should be administered and compared to previously collected data in an effort to specify which behaviors have actually worsened and to quantify the amount of behavioral change. After this is done, if there are no side effects, a cautious increment in dosage may be tried.

The presence and severity of side effects should be ascertained at every monthly contact, and the parents should be informed in advance about possible side effects, including depressed mood, weight loss, induction of tics or, with pemoline, symptoms of hepatic damage. When children are receiving pemoline, every 6 months, or whenever suspicions are prompted by symptoms, blood should be drawn for liver function tests, given the findings that this drug may rarely and idiosyncratically adversely affect liver functions. The latter is no substitute for a review of possible presenting symptoms of such dysfunction at each monthly visit.

Approximately every 3 to 4 months while a child is on medication, it is advisable for physicians to administer a more thorough follow-up clinic examination. During this time, height, weight, blood pressure, and heart rate can be recorded to determine potential side effects. Also, any necessary blood tests can be conducted at this time. Parent and teacher ratings should be collected concurrent with this visit as well. Difficulties (e.g., significant side

---

1. What dose have you been regularly giving to this child over the past month?
2. Have you noticed any of the following side effects this month?

Loss of appetite	Rashes
Insomnia	Dizziness
Irritability in late morning or late afternoon	Dark circles under eyes
Unusual crying	Fearfulness
Tics or nervous habits	Social withdrawal
Headache/stomachache	Drowsiness
Sadness	Anxiety

3. If so, please describe how often and when the side effects occurred.
4. Have you spoken with the child's teacher lately? How is the child performing in class? What have been his or her test grades? Have there been any problems with completion of homework?
5. Did your child complain about taking the medication or avoid its use?
6. Does the medication seem to be helping the child as much this month as it did last month? If not, what seems to have changed?
7. When was your child last examined by the doctor? (If more than 6 months, schedule the child for a clinic visit and exam.)
8. Have there been any problems in giving the medication at school?

FIGURE 17.5. A checklist of questions to be reviewed monthly with parents of children taking stimulant medication. Adapted from Barkley (1981). Copyright 1981 by The Guilford Press. Adapted by permission.

effects or behaviors that are not responsive to medication) that continue to plague the child or family can be discussed, and referrals to appropriate professionals can be made as necessary. When parents are called for the appointment, they should be encouraged to write down any concerns or questions they might have in advance, so that the visit can be as useful as possible.

Terminating Stimulant Treatment

There are no firm guidelines regarding when to discontinue pharmacotherapy other than a determination that it no longer seems to be necessary. Up to 20% of children may be able to have medication stopped after a year or so. Stimulant medications do not need to be discontinued at onset of puberty, as their efficacy with adolescents and adults has been established (Coons et al., 1987; Spencer et al., 1995). Further, chronic administration of these compounds does not appear to increase the probability of substance abuse and may, in fact, decrease it (Weiss & Hechtman, 1993).

Treatment can be discontinued annually for a short time (e.g., a few days to 2 weeks) usually midway into the school year. At that time, standardized measures, such as the aforementioned behavior rating scales, can be collected during both medication and nonmedication periods. We recommend that children who have been successful with pharmacotherapy during the previous school year begin a new academic year on that medication. This cirumvents a situation wherein the child begins to fail at the beginning of a new school year before medication is resumed. The reassessment of drug responding should not take place right at the beginning of the school year to ensure that the child has acclimated to the new classroom and to prevent erroneous decisions being made on the basis of a "honeymoon" effect with a new teacher which may occur during the initial stages of the academic year. If there is no significant difference in the child's behavior when he or she is on or off medication, treatment may be discontinued for a longer period. If there is no appreciable difference with treatment and the child continues to display behavioral control difficulties, it may be time to reevaluate the dosage or switch to a different medication.

STIMULANTS IN COMBINATION WITH OTHER MEDICATIONS

In rare cases, it may be necessary to combine the stimulants with other medications to achieve greater therapeutic management of individuals with ADHD. Polypharmacy may be more likely when comorbid disorders are present that may not respond satisfactorily to stimulants. For example, comorbid disorders might include Major Depressive Disorder, Generalized Anxiety Disorder, juvenile-onset Bipolar Disorder, Tourette's Disorder, or enuresis. In recent years, two types of drug combinations have increased in frequency in the clinical management of children with ADHD: combined stimulant/antidepressant therapy and combined stimulant/clonidine therapy. Although these other medications are discussed in detail in other chapters in this text, some special considerations involved in these medication combinations are briefly discussed next.

Combined Stimulant/Antidepressant Therapy

Combinations of stimulant medications with tricyclic antidepressants can be considered when ADHD presents with comorbid, socially serious enuresis that remains refractory to behavioral treatment, or with comorbid affective (mood and anxiety) disorders. In a series of studies, the separate and combined effects of methylphenidate and desipramine on ADHD and comorbid affective disorders have been investigated (Pataki, Carlson, Kelly, Rapport, & Biancaniello, 1993; Rapport, Carlson, Kelly, & Pataki, 1993). Although methylphenidate and desipramine in isolation produced reductions in ADHD symptoms, the combination of these compounds led to positive effects on learning over and above the efficacy of each single agent. Although the combination of medications was associated with a greater number of side effects than either compound alone, there was no evidence that combined use was associated with any unique or serious side effects. Stimulants also have been successfully combined with fluoxetine (a selective serotonin reuptake inhibiting antidepressant) in the management of ADHD and depression (Gammon & Brown, 1993). As was the case for the combination of methylphenidate and desipramine, the combination of methylphenidate and fluoxetine has not been found to produce unique or serious side effects apart from those side effects associated with either medication used individually. Data are sparse on the behavioral and side effects of this medication combination; thus, continued vigilance in such cases appears prudent.

Combined Stimulant–Clonidine Therapy

Clonidine is a presynaptic alpha-adrenergic receptor agonist that downregulates norepinephrine outflow from the CNS. This medication has been combined with stimulants when children with ADHD exhibit comorbid conduct disorder, extreme hyperactivity–impulsivity, and/or aggression. Clonidine does not significantly improve attention span or academic productivity, but it may be helpful in decreasing overarousal that contributes to behavioral problems in these children (Gunning, 1992). Because of its acute sedative properties, clonidine may also be used with stimulants for delayed sleep onset or other sleep disturbances that may be associated with ADHD or with stimulant treatment (Spencer, Biederman, Wilens, et al., 1996). Clonidine decreases blood pressure and pulse; thus, patients with preexisting syncope, bradycardic arrhythmias, or cardiac conditions are not candidates for clonidine therapy. Recently, three cases of sudden death were reported in children taking the combination of methylphenidate and clonidine (Popper, 1995). Although the association of medication treatment and these deaths may have been coincidental, prudence suggests that practitioners be cautious in prescribing the combination of methylphenidate and clonidine and in monitoring any physical effects (Swanson et al., 1996). In addition, abrupt clonidine withdrawal (e.g., from noncompliance with dosage administration) can result in adrenergic rebound and associated treatment emergent symptoms of hypertension, diaphoresis, tachycardia, diarrhea, and anxiety. A baseline child and family cardiac history, recent physical examination, baseline and on-drug electrocardiogram, pulse, and blood pressure monitoring are recommended when clonidine is combined with stimulants.

CONTRAINDICATIONS FOR STIMULANT PRESCRIPTION AND DRUG INTERACTIONS

As stated earlier, individuals with a history of tics, Tourette's Disorder, or psychosis should be given stimulant medications with great caution, for the latter may exacerbate the symptoms of such disorders. Children with high levels of anxiety (e.g., Generalized Anxiety Disorder) have a higher potential to respond poorly to these medications than do their nonanxious counterparts with ADHD. Furthermore, children under 4 years of age tend to be less responsive to stimulant compounds and there are few research studies investigating behavior and side effects in this age group. There is some controversy over whether stimulants should be given to children with seizures or epilepsy; doubts about the practice are based on the possibility that these drugs may lower seizure thresholds. Alternatively, empirical studies indicate that this does not often occur (Crumrine et al., 1987; Spencer et al., 1995). Stimulant-induced seizure activity is rarely, if ever, seen clinically and it can be avoided by a slight increase in the level of anticonvulsants. High blood pressure and cardiac or cardiovascular problems in children may also be contraindications for the stimulants given their mild but significant cardiac pressor effects, but a pediatric cardiologist should be consulted in such cases.

Stimulant medications can alter the actions of other compounds. Though such interactions are unusual, some are potentially serious. The sedating effects of antihistamines and benzodiazepines may be inhibited by stimulants, and the latter can potentiate the effect of all sympathomimetic drugs, including street drugs such as cocaine. The effect of combining heterocyclic antidepressants with stimulants may be beneficial, and in small doses this combination may give better and more consistent control of ADHD symptoms. However, cardiac arrythmias and hypertensive crises have been reported with this drug combination, as have unusual cognitive and mood disturbances (Gadow, Nolan, Paolicelli, & Sprafkin, 1991). Stimulant and antidepressant drugs also may accentuate the effects of one another. The combination of monoamine oxidase inhibitors (MAOIs), sometimes used as antidepressants, with stimulants is dangerous and has the potential to lead to a fatal hypertensive crisis. If an MAOI has been used, a minimum 2-week washout interval should be allowed before initiating treatment with stimulants. Lithium inhibits the stimulatory effects of amphetamines and probably those of other stimulants. It has been suggested that amphetamines may act synergistically with phenytoin and phenobarbital to increase anticonvulsant activity. Other interactions have been documented with medications unlikely to be used in clinical practice.

MANAGEMENT OF STIMULANT OVERDOSE

An overdose of stimulant medication is rarely, if ever, fatal on its own. In fact, we are aware of no cases of fatalities from oral administration of the stimulant compounds. Signs and symptoms of acute overdose result from overstimulation of the CNS and from excessive sympathomimetic effects. Indicators of overdose may include symptoms such as vomiting, agitation, tremor, convulsions, confusion, hallucinations, hyperpyrexia, tachycardia, arrhythmias, hypertension, and delirium. Treatment consists of prompt medical referral and appropriate supportive measures. The patient must be protected from self-injury and from environmental overstimulation that would aggravate heightened sympathomimetic arousal. Chlorpromazine has been reported in the literature to be useful in decreasing CNS stimulation and sympathomimetic effects. Sedation with a barbiturate may also be helpful. If the patient is alert and conscious, gastric contents may be evacuated by induction of emesis or gastric lavage. For amphetamine intoxication, acidification of the urine will increase excretion. For more severe overdose, intensive care must be provided to maintain adequate cardiopulmonary function and treat hyperpyrexia. The efficacy of peritoneal dialysis or extracorporeal hemodialysis for stimulant overdosage has not been established.

SUMMARY OF CLINICAL EFFECTS
OF STIMULANT MEDICATION

This chapter provided an overview of the clinical effects and side effects of stimulant medications. Several important conclusions regarding the use of these medications for the treatment of ADHD are supported by the empirical literature.

1. Up to 70–80% of children with carefully diagnosed ADHD appear to exhibit a positive response to CNS stimulants. Although the percentage of positive responders is lower, CNS stimulants also are the medication of choice for adolescents and adults with ADHD. Primary effects are the improvement of attention span and the reduction of disruptive, inappropriate, and impulsive behavior. Compliance with authority-figure commands is increased and children's peer relations may also improve, primarily through reductions in aggression. If the medication is titrated according to changes in academic performance, improvements may also be seen in productivity and accuracy, at least in the short term. Dosages and regimens should be individualized and adjusted slowly to suit each individual and never given solely according to some formula (e.g., based on body weight). Many of the problems attributed to stimulants may be the result of excessive dose levels and schedules for a particular child, as well as to unrealistic clinical objectives in inadequately assessed and monitored children.

2. Although stimulant medications are certainly helpful in the day-to-day management of ADHD, they have not been demonstrated to lead to enduring positive changes after their cessation. Thus, this treatment is not a quick solution to ADHD but rather an intervention that must often be employed on a continuing basis to maintain positive effects.

3. The short- and long-term side effects of stimulant medications are generally mild, often transient, and diminish with reduction or discontinuance of pharmacotherapy. Children with ADHD who also have a personal or family history of tics or Tourette's Disorder may be prescribed stimulants but closer monitoring of such children and the use of lower doses during initial titration may be in order. Tics may be induced or exacerbated by the stimulants in some children, although recent studies indicate that such reactions are less likely than early reports had indicated. Whether such tics may prove irreversible seems unlikely but is not yet known.

4. Despite the lack of established long-term success of these medications, they are useful in managing the behavior of indivdiuals with ADHD. Although the issue of controlling the behavior of children with psychotropic drugs is highly controversial, the difficulties these youngsters present to others who must live, work, or attend school with them must not be overlooked. Not only do such children frustrate parents and teachers, but the effect of their disruptive behavior on the ability of their classmates to receive adequate instruction is, at times, considerable. If stimulants can temporarily ameliorate these difficulties, while reducing the level of ostracism, censure, and punishment that children with ADHD receive, they seem certainly worthwhile.

5. Stimulant medications are not a panacea for ADHD symptoms and should not be the sole treatment employed. Other therapies focusing on the myriad social, psychological, educational, and physical problems these children often display are necessary. *Medications do not teach the child anything;* they merely alter the likelihood of occurrence of behaviors already in the child's repertoire. The numerous skill deficits that these children may present with will still require attention. Thus, the medication may enhance the efficacy of other interventions by aiding the child to attend and respond to the environment in a more successful fashion. Further, parents require child management training and other forms of counseling to cope with the children during periods when the medication cannot be used. Each professional must, therefore, be knowledgeable about the resources within the community that will be necessary to treat the "total child."

CONCLUSION

The stimulant medications are effective and safe treatments for the symptomatic management of individuals with ADHD. Indeed, CNS stimulants are the best-studied treatment applied to this disorder and are among the safest and most effective symptomatic treatments in medicine. Most children who receive stimulants show improvement in their attention, impulse control, task-irrelevent activity, academic productivity and accuracy, handwriting, play, social conduct, and/or compliance to commands and rules. These effects result in a diminution of the supervision, reprimands, punishment, and censure from those adults and peers who must frequently interact with them. Changes in the long-term outcome of children on stimulants have not been reliably obtained to date. Even though the stimulants are quite useful in the day-to-day management of symptoms of ADHD, other treatments are usually required to maximize the chances for better short- and long-term adjustment. This is because the stimulants do not teach appropriate or prosocial behavior but increase the probabilities of a child displaying "good" behavior that is already in the child's repertoire. Such displays of behavior require the right environment to be present to reinforce and maintain their occurrence. Although the absence of such positive environments or adjunctive treatments cannot be a sole reason to give medication to children, neither is it a reason to withhold it.

REFERENCES

Abikoff, H., & Gittelman, R. (1984). Does behavior therapy normalize the classroom behavior of hyperactive children? *Archives of General Psychiatry, 41,* 449–454.

Ahmann, P. A., Waltonen, S. J., Olson, K. A., et al. (1993). Placebo-controlled evaluation of Ritalin side effects. *Pediatrics, 91,* 1101–1106.

Aman, M. G. (1982). Stimulant drug effects in developmental disorders and hyperactivity: Toward a resolution of disparate findings. *Journal of Autism and Developmental Disorders, 12,* 385–398.

Aman, M. G. (1996). Stimulant drugs in developmental disabilities revisited. *Journal of Developmental and Physical Disabilities, 8,* 347–365.

Aman, M. G., Kern R. A., Osborne P., et al. (1997). Fenfluramine and methylphenidate in children with mental retardation and borderline IQ: Clinical effects. *American Journal of Mental Retardation, 101,* 521–534.

Aman, M. G., Marks, R. E., Turbott, S. H., Wilsher, C. P., & Merry, S. N. (1991). Clinical effects of methylphenidate and thioridazine in intellectually subaverage children. *Journal of the American Academy of Child and Adolescent Psychiatry, 30,* 246–256.

Aman, M. G., & Turbott, S. H. (1991). Prediction of clinical response in children taking methylphenidate. *Journal of Autism and Developmental Disorders, 21,* 211–227.

Aman, M. G., & Werry, J. S. (1975). The effects of methylphenidate and haloperidol on the heart rate and blood pressure of hyperactive children with special reference to time of action. *Psychopharmacology, 43,* 163–168.

American Psychiatric Association. (1994). *Diagnostic and statistical manual of mental disorders* (4th ed., rev.). Washington, DC: Author.

Barkley, R. A. (1976). Predicting the response of hyperactive children to stimulant drugs: A review. *Journal of Abnormal Child Psychology, 4,* 327–348.

Barkley, R. A. (1977). A review of stimulant drug research with hyperactive children. *Journal of Child Psychology and Psychiatry, 18,* 137–165.

Barkley, R. A. (1981). *Hyperactive children: A handbook for diagnosis and treatment.* New York: Guilford Press.

Barkley, R. A. (1988a). Tic disorders and Gilles de la Tourette syndrome. In E. J. Mash & L. A. Terdal (Eds.), *Behavioral assessment of childhood disorders* (2nd ed., pp. 69–104). New York: Guilford Press.

Barkley, R. A. (1988b). The effects of methylphenidate on the interactions of preschool ADHD children with their mothers. *Journal of the American Academy of Child and Adolescent Psychiatry, 27,* 336–341.

Barkley, R. A. (1990). Hyperactive girls and boys: Stimulant drug effects on mother–child interactions. *Child Psychology and Psychiatry, 30,* 379–390.

Barkley, R. A., & Cunningham, C. E. (1978). Do stimulant drugs improve the academic performance of hyperkinetic children? A review of outcome research. *Clinical Pediatrics, 17*, 85–92.

Barkley, R. A., & Cunningham, C. E. (1979). The effects of methylphenidate on the mother–child interactions of hyperactive children. *Archives of General Psychiatry, 36*, 201–208.

Barkley, R. A., DuPaul, G. J., & Connor, D. F. (in press). Stimulants. In J. S. Werry & M. G. Aman (Eds.), *Practitioner's guide to psychoactive drugs for children and adolescents* (2nd ed.). New York: Plenum.

Barkley, R. A., DuPaul, G. J., & McMurray, M. B. (1991). Attention deficit disorder with and without Hyperactivity: Clinical response to three dose levels of methylphenidate. *Pediatrics, 87*, 519–531.

Barkley, R. A., Fischer, M., Newby, R., & Breen, M. (1988). Development of a multi-method clinical protocol for assessing stimulant drug responses in ADHD children. *Journal of Clinical Child Psychology, 17*, 14–24.

Barkley, R. A., & Jackson, T. Jr. (1977). Hyperkinesis, autonomic nervous system activity, and stimulant drug effects. *Journal of Child Psychology and Psychiatry, 18*, 347–357.

Barkley, R. A., Karlsson, J., Pollard, S., & Murphy, J. (1985). Developmental changes in the mother–child interactions of hyperactive boys: effects of two doses of Ritalin. *Journal of Child Psychology and Psychiatry, 26*, 705–715.

Barkley, R. A., McMurray, M. B., Edelbrock, C. S., & Robbins, K. (1990). The side effects of Ritalin: A systematic placebo controlled evaluation of two doses. *Pediatrics, 86*, 184–192.

Becker-Mattes, A., Mattes, J. A., Abikoff, H., & Brandt, L. (1985). State-dependent learning in hyperactive children receiving methylphenidate. *American Journal of Psychiatry, 142*, 455–459.

Bergman, A., Winters, L., & Cornblatt, B. (1991). Methylphenidate: Effects on sustained attention. In L. L. Greenhill & B. B. Osmon (Eds.), *Ritalin: Theory and patient management* (pp. 223–232). New York: Mary Ann Liebert.

Birmaher, B., Greenhill, L. L., Cooper, T. B., Fried, J., & Maminski, B. (1989). Sustained release methylphenidate: Pharmacokinetic studies in ADDH males. *Journal of the American Academy of Child and Adolescent Psychiatry, 28*, 768–772.

Brown, G. L., Hunt, R. D., Ebert, M. H., et al. (1979). Plasma levels of D-amphetamine in hyperactive children. *Psychopharmacology, 62*, 133–140.

Brown, R. T., & Sexson, S. B. (1989). Effects of methylphenidate on cardiovascular responses in attention deficit hyperactivity disordered adolescents. *Journal of Adolescent Health Care, 10*, 179–183.

Caine, E. D., Ludlow, C. L., Polinsky, R. J., & Ebert, M. H. (1984). Provocative drug testing in Tourette's syndrome: D- and L-amphetamine and haloperidol. *Journal of the American Academy of Child Psychiatry, 23*, 147–152.

Cantwell, D., & Carlson, G. (1978). Stimulants. In J. Werry (Ed.), *Pediatric psychopharmacology* (pp. 171–207). New York: Brunner/Mazel.

Carlson, C. L., Pelham, W. E., Milich, R., & Hoza, B. (1993). ADHD boys' performance and attributions following success and failure: Drug effects and individual differences. *Cognitive Therapy Research, 17*, 269–287.

Castellanos, F. X., Giedd, J. N., Elia, J., Marsh, W. L., Ritchie, G. F., Hamburger, S. D., & Rapoport, J. L. (1997). Controlled stimulant treatment of ADHD and comorbid Tourette's syndrome: Effects of stimulant and dose. *Journal of the American Academy of Child and Adolescent Psychiatry, 36*, 589–596.

Chan, Y. M., Swanson, J. M., Soldin, S. S., et al. (1983). Methylphenidate hydrochloride given with or before breakfast: II. Effects on plasma concentrations of methylphenidate and ritalinic acid. *Pediatrics, 72*, 56–59.

Cohen, D., Bruun, R. D., & Leckman, J. F. (1987). *Tourette syndrome and tic disorders.* New York: Wiley.

Conners, C. K., & Taylor, E. (1980). Pemoline, methylphenidate, and placebo in children with minimal brain dysfunction. *Archives of General Psychiatry, 37*, 922–932.

Coons, H. W., Klorman, R., & Borgstedt, A. D. (1987). Effects of methylphenidate on adolescents with a childhood history of attention deficit disorder: II. Information processing. *Journal of the American Academy of Child and Adolescent Psychiatry, 26*, 368–374.

Crumrine, P. K., Feldman, H. M., Teodori, J., et al. (1987, October). *The use of methylphenidate in children with seizures and attention deficit disorder.* Paper presented at the meeting of the Child Neurology Society.

Cunningham, C. E., Siegel, L. S., & Offord, D. R. (1985). A developmental dose response analysis of the effects of methylphenidate on the peer interactions of attention deficit disordered boys. *Journal of Child Psychology and Psychiatry, 26,* 955–971.

Diener, R. M. (1991). Toxicology of Ritalin. In L. L. Greenhill & B. B. Osmon (Eds.), *Ritalin: Theory and patient management* (pp. 34–43). New York: Mary Ann Liebert.

Donnelly, M., & Rapoport, J. L. (1985). Attention deficit disorders. In J. M. Wiener (Ed.), *Diagnosis and psychopharmacology of childhood and adolescent disorders* (pp. 178–198). New York: Wiley.

Douglas, V. I., Barr, R. D., Desilets, J., & Sherman, E. (1995). Do high doses of stimulants impair flexible thinking in attention-deficit hyperactivity disorder? *Journal of the American Academy of Child and Adolescent Psychiatry, 34,* 877–885.

Douglas, V. I., Barr, R. G., O'Neill, M. E., & Britton, B. G. (1988). Dosage effects and individual responsivity to methylphenidate in attention deficit disorder. *Journal of Child Psychology and Psychiatry, 29,* 453–475.

Dulcan, M. K. (1990). Using psychostimulants to treat behavioral disorders of children and adolescents. *Journal of Child and Adolescent Psychopharmacology, 1,* 7–20.

DuPaul, G. J., Anastopoulos, A. D., Kwasnik, D., Barkley, R. A., & McMurray, M. B. (1996). Methylphenidate effects on children with attention deficit hyperactivity disorder: Self-report of symptoms, side-effects, and self-esteem. *Journal of Attention Disorders, 1,* 3–15.

DuPaul, G. J., & Barkley, R. A. (1990). Medication therapy. In R. A. Barkley, *Attention-deficit hyperactivity disorder: A handbook for diagnosis and treatment* (pp. 573–612). New York: Guilford Press.

DuPaul, G. J., & Barkley, R. A. (1993). Behavioral contributions to pharmacotherapy: The utility of behavioral methodology in medication treatment of children with attention deficit hyperactivity disorder. *Behavior Therapy, 24,* 47–65.

DuPaul, G. J., Barkley, R. A., & McMurray, M. B. (1994). Response of children with ADHD to methylphenidate: Interaction with internalizing symptoms. *Journal of the American Academy of Child and Adolescent Psychiatry, 33,* 894–903.

DuPaul, G. J., & Rapport, M. D. (1993). Does methylphenidate normalize the classroom performance of children with attention deficit disorder? *Journal of the Amercian Academy of Child and Adolescent Psychiatry, 32,* 190–198.

Dyme, I. Z., Sahakian, B. J., Golinko, B., & Rabe, E. F. (1982). Perseveration induced by methylphenidate in children: Preliminary findings. *Progress in Neuropsychopharmacology and Biological Psychiatry, 6,* 269–273.

Elia, J., Borcherding, B. G., Rapoport, J. L., & Keysor, C. S. (1991). Methylphenidate and dextroamphetamine treatments of hyperactivity: Are there true nonresponders? *Psychiatry Research, 36,* 141–155.

Elia, J., & Rapoport, J. L. (1991). Ritalin versus dextroamphetamine in ADHD: Both should be tried. In L. L. Greenhill & B. B. Osmon (Eds.), *Ritalin: Theory and patient management* (pp. 69–74). New York: Mary Ann Liebert.

Erenberg, G., Cruse, R. P., & Rothner, A. D. (1984). The effect of stimulant drugs on Tourette syndrome. *Neurology, 34,* 84.

Fiedler, N., & Ullman, D. G. (1983). The effects of stimulant drugs on curiosity behaviors of hyperactive boys. *Journal of Abnormal Child Psychology, 11,* 193–206.

Fine, S., & Johnston, C. (1993). Drug and placebo side effects in methylphenidate–placebo trial for attention deficit hyperactivity disorder. *Child Psychiatry and Human Development, 24,* 25–30.

Fitzpatrick, P. A., Klorman, R., Brumaghim, J. T., & Borgstedt, A. D. (1992). Effects of sustained-release and standard preparations of methylphenidate on attention deficit disorder. *Journal of the American Academy of Child and Adolescent Psychiatry, 31,* 226–234.

Gadow, K. (1986). *Children on medication: Vol.1. Hyperactivity, learning disabilities, and mental retardation.* Boston: Little, Brown.

Gadow, K. D., Nolan, E. E., Paolicelli, L. M., & Sprafkin, J. (1991). A procedure for assessing the effects of methylphenidate on hyperactive children in public school settings. *Journal of Clinical Child Psychology, 20,* 268–276.

Gadow, K. D., Nolan, E. E., & Sverd, J. (1992). Methylphenidate in hyperactive boys with comorbid tic disorder: II. Short-term behavioral effects in school settings. *Journal of the American Academy of Child and Adolescent Psychiatry, 31,* 462–471.

Gadow, K. D., Sverd, J., Sprafkin, J., Nolan, E. E., & Ezor, S. N. (1995). Efficacy of methylphenidate for attention-deficit hyperactivity disorder in children with tic disorder. *Archives of General Psychiatry, 52,* 444–455.

Gammon, B. D., & Brown, T. E. (1993). Fluoxetine and methylphenidate in combination for treatment of attention deficit disorder and comorbid depressive disorder. *Journal of Child and Adolescent Psychopharmacology, 3,* 1–10.

Gittelman, R., Klein, D. F., & Feingold, I. (1983). Children with reading disorders. II: Effects of methylphenidate in combination with reading remediation. *Journal of Child Psychology and Psychiatry, 24,* 193–212.

Gittelman, R., Landa, B., Mattes, J. A., & Klein, D. F. (1988). Methylphenidate and growth in hyperactive children. *Archives of General Psychiatry, 45,* 1127–1130.

Golden, G. S. (1974). Gilles de la Tourette's syndrome following methylphenidate administration. *Developmental Medicine and Child Neurology, 16,* 76–78.

Golden, G. S. (1988). The use of stimulants in the treatment of Tourette's syndrome. In D. J. Cohen, R. D. Bruun, & J. F. Leckman (Eds.), *Tourette's syndrome and tic disorders: Clinical understanding and treatment.* New York: Wiley.

Goyette, C. H., Conners, C. K., & Ulrich, R. F. (1978). Normative data on Revised Conners Parent and Teacher Rating Scales. *Journal of Abnormal Child Psychology, 6,* 221–236.

Granger, D. A., Whalen, C. K., & Henker, B. (1993). Perceptions of methylphenidate effects on hyperactive children's peer interactions. *Journal of Abnormal Child Psychology, 21,* 535–549.

Granger, D. A., Whalen, C. K., Henker, B., & Cantwell, C. (1996). ADHD boys' behavior during structured classroom social activities: Effects of social demands, teacher proximity, and methylphenidate. *Journal of Attention Disorders, 1,* 16–30.

Greenhill, L. L. (1991). Methylphenidate in the clinical office practice of child psychiatry. In L. L. Greenhill & B. B. Osmon (Eds.), *Ritalin: Theory and patient management* (pp. 97–118). New York: Mary Ann Liebert.

Grob, C. S., & Coyle, J. T. (1986). Suspected adverse methylphenidate–imipramine interactions in children. *Journal of Developmental and Behavioral Pediatrics, 7,* 265.

Gualtieri, C. T. (1991). Psychostimulants in traumatic brain injury. In L. L Greenhill & B. B. Osmon (Eds.), *Ritalin: Theory and patient management* (pp. 171–176). New York: Mary Ann Liebert.

Gualtieri, C. T., Hicks, R. E., & Mayo, J. P. (1983). Hyperactivity and homeostasis. *Journal of the American Academy of Child and Adolescent Psychiatry, 22,* 382–384.

Gunning, B. (1992). *A controlled trial of clonidine in hyperkinetic children.* Unpublished master's thesis, Department of Child and Adolescent Psychiatry, Academic Hospital Rotterdam, Sophia Children's Hospital Rotterdam, The Netherlands.

Haenlein, M., & Caul, W. F. (1987). Attention deficit disorder with hyperactivity: A specific hypothesis of reward dysfunction. *Journal of the American Academy of Child and Adolescent Psychiatry, 26,* 356–362.

Handen, B. L., Breaux, A. M., Janosky, J., McAuliffe, S., Feldman, H., & Gosling, A. (1992). Effects and noneffects of methylphenidate in children with mental retardation and ADHD. *Journal of the American Academy of Child and Adolescent Psychiatry, 31,* 455–461.

Handen, B. L., Feldman, H., Gosling, A., Breaux, A. M., & McAuliffe, S. (1991). Adverse side effects of methylphenidate among mentally retarded children with ADHD. *Journal of the American Academy of Child and Adolescent Psychiatry, 30,* 241–245.

Handen, B. L., Janosky, J., McAuliffe, S., Breaux, A. M., & Feldman, H. (1994). Prediction of response to methylphenidate among children with ADHD and mental retardation. *Journal of the American Academy of Child and Adolescent Psychiatry, 33,* 1185–1193.

Hastings, J. E., & Barkley, R. A. (1978). A review of psychophysiological research with hyperactive children. *Journal of Abnormal Child Psychology, 7,* 413–447.

Hinshaw, S. P. (1991). Stimulant medication and the treatment of aggression in children with attentional deficits. *Journal of Clinical Child Psychology, 20,* 301–312.

Hinshaw, S. P., Buhrmester, D., & Heller, T. (1989). Anger control in response to verbal provocation: Effects of stimulant medication for boys with ADHD. *Journal of Abnormal Child Psychology, 17,* 393–407.

Hinshaw, S. P., Heller, T., & McHale, J. P. (1992). Covert antisocial behavior in boys with attention-deficit hyperactivity disorder: External validation and effects of methylphenidate. *Journal of Consulting and Clinical Psychology, 60,* 274–281.

Hinshaw, S. P., Henker, B., Whalen, C. K., Erhardt, D., & Dunnington, R. E. (1989). Aggressive, prosocial, and nonsocial behavior in hyperactive boys: Dose effects of methylphenidate in naturalistic settings. *Journal of Consulting and Clinical Psychology, 57,* 636–643.

Humphries, T., Kinsbourne, M., & Swanson, J. (1978). Stimulant effects on cooperation and social interaction between hyperactive children and their mothers. *Journal of Child Psychology and Psychiatry, 19,* 13–22.

Ialongo, N. S., Lopez, M., Horn W. F., Pascoe, J. M., & Greenberg, G. (1994). Effects of psychostimulant medication on self-perceptions of competence, control, and mood in children with attention deficit hyperactivity disorder. *Journal of Clinical Child Psychology, 23,* 161–173.

Jacobsen, N. S., & Truax, P. (1991). Clinical significance: A statistical approach to defining meaningful change in psychotherapy research. *Journal of Consulting and Clinical Psychology, 59,* 12–19.

Johnston, C., Pelham, W. E., Hoza, J., & Sturges, J. (1988). Psychostimulant rebound in attention deficit disordered boys. *Journal of the American Academy of Child and Adolescent Psychiatry, 27,* 806–810.

Kalikow, K. T., & Blumencranz, H. (1996). Severe weight loss induced by Adderall in a child with ADHD. *Journal of Child and Adolescent Psychopharmacology, 6,* 81–82.

Kaufman, R. E., Smith-Wright, D., Reese, C. A., Simpson, R., & Jones, F. (1981). Medication compliance in hyperactive children. *Pediatric Pharmacology, 1,* 231–237.

Kavale, K. (1982). The efficacy of stimulant drug treatment for hyperactivity: A meta-analysis. *Journal of Learning Disabilities, 15,* 280–289.

Kelly, K. L., Rapport, M. D., & DuPaul, G. J. (1988). Attention deficit disorder and methylphneidate: A multi-step analysis of dose response effects on children's cardiovascular functioning. *International Clinical Psychopharmacology, 3,* 167–181.

Kent, J. D., Blader, J. C., Koplewicz, H. S., Abikoff, H., & Foley, C. A. (1995). Effects of late-afternoon methylphenidate administration on behavior and sleep in attention-deficit hyperactivity disorder. *Pediatrics, 96,* 320–325.

Klein, R. G., & Mannuzza, S. (1988). Hyperactive boys almost grown up: III. Methylphenidate effects on ultimate height. *Archives of General Psychiatry, 45,* 1131–1134.

Knights, R. M., & Viets, A. (1975). Effects of pemoline on hyperactive boys. *Pharmacology, Biochemistry and Behavior, 3,* 1107–1114.

Kupietz, S. S. (1991). Ritalin blood levels and their correlations with measures of learning. In L. L. Greenhill & B. B. Osmon (Eds.), *Ritalin: Theory and patient management* (pp. 247–256). New York: Mary Ann Liebert.

Lou, H. C., Henriksen, L., & Bruhn, P. (1984). Focal cerebral hypoperfusion in children with dysphasia and/or attention deficit disorder. *Archives of Neurology, 41,* 825–829.

Lou, H. C., Henriksen, L., Bruhn, P., Borner, H., & Neilsen, J. B. (1989). Striatal dysfunction in attention deficit and hyperkinetic disorder. *Archives of Neurology, 46,* 48–52.

Mattes, J. A., & Gittelman, R. (1983). Growth of hyperactive children on maintenance regimen of methylphenidate. *Archives of General Psychiatry, 40,* 317–321.

McBurnett, K., Lahey, B. B., & Swanson, J. M. (1991). Ritalin treatment in attention deficit disorder without hyperactivity. In L. L. Greenhill & B. B. Osmon (Eds.), *Ritalin: Theory and patient management* (pp. 257–265). New York: Mary Ann Liebert.

Milich, R., Carlson, C. L., Pelham, W. E., & Licht, B. G. (1991). Effects of methylphenidate on the persistence of ADHD boys following failure experiences. *Journal of Abnormal Child Psychology, 19,* 519–536.

Mino, Y., & Ohara, H. (1991). Methylphenidate and interpersonal relationships of children with attention deficit hyperactivity disorder. *Japanese Journal of Psychiatry and Neurology, 45,* 45–51.

Murphy, D. A., Pelham, W. E., & Lang, A. R. (1992). Aggression in boys with attention deficit-hyperactivity disorder: Methylphenidate effects on naturalistically obsered aggression, response to provocation, and social information processing. *Journal of Abnormal Child Psychology, 20,* 451–465.

Pataki, C., Carlson, G., Kelly, K., Rapport, M. D., & Biancaniello, T. (1993). Side effects of methylphenidate and desipramine alone and in combination in children. *American Journal of Psychiatry, 32*, 1065–1072.

Patrick, K. S., Mueller, R. A., Gualtieri, C. T., et al. (1987). Pharmacokinetics and actions of methylphenidate. In H.Y. Meltzer (Ed.), *Psychopharmacology: The third generation of progress*. New York: Raven Press.

Pelham, W. E. (1985). The effects of stimulant drugs on learning and achievement in hyperactive and learning disabled children. In J. K. Torgesen & B. Wong (Eds.), *Psychological and educational perspectives on learning disabilities* (pp. 259–295). New York: Academic Press.

Pelham, W. E. (1993). Pharmacotherapy for children with attention-deficit hyperactivity disorder. *School Psychology Review, 22*, 199–227.

Pelham, W. E., Greenslade, K. E., Vodde-Hamilton, M., Murphy, D. A., Greenstein, J. J., Gnagy, E. M., & Dahl, R. E. (1990). Relative efficacy of long-acting stimulants on children with attention deficit-hyperactivity disorder: A comparison of standard methylphenidate, sustained-release methylphenidate, sustained-release dextroamphetamine, and pemoline. *Pediatrics, 86*, 226–237.

Pelham, W. E., McBurnett, K., Harper, G. W., Milich, R., Murphy, D. A., Clinton, J., & Thiel, C. (1990). Methylphenidate and baseball playing in ADHD children: Who's on first? *Journal of Consulting and Clinical Psychology, 58*, 130–133.

Pelham, W. E., & Milich, R. (1991). Individual differences in response to Ritalin in classwork and social behavior. In L. L Greenhill & B. B. Osmon (Eds.), *Ritalin: Theory and patient management* (pp. 203–221). New York: Mary Ann Liebert.

Pelham, W. E., Murphy, D. A., Vannatta, K., Milich, R., Licht, B. G., Gnagy, E. M., Greenslade, K. E., Greiner, A. R., & Vodde-Hamilton, M. (1992). Methylphenidate and attributions in boys with attention-deficit hyperactivity disorder. *Journal of Consulting and Clinical Psychology, 60*, 282–292.

Pelham, W. E., Sturges, J., Hoza, J., Schmidt, C., Biijlsma, J. J., Milich, R., & Moorer, S. (1987). Sustained release and standard methylphenidate effects on cognitive and social behavior in children with attention deficit disorder. *Pediatrics, 4*, 491–501.

Pelham, W. E., Swanson, J. M., Furman, M. B., & Schwindt, H. (1995). Pemoline effects on children with ADHD: A time-response by dose-response analysis on classroom measures. *Journal of the American Academy of Child and Adolescent Psychiatry, 34*, 1504–1513.

Pelham, W. E., Walker, J. L., Sturges, J., & Hoza, J. (1989). Comparative effects of methylphenidate on ADD girls and ADD boys. *Journal of the American Academy of Child and Adolescent Psychiatry, 28*, 773–776.

Peloquin, L. J., & Klorman, R. (1986). Effects of methylphenidate on normal children's mood, event-related potentials, and performance in memory scanning and vigilance. *Journal of Abnormal Psychology, 95*, 88–98.

Pliszka, S. R. (1989). Effect of anxiety on cognition, behavior, and stimulant response in ADHD. *Journal of the American Academy of Child and Adolescent Psychiatry, 28*, 882–887.

Popper, C. (1995). Combining methylphenidate and clonidine: Pharmacologic questions and new reports about sudden death. *Journal of Child and Adolescent Psychopharmacology, 5*, 157–166.

Rapoport, J. L., Buchsbaum, M. S., Weingartner, H. Zahn, T. P., Ludlow, C. Bartko, J., Mikkelson, E., Langer, D., & Bunney, W. (1980). Dextroamphetamine: Cognitive and behavioral effects in normal and hyperactive boys and normal adult males. *Archives of General Psychiatry, 37*, 933–946.

Rapport, M. D., Carlson, G. A., Kelly, K. L., & Pataki, C. (1993). Methylphenidate and desipramine in hospitalized children: I. Separate and combined effects on cognitive function. *Journal of the American Academy of Child and Adolescent Psychiatry, 32*, 333–342.

Rapport, M. D., & Denney, C. (1997). Titrating methylphenidate in children with attention-deficit/hyperactivity disorder: Is body mass predictive of clinical response? *Journal of the American Academy of Child and Adolescent Psychiatry, 36*, 523–530.

Rapport, M. D., Denney, C., DuPaul, G. J., & Gardner, M. J. (1994). Attention deficit disorder and methylphenidate: Normalization rates, clinical effectiveness, and response prediction in 76 children. *Journal of the American Academy of Child and Adolescent Psychiatry, 33*, 882–893.

Rapport, M. D., & DuPaul, G. J. (1986). Attention deficit disorder and methylphenidate: Rate-dependent effects on attention. *International Clinical Psychopharmacology, 1*, 45–52.

Rapport, M. D., DuPaul, G. J., & Kelly, K. L. (1989). Attention-deficit hyperactivity disorder and methylphenidate: The relationship between gross body weight and drug response in children. *Psychopharmacology Bulletin, 25*, 285–290.

Rapport, M. D., DuPaul, G. J., & Smith, N. F. (1985). Rate-dependency and hyperactivity: Methylphenidate effects on operant responding. *Pharmacology, Biochemistry and Behavior, 23*, 77–83.

Rapport, M. D., DuPaul, G. J., Stoner, G., & Jones, J. T. (1986). Comparing classroom and clinic measures of attention deficit disorder: Differential, idiosyncratic, and dose-response effects of methylphenidate. *Journal of Consulting and Clinical Psychology, 54*, 334–341.

Rapport, M. D., Jones, J. T., DuPaul, G. J., Kelly, K. L., Gardner, M. J., Tucker, S. B., & Shea, M. S. (1987). Attention deficit disorder and methylphenidate: Group and single-subject analyses of dose effects on attention in clinic and classroom settings. *Journal of Consulting and Clinical Psychology, 16*, 329–338.

Rapport, M. D., & Kelly, K. L. (1991). Psychostimulant effects on learning and cognitive function: Findings and implications for children with attention-deficit hyperactivity disorder. *Clinical Psychology Review, 11*, 61–92.

Redman, C. A., & Zametkin, A. J. (1991). Ritalin and brain metabolism. In L. L. Greenhill & B. B. Osmon (Eds.), *Ritalin: Theory and patient management* (pp. 301–309). New York: Mary Ann Liebert.

Reeve, E., & Garfinkel, B. (1991). Neuroendocrine and growth regulation: The role of sympathomimetic medication. In L. L. Greenhill & B. B. Osmon (Eds.), *Ritalin: Theory and patient management* (pp. 289–300). New York, Mary Ann Liebert, 1991.

Rosenthal, R. H., & Allen, T. W. (1978). An examination of attention, arousal, and learning dysfunctions of hyperkinetic children. *Psychological Bulletin, 85*, 689–715.

Safer, D. J. (1992). Relative cardiovascular safety of psychostimulants used to treat attention-deficit hyperactivity disorder. *Journal of Child and Adolescent Psychopharmacology, 2*, 279–290.

Safer, D. J., & Allen, D. J. (1973). Factors influencing the suppressant effects of two stimulant drugs on the growth of hyperactive children. *Pediatrics, 51*, 660–667.

Safer, D. J., Allen, R. P., & Barr, E. (1972). Depression of growth in hyperactive children on stimulant drugs. *New England Journal of Medicine, 287*, 217–220.

Safer, D. J., Zito, J. M., & Fine, E. M. (1986). Increased methylphenidate usage for attention deficit disorder in the 1990s. *Pediatrics, 98*, 1084–1088.

Sallee, F., Stiller, R., Perel, J., et al. (1985). Oral pemoline kinetics in hyperactive children. *Clinical Pharmacological Therapeutics, 37*, 606–609.

Sallee, F. R., Stiller, R. L., Perel, J. M., et al. (1989). Pemoline-induced abnormal involuntary movements. *Journal of Clinical Psychopharmacology, 9*, 125–129.

Satterfield, J. H., & Dawson, M. E. (1971). Electrodermal correlates of hyperactivity in children. *Psychophysiology, 8*, 191–197.

Schachar, R., & Tannock, R. (1993). Childhood hyperactivity and psychostimulants: A review of extended treatment studies. *Journal of Child and Adolescent Psychopharmacology, 3*, 81–97.

Schachar, R. J., Tannock, R., Cunningham, C., & Corkum, P. V. (1997). Behavioral, situational, and temporal effects of treatment of ADHD with methylphenidate. *Journal of the American Academy of Child and Adolescent Psychiatry, 36*, 754–763.

Sergeant, J., & van der Meere, J. J. (1991). Ritalin effects and information processing in hyperactivity. In L. L. Greenhill & B. B. Osmon (Eds.), *Ritalin: Theory and patient management* (pp. 1–13). New York, Mary Ann Liebert.

Shah, M. R., Seese, L. M., Abikoff, H., & Klein, R. G. (1994). Pemoline for children and adolescents with conduct disorder: A pilot investigation. *Journal of Child and Adolescent Psychopharmacology, 4*, 255–261.

Shaywitz, S. E., & Shaywitz, B. A. (1991). Attention deficit disorder: Diagnosis and role of Ritalin in management. In L. L. Greenhill & B. B. Osmon (Eds.), *Ritalin: Theory and patient management* (pp. 45–68). New York: Mary Ann Liebert.

Solanto, M. V. (1991). Dosage effects of Ritalin on cognition. In L. L. Greenhill & B. B. Osmon (Eds.), *Ritalin: Theory and patient management* (pp. 233–246). New York: Mary Ann Liebert.

Solanto, M. V., & Wender, E. K. (1989). Does methylphenidate constrict cognitive functioning? *Journal of the American Academy of Child and Adolescent Psychiatry, 28*, 897–902.

Spencer, T. J., Biederman, J., Harding, M., O'Donnell, D., Faraone, S. V., & Wilens, T. W. (1996). Growth deficits in ADHD children revisited: Evidence of disorder-associated growth delays? *Journal of the American Academy of Child and Adolescent Psychiatry, 35*, 1460–1469.

Spencer, T., Biederman, J., Wilens, T., Harding, M., O'Donnell, D., & Griffin, S. (1996). Pharmacotherapy of attention-deficit hyperactivity disorder across the life cycle. *Journal of the American Academy of Child and Adolescent Psychiatry, 35*, 409–432.

Spencer, T., Wilens, T., Biederman, J., Faraone, S.V., Ablon, S., & Lapey, K. (1995). A double-blind, crossover comparison of methylphenidate and placebo in adults with childhood-onset attention deficit hyperactivity disorder. *Archives of General Psychiatry, 52*, 434–443.

Sprague, R., & Sleator, E. (1976). Drugs and dosages: Implications for learning disabilities. In R. M. Knights & D. J. Bakker (Eds.), *The neuropsychology of learning disorders* (pp. 351–366). Baltimore: University Park Press.

Sprague, R., & Sleator, E. (1977). Methylphenidate in hyperkinetic children: Differences in dose effects on learning and social behavior. *Science, 198*, 1274–1276.

Stein, M. A., Blondis, T. A., Schnitzler, E. R., O'Brien, T., Fishkin, J., Blackwell, B., Szumowski, E., & Roizen, N. J. (1996). Methylphenidate dosing: Twice daily versus three times daily. *Pediatrics, 98*, 748–756.

Stephens, R. S., Pelham, W. E., & Skinner, R. (1984). State-dependent and main effects of methylphenidate and pemoline on paired-associate learning and spelling in hyperactive children. *Journal of Consulting and Clinical Psychology, 52*, 104–113.

Stoner, G., Carey, S. P., Ikeda, M. J., & Shinn, M. R. (1994). The utility of curriculum-based measurement for evaluating the effects of methylphenidate on academic performance. *Journal of Applied Behavior Analysis, 27*, 101–114.

Swanson, J. M. (1988a). Measurement of serum concentrations and behavioral response in ADDH children to acute doses of methylphenidate. In L. B. Bloomingdale (Ed.), *Attention deficit disorder: New research in attention, treatment, and psychopharmacology* (pp. 107–226). New York: Pergamon Press.

Swanson, J. M. (1988b). What do psychopharmacological studies tell us about information processing deficits in ADDH? In L. M. Bloomingdale & J. Sergeant (Eds.), *Attention deficit disorder: Criteria, cognition, intervention* (pp. 97–116). New York, Pergamon Press.

Swanson, J. M. (1989). Paired-associate learning in the assessment of ADD-H children. In L. M. Bloomingdale & J. Swanson (Eds.), *Attention deficit disorder: Current concepts and emerging trends in attentional and behavioral disorders of childhood* (pp. 87–123). New York: Pergamon Press.

Swanson, J. M., Flockhart, D., Udrea, D., Cantwell, D., Connor, D., & Williams, L. (1996). Clonidine in the treatment of ADHD: Questions about safety and efficacy. *Journal of Child and Adolescent Psychopharmacology, 5*, 301–304.

Swanson, J., & Kinsbourne, M. (1978). The cognitive effects of stimulant drugs on hyperactive children. In G. A. Hale & M. Lewis (Eds.), *Attention and cognitive development* (pp. 249–274). New York: Plenum.

Swanson, J., Kinsbourne, M., Roberts, W., & Zucker, K. (1978). Time-response analysis of the effect of stimulant medication on the learning ability of children referred for hyperactivity. *Pediatrics, 61*, 21–29.

Swanson, J. M., McBurnett, K., Christian, D. L., & Wigal, T. (1995). Stimulant medications and the treatment of children with ADHD. In T. H. Ollendick & R. J. Prinz (Eds.), *Advances in clinical child psychology* (vol. 17, pp. 265–322). New York: Plenum.

Taylor, E. A. (1983). Drug response and diagnostic validation. In M. Rutter (Ed.), *Developmental neuropsychiatry* (pp. 348–368). New York: Guilford Press.

Taylor, E. A. (1986). *The overactive child.* Philadelphia: Lippincott.

Voelker, S., Lachar, D., & Gdowski, C. (1983). The Personality Inventory for Children and response to methylphenidate: Preliminary evidence for predictive validity. *Journal of Pediatric Psychology, 8*, 161–169.

Vyse, S. A., & Rapport, M. D. (1989). The effects of methylphenidate on learning in children with ADDH: The stimulus-equivalence paradigm. *Journal of Consulting and Clinical Psychology, 57*, 425–435.

Wargin, W., Patrick, K., Kilts, C., Gualtieri, C. T., Ellington, K., Mueller, R. A., Kraemer, G., & Breese, G. R. (1983). Pharmacokinetics of methylphenidate in man, rat, and monkey. *Journal of Pharmacology and Experimental Therapeutics, 226,* 382–386.

Weiner, W. J., Nauseida, P. J., & Klawans, H. L. (1978). Methylphenidate-induced chorea: Case report and pharmacologic implications. *Neurology, 28,*1041–1044.

Weiss, G., & Hechtman, L. (1993). *Hyperactive children grown up: ADHD in children, adolescents, and adults* (2nd ed.). New York: Guilford Press.

Werry, J. (1978). *Pediatric psychopharmacology.* New York: Brunner/Mazel.

Whalen, C. K., Henker, B., Collins, B. E., Finck, D., & Dotemoto, S. (1979). Peer interaction in structured communication task: Comparisons of normal and hyperactive boys and of methylphenidate (Ritalin) and placebo effects. *Child Development, 50,* 388–401.

Whalen, C. K., Henker, B., & Dotemoto, S. (1980). Methylphenidate and hyperactivity: Effects on teacher behaviors. *Science, 208,* 1280–1282.

Whalen, C. K., Henker, B., Hinshaw, S. P., Heller, T., & Huber-Dressler, A. (1991). Messages of medication: Effects of actual versus informed medication status on hyperactive boys expectancies and self-evaluations. *Journal of Consulting and Clinical Psychology, 59,* 602–606.

Whalen, C. K., Henker, B., Swanson, J. M., Granger, D., Kliewer, W., & Spencer, J. (1987). Natural social behaviors in hyperactive children: Dose effects of methylphenidate. *Journal of Consulting and Clinical Psychology, 55,* 187–193.

Zametkin, A., Nordahl, T., Gross, M., King, A. C., Semple, W. E., Rumsey, J., Hamburger, S., & Cohen, R. M. (1990). Cerebral glucose metabolism in adults with hyperactivity of childhood onset. *New England Journal of Medicine, 323,* 1361–1366.

Zeiner, P. (1995). Body growth and cardiovascular function after extended (1.75 years) with methylphenidate in boys with attention-deficit hyperactivity disorder. *Journal of Child and Adolescent Psychopharacology, 5,* 129–138.

Chapter 18

PHARMACOTHERAPY OF ADHD WITH ANTIDEPRESSANTS

Thomas J. Spencer
Joseph Biederman
Timothy Wilens

ઠ્વ

Although the stimulants are the most established treatment for Attention-Deficit/Hyperactivity Disorder (ADHD), as many as 30% of affected individuals do not respond or may not tolerate such treatments (Spencer et al., 1996). Effective alternatives have included medications traditionally considered antidepressants. In the last two decades, a considerable research literature has emerged addressing the effectiveness, tolerability, and safety of these compounds. However, because of the rapid introduction of novel medications, there are fewer data on more recently available agents.

Increasingly we recognize that ADHD is a heterogeneous disorder with a considerable incidence of additional (comorbid) psychiatric and cognitive disorders. The most frequently co-occurring psychiatric disorders include conduct, substance use, mood, and anxiety disorders (Biederman, Newcorn, & Sprich, 1991) as well as tic disorders (Comings & Comings, 1988). We are only beginning to understand whether these subgroups respond preferentially to different psychotropics and whether it is preferable to use a single, broad-spectrum agent or to shift to combination treatments for these complex conditions.

ADHD is defined by a limited set of symptoms. However, the translation of these symptoms into adaptive or impaired function varies widely among individuals so diagnosed. A comprehensive treatment approach to the ADHD patient of any age should attempt to address three main areas of potential dysfunction: behavioral, social, and cognitive. Pharmacotherapy of ADHD can help not only abnormal behaviors in school or work but, equally important, the individual's social, and family life (Whalen & Henker, 1992). In some but not all patients, medication should be paired with cognitive-behavioral interventions that may include training in self-instruction, self-evaluation, attribution, social skills, and anger management (Hinshaw & Erhardt, 1991). Because at least 30% of ADHD children may suffer from learning disabilities, and because learning disorders are not drug sensitive, learning-disabled ADHD patients require additional remediation, such as tutoring or placement in special classes and, occasionally, specialized schools.

TRICYCLIC ANTIDEPRESSANTS

Medications in the class of tricyclics antidepressants (TCAs) are the most established non-stimulant agents used in the treatment of ADHD. This class of medications is divided into the tertiary amines—amitriptyline, imipramine, doxepin, and trimipramine—and the secondary amines—desipramine, nortriptyline, and protriptyline. The common mechanism of action appears to be a result of the inhibition of reuptake of selected brain neurotransmitters, especially norepinephrine and serotonin. However, these agents have variable effects on additional neurotransmitter systems, resulting in differing positive and adverse effect profiles. Unwanted side effects may emerge from modulation of histaminic (sedation, weight gain), cholinergic (dry mouth, constipation), alpha-adrenergic (postural hypotension), and serotonergic (sexual dysfunction) neuronal systems. Accordingly, more selective (noradrenergic) secondary amines have less side effects in sensitive populations such as juvenile and geriatric.

There have been 31 TCA studies (58% controlled) of more than 1,000 children, adolescents, and adults with ADHD. The vast majority of these studies (87%) reported substantial improvement. However, as with the stimulants, the vast majority of studies were relatively brief and included primarily latency-age children. A number of recent studies have examined extended treatment for up to 2 years and noted sustained improvement (Biederman, Gastfriend, & Jellinek, 1986; Gastfriend, Biederman, & Jellinek 1985; Wilens, Biederman, Geist, Steingard, & Spencer, 1993). This is in contrast to an earlier study (Quinn & Rapoport, 1975) that reported poor long-term outcome. In that study, 50% of subjects dropped out because of side effects; however, of those who remained on imipramine, improvement was sustained for over 1 year. The issue of lost efficacy due to tolerance or side effects is receiving increasing research interest but has rarely been addressed in existing studies. As with the stimulants, sustained improvement of ADHD symptoms in juveniles on TCAs appears to require periodic clinical reevaluation with the upward adjustment of daily doses to maintain therapeutic blood levels in growing children. (Biederman et al., 1986; Gastfriend et al., 1985; Wilens et al., 1993; Biederman, Baldessarini, Wright, Knee, & Harmatz, 1989). There have been contradictory reports on recommended dosing of the TCA's in ADHD. Some studies have touted the benefits of low-dose TCAs in the treatment of ADHD. In contrast, in our clinical experience and in several long-term studies, our group has consistently found that relatively higher doses, consistent with dosing recommended for depression, have been more effective. For example, studies using aggressive doses of TCAs have reported sustained improvement for up to 1 year with desipramine (>4 mg/kg) (Beiderman et al., 1986; Gastfriend et al., 1985) and nortriptyline (2.0 mg/kg) (Wilens et al., 1993). It could be that the apparent short-lived effects reported in several previous studies of TCAs in ADHD children could have been due to the use of relatively low (<3 mg/kg) daily doses.

In the largest controlled study of TCAs in children, our group reported dramatic improvement with desipramine (DMI) in 62 clinically referred ADHD children, most of whom had previously failed psychostimulant treatment (Biederman, Baldessarini, Wright, Knee, & Harmatz, 1989). Meaningful behavioral improvements were found in 68% of DMI-treated patients compared to only 10% of patients on placebo. In addition to parent-endorsed positive benefits, classroom improvement was reported by teachers only in the DMI-treated group. In further analyses we examined whether the children with comorbid conduct disorder, anxiety or depression, or a family history of ADHD responded differently to DMI treatment (Biederman, Baldessarini, Wright, Keenan, & Faraone, 1993). In this study none of these comorbidities or a family history of ADHD yielded differential responses to DMI treatment. These findings contrast to a body of literature that suggests that comorbidity with depression and anxiety predicts a poorer response to the stimulants (Swanson, Kinsbourne, Roberts, & Zucker, 1978; Voelker, Lachar, & Gdowski, 1983; Taylor et al., 1987; Pliszka, 1989; DuPaul, Barkley, & McMurray, 1994; Tannock, Ickowicz, & Schachar, 1995). In addition, DMI-treated ADHD patients showed a substantial reduction in depressive symptoms compared with placebo-treated patients (Biederman, Baldessarini, Wright, Knee, & Harmatz, 1989). These data suggest that DMI may be a particularly appropriate choice of treatment in depressed or anxious children with ADHD.

Similar results were obtained in a rigorously controlled trial of DMI in adult ADHD (Wilens, Biederman, Prince, et al., 1996). At a daily DMI dose of 150 mg (serum levels of 113 ng/ml), we documented an identical level of therapeutic response for DMI compared with placebo (68% vs. 0%). In this study the magnitude of the response was sufficient that most subjects no longer had enough ADHD symptoms to meet criteria for the diagnosis of ADHD (clinically subthreshold). There have been reports of an immediate response of ADHD symptoms to TCAs unlike the lag typically found in depression studies. Importantly, in our study, full improvement required an extended period on medication. The full dose was achieved at week 2, but the clinical response improved further over the following 4 weeks, indicating a considerable latency of response. Also akin to the pediatric study, the response of ADHD adults to DMI was independent of lifetime psychiatric comorbidity with anxiety or depressive disorders.

A frequently asked question in evaluating alternative treatments is how they compare in efficacy with the more established stimulants. Technically this is a hard question to answer because it requires a much larger study size rarely achieved in pediatric investigations. In addition, different medications may be effective for different symptoms and for various subgroups. Although studies of TCAs demonstrate clear efficacy in ADHD, comparisons of TCAs to stimulants have not found a clear advantage of either treatment. Some studies reported that stimulants were superior to TCAs (Gittelman-Klein, 1974; Greenberg, Yellin, Spring, & Metcalf, 1975; Garfinkel, Wender, Sloman, & O'Neill, 1983; Rapoport, Quinn, Bradbard, Riddle, & Brooks, 1974); others that stimulants were equal to TCAs (Gross, 1973; Huessy & Wright, 1970; Rapport, Carlson, Kelly, & Pataki, 1993; Yepes, Balka, Winsberg, & Bialer, 1977; Kupietz & Balka, 1976). Three studies reported that TCAs were superior to stimulants (Werry, 1980; Walter & Dreyfus, 1973; Winsberg, Bialer, Kupietz, & Tobias, 1972).

The available literature seems to indicate that TCAs are as efficacious in controlling abnormal behaviors associated with ADHD but are less effective in improving cognitive impairments relative to the stimulants (Quinn & Rapoport, 1975; Rapport et al., 1973; Werry, 1980; Gualtieri & Evans, 1988). However, one study found that DMI and methylphenidate affected different cognitive tasks and were synergistic in combination (Rapport et al., 1993). Despite the considerable literature on TCAs and stimulants in ADHD children, more work is needed to better define the cognitive effects of both classes of agents.

High doses (up to 5 mg/kg) of imipramine (IMI) and DMI have been used to treat school phobia, Major Depressive Disorder, and ADHD (Biederman, Baldessarini, Wright, Knee, & Harmatz, 1989; Biederman, Baldessarini, Wright, Knee, Harmatz, & Goldblatt, 1989) in children. Because children and adolescents are more efficient in metabolizing TCAs compared to adults, they frequently require higher weight-corrected dosing, to achieve similar TCA blood levels as adults (Wilens, Biederman, Baldessarini, Pupolo, & Flood, 1992). However, because of genetic variability in the enzymes that metabolize TCAs (p450), the relationship between dose and blood level is highly variable. Therefore, some children require only low doses and others relatively high doses. TCA treatment should always be carefully individualized with blood levels periodically obtained for dosage guidance.

At our center, we obtain baseline vital signs, blood tests, and an electrocardiogram (EKG). Treatment is initiated with a low dose and titrated upward slowly every 4 to 5 days by 20% to 30% while monitoring side effects. After reaching a dose of approximately 2 to 3 mg/kg (~1 mg/kg for nortriptyline) we systematically review whether the medication is tolerated and obtain a second EKG and a steady-state blood level. This blood level can be used as a guide to estimate the ultimate therapeutic dose. After any substantial change in dose or with the advent of additional psychotropics or other medications that may be expected to affect TCA metabolism, we obtain repeat steady-state serum levels and EKGs.

Common short-term adverse effects of the TCAs include anticholinergic effects, such as dry mouth, blurred vision, and constipation. However, there are no known long-term deleterious effects associated with chronic administration of these drugs. Although it is not dangerous to discontinue the drugs abruptly, unpleasant side effects such as gastrointestinal symptoms or even vomiting may ensue unless tapered. Because the anticholinergic effects of TCAs limit salivary flow, they may promote tooth decay in some children. TCA serum level monitoring is useful not only to predict clinical response but also to determine the limits of serum TCA concentration associated with adverse cardiovascular effects. In contrast, some subjective adverse effects such as dry mouth or dizziness appear unrelated to drug serum levels.

There have been concerns about potential serious risks with the use TCAs in children because of reports of sudden unexplained death in four ADHD children treated with DMI (Abramowicz, 1990). The causal link between DMI and these deaths remains uncertain. A recent report estimated that the magnitude of DMI-associated risk of sudden death in children may not be much larger than the baseline risk of sudden death in this age group (Biederman, Thisted, Greenhill, & Ryan, 1995). Moreover, these deaths have been difficult to reconcile with the rather extensive literature evaluating cardiovascular parameters in TCA-exposed patients of all ages and the extraordinary worldwide use of TCAs in all age groups. In most studies, TCA treatment has been associated with asymptomatic, minor increases in heart rate and EKG measures of cardiac conduction times consistent with that seen in adults (Biederman, Baldessarini, Goldblatt, et al., 1993; Wilens, Biederman, Baldessarini, et al., 1996). However, because of this uncertainty, TCAs should be used as second-line treatment for uncomplicated ADHD in juveniles and only after carefully weighing the risks and benefits of treating or not treating an affected child.

OTHER ANTIDEPRESSANTS

Bupropion

Bupropion hydrochloride is a novel-structured antidepressant of the aminoketone class related to the phenylisopropylamines but pharmacological distinct from known antidepressants (Casat, Pleasants, Schroeder, & Parler, 1989). Bupropion appears to possess both indirect dopamine agonist and noradrenergic effects. Bupropion has been shown to be effective for ADHD in children, in a large, controlled multisite study ($N = 72$) (Casat et al., 1989; Casat, Pleasants, & Van Wyck Fleet, 1987; Conners et al., 1996) and in a comparison with methylphenidate ($N = 15$) (Barrickman et al., 1995). In an open study of ADHD adults, sustained improvement was documented at 1 year (Wender & Reimherr, 1990). In that study, dosing for ADHD, an average of 360 mg of bupropion for 6 to 8 weeks, appeared to be similar to that recommended for depression.

Although bupropion is metabolized at a similar rate as the TCAs with a half-life of 14 hours, it is taken in divided doses to minimize the slightly increased risk (0.4%) for drug-induced seizures relative to other antidepressants. However, this risk has been linked to high doses, a previous history of seizures, and eating disorders. Thus, by avoiding these risk factors, and by dividing the daily dose or using the long-acting preparation, the risk of seizures may be comparable to other antidepressants. Although the medication is generally well tolerated, other potential side effects include edema, rashes, nocturia, irritability, anorexia, and insomnia.

Monoamine Oxidase Inhibitors

The monoamine oxidase inhibitor (MAOI) antidepressants have also been shown to be effective in the treatment of ADHD (Zametkin, Rapoport, Murphy, Linnoila, & Ismond, 1985). However, because of potentially severe reactions in most MAOIs due to dietetic restrictions and potential drug–drug interactions, their use is severely restricted in children. One MAOI, seligiline has been successfully used in children with tic disorders (discussed later) (Jankovic, 1993). Preliminary evidence indicates that this agent at low doses may have less of the potentially severe side effects of the other MAOIs.

Major general limitations to the use of MAOIs are the dietetic restrictions of tyramine-containing foods (i.e., most cheeses), pressor amines (i.e., sympathomimetic substances), or drug interactions (i.e., most cold medicines and amphetamines), which can induce a hypertensive crisis or the serotonergic syndrome when MAOIs are combined with predominantly serotonergic drugs. Short-term adverse effects may also include orthostatic hypotension, weight gain, drowsiness, and dizziness. Although the use of MAOIs in this clinical population is complicated, nonetheless, they may be important to consider in treatment refractory ADHD individuals.

Selective Serotonin Reuptake Inhibitors

Currently available selective serotonin reuptake inhibitors (SSRIs) include fluoxetine, paroxetine, sertraline and fluvoxamine. Emerging evidence suggests that these medications are the most effective for childhood depression and Obsessive–Compulsive Disorder (along with clomipramine) and are promising agents for childhood anxiety. SSRIs have not been systematically evaluated in the treatment of ADHD. A small open study (Barrickman, Noyes, Kuperman, Schwmacher, & Verda, 1991) suggested that fluoxetine may be beneficial in the treatment of ADHD children; however, the consensus of ADHD experts at a National Institute of Mental Health conference on the use of alternative agents for ADHD did not support the usefulness of these compounds in the treatment of core ADHD symptoms (National Institute of Mental Health, 1996). Nevertheless, because of the high rates of comorbidity in ADHD, these compounds are frequently combined with effective anti-ADHD agents (see discussion later).

Because of their pharmacological profile, these medications have fewer anticholinergic, sedative, cardiovascular (blood pressure and EKG changes), and weight-affecting adverse side effects than the TCAs. Unlike TCAs, SSRIs are structurally dissimilar to each other. Further, these agents vary in their pharmacokinetics and side effect profiles.

Suggested daily doses in pediatric patients are approximately 0.5 to 1.0 mg/kg. Fluoxetine and its active metabolite have a long half life of 7 to 9 days. In contrast, paroxetine (dose range = 0.25 to 0.70 mg/kg daily), sertraline (dose range = 1.5 to 3.0 mg/kg daily [≤ 200 mg/day]) and fluvoxamine (dose range = 1.0 to 4.5 mg/kg [≤ 300 mg/day]) have moderately long half lives of approximately 24 hours (fluvoxamine approximately 15 hours). Common adverse effects of SSRIs include irritability, insomnia, gastrointestinal symptoms, sexual dysfunction, and headaches. Paroxetine and sertraline have also been associated with a higher incidence of headache, sedation, dry mouth, and constipation than fluoxetine but less anxiety and agitation (Grimsley & Jann, 1992). Antidepressants and many other psychotropics are metabolized in the liver by the cytochrome P450 system (Nemeroff, DeVare, & Pollock, 1996). The coadministration of TCAs (and similar compounds) and SSRIs may result in increased levels of the TCAs; thus, great caution should be exercised when using TCAs and the SSRIs.

Venlafaxine

Venlafaxine (Effexor) is chemically unrelated to other antidepressants. It has both SSRI and TCA properties (noradrenergic and serotonergic). Venlafaxine is an established antidepressant in adults and controlled studies are under way in the treatment of juvenile mood disorders. There are four open studies of venlafaxine in ADHD adults ($N = 59$) reporting an overall response of 79% in completers with a 20% rate of dropout due to side effects (Hornig-Rohan & Amsterdam, 1995; Findling, Schwartz, Flannery, & Manos, 1996; Adler, Resnick, Kunz, & Devinsky, 1995; Reimherr, Hedges, Strong, & Wender, 1995). In addition, an open study of 16 ADHD children reported a 50% response rate in completers with a 29% rate of dropout due to side effects, most prominently increased hyperactivity (Luh, Pliszka, Olvers, & Tatum, 1996).

Venlafaxine has a medium half-life of approximately 5 hours (*O*-desmethylvenlafaxine approximately 11 hours) with an increased clearance in children and adolescents. The usual dose range is 2.0 to 5.0 mg/kg daily given in three divided doses. Tolerance is improved by slow upward titration. Venlafaxine lacks significant activity at muscarinic/cholinergic, alpha-adrenergic and histaminergic sites thus have less side effects (sedation, anticholinergic) than other antidepressants. However, when using venlafaxine, unlike the SSRIs, there is a need to monitor for potential cardiac effects such as diastolic hypertension.

IMPACT OF PSYCHIATRIC COMORBIDITY IN THE PHARMACOTHERAPY OF ADHD

Comorbidity with Conduct Disorder and Aggression

There is a substantial literature documenting the effectiveness of stimulants in aggressive ADHD children both for ADHD symptoms and comorbid aggression (Spencer et al., 1996). However, the heightened risk of abuse in this population indicates a need to consider alternative agents. Several studies of antidepressants for ADHD children with comorbid conduct disorder ($N = 4$ studies, $N = 137$ children) also indicate improvement of ADHD (Wilens et al., 1993; Biederman et al., 1993; Winsberg et al., 1972; Simeon, Ferguson, Van Wyck, & Fleet, 1986) and aggressive symptoms in these subjects (Winsberg et al., 1972; Simeon et al., 1986). Although no class of therapeutic agents has been found to be effective for the diagnosis of conduct disorder per se, reduction of ADHD symptoms may be critical to allow the social learning necessary for successful psychosocial treatments. In addition, ADHD children with Conduct Disorder are at an even higher risk for additional mood disorders that may be best addressed with antidepressant medications.

Comorbidity with Anxiety and Depression

An emerging literature suggests that anxious and depressed ADHD children respond more poorly to stimulants than do ADHD children without these additional symptoms. As discussed earlier, studies of TCAs have shown this class of compounds to be equally effective for ADHD symptoms in children or adults with a lifetime history of depression or anxiety. Several studies have documented that TCA treatment improved both ADHD and depressive symptoms (Biederman et al., 1993; Garfinkel et al., 1983). However, these studies have examined few subjects with current mood or anxiety symptoms judged to be in the clinically severe range. At this point, current practice would suggest prioritizing treatment so that severe mood or anxiety disorders are first stabilized and then ADHD symptoms are addressed. In this regard, there is one promising report of the use of venlafaxine for ADHD adults (Hornig-Rohan & Amsterdam, 1995) with depression and two open reports of the successful use of combined SSRIs and stimulants in this comorbid population (see discussion later) (Grammon & Brown, 1993; Findling, 1996).

Comorbidity with Bipolar Disorder

Despite increasing recognition of the co-occurrence of ADHD and bipolarity (West, McElroy, Strakowski, Keck, & McConville, 1995; Wozniak et al., 1995), little is known about the pharmacotherapy of the combined condition. Considering the potential for activation of individuals with ADHD and mania with TCAs and stimulants, caution should be used in treating ADHD and mania with stimulants and antidepressants in the absence of mood stabilzers (Wozniak & Biederman, 1996). Because mania can produce severe cognitive and behavioral symptoms, it is crucial first to stabilize the manic symptoms in ADHD children with this comorbidity (Biederman et al., in press).

Comorbidity with Tic Disorders

Recent studies have documented chronic tic disorder or Tourette syndrome in over 30% of ADHD children. Traditionally, stimulants have been contraindicated in the treatment of patients with tics and ADHD; however, a recent literature has challenged this position. Recent investigations at our center have found similar rates of tic disorders in treated and untreated ADHD children, suggesting little contribution of the stimulants to the precipitation of tics that would not have otherwise emerged. In ADHD patients who already have a tic disorder, studies report tics worsening in 20–30% of patients; however, there is reassuring evidence that such exacerbations may have little long-term consequence (Castellanos et al., 1997). Until more is known, clinicians should continue to exercise caution in the use of stimulants in this population.

There is an emerging literature on the use of TCAs in the treatment of children and adolescents with ADHD and tic disorders. Recent case reports and case series of imipramine (Dillon, Salzman, & Schulsinger, 1985), nortriptyline (Spencer, Biederman, Wilens, Steingard, & Geist, 1993), and desipramine (Spencer, Biederman, Kerman, Steingard, & Wilens, 1993; Hoge & Biederman, 1986; Riddle, Harding, Cho, Woolston, & Leckman, 1988) have reported a high rate (82%) of improvement of ADHD symptoms with no change or improvement of the tic disorder over an extended follow-up period (Spencer, Biederman, Wilens, et al., 1993; Spencer, Biederman, Kerman, et al., 1993). Two controlled studies have documented that desipramine was highly effective in its ability to improve ADHD symptoms associated with chronic tics or the full Tourette syndrome. In the report by Singer et al. (1994), desipramine was tic neutral and clonidine also did not improve tics. In contrast, Spencer, Biedermanm, Kerman, et al. (1993) found that desipramine had a moderately positive effect on the tic symptoms themselves. Therefore the TCAs may be a particularly useful choice in this population.

COMBINED PHARMACOTHERAPY

In clinical practice, many ADHD patients receive multiple treatments; however, the development of clear therapeutic guidelines is only now emerging. In contrast to polypharmacy, rational combined pharmacological approaches can be used for the treatment of comorbid ADHD, as augmentation strategies for patients with insufficient response to a single agent, and for the management of treatment emergent adverse effects. Examples of the rational use of combined treatment include the use of an antidepressant plus a stimulant for ADHD and comorbid depression, the use of clonidine to ameliorate stimulant-induced insomnia, and the use of a mood stabilizer plus an anti-ADHD agent to treat ADHD comorbid with Bipolar Disorder (Wilens, Spencer, Biederman, Wozniak, & Connor, 1994).

Historically, the first reports of combined pharmacotherapy in ADHD were of antipsychotics and stimulants. Despite the theoretic concern of contradictory dopaminergic mechanisms of action, there have been two controlled studies ($N = 181$) of combined neuroleptic and stimulant treatment of ADHD children (Weizman, Weitz, Szekely, Tyano, & Belmaker, 1984; Gittelman-Klein, Klein, Katz, Saraf, & Pollack, 1976). In both studies the combination was superior to stimulant medication alone, though only a trend in the larger study. Because of the potentially severe side effects of the neuroleptics, their use is generally not indicated for uncomplicated ADHD but may be quite useful in comorbid severe mood disorders not response to typical mood stabilizers (see earlier discussion).

In one of the few studies of its kind, Rapport et al. (1993) evaluated the separate and combined effects of methylphenidate and desipramine in 16 hospitalized children. These investigators found that methylphenidate alone improved vigilance, both methylphenidate and desipramine alone produced positive affects on short-term memory and visual problem solving, and their combination produced positive affects on learning of higher-order relationships. The authors speculated that performance on different cognitive measures may be modulated by separate neurotransmitter systems. Of note, the subjects in this study were children with ADHD and comorbid major depression, dysthymia, and anxiety. These investigators (Pataki, Carlson, Kelly, Rapport, & Biancaniello, 1993) also reported that, although this combined pharmacotherapy was associated with more side effects than monotherapy, there was no evidence that the combined use of both drugs was associated with unique or serious side effects.

There are several other reports on the use of multiple agents in the treatment of concurrent disorders with ADHD. There are two open reports of the successful use of SSRIs with stimulants in the management of concurrent depressive disorders (Gammon & Brown, 1993; Findling, 1996). Although anti-ADHD drugs (stimulants or TCAs) may worsen comorbid bipolar disorders, they may be used successfully when combined with mood stabilizers or neuroleptics (Biederman et al., in press).

There are open reports of the successful use of clonidine with stimulants for sleep disorders (Brown & Gammon, 1992; Prince, Wilens, Biederman, Spencer, & Wozniak, 1996) in ADHD children. Although the combined use of anti-ADHD drugs with benzodiazepines or antidepressants for anxiety has not been systematically evaluated, anecdotal evidence is promising.

CONCLUSIONS

The available literature strongly indicates an important role for the antidepressants in the treatment of individuals with ADHD not only for core behavioral symptoms but also on associated impairments including social skills and family function. Effective antidepressants seem to share noradrenergic and dopaminergic mechanisms of action. Stimulant medications continue to be the first-line drug of choice for uncomplicated ADHD at any age, with antidepressants for nonresponders or patients with concurrent psychiatric disorders. There is increasing recognition that ADHD is a heterogeneous disorder with considerable and varied comorbidity. Because stimulants may be less effective in the presence of comorbid disorders or may even exacerbate these conditions, antidepressants may be particularly useful in these complex cases. Other potential advantages of antidepressants over stimulants include a longer duration of action, the feasibility of once-daily dosing without symptom rebound or insomnia, greater flexibility in dosage, the readily available option of monitoring plasma drug-levels (Preskorn, Weller, Weller, & Glotzbach, 1983), and minimal risk of abuse or dependence (Rapoport & Mikkelsen, 1978; Gittelman, 1980). Although all medications have associated short-term adverse effects and our experience with the newer compounds is limited, there are no known long-term deleterious effects associated with chronic administration of these drugs. Current clinical experience suggests that multiple agents may be necessary in the successful treatment of some complex ADHD patients with partial responses or psychiatric comorbidity.

REFERENCES

Abramowicz, M. (1990). Sudden death in children treated with a tricyclic antidepressant. *Medical Letter on Drugs and Therapeutics, 32,* 53.

Adler, L., Resnick, S., Kunz, M., & Devinsky, O. (1995). *Open-label trial of venlafaxine in attention deficit disorder.* New Clinical Drug Evaluation Unit Program, Orlando, FL.

Barrickman, L., Noyes, R., Kuperman, S., Schumacher, E., & Verda, M. (1991). Treatment of ADHD with fluoxetine: A preliminary trial. *Journal of the American Academy of Child and Adolescent Psychiatry, 30,* 762–767.

Barrickman, L., Perry, P., Allen, A., Kuperman, S., Arndt, S., Herrman, K., & Schumacher, E. (1995). Bupropion versus methylphenidate in the treatment of attention-deficit hyperactivity disorder in adults. *Journal of the American Academy of Child and Adolescent Psychiatry, 34,* 649–657.

Biederman, J., Baldessarini, R., Goldblatt, A., Lapey, K., Doyle, A., & Hesslein, P. (1993). A naturalistic study of 24-hour electrocardiographic recordings and echocardiographic finding in children and adolescents treated with desipramine. *Journal of the American Academy of Child and Adolescent Psychiatry, 32,* 805–813.

Biederman, J., Baldessarini, R. J., Wright, V., Keenan, K., & Faraone, S. (1993). A double-blind placebo controlled study of desipramine in the treatment of attention deficit disorder: III. Lack of impact of comorbidity and family history factors on clinical response. *Journal of the American Academy of Child and Adolescent Psychiatry, 32,* 199–204.

Biederman, J., Baldessarini, R. J., Wright, V., Knee, D., & Harmatz, J. (1989). A double-blind placebo controlled study of desipramine in the treatment of attention deficit disorder: I. Efficacy. *Journal of the American Academy of Child and Adolescent Psychiatry, 28,* 777–784.

Biederman, J., Baldessarini, R. J., Wright, V., Knee, K., Harmatz, J., & Goldblatt, A. (1989). A double-blind placebo controlled study of desipramine in the treatment of attention deficit disorder: II. Serum drug levels and cardiovascular findings. *Journal of the American Academy of Child and Adolescent Psychiatry, 28,* 903–911.

Biederman, J., Gastfriend, D. R., & Jellinek, M. S. (1986). Desipramine in the treatment of children with attention deficit disorder. *Journal of Clinical Psychopharmacology, 6,* 359–363.

Biederman, J., Mick, E., Bostic, J. Q., Prince, J., Daly, J., Wilens, T. E., Spencer, T., Garcia-Jetton, J., Russell, R. L., Wozniak, J., & Faraone, S. V. (in press). The naturalistic course of pharmacologic treatment of children with manic-like symptoms. A systematic chart review. *Journal of Clinical Psychiatry.*

Biederman, J., Newcorn, J., & Sprich, S. (1991). Comorbidity of attention deficit hyperactivity disorder with conduct, depressive, anxiety, and other disorders. *American Journal of Psychiatry, 148,* 564–577.

Biederman, J., Thisted, R., Greenhill, L., & Ryan, N. (1995). Estimation of the association between desipramine and the risk for sudden death in 5- to 14-year-old children. *Journal of Clinical Psychiatry, 56,* 87–93.

Brown, T. E., & Gammon, G. D. (1992). ADHD-associated difficulties falling asleep and awakening: Clonidine and methylphenidate treatments. *Scientific Proceedings of the Annual Meeting: American Academy of Child and Adolescent Psychiatry*, p. 76.

Casat, C. D., Pleasants, D. Z., Schroeder, D. H., & Parler, D. W. (1989). Bupropion in children with attention deficit disorder. *Psychopharmacology, 25*, 198–201.

Casat, C. D., Pleasants, D. Z., & Van Wyck Fleet, J. (1987). *Psychopharmacology, 23*, 120–122.

Castellanos, F., Giedd, J., Elia, J., Marsh, W., Ritchie, G., Hamburger, S., & Rapoport, J. (1997). Controlled stimulant treatment of ADHD and comorbid Tourette's syndrome: Effects of stimulant and dose. *Journal of the American Academy of Child and Adolescent Psychiatry, 36*, 589–596.

Comings, D. E., & Comings, B. G. (1988). Tourette's syndrome and attention deficit disorder. In D. J. Cohen, R. D. Bruhn, & J. F. Leckman (Eds.), *Tourette's syndrome and tic disorders: Clinical understanding and treatment*. New York: Wiley.

Conners, C., Casat, C., Gualtieri, C., Weller, E., Reader, M., Reiss, A., Weller, R., Khayrallah, M., & Ascher, J. (1996). Bupropion hydrochloride in attention deficit disorder with hyperactivity. *Journal of the American Academy of Child and Adolescent Psychiatry, 35*, 1314–1321.

Dillon, D. C., Salzman, I. J., & Schulsinger, D. A. (1985). The use of imipramine in Tourette's syndrome and attention deficit disorder: Case report. *Journal of Clinical Psychiatry, 46*, 348–349.

DuPaul, G., Barkley, R., & McMurray, M. (1994). Response of children with ADHD to methylphenidate: Interaction with internalizing symptoms. *Journal of the American Academy of Child and Adolescent Psychiatry, 33*, 894–903.

Findling, R. (1996). Open-label treatment of comorbid depression and attentional disorder with co-administration of SRI's and psychostimulants in children, adolescents, and adults: A case series. *Journal of Child and Adolescent Psychopharmacology, 6*, 165–175.

Findling, R., Schwartz, M., Flannery, D., & Manos, M. (1996). Venlafaxine in adults with ADHD: An open trial. *Journal of Clinical Psychiatry, 57*, 184–189.

Gammon, G. D., & Brown, T. E. (1993). Fluoxetine and methylphenidate in combination for treatment of attention deficit disorder and comorbid depressive disorder. *Journal of Child and Adolescent Psychopharmacology, 3*, 1–10.

Garfinkel, B. D., Wender, P. H., Sloman, L., & O'Neill, I. (1983). Tricyclic antidepressant and methylphenidate treatment of attention deficit disorder in children. *Journal of the American Academy of Child and Adolescent Psychiatry, 22*, 343–348.

Gastfriend, D. R., Biederman, J., & Jellinek, M. S. (1985). Desipramine in the treatment of attention deficit disorder in adolescents. *Psychopharmacology, 21*, 144–145.

Gittelman, R. (1980). Childhood disorders. In D. Klein, F. Quitkin, A. Rifkin, & R. Gittelman (Eds.), *Drug treatment of adult and child psychiatric disorders*. Baltimore: Williams & Wilkins.

Gittelman-Klein, R. (1974). Pilot clinical trial of imipramine in hyperkinetic children. In C. Conners (Ed.), *Clinical use of stimulant drugs in children*. The Hague, Netherlands: Excerpta Medica.

Gittelman-Klein, R., Klein, D. F., Katz, S., Saraf, K., & Pollack, E. (1976). Comparative effects of methylphenidate and thioridazine in hyperkinetic children. *Archives of General Psychiatry, 33*, 1217–1231.

Greenberg, L., Yellin, A., Spring, C., & Metcalf, M. (1975). Clinical effects of imipramine and methylphenidate in hyperactive children. *International Journal of Mental Health, 4*, 144–156.

Grimsley, S., & Jann, M. (1992). Paroxetine, sertraline, and fluvoxamine: New selective serotonin reuptake inhibitors. *Clinical Pharmacy, 11*, 930–957.

Gross, M. (1973). Imipramine in the treatment of minimal brain dysfunction in children. *Psychosomatics, 14*, 283–285.

Gualtieri, C. T., & Evans, R. W. (1988). Motor performance in hyperactive children treated with imipramine. *Perceptual and Motor Skills, 66*, 763–769.

Hinshaw, S., & Erhardt, D. (1991). Attention-Deficit Hyperactivity Disorder. In P. Kendall (Ed.), *Child and adolescent therapy: Cognitive-behavioral procedures*. New York: Guilford Press.

Hoge, S. K., & Biederman, J. (1986). A case of Tourette's syndrome with symptoms of attention deficit disorder treated with desipramine. *Journal of Clinical Psychiatry, 47*, 478–479.

Hornig-Rohan, M., & Amsterdam, J. (1995). *Venlafaxine vs. stimulant therapy in patients with dual diagnoses of ADHD and depression*. New Clinical Drug Evaluation Unit Program, Orlando, FL.

Huessy, H., & Wright, A. (1970). The use of imipramine in children's behavior disorders. *Acta Psaedosychiatre, 37,* 194–199.

Jankovic, J. (1993). Deprenyl in attention deficit associated with Tourette's syndrome. *Archives of Neurology, 50,* 286–288.

Luh, J., Pliszka, S., Olvers, R., & Tatum, R. (1996). *An open trial of venlafaxine in the treatment of attention deficit hyperactivity disorder: A pilot study.* University of Texas Health Science Center at San Antonio.

Kupietz, S. S., & Balka, E. B. (1976). Alterations in the vigilance performance of children receiving amitriptyiline and methylphenidate pharmacotherapy. *Psychopharmacology, 50,* 29–33.

National Institute of Mental Health. (1996). [Unpublished findings from conference on Alternative Pharmacology of ADHD]. Washington, DC: Author.

Nemeroff, C., DeVane, L., & Pollock, B. (1996). Newer antidepressants and the cytochrome P450 system. *American Journal of Psychiatry, 153,* 311–320.

Pataki, C., Carlson, G., Kelly, K., Rapport, M., & Biancaniello, 1. (1993). Side effects of methylphenidate and desipramine alone and in combination in children. *American Journal of Psychiatry, 32,* 1065–1072.

Pliszka, S. R. (1989). Effect of anxiety on cognition, behavior, and stimulant response in ADHD. *Journal of the American Academy of Child and Adolescent Psychiatry, 28,* 882–887.

Preskorn, S. H., Weller, E. B., Weller, R. A., & Glotzbach, E. (1983). Plasma levels of imipramine and adverse effects in children. *American Journal of Psychiatry, 140,* 1332–1335.

Prince, J., Wilens, T., Biederman, J., Spencer, T., & Wozniak, J. (1996). Clonidine for ADHD related sleep disturbances: A systematic chart review of 62 cases. *Journal of the American Academy of Child and Adolescent Psychiatry, 35,* 599–605.

Quinn, P. O., Rapoport, J. L. (1975). One-year follow-up of hyperactive boys treated with imipramine or methylphenidate. *American Journal of Psychiatry, 132,* 241–245.

Rapoport, J., & Mikkelsen, E. (1978). Antidepressants. In J. Werry (Ed.), *Pediatric psychopharmacology.* New York: Brunner/Mazel.

Rapoport, J. L., Quinn, P., Bradbard, G., Riddle, D., & Brooks, E. (1974). Imipramine and methylphenidate treatment of hyperactive boys: A double-blind comparison. *Archives of General Psychiatry, 30,* 789–793.

Rapport, M., Carlson, G., Kelly, K., & Pataki, C. (1993). Methylphenidate and desipramine in hospitalized children: I. Separate and combined effects on cognitive function. *Journal of the American Academy of Child and Adolescent Psychiatry, 32,* 333–342.

Reimherr, F., Hedges, D., Strong, R., & Wender, P. (1995). *An open trial of venlafaxine in adult patients with attention deficit hyperactivity disorder.* New Clinical Drug Evaluation Unit Program, Orlando, FL.

Riddle, M. A., Hardin, M. T., Cho, S. C., Woolston, J. L., & Leckman, J. F. (1988). Desipramine treatment of boys with attention-deficit hyperactivity disorder and tics: Preliminary clinical experience. *Journal of the American Academy of Child and Adolescent Psychiatry, 27,* 811–814.

Simeon, J. G., Ferguson, H. B., & Van Wyck Fleet, J. (1986). Bupropion effects in attention deficit and conduct disorders. *Canadian Journal of Psychiatry, 31,* 581–585.

Singer, S., Brown, J., Quaskey, S., Rosenberg, L., Mellits, E., & Denckla, M. (1994). The treatment of attention-deficit hyperactivity disorder in Tourette's syndrome: A double-blind placebo-controlled study with clonidine and desipramine. *Pediatrics, 95,* 74–81.

Spencer, T. J., Biederman, J., Kerman, K., Steingard, R., & Wilens, T. (1993). Desipramine in the treatment of children with tic disorder or Tourette's syndrome and attention deficit hyperactivity disorder. *Journal of the American Academy of Child and Adolescent Psychiatry, 32,* 354–360.

Spencer, T. J., Biederman, J., Wilens, T., Harding, M., O'Donnell, D., & Griffin, S. (1996). Pharmacotherapy of ADHD across the lifecycle: A literature review. *Journal of the American Academy of Child and Adolescent Psychiatry, 35,* 409–432.

Spencer, T. J., Biederman, J., Wilens, T., Steingard, R., & Geist, D. (1993). Nortriptyline in the treatment of children with attention deficit hyperactivity disorder and tic disorder or Tourette's syndrome. *Journal of the American Academy or Child and Adolescent Psychiatry, 32,* 205–210.

Swanson, J., Kinsbourne, M., Roberts, W., & Zucker, K. (1978). Time-response analysis of the effect of stimulant medication on the learning ability of children referred for hyperactivity. *Pediatrics, 61,* 21–24.

Tannock, R., Ickowicz, A., & Shachar, R. (1995). Differential effects of methylphenidate on working memory in ADHD children with and without comorbid anxiety. *Journal of the American Academy of Child and Adolescent Psychiatry, 34,* 886–896.

Taylor, E., Schachar, R., Thorley, G., Wieselberg, H. M., Everitt, B., & Rutter, M. (1987). Which boys respond to stimulant medication? A controlled trial of methylphenidate in boys with disruptive behaviour. *Psychology and Medicine, 17,* 121–143.

Voelker. S. L., Lachar. D., & Gdowski. L. L. (1983). The personality inventory for children and response to methylphenidate: Preliminary evidence for predictive validity. *Journal of Pediatric Psychology, 8,* 161–169.

Watter, N., & Dreyfuss, F . E. (1973). Modifications of hyperkinetic behavior by nortriptyline. *Virginia Medical Monthly, 100,* 123–126.

Weizman, A., Weitz, R., Szekely, F., Tyano, S., & Belmaker, R. (1984). Combination of neuroleptic and stimulant treatment in ADHD. *Journal of the American Academy of Child Psychiatry, 23,* 295–298.

Wender, P. H., & Reimherr, F. W. (1990). Bupropion treatment of attention-deficit hyperactivity disorder in adults. *American Journal of Psychiatry, 147,* 1018–1020.

Werry, J. (1980). Imipramine and methylphenidate in hyperactive children. *Journal of Child Psychology and Psychiatry, 21,* 27–35.

West, S., McElroy, S., Strakowski, S., Keck, P., & McConville, B. (1995). Attention deficit hyperactivity disorder in adolescent mania. *American Journal of Psychiatry, 152,* 271–274.

Whalen, C. K., & Henker, B . (1992). The social profile of attention-deficit hyperactivity disorder. *Child and Adolescent Psychiatric Clinics of North America, 1,* 395–410.

Wilens, T., Biederman, J., Baldessarini, R., Geller, B., Schliefer, D., Spencer, T., Birmaher, B., & Goldblatt, A. (1996). Cardiovascular effects of therapeutic doses of tricyclic antidepressants in children and adolescents. *Journal of the American Academy of Child and Adolescent Psychiatry, 35,* 1491–1501.

Wilens, T. E., Biederman, J., Baldessarini, R. J., Pupolo, P. R., & Flood, J. G. (1992). Developmental changes in serum concentrations of desipramine and 2-Hydroxydesipramine during treatment with desipramine. *Journal of the American Academy of Child and Adolescent Psychiatry, 31,* 691–698.

Wilens, T. E., Biederman, J., Geist, D. E., Steingard, R., & Spencer, T. (1993). Nortriptyline in the treatment of attention deficit hyperactivity disorder: A chart review of 58 cases. *Journal of the American Academy of Child and Adolescent Psychiatry, 32,* 343–349.

Wilens, T. E., Biederman, J., Prince, J., Spencer, T. J., Faraone, S. V., Warburton, R., Schleifer, D., Harding, M., Linehan, C., & Geller, D. (1996). Six week, double blind, placebo controlled study of desipramine for adult attention deficit hyperactivity disorder. *American Journal of Psychiatry, 153,* 1147–1153.

Wilens, T. E., Spencer, T. J., Biederman, J., Wozniak, J., & Connor, D. (1994). Combined pharmacotherapy: An emerging trend in pediatric psychopharmacology. *Journal of the American Academy of Child and Adolescent Psychiatry, 34,* 110–112.

Winsberg, B. G., Bialer, I., Kupietz, S., & Tobias, J. (1972). Effects of imipramine and dextroamphetamine on behavior of neuropsychiatrically impaired children. *American Journal of Psychiatry, 128,* 1425–1431.

Wozniak, J., & Biederman, J. (1996). A pharmacological approach to the quagmire of comorbidity in juvenile mania. *Journal of the American Academy of Child and Adolescent Psychiatry, 35,* 826–828.

Wozniak, J., Biederman, J., Kiely, K., Ablon, S., Faraone, S., Mundy, E., & Mennin, D. (1995). Mania-like symptoms suggestive of childhood onset bipolar disorder in clinically referred children. *Journal of the American Academy of Child and Adolescent Psychiatry, 34,* 867–876.

Yepes, L. E., Balka, E. B., Winsberg, B. G., & Bialer, I. (1977). Amitriptyline and methylphenidate treatment of behaviorally disordered children. *Journal of Child Psychology and Psychiatry, 18,* 39–52.

Zametkin, A., Rapoport, J. L., Murphy, D. L., Linnoila, M., & Ismond, D. (1985). Treatment of hyperactive children with monoamine oxidase inhibitors: I. Clinical efficacy. *Archives of General Psychiatry, 42,* 962–966.

Chapter 19

OTHER MEDICATIONS IN THE TREATMENT OF CHILD AND ADOLESCENT ADHD

Daniel F. Connor

ع

A considerable literature on the clinical use of nonstimulant, nonantidepressant medication in treating children and adolescents with Attention-Deficit/Hyperactivity Disorder (ADHD) has accrued over the past 20 years. Stimulants such as methylphenidate (Ritalin) and dextroamphetamine (Dexedrine) are generally considered first-line medications for uncomplicated ADHD (ADHD Simplex). Antidepressants (ADs), especially tricyclic antidepressants (TCAs), are considered by most clinicians to be second-line drugs of choice and possibly first-choice agents in ADHD complicated by tics, anxiety, or depression. However, for a variety of reasons, about 20% to 30% of ADHD children and adolescents do not respond satisfactorily to these agents.

Several possible reasons exist for lack of response. As defined by the fourth edition of the *Diagnostic and Statistical Manual of Mental Disorders* (DSM-IV; American Psychiatric Association, 1994), ADHD is a heterogeneous disorder of unknown etiology that can result from a multitude of biopsychosocial risk factors. Comorbidity with conduct, depressive, anxiety, and tic disorders is common (Biederman, Newcorn, & Sprich, 1991). These ADHD subgroups may have differing pharmacological responses as well as differing risk factors and clinical prognoses. Some children may have difficulty tolerating the side effects of stimulants or TCA. For example, children with ADHD who are also very anxious may have a less satisfactory treatment response to stimulants, which can increase anxiety because of sympathomimetic effects on the central nervous system (CNS). Children with preexisting cardiac disease or a family history significant for early-onset cardiac disease may be at increased risk for cardiovascular side effects of TCAs. In addition, some children and adolescents may have only a partial response to standard medication treatment for ADHD.

For these reasons there has been clinical interest in the possible efficacy of other medications in the treatment of ADHD. It should be noted that none of the nonstimulant medications discussed in this chapter have been approved by the Food and Drug Administration

(FDA) for pharmaceutical manufacturer advertising as safe and effective for the treatment of ADHD. However, the FDA does not limit physician prescribing of a drug for an off-label indication if rational scientific theory, expert medical opinion, or evidence from controlled clinical trials exists that the drug may be safe and effective for the unapproved condition. None of the medications reviewed herein are "experimental" treatments in the sense of being new, untried, or untested. All the following medications are well-known to clinicians and FDA approved for manufacturer advertising in conditions other than ADHD. Some of these medications have been used for ADHD for the past two decades and much experience has accumulated about their use.

This chapter reviews the clinical use of antihypertensive agents, including clonidine, guanfacine, and beta-adrenergic blockers and anticonvulsants (predominantly carbamazepine) in the treatment of ADHD. For each medication, a brief review of the evidence for efficacy is followed by a discussion of mechanism of action and pharmacokinetics, short- and long-term treatment effects, procedures for a clinical trial, and treatment-emergent side effects. The current place of neuroleptics and combined pharmacotherapy in the treatment of ADHD is discussed next. Finally, a brief discussion alerts the reader to medications not considered effective in the treatment of ADHD.

WHEN TO CONSIDER USING NONSTIMULANT, NONANTIDEPRESSANT MEDICATIONS IN THE TREATMENT OF ADHD

Following is a list of some reasons to consider prescribing these "other medications'" to children and adolescents diagnosed with ADHD.

1. Unsatisfactory clinical response to stimulants or ADs (after clinical trials of two or three different stimulants, TCAs, or other ADs).
2. Inability to tolerate treatment-emergent side effects of stimulants or antidepressants.
3. At-risk children because of tics or Tourette syndrome (stimulants, bupropion) or a worrisome cardiac history in the child or family (TCAs).
4. Development of tolerance to the therapeutic benefits of stimulants or ADs.
5. ADHD symptoms in special populations: psychoses, schizophrenia, bipolar illness, borderline personality disorder, seizure disorder, or pervasive developmental disorder.
6. Presence of severe mental retardation (IQ $\leq$ 45 or mental age $\leq$ 4.5 years).
7. Use in combination with a stimulant or AD to augment a partial but inadequate response to monotherapy.
8. Use in combination with a stimulant or AD to treat a comorbid diagnostic condition.

As with the prescribing of any medication, documentation of valid reasons for the use of a nonstimulant, nonantidepressant drug for the treatment of ADHD in the medical record, discussion of the risk/benefit ratio with child and family, and education as to clinical procedures, follow-up, and time course of a medication trial are to be completed by the physician prior to initiating medication therapy. Clinicians who prescribe these other medications for ADHD are generally on firm clinical ground if a previous trial of stimulant or AD medication has failed or if they document scientifically valid reasons for preferring these drugs (Green, 1995).

ANTIHYPERTENSIVE MEDICATION
IN THE TREATMENT OF ADHD

Clonidine

Evidence for Efficacy in ADHD

Clonidine has been FDA approved for use in hypertension since the early 1970s. Because of its well-recognized ability to downregulate noradrenergic output from the CNS, its possible use in psychiatric disorders characterized by excessive autonomic nervous system overarousal, hyperactivity, and impulsivity, including ADHD, has been explored. In child and adolescent psychiatry, clonidine was first used to treat tics in children with Tourette syndrome (Cohen, Young, Nathanson, & Shaywitz, 1979). The clonidine challenge test was used in the early 1980s to investigate noradrenergic receptor sensitivity changes associated with methylphenidate treatment (Hunt, Cohen, Anderson, & Clark, 1984). A recent literature review (Connor & Fletcher, 1998) identified 39 reports of clonidine use in child/adolescent ADHD and associated conditions since 1980. Clonidine use has been investigated in ADHD, ADHD comorbid with Tourette syndrome and tic disorders, ADHD and aggression associated with conduct disorder, conduct disorder without ADHD, sleep disorders associated with ADHD, overarousal and aggression in posttraumatic stress disorder in preschool children, ADHD symptoms in autism, and ADHD symptoms in children and adolescents with fragile-X syndrome.

The majority of reports are single case descriptions or open pilot studies. Two methodologically controlled studies of clonidine use in ADHD both report benefits of clonidine 0.1 to 0.3 mg/day as compared to placebo on parent and teacher rating scales of ADHD symptoms (Hunt, Minderaa, & Cohen, 1985; Gunning, 1992). Two controlled studies of clonidine use in Tourette syndrome comorbid with ADHD found differing results. Benefits on both ADHD symptoms and tic frequency were reported in one study (Leckman et al., 1991). Singer et al. (1995) found little benefit for clonidine as compared to placebo in 34 children with Tourette syndrome and ADHD. Two controlled studies in autistic children with symptoms of inattention, impulsivity, and hyperactivity also reported benefits with clonidine therapy, but frequent side effects caused many patients to discontinue clonidine (Jaselskis, Cook, Fletcher, & Leventhal, 1992; Frankenhauser, Karumanchi, German, Yates, & Karumanchi, 1992).

These studies generally describe benefits for behavioral target symptoms of aggression, hyperactivity, overarousal, impulsivity, and sleep disturbance as assessed by observer completed rating scales. Fewer benefits are reported with clonidine for sustained attentional deficits and cognitive symptoms of ADHD. This literature continues to evolve. Presently, some support is found for clonidine's efficacy in ADHD. However, claims of equal efficacy to the stimulants should not be accepted until more methodologically controlled studies are completed. In addition, clinical research has not yet shown clonidine's efficacy in ADHD to be independent of its sedative side effects. Until such research is completed, clonidine should not yet be considered a first- or second-line medication treatment for ADHD.

Mechanism of Action/Pharmacokinetics

Clonidine stimulates presynaptic alpha-2-adrenergic receptors in the brain stem (locus coeruleus), resulting in a reduction in sympathetic outflow from the CNS. The decrease in plasma norepinephrine (NE) is directly related to clonidine's hypotensive action. In the prefrontal cortex (PFC), clonidine may also influence postsynaptic alpha-2-adrenergic receptors. Three subtypes of alpha-2-adrenergic receptors have recently been cloned in humans:

the alpha-2-A, alpha-2-B, and alpha-2-C. Genes for these receptors reside on chromosomes 10, 2, and 4, respectively. Postsynaptic alpha-2-A receptors may mediate NE neurotransmission in the PFC to enhance inhibition over lower CNS structures and enhance working memory under distracting conditions (see Arnsten, Steere, & Hunt, 1996). Because deficits in behavioral inhibition and working memory are two neuropsychological constructs thought to be crucial in the pathoetiology of ADHD (Barkley, 1997), scientific reasons exist to think that clonidine may be effective in ADHD.

Clonidine is well absorbed after oral administration. In adults, peak plasma concentrations (and maximal hypotensive effects) are observed 1 to 3 hours after dose administration. Metabolism occurs both by hepatic mechanisms (50%) and by unchanged renal excretion (50%). There are no active metabolites. The excretion half-life of oral clonidine in children averages 8 to 12 hours with considerable individual variability. In contrast to the pharmacokinetic half-life described earlier, the behavioral effects of clonidine last only 3 to 6 hours. Three or four divided daily dosings are thus required in children and adolescents to maintain plasma levels, prevent clonidine withdrawal symptoms, and preserve behavioral effects.

Clonidine is also available as a skin patch called the transdermal therapeutic system (TTS). This patch allows administration of clonidine without the use of pills. Clonidine is delivered by diffusion and absorption through the skin. Dosing is a function of the area of the patch. A more steady plasma level is achieved which can result in decreased frequency and intensity of side effects, which are often related to peak serum levels after oral absorption. The patch should be replaced every 5 days.

Treatment Effects

Clonidine appears partially effective in decreasing the frequency, intensity, and severity of impulsivity and hyperactivity and improving frustration tolerance in children and adolescents with ADHD, Combined Type or ADHD, Predominantly Hyperactive–Impulsive Type (DSM-IV). Although there are theoretical reasons to believe that clonidine may improve cognitive functioning in ADHD patients, this has not yet been shown clinically. Therefore, clonidine should not be used for ADHD, Predominantly Inattentive Type (DSM-IV). ADHD children presenting clinically with high levels of arousal, impulsivity, explosive aggression to minimal environmental provocation, motor overactivity, and associated comorbid conduct disorder appear to respond best. It should be noted that clonidine is not a treatment for the more covert forms of aggression frequently found in conduct disorder (cheating, lying, stealing, vandalism).

Clonidine is also useful for tic disorders which often present clinically with ADHD. Many studies (although not all) have reported a reduction in frequency and severity of motor and vocal tics with clonidine treatment when tics occur either with or without accompanying ADHD.

Sleep disturbances frequently accompany both ADHD and the treatment of ADHD (stimulants). A growing body of clinical case reports suggest that clonidine can help reduce initial insomnia either caused by difficulties settling for sleep in the hyperactive ADHD child or as a result of lingering stimulants in the plasma at bedtime that cause insomnia. In normal young adult volunteers, a single dose of clonidine 0.25 mg to 0.3 mg was significantly associated with electroencephelograph-documented reduced Stage 1 and rapid-eye-movement (REM) sleep and increased Stage 2 (deeper) sleep (Carskadon, Cavallo, & Rosekind, 1989).

Clonidine has also found some clinical success in treating target symptoms of adrenergic overarousal, impulsivity, hyperactivity, and explosive aggression and temper tantrums in special populations of children. These include pervasive developmental disorders, fragile-X syndrome (X-linked mental retardation), and posttraumatic stress disorders.

Procedures for a Clinical Trial

Indications for clonidine use in child and adolescent psychiatry are not firmly established and continue to evolve with ongoing clinical research. Clonidine may be considered as follows: (1) as a third-line medication for overarousal, impulsivity, excessive hyperactivity, and explosive outbursts of aggression in ADHD children and adolescents who have not responded satisfactorily to previous trials of stimulants or TCAs; (2) as combination therapy with stimulants to decrease motoric overarousal and impulsivity not fully responsive to stimulant monotherapy; (3) as combination therapy with stimulants to treat sleep disturbances associated with ADHD or stimulant therapy; (4) in special populations such as pervasive developmental disorders, fragile-X syndrome, or posttraumatic stress disorder when these conditions are accompanied by excessive and impairing adrenergic overarousal, impulsivity, hyperactivity, sleep disturbance, or aggression; and (5) in ADHD children with comorbid tic disorders or Tourette syndrome.

There are several exclusion criteria for a clonidine trial. Because of clonidine's known cardiovascular effects, children and adolescents with preexisting cardiac disease, especially sinus or atrioventricular node dysfunction and bradycardic arrhythmias, syncope, vascular disease such as Raynaud syndrome, and a family history of early-onset cardiac disease or syncope in first-degree relatives, are not candidates for a clonidine trial. Children and adolescents with a history of melancholic depression (Major Depressive Disorder) also should not receive clonidine because of clonidine's known risk in exacerbating an underlying vulnerability to depression.

Prior to initiating a trial of clonidine, the child should have a baseline physical examination completed within 1 year of drug initiation, baseline electrocardiogram (EKG), baseline pulse, and baseline blood pressure. The standard daily dose range of clonidine for ADHD, Tourette syndrome, and disturbances of adrenergic overarousal is 0.10 mg to 0.30 mg. Rarely, higher doses up to 0.5 mg to 0.8 mg have been reported in the literature. Sleep disturbances can sometimes be treated with lower doses of 0.05 mg to 0.20 mg given one hour before bedtime. Oral clonidine is commonly given to 6- to 13-year-old children in three to four divided daily doses to prevent withdrawal effects. In older adolescents who exhibit slower drug metabolism, oral clonidine can be given two or three times daily. Clonidine, both oral and patch must be given 7 days a week to avoid withdrawal symptoms.

Oral clonidine is initiated at low doses of 0.025 mg in smaller children and 0.05 mg in larger children and adolescents, given first in the evening (because of sedative side effects). The dose is titrated upwards by 0.025 mg to 0.05 mg every 4 to 5 days, given twice, then three times, then four times per day in divided doses until therapeutic benefit, unacceptable side effects, or the upper limit of dose titration is reached. Sedation and occasional irritability limit the rate of dose titration. A useful rule of thumb to limit these side effects is to "start low and go slow." A stable full dose can generally be achieved in 2 to 5 weeks after oral clonidine initiation.

Treatment effects, independent of sedation, are noticeable after 1 month of therapy at full dose. Therefore, a clonidine initiation trial to determine efficacy in a child or adolescent will take 1 to 3 months to achieve. Parents and children need to be informed about the expected time course of treatment with clonidine. If, at the end of the clonidine initiation phase, benefit on drug is established, the length of a clonidine maintenance phase can be discussed with the child and family. It is useful to think in school-year units with consideration given to drug holidays, if possible, during the summer to establish continuing need for clonidine treatment and drug efficacy and to document any treatment-emergent side effects that may become noticeable in retrospect when clonidine therapy is suspended. If, at the end of the clonidine initiation phase, benefit on drug is not established, clonidine can be tapered off slowly to prevent withdrawal symptoms and reassessment can take place.

During the clonidine initiation phase, contact with the prescribing physician should occur regularly. Blood pressure and pulse should be obtained weekly during dose titration. Pulse < 55 bpm (beats per minute) or blood pressure < 80/50 mm Hg should prompt re-evaluation and possibly lowering of dose. The physician should inquire about side effects, especially exercise-related dizziness, shortness of breath, or syncope. These may be secondary to clonidine-induced adrenergic blockade preventing the cardiovascular system from adequately responding to increased exercise-mediated metabolic demands. Exercise-related treatment-emergent clonidine side effects require immediate evaluation by the child's physician. At full dose, a repeat EKG is recommended to rule out bradycardic arrhythmias secondary to clonidine use. During the maintenance phase, regular physician contact should occur every 2 months. Pulse and blood pressure should be checked at this time. Height and weight should be followed every 4 to 5 months. Assessment of continuing efficacy on clonidine should be determined from child, parent, and teacher reports and rating scales at each visit. For long-term use, an EKG should be completed on a yearly basis.

As an alternative to oral clonidine therapy, the transdermal (patch) system may be utilized. This system is available in a brand-name formulation labeled Catapress-TTS 1, 2, or 3, which corresponds approximately to daily doses of 0.1, 0.2, and 0.3 mg, respectively. Children and adolescents are generally begun on oral clonidine to establish efficacy (initiation phase). If effective and desired, they are then shifted to the TTS (maintenance phase). The clonidine skin patch is placed on a hairless and inaccessible area such as the back. It generally tolerates brief exposure to moisture (perspiration, shower, bath) but may need replacement after swimming. The patch maintains a constant plasma level for about 5 days in children and adolescents. It must then be replaced. Because absorption to plasma is constant and does not peak as with oral dosing, side effects may be less with the transdermal preparation.

Side Effects

Table 19.1 lists frequent treatment-emergent side effects from oral clonidine and compares them with the side effect profiles of other antihypertensive agents occasionally used in ADHD. Most side effects are mild and tend to diminish over time with continued therapy. The most frequent are drowsiness, dizziness, and sedation. These can be problematic in the first 4 to 6 weeks of dose titration. They are occasionally accompanied by increased irritability. Side effects can be helped by a slower rate of dose titration and by dose reduction. Early-morning awakening, perhaps a consequence of nighttime clonidine withdrawal, can also be seen. Children may be less susceptible to the anticholinergic effects of clonidine (constipation, dry mouth) than adults. A contact dermatitis is seen under the patch in 15% to 20% when the transdermal system is used. Switching to a different location, use of a topical steroid cream, and returning to oral administration are effective strategies for management.

A potentially serious side effect of clonidine use (and with all antihypertensives discussed in this chapter) is a withdrawal syndrome upon abrupt medication discontinuation. This syndrome is characterized by rebound adrenergic overdrive leading to symptoms of hypertension, agitation, fever, headache, chest pain, sleep disturbance, nausea, and vomiting. Two types of clonidine-adverse cardiovascular treatment-emergent side effect patterns have been described (Cantwell, Swanson, & Connor, 1997). In the first type, abrupt clonidine discontinuation leads to the previously mentioned signs of adrenergic overdrive, which is ameliorated by clinical recognition of the withdrawal syndrome and reintroduction of clonidine. In the second type, high dose and possibly prolonged time on the drug lead to bradycardic arrhythmias, fatigue, lethargy, and hypotension. This type can be identified by EKG and vital sign monitoring and responds to dose reduction or clonidine discontinuation.

TABLE 19.1. Common Treatment-Emergent Side Effects of Oral
Antihypertensive Agents

Side effect	Clonidine	Guanfacine	Beta blockers (CNS acting)
Drowsiness	33%	13%	25%
Dizziness	16%	8%	8%
Sedation	10%	8%	28%
Weakness	10%	7%	17%
Sleep disturbance	10%	5%	18%
Depression	5%	<1%	8%
Cardiac arrhythmia	5%	<1%	5%
Nausea/vomiting	5%	>1%	18%
Irritability	3%	<1%	10%
Orthostatic hypotension	3%	<1%	18%
Weight gain	1%	<1%	<1%
Hallucinations	1%	<1%	9%

To prevent withdrawal, clonidine should be discontinued gradually when stopping the medication. Tapering can be accomplished by decreasing clonidine 0.05 mg every 3 days. Caution must be taken by physician and family to prevent sudden discontinuation (e.g., prescription running out, missed appointments).

Guanfacine

Evidence for Efficacy in ADHD

Guanfacine is an orally administered centrally acting antihypertensive agent that also stimulates CNS alpha-2-adrenergic autoreceptors to downregulate sympathomimetic outflow from the brainstem. It possesses a more selective receptor-binding profile, which may confer less risk of sedation and hypotensive side effects than clonidine. Clinical experience with this agent to treat ADHD is only just beginning. Hunt, Arnsten, and Asbell (1995) reported the results of an open clinical trial of guanfacine in 13 children and adolescents (mean age 11.1 years) with ADHD. At an average dose of 3.2 mg/day, parent rating scales documented significant improvement in hyperactivity, inattention, and immaturity, but not for mood or aggression. In another prospective open-label clinical trial, guanfacine 0.5 mg/day to 3.0 mg/day was found significantly effective in reducing ADHD target symptoms in 15 boys ages 7 to 17 years as assessed by parent completed rating scales and physician assessed global clinical impression (Horrigan & Barnhill, 1995). In a third open clinical trial, 10 patients with ADHD and comorbid Tourette syndrome received guanfacine (average dose 1.5 mg/day) (Chappell et al., 1995). Some efficacy in decreasing motor and vocal tics was found. Parent ratings of ADHD symptoms were not significantly reduced on guanfacine. Interestingly, some effects were reported on cognitive measures of ADHD. A reduction in commission errors and omission errors on a continuous performance test were found. This is in contrast to the lack of cognitive effects reported for clonidine. To date, there are no controlled studies of guanfacine in ADHD.

Mechanism of Action/Pharmacokinetics

Guanfacine is an orally administered, centrally acting antihypertensive with alpha-2-adrenergic receptor agonist properties. Receptor binding studies have shown a greater receptor specificity for guanfacine as compared to clonidine for the adrenergic alpha-2-A receptor. This receptor may be involved in mediating norepinephrine effects in the PFC involving inhibition and working memory. Guanfacine also interacts less with alpha-1, beta-adrenergic, histaminergic, and possibly dopaminergic receptors than clonidine (Cornish, 1988). As a result, there is theoretically less risk of side effects with guanfacine as compared to clonidine, especially sedation and rebound hypertension on abrupt discontinuation.

Guanfacine is well absorbed after oral administration. In adults, peak plasma concentrations occur on average 2.6 hours after a single oral dose. About 50% is excreted unchanged in the urine and 50% is hepatically metabolized. There are no active metabolites. The pharmacokinetic half-life in children is 13 to 14 hours, leading to clinical dosing recommendations of twice to three times daily divided doses in younger patients (Horrigan & Barnhill, 1995). This is a longer excretion half-life than reported for clonidine.

Treatment Effects

The place for guanfacine in the clinical treatment of children and adolescents with ADHD is not yet established. Although open pilot studies report encouraging results with less side effects than clonidine, no controlled studies have been completed to date. Much like clonidine, improvement in hyperactive, impulsive, overarousal symptoms are reported on observer completed rating scales. Unlike clonidine, some cognitive benefits on attention may occur with guanfacine treatment. Preliminary indications also suggest some benefit in tic disorders.

Procedures for a Clinical Trial

Indications for guanfacine use in child and adolescent psychiatry are not yet established. Further clinical research is presently ongoing. Guanfacine might be considered in an ADHD child (older than 7 years) or adolescent with comorbid tic disorder and/or impulsivity/hyperactivity after treatment failures with more established ADHD medications (stimulants, ADs); especially if they might benefit from decreased adrenergic overarousal but might not tolerate the side effects of clonidine. Guanfacine is not indicated in children with preexisting cardiac, renal, or vascular disease.

In open pilot research, the dose range for guanfacine is 0.5 mg/day to 3.0 mg/day (Horrigan & Barnhill, 1995) or 4.0 mg/day (Hunt et al., 1995). Therapeutic administration at peak dose is most often divided into two (for adolescents) to four (for young children) daily dosings. Guanfacine is initiated at 0.5 mg given at bedtime and titrated upwards by 0.25 mg to 0.5 mg increments every 5 to 7 days. Vital signs, side effects, and treatment benefits are checked by the prescribing physician in follow-up every 2 weeks during dose titration. Currently, there is too little experience with guanfacine in children to make EKG recommendations at the present time. If treatment benefits occur and a stable maintenance dose is achieved, a reasonable frequency of follow-up visits would be once every 2 months.

Side Effects

Table 19.1 lists frequent treatment-emergent side effects of guanfacine and compares them with other antihypertensive agents occasionally used in ADHD. In general, the side effect profile is similar to clonidine. However, because of increased receptor specificity, side effects with guanfacine are generally less frequent or severe when compared to clonidine. Similar to clonidine, there is a risk of rebound hypertension upon abrupt guanfacine discontinuation. Dose changes should be accomplished slowly (0.5 mg changes every 2 to 3 days) to prevent adrenergic rebound and withdrawal symptoms when guanfacine dose is reduced or the medication will be stopped.

Beta-Adrenergic Blockers

Evidence for Efficacy in ADHD

Beta-blockers are a family of agents that competitively inhibit norepinephrine and epinephrine actions at beta-adrenergic receptor sites both centrally and in the periphery. Clinical studies of beta-blockers in child and adolescent psychiatry are limited to open designs, generally in subjects with CNS damage, pervasive developmental disorders, or mental retardation (for review, see Connor, 1993). In ADHD, there presently exists one methodologically controlled study of pindolol (a centrally acting beta-blocker) in comparison with placebo and methylphenidate (MPH) (Buitelaar, van de Gaag, Swaab-Barneveld, & Kuiper, 1996). Fifty-two children, ages 7 to 13 years, received either pindolol and MPH, MPH 10 mg twice a day alone, or pindolol 20 mg twice a day alone under blinded conditions for 4 weeks. Outcome was assessed by parent-, teacher-, and clinician-completed rating scales. Pindolol was found modestly effective in ADHD and just as effective as MPH in decreasing impulsivity/hyperactivity but less effective than MPH for cognitive symptoms of ADHD. However, because of a high incidence of side effects, including nightmares, hallucinations, and paraesthesias, pindolol was stopped in all 32 children receiving this drug. In an open prospective study of 12 children, adolescents, and young adults with CNS deficits, significant aggression, and ADHD symptoms, nadolol (a peripherally acting beta-blocker with little penetration into the CNS) 2.5 mg/kg/day was not found to significantly reduce parent- and teacher-rated ADHD symptoms. Significant improvements in aggression were found (Connor, Ozbayrak, Benjamin, Ma, & Fletcher, 1997). Nadolol was very well tolerated with few side effects. This study suggests that peripherally acting beta-blockers may be effective for some aggressive/hyperactive symptoms without inducing the side effects seen with more CNS acting beta-blockers. However, much more controlled research is needed before beta-blockers can be recommended as treatment for ADHD.

Mechanism of Action/Pharmacokinetics

In the brain, the predominant beta-adrenergic receptors are beta-1-noradrenergic receptors. In the peripheral nervous system, beta-1 receptors mediate cardiac effects and beta-2 receptors mediate bronchodilation and vasodilation. Beta blockers are classified as to whether they are central and peripheral acting (propranolol, metoprolol, pindolol) or peripheral acting with little CNS penetration (nadolol, atenolol). The family of beta-blockers is also classified as to what types of beta adrenergic receptors are competitively antagonized: nonselective beta-blockers block both beta-1 and beta-2 receptors (propranolol, nadolol, pindolol) and selective beta-blockers inhibit only beta-1 (cardiac) receptors (atenolol, metoprolol).

Beta-blockers are well absorbed after oral administration. The pharmacokinetic half-life varies with the different types of beta-blockers. Nadolol is a long-acting agent which may require two daily doses in children and adolescents. Propranolol and metoprolol are short-acting agents requiring multiple daily doses. Metabolism also varies with the different agents. Nadolol and atenolol undergo no hepatic biotransformation and are largely cleared from the body unchanged by renal mechanisms. Propranolol undergoes extensive hepatic metabolism. The risk of drug–drug interactions in children receiving beta-blockers and other medications is minimized with nadolol or atenolol use and maximized with propranolol use.

Treatment Effects

Children and adolescents with signs of disinhibition and adrenergic overarousal, from CNS disease, developmental disorders, posttraumatic stress disorders, or ADHD, may benefit from beta-blocker therapy. The pediatric treatment literature remains scarce but does suggest some efficacy for severe impulsivity/hyperactivity and explosive outbursts of aggression and temper tantrums. No support for beneficial effects on cognition have been currently reported.

Procedures for a Clinical Trial

Indications for beta-blockers in child psychiatry are generally those noted in the preceding paragraph. Several exclusion criteria exist, which, if present, preclude beta-blocker use. These are preexisting asthma, reactive airway disease, insulin-dependent diabetes mellitus, hyperthyroidism, bradycardic arrhythmias, cardiac disease, renal disease, and melancholic depression (Major Depressive Disorder). The general dose range in child and adolescent psychiatry is around 1.0 mg/kg/day to 5.5 mg/kg/day, with an average daily dose of roughly 2.5 mg/kg/day. The starting dose of beta-blockers is low. Nadolol is begun at 10 mg twice a day and titrated upwards by 10 to 20 mg every 3 to 4 days. In younger children with faster metabolic rates it is generally given in two or three divided daily doses. In adolescents it can be given twice daily. Propranolol can begin at 10 mg twice a day with dose escalation of 10 mg every 3 or 4 days. Because of its shorter half-life, propranolol is given three to four times daily.

Because beta-blockers cause hypotension and lower the heart rate, cardiovascular monitoring is recommended. Baseline pulse, blood pressure, EKG, and physical examination should be completed prior to dose introduction. Exclusion criteria should be reviewed with the child and family. Physician monitoring should take place every 2 weeks during dose titration including monitoring pulse and blood pressure. A dose should be held if pulse falls below 55 bpm or blood pressure is less than 80/55 mm Hg. Once a stable dose is reached, monitoring can take place every 2 months. It is reasonable to repeat the EKG once yearly in patients with ongoing long-term beta-blocker therapy for behavioral reasons.

Side Effects

Table 19.1 lists frequent treatment-emergent side effects of beta blockers and compares them with the side effect profiles of other antihypertensive agents occasionally used in ADHD. CNS-acting beta-blockers have a higher incidence of side effects than peripherally acting agents. These treatment-emergent side effects may include vivid nightmares, hallucinations, depression, numbness and tingling in the extremities (paraesthesias), lethargy, and weakness. Beta-blockers may slow the heart rate to less than 50 bpm. Exacerbation of asthma and bronchospastic disease may occur if exclusion criteria are not followed.

Rebound hypertension and signs of adrenergic hyperactivity can occur if beta-blocker therapy is abruptly discontinued. This may be especially true if combined pharmacotherapy with clonidine is prescribed. Beta-blocker dosages must be tapered gradually to minimize the risk of withdrawal effects.

ANTICONVULSANT MEDICATION IN THE TREATMENT OF ADHD

Anticonvulsants are traditionally used in the management of epilepsy. The primary anticonvulsants in current neurological use are phenytoin, phenobarbital, primadone, carbamazepine, valproic acid, and ethosuximide. Their value in treating behavior disorders, primarily ADHD and conduct disorders, in nonepileptic children and adolescents has been explored since the 1970s. Carbamazepine is the anticonvulsant with the most research and clinical support for the treatment of disruptive behavior disorders.

Carbamazepine

Evidence for Efficacy in ADHD

Carbamazepine (CBZ) is an anticonvulsant found useful in children with generalized tonic–clonic seizures and partial complex seizures and for relief of pain in trigeminal and glossopharyngeal neuralgias. CBZ is also frequently used in Europe for treating ADHD and ADHD comorbid with conduct disorders. Although it has been largely ignored in the United States for the treatment of ADHD, a recent meta-analysis of 10 reports from the world literature, including three controlled studies comparing CBZ to placebo, suggests some efficacy in children with ADHD (Silva, Munoz, & Alpert, 1996). Response rates in open studies were found to be 70% and in controlled studies, 71%. Efficacy correlated with treatment duration suggesting time on drug is important in CBZ treatment of ADHD. Doses ranged from 50 mg to 800 mg/day. Only one study reported CBZ plasma levels, with optimal levels for therapeutic response ranging from 4.8 µg/ml to 10.4 µg/ml (mean 6.2 µg/ml) (Kafantaris et al., 1992).

It remains unclear if conduct disorders independent of comorbid ADHD will respond to CBZ. A double-blind, placebo-controlled study with a parallel groups design and random assignment to placebo or CBZ 400 to 800 mg/day found no significant reduction in overt categorical aggression in 22 children diagnosed with conduct disorder and frequent aggression (Cueva et al., 1996). This is in contrast to open pilot studies which have reported benefits for CBZ in reducing aggressive conduct disorder symptoms. It should be emphasized that these children did not have comorbid ADHD symptoms.

Mechanism of Action/Pharmacokinetics

CBZ is an anticonvulsant with a tricyclic chemical structure that is orally administered. It is a partial agonist of adenosine receptors and appears relatively more selective in its anticonvulsant properties for inhibiting amygdala-kindled seizures, suggesting some possible limbic system specificity over other anticonvulsants. Its anticonvulsant mechanism of action (and possible mechanism of action in ADHD) is unknown. Possibilities include enhancement of CNS inhibition by facilitating gamma aminobutyric acid (GABA, an inhibitory neurotransmitter), inhibition of excitatory amino acid neurotransmission (by blockade of N-methyl-D-aspartate [NMDA] receptors), and/or increasing neuronal membrane stabilization by influencing calcium channels and transcellular transport of sodium and other ions across cell membranes. Possible treatment effects in ADHD may also be partially explained by carbamazepine's weak dopamine and norepinephrine reuptake inhibiting effects as a result of its tricyclic chemical structure.

Carbamazepine comes as both a tablet and suspension formulation available for oral use. Both preparations deliver equivalent amounts of drug to the systemic circulation, but the suspension is absorbed faster. Plasma levels peak at 1½ hours with use of the suspension compared to 4 to 5 hours after ingestion of the oral tablet. Because CBZ induces its own hepatic metabolism, the pharmacokinetic half-life is variable and progressively shortens over the first 4 to 6 weeks of therapy (metabolic autoinduction). Autoinduction may lead to a 50% decline in CBZ serum levels over the first 6 weeks of therapy under constant dosing conditions. Serum levels (and daily dose) must be monitored and continually readjusted during the first 2 months of CBZ therapy (Trimble, 1990). CBZ is metabolized to an active 10,11 epoxide, which also exhibits anticonvulsant activity.

Because hepatic biotransformation and renal clearance are fastest in prepubertal children and faster than adult rates in adolescents, CBZ (and other anticonvulsants) will exhibit a shorter half-life, a higher clearance rate, and a higher mg/kg dosage requirement in young patients than in adults. CBZ has a half-life of 12 hours and it takes 3 to 4 weeks for complete autoinduction to occur. CBZ is generally given two to three times daily to children and adolescents, and plasma monitoring and dose adjustment are required especially during the time of autoinduction.

Treatment Effects

Much further research on CBZ in ADHD is needed before firm conclusions can be drawn about treatment effects in ADHD. Presently, CBZ is not considered a standard treatment for children and adolescents with ADHD. Open and controlled studies generally document some significant benefit for overarousal, aggression, impulsivity, hyperactivity, restlessness, and excitability in children and adolescents with ADHD and no neurological abnormalities. CBZ effects on cognition in ADHD have not yet been studied.

Procedures for a Clinical Trial

Indications for CBZ use in child and adolescent psychiatry and ADHD are not firmly established. CBZ might be considered in the following: (1) in children and adolescents with a comorbid generalized tonic–clonic epilepsy, partial complex epilepsy, or focally abnormal electroencephalograph and accompanying symptoms of ADHD and (2) as a third-line medication for overarousal, impulsivity, hyperactivity, and aggression in ADHD patients who have not responded satisfactorily to several previous trials of more established agents in the treatment of ADHD. Exclusion criteria that preclude the use of CBZ include preexisting hepatic disease, severe allergic responses or skin rashes to previous trials of tricyclic agents, preexisting bone marrow disease, or concomitant clozapine use (an atypical neuroleptic with a 1% risk of inducing agranulocytosis), because of the potential of both medicines to cause bone marrow suppression.

Prior to anticonvulsant therapy, a baseline medical workup is recommended. This should include a screening physical examination completed within the preceding year, complete blood count with differential and platelet count (hematological function tests), liver function tests, and blood urea nitrogen and creatinine clearance (renal function tests). An EKG might be considered because tricyclic agents can cause cardiac intraventricular conduction delay. CBZ is initiated at a dose of 50 mg twice a day and increased in weekly increments of 100 mg up to a daily dose of 10 to 30 mg/kg/day. CBZ is generally prescribed to children and adolescents in three divided daily dosages. Serum levels 4 to 12 µg/ml are considered within the therapeutic range for epilepsy. However, serum levels have not been shown to reliably correlate with treatment response for behavioral disorders. As noted previously, one study of CBZ in ADHD suggested levels above 6.2 µg/ml might be optimal (Kafantaris et al., 1992), but further research is necessary before clinical recommendations can be made.

CBZ shows a narrow therapeutic range before toxic effects are seen. Therapeutic drug monitoring is therefore recommended. Blood levels of anticonvulsants are sampled at trough, at the end of one half-life. Because of autoinduction, levels should be sampled more frequently during the first 2 months of therapy. Generally, sampling after the first week of CBZ use and then again after the first and second month of use will allow adequate dose adjustment in the face of metabolic induction. Levels can then be sampled every 6 to 12 months on a constant dosing schedule. Because of rare risks of bone marrow suppression and hepatotoxicity (see section on side effects, next), blood counts and hepatic enzymes should be followed once every 6 to 12 months. Blood monitoring should occur more frequently if signs and symptoms referable to hematologic, renal, or hepatic disease become clinically manifest (Trimble, 1990; Pellock & Willmore, 1991).

Side Effects

Table 19.2 lists frequent treatment-emergent side effects of oral CBZ. Side effects referable to the CNS are frequent at serum concentrations above 9 µg/ml. Many acute side effects can be avoided by starting at a low dose and titrating slowly. Untoward effects increase with dose noncompliance and intermittent therapy. CBZ therapy should be withdrawn slowly when treatment is discontinued to prevent mild withdrawal effects. Behavioral toxicity has also been reported with CBZ use. Paradoxically, increased hyperactivity, aggression, and impulsivity have been reported in children and adolescents treated with CBZ for aggression (Pleak, Birmaher, Gavrilescu, Abichandani, & Williams, 1988).

Initial concerns that severe and potentially life-threatening side effects of CBZ were common with long-term treatment have not materialized. Although routine monitoring of hepatic functioning reveals elevations in 5% to 15% of CBZ-treated patients, less than 20 cases of significant hepatic complications were reported in the United States from 1978 to 1989 (Pellock & Willmore, 1991). Transient leukopenia occurs commonly in children and adults treated with CBZ. Unrelated to benign leukopenia, agranulocytosis occurs rarely in only 2 cases per 575,000 (Pellock & Willmore, 1991). Severe exfoliative dermatitis alone or as part of a hypersensitivity reaction can seldom occur. The appearance of rash on CBZ should prompt abrupt drug discontinuation and careful ongoing clinical monitoring. The best way

TABLE 19.2. Common Treatment-Emergent Side Effects
of Carbamazepine

Side effect	Percent reporting
CNS	
Dizziness	54%
Headache	46%
Diplopia	38%
Drowiness	31%
Ataxia	23%
Blurred vision	23%
Fatigue	15%
Dysarthria	8%
Irritability	8%
Gastrointestinal	
Nausea	31%
Vomiting	23%
Stomachache	23%
Decreased appetite	8%
Dermatological	
Rash	46%
Hematological	
Leukopenia	46%

to minimize the development of major adverse side effects of CBZ is for the prescribing physician to provide repeated and ongoing education to the patient and family that any indication of systemic illness should lead to prompt medical consultation.

ANTIPSYCHOTIC MEDICATION IN THE TREATMENT OF ADHD

The majority of studies comparing antipsychotic medications with stimulants have reported that stimulants are more effective than antipsychotics in the treatment of ADHD (see Green, 1995). Antipsychotics carry a substantial risk of neurological side effects, including extrapyramidal symptoms (acute dystonia, parkinsonian symptoms, akathisia) and tardive dyskinesia with chronic use. In addition, the sedative effects of antipsychotics may interfere with cognition and learning. Because of these risks, routine neuroleptic therapy for ADHD children and adolescents should be minimized.

However, some exceptions should be noted. Special populations of children and adolescents with ADHD may benefit from antipsychotics. These include ADHD comorbid with severe Tourette syndrome or tic disorder for which an antipsychotic may be indicated. Pervasive developmentally delayed and mentally retarded children often present with symptoms of excessive hyperactivity, impulsivity, and attentional deficits. Thioridazine, chlorpromazine, and haloperidol have been most studied in these populations and generally found significantly effective in controlled investigations when compared to placebo (see Green, 1995, for review). The new atypical antipsychotics including clozapine, risperidone, olanzapine, sertindole, and quetiapine have not been studied for disruptive behavior disorders and ADHD in child and adolescent psychiatry.

COMBINED PHARMACOTHERAPY IN THE TREATMENT OF ADHD

The concurrent use of more than one medication in the treatment of ADHD is increasingly common in clinical practice. However, this remains a poorly researched area and few data from controlled studies are presently available to guide the clinician. The use of more than one agent might be considered in the following circumstances: (1) significant ADHD symptoms only partially responsive to monotherapy; (2) potentiating effects of combined medications on ADHD symptoms (e.g., MPH and TCA); (3) use of lower doses of each agent when combined, reducing the risk of side effects from each agent alone if used in higher doses; and (4) CPT for treatment of ADHD and common medication-responsive comorbid conditions (e.g., Tourette syndrome, severe anxiety or depression, explosive aggression in Conduct Disorder).

Systematic study of the use of combined psychopharmacotherapy in ADHD is only just beginning. Stimulants have been combined with desipramine (Rapport, Carlson, Kelly, & Pataki, 1993). In a placebo-controlled study comparing desipramine alone, MPH alone, and the combination, MPH alone improved vigilance, both drugs alone improved short-term memory and visual problem solving, and the combination improved learning of higher-order relationships. The side effects of the combination were not significantly greater than those for desipramine alone (Pataki, Carlson, Kelly, Rapport, & Biancaniello, 1993). In a retrospective study of the efficacy of nortriptyline in ADHD, Wilens, Biederman, Geist, Steingard, and Spencer (1993) noted that 47% of 58 children and adolescents were receiving adjunctive medications in addition to nortriptyline. Stimulants have also been combined with selective serotonin reuptake inhibiting antidepressants in the treatment of ADHD comorbid with affective disorders or other disruptive behavioral disorders. Gammon and Brown (1993) added fluoxetine to ongoing MPH therapy in 32 child and adolescent patients with ADHD and comorbid Affective Disorder, Oppositional Defiant Disorder (ODD), or Conduct Disorder (CD) and found significant improvements on the combination. No significant or lasting untoward effects of MPH and fluoxetine were reported.

Antihypertensive agents have also been used in combination with stimulants for ADHD comorbid with highly overaroused, impulsive, hyperactive, and explosively aggressive symptoms comorbid with ODD or CD. Clonidine is often added to ongoing MPH therapy (Hunt, Capper, & O'Connell, 1990). No controlled research on this combination is presently available. Several case reports have raised questions about the safety of this combination in subgroups of children (Cantwell et al., 1997), but in general it appears well tolerated if properly monitored by a physician. In adults with ADHD and explosive rage attacks, a small case series found efficacy for the combination of a stimulant and nadolol (Ratey, Greenberg, & Lindem, 1991).

MEDICATIONS NOT FOUND USEFUL IN THE TREATMENT OF ADHD

Several medications have been studied and found not helpful in the clinical treatment of children and adolescents diagnosed with ADHD.

Fenfluramine

In comparison with dextroamphetamine, fenfluramine showed no benefit in treating motor and behavior symptoms in noncognitively delayed children with ADHD (Donnelly et al., 1989). However, in a special population of children with ADHD, mental retardation, and IQ < 45, some support for fenfluramine in comparison to MPH was found for children with more severe mental retardation (Aman, Kern, McGhee, & Arnold, 1993). Fenfluramine must be used cautiously as it depletes CNS serotonin with chronic use.

Antihistamines

Little support is found for efficacy of commonly used antihistamines such as diphenhydramine in the treatment of ADHD.

Benzodiazepines

Studies comparing benzodiazepines such as chlordiazepoxide or diazepam to stimulants and placebo have reported that benzodiazepines lack efficacy in ADHD (see Green, 1995).

Lithium

Lithium has not proved effective in the treatment of ADHD (see Green, 1995). Recently however, phenomenological studies in child and adolescent psychiatry have described comorbidity between ADHD and bipolar disorders in adolescents and raised questions about possible prepubertal onset of Bipolar Disorder being mistaken for ADHD (Wozniak, Biederman, Kiely, Ablon, & Faraone, 1993). Because lithium may be an effective treatment for pediatric bipolar illness and stimulants may exacerbate mania, this possible overlap requires much further clinical research. Currently, lithium is not considered a treatment for ADHD.

Caffeine

Although caffeine is a stimulant, it is not considered a routine treatment for ADHD.

CONCLUSION

This chapter considered the use of "other medications" in the treatment of ADHD. These medications continue to be a focus of clinical research because a not insignificant percentage of ADHD children and adolescents fail to satisfactorily respond to more established agents. Although not FDA approved for pharmaceutical manufacturers advertising as effective in ADHD, these are clinically well-known medications, FDA approved for other indications in medicine, and should not be considered experimental medications. Their judicious and careful clinical use offers hope that ADHD patients not responding to conventional therapies or who possess significant comorbid conditions may be further helped with this often complex, chronic, and disabling disorder.

REFERENCES

Aman, M. G., Kern, R. A., McGhee, D. E., & Arnold, L. E. (1993). Fenfluramine and methylphenidate in chidren with mental retardation and ADHD: Clinical and side effects. *Journal of the American Academy of Child and Adolescent Psychiatry, 32*, 851–859.

American Psychiatric Association. (1994). *Diagnostic and statistical manual of mental disorders* (4th ed.). Washington, DC: Author.

Arnsten, A. F., Steere, J. C., & Hunt, R. D. (1996). The contribution of alpha-2-noradrenergic mechanisms to prefrontal cortical cognitive function. *Archives of General Psychiatry, 53*, 448–455.

Barkley, R. A. (1997). Behavioral inhibition, sustained attention, and executive functions: Constructing a unifying theory of ADHD. *Psychological Bulletin, 121*, 65–94.

Biederman, J., Newcorn, J., & Sprich, S. (1991). Comorbidity of attention deficit hyperactivity disorder with conduct, depressive, anxiety, and other disorders. *American Journal of Psychiatry, 148*, 564–577.

Buitelaar, J. K., van de Gaag, R. J., Swaab-Barneveld, H., & Kuiper, M. (1996). Pindolol and methylphenidate in children with attention-deficit hyperactivity disorder. Clinical efficacy and side effects. *Journal of Child Psychology and Psychiatry, 37*, 587–595.

Cantwell, D. P., Swanson, J., & Connor, D. F. (1997). Adverse response to clonidine. *Journal of the American Academy of Child and Adolescent Psychiatry, 36*, 539–544.

Carskadon, M. A., Cavallo, A., & Rosekind, M. R. (1989). Sleepiness and nap sleep following a morning dose of clonidine. *Sleep, 12*, 338–344.

Chappell, P. B., Riddle, M. A., Scahill, L., Lynch, K. A., Schultz, R., Arnsten, A., Leckman, J. F., & Cohen, D. J. (1995). Guanfacine treatment of comorbid attention deficit hyperactivity disorder and Tourette's syndrome: Preliminary clinical experience. *Journal of the American Academy of Child and Adolescent Psychiatry, 34*, 1140–1146.

Cohen, D. J., Young, J. G., Nathanson, J. A., & Shaywitz, B. A. (1979). Clonidine in Tourette's syndrome. *Lancet, 2*, 551–553.

Connor, D. F. (1993). Beta blockers for aggression: A review of the pediatric experience. *Journal of Child and Adolescent Psychopharmacology, 3*, 99–114.

Connor, D. F., Ozbayrak, K. R., Benjamin, S., Ma, Y., & Fletcher, K. E. (1997). A pilot study of nadolol for overt aggression in developmentally delayed individuals. *Journal of the American Academy of Child and Adolescent Psychiatry, 36*, 826–834.

Connor, D. F., & Fletcher, K. E. (1998). *Clonidine in the treatment of children with ADHD and associated conditions: A critical review of efficacy.* Manuscript submitted for publication.

Cornish, L. A. (1988). Guanfacine hydrochloride: A centrally acting antihypertensive agent. *Journal of Clinical Pharmacology, 7*, 187–197.

Cueva, J. E., Overall, J. E., Small, A. A., Armenteros, J. L., Perry, R., & Campbell, M. (1996). Carbamazepine in aggressive children with conduct disorder: A double-blind and placebo-controlled study. *Journal of the American Academy of Child and Adolescent Psychiatry, 35*, 480–490.

Donnelly, M., Rapoport, J. L., Potter, W. Z., Oliver, J., Keysor, C. S., & Murphy, D. L. (1989). Fenfluramine and dextroamphetamine treatment of childhood hyperactivity. *Archives of General Psychiatry, 46*, 205–212.

Frankenhauser, M., Karumanchi, V., German, M., Yates, A., & Karumanchi, S. (1992). A double-blind placebo-controlled study of the efficacy of transdermal clonidine in autism. *Journal of Clinical Psychiatry, 53*, 77–82.

Gammon, G. D., & Brown, T. E. (1993). Fluoxetine and methylphenidate in combination for treatment of attention deficit disorder and comorbid depressive disorder. *Journal of Child and Adolescent Psychopharmacology, 3*, 1–10.

Green, W. H. (1995). The treatment of attention-deficit hyperactivity disorder with nonstimulant medications. *Child and Adolescent Psychiatric Clinics of North America, 4*, 169–195.

Gunning, B. (1992). *A controlled trial of clonidine in hyperkinetic children.* Doctoral dissertation, Department of Child and Adolescent Psychiatry, Academic Hospital, Erasmus University, Rotterdam, The Netherlands.

Horrigan, J. P., & Barnhill, L. J. (1995). Guanfacine treatment of attention-deficit hyperactivity disorder in boys. *Journal of Child and Adolescent Psychopharmacology, 5*, 215–223.

Hunt, R. D., Arnsten, A. F. T., & Asbell, M. D. (1995). An open trial of guanfacine in the treatment of attention-deficit hyperactivity disorder. *Journal of the American Academy of Child and Adolescent Psychiatry, 34*, 50–54.

Hunt, R. D., Capper, L., & O'Connell, P. (1990). Clonidine in child and adolescent psychiatry. *Journal of Child and Adolescent Psychopharmacology, 1*, 87–102.

Hunt, R. D., Cohen, D. J., Anderson, G., & Clark, L. (1984). Possible changes in noradrenergic receptor sensitivity following methylphenidate treatment: Growth hormone and MHPG response to clonidine challange in children with attention deficit disorder and hyperactivity. *Life Sciences, 35*, 885–897.

Hunt, R. D., Minderaa, R. B., & Cohen, D. J. (1985). Clonidine benefits children with attention deficit disorder and hyperactivity: Report of a double-blind placebo-crossover therapeutic trial. *Journal of the American Academy of Child and Adolescent Psychiatry, 24*, 617–629.

Jaselskis, C. A., Cook, E. H., Fletcher, K. E., & Leventhal, B. L. (1992). Clonidine treatment of hyperactive and impulsive children with autistic disorder. *Journal of Clinical Psychopharmacology, 12*, 322–327.

Kafantaris, V., Campbell, M., Padron-Gayol, M. V., Small, A. M., Locascio, J. J., & Rosenberg, C. R. (1992). Carbamazepine in hospitalized aggressive conduct disorder children: An open pilot study. *Psychopharmacology Bulletin, 28*, 193–199.

Leckman, J. F., Hardin, M. T., Riddle, M. A., Stevenson, J., Ort, S. I., & Cohen, D. J. (1991). Clonidine treatment of Gilles de la Tourette's syndrome. *Archives of General Psychiatry, 48*, 324–328.

Pataki, C. S., Carlson, G. A., Kelly, K. L., Rapport, M. D., & Biancaniello, T. M. (1993). Side effects of methylphenidate and desipramine alone and in combination in children. *Journal of the American Academy of Child and Adolescent Psychiatry, 32*, 1065–1072.

Pellock, J. M., & Willmore, L. J. (1991). A rational guide to routine blood monitoring in patients receiving antiepileptic drugs. *Neurology, 41*, 961–964.

Pleak, R. R., Birmaher, B., Gavrilescu, A., Abichandani, C., & Williams, D. T. (1988). Mania and neuropsychiatric excitation following carbamazepine. *Journal of the American Academy of Child and Adolescent Psychiatry, 27*, 500–503.

Rapport, M. D., Carlson, G. A., Kelly, K. L., & Pataki, C. (1993). Methylphenidate and desipramine in hospitalized children: I. Separate and combined effects on cognitive function. *Journal of the American Academy of Child and Adolescent Psychiatry, 32*, 333–342.

Ratey, J. J., Greenberg, M. S., & Lindem, K. J. (1991). Combination of treatments for attention deficit hyperactivity disorder in adults. *Journal of Nervous and Mental Disease, 179*, 699–701.

Silva, R. R., Munoz, D. M., & Alpert, M. (1996). Carbamazepine use in children and adolescents with features of attention-deficit hyperactivity disorder: A meta-analysis. *Journal of the American Academy of Child and Adolescent Psychiatry, 35,* 352–358.

Singer, H. S., Brown, J., Quaskey, S., Rosenberg, L. A., Mellits, E. D., & Denckla, M. B. (1995). The treatment of attention-deficit hyperactivity disorder in Tourette's syndrome: A double-blind placebo-controlled study with clonidine and desipramine. *Pediatrics, 95,* 74–80.

Trimble, M. R. (1990). Anticonvulsants in children and adolescents. *Journal of Child and Adolescent Psychopharmacology, 1,* 107–124.

Wilens, T. E., Biederman, J., Geist, D. E., Steingard, R., & Spencer, T. (1993). Nortriptyline in the treatment of ADHD: A chart review of 58 cases. *Journal of the American Academy of Child and Adolescent Psychiatry, 32,* 343–349.

Wozniak, J., Biederman J., Kiely, K., Ablon, J. S., & Faraone, S. (1993). Prepubertal mania revisited. *Scientific Proceedings of the American Academy of Child and Adolescent Psychiatry, 9,* 36.

Chapter 20

PSYCHOLOGICAL COUNSELING OF ADULTS WITH ADHD

Kevin R. Murphy

ૐ

Most adults with Attention-Deficit/Hyperactivity Disorder (ADHD) have suffered years of feeling demoralized, discouraged, and ineffective because of a long-standing history of frustrations and failures in school, work, family, and social domains. Many report a chronic and deep-seated sense of underachievement and intense frustration over squandered opportunities and are at a loss to explain why they cannot seem to translate their obvious assets into more positive outcomes. Further, many report having heard a consistent barrage of complaints about themselves from parents, teachers, spouses, friends, or employers regarding their behavioral, academic, interpersonal, or productivity shortcomings. The cumulative effect of such a history can sometimes lead to feelings of intense frustration and demoralization and a sense of anticipating failure as the predictable outcome to their efforts. Sadly, some appear so wedded to this belief system that they eventually give up believing life could be different for them. Many are completely unaware that their condition is a highly treatable one.

One of the aims of this chapter is to describe the importance of instilling hope, optimism, and motivation during the counseling of adults with ADHD so they can better understand their condition and be more inclined to engage in and follow through with a multimodal treatment plan. Our philosophy at the University of Massachusetts Medical Center Adult ADHD Clinic is to help patients view their disorder from a perspective that empowers them to believe their lives can be different and encourages their active and enthusiastic involvement in treatment. The principles described are not new and in many ways are generic to psychosocial counseling with any psychiatric population. The concepts of such things as education about the disorder, cognitive restructuring, reframing the past, empowering, and instilling hope seem to lend themselves particularly well to the treatment of ADHD in adults. Although there are as yet no controlled empirical studies demonstrating the efficacy of these approaches with ADHD adults, they appear to have been beneficial to many in our clinic population.

l

This chapter is adapted from Murphy (1995). Copyright 1995 by Brunner/Mazel. Adapted by permission.

This chapter also describes some common emotional, attitudinal, and psychological consequences of living with ADHD in adulthood and discusses a range of other non-pharmacological treatment approaches currently being used in treating ADHD in adults. It must be emphasized that the psychosocial treatment of ADHD in adults does not rest on an empirical database. In fact, to date there have been no controlled scientific studies published in this domain. Unfortunately, we remain at the level of using interventions based on intuition and common sense, clinical case studies, and anecdotal clinician accounts of what seems to be efficacious for this population (Nadeau, 1995). However, most would agree that pragmatic, behavioral skill building, and self-management strategies are more useful for the types of issues adults with ADHD encounter rather than more traditional nondirective, insight-oriented, psychodynamic approaches.

ADULT CONSEQUENCES OF GROWING UP WITH ADHD

Some of the more common correlates associated with ADHD in adults, as noted in Chapter 6 (this volume), are low self-esteem, avoidance/anxiety, depression, school and job performance problems, marital discord, poorer driving outcomes, and substance abuse. Many adults treated at our clinic have admitted to having low self-esteem as a result of years of frustration with their academic, work, social, and day-to-day family lives. They often report a long-standing and nagging sense of knowing something was wrong but never knowing exactly what it was. In many cases they sought help from multiple mental health professionals who overlooked ADHD and instead conceptualized their problems as related solely to mood, anxiety, or character disorders. Treatment for their underlying neurobiological condition (ADHD) that may be driving at least some of their behavior/symptoms may never have even been considered, which may explain why a good percentage of our adult patients report past counseling experiences as not being especially helpful. Consequently, some end up attributing their problems to a character or moral defect in themselves and pay a heavy emotional price as a result. This underscores the importance of reframing the disorder as neurobiological and not characterological, of rebuilding self-esteem and self-confidence, and of instilling hope for the future.

Another common consequence of having ADHD is anxiety and avoidance of situations that have historically been unsuccessful or troublesome for the patient. One example of this avoidance concerns the idea of returning to school. Some of our clinic population have expressed a desire to return to school but are understandably hesitant because of their prior record of school struggles. They fear they will fail again and wish to avoid another setback. They report that if they had reason to believe that their school experience might be different this time, they would be more willing to attempt it. But to many, it is safer not to try, so they avoid school even though deep down they have a strong desire to go. This is indeed unfortunate for some because proper diagnosis, treatment, and motivation can open new possibilities and potentially make the difference between success and failure in school.

Another example concerns social/interpersonal relationships. In part because of their impulsivity, interrupting, forgetfulness, inattentiveness, hyperactivity, difficulty reading social cues, temper, or mood swings, adults with ADHD frequently report having difficulty maintaining friendships. Their behavior may be viewed by others as rude, insensitive, irresponsible, or obnoxious and they may sometimes be ostracized by others. Some associate social interaction with embarrassment, disappointment, criticism, or failure. When confronted with future opportunities for social interaction, these ADHD adults sometimes withdraw or avoid others to protect themselves. Again, treatment can sometimes improve their verbal and behavioral impulsivity, disinhibition, and focusing/listening ability and as a result improve their overall social functioning.

Depression is another relatively common consequence associated with adult ADHD. Approximately 35% of our adult ADHD patients meet criteria for either major depression or Dysthymia at sometime in their lives. In a recent study (Murphy & Barkley, 1996) comparing 172 adults diagnosed with ADHD with 30 adults referred to our clinic who were not so diagnosed, we found that the ADHD group showed a significantly greater prevalence of oppositional, conduct, and substance abuse disorders, and greater illegal substance abuse than did control adults. Moreover, adults with ADHD displayed greater self-reported psychological maladjustment, more driving risks (speeding violations), and more frequent changes in employment. Significantly more ADHD adults experienced suspension of their driver's license, performed poorly, quit or were fired from their job, had a history of poorer educational performance, and had more frequent school disciplinary actions against them than did adults without ADHD. Multiple marriages were more likely in the ADHD group as well. Some adults with ADHD have become so demoralized over their past failures, and from being misunderstood and mistreated by others, that they require concurrent treatment for a mood disorder.

Finally, a substantial minority of ADHD adults gravitate toward substance abuse, possibly as a way of relaxing or calming the mental restlessness they often experience. Recent studies have suggested that those with ADHD are at increased risk for developing substance abuse problems (Weiss & Hechtman, 1993; Mannuzza, Gittelman-Klein, Bessler, Malloy, & LaPadula, 1993; Murphy & Barkley, 1996). Approximately 33% of our clinic population have met criteria for substance abuse or dependence either in the present or in the past. Many appear to be self-medicating in an attempt to soothe their underlying ADHD symptoms. Most report using alcohol and/or marijuana as their primary drugs of choice. Our clinic has found that after being treated with stimulant medication, a fair number of our substance-abusing ADHD patients report improvement not only in their ADHD symptoms but also in their substance abuse. Others have also found this to be true (Schubiner et al., 1995). One possible hypothesis is that the stimulant medication may quell the desire to self-medicate. We therefore do not routinely disqualify an ADHD substance *abuser* from medication treatment. To do so may be depriving these patients of a potentially important and needed treatment. We do not immediately medicate those with active substance *dependence*; they get referred for substance abuse treatment before undergoing any treatment for ADHD. In most cases, we would want to see at least 1 to 2 months of stable sobriety before introducing medication for ADHD. Those with comorbid substance abuse and ADHD require close follow-up to monitor progress and safety. Clearly, the relationship between ADHD and substance abuse warrants further scientific investigation.

An important goal for professionals who treat adults with ADHD is to respond to these and any other negative sequelae of living with ADHD in a way that instills hope, fosters personal potency, and empowers them to believe that with a combination of treatment, support, perseverance, and hard work, their lives *can* be improved. Despite the absence of data to back up this suggestion, common sense would suggest it to be a reasonable place to start.

EXPLAINING THE ADHD DIAGNOSIS

Treatment for adults with ADHD begins at the time they are diagnosed. How clinicians communicate the diagnosis to them is critical to both their understanding of the disorder and their willingness to engage in and follow through with treatment. If clinicians can help patients understand the disorder, offer a plausible rationale as to how it causes their symptoms, frame it as something that is treatable, and instill hope and optimism for their future, patients are more likely to feel motivated to work at and follow through with treatment. Increased knowledge and understanding of the disorder and staying involved in treatment would likely increase the chances of more positive outcomes. Conversely, if patients are left with only a vague notion of what ADHD is, are confused or unsure of how they might be helped, and are not activated to feel hope, they are far less likely to embrace treatment, persevere, and achieve a positive outcome. Many adult patients who visit our clinic have had prior ADHD evaluations and yet report very little understanding of ADHD, do not understand the implications it has on their lives, and are unaware of the range of treatment possibilities that exist. Their disorder was never adequately explained to them. Clinicians can have substantial control over the feedback process and have an opportunity to influence whether patients become actively engaged or disengaged from treatment. The framework described next may assist clinicians in developing strategies and skills to more effectively explain the diagnosis to adults.

Rationale for ADHD and Comorbid Diagnoses

Perhaps the most important nonpharmacological strategy for ADHD adults is to educate themselves as much as possible about the disorder. Most adults have little knowledge of ADHD and do not fully understand the implications it may have on their day-to-day lives. Having a sound and informed knowledge base can help adults make sense of what has been troubling them, help them set realistic and attainable goals, and ease their frustration. Just knowing that there is a name and neurobiological reason for much of their struggles is, in itself, therapeutic. Once they have been accurately diagnosed by a professional who understands ADHD, there is often a sense of tremendous relief at finally having an explanation for their long-standing difficulties. The clinician can begin by explaining the rationale for arriving at the ADHD diagnosis and any other comorbid conditions. It is helpful for patients to understand the reasons they qualify for the diagnosis. For example, explaining that (1) they (and a spouse or parent) endorsed a sufficient number of the symptoms of ADHD according to the fourth edition of the *Diagnostic and Statistical Manual of Mental Disorders* (DSM-IV; American Psychiatric Association, 1994); (2) had an onset of symptoms in early childhood; (3) their symptoms have caused significant impairment in academic, social, vocational, or daily adaptive functioning; (4) they have no other psychiatric or medical condition that could better explain their symptoms; and (5) have behavioral, school, and/or work histories that reflect typical impairments associated with the diagnosis, all of this can help them begin to understand ADHD.

Reframing the Past

An important next step is to continue educating the patient about what ADHD is and how it affects their life. Patients need to have at least a general understanding that they have a neurological condition, not a character defect or moral weakness. The realization that many of the problems they have experienced stem from neurological causes rather than from laziness or low intelligence can begin the process of repairing self-esteem. Often they have internalized negative messages over the years from parents, teachers, spouses, and employers who have concluded they are either stupid, lazy, incompetent, immature, or unmotivated. If valid and appropriate, it should be explained that the likely reason for many of the problems they experienced in school, work, and/or social relationships was largely due to a subtle neurological deficit in the brain over which they had little control. Their problems were not the result of deliberate misbehavior, low intelligence, or lack of effort. These misguided and damaging perceptions should be recast in a more positive and hopeful light so patients can begin to rebuild their self-confidence and believe successful treatment is possible. As a consequence, patients would hopefully be in a better position to break out of the shackles of feeling stuck, demoralized, and chronically frustrated. Educating spouses, family members, and friends is also important so that they can understand and be better able to help.

Hope and Genuineness

Hope is a necessary ingredient. Whether it is battling a life-threatening illness, facing difficult surgery, recovering from physical or psychological trauma, or learning to cope with ADHD, patients need to feel hope. Without hope, it seems there is little chance of significant change, consistent effort, or positive outcome. To achieve an optimal outcome, patients need to feel their clinician is a partner with them and sincerely believes they can be helped. If clinicians are genuine in their desire to become involved in helping, and this is clearly evident to the patient, it can go a long way toward instilling hope and motivation in the patient. Conversely, if clinicians are perceived by patients as merely technicians performing their routine in a relatively uninvolved manner, the opposite is true. Caring, support, compassion, and encouragement are crucial ingredients and their importance should never be underestimated. The pressures of the managed care environment and the reality of doing more in less time with fewer resources can make this a real challenge in today's health care environment. Nevertheless, the message that should come through loud and clear is that with proper treatment including education, counseling, medication, behavioral strategies, hard work, and the support of family and friends, adults with ADHD can make significant and sometimes dramatic improvements in their lives.

As an additional educational resource, the University of Massachusetts Adult ADHD Clinic provides a packet of educational literature to all patients at the end of the evaluation. This packet typically includes a fact sheet about ADHD; a list of books, magazines, or newsletters that may be useful for them; and information on medication (i.e., copies of the fact sheets on medication from the *Journal of Child and Adolescent Psychopharmacology*, Winter 1992 issue). Although we have no scientific proof that such educational literature is useful (or even actually read), it is hoped that providing this type of immediately relevant educational material can promote better understanding and help motivate some patients to engage in ongoing treatment.

It can also be helpful to provide some specific examples of treatment strategies that are relevant to the problems the patient is currently experiencing. For example, patients who are disorganized and forgetful may benefit from training in prioritizing and list making, keeping an appointment calendar, posting visual reminders in strategic locations, blocking out time in schedules for priority tasks, breaking large tasks down into smaller units, building mini-rewards into projects, and the like. Or, if the patient is a college student, it could be useful to describe some specific types of classroom modifications, lifestyle or class schedule adjustments, study skills, or other accommodations that are appropriate and justified given the nature of their difficulties.

Providing education to patients about medication also seems important. Explaining how medication might help patients improve the quality of their lives by enhancing their ability to focus and concentrate and curb their impulsivity may provide further hope. Explaining how their life may be different if they respond well to medication by using actual examples from their personal history may be useful. Taking the time to answer questions about side effects and providing enough factual information so patients can make informed decisions regarding medication also appears useful. Patients often have mistaken notions and unrealistic fears/myths about medication that need to be addressed before agreeing to try it. Providing fact sheets (as mentioned earlier) in addition to these verbal explanations can give them further information to share with family or friends.

Although there is no "cure" for ADHD and treatment is aimed at symptom reduction via a variety of coping strategies, an overriding principal is to assist patients in becoming the best that they can be by helping them to focus and build on their strengths and learn to better compensate for their weaknesses.

Instilling hope for the future, balanced with the reality that changing habits and behavioral patterns requires hard work and sustained effort, can foster a realistic attitude toward treatment. Clinicians can exert a strong influence in constructing a therapeutic atmosphere of hope and optimism to counter the demoralization and pessimism that so often accompany adults with ADHD. Equipped with this combination of hope, knowledge, and awareness of ADHD, adults with ADHD should be in a much better position to benefit from treatment, to learn to adapt better to current tasks and responsibilities, and to lead more fulfilling lives than had previously been the case.

PSYCHOSOCIAL TREATMENT APPROACHES

A combination of treatments is usually recommended for adults with ADHD. Again, treatment of the individual with ADHD does not produce a cure for the underlying cause of the disorder. Treatment is aimed at symptom reduction and minimizing the negative effects of the disorder to improve one's overall quality of life. Despite the fact that prior research has demonstrated that clinic-based treatments that focused on skill training, such as social skills, self-control, or cognitive-behavioral training have not been of much benefit to those with ADHD (Abikoff, 1985, 1987; Barkley, 1990; Diaz & Berk, 1995), and that short-term psychosocial treatment effects do not generalize outside the context in which they are applied (Abikoff & Gittelman, 1984; Barkley, 1987, 1990; Barkley, Copeland, & Sivage, 1980), the management of behavior in the immediate environments in which it is problematic for those with ADHD is a laudable goal (Barkley, 1997). As Barkley (1997) states:

> Only a treatment which can result in improvement or normalization of the underlying neuropsychological deficit in behavioral inhibition is likely to result in an improvement or normalization of the executive functions dependent on such inhibition. To date, the only treatment that exists that has any hope of achieving this end is stimulant medication or other pharmacological agents that improve or normalize the neural substrates in the prefrontal regions that likely underlie this disorder. (p. 60)

Does this mean that all psychosocial treatment approaches have no value in assisting adults in coping with their ADHD? I think not. Psychosocial treatment may not "cure" the underlying brain dysfunction that gives rise to core ADHD symptoms, but it may well help to improve the side effects, emotional sequelae, and/or comorbid conditions often associated with ADHD. Further, some psychosocial approaches may prove useful under scientific scrutiny in the future.

The most common types of psychosocial treatments used in treating adults with ADHD include individual counseling, group counseling, family/marriage counseling, vocational counseling, and coaching.

INDIVIDUAL COUNSELING

The initial stage of individual counseling usually includes information/education about ADHD, outlining goals, and developing strategies to meet those goals. Follow-up meetings monitor progress, discuss medication issues, add or alter treatment approaches, and work on improving specific areas of difficulty. Individual counseling can bring increased awareness of how the disorder affects their lives and can thereby help to identify appropriate behavioral/self-management strategies to better manage symptoms. Understanding the disorder can also influence immediate and future life decisions. For example, knowledge of one's ADHD can influence job choice, choice of spouse, choice of major in school, or decisions about whether to return to school and where (preferably one with an established program for assisting ADHD/learning-disabled students). Acquiring this kind of self-knowledge can assist adults with ADHD in making better choices and goodness-of-fit decisions.

Adults with ADHD may also benefit from individual counseling on behavior modification principles and strategies. Treatment for ADHD appears to respond best to an active and pragmatic approach on the part of both therapist and patient. Most often, the goals of treatment are to change disruptive behavior and thought patterns that consistently interfere in day-to-day functioning. Behavioral therapy and cognitive therapy are two forms of individual counseling thought to be particularly useful to adults with ADHD. Specifically, training in methods of time management, organizational skills, communication skills, anger control, decision making, self-monitoring and reward, chunking large tasks into a series of smaller steps, and changing faulty cognitions are thought to be potentially helpful in more efficiently meeting the demands of daily work, family, and social life. In essence, the same sorts of suggestions that may prove useful to ADHD children in school may also be of value to the ADHD adult when upgraded to their performance contexts (see Chapter 15, this volume). Preparing patients for the expected and inevitable feelings of disappointment and frustration when setbacks occur by framing setbacks as normal—and as opportunities for learning and personal growth may reduce discouragement. For example, an adult with ADHD may conclude that making lists or using an appointment book is fruitless because they frequently lose them. Explaining that habit change and learning new strategies require ongoing practice and are not one-trial learning may help them to keep trying. The goal is to continue practicing until the skill becomes an automatic and natural part of a daily routine. Individual counseling aimed at erasing long-standing negative messages from teachers, parents, spouses, and employers and replacing them with more rational and optimistic messages is another area of potential benefit to adults with ADHD.

It also seems important to emphasize and make explicit the strengths and positive traits the patient possesses. For example, informing a patient that their testing results indicated average, above-average, or superior native intelligence can sometimes be a powerful revelation. Explaining that their lower-than-expected grades throughout their school history had nothing to do with low intelligence can provide a strong measure of relief to someone who may well have lived his or her life believing the opposite. Another example is to point out positive character traits observed in the patient such as tenacity, willingness to keep trying despite many setbacks, boundless energy and drive, assertiveness, sense of humor, or whatever else is appropriate. This may serve to counterbalance negative self-perceptions, reinforce strengths, and help to promote self-acceptance.

In summary, individual counseling may be helpful in assisting adults with ADHD to cope with a variety of coexisting problems including depression, anxiety, low self-esteem, interpersonal problems, and disorganization.

GROUP TREATMENT

Although again no scientific data as yet support the efficacy of group therapy, it seems a potentially useful intervention for this population. Patients can learn a great deal from each other, feel accepted, and feel less isolated and alone. One patient who participated in a support group at our clinic who had refused to take medication ended up changing his mind after discussing the issue with fellow group members and receiving their input. Clearly, the group influenced him to try the medication where his counselor was previously unsuccessful. Hearing how others cope and manage their symptoms, realizing there are others with similar problems, and having a "laboratory" for learning and trying out new social and interpersonal skills, as well as the support and validation offered by the group, can all be helpful to group members. In my experience, it is best to have a time-limited and semistructured format with target goals and themes for each session. Balancing a mixture of some didactic instruction with time for open-ended discussion works best. Ongoing, open-ended, "here and now" types of groups can rapidly become diffuse and disorganized and be difficult to lead and manage. Among the topics that we and our colleagues at Wayne State University, Angela Tzelepis and Howard Schubiner, have utilized include medication issues, organizational skills, listening/interpersonal skills, anger control, decision making, stress reduction, vocational/workplace issues, and personal coping strategies. With a skilled group therapist and a motivated and carefully screened group of preferably no more than 10, group therapy can be a useful adjunct to other forms of treatment. Participating in local support group organizations such as CHADD (Children and Adults with Attention Deficit Disorder) is another avenue for support and education.

FAMILY/MARRIAGE COUNSELING

Family and marital therapy may also be potentially useful for resolving difficulties that affect relationships in family members and spouses. A significant percentage of the non-ADHD spouses who come to our clinic report severe marital dissatisfaction as measured by their Locke–Wallace Marital Inventory scores. Non-ADHD spouses often report feeling confused, angry, and frustrated. They may complain that their spouse is a poor listener, is unreliable, is forgetful, is self-centered or insensitive, often seems distant or preoccupied, is messy, does not finish household projects, or behaves irresponsibly. Gaining a greater understanding of the disorder, and realizing that many of these problems may not necessarily stem from "willful misconduct," may enable the couple to take a fresh look at their problems from an ADHD perspective, stop blaming each other, and begin to align together as a team to reduce conflict. To be successful, however, the non-ADHD spouse must perceive their partner to be making a sincere and legitimate effort at behavioral change. If the patient uses the ADHD as an excuse to justify continued behavioral problems without demonstrating an observable commitment to behavioral change, there will be little chance for improvement in the relationship. Without a mutual understanding of how ADHD affects marital and family functioning, the chances for a positive outcome are greatly diminished. (For a more detailed discussion on marital and family issues, readers are referred to Dixon, 1995; Ratey, Hallowell, & Miller, 1995; Hallowell, 1995.)

VOCATIONAL COUNSELING

Workplace problems can be particularly troublesome to many adults with ADHD. Impulsivity, inattention, careless mistakes, disorganization, poor time management, and inconsistency are just some of the things that can interfere in job performance. Most who experience workplace problems do so not because of incompetence but because their jobs are ill-suited to their strengths. They frequently leave jobs because of boredom or inability to tolerate what they perceive as a boring and tedious daily routine. Vocational counseling aimed at identifying strengths and limitations in matching patients to jobs that "fit" for them is of critical importance for many adults with ADHD. It may involve vocational testing to identify interests and aptitudes, job coaching and training, or advocacy with potential employers. Unfortunately, the need for such services seems to greatly outweigh the availability of skilled resources. Nevertheless, successful vocational adjustment can have a positive effect on self-esteem, family and marital functioning, and financial well-being. If the adult ADHD patient can find a successful niche, it will likely increase chances for ongoing vocational success, reduce boredom, and, ideally, result in a greater sense of confidence, self-esteem, and personal satisfaction.

COACHING

Another relatively new area of intervention for adults with ADHD is coaching. Although again no empirical data support the efficacy of coaching with adults, it appears to be growing as an adjunctive treatment for adults. The Personal and Professional Coaches Association defines coaching as "an ongoing relationship which focuses on the client taking action toward the realization of their vision, goals, or desires." It further states that "coaching uses a process of inquiry and personal discovery to build the client's level of awareness and responsibility, and provides the client with structure, support, and feedback." Coaching is a supportive, pragmatic, and collaborative process in which the coach and adult with ADHD work together usually via daily 10- to 15-minute telephone conversations to identify goals and strategies to meet those goals. Because most adults with ADHD have difficulty persisting in effort over long periods and often cannot sustain ongoing motivation to complete tasks, the coach can assist them in staying on task by offering encouragement, support, structure, accountability, and, at times, gentle confrontation. There is no standard methodology. The coaching relationship is tied to the needs and desires of each patient and can be structured in any way that is acceptable to the coach and person being coached. Some may talk with their coach on a daily basis and others far less frequently. Some may correspond via e-mail. The intended outcome is to assist adults with ADHD to take charge and better manage their lives by learning to set realistic goals and stay on task to reach those goals, in an atmosphere of encouragement and supportive understanding. While we await future results of scientific inquiry into the effectiveness of coaching, it is likely to continue to be a frequent treatment recommendation for the adult ADHD population.

Other practical and commonsense coping strategies that may prove helpful for some include the use of a color-coded file system, posting visual reminders in strategic locations, use of a daytimer schedule book, learning how to prioritize and make lists, using a wristwatch with an alarm set to go off at regular intervals to better manage time, having duplicate sets of keys available, and becoming proficient in the use of the various technologies available today such as e-mail, word processing, spell checkers, and grammar checkers. Another option is to hire a personal organizational consultant to provide pragmatic one-to-one training in organizational skills, time management skills, managing mail and other paperwork, balancing a checkbook, or general clutter management.

A subgroup of the adult ADHD population may need additional treatment for specific problems that may coexist with ADHD such as substance abuse/dependence, credit counseling/money management, eating disorders, or anxiety and mood disorders. Because those with ADHD are at greater risk for developing comorbid problems, treatment efforts need to take into account the totality of the patient's problems.

Whatever combination of treatments is used for a given patient, it is likely that intervention needs to be extended over long time intervals, much like the management of a chronic medical illness such as diabetes (Barkley, 1994). Periodic follow-up for support, adjustment to treatment, academic or workplace advocacy, or new intervention as needed will likely be necessary and beneficial for most ADHD adults in the ongoing management of their disorder.

REFERENCES

Abikoff, H. (1985). Efficacy of cognitive training interventions in hyperactive children: A critical review. *Clinical Psychology Review, 5,* 479–512.

Abikoff, H. (1987). An evaluation of cognitive behavior therapy for hyperactive children. In B. B. Lahey & A. E. Kazdin (Eds.), *Advances in clinical child psychology* (Vol. 10, pp. 171–216). New York: Plenum.

Abikoff, H., & Gittelman, R. (1984). Does behavior therapy normalize the classroom behavior of hyperactive children? *Archives of General Psychiatry, 41,* 449–454.

American Psychiatric Association. (1994). *Diagnostic and statistical manual of mental disorders* (4th ed.). Washington, DC: Author.

Barkley, R. A. (1987). *Defiant children: A clinician's manual for parent training.* New York: Guilford Press.

Barkley, R. A. (1990). *Attention-deficit hyperactivity disorder: A handbook for diagnosis and treatment.* New York: Guilford Press.

Barkley, R. A. (1994). *ADHD in adults* [Manual to accompany videotape]. New York: Guilford Press.

Barkley, R.A. (1997). *ADHD and the nature of self-control.* New York: Guilford Press.

Barkley, R. A., Copeland, A. P., & Sivage, C. (1980). A self-control classroom for hyperactive children. *Journal of Autism and Developmental Disorders, 10,* 75–89.

Diaz, R. M., & Berk, L. E. (1995). A Vygotskian critique of self-instructional training. *Development and Psychopathology, 7,* 369–392.

Dixon, E. B. (1995). Impact of adult ADD on the family. In K. Nadeau (Ed.), *A comprehensive guide to attention deficit disorder in adults* (pp. 236–259). New York: Brunner/Mazel.

Hallowell, E. M. (1995). Psychotherapy of adult attention deficit disorder. In K. G. Nadeau (Ed.), *A comprehensive guide to attention deficit disorder in adults: Research, diagnosis, and treatment* (pp. 144–167). New York: Brunner/Mazel.

Mannuzza, S., Gittelman-Klein, R., Bessler, A., Malloy, P., & LaPadula, M. (1993). Adult outcome of hyperactive boys: Educational achievement, occupational rank, and psychiatric status. *Archives of General Psychiatry, 50,* 565–576.

Murphy, K. R. (1995). Empowering the adult with ADHD. In K. G. Nadeau (Ed.), *A comprehensive guide for attention deficit disorder in adults: Research, diagnosis, and treatment* (pp. 135–145). New York: Brunner/Mazel.

Murphy, K. R., & Barkley, R. A. (1996). Parents of children with attention-deficit/hyperactivity disorder: Psychological and attentional impairment. *American Journal of Orthopsychiatry, 66,* 93–102.

Nadeau, K. G. (Ed.). (1995). *A comprehensive guide for attention deficit disorder in adults: Research, diagnosis, and treatment.* New York: Brunner/Mazel.

Ratey, J. J., Hallowell, E. M., & Miller, A. C. (1995). Relationship dilemmas for adults with ADD. In K. G. Nadeau (Ed.), *A comprehensive guide to attention deficit disorder in adults: Research, diagnosis, and treatment* (pp. 218–235). New York: Brunner/Mazel.

Schubiner, H., Tzelepis, A., Isaacson, H., Warbasse, L., Zacharek, M., & Musial, J. (1995). The dual diagnosis of attention-deficit hyperactivity disorder and substance abuse: Case reports and literature review. *Journal of Clinical Psychiatry, 56*(4), 146–150.

Weiss, G., & Hechtman, L. T. (1993). *Hyperactive children grown up* (2nd ed.): *ADHD in children, adolescents, and adults.* New York: Guilford Press.

Chapter 21

PHARMACOTHERAPY OF ADULT ADHD

Timothy E. Wilens
Thomas J. Spencer
Joseph Biederman

ॐ

Attention-Deficit/Hyperactivity Disorder (ADHD) is a prevalent disorder estimated to affect 2% to 9% of school-age children and up to 5% of adults (Bauermeister, Canino, & Bird, 1994; Murphy & Barkley, 1996). Although its precise etiology remains unknown, family, adoption, and twin studies suggest that genetic risk factors are operant in this disorder (Faraone et al., 1992). Although historically ADHD was not thought to continue beyond adolescence, long-term controlled follow-up studies have shown the persistence of the syndrome in 10% to 60% of young adults diagnosed as having ADHD in childhood (Weiss & Hechtman, 1986; Mannuzza, Klein, Bessler, Malloy, & LaPadula, 1993).

Compared to their non-ADHD peers, adults with ADHD have been reported to have higher rates of anxiety, depression, and substance use disorders; more conflicts in social and marital relations; and underachievement in their careers and academics despite adequate intellectual abilities (Weiss & Hechtman, 1986; Biederman et al., 1993, 1995; Mannuzza et al., 1993). Although the diagnosis of adult ADHD has been questioned, evidence supports the descriptive, face, predictive, and concurrent validity of diagnosing ADHD in adults (Spencer, Biederman, Wilens, Faraone, & Li, 1994).

CLINICAL FEATURES, ASSESSMENT, AND DIAGNOSTIC CONSIDERATIONS

ADHD can be diagnosed in adults by carefully querying for developmentally appropriate criteria, according to the fourth edition of the *Diagnostic and Statistical Manual of Mental Disorders* (DSM IV; American Psychiatric Association; 1994), that attend to the childhood onset, persistence, and current presence of these symptoms. In addition, adult self-report scales such as the Brown-ADD (Brown, 1995) and the Wender rating scales (Ward, Wender, & Reimherr, 1993) may also assist in making the diagnosis. Adults with ADHD most often describe the core attentional symptoms of ADHD, including poor attention and concentration, easy distractibility, shifting activities frequently, daydreaming, and forgetfulness, followed more distantly by impulsivity, impatience, boredom, fidgetiness, and intrusiveness (Millstein, Wilens, Spencer, & Biederman, 1998). ADHD symptoms in adults appear to be related to those in children and adolescents. ADHD adults often do not manifest these symptoms during their interview and may have developed cognitive-behavioral strategies to compensate for their deficiencies related to ADHD. Neuropsychological testing should be used in cases in which learning disabilities are suspected or learning problems persist in the presence of a treated ADHD adult (Barkley, 1990). ADHD adults are thought to have working-memory deficits as exemplified by less ability to attend, encode, and manipulate information (Seidman, Biederman, Weber, Hatch, & Faraone, in press). Although less defined within ADHD, organizational difficulties and procrastination appear common.

Despite the increasing recognition that children with ADHD commonly grow up to be adults with the same disorder, the treatment of this disorder in adults remains under intense study. In addition, complicating the diagnostics and treatment strategy, many adults with ADHD seeking treatment have depressive and anxiety symptoms, as well as histories of drug and alcohol dependence or abuse (Tarter, McBride, Buonpane, & Schneider, 1977; Eyre, Rounsaville, & Kleber, 1982; Wood, Wender, & Reimherr, 1983; Biederman et al., 1993; Wilens, Spencer, & Biederman, 1995). Thus, with the increasing recognition of the complex presentation of adults with ADHD, there is a need to develop effective pharmacotherapeutic strategies. In the following sections, guidelines for pharmacotherapy will be delineated, the available information on the use of medications for adult ADHD will be reviewed, and pharmacological strategies suggested for the management of ADHD symptoms with accompanying comorbid conditions.

TREATMENT

Pharmacotherapy should be part of a treatment plan in which consideration is given to all aspects of the patient's life. Hence, it should not be used exclusive of other interventions. The administration of medication in adults with ADHD should be undertaken as a collaborative effort with the patient, with the physician guiding the use and management of efficacious anti-ADHD agents. The use of medication should follow a careful evaluation of the adult including psychiatric, social, and cognitive assessments. Diagnostic information should be gathered from the patient and, whenever possible, from significant others such as partners, parents, siblings, and close friends. If ancillary data are not available, information from an adult is acceptable for diagnostic and treatment purposes as adults with ADHD, as they are with other disorders, are appropriate reporters of their own condition. Careful attention should be paid to the childhood onset of symptoms, longitudinal history of the disorder, and differential diagnosis including medical/neurological, as well psychosocial factors contributing to the clinical presentation. In the ADHD adult, issues of comorbidity with learning disabilities and other psychiatric disorders need to be addressed. Because learning disabilities do not respond to pharmacotherapy, it is important to identify these deficits to help define remedial interventions. For instance, this evaluation may assist in the design and implementation of an educational plan for the adult who may be returning to school or serve as an aid for structuring the current work environment. Because alcohol and drug use disorders are frequently encountered in adults with ADHD (Wilens, Spencer, & Biederman, 1995), a careful history of substance use should be completed. Patients with ongoing substance abuse or dependence should generally not be treated until appropriate addiction treatments have been undertaken and the patient has maintaied a drug- and alcohol-free period. Other concurrent psychiatric disorders also need to be assessed, and if possible the relationship of the ADHD symptoms with these other disorders needs to be delineated. In subjects with ADHD plus bipolar mood disorders, for example, the risk of mania needs be addressed and closely monitored during the treatment of the ADHD. In cases such as these, the conservative introduction of anti-ADHD medications along with mood-stabilizing agents should be considered.

Although the efficacy of various psychotherapeutic interventions remain to be established, a retrospective assessment of adults with ADHD indicated that traditional insight-oriented psychotherapies were not helpful for ADHD adults (Ratey, Greenberg, Bemporad, & Lindem, 1992). A cognitive therapy protocol adapted for adults with ADHD has been developed (McDermott & Wilens, in press), which, preliminary data suggest, is effective when used with pharmacotherapy (Wilens, McDermott, Biederman, Abrantes, & Spencer, in press). As for juveniles with ADHD, medications appear to be the mainstay of treatment for adults with ADHD. In the following sections, guidelines for pharmacotherapy will be delineated, the available information on the use of medications for adult ADHD will be reviewed, and pharmacological strategies will be suggested for the management of ADHD symptoms with accompanying comorbid conditions.

Stimulants

The stimulant medications remain the mainstay treatment in children, adolescents, and adults with ADHD. In comparison to the more than 200 controlled studies of stimulant efficacy in pediatric ADHD (Spencer et al., 1996), there are only two open and eight controlled stimulant trials in adults with ADHD (Wood, Reimherr, Wender, & Johnson, 1976; Wender, Reimherr, & Wood, 1981; Mattes, Boswell, & Oliver, 1984; Gualtieri, Ondrusek, & Finley, 1985; Wender, Reimherr, Wood, & Ward, 1985; Shekim, Asarnow, Hess, Zaucha, & Wheeler, 1990; Spencer et al., 1995; Iaboni, Bouffard, Minde, & Hechtman, 1996) (Table 21.1). In contrast to consistent robust responses (approximately 70%) to stimulants in children and adolescents (Wilens & Biederman, 1992), controlled studies in adults have shown more equivocal responses to stimulants ranging from 25% (Mattes et al., 1984) to 78% (Spencer et al., 1995) of adults responding to treatment. In controlled trials, there appears to be more robust response to methylphenidate (MPH) (Wood et al., 1976; Mattes et al., 1984; Gualtieri et al., 1985; Wender et al., 1985a; Spencer et al., 1995) compared to pemoline (Wender et al., 1981; Wilens, Frazier, et al., 1996). There are no studies of the sustained release preparations of MPH or dextroamphetamine available in ADHD adults.

Variability in the response rate appears to be related to several factors including the diagnostic criteria utilized to determine ADHD, varying stimulant doses, high rates of comorbidity, and differing methods of assessing overall response. Dosing of the stimulants, for example, appears important in outcome: (1) controlled investigations using higher-stimulant dosing (> 1.0 mg/kg/day) resulted in more robust outcomes (Spencer et al., 1995; Iaboni et al., 1996) than those using lower-stimulant dosing (< 0.7 mg/kg/day) (Wender et al., 1981; Mattes et al., 1984), and (2) A dose-dependent response to stimulants was found in two studies of adults with ADHD (Spencer et al., 1995; Wilens, Frazier, et al., 1996). Although commonly used, the utility of amphetamines (Dexedrine, Adderall, and others) for ADHD in adults remains unstudied. Although long-term data are generally lacking, preliminary data from one controlled trial of 117 adults suggests that the response to MPH is sustained at 6-month follow-up (Wender et al., 1995).

Plasma levels of the stimulants have not been shown to correlate with response in ADHD in adults (Gualtieri, Hicks, Patrick, Schroeder, & Breese, 1984; Spencer et al., 1995). More-

TABLE 21.1. Studies of Nonstimulant Pharmacotherapy in Adult ADHD

Study (year)	N	Design	Medication	Duration	Total dose (weight corrected)	Response rate	Comments
Wood et al. (1976)	15	Double-blind	MPH	4 weeks	27 mg (04.mg/kg[a])	73%	Diagnostic criteria not well defined; low doses of pemoline; mild side effects
		Open	Pemoline	4 weeks	37.5–70 mg (0.5–1.0 mg/kg[a])	33%	
Wender et al. (1981)	51	Double-blind placebo crossover	Pemoline	6 weeks	65 mg (0.9 mg/kg[a])	50% (childhood onset)	Diagnostic criteria not well defined; high rates of dysthymia; moderate side effects
Mattes et al. (1984)	26	Double-blind placebo crossover	MPH	6 weeks	48 mg (0.7 mg/kg[a])	25%	Moderate rate of comorbidity; mild state effects
Wender, Reimherr, et al. (1985)	37	Double-blind placebo crossover	MPH	5 weeks	43 mg (0.6 mg/kg[a])	57%	68% dysthymia; 22% cyclothymia; mild side effects
Gualtieri et al. (1985)	8	Double-blind placebo crossover	MPH	2 weeks	42 mg[a] (0.6 mg/kg)	Mild–moderate	No plasma level–response associations
Shekim, Asarnow, et al. (1990)	33	Open	MPH	8 weeks	40 mg (0.6 mg/kg[a])	70%	Problematic outcome measures
Spencer et al. (1995)	23	Double-blind placebo crossover	MPH	7 weeks	30–100mg (0.5, 0.75, and 1.0 mg/kg)	78%, dose relationship	No plasma level associations; no effect of gender or comorbidity
Iaboni et al. (1996)	30	Double-blind placebo crossover	MPH	4 weeks	30–45 mg (≤0.6 mg/kg[a])	Moderate	Improvement in neuropsychological function and anxiety
Wilens, Frazier, et al. (1996)	42	Double-blind placebo crossover	Pemoline	10 weeks	150 mg (2 mg/kg)	61%	35% reduction in ADHD symptoms; moderate side effects > 2 mg/kg
TOTAL	265	8 double-blind, 2 open studies	MPH and pemoline	2–10 weeks	40 mg MPH (0.6 mg/kg[a]); 105 mg pemoline (1.5 mg/kg[a])	Variable	Diagnostic criteria not well defined; high rate of comorbidity; side effects in 30%

Note. Duration of medication trial includes placebo phase. MPH, methylphendiate.
[a]Weight-normalized dose using 50th percentile weight for age.

over, comorbidity with ADHD and gender have not been associated with variable response (Spencer et al., 1995; Wilens, Frazier, et al., 1996); however, sample sizes have not been large enough to address this issue adequately.

The effects of the stimulants in the brain are variable. Preclinical studies have shown that the stimulants block the reuptake of dopamine and norepinephrine into the presynaptic neuron, and that both drugs increase the release of these monoamines into the extraneuronal space (Elia et al., 1990). Although not entirely sufficient, alteration in dopaminergic and noradrenergic function appear necessary for clinical efficacy of the anti-ADHD medications, including the stimulants (Zametkin & Rapoport, 1987). There may be differential responses to the chemically distinct available stimulants as each may have a different mode of action. For example, although MPH and amphetamines alter dopamine transmission, they appear to have different mechanisms on release of dopamine from neuronal pools (Elia et al., 1990). The different mechanisms of actions of the amphetamines may explain why adults not responding to one stimulant may respond favorably to another.

There is a paucity of data available to guide the dosing parameters of the stimulants. Food and Drug Administration (FDA) guidelines for dosing reflect general cautiousness and should not be the only guide for clinical practice. For instance, absolute dose limits (in mg) do not adequately consider a patient's height, weight, and use in refractory cases or adults. The dose should be individually titrated based on therapeutic efficacy and side effects. Treatment should be started with short-acting preparations at the lowest possible dose. Initiation of treatment with once-daily dosing in the morning is advisable until an acceptable response is noted. Treatment generally starts at 5 mg of MPH or amphetamine, or 37.5 mg of pemoline once daily, and is titrated upward every 3 to 5 days until an effect is noted or adverse effects emerge. Repeat dosing through the day is dependent on duration of effectiveness, wear-off, and side effects. Typically, the half-life of the short-acting stimulants necessitates at least twice-daily dosing with the addition of similar or reduced afternoon doses dependent on breakthrough symptoms. In a typical adult, dosing of MPH is generally up to 30 mg three to four times daily, amphetamine 15 to 20 mg three to four times a day, and pemoline 75 to 225 mg daily. Consideration of another stimulant or class of agents is recommended if an ADHD adult is unresponsive or has intolerable side effects from the initial medication. Once pharmacotherapy is initiated, monthly contact with the patient is suggested during the initial phase of treatment to carefully monitor response to the intervention and adverse effects.

The side effects of the stimulants in ADHD adults have been reported to be mild; the following side effects are most frequently reported: insomnia, edginess, diminished appetite, weight loss, dysphoria, obsessiveness, tics, and headaches (Wilens & Biederman, 1992). No cases of stimulant-related psychosis at therapeutic doses have been reported in adults (Wilens & Biederman, 1992). Likewise, despite the theoretical abuse potential of the stimulants, there have been no reports of stimulant abuse in controlled or retrospective studies of adults with ADHD (Langer, Sweeney, Bartenbach, Davis, & Menander, 1986). The cardiovascular adverse effects in adults are benign with minimal elevations of heart rate and blood pressure weakly correlated with dose (Spencer et al., 1995). The addition of low-dose beta-blockers (i.e. propanolol at 10 mg up to three times daily) or busipirone (5 to 10 mg up to three times daily) may be helpful in reducing the edginess/agitation associated with stimulant administration (Ratey, Greenberg, & Lindem, 1991). Although not observed in short-term studies of pemoline in ADHD adults (Wilens, Frazier, et al., 1996), elevated liver function tests remain a concern when using this medication. Discussion and close observation of hepatitis symptoms, including change in urine/stool characteristic, abdominal pain, persistent flu-like symptoms, or jaundice are more useful in monitoring for hepatic dysfunction with pemoline than liver function tests.

The interactions of the stimulants with other prescription and nonprescription medications are generally mild and not a source of concern (Wilens & Biederman, 1992). Whereas coadministration of sympathomimetics (i.e., pseudoephedrine) may potentiate both medications effects, the antihistamines may diminish the stimulant's effectiveness. Caution should be exercised when using stimulants and antidepressants of the monoamine oxidase inhibitor (MAOI) type because of the potential for hypertensive reactions with this combination. The concomitant use of stimulants and tricyclic antidepressants is common practice with a recent study not indicating significant drug interactions (Prince, Wilens, Biederman, & Spencer, 1995).

Despite the increasing use of stimulants for adults with ADHD, up to 50% do not respond, have untoward side effects, or manifest comorbidity which stimulants may exacerbate or be ineffective in treating (Taylor et al., 1987; Shekim et al., 1990; Biederman et al., 1993). Reports of nonstimulant treatments for ADHD adults have included the use of antidepressants, antihypertensives, and amino acids (Table 21.2).

Antidepressants

Within the past two decades, the tricyclic antidepressants (TCAs) have been used as alternatives to the stimulants for ADHD in pediatrics (Spencer et al., 1996). Despite an extensive experience in children and adolescents (Spencer et al., 1996), there are only two studies of these agents in adult ADHD. Compared to the stimulants, TCAs have negligible abuse liability, single daily dosing, and efficacy for comorbid anxiety and depression.

An initial chart review indicated that desipramine or nortriptyline often in combination with other psychotropics including stimulants resulted in moderate improvement which was sustained at 1 year (Wilens, Biederman, Mick, & Spencer, 1995). A controlled trial of desipramine with a target dose of 200 mg daily resulted in significant reductions in ADHD symptoms in adults (Wilens, Biederman, et al., 1996). In that study, response was noted during the initial titration at 2 weeks which continued to improve at the 6-week end point. Whereas a minority of subjects responded to < 100 mg daily, the majority required more robust dosing (mean of 150 mg daily) for efficacy.

Generally, TCA daily doses of 50 to 250 mg are required with a relatively rapid response to treatment (i.e., 2 weeks) when the appropriate dose is reached. TCAs should be initiated at 25 mg and slowly titrated upward within dosing and serum-level parameters until an acceptable response or intolerable adverse effects are reported. Common side effects of the TCAs include dry mouth, constipation, blurred vision, weight gain, and sexual dysfunction. Although cardiovascular effects of reduced cardiac conduction, elevated blood pressure, and heart rates are not infrequent, if monitored, they rarely prevent treatment. As serum TCA levels are variable, they are best used as guidelines for efficacy and to reduce central nervous system and cardiovascular toxicity.

More recently, the atypical, stimulant-like antidepressant bupropion (Wellbutrin) has been reported to be moderately helpful in reducing ADHD symptoms in children (Casat, Pleasants, & Fleet, 1987) and adults (Wender & Reimherr, 1990). In an open study of 19 adults treated with an average of 360 mg of bupropion for 6 to 8 weeks, Wender and Reimherr (1990) reported a moderate to marked response in 74% of adults in the study (five dropouts) with sustained improvement at 1 year noted in 10 subjects. Despite the small numbers of adults studied, bupropion may be helpful in ADHD, particularly when associated with comorbid mood instability or in adults with cardiac abnormalities (Gelenberg, Bassuk, & Schoonover, 1991). Bupropion should also be started at very low doses (37.5 mg) and titrated upward weekly to a maximal dose of 450 mg per day. ADHD adults may benefit from the

TABLE 21.2. Studies of Nonstimulant Pharmacotherapy in Adult ADHD

Study (year)	N	Design	Medication	Duration	Dose (mean)	Response	Comments
Wood et al. (1982)	8	Open	L-Dopa (+ carbidopa)	3 weeks	625 mg (63 mg)	No benefit	Side effects: nausea, sedation, low doses
Wender et al. (1983)	22	Open	Pargyline	6 weeks	30 mg	13/22 moderate improvement	Delayed onset; brief behavioral action
Wender, Wood, et al. (1985)	11	Open	Deprenyl	6 weeks	30 mg	6/9 reponded, 2 dropouts	Amphetamine metabolite
Wood et al. (1985)	19	Double-blind crossover	Phenylalanine	2 weeks	587 mg	Poor	Transient mood improvement only
Mattes (1986)	13	Open, retrospective	Propanolol	3–50 weeks	528 mg	11/13 improved	Part of "temper" study
Reimherr et al. (1987)	12	Open	Tyrosine	8 weeks	150 mg	Poor response, 4 dropouts	14-day onset of action; tolerance developed
Shekim et al. (1989)	18	Open	Nomifensine maleate	4 weeks	<300 mg	18/18-responded Reduction in ADHD symptoms	Immediate response; one patient with allergic reaction
Shekim, Antun, et al. (1990)	8	Open	S-Adenosyl-L-methionine	4 weeks	<2,400 mg	75% of patients responded	Mild adverse effects
Wender & Reimherr (1990)	19	Open	Bupropion	6-8 weeks	360 mg	Moderate response, 5 dropouts	10 subjects with improvement at 1 year
Wilens, Biederman, et al. (1995)	37	Retrospective	Desipramine, nortriptyline	50 weeks	183 mg 92 mg	68% response rate, response sustained	Comorbidity unrelated to response; 60% on stimulants
Adler et al. (1995)	12	Open	Venlafaxine	8 weeks	110 mg	10/12 responded	4 subjects on other medications
Reimherr et al. (1995)	20	Open	Venlafaxine	N.A.	109 mg	8/12 responded	Side effects led to 40% dropout rate
Spencer et al. (1995)	22	Double-blind crossover	Tomoxetine	7 weeks	76 mg	52% response rate	Adrenergic agent; well tolerated
Findling et al. (1996)	9	Open	Venlafaxine	8 weeks	150 mg	7/9 responded, reduction in ADHD	Improved anxiety scores
Ernst et al. (1996)	24	Double-blind parallel	Selegeline	6 weeks	20 mg and 60 mg	Mild improvement; 60-mg dose better	High placebo reponse; mild side effects
Wilens, Biederman, et al. (1996)	43	Double-blind parallel	Desipramine	6 weeks	147 mg	68% response rate	Comorbidity or levels not related to response
TOTAL	297	4 controlled, 10 open, 2 retrospective	Mixed	2–50 weeks	Moderate doses	Variable response	Side effects common; often loss of effect; inconsistent ADHD diagnosis

Note. Duration of medication trial includes placebo phase. N.A., not available.

long-acting bupropion preparation. Bupropion appears to be more stimulating than other antidepressants and is associated with higher rate of drug-induced seizures than other antidepressants (Gelenberg et al., 1991). These seizures appear to be dose related (> 450 mg/day) and elevated in patients with bulimia or a previous seizure history. Bupropion has also been associated with excitement, agitation, increased motor activity, insomnia, and tremor.

The MAOI antidepressants have also been studied for the treatment of ADHD. Whereas open studies with pargyline and Deprenyl in adult ADHD showed moderate improvements (Wender, Wood, Reimherr, & Ward, 1983; Wender, Wood, & Reimherr, 1985), a more recent controlled trial of selegeline (Deprenyl) yielded less enthusiastic findings (Ernst et al., 1996). Ernst et al. (1996) reported dose-dependent improvements in ADHD symptoms on selegeline, which were not significant when compared to a high placebo response. Although a pilot child-based study demonstrated efficacy of the reversible MAOI, moclobemide, data of its effectiveness for ADHD are not available in adults. The MAOIs may have a role in the management of treatment refractory, nonimpulsive, adult ADHD subjects with comorbid depression and anxiety, who are able to comply with the stringent requirements of these agents. The concerns of diet- or medication-induced hypertensive crisis limits are the usefulness and safety of these medications, especially in a group of ADHD patients vulnerable to impulsivity. In addition, other adverse effects associated with the MAOIs include agitation or lethargy, orthostatic hypotension, weight gain, sexual dysfunction, sleep disturbances, and edema often leading to the discontinuation of these agents (Gelenberg et al., 1991).

An investigational antidepressant with noradrenergic properties, tomoxetine, has been shown in one controlled trial to have mild to moderate effectiveness for ADHD, although the authors noted that the short duration of the study may have limited its full therapeutic benefit (Spencer et al., 1998). The investigational antidepressants *S*-adenosylmethionine and nomifensen have also been shown to be effective for ADHD in adults, although they remain unstudied under controlled conditions (Shekim, Masterson, Cantwell, Hanna, & McCracken, 1989; Shekim, Antun, Hanna, McCracken, & Hess, 1990).

The selective serotonin reuptake inhibitors (SSRIs) do not appear to be effective for ADHD (Spencer et al., 1996); however, venlafaxine, an antidepressant with both serotonin and noradrenergic properties, may have anti-ADHD efficacy. In three open studies totaling 41 adults, 75% of adults who tolerated venlafaxine had a measurable reduction in their ADHD at doses of 75 to 150 mg daily (Adler, Resnick, Kunz, & Devinsky, 1995; Findling, Schwartz, Flannery, & Manos, 1995; Reimherr, Hedges, Strong, & Wender, 1995). Although further controlled trials are necessary to determine its optimal dosing and efficacy, venlafaxine is generally titrated from 25 mg daily to more typical antidepressant dosing between 150 and 225 mg daily for ADHD control. Side effects to venlafaxine in adults include nausea, gastrointestinal distress, and concerns of elevated blood pressure at relatively higher dosing. Venlafaxine is often used conjointly with stimulants for control of ADHD in adults.

Miscellaneous Medications

Antihypertensives

The antihypertensives clonidine and guanfacine have been used in childhood ADHD, especially in cases with a marked hyperactive or aggressive component (Spencer et al., 1996). However, because of a lack of efficacy of data and concerns of their sedative and hypotensive effects, their use in adults remains dubious. Beta-blockers may be helpful in adult ADHD but remain unstudied under controlled conditions (Mattes, 1986; Ratey et al., 1991). One small open study of propanolol for adults with ADHD and temper outbursts indicated improvement in both the ADHD symptoms and outbursts at daily doses of up to 640 mg/day

(Mattes, 1986). Beta-blockers when added to stimulants have also been reported to be helpful for ADHD in three adults (Ratey et al., 1991), although it may be that this combination was helpful by reducing the stimulant-induced adverse effects.

Amino Acids

Trials with the amino acids were in part undertaken with the assumptions that ADHD may be related to a deficiency in the catecholaminergic system and that administration of precursors of these systems would reverse these deficits. The results of open studies with L-DOPA and tyrosine and controlled studies of phenylalanine in adults with ADHD have generally been disappointing despite robust dosing and adequate trial duration (Table 21.2) (Wood, Reimherr, & Wender, 1982; Wood, Reimherr, & Wender, 1985; Reimherr, Wender, Wood, & Ward, 1987). In these studies, transient improvement in ADHD was lost after 2 weeks of treatment.

More recently, the relationship of nicotine and ADHD has attracted attention, including findings of higher than expected overlap of cigarette smoking in ADHD children (Milberger, Biederman, Faraone, Chen, & Jones, 1997) and adults (Pomerleau, Downey, Stelson, & Pomerleau, 1996). One small study of 2 days' duration showed a significant reduction in ADHD symptoms in adults wearing standard-size nicotine patches (Conners et al., 1996). Moreover, the authors have observed the efficacy of the nicotine patch in reducing ADHD symptoms in smokers who report the emergence of ADHD symptoms with cigarette cessation. Although compelling based on efficacy in Alzheimer's disease, there are no data on the cognitive-enhancing cholinergic agents in ADHD adults, but studies are currently under way.

Combined Pharmacotherapy

Although systematic data assessing the efficacy and safety profile of combining agents for ADHD in adults are lacking, combination treatment may be necessary in those who have residual symptomatology with single agents or psychiatric comorbidity. For example, in a recent naturalistic report on TCAs for adults with ADHD, 84% of adults were receiving additional psychoactive medications with 59% receiving adjunctive stimulants (Wilens, Biederman, Mick, & Spencer, 1995). These findings are similar to controlled data in juvenile ADHD in which the combination of MPH and desipramine improved the ADHD response more than either agent singly (Rapport, Carlson, Kelly, & Pataki, 1993). The use of MPH conjointly with fluoxetine has been reported to be well tolerated and useful in improving depression in ADHD adolescents (Gammon & Brown, 1993) and appears useful in adults with the same comorbidity. In cases of partial response or adverse effects with stimulants, the addition of low-dose SSRIs, TCAs, or beta-blockers have been reported to be helpful (Ratey et al., 1991; Gammon & Brown, 1993). When combining agents, one needs to consider potential drug interactions such as has been described between TCAs and some SSRIs (Aranow et al., 1989).

Treatment-Refractory Patients

Despite the availability of various agents for adults with ADHD, a number of individuals either do not respond or are intolerant of adverse effects of medications used to treat their ADHD. In managing difficult cases, several therapeutic strategies are available (Table 21.3). If psychiatric adverse effects develop concurrent with a poor medication response, alternate treatments should be pursued. Severe psychiatric symptoms that emerge during the acute

TABLE 21.3. **Strategies in Difficult Adult ADHD Cases**

Symptoms	Intervention
Worsened or unchanged ADHD	• Increase medication dose • Change timing of administration • Change preparation, substitute stimulant • Consider adjunctive treatment (add antidepressant, stimulants) • Consider nonpharmacological treatment (e.g., cognitive-behavioral therapy)
Emergence of side effect	• Evaluate if side effect is drug-induced • Manage side effects aggressively: usually change timing of dose, preparation; stimulant or antidepressant substitution • Use of adjunctive medication (e.g., propanolol)
Marked rebound phenomena	• Change timing of administration • Change preparation • Add multiple dosings
Emergence of dysphoria, anxiety, agitation, irritability	• Assess for toxicity or withdrawal • Evaluate for return of ADHD symptoms • Evaluate for comorbidity • Change preparations, substitute type of agent • Discontinue stimulants, add antidepressants • Consider adjunct treatment (e.g., benzodiazepines, mood stabilizers) • Consider nonpharmacological intervention
Emergence of psychosis	• Discontinue medication • Assess for comorbidity (e.g., Bipolar Disorder) • Consider alternative treatment

Note. ADHD adults should be assessed for their ADHD response. If no response is noted, alternative agents should be considered.

phase can be problematic, irrespective of the efficacy of the medications for ADHD. These symptoms may require reconsideration of the diagnosis of ADHD and careful reassessment of the presence of comorbid disorders. For example, it is common to observe depressive symptoms in an ADHD adult which are independent of the ADHD or treatment. If reduction of dose or change in preparation (i.e., regular vs. slow-release stimulants) do not resolve the problem, consideration should be given to alternative treatments. Concurrent nonpharmacological interventions such as behavioral or cognitive therapy may assist with symptom reduction.

SUGGESTED MANAGEMENT STRATEGIES

Once having diagnosed ADHD, the clinician needs to familiarize the adult with the risks and benefits of pharmacotherapy, the availability of alternative treatments, and the likely adverse effects. The clinician needs to explore patient expectations and clearly delineate realistic goals of treatment. Likewise, the clinician should review with the patient the various pharmacological options available and that each will require systematic trials of the anti-ADHD medications for reasonable durations of time and at clinically meaningful doses. Treatment-seeking ADHD adults who manifest substantial psychiatric comorbidity, have residual symptomatology with treatment, or report psychological distress related to their ADHD (i.e., self-esteem issues, self-sabotaging patterns, or interpersonal disturbances) should be directed to appropriate psychotherapeutic intervention with clinicians knowledgeable in ADHD treatment.

The stimulant medications continue to be the most rigorously investigated pharmacotherapy (Table 21.1) and are considered the first-line therapy for ADHD in adults. Consideration of another stimulant or class of agents is recommended if an ADHD adult is unresponsive or has intolerable side effects to the initial medication. The use of TCAs and bupropion can improve anti-ADHD response to the stimulants, whereas the SSRI and other antidepressants can be used adjunctly for comorbid depression, anxiety, or obsessiveness. The effect of age, long-term adverse effects, and stimulant use in substance-abusing subgroups of ADHD remains unstudied. Monitoring routine side effects, vital signs, and the misuse of the medication are warranted.

The antidepressants, namely, TCAs and bupropion, are less well studied, appearing useful for stimulant nonresponders or adults with concurrent psychiatric disorders including depression, anxiety, or active or recent substance abuse (Wender & Reimherr, 1990; Wilens, Biederman, et al., 1996). Comparative data between the antidepressants and stimulants coupled with studies in children support the view that stimulants are generally more effective in reducing ADHD symptoms (Spencer et al., 1996). In addition, the response to the stimulants is immediate (Wood et al., 1976; Spencer et al., 1995), whereas the antidepressants have continued improvement up to 4 weeks after titration (Wilens, Biederman, et al., 1996). Although some adults may respond to relatively low doses of the TCAs (Ratey et al., 1992), the majority of adults appear to require solid antidepressant dosing of these agents (i.e. desipramine >150 mg daily). MAOIs are mildly effective and are generally reserved for treatment-refractory adults who can reliably follow the dietary requirements. The antihypertensives may be useful in adults with ADHD and aggressive outbursts (Mattes, 1986) or those with adverse effects to the stimulants. The amino acids have not been shown effective and the cholinergic-enhancing compounds remain to be studied comprehensively in ADHD adults.

ADHD adults often require more comprehensive treatment for their ADHD given the sequalae associated with a chronic disorder, its effect on psychological development, and residual psychiatric and ADHD symptoms even with aggressive pharmacotherapy. To this end, the use of structured cognitive-based psychotherapies appear helpful, especially when used conjointly with pharmacotherapy. In our center, we utilize an ADHD-adapted cognitive therapy protocol (McDermott & Wilens, in press), as recent data indicate that when combined with medication, two-thirds of 26 ADHD adults previously unresponsive to treatment were found to manifest clinically significant improvement (Wilens et al., in press). Groups focused on coping skills, support, and interpersonal psychotherapy may also be very useful for these adults. For adults considering advanced schooling, educational planning and alterations in the school environment may be necessary.

The pharmacology of ADHD is directly related to the pathogenesis of ADHD. The neurochemical dysfunction in ADHD appears to be mediated by dopaminergic and adrenergic systems with little direct influence by the serotonergic systems (Zametkin & Rapoport, 1987). For instance, stimulants block the reuptake of dopamine and norepinephrine presynaptically and simultaneously increase the release of these monoamines into the extraneuronal space (Elia et al., 1990). Similar biochemical findings have been reported with those antidepressants (TCAs and bupropion) also shown effective for ADHD. Serotonin does not appear integral in ADHD, and conversely, serotonin-based agents have not been shown to be useful for core ADHD symptomatology. Although cholinergic modulation of temporal memory has been investigated (Meck & Church, 1987), the effect of cholinergic-enhancing agents on ADHD, as well as dopaminergic and other neurotransmitter systems, is currently under investigation.

In summary, the aggregate literature supports the view that pharmacotherapy provides an effective treatment for adults with ADHD. Effective pharmacological treatments for ADHD adults to date have included the use of the psychostimulants and antidepressants with unclear efficacy of cognitive enhancers. Structured psychotherapy may be effective when used adjunctly with medications. Further controlled investigations assessing the efficacy of single and combination agents for adults with ADHD are necessary with careful attention to diagnostics, symptom and neuropsychological outcome, long-term tolerability and efficacy, and use in specific ADHD subgroups.

REFERENCES

American Psychiatric Association. (1994). *Diagnostic and statistical manual of mental disorders* (4th ed.). Washington, DC: Author.

Adler, L. A., Resnick, S., Kunz, M., & Devinsky, O. (1995). Open label trial of venlafaxine in adults with attention deficit disorder. *Psychopharmacology Bulletin, 31*, 785–788.

Aranow, R. B., Hudson, J. L., Pope, H. G., Grady, T. A., Laage, T. A., Bell, I. R., & Cole, J. O. (1989). Elevated antidepressant plasma levels after addition of fluoxetine. *American Journal of Psychiatry, 146*, 911–913.

Barkley, R. A. (1990). *Attention-deficit hyperactivity disorder: A handbook for diagnosis and treatment.* New York: Guilford Press.

Bauermeister, J. J., Canino, G., & Bird, H. (1994). Epidemiology of disruptive behavior disorders. In L. Greenhill (Eds.), *Child and adolescent psychiatric clinics of North America* (pp. 177–194). Philadelphia: W.B. Saunders.

Biederman, J., Faraone, S. V., Spencer, T., Wilens, T. E., Norman, D., Lapey, K. A., Mick, E., Lehman, B., & Doyle, A. (1993). Patterns of psychiatric comorbidity, cognition, and psychosocial functioning in adults with attention deficit hyperactivity disorder. *American Journal of Psychiatry, 150*, 1792–1798.

Biederman, J., Wilens, T. E., Mick, E., Milberger, S., Spencer, T. J., & Faraone, S. V. (1995). Psychoactive substance use disorders in adults with attention deficit hyperactivity disorder (ADHD): Effects of ADHD and psychiatric comorbidity. *American Journal of Psychiatry, 152*(11), 1652–1658.

Brown, T. (1995). *Brown Attention Deficit Disorder Scales.* San Antonio, TX: Psychological Corporation.

Casat, C. D., Pleasants, D. Z., & Fleet, J. V. W. (1987). A double blind trial of bupropion in children with attention deficit disorder. *Psychopharmacology Bulletin, 23*, 120–122.

Conners, C., Levin, E. D., Sparrow, E., Hinton, S., Erhardt, D., Meck, W., Rose, J., & March, J. (1996). Nicotine and attention in adult attention deficit hyperactivity disorder. *Psychopharmacology Bulletin, 32*, 67–73.

Elia, J., Borcherding, B. G., Potter, W. Z., Mefford, I. N., Rapoport, J. L., & Keysor, C. S. (1990). Stimulant drug treatment of hyperactivity: Biochemical correlates. *Clinical Pharmacology Therapy, 48*, 57–66.

Ernst, M., Liebenauer, L., Jons, P., Tebeka, D., Cohen, R., & Zametkin, A. (1996). Selegiline in adults with attention deficit hyperactivity disorder: Clinical efficacy and safety. *Psychopharmacology Bulletin, 32*, 327–334.

Eyre, S. L., Rounsaville, B. J., & Kleber, H. D. (1982). History of childhood hyperactivity in a clinic population of opiate addicts. *Journal of Nervous and Mental Disorders, 170*, 522–529.

Faraone, S. V., Biederman, J., Chen, W. J., Krifcher, B., Keenan, K., Moore, C., Sprich, S., & Tsuang, M. T. (1992). Segregation analysis of attention deficit hyperactivity disorder. *Psychiatric Genetics, 2*, 257–275.

Findling, R. L., Schwartz, M. A., Flannery, D. J., & Manos, M. J. (1995). Venlafaxine in adults with attention-deficit /hyperactivity disorder: An open clinical trial. *Journal of Clinical Psychiatry, 57*(5), 184–189.

Gammon, G. D., & Brown, T. E. (1993). Fluoxetine and methylphenidate in combination for treatment of attention deficit disorder and comorbid depressive disorder. *Journal of Child and Adolescent Psychopharmacology, 3*(1), 1–10.

Gelenberg, A. J., Bassuk, E. L., & Schoonover, S. C. (1991). *The practitioner's guide to psychoactive drugs* (3rd ed.). New York: Plenum.

Gualtieri, C. T., Hicks, R. E., Patrick, K., Schroeder, S. R., & Breese, G. R. (1984). Clinical correlates of methylphenidate blood levels. *Therapeutic Drug Monitoring, 6*(4), 379–392.

Gualtieri, C. T., Ondrusek, M. G., & Finley, C. (1985). Attention deficit disorder in adults. *Clinical Neuropharmacology, 8,* 343–356.

Iaboni, F., Bouffard, R., Minde, K., & Hechtman, L. (1996). The efficacy of methylphenidate in treating adults with attention-deficit/hyperactivity disorder. In *Scientific Proceedings of the American Academy of Child and Adolescent Psychiatry,* Philadelphia, PA.

Langer, D. H., Sweeney, K. P., Bartenbach, D. E., Davis, P. M., & Menander, K. B. (1986). Evidence of lack of abuse or dependence following pemoline treatment: results of a retrospective survey. *Drug and Alcohol Dependency, 17,* 213–227.

Mannuzza, S., Klein, R. G., Bessler, A., Malloy, P., & LaPadula, M. (1993). Adult outcome of hyperactive boys: Educational achievement, occupational rank, and psychiatric status. *Archives of General Psychiatry, 50,* 565–576.

Mattes, J. A. (1986). Propanolol for adults with temper outbursts and residual attention deficit disorder. *Journal of Clinical Psychopharmacology, 6,* 299–302.

Mattes, J. A., Boswell, L., & Oliver, H. (1984). Methylphenidate effects on symptoms of attention deficit disorder in adults. *Archives of General Psychiatry, 41,* 1059–1063.

McDermott, S. P., & Wilens, T. E. (in press). Cognitive and emotional impediments to treating the adult with ADHD: A cognitive therapy perspective. In T. Brown (Ed.), *Subtypes of attention deficit disorders in children, adolescents, and adults.* Washington, DC: American Psychiatric Press.

Meck, W. H., & Church, R. M. (1987). Cholinergic modulation of the content of temporal memory. *Behavioral Neuroscience, 101,* 207–214.

Milberger, S., Biederman, J., Faraone, S., Chen, L., & Jones, J. (1997). ADHD is associated with early initiation of cigarette smoking in children and adolescents. *Journal of the American Academy of Child and Adolescent Psychiatry, 36,* 37–43.

Millstein, R., Wilens, T., Spencer, T., & Biederman, J. (1998). Presenting ADHD symptoms and subtypes in clinically referred adults with ADHD. *Journal of Attention Disorders, 2,* 159–165.

Murphy, K., & Barkley, R. (1996). Prevalence of DSM-IV symptoms of ADHD in adult licensed drivers: Implications for clinical diagnosis. *Journal of Attention Disorders, 1,* 147–161.

Pomerleau, O., Downey, K., Stelson, F., & Pomerleau, C. (1996). Cigarette smoking in adult patients diagnosed with ADHD. *Journal of Substance Abuse, 7,* 373–378.

Prince, J., Wilens, T., Biederman, J., & Spencer, T. (1995). *A naturalistic study of the coadministration of psychostimulants and desipramine: Effects on serum desipramine levels.* Scientific Proceedings of the American Academy of Child and Adolescent Psychiatry, 11, New Orleans.

Rapport, M. D., Carlson, G. A., Kelly, K. L., & Pataki, C. (1993). Methylphenidate and desipramine in hospitalized children: I. Separate and combined effects on cognitive function. *Journal of the American Academy of Child and Adolescent Psychiatry, 32,* 333–342.

Ratey, J., Greenberg, M., & Lindem, K. (1991). Combination of treatments for attention deficit disorders in adults. *Journal of Nervous and Mental Disease, 176,* 699–701.

Ratey, J. J., Greenberg, M. S., Bemporad, J. R., & Lindem, K. J. (1992). Unrecognized attention-deficit hyperactivity disorder in adults presenting for outpatient psychotherapy. *Journal of Child and Adolescent Psychopharmacology, 2*(4), 267–275.

Reimherr, F. W., Hedges, D. W., Strong, R. E., & Wender, P. H. (1995). *An open trial of venlafaxine in adult patients with attention deficit hyperactivity disorder.* New Clinical Drug Evaluation Unit Program, Orlando, FL.

Reimherr, F. W., Wender, P. H., Wood, D. R., & Ward, M. (1987). An open trial of L-tyrosine in the treatment of attention deficit hyperactivity disorder, residual type. *American Journal of Psychiatry, 144,* 1071–1073.

Seidman, L. J., Biederman, J., Weber, W., Hatch, M., & Faraone, S. (in press). Neuropsychological functioning in adults with ADHD. *Biological Psychiatry.*

Shekim, W. O., Antun, F., Hanna, G. L., McCracken, J. T., & Hess, E. B. (1990). S-adenosyl-l-methionine (SAM) in adults with ADHD, RS: Preliminary results from an open trial. *Psychopharmacology Bulletin, 26,* 249–253.

Shekim, W. O., Asarnow, R. F., Hess, E., Zaucha, K., & Wheeler, N. (1990). A clinical and demographic profile of a sample of adults with attention deficit hyperactivity disorder, residual state. *Comprehensive Psychiatry, 31,* 416–425.

Shekim, W. O., Masterson, A., Cantwell, D. P., Hanna, G. L., & McCracken, J. T. (1989). Nomifensine maleate in adult attention deficit disorder. *Journal of Nervous and Mental Disease, 177,* 296–299.

Spencer, T., Wilens, T. E., Biederman, J., Faraone, S. V., Ablon, S., & Lapey, K. (1995). A double blind, crossover comparison of methylphenidate and placebo in adults with childhood onset attention deficit hyperactivity disorder. *Archives of General Psychiatry, 52,* 434–443.

Spencer, T., Biederman, J., Wilens, T. E., Faraone, S. V., & Li, T. (1994). Is attention deficit hyperactivity disorder in adults a valid diagnosis. *Harvard Review of Psychiatry, 1,* 326–335.

Spencer, T., Biederman, J., Wilens, T., Faraone, S., Prince, J., Hatch, M., & Harding, M. (1998). Tolerability and efficacy of tomoxetine for adults with attention deficit hyperactivity disorder. *American Journal of Psychiatry, 155,* 693–695.

Spencer, T., Biederman, J., Wilens, T., Harding, M., O'Donnell, D., & Griffin, S. (1996). Pharmacotherapy of attention deficit disorder across the life cycle. *Journal of the American Academy of Child and Adolescent Psychiatry, 35*(4), 409–432.

Tarter, R. E., McBride, H., Buonpane, N., & Schneider, D. U. (1977). Differentiation of alcoholics. *Archives of General Psychiatry, 34,* 761–768.

Taylor, E., Schachar, R., Thorley, G., Wieselberg, H. M., Everitt, B., & Rutter, M. (1987). Which boys respond to stimulant medication? A controlled trial of methylphenidate in boys with disruptive behaviour. *Psychological Medicine, 17,* 121–143.

Ward, M. F., Wender, P. H., & Reimherr, F. W. (1993). The Wender Utah rating scale: An aid in the retrospective diagnosis of childhood attention deficit hyperactivity disorder. *American Journal of Psychiatry, 150,* 885–890.

Weiss, G., & Hechtman, L. T. (1986). *Hyperactive children grown up.* New York: Guilford Press.

Wender, P. H., & Reimherr, F. W. (1990). Bupropion treatment of attention deficit hyperactivity disorder in adults. *American Journal of Psychiatry, 147,* 1018–1020.

Wender, P., Reimherr, F., Czajkowski, L., Sanford, E., Rogers, A., Gardner, L., & Eden, J. (1995). A long-term trial of methlphenidate in the treatment of adhd adults: A placebo-controlled trial and six-month followup. In *Scientific Proceedings of the American College of Neuropharmacology* (p. 209).

Wender, P. H., Reimherr, F. W., & Wood, D. R. (1981). Attention deficit disorder ("minimal brain dysfunction") in adults: A replication study of diagnosis and drug treatment. *Archives of General Psychiatry, 38,* 449–456.

Wender, P. H., Reimherr, F. W., Wood, D., & Ward, M. (1985). A controlled study of methylphenidate in the treatment of attention deficit disorder, residual type, in adults. *American Journal of Psychiatry, 142,* 547–552.

Wender, P. H., Wood, D. R., & Reimherr, F. W. (1985). Pharmacological treatment of attention deficit disorder residual type (ADD, RT, "minimal brain dysfunction," "hyperactivity") in adults. *Psychopharmacology Bulletin, 21,* 222–230.

Wender, P. H., Wood, D. R., Reimherr, F. W., & Ward, M. (1983). An open trial of pargyline in the treatment of attention deficit disorder, residual type. *Psychiatry Research, 9,* 329–336.

Wilens, T., & Biederman, J. (1992). The stimulants. In D. Shafer (Ed.), *The psychiatric clinics of North America* (pp. 191–222). Philadelphia: W.B. Saunders.

Wilens, T., Biederman, J., Mick, E., & Spencer, T. (1995). A systematic assessment of tricyclic antidepressants in the treatment of adult attention-deficit hyperactivity disorder. *Journal of Nervous and Mental Disease, 184,* 48–50.

Wilens, T., Biederman, J., Prince, J., Spencer, T., Schleifer, D., Harding, M., Linehan, C., & Hatch, M. (1996). A double blind, placebo controlled trial of desipramine for adults with ADHD. *American Journal of Psychiatry, 153,* 1147–1153.

Wilens, T., Frazier, J., Prince, J., Spencer, T., Bostic, J., Hatch, M., Abrantes, A., Sienna, M., Soriano,

J., Millstein, R., & Biederman, J. (1996). *A double blind comparison of pemoline in adults with ADHD: Preliminary results.* Scientific Proceedings of the American Academy of Child and Adolescent Psychiatry, Philadelphia.

Wilens, T., McDermott, S., Biederman, J., Abrantes, A., & Spencer, T. (in press). Combined cognitive therapy and pharmacotherapy for adults with attention deficit hyperactivity disorder: A systematic chart review of 26 cases. *Journal of Cognitive Psychotherapy.*

Wilens, T., Spencer, T., & Biederman, J. (1995). Are attention-deficit hyperactivity disorder and the psychoactive substance use disorders really related? *Harvard Review of Psychiatry, 3,* 260–262.

Wood, D. R., Reimherr, J., & Wender, P. H. (1982). Effects of levodopa on attention deficit disorder, residual type. *Psychiatry Research, 6,* 13–20.

Wood, D. R., Reimherr, F. W., & Wender, P. H. (1985). The treatment of attention deficit disorder with d,l-phenylalanine. *Psychiatry Research, 16,* 21–26.

Wood, D. R., Reimherr, F. W., Wender, P. H., & Johnson, G. E. (1976). Diagnosis and treatment of minimal brain dysfunction in adults. *Archives of General Psychiatry, 33,* 1453–1460.

Wood, D. R., Wender, P. H., & Reimherr, F. W. (1983). The prevalence of attention deficit disorder, residual type, or minimal brain dysfunction, in a population of male alcoholic patients. *American Journal of Psychiatry, 140,* 95–98.

Zametkin, A. J., & Rapoport, J. L. (1987). Neurobiology of attention deficit disorder with hyperactivity: Where have we come in 50 years? *Journal of the American Academy of Child and Adolescent Psychiatry, 26,* 676–686.

AUTHOR INDEX

SUBJECT INDEX